Some penguins swim at about **15 MPH** underwater.

The deepest recorded dive by a penguin is **565 m.** It was made by an Emperor Penguin.

Some penguins will spend **75%** of their lives underwater.

Some penguins travel up to 3,000 miles to breed.

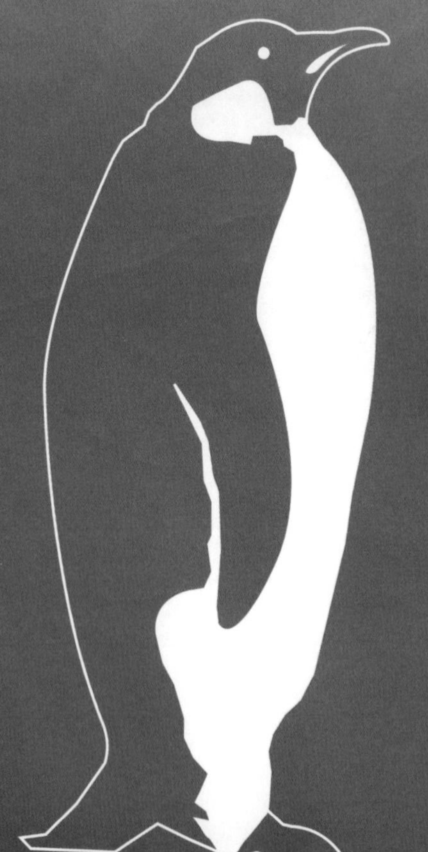
Emperor Penguin
122 cm
27 to 41 kg

Fairy Penguin
30 cm
1 to 3.3 kg

KENTUCKY Math

HOUGHTON MIFFLIN HARCOURT
School Publishers

Visit *The Learning Site!*
www.harcourtschool.com

Printed in the U.S.A.

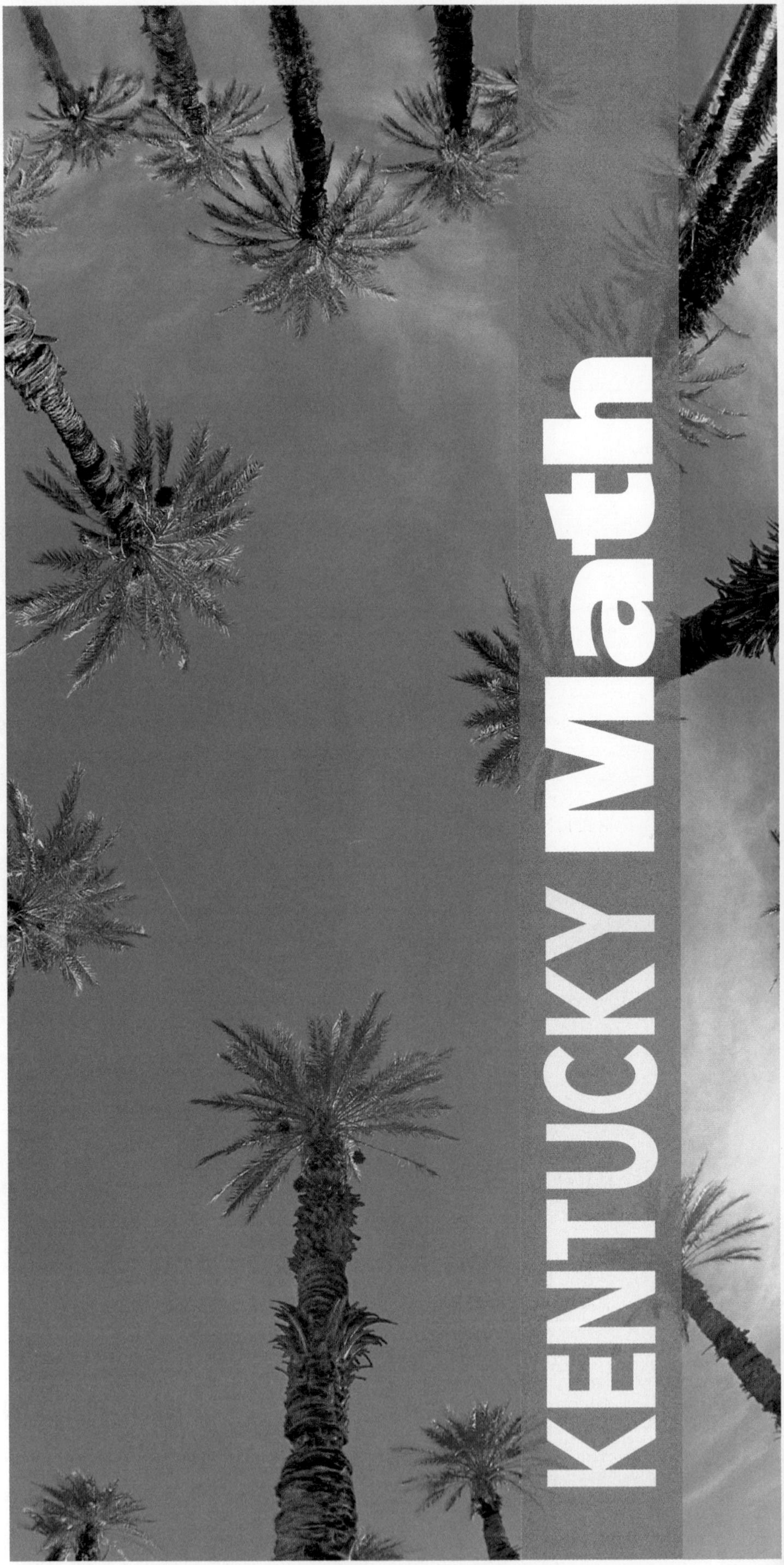

ISBN 13: 978-0-15-378496-5
ISBN 10: 0-15-378496-2

2 3 4 5 6 7 8 9 10 0868 17 16 15 14 13 12 11 10

4500255256

KENTUCKY Math

Senior Authors

Evan M. Maletsky
Professor Emeritus
Montclair State University
Upper Montclair, New Jersey

Joyce McLeod
Visiting Professor, Retired
Rollins College
Winter Park, Florida

Authors

Karen S. Norwood
Associate Professor of Mathematics Education
North Carolina State University
Raleigh, North Carolina

Tom Roby
Associate Professor of Mathematics
Director, Quantitative Learning Center
University of Connecticut
Storrs, Connecticut

James A. Mendoza Epperson
Associate Professor
Department of Mathematics
The University of Texas at Arlington
Arlington, Texas

Juli K. Dixon
Associate Professor of Mathematics Education
University of Central Florida
Orlando, Florida

Janet K. Scheer
Executive Director
Create-A-Vision
Foster City, California

David G. Wright
Professor
Department of Mathematics
Brigham Young University
Provo, Utah

David D. Molina
Program Director, Retired
The Charles A. Dana Center
The University of Texas at Austin

Jennie M. Bennett
Mathematics Teacher
Houston Independent School District
Houston, Texas

Lynda Luckie
Director, K-12 Mathematics
Gwinnett County Public Schools
Suwanee, Georgia

Angela G. Andrews
Assistant Professor of Math Education
National Louis University
Lisle, Illinois

Vicki Newman
Classroom Teacher
McGaugh Elementary School
Los Alamitos Unified School District
Seal Beach, California

Barbara Montalto
Mathematics Consultant
Assistant Director of Mathematics, Retired
Texas Education Agency
Austin, Texas

Minerva Cordero-Epperson
Associate Professor of Mathematics and Associate Dean of the Honors College
The University of Texas at Arlington
Arlington, Texas

Program Consultants and Specialists

Michael DiSpezio
Writer and On-Air Host, JASON Project
North Falmouth, Massachusetts

Valerie Johse
Elementary Math Specialist
Office of Curriculum & Instruction
Pearland I.S.D.
Pearland, Texas

Concepion Molina
Southwest Educational Development Lab
Austin, Texas

Lydia Song
Program Specialist–Mathematics
Orange County Department of Education
Costa Mesa, California

Rebecca Valbuena
Language Development Specialist
Stanton Elementary School
Glendora, California

Robin C. Scarcella
Professor and Director
Program of Academic English and ESL
University of California, Irvine
Irvine, California

Tyrone Howard
Assistant Professor
UCLA Graduate School of Education
Information Studies
University of California at Los Angeles
Los Angeles, California

Russell Gersten
Director, Instructional Research Group
Long Beach, California
Professor Emeritus of Special Education
University of Oregon
Eugene, Oregon

Use Whole Numbers

1 Place Value, Addition, and Subtraction 2

2 Multiply Whole Numbers 34

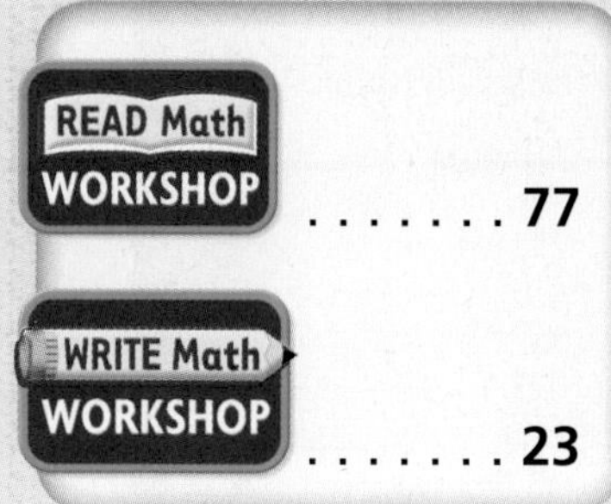

GO ONLINE Technology

Harcourt Mega Math: Chapter 1, p. 12; Chapter 2, p. 42; Chapter 3, p. 64; Chapter 4, p. 111; Extra Practice, pp. 28, 52, 84, 120
The Harcourt Learning Site: www.harcourtschool.com
Multimedia Math Glossary www.harcourtschool.com/hspmath

Use Decimals

5 Understand Decimals 130

6 Add and Subtract Decimals 148

7 Multiply Decimals 168

8 Divide Decimals by Whole Numbers 192

MATH ON LOCATION

GO ONLINE Technology

Harcourt Mega Math: Chapter 5, p. 133; Chapter 6, p. 153; Chapter 7, p. 175; Chapter 8, p. 200; Extra Practice, pp. 142, 162, 186, 204

The Harcourt Learning Site: www.harcourtschool.com

Multimedia Math Glossary www.harcourtschool.com/hspmath

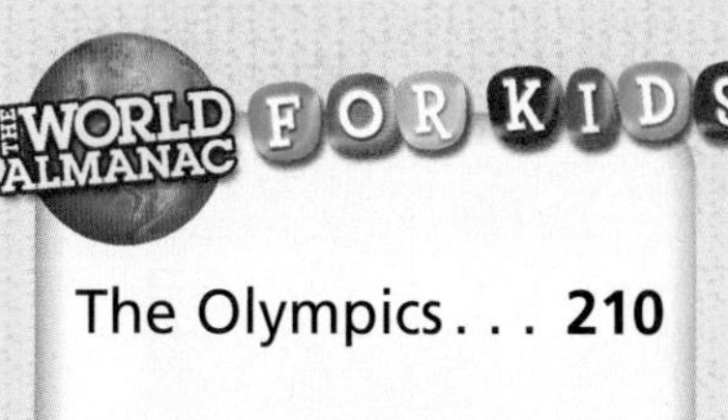

Data and Graphing

9 Data and Statistics 214

10 Make Graphs 240

MATH ON LOCATION

GO ONLINE Technology

Harcourt Mega Math: Chapter 9, p. 227; Chapter 10, p. 250; Extra Practice, pp. 234, 264
The Harcourt Learning Site: www.harcourtschool.com
Multimedia Math Glossary www.harcourtschool.com/hspmath

THE WORLD ALMANAC FOR KIDS

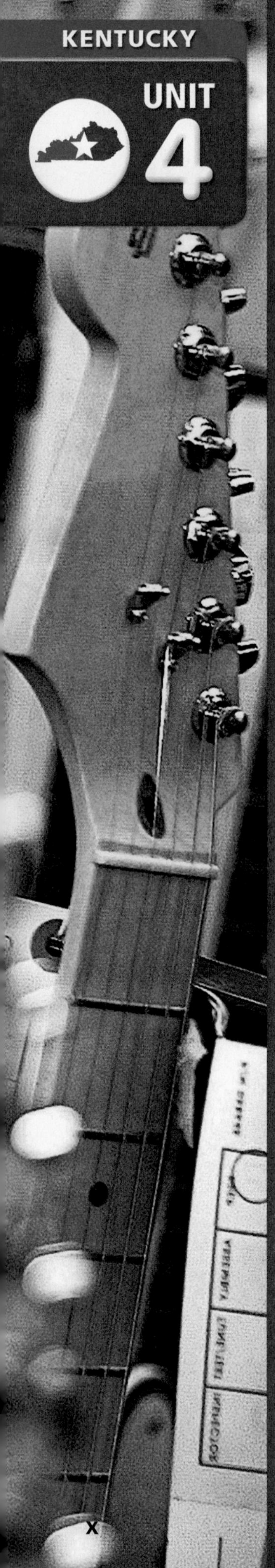

Number Theory and Fraction Concepts

11 Number Theory 274

12 Fraction Concepts 306

MATH ON LOCATION

DVD from  with Chapter Projects 273

GO ONLINE Technology

Harcourt Mega Math: Chapter 11, p. 293; Chapter 12, p. 314; Extra Practice, pp. 300, 330
The Harcourt Learning Site: www.harcourtschool.com
Multimedia Math Glossary www.harcourtschool.com/hspmath

Fraction Operations

13 Add and Subtract Fractions 340

14 Add and Subtract Mixed Numbers 364

15 Multiply and Divide Fractions 386

MATH ON LOCATION

GO ONLINE Technology

Harcourt Mega Math: Chapter 13, p. 347; Chapter 15, p. 400; Extra Practice, pp. 358, 380, 410
The Harcourt Learning Site: www.harcourtschool.com
Multimedia Math Glossary www.harcourtschool.com/hspmath

Ratios, Percents, and Probability

16 Ratios and Percents 420

17 Probability 452

GO ONLINE Technology

Harcourt Mega Math: Chapter 17, p. 440; Chapter 18, p. 453; Extra Practice, pp. 446, 470
The Harcourt Learning Site: www.harcourtschool.com
Multimedia Math Glossary www.harcourtschool.com/hspmath

KENTUCKY

UNIT 7

Geometry and Algebra

18 Geometric Figures 480

19 Plane and Solid Figures 512

20 Patterns 540

21 Integers and the Coordinate Plane 560

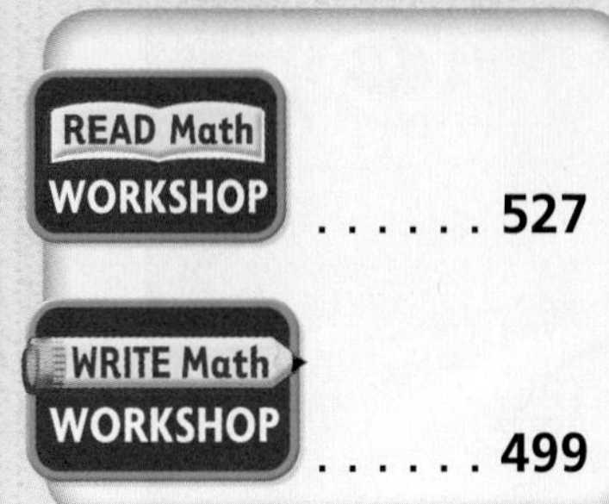

GO ONLINE Technology

Harcourt Mega Math: Chapter 18, p. 483; Chapter 19, p. 524; Chapter 20, p. 545; Chapter 21, p. 572; Extra Practice, pp. 506, 534, 554, 580
The Harcourt Learning Site: www.harcourtschool.com
Multimedia Math Glossary www.harcourtschool.com/hspmath

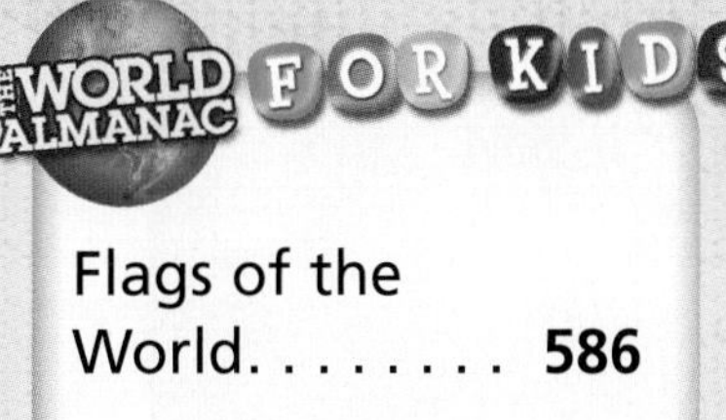

Measurement

24 Area and Volume 638

Student Handbook

GO ONLINE Technology

Harcourt Mega Math: Chapter 22, p. 591, Chapter 23, p. 622; Chapter 24, p. 642; Extra Practice, pp. 614, 632, 674
The Harcourt Learning Site: www.harcourtschool.com
Multimedia Math Glossary www.harcourtschool.com/hspmath

TALK, READ, and WRITE About Math

Mathematics is a language of numbers, words, and symbols.

This year you will learn ways to communicate about math as you **talk**, **read**, and **write** about what you are learning.

The line graph shows the average maximum temperature [illegible] the airport in San Diego, California.

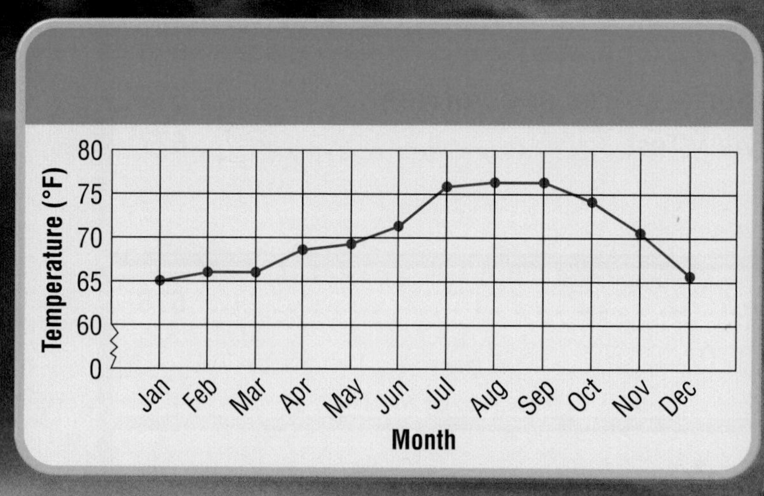

TALK Math

Talk about the line graph.

1. What do the words *average* and *maximum* in the title tell you about the data?
2. What do the numbers along the left side of the graph represent?
3. What is the interval on the graph scale?
4. What can you tell about the data by looking at the line on the graph?

READ Math

Read the data on the graph.

5. Which months have the highest temperatures?

6. What is the greatest temperature difference shown between any two months? Which months are they?

7. Which two consecutive months have a difference of 4°F in the average maximum temperatures?

8. How much greater is the temperature shown for November than for December?

WRITE Math

Write a problem about the graph.

This year you will write many problems. When you see **Pose a Problem**, you look at a problem on the page and use it to write your own problem.

In your problem you can
- change the numbers or some of the information.
- exchange the known and unknown information.
- write an open-ended problem that can have more than one correct answer.

These problems are examples of ways you can pose your own problem. Solve each problem.

Problem What is the difference in the average maximum temperatures of May and August?

- **Change the numbers or information**
  What is the difference in the average maximum temperatures of January and April?

- **Exchange the known and unknown information**
  Which two months have a difference of 8°F in the average maximum temperatures?

- **Open-Ended**
  What are two consecutive months that have a difference of 1°F in the average maximum temperatures?

Pose a Problem Choose one of three ways to write a new problem. Use the information on the line graph.

UNIT 1

Use Whole Numbers

Math on Location

with
Chapter Projects

1

As old computers are taken apart, the numbers of cases, circuit boards, and keyboards multiply.

2

Equal numbers of CRTs (cathode ray tubes) are placed on wood pallets for safe handling.

3

Three men can recycle 600 computers a day. That is 75 computers an hour in an 8-hour day.

VOCABULARY POWER

TALK Math

What math do you see in the **Math on Location** photographs? How are multiplication and division used?

READ Math

REVIEW VOCABULARY You will learn the words below when you learn about whole numbers. How do these words relate to **Math on Location**?

estimate a number close to an exact amount

Distributive Property the property that states that multiplying a sum by a number is the same as multiplying each addend in the sum by the number and then adding the products

evaluate to find the value of a numerical or algebraic expression

WRITE Math

Copy a Venn diagram like the one below. Use what you know about multiplication and division to add more words.

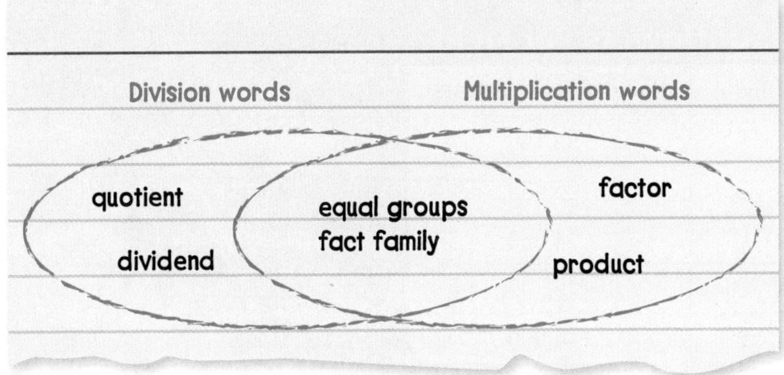

Technology
Multimedia Math Glossary link at
www.harcourtschool.com/hspmath

CHAPTER 1

Place Value, Addition, and Subtraction

Investigate

Suppose you are a sunflower farmer. This week, you need to harvest the flowers from three of your fields. Choose three fields from the table for harvesting. Write the number of sunflowers in those fields in order from least to greatest. Tell how many sunflowers will be harvested from the three fields you chose.

Sunflowers Per Field

Field	Number of Sunflowers
A	99,150
B	125,450
C	74,850
D	149,700
E	174,000

FAST FACT

Each sunflower actually is made up of as many as 2,000 smaller flowers within its center. The leaves of a sunflower are *phototropic,* which means they follow the rays of the sun.

GO ONLINE **Technology** Student pages are available in the Student eBook.

Show What You Know

Check your understanding of important skills needed for success in Chapter 1.

▶ Place Value Through Hundred Thousands

Write the value of the underlined digit.

1. 32$\underline{8}$,406 **2.** $\underline{4}$19,003 **3.** 16,$\underline{2}$97 **4.** 152,4$\underline{1}$9

5. 4$\underline{5}$6,107 **6.** 9,3$\underline{4}$2 **7.** $\underline{2}$04,593 **8.** $\underline{3}$8,452

▶ Round to Thousands

Round each number to the nearest thousand.

9. 837 **10.** 6,409 **11.** 13,526 **12.** 70,143

13. 4,810 **14.** 238,456 **15.** 42,718 **16.** 354,630

▶ Add and Subtract up to 4-Digit Numbers

Find the sum or difference.

17. $\begin{array}{r} 258 \\ +437 \\ \hline \end{array}$ **18.** $\begin{array}{r} 984 \\ -562 \\ \hline \end{array}$ **19.** $\begin{array}{r} 739 \\ -271 \\ \hline \end{array}$ **20.** $\begin{array}{r} 3,926 \\ +1,451 \\ \hline \end{array}$

21. $\begin{array}{r} 4,025 \\ +2,933 \\ \hline \end{array}$ **22.** $\begin{array}{r} 8,059 \\ -5,426 \\ \hline \end{array}$ **23.** $\begin{array}{r} 1,294 \\ +\ \ 638 \\ \hline \end{array}$ **24.** $\begin{array}{r} 9,162 \\ -2,543 \\ \hline \end{array}$

25. 67 + 45 + 83 **26.** 134 + 72 + 250

27. 563 − 209 **28.** 7,652 − 3,114

VOCABULARY POWER

CHAPTER VOCABULARY

billion
compatible numbers
difference
estimate
inverse operations
million
overestimate
period
round
sum
underestimate

WARM-UP WORDS

billion 1,000 million; written as 1,000,000,000

estimate a number close to an exact amount

overestimate an estimate that is greater than the exact answer

Place Value Through Millions

OBJECTIVE: Read and write whole numbers through millions.

Quick Review

Write the number that is 1,000 more than the given number.

1. 336
2. 1,230
3. 1,580
4. 3,975
5. 8,627

Vocabulary

period million

Learn

The diameter of the sun is 1,392,000 kilometers. To understand this distance, you need to understand the place value of each digit in 1,392,000.

A place-value chart contains periods. A **period** is a group of three digits separated by commas in a multi-digit number. The millions period is left of the thousands period. One **million** is written as 1,000,000.

Periods

MILLIONS			THOUSANDS			ONES		
Hundreds	Tens	Ones	Hundreds	Tens	Ones	Hundreds	Tens	Ones
		1,	3	9	2,	0	0	0
		$1 \times 1{,}000{,}000$	$3 \times 100{,}000$	$9 \times 10{,}000$	$2 \times 1{,}000$	0×100	0×10	0×1
		1,000,000	300,000	90,000	2,000	0	0	0

The place value of the digit 1 in 1,392,000 is millions. The value of 1 in 1,392,000 is $1 \times 1{,}000{,}000 = 1{,}000{,}000$.

Standard Form: 1,392,000

Word Form: one million, three hundred ninety-two thousand

Expanded Form: 1,000,000 + 300,000 + 90,000 + 2,000

More Examples

A **Standard Form:** 582,031

Word Form: five hundred eighty-two thousand, thirty-one

Expanded Form: 500,000 + 80,000 + 2,000 + 30 + 1

B **Standard Form:** 7,644,000

Word Form: seven million, six hundred forty-four thousand

Expanded Form: 7,000,000 + 600,000 + 40,000 + 4,000

KY MA-05-1.1.1 Students will: apply multiple representations (e.g., drawings, manipulatives, base-10 blocks, number lines, expanded form, symbols) to represent whole numbers (0 to 99,999,999); DOK 2 *also MA-05-1.1.2*

Place-Value Patterns

Mercury's speed as it orbits the sun is about 100,000 miles per hour. Pluto's speed is about 10,000 miles per hour. Compare the two speeds.

Example 1 Use a place-value chart.

Step 1

Write the numbers in a place-value chart.

MILLIONS			THOUSANDS			ONES		
Hundreds	Tens	Ones	Hundreds	Tens	Ones	Hundreds	Tens	Ones
			1	0	0,	0	0	0
				1	0,	0	0	0

×10

Step 2

Count the number of places in each number.
100,000 has 1 more place than 10,000.
100,000 is 10 times greater than 10,000.

So, Mercury's speed is 10 times greater than Pluto's speed.

You can use place-value patterns to rename a number.

Math Idea
As you move to the left in a place-value chart, the value of each place is ten times the value of the place to the right.

Example 2 Use place-value patterns.

Rename 10,000 using other place values.

10,000	**1 ten thousand**	**1 × 10,000**
10,000	**10 thousands**	**10 × 1,000**
10,000	**100 hundreds**	**100 × 100**

Guided Practice

1. Copy and complete the place-value chart to find the value of each digit.

MILLIONS			THOUSANDS			ONES		
Hundreds	Tens	Ones	Hundreds	Tens	Ones	Hundreds	Tens	Ones
		7,	3	3	3,	8	2	0
		7 × 1,000,000	3 × ■	3 × 10,000	■ × 1,000	8 × 100	■	0 × 1
		■	■	30,000	3,000	■	20	0

Write the value of the underlined digit.

2. 189,65$\underline{4}$,023
3. 925,$\underline{7}$07,436
4. 7$\underline{6}$,283
5. $\underline{3}$01,256,878

Write the number in two other forms.

6. 1,000,000 + 800,000 + 80,000 + 4,000 + 40 + 6
7. seven million, five hundred twenty thousand, thirty-two
8. 15,000,000
9. 991,030,000
10. TALK Math **Explain** how you would help someone understand why 230,100 is 100 times greater than 2,301.

Independent Practice and Problem Solving

Write the value of the underlined digit.

11. 8$\underline{4}$9,567,043
12. 118,0$\underline{5}$5,348
13. 9,$\underline{4}$22,850
14. 1$\underline{7}$,651,034
15. $\underline{9}$6,283
16. $\underline{6}$3,293,923
17. $\underline{4}$98,354,021
18. 28,2$\underline{5}$0,420

Write the number in two other forms.

19. 345,000
20. 199,100,003
21. 57,060,077
22. 3,000,916
23. 30,000,000 + 100,000 + 5,000 + 20
24. 400,000,000 + 9,000 + 60 + 2
25. eighteen million, seven hundred fifty-nine thousand
26. seventy million, two hundred fifty-eight thousand, six hundred twelve

What number makes the statement true?

27. 230,000 = 23 × ■
28. 8,550,000 = 855 × ■
29. 70,000,000 = ■ × 100
30. 600,000,000 = ■ × 1,000

USE DATA For 31–32, use the table.

31. Which planet is about 10 times as far as Earth is from the sun?
32. **Pose a Problem** Use the information in the table to write a problem. Have a classmate solve the problem.
33. **What's the Error?** Matt wrote the number four million, three hundred five thousand, seven hundred sixty-two as 4,350,762. Describe his error. Write the number in standard form.

Average Distance from the Sun (in thousands of km)			
Mercury	57,910	Saturn	1,429,000
Venus	108,200	Uranus	2,870,990
Earth	149,600	Neptune	4,504,300
Mars	227,940	Pluto	5,913,520
Jupiter	778,000		

34. WRITE Math **Explain** how you know that the value of the digit 5 in the numbers 150,000 and 100,500 is not the same.

Extra Practice on page 28, Set A

Learn About Benchmark Numbers

A **benchmark** is used as a point of reference. You can use a benchmark number to determine a reasonable estimate.

Example

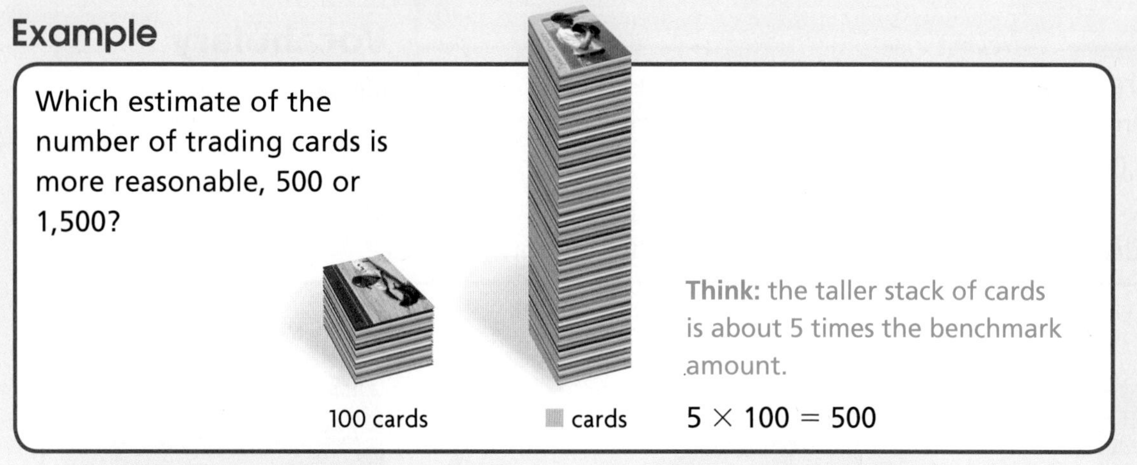

Which estimate of the number of trading cards is more reasonable, 500 or 1,500?

100 cards ■ cards

Think: the taller stack of cards is about 5 times the benchmark amount.

$5 \times 100 = 500$

So, the more reasonable estimate is 500.

Try It

Use the benchmark to find a reasonable estimate.

35. jelly beans in a full jar

100 jelly beans ■ jelly beans

36. tennis balls in a full carton

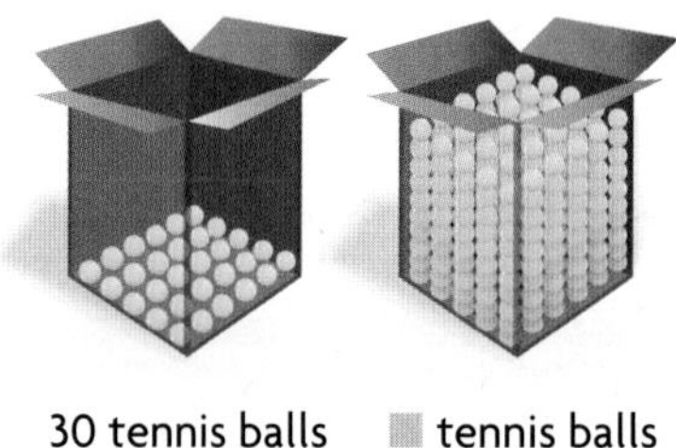

30 tennis balls ■ tennis balls

Mixed Review and Test Prep

37. Mr. Williams starts a movie at 2:30 P.M. The movie is 35 minutes long. What time will the movie end? (Grade 4)

38. **Test Prep** What is the value of the underlined digit in $34\underline{8},912,605$?

A 800,000,000 **C** 8,000,000

B 80,000,000 **D** 800,000

39. Kaitlin bought a movie ticket for \$6, a drink for \$3, and a snack for \$3. She started with \$20, how much money does she have left? (Grade 4)

40. **Test Prep** In 875,693,214, which digit is in the ten millions place?

A 8 **C** 9

B 7 **D** 1

LESSON 2

Understand Billions

OBJECTIVE: Read and write whole numbers through billions.

Quick Review

Carla says that the value of the digit 4 in 340,592 is 40. Is she correct? Explain.

Vocabulary

billion

Learn

PROBLEM Picture 1 billion pennies. How much space would they fill? One **billion** is 1,000 million. You can write 1 billion as 1,000,000,000.

Look at the pictures to understand the space filled by 1 billion pennies.

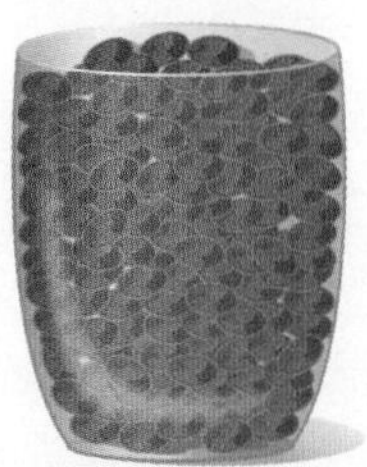

About 1,000 pennies could fill a small vase.

About 1,000,000 pennies could fill a car trunk.

About 1,000,000,000 pennies could fill half a basketball court to a height of 10 feet.

Example What is the value of the digit 3 in 3,205,720,000?

BILLIONS			MILLIONS			THOUSANDS			ONES		
Hundreds	Tens	Ones	Hundreds	Tens	Ones	Hundreds	Tens	Ones	Hundreds	Tens	Ones
		3,	2	0	5,	7	2	0,	0	0	0

The digit 3 is in the billions place, so its value is 3 × 1,000,000,000 or 3,000,000,000.

A number can be written in standard form, word form, or expanded form.

Standard Form: 13,181,260,000

Word Form: thirteen billion, one hundred eighty-one million, two hundred sixty thousand

Expanded Form: 10,000,000,000 + 3,000,000,000 + 100,000,000 + 80,000,000 + 1,000,000 + 200,000 + 60,000

ERROR ALERT

Remember when writing a number in expanded form that you do not need to include the values for places that have the digit 0.

Guided Practice

1. How can you use the place-value chart to find the value of the digit 4 in 38,752,491,050?

BILLIONS			MILLIONS			THOUSANDS			ONES		
Hundreds	Tens	Ones	Hundreds	Tens	Ones	Hundreds	Tens	Ones	Hundreds	Tens	Ones
	3	8,	7	5	2,	4	9	1,	0	5	0

Write the number in two other forms.

2. 2,000,000,000 + 20,000,000 + 3,000,000 + 30,000 + 500 + 6

3. TALK Math About how many pennies are shown at the right—1,000 pennies, 1,000,000 pennies, or 1,000,000,000 pennies? **Explain.**

Independent Practice and Problem Solving

Write the value of the underlined digit.

4. 1$\underline{2}$6,568,657,003
5. 3,$\underline{5}$83,007,165
6. $\underline{9}$,848,012,112
7. 3,20$\underline{5}$,772,994

Write the number in two other forms.

8. 4,000,000,000 + 60,000,000 + 5,000,000 + 40,000 + 200 + 8
9. seven billion, nine hundred three thousand, six hundred thirteen
10. 562,000
11. 7,000,145
12. 165,320,912
13. 40,920,001,000

USE DATA For 14–15, use the table.

Nickel Mass	
Number of Nickels	Mass (in grams)
1	5
10	50
100	500

14. How does the mass change from 1 nickel to 10 nickels to 100 nickels?
15. What is the mass of 1,000 nickels? **Explain.**
16. WRITE Math **Explain** which one of the following numbers cannot be a product of multiplying 1,087 repeatedly by 10.

    10,870; 180,700; 1,087,000

Mixed Review and Test Prep

17. John bought 5 packs of 8 collector cards and 1 pack of 3 cards. How many collector cards did John buy? (Grade 4)
18. The referee tosses a quarter to decide which football team kicks first. What is the probability of tossing tails? (Grade 4)
19. **Test Prep** What is the standard form of sixteen billion, three hundred seven thousand, forty-five?

    A 16,000,307,045
    B 16,000,370,045
    C 16,307,000,045
    D 16,307,045,000

Extra Practice on page 28, Set B

LESSON 3

Compare and Order Whole Numbers

OBJECTIVE: Use place value and number lines to compare and order whole numbers.

Quick Review

Compare. Write <, >, or =.

1. 132 ● 140
2. 1,541 ● 2,038
3. 17,008 ● 17,008
4. 5,612 ● 5,613
5. 62,100 ● 62,001

Learn

PROBLEM The United States Mint's 50 State Quarters program began in 1999. How does the number of minted Pennsylvania quarters compare with the number of minted Delaware quarters?

774,824,000 coins minted

707,332,000 coins minted

662,228,000 coins minted

939,932,000 coins minted

1,346,624,000 coins minted

ONE WAY **Use place value to compare. Start at the left. Compare the digits in each place-value position until the digits are different.**

Step 1	Step 2
Compare the hundred millions. 707,332,000 ↓ same 774,824,000	Compare the ten millions. 707,332,000 ↓ $7 > 0$ 774,824,000

So, 774,824,000 > 707,332,000, and 707,332,000 < 774,824,000. There were more Delaware quarters minted than Pennsylvania quarters.

Math Idea
On a number line, the greater number is to the right.

ANOTHER WAY **Use a number line to compare.**

Compare 99,638 and 100,204.

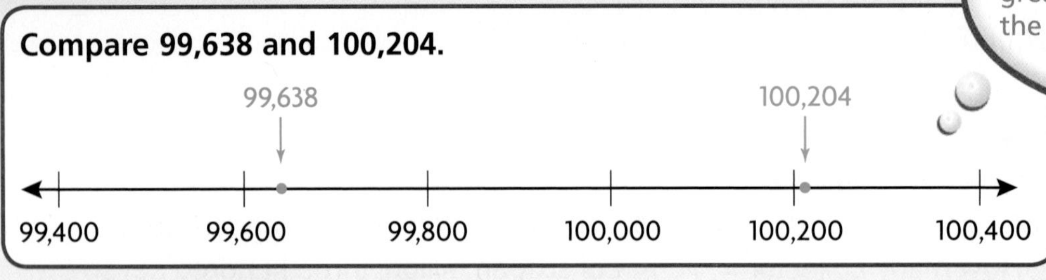

So, 99,638 < 100,204.

- Tell how the numbers 69,786,532 and 69,872,291 compare using words.

FAST TRACK

KY MA-05-1.1.3 Students will compare (<, >, =) and order whole numbers, fractions and decimals, and explain the relationships (equivalence, order) between and among them. DOK 2 *also* MA-05-1.1.1; *MA-05-1.1.2*

Order Whole Numbers

The Maryland quarter was released in 2000, and the New York quarter was released in 2001. Order from least to greatest the numbers of Connecticut, Maryland, and New York quarters minted.

1,234,732,000
coins minted

1,275,040,000
coins minted

1,346,624,000
coins minted

ONE WAY **Use place value.**

Step 1

Compare the billions.

1,234,732,000
1,275,040,000
1,346,624,000 same

Step 2

Compare the hundred millions.

1,234,732,000
1,275,040,000 $2 < 3$
1,346,624,000 ← greatest

Step 3

Compare the other two numbers at ten millions.

1,234,732,000 ← least
1,275,040,000 $3 < 7$
1,346,624,000

So, the states listed in order of quarters minted from least to greatest are Maryland, New York, and Connecticut.

ANOTHER WAY **Use a number line.**

A **Order from least to greatest.**

1,002; 1,091; 997

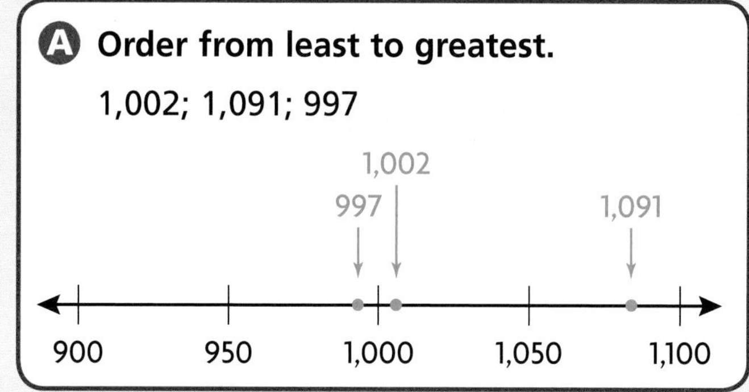

So, $997 < 1{,}002 < 1{,}091$.

B **Order from greatest to least.**

2,335,000; 2,381,000; 2,359,000

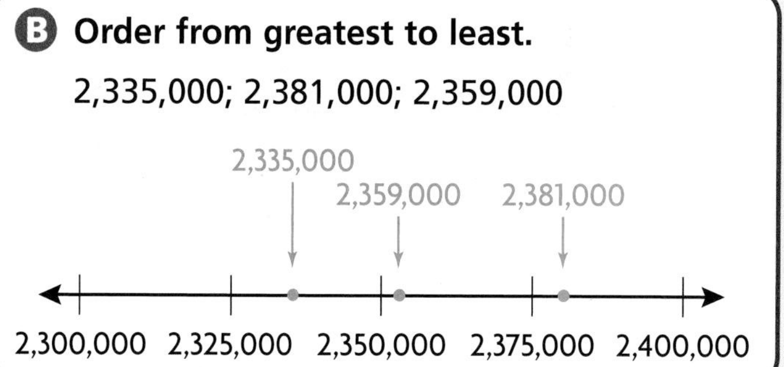

So, $2{,}381{,}000 > 2{,}359{,}000 > 2{,}335{,}000$.

Guided Practice

1. Use the place-value chart to compare the two numbers. What is the greatest place-value position where the digits differ?

THOUSANDS			ONES		
Hundreds	Tens	Ones	Hundreds	Tens	Ones
5	4	2,	9	0	0
5	4	4,	7	2	0

Compare. Write <, >, or = for each ●.

2. 32,403 ● 32,304

3. 102,405 ● 102,405

✓4. 2,306,821 ● 2,310,084

Name the greatest place-value position where the digits differ. Name the greater number.

5. 2,318; 2,328

6. 93,462; 98,205

✓7. 664,592,031; 664,598,347

Order from least to greatest.

8. 36,615; 36,015; 35,643

9. 5,421; 50,231; 50,713

10. 707,821; 770,821; 700,821

11. **TALK Math** Do you think it is easier to use place value or a number line to compare and order numbers? **Explain** your choice.

Independent Practice and Problem Solving

Compare. Write <, >, or = for each ●.

12. 8,942 ● 8,492

13. 603,506 ● 603,506

14. 7,304,552 ● 7,430,255

15. 1,908,102 ● 1,890,976

16. 530,240 ● 540,230

17. 10,670,210 ● 10,670,201

Order from least to greatest.

18. 503,203; 530,230; 305,320

19. 561,682,500; 561,862,500; 561,628,600

20. 1,092,303; 1,173,303; 1,292,210

21. 97,395; 98,593; 97,359

Order from greatest to least.

22. 85,694; 82,933; 85,600

23. 21,390,208; 21,309,280; 21,309,820

24. 5,505,055; 5,402,987; 5,577,001

25. 696,031; 966,301; 696,103

Algebra **Find the missing digit to make each statement true.**

26. $35{,}938 < 35{,}9\blacksquare 0 < 35{,}941$

27. $134{,}862 > 134{,}8\blacksquare 0 > 134{,}857$

USE DATA For 28–30, use the table.

28. In comparing the numbers of coins minted, what is the greatest place value where the digits differ?

29. How does the number of Turban Head coins minted compare for 1795 and 1796? Compare the numbers using words.

30. **WRITE Math** **Explain** how to order the numbers of coins minted from least to greatest.

Turban Head Ten-Dollar Coins

Year	Number of Coins Minted
1795	5,583
1796	4,416
1797	3,615

CD ROM Technology
Use Harcourt Mega Math, Fraction Action, *Number Line Mine*, Level B.

Extra Practice on page 28, Set C

Learn About Distance on a Number Line

You can use a number line to find the distance between two points.

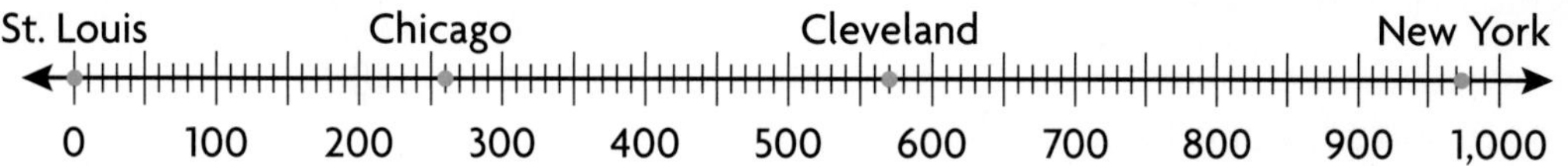

A Find the distance: Chicago to Cleveland.

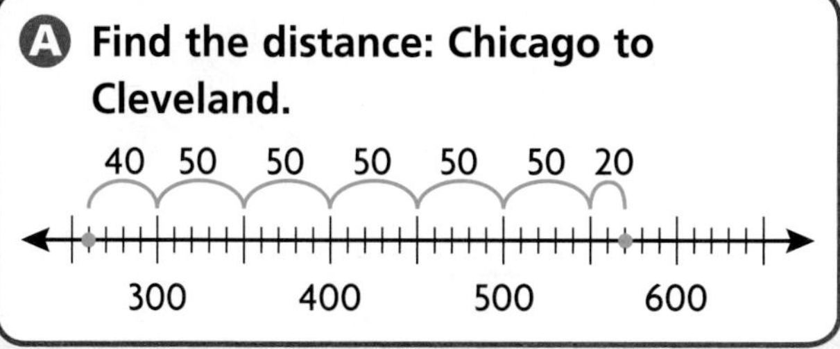

So, the distance is 310 miles.

B Find the distance: Cleveland to New York.

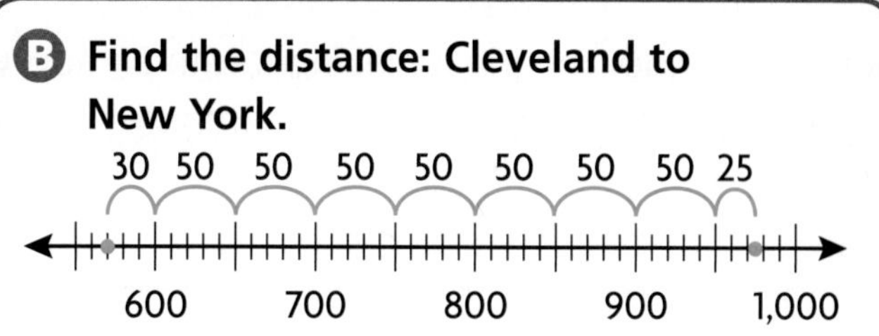

So, the distance is 405 miles.

Try It

Find the distance between each pair of points.

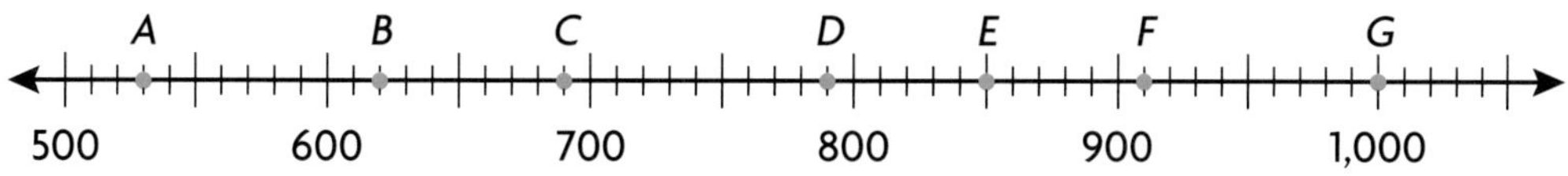

31. *A* and *B*; *A* and *C* **32.** *D* and *E*; *C* and *D* **33.** *D* and *G*; *C* and *E* **34.** *A* and *D*; *C* and *F*

35. **Explain** how you can use the number line to compare the distance between points *B* and *C* and points *B* and *D*.

Mixed Review and Test Prep

36. Mr. Bradshaw bought 3 dozen bagels. He gave his neighbor 6 bagels. How many bagels does he now have? (Grade 4)

37. **Test Prep** Which number is less than 46,726?

A 46,821

B 46,746

C 46,412

D 48,999

38. Write 1,000,750,000 in word form. (p. 8)

39. **Test Prep** Which shows the numbers in order from greatest to least?

A 8,107,450; 8,071,504; 8,059,631

B 8,059,631; 8,071,504; 8,107,450

C 8,071,504; 8,059,631; 8,107,450

D 8,107,450; 8,059,631; 8,071,504

4 Round Whole Numbers

OBJECTIVE: Round whole numbers to a given place value.

Quick Review

Tell whether the number is closer to 10,000 or 20,000.

1. 13,579 **2.** 18,208
3. 15,781 **4.** 11,627
5. 19,488

Learn

PROBLEM A newspaper reported that 43,855 people attended a baseball game at Camden Yard. During the game, a TV sportscaster rounded that number to 40,000. Is the sportscaster's estimate reasonable? Why?

Rounding a number means replacing it with an approximate number. A rounded number is often easier to compute.

ONE WAY **Use a number line.**

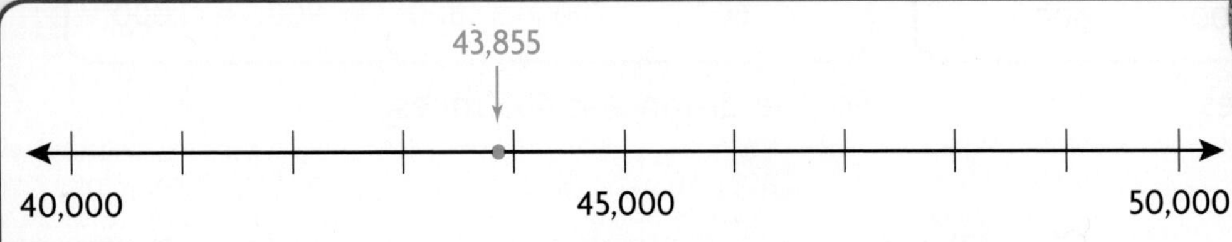

On the number line, 43,855 is between 40,000 and 50,000 but closer to 40,000.

So, the sportscaster's estimate is reasonable.

ANOTHER WAY **Use place value.**

Round 4,835,971 to the place of the underlined digit.

A Million

<u>4</u>,835,971
↓ 8 > 5
5,000,000 Round up.

4,835,971 rounded to the nearest million is 5,000,000.

B Hundred thousand

4,<u>8</u>35,971
↓ 3 < 5
4,800,000 Round down.

4,835,971 rounded to the nearest hundred thousand is 4,800,000.

Remember

When rounding, look at the digit to the right of the place to which you are rounding.

- If that digit is 5 or greater, round up.
- If that digit is less than 5, round down.
- Change each digit after the place being rounded to 0.

Guided Practice

1. Use the number line to round 38,778 to the nearest thousand.

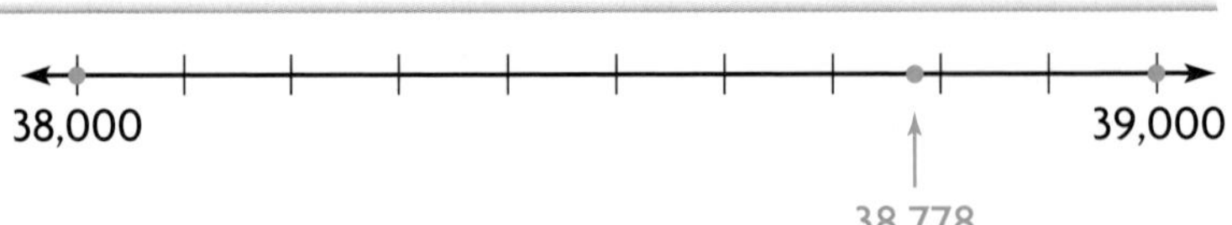

FAST TRACK

KY MA-05-1.2.1 Students will apply and describe appropriate strategies for estimating quantities of objects and computational results in real-world problems. DOK 2 *also* MA-05-1.1.1; *MA-05-1.1.2*

Round each number to the place of the underlined digit.

2. 6<u>7</u>,348 3. 141,<u>7</u>42 4. <u>8</u>,304,952 5. 1<u>2</u>,694,022 6. <u>3</u>6,402,695

7. TALK Math **Explain** why rounding 428,024 and 425,510 to the nearest ten thousand results in the same number.

Independent Practice and Problem Solving

Round each number to the place of the underlined digit.

8. 6<u>7</u>5,345,803
9. <u>3</u>,981
10. 26,<u>9</u>39,676
11. 500,35<u>7</u>,836
12. 56,<u>4</u>69
13. <u>2</u>4,508,349
14. 792,<u>4</u>06,314
15. <u>2</u>76,405,651

Name the place to which each number was rounded.

16. 56,037 to 60,000
17. 919,919 to 900,000
18. 65,308,976 to 65,309,000

Round 4,813,726 to the place named.

19. millions
20. ten thousands
21. thousands
22. hundred thousands

USE DATA For 23–24, use the table.

23. The total attendance of two basketball teams, rounded to the nearest ten thousand, are the same. Name the two teams.

24. **What's the Error?** Travis says that the total attendance at the Syracuse games, rounded to the nearest thousand, is 411,000. Is he correct? If not, what is his error?

25. WRITE Math A rounded number for the distance between two cities is 540 miles. What are the highest and the lowest numbers that round to 540? **Explain.**

2006 NCAA Men's Basketball

School	Total Attendance
Syracuse	410,153
Kansas	260,800
Illinois	265,888
Michigan State	206,626
Ohio State	261,622

Mixed Review and Test Prep

26. Hannah had $3,800. She bought a computer for $2,345 and a printer for $350. How much money did Hannah have left? (Grade 4)

27. Order the numbers from greatest to least. (p. 10)

18,493; 18,942; 18,053

28. **Test Prep** Name the place to which the number was rounded.

329,605,477 to 330,000,000

A hundred million
B ten million
C million
D hundred thousand

Extra Practice on page 29, Set D

Estimate Sums and Differences

OBJECTIVE: Estimate sums and differences of whole numbers.

Quick Review

Round each number to the place of the underlined digit.

1. <u>1</u>78,902
2. 34,<u>9</u>98
3. 2,5<u>0</u>3,499
4. 90<u>1</u>,694
5. <u>1</u>5,500,000

Vocabulary

estimate **underestimate**
compatible numbers **overestimate**

Learn

PROBLEM The continent of South America has many countries. The countries shown on the map have the greatest populations. About how many people live in Brazil and Colombia?

You can estimate sums and differences of whole numbers. An **estimate** is a number close to an exact amount.

Example 1 Use rounding.

Round the population of each country to the nearest ten million. Then add.

Brazil:	186,112,794 →	190,000,000
Colombia:	+ 42,954,279 →	+ 40,000,000
		230,000,000

So, about 230,000,000 people live in Brazil and Colombia.

More Examples

A **Round to the nearest hundred thousand.**

8,456,510 →	8,500,000
− 276,840 →	− 300,000
	8,200,000

B **Round to the nearest ten thousand.**

55,455 →	60,000
− 6,720 →	− 10,000
	50,000

C **Round to the nearest thousand.**

55,455 →	55,000
6,720 →	7,000
+ 30,200 →	+ 30,000
	92,000

You can also use compatible numbers to estimate.
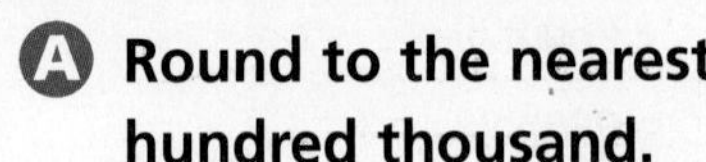
Compatible numbers are numbers that are easy to compute mentally.

Example 2 Use compatible numbers.

About how many more people live in Brazil than in Argentina?

Brazil:	186,112,794 →	200,000,000
Argentina:	− 39,537,943 →	− 50,000,000
		150,000,000

So, about 150,000,000 more people live in Brazil than in Argentina.

FAST TRACK

KY MA-05-1.2.1 Students will apply and describe appropriate strategies for estimating quantities of objects and computational results in real-world problems. DOK 2 *also* MA-05-1.1.1; MA-05-1.3.1

Overestimates and Underestimates

When an estimate is greater than the exact answer, it is called an **overestimate.** When an estimate is less than the exact answer, it is called an **underestimate.**

Example 3

Determine whether the estimate is an overestimate or an underestimate.

A Estimate:

$$\begin{array}{rcrl} 462{,}125 & \rightarrow & 400{,}000 & \leftarrow \text{Round down.} \\ +125{,}016 & \rightarrow & +100{,}000 & \leftarrow \text{Round down.} \\ \hline & & 500{,}000 & \end{array}$$

Since both addends are rounded down, the estimate, 500,000, is an underestimate.

B Estimate:

$$\begin{array}{rcrl} 17{,}705 & \rightarrow & 18{,}000 & \leftarrow \text{Round up.} \\ +21{,}868 & \rightarrow & +22{,}000 & \leftarrow \text{Round up.} \\ \hline & & 40{,}000 & \end{array}$$

Since both addends are rounded up, the estimate, 40,000, is an overestimate.

Math Idea

If each number is rounded up, the estimate will be an overestimate. If each number is rounded down, the estimate will be an underestimate.

Example 4 Find the range the answer will be within.

C **83,421 + 76,804**

underestimate	overestimate
80,000	90,000
+70,000	+80,000
150,000	170,000

The answer will be within the range of 150,000 to 170,000.

D **12,485 + 7,839**

underestimate	overestimate
12,000	13,000
+ 7,000	+ 8,000
19,000	21,000

The answer will be within the range of 19,000 to 21,000.

Guided Practice

1. Round each addend to the nearest thousand. Then estimate the sum.

   2,478 + 3,258

2. Use compatible numbers to estimate the difference.

   52,168 − 25,056

Estimate by rounding.

3. 2,490 − 1,053
4. 24,619 + 45,998
5. 67,209 + 28,584
6. 560,051 − 237,845
7. $51,922 − $39,104

Estimate by using compatible numbers.

8. $75,578 + $123,807   9. 24,796 + 38,879   10. $1,936 − $1,204   11. 89,494 − 18,302   ✓12. 103,883 + 71,852

13. TALK Math **Explain** why the estimate will be greater than the exact sum if each addend is rounded up.

Independent Practice and Problem Solving

Estimate by rounding.

14. $5,684 + $1,922   15. 506,108 − 397,281   16. 18,292 − 12,496   17. 93,386 + 76,194   18. 503,290 − 261,997

Estimate using compatible numbers or other methods.

19. 565,606 + 124,592   20. 39,402 + 61,695   21. $2,881 − $1,362   22. 90,203 + 87,392   23. 123,786 − 82,004

For 24–28, find the range the answer will be within.

24. 5,847 + 7,931   25. 55,723 + 27,205   26. 387 + 396   27. 1,387 + 5,396   28. 8,941 + 2,348

Estimate to compare. Write < or > for each ●.

29. 32,306 + 18,814 ● 40,000   30. 56,306 + 38,971 ● 90,000   31. 98,314 − 8,541 ● 80,000

32. 3,890 − 490 ● 3,000   33. 35,484 + 14,422 ● 50,000   34. 89,378 − 13,725 ● 75,000

USE DATA **For 35–37, use the table.**

35. About how much higher is the highest point in the Guiana Highlands than the highest point in the Brazilian Highlands?

36. What if the Coastal South America region were added to the table? Its area is 327,764 square miles. Estimate the total area of all four regions.

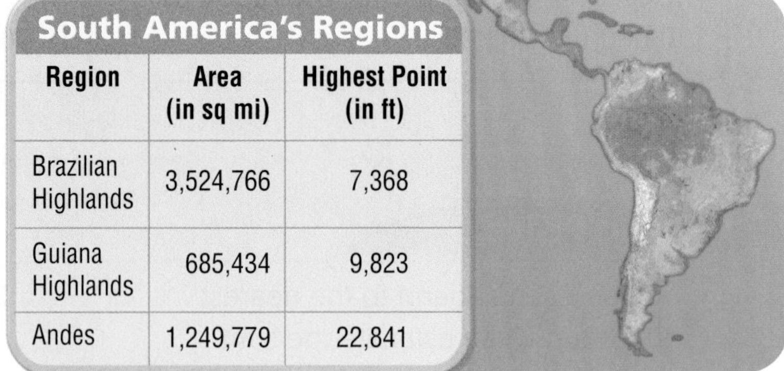

South America's Regions

Region	Area (in sq mi)	Highest Point (in ft)
Brazilian Highlands	3,524,766	7,368
Guiana Highlands	685,434	9,823
Andes	1,249,779	22,841

37. The tallest waterfall in the world, Angel Falls, is in the Guiana Highlands. It is 3,212 feet tall. Estimate the difference of this height and the highest point in the Guiana Highlands.

38. WRITE Math Marci's estimate for 1,384 + 742 is 2,000. **Explain** how she might have found her estimate.

Extra Practice on page 29, Set E

Learn About Front-end Estimation

Another useful estimation strategy is front-end estimation. When you use front-end estimation, you add or subtract the front, or leading, digits of each number. To get a closer estimate, you can adjust.

Example

Use front-end estimation to estimate 4,296 + 5,510.

Step 1	Step 2	Step 3
Add the values of the front digits of each number.	Estimate the remaining digits.	Adjust the estimate.
$4{,}296 \rightarrow 4{,}000$ $+5{,}510 \rightarrow +5{,}000$ $9{,}000$	296 $+510$ 800 296 + 510 is about 800	$9{,}000 + 800 = 9{,}800$

Try It

Use front-end estimation to estimate the sum or difference.

39. 6,481 + 557 + 1,935 **40.** 9,692 − 3,024 **41.** 963 + 540 **42.** $7,701 − $3,382

43. Explain how to use front-end estimation to find an estimate for 4,381 + 321 + 6,918.

Mixed Review and Test Prep

44. A painting is 3 feet wide and 2 feet long. What is its area? (Grade 4)

45. Write two thousand, eight hundred four kilometers in standard form. (p. 10)

46. Test Prep Estimate. Round to the nearest ten-thousand.

$$\begin{array}{r} 654{,}399 \\ +\,287{,}571 \\ \hline \end{array}$$

A 1,000,000 **C** 930,000

B 940,000 **D** 94,000

47. Test Prep Wendi went biking 4 days last week. The longest distance she rode in one day was 7 miles, and the shortest distance she rode was 5 miles. What is a reasonable total number of miles Wendi biked during the 4 days?

A Less than 7 mi

B Between 3 mi and 7 mi

C Between 5 mi and 9 mi

D More than 20 mi

LESSON 6

Add and Subtract Whole Numbers

OBJECTIVE: Add and subtract whole numbers.

Quick Review

Estimate the sum or difference.

1. \$379 + \$298
2. 14,668 − 8,015
3. \$2,359 − \$1,131
4. 74,952 + 3,883
5. 20,141 + 912 + 11,018

Vocabulary

inverse operations

Learn

PROBLEM Michigan's land area is 56,804 square miles. Its water surface area is 39,912 square miles. Find the total area of Michigan.

Example 1

Add. 56,804 + 39,912

Estimate. 60,000 + 40,000 = 100,000

$$\begin{array}{r} \scriptstyle 1\,1 \\ 56{,}804 \\ +\,39{,}912 \\ \hline 96{,}716 \end{array}$$

Start with the ones.
Regroup as needed.

So, the total area of Michigan is 96,716 square miles. This is close to the estimate of 100,000, so it is reasonable.

New York State has an area of 54,556 square miles. Its neighbor, New Jersey, has an area of 8,721 square miles. How much greater is New York's area than New Jersey's?

Example 2

Subtract. 54,556 − 8,721

Estimate. 50,000 − 10,000 = 40,000

$$\begin{array}{r} \scriptstyle 13 \\ \scriptstyle 4\ \not{3}\ 15 \\ \not{5}\not{4}{,}\not{5}56 \\ -\quad 8{,}721 \\ \hline 45{,}835 \end{array}$$

Start with the ones.
Regroup as needed.

So, New York's area is 45,835 square miles greater than New Jersey's area. Since 45,835 is close to the estimate of 40,000, it is reasonable.

- Explain the regrouping in Example 2.

FAST TRACK KY MA-05-1.3.1 Students will analyze real-world problems to identify appropriate representations using mathematical operations, and will apply operations to solve real-world problems with the following constraints: add, subtract, multiply and divide whole numbers (less than 100,000,000), using technology where appropriate. DOK 2 *also* MA-05-1.1.1

Add and Subtract Greater Numbers

The area of North America is 8,260,174 square miles. The area of South America is 6,765,422 square miles. How much greater is the area of North America than the area of South America?

ONE WAY **Use paper and pencil.**

Subtract. 8,260,174 − 6,765,422

Estimate. 8,000,000 − 7,000,000 = 1,000,000

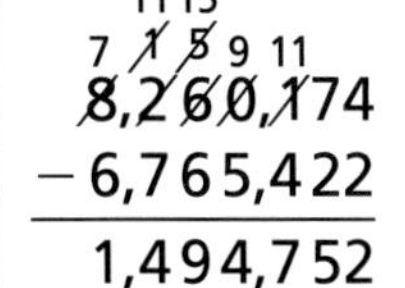

Start with the ones.
Regroup as needed.

ANOTHER WAY **Use a calculator.**

A calculator is very useful when computing with greater numbers.

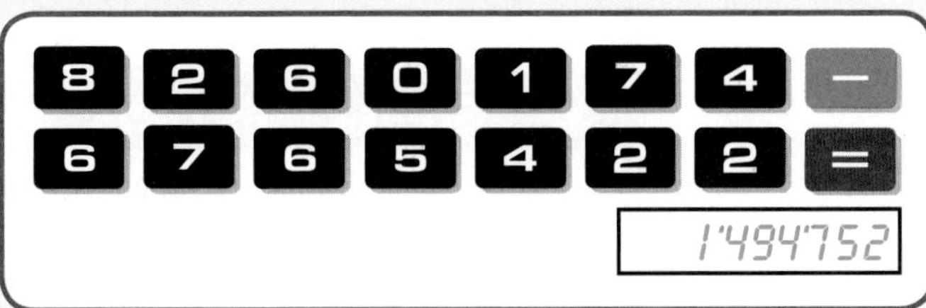

So, the area of North America is 1,494,752 square miles greater than the area of South America. Since this is close to the estimate of 1,000,000, it is reasonable.

Inverse operations are operations that undo each other. The inverse relationship allows you to check addition by using subtraction and to check subtraction by using addition.

- How can you check your answer in the example above?

Guided Practice

Copy and complete to find the sum or difference.

1. 32,146 + 18,219 = ■0,■65
2. 516,828 − 198,756 = ■1■,0■2
3. 6,941 + 9,387 = 1■,■2■
4. 702,418 − 319,295 = ■■3,12■

Estimate. Then find the sum or difference.

5. 3,794 + 2,073
6. 54,042 + 21,394
7. 409,232 − 403,243
8. 3,593,209 − 1,254,155
9. 789,039 + 325,155

10. **TALK Math** **Explain** how to find 92,010 − 61,764.

Independent Practice and Problem Solving

Estimate. Then find the sum or difference.

11. $4{,}596 + 9{,}293$ **12.** $39{,}515 + 69{,}036$ **13.** $109{,}958 - 102{,}989$ **14.** $480{,}084 + 515{,}765$ **15.** $2{,}308{,}027 - 1{,}456{,}328$

16. $8{,}023{,}154 + 731{,}636$ **17.** $129{,}993 + 74{,}875$ **18.** $67{,}846 - 38{,}559$ **19.** $1{,}009{,}875 - 872{,}945$ **20.** $6{,}693{,}071 + 2{,}381{,}305 + 1{,}043{,}829$

21. $43{,}831 + 8{,}375 + 30{,}294$ **22.** $4{,}801{,}123 - 1{,}956{,}627$ **23.** $100{,}230 - 76{,}834$

Algebra Find each missing value.

24. ■ − 2,346 = 9,638 **25.** 93,010 − ■ = 61,871 **26.** ■ + 197,794 = 200,010

27. **Reasoning** How can you use inverse operations to check your answers in Problems 24–26?

USE DATA For 28–31, use the table.

28. How many more square miles of surface area does Lake Superior have than Lake Erie?

29. What is the total water surface area of the Great Lakes?

30. The maximum depth of Lake Erie is 210 feet. Find the maximum depth of Lake Superior if its maximum depth is 1,122 feet greater than that of Lake Erie.

31. WRITE Math **What's the Question?** Tami and Paul compared the water surface areas of two lakes. The answer is 24,360 sq mi.

Great Lakes Facts

Lake	Water Surface Area (in sq mi)
Superior	31,700
Michigan	22,300
Ontario	7,340
Erie	9,910
Huron	23,000

Mixed Review and Test Prep

32. Write in standard form, the number that is 100,000 less than three hundred fifty thousand, seven hundred eighty-nine. (Grade 4)

33. **Test Prep** 628,315 + 547,906 =

A 1,761,221 **C** 1,176,221

B 1,716,212 **D** 1,176,211

34. Mr. Hudson has 8 boxes of 7 cups each. He can display 4 cups on each shelf. How many shelves does Mr. Hudson need for his cups? (Grade 4)

35. **Test Prep** The Summit Theater sold 35,890 tickets and the Capital Theater sold 59,741. How many more tickets did the Capital Theater sell?

 Extra Practice on page 29, Set F

Write to Explain

Pennsylvania ranks fifth in the United States for producing apples. In 2002, there were nearly 3,000,000 apple trees in 373 orchards in Pennsylvania. How many of those trees were 21 years old or less in 2002? **Explain** how to solve the problem.

There are important things you can do when explaining how to solve a problem. Writing a good explanation means learning how to carefully describe a process.

Pennsylvania's Apple Trees 2002	
Age (in yr)	**Number of Trees**
1–3	394,021
4–6	478,455
7–21	1,322,786
22+	619,177

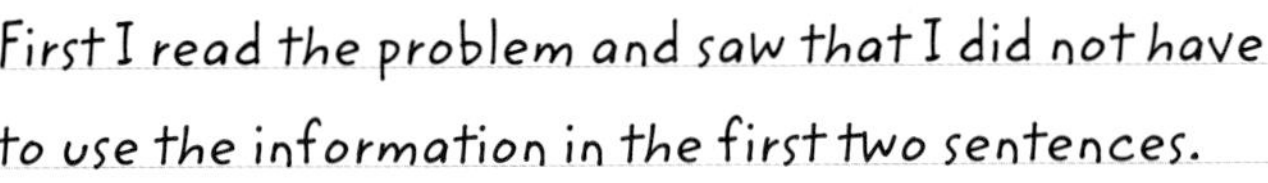

First I read the problem and saw that I did not have to use the information in the first two sentences.

Then I looked at the table and saw that I needed to add three of the numbers to find the number of trees 21 years old or less in 2002.

I added the numbers of trees that are 21 years or less to find the total.

Estimate: $400{,}00 + 500{,}000 + 1{,}300{,}000 = 2{,}200{,}000$

$394{,}021 + 478{,}455 + 1{,}322{,}786 = 2{,}195{,}262.$

The answer, 2,195,262, is reasonable because the estimate is about 2,200,000.

Tips

- Include only information needed.
- Write complete sentences, using transition words such as *first* and *then*.
- Break the explanation into steps to make it clear.
- Use math vocabulary to describe how to solve the problem.
- Draw a picture or a diagram if needed.
- Check that the answer is reasonable.

Problem Solving Explain how to solve the problem.

1. The Kane family travels on a 1,238-mile trip from New York City to Miami. The first day, the Kanes travel 405 miles, and the second day 390 miles. How many more miles must the Kane family travel to reach Miami?

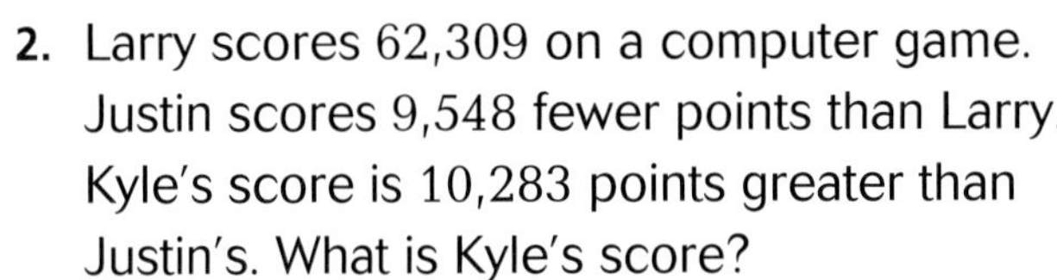

2. Larry scores 62,309 on a computer game. Justin scores 9,548 fewer points than Larry. Kyle's score is 10,283 points greater than Justin's. What is Kyle's score?

Problem Solving Workshop
Strategy: Work Backward

OBJECTIVE: Solve problems by using the strategy *work backward*.

Learn the Strategy

To work backward, identify the missing amount and decide the sequence of the information you are given.

Work backward when you know the result but are missing information from the beginning.

Mr. Warren teaches one piano lesson that lasts 45 minutes, two lessons that last 30 minutes each, and one lesson that lasts an hour. He finishes at 7:30. At what time does Mr. Warren begin piano lessons?

Work backward to find a missing amount.

James bought a watch for \$12, a pair of sneakers for \$23, and 4 CDs at \$11 each. He has \$15 left. How much money did James have before he went shopping?

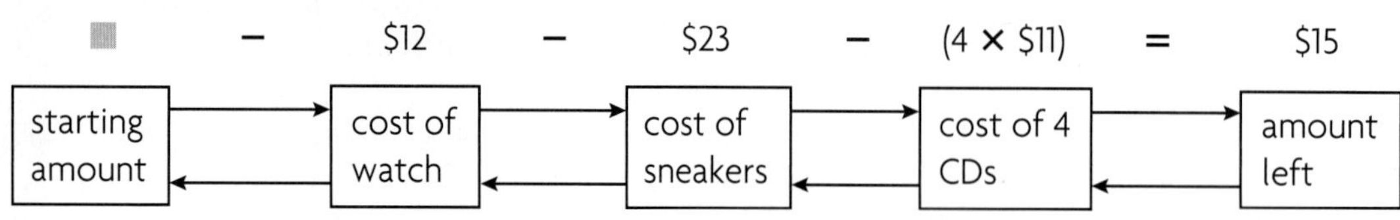

Work backward to check your solution.

Rebecca had 23 homework problems. She finished 5 problems after school. Then she finished 6 more before dinner. Rebecca thought she had 12 problems left to do to complete her homework. Was she correct?

$$23 - 5 - 6 = ■$$

Does $12 + 5 + 6 = 23$?

TALK Math

How do inverse operations help you *work backward* to find the answer?

FAST TRACK

KY MA-05-1.1.1 Students will: apply these numbers to represent real-world problems. DOK 2

Use the Strategy

PROBLEM Since 1974, the number of American bald eagle pairs has increased. From 1974 to 1990, the number of bald eagle pairs increased by 2,244. From 1990 to 2000, the number increased by 3,436. In 2000, 6,471 pairs of bald eagles were counted. How many bald eagle pairs were counted in 1974?

The American bald eagle was near extinction when the Endangered Species Act was passed in 1973.

- Read to Understand
- Plan
- Solve
- Check

Read to Understand

- **What information is not given?**
- **What is the sequence of the information?**

Plan

- **What strategy can you use to solve the problem?**

  You can *work backward* to solve the problem.

Solve

- **How can you use the strategy to solve the problem?**

  Identify the unknown amount and decide the sequence of the information. Determine the operations that you need to use and write a number sentence to model the problem.

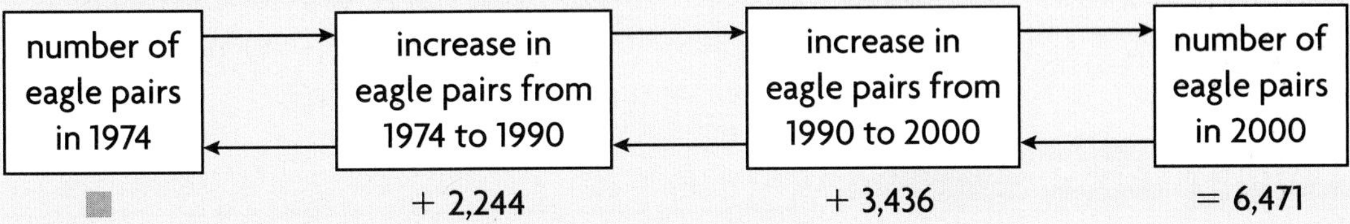

Begin at the end of the problem and use inverse operations. Work backward to solve for the missing number.

$6{,}471 - 3{,}436 - 2{,}244 = \blacksquare$

$6{,}471 - 3{,}463 - 2{,}244 = 791$

So, 791 bald eagle pairs were counted in 1974.

Check

- **How can you check your answer?**
- **Is your answer reasonable? Explain.**

Guided Problem Solving

1. The Iberian Lynx is one of the most endangered species of wild cats in the world. From 1995 to 2000, this lynx population decreased by 700. From 2000 to 2004, the Iberian Lynx population decreased again by 465. In 2004, only 135 Iberian Lynx remained. How many Iberian Lynx were counted in 1995?

First, identify the unknown amount. Decide the sequence of the information.

number of lynx in 1995	decrease in lynx from 1995 to 2000	decrease in lynx from 2000 to 2004	number of lynx in 2004
■	700	465	135

Then, decide which operations you need to use. Write a number sentence to model the problem.

$$■ - 700 - 465 = 135$$

Finally, use inverse operations to work backward to solve the number sentence.

$$135 + 465 + 700 = ■$$

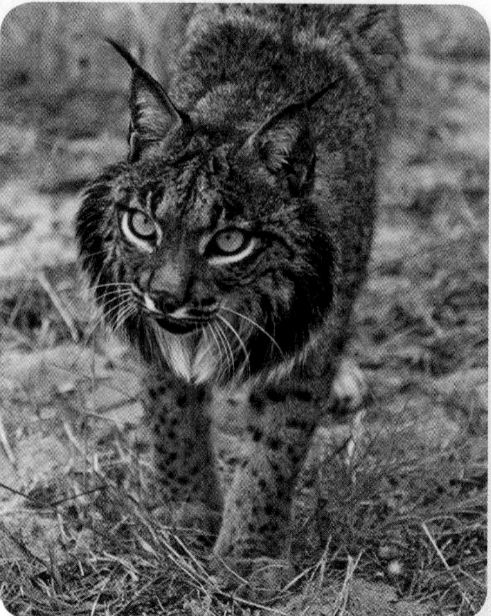

▲ **The Iberian Lynx, found in Spain and Portugal, is nearly extinct.**

2. **What if** the Iberian Lynx population had only decreased by 500 from 1995 to 2000? How many Iberian Lynx would have been counted in 1995?

3. On Saturdays, Samantha has stretching class for 45 minutes and ballet for an hour and a half. After a 30-minute break, she has jazz class for 1 hour, which is over at 1:45 P.M. At what time does she begin?

Problem Solving Strategy Practice

Work backward to solve.

4. A number is divided by 2, then 17 is added to the result. The answer is 41. What is the number?

5. Allison's field hockey team spent $438 of its budget on new equipment. After spending $87 to print programs, $112 of the budget remained. What was the budget before?

USE DATA For 6–7, use the table.

6. Richard spent 95¢. He bought 3 pencils, an eraser and some folders. How many folders did Richard buy?

7. Emily bought a notebook, a folder, and an eraser. Her change was 10¢. How much money did Emily have to start?

School Store

Item	Cost
Pencil	10¢
Eraser	5¢
Notebook	50¢
Folder	20¢

Mixed Strategy Practice

USE DATA **For 8–12, use the information in the table.**

Rhinos in 2005			
Type of Rhino	Number in the Wild	Number in Captivity	Total
Black	3,100	■	3,350
White	■	750	12,050
Indian	2,400	150	■
Sumatran	300	■	309
Javan	60	■	60
Total	■	■	18,319

8. Copy and complete the table.
9. How many more white rhinos are in the wild than in captivity?
10. The number of black rhinos in captivity is 50 less than 2 times the number of Indian rhinos in captivity. How many black rhinos are in captivity?
11. **Pose a Problem** Use the data in the table to write a problem. **Explain** how to find the answer to your problem.
12. **Open-Ended** How could you find the total number of rhinos in captivity without finding the numbers of black, Sumatran, and Javan rhinos in captivity?

CHALLENGE YOURSELF

Suppose a male white rhino at a zoo weighs 5,015 pounds and gained 493 pounds each year since he was born.

13. If the male white rhino is 10 years old, how much did he weigh when he was born?
14. Suppose a female white rhino at the zoo weighed 1,250 pounds less than the male rhino at her previous check-up. If the female rhino gained 389 pounds, what is her current weight?

Choose a STRATEGY

- Draw a Diagram or Picture
- Make a Model or Act It Out
- Make an Organized List
- Find a Pattern
- Make a Table or Graph
- Predict and Test
- Work Backward
- Solve a Simpler Problem
- Write an Equation
- Use Logical Reasoning

Extra Practice

Set A Write the value of the underlined digit. (pp. 4–7)

1. 5<u>6</u>,240
2. 19,<u>2</u>34,587
3. 328,264,5<u>8</u>2
4. <u>7</u>,694,560

Write each number in two other forms.

5. 618,268
6. 25,698,045
7. 1,965,038
8. 64,238,045
9. fifty-three million, four hundred sixty-one thousand, two hundred twelve
10. 6,000,000 + 200,000 + 30,000 + 4,000 + 100 + 90 + 7

What number makes the statement true?

11. 940,000 = 94 × ■
12. 30,000,000 = ■ × 100

Set B Write the value of the underlined digit. (pp. 8–9)

1. <u>7</u>,934,098,913
2. 2<u>3</u>6,957,483,538
3. 6,285,1<u>3</u>5,696
4. 314,<u>8</u>57,809,847

Write the number in two other forms.

5. 1,000,000,000 + 300,000,000 + 30,000,000 + 7,000,000 + 500,000 + 7
6. Eight billion, nine hundred seventy million, two hundred thousand, eighty

Set C Compare. Write <, >, or = for each ●. (pp. 10–13)

1. 106,447 ● 106,242
2. 514,659 ● 524,659

Order from least to greatest.

3. 705,984; 750,948; 700,937
4. 451,845,948; 415,945,058; 4,159,450,580

Order from greatest to least.

5. 567,867,585; 675,887,585; 576,687,855
6. 821,067; 812,958; 821,076
7. At a Saturday game, there were 54,905 people at the stadium. At the Sunday game there were 54,095 people. Which game had more people in attendance?
8. The population of deer in Louisiana in 2005 was 4,523,628. In Alabama the deer population was 4,557,808. Which state had a greater population of deer?

CD ROM **Technology**
Use Harcourt Mega Math, The Number Games, *Tiny's Think Tank*, Level A

Set D Round each number to the place of the underlined digit. (pp. 14–15)

1. 9<u>5</u>8,676,960
2. <u>2</u>03,968,685
3. 424,5<u>8</u>6,686
4. 12,955,<u>9</u>60

Name the place to which each number was rounded.

5. 76,960 to 77,000
6. 687,684 to 690,000
7. 1,284,955 to 1,284,960

Round 7,596,459,456 to the place named.

8. ten thousands
9. millions
10. hundreds
11. thousands

Set E Estimate using compatible numbers or other methods. (pp. 16–19)

1. 845,686 + 659,342
2. 76,789 − 32,964
3. $5,748 − $2,466
4. 157,658 + 585,057
5. 45,912 + 24,610

For 6–10, find the range the answer will be within.

6. 6,473 + 3,234
7. 32,959 + 15,568
8. 79,484 + 8,933
9. 56,394 + 23,696
10. 4,586 + 2,485

Estimate to compare. Write < or > for each ●.

11. 32,860 + 20,100 ● 60,000
12. 10,976 + 9,805 ● 18,000
13. 54,406 − 5,032 ● 40,000

14. In 2005, 25,347 baby boys were named Jacob in the United States. 14,116 boys were named Nathan. About how many more boys were named Jacob than Nathan?

15. In 2005, 23,544 baby girls were named Emily in the United States. In 2004, 24,897 girls were named Emily. About how many fewer girls were named Emily in 2005 than in 2004?

Set F Estimate. Then find the sum or difference. (pp. 20–23)

1. 3,496 + 4,714
2. 245,965 − 124,849
3. 2,475,585 + 3,494,083
4. 2,394,596 − 56,394
5. 45,759 − 12,368

6. 21,658 + 85,262
7. 438,932 − 264,588
8. 2,614,525 + 156,943

9. Jerry has put together 3,921 pieces of a puzzle. He has 1,579 pieces left in the box. How many pieces are there in all of the puzzle?

10. A male elephant at the zoo weighs 13,894 pounds. A female elephant weighs 12,907 pounds. How much more does the male elephant weigh?

MATH POWER

Other Ways to Add and Subtract

Fitness Fun!

Field Day at Stewart Elementary includes Grades 3, 4, and 5. There were 237 Grade 3 students, 369 Grade 4 students, and 409 Grade 5 students.

Examples

A Partial-Sums Method for Addition

How many students at Stewart Elementary participated in Field Day?

$237 + 369 + 409 = ?$

Add hundreds.	200 + 300 + 400 =	900
Add tens.	30 + 60 + 0 =	90
Add ones.	7 + 9 + 9 =	+ 25
Add partial sums.		1,015

So, 1,015 students participated in Field Day at Stewart Elementary.

B Counting-Up Method for Subtraction

How many more Grade 5 students than Grade 3 students participated in Field Day?

$409 - 237 = ?$

Start with the smaller number.	237	
Count up to the next ten.	+ 3 → 240	3
Count up to the next hundred.	+ 60 → 300	60
Count up to match hundreds.	+ 100 → 400	100
Count up to the larger number.	+ 9 → 409	+ 9
Find the sum of the numbers you added.		172

So, 172 more Grade 5 students than Grade 3 students participated in Field Day.

Try It

Use the partial-sums or the counting-up method to find the sum or difference.

1. 185 + 427
2. 376 + 152 + 827
3. 386 − 228
4. 802 − 655
5. 29 + 305 + 912

6. The cafeteria served 567 lunches on Wednesday and 492 lunches on Thursday. How many lunches were served on both days?

7. WRITE Math Use the method from page 20 and the partial-sums method to find 325 + 107 + 416. Which method do you prefer? **Explain.**

Chapter 1 Review/Test

Check Vocabulary and Concepts

Choose the best term from the box.

1. A group of three digits in a multi-digit number. KY MA-05-1.1.1 (p. 4)
2. Numbers that are easy to compute mentally. KY MA-05-1.2.1 (p. 16)
3. Operations that undo each other. KY MA-05-1.3.1 (p. 21)

VOCABULARY
- compatible numbers
- period
- inverse operations
- estimate

Check Skills

Write the value of the underlined digit. KY MA-05-1.1.1 (pp. 4–7)

4. $6\underline{7},049,595$
5. $34,\underline{6}89,431$
6. $4,869,\underline{3}87$
7. $2\underline{1},214,509$

Compare. Write <, >, or = for each ●. KY MA-05-1.1.3 (pp. 10–13)

8. 86,565 ● 86,556
9. 54,613 ● 56,413
10. 90,342 ● 900,342

Estimate using compatible numbers or other methods. KY MA-05-1.2.1 (pp. 16–19)

11. 54,960 + 29,494
12. 414,953 − 238,548
13. 45,960 + 23,438
14. \$3,952 + \$2,405

Estimate. Then find the sum or difference. KY MA-05-1.3.1 (pp. 20–23)

15. 5,903,329 + 2,942,712
16. 23,483 − 13,201
17. 8,487,284 − 3,592,871
18. 34,593 + 11,278

Check Problem Solving

Solve. KY MA-05-1.1.1 (pp. 24–27)

19. During practice a football team stretches for 15 minutes, sprints for 35 minutes, and plays a practice game for 1 hour and 10 minutes. If practice ends at 4:15 P.M., what time does it begin?

20. **WRITE Math** Jack and his mother paid \$11.50 for tickets to the movies. An adult's ticket costs \$4.50 more than a child's ticket. What was the cost of each ticket? **Explain** how you can decide if your answer makes sense.

Technology Use *Online Assessment.*

Practice for the KCCT
Chapter 1

Number Properties and Operations

1. Order the numbers from least to greatest. KY MA-05-1.1.3 (p. 10)

   79,138; 77,630; 78,959; 78,754

   A 77,630; 78,754; 78,959; 79,138

   B 77,630; 78,959; 78,754; 79,138

   C 78,754; 78,959; 79,138; 77,630

   D 79,138; 78,959; 78,754; 77,630

Eliminate Choices.

See item 2. Look at the hundreds place of each number. Decide whether you should round up or down.

2. The zoo made a table to show the number of visitors each year. In what year was the number of visitors about 16,000? KY MA-05-1.2.1 (p. 14)

Visitors to the Zoo	
Year	**Number of Visitors**
2003	16,919
2004	15,420
2005	16,845
2006	15,735

   A 2003 C 2005

   B 2004 D 2006

3. WRITE Math **Explain** how you know that the value of the digit 3 in the numbers 305,000 and 503,000 are not the same. KY MA-05-1.1.1 (p. 4)

Algebraic Thinking

4. Angela drew this diagram of her bedroom. What is the area of her bedroom? KY Grade 4

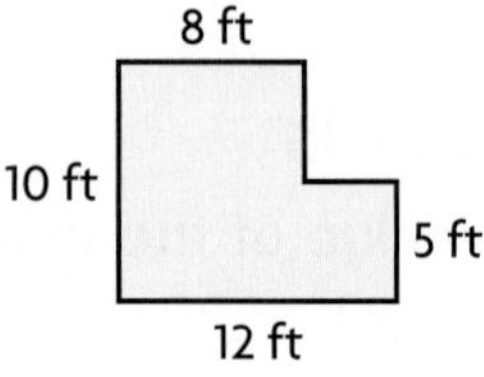

   A 92 square feet

   B 100 square feet

   C 140 square feet

   D 146 square feet

5. It took Kiera 300 seconds to walk home from her friend's house. How many minutes did it take Kiera to walk home? KY Grade 4

   A 5 minutes C 30 minutes

   B 15 minutes D 50 minutes

6. WRITE Math Robyn wants to buy a new bicycle that costs \$99. She has saved \$58. Let m represent the amount of money she still needs to buy the bicycle. What equation could Robyn write to find how much money she still needs? **Explain** how you can check your answer. KY Grade 4

Geometry

7. Which figure below is a ray? KY Grade 4

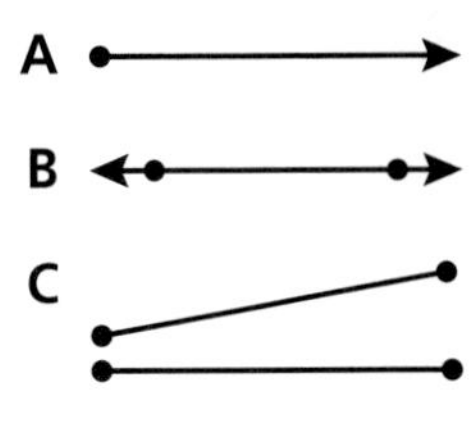

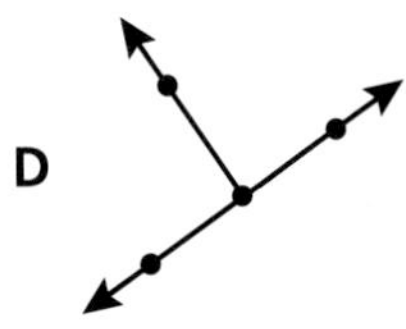

8. Ella drew this figure. Then she turned the figure 90°. Choose the figure below that shows a 90° turn. KY Grade 4

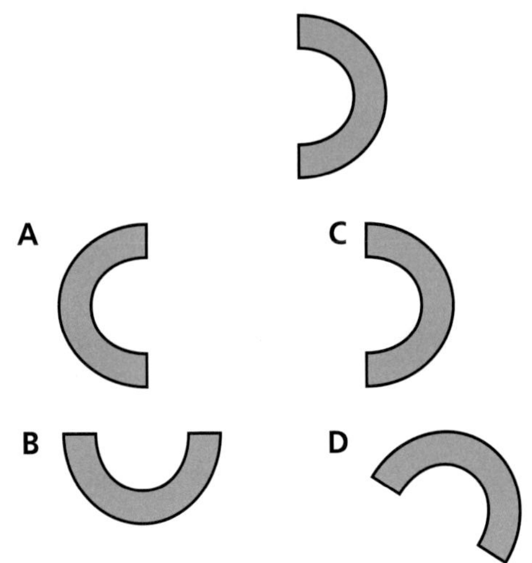

9. WRITE Math How many edges are there on a square pyramid? **Explain** how you know. KY Grade 4

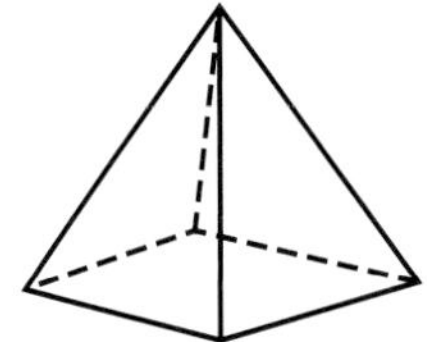

Data Analysis and Probability

10. Marcia made a table to show the clothes she is packing for a trip. How many combinations of skirts and sweaters can Marcia make? KY Grade 4

Clothes to Pack	
red skirt	white sweater
blue jeans	orange T-shirt
blue skirt	green sweater
brown pants	black sweater
black skirt	blue sweater

A 7 **C** 12

B 8 **D** 16

11. Jamie can buy milk or orange juice. Each comes in a pint, quart, or gallon. How many choices does Jamie have? KY Grade 4

A 3 **C** 6

B 5 **D** 9

12. WRITE Math What is the probability that Micah will pull a red marble from this bag? Write your answer as a fraction in simplest form. **Explain** how you know. KY Grade 4

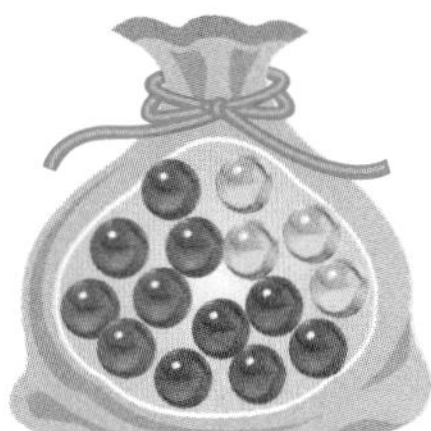

CHAPTER 2

Multiply Whole Numbers

Investigate

You are a scientist studying penguin populations. You have noticed that the population of Adelie penguins is about 4 times as great as the population of southern rockhopper penguins. Choose two species of penguins. Estimate how many times as great as one population is than the other.

Penguin Populations Worldwide

Species	Estimated Population (in pairs)
Adelie	2,500,000
Northern Rockhopper	350,000
Southern Rockhopper	650,000
Macaroni	9,000,000
Emperor	220,000

FAST FACT

Emperor penguins are the largest of all penguins and can grow to a height of nearly 4 feet. Emperor penguins live an average of about 20 years.

GO ONLINE

Technology
Student pages are available in the Student eBook.

Show What You Know

Check your understanding of important skills needed for success in Chapter 2.

▶ Multiply Basic Facts and Multiples of 10

Find the product.

1. 90×7

2. 40×6

3. 50×7

4. 20×8

5. 30×9

6. 60×6

7. 80×4

8. 70×8

9. 5×40

10. 9×60

11. 6×30

12. 80×3

▶ Mutiply 2-Digit Numbers

Find the product.

13. 14×6

14. 23×4

15. 19×5

16. 31×8

17. 56×3

18. 97×2

19. 37×9

20. 69×4

21. 72×5

22. 86×7

23. 63×5

24. 96×3

25. 62×2

26. 76×3

27. 48×6

28. 88×4

VOCABULARY POWER

CHAPTER VOCABULARY

basic fact
Distributive Property
multiple
partial product
pattern
product
regroup

WARM-UP WORDS

Distributive Property the property that states that multiplying a sum by a number is the same as multiplying each addend in the sum by the number and then adding the products

multiple The product of two counting numbers is a multiple of each of those numbers.

product the answer to a multiplication problem

MENTAL MATH
Patterns in Multiples

OBJECTIVE: Multiply basic facts using mental math and patterns of zeros.

Quick Review

1. 5×10
2. 6×20
3. 9×40
4. 80×3
5. 7×70

Learn

PROBLEM A colony of Macaroni penguins may contain thousands of nests. The colony population is found by counting the nests. Suppose a Macaroni penguin colony has 12,000 nests, each with two adults and one chick. About how many penguins are there in the colony?

▲ The Macaroni penguin got its name because its head feathers look like the hat made famous by the song "Yankee Doodle".

Example Multiply. 3 × 12,000

You can use basic facts and patterns in factors that are multiples of 10 to find products.

$3 \times 12 = 36$ basic fact
$3 \times 120 = 3 \times 12 \times 10 = 360$ basic fact times 10
$3 \times 1{,}200 = 3 \times 12 \times 100 = 3{,}600$ basic fact times 100
$3 \times 12{,}000 = 3 \times 12 \times 1{,}000 = 36{,}000$ basic fact times 1,000

So, the colony has about 36,000 Macaroni penguins in all.

- Count the number of zeros in a factor that is a multiple of 10. How is it related to the number of zeros in the product?

More Examples Use basic facts and a pattern.

A
$4 \times 5 = 20$
$4 \times 50 = 200$
$4 \times 500 = 2{,}000$
$4 \times 5{,}000 = 20{,}000$

B
$6 \times 8 = 48$
$6 \times 80 = 480$
$6 \times 800 = 4{,}800$
$60 \times 800 = 48{,}000$

Math Idea
You can use mental math to find the product. Start with the basic fact. Then count the number of zeros in each multiple of 10. Add the same number of zeros to the end of the product.

Guided Practice

Find the missing numbers.

1. $4 \times 4 = ■$
   $4 \times 40 = ■$
   $40 \times 40 = ■$
2. $5 \times 2 = ■$
   $5 \times 20 = ■$
   $5 \times 200 = ■$
3. $2 \times 3 = ■$
   $2 \times 30 = ■$
   $20 \times 30 = ■$
4. $8 \times 7 = ■$
   $8 \times 70 = ■$
   $8 \times 700 = ■$

Find the product.

5. 3×40
6. 2×500
7. 60×70
✓8. 80×100
✓9. 3×30

10. TALK Math **Explain** how 5×7 and patterns of zeros can help you find the product of a very large number like $500 \times 70{,}000$.

KY MA-05-1.3.1 Students will analyze real-world problems to identify appropriate representations using mathematic operations, and will apply operations to solve real-world problems with the following constraints: add, subtract, multipl and divide whole numbers (less than 100,000,000), using technology where appropriate. DOK 2 *also* MA-05-1.1.

Independent Practice and Problem Solving

Find the product.

11. 40×80 **12.** 8×200 **13.** 3×400 **14.** 9×700 **15.** 10×500

16. 11×100 **17.** 60×300 **18.** 90×120 **19.** $7 \times 6{,}000$ **20.** $1{,}100 \times 12$

Algebra **Find the missing number.**

21. $3 \times 7{,}000 = ■$ **22.** $50 \times ■ = 4{,}500$ **23.** $■ \times 600 = 5{,}400$ **24.** $8 \times 3{,}000 = ■$

25. $70 \times 80 = ■$ **26.** $20 \times ■ = 8{,}000$ **27.** $■ \times 500 = 3{,}000$ **28.** $■ \times 50 = 200$

USE DATA **For 29–31, use the krill facts.**

29. Krill lay eggs, or spawn, several times in one season. If a krill lays eggs 4 times, about how many eggs will it lay?

30. Suppose a penguin eats about 5 pounds of krill a day. About what number of krill does the penguin eat in 100 days? (Hint: 1 pound = 16 ounces.)

31. **Reasoning** Researchers discovered a large group of krill that was more than 30,000 feet long. About how long is 30,000 feet, measured in the number of krill?

32. WRITE Math **Explain** how you can tell without multiplying that $700 \times 60{,}000$ and $7{,}000 \times 6{,}000$ have the same value.

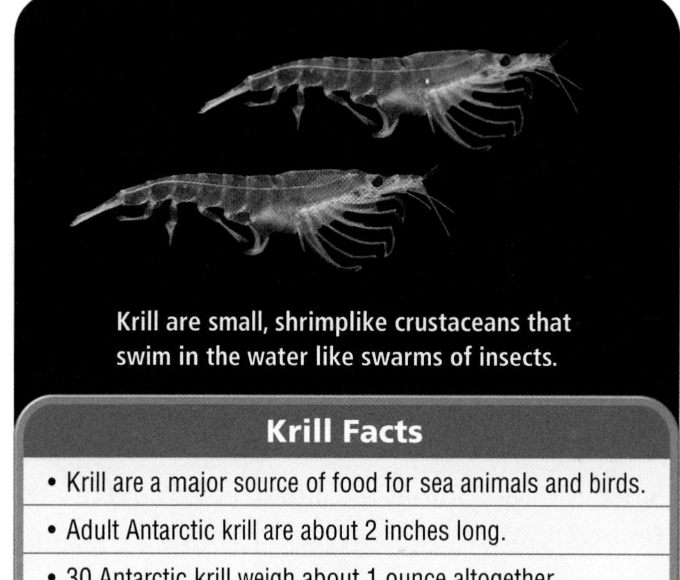

Krill are small, shrimplike crustaceans that swim in the water like swarms of insects.

Krill Facts
• Krill are a major source of food for sea animals and birds.
• Adult Antarctic krill are about 2 inches long.
• 30 Antarctic krill weigh about 1 ounce altogether.
• A krill lays about 8,000 eggs at a time.

Mixed Review and Test Prep

33. While visiting South Georgia Island in the South Atlantic Ocean, a biologist took 783 photos of penguins and 224 photos of seals. About how many photographs did the biologist take? (p. 16)

34. The side of a square is 2 meters long. What is the area of the square? What is the perimeter of the square in centimeters? (Grade 4)

35. **Test Prep** Tickets to an exhibition basketball game cost \$80 each. How much money will be made from ticket sales if 9,000 tickets are sold?

A \$72,000

B \$720,000

C \$7,200,000

D \$72,000,000

Extra Practice on page 52, Set A

LESSON 2

Estimate Products

OBJECTIVE: Estimate products by rounding and using the expanded form of numbers.

Quick Review

1. 3×600
2. $5 \times 3{,}000$
3. 70×900
4. 80×50
5. 90×400

Learn

PROBLEM A company wants to buy 58,000 board feet of lumber to build 4 houses. Mr. Nelson has 23 acres of land. Each acre has enough trees to make an average of about 3,245 board feet of lumber. Does Mr. Nelson have enough trees to sell the company to build the 4 houses?

You do not need to know the exact number of board feet of lumber in 23 acres, so you can estimate.

▲ A board foot usually measures 1 foot by 1 foot by 1 inch.

Example Estimate. 3,245 × 23

Step 1

Round both factors to the greatest place value.

$$\begin{array}{c} 23 \times 3{,}245 \\ \downarrow \quad \downarrow \\ 20 \times 3{,}000 \end{array}$$

Step 2

Use the basic fact and patterns of multiples of 10 to find the estimate.

$$\begin{aligned} 20 \times 3{,}000 &= 2 \times 10 \times 3 \times 1{,}000 \\ &= 6 \times 10{,}000 \\ &= 60{,}000 \end{aligned}$$

Since Mr. Nelson has enough trees to make about 60,000 board feet of lumber, he could sell them to the company.

- Is 60,000 an overestimate of 23 × 3,245 or an underestimate? Explain.

More Examples

A Basic fact and a multiple of 10

$$\begin{array}{c} 6 \times 593 \\ \downarrow \\ 6 \times 600 = 3{,}600 \end{array}$$

B Basic fact and two multiples of 10

$$\begin{array}{c} 480 \times 422 \\ \downarrow \quad \downarrow \\ 500 \times 400 = 200{,}000 \end{array}$$

C Basic fact with greater numbers

$$\begin{array}{c} 90{,}189 \times 794 \\ \downarrow \quad \downarrow \\ 90{,}000 \times 800 = 72{,}000{,}000 \end{array}$$

D Nearest dollar

$$\begin{array}{c} 7 \times \$9.16 \\ \downarrow \\ 7 \times \$9.00 = \$63.00 \end{array}$$

FAST TRACK

KY MA-05-1.2.1 Students will apply and describe appropriate strategies for estimating quantities of objects and computational results in real-world problems. DOK 2 *also* MA-05-1.1.1; MA-05-1.3.1

Guided Practice

1. Copy and complete the problem to estimate the product.

$$28 \times 4{,}125$$
$$\downarrow \quad \downarrow$$
$$\blacksquare \times 4{,}000 = \blacksquare \times 10 \times 4 \times \blacksquare$$
$$= \blacksquare \times 10{,}000$$
$$= \blacksquare$$

Estimate the product.

2. 76 × 41
3. 122 × 67
4. $9.65 × 18
5. 32 × 723
6. 48 × 612

7. **TALK Math** **Explain** why you can sometimes estimate instead of finding an exact answer.

Independent Practice and Problem Solving

Estimate the product.

8. 53 × 22
9. 96 × 51
10. 37 × 13
11. 626 × 94
12. 82 × $5.86
13. 28 × 491
14. 76 × 927
15. 5,678 × 31
16. 29 × 7,059
17. 2,492 × 65
18. 1,682 × 73
19. 2,351 × 505
20. 589 × 3,208
21. $21.07 × 29
22. 32 × 89,075

USE DATA For 23–25, use the table.

23. The Conservation Society raised $17,000 to buy 38 magnolia trees for a city park. Estimate to find whether the group raised enough money to buy the trees.

24. The Conservation Society has $6,000 to spend on oleander bushes to plant along a bike trail. Estimate to find whether it has enough money to buy 215 bushes.

25. **Pose a Problem** Look back at Problem 23. Write a similar problem by changing the type of plant and the numbers.

Conservation Society Expenses

Item	Cost
Magnolia tree	$412
Oleander bush	$33
Camellia tree	$129
Hibiscus bush	$54

26. **WRITE Math** Estimate the product 2,788 × 48. **Explain** whether it is an overestimate or an underestimate.

Mixed Review and Test Prep

27. The Conservation Society planted 8,147 flowers in the spring and 3,821 flowers in the summer. Estimate the total number of flowers they planted. (p. 18)

28. Find the median of the data set. (Grade 4)

    63, 48, 56, 60, 51

29. **Test Prep** Which would give the best estimate for 38 × 727?

    A 30 × 700
    B 30 × 800
    C 40 × 700
    D 40 × 800

Extra Practice on page 52, Set B

LESSON 3 Multiply by 1-Digit Numbers

OBJECTIVE: Multiply by a 1-digit number.

Quick Review

Estimate the product.

1. 4 × 672
2. 335 × 3
3. 1,806 × 7
4. 5 × 7,891
5. 8,288 × 4

Vocabulary

Distributive Property

Learn

PROBLEM An airline flies six 747 jets from New York to Paris every day. If each flight carries an average of 238 passengers, how many passengers fly on this airline from New York to Paris every day?

◀ **The cruising altitude of a 747 jet is 35,000 feet. The flying time from New York to Paris is about 7 hours 13 minutes.**

Use the Distributive Property.

Example **Multiply.** 6 × 238 **Estimate.** 6 × 200 = 1,200

The **Distributive Property** states that multiplying a sum by a number is the same as multiplying each addend in the sum by the number and then adding the products.

Step 1

Write the greater factor in expanded form.

6 × 238 = 6 × (200 + 30 + 8)

Step 2

Multiply each addend by 6.

6 × 238 = 6 × (200 + 30 + 8)
= (6 × 200) + (6 × 30) + (6 × 8) Multiply to find the partial products.
= 1,200 + 180 + 48 Add the partial products.
= 1,428

Compare the product to the estimate.
Since 1,428 is close to 1,200, it is a reasonable answer.

So, the airline flies an average of 1,428 passengers from New York to Paris each day.

READ Math

The expression 6 × 238 can be read in different ways:

- 6 groups of 238
- the product of 6 and 238
- 6 times 238

FAST TRACK KY MA-05-1.3.1 Students will analyze real-world problems to identify appropriate representations using mathematic operations, and will apply operations to solve real-world problems with the following constraints: add, subtract, multipl and divide whole numbers (less than 100,000,000), using technology where appropriate. DOK 2 *also* MA-05-1.1.1

ANOTHER WAY Use place value and regrouping.

Step 1	Step 2	Step 3
Multiply the ones. $6 \times 8 = 48$ ones Regroup. $\begin{array}{r} \scriptstyle 4 \\ 238 \\ \times \quad 6 \\ \hline 8 \end{array}$	Multiply the tens. 6×3 tens $= 18$ tens Add the 4 regrouped tens. 18 tens + 4 tens = 22 tens $\begin{array}{r} \scriptstyle 24 \\ 238 \\ \times \quad 6 \\ \hline 28 \end{array}$	Multiply the hundreds. 6×2 hundreds $= 12$ hundreds Add the 2 regrouped hundreds. 12 hundreds + 2 hundreds = 14 hundreds $\begin{array}{r} \scriptstyle 24 \\ 238 \\ \times \quad 6 \\ \hline 1{,}428 \end{array}$

- How is multiplying with regrouping like using the Distributive Property? How is it different?

More Examples

A Place value and regrouping

$$\begin{array}{r} \scriptstyle 1\ \ 2 \\ 5{,}628 \\ \times \qquad 3 \\ \hline 16{,}884 \end{array}$$

B Place value and regrouping

$$\begin{array}{r} \scriptstyle 3\ \ \ 24 \\ 44{,}036 \\ \times \qquad 8 \\ \hline 352{,}288 \end{array}$$

C Distributive Property

$$\begin{aligned} 7 \times 9{,}184 &= 7 \times (9{,}000 + 100 + 80 + 4) \\ &= (7 \times 9{,}000) + (7 \times 100) + (7 \times 80) + (7 \times 4) \\ &= 63{,}000 + 700 + 560 + 28 \\ &= 64{,}288 \end{aligned}$$

Math Idea
To multiply a greater number by a 1-digit number, use the same method you use for a 2- or 3-digit number. Just repeat the steps for all of the digits in the greater number.

Guided Practice

Copy and complete.

1. $4 \times 283 = 4 \times (200 + 80 + ■)$
   $= (4 \times 200) + (■ \times 80) + (4 \times 3)$
   $= 800 + ■ + 12$
   $= ■$

2. $5 \times 769 = ■ \times (■ + 60 + 9)$
   $= (5 \times ■) + (5 \times ■) + (5 \times ■)$
   $= ■ + 300 + ■$
   $= ■$

Estimate. Then find the product.

3. 36×7
4. 497×3
5. 208×8
6. ✓ 556×4
7. 821×5
8. 4×915
9. $3{,}006 \times 9$
10. ✓ $9{,}682 \times 2$

11. **TALK Math** **Explain** how to find the digit in the hundreds place of the product of 731×7.

Independent Practice and Problem Solving

Estimate. Then find the product.

12. 32×4 **13.** 85×5 **14.** 709×2 **15.** 573×4 **16.** 625×3

17. 423×7 **18.** 716×5 **19.** $11{,}808 \times 8$ **20.** $32{,}045 \times 6$ **21.** $42{,}531 \times 9$

22. 632×4 **23.** 709×9 **24.** $4{,}625 \times 3$ **25.** $5{,}473 \times 2$

26. $5 \times 3{,}954$ **27.** $1{,}739 \times 8$ **28.** $8{,}576 \times 7$ **29.** $34{,}253 \times 6$

Algebra Solve for the missing number.

30. $6 \times 5{,}396 = \blacksquare$ **31.** $8 \times 5{,}179 = \blacksquare$ **32.** $5 \times 42{,}736 = \blacksquare$ **33.** $7 \times 135{,}819 = \blacksquare$

USE DATA For 34–40, use the table.

Round-trip Airfares from New York, NY

Destination	Cost in Dollars
Detroit, MI	239
Chicago, IL	140
London, England	591
Paris, France	883
Tokyo, Japan	1,237
Sydney, Australia	1,329

34. How much would it cost a family of four to fly round-trip from New York to Detroit?

35. There are 6 Dance Team members and 3 chaperones flying from New York to Chicago. How much will the plane tickets cost in all?

36. If a family of three brought two suitcases per person that weighed 44 pounds each, what is the total weight of their luggage?

37. Mr. Abrams went on several business trips. Flying from New York, he went to Sydney and Chicago once, to Tokyo and Paris twice, and to London four times. What was the total cost of Mr. Abrams's plane tickets?

38. Zach drove from New York to Detroit and back. He paid \$452 for gas and a one-night stay at a hotel. How much less would Zach have paid if he had flown round-trip from New York to Detroit in one day?

39. How many times could a person fly round-trip from New York to Chicago before the cost was greater than the cost to fly from New York to Sydney, Australia, one time?

40. How much more does it cost 3 people to fly round-trip from New York to Tokyo than to fly from New York to Paris?

41. WRITE Math **What's the Error?** Paxton wrote $5 \times 2{,}047 = (5 \times 20) + (5 \times 4) + (5 \times 7)$. Describe his error. Then write the equation correctly.

CD ROM Technology
Use Harcourt Mega Math, The Number Games, *Up, Up, and Array,* Level J.

Extra Practice on page 53, Set C

Learn About Multiplication Patterns

Carl Friedrich Gauss, a mathematician, was born in Germany in 1777. A famous story is told about Gauss when he was 10 years old.

Gauss's teacher asked Gauss and his classmates to add the numbers from 1 to 100. The teacher was surprised when, in only moments, Gauss came up with the correct answer of 5,050.

Carl Friedrich Gauss

Here is one way Gauss could have answered the question.

$1 + 100 = 101$ Start with the greatest and the least numbers.
$2 + 99 = 101$ Continue to add the next greatest and next least numbers.
$3 + 98 = 101$ The sum of each pair is 101.
⋮
$49 + 52 = 101$
$50 + 51 = 101$ This is the last pair because they are consecutive addends with a sum of 101. There are 50 pairs. The first addend of each sum counts the number of pairs.

There are 50 sums of 101, so multiply 50×101. $50 \times 101 = 5{,}050$

Try It

Use the method above to find the sum of the numbers.

42. from 1 to 50
43. from 1 to 80
44. from 1 to 200
45. from 1 to 500

Mixed Review and Test Prep

46. Carlos buys pencils in packages. The table shows how many pencils there are in 3, 5, and 6 packages.

Number of Packages	3	5	6	8
Number of Pencils	24	40	48	■

How many pencils are in 8 packages?
(Grade 4)

47. The total population of the United States in 1900 was 75,994,575. In 2000, the total population of the United States was 281,421,906. Estimate the difference in the United States population in 1900 and 2000.
(p. 16)

48. Test Prep Which expression has the same value as $5 \times (900 + 60 + 4)$?

A $5 \times 900{,}604$
B $45 + 30 + 20$
C $4{,}500 + 60 + 4$
D $4{,}500 + 300 + 20$

49. Test Prep Mr. Stewart bought 7 computers for the mathlab. The computers cost $938 each. How much did Mr. Stewart pay for the computers in all?

A $6,316
B $6,366
C $6,566
D $6,666

LESSON 4

Multiply by Multi-Digit Numbers

OBJECTIVE: Multiply by multi-digit numbers.

Quick Review

1. 48×4
2. 5×23
3. 85×4
4. 50×70
5. 839×2

Learn

PROBLEM Ana lives in San Francisco, California, and plans to cycle to Cape May, New Jersey. She wants to take a few side trips along the way. She plans to travel about 24 miles each day for 124 days. How many miles in all is Ana planning to cycle?

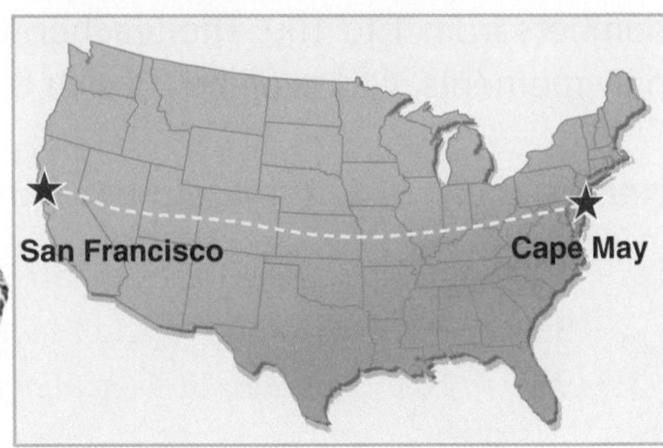

Example **Multiply.** 24×124 **Estimate.** $20 \times 120 = 2,400$

Step 1	Step 2	Step 3
Multiply by the ones.	Multiply by the tens.	Add the partial products.
$\begin{array}{r} \overset{1}{124} \\ \times\ 24 \\ \hline 496 \end{array}$ ← 4 × 124	$\begin{array}{r} 124 \\ \times\ 24 \\ \hline 496 \\ 2480 \end{array}$ ← 20 × 124	$\begin{array}{r} 124 \\ \times\ 24 \\ \hline 496 \\ +\ 2480 \\ \hline 2,976 \end{array}$ partial products

So, Ana plans to cycle 2,976 miles. Since it is close to the estimate of 2,400, it is a reasonable answer.

More Examples

A Money

$$\begin{array}{r} \overset{5}{\overset{3}{}}\$208 \\ \times\ 74 \\ \hline 832 \\ +\ 14560 \\ \hline \$15,392 \end{array}$$

832 ← 4 × 208; 14560 ← 70 × 208

B 4-digit factor

$$\begin{array}{r} 8,164 \\ \times\ 95 \\ \hline 40820 \\ +\ 734760 \\ \hline 775,580 \end{array}$$

Regrouped digits: 1 5 3 / 3 2. 40820 ← 5 × 8,164; 734760 ← 90 × 8,164

C Two 3-digit factors

$$\begin{array}{r} 619 \\ \times\ 372 \\ \hline 1238 \\ 43330 \\ +\ 185700 \\ \hline 230,268 \end{array}$$

Regrouped digits: 2 / 1 6 / 1. 1238 ← 2 × 619; 43330 ← 70 × 619; 185700 ← 300 × 619

- In Example A, what happens to the regrouped digits 3 and 5, since there is a zero in the factor?

KY MA-05-1.3.1 Students will analyze real-world problems to identify appropriate representations using mathematical operations, and will apply operations to solve real-world problems with the following constraints: add, subtract, multiply and divide whole numbers (less than 100,000,000), using technology where appropriate. DOK 2 *also* MA-05-1.1.1

Guided Practice

Find the missing numbers.

1.
$$\begin{array}{r} 453 \\ \times\ 17 \\ \hline 3171 \leftarrow 453 \times \blacksquare \\ +4530 \leftarrow 453 \times \blacksquare \\ \hline 7{,}701 \end{array}$$

2.
$$\begin{array}{r} 608 \\ \times\ 29 \\ \hline 5472 \leftarrow \blacksquare \times \blacksquare \\ +12160 \leftarrow \blacksquare \times \blacksquare \\ \hline 17{,}632 \end{array}$$

3.
$$\begin{array}{r} 571 \\ \times\ 38 \\ \hline 4568 \leftarrow \blacksquare \times \blacksquare \\ +17130 \leftarrow \blacksquare \times \blacksquare \\ \hline \blacksquare\blacksquare\blacksquare\blacksquare\blacksquare \end{array}$$

Estimate. Then find the product.

4. 221×19
5. 308×36
6. 416×54
7. $\$533 \times 85$
8. 688×67

9. **TALK Math** **Explain** why the second partial product is always greater than the first partial product when you multiply a 3-digit number by a 2-digit number.

Independent Practice and Problem Solving

Estimate. Then find the product.

10. 295×53
11. 604×72
12. 724×46
13. $\$4{,}151 \times 81$
14. 307×197

15. 22×348
16. 436×50
17. $25 \times 1{,}803$
18. $52 \times 7{,}009$
19. 938×254

20. While Brandon is cycling, his heart rate rises to 185 beats per minute for 25 minutes. During this 25-minute time period, how many times does Brandon's heart beat?

21. Sandra trained for a bike race by riding 108 miles per day, 4 days a week, for 8 weeks. What is the total number of miles that Sandra rode while training?

22. **WRITE Math** **What's the Question?** A cyclist on a bike with 27-inch wheels travels about 85 inches for each revolution the wheels make. The wheels make 325 revolutions. The answer is 27,625 inches.

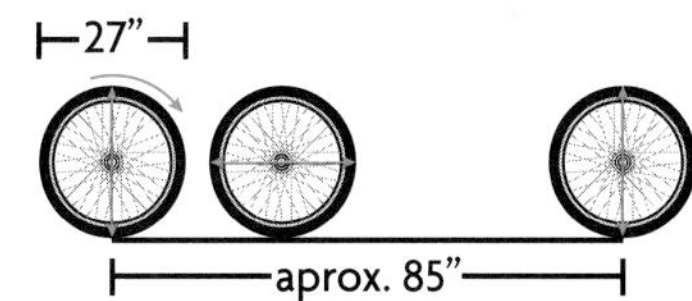

Mixed Review and Test Prep

23. Sponsors donated $6 for each student that participated in a Bike-a-thon. If 473 students participated, how much did the sponsors donate? (p. 40)

24. There are 89 fifth graders at Dover School. How much will the fifth grade make if each student sells ten coupon books for $10. (p. 36)

25. **Test Prep** Carol is training for a cycling event on a track in which one lap is 440 yards. So far, she has cycled 15 laps. What distance has she cycled?

A 6,600 yards
B 6,400 yards
C 4,400 yards
D 2,640 yards

Extra Practice on page 53, Set D

LESSON 5

Problem Solving Workshop
Strategy: Find a Pattern

OBJECTIVE: Solve problems by using the strategy *find a pattern*.

Learn the Strategy

Patterns sometimes repeat details in the same order over and over again. Finding a pattern can help you extend it. You can use different types of patterns to show different types of problems.

A pattern can help you identify the details that repeat.

Maria's pattern has three numbers that repeat. The numbers are 5, 6, and 7.

5, 6, 7, 5, 6, 7, 5, 6, 7, 5, 6, 7, …

A pattern can help you predict what will happen next.

Each number in Nadeem's pattern is 2 times the number before it.

1, 2, 4, 8, 16, ■

The missing term is 32.

A pattern can help you draw conclusions.

The second factor contains all 5s, which produces a product in which the first digit is always 3, the last digit is always 5, and the digits in the middle are always 8.

$7 \times 55 = 385$

$7 \times 555 = 3{,}885$

$7 \times 5{,}555 = 38{,}885$

$7 \times 55{,}555 = 388{,}885$

TALK Math

Describe some other patterns you have seen.

To find a pattern, look for details that repeat. However, repeating details do not always mean that a pattern exists.

KY MA-05-5.1.1 Students will extend patterns, find the missing term(s) in a pattern or describe rules for patterns (numbers, pictures, tables, words) from real-world and mathematical problems. DOK 3

Use the Strategy

PROBLEM Portraits of famous people often sell for large amounts of money. Suppose a series of 8 portraits of George Washington were sold at an art gallery. If the gallery made $3,999,999 for each portrait it sold, how much money did it make if it sold all 8 paintings?

"George Washington at Princeton" was painted in 1779 by Charles Willson Peale. It sold in 2006 for more than $21,000,000.

Read to Understand

- **What information is given?**
- **How can you generalize the information to make the problem easier to solve?**

Plan

- **What strategy can you use to solve the problem?**
  You can find a pattern to help you solve the problem.

Solve

- **How can you use the strategy to help you solve the problem?**
  Use a calculator or pencil and paper to find the multiplication pattern for $3,999,999 × 8.

  Find 39 × 8.
  Then find 399 × 8.
  Use the calculator to find the product for each increase in place value. Make a table to record each product.

Press	Display
3 9 × 8 =	312.
3 9 9 × 8 =	3192.
3 9 9 9 × 8 =	31992.
3 9 9 9 9 × 8 =	319992.

  Look for a pattern. In this pattern, the first two digits and the last digit stay the same. The digits in the middle stay the same, but the number of them increases as the digits in the greater factor increase.

  Once you have found the pattern, it is not necessary to use the calculator to find the final product. You can use the pattern to determine the answer.

  So, if the art gallery sold 8 paintings, it made $31,999,992.

Check

- **What other strategies could you use to solve the problem?**
- **Is your answer reasonable? Explain.**

Read to Understand
Plan
Solve
Check

Guided Problem Solving

1. A group of 6 oil paintings by a famous artist will be sold for $599,999 each. How much will 6 paintings cost?

First, use a pencil and paper or a calculator to multiply part of the problem.

Then, make a table to record the results. Look for a pattern.

Finally, use the pattern to find the product.

Press	Display
5 9 × 6 =	354.
5 9 9 × 6 =	3594.
5 9 9 9 × 6 =	35994.

2. **What if** another artist's painting sold for $377,777? How much would 6 paintings cost?

3. A large art museum is planning a show of famous oil paintings. The show will last for 4 days. If 38,888 people attend the show each day, how many people will attend the show in all?

Problem Solving Strategy Practice

Find a pattern to solve.

4. A group of 8 photographs by a famous photographer will be sold for $155,555 each. How much will 8 photographs cost?

5. Paintbrushes come in five different sizes. Size A costs $1, size B $4, size C $7, and size D $10. What rule can you use to find the cost of size E?

6. An art gallery sold 3 paintings in January, 7 paintings in February, 15 paintings in March, 31 paintings in April, and 63 paintings in June. If the pattern continues, how many paintings will they sell in July?

7. Eric will paint a house this summer. He has the option of being paid $5 an hour for 4 hours or $1 the first day, $2 the second, $3 the third and so on for 8 days. For which option will Eric be paid more?

8. An art studio is offering an oil painting class. The cost of the class is $101. Use a calculator to find how much money the studio will make if 14, 23, or 33 people take the class. Then, without using a calculator, figure out how much the studio will make if 58, 73, or 84 people take the class.

9. WRITE Math Use a calculator to multiply the numbers 1, 12, 123, 1,234, and so on, by any 1-digit number. What patterns can you find? Repeat the process with a different multiplier, using a calculator, multiplying up to at least 123,456. Describe how the pattern is formed. Subtract a product from the next greater product, such as $(123{,}456 \times 8) - (12{,}345 \times 8)$. What patterns can you find?

Mixed Strategy Practice

10. Matt's dad plans to cook 2 hamburgers for every 3 people at a picnic. How many hamburgers should Matt's dad cook for 15 people?

11. Emma rode her bike 3 miles round-trip to the art museum one day. She also rode her bike to the art supply store for supplies 2 miles round-trip each day for 4 days. How many miles did Emma ride her bike?

USE DATA For 12–15, use the information in the pictures.

12. Ryan is 4 feet tall. How does Ryan's height compare to the heights of the paintings shown?

13. Which painting has an area of about 6 square feet?

14. **Pose a Problem** Use the information in the picture to write a problem that involves estimation. **Explain** how to solve your problem.

15. **Open-Ended** Write two different expressions that equal the width of Whistler's Mother in inches. Remember 1 foot = 12 inches.

CHALLENGE YOURSELF

Jakob is 10 inches shorter than his sister, Anna. Anna is 42 inches tall.

16. Anna and Jakob's dad is 2 inches shorter than their heights combined. How tall is Anna and Jakob's dad?

17. Suppose Jakob grew 2 more inches each year. How tall would Jakob be 4 years from now?

Choose a STRATEGY

- Draw a Diagram or Picture
- Make a Model or Act It Out
- Make an Organized List
- Find a Pattern
- Make a Table or Graph
- Predict and Test
- Work Backward
- Solve a Simpler Problem
- Write an Equation
- Use Logical Reasoning

width 1 ft $8\frac{7}{8}$ in.

height 2 ft 6 in.

▲ "Mona Lisa"

width 5 ft 4 in.

height 4 ft $8\frac{3}{4}$ in.

▲ "Whistler's Mother"

LESSON 6

Choose a Method

OBJECTIVE: Choose mental math, paper and pencil, or a calculator to multiply whole numbers.

Quick Review

1. 90×40
2. 4×618
3. $2,794 \times 5$
4. 96×27
5. 38×405

Learn

PROBLEM An adult lion sleeps as much as 21 hours a day. How many minutes a day might a lion sleep?

A lion needs to conserve its energy for the bursts of activity needed for stalking and capturing prey.

Use Mental Math

If the numbers are easy to compute, use mental math.

Multiply. 21×60 Think: 1 hour = 60 minutes

$21 \times 60 = (20 + 1) \times 60 = (20 \times 60) + (1 \times 60) = 1,200 + 60 = 1,260$

So, a lion might sleep about 1,260 minutes per day.

Use Paper and Pencil

When mental math is too difficult, use paper and pencil.

A giant armadillo sleeps about 18 hours a day. How many hours might an armadillo sleep in a month with 31 days?

Multiply. 18×31

Step 1	Step 2	Step 3
Multiply by the ones.	Multiply by the tens.	Add the partial products.
$\begin{array}{r} 18 \\ \times 31 \\ \hline 18 \end{array}$ 1×18	$\begin{array}{r} {}^{2}\ \\ 18 \\ \times 31 \\ \hline 18 \\ 540 \end{array}$ 30×18	$\begin{array}{r} {}^{2}\ \\ 18 \\ \times 31 \\ \hline 18 \\ +540 \\ \hline 558 \end{array}$

So, a giant armadillo might sleep 558 hours in a month with 31 days.

Use a Calculator

For greater numbers or several calculations, use a calculator.

A giraffe may sleep as little as 2 hours a day.

How many minutes per year might a giraffe sleep?

Multiply. $2 \times 60 \times 365$ Think: 1 year = 365 days

         43,800

So, a giraffe might sleep 43,800 minutes per year.

A giraffe sleeps about five minutes at a time, standing up with one eye open.

KY MA-05-1.3.1 Students will . . . multiply whole numbers (less than 100,000,000), using technology where appropriate. DOK 2 *also* MA-05-1.1.1

Guided Practice

1. Choose a method for multiplying 15×300.
   - Are the numbers greater or are there several calculations?
   - Is mental math too difficult?
   - Are the numbers easy to compute with paper and pencil?

Find the product. Choose mental math, paper and pencil, or a calculator.

2. 400×21
3. 54×203
4. 500×26
5. 429×8
6. 368×77

7. TALK Math **Explain** how you decide whether to use mental math, a calculator, or paper and pencil.

Independent Practice and Problem Solving

Find the product. Choose mental math, paper and pencil, or a calculator.

8. 409×64
9. 973×438
10. $8,000 \times 50$
11. 423×128
12. 796×32

13. $9 \times 3,587$
14. 700×40
15. $82 \times 32 \times 22$
16. $10 \times 60 \times 600$

USE DATA For 17–18, use the table.

17. How many hours does a pig sleep in one year?
18. In minutes, how much longer does a tiger sleep in one week than a cow?
19. WRITE Math **What's the Error?** Allison reads 12 books per month. She says that if she reads 12 books each month for the next 5 years, she will have read 149 books. What is Allison's error? What is the correct answer?

Animal Sleep

Animal	Time (hours per day)
Tiger	16
Pig	8
Cow	4

Mixed Review and Test Prep

20. In 1975, the number of lions in Africa was about 5 times as great as the number in 2005. In 2005, there were about 40,000 lions in Africa. About how many lions were there in 1975? (p. 36)
21. An elephant can hold about 6 quarts of water in its trunk. How many cups of water is this? (Hint: 4 cups = 1 quart) (Grade 4)
22. **Test Prep** A typical hippopotamus may weigh about 96 pounds at birth. At maturity, its weight is 50 times as great. What does a typical hippopotamus weigh at maturity?

    A 960 pounds
    B 4,800 pounds
    C 9,600 pounds
    D 48,000 pounds

Extra Practice on page 53, Set E

Extra Practice

Set A Find the product. (pp. 36–37)

1. $\begin{array}{r} 20 \\ \times 90 \\ \hline \end{array}$
2. $\begin{array}{r} 700 \\ \times \ \ 6 \\ \hline \end{array}$
3. $\begin{array}{r} 800 \\ \times \ \ 5 \\ \hline \end{array}$
4. $\begin{array}{r} 120 \\ \times \ 40 \\ \hline \end{array}$
5. $\begin{array}{r} 200 \\ \times \ 60 \\ \hline \end{array}$
6. $\begin{array}{r} 5{,}000 \\ \times \ \ \ \ 7 \\ \hline \end{array}$
7. $\begin{array}{r} 900 \\ \times \ \ 9 \\ \hline \end{array}$
8. $\begin{array}{r} 7{,}000 \\ \times \ \ \ \ 3 \\ \hline \end{array}$
9. $\begin{array}{r} 500 \\ \times \ 60 \\ \hline \end{array}$
10. $\begin{array}{r} 300 \\ \times \ 11 \\ \hline \end{array}$
11. $8 \times 7{,}000$
12. $5 \times 6{,}000$
13. 70×300
14. 50×80
15. $2 \times 9{,}000$
16. $30 \times 1{,}300$
17. $90 \times 6{,}000$
18. $5{,}000 \times 14$
19. 30×60
20. 20×80
21. There are 50 rows of seats in the auditorium where the theater group performs. Each row contains 200 seats. How many seats are in the auditorium?
22. The theater group performed 3 shows this weekend. If 400 people were at each show, how many people saw the theater group's performance in total?

Set B Estimate the product. (pp. 38–39)

1. $\begin{array}{r} 78 \\ \times 21 \\ \hline \end{array}$
2. $\begin{array}{r} 53 \\ \times 61 \\ \hline \end{array}$
3. $\begin{array}{r} 34 \\ \times 18 \\ \hline \end{array}$
4. $\begin{array}{r} 512 \\ \times \ 84 \\ \hline \end{array}$
5. $\begin{array}{r} 92 \\ \times 785 \\ \hline \end{array}$
6. $\begin{array}{r} \$3.96 \\ \times \ \ \ 52 \\ \hline \end{array}$
7. $\begin{array}{r} 832 \\ \times \ 66 \\ \hline \end{array}$
8. $\begin{array}{r} 4{,}295 \\ \times \ \ \ 39 \\ \hline \end{array}$
9. $\begin{array}{r} 6{,}077 \\ \times \ \ \ 43 \\ \hline \end{array}$
10. $\begin{array}{r} \$18.76 \\ \times \ \ \ \ 27 \\ \hline \end{array}$
11. $59 \times 2{,}731$
12. $1{,}743 \times 518$
13. $\$71.84 \times 82$
14. 211×439
15. $49 \times 6{,}912$
16. $23 \times 6{,}198$
17. $\$46 \times 58$
18. 18×47
19. 429×88
20. 31×759
21. There are 56 players on the township baseball league. New baseball uniforms cost $32.87 each. Estimate the cost to buy uniforms for all the baseball players.
22. The township baseball league has a total of 37 baseball bats. Each baseball bat is 29 inches long. Estimate the total length if each bat is placed end to end.
23. A baseball league is having training clinics. The league is offering 12 different clinics that each have a capacity of 78 students. About how many students can attend these clinics?

CD ROM **Technology**
Use Harcourt Mega Math, The Number Games, *Tiny's Think Tank*, Level F.

Set C Estimate. Then find the product. (pp. 40–43)

1. $\begin{array}{r} 47 \\ \times\ 4 \\ \hline \end{array}$ 2. $\begin{array}{r} 72 \\ \times\ 6 \\ \hline \end{array}$ 3. $\begin{array}{r} 318 \\ \times\ 5 \\ \hline \end{array}$ 4. $\begin{array}{r} 492 \\ \times\ 3 \\ \hline \end{array}$ 5. $\begin{array}{r} 703 \\ \times\ 9 \\ \hline \end{array}$

6. $\begin{array}{r} 253 \\ \times\ 8 \\ \hline \end{array}$ 7. $\begin{array}{r} 645 \\ \times\ 7 \\ \hline \end{array}$ 8. $\begin{array}{r} 1{,}904 \\ \times\ 3 \\ \hline \end{array}$ 9. $\begin{array}{r} 36{,}497 \\ \times\ 5 \\ \hline \end{array}$ 10. $\begin{array}{r} 12{,}417 \\ \times\ 6 \\ \hline \end{array}$

11. 744×8 12. 297×3 13. $4{,}205 \times 9$ 14. $6{,}911 \times 5$ 15. $3{,}281 \times 6$

16. $4 \times 9{,}026$ 17. $3{,}917 \times 9$ 18. $5 \times 18{,}204$ 19. $26{,}476 \times 8$ 20. $50{,}914 \times 3$

21. Claire sold 6 books of raffle tickets. Each book contains 32 raffle tickets. How many raffle tickets did she sell altogether?

22. Travis read all 8 books in a detective series. If each book has 245 pages, how many pages did he read in all?

Set D Estimate. Then find the product. (pp. 44–45)

1. $\begin{array}{r} 318 \\ \times\ 26 \\ \hline \end{array}$ 2. $\begin{array}{r} 704 \\ \times\ 53 \\ \hline \end{array}$ 3. $\begin{array}{r} 673 \\ \times\ 31 \\ \hline \end{array}$ 4. $\begin{array}{r} 3{,}926 \\ \times\ 72 \\ \hline \end{array}$ 5. $\begin{array}{r} 415 \\ \times 293 \\ \hline \end{array}$

6. 34×927 7. 381×22 8. $1{,}675 \times 85$ 9. 549×311 10. 168×145

11. Kathy's family uses 138 gallons of water doing laundry each week. How many gallons of water does Kathy's family use for laundry in 1 year? (**Hint:** 1 year = 52 weeks)

12. A dishwasher uses 18 gallons of water for each load. If a family runs the dishwasher once a day, how many gallons of water would the family use in a year? (**Hint:** 1 year = 365 days)

Set E Find the product. Choose mental math, paper and pencil, or a calculator. (pp. 50–51)

1. $\begin{array}{r} 318 \\ \times\ 93 \\ \hline \end{array}$ 2. $\begin{array}{r} 502 \\ \times 176 \\ \hline \end{array}$ 3. $\begin{array}{r} 300 \\ \times 120 \\ \hline \end{array}$ 4. $\begin{array}{r} 72 \\ \times 19 \\ \hline \end{array}$ 5. $\begin{array}{r} 90 \\ \times 46 \\ \hline \end{array}$

6. $50 \times 4{,}000$ 7. 283×624 8. $30 \times 800 \times 10$ 9. 82×77 10. 594×967

11. Mr. Smith's car averages 23 miles per gallon of gas. The gas tank holds 14 gallons of gas. How many miles can Mr. Smith travel on a full tank of gas?

12. Mr. Smith drove from Pennsylvania to Georgia. He drove for 12 hours at an average rate of 60 miles per hour. How many total miles did he drive?

MATH POWER **Distributive Property**

Compatible Numbers

Students in the science club are looking at fossils arranged in 4 display cases. Each case holds 140 fossils. How many fossils are there?

You can use **compatible numbers** and the Distributive Property to find the product mentally.

Example 1 Find 4 × 140.

$4 \times 140 = 4 \times (100 + 40)$	Break apart 140 into compatible numbers. **Think:** $140 = 100 + 40$
$= (4 \times 100) + (4 \times 40)$	Use the Distributive Property. Multiply mentally.
$= 400 + 160$	Add mentally.
$= 560$	

So, there are 560 fossils.

Example 2 Find 6 × 48.

$6 \times 48 = 6 \times (50 - 2)$	Break apart 48 into compatible numbers. **Think:** $48 = 50 - 2$
$= (6 \times 50) - (6 \times 2)$	Use the Distributive Property. Multiply mentally.
$= 300 - 12$	Subtract mentally.
$= 288$	

Try It

Use compatible numbers and the Distributive Property to find the product mentally.

1. 2×156
2. 3×197
3. 5×210
4. 8×525
5. 6×395
6. 4×550
7. 2×176
8. 4×485
9. **Challenge** Sticker books in the museum gift shop cost \$6.50 each. How much do 4 sticker books cost?
10. WRITE Math **Explain** how you would find $3 \times 9{,}998$ mentally.

KENTUCKY Chapter 2 Review/Test

Check Concepts

1. Explain how to use basic facts and patterns to estimate the product of 19×382. KY MA-05-1.2.1 (p. 38)
2. What is the Distributive Property? Give an example. KY MA-05-1.2.1 (p. 40)

Check Skills

Find the product. KY MA-05-1.3.1 (pp. 36–37)

3. 600×7
4. $9 \times 4{,}000$
5. 800×12
6. 50×400

Estimate the product. KY MA-05-1.2.1 (pp. 38–39)

7. $72 \times 3{,}149$
8. 115×33
9. $19 \times \$29.95$
10. 520×682

Estimate. Then find the product. KY MA-05-1.2.1; MA-05-1.3.1 (pp. 40–43, 44–45)

11. 91×7
12. 582×5
13. 324×6
14. $4{,}681 \times 3$
15. 418×28
16. 762×31
17. $\$3{,}760 \times 21$
18. 439×167
19. 33×275
20. $1{,}698 \times 54$
21. 204×711
22. $46 \times 8{,}239$

Check Problem Solving

Solve. KY MA-05-5.1.1 (pp. 46–49)

23. Kip made \$15 after one week of mowing lawns. At the end of the second week, Kip had a total of \$30. After the third week, Kip had \$45. If this pattern continues, how much money will Kip have after 8 weeks?
24. Rosa is making a beaded bracelet using this pattern: 3 red beads, 2 pink beads, and one white bead. If she repeats the pattern 6 times, how many pink beads will Rosa have used?
25. **WRITE Math** Troy drew a pattern of 4 dots, 8 dots, 12 dots and then 16 dots. He says he should draw 24 dots next. **Explain** Troy's error and tell how many dots he should draw next.

GO ONLINE **Technology** Use *Online Assessment.*

Practice for the KCCT
Chapters 1–2

Number Properties and Operations

Decide on a plan.

See item 1. First round each factor to the greatest place value. Then use basic facts and patterns of zero to find the product. Choose the product with the correct number of places.

1. The art teacher is gathering supplies for a knitting project. She needs 172 inches of yarn for each student. There are 67 students enrolled in the class. Which is the best estimate of the total amount of yarn the teacher needs? KY MA-05-1.2.1 (p. 38)

   A 140 inches

   B 1,400 inches

   C 14,000 inches

   D 140,000 inches

2. For a social studies project, Malaka researched her city. She found that the population was three hundred fifty-two thousand, six hundred nine. Which is the population written in standard form?
   KY MA-05-1.1.1 (p. 4)

   A 352,690 **C** 352,069

   B 352,609 **D** 305,269

3. **WRITE Math** What is 176×32? **Explain** the steps to find the product.
   KY MA-05-1.3.1 (p. 44)

Algebraic Thinking

4. What number makes this number sentence true? KY Grade 4

   $$6 \times n = (6 \times 70) + (6 \times 2)$$

   A $n = 432$

   B $n = 140$

   C $n = 72$

   D $n = 27$

5. Write a rule for the table using an equation and the variables x and y.
   KY Grade 4

Input, x	5	10	15	20	25
Output, y	10	20	30	40	50

   A $x + 10 = y$

   B $x + 5 = y$

   C $2y = x$

   D $2x = y$

6. What is the value of the expression below? KY Grade 4

   $$7 \times (6 - 2)$$

   A 28 **C** 63

   B 45 **D** 126

7. **WRITE Math** **Explain** how to find the value of the variable in the number sentence $5 \times n = 50$. KY Grade 4

Measurement

8. What is the length of this piece of string measured to the nearest $\frac{1}{4}$ inch? KY Grade 4

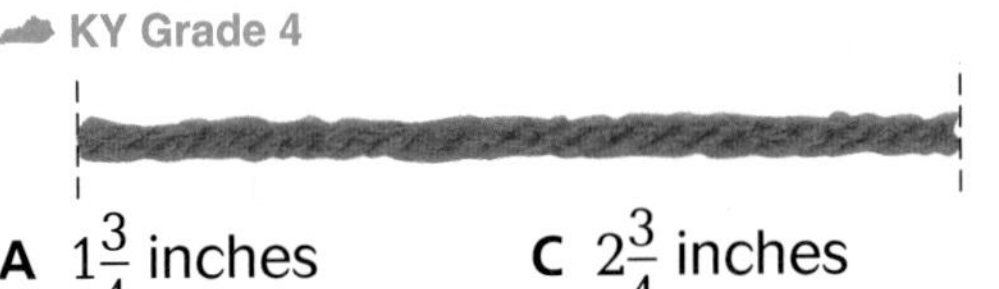

A $1\frac{3}{4}$ inches
B $2\frac{1}{4}$ inches
C $2\frac{3}{4}$ inches
D $3\frac{3}{4}$ inches

9. Jackie is making curtains for her window. Each curtain will be 108 inches long. Fabric is sold in yards. What is the length of each curtain in yards? KY Grade 4

A 3 yards
B 9 yards
C 27 yards
D 36 yards

10. Mr. Vega drew the diagram below of his classroom. What is the perimeter of the classroom? KY Grade 4

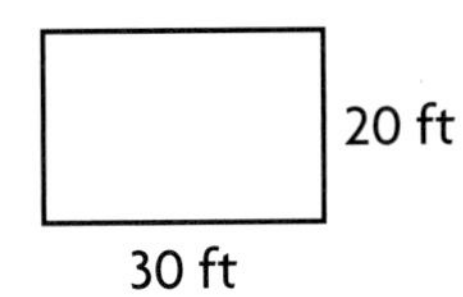

A 50 ft
B 60 ft
C 100 ft
D 600 ft

11. **WRITE Math** What is the relationship between centimeters and meters? How do you convert from one unit to the other? **Explain.** KY Grade 4

Data Analysis and Probability

12. The bar graph shows the number of each type of lunch the cafeteria sold. How many more pizzas were sold than hot dogs? KY Grade 4

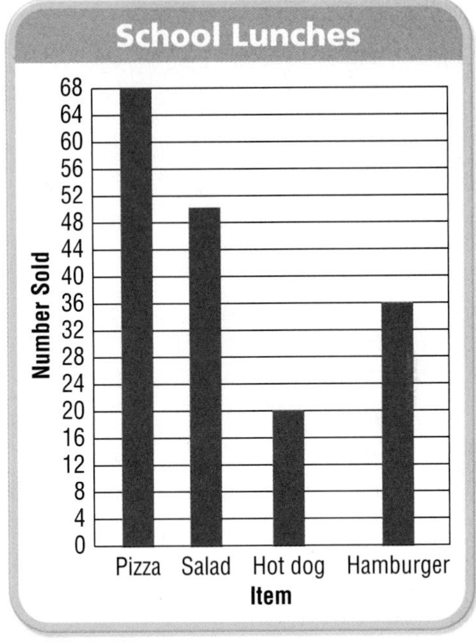

A 11
B 24
C 48
D 68

13. Here are Liz's scores on her last seven math tests. What is her mean score? KY Grade 4

72, 84, 76, 94, 86, 94, 82

A 22
B 84
C 86
D 94

14. **WRITE Math** A bag is filled with 6 red marbles, 4 blue marbles, and 2 yellow marbles. You reach into the bag without looking and pick a marble. What is the probability of picking a blue marble? Write your answer as a fraction. **Explain.** KY Grade 4

CHAPTER

3 Divide by 1- and 2-Digit Divisors

FAST FACT

The *Great American Scream Machine*, located at Six Flags Great Adventure in Jackson, New Jersey, was introduced in 1989. This steel coaster thrills riders by achieving a top speed of 68 mph.

Investigate

Choose three roller coasters from the table. Find the number of trips that each roller coaster makes each hour to carry the maximum number of riders. Round your answer to the nearest whole number.

Roller Coasters at Six Flags, New Jersey

Coaster	Riders per Trip	Maximum Riders per Hour
El Toro	36	1,500
Great American Scream Machine	28	1,680
Kingda Ka	18	1,400
Rolling Thunder	24	1,920
Batman: The Ride	32	1,280

Technology
Student pages are available in the Student eBook.

Show What You Know

Check your understanding of important skills needed for success in Chapter 3.

Estimate Quotients

Estimate the quotient.

1. $4\overline{)130}$ **2.** $6\overline{)230}$ **3.** $3\overline{)280}$ **4.** $5\overline{)340}$

5. $8\overline{)500}$ **6.** $9\overline{)520}$ **7.** $4\overline{)390}$ **8.** $7\overline{)640}$

9. $400 \div 6$ **10.** $370 \div 6$ **11.** $610 \div 8$ **12.** $200 \div 3$

Place the First Digit

Name the position of the first digit of the quotient.

13. $5\overline{)428}$ **14.** $2\overline{)361}$ **15.** $7\overline{)403}$ **16.** $9\overline{)572}$

17. $3\overline{)645}$ **18.** $4\overline{)793}$ **19.** $8\overline{)622}$ **20.** $6\overline{)917}$

Multiply by 1- and 2-Digit Numbers

Find the product.

21. 78×6 **22.** 413×9 **23.** 826×5 **24.** 673×8

25. 329×12 **26.** 168×33 **27.** $2{,}716 \times 25$ **28.** $3{,}118 \times 34$

VOCABULARY POWER

CHAPTER VOCABULARY

compatible numbers
dividend
divisor
quotient
remainder

WARM-UP WORDS

compatible numbers numbers that are easy to compute mentally

dividend the number that is to be divided in a division problem

quotient the number, not including the remainder, that results from dividing

LESSON 1

Estimate with 1-Digit Divisors

OBJECTIVE: Estimate quotients by using compatible numbers and rounding.

Quick Review

1. 15 ÷ 3
2. 24 ÷ 4
3. 32 ÷ 8
4. 49 ÷ 7
5. 54 ÷ 6

Vocabulary

compatible numbers

Learn

PROBLEM Tractor trailer trucks move cars from factories to dealerships. A truck can hold 9 cars. Last month, a dealership sold 435 cars. About how many truckloads of cars were sold?

You can use compatible numbers or round to estimate quotients.

Compatible numbers are numbers that are easy to compute mentally.

ONE WAY **Use compatible numbers. Estimate.** 435 ÷ 9

Step 1 Determine the place-value of the first digit.

9)435

Look at the beginning digits. Since 9 > 4, the first digit will be in the tens place and the quotient will be a 2-digit number.

Step 2 Change to compatible numbers.

9)435 → 9)450 = 50

Think: What division expression looks like a basic division fact and is close to 435 ÷ 9?

ANOTHER WAY **Use rounding and patterns in multiples of 10.**

Step 1

Round the dividend and the divisor to the first or second digit.

435 ÷ 9
↓ ↓
400 ÷ 10

Step 2

Divide. 400 ÷ 10

Think: What can I multiply by 10 to get the product 400?

10 × ■ = 400
10 × 40 = 400
400 ÷ 10 = 40

So, between 40 and 50 truckloads of cars were sold.

- Which estimate is closer to the actual answer, 40 or 50? Explain.

More Examples

A **Use compatible numbers.**

256 ÷ 4
↓ ↓
240 ÷ 4 = 60

or

256 ÷ 4
↓ ↓
280 ÷ 4 = 70

B **Use rounding.**

267 ÷ 3
↓ ↓
300 ÷ 3 = 100

FAST TRACK

KY MA-05-1.2.1 Students will apply and describe appropriate strategies for estimating quantities of objects and computational results in real-world problems. DOK 2 *also* MA-05-1.3.1

Guided Practice

1. Estimate 604 ÷ 8 using compatible numbers. 560 ÷ 8 = ■ 640 ÷ 8 = ■

Estimate the quotient.

2. $9\overline{)333}$
3. $6\overline{)148}$
4. $7\overline{)455}$
5. $6\overline{)216}$
6. $8\overline{)598}$
7. TALK Math **Explain** how you know that 40 is an overestimate for 351 ÷ 9.

Independent Practice and Problem Solving

Estimate the quotient.

8. $2\overline{)704}$
9. $5\overline{)430}$
10. $8\overline{)208}$
11. $4\overline{)296}$
12. $6\overline{)534}$
13. 268 ÷ 6
14. 727 ÷ 9
15. 324 ÷ 9
16. 832 ÷ 4
17. 595 ÷ 7

USE DATA For 18–20, use the table.

18. A motorcycle repair shop received a shipment of motors that included 7 Wind Rider motors. About how much does each Wind Rider motor weigh?
19. There are 6 Open Road motors in the shipment. About how much does each Open Road motor weigh?
20. The shipment included 6 Strada Sprint motors. About how much more does an Open Road motor weigh than a motor for a Strada Sprint?
21. WRITE Math **Explain** how to estimate 478 ÷ 7 using compatible numbers.

Motorcycle Motors in One Shipment by Total Weight

Kind of Motorcycle Motor	Total Weight (in pounds)
Open Road	936
Strada Sprint	684
Wind Rider	945

Mixed Review and Test Prep

22. How many faces and edges does a sphere have? (Grade 4)
23. If a cow produces about 250 gallons of milk in one month, about how many gallons can it produce in one year? (p. 44)
24. **Test Prep** Mr. Stone drove 458 miles in 3 days. If he drove the same number of miles each day, what is the best estimate of how far Mr. Stone drove on the first day?

A 200 mi **C** 100 mi

B 150 mi **D** 90 mi

Extra Practice on page 84, Set A

LESSON 2

Divide by 1-Digit Divisors

OBJECTIVE: Divide 3-digit and 4-digit dividends by 1-digit divisors.

Quick Review

1. 5×9
2. 4×70
3. 6×60
4. 8×300
5. 7×800

▲ The California gold rush began in 1848.

Learn

PROBLEM In 1854, a gold nugget weighing 195 pounds was found in Carson Hill, California. Suppose the gold nugget was melted down and made into 5 gold bricks of equal size. How many pounds would each gold brick weigh?

ONE WAY Use estimation to place the first digit.

Divide. $195 \div 5$.

Step 1

Estimate.

$$5\overline{)200} = 40$$

Since 5 > 2, the first digit will be in the tens place. The quotient will be a 2-digit number.

$5\overline{)195}$ (■ in the tens place)

Step 2

Divide the 19 tens.

```
    3
5)195
 -15
   4
```

Divide.	$5\overline{)19}$
Multiply.	5×3
Subtract.	$19 - 15$
Compare.	$4 < 5$

Step 3

Bring down the 5 ones. Divide the 45 ones.

```
   39
5)195
 -15↓
   45
  -45
    0
```

Divide.	$5\overline{)45}$
Multiply.	5×9
Subtract.	$45 - 45$
Compare.	$0 < 5$

So, each gold brick would weigh 39 pounds.

More Examples Divide.

A $8\overline{)4,872}$

Estimate: $4,800 \div 8 = 600$

```
    609
8)4,872
 -48
   07
   -0
    72
   -72
     0
```

Since 7 < 8, write 0 in the quotient in the tens place.

Check ✓

```
   7
  609
×   8
4,872
```

B $9\overline{)1,700}$

Estimate: $1,800 \div 9 = 200$

```
    188 r8
9)1,700
  -9
   80
  -72
    80
   -72
     8
```

Check ✓

```
   77
   188
×    9
 1,692

   11
 1,692
+    8
 1,700
```

Remember

The remainder is the amount left over when a number cannot be divided evenly.

To check your answer, multiply the quotient by the divisor. Then add the remainder to get the dividend.

FAST TRACK

KY MA-05-1.3.1 Students will analyze real-world problems to identify appropriate representations using mathematical operations, and will apply operations to solve real-world problems with the following constraints: add, subtract, multiply, and divide whole numbers (less than 100,000,000), using technology where appropriate. DOK

ANOTHER WAY **Use place value to place the first digit.**

Divide. $637 \div 7$.

Step 1

Look at the hundreds.

$7\overline{)637}$ 6 < 7, so look at the tens.

$7\overline{)637}$ 63 > 7, so use 63 tens.

Place the first digit in the tens place.

Step 2

Divide the 63 tens.

$$\begin{array}{r} 9 \\ 7\overline{)637} \\ -63 \\ \hline 0 \end{array}$$

Divide. $7\overline{)63}$
Multiply. 9×7
Subtract. $63 - 63$
Compare. $0 < 7$

Step 3

Bring down the 7 ones. Divide the 7 ones.

$$\begin{array}{r} 91 \\ 7\overline{)637} \\ -63\downarrow \\ \hline 07 \\ -7 \\ \hline 0 \end{array}$$

Divide. $7\overline{)7}$
Multiply. 1×7
Subtract. $7 - 7$
Compare. $0 < 7$

So, the quotient is 91.

More Examples

C $5\overline{)2,654}$

$$\begin{array}{r} 530 \text{ r4} \\ 5\overline{)2,654} \\ -25 \\ \hline 15 \\ -15 \\ \hline 04 \end{array}$$

D $7\overline{)3,702}$

$$\begin{array}{r} 528 \text{ r6} \\ 7\overline{)3,702} \\ -35 \\ \hline 20 \\ -14 \\ \hline 62 \\ -56 \\ \hline 6 \end{array}$$

Check ✓

$$\begin{array}{r} 528 \\ \times \quad 7 \\ \hline 3,696 \end{array} \qquad \begin{array}{r} 3,696 \\ + \quad 6 \\ \hline 3,702 \end{array}$$

E $4\overline{)547}$

$$\begin{array}{r} 136 \text{ r3} \\ 4\overline{)547} \\ -4 \\ \hline 14 \\ -12 \\ \hline 27 \\ -24 \\ \hline 3 \end{array}$$

Check ✓

$$\begin{array}{r} 136 \\ \times \quad 4 \\ \hline 544 \end{array} \qquad \begin{array}{r} 544 \\ + \quad 3 \\ \hline 547 \end{array}$$

- Explain how you would check the answer to Example C.

Guided Practice

1. Use the estimate to find the position of the first digit of the quotient for $4\overline{)236}$.

   Estimate: $200 \div 4 = 50$.

Name the position of the first digit of the quotient. Then find the first digit.

2. $3\overline{)579}$ 3. $5\overline{)1,035}$ 4. $6\overline{)282}$ ✓5. $8\overline{)1,766}$ ✓6. $4\overline{)1,027}$

7. **TALK Math** **Explain** how you can tell without dividing whether a 3-digit number divided by a 1-digit number will have a quotient of 2 or 3 digits.

Independent Practice and Problem Solving

Name the position of the first digit of the quotient. Then find the first digit.

8. $5\overline{)275}$	**9.** $8\overline{)624}$	**10.** $3\overline{)468}$	**11.** $2\overline{)810}$	**12.** $8\overline{)546}$
13. $7\overline{)966}$	**14.** $4\overline{)3,220}$	**15.** $9\overline{)1,157}$	**16.** $6\overline{)6,723}$	**17.** $7\overline{)8,567}$

Divide. Check by multiplying.

18. $2\overline{)518}$	**19.** $6\overline{)618}$	**20.** $8\overline{)736}$	**21.** $4\overline{)716}$	**22.** $5\overline{)875}$
23. $3\overline{)223}$	**24.** $5\overline{)693}$	**25.** $4\overline{)762}$	**26.** $8\overline{)2,012}$	**27.** $2\overline{)1,729}$
28. $693 \div 9$	**29.** $2,203 \div 4$	**30.** $341 \div 2$	**31.** $3,632 \div 6$	**32.** $8,524 \div 7$

Algebra Write the missing number for each ■.

33. $568 \div 8 =$ ■ **34.** ■ $\div 3 = 317$ r2 **35.** ■ $\div 5 = 66$ r4 **36.** $685 \div$ ■ $= 97$ r6

USE DATA For 37–38, use the table.

37. If the Welcome gold nugget were turned into 3 equal-sized gold bricks, how much would each brick weigh?

38. **Pose a Problem** Look back at Problem 37. Write a similar problem by changing the numbers and information. Then solve the problem.

Large Gold Nuggets Found

Name	Weight	Location
Welcome Stranger	2,284 troy ounces	Australia
Welcome	2,217 troy ounces	Australia
Willard	788 troy ounces	California

Gold and other precious metals are measured in troy ounces.

39. There are 246 students going on a field trip to pan for gold. If each van holds 9 students, how many vans are needed if all but the last van is filled? How many students will ride in the van that isn't full?

40. **FAST FACT** The United States Bullion Depository in Fort Knox, Kentucky, holds approximately 4,570 tons of gold. Some estimates place the value of the gold at Fort Knox to be about \$5 billion. How many tons of gold would be in about \$1 billion worth of gold?

41. **WRITE Math** **Explain** how you know where to place the first digit of the quotient in $374 \div 4$.

Technology
CD ROM Use Harcourt Mega Math, The Number Games, *Up, Up, and Array,* Levels M, N, and O.

Extra Practice on page 84, Set B

Learn About Number Pyramids

The puzzles below are called number pyramids.
You can use multiplication and division formulas to solve the puzzles.

To find the number in the top box, use the formula $A \times B = C$.

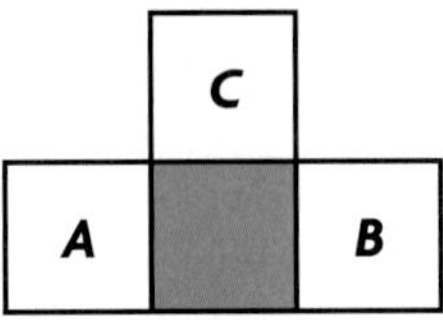

To find the number in the lower right box, use the formula $C \div A = B$.

Example

$10 \times 14 = 140$

140

10 | 14

5 | 2 | 7

$14 \div 2 = 7$

Try It

Copy and complete the number pyramids. Use the multiplication and division formulas.

42.

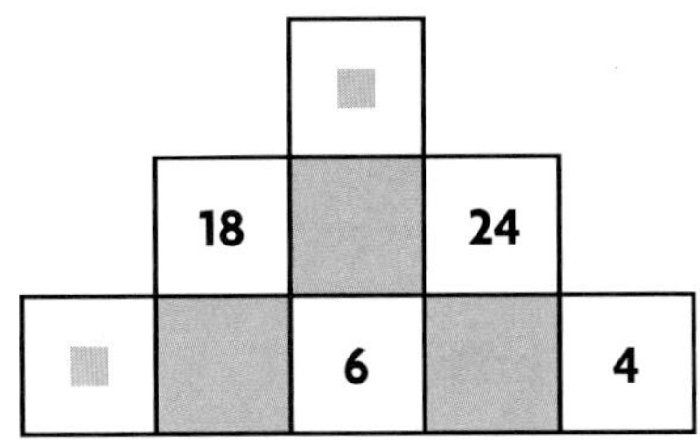

43.

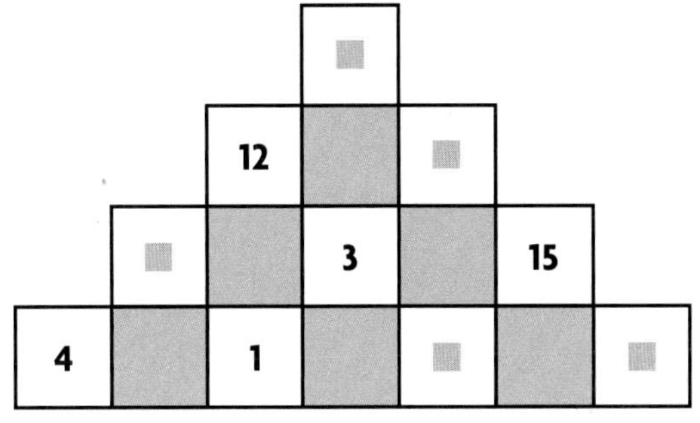

Mixed Review and Test Prep

44. A computer keyboard has 114 keys. How many keys would 100 computer keyboards have? (p. 36)

45. Test Prep One carton can hold 8 boxes of cereal. How many cartons are needed for 128 boxes of cereal?

A 1,024 **C** 16

B 17 **D** 8

46. Vincent is 37 years old. His sister, Maggie, is 9 years younger. How old is Maggie? Write a numerical expression. Then find the value. (Grade 4)

47. Test Prep For a bake sale, a fifth-grade class made 324 cupcakes, sold in packages of 6. How many packages did the class make?

A 1,944 **C** 64

B 108 **D** 54

Problem Solving Workshop
Skill: Interpret the Remainder

OBJECTIVE: Solve problems by using the skill *interpret the remainder.*

This footpath is part of the Appalachian Trail.

Use the Skill

PROBLEM The Appalachian Trail is a 2,160-mile-long hiking trail that goes from Maine to Georgia. Suppose the Jacksons want to hike 9 miles per day along an 857-mile section of the trail from New York to Georgia. Each of the division problems below uses this information.

When you solve a division problem with a remainder, the way you interpret the remainder depends on the situation and the question.

A The quotient stays the same. Drop the remainder.

On how many days will the Jacksons hike exactly 9 miles?

$$\begin{array}{r} 95 \\ 9\overline{)857} \\ -81 \\ \hline 47 \\ -45 \\ \hline 2 \end{array}$$

The miles left over are not enough for another 9-mile day. So, they will hike 9 miles a day for 95 days.

B Increase the quotient by 1.

At 9 miles per day, how many days will it take the Jacksons to hike the entire 857 miles?

To hike the remaining 2 miles will take 1 more day. So, it will take 96 days to hike the entire 857 miles.

C Use the remainder as the answer.

If the Jacksons hike exactly 9 miles each day except the last day, how many miles will they hike on the last day?

The remainder is 2. So, they will hike just 2 miles on the last day.

D Use the quotient and the remainder written as a fraction.

If the Jacksons' average hiking speed for 9 miles is 2 miles per hour, about how long will it take for them to hike 9 miles?

$$\begin{array}{r} 4\frac{1}{2} \\ 2\overline{)9} \\ -8 \\ \hline 1 \end{array}$$

← Write the remainder as a fractional part of the divisor. Use the remainder as the numerator and the divisor as the denominator.

So, it will take the Jacksons about $4\frac{1}{2}$ hours to hike 9 miles.

FAST TRACK

KY MA-05-1.3.1 Students will analyze real-world problems to identify appropriate representations using mathematic operations, and will apply operations to solve real-world problems with the following constraints: add, subtract, multipl and divide whole numbers (less than 100,000,000), using technology where appropriate. DOK 2 *also* MA-05-1.1.1

Think and Discuss

Read to Understand
Plan
Solve
Check

Tell how you would interpret the remainder. Then give the answer.

A warehouse has 1,239 books to be shipped. Each shipping carton can hold 8 books.

a. How many cartons will be full?

b. How many cartons are needed for all of the books?

c. How many books will be in the last carton?

Guided Problem Solving

1. Amy and her family want to bike on Missouri's Katy Trail. They will bike a total of 224 miles along the Missouri river, and want to bike only 9 miles per day. On how many days will Amy and her family bike exactly 9 miles? How many days will their trip last in all?

   First, divide to find the quotient and remainder. $\begin{array}{r} \blacksquare\blacksquare \text{ r}\blacksquare \\ 9\overline{)224} \end{array}$

   Then, decide how to use the quotient and remainder in your answer.

2. **What if** Amy's family wanted to bike only 165 miles at a rate of 9 miles per day? How long would it take for them to bike the entire distance? How many miles would they bike on the last day?

3. A total of 75 fifth-grade students are going on a field trip to a local park. The school is providing minivans to take the students to the park. If each minivan holds 7 students, how many minivans are needed?

Mixed Applications

4. Andrew is going hiking with 4 friends. He is making trail mix to take on the hike. He is using 5 ounces of peanuts, 6 ounces of cashews, and 12 ounces of raisins. If each hiker got the same amount of trail mix, how much would be left over?

5. A music store wants to hire a salesperson to work on weekends. The salesperson would work 10 hours on Saturday and 8 hours on Sunday. If the pay rate is $8 per hour, how much would the salesperson earn each weekend?

6. WRITE Math Mrs. Smith wants to give each of her 36 students outstanding achievement certificates. If there are 8 certificates in one package, is it reasonable to say that Mrs. Smith will need to buy 4 packages of certificates? **Explain.**

7. A restaurant can seat 228 people inside and 88 people outside on its patio. If each table inside can seat 6 people and each table outside can seat 4 people, how many tables are inside and outside the restaurant?

LESSON 4

Zeros in Division

OBJECTIVE: Use zeros in division.

Quick Review

1. 2)80
2. 3)210
3. 4)360
4. 6)480
5. 9)720

Learn

PROBLEM The Leaf Nursery has 624 tomato plants and The Seedling Nursery has 665 tomato plants. How many 6-pack containers can each nursery sell?

Examples Divide. 6)624 6)665

Step	A The Leaf Nursery	B The Seedling Nursery
Step 1 Estimate.	624 ÷ 6 → 600 ÷ 6 = 100 Use rounding.	665 ÷ 6 → 660 ÷ 6 = 110 Use compatible numbers.
Step 2 Place the first digit of the quotient. Since 6 = 6, the quotient for each problem will be a 3-digit number.	Divide the 6 hundreds. 1 6)624 −6 0 Divide. Multiply. Subtract. Compare. $0 < 6$	Divide the 6 hundreds. 1 6)665 −6 0 Divide. Multiply. Subtract. Compare. $0 < 6$
Step 3 Bring down the tens. Place the next digit of the quotient.	Divide the 2 tens. 10 6)624 −6 02 −0 2 Since $2 < 6$, write 0 in the tens place.	Divide the 6 tens. 11 6)665 −6 06 −6 0 Divide. Multiply. Subtract. Compare. $0 < 6$
Step 4 Bring down the ones. Place the last digit of the quotient. If there is an amount left over find the remainder.	Divide the 24 ones. 104 6)624 −6 02 −0 24 −24 0 Divide. Multiply. Subtract. Compare. $0 < 6$	Divide the 5 ones. 110 r5 6)665 −6 06 −6 05 −0 5 Since $5 < 6$, write 0 in the ones place.

So, The Leaf Nursery can sell 104 six-pack containers and The Seedling Nursery can sell 110 six-pack containers.

ERROR ALERT

To check your answer for missing or misplaced zeros, multiply the quotient by the divisor, then add the remainder.

FAST TRACK

KY MA-05-1.3.1 Students will analyze real-world problems to identify appropriate representations using mathemati operations, and will apply operations to solve real-world problems with the following constraints: add, subtract, multi and divide whole numbers (less than 100,000,000), using technology where appropriate. DOK 2 *also* MA-05-1.1.

Guided Practice

1. Copy the following problem. Then complete the division.

   a. $\begin{array}{r} 1\square\square \\ 4\overline{)436} \\ -4 \\ \hline 0 \end{array}$

   b. $\begin{array}{r} 1\square\square\text{ r}\square \\ 7\overline{)708} \end{array}$

Divide.

2. $5\overline{)545}$
3. $3\overline{)318}$
4. $2\overline{)221}$
5. $7\overline{)714}$
6. $5\overline{)553}$
7. TALK Math **Explain** how you know when to write a zero in the quotient.

Independent Practice and Problem Solving

Divide.

8. $7\overline{)721}$
9. $4\overline{)404}$
10. $2\overline{)341}$
11. $9\overline{)958}$
12. $6\overline{)843}$
13. $8\overline{)856}$
14. $5\overline{)540}$
15. $8\overline{)846}$
16. $3\overline{)605}$
17. $5\overline{)402}$
18. $810 \div 2$
19. $818 \div 9$
20. $905 \div 4$
21. $724 \div 6$
22. $812 \div 3$

Solve.

23. If there are 836 individual pepper plants, how many 4-pack containers of peppers can be sold?
24. If there are 960 individual petunia plants, how many 6-pack containers of petunias can be sold?
25. The marigolds are put in 8-pack containers. If there are 723 marigold plants, how many marigolds are left over? How many more marigolds are needed to fill an 8-pack container?
26. WRITE Math **Explain** why you need to write a zero in the tens place when you divide 912 by 3.

Mixed Review and Test Prep

27. The population of the world in July 2007 was about 6,602,224,175. What is the value of the digit 4 in that number? (p. 8)
28. There are 384 passengers on three airplanes. Each plane has the same number of passengers. How many passengers are on each plane? (p. 62)
29. **Test Prep** A dog bakery sells treats in packages of 7. How many packages can they make from 749 treats?

    A 5,243

    B 749

    C 170

    D 107

Extra Practice on page 84, Set C

LESSON 5

ALGEBRA

Patterns in Division

OBJECTIVE: Use patterns to divide.

Quick Review

1. 10 ÷ 2
2. 18 ÷ 3
3. 24 ÷ 4
4. 15 ÷ 5
5. 32 ÷ 8

Learn

PROBLEM A fifth-grade class wrote a book about the history of its school. The book has 40 sheets of paper. The class has 8,000 sheets of paper to make copies of the book. How many copies of the book can the class make?

To find the quotient, start with a basic division fact and look for a pattern.

Example Divide. 8,000 ÷ 40

8 ÷ 4 = 2 ← basic fact
80 ÷ 40 = 2
800 ÷ 40 = 20
8,000 ÷ 40 = 200

So, the class can make 200 copies.

Math Idea
If the dividend increases by a power of 10, then the quotient increases by a power of 10.

More Examples

A
27 ÷ 3 = 9 ← basic fact
270 ÷ 3 = 90
2,700 ÷ 3 = 900
27,000 ÷ 3 = 9,000

B
\$35 ÷ 5 = \$7 ← basic fact
\$350 ÷ 50 = \$7
\$3,500 ÷ 50 = \$70
\$35,000 ÷ 50 = \$700

C
6 ÷ 1 = 6 ← basic fact
6,000 ÷ 10 = 600
6,000 ÷ 100 = 60
6,000 ÷ 1,000 = 6

D
63 ÷ 7 = 9 ← basic fact
630 ÷ 70 = 9
6,300 ÷ 700 = 9
63,000 ÷ 7,000 = 9

- Explain the difference between the patterns in Examples B and C.

Guided Practice

Find the missing numbers.

1. 9 ÷ 3 = 3
90 ÷ 3 = 30
900 ÷ 3 = ■
9,000 ÷ 3 = 3,000

2. 24 ÷ 6 = 4
240 ÷ 6 = 40
2,400 ÷ 6 = 400
24,000 ÷ 6 = ■

3. 40 ÷ 5 = ■
400 ÷ 50 = ■
4,000 ÷ 500 = ■
40,000 ÷ 5,000 = ■

FAST TRACK

KY MA-05-1.3.1 Students will analyze real-world problems to identify appropriate representations using mathematic operations, and will apply operations to solve real-world problems with the following constraints: add, subtract, multip and divide whole numbers (less than 100,000,000), using technology where appropriate. DOK 2 *also* MA-05-1.1.1

Use basic facts and patterns to find the quotient.

4. 80 ÷ 2 **5.** 140 ÷ 20 **6.** $3,200 ÷ 8 **7.** 36,000 ÷ 60

8. TALK Math **Explain** why the quotient decreases as the number of zeros in the divisor increases.

Independent Practice and Problem Solving

Use basic facts and patterns to find the quotient.

9. 20 ÷ 10 **10.** 180 ÷ 9 **11.** $160 ÷ 40 **12.** 420 ÷ 7

13. 300 ÷ 50 **14.** 640 ÷ 80 **15.** $810 ÷ 9 **16.** 540 ÷ 60

17. 1,200 ÷ 4 **18.** $1,000 ÷ 10 **19.** 5,600 ÷ 70 **20.** 3,600 ÷ 90

21. 49,000 ÷ 70 **22.** 60,000 ÷ 2 **23.** 40,000 ÷ 20 **24.** $25,000 ÷ 50

Compare. Use <, >, or = for each ●.

25. 560 ÷ 80 ● 5,600 ÷ 8 **26.** 3,000 ÷ 5 ● 300 ÷ 5 **27.** 32,000 ÷ 40 ● 3,200 ÷ 4

28. 11,000 ÷ 110 ● 500 ÷ 5 **29.** 360 ÷ 6 ● 3,600 ÷ 600 **30.** 24,000 ÷ 80 ● 1,800 ÷ 6

31. A school ordered 40 cartons of paper weighing a total of 2,000 pounds. How much does 1 carton of paper weigh?

32. One carton holds 10 reams of paper, which is 5,000 sheets of paper. How many sheets of paper are in 1 ream?

33. A company is buying 4 laser printers for $800. If each printer comes with a $25 mail-in rebate, what is the cost of a single printer?

34. It takes about 3 trees to make 24,000 sheets of paper. About how many sheets of paper can be made out of one tree?

35. **Algebra** How would you find the value of n for $2{,}400 \div n = 80$?

36. WRITE Math **What's the Error?** Mela says that 66,000 ÷ 6 is 1,100. What is her error? What should her answer be?

Mixed Review and Test Prep

37. If 10 people swim 25 laps each, what is the total number of laps they swim? (p. 36)

38. Mount Everest is 29,035 feet high. What is its height rounded to the nearest hundred feet? (p. 14)

39. **Test Prep** A hotel owner spends $20,000 on 40 new television sets. How much does she spend on each television set if each costs the same amount?

A $400 **C** $4,000

B $500 **D** $5,000

Extra Practice on page 84, Set D

LESSON 6

Estimate with 2-Digit Divisors

OBJECTIVE: Estimate quotients when dividing by 2-digit numbers.

Quick Review

1. 16 ÷ 2
2. 28 ÷ 4
3. 30 ÷ 5
4. 72 ÷ 8
5. 36 ÷ 12

Learn

PROBLEM The Transamerica Pyramid in San Francisco, California, is 853 feet tall and has 48 floors. If each floor is the same height, about what difference, in feet, is between one floor level and the next?

You can use compatible numbers to estimate quotients.

Example 1 **Estimate.** 853 ÷ 48

853 ÷ 48 ↓ ↓ 850 ÷ 50 = 17	Determine the place-value of the quotient. Since $48 > 8$ but $48 < 85$, the first digit will be in the tens place. 850 and 50 are compatible numbers since 85 ÷ 5 = 17.

So, the difference between one floor level and the next is about 17 feet.

You can also estimate a quotient by using two sets of compatible numbers to find two different reasonable estimates.

Example 2 **Estimate.** 2,720 ÷ 32

Think: 2,720 is between 2,700 and 3,000.

Use 2,700.	Use 3,000.
2,720 ÷ 32 ↓ ↓ 2,700 ÷ 30 = 90 ← 2,700 and 30 are compatible numbers since 27 ÷ 3 = 9.	2,720 ÷ 32 ↓ ↓ 3,000 ÷ 30 = 100 ← 3,000 and 30 are compatible numbers since 3 ÷ 3 = 1.

So, two reasonable estimates for 2,720 ÷ 32 are 90 and 100.

Math Idea
Choose compatible numbers that are easy to solve using patterns and basic facts.

Guided Practice

1. Estimate 149 ÷ 43 using two sets of compatible numbers.

   120 ÷ 40 = ■ or ■ ÷ 40 = 4

Write two sets of compatible numbers for each. Then give two possible estimates.

2. 22)94
3. 68)523
4. 81)705
5. 43)2,326
6. 23)1,260

FAST TRACK KY MA-05-1.2.1 Students will apply and describe appropriate strategies for estimating quantities of objects and computational results in real-world problems. DOK 2 *also* MA-05-1.1.1; MA-05-1.3.1

Estimate the quotient.

7. $33\overline{)291}$ 8. $49\overline{)427}$ 9. $85\overline{)\$618}$ 10. $91\overline{)1{,}805}$ 11. $31\overline{)6{,}468}$

12. TALK Math Explain whether 60 or 70 is a more reasonable estimate for $4{,}158 \div 58$.

Independent Practice and Problem Solving

Write two sets of compatible numbers for each. Then give two possible estimates.

13. $42\overline{)396}$ 14. $56\overline{)413}$ 15. $71\overline{)580}$ 16. $21\overline{)1{,}716}$ 17. $59\overline{)4{,}636}$

18. $\$375 \div 63$ 19. $2{,}302 \div 34$ 20. $4{,}337 \div 74$ 21. $\$3{,}426 \div 47$ 22. $8{,}199 \div 77$

Estimate the quotient.

23. $19\overline{)228}$ 24. $25\overline{)\$595}$ 25. $27\overline{)914}$ 26. $96\overline{)831}$ 27. $31\overline{)6{,}468}$

28. $462 \div 83$ 29. $1{,}319 \div 41$ 30. $5{,}535 \div 74$ 31. $33{,}842 \div 36$ 32. $48{,}574 \div 53$

USE DATA For 33–34, use the picture.

33. About what distance, in meters, is between one floor level and the next at the Chrysler Building?

34. Estimate the difference between the distance in meters between one floor level and the next at the Columbia Center and at the Aon Center.

35. **Reasoning** George ran for 45 minutes. Lily ran for 3,180 seconds. Estimate who ran for the shorter amount of time.

36. WRITE Math Explain how you know the quotient $298 \div 31$ will be between 9 and 10.

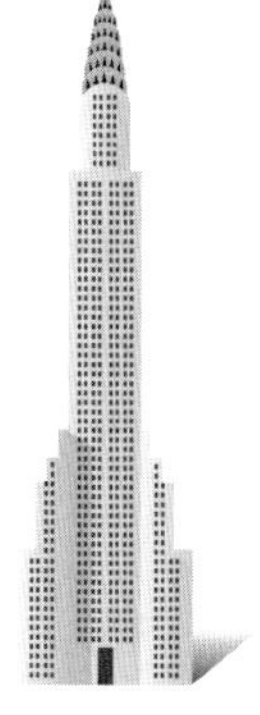

319 meters
77 floors
Chrysler Building
New York City

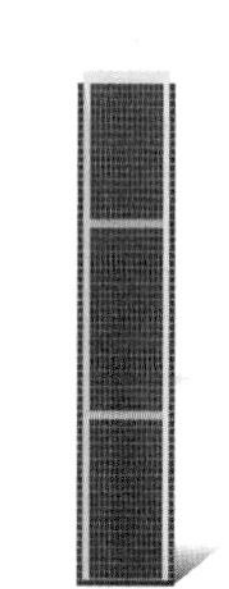

262 meters
62 floors
Aon Center
Los Angeles

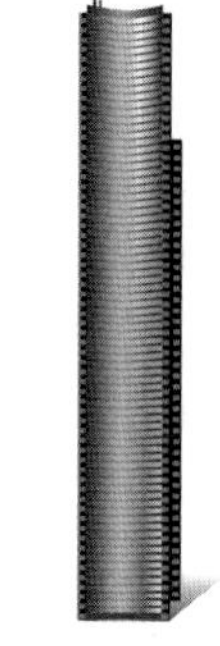

295 meters
76 floors
Columbia Center
Washington

Mixed Review and Test Prep

37. Erin drew a quadrilateral with only one pair of parallel sides. What type of quadrilateral did she draw? (Grade 4)

38. Leo wrote the following pattern: $36 \div 6 = 6$, $360 \div 6 = 60$, $3{,}600 \div 6 = 600$. What might come next in his pattern? (p. 70)

39. **Test Prep** Jorja built a tower out of cubes. It was 654 centimeters tall. The height of each cube was about 16 centimeters. About how many cubes did Jorja use?

A 4
B 14
C 40
D 400

Extra Practice on page 84, Set E

LESSON 7

Divide by 2-Digit Divisors

OBJECTIVE: Divide by 2-digit numbers.

Quick Review

1. 4×30
2. 6×19
3. 25×10
4. 46×20
5. 60×16

Learn

PROBLEM The average person in the United States eats about 23 pounds of pizza every year. How many years would it take the average person to eat 1,000 pounds of pizza?

To solve the problem, you can divide using place value.

Surveys of kids between the ages of 3 and 11 show that they prefer pizza for lunch and dinner to all other foods. ▼

ONE WAY Use place value.

Divide. $1{,}000 \div 23$ $\quad 23\overline{)1{,}000}$

Step 1

Estimate to place the first digit in the quotient.

Think: $25\overline{)1{,}000}$ = 40 $\qquad 23\overline{)1{,}000}$ ■

So, place the first digit of the quotient in the tens place.

Step 2

Divide the 100 tens by 23.

```
     4
23)1,000
  -92
    8
```

Divide. $23\overline{)100}$
Multiply. 23×4
Subtract. $100 - 92$
Compare. $8 < 23$

Step 3

Bring down the 0 ones.
Divide 80 by 23.

```
     43 r11
23)1,000
  -92↓
    80
   -69
    11
```

Divide. $23\overline{)80}$
Multiply. 23×3
Subtract. $80 - 69$
Compare. $11 < 23$

Step 4

To check your answer, multiply the quotient by the divisor. Then add the remainder.

```
   43
  ×23
  129
 +860
  989
```

$989 + 11 = 1{,}000$

So, it would take more than 43 years to eat 1,000 pounds of pizza.

A $2{,}394 \div 63$ $\quad 63\overline{)2{,}394}$

Estimate. $2{,}400 \div 60 = 40$

```
      38
63)2,394
  -189↓
    504
   -504
      0
```

Check ✓

```
   63
  ×38
2,394
```

B $1{,}506 \div 22$ $\quad 22\overline{)1{,}506}$

Estimate. $1{,}500 \div 25 = 60$

```
      68 r10
22)1,506
  -132↓
    186
   -176
     10
```

Check ✓

```
   68
  ×22
1,496
```

$1{,}496 + 10 = 1{,}506$

FAST TRACK KY MA-05-1.3.1 Students will analyze real-world problems to identify appropriate representations using mathematic operations, and will apply operations to solve real-world problems with the following constraints: add, subtract, multip and divide whole numbers (less than 100,000,000), using technology where appropriate. DOK 2 *also* MA-05-1.1.

ANOTHER WAY **Use repeated subtraction.**

If the average person eats 23 pounds of pizza each year, how many years would it take the average person to eat 775 pounds of pizza?

Divide. 775 ÷ 23 $\quad 23\overline{)775}$

Step 1

Subtract multiples of the divisor until the remaining number is less than the divisor. Start by subtracting 10 times the divisor 3 times.

```
23)775
  −230  ← 10 × 23
   545
  −230  ← 10 × 23
   315
  −230  ← 10 × 23
    85
```

Step 2

Then subtract smaller multiples of the divisor, such as 5, 2, or 1 times the divisor. Add the multiples to find the quotient.

```
    33 r16
23)775
  −230  ← 10 × 23      10
   545                 10
  −230  ← 10 × 23      10
   315                  2
  −230  ← 10 × 23     + 1
    85                 33
   −46  ← 2 × 23
    39
   −23  ← 1 × 23
    16
```

So, it would take over 33 years to eat 75 pounds of pizza.

Example **Divide.** 622 ÷ 47

```
   13 r11                         Check ✓
47)622
  −470  ← 10 × 47                   13
   152                 10          ×47
  −141  ← 3 × 47      + 3           91
    11                 13         +520
                                   611   611 + 11 = 622
```

Guided Practice

1. Copy and complete the problem below to find 328 ÷ 31.

Estimate: $30\overline{)300}$ (quotient: ■■)

```
     ■■ r18
31)328
  −31↓
    18
   − 0
    18
```

Divide.

2. $18\overline{)648}$ 3. $22\overline{)929}$ ✓4. $53\overline{)2,369}$ ✓5. $62\overline{)3,774}$ 6. $47\overline{)7,395}$

7. TALK Math Explain how you would find 2,044 ÷ 28.

Independent Practice and Problem Solving

Divide. Check your answer.

8. $24\overline{)744}$ 9. $46\overline{)874}$ 10. $39\overline{)975}$ 11. $73\overline{)584}$ 12. $57\overline{)855}$

13. $37\overline{)862}$ 14. $82\overline{)964}$ 15. $56\overline{)2,492}$ 16. $91\overline{)3,276}$ 17. $89\overline{)8,969}$

18. 916 ÷ 41 19. 707 ÷ 96 20. 298 ÷ 12 21. 1,117 ÷ 53 22. 2,816 ÷ 56

Algebra **Write the missing number for each ■.**

23. 263 ÷ 13 = ■ r3 24. ■ ÷ 35 = 3 r24 25. 648 ÷ ■ = 24 26. 416 ÷ 67 = 6 r■

USE DATA For 27–30, use the list.

Each year, the average person in the U.S. eats...
• 68 quarts of popcorn
• 53 pounds of bread
• 19 pounds of apples
• 14 pounds of turkey
POPCORN

27. How many years would it take for the average person in the U.S. to eat 855 pounds of apples?

28. How many pounds of bread would the average person in the U.S. eat in 25 years?

29. How many quarts of popcorn would 6 average people in the U.S. eat in 5 years?

30. **Reasoning** Will the average person in the U.S. eat more pounds of turkey in 20 years or more pounds of apples in 15 years?

31. WRITE Math **Sense or Nonsense** The average person in the U.S. will eat more than 40,000 pounds of bread in his or her lifetime.

Mixed Review and Test Prep

32. One acre is 4,480 square yards. How many square yards are in 8 acres? (p. 40)

33. A parking garage holds 680 cars. The garage has 8 levels. If each level holds the same number of cars, how many cars does each level hold? (p. 62)

34. **Test Prep** The school auditorium has 448 seats arranged in 32 equal rows. How many seats are in each row?

A 14,336 **C** 416

B 480 **D** 14

 Extra Practice on page 84, Set F

Up, Up, and Away!

Summarize

Over the years, many hot-air balloon distance records have been set. The first time that the Atlantic Ocean was crossed in a propane-fueled hot-air balloon was in 1987. This flight covered a distance of 2,900 miles and took the two pilots 33 hours. In 1991 the same two pilots crossed the Pacific, a distance of 6,700 miles, in 47 hours. In 1999, the first flight around the world covered a distance of 26,542 miles and took about 472 hours. Which balloon flight had the fastest average speed in miles per hour?

When you summarize, you restate the most important information in a shortened form to understand what you have read.

ONE WAY **Rewrite the paragraph in a shortened form.**

Summary: Several distance records have been set in hot-air balloons. In 1987, the record was 2,900 miles in 33 hours; in 1991, it was 6,700 miles in 47 hours; and in 1999, it was 26,542 miles in 472 hours. Which balloon flight had the fastest average speed?

ANOTHER WAY **Use a table for important information.**

Hot-Air Balloon Distance Records		
Year	**Distance Traveled (miles)**	**Time (in hours)**
1987	2,900	33
1991	6,700	47
1999	26,542	472

- The title of the table tells the main idea of the word problem.
- The table shows the information needed to solve the problem.

Problem Solving Summarize to understand the problem.

1. Solve the problem above.
2. Hot-air balloons once used helium gas. In 1978, the *Double Eagle II* used helium gas to cross the Atlantic, a distance of 3,120 miles, in 137 hours. Three years later, the *Double Eagle V* crossed the Pacific Ocean, setting a new distance record of 3,535 miles. The flight took 84 hours. Which balloon flight had the faster average speed in miles per hour? Solve the problem.

LESSON 8

Correcting Quotients

OBJECTIVE: Adjust the quotient if the estimate is too high or too low.

Quick Review

Compare. Use <, >, or =.

1. 37 ● 35 **2.** 16 ● 19
3. 55 ● 55 **4.** 28 ● 48
5. 92 ● 29

Learn

PROBLEM An art class is using 336 crayons. All of the crayons are from 48-crayon boxes. How many boxes of crayons does the art class have?

Example **Divide.** 336 ÷ 48 $48\overline{)336}$

Step 1

Use compatible numbers to estimate to place the first digit.

300 ÷ 50 = 6 or 350 ÷ 50 = 7

Divide, using your first estimate.

$$\begin{array}{r} 6 \\ 48\overline{)336} \\ -288 \\ \hline 48 \end{array}$$

Divide. 336 ÷ 48
Multiply. 48 × 6
Subtract. 336 − 288
Compare. 48 = 48

Since 48 = 48, the estimate of 6 is too low.

Step 2

Adjust the quotient. Divide, using your second estimate.

$$\begin{array}{r} 7 \\ 48\overline{)336} \\ -336 \\ \hline 0 \end{array}$$

Divide. 336 ÷ 48
Multiply. 48 × 7
Subtract. 336 − 336
Compare. $0 < 48$

So, the art class has 7 boxes of crayons.

More Examples **Divide.**

A 536 ÷ 64 $64\overline{)536}$

Use compatible numbers to estimate to place the first digit.

540 ÷ 60 = 9 or 480 ÷ 60 = 8

Try 9. Divide.

$$\begin{array}{r} 9 \\ 64\overline{)536} \\ -576 \\ \hline \end{array}$$

$576 > 536$

The estimate of 9 is too high.

Adjust the estimate.

$$\begin{array}{r} 8\text{ r24} \\ 64\overline{)536} \\ -512 \\ \hline 24 \end{array}$$

B 4,563 ÷ 37 $37\overline{)4{,}563}$

Use compatible numbers to estimate to place the first digits.

4,400 ÷ 40 = 110 or 4,800 ÷ 40 = 120

Try 11 tens. Divide.

$$\begin{array}{r} 11 \\ 37\overline{)4{,}563} \\ -37 \\ \hline 86 \\ -37 \\ \hline 49 \end{array}$$

$49 > 37$

The estimate of 110 is too low.

Adjust the estimate.

$$\begin{array}{r} 123\text{ r12} \\ 37\overline{)4{,}563} \\ -37 \\ \hline 86 \\ -74 \\ \hline 123 \\ -111 \\ \hline 12 \end{array}$$

KY MA-05-1.3.1 Students will analyze real-world problems to identify appropriate representations using mathematical operations, and will apply operations to solve real-world problems with the following constraints: add, subtract, multiply and divide whole numbers (less than 100,000,000), using technology where appropriate. DOK 2 *also* MA-05-1.1.1

Guided Practice

1. Use compatible numbers to estimate the quotient.

   $74\overline{)528}$ $\quad 490 \div 70 = ■ \quad ■ \div 70 = 8$

Adjust the estimated digit in the quotient, if needed. Then divide.

2. $\begin{array}{r} 4 \\ 4\overline{)1,546} \end{array}$ **3.** $\begin{array}{r} 3 \\ 27\overline{)810} \end{array}$ **4.** $\begin{array}{r} 9 \\ 34\overline{)2,831} \end{array}$ ✓**5.** $\begin{array}{r} 2 \\ 16\overline{)416} \end{array}$ ✓**6.** $\begin{array}{r} 5 \\ 67\overline{)3,350} \end{array}$

7. TALK Math **Explain** how you know if an estimated quotient is too low or too high.

Independent Practice and Problem Solving

Adjust the estimated digit in the quotient, if needed. Then divide.

8. $\begin{array}{r} 2 \\ 26\overline{)541} \end{array}$ **9.** $\begin{array}{r} 3 \\ 53\overline{)1,592} \end{array}$ **10.** $\begin{array}{r} 9 \\ 38\overline{)327} \end{array}$ **11.** $\begin{array}{r} 1 \\ 43\overline{)688} \end{array}$ **12.** $\begin{array}{r} 6 \\ 67\overline{)4,873} \end{array}$

Choose the better estimate to use for the quotient. Write *a or b*.

13. $29\overline{)117}$ **a.** 3 **b.** 4 **14.** $18\overline{)786}$ **a.** 30 **b.** 40 **15.** $75\overline{)3,300}$ **a.** 40 **b.** 50

Divide.

16. $15\overline{)975}$ **17.** $37\overline{)264}$ **18.** $22\overline{)6,837}$ **19.** $59\overline{)126}$ **20.** $83\overline{)5,146}$

21. $2,135 \div 42$ **22.** $452 \div 31$ **23.** $1,067 \div 97$ **24.** $8,610 \div 82$ **25.** $592 \div 74$

26. Liz needs to buy 675 candles for a wedding reception. Each package contains 24 candles. How many packages should Liz buy?

27. A car repair shop ordered 192 ounces of a special hand cleaner. The cleaner comes in 16-ounce containers that cost $4 each. How much did the order cost?

28. WRITE Math **Explain** how you know that $785 \div 21$ will have a quotient that is less than 40.

Mixed Review and Test Prep

29. A frame is 14 inches wide. How wide is a frame that is 10 times as large? Write a number sentence. (p. 36)

30. At a school fair, 456 students are working in teams of 12. How many teams are there? (p. 74)

31. **Test Prep** The Box of Socks Company packs 18 pairs of socks in a box. How many boxes will the company need to pack 810 pairs of socks?

A 40 **C** 50

B 45 **D** 56

Extra Practice on page 84, Set G

Practice Division

OBJECTIVE: Practice division by 1- and 2-digit divisors.

Quick Review

1. $5\overline{)155}$
2. $7\overline{)287}$
3. $4\overline{)368}$
4. $6\overline{)426}$
5. $8\overline{)648}$

Learn

PROBLEM A cube can be made from 6 square cards. How many cubes can be made out of 1,896 cards?

Example Divide. 1,896 ÷ 6 $\quad 6\overline{)1{,}896}$

Step 1

Estimate to place the first digit.

$6\overline{)1{,}800}$ = 300 $\qquad 6\overline{)1{,}896}$ = ■

Place the first digit in the hundreds place.

Step 2

Divide the 18 hundreds.

```
     3
6)1,896
 -18
   0
```

Step 3

Divide the 9 tens.

```
     31
6)1,896
 -18
    9
   -6
    3
```

Step 4

Bring down the 6 ones. Divide the 36 ones.

```
     316
6)1,896
 -18
   09
   -6
    36
   -36
     0
```

Check ✓

```
  316
×   6
1,896
```

So, 316 cubes can be made out of 1,896 cards. Multiply to check your answer.

More Examples Divide.

A $18\overline{)419}$

Estimate. 400 ÷ 20 = 20

```
     23 r5
18)419
  -36
    59
   -54
     5
```

B $9\overline{)753}$

Estimate. 720 ÷ 9 = 80

```
    83 r6
9)753
 -72
   33
  -27
    6
```

Think Math

You can use multiplication to check your answer in division problems. Or, to simply check if your answer is reasonable, estimate using compatible numbers or rounding.

FAST TRACK

KY MA-05-1.3.1 Students will analyze real-world problems to identify appropriate representations using mathematical operations, and will apply operations to solve real-world problems with the following constraints: add, subtract, multiply and divide whole numbers (less than 100,000,000), using technology where appropriate. DOK 2 *also* MA-05-1.1.1

Guided Practice

1. Estimate to place the first digit of the quotient for $232 \div 5$. $\blacksquare \div 5 = \blacksquare$

Divide. Multiply to check your answer.

2. $3\overline{)177}$
3. $28\overline{)2,688}$
4. $4\overline{)353}$
5. $41\overline{)3,085}$

6. TALK Math **Explain** how you can use division to find the missing number in $9 \times n = 1,332$.

Independent Practice and Problem Solving

Divide. Multiply to check your answer.

7. $8\overline{)2,744}$
8. $9\overline{)5,047}$
9. $25\overline{)15,325}$
10. $44\overline{)310,375}$
11. $9,088 \div 3$
12. $12,422 \div 6$
13. $45,090 \div 9$
14. $74,608 \div 12$

Algebra **Write the missing number for each $\blacksquare$.**

15. $532 \div \blacksquare = 28$
16. $2,493 \div 9 = \blacksquare$
17. $863 \div 23 = 37 \text{ r}\blacksquare$

USE DATA **For 18–20, use the table.**

Making Origami Cranes and Boxes

- By using a certain computer program, you can follow the instructions to fold an origami box in about 4 minutes.
- Using the same computer program, you can follow the instructions to fold an origami crane in about 12 minutes.

18. Using the method taught by the computer program, what is the greatest number of origami boxes that can be folded in 336 minutes?
19. Ki spent 528 minutes making paper cranes for a party. What is the greatest number of cranes that Ki could have made?
20. WRITE Math **What's the Question?** Jed used the computer program to learn how to fold origami boxes. Jed folded the greatest number of boxes in the given amount of time. The answer is 140 minutes.

Mixed Review and Test Prep

21. Luis makes 4 stacks of cards. Each stack has 23 cards in it. How many cards does Luis use? (p. 40)
22. Gen had \$42.72. She earned \$19.50 for pet sitting. How much money does Gen have now? (Grade 4)
23. **Test Prep** A school cafeteria used 1,300 flour tortillas in one week. There are 24 tortillas in a package. How many packages of tortillas did the cafeteria open?

    A 6 **C** 54

    B 24 **D** 55

Extra Practice on page 84, Set H

Problem Solving Workshop
Skill: Relevant or Irrelevant Information

OBJECTIVE: Solve problems by using the skill *relevant or irrelevant information.*

Use the Skill

PROBLEM Mr. Ramirez drove from New York City, New York, to Miami, Florida, a distance of about 1,320 miles. He drove for a total of 24 hours. His car got 22 miles per gallon of gas used. If Mr. Ramirez drove about the same number of miles each hour, how many miles did he drive in 1 hour? How many gallons of gas did he use?

▲ Cars get more miles to the gallon when driving on a major highway than when driving in a town.

Sometimes a problem contains information you need for one question and not another. Sometimes there is more information than you need for either question. You must decide which information is relevant, or needed, to answer each question.

Fact	How many miles did Mr. Ramirez drive in 1 hour?	How many gallons of gas did he use?
Mr. Ramirez drove a distance of about 1,320 miles.	relevant	relevant
Mr. Ramirez drove for a total of 24 hours.	relevant	irrelevant
Mr. Ramirez's car got 22 miles to the gallon.	irrelevant	relevant

Use the relevant information to answer each question.

So, Mr. Ramirez drove 1,320 ÷ 24, or about 55, miles each hour. He used 1,320 ÷ 22, or 60, gallons of gas.

Think and Discuss

Tell which information is relevant to solve the problem. Explain your choice. Solve the problem.

a. The Christophers drove 1,197 miles from their house to a cousin's house. They drove 565 miles on Friday and 632 miles on Saturday. They drove about 57 miles each hour. How many hours were they driving?

b. A warehouse has 45 cartons of books with the same number of books in each carton. There are 3,060 books in the cartons. Each book costs $5.95. How many books are in each carton?

 FAST TRACK KY MA-05-1.1.1 Students will: apply these numbers to represent real-world problems. DOK 2

Guided Problem Solving

Tell which information is relevant and irrelevant to solve the problem. Then solve the problem.

1. Rashid earns $25 per week walking his neighbor's dog. His goal is to save $1,200 to buy a new computer. Every week, Rashid saves $15 of his earnings and he spends $10. How many weeks must Rashid save $15 per week to reach his goal? If he saved all his earnings every week, how many weeks would it take him to reach his goal?

Fact	How many weeks must Rashid save $15 to reach his goal?	How many weeks must Rashid save all his earnings to reach his goal?
Rashid earns $25 per week.	irrelevant	relevant
Rashid saves $15 per week.	■	irrelevant
Rashid's goal is to save $1,200.	relevant	relevant
Rashid spends $10 per week.	irrelevant	■

So, Rashid must save $15 per week for $1,200 ÷ $15, or ■ weeks.
He must save $25 per week for $1,200 ÷ ■, or 48 weeks.

2. **What if** Rashid's parents gave him an additional $15 per week towards his goal? If he adds it to the $15 he already saves, how many weeks will it take him to reach his goal of $1,200?

3. A total of 48 fifth graders and 4 teachers went on a trip to the museum. The total cost for the students' tickets was $576. The total cost for the teachers' tickets was $60. What was the price for each student ticket?

Mixed Applications

USE DATA For 4–6, use the table.

4. Jennifer drove from Chicago to St. Louis. She drove about 65 miles each hour and used 15 gallons of gas. For how many hours was Jennifer driving?

5. Bill drove from Atlanta, GA, to Phoenix, AZ. He drove about 62 miles each hour. For how many hours did Bill drive?

6. Li and Jon wanted to meet in Raleigh, NC. Li drove from Atlanta, GA, and Jon drove from Louisville, KY. Li drove about 52 miles each hour and Jon drove about 70 miles each hour. If they left at the same time and took the same amount of time for breaks, who arrived in Raleigh first?

Distances Between Cities (in miles)

	Atlanta, GA	St. Louis, MO	Louisville, KY
Chicago, IL	710	260	297
Phoenix, AZ	1,860	1,506	1,764
Raleigh, NC	416	827	560

7. **WRITE Math** During the last 6 months, a pizza restaurant sold 526 large pizzas and 416 small pizzas. Is it reasonable to say that the restaurant sold about 1,000 pizzas per month? **Explain.**

Extra Practice

Set A Estimate the quotient. (pp. 60–61)

1. $6\overline{)250}$ 2. $8\overline{)319}$ 3. $9\overline{)452}$ 4. $4\overline{)359}$ 5. $8\overline{)650}$

Set B Divide. Check by multiplying. (pp. 62–65)

1. $2\overline{)156}$ 2. $4\overline{)563}$ 3. $7\overline{)2,308}$ 4. $5\overline{)5,823}$ 5. $6\overline{)2,099}$

6. $4\overline{)252}$ 7. $9\overline{)729}$ 8. $3\overline{)1,640}$ 9. $7\overline{)3,627}$ 10. $3\overline{)5,210}$

Set C Divide. (pp. 68–69)

1. $5\overline{)620}$ 2. $4\overline{)416}$ 3. $8\overline{)853}$ 4. $3\overline{)1,052}$ 5. $6\overline{)4,240}$

Set D Use basic facts and patterns to find the quotient. (pp. 70–71)

1. $300 \div 3$ 2. $240 \div 8$ 3. $\$2,500 \div 5$ 4. $10,000 \div 10$

5. A printing company ordered 60 cases of printer ink containing 1,440 ink cartridges. How many cartridges are in a single case?

6. The Sanchez family drove about 10,800 miles last year. If they drove about the same distance each month, how many miles did they drive in one month?

Set E Estimate the quotient. (pp. 72–73)

1. $21\overline{)489}$ 2. $43\overline{)832}$ 3. $72\overline{)285}$ 4. $38\overline{)1,615}$ 5. $59\overline{)5,470}$

6. $24\overline{)502}$ 7. $62\overline{)1,308}$ 8. $13\overline{)2,424}$ 9. $61\overline{)5,432}$ 10. $38\overline{)1,197}$

Set F Divide. Check your answer. (pp. 74–77)

1. $21\overline{)861}$ 2. $13\overline{)637}$ 3. $56\overline{)5,618}$ 4. $26\overline{)658}$ 5. $63\overline{)3,876}$

Set G Adjust the estimate in the quotient, if needed. Then divide. (pp. 78–79)

1. $\begin{array}{r}2\\31\overline{)607}\end{array}$ 2. $\begin{array}{r}3\\12\overline{)487}\end{array}$ 3. $\begin{array}{r}3\\8\overline{)2,509}\end{array}$ 4. $\begin{array}{r}9\\40\overline{)423}\end{array}$ 5. $\begin{array}{r}2\\16\overline{)312}\end{array}$

Set H Divide. Multiply to check your answer. (pp. 80–81)

1. $8\overline{)424}$ 2. $16\overline{)329}$ 3. $30\overline{)3,890}$ 4. $43\overline{)8,452}$ 5. $24\overline{)781}$

6. Carson collects 241 cans to recycle. He can fit 14 cans in a bag. How many bags will Carson need for all of the cans?

CD ROM **Technology**
Use Harcourt Mega Math, The Number Games, *Up, Up, and Array,* Levels Q, R, S.

PRACTICE GAME

What's Left?

Ready!

2 players

Set!

- 2 sets of 10 counters, each set a different color

19 17 11 20 13 6 3 1 16 18 12 8 14 2 7 4 9 10 5 15

Begin!

- Each player selects a set of counters.
- Player 1 chooses a number from 1 to 20. This will be the remainder.
- Player 2 should write a division problem that, when solved, has the remainder that Player 1 chose.
- Player 1 finds the quotient and remainder of the division problem.
- If the division problem is correct, Player 2 places a counter on the remainder located on the board.
- If the problem is incorrect, Player 1 places a counter on the remainder located on the board.
- Players reverse roles to complete the round.
- After 10 rounds, the player with the greater number of counters on the board wins.

MATH POWER Rate, Distance, Time

On Your Mark, Get Set, Go!

In the first three stages of the Tour de France, one racer covered a distance of 630 kilometers in 15 hours. What was this racer's rate of speed?

You can use the basic formula, distance = rate × time, to solve the problem. Dividing distance by time will give the rate, or speed.

Math Idea
distance = rate × time
rate = distance ÷ time
time = distance ÷ rate

Examples

Find the rate for covering 630 km in 15 hours.

Write the distance and time. distance = 630 km, time = 15 hr
Divide distance by time.

$$\begin{array}{r} 42 \\ 15\overline{)630} \\ -60 \\ \hline 30 \\ -30 \\ \hline 0 \end{array}$$

So, the racer's rate of speed was 42 kilometers per hour.

You can find the time by dividing the distance by rate. The racer covered the next 703 kilometers of the race at an average speed of 37 kilometers per hour. How long did this take?

Find the time.

Write the distance and rate. distance = 703 km, rate = 37 km/hr
Divide distance by rate.

$$\begin{array}{r} 19 \\ 37\overline{)703} \\ -37 \\ \hline 333 \\ -333 \\ \hline 0 \end{array}$$

So, it took 19 hours to ride 703 kilometers.

Try It

Find the rate, time, or distance.

1. rate: 12 km/hr
   distance: 96 km
   time: ■
2. rate: ■
   distance: 1,044 mi
   time = 36 hr
3. rate: 59 km/hr
   distance: ■
   time: 21 hr
4. rate: 85 m/s
   distance: 935 m
   time = ■
5. WRITE Math **Explain** how to find how long it took Dave to read a 208-page book if he read at a rate of 26 pages per hour.

KENTUCKY Chapter 3 Review/Test

Check Concepts

1. How can you check your quotient when there is a remainder? Describe the steps. KY MA-05-1.3.1 (p. 68)
2. Explain how to use compatible numbers to estimate $2,456 \div 13$. KY MA-05-1.2.1 (p. 72)
3. Explain how you know that an estimate of 5 is too low for $115 \div 19$. KY MA-05-1.2.1 (p. 78)

Check Skills

Estimate. Then divide. KY MA-05-1.2.1; MA-05-1.3.1 (pp. 68–69)

4. $6\overline{)302}$
5. $2\overline{)1,423}$
6. $5\overline{)518}$
7. $14\overline{)2,867}$
8. $31\overline{)786}$

Use basic facts and patterns to find the quotient. KY MA-05-1.3.1 (pp. 70–71)

9. $50 \div 10$
10. $720 \div 9$
11. $3,600 \div 600$
12. $60,000 \div 3,000$
13. $49,000 \div 70$

Estimate the quotient. KY MA-05-1.2.1 (pp. 60–61, 72–73)

14. $7\overline{)418}$
15. $9\overline{)5,539}$
16. $14\overline{)624}$
17. $43\overline{)1,025}$
18. $76\overline{)3,229}$

Divide. Check your answer by multiplying. KY MA-05-1.3.1 (pp. 62–65, 74–77, 80–81)

19. $3\overline{)309}$
20. $7\overline{)444}$
21. $6\overline{)634}$
22. $22\overline{)3,972}$
23. $47\overline{)366}$
24. $17\overline{)981}$
25. $60\overline{)715}$
26. $34\overline{)1,510}$
27. $22\overline{)1,244}$
28. $47\overline{)5,781}$
29. $50\overline{)9,950}$
30. $85\overline{)3,276}$

Check Problem Solving

Solve. KY MA-05-1.3.1 (pp. 82–83)

31. Students at Dodson Middle School raised $1,344 during a charity drive. The fundraiser was held for 6 weeks, and the money will be divided evenly among 4 different charities. How much money will each charity receive? Tell which information is relevant and irrelevant. Then solve.
32. Kyle earned $25 for each lawn that he mowed. If he earned $675 for the summer, how many times did Kyle mow lawns during that period?
33. **WRITE Math** Ms. Quincy needs 328 yards of fabric to make quilts for a craft fair. The fabric comes in rolls of 15 yards. How many rolls should Ms. Quincy buy? **Explain** your answer.

GO ONLINE **Technology** Use *Online Assessment.*

Practice for the KCCT
Chapters 1–3

Number and Operations

1. Which number has the digit 4 in the tens place? KY MA-05-1.1.1 (p. 6)

   A 3,096,432 C 3,096,324

   B 3,094,320 D 3,096,342

2. A concert hall has 432 seats. There are 24 rows. Each row has the same number of seats. How many seats are in each row? KY MA-05-1.3.1 (p. 74)

   A 17 C 22

   B 18 D 24

Choose the answer.

See item 2. If your answer doesn't match one of the choices, check your computation.

3. Which is 54,965 written in expanded form? KY MA-05-1.1.1 (p. 4)

   A 5,400 + 900 + 60 + 5

   B 50,000 + 4,000 + 900 + 65

   C 50,000 + 4,000 + 960 + 5

   D 50,000 + 4,000 + 900 + 60 + 5

4. WRITE Math Estimate the product 472 × 11. Then find the exact product. Was your estimate reasonable? **Explain.** KY MA-05-1.2.1 (p. 38)

Algebraic Thinking

5. The table shows a number pattern. If the pattern continues, what might the missing number be? KY Grade 4

Input	1	2	3	4	5
Output	7	■	11	13	15

   A 6 C 8

   B 7 D 9

6. Joan is *n* years older than her brother Peter. If Peter is 15, which expression represents Joan's age? KY Grade 4

   A $15 + n$

   B $15n$

   C $15 - n$

   D $15 \div n$

7. Which is an example of the Distributive Property? KY Grade 4

   A $7 \times (6 \times 5) = (7 \times 6) \times 5$

   B $3 + 5 = 5 + 3$

   C $4 \times 1 = 4$

   D $6 \times 15 = 6 \times (10 + 5)$

8. WRITE Math Jessie solved the division problem below. How can she use multiplication to check her work? **Explain.** KY Grade 4

$$369 \div 9 = 41$$

Geometry

9. Which of the following is an obtuse angle? KY Grade 4

A 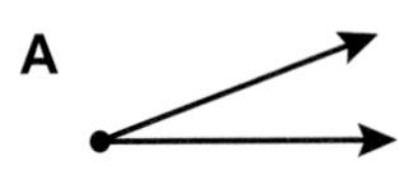

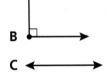

B 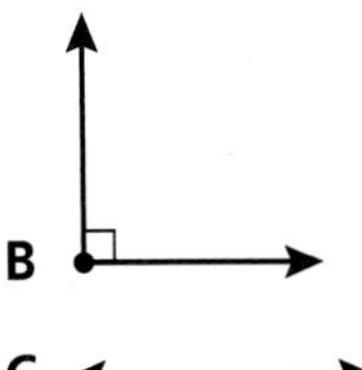

C 

D

10. Which term best describes the triangle shown below? KY Grade 4

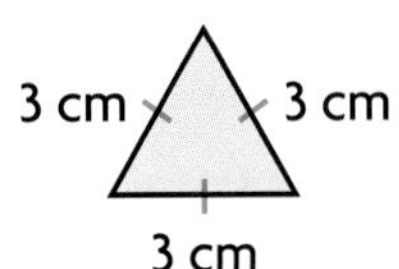

A right

B obtuse

C isosceles

D equilateral

11. WRITE Math Philippe says the figures below are congruent because they are both rectangles. Is he correct? **Explain.** KY Grade 4

Data Analysis and Probability

12. A bag contains 3 red marbles, 2 blue marbles, and 1 green marble. What is the likelihood of randomly choosing a green marble? KY Grade 4

A certain

B likely

C unlikely

D impossible

13. Connie asked her classmates who they voted for as class president. Her results are shown in the table below. What type of graph works best for the data? KY Grade 4

Candidates	Number of Votes
Horatio	32
Lin	27
Tyrone	24
Ashley	17

A stem-and-leaf plot

B line plot

C double-bar graph

D circle graph

14. WRITE Math Tyrell performed an experiment. He put 40 tiles into a bowl. Half of the tiles were red and half were blue. Tyrell chose 1 tile out of the bowl without looking. What is the probability that Tyrell chose a red tile? **Explain.** KY Grade 4

CHAPTER

4 Algebra: Expressions and Equations

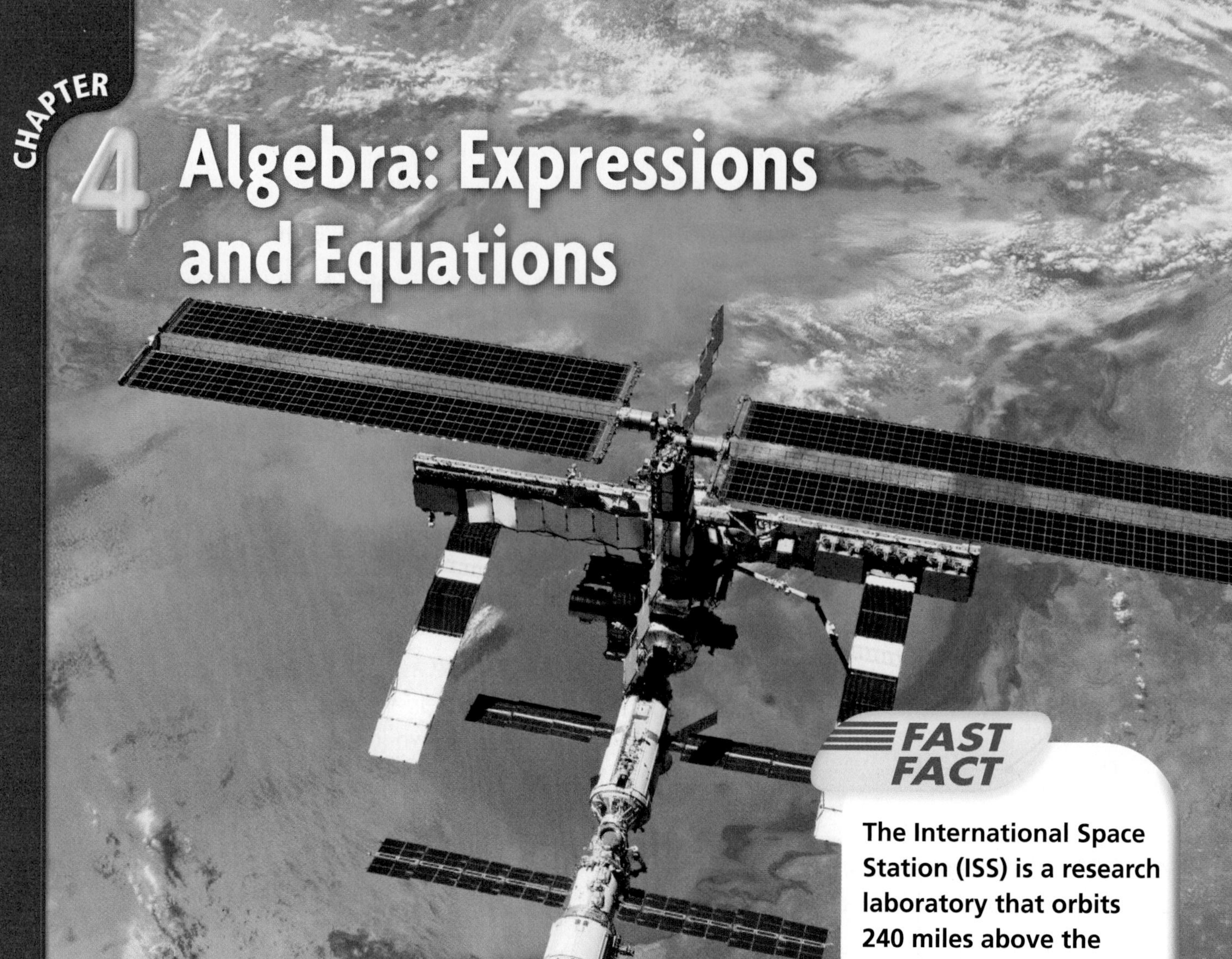

FAST FACT

The International Space Station (ISS) is a research laboratory that orbits 240 miles above the Earth's surface. The station weighs more than 400,000 pounds and has as much living area as a 3-bedroom home!

Investigate

Each crew of astronauts on the ISS completes a variety of experiments during its expedition. Choose two expeditions from the table. Show how you would write an equation to compare the number of experiments using a variable. Tell what the variable represents, and then find the value of the variable.

ISS Expedition Experiments

Expedition	Number of Experiments
1	7
2	22
3	29
4	33
5	33
6	23
7	24

GO ONLINE **Technology** Student pages are available in the Student eBook.

Show What You Know

Check your understanding of important skills needed for success in Chapter 4.

▶ Multiplication Properties

Write the letter of the multiplication property used in each equation.

A. Commutative Property **C.** Identity Property
B. Associative Property **D.** Zero Property

1. $43 \times 1 = 43$ **2.** $6 \times 9 = 9 \times 6$ **3.** $(8 \times 2) \times 4 = 8 \times (2 \times 4)$

4. $7 \times 12 = 12 \times 7$ **5.** $3 \times (9 \times 5) = (3 \times 9) \times 5$ **6.** $62 \times 0 = 0$

▶ Addition Properties

Write the letter of the addition property used in each equation.

A. Commutative Property **B.** Associative Property **C.** Identity Property

7. $8 + 5 = 5 + 8$ **8.** $25 + 0 = 25$ **9.** $(6 + 7) + 2 = 6 + (7 + 2)$

10. $0 + 37 = 37$ **11.** $9 + (3 + 5) = (9 + 3) + 5$ **12.** $15 + 29 = 29 + 15$

▶ Expressions

Find each value.

13. $(6 + 9) - 3$ **14.** $4 + (16 - 5)$ **15.** $12 + (25 - 3)$

16. $(32 + 8) - 10$ **17.** $(9 + 8) - 7$ **18.** $20 - (3 + 4)$

19. $15 + (22 - 3)$ **20.** $36 - (9 + 3)$ **21.** $41 - (20 - 5)$

VOCABULARY POWER

CHAPTER VOCABULARY

algebraic expression
Associative Property
Commutative Property
Distributive Property
equation
evaluate
expression
function
Identity Property
inequality
numerical expression
order of operations
solution
variable
Zero Property of Multiplication

WARM-UP WORDS

equation an algebraic or numerical sentence that shows that two quantities are equal

evaluate to find the value of a numerical or algebraic expression

order of operations a special set of rules which gives the order in which calculations are done in an expression

Write Expressions

OBJECTIVE: Write numerical and algebraic expressions.

Quick Review

Teresa has 8 pieces of pottery, and Erin has 13 pieces of pottery. What operation would you use to find how many more pieces Erin has?

Vocabulary

expression
variable
numerical expression
algebraic expression

Learn

An **expression** is a mathematical phrase that combines numbers, operation signs, and sometimes variables, but does not have an equal sign. A **numerical expression** has only numbers and operation signs.

PROBLEM Tyler's camp group caught 15 sand bass and 12 stripers. Write a numerical expression to represent how many fish the group caught in all.

First, identify the operation to use. In this example, it is addition.

15 sand bass	plus	12 stripers
↓		↓
15	+	12

So, 15 + 12 represents how many fish the group caught in all.

Examples Write a numerical expression for each situation.

A Addition

Emma has 11 fish in her aquarium. She bought 4 more fish.

fish	plus	new fish
↓		↓
11	+	4

B Subtraction

Alexi had 128 stamps. She used 38 stamps on party invitations.

stamps	minus	stamps
↓		↓
128	−	38

C Multiplication

Kayla bought 5 books. Each book cost $3.

books	multiplied by	cost per book
↓		↓
5	×	3

D Division

Four players share 52 cards equally.

cards	divided by	players
↓		↓
52	÷	4

- In Examples A–D, what does each expression represent?

FAST TRACK KY MA-05-5.3.1 Students will model real-world and mathematical problems with simple number sentences (equations and inequalities) with a variable or missing value (e.g., 4 = 2 × N, ___ + 5 > 14) and apply simple number sentences to solve mathematical and real-world problems. DOK 2 *also* MA-05-1.1.1; MA-05-5.2.1

Algebraic Expressions

A **variable** is a letter or symbol that stands for one or more numbers. An **algebraic expression** contains at least one variable.

At Pets for Less, a blue peacock fish costs $7. Brian bought some blue peacocks. What expression can you write to represent the cost?

Example 1 Write an algebraic expression. Tell what the variable represents.

Step 1

Choose a variable and tell what it represents.

Let n = the number of blue peacocks.

Step 2

Write the expression.

cost per fish	multiplied by	number of blue peacocks
↓		↓
7	×	n

So, $7 \times n$ represents the cost of the blue peacocks.

In algebraic expressions, there are several ways to show multiplication. The expression $7 \times n$ can also be written as $7 \cdot n$, $7(n)$, or $7n$.

More Examples Write an algebraic expression for each situation.

A Jim is thinking of a number. He doubles the number and then adds 7.

Let n = the number.

$2n + 7$

B Raye has some hats. She gave 2 hats to her sister.

Let h = the number of hats Raye had.

$h - 2$

C The coach gave Seth 10 soccer balls to add to the soccer balls the team already had.

Let s = the soccer balls the team already had.

$s + 10$

Write the algebraic expression in words.

D $3c - 8$

8 less than 3 times a number, c

E $p \times 5$

the number, 5, p times.

F $6 + \frac{t}{5}$

6 plus the quotient of t divided by 5

Guided Practice

1. Movie tickets cost $8 each. Some friends buy tickets to see a movie. Copy and complete the expression.

cost for each ticket	multiplied by	number of friends
↓		↓
■	×	f

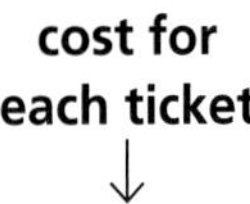

Write a numerical expression. Tell what the expression represents.

2. Terri drives 26 miles on Monday and 90 miles on Tuesday.
3. 27 less than 80
4. 7 plus the quotient of 72 divided by 9

Write an algebraic expression. Tell what the variable represents.

5. Nathan had 11 shirts. He grew out of some of them and bought 2 more.
6. Callie paid money to the kennel to board her cat for 13 days.
7. Dee had some books. She was given 9 more books.

8. TALK Math **Explain** how to write an expression for this situation: Ben had 24 pencils and then gave some to his sister.

Independent Practice and Problem Solving

Write a numerical expression. Tell what the expression represents.

9. Jose divides 12 party favors equally among 6 friends.
10. Monique had $20. She spent $5 on lunch and $10 at the book store.
11. Isabelle bought a dozen bottles of water at 95 cents each.

Write an algebraic expression. Tell what the variable represents.

12. Walter made some granola bars. He divided them equally among 8 bags.
13. Tina has some shells from the beach. Her sister has twice as many shells.
14. Erica is 7 years younger than Paul.

Write each algebraic expression in words.

15. $p \times 12$
16. $7c + 8$
17. $28 - \frac{w}{3}$

USE DATA For 18–20, use the table.

18. Write a numerical expression to represent the total number of lemon tetras that could be in a 20-gallon tank.
19. **Pose a Problem** Look at Problem 18. Write a similar problem by changing the type of fish and the size of the tank.
20. WRITE Math **Explain** how to represent the cost of some tiger barbs if the cost of each one is $4.

Aquarium Fish

Type of Fish	Length (in inches)
Lemon tetra	2
Strawberry tetra	3
Giant danio	5
Tiger barb	3
Swordtail	5

The rule for the number of fish in an aquarium is to allow 1 gallon of water for each inch of fish.

 Extra Practice on page 120, Set A

Learn About Models and Expressions

You can use models to represent algebraic expressions.

Examples

Use pattern blocks to model each situation. Use the yellow hexagon to represent the variable and the orange square to represent 1.

A At 3 months, Glen's dog, Kody, weighed 6 more pounds than he did at birth.

Let ⬡ represent the number of pounds Kody weighed at birth.

Then, ⬡ ■ ■ ■ ■ ■ ■ represents the number of pounds he weighed at 3 months.

B A home builder built 5 times as many homes this year as last year.

Let ⬡ represent the number of homes built last year.

Then, ⬡⬡⬡⬡⬡ represents the number of homes built this year.

Try It

Use pattern blocks to model each situation.

21. James did 2 loads of laundry. Then his brother did the rest.

22. The mail carrier has 3 times as many letters to deliver today as yesterday.

23. Randy had some money. Then he earned $10.

24. Erica has 2 times as many shells as her sister.

25. Chris has saved $7 more than Adam.

26. Monica jogged 5 miles more this week than she jogged last week.

Mixed Review and Test Prep

27. There are 6 marbles. Two are red, one is blue, and 3 are green. If Mark picks a marble without looking, which color is Mark most likely to pull? (Grade 4)

28. **Test Prep** Alicia has some CDs. Her older brother has 3 times as many CDs. Write an expression to represent the number of CDs Alicia's brother has. Tell what the variable represents.

29. Each bus can seat 38 people. How many buses will be needed for 532 people? (p. 74)

30. **Test Prep** The temperature dropped from a high of 48 degrees. Which expression best describes the new temperature?

A $48 - t$

B $48 + t$

C $48t$

D $t - 48$

LESSON 2

Evaluate Expressions

OBJECTIVE: Evaluate numerical and algebraic expressions using order of operations.

Quick Review

Find the value.

1. $12 + 5 - 8$
2. $10 - (8 - 4)$
3. $18 - 7 + 4$
4. $16 + (7 - 2)$
5. $21 + 9 - 25$

Vocabulary

evaluate **terms**

order of operations

Learn

Some expressions may have more than one operation.

PROBLEM Simone went to a museum of natural history. To remember the butterfly exhibit, she bought 3 postcards at 25¢ each and 2 postcards at 45¢ each. How much did Simone spend on postcards?

$$(3 \times 25) + (2 \times 45)$$

To **evaluate** an expression, you find its value. When you evaluate an expression that has more than one operation, you need to use rules called the **order of operations**.

1. First, operate inside parentheses.
2. Next, multiply and divide from left to right.
3. Then, add and subtract from left to right.

▲ Butterfly wings show many different shapes and colors.

Example 1 Evaluate. $(3 \times 25) + (2 \times 45)$

$(3 \times 25) + (2 \times 45)$	Operate inside parentheses.
$75 + 90$	Add.
165	

So, Simone spent 165¢, or $1.65, for postcards.

More Examples

A Evaluate. $70 - 4 \times (12 + 4)$

$70 - 4 \times (12 + 4)$
$70 - 4 \times 16$
$70 - 64$
6

B Evaluate. $27 - 9 \div 3 \times 5$

$27 - 9 \div 3 \times 5$
$27 - 3 \times 5$
$27 - 15$
12

- **What if** the expression in Example A were $70 - 4 \times 12 + 4$? What is the new value?
- In Example B, why would the answer be the same if parentheses enclosed $9 \div 3$?

FAST TRACK KY MA-05-5.3.1 Students will model real-world and mathematical problems with simple number sentences (equations and inequalities) with a variable or missing value (e.g., $4 = 2 \times N$, ___ $+ 5 > 14$) and apply simple number sentences to solve mathematical and real-world problems. DOK 2 *also* MA-05-5.2.1

Expressions with Variables

To evaluate an algebraic expression with a variable, replace the variable with a number. Then follow the order of operations to find the value of the expression.

Example 2 **Evaluate $(18 + n) \times 6 - 4$ if $n = 12$.**

$(18 + n) \times 6 - 4$	Replace n with 12.
$(18 + 12) \times 6 - 4$	Operate inside the parentheses.
$30 \times 6 - 4$	Multiply.
$180 - 4$	Subtract.
176	

So, the expression $(18 + n) \times 6 - 4$ has a value of 176 when $n = 12$.

More Examples

A **Evaluate $7 \times (n - 3)$ if $n = 6$.**

$7 \times (n - 3)$
$7 \times (6 - 3)$
7×3
21

B **Evaluate $3c + 5$ if $c = 5$.**

$3c + 5$
$(3 \times 5) + 5$
$15 + 5$
20

- Find the value of the expression in Example B if $c = 10$.

Guided Practice

1. Tell which operation you would do first, second, and third to evaluate the expression.

$49 - 45 \div 5 \times 3$

Evaluate each expression.

2. $30 \div (8 + 7)$
3. $32 - (7 \times 3)$
4. $20 \times 4 - 2$
5. $(6 \div 3) \times 4 + 8$

Evaluate the algebraic expression for the given value of the variable.

6. $n + 2 - 3$ if $n = 8$
7. $9 - (n + 2)$ if $n = 3$
8. $(n \times 6) - 12$ if $n = 4$
9. $8 \times (28 \div n)$ if $n = 4$

10. **TALK Math** Explain how to evaluate the expression $9m + (50 \div m)$ if $m = 10$.

Independent Practice and Problem Solving

Evaluate each expression.

11. $27 - (12 + 9)$

12. $41 - (42 \div 14)$

13. $13 \times 3 - 7$

14. $(56 \div 4) - 9$

Evaluate the algebraic expression for the given value of the variable.

15. $4 + (n + 3)$ if $n = 6$

16. $17 + d - 5$ if $d = 3$

17. $2c - 4$ if $c = 8$

18. $8 + \frac{24}{n}$ if $n = 3$

19. $3k - 1$ if $k = 5$

20. $7 + 5d$ if $d = 12$

21. $12 - n \times 3$ if $n = 2$

22. $5t + 2$ if $t = 4$

23. $6 + (q - 4)$ if $q = 10$

24. $15 - b + 7$ if $b = 5$

25. $3h - (2 + 17)$ if $h = 8$

26. $5 \times (r - 4)$ if $r = 6$

27. $37 - 4m$ if $m = 6$

28. $(15 + n) - 6$ if $n = 7$

Write an algebraic expression using a variable. Then find the value.

29. Darius saw 5 monarch butterflies and some painted lady butterflies. Then 3 of the butterflies flew away. How many butterflies were left if Darius saw 4 painted lady butterflies?

30. Josie's camera had space for 36 more pictures in its memory. She took some pictures in the butterfly exhibit. Then she took 16 more pictures in the African Mammal Hall. If Josie took 13 pictures in the butterfly exhibit, how many of the 36 pictures can she still take?

31. Cynthia bought bottles of water at the museum. Each bottle of water cost \$3. She had \$10 to start with. How much money did Cynthia have left if she bought 3 bottles of water?

32. WRITE Math A class of 24 students will be divided into equal groups at the museum. Each group will have 2 guides. The total number of people in each group must be less than 10. **Explain** whether the students should be divided into 2, 3, or 4 groups.

 Extra Practice on page 120, Set B

Learn About Like Terms in Expressions

Sometimes an algebraic expression uses the same variable more than once.

ONE WAY **Evaluate. $4x + x - 6$ if $x = 7$**

$4x + x - 6$	Replace x with 7.
$(4 \times 7) + 7 - 6$	Operate inside the parentheses.
$28 + 7 - 6$	Add.
$35 - 6$	Subtract.
29	

Another way to find the value of an expression that uses the same variable more than once is to combine like terms. The parts of an algebraic expression that are separated by an addition or subtraction sign are called **terms**.

Algebraic Expression	Like Terms
$4m + 2m - 7$	$4m$ and $2m$
$9c + 5 - c$	$9c$ and c

ANOTHER WAY **Evaluate. $4x + x - 6$ if $x = 7$**

$4x + x - 6$	Combine like terms.
$5x - 6$	Replace x with 7.
$(5 \times 7) - 6$	Multiply.
$35 - 6$	Subtract.
29	

Try It

Evaluate the algebraic expression for the given value of the variable.

33. $9y - 7 + 3y$ if $y = 7$

34. $12s - 10s + 6$ if $s = 10$

35. $x - 4 + 9x$ if $x = 6$

36. $5d + 18 + 2d$ if $d = 4$

Mixed Review and Test Prep

37. What is the median of these driving speeds: 55 mph, 65 mph, 75 mph, 60 mph, 55 mph, 65 mph, 55 mph? (Grade 4)

38. **Test Prep** The expression $6m$ shows the cost of lunch for 6 people. If $m = \$4$, what was the total cost of the lunch?

39. The pastry chef baked 175 brownies. Each serving is 3 brownies. How many people can have one serving of brownies? (p. 62)

40. **Test Prep** If $d = 7$, what is the value of $5d + 2$?

A 35 **B** 37 **C** 39 **D** 41

LESSON 3

Properties

OBJECTIVE: Identify the properties of addition and multiplication.

Quick Review

Find the missing number.

1. ■ + 52 = 52
2. 16 + 8 = 8 + ■
3. 6 + (3 + 7) = (■ + 3) + 7
4. ■ × 5 = 5 × 7
5. 3 × (4 × ■) = (3 × 4) × 9

Vocabulary

Commutative Property

Associative Property

Identity Property

Zero Property of Multiplication

Learn

The operations of addition and multiplication have special properties.

Examples

A Commutative Property

If the order of the addends or factors is changed, the sum or product stays the same.

Addition		Multiplication	
$4 + 9 = 9 + 4$	$a + b = b + a$	$2 \times 8 = 8 \times 2$	$a \times b = b \times a$

B Associative Property

The way addends are grouped or factors are grouped does not change the sum or product.

Addition	Multiplication
$(8 + 1) + 5 = 8 + (1 + 5)$	$(6 \times 2) \times 4 = 6 \times (2 \times 4)$
$(a + b) + c = a + (b + c)$	$(a \times b) \times c = a \times (b \times c)$

C Identity Property

The sum of zero and any number equals that number. The product of one and any number equals that number.

Addition		Multiplication	
$6 + 0 = 6$	$a + 0 = a$	$5 \times 1 = 5$	$a \times 1 = a$

D Distributive Property

Multiplying a sum by a number is the same as multiplying each addend in the sum by the number and then adding the products.

$3 \times (5 + 10) = (3 \times 5) + (3 \times 10)$ $\quad$ $a \times (b + c) = (a \times b) + (a \times c)$

E Zero Property of Multiplication

The product of any number and zero is zero.

$12 \times 0 = 0$ $\quad$ $a \times 0 = 0$

FAST TRACK

KY MA-05-1.5.2 Students will use the commutative properties of addition and multiplication, the associative properties of addition and multiplication, the identity properties of addition and multiplication and the zero property of multiplication in written and mental computation. also **MA-05-5.3.1**

Guided Practice

1. Which multiplication property is shown by $12 \times (6 \times 8) = (12 \times 6) \times 8$?
   a. Identity Property
   b. Commutative Property
   c. Associative Property
   d. Distributive Property

Find the value of n. Identify the property used.

2. $24 + 57 = 57 + n$
3. $81 \times n = 81$
4. $13 \times (n \times 5) = (13 \times 4) \times 5$
5. TALK Math **Explain** how you would use the Distributive Property to find the value of n for $7 \times (4 + 8) = (n \times 4) + (n \times 8)$.

Independent Practice and Problem Solving

Find the value of n. Identify the property used.

6. $67 \times 34 = n \times 67$
7. $n = 35 + 0$
8. $4 \times (7 + n) = (4 \times 7) + (4 \times 9)$
9. $14 \times n = 23 \times 14$
10. $n \times 56 = 0$
11. $(41 + n) + 9 = 41 + (18 + 9)$
12. $(15 + 8) + 20 = n + (8 + 20)$
13. $1 \times n = 70$
14. $n \times (6 \times 8) = (4 \times 6) \times 8$

USE DATA For 15–16, use the graph.

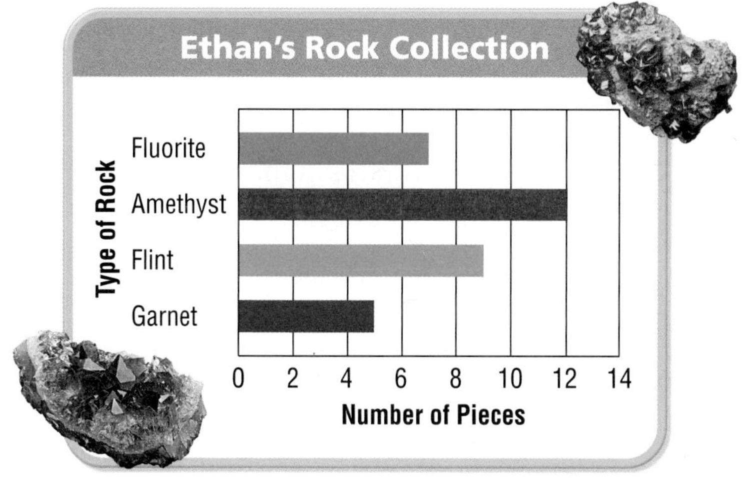

15. Use Ethan's collection of fluorite, amethyst, and flint pieces to write a number sentence that shows the Associative Property.
16. The total number of flint and garnet pieces Beth has is the same as the total number Ethan has. However, Beth has 9 garnet pieces. Use the Commutative Property to find the number of flint pieces Beth has.
17. WRITE Math Pam said that she can use the Associative Property for subtraction. Do you agree? Give an example to support your answer.

Mixed Review and Test Prep

18. What is 6,852 rounded to the nearest thousand? (p. 14)
19. On Monday, Burton earned \$9 per hour for 5 hours. On Tuesday, he earned \$12 per hour for 3 hours. How much did Burton earn in all? (p. 40)
20. **Test Prep** The expression $20 \times (6 + 7)$ shows the amount of money Olivia earned. Which expression represents the same amount of money?
    A $(20 \times 6) \times 7$
    B $20 + (6 \times 7)$
    C $(20 + 6) \times (20 + 7)$
    D $(20 \times 6) + (20 \times 7)$

Extra Practice on page 120, Set C

MENTAL MATH

Use the Properties

OBJECTIVE: Use the properties and mental math to solve problems.

Quick Review

Identify the property used.

1. $(6 + 4) + 7 = 6 + (4 + 7)$
2. $15 \times 9 = 9 \times 15$
3. $1 \times 34 = 34$
4. $0 + 302 = 302$
5. $4 \times 37 = (4 \times 30) + (4 \times 7)$

Learn

PROBLEM At the Point Defiance Zoo and Aquarium in Tacoma, Washington, Bruce and Tani saw 4 sea otters in one of the exhibit pools. Then they saw 6 tufted puffins and 3 walruses. How many sea animals did Bruce and Tani see?

Use mental math to find the total number of sea animals they saw. You can use the Associative Property to help you find the sum mentally.

Example 1 Use the Associative Property.

$4 + (6 + 3) = (4 + 6) + 3$ Associative Property of Addition
$= 10 + 3$ Use mental math.
$= 13$

So, Bruce and Tani saw 13 sea animals.

- Why does grouping the numbers differently make it easier to find the value mentally?

You can use other properties to help you mentally solve problems.

More Examples Use the Commutative and Associative Properties.

A $(13 + 2) + 7 = (2 + 13) + 7$ Commutative Property of Addition
$= 2 + (13 + 7)$ Associative Property of Addition
$= 2 + 20$ Use mental math.
$= 22$

B $5 \times (2 \times 75) = (5 \times 2) \times 75$ Associative Property of Multiplication
$= 10 \times 75$ Use mental math.
$= 750$

- Does the Commutative Property work for subtraction? Explain.

A sea otter's fur is the thickest and finest of any mammal. Sea otters have 850,000 to 1,000,000 hairs per square inch and two coats of hairs. ▼

 FAST TRACK

KY *MA-05-1.5.2 Students will use the commutative properties of addition and multiplication, the associative properties of addition and multiplication, the identity properties of addition and multiplication and the zero property of multiplication in written and mental computation. also* **MA-05-1.1.1; MA-05-5.3.1**

Use the Distributive Property

You can also use the Distributive Property to mentally solve a problem.

Example 2 Use the Distributive Property.

Find 4×29.

4×29

$4 \times 29 = 4 \times (25 + 4)$	Break 29 into parts.
$= (4 \times 25) + (4 \times 4)$	Use the Distributive Property.
$= 100 + 16$	Use mental math.
$= 116$	

So, $4 \times 29 = 116$.

- In Example 2, why might it be easier to break 29 into 25 and 4 than into 20 and 9 when doing mental math?

You can also use the Distributive Property with subtraction.

Example 3 Use the Distributive Property.

Find 6×17.

6×17

$6 \times 17 = 6 \times (20 - 3)$	Use $20 - 3$.
$= (6 \times 20) - (6 \times 3)$	Use the Distributive Property. Multiply mentally.
$= 120 - 18$	Subtract.
$= 102$	

More Examples

A 8×38

$$\begin{aligned} 8 \times 38 &= 8 \times (40 - 2) \\ &= (8 \times 40) - (8 \times 2) \\ &= 320 - 16 \\ &= 304 \end{aligned}$$

B 4×275

$$\begin{aligned} 4 \times 275 &= 4 \times (300 - 25) \\ &= (4 \times 300) - (4 \times 25) \\ &= 1{,}200 - 100 \\ &= 1{,}100 \end{aligned}$$

Guided Practice

Copy and complete. Name the property used.

1. $(29 + 8) + 24 = 29 + (8 + 24)$
   $= 29 + ■$
   $= ■$

2. $2 \times 8 \times 5 = 2 \times 5 \times 8$
   $= ■ \times 8$
   $= ■$

Use properties and mental math to find the value.

3. $4 \times 17 \times 50$ **4.** $7 + 63 + 25$ **5.** 5×29 **6.** 108×6

7. TALK Math **Explain** how to use the Commutative Property to find the value of $4 \times 7 \times 5$. How does this property make this problem easier to solve mentally?

Independent Practice and Problem Solving

Use properties and mental math to find the value.

8. $19 + (28 + 21)$ **9.** 3×270 **10.** $(86 + 27) + 3$ **11.** $(10 \times 8) \times 3$

12. $8 \times (3 \times 5)$ **13.** $(36 + 42) + 24$ **14.** $4 \times (9 \times 5)$ **15.** 4×23

16. $78 + (64 + 2)$ **17.** 9×510 **18.** $(47 + 58) + 13$ **19.** $50 \times (7 \times 2)$

20. $25 \times (3 \times 4)$ **21.** 28×8 **22.** $29 + (18 + 32)$ **23.** 19×6

24. 24×9 **25.** 6×18 **26.** $7 \times 8 \times 6$ **27.** 17×9

USE DATA For 28–31, use the table.

28. An aquarium has 6 California sea lions in one tank. How many pounds of food do the sea lions eat in one day?

29. A harbor seal made 2 dives that lasted the greatest amount of time it can stay underwater. It also made a 14-minute dive and an 11-minute dive. How much time was the harbor seal underwater?

30. ***FAST FACT*** Dolphins travel in social groups called pods with as many as 15 dolphins. Pods work together to catch food. About how many pounds of food would a pod of 14 dolphins eat in one day?

31. A bottlenose dolphin made 3 dives in an hour. On the first dive, it swam to a depth of 58 feet. The second dive was to 32 feet and the third dive was to the dolphin's maximum depth. What is the total distance for all 3 dives?

Sea Mammal Facts

Sea Mammal	Maximum Dive Depth (in ft)	Average Daily Food Intake (in lb)	Greatest Time Underwater (in min)
California sea lion	899	27	10
Bottlenose dolphin	150	23	8
Harbor seal	1,450	14	28

32. A California sea lion's exhibit time is 24 minutes, 3 times per day. How many minutes is the sea lion's total exhibit time in a 7-day week?

33. Tell which property you would use to mentally find the value of 35×12. Then find the value.

34. WRITE Math To multiply 4×97 Trevor wrote $4 \times (99 - 2)$. Will writing it this way allow him to use mental math? **Explain** how Trevor can solve the problem mentally.

 Extra Practice on page 120, Set D

Learn About Decomposing and Composing Numbers

To decompose a number, break the number into addends or factors to form an equivalent representation.

Examples

A Use expanded notation.

624

$624 = 600 + 20 + 4$

B Use the Distributive Property.

12×52

$12 \times 52 = (12 \times 50) + (12 \times 2)$

To compose a number, use addition or multiplication to put a set of numbers together to form an equivalent representation.

Examples

C Add.

$3{,}000 + 500 + 20$

$3{,}000 + 500 + 20 = 3{,}520$

D Multiply and then add.

$(35 \times 40) + (35 \times 4)$

$(35 \times 40) + (35 \times 4) =$
$1{,}400 + 140 = 1{,}540$

Try It

For each, write an equivalent representation. Tell whether you decomposed or composed.

35. 18×48

36. $(16 \times 20) + (16 \times 3)$

37. 7,839

38. $10{,}000 + 700 + 30 + 8$

39. 99,750

40. $(12 \times 30) + (12 \times 5)$

Mixed Review and Test Prep

41. Students have collected 348 pounds of paper to recycle. They put the paper in bundles that weigh 12 pounds each. How many bundles did they make? (p. 74)

42. **Test Prep** There are 5 bookcases containing 4 shelves each. Each shelf holds 25 books. Find the total number of books in the bookcases.

A 450

B 500

C 550

D 600

43. Ray's bowling scores are 78, 84, 95, 87, 91, and 95. What is the mode of Ray's bowling scores? (Grade 4)

44. **Test Prep** Concert tickets cost $27 each. Mr. Casey buys 5 tickets. **Explain** how to use mental math to find the total cost of the tickets.

LESSON 5

Write Equations

OBJECTIVE: Write equations for words and word problems for equations.

Quick Review

Write an expression.

A baker divides some cookies evenly among 4 trays.

Vocabulary

equation

Learn

PROBLEM Ben has $150 in his checking account. After making a deposit, he will have a total of $220 in the account. How much money will Ben deposit in his checking account? Write an equation with a variable to represent the problem.

An **equation** is a number sentence that shows that two quantities are equal. Use the variable *d* for the amount of the deposit.

amount in account		deposit		total in account
↓		↓		↓
$150	+	d	=	$220

So, the equation is $150 + d = 220$.

Example Write an equation for this sentence: a number decreased by twenty-six is four.

Choose a variable. Let *n* represent the number.

a number		twenty-six		four
↓		↓		↓
n	−	26	=	4

More Examples

A Write an equation for the problem.

Andrea has 10 collector cards. How many more cards does Andrea need to collect to have all 60 cards in the set? Let *m* represent the number of cards left to collect.

cards collected		cards left to collect		total number of cards
↓		↓		↓
10	+	m	=	60

B Write a problem for the equation.

y	÷	12	=	18
↓		↓		↓
berries to start with		number of boxes		berries in each box

Ken divides berries into 12 boxes. Each box has 18 berries. How many berries did he start with?

Guided Practice

1. A bike tour is 35 miles. There is a break after 15 miles. Which equation shows *d*, the distance left after the break?

   a. $d - 15 = 35$ **c.** $15 + d = 35$

   b. $d \times 15 = 35$ **d.** $35 \div d = 15$

 FAST TRACK

KY MA-05-5.3.1 Students will model real-world and mathematical problems with simple number sentences (equations and inequalities) with a variable or missing value (e.g., $4 = 2 \times N$, ___ $+ 5 > 14$) and apply simple number sentences to solve mathematical and real-world problems. DOK 2 *also* MA-05-5.2.1

Write an equation for each. Tell what the variable represents.

2. Tia has 5 fewer keys than Omar. If Tia has 7 keys, how many does Omar have?

3. The cafeteria has 156 plates. It has 3 times as many plates as trays. How many trays are there?

4. TALK Math **Explain** how to write an equation for this word problem. Dylan has 520 books. He packs 20 books in each carton. How many cartons will he pack?

Independent Practice and Problem Solving

Write an equation for each. Tell what the variable represents.

5. Hunter had 16 CDs. He received more CDs for his birthday. Now he has 23 CDs. How many CDs did Hunter get for his birthday?

6. Hilary paid $4 for breakfast and $6 for lunch. Then she bought dinner. Hilary spent a total of $25. How much did dinner cost?

Write a problem for each equation. Tell what the variable represents.

7. $5 + n = 16$
8. $x - 4 = 7$
9. $3y = 24$
10. $2a + 1 = 7$

For 11–13, use the information in the picture to write an equation with a variable. Tell what the variable represents.

11. Tim spent $89 on a bicycle seat and another item from Bruce's Bike Shop. How much did the other item cost?

12. Whitney had $53 and bought two of the same item. She had $19 left. How much did one of the items cost?

13. WRITE Math Hoshi has saved some money. After he buys a new bicycle seat, he has $26 left. **Explain** how to write an equation with a variable to show the amount of money Hoshi started with.

Mixed Review and Test Prep

14. Jackson is the largest city in Mississippi. In 2003, its population was 179,599. What is the place value of the digit 7 in 179,599? (p. 4)

15. Evan had 18 baseball cards. He gave some to his brother and then bought 6 more. Write an algebraic expression to represent this problem. (p. 92)

16. **Test Prep** The Boomerang roller coaster's height is 125 feet. It is 40 feet higher than the Cyclone roller coaster. Which equation shows n, the height of the Cyclone?

A $125 = n - 40$
B $n = 165 - 40$
C $125 = n + 40$
D $165 = n + 125$

Extra Practice on page 121, Set E

LESSON 6 Solve Equations

OBJECTIVE: Write and solve equations.

Quick Review

Find the missing number.

1. ■ + 8 = 13
2. 24 ÷ ■ = 4
3. ■ × 9 = 27
4. 32 − ■ = 20
5. ■ × 7 = 42

Vocabulary

solution

Learn

PROBLEM The American black bear is active for 7 months of the year. It usually rests part of the year. How many months does the bear rest?

Write an equation to represent the problem.

months active		months resting		months in year
↓		↓		↓
7	+	m	=	12

To solve an equation, you find a value for the variable that makes the equation true. That value is called the **solution**.

▲ The American black bear is found only in North America.

HANDS ON

Activity

Materials ■ Equabeam™ balance ■ weights

You can use an Equabeam balance to show which of the numbers 4, 5, or 6 is the solution of the equation $7 + m = 12$.

Step 1

Show 7 on the left and 12 on the right.

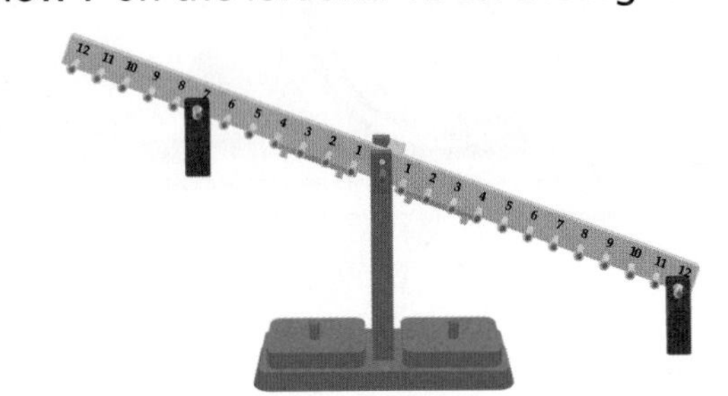

Step 2

Replace m with 4.	Place 4 on the left side.
$7 + 4 \stackrel{?}{=} 11$	$11 \stackrel{?}{=} 12$ false
Replace m with 5.	Place 5 on the left side.
$7 + 5 \stackrel{?}{=} 12$	$12 \stackrel{?}{=} 12$ true
Replace m with 6.	Place 6 on the left side.
$7 + 6 \stackrel{?}{=} 13$	$13 \stackrel{?}{=} 12$ false

The solution is 5. The values on both sides of the Equabeam balance are equal. So, the black bear rests 5 months of the year.

Example **Is 3, 5, or 9 the solution of $23 - x = 14$?**

Try 3.	Try 5.	Try 9.
$23 - 3 \stackrel{?}{=} 14$ Replace x with 3.	$23 - 5 \stackrel{?}{=} 14$ Replace x with 5.	$23 - 9 \stackrel{?}{=} 14$ Replace x with 9.
$20 \stackrel{?}{=} 14$ false	$18 \stackrel{?}{=} 14$ false	$14 \stackrel{?}{=} 14$ true

FAST TRACK

KY MA-05-5.3.1 Students will model real-world and mathematical problems with simple number sentences (equations and inequalities) with a variable or missing value (e.g., 4 = 2 × N, ___ + 5 > 14) and apply simple number sentences to solve mathematical and real-world problems. DOK 2 *also* MA-05-1.1.1; MA-05-5.2.1

Mental Math

A 2-year-old black bear weighs about 4 times as much as it weighed as a 6-month-old cub. If the bear weighs 120 pounds, how much did it weigh as a cub?

Write an equation to solve the problem.

6–month weight	$\times$	**4**	=	**weight**
↓		↓		↓
w	$\times$	4	$=$	120

Solve the equation using mental math.

$4w = 120$ **Think:** 4 times what number equals 120?
$w = 30$

Check: $4 \times 30 = 120$ Replace w with 30.

$120 = 120$ ✓ The equation checks. The value of w is 30.

More Examples **Use mental math to solve each equation.**

A $a + 16 = 20$

$a + 16 = 20$ **Think:** What number plus 16 equals 20?
$a = 4$

Check: $4 + 16 = 20$
$20 = 20$ ✓

B $n - 17 = 8$

$n - 17 = 8$ **Think:** What number minus 17 equals 8?
$n = 25$

Check: $25 - 17 = 8$
$8 = 8$ ✓

C $6h = 54$

$6h = 54$ **Think:** What number times 6 equals 54?
$h = 9$

Check: $6 \times 9 = 54$
$54 = 54$ ✓

D $36 \div x = 3$

$36 \div x = 3$ **Think:** 36 divided by what number equals 3?
$x = 12$

Check: $36 \div 12 = 3$
$3 = 3$ ✓

- How do you know that the value of a is less than 20 in Example A?

Guided Practice

1. Which equation has a solution of 6?

a. $9 + n = 17$
$9 + 6 \stackrel{?}{=} 17$

b. $11 - n = 6$
$11 - 6 \stackrel{?}{=} 6$

c. $6n = 36$
$6 \times 6 \stackrel{?}{=} 36$

d. $\frac{72}{9} - n = 4$
$8 - 6 \stackrel{?}{=} 4$

Which of the numbers 5, 8, or 10 is the solution of the equation?

2. $11 + n = 19$ **3.** $y - 3 = 7$ **4.** $s \div 5 = 2$ ✓**5.** $7 \times a = 35$

Use mental math to solve each equation. Check your solution.

6. $14 - x = 5$ **7.** $m + 8 = 15$ **8.** $4 \times n = 24$ **9.** $15 \div r = 5$

10. TALK Math **Explain** why $x = 186$ is the solution of the equation $x \div 6 = 31$.

Independent Practice and Problem Solving

Which of the numbers 6, 9, or 14 is the solution of the equation?

11. $k \div 2 = 7$ **12.** $10 \times b = 60$ **13.** $34 - z = 25$ **14.** $18 + s = 24$

15. $n \times 6 = 54$ **16.** $42 - w = 28$ **17.** $25 + q = 31$ **18.** $27 \div x = 3$

Use mental math to solve each equation. Check your solution.

19. $12 = 10 + r$ **20.** $9 = h \div 2$ **21.** $4 \times n = 28$ **22.** $x - 4 = 4$

23. $36 \div t = 6$ **24.** $15 = c + 7$ **25.** $7 = 10 - a$ **26.** $w \times 8 = 40$

27. $3 \times b = 15$ **28.** $\$26 - m = \$20$ **29.** $f \div 5 = 7$ **30.** $\$24 + s = \$29$

For 31–34, each variable represents one number. Find the value of each variable.

31. $x + 4 = 9$
$3 + y = x$

32. $a + 5 = 11$
$a - b = 2$

33. $3 \times c = 12$
$c \div d = 4$

34. $6 + s = 14$
$s \div t = 4$

USE DATA For 35–36, use the table to write an equation. Then solve.

Black Bears

	Average Weight Male	Average Weight Female
1-year-old	70	f
Adult	250	a

35. The average 1-year-old male bear weighs 20 pounds more than the average 1-year-old female bear. What is the average weight of the 1-year-old female bear?

36. The average adult female bear weighs more than the average adult male bear. The difference between their average weights is 50 pounds. What is the average weight of the adult female bear?

37. WRITE Math A black bear cub usually stays with its mother for about 17 months. If a cub has been with its mother for 11 months, how much longer will the cub stay with its mother? **Explain** how to use an equation to solve the problem.

 Extra Practice on page 121, Set F

Learn About Like Terms in Equations

Before you solve equations, you should check to see if they can be simplified by adding or subtracting like terms.

Equation	Like Terms	Simplified
$4x + 2x = 24$	$4x$ and $2x$	$6x = 24$
$7y - 3y = 32$	$7y$ and $3y$	$4y = 32$

Examples

Simplify by combining like terms. Then solve.

A $8x - 2x = 18$ Combine like terms.
$6x = 18$ **Think:** 6 times what number equals 18?
$x = 3$

B $5h + 2h = 42$ Combine like terms.
$7h = 42$ **Think:** 7 times what number equals 42?
$h = 6$

Try It

Simplify by combining like terms. Then solve.

38. $5y + 2y = 63$ **39.** $9n - 4n = 35$ **40.** $6x + 3x = 81$

41. $8m + 3m = 55$ **42.** $15c - 8c = 28$ **43.** $x + 2x = 30$

Mixed Review and Test Prep

44. Jeff took 36 pictures. He put some of the pictures in an album. Write an expression with a variable to model the situation. (p. 92)

45. **Test Prep** The equation $6 \times c = \$48$ represents the total cost of 6 T-shirts. How much does each T-shirt cost?

A \$8 **C** \$42

B \$12 **D** \$54

46. Ten cards are numbered 1 to 10. The cards are mixed and then placed in a bag. What is the probability that Bill will pull an odd number out of the bag? (Grade 4)

47. **Test Prep** During a spelling bee, Lee has to spell 15 words. After spelling some of the words, he has 6 words left. Write and solve an equation to find the number of words Lee has already spelled.

Technology
Use Harcourt Mega Math, Ice Station Exploration, *Arctic Algebra,* Levels S, T, Y, Z, AA, BB.

Functions

OBJECTIVE: Represent a function with a table and an equation.

Quick Review

Complete.

1. 10, 15, ■, 25, ■
2. 48, 56, 64, ■, ■
3. ■, 8, 12, ■, ■, 24
4. 12, 24, ■, ■, 60
5. ■, 18, 27, 36, ■

Vocabulary

function

Learn

PROBLEM Karen takes karate lessons at the Little Dragon Center. Lessons cost \$30 per month. How much will 5 months of karate lessons cost? Look for a pattern.

Month, m	1	2	3	4	5
Cost, c	30	60	90	120	■

← Rule: Multiply by 30.

$5 \times 30 = 150$, so 5 months of karate lessons will cost \$150.

A **function** is a relationship between two quantities in which one quantity depends upon the other. In the problem above, the total cost of the lessons depends upon the number of months. So, the table above represents a function.

number of months		lesson cost		total cost
↓		↓		↓
m	$\times$	30	$=$	c

More Examples **Write an equation to represent the function. Then complete the function table.**

 Find a possible rule.

Input, x	28	32	36	40
Output, y	7	8	9	■

Rule: Divide by 4.
Equation: $x \div 4 = y$

$40 \div 4 = y$ Replace x with 40. Divide.
$10 = y$

So, when $x = 40$ in this function, $y = 10$.

 Find a possible rule.

Input, p	5	8	15	■
Output, r	12	15	22	36

Rule: Add 7.
Equation: $p + 7 = r$

$p + 7 = 36$ Replace r with 36. **Think:** What number plus 7 equals 36?
$p = 29$

So, when $r = 36$ in this function, $p = 29$.

Guided Practice

1. **Complete the function table.**

Input, w	6	7	8	9
Output, t	■	12	13	■

$w + 5 = t$
$6 + 5 = t$
■ $= t$

$w + 5 = t$
$9 + 5 = t$
■ $= t$

FAST TRACK

KY MA-05-5.1.2 Students will describe functions (input-output) through pictures, tables, or words and will construct tables to analyze functions based on real-world or mathematical problems. DOK 2 *also* MA-05-1.1.1; *MA-05-1.3.2;* MA-05-5.2.1

Write an equation to represent each function. Then complete the table.

2.

Input, r	1	2	3	4
Output, d	5	10	15	■

3.

Input, x	30	36	42	48
Output, y	5	6	■	8

4.

Input, m	12	14	■	18
Output, n	6	8	10	12

5. TALK Math In a function, every input has exactly one output. In the equation $y = 12x$, x is the input and y is the output. Does the equation represent a function? **Explain.**

Independent Practice and Problem Solving

Write an equation to represent each function. Then complete the table.

6.

Input, v	2	4	6	8
Output, w	23	25	■	29

7.

Input, a	4	8	12	16
Output, b	20	40	■	80

8.

Input, x	1	2	3	4
Output, y	■	16	17	18

9.

Input, c	54	63	72	81
Output, d	6	7	8	■

10.

Input, f	100	200	220
Output, g	15	115	■

11.

Input, m	8	12	13	14
Output, n	56	84	■	98

Use the rule and the equation to make a function table.

12. **Rule:** Subtract 5.
$x - 5 = y$

13. **Rule:** Divide by 3.
$m \div 3 = n$

14. **Rule:** Add 12.
$c + 12 = d$

15. **Rule:** Multiply by 7.
$p \times 7 = r$

16. At Kerri's Karate, the cost is $12 per lesson. How much does it cost for 6 weeks of lessons if you take one lesson per week? Make a function table for the first 6 weeks.

17. WRITE Math Rodney takes 2 hours of karate per week for 4 weeks. Each hour costs $12. **Explain** how to write an equation to show how the number of hours relates to the total cost of the lessons.

Mixed Review and Test Prep

18. Anna needs 2 pints of milk. She has 3 cups of milk. How much more milk does Anna need? (Grade 4)

19. Ray has 150 stamps. He can put 20 stamps on one page. How many pages will Ray need for 150 stamps? (p. 74)

20. **Test Prep** The function $y = 20x$ shows the amount of money in Marcy's bank account after x weeks. How much money will be in the account after 6 weeks?

A $120 **C** $800

B $600 **D** $1,200

Extra Practice on page 121, Set G

LESSON 8

Inequalities

OBJECTIVE: Find whole-number solutions of inequalities.

Quick Review

Write <, >, or = for each ●.

1. 9 ● 15
2. 14 ● 12 + 5
3. 16 ● 6 + 8
4. 17 − 5 ● 10
5. 7 + 2 ● 18

Vocabulary

inequality

Learn

Look at the admission sign below. You can write the age requirements for each price as an inequality. An **inequality** is a mathematical sentence that uses the symbols $<$, $>$, $\leq$, $\geq$, or $\neq$ and shows a relationship between two quantities that are not equivalent.

Admission	
10 and under	$24
Over 60	$30
Regular Admission	$35

Let a = age.

$a \leq 10$

a is less than or equal to 10.

$a > 60$

a is greater than 60.

Math Idea

When graphing whole-number solutions of an inequality, some of the many solutions can be shown. The blue arrow in the example below indicates that whole numbers to the right are also solutions.

A solution of an inequality is a value for the variable that makes it true.

$a \leq 10$

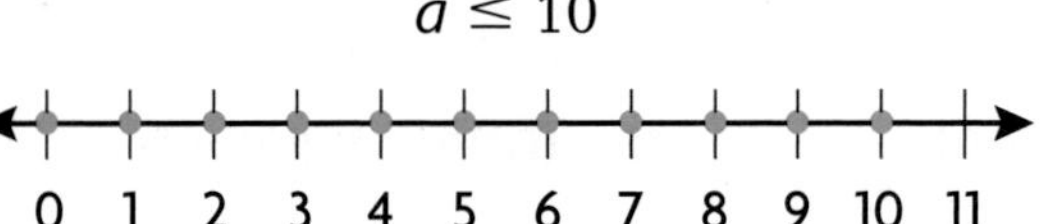

So, 0, 1, 2, 3, 4, 5, 6, 7, 8, 9, and 10 are whole-number solutions to the inequality.

$a > 60$

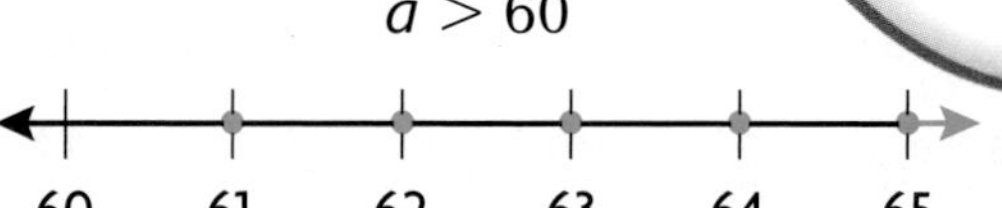

So, 61, 62, 63, 64, and 65 are some of the whole-number solutions to the inequality.

Examples Are 8, 9, and 10 solutions of $x + 4 > 12$?

A Model

Show 4 on the left and 12 on the right.

Think: The left side should be greater than the right side, so the balance should tilt to the left.

Try 8: false

Try 9: true

Try 10: true

B Evaluate

$8 + 4 \overset{?}{>} 12$ Replace x with 8.
$12 > 12$ false

$9 + 4 > 12$ Replace x with 9.
$13 > 12$ true

$10 + 4 > 12$ Replace x with 10.
$14 > 12$ true

So, $x = 9$ and $x = 10$ are solutions, but $x = 8$ is not a solution.

FAST TRACK

KY MA-05-5.3.1 Students will model real-world and mathematical problems with simple number sentences (equations and inequalities) with a variable or missing value (e.g., 4 = 2 × N, ___ + 5 > 14) and apply simple number sentences to solve mathematical and real-world problems. DOK 2 *also* MA-05-5.2.1

Guided Practice

1. Copy the number line. Use it to show the whole-number solutions of the inequality $m \geq 7$.

Which of the numbers 8, 9, and 10 are solutions of each inequality?

2. $f \leq 9$
3. $p + 2 > 11$
4. $x - 5 < 6$
5. $r + 7 \geq 16$

6. TALK Math **Explain** why $x = 2$ is a solution of the inequality $x + 6 \geq 8$, but $x = 1$ is not a solution of the inequality.

Independent Practice and Problem Solving

Which of the numbers 12, 13, and 14 are solutions of each inequality?

7. $x > 10$
8. $t + 4 \leq 17$
9. $c - 7 \geq 7$
10. $y + 5 < 18$

Draw a number line from 0 to 8. Locate points to show the whole-number solutions from 0 to 8 for each inequality.

11. $d > 3$
12. $h + 9 \leq 13$
13. $a - 2 > 4$
14. $m + 5 \leq 7$

Write an inequality to match the words. Choose the variable for the unknown. Tell what the variable represents.

15. The height requirement for riding a coaster is at least 52 inches.
16. An adult elephant weighs more than 5 tons.

USE DATA For 17–18, use the table.

17. Let a = age. What ticket price does $a > 12$ represent?
18. Let a = age. What ticket price does $a \leq 12$ and $a \geq 2$ represent?
19. WRITE Math Draw a number line from 0 to 10. **Explain** how to use the number line to show the whole-number solutions of the inequality $n + 3 < 10$.

CIRCUS ADMISSION

Age	Price
Under 2	Free
2 - 12 / Child	\$5.00
Over 12 / Adult	\$8.00

Mixed Review and Test Prep

20. What is the value of the 4 in 24,870,500? (p. 4)
21. The function $d = 10t$ shows distance in miles Jeff travels in t hours. How many miles does he travel in 4 hours? (p. 112)
22. **Test Prep** The inequality $m + 1 \geq 5$ represents the least amount of money a ticket costs at the school show. Which amount is *not* a solution of the inequality?

A 3 **B** 4 **C** 5 **D** 6

Extra Practice on page 121, Set H

Problem Solving Workshop
Strategy: Predict and Test

OBJECTIVE: Solve problems by using the strategy *predict and test.*

Learn the Strategy

Predict and test is one strategy you can use to solve a problem. First, predict a reasonable answer. Then, test and revise your predictions, trying to get closer to the correct answer.

Predict and test to find two numbers.

Nicole is thinking of two numbers. One number is two times as great as the second number. The sum of the numbers is 24. What are the two numbers?

Think: One number is half as great as the other number. Together they total 24.

Predict	Test	
6 and 12	$6 + 12 = 18$	too low
7 and 14	$7 + 14 = 21$	too low
8 and 16	$8 + 16 = 24$	just right

Predict and test to solve a perimeter problem.

Mr. Andrews wants to enclose a rectangular area using 52 feet of fencing for a dog. He wants the length to be 12 feet. How many feet of fencing will Mr Andrews use for the width? Use the expression $12 + 12 + w + w$ when you predict and test.

Predict	Test	
10	$12 + 12 + w + w$ $12 + 12 + 10 + 10 = 44$	too low
13	$12 + 12 + w + w$ $12 + 12 + 13 + 13 = 50$	too low
14	$12 + 12 + w + w$ $12 + 12 + 14 + 14 = 52$	just right

So, Mr. Andrews will use 14 feet for each of the two remaining sides.

TALK Math

How does testing your prediction help you make new predictions?

FAST TRACK

KY MA-05-5.3.1 Students will model real-world and mathematical problems with simple number sentences (equations and inequalities) with a variable or missing value (e.g., $4 = 2 \times N$, ___ $+ 5 > 14$) and apply simple number sentences to solve mathematical and real-world problems. DOK 2 *also* MA-05-1.1.1

Use the Strategy

PROBLEM Sean has an aquarium with several kinds of tropical fish. Of those fish, 10 are tetras and mollies. If Sean has 2 more tetras than mollies, how many of each are in his aquarium? Use the equation $m + (m + 2) = 10$ where m represents the number of mollies and $m + 2$ represents the number of tetras.

Read to Understand

- **Summarize what you are asked to find.**
- **Is there information you will not use? If so, what?**

Plan

- **What strategy can you use to solve the problem?**

  You can predict and test to help you solve the problem.

Solve

- **How can you use the strategy to solve the problem?**

Predict a value for m.

Try 3 mollies.

$$m + (m + 2) = 10$$

$$3 + (3 + 2) \stackrel{?}{=} 10$$

$$3 + 5 \stackrel{?}{=} 10$$

$3 + 5 \neq 10$ is false.

Predict again. Try another number.

Try 4 mollies.

$$m + (m + 2) = 10$$

$$4 + (4 + 2) \stackrel{?}{=} 10$$

$$4 + 6 \stackrel{?}{=} 10$$

$4 + 6 = 10$ is true.

So, there are 4 mollies and 6 tetras in Sean's aquarium.

Check

- **How can you check your answer?**
- **What other strategy could you use to solve the problem?**

Guided Problem Solving

Read to Understand
Plan
Solve
Check

1. In Alexa's aquarium there are 20 swordtails and danios. If there are 3 times as many swordtails as danios, how many of each are in Alexa's aquarium? Use the equation $d + (3 \times d) = 20$.

First, predict a number of danios.

Then, check and revise your prediction.

Continue to predict and test until you have a solution.

Try 6 danios.

$d + (3 \times d) = 20$

$6 + (3 \times 6) \stackrel{?}{=} 20$

$6 + 18 \stackrel{?}{=} 20$ false

2. **What if** there were a total of 8 swordtails and danios in Alexa's aquarium? How many of each would there be?

3. The capacity of a large aquarium is 12 gallons more than the capacity of a small aquarium. The aquariums hold a total of 52 gallons of water. What is the capacity of each aquarium?

Problem Solving Strategy Practice

Predict and test to solve.

4. Marcella bought a total of 25 fish for her aquarium. She bought 5 fewer tiger barbs than bala sharks. How many tiger barbs and bala sharks did Marcella buy?

USE DATA For 5 and 7, use the table.

5. Lisa bought black skirt tetras and silver dollars for her fish tank. She bought the same number of each type and spent a total of $18.00. How many of each fish did she buy?

6. Peter has 2 types of fish in his aquarium. There are a total of 18 of them. The product of the numbers of each type is 56. What are the two numbers?

7. WRITE Math James has selected 2 tiger barbs, 1 silver dollar, 1 bala shark, and 1 clown loach to buy. He wants to buy 2 more fish and has a total of $30 to spend. **Explain** how James should decide which fish to select if he plans to spend $30.

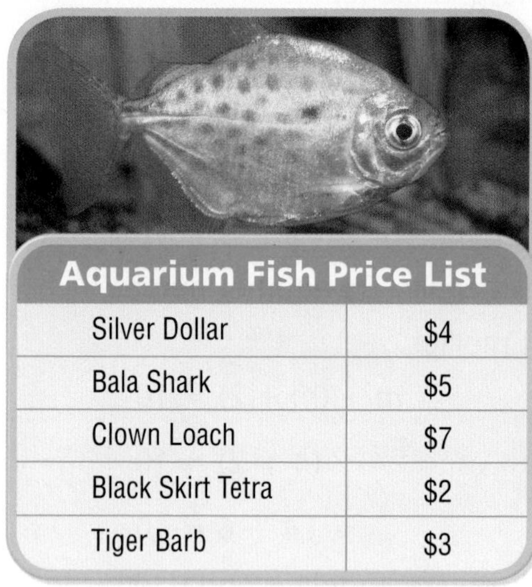

Aquarium Fish Price List	
Silver Dollar	$4
Bala Shark	$5
Clown Loach	$7
Black Skirt Tetra	$2
Tiger Barb	$3

Mixed Strategy Practice

USE DATA For 9–12, use the table.

8. Kevin is starting a saltwater aquarium with 14 fish. He wants to start with 4 more damselfish than clownfish. How many of each kind of fish will he use?

9. Kevin bought 3 bags of gravel to cover the base of the tank. He has 10 pounds of gravel left over. How much gravel did he use to cover the base of the tank?

10. Kevin used a store coupon to buy a 30-gallon tank, an aquarium light, and a filtration system. He paid a total of $240. How much did Kevin save by using the coupon?

11. **Pose a Problem** Look back at Problem 9. Write a similar problem by changing the number of bags of gravel and the amount of gravel left.

12. **Open-Ended** Kevin's older brother has saved $300 to start a saltwater aquarium. Make a list of the items he could buy with $300.

CHALLENGE YOURSELF

To start his saltwater aquarium, Kevin has to add about 4 ounces of marine salt to each gallon of fresh water. A $17 bag of marine salt has enough for 25 gallons of water.

13. After all of the rocks are in the tank, the tank will hold about 6 gallons of water less than its total capacity. How much salt will Kevin need to use for the water in his tank?

14. Kevin will replace half the water in his tank 5 times during the first year. **Explain** how to find the total cost of buying enough marine salt to replace the water 5 times.

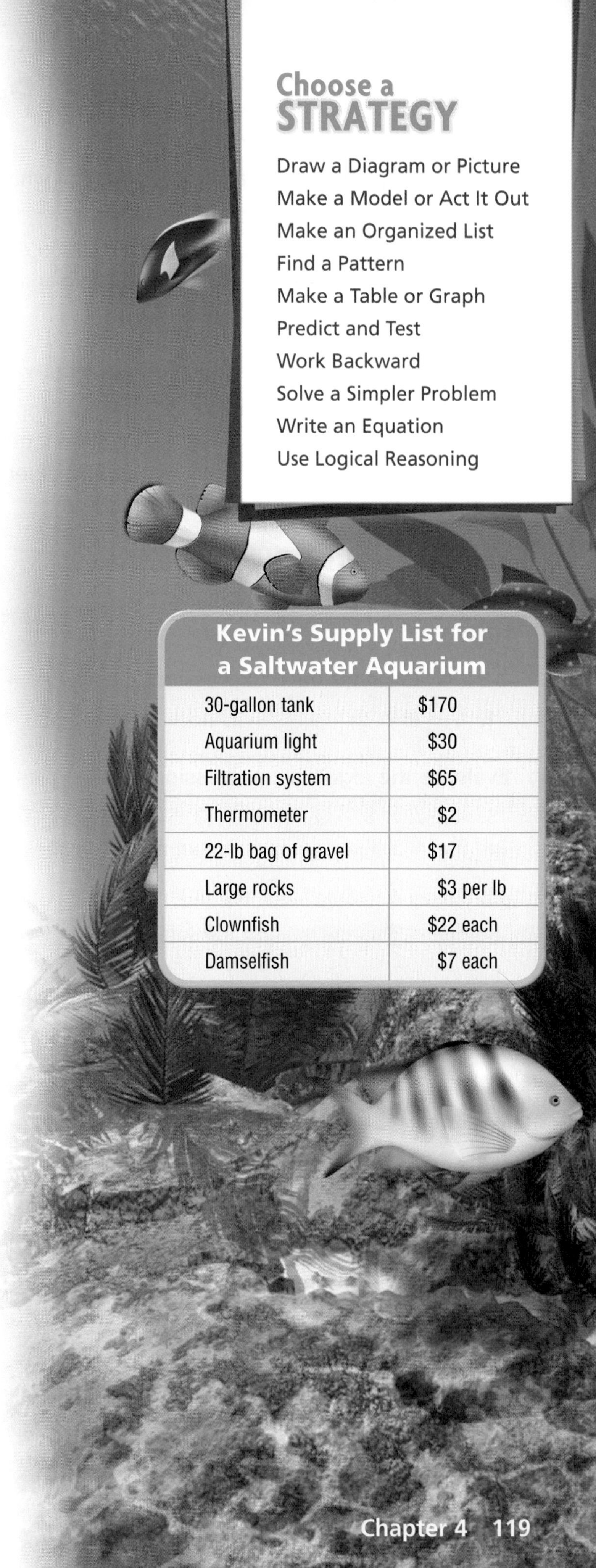

Choose a STRATEGY

Draw a Diagram or Picture
Make a Model or Act It Out
Make an Organized List
Find a Pattern
Make a Table or Graph
Predict and Test
Work Backward
Solve a Simpler Problem
Write an Equation
Use Logical Reasoning

Kevin's Supply List for a Saltwater Aquarium

Item	Cost
30-gallon tank	$170
Aquarium light	$30
Filtration system	$65
Thermometer	$2
22-lb bag of gravel	$17
Large rocks	$3 per lb
Clownfish	$22 each
Damselfish	$7 each

Extra Practice

Set A Write a numerical expression. Tell what the expression represents. (pp. 92–95)

1. Cal had \$15. He spent \$3 on pens and \$8 on a book.
2. Mr. Carson divides 28 chairs into 4 equal rows.
3. Emily bought 9 color pencils at 60 cents each.

Write an algebraic expression. Tell what the variable represents.

4. Leslie has some marbles. Her brother has three times as many marbles.
5. At a bus stop, 8 of the 33 passengers got off the bus and other people got on.
6. Some skiers are on a slope when 3 more skiers arrive at the slope.

Write each algebraic expression in words.

7. $t + 4$
8. $w \times 8$
9. $10 - 3y$

Set B Evaluate each expression. (pp. 96–99)

1. $5 + (8 - 2)$
2. $45 - 7 + 5$
3. $7 \times 2 + 1$
4. $(6 + 3) \div 3$

Evaluate the algebraic expression for the given value of the variable.

5. $4 + n \times 8$ if $n = 5$
6. $(3 \div d) + 9$ if $d = 3$
7. $8 + 2t$ if $t = 9$
8. $2 + 4 \times (n + 5)$ if $n = 7$
9. $7m - 4$ if $m = 8$
10. $(49 \div 7) \times s$ if $s = 3$
11. $11 + (15 \div c)$ if $c = 3$
12. $94 - (10 + y)$ if $y = 57$

Set C Find the value for *n*. Identify the property used. (pp. 100–101)

1. $5 \times (8 + 3) = (5 \times 8) + (5 \times n)$
2. $98 \times n = 98$
3. $27 + 13 = n + 27$
4. $n + 21 = 21 + 14$
5. $n \times 82 = 0$
6. $31 + (8 - 2) = (31 + n) - 2$

Set D Use properties and mental math to find the value. (pp. 102–105)

1. 75×3
2. $5 \times 7 \times 8$
3. $(26 + 9) + 4$
4. $30 \times (6 \times 2)$
5. $(13 + 5) + 17$
6. $6 \times 9 \times 5$
7. 42×8
8. $(33 + 4) + 7$

CD ROM **Technology**
Use Harcourt Mega Math, Ice Station Exploration, *Arctic Algebra*, Levels F, G, H.

Set E Write an equation for each. Tell what the variable represents. (pp. 106–107)

1. Jayden had 14 baseball cards. He bought more cards. Now he has 23 cards. How many cards did Jayden buy?

2. Todd spent $51 on a video game and another item. If the video game cost $33, how much was the other item?

Write a problem for each equation. Tell what the variable represents.

3. $7 + n = 23$ 4. $8d - 4 = 20$ 5. $3s + 1 = 19$ 6. $c - 4 = 78$

Set F Which of the numbers 5, 7, or 11 is the solution to the equation? (pp. 108–111)

1. $z - 5 = 2$ 2. $x + 23 = 34$ 3. $22 \div 2 = m$ 4. $b \times 15 = 75$

Use mental math to solve each equation. Check your solution.

5. $f - 8 = 17$ 6. $5 + p = 16$ 7. $40 = b + 18$ 8. $25 \div 5 = k$

9. $x + 12 = 33$ 10. $4m = 56$ 11. $99 \div r = 9$ 12. $72 - d = 50$

Set G Write an equation to represent each function. Then complete the table. (pp. 112–113)

1.

Input, y	2	4	6	8
Output, d	6	12	18	■

2.

Input, x	1	■	3	4
Output, y	5	6	7	8

3.

Input, w	10	12	14	16
Output, p	8	10	■	14

Use the rule and the equation to make a function table.

4. **Rule:** Add 7.
$x + 7 = y$

5. **Rule:** Multiply by 2.
$2m = n$

6. **Rule:** Divide by 5.
$c \div 5 = d$

Set H Which of the numbers 10, 12, and 14 are solutions of each inequality? (pp. 114–115)

1. $x < 11$ 2. $f + 3 \leq 15$ 3. $a - 2 > 5$ 4. $d + 8 \leq 20$

Draw a number line from 0 to 8. Locate points to show the whole number solutions for each inequality.

5. $y > 6$ 6. $c - 1 < 8$ 7. $m + 1 > 5$ 8. $x + 4 \leq 10$

MATH POWER **One-Step Equations**

Counter Opposites

Marnie installed 39 tiles on the kitchen counter. Marnie used all but 13 tiles from a full box of tiles. How many tiles were in a full box?

To solve the problem, you can write the equation $n - 13 = 39$, where n stands for the number of tiles in a full box. To solve the equation, use the inverse operation of subtraction to get the variable alone on one side of the equation.

Identify the operation: subtraction.	$n - 13 = 39$
Identify the inverse operation: addition. Add 13 to both sides.	$n - 13 + 13 = 39 + 13$
Simplify and solve.	$n = 52$

So, a full box contained 52 tiles.

You can use inverse operations to solve any equation.

Examples

Solve using the inverse operation.

A $a + 6 = 11$

inverse operation: subtraction

$a + 6 - 6 = 11 - 6$

Subtract 6 from both sides.

$a = 5$

B $3b = 51$

inverse operation: division

$\frac{3b}{3} = \frac{51}{3}$

Divide both sides by 3.

$b = 17$

C $\frac{c}{5} = 7$

inverse operation: multiplication

$\frac{5}{1} \cdot \frac{c}{5} = \frac{7}{1} \cdot \frac{5}{1}$

Multiply both sides by 5.

$c = 35$

Try It

Use the inverse operation to solve the equation.

1. $d + 9 = 12$

2. $4e = 20$

3. $f - 6 = 15$

4. $\frac{g}{7} = 6$

5. $w - 19 = 11$

6. $\frac{x}{12} = 6$

7. $9y = 72$

8. $z + 14 = 24$

9. WRITE Math **Explain** how you know which inverse operation to use to solve the equation $8n = 56$.

KENTUCKY Chapter 4 Review/Test

Check Vocabulary and Concepts

Choose the best term from the box.

VOCABULARY
equation
inequality
variable

1. A letter or symbol that stands for one or more numbers is a __?__. KY MA-05-5.2.1 (p. 93)
2. A number sentence that shows two equal quantities is an __?__. KY MA-05-5.3.1 (p. 106)

Check Skills

Write an algebraic expression. Tell what the variable represents. KY MA-05-5.3.1 (pp. 92–95, 96–99)

3. Shelly had 12 pears. She ate some and bought 5 more.
4. Jack is 9 years older than his brother Aidan.
5. Ann has 2 boxes of pictures with *b* pictures in each box.
6. If the variable in Exercises 3–5 is equal to 3, what is the value of each expression?

Use the properties and mental math to find the value. KY MA-05-1.5.2 (pp. 102–105)

7. $15 + (32 + 5)$
8. 22×8
9. $(18 \times 5) \times 4$

Use mental math to solve each equation. Check your solution. KY MA-05-5.3.1 (pp. 108–111)

10. $h - 6 = 4$
11. $f \times 3 = 15$
12. $k + 11 = 23$
13. $12 = c \div 4$

Write an equation to represent each function.
Then complete the table. KY MA-05-5.1.2 (pp. 112–113)

14.

Input, *m*	5	8	12	15
Output, *n*	17	20	■	27

15.

Input, *c*	4	7	■	13
Output, *d*	20	35	50	65

Which of the numbers 15, 16, and 20 are solutions of each inequality?
KY MA-05-5.3.1 (pp. 114–115)

16. $x > 12$
17. $x + 2 < 20$
18. $x - 5 \leq 24$

Check Problem Solving

Solve. KY MA-05-5.3.1 (pp. 116–119)

19. Mia has 2 types of stickers. There are a total of 26. The product of the numbers of each type is 153. What are the two numbers?
20. WRITE Math Luis bought a total of 18 baseball cards for his collection. He bought 4 fewer rookie cards than hologram cards. How many rookie cards and hologram cards did Luis buy? **Explain.**

GO ONLINE **Technology** Use *Online Assessment.*

Unit Review/Test
Chapters 1–4

Multiple Choice

1. What is the value of the 8 in the number 5,800,072,035? KY MA-05-1.1.1 (p. 8)

   A. 8,000,000

   B. 80,000,000

   C. 800,000,000

   D. 8,000,000,000

2. A printing company is making a picture book. There are 30 pages in the book. The printing company has 600,000 sheets of paper. How many copies of the picture book can be made? KY MA-05-1.3.1 (p. 70)

   A. 2,000

   B. 20,000

   C. 200,000

   D. 2,000,000

3. Al is putting jars of pasta sauce into boxes to send to his customers. There are 672 jars of pasta sauce. Each box can hold 8 jars. How many boxes does Al need? KY MA-05-1.3.1 (p. 62)

   A. 81

   B. 82

   C. 83

   D. 84

4. The Ecology Club is planting trees in the park next to the school. One tree costs \$29. About how much money does the club need in order to plant 15 trees? KY MA-05-1.2.1 (p. 38)

   A. \$455

   B. \$450

   C. \$375

   D. \$300

5. Julia needs 128 plates for a party. Each package contains 9 plates. How many packages should Julia buy? KY MA-05-1.3.1 (p. 62)

   A. 14 packages

   B. 15 packages

   C. 16 packages

   D. 17 packages

6. Meredith swam 8 miles on Saturday and 10 miles on Sunday. Write a numerical expression to represent the total number of miles she swam in all. KY MA-05-5.3.1 (p. 92)

   A. $8 + 10$

   B. 8×10

   C. $10 - 8$

   D. $10 \div 8$

7. Round 8,437,912 to the thousands place. KY MA-05-1.2.1 (p. 14)

A. 8,438,000

B. 8,400,000

C. 8,438,900

D. 8,500,912

8. Evaluate the expression below if $y = 5$. KY MA-05-5.3.1 (p. 96)

$$y + 12 \times 2 - 4$$

A. 60 C. 30

B. 58 D. 25

9. Eric is riding his motorcycle from Murray, Kentucky to Miami, Florida. He plans to ride 25 miles a day for 55 days. How many miles is Eric planning to ride his motorcycle? KY MA-05-1.3.1 (p. 44)

A. 1,000 miles

B. 1,100 miles

C. 1,250 miles

D. 1,375 miles

10. Marshall's bookstore ordered 6 boxes of a bestselling mystery. There are 42 books in each box. How many books are there in all? KY MA-05-1.3.1 (p. 40)

A. 242 C. 252

B. 248 D. 258

Open Response WRITE Math

11. Ava made the function table below to show how much her dance lessons cost. Complete the table to find how much 6 dance lessons cost. KY MA-05-5.1.2 (p. 112)

Class, c	1	2	3	4	5	6
Cost, m	\$15	\$30	\$45	■	■	■

12. Alex has swim practice 3 times a week. How many times does he have swim practice in 12 weeks? **Explain** the method you used to solve this problem. KY MA-05-1.3.1 (p. 40)

13. Sharice had \$15. She spent \$5 on breakfast and \$3 on a snack. Then, she spent the rest of her money on lunch. How much did lunch cost? **Explain.** KY MA-05-1.3.1 (p. 20)

THE WORLD ALMANAC FOR KIDS

Populations

Counting People

Every 10 years the United States conducts a census to count the number of people in each state and to determine the total population. You were probably counted when your family filled out a form or talked to a census taker.

10 Most Populated States

State	Population
California	36,132,147
Florida	17,789,864
Georgia	9,072,576
Illinois	12,763,371
Michigan	10,120,860
New Jersey	8,717,925
New York	19,254,630
Ohio	11,464,042
Pennsylvania	12,429,616
Texas	22,859,968

10 Least Populated States

State	Population
Alaska	663,661
Delaware	843,524
Hawaii	1,275,194
Montana	935,670
New Hampshire	1,309,940
North Dakota	636,677
Rhode Island	1,076,189
South Dakota	775,933
Vermont	623,050
Wyoming	509,294

Cleveland
POPULATION 458,684

FACT·ACTIVITY

Use the tables to answer questions and make decisions.

1. You are moving to the most populated state. In which state will you live?
2. You are going to visit the state that has the fewest people. Which state will you visit?
3. What is the difference in populations between the most and least populated states?
4. Your friend lives in the state that has about 10 times the population of Delaware. Which state is this?
5. WRITE Math You want to vacation in the state that is 42nd in total population. Where will you go? **Explain** how you found your answer.

Big Cities . . . Small Towns . . . Your Town

Do you live in the country, a town, a suburb, or a large city? How many people live there? Almost 3,000,000 people live in Chicago, Illinois. Glen Ridge, New Jersey, has a population of about 7,000.

ALMANAC Fact

New York City has a greater population than most states. In fact, only 11 out of the 50 states have more people than New York City.

New York City's population is about 8,000,000.

FACT • ACTIVITY

Use the map and other information to make comparisons.

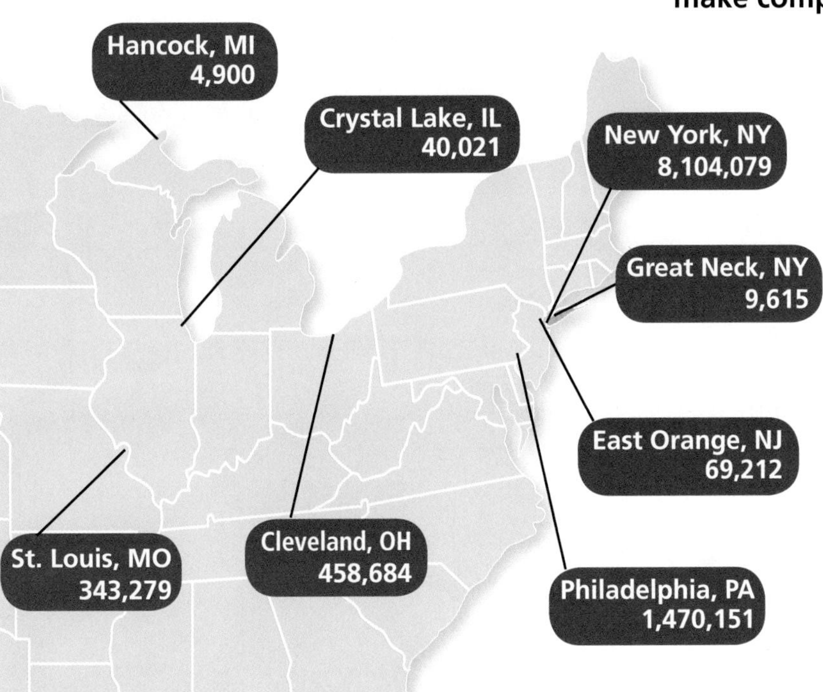

- Use your school or town library, city or town hall, or the *World Almanac* to find the population of the city or town where you live.
- Between which two populations on the map is the population of your city or town? List the three places in order from least to greatest population.
- Use the resources you used before. Find the populations of two more cities or towns in your state.
- List the five cities or towns in order of population from least to greatest.
- Make a bar graph using the five cities. Round the populations to an appropriate place value: thousands, ten thousands, hundred thousands, or millions.

UNIT 2 Use Decimals

Math on Location

with
Chapter Projects

1

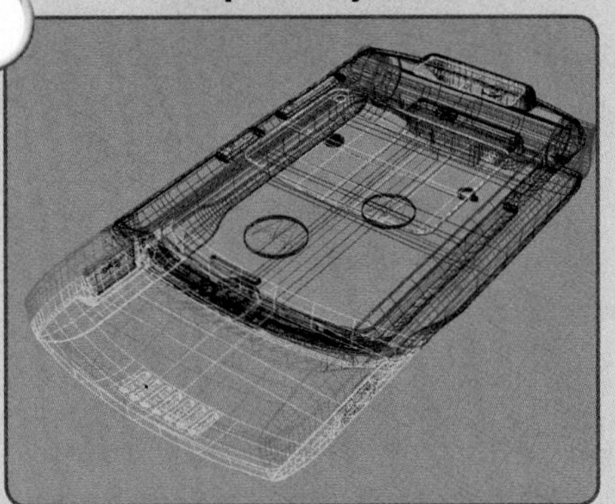

A new cell phone design begins with a drawing that shows how the pieces fit together so it is easy to use and hold.

2

Cell phones are much smaller than before, even though many new functions have been added.

3

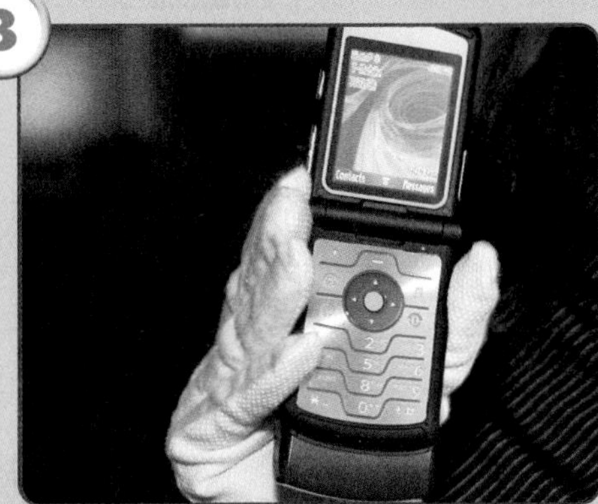

Decimal units are needed to measure the buttons on the key pad and the thinness of the metal case.

VOCABULARY POWER

TALK Math

What math is used in the **Math on Location**? How can you find a precise measurement of the width of the cell phones shown?

READ Math

REVIEW VOCABULARY You will learn the words below when you learn about decimals and place value. How do these words relate to **Math on Location**?

thousandth one of one thousand equal parts

equivalent decimals decimals that name the same number or amount

round to replace a number with another number that is simpler and is approximately the same size as the original number

WRITE Math

Copy and continue the category map below. Use what you know about decimals.

	Whole numbers	Fractions	Decimals
Can represent counting numbers	YES	YES	YES
Can represent parts of numbers less than 1	NO	YES	YES
Can make precise measurements			

Technology
Multimedia Math Glossary link at
www.harcourtschool.com/hspmath

CHAPTER

5 Understand Decimals

FAST FACT

Missouri is home to more than 40 species of damselflies. Damselflies use their two sets of wings to fly at speeds of 10 kilometers per hour.

Investigate

You are a researcher studying the damselflies of Missouri. The table shows the body lengths of some of the damselflies you have observed. Choose and compare the body lengths of two species of damselflies. Which damselfly has the greater length?

Missouri Damselfly Research Study

Species	Body Length (m)
American Rubyspot	0.046
Azure Bluet	0.026
Common Spreadwing	0.050
Double-Striped Bluet	0.027
Eastern Forktail	0.038
Powdered Dancer	0.040

GO ONLINE

Technology
Student pages are available in the Student eBook.

Show What You Know

Check your understanding of important skills needed for success in Chapter 5.

▶ Compare and Order Whole Numbers

Compare. Write <, >, or = for each ●.

1. 572 ● 800 **2.** 635 ● 599 **3.** 706 ● 760 **4.** 3,926 ● 3,906

5. 3,404 ● 3,440 **6.** 52,008 ● 52,100 **7.** 90,523 ● 90,098 **8.** 146,025 ● 146,025

Write the numbers in order from least to greatest.

9. 4,032; 4,203; 3,402; 4,320 **10.** 25,046; 25,406; 50,256; 45,620

11. 73,801; 38,710; 187,039 **12.** 182,950; 208,109; 102,985

▶ Decimal Models

Write as a decimal.

13. 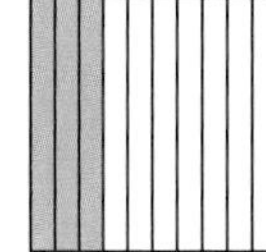 **14.** 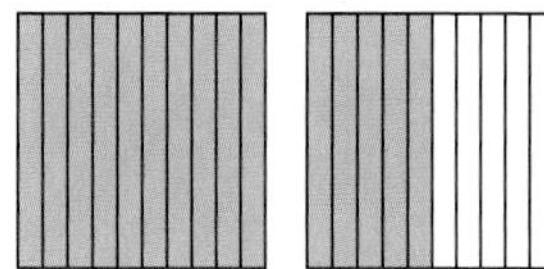 **15.** 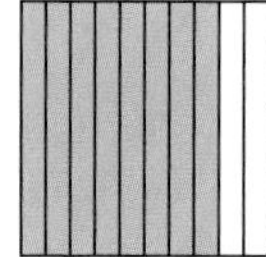

Write the numbers in two other forms.

16. four and seven tenths **17.** 10 + 0.3 **18.** 0.7

19. 200 + 5 + 0.9 **20.** 5.2 **21.** three and two tenths

VOCABULARY POWER

CHAPTER VOCABULARY

decimal
equivalent decimals
hundredth
tenth
thousandth

WARM-UP WORDS

equivalent decimals decimals that name the same number or amount

hundredth one of one hundred equal parts

thousandth one of one thousand equal parts

Decimal Place Value

OBJECTIVE: Read and write decimals through thousandths.

Quick Review

A soccer stadium holds one hundred thirty-five thousand people. Write the number in standard form.

Vocabulary

thousandth

Learn

You can make a model to understand decimals through thousandths.

HANDS ON Activity

Materials ■ 3 decimal squares ■ straightedge

A decimal square represents 1 whole.

Step 1

Divide the square into tenths. Shade one tenth.

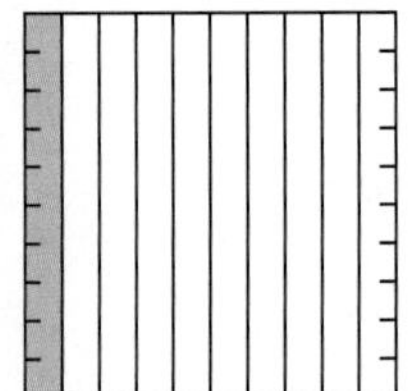

The model shows $\frac{1}{10}$, 0.1, and one tenth.

Step 2

Divide a second square into hundredths. Shade one hundredth.

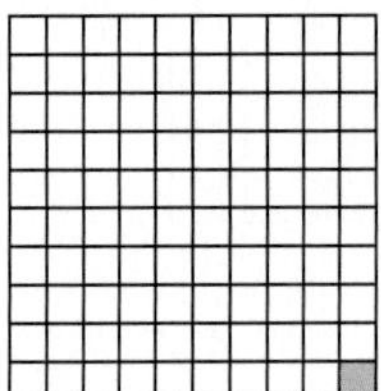

The model shows $\frac{1}{100}$, 0.01, and one hundredth.

Step 3

Using a third square, divide one hundredth into ten parts. Shade one thousandth.

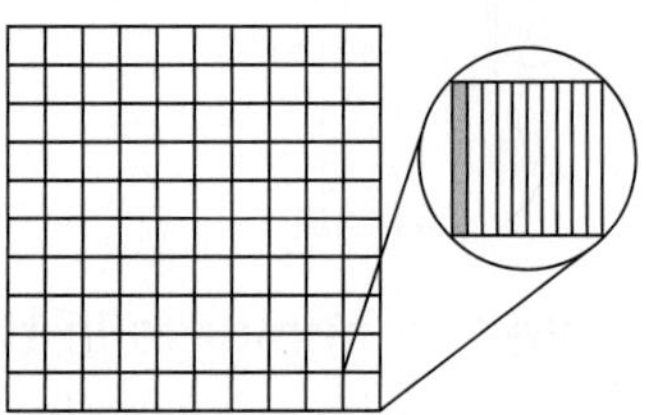

The model shows $\frac{1}{1,000}$, 0.001, and one thousandth.

When you divide one whole by 1,000, you get one **thousandth**.

PROBLEM Honeybees were brought to North America by European colonists. A honeybee is about 0.017 meter long. What is the value of the digit 7 in 0.017?

▲ European honeybee

Example 1 Use a place-value chart.

Ones	Tenths	Hundredths	Thousandths
0 .	0	1	7
$0 \times 0 = 0$	$0 \times 0.0 = 0$	$1 \times 0.01 = 0.01$	$7 \times 0.001 = 0.007$

So, the value of the digit 7 is 7 thousandths, or 0.007.

You can write a decimal in standard form, word form, and expanded form.

Standard Form: 3.592 **Expanded Form:** 3 + 0.5 + 0.09 + 0.002

Word Form: three and five hundred ninety-two thousandths

FAST TRACK

KY MA-05-1.1.1 Students will: apply multiple representations (e.g., drawings, manipulatives, base-10 blocks, number lines, symbols) to describe commonly-used fractions, mixed numbers and decimals through thousandths; DOK 2 *also MA-05-1.1.2*

Place-Value Patterns

To understand the size of numbers, look for a pattern in a place-value chart. For the number 2.222, how does the value of the 2 in the hundredths place compare to the value of the 2 in the thousandths place?

Example 2 **Use a place-value chart.**

Write the number in the place-value chart and look for a pattern.

Ones	Tenths	Hundredths	Thousandths
2 .	2	2	2

2×1	2×0.1	2×0.01	2×0.001	
2	0.2	0.02	0.002	←Value

Math Idea
The value of each place of a decimal is ten times the value of the place to its right.

So, the value of the 2 in the hundredths place is ten times as great as the value of the 2 in the thousandths place.

- How does the value of the 2 in the tenths place compare to the value of the 2 in the thousandths place?

Guided Practice

1. Copy the place-value chart, and write 8.305 in your chart. What is the value of the digit 3?

Ones	Tenths	Hundredths	Thousandths
■ .	■	■	■

Write the decimal shown by the shaded part of each model.

2. 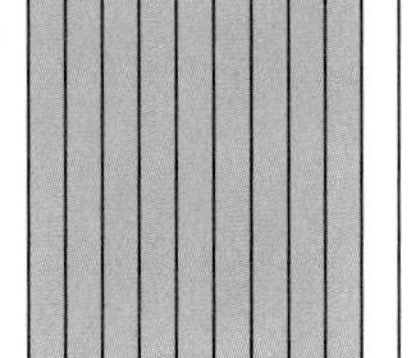

3. 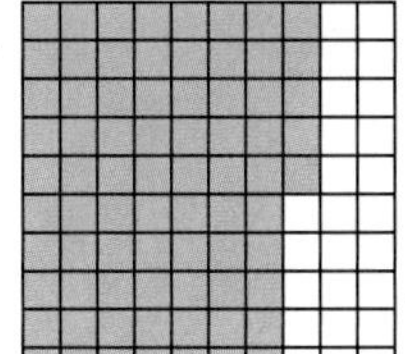

4. 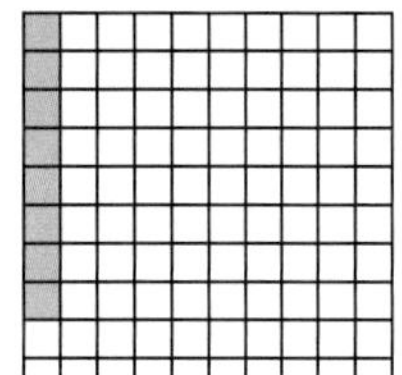

✓5. 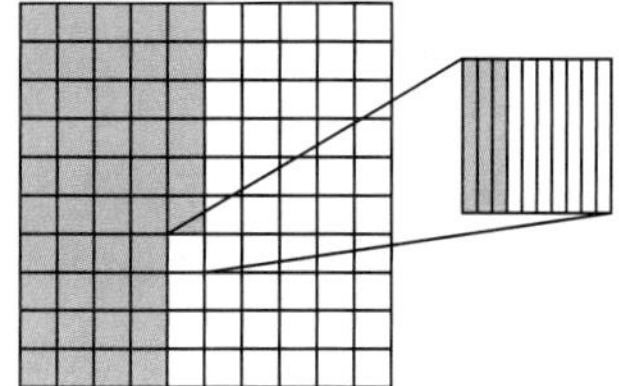

Find the value of the underlined digit.

6. 2.32<u>6</u>
7. 0.6<u>7</u>8
8. 5.00<u>1</u>
9. 12.<u>9</u>5
10. 19.<u>7</u>34
11. 0.00<u>7</u>
12. 5.2<u>3</u>
13. 33.<u>8</u>75
14. 9.4<u>9</u>9
✓15. 4.0<u>7</u>2

16. **TALK Math** **Explain** why, in the decimal 3.665, the value of the 6 in the tenths place is 10 times as great as the value of the 6 in the hundredths place.

CD ROM **Technology**
Use Harcourt Mega Math, Fraction Action, *Number Line Mine*, Level M.

Independent Practice and Problem Solving

Write the decimal shown by the shaded part of each model.

17. 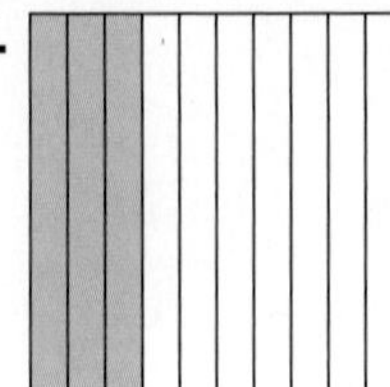

18. 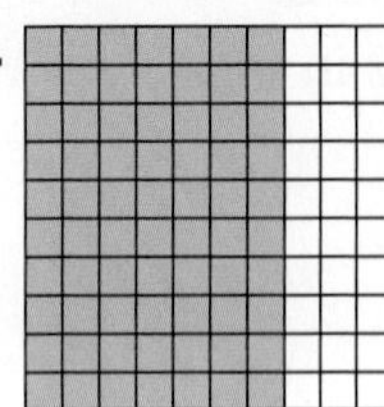

19. 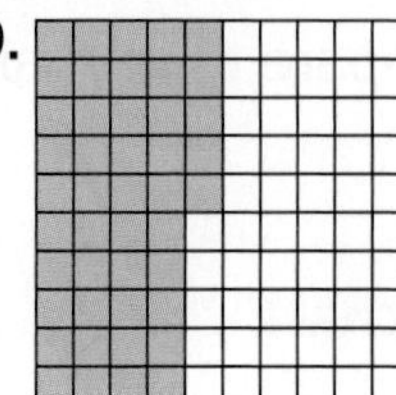

20. 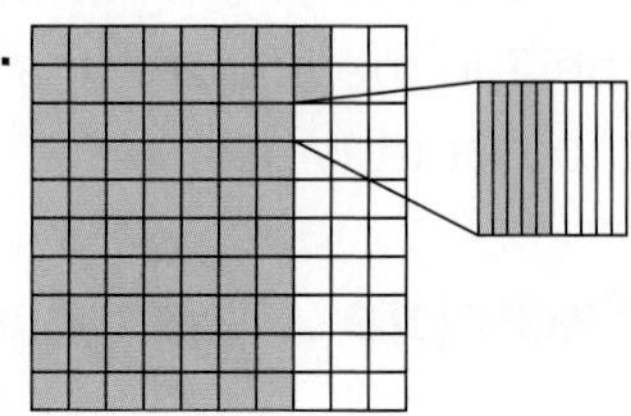

Find the value of the underlined digit.

21. $5.8\underline{1}2$ **22.** $28.32\underline{4}$ **23.** $0.\underline{2}83$ **24.** $1.2\underline{5}0$ **25.** $3.23\underline{8}$

26. $52.\underline{9}64$ **27.** $7.9\underline{2}7$ **28.** $0.28\underline{1}9$ **29.** $7.29\underline{8}$ **30.** $41.\underline{7}04$

Write each number in two other forms.

31. four and one hundred nine thousandths

32. two and forty-two hundredths

33. seventy-three hundredths

34. twelve and eighty-five hundredths

35. $0.6 + 0.07$ **36.** 0.725 **37.** $3 + 0.1 + 0.01$ **38.** 0.552

Algebra **Complete the expanded notation.**

39. $0.872 = (8 \times 0.1) + (7 \times 0.01) + (■ \times ■)$

40. $5.97 = (5 \times 1) + (■ \times ■) + (7 \times 0.01)$

USE DATA **For 41–45, use the table.**

41. Write the length of the orchid bee in expanded form.

42. What is the value of the digit 2 in the carpenter bee's length?

43. The atlas beetle is about 10 times as long as the leafcutting bee. About how long is an atlas beetle?

44. Write the length of the bumblebee in two other forms.

45. **Pose a Problem** Look back at Problem 42. Write a similar problem by changing the type of bee.

46. WRITE Math **What's the Error?** Erica has the number 0.303 in a Guess My Number game. She says that the hundredths digit is 0 and the value of the digit in the tenths place, 3, is 10 times the value of the digit in the thousandths place. Describe Erica's error.

Bee Lengths (in meters)	
Bumblebee	0.019
Carpenter Bee	0.025
Leafcutting Bee	0.014
Orchid Bee	0.028
Sweat Bee	0.006

 Extra Practice on page 142, Set A

Learn About Measurement and Place Value

The metric measurement system is related to our base-10 number system.

In the metric system: 1 meter = 10 decimeters
1 decimeter = 10 centimeters
1 centimeter = 10 millimeters

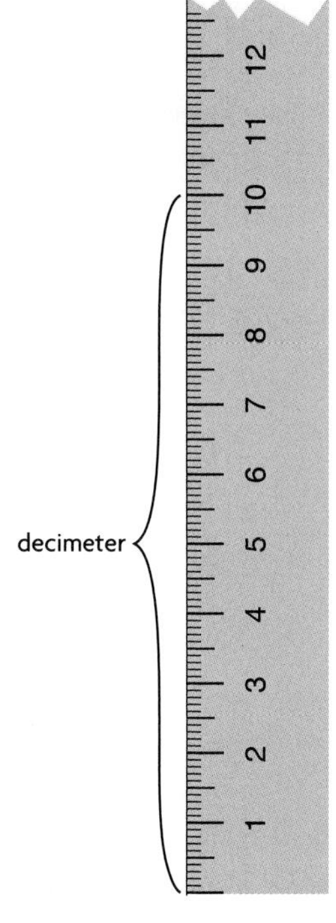

Example **Write 4.375 meters in expanded form, using the units of measure.**

Write the number of meters, decimeters, centimeters, and millimeters in a place-value chart.

Meters (Ones)	Decimeters (Tenths)	Centimeters (Hundredths)	Millimeters (Thousandths)
4 .	3	7	5
4.000	0.300	0.070	0.005

So, in expanded form 4.375 meters is 4 meters + 3 decimeters + 7 centimeters + 5 millimeters.

Try It

Use a place-value chart to solve.

47. Write 3.641 meters in expanded form, as a sum of meters, decimeters, centimeters, and millimeters.

48. Write 5 meters + 4 decimeters + 8 centimeters in standard form.

Mixed Review and Test Prep

49. Elliot bought 4 cartons of juice for a party. Each carton holds 64 ounces. How many ounces of juice did Elliot buy? (p. 40)

50. **Test Prep** What is the value of the underlined digit in 5.92<u>6</u>?

A 0.0006 **C** 0.06
B 0.006 **D** 0.6

51. Brad wants to run a 3-mile race in 24 minutes. Write an equation that can be used to find the number of minutes, *m*, he needs to run each mile. (p. 106)

52. **Test Prep** How many times greater is 0.05 than 0.005?

A 5 **C** 100
B 10 **D** 1,000

LESSON 2

Equivalent Decimals

OBJECTIVE: Identify and write equivalent decimals.

Quick Review

1. 3.■ = $3\frac{4}{10}$
2. 1.9 = $1\frac{■}{10}$
3. 7.■ = $7\frac{52}{100}$
4. 9.84 = $9\frac{■}{100}$
5. 12.■ = $12\frac{3}{10}$

Vocabulary

equivalent decimals

Learn

PROBLEM The whooping crane is the tallest bird in North America. An adult whooping crane can reach a height of 1.5 meters. Write an equivalent decimal for 1.5.

Equivalent decimals are decimals that name the same number or amount. In the place-value chart below, zeros have been placed to the right of the digit 5 to make equivalent decimals.

Ones .	Tenths	Hundredths	Thousandths
1	5		
1	5	0	
1	5	0	0

So, the decimals 1.50 and 1.500 are equivalent to 1.5.

Math Idea
You can add zeros to the right of the last digit in a decimal without changing the value of the decimal.

You can use models to determine if two decimals are equivalent.

Examples **Draw a model for each decimal. Write *equivalent* or *not equivalent* to describe each pair of decimals.**

A 0.3 and 0.30

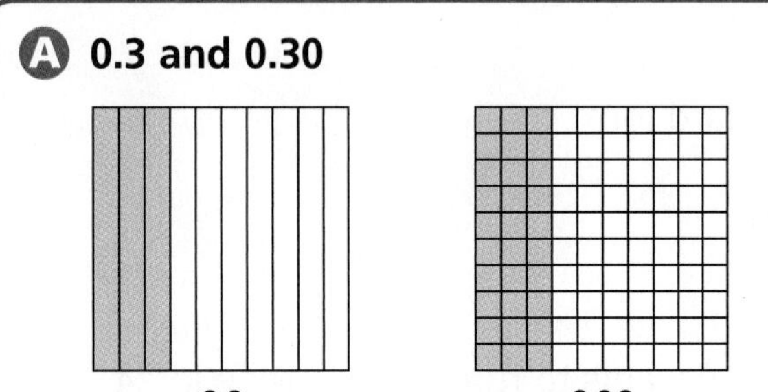

0.3 0.30

The shaded area for both models is the same size. So, 0.3 is equivalent to 0.30.

B 0.5 and 0.05

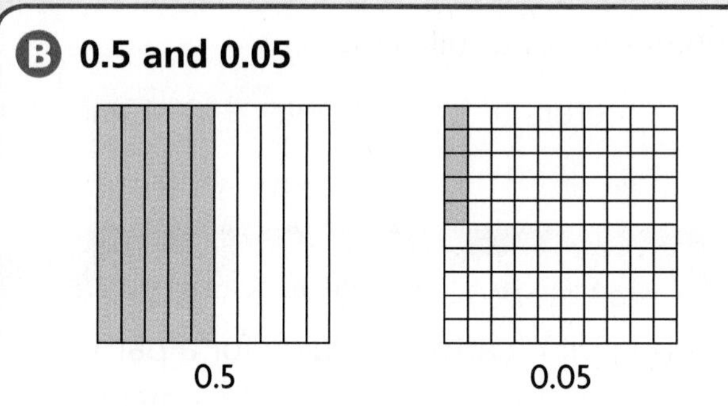

0.5 0.05

The shaded area for both models is **not** the same size. So, 0.5 is **not** equivalent to 0.05.

- Ten hundredths are equivalent to one tenth. How many tenths are equivalent to 1? Use a model to explain your answer.

Guided Practice

1. Make a model for 0.4 and 0.40. Then explain how the models help you decide if the decimals are equivalent. Are the decimals equivalent?

KY MA-05-1.1.3 Students will compare (<, >, =) and order whole numbers, fractions and decimals, and explain the relationships (equivalence, order) between and among them. DOK 2 *also* MA-05-1.1.1; *MA-05-1.1.2*

Write *equivalent* or *not equivalent* to describe each pair of decimals.

2. 3.7 and 3.70 **3.** 0.06 and 0.006 **4.** 8.90 and 8.09 **5.** 2.5 and 2.5

6. 0.52 and 0.520 **7.** 7.8 and 7.08 **8.** 0.9 and 0.09 **9.** 0.42 and 0.420

10. TALK Math **Explain** how you can determine if 1.206 is equivalent to 1.026.

Independent Practice and Problem Solving

Write *equivalent* or *not equivalent* to describe each pair of decimals.

11. 2.09 and 2.90 **12.** 5.003 and 5.03 **13.** 12 and 12.0 **14.** 9.01 and 9.010

15. 3.26 and 3.260 **16.** 4.01 and 4.011 **17.** 6.004 and 6.04 **18.** 7.08 and 7.80

Write an equivalent decimal for each number.

19. 0.09 **20.** 1.430 **21.** 0.6 **22.** 2.400

23. 5.08 **24.** 0.700 **25.** 4.08 **26.** 8.90

Write the two decimals that are equivalent.

27. 6.03
6.300
6.030

28. 0.041
0.0401
0.0410

29. 1.006
1.600
1.6000

30. 0.5900
0.059
0.59

USE DATA For 31–33, use the table.

31. Write two equivalent decimals for the mass of the demoiselle crane.

32. Which two cranes have an equivalent mass? Are the heights of these two cranes equivalent?

33. WRITE Math **What's the Question?** The blue crane has an average height of 1.23 meters. The answer is sandhill.

Cranes' Average Height and Mass

Kind of Crane	Height (in meters)	Mass (in kilograms)
Sandhill	1.23	4.55
Wattled	1.85	6.36
Demoiselle	0.92	2.50
Sarus	1.85	6.36

Mixed Review and Test Prep

34. Ann scored 163,425 points and Ross scored 149,896 points in a video game. Who scored more points? (p. 10)

35. The average distance from Mars to the Sun is two hundred twenty million, nine hundred thousand kilometers. Write the distance in standard form. (p. 4)

36. **Test Prep** Jamie hiked 2.75 miles to the waterfall. Which decimal is equivalent?

A 2.075

B 2.705

C 2.750

D 2.755

Extra Practice on page 142, Set B

LESSON 3

Compare and Order Decimals

OBJECTIVE: Use models and place value to compare and order decimals.

Quick Review

Write *equivalent* or *not equivalent* to describe each pair.

1. 0.06 and 0.60
2. 3.5 and 3.50
3. 4.09 and 4.090
4. 5.201 and 5.021
5. 0.78 and 0.780

Learn

PROBLEM An entomologist, a scientist who studies insects, is comparing the lengths of two ladybird beetles, also called ladybugs. The ladybugs are 0.528 and 0.534 centimeter long. Which ladybug has the greater length?

ONE WAY Use a number line.

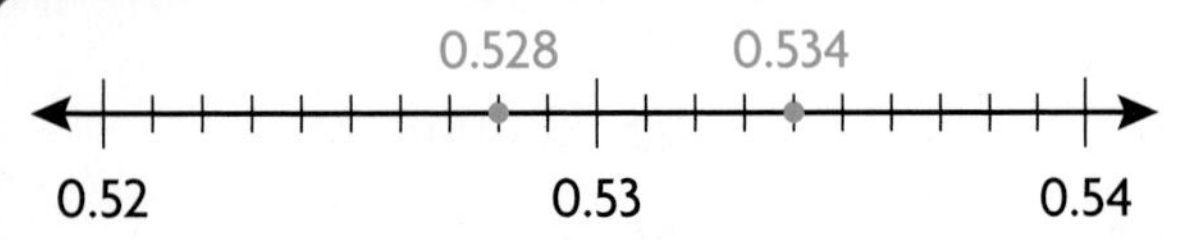

Since 0.534 is to the right of 0.528, 0.534 > 0.528.

Remember
On a number line, the greater number is to the right.

So, the ladybug that is 0.534 centimeter long has the greater length.

ANOTHER WAY Use place value. Compare 3.25 and 3.254.

Step 1	Step 2	Step 3	Step 4
Line up the decimal points. Begin at the left. Compare the ones.	Compare the tenths.	Compare the hundredths.	To compare thousandths, write an equivalent decimal for 3.25. Then compare.
3.25 3.254 same	3.25 3.254 same	3.25 3.254 same	3.250 3.254 0 < 4

So, 3.25 < 3.254, or 3.254 > 3.25.

Example Use place value. Order 4.137, 4, and 4.19 from least to greatest.

Step 1	Step 2	Step 3
Line up the decimal points. Write equivalent decimals.	Begin at the left. Compare the digits until they are different.	Continue comparing.
4.137 4.000 4.190	4.137 4.000 ← 0 < 1 4.190 4.000 is least.	4.137 3 < 9 4.190 ← 4.190 is greatest.

So, the order from least to greatest is 4, 4.137, 4.19.

FAST TRACK

KY MA-05-1.1.3 Students will compare (<, >, =) and order whole numbers, fractions and decimals, and explain the relationships (equivalence, order) between and among them. DOK 2 *also* MA-05-1.1.1; *MA-05-1.1.2*

Guided Practice

1. Copy the number line. Locate 0.72 and 0.7 on the number line. Then, compare the decimals.

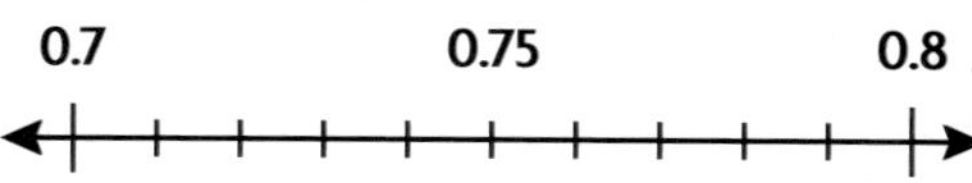

Compare. Write $<$, $>$, or $=$ for each ●.

2. 5.43 ● 5.432
3. 0.28 ● 0.208
4. 9.39 ● 9.9

5. TALK Math **Explain** how to use place value to order 1.567, 1.571, and 1.556 from greatest to least.

Independent Practice and Problem Solving

Compare. Write $<$, $>$, or $=$ for each ●.

6. 0.972 ● 0.98
7. 4 ● 0.79
8. 3.602 ● 3.082
9. 10.3 ● 1.898
10. 6.7 ● 6.701
11. 0.749 ● 0.769

Order from least to greatest.

12. 0.123, 0.32, 0.113, 0.2
13. 6.0, 6.498, 6.52, 6.490
14. 5.6, 9, 6.8, 8.005

Algebra **Find all of the digits that can replace each ■.**

15. $9.7■7 < 9.770$
16. $0.28■ > 0.284$
17. $2.356 > 2.■83$

USE DATA For 18–20, use the table.

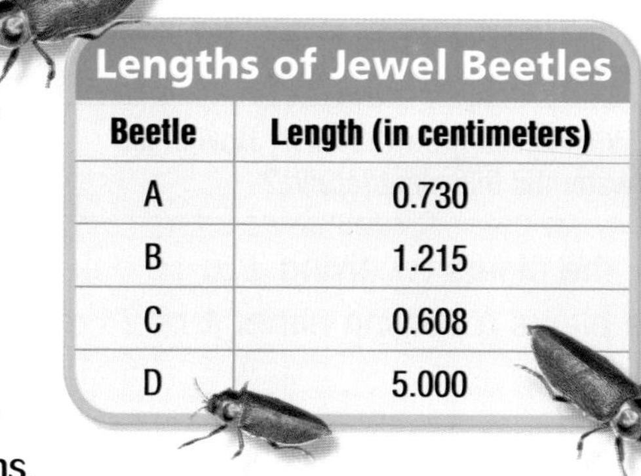

Lengths of Jewel Beetles

Beetle	Length (in centimeters)
A	0.730
B	1.215
C	0.608
D	5.000

18. Which beetle is the longest? Which beetle is the shortest?

19. **Reasoning** Suppose another beetle was measured with a length of 0.84 centimeter. Between which two beetles' lengths does the length of this beetle fall?

20. WRITE Math Order the lengths of the beetles in the table from least to greatest. **Explain** how you ordered the lengths.

Mixed Review and Test Prep

21. Karl's backyard is rectangular. The length is 42 feet and the width is 18 feet. What is the perimeter? (Grade 4)

22. A trail at the park is 0.215 mile long. Write 0.215 in word form. (p. 132)

23. **Test Prep** Taylor received the scores below in a diving competition. The lowest score is tossed out. Which score will be tossed out?

    A 8.495
    B 8.625
    C 8.175
    D 8.905

Extra Practice on page 142, Set C

Problem Solving Workshop
Skill: Draw Conclusions

OBJECTIVE: Solve problems by using the skill *draw conclusions.*

Use the Skill

PROBLEM Samantha conducted an experiment to see how the amount of water that a bamboo plant receives daily affects its growth. The 5 plants had the same soil and received the same amount of sunlight. How did the amount of water each bamboo plant received affect its growth?

Amount of Water Per Day	
Plant	**Number of Fluid Ounces of Water**
A	1
B	4
C	8
D	16
E	24

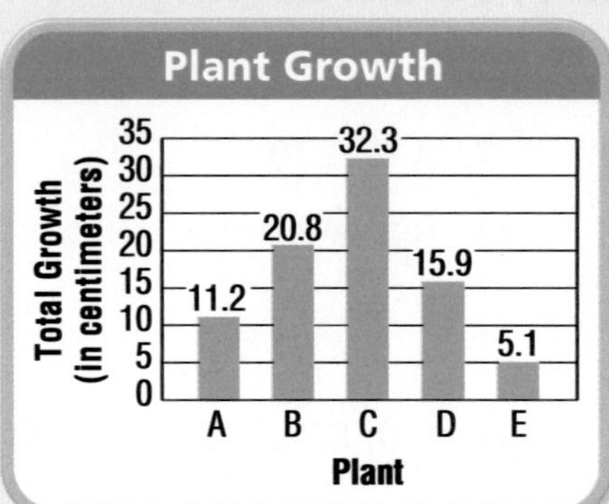

You can analyze data to draw a conclusion.

Analyze	Conclusion
• Which plant grew the most? How much water did this plant receive?	Plant C grew the most. Plant C received 8 fluid ounces of water.
• Which plant grew the least? How much water did this plant receive?	Plant E grew the least. Plant E received 24 fluid ounces of water.

So, the plants receiving 4 to 16 ounces each day grew the most, and the plants receiving either 1 or 24 ounces each day grew the least.

Think and Discuss

Read each conclusion about Samantha's experiment. Tell whether it can be drawn from the data in the table and graph. Write *yes* or *no*. Explain your reasoning.

a. The more water given, the taller the plants grew.

b. One plant grew to be 15.9 centimeters tall.

c. Plant E received twice as much water daily as Plant C.

FAST TRACK

KY MA-05-1.1.3 Students will compare (<, >, =) and order whole numbers, fractions and decimals, and explain the relationships (equivalence, order) between and among them. DOK 2

Guided Problem Solving

1. Albert conducted an experiment on plant growth. One plant received 8 hours of sunlight each day and grew to a height of 9.5 centimeters. A second plant received 6 hours of sunlight each day and grew to a height of 14 centimeters. A third plant received 2 hours of sunlight each day and grew to a height of 4.25 centimeters. What conclusion can you draw about the amount of sunlight a plant needs for it to have the greatest growth?

   First, identify the details in the problem.

   Plant 1: 8 hrs ⟶ 9.5 centimeters

   Plant 2: 6 hrs ⟶ 14 centimeters

   Plant 3: 2 hours ⟶ 4.25 centimeters

   Then, make comparisons by ordering the plants from greatest to least amount of sunlight. Then, order the plants' heights from greatest to least.

   Draw a conclusion to solve the problem.

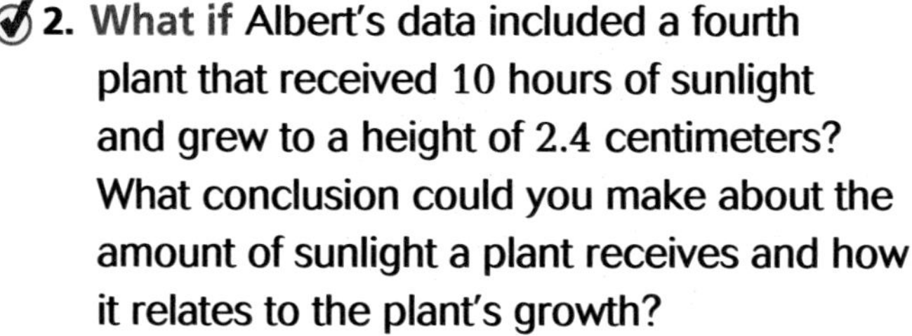

2. **What if** Albert's data included a fourth plant that received 10 hours of sunlight and grew to a height of 2.4 centimeters? What conclusion could you make about the amount of sunlight a plant receives and how it relates to the plant's growth?

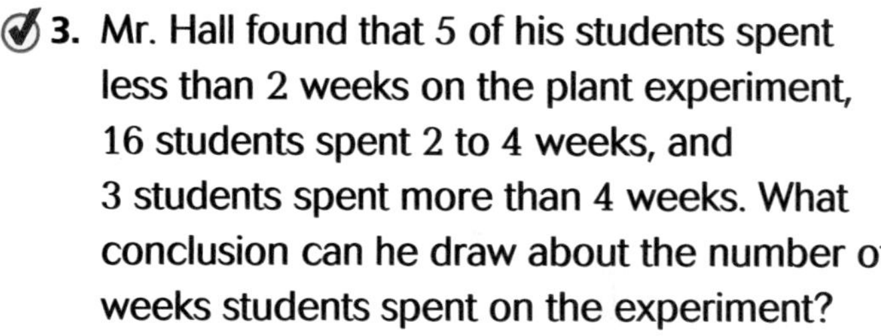

3. Mr. Hall found that 5 of his students spent less than 2 weeks on the plant experiment, 16 students spent 2 to 4 weeks, and 3 students spent more than 4 weeks. What conclusion can he draw about the number of weeks students spent on the experiment?

Mixed Applications

4. On average, 235 pizzas are sold each month at a store. Ed says about 25,000 pizzas are sold in a year. Brian says about 3,000 pizzas are sold in a year. Whose answer is reasonable?

5. The fifth-grade classes are going on a field trip. They plan to use buses for the 128 students, 3 teachers, and 6 other adults. Each bus holds 55 people. How many buses will they need?

6. Shawn worked for 12 hours over two days. He earned $6.00 each hour. He paid $1 every 4 hours to park his car. How much money did Shawn make after paying for parking?

7. Elizabeth is planning an outfit to wear. She has a red top and a black top. She has shorts, jeans, and a skirt. How many different outfits can she wear?

8. **WRITE Math** Hicham El Guerrouj from Morocco ran a mile in a record-breaking time, 3 minutes and 43.13 seconds. A mile is run with 4 laps around a track. **Explain** how to find the number of seconds El Guerrouj would have taken to run each lap if he had run each of his laps in the same time.

Extra Practice

Set A Write the decimal shown by the shaded part of each model. (pp. 132–135)

1. 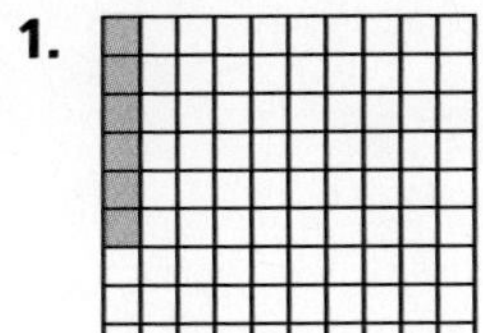
2.
3.
4.

Find the value of the underlined digit in each number.

5. $3.\underline{6}45$
6. $51.82\underline{9}3$
7. $0.6\underline{1}47$
8. $1.07\underline{6}$
9. $29.\underline{5}28$
10. $7.\underline{8}94$
11. $0.54\underline{9}$
12. $5.\underline{7}50$
13. $12.88\underline{3}$
14. $9.6\underline{4}7$

Write each number in two other forms.

15. three and two hundred six thousandths
16. sixty-four hundredths
17. 15 + 0.1 + 0.003
18. 1.392
19. A monarch butterfly had a wingspan of 9.65 cm. Write this length in word form.

Set B Write *equivalent* or *not equivalent* to describe each pair of decimals. (pp. 136–137)

1. 3.60 and 3.6
2. 5.07 and 5.70
3. 7.104 and 7.014
4. 1.002 and 1.200

Write an equivalent decimal for each number.

5. 0.03
6. 2.5
7. 6.180
8. 0.49

Set C Compare. Write <, >, or = for each ●. (pp. 138–139)

1. 0.348 ● 0.36
2. 9.71 ● 9.17
3. 2.093 ● 2.93
4. 7.58 ● 7.5
5. 10.7 ● 10.07
6. 4.33 ● 4.330

Order from least to greatest.

7. 3.28, 3.109, 3.5, 3.218
8. 0.7, 0.296, 0.61, 0.402
9. 4.82, 4.790, 4.0, 4,798
10. 0.9, 0.98, 9.8, 0.5
11. 12.775, 12.43, 1.243, 12.7
12. 3.527, 3.52, 3.528, 3.6
13. There are three hiking trails at the park. On the map, the red trail is 3.75 miles long. The blue trail is 3.38 miles long, and the green trail is 3.9 miles long. Order the trails from shortest to longest.

CD ROM **Technology**
Use Harcourt Mega Math, Fraction Action, *Number Line Mine,* Level R

PRACTICE GAME

DECIMAL CHALLENGE

Players

2–4 players

Materials

- 4 sets of symbol cards (<, >, =)
- number cube labeled 1, 1, 1, 2, 2, 3
- game pieces

Compare!

- Shuffle the symbol cards and place them facedown in a pile.
- Each player selects a different game piece and places it on *START*.
- Player 1 tosses the number cube and moves that many spaces on the board. Then Player 1 draws a symbol card.
- Depending on the card, they must think of a decimal that is greater than, less than, or equal to the decimal they landed on.
- If a player is correct, it is the next player's turn. If a player gives an incorrect answer, he or she loses a turn.
- The first player to reach *FINISH* wins.

MATH POWER Ten-Thousandths

The Tiniest Insect

The Fairyfly wasp is the tiniest insect in the world. The insect is so small that it can fly through the eye of a needle! Scientists estimate that the wingspan of the Fairyfly wasp is 0.0067 inch. What is the value of the digit 7 in 0.0067?

You can use a place-value chart to find the value.

Ones	Tenths	Hundredths	Thousandths	Ten-thousandths
0	0	0	6	7
$0 \times 0 = 0$	$0 \times 0.1 = 0$	$0 \times 0.01 = 0$	$6 \times 0.001 = 0.006$	$7 \times 0.0001 = 0.0007$

So, the value of the digit 7 is 7 ten-thousandths, or 0.0007.

You can write decimals in different forms.

Examples

Write 0.0067 in different forms.

A Standard Form: 0.0067

B Word Form: sixty-seven ten-thousandths

C Expanded Form:

- $0.006 + 0.0007$
- $(6 \times 0.001) + (7 \times 0.0001)$

Try It

What is the value of the underlined digit?

1. $1.388\underline{2}$ **2.** $0.\underline{7}514$ **3.** $6.094\underline{0}$ **4.** $0.00\underline{1}2$

5. $10.000\underline{9}$ **6.** $2.8\underline{1}83$ **7.** $0.0\underline{6}01$ **8.** $19.734\underline{1}$

9. $0.00\underline{4}1$ **10.** $5.\underline{5}762$ **11.** $24.008\underline{9}$ **12.** $8.22\underline{9}8$

Write each number in two other forms.

13. 0.0034 **14.** 0.2169 **15.** 1.0005 **16.** 3.1008

17. $0.001 + 0.0006$ **18.** $0.4 + 0.05 + 0.0007$

19. one and ninety-six ten-thousandths **20.** two thousand thirty-five ten-thousandths

21. WRITE Math **Explain** how you would compare 2.9075 and 2.9073.

Chapter 5 Review/Test

Check Vocabulary and Concepts

Choose the best term from the box.

VOCABULARY
thousandth
hundredth
equivalent decimals

1. Decimals that name the same number or amount are __?__.
   KY MA-05-1.1.3 (p. 136)
2. When you divide one whole by 1,000 you get one __?__.
   KY MA-05-1.1.1 (p. 132)

Check Skills

Find the value of the underlined digit. KY MA-05-1.1.1 (pp. 132–135)

3. $0.78\underline{2}$
4. $2.0\underline{5}13$
5. $35.\underline{2}89$
6. $1.\underline{4}07$
7. $9.12\underline{7}$

Write each number in two other forms. KY *MA-05-1.1.2* (pp. 132–135)

8. 2.105
9. 5 + 0.3 + 0.08
10. 0.7 + 0.01 + 0.004
11. 0.646

Write an equivalent decimal for each number. KY MA-05-1.1.3 (pp. 136–137)

12. 0.5
13. 2.690
14. 0.01
15. 3.400

Compare. Write <, >, or = for each ●. KY MA-05-1.1.3 (pp. 138–139)

16. 0.5 ● 0.050
17. 2.427 ● 2.61
18. 7.19 ● 7.190

Check Problem Solving

Solve. KY MA-05-1.1.3 (pp. 140–141)

19. The table shows the training schedules for Eric, Aliyah, and Gina. At the last track meet, Eric ran the mile in 7.5 minutes. Aliyah ran the mile in 7.25 minutes, and Gina ran the mile in 8.1 minutes. What conclusion can you draw about the number of training days and the fastest time?

Training Schedules

	Mon	Tues	Wed	Thurs	Fri	Sat	Sun
Eric	run	run	run	run	run	run	run
Aliyah	run	weights	run	weights	run		run
Gina	run		run		run		

20. WRITE Math Kyle lives 2.8 miles from the school. Jordan lives 2.45 miles from the school. The distance Colleen lives from the school is between these two distances. Give a possible distance that Colleen lives from the school. **Explain** your answer.

GO ONLINE **Technology** Use *Online Assessment.*

Practice for the KCCT
Chapters 1–5

Number and Operations

1. Which is three and seventy-two thousandths written in standard form? KY MA-05-1.1.1 (p. 132)

   A 0.372

   B 3.072

   C 3.702

   D 3.72

2. Hayley's Girl Scout troop went to the amusement park. There were 34 children and 5 adults. KY MA-05-1.3.1 (p. 44)

Amusement Park Tickets	
Age	**Price**
Children (ages 2–17)	$26
Adults	$32

   What was the total cost for the tickets?

   A $884

   B $916

   C $1,044

   D $2,262

3. Which list shows decimals ordered from greatest to least? KY MA-05-1.1.3 (p. 138)

   A 0.74, 0.70, 0.47

   B 0.70, 0.47, 0.74

   C 0.47, 0.74, 0.70

   D 0.74, 0.47, 0.70

4. **WRITE Math** **Explain** how to write equivalent decimals. Give an example. KY MA-05-1.1.3 (p. 136)

Algebraic Thinking

5. Which decimal number makes the inequality true? KY MA-05-1.1.3 (p. 138)

   $1.68 < \blacksquare$

   A 0.75 **C** 1.675

   B 1.372 **D** 1.7

Eliminate Choices.

See item 5. You need to find a number that is greater than 1.68. Begin by looking at the ones digit. Compare digits from left to right. Choose the answer choice with the greatest value.

6. Jenny has 12 CDs. Her brother has 4 times as many. Which expression shows how many CDs Jenny's brother has? KY MA-05-5.2.1 (p. 92)

   A $12 - 4$ **C** 12×4

   B $12 + 4$ **D** $12 \div 4$

7. Jada is 3 years older than twice the age of her sister Lexi. Which equation shows this relationship if x represents Jada's age and y represents Lexi's age? KY MA-05-5.2.1 (p. 106)

   A $x = 2y + 3$

   B $x + 3 = 2y$

   C $x + 3 = y + 2$

   D $x = y + 3$

8. **WRITE Math** **Explain** how to find the value of the expression $3 \times (6 + a)$ if $a = 4$. KY MA-05-5.3.1 (p. 96)

Measurement

9. Mr. Fry is building a deck. He nails together 12 boards. Each board is 12 feet long and 1 foot wide. What is the perimeter of the deck? KY Grade 4

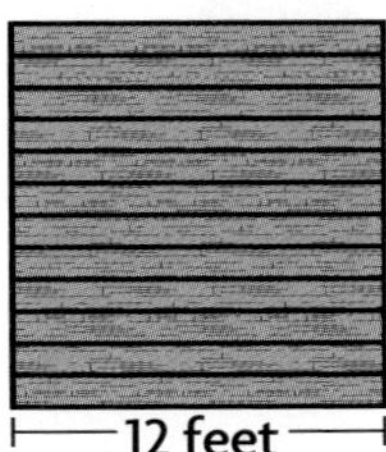

A 12 feet

B 24 feet

C 48 feet

D 144 feet

10. What is the best estimate for the capacity of a cereal bowl? KY Grade 4

A 450 mL **C** 450 L

B 450 oz **D** 450 gal

11. The volleyball tournament began at 10:45 A.M. When the last game of the tournament ended, Corbin looked at the clock on the wall. The time was 3:21 P.M. How long did the volleyball tournament last? KY Grade 4

A 7 hours 24 minutes

B 5 hours 36 minutes

C 5 hours 24 minutes

D 4 hours 36 minutes

12. WRITE Math The side lengths of a square are doubled. **Explain** how the area of the square changes. KY Grade 4

Data Analysis and Probability

13. The line plot shows the ages of students in Maria's dance class. What is the median of the ages? KY Grade 4

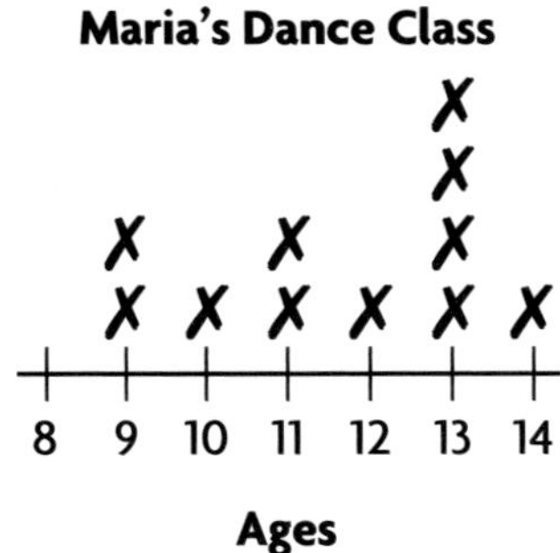

A 11

B 11.6

C 12

D 13

14. Leo tosses a cube numbered 1–6. What is the probability that he will toss an odd number? KY Grade 4

A $\frac{1}{6}$

B $\frac{1}{3}$

C $\frac{1}{2}$

D 1

15. WRITE Math Carly made a line graph to display the results of her experiment. **Explain** the type of data shown on a line graph. KY Grade 4

CHAPTER 6

Add and Subtract Decimals

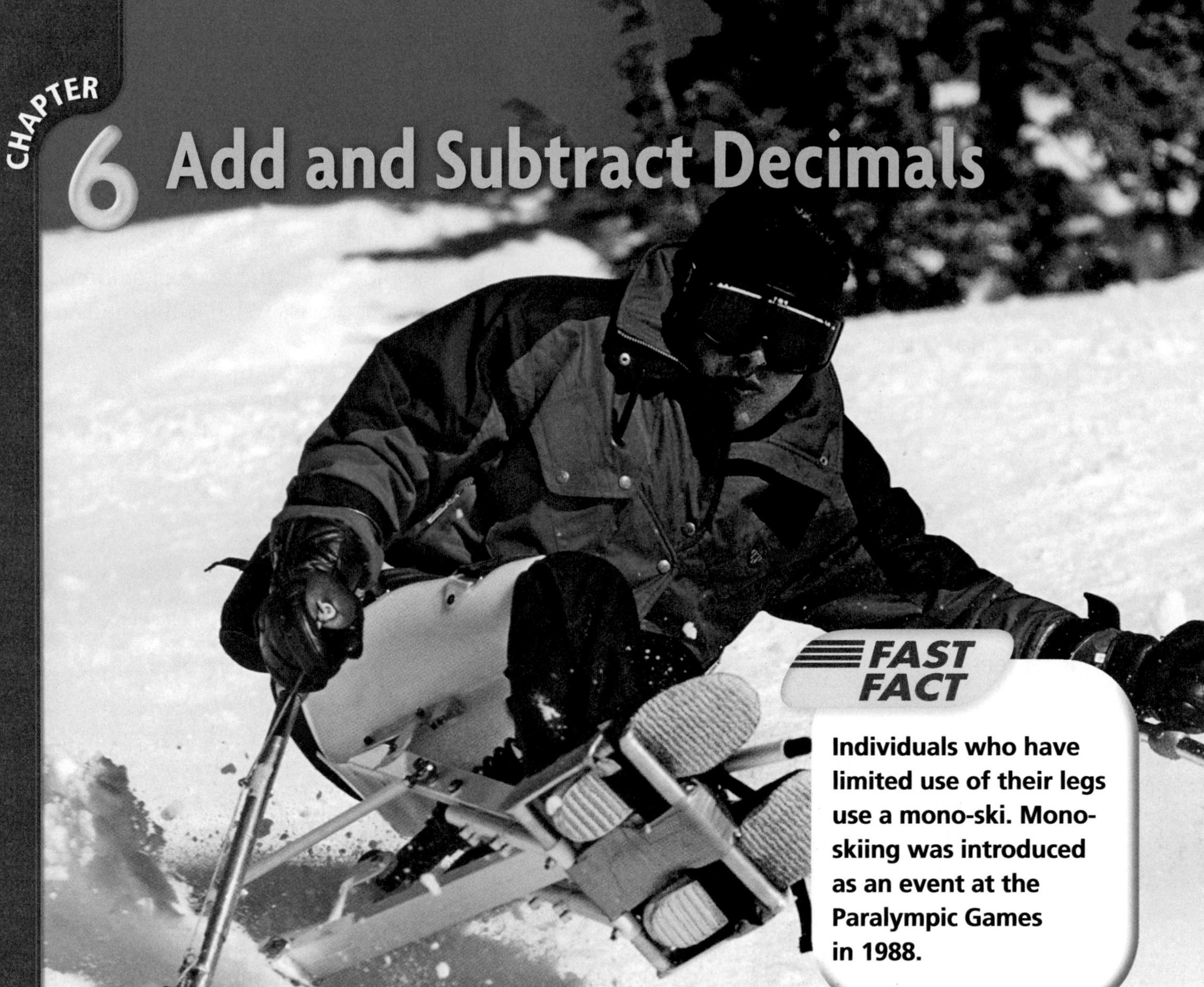

FAST FACT

Individuals who have limited use of their legs use a mono-ski. Mono-skiing was introduced as an event at the Paralympic Games in 1988.

Investigate

While on vacation in central New York, you decide to ski on two different ski runs in the area. Write three equations that show the combined lengths of two different runs that you could choose to ski.

New York Ski Runs

Ski Resort	Longest Run (in miles)
Belleayre	2.27
Hickory Ski Center	2.5
Plattekill Mountain	2.3
Willard Mountain	1.1
Windham Mountain	2.25

GO ONLINE **Technology**
Student pages are available in the Student eBook.

Show What You Know

Check your understanding of important skills needed for success in Chapter 6.

▶ Rounding

Round each number to the nearest hundred.

1. 562 **2.** 407 **3.** 638 **4.** 153

5. 4,709 **6.** 8,371 **7.** 6,881 **8.** 7,349

9. 16,535 **10.** 38,271 **11.** 42,764 **12.** 54,098

▶ Model Decimals

Write the decimal for the shaded part.

13. 

14. 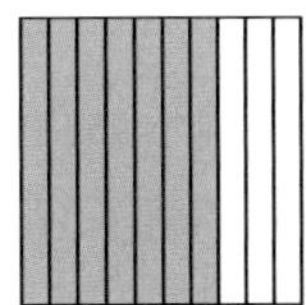

15. 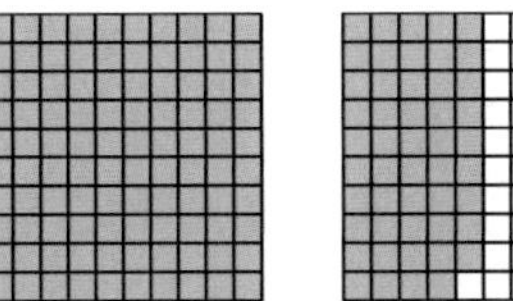

16. 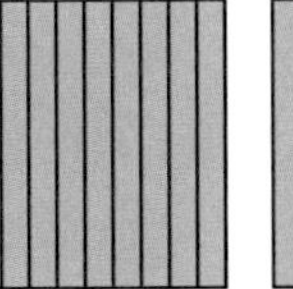

17. 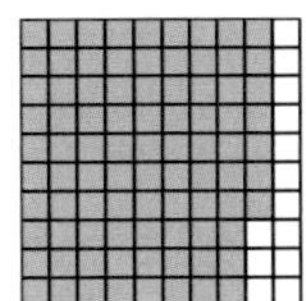

18. 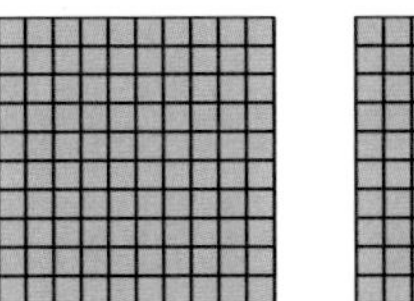

19. 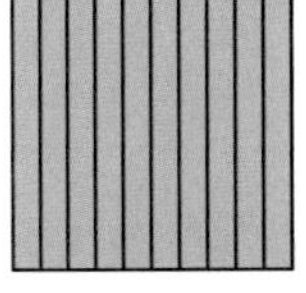 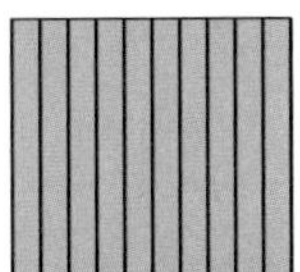 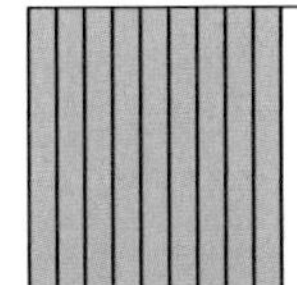

20. 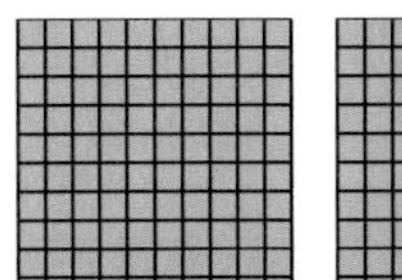 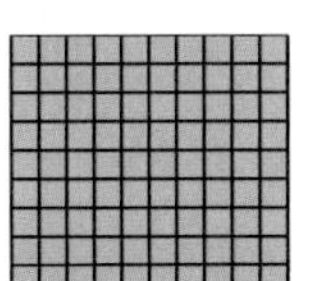 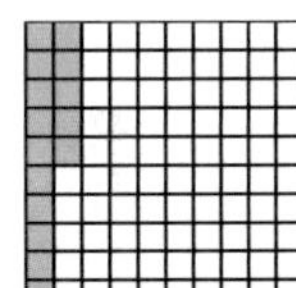

VOCABULARY POWER

CHAPTER VOCABULARY

decimal
decimal point
equivalent decimals
hundredth
tenth
thousandth

WARM-UP WORDS

decimal a number with one or more digits to the right of the decimal point

hundredth one of one hundred equal parts

tenth one of ten equal parts

Round Decimals

OBJECTIVE: Round decimals to a given place value.

Quick Review

Round each number to the place of the underlined digit.

1. 391
2. 5,045
3. 28,036
4. 34,578
5. 169,822

Learn

PROBLEM In Ms. Cosa's science class, students found that grated carrots have an average of 0.039 gram of salt per cup. Rounded to the nearest hundredth of a gram, what is the salt content of one cup of grated carrots?

ONE WAY **Use a number line.**

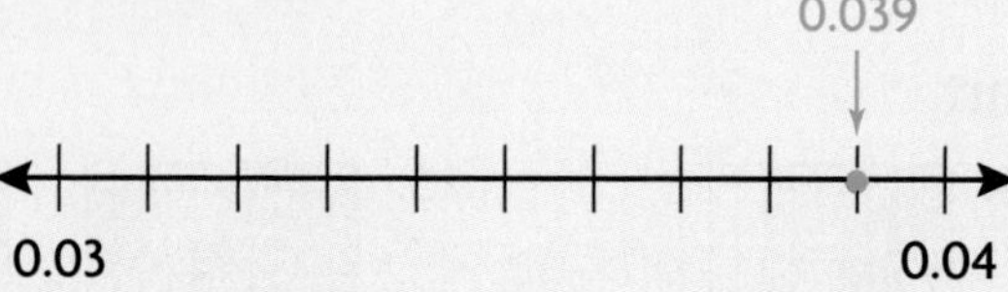

0.039 is closer to 0.04 than to 0.03. So, 0.039 rounded to the nearest hundredth of a gram is 0.04 grams.

ANOTHER WAY **Use the rounding rules.**

Round to the place of the underlined digit. Use the rounding rules.

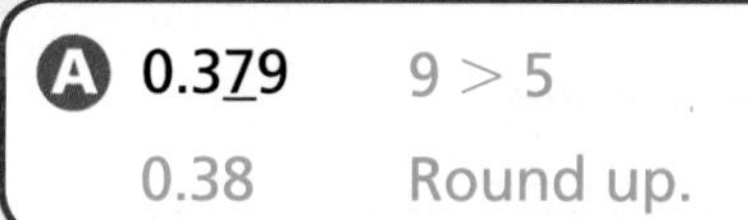

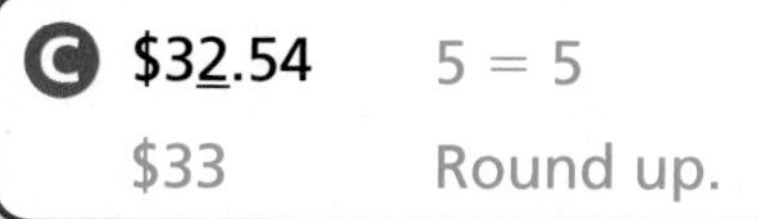

Guided Practice

1. Use the number line to round 0.486 to the nearest hundredth.

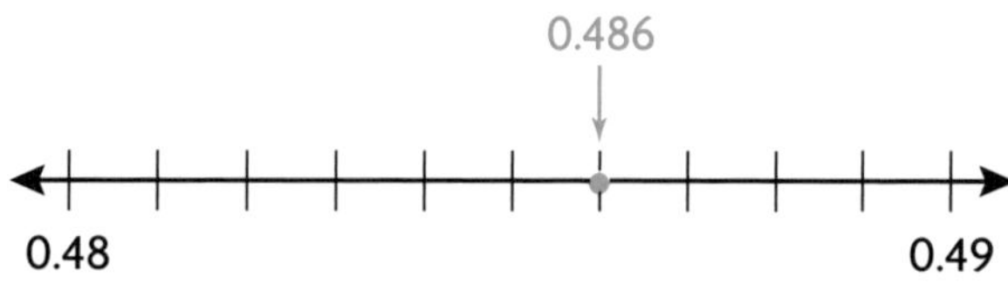

Remember

Rounding rules:

- Find the place to which you want to round.
- If the digit to the right is < 5, round down.
- If the digit to the right is ≥ 5, round up.

Round each number to the place of the underlined digit.

2. 0.355
3. 0.672
4. 0.807
5. 0.134

Round 0.859 to the place named.

6. tenths
7. hundredths
8. ones

9. **TALK Math** **Explain** how to round 7.86 to the nearest tenth.

FAST TRACK

KY MA-05-1.2.1 Students will apply and describe appropriate strategies for estimating quantities of objects and computational results in real-world problems. DOK 2 *also* MA-05-1.1.1; *MA-05-1.1.2*

Independent Practice and Problem Solving

Round each number to the place of the underlined digit.

10. $0.9\underline{3}4$ **11.** $23.\underline{1}73$ **12.** $\underline{0}.481$ **13.** $137.5\underline{4}5$ **14.** $42.\underline{8}57$

Round 2.306 to the place named.

15. tenths **16.** hundredths **17.** ones

Name the place to which each number was rounded.

18. 0.625 to 0.63 **19.** 7.846 to 7.85 **20.** 12.87 to 12.9

Round to the nearest tenth of a dollar and to the nearest dollar.

21. \$10.35 **22.** \$0.49 **23.** \$0.98 **24.** \$3.22 **25.** \$13.28

Round each number to the nearest hundredth.

26. seven hundred twenty-six thousandths

27. one and six hundred twelve thousandths

28. $10 + 4 + 0.5 + 0.009$

29. $3 + 0.4 + 0.06 + 0.008$

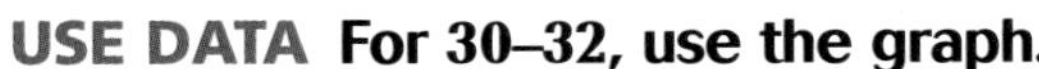

USE DATA For 30–32, use the graph.

30. Round the salt content of the blueberry muffin to the nearest hundredth of a gram.

31. Which muffin has a salt content of 0.30 gram when rounded to the nearest hundredth of a gram?

32. WRITE Math Explain how to round the salt content of a bran muffin to the nearest tenth of a gram.

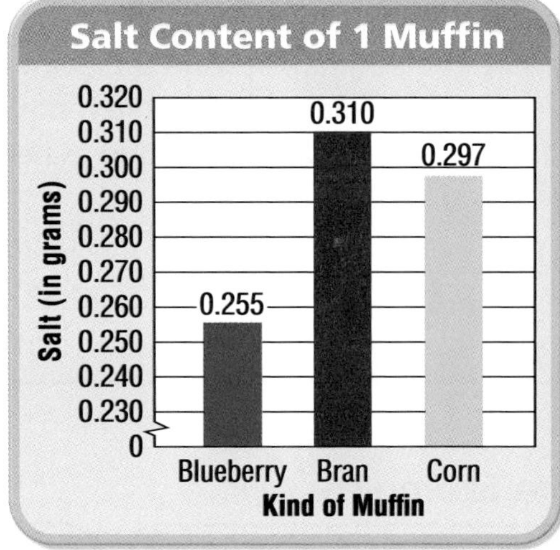

Mixed Review and Test Prep

33. Write the sandwiches in order from least expensive to most expensive. (p. 138)

Chicken salad	\$3.69
Roast beef	\$4.85
Peanut butter & jelly	\$3.25

34. Write the next two numbers in the pattern.

0.2, 0.20, 0.200, ■, ■ (p. 46)

35. **Test Prep** Darrin rounded 5.849 pounds to 5.8 pounds. To which place did he round?

A ones

B tenths

C hundredths

D thousandths

Extra Practice on page 162, Set A

LESSON 2

Add and Subtract Decimals

OBJECTIVE: Find the sums and differences of decimals.

Quick Review

Write an equivalent decimal for each number.

1. 0.34
2. 1.80
3. 8.09
4. 0.01
5. 19.4

Learn

PROBLEM At the 2006 Winter Olympics, Armin Zoeggeler won the gold medal in the men's luge event. He set a track record in one of his four medal-winning runs. After a slow start, he passed the first interval at 23.835 seconds and moved into first position. From the first interval, it took him 27.883 seconds to reach the finish line. What was Zoeggeler's finish time?

Adding and subtracting decimals is done in the same way as adding and subtracting whole numbers. Use place value to place the decimal point.

Math Idea
When finding the sum or difference, be sure to place the decimal point between the ones place and the tenths place.

Example **Add. 23.835 + 27.883**

Step 1	Step 2	Step 3
Line up the decimal points to align place-value positions. Add the thousandths.	Add the hundredths. Add the tenths. Regroup as needed.	Add the ones and tens. Place the decimal point in the sum.
23.835 +27.883 8	1 1 23.835 +27.883 718	1 1 1 23.835 +27.883 51.718

So, the time of Zoeggeler's run was 51.718 seconds.

More Examples

A 2.5 + 4.72 + 8.091

```
  1 1
  2.500 ← Place zeros
  4.720 ← to make
+ 8.091   equivalent
 15.311   decimals.
```

B \$12.48 + \$3.93

```
  1 1
 $12.48   Line up decimal points.
+ $3.93
 $16.41   Place the decimal point in the sum.
```

• Why do you use equivalent decimals in Example A?

▲ A luge sledder can reach speeds of 86 miles per hour.

FAST TRACK KY MA-05-1.3.1 Students will analyze real-world problems to identify appropriate representations using mathematical operations, and will apply operations to solve real-world problems with the following constraints: add and subtract decimals through hundredths. DOK 2 *also* MA-05-1.1.1

Subtraction

Zoeggeler finished the first half of the run in 34.535 seconds. The second half took only 17.183 seconds. How many seconds faster was the last half of the run?

Example Subtract. 34.535 − 17.183

Step 1	Step 2	Step 3
Line up the decimal points to align place-value positions. Subtract the thousandths.	Subtract the hundredths. Subtract the tenths. Regroup as needed.	Subtract the ones and tens. Place the decimal point in the difference.
$\begin{array}{r} 34.535 \\ -17.183 \\ \hline 2 \end{array}$	$\begin{array}{r} \scriptstyle 4\ 13 \\ 34.\not{5}\not{3}5 \\ -17.183 \\ \hline 352 \end{array}$	$\begin{array}{r} \scriptstyle 2\ 14\ 4\ 13 \\ \not{3}\not{4}.\not{5}\not{3}5 \\ -17.183 \\ \hline 17.352 \end{array}$ Place the decimal point.

So Zoeggeler was 17.352 seconds faster in the second half of the run.

You can also use a calculator to add or subtract decimals.

17.352

More Examples

C \$8 − \$5.63

$$\begin{array}{r} \scriptstyle 9 \\ \scriptstyle 7\ \not{10}\ 10 \\ \$\not{8}.\not{0}0 \\ -\$5.63 \\ \hline \$2.37 \end{array}$$

D 1.5 − 0.259

$$\begin{array}{r} \scriptstyle 9 \\ \scriptstyle 4\ \not{10}\ 10 \\ 1.\not{5}\not{0}\not{0} \\ -0.259 \\ \hline 1.241 \end{array}$$

E 12.193 − 9.65

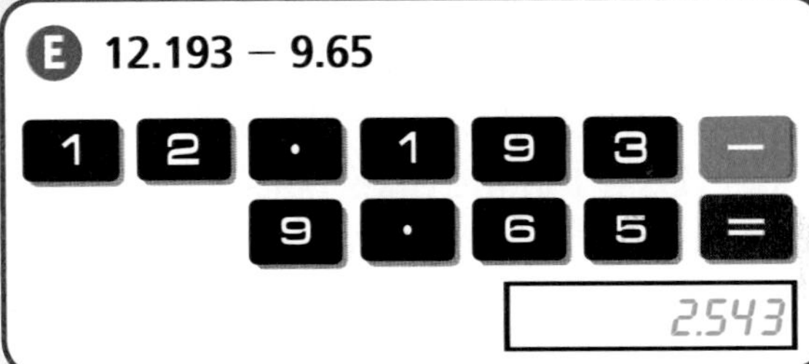

Guided Practice

1. Copy the problem at the right. Explain each step.

$$\begin{array}{r} 0.327 \\ +0.950 \\ \hline 7 \end{array} \quad \begin{array}{r} 0.327 \\ +0.950 \\ \hline 77 \end{array} \quad \begin{array}{r} \scriptstyle 1 \\ 0.327 \\ +0.950 \\ \hline 1.277 \end{array}$$

Find the sum or difference.

2. $\begin{array}{r} 0.423 \\ +0.8 \\ \hline \end{array}$

3. $\begin{array}{r} 16.3 \\ -\ 4.05 \\ \hline \end{array}$

4. $\begin{array}{r} 21.87 \\ +16.34 \\ \hline \end{array}$

✓5. \$13 − \$0.95

✓6. 2.5 + 6.88 + 0.19

7. **TALK Math** **Explain** the role of place value in adding and subtracting decimals.

Technology
Use Harcourt Mega Math, The Number Games, *Buggy Bargains,* Levels E, F, G, I.

Independent Practice and Problem Solving

Find the sum or difference.

8. $\begin{array}{r} 0.991 \\ -0.45 \\ \hline \end{array}$

9. $\begin{array}{r} 14.467 \\ +12.312 \\ \hline \end{array}$

10. $\begin{array}{r} \$16.06 \\ -\$10.10 \\ \hline \end{array}$

11. $\begin{array}{r} 32.98 \\ +18.25 \\ \hline \end{array}$

12. $\begin{array}{r} 5 \\ -2.391 \\ \hline \end{array}$

13. $\begin{array}{r} 1.18 \\ +2.039 \\ \hline \end{array}$

14. $\begin{array}{r} 3.704 \\ -1.325 \\ \hline \end{array}$

15. $\begin{array}{r} 0.75 \\ 0.359 \\ +1.4 \\ \hline \end{array}$

16. $\begin{array}{r} 23.002 \\ -\ 1.74 \\ \hline \end{array}$

17. $\begin{array}{r} 9.94 \\ 0.318 \\ +1.283 \\ \hline \end{array}$

Algebra **Find a rule for the pattern. Use your rule to find the missing numbers in the pattern.**

18. 2.1, 3.3, 4.5, 5.7, ■, 8.1, ■

19. 4.10, 4.05, 4.00, 3.95, ■, 3.85, ■

20. 1.25, 1.50, 1.75, 2.00, ■, ■

Solve.

21. Nathan and his uncle paid $9.50 for tickets to a bike race. They bought one adult's ticket and one child's ticket. The adult's ticket cost $5.75. What was the cost of Nathan's ticket?

22. Babe Ruth had a batting average of .308 while playing for the Boston Red Sox. He later played for the New York Yankees, where his batting average was .349. Find the difference in those batting averages.

23. **Reasoning** The sum of two numbers is 4.004. One number has a 4 in the tenths place and a 3 in the thousandths place. The other number has a 1 in the ones place and an 8 in the hundredths place. What are the two numbers?

24. **WRITE Math** **What's the Question?** At the 2006 Winter Olympics, after competing in the ski jump, Georg Hettich was in first place with 262.5 points. Magnus Moan was in ninth place with 237.5 points. The answer is 25.0.

Mixed Review and Test Prep

25. What number times 90 equals 45,000? (p. 36)

26. Tyler uses this table to record the number of miles he runs each week. If the pattern continues, how many miles would Tyler run in Week 5? (p. 46)

Week	1	2	4	5
Miles Run	20	25	30	■

27. **Test Prep** Mark buys a notebook for $3.55 and a pen for $0.89. How much change will Mark receive from a $5.00 bill?

A $0.56 **B** $1.45 **C** $1.55 **D** $4.44

28. **Test Prep** Toni has a ribbon that is 2.75 meters long. She cuts off 0.345 meter. How much of the ribbon does Toni have left?

A 3.095 m **C** 2.715 m

B 3.785 m **D** 2.405 m

 Extra Practice on page 162, Set B

Speedy Skates

Identify the Details

▲ Speed skating was one of the events at the first-ever Winter Olympics in 1924.

Speed skating is a popular event in the Winter Olympic Games. Athletes race on ice skates around a frozen track. In the 2006 Winter Olympics, there were three skaters in Race 9 of the women's 500-meter short-track heats: K. Novotna, C. Tanaka, and E. Radanova. Their times are shown in the table. How much faster was the first-place time than the third-place time?

Sometimes a problem has more information than you need. To solve the problem correctly, you must identify the details you need to answer the question. Start by rereading the question. Then ask yourself what details you need to solve the problem. For example:

- Which column contains the skaters' times?
- What is the first-place time—that is, the least time?
- What is the third-place time—that is, the greatest time?

Race 9 of Women's 500-meter Short-Track Speed Skating Heats

Skater	Time (in seconds)
K. Novotna	46.279
C. Tanaka	46.387
E. Radanova	45.703

Problem Solving Identify the details you need to solve the problem.

1. Solve the problem above.
2. Only the skaters with the two best times in each heat advance to the next race. Which two skaters advanced to the next race? **Explain** how you know.

LESSON 3

Estimate Sums and Differences

OBJECTIVE: Estimate the sums and differences of decimals to check reasonableness.

Quick Review

Round each number to the nearest tenth.

1. 0.45 **2.** 3.16
3. 0.284 **4.** 10.349
5. 6.727

Learn

PROBLEM A singer is recording a CD. He says the total recording time is 10.37 minutes. The lengths of the three songs are 3.4 minutes, 2.78 minutes, and 4.19 minutes. How can you tell whether the singer's statement is reasonable?

You can estimate to check reasonableness.

Example **Estimate. 3.4 + 2.78 + 4.19**

Round to the nearest whole number. Then add.

$$\begin{array}{rcr} 3.4 & \rightarrow & 3 \\ 2.78 & \rightarrow & 3 \\ +4.19 & \rightarrow & +\ 4 \\ \hline & & 10 \end{array}$$

So, the total recording time is about 10 minutes. The estimate is close to 10.37, so the singer's statement is reasonable.

- Is the estimate greater than or less than the exact sum? Explain.

Math Idea
When estimating the total cost, it sometimes makes more sense to round up to the next whole dollar.

More Examples

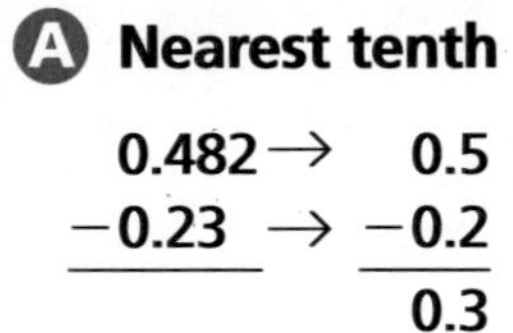

A Nearest tenth

$$\begin{array}{rcr} 0.482 & \rightarrow & 0.5 \\ -0.23 & \rightarrow & -0.2 \\ \hline & & 0.3 \end{array}$$

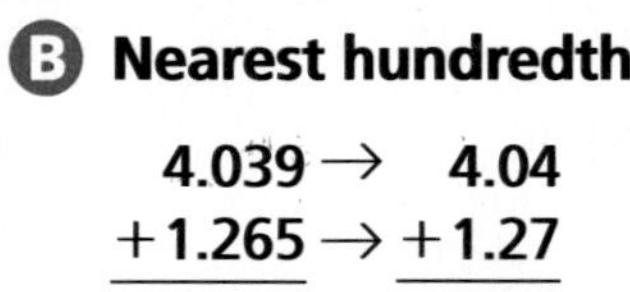

B Nearest hundredth

$$\begin{array}{rcr} 4.039 & \rightarrow & 4.04 \\ +1.265 & \rightarrow & +1.27 \\ \hline & & 5.31 \end{array}$$

C Next whole dollar

$$\begin{array}{rcr} \$12.45 & \rightarrow & \$13 \\ +\$\ 9.72 & \rightarrow & +\$10 \\ \hline & & \$23 \end{array}$$

Guided Practice

1. Copy and complete the problems at the right to estimate the sum and the difference.

Round to the nearest whole number. Then add.

$$\begin{array}{r} 78.7 \\ +\ 2.58 \\ \hline \end{array}$$

Round up to the next whole dollar. Then subtract.

$$\begin{array}{r} \$42.35 \\ -\$18.79 \\ \hline \end{array}$$

FAST TRACK

KY MA-05-1.2.1 Students will apply and describe appropriate strategies for estimating quantities of objects and computational results in real-world problems. DOK 2 *also* MA-05-1.1.1; MA-05-1.3.1

Estimate by rounding.

2. $0.348 + 0.1 + 0.25$

3. $10.39 - 4.28$

4. $\$19.75 + \$3.98$

✓5. $0.78 - 0.305$

✓6. $1.247 + 0.82 + 3.4$

7. TALK Math Andrew wants to buy three shirts that cost $19.98, $34.79, and $25.25. What is a reasonable estimate of the total cost? **Explain.**

Independent Practice and Problem Solving

Estimate by rounding.

8. $52.63 - 38.4$

9. $\$57.88 + \$39.80$

10. $7.36 - 4.19$

11. $0.482 + 0.305$

12. $18.88 - 10.24$

13. $5.57 - 1.8$

14. $1.26 + 1.8 + 2.795$

15. $\$1.93 - \$0.85$

16. $18.7 + 52.53$

17. $\$19.05 - \$8.32$

18. $4.52 + 0.86$

19. $\$20.82 - \$13.66$

20. $30.406 + 20.894$

21. $0.325 + 0.149$

22. $81.06 - 19.57$

23. $\$17.45 + \$7.99$

Algebra **Estimate to compare. Write < or > for each ●.**

24. 0.574 − 0.32 ● 0.2

25. 1.78 + 2.34 ● 4

26. 5.25 − 2.39 ● 3

USE DATA **For 27–29, use the table.**

27. For the week of April 4, 1964, the Beatles had the top four songs. About how long would it take to listen to these four songs?

28. WRITE Math **What's the Error?** Isabelle has 10 minutes to listen to music. She says she can listen to the first three songs in the table in 7 minutes. Estimate to check if that is reasonable.

Hot 100 Songs Week of April 4, 1964

Number	Song Title	Song Length (in minutes)
1	"Can't Buy Me Love"	2.30
2	"She Loves You"	2.50
3	"I Want to Hold Your Hand"	2.75
4	"Please, Please Me"	2.00

Mixed Review and Test Prep

29. Which two songs in the table are the closest in length? (p. 138)

30. Round 2 + 0.07 + 0.004 to the nearest hundredth. (p. 150)

31. **Test Prep** Chau bought sneakers for $54.26 and a shirt for $34.34. If she had $100, about how much money does she have left?

A $10

B $20

C $35

D $90

Extra Practice on page 162, Set C

LESSON 4

Choose a Method

OBJECTIVE: Choose mental math, paper and pencil, or a calculator to find decimal sums and differences.

Quick Review

Find the sum or difference.

1. 2.1 + 4.2
2. 3.3 + 3.35
3. 0.6 − 0.4
4. 1.0 − 0.5
5. 5.41 − 2.41

Learn

PROBLEM At a track meet, Steven entered the triple jump. His jumps were 2.25 meters, 1.81 meters, and 3.75 meters. What was the total distance Steven jumped?

You can use mental math, a calculator, or paper and pencil to find decimal sums and differences.

▲ In the 1924 Olympics, William DeHart Hubbard from Ohio won a gold medal for the long jump.

Use Mental Math **Find the sum of the distances Steven jumped.**

Write the equation as the sum of whole numbers and decimal parts.

2.25 + 1.81 + 3.75 = 2 + 0.25 + 1 + 0.81 + 3 + 0.75

2 + 1 + 3 = 6	Add the whole number parts first.
(0.25 + 0.75) + 0.81	Next, add the decimals that are easy to add mentally.
1.00 + 0.81 = 1.81	Make a whole number. Then add the other decimal.
6.00 + 1.81 = 7.81	Add the whole number and decimal parts to find the sum.

So, Steven jumped a total distance of 7.81 meters.

In 1924, William DeHart Hubbard won a gold medal with a long jump of 7.44 meters. In 2000, Roman Churenko won the bronze medal with a jump of 8.31 meters. How much longer was Churenko's jump than Hubbard's?

Use Paper and Pencil **Compute using paper and pencil.**

Subtract. 8.31 − 7.44
Estimate. 8 − 7 = 1

$$\begin{array}{r} 8.31 \\ -7.44 \\ \hline 0.87 \end{array}$$

Regroup as needed.

ERROR ALERT When entering a decimal on a calculator, be sure to enter the decimal point between the ones and tenths places.

Use a Calculator **Calculators can simplify the addition and subtraction of decimals that are difficult to compute using paper and pencil.**

So, Churenko's jump was 0.87 meter longer than Hubbard's jump. This difference is close to the estimate, so the answer is reasonable.

 FAST TRACK

KY MA-05-1.3.1 Students will analyze real-world problems to identify appropriate representations using mathematical operations, and will apply operations to solve real-world problems with the following constraints: add and subtract decimals through hundredths. DOK 2 *also* MA-05-1.1.1

Guided Practice

1. Find 5.15 + 1.10. Use mental math.

$5.15 + 1.10 = 5 + \blacksquare + \blacksquare + 0.10$
$5 + 1 = \blacksquare$
$0.15 + \blacksquare = \blacksquare$

$$\begin{array}{r} 5.15 \\ +1.10 \\ \hline \end{array}$$

Choose a method. Find the sum or difference.

2. $\begin{array}{r} 4.19 \\ +0.584 \\ \hline \end{array}$
3. $\begin{array}{r} 9.99 \\ -4.10 \\ \hline \end{array}$
4. $\begin{array}{r} 5.7 \\ 2.25 \\ +1.3 \\ \hline \end{array}$
5. $\begin{array}{r} 38.445 \\ -25.86 \\ \hline \end{array}$
6. $\begin{array}{r} \$15.79 \\ +\$32.81 \\ \hline \end{array}$
7. TALK Math **Explain** which method you would choose to solve 1.281 + 3.095.

Independent Practice and Problem Solving

Choose a method. Find the sum or difference.

8. $\begin{array}{r} \$18.39 \\ +\$\ 7.56 \\ \hline \end{array}$
9. $\begin{array}{r} 8.202 \\ -4.39 \\ \hline \end{array}$
10. $\begin{array}{r} 3.12 \\ 2.891 \\ +3.405 \\ \hline \end{array}$
11. $\begin{array}{r} 7.8 \\ -5.2 \\ \hline \end{array}$
12. $\begin{array}{r} 1.82 \\ +2.28 \\ \hline \end{array}$
13. 9.735 − 2.52
14. \$18 − \$3.55
15. \$14.98 + \$6.83
16. 7.25 + 0.25 + 1.50

USE DATA For 17–19, use the table.

17. How much farther did the gold medal winner jump than the silver medal winner?
18. **Pose a Problem** Look back at Problem 17. Write and answer a similar problem by choosing different medal distances.
19. WRITE Math The fourth-place competitor's jump measured 8.31 meters. If his jump had been 0.25 meter greater, what medal would he have received? **Explain** how you solved the problem.

2004 Olympics Men's Long Jump Results

Medal	Distance (in meters)
Gold	8.59
Silver	8.47
Bronze	8.32

Mixed Review and Test Prep

20. Which is longer, a length of 5.3 meters or a length of 53 centimeters? (Grade 4)
21. Jake cuts a length of 1.12 meters from a 3-meter board. About how long is the board now? (p. 156)
22. **Test Prep** Mika has a dime, a quarter, a dollar, and 2 nickels. How much money does Mika have? Show your work.

Extra Practice on page 162, Set D

Problem Solving Workshop
Skill: Estimate or Find Exact Answer

OBJECTIVE: Solve problems by using the skill *estimate or find exact answer.*

Read to Understand
Plan
Solve
Check

Use the Skill

PROBLEM Lexi has $25 to buy gym shorts for $7.95, a T-shirt for $8.29, and a pair of socks for $3.50. Does Lexi have enough money to pay for all three items? All prices include sales tax.

Sometimes you need to find an exact answer. Other times, an estimate is all you need to solve a problem.

Estimate.

Round each item up to the next whole dollar. Then add.

$$\begin{array}{rcr} \$7.95 & \rightarrow & \$8.00 \\ \$8.29 & \rightarrow & \$9.00 \\ +\,\$3.50 & \rightarrow & +\,\$4.00 \\ \hline & & \$21.00 \end{array}$$

Since $21 < $25, Lexi has enough money to pay for all three items. If Lexi gives the cashier $25, how much change will she receive?

Find an exact answer.

To find the amount of change, you need an exact answer.

$$\begin{array}{r} \$7.95 \\ \$8.29 \\ +\,\$3.50 \\ \hline \$19.74 \end{array} \qquad \begin{array}{r} \$25.00 \\ -\,\$19.74 \\ \hline \$5.26 \end{array}$$

The exact cost is $19.74, so Lexi's change will be $5.26.

Think and Discuss

Tell whether you need an estimate or an exact answer. Explain your choice. Solve the problem.

a. A hamburger costs $2.95 with tax. Julian has $10. Does Julian have enough money to buy 3 hamburgers?

b. Taylor's time for the swimming race was 53.12 seconds and Alex's time was 50.59 seconds. How much faster was Alex's time?

 FAST TRACK

KY MA-05-1.2.1 Students will apply and describe appropriate strategies for estimating quantities of objects and computational results in real-world problems. DOK 2 *also* MA-05-1.1.1; MA-05-1.3.1

Guided Problem Solving Practice

Tell whether you need an estimate or an exact answer. Then solve the problem.

1. In a baseball-throwing contest, the distances of a person's three throws are added to determine the person's final score. A score of 50 or more is needed to advance to the final round. Carson had throws of 16.35 meters, 18.44 meters, and 17.97 meters. Will Carson advance to the final round?

   First, decide if you need an estimate or an exact answer. You need to determine if Carson's score is greater than or less than 50. So, find an estimate.

   Then, compare it to 50.

$$\begin{array}{ccccccccc} 16.35 & + & 18.44 & + & 17.97 & & \\ \downarrow & & \downarrow & & \downarrow & & \\ 16 & + & 18 & + & \blacksquare & = & \blacksquare \end{array}$$

2. **What if** Carson's second throw had been 16.44 meters instead of 18.44 meters? Would finding an estimate be a good way to determine whether Carson should advance to the final round? **Explain.**

3. Jenna's first two throws were 16.64 meters and 15.33 meters. How long does her last throw need to be for her to advance to the final round?

Mixed Applications

USE DATA For 4 and 5, use the table.

4. Olivia is buying a pair of ballet shoes and a pair of tights. She has a discount coupon for $10.00 off her total purchase. How much will Olivia pay for the tights and shoes?

5. Jackie has $60 to spend on clothing for ballet class. She has to buy a leotard and wants to buy either 2 pairs of tights or a pair of shoes. Which items can Jackie buy?

Tip-Toe Ballet Shop

Item	Cost
Tights	$11.98
Leotard	$36.50
Ballet Shoes	$23.48

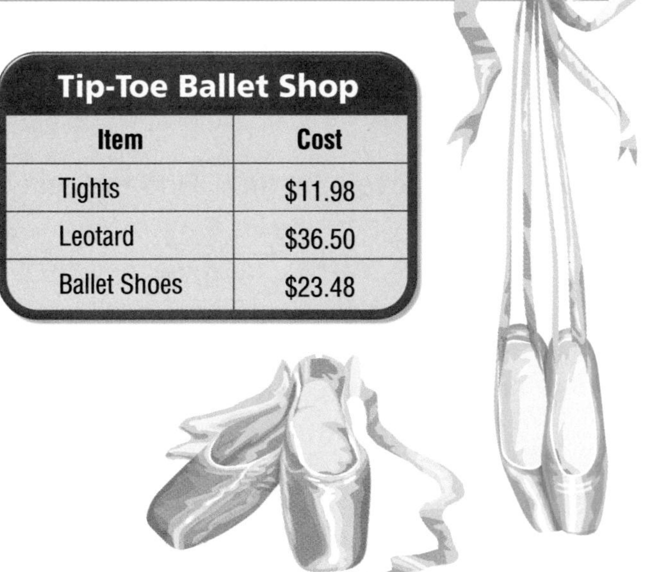

6. Joe's backpack weighs 6.5 kilograms. Tino's backpack is 2.4 kilograms heavier than Joe's. Rod's backpack is 1.7 kilograms lighter than Joe's. About how much do the three backpacks weigh in all?

7. WRITE Math Wayne is buying wood trim that goes all around his room. He needs trim for sections that are 17, 12.5, 11, 10.75, and 4.5 feet in length. He can buy 5 trim pieces that are 12 feet long each. Will Wayne have enough to make all the trim sections for his room? **Explain.**

Extra Practice

Set A Round each number to the place of the underlined digit. (pp. 150–151)

1. $2.7\underline{3}5$
2. $0.\underline{4}19$
3. $5\underline{1}.076$
4. $\$0.\underline{3}9$
5. $\$1\underline{2}.25$

Name the place to which each number was rounded.

6. 1.734 to 1.7
7. 0.526 to 0.53
8. 39.481 to 39.5

Round each number to the nearest hundredth.

9. three hundred five thousandths
10. 200 + 5 + 0.3 + 0.01 + 0.007

Set B Find the sum or difference. (pp. 152–155)

1. $\begin{array}{r} \$13.72 \\ +\$28.49 \\ \hline \end{array}$
2. $\begin{array}{r} 2.37 \\ +5.8 \\ \hline \end{array}$
3. $\begin{array}{r} 9.82 \\ -1.914 \\ \hline \end{array}$
4. $\begin{array}{r} 20 \\ -\ 7.4 \\ \hline \end{array}$
5. $\begin{array}{r} 1.625 \\ 0.3 \\ +0.61 \\ \hline \end{array}$

6. Gina competed in a gymnastics competition. Her total score for the balance beam and the vault was 16.75. She scored 9.3 on the vault. What was her score for the balance beam?
7. Simon scored 7.23, 6.94, and 8.32 points for his three dives at the competition. What was his total score for the three dives?

Set C Estimate by rounding. (pp. 156–157)

1. $\begin{array}{r} 9.42 \\ +8.71 \\ \hline \end{array}$
2. $\begin{array}{r} 1.842 \\ -0.31 \\ \hline \end{array}$
3. $\begin{array}{r} 18.2 \\ +\ 6.57 \\ \hline \end{array}$
4. $\begin{array}{r} \$43.82 \\ +\$\ 7.14 \\ \hline \end{array}$
5. $\begin{array}{r} 75.12 \\ -42.8 \\ \hline \end{array}$

Set D Choose a method. Find the sum or difference. (pp. 158–159)

1. $\begin{array}{r} 9.5 \\ -1.42 \\ \hline \end{array}$
2. $\begin{array}{r} 4.93 \\ +0.78 \\ \hline \end{array}$
3. $\begin{array}{r} \$47.50 \\ -\$15.22 \\ \hline \end{array}$
4. $\begin{array}{r} 3.6 \\ +2.1 \\ \hline \end{array}$
5. $\begin{array}{r} 4.28 \\ 0.715 \\ +2.34 \\ \hline \end{array}$

6. Ellie buys some craft supplies. The supplies cost a total of $6.43. She pays with a $20 bill. How much change does she receive?
7. Colleen paid $3.20 for a magazine and $5.80 for a book at the bookstore. How much more did the book cost than the magazine?

CD ROM **Technology**
Use Harcourt Mega Math, Fraction Action, *Number Line Mine*, Level R

TECHNOLOGY CONNECTION

Spreadsheet Formulas

For one month, Home Pies spent $6.51 on flour, $3.89 on spices, $31.17 on fruit, $4.25 on baking powder, $8.70 on eggs, $4.91 on sugar, and $24.50 on butter. How can Home Pies use a spreadsheet to organize its expenses from most expensive to least expensive and find the total cost?

Step 1	Open a new document in the spreadsheet program. Enter the ingredients in column A and the costs in column B.
Step 2	To sort by price, highlight both columns starting with column B. Click [Z↓A] to sort the data from greatest to least value.
Step 3	To find the total, go to the cell below the lowest value in column B. Click [*fx*], and then select *SUM*. Click *OK*. The total will appear in that cell.
Step 4	In some spreadsheet programs, you can find the total by highlighting the values you want to find a sum of and then click [Σ], or autosum.

unsorted data

	A	B
1	Flour	$6.51
2	Spices	$3.89
3	Fruit	$31.17
4	Baking Powder	$4.25
5	Eggs	$8.70
6	Sugar	$4.91
7	Butter	$24.50
8		

same data sorted from high to low

	A	B
1	Fruit	$31.17
2	Butter	$24.50
3	Eggs	$8.70
4	Flour	$6.51
5	Sugar	$4.91
6	Baking Powder	$4.25
7	Spices	$3.89
8		$83.93

total

Try It

For 1–3, use a spreadsheet to organize the data from greatest to least. Then, find the total of each data set.

1. Winston earned the following amounts for doing lawn work: $7.00 on Monday, $16.00 on Tuesday, $14.50 on Wednesday, $4.75 on Thursday, and $13.50 on Friday.

2. Candy bought the following items at a computer store: a flash drive for $49.98, cable for $8.49, a microphone for $29.12, and a game for $78.98.

3. Jorgé received these scores in a skating competition: Judge 1: 6.34, Judge 2: 5.9, Judge 3: 6.75, Judge 4: 5.78, Judge 5: 6.0, Judge 6: 7.1.

4. **Explore More** The [A↓Z] button on a spreadsheet is used to sort data from least to greatest. **Explain** how your data display for Problem 1 would change if you clicked on this button.

Addition Properties and Decimals

What's the Total?

You can find a decimal sum mentally by using the Commutative or Associative Properties of Addition.

Mr. Anderson stops at the grocery store after work. He has \$15 to buy chicken for \$6.25, cheese for \$5.15, and lettuce for \$2.75. Does he have enough money to pay for the groceries? Find the total cost of the groceries.

Example 1 **Add. \$6.25 + \$5.15 + \$2.75**

Use the Commutative Property.

Think: \$0.25 + \$0.75 = \$1.	\$6.25 + **\$5.15** + \$2.75 =
Use the Commutative Property.	\$6.25 + \$2.75 + **\$5.15** =
Add. Use mental math.	**\$9** + **\$5.15** = **\$14.15**

The total cost of the groceries is **\$14.15**.

Since \$15 is greater than \$14.15, Mr. Anderson has enough money.

Example 2 **Add. 15.4 + (0.6 + 10.8)**

Use the Associative Property.

Think: 0.4 + 0.6 = 1.	15.4 + (0.6 + 10.8) =
Use the Associative Property.	(15.4 + 0.6) + 10.8 =
Add. Use mental math.	16 + 10.8 = 26.8

Remember

The Commutative Property states that if the order of addends is changed, the sum stays the same.

The Associative Property states that addends can be grouped in different ways, and the sum does not change.

Try It

Use the Commutative or Associative Property to find the sum.

1. \$12.50 + \$4.29 + \$5.50
2. 36.3 + (12.7 + 12.1)
3. (56.3 + 8.9) + 121.1
4. 0.91 + 1.15 + 2.09
5. \$5.65 + \$5.18 + \$4.35
6. 5.3 + (1.25 + 12.7)
7. WRITE Math **Explain** how you can use the properties to find decimal sums mentally.

Chapter 6 Review/Test

Check Concepts

1. Explain how to use the rounding rules to round a decimal to the nearest tenth. KY MA-05-1.2.1 (p. 150)
2. Explain the steps for adding two decimal numbers. KY MA-05-1.3.1 (p. 152)

Check Skills

Round each number to the place of the underlined digit. KY MA-05-1.2.1 (pp. 150–151)

3. $1.3\underline{2}8$ 4. $17.\underline{6}74$ 5. $0.\underline{9}36$ 6. $2\underline{4}.512$ 7. $80.\underline{1}26$

Find the sum or difference. KY MA-05-1.3.1 (pp. 152–155)

8. $\begin{array}{r} 14.9 \\ +10.61 \\ \hline \end{array}$ 9. $\begin{array}{r} 0.85 \\ -0.07 \\ \hline \end{array}$ 10. $\begin{array}{r} \$9.54 \\ +\$2.85 \\ \hline \end{array}$ 11. $\begin{array}{r} 37.5 \\ -\ \ 5.36 \\ \hline \end{array}$ 12. $\begin{array}{r} 2.85 \\ +8.1 \\ \hline \end{array}$

Estimate by rounding. KY MA-05-1.2.1 (pp. 156–157)

13. $\begin{array}{r} \$28.41 \\ -\$\ \ 5.23 \\ \hline \end{array}$ 14. $\begin{array}{r} 6.18 \\ +9.7 \\ \hline \end{array}$ 15. $\begin{array}{r} 4.08 \\ -0.72 \\ \hline \end{array}$ 16. $\begin{array}{r} 1.8 \\ -0.63 \\ \hline \end{array}$ 17. $\begin{array}{r} 5.72 \\ +8.34 \\ \hline \end{array}$

Check Problem Solving

Solve. KY MA-05-1.2.1 (pp. 160–161)

18. Verna has $20 to buy knitting supplies. She picks out yarn that costs $4.88, a book that costs $9.05, and knitting needles that cost $4.90. All prices include sales tax. Does Verna have enough money to buy all three items? Tell whether you need to find an estimate or exact answer. Then solve.

19. Verna is knitting a scarf. When finished, the scarf will be 1.65 meters long. Right now the scarf measures 0.94 meters. How much more does Verna need to knit? Tell whether you need to find an estimate or an exact answer. Then solve.

20. **WRITE Math** The table at the right shows the costs of different jewelry supplies. Fred has $10. He needs to buy cord, a pack of wooden beads, and 2 pendants. Would finding an estimate be a good way to determine whether Fred has enough money to buy the supplies he needs? **Explain.**

Jewelry Supplies

Item	Price
Nylon cord	$1.35
Wooden beads	$1.79 a pack
Pendants	$3.29 each
Glass beads	$4.19 a pack

GO ONLINE **Technology** Use *Online Assessment.*

 Practice for the KCCT
Chapters 1–6

Number and Operations

1. Jenisha and her friends went to the Ice Cream Café. Jenisha ordered a medium ice cream cone with sprinkles. She paid with a $5 bill. How much change did Jenisha receive? KY MA-05-1.3.1 (p. 152)

Ice Cream Café	
Item	**Price**
Cone	
Small	$1.19
Medium	$2.35
Large	$3.15
Toppings (sprinkles, nuts, fruit)	$0.50 each

A $3.15 **C** $2.65

B $2.85 **D** $2.15

2. The students at Clearview Middle School are taking a trip to the zoo. A total of 369 people are going on the trip. Each bus can hold 78 people. How many buses do they need? KY MA-05-1.3.1 (p. 74)

A 4

B 5

C 6

D 7

3. WRITE Math **Explain** how to round 24.763 to the nearest tenth. KY MA-05-1.2.1 (p. 150)

Algebraic Thinking

Test Tip

Decide on a plan.

See item 4. Use the function table to find the rule. Then, find the answer choice below that matches the rule.

4. Which is the rule for the function table? KY MA-05-5.1.2 (p. 112)

x	90	80	60	50	40
y	9	8	6	5	4

A add 81 to y

B divide y by 10

C divide x by 10

D multiply x by 10

5. Solve for n. KY MA-05-5.3.1 (p. 108)

$$3n - 2 = 16$$

A $n = 18$

B $n = 14$

C $n = 6$

D $n = 5$

6. WRITE Math Look at the function table. **Explain** the relationship between the x- and y-values. KY MA-05-5.1.2 (p. 112)

x	6	8	10	12
y	13	17	21	25

Geometry

7. Which best describes the angle, *R*, formed by the intersection of Market Street and Grant Avenue? KY Grade 4

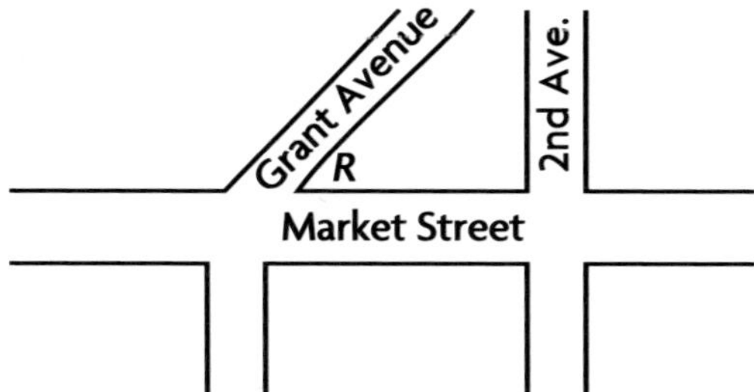

A acute

B obtuse

C right

D straight

8. Which figures below are rhombuses? KY Grade 4

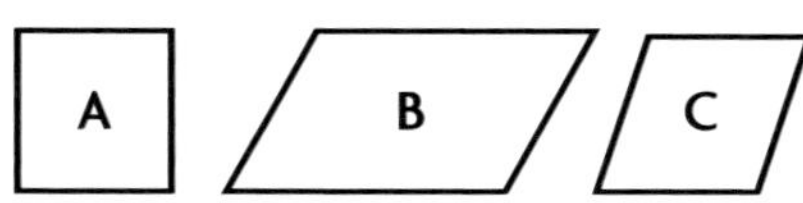

A Figure A only.

B Figure B only.

C Figures A and C.

D Figures A, B, and C.

9. WRITE Math Billy drew an obtuse scalene triangle. **Explain** the characteristics of Billy's triangle. KY Grade 4

Data Analysis and Probability

10. Fran and her sisters are playing a game with these two spinners. If a player spins both spinners, how many possible outcomes are there? KY Grade 4

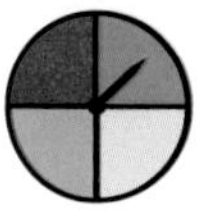 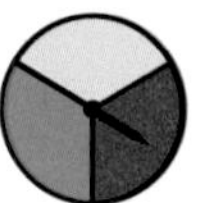

A 4

B 7

C 12

D 14

11. Evan has 8 white socks, 4 black socks, and 2 red socks in a drawer. Without looking, Evan reaches in and pulls out a white sock. Without placing the sock back into the drawer, Evan reaches in again and pulls out another sock. What is the probability that it will also be white? KY Grade 4

A $\frac{1}{3}$

B $\frac{4}{7}$

C $\frac{1}{2}$

D $\frac{7}{13}$

12. WRITE Math Sue received the following scores on her 10-point math quizzes.

8, 6, 7, 9, 10, 7, 9

Explain how to find Sue's mean quiz score. KY Grade 4

CHAPTER 7

Multiply Decimals

During the 2001 World of Speed Finals held at the Bonneville Salt Flats, Don Vesco set the world land speed record for wheel-driven automobiles with a speed of 458 mph.

Investigate

The table shows the rate and time of some automobiles tested at the Bonneville Salt Flats. Choose any two cars and show how to find the total distance, in miles, each traveled during the tests. Use the formula $d = rt$, where d is distance, r is rate, and t is time.

Bonneville Salt Flats Testing

Car Number	Rate (mph)	Time (hours)
1478	110	0.045
225	89	0.056
99	295	0.034
55	206	0.048
519	219	0.046

Technology
Student pages are available in the Student eBook.

Show What You Know

Check your understanding of important skills needed for success in Chapter 7.

Estimate Products

Estimate the product.

1. $\begin{array}{r} 57 \\ \times\ 4 \\ \hline \end{array}$
2. $\begin{array}{r} 32 \\ \times\ 8 \\ \hline \end{array}$
3. $\begin{array}{r} 74 \\ \times\ 5 \\ \hline \end{array}$
4. $\begin{array}{r} 426 \\ \times\ \ 7 \\ \hline \end{array}$
5. 926×2
6. 268×9
7. 97×3
8. 629×8

Multiply by 2-Digit Numbers

Find the product.

9. $\begin{array}{r} 94 \\ \times\ 3 \\ \hline \end{array}$
10. $\begin{array}{r} \$47 \\ \times\ \ 5 \\ \hline \end{array}$
11. $\begin{array}{r} 83 \\ \times\ 7 \\ \hline \end{array}$
12. $\begin{array}{r} 343 \\ \times\ 28 \\ \hline \end{array}$
13. 72×9
14. $\$218 \times 71$
15. 56×43
16. 25×81

Multiply Money

Multiply.

17. $\begin{array}{r} \$0.25 \\ \times\ \ \ \ 6 \\ \hline \end{array}$
18. $\begin{array}{r} \$0.05 \\ \times\ \ \ \ 4 \\ \hline \end{array}$
19. $\begin{array}{r} \$0.10 \\ \times\ \ \ \ 5 \\ \hline \end{array}$
20. $\begin{array}{r} \$0.50 \\ \times\ \ \ \ 9 \\ \hline \end{array}$
21. $\$0.10 \times 3$
22. $\$0.01 \times 8$
23. $\$0.25 \times 7$
24. $\$0.05 \times 9$

VOCABULARY POWER

CHAPTER VOCABULARY

decimal
decimal point
factor
hundredth
tenth

WARM-UP WORDS

factor a number multiplied by another number to find a product

hundredth one of one hundred equal parts

tenth one of ten equal parts

LESSON 1 HANDS ON

Model Multiplication by a Whole Number

OBJECTIVE: Use models to multiply whole numbers and decimals.

Quick Review

1. 15×5
2. 22×8
3. 86×3
4. 64×6
5. 71×9

Investigate

Materials ■ 3 decimal models ■ color pencils

You can use models to help you multiply decimals and whole numbers.

A Find 3×0.61. Use the decimal models. Shade 0.61 three times.

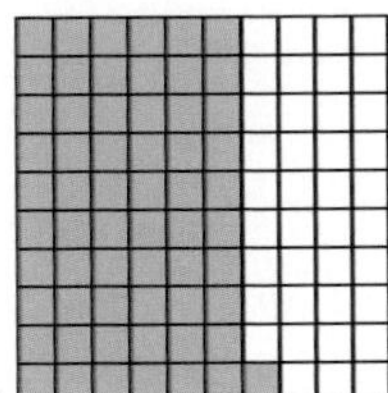

B Count the number of shaded hundredths. How many hundredths are shaded?

C Write 3×0.61 as repeated addition. Find the sum. How does the sum compare to your answer in B?

D Write the multiplication equation and the addition equation that represent your model.

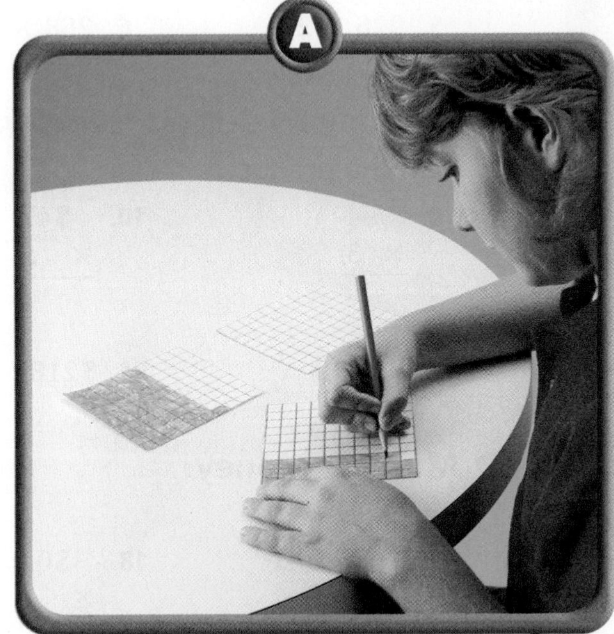

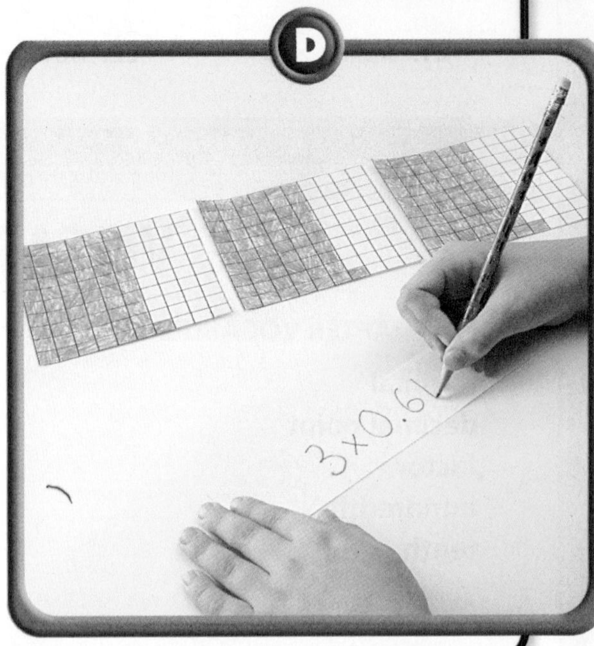

Draw Conclusions

1. What is the value of one square in the decimal model? What is the value of one column or one row?
2. How is multiplying 3×0.61 like multiplying 3×61?
3. Is the product 3×0.61 greater than or less than 3? **Explain** why.
4. **Synthesis** In what other ways can you express the product 3×0.61?

KY MA-05-1.3.3 Students will multiply decimals through tenths.

Connect

You can use a model to record multiplication.

Step 1

Find 4×0.27.

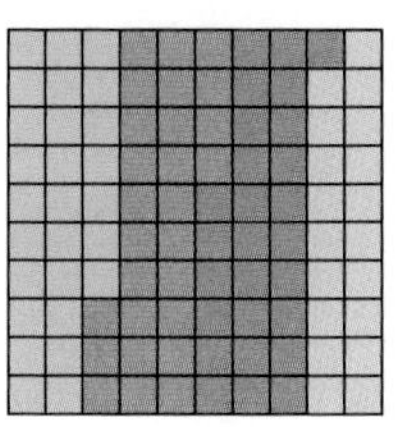

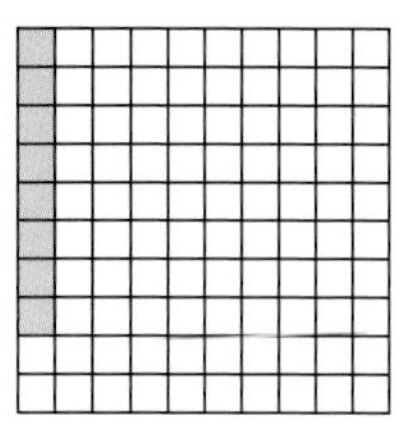

Use decimal models. Shade 0.27 four times, using a different color each time. Count the number of colored squares. There are 108 hundredths, or 1 whole and 8 hundredths.

Step 2

Record.

$$\begin{array}{r} \scriptstyle{1\,2} \\ 0.27 \\ \times \quad 4 \\ \hline 1.08 \end{array}$$

Use the model to place the decimal point. 4×0.27 is 1 whole and 8 hundredths, so place the decimal point after the 1.

TALK Math

Explain how the model helps you place the decimal point.

Practice

Copy and complete the multiplication expression for each model. Find the product.

1. 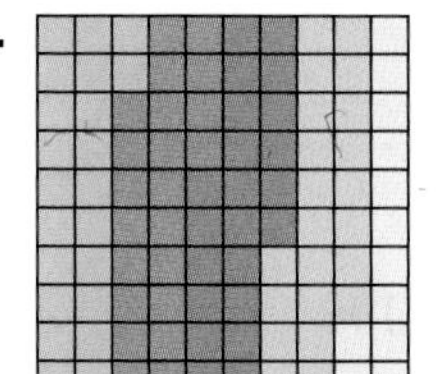

$\blacksquare \times 0.22$

2. 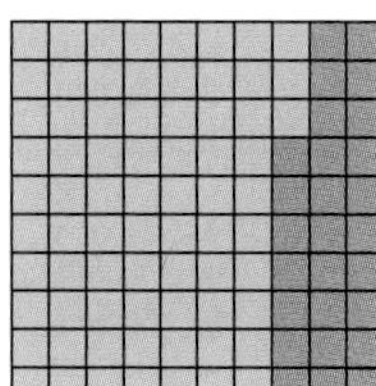 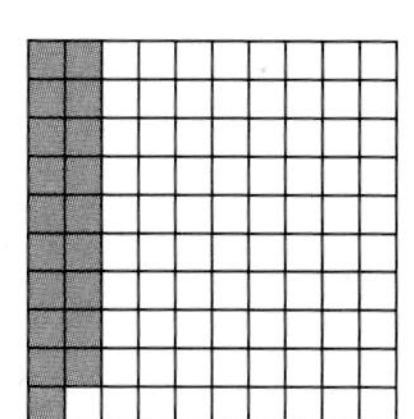

$3 \times \blacksquare$

Find the product. You may use decimal models.

3. 4×0.42
4. 0.13×5
5. 3×0.36
6. 0.33×6
7. 2×0.28
8. 0.48×5
9. 5×0.92
10. 2×0.96
11. 0.44×3
12. 0.67×4
13. 6×0.45
14. 8×0.04
15. 0.64×2
16. 0.51×3
17. 0.39×4
18. 7×0.61

19. **WRITE Math** **Explain** why the product of a decimal between 0 and 1 and a whole number greater than 1 is a number that is between both factors.

ALGEBRA

Patterns in Decimal Factors and Products

OBJECTIVE: Use patterns in decimal factors to find products.

Quick Review

1. 8 × 1
2. 8 × 10
3. 8 × 100
4. 8 × 1,000
5. 8 × 10,000

Learn

PROBLEM The length of a day is the amount of time it takes a planet to make a complete rotation on its axis. A true Earth day is about 23.93 hours. How many hours are in 1,000 days on Earth? How many hours are in 1,000 days on Mars?

You can use basic facts and place-value patterns to find products.

▲ A day on Mars is 24.62 Earth hours.

Example

Earth	Mars
23.93 × 1 = 23.93	24.62 × 1 = 24.62
23.93 × 10 = 239.3	24.62 × 10 = 246.2
23.93 × 100 = 2,393.	24.62 × 100 = 2,462.
23.93 × 1,000 = 23,930.	24.62 × 1,000 = 24,620.

So, on Earth, there are about 23,930 hours in 1,000 days. On Mars, there are about 24,620 Earth hours in 1,000 days.

More Examples

A

$6.75 × 1 = $6.75
$6.75 × 10 = $67.50
$6.75 × 100 = $675.00
$6.75 × 1,000 = $6,750.00
$6.75 × 10,000 = $67,500.00

B

0.769 × 1 = 0.769
0.769 × 10 = 7.69
0.769 × 100 = 76.9
0.769 × 1,000 = 769
0.769 × 10,000 = 7,690

C

0.004 × 1 = 0.004
0.004 × 10 = 0.04
0.004 × 100 = 0.4
0.004 × 1,000 = 4
0.004 × 10,000 = 40

- What rule can you use to describe the pattern to place the decimal point in the products above?

Guided Practice

Copy and complete the pattern to find the missing products.

1. 1 × 0.4 = 0.4
   10 × 0.4 = 4
   100 × 0.4 = 40
   1,000 × 0.4 = ■

2. 1 × 9.81 = 9.81
   10 × 9.81 = ■
   100 × 9.81 = 981
   1,000 × 9.81 = ■

3. 1 × $0.07 = $0.07
   10 × $0.07 = ■
   100 × $0.07 = $7.00
   1,000 × $0.07 = ■

KY *MA-05-1.3.3 Students will multiply decimals through tenths. also* MA-05-1.1.1

Use patterns to find the product.

4. $3.19 × 1
   $3.19 × 10
   $3.19 × 100
   $3.19 × 1,000

5. 0.298 × 1
   0.298 × 10
   0.298 × 100
   0.298 × 1,000

6. 0.005 × 1
   0.005 × 10
   0.005 × 100
   0.005 × 1,000

7. 1.017 × 1
   1.017 × 10
   1.017 × 100
   1.017 × 1,000

8. TALK Math **Explain** why the product 2.78 × 10 is the same as the product 0.278 × 100.

Independent Practice and Problem Solving

Use patterns to find the products.

9. 9.35 × 1
   9.35 × 10
   9.35 × 100
   9.35 × 1,000

10. 0.002 × 1
    0.002 × 10
    0.002 × 100
    0.002 × 1,000

11. 3.105 × 1
    3.105 × 10
    3.105 × 100
    3.105 × 1,000

12. $12.65 × 1
    $12.65 × 100
    $12.65 × 1,000
    $12.65 × 10,000

Multiply each number by 10, 100, 1,000, and 10,000.

13. 1.146
14. $6.32
15. 33.52
16. 0.009
17. 0.78
18. 0.1
19. $0.50
20. 483.2
21. 2.14
22. $81.75

Find the value of *n*.

23. 10 × 16.49 = *n*
24. $3.24 × *n* = $324.00
25. 1.41 × *n* = 14,100
26. *n* × 0.095 = 95

USE DATA For 27–29, use the table.

27. How many hours are in 10 days on Neptune?
28. How many hours are in 1,000 days on Saturn?
29. **Reasoning** How many more hours are in 100 days on Uranus than on Jupiter?
30. WRITE Math **Explain** how you know where to place the decimal point in 75.95 × 10.

Length of Planet Days

Planet	Length of Day (in Earth hours)
Jupiter	9.8
Saturn	10.2
Uranus	15.5
Neptune	15.8

Mixed Review and Test Prep

31. What digit is in the millions place in the number 146,378,920? (p. 4)
32. Eli has $7.30. He spends $2.90. About how much money does Eli have left? (p. 156)
33. **Test Prep** A car gets 28.2 miles per gallon of gas. How many miles can it go on 100 gallons of gas?
    A 2.82 miles
    B 28.2 miles
    C 282 miles
    D 2,820 miles

Extra Practice on page 186, Set A

LESSON 3

Record Multiplication by a Whole Number

OBJECTIVE: Multiply a decimal by a whole number.

Quick Review

1. 123×4
2. 363×15
3. $4,409 \times 6$
4. $6,591 \times 19$
5. $7,092 \times 31$

Learn

PROBLEM The moon is slowly spiraling away from Earth's orbit, drifting away at a rate of about 3.8 centimeters each year.

Astronauts from the United States walked on the surface of the moon for the first time in 1969. In 2006, 37 years later, the United States, China, India, and Japan were all planning missions to the moon. How much farther away from Earth was the moon in 2006 than in 1969?

You can use an estimate to place the decimal point in a decimal product.

▼ The moon is about 384,400 kilometers from Earth.

Example Multiply. 3.8 × 37

Step 1

Estimate the product. Round each factor.

$$3.8 \times 37$$
$$\downarrow \quad \downarrow$$
$$4 \times 40 = 160$$

Step 2

Multiply as with whole numbers.

$$\begin{array}{r} \overset{2}{\overset{5}{3.8}} \\ \times\ 3\,7 \\ \hline 26\,6 \\ +\,114\,0 \\ \hline 140\,6 \end{array}$$

Step 3

Use the estimate to place the decimal point in the product.

$$\begin{array}{r} \overset{2}{\overset{5}{3.8}} \\ \times\ 3\,7 \\ \hline 26\,6 \\ +\,114\,0 \\ \hline 140.6 \end{array}$$

Math Idea
Place the decimal so that the product has the closest value to the estimate.

So, the moon was 140.6 centimeters farther away from Earth in 2006 than in 1969.

More Examples

A Multiply. 8 × 0.94

Estimate. 10 × 1 = 10

$$\begin{array}{r} \overset{7\ 3}{0.94} \\ \times\quad 8 \\ \hline 7.52 \end{array}$$

B Multiply. 0.856 × 19

Estimate. 1 × 19 = 19

$$\begin{array}{r} \overset{7\ 5\,5}{0.856} \\ \times\quad 19 \\ \hline 7704 \\ +\ \ 8560 \\ \hline 16.264 \end{array}$$

C Multiply. 2.815 × 7

Estimate. 3 × 7 = 21

$$\begin{array}{r} \overset{5\ 1\,3}{2.815} \\ \times\quad\ 7 \\ \hline 19.705 \end{array}$$

KY *MA-05-1.3.3 Students will multiply decimals through tenths.* *also* **MA-05-1.1.1**

Guided Practice

Complete the estimate. Then use the estimate to place the decimal point in the product.

1. Estimate: $7 \times 7 = \blacksquare$

$$\begin{array}{r} 6.81 \\ \times \quad 7 \\ \hline 4767 \end{array}$$

2. Estimate: $\blacksquare \times 30 = 90$

$$\begin{array}{r} 3.24 \\ \times \quad 28 \\ \hline 9072 \end{array}$$

3. Estimate: $\blacksquare \times 4 = 24$

$$\begin{array}{r} 6.019 \\ \times \quad 4 \\ \hline 24076 \end{array}$$

Find and record the product.

4. 6.32×3 **5.** 0.307×9 **6.** 2.15×21 **7.** 4.88×26 **8.** 40.7×5

9. TALK Math **Explain** how estimating helps you place the decimal point in the product.

Independent Practice and Problem Solving

Find and record the product.

10. $\begin{array}{r} 4.93 \\ \times \quad 7 \\ \hline \end{array}$ **11.** $\begin{array}{r} 1.21 \\ \times \quad 35 \\ \hline \end{array}$ **12.** $\begin{array}{r} 2.209 \\ \times \quad 61 \\ \hline \end{array}$ **13.** $\begin{array}{r} 87.18 \\ \times \quad 4 \\ \hline \end{array}$ **14.** $\begin{array}{r} 575.7 \\ \times \quad 44 \\ \hline \end{array}$

15. 55.9×9 **16.** 6.31×22 **17.** 10.02×9 **18.** 24.7×53 **19.** 9.09×4

Algebra **Find the value of *n*.**

20. $1.6 \times 3 = n$ **21.** $1.1 \times n = 13.2$ **22.** $372.9 \times 5 = n$ **23.** $0.9 \times n = 6.3$

24. A planet's orbital speed is its average speed as it revolves around the sun. Mercury's orbital speed is 29.76 miles per second. How many miles does Mercury travel in 1 minute?

25. The orbital speed of Earth is 18.52 miles per second. Pluto's orbital speed is 2.92 miles per second. How much farther does Earth travel in 1 minute than Pluto?

26. WRITE Math **What's the Error?** Jupiter's orbital speed is 8.14 miles per second. Frank calculated that the distance Jupiter travels in 1 hour is 488.4 miles. What is Frank's error? What should Frank's answer have been?

Mixed Review and Test Prep

27. Tyra arrived at the library at 3:45 P.M. She left at 6:20 P.M. How long was Tyra at the library? (Grade 4)

28. On Monday, Cal drove 218.1 miles. On Tuesday, he drove 197.9 miles. How many more miles did Cal drive on Monday? (p. 156)

29. **Test Prep** The trail around Sun Lake is 10.56 km long. If Elena walks around the lake 4 times, how far does she walk?

A 4,244 km
B 422.4 km
C 42.24 km
D 4.224 km

Extra Practice on page 186, Set B

LESSON 4 HANDS ON

Model Multiplication by a Decimal

OBJECTIVE: Model multiplication by decimals.

Quick Review

1. 4×0.3
2. 1.2×7
3. 6×21.5
4. 0.08×10
5. 100×75.1

Investigate

Materials ■ grid paper ■ color pencils

You can use a model to multiply decimals.

Find 0.7×0.4.

A Draw a square on grid paper. Divide the square into 10 equal columns.

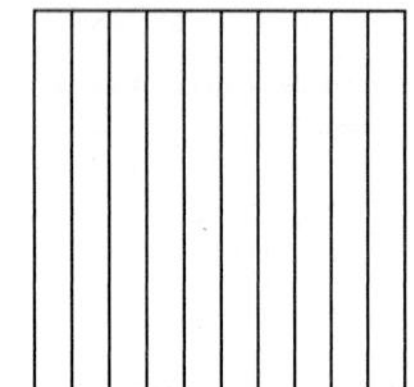

B Use a color pencil to shade 7 columns to represent the first factor.

C Divide the square into 10 equal rows to make 100 equal parts. Use a different color to shade 4 parts of 7 columns to show the second factor.

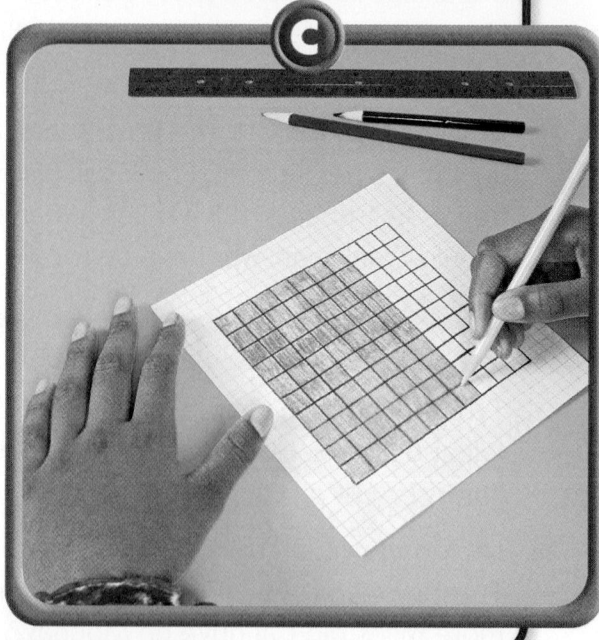

D Count the squares in the area in which the color shading overlaps. Record your answer. Write the equation that represents the model.

Draw Conclusions

1. Which product will be greater: 0.8×0.9 or 0.8×0.10? Explain your reasoning.
2. If the model represents one whole, how much does one column or one row represent? How much does each square represent?
3. **Comprehension** Why is the part of the model representing the product less than either factor?

Connect

You can model multiplication for decimals greater than 1.

A **Find 1.3 × 0.3.**

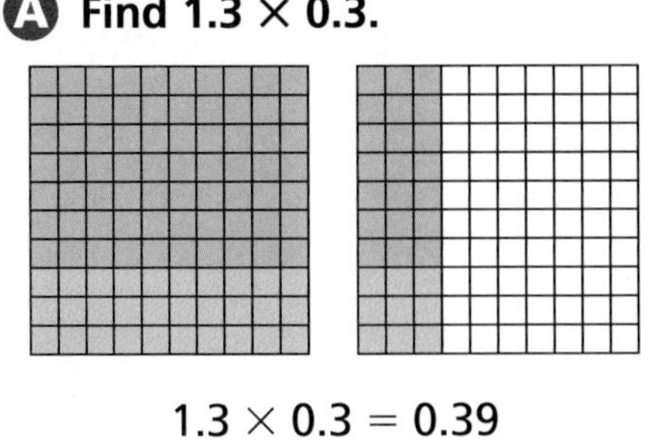

$1.3 \times 0.3 = 0.39$

B **Find 1.9 × 0.6.**

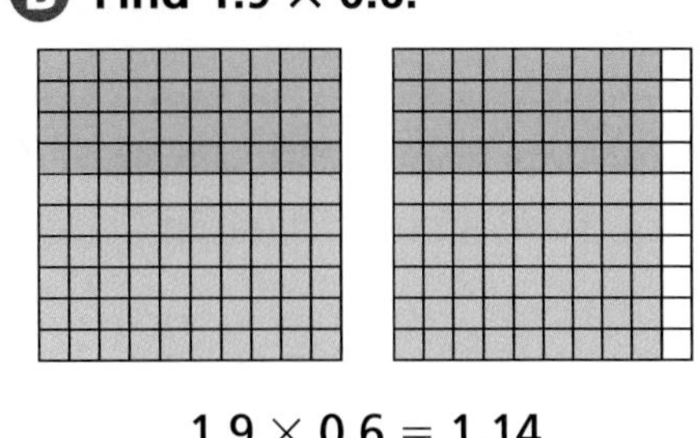

$1.9 \times 0.6 = 1.14$

Count the squares in the area in which the color shading overlaps to find the product.

TALK Math

How many digits do you think will follow the decimal for the product 1.2×1.1? **Explain** your thinking.

Practice

Use the model to find the product.

1. 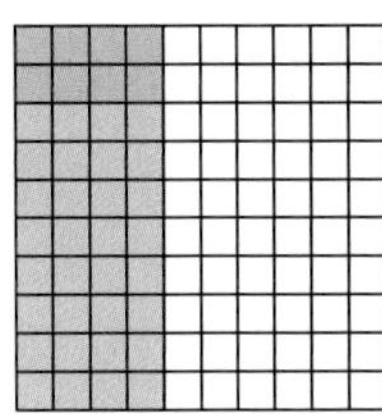

0.4×0.8

2. 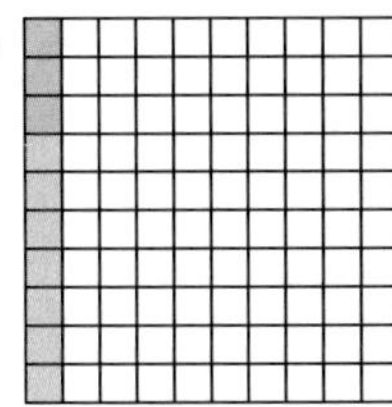

0.1×0.7

3. 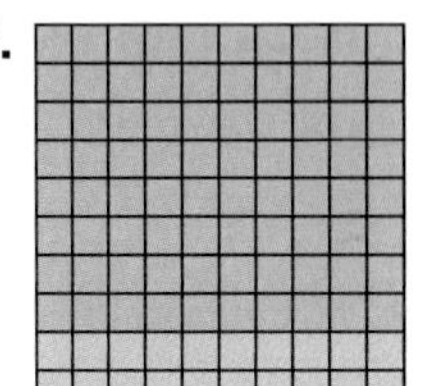

1.4×0.2

Make a model to find the product.

4. 0.3×0.2
5. 0.2×0.4
6. 0.6×0.9
7. 0.6×0.8
8. 0.9×0.1
9. 0.5×0.9
10. 1.5×0.3
11. 1.1×0.6
12. 1.2×0.4
13. 1.6×0.5

Find the product.

14. 0.8×0.3
15. 0.2×0.7
16. 0.9×0.5
17. 0.3×0.6
18. 0.9×0.9
19. 0.9×0.8
20. 1.7×0.3
21. 1.5×0.5
22. 1.4×0.7
23. 1.3×0.8
24. **WRITE Math** **Explain** why you need a zero between the decimal point and the 1 in the product of the equation $0.1 \times 0.1 = 0.01$.

CD ROM Technology
Use Harcourt Mega Math, The Number Games, *Buggy Bargains*, Level J.

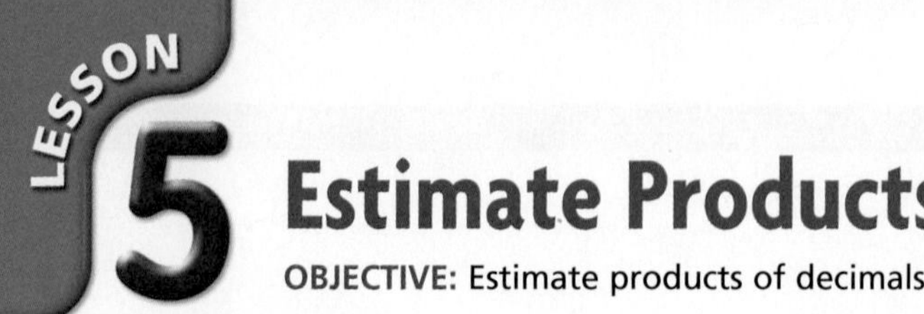

LESSON 5 Estimate Products

OBJECTIVE: Estimate products of decimals.

Quick Review

Round to the nearest whole number.

1. 2.3 **2.** 5.7
3. 7.8 **4.** 9.9
5. 11.4

Learn

PROBLEM A California condor eats about 0.91 kilogram of food each day. About how much food will a condor eat in 4 weeks, or 28 days?

▲ The head of a California condor is bald and pink. When the condor is scared or excited, its head turns bright red.

Example 1 Use compatible numbers. Estimate. 0.91 × 28

Step 1	Step 2	Step 3
Use compatible numbers. 0.91 × 28 ↓ ↓ 0.9 × 30	Multiply as with whole numbers. 30 × 0.9 270	Use whole numbers to place the decimal point. 30 × 1 = 30 → 30 × 0.9 = 27.0 Use the product 30 × 1 to place the decimal point in the estimate.

So, a condor eats about 27 kilograms of food in 4 weeks.

Example 2 Use rounding. Estimate. 27 × 2.205

One kilogram is equal to about 2.205 pounds. If a California condor eats 27 kilograms of food in 4 weeks, about how many pounds of food does a condor eat in 4 weeks?

Step 1	Step 2
Round to the nearest whole numbers. 27 × 2.205 ↓ ↓ 27 × 2	Multiply. 27 × 2 54

So, a condor eats about 54 pounds of food in 4 weeks.

Remember
Overestimate cost by rounding money amounts up to the next whole dollar amount.

More Examples Estimate.

A Rounding

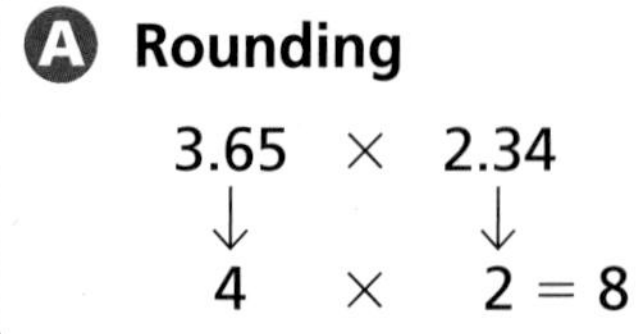

3.65 × 2.34
↓ ↓
4 × 2 = 8

B Compatible numbers

7.2 × 4.8
↓ ↓
7 × 5 = 35

C Rounding money

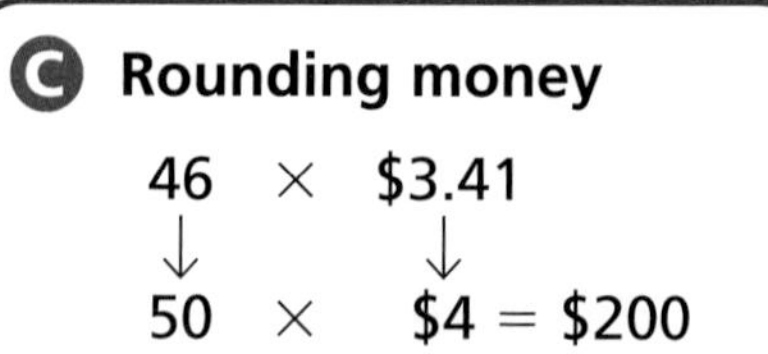

46 × \$3.41
↓ ↓
50 × \$4 = \$200

FAST TRACK

KY MA-05-1.2.1 Students will apply and describe appropriate strategies for estimating quantities of objects and computational results in real-world problems. DOK 2 *also MA-05-1.3.3;* MA-05-1.1.1

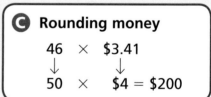

Guided Practice

Find the missing number or numbers in the estimate.

1. 2.6×1.8 Estimate: $3 \times ■ = 6$
2. 8.9×8.7 Estimate: $■ \times ■ = 81$
3. 2.39×3.1 Estimate: $2.4 \times ■ = 7.2$
4. $\$6.61 \times 52$ Estimate: $■ \times 50 = \$350$

Estimate the product.

5. 7.9×2.2
6. 13.1×6.5
7. $6 \times \$4.25$
8. 2.15×3.92
9. $\$89.73 \times 12$

10. TALK Math **Explain** how you know that 27 is an overestimate for 8.78×2.7.

Independent Practice and Problem Solving

Estimate the product.

11. 4.2×6.8
12. 5.3×7.4
13. $\$7.85 \times 5$
14. $\$2.98 \times 6$
15. 2.9×6.6
16. 21.13×9
17. $8 \times \$14.10$
18. 3.66×8.12
19. 3.7×19.5
20. $\$13.74 \times 19$

USE DATA For 21–23, use the table.

21. A condor has a wingspan that is about 2.6 times as great as the greatest wingspan of a peregrine falcon. Estimate the wingspan of the condor.

22. The female peregrine falcon is heavier than the male. The average male peregrine falcon has a weight that is about 0.67 times as great as the maximum weight. What is the average weight of a male peregrine falcon?

23. **Pose a Problem** Use the data in the table to write an estimation problem. Have a classmate solve the problem.

North American Birds of Prey

Bird	Maximum Weight (in kg)	Maximum Wingspan (in m)
Condor	14.1	■
Peregrine falcon	1.19	1.1

24. WRITE Math **Explain** whether the answer given is reasonable or unreasonable.

$$21.4 \times 6.71 = 114.265$$

Mixed Review and Test Prep

25. Lily made 7 stacks of paper with 125 sheets of paper in each stack. How many sheets of paper did Lily use? (p. 42)

26. Jorie scored 94, 89, 85, 87, and 88 on her math tests. What was Jorie's median score? (Grade 4)

27. **Test Prep** Dave sold 22 snow cones for $1.75 each. Which expression gives the closest estimate for the amount of money Dave made selling snow cones?

A $20 \times \$1.00$
B $22 \times \$1.00$
C $22 \times \$2.00$
D $30 \times \$2.00$

Extra Practice on page 186, Set C

LESSON 6

Practice Decimal Multiplication

OBJECTIVE: Place the decimal point in decimal multiplication.

Quick Review

Round to the nearest whole number.

1. 7.4 **2.** 22.8
3. 0.63 **4.** 5.59
5. 3.398

Learn

PROBLEM Leopard seals and elephant seals live on island coasts between southern Australia and Antarctica. An average male leopard seal is about 2.8 meters in length. An average male elephant seal is about 1.5 times as long. About what length is a male elephant seal?

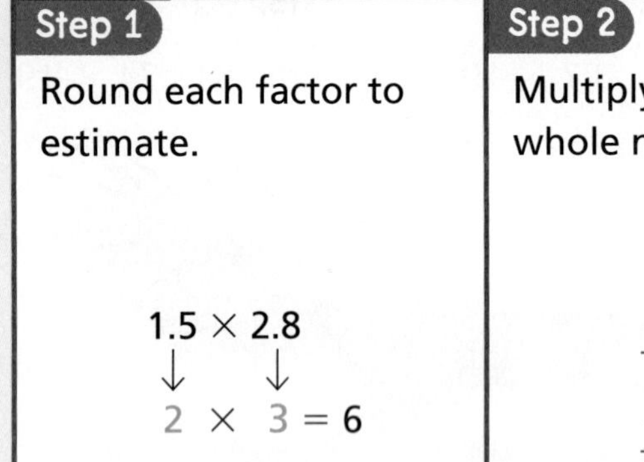

▲ **Elephant seals are fiercely territorial and protect their home and their young.**

ONE WAY **Use estimation.**

Multiply. 1.5×2.8

Step 1	Step 2	Step 3
Round each factor to estimate. 1.5×2.8 $\downarrow \quad \downarrow$ $2 \times 3 = 6$	Multiply as with whole numbers. $\begin{array}{r} \overset{1}{\overset{4}{}} \\ 1.5 \\ \times 2.8 \\ \hline 120 \\ +300 \\ \hline 420 \end{array}$	Use the estimate to place the decimal point. $\begin{array}{r} \overset{1}{\overset{4}{}} \\ 1.5 \\ \times 2.8 \\ \hline 120 \\ +300 \\ \hline 4.20 \end{array}$ Since the estimate is 6, the product should have one digit before the decimal point.

So, the length of a male elephant seal is about 4.2 meters.

ERROR ALERT

The zeros at the end of a product should not be dropped until after you place the decimal point.

The length of a female leopard seal is about 1.1 times that of a male leopard seal. About how long is a female leopard seal?

ANOTHER WAY **Count decimal places.**

Multiply. 1.1×2.8 **Estimate.** $1 \times 3 = 3$

Step 1	Step 2
Multiply as with whole numbers. $\begin{array}{r} 1.1 \\ \times 2.8 \\ \hline 88 \\ +220 \\ \hline 308 \end{array}$	Count the number of decimal places in both factors. Place the decimal point that number of places from the right in the product. $\begin{array}{rl} 1.1 & \leftarrow \text{1 decimal place in 1.1} \\ \times 2.8 & \leftarrow \text{1 decimal place in 2.8} \\ \hline 88 & \\ +220 & \\ \hline 3.08 & \leftarrow 1 + 1\text{, or 2 decimal places in the product} \end{array}$

So, the length of a female leopard seal is about 3.08 meters.

KY *MA-05-1.3.3 Students will multiply decimals through tenths.* *also* **MA-05-1.1.1**

Zeros in the Product

Sometimes, you may have to add zeros to the product when placing the decimal point.

Example

Multiply. 0.05×0.84 **Estimate.** $0.05 \times 1 = 0.05$

Step 1	Step 2	Step 3
Multiply as with whole numbers.	Count the number of decimal places in both factors.	Write a zero to the left of the product to place the decimal point.
$\begin{array}{r} 0.84 \\ \times 0.05 \\ \hline 420 \end{array}$	$\begin{array}{rl} 0.84 & \leftarrow \text{2 places} \\ \times 0.05 & \leftarrow \underline{+\text{ 2 places}} \\ \hline 420 & \end{array}$	$\begin{array}{rl} 0.84 & \\ \times 0.05 & \\ \hline 0.0420 & \leftarrow \text{4 places} \end{array}$

So, 0.05×0.84 is equal to 0.0420.

More Examples

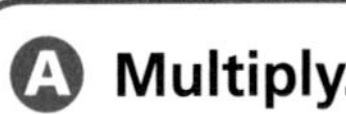

A Multiply.

7.3×0.004

$$\begin{array}{rl} 7.3 & \\ \times 0.004 & \\ \hline 0.0292 & \leftarrow \text{4 places} \end{array}$$

Write one zero to the left of the product.

B Multiply.

$\$16 \times 0.006$

$$\begin{array}{rl} \$16 & \\ \times 0.006 & \\ \hline \$0.096 & \leftarrow \text{3 places} \end{array}$$

Round the product to $0.10.

Math Idea
When multiplying money amounts, round your answer to two decimal places.

Guided Practice

Complete the estimate. Then use the estimate to place the decimal point in the product.

1. 6.87×2.4
   Estimate: ■ × 2 = ■ $\begin{array}{r} 6.87 \\ \times\ 2.4 \\ \hline 16488 \end{array}$

2. 1.27×0.03
   Estimate: ■ × 0.03 = 0.03 $\begin{array}{r} 1.27 \\ \times 0.03 \\ \hline \end{array}$

Find the number of decimal places in each product.

3. 0.09×3
4. 8×0.004
5. 0.02×0.6
6. 0.03×0.01
7. 0.07×0.006

Estimate. Then find the product.

8. $\begin{array}{r} 32.3 \\ \times\ 0.4 \\ \hline \end{array}$
9. $\begin{array}{r} 0.07 \\ \times\ 62 \\ \hline \end{array}$
10. $\begin{array}{r} 8.5 \\ \times 0.3 \\ \hline \end{array}$
11. $\begin{array}{r} 1.09 \\ \times 0.02 \\ \hline \end{array}$
12. $\begin{array}{r} 0.41 \\ \times 0.56 \\ \hline \end{array}$

13. **TALK Math** **Explain** how you know that 77.7 isn't a reasonable answer for 3.7×2.1.

Independent Practice and Problem Solving

Find the number of decimal places in each product.

14. 0.004×0.02 **15.** $\$6 \times 0.003$ **16.** 5.16×0.08 **17.** 0.04×0.07 **18.** 1.009×0.15

19. 0.9×0.11 **20.** 0.14×0.012 **21.** 0.13×0.007 **22.** 1.001×1.01 **23.** 2.92×0.207

Estimate. Then find the product.

24. 0.2×26 **25.** 0.9×0.8 **26.** 3.7×0.4 **27.** 31.2×0.5 **28.** 6.06×7.3

29. 7.25×3.4 **30.** 5.1×2.7 **31.** 0.201×0.8 **32.** 436.3×1.81 **33.** 12.92×7.3

34. $\$2.90 \times 0.8$ **35.** 442.4×0.8 **36.** 1.638×182 **37.** 97.5×7.13 **38.** $\$14.25 \times 1.8$

39. 34.7×5.29 **40.** 21×7.164 **41.** 0.331×1.2 **42.** 0.45×0.65 **43.** 282.6×0.403

USE DATA For 44–45, use the table.

Sizes of Seals

Type of Seal	Length (in meters)	Mass (in kilograms)
Leopard	up to 3.6 m	up to 450 kg
Harbor	from 1.2 m to 2.0 m	from 50 kg to 170 kg
Ross	up to 2.5 m	up to 200 kg
Monk	up to 2.8 m	from 240 to 400 kg

44. A monk seal at an aquarium has a mass 1.67 times as great as the heaviest Ross seal. What is the mass of the monk seal?

45. The length of one of the aquarium's leopard seals is 2.5 times as great as the length of the smallest harbor seal. What is the length of the aquarium's leopard seal?

46. **Reasoning** Why would you not use 4 decimal places in the product $2.98 × 1.07? How would you write your answer?

47. WRITE Math **What's the Error?** A pound of fish costs $7.50. Jon says 62.2 pounds of fish will cost $4,665.00. What is his error? What should Jon's answer have been?

Mixed Review and Test Prep

48. A school cafeteria can hold 864 students. Each table can hold 8 students. How many tables are in the cafeteria? (p. 42)

49. The standard mass of a United States quarter is 5.67 grams. What is the mass of a quarter rounded to the nearest tenth? (p. 150)

50. **Test Prep** Trisha put $1.25 in her bank each week for one year. How much money did she put in her bank?

A $65.00 **C** $6.50

B $62.50 **D** $6.25

 Extra Practice on page 186, Set D

Justify an Answer

WRITE Math WORKSHOP

Sometimes you need to provide an explanation to justify an answer. If there are two possible ways to find an answer, explain both ways.

Tina's teacher asked her to solve the following problem and to justify the placement of the decimal point in her answer.

In 2003, young people between the ages of 13 and 24 said they spent an average of 16.7 hours per week surfing the Internet. How many hours will a young person spend surfing the Internet in one year?

Read Tina's solution and justification of her answer.

How I Knew Where to Place the Decimal Point

Multiply the number of hours per week times the number of weeks in the year to find the number of hours a young person spends surfing the Internet in one year.

$$16.7 \times 52 = 868.4$$

One way is to use estimation to check placement of the decimal point. Round both factors to the nearest ten and then multiply: $20 \times 50 = 1{,}000$. The estimate shows that the product is close to 1,000. Since 868.4 is much closer to 1,000 than 8,684 is, 868.4 must be the product.

Another way to check placement of the decimal point is to count the number of decimal places in the factors. Since there is only one decimal place, the product will have only one decimal place.

Tips

To justify an answer:

- explain how you found the answer.
- explain each way you checked the answer.
- use correct math vocabulary.
- check all computations.
- write a conclusion to justify your answer in the last sentence.

Problem Solving Solve. Then justify each answer.

1. People between the ages of 13 and 24 spend an average of 12 hours a week listening to the radio. About how many hours does the average young person spend listening to the radio in 6.5 weeks?

2. In one week, young people between the ages of 13 and 24 watch TV for an average of 13.6 hours. About how many hours does an average young person spend watching TV in 52 weeks?

Problem Solving Workshop Skill: Multistep Problems

OBJECTIVE: Solve problems by using the skill *multistep problems*.

Read to Understand
Plan
Solve
Check

Use the Skill

PROBLEM The Chester Elementary fifth graders are taking a field trip to the Mystic Seaport Museum. Admission costs $8.00 for each student and $10.00 for each chaperone. There are 74 students and 15 adults.

While at the museum, 22 students from the Science Club will visit the planetarium. Members of the Chorus will attend the Chantey Music program. The planetarium costs $2.50 per person. The music program has a group rate of $80.00. How much will admissions to the museum and the activities cost the fifth–grade class?

▲ Visitors to Mystic Seaport can climb aboard the *Charles W. Morgan*, which was built in 1841.

A multistep problem requires more than one step to solve. You can solve multistep problems by breaking them down into single steps.

Step 1	Step 2
Find the total cost of the student tickets. $74 \times \$8.00 = \$592.00$	Find the total cost of the adult tickets. $15 \times \$10.00 = \$150.00$

Step 3	Step 4
Find the costs of the activities. Planetarium: $22 \times \$2.50 = \$55.00$ Music Program: $80.00 $\$55.00 + \$80.00 = \$135.00$	Find the combined amount of all costs. $\$592.00 + \$150.00 + \$135.00 = \$877.00$ student tickets + adult tickets + activities = combined amount

So, the total cost of admissions to the museum with activities is $877.00.

Think and Discuss

Describe the steps required to solve. Then solve the problem.

a. The students raised money for the trip by washing cars. They washed 169 cars and made $3.00 for each car. The money from the car wash was applied to the total cost of the trip, which was $877.00. The remaining cost of the trip was divided equally among the 74 students. How much did each student have to pay?

b. Students can choose to buy a lunch for an additional $2.25. The cost of an adult lunch is $3.00. If all 74 students and 15 adults buy lunch, how much extra will it add to the total cost of the field trip?

Guided Problem Solving

▲ The *Emma C. Berry* was launched in 1866.

Describe the steps required to solve. Then solve the problem.

1. Mystic Seaport displays a fishing boat named the *Emma C. Berry*. Boats such as the *Emma* were used to catch lobster and fish like halibut and cod in the late 1800s.

   Suppose the crew of a fishing boat in 1872 caught 465 lobsters, 190 cod, and 400 pounds of halibut. The crew received $0.02 for each lobster, $0.13 for each cod, and $200 for all of the halibut. If the crew of 3 men divided the total amount equally, how much money did each man earn?

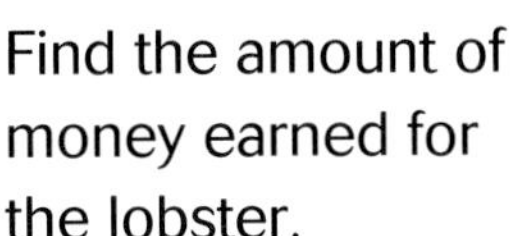

Find the amount of money earned for the lobster.	Find the amount of money earned for the cod.	Add the amounts of money for the lobster, the cod, and the halibut.	Divide the total amount of money by the number of men in the crew.
■ × \$0.02 = \$9.30	■ × \$0.13 = \$24.70	\$9.30 + \$24.70 + ■ = \$234.00	\$234 ÷ 3 = \$■

2. **What if** the crew had caught 516 lobsters, 136 cod, and $194.00 worth of halibut? How much money would each man have earned?

3. A fishing boat caught a total of 4,012 lobsters in one season, selling the lobsters to fish markets for $0.05 each. How much money did the boat earn for the season?

Mixed Applications

For 4–8, use the camp flyer.

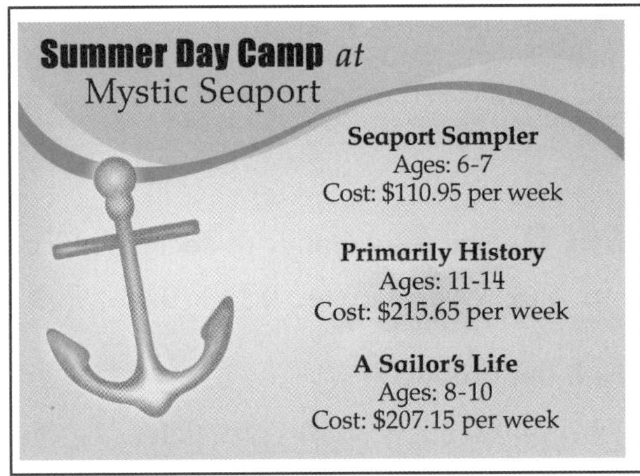

Summer Day Camp *at*
Mystic Seaport
Seaport Sampler
Ages: 6-7
Cost: $110.95 per week
Primarily History
Ages: 11-14
Cost: $215.65 per week
A Sailor's Life
Ages: 8-10
Cost: $207.15 per week

4. It will cost $422.80 for the 2 Linden children to attend the Mystic summer camps for 1 week. Between what ages is each child?

5. How much will it cost for two 7-year-olds, an 8-year-old, three 11-year-olds and a 12-year-old to attend a week of camp at Mystic Seaport?

6. **Pose a Problem** Use the information about the Mystic Seaport day camps to write and solve a multistep problem.

7. The Bristol family has 2 children attending camp at Mystic Seaport. One child is 7 years old and the other child is 12 years old. There are 3 children in the Mayer family that are also going to Mystic's summer camp. Their ages are 8, 11, and 14. How much more will the Mayer family pay?

8. **WRITE Math** Mrs. Jones paid $854.10 for her 4 children to attend summer camp at Mystic Seaport. If 3 of her children are between the ages of 11 and 14, is her fourth child between the ages of 6 and 7 or 8 and 10? **Explain** how you know.

Extra Practice

Set A Use patterns to find the products. (pp. 172–173)

1. 0.625×1
0.625×10
0.625×100
$0.625 \times 1{,}000$
2. 1.37×1
1.37×10
1.37×100
$1.37 \times 1{,}000$
3. 0.081×1
0.081×10
0.081×100
$0.081 \times 1{,}000$
4. $\$22.50 \times 1$
$\$22.50 \times 100$
$\$22.50 \times 1{,}000$
$\$22.50 \times 10{,}000$

Multiply each number by 10, 100, 1,000, and 10,000.

5. 0.49
6. 3.288
7. 0.007
8. $15.25
9. 236.4
10. A half dollar is 0.50 of a dollar. What is the value of 100 half dollars? of 1,000 half dollars?

Set B Find and record the product. (pp. 174–175)

1. 3.15×4
2. 50.2×21
3. 33.76×8
4. 418.2×7
5. 6.075×33
6. As part of a fitness program, Franklin walks 3.3 miles every day. How many miles will Franklin have walked in 7 days?
7. Jameson bought 3 packs of batteries. If each pack of batteries cost $2.89, how much did Jameson spend on batteries?

Set C Estimate the product. (pp. 178–179)

1. 1.4×0.4
2. 3.7×2.8
3. 1.3×9.2
4. 1.43×2.6
5. 2.37×1.5
6. 1.6×2.2
7. 4.13×0.8
8. $\$12.38 \times 1.4$
9. 0.231×0.9
10. 52.3×2.47

Set D Find the number of decimal places in the product. (pp. 180–183)

1. 0.07×0.2
2. 0.15×0.6
3. 7.05×1.4
4. 0.105×0.3
5. 0.09×0.9

Find the product.

6. 0.003×5
7. 0.08×0.05
8. 1.65×0.002
9. 0.21×0.045
10. 3.7×0.09
11. Bananas are on sale for $0.48 a pound. How much will 1.25 pounds of bananas cost?
12. Tabitha is making an apple pie. The recipe calls for 2.25 pounds of apples. Apples are $1.60 per pound. How much will Tabitha spend on apples?

CD ROM **Technology**
Use Harcourt Mega Math, The Number Games, *Tiny's Think Tank*, Level R

PRACTICE GAME Powerful Products

Ready!
2 players

Set!
- number cards (0–9)
- decimal product outline
- two-player chart
- paper bag

Player 1			Player 2		
Product	Correct?	Points	Product	Correct?	Points

Play!

- Player 1 puts the number cards in the paper bag, shakes it, and then draws four cards. Player 1 uses the cards to make two decimal factors that will make the greatest product possible.
- Player 1 puts the cards on the decimal product outline to display the factors and finds the product. Player 1 records the product in the chart.
- Player 2 checks Player 1's product and writes yes or no after the product in the chart.
- If the product is incorrect, a zero is placed in the chart in the points column.
- The cards are returned to the bag. Player 2 then draws four cards and repeats the process.
- At the end of each round, players compare their products. The player who has the greater product gets 1 point. The first player to earn 5 points wins the game.

MATH POWER **Expressions**

Balancing Act

An expression is a mathematical phrase that combines numbers, operation signs, and sometimes variables.

$1.4 \times 4 = 5.6$

Example

0.7×8 is an expression. 1.4×4 is an expression. Are the expressions equal?

Find the value of each expression.

$0.7 \times 8 = 5.6 \quad 1.4 \times 4 = 5.6$

$5.6 = 5.6$, so $0.7 \times 8 = 1.4 \times 4$.

$0.7 \times 8 = 5.6$

Try It

Choose one expression from Box A and an equivalent expression from Box B to balance each scale. Use each expression only once.

A	B
0.15×5	0.7×0.8
9×1.2	0.25×3
7×0.6	2×0.15
0.3×8	6×0.4
0.05×6	1.4×3
4×0.14	2.7×4

1. 

2. 

3. 

4. 

5. 

6. 

7. WRITE Math **Explain** how to find the number of decimal places in a product.

Chapter 7 Review/Test

Check Concepts

1. Explain how to use a pattern to find the product of $0.007 \times 1,000$. KY MA-05-1.3.3 (p. 172)
2. How many decimal places are in the product of 3.2×0.16? Explain how you know. KY MA-05-1.3.3 (p. 178)

Check Skills

Multiply each number by 10, 100, 1,000, and 10,000. KY MA-05-1.3.3 (pp. 172–173)

3. 0.7
4. 1.8
5. 5.9
6. 4.1
7. 3.6

Find the product. KY MA-05-1.3.3 (pp. 174–175)

8. 5.8×3
9. 1.1×7
10. 23.5×28
11. 3.6×57
12. 31.9×14
13. 43.7×0.6
14. 4.2×0.9
15. 2.8×3.5
16. 0.7×0.2
17. 15.7×4.7
18. 9.5×3.2
19. 27.1×5.6
20. 0.6×0.4
21. 15.9×14.6
22. 6.5×1.2

Check Problem Solving

Solve. KY MA-05-1.3.3 (pp. 184–185)

23. Mrs. Bennet visited the market. She bought 3.2 pounds of apples, 4.5 pounds of grapes and a watermelon that weighed 13 pounds. She paid with a $20 bill. How much change did Mrs. Bennet receive?
24. At the market, Nickie bought a bag of grapefruit, 3 pounds of oranges, and 3 pounds of grapes. She spent a total of $12.28. What was the cost for the bag of grapefruit?
25. WRITE Math Mr. Charles bought a total of 5 pounds of fruit. He spent $6.58 and he bought apples, oranges, and grapes. How much of each fruit did Mr. Charles buy? **Explain** how you found your answer.

Practice for the KCCT
Chapters 1–7

Number and Operations

1. The total area of the United States is about three million seven hundred ninety-four thousand square miles. Which is the area written in standard form? KY MA-05-1.1.1 (p. 4)

   A 3,700,940 sq. mi

   B 3,794,000 sq. mi

   C 3,700,094,000 sq. mi

   D 3,000,794,000 sq. mi

Understand the problem.

See item 2. You need to find the amount Gwen saved which is equal to the total cost of the chips and drink. You add to find total cost.

2. At Chris's Sandwich Shop, sandwiches cost \$5.69 each, a bag of chips costs \$0.89, and drinks cost \$1.56. Gwen ordered a sandwich, a bag of chips, and a drink and she used this coupon. How much did she save on her lunch? KY MA-05-1.3.1 (p. 152)

   Chris's Sandwich Shop

   FREE bag of chips and a FREE drink when you buy any sandwich.

   A \$8.14 **C** \$2.45

   B \$3.24 **D** \$0.67

3. **WRITE Math** Explain how to add $4.54 + 5.4$. KY MA-05-1.3.1 (p. 152)

Algebraic Thinking

4. The dance studio has registration this weekend. To sign up for a class, there is a \$25 registration fee. Each class costs \$7. Which expression shows the total cost to register for dance classes if *d* is the number of classes? KY MA-05-5.2.1 (p. 92)

   A $7d - 25$

   B $25 - 7d$

   C $7d + 25$

   D $25d + 7$

5. What is the rule for this function table? KY MA-05-5.1.2 (p. 112)

Input, x	Output, y
2	30
3	45
5	75
10	150

   A $y = 8x$

   B $y = 10x$

   C $y = 12x$

   D $y = 15x$

6. **WRITE Math** **Explain** how to solve for *n*. KY MA-05-5.3.1 (p. 108)

$$n - 5 = 19$$

Measurement

7. The thermometer shows the temperature outside. The temperature inside is 18°F warmer. What is the temperature inside? KY Grade 4

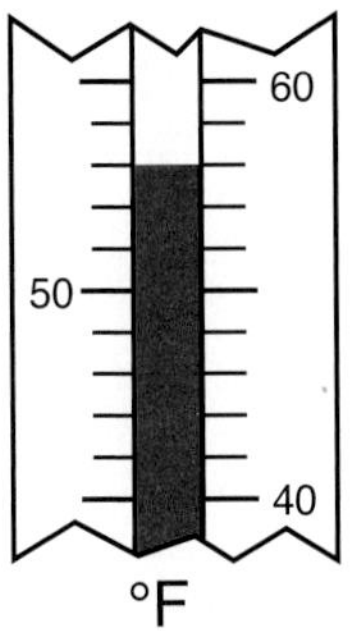

A 38°F

B 56°F

C 71°F

D 74°F

8. In gym class, the students run the 100 meter dash. What is this distance written in kilometers? KY Grade 4

A 1,000 kilometers

B 1 kilometer

C 0.1 kilometer

D 0.01 kilometer

9. WRITE Math How many inches equal 3 yards? **Explain** how you found your answer. KY Grade 4

Data Analysis and Probability

10. Malika surveyed her class about their favorite subject. If Malika surveyed 40 students, how many students voted for Science? KY Grade 4

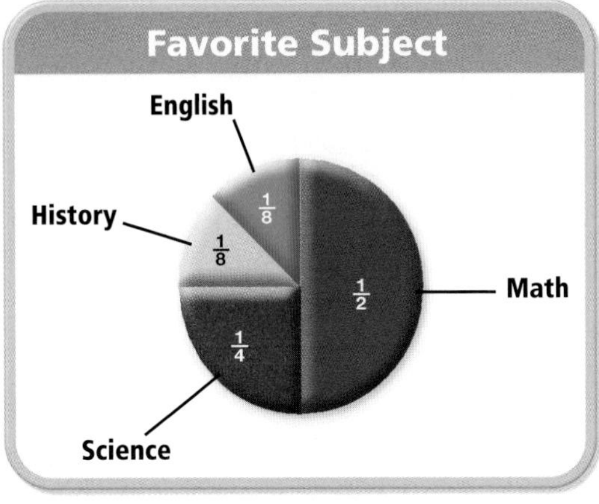

A 4 C 14

B 10 D 20

11. Lee surveyed students about their favorite snack. How many students voted? KY Grade 4

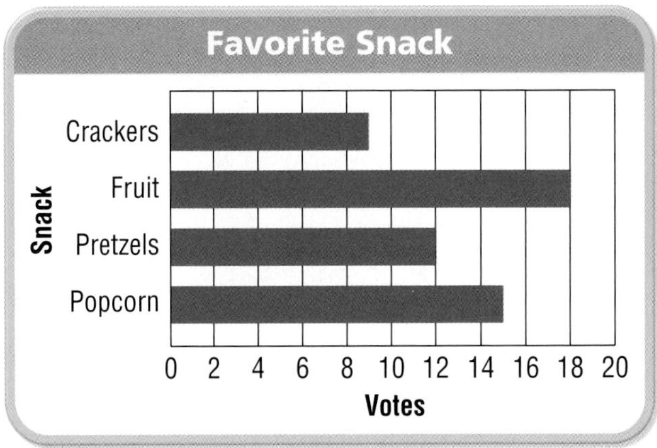

A 18 C 38

B 20 D 54

12. WRITE Math You toss a coin and a number cube labeled 1, 2, 3, 4, 5, and 6. What is the probability of tossing heads and an even number? Write your answer as a fraction. **Explain.** KY Grade 4

CHAPTER

8 Divide Decimals by Whole Numbers

FAST FACT

The Kovler Sea Lion Pool at the Lincoln Park Zoo, in Illinois, is home to grey seals and harbor seals. Seals and their relatives, sea lions and walruses, are *pinnipeds*, which means "fin-footed."

Investigate

Harbor seal pups are light compared to adult seals. Choose a weight, to a tenth of a kilogram, within the ranges shown for a newborn pup and an adult male. How many times as great is the weight of the adult compared to the weight of the pup? Round your answer to the nearest tenth of a kilogram.

Weights of Harbor Seals

GO ONLINE **Technology** Student pages are available in the Student eBook.

Show What You Know

Check your understanding of important skills needed for success in Chapter 8.

Division Patterns

Complete the pattern.

1. $24 \div 6 = 4$
$240 \div 6 = 40$
$2,400 \div 6 = n$

2. $21 \div 7 = 3$
$210 \div 7 = n$
$2,100 \div 7 = 300$

3. $32 \div 4 = n$
$320 \div 4 = 80$
$3,200 \div 4 = 800$

4. $30 \div 5 = 6$
$300 \div n = 60$
$3,000 \div 5 = 600$

5. $54 \div 9 = 6$
$n \div 9 = 60$
$5,400 \div 9 = 600$

6. $40 \div 8 = 5$
$400 \div n = 50$
$4,000 \div 8 = 500$

Estimate Quotients

Estimate the quotient.

7. $8\overline{)316}$ **8.** $3\overline{)88}$ **9.** $5\overline{)437}$ **10.** $6\overline{)402}$

11. $956 \div 3$ **12.** $96 \div 4$ **13.** $479 \div 8$ **14.** $312 \div 6$

Divide 3-Digit Dividends by 1-Digit

Divide.

15. $3\overline{)258}$ **16.** $5\overline{)210}$ **17.** $8\overline{)912}$ **18.** $4\overline{)276}$

19. $6\overline{)882}$ **20.** $9\overline{)342}$ **21.** $7\overline{)448}$ **22.** $3\overline{)651}$

23. $630 \div 5$ **24.** $924 \div 4$ **25.** $354 \div 6$ **26.** $584 \div 8$

VOCABULARY POWER

CHAPTER VOCABULARY

decimal
estimate
hundredth
quotient
tenth

WARM-UP WORDS

estimate to find a number that is close to an exact amount

hundredth one of one hundred equal parts

tenth one of ten equal parts

LESSON 1 HANDS ON

Decimal Division

OBJECTIVE: Use models to divide decimals by whole numbers.

Quick Review

1. $329 \div 7$
2. $475 \div 5$
3. $804 \div 6$
4. $756 \div 4$
5. $891 \div 9$

Investigate

Materials ■ decimal models ■ color pencils ■ scissors ■ play bills and coins

Make a model to divide a decimal by a whole number.

Find $2.4 \div 3$.

A Shade the decimal model to show 2.4.

 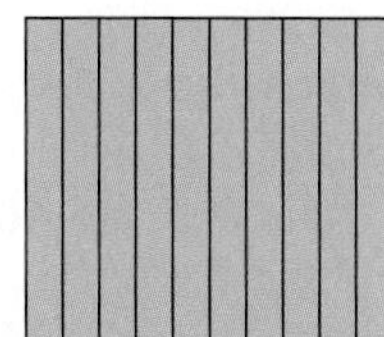 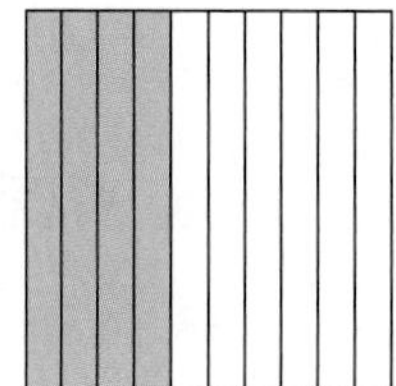

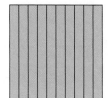

B Cut your model apart to show the number of tenths.

C Divide the tenths into 3 groups of the same size.

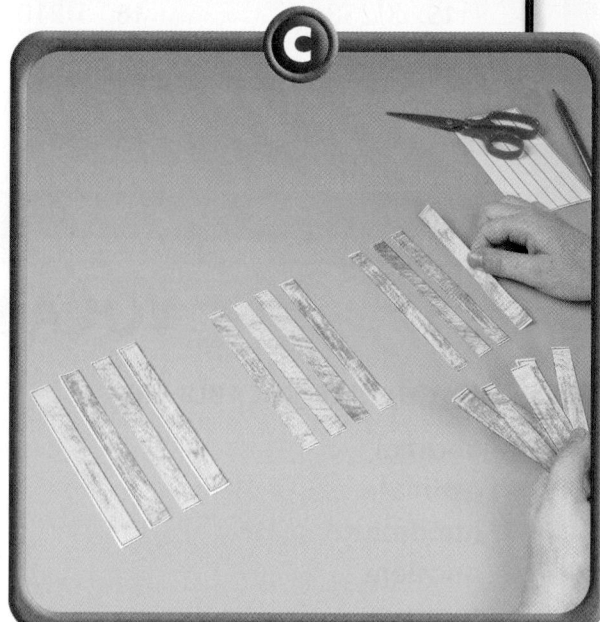

D Use your model to solve the division equation.

$2.4 \div 3 = ■$

Draw Conclusions

1. Why did you cut the model into tenths?
2. How can you use your materials to find $1.4 \div 2$? Use your model to solve the new expression.
3. **Synthesis** Explain how your model would be different for the problem $0.24 \div 3$.

Connect

You can also use money to model division of a decimal by a whole number.

Find 7.32 ÷ 6.

Step 1

Use $1 bills, dimes, and pennies to show $7.32.

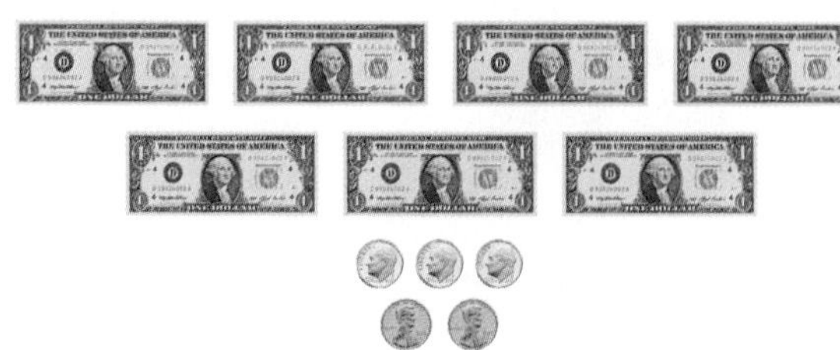

Step 2

Divide the $1 bills into 6 equal groups. Exchange the remaining $1 bill for dimes.

Step 3

Divide the dimes into 6 equal groups. Exchange the remaining dime for pennies.

Step 4

Divide the pennies into 6 equal groups.

$7.32 ÷ 6 = $1.22, so 7.32 ÷ 6 = 1.22.

TALK Math

Why wouldn't you use quarters or nickels to model division of decimals?

Practice

Use decimal models or play money to model the quotient. Record your answer.

1. 1.5 ÷ 3 **2.** 3.2 ÷ 4 **3.** 0.18 ÷ 9 ✓**4.** 0.28 ÷ 4

5. $6.96 ÷ 6 **6.** $6.45 ÷ 5 **7.** 4.68 ÷ 3 ✓**8.** 5.11 ÷ 7

9. $1.32 ÷ 4 **10.** 4.98 ÷ 6 **11.** 2.24 ÷ 7 **12.** $0.18 ÷ 3

13. **WRITE Math** Describe how you can use a model to find 0.39 ÷ 3.

LESSON 2

Estimate Quotients

OBJECTIVE: Estimate decimal quotients.

Quick Review

Estimate.

1. 743 ÷ 84
2. 362 ÷ 5
3. 276 ÷ 39
4. 195 ÷ 7
5. 451 ÷ 63

Learn

PROBLEM Diana lives in Duluth, Minnesota, and she likes to ski. She found out that 3.3 feet was the greatest amount of snow Duluth has ever received during a 7-day period. This occurred in 1991. Estimate the daily snowfall, if about the same amount of snow fell each day for that 7-day period.

The greatest recorded snowfall for one year in the United States was 1,069.8 inches, on Mount Rainier in Washington from August 1973 through July 1974.

Example Use compatible numbers.

Estimate. 3.3 ÷ 7.

Think: 3.3 is 33 tenths.
28 and 7 are compatible numbers.
28 tenths divided by 7 is 4 tenths or 0.4.
35 and 7 are compatible numbers.
35 tenths divided by 7 is 5 tenths or 0.5.

So, if about the same amount of snow fell each day, the daily snowfall was between 0.4 foot and 0.5 foot.

More Examples Estimate the quotients.

A Use two estimates.

Estimate 263.51 ÷ 62.

263.51 ÷ 62
240 ÷ 60 = 4
300 ÷ 60 = 5

So, 263.51 ÷ 62 is between 4 and 5.

B Use one estimate.

Estimate 70.61 ÷ 9.

70.61 ÷ 9 ≈ 72 ÷ 9

So, 70.61 ÷ 9 ≈ 8.

READ Math

The symbol ≈ is read "is approximately equal to." Use it when your solution to a problem is an estimate and not an exact answer.

- Explain the compatible numbers used in Examples A and B.

Guided Practice

Find two estimates for the quotient.

1. 52 ÷ 8
   64 ÷ 8 = ■
   56 ÷ 8 = ■
2. 26 ÷ 3
   27 ÷ 3 = ■
   24 ÷ 3 = ■
3. 124.6 ÷ 34
   120 ÷ 30 = ■
   120 ÷ 40 = ■
4. 45.12 ÷ 7
   42 ÷ 7 = ■
   49 ÷ 7 = ■

Use compatible numbers to estimate the quotient.

5. $44.7 \div 6$
6. $68.32 \div 9$
7. $22.6 \div 4$
8. $34.09 \div 83$

9. TALK Math **Explain** how you could estimate $4 \div 5$ without using compatible numbers.

Independent Practice and Problem Solving

Find two estimates for the quotient.

10. $2.36 \div 5$
11. $502.9 \div 8$
12. $13.1 \div 3$
13. $5.621 \div 6$

Use compatible numbers to estimate the quotient.

14. $39.6 \div 9$
15. $21.8 \div 4$
16. $336.4 \div 7$
17. $20.72 \div 3$
18. $43.7 \div 5$
19. $67.9 \div 84$
20. $345.1 \div 46$
21. $154.9 \div 19$

USE DATA For 22–24, use the table.

22. Jesse's mom made ski hats for all 12 members of the school winter sports club. She spent $71.88 for materials. About how much did each hat cost?

23. Andrea spent $199.50 for yarn to make mittens to donate to the Children's Shelter. How many mittens did Andrea make?

24. **Algebra** Janie's grandmother bought $113.88 of yarn to make scarves for all of her grandchildren. How many grandchildren does Janie's grandmother have?

25. WRITE Math How does estimation help you when you divide a decimal by a whole number?

Winter Wear Knitting Costs

Project	Yarn Cost per Project
Ski hat	■
Scarf	$9.49
Mittens, pair	$7.98

Mixed Review and Test Prep

26. What is the total of these snowfall amounts? (p. 152)

    6.3 in. 3.7 in. 4.3 in. 5.6 in.
    8.6 in. 2.4 in. 3.7 in.

27. A meteorologist found that 1 inch of melted snow equaled 0.12 inch of water. If a storm with 7.4 inches of snowfall had been rain instead of snow, how much rain would have fallen? (p. 180)

28. **Test Prep** Which shows how you can best use compatible numbers to estimate $53.4 \div 8$?

    A $48 \div 6$
    B $50 \div 8$
    C $53 \div 9$
    D $56 \div 8$

Extra Practice on page 204, Set A

LESSON 3

Divide Decimals by Whole Numbers

OBJECTIVE: Divide decimals by whole numbers.

Quick Review

1. $827 \div 7$
2. $946 \div 23$
3. $2{,}851 \div 9$
4. $5{,}225 \div 4$
5. $3{,}216 \div 57$

Learn

PROBLEM Donita's swim team participated in a swim-a-thon to raise money for charity. Each team member swam an equal part of the total distance. Donita's team swam a total of 5.24 kilometers. There are 4 swimmers on Donita's team. What distance did each team member swim?

ONE WAY Use a model.

Step 1

Shade the decimal models to show 5.24.

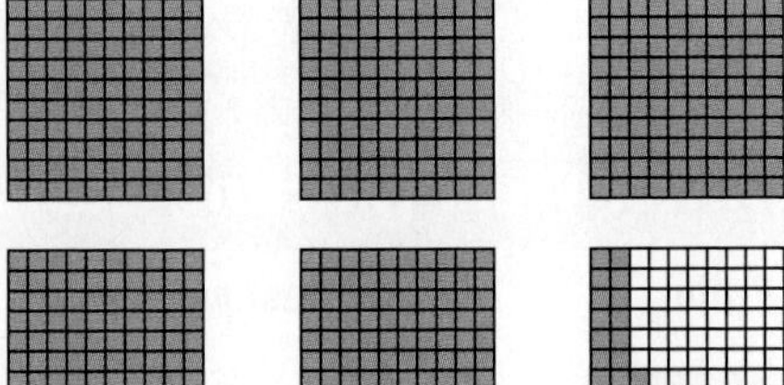

Step 2

Divide the models into 4 groups of the same size.

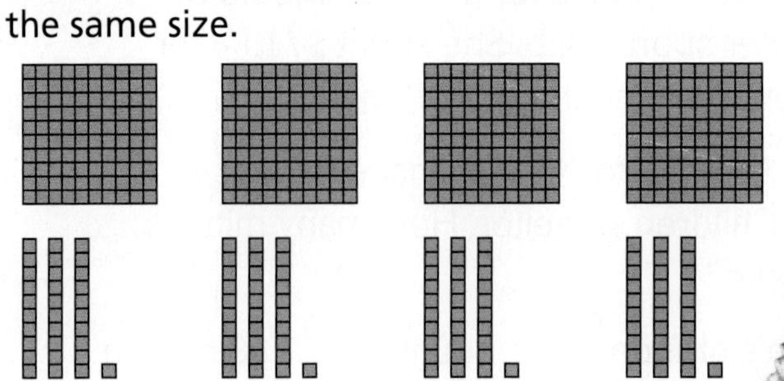

ANOTHER WAY Use paper and pencil.

Step 1

Write the decimal point of the quotient above the decimal point of the dividend.

$$4\overline{)5.24} \quad \text{(decimal point placed above)}$$

Step 2

Divide as you would with whole numbers. Check by multiplying.

```
   1.31
4)5.24
 -4
  12
 -12
   04
  - 4
    0
```

Check ✓

```
  1
  1.31
×    4
  5.24
```

So, each team member swam 1.31 kilometers.

More Examples

A Money

Find $22.95 ÷ 15.

```
      $1.53
15)$22.95
   −15
     79
    −75
     45
    −45
      0
```

Check ✓

```
   $1.53
 ×    15
     765
 + 1530
  $22.95
```

B Divisor greater than dividend

Find 2.61 ÷ 3.

```
   0.87
3)2.61
  −24
    21
   −21
     0
```

Check ✓

```
  0.87
 ×   3
  2.61
```

C Zeros placed in the dividend

Find 9.08 ÷ 8.

```
   1.135
8)9.080
  −8
   10
  − 8
    28
   −24
     40
    −40
      0
```

Check ✓

```
  1.135
 ×    8
  9.080
```

To check your answer, multiply the quotient by the divisor.

- In Example B, why do you place a zero in the ones place of the quotient?
- In Example C, why is a zero placed to the right of 9.08?

When dividing decimals, be sure to place zeros in the dividend until the remainder is zero.

Guided Practice

Use the model to find the quotient.

1. 3.12 ÷ 3

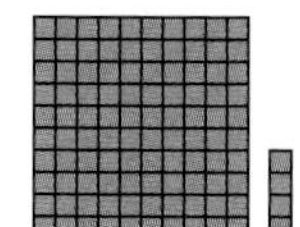
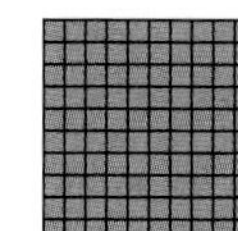
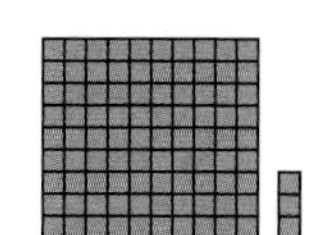

2. 1.48 ÷ 2

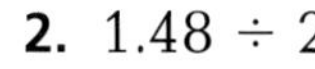
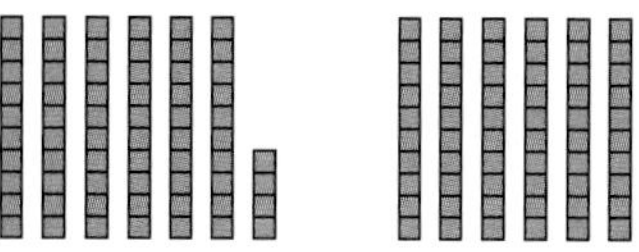

Copy the quotient and correctly place the decimal point.

3. 5)8.65 quotient 173

4. 9)4.14 quotient 046

5. 7)0.056 quotient 0008

6. 38)$51.30 quotient 135

Divide. Check by multiplying.

7. 3)224.7

8. 8)$38.88

✓**9.** 5)3.15

✓**10.** 9)0.072

11. 27)97.2

12. 72)64.08

13. 54)$93.42

14. 36)8.82

15. TALK Math **Explain** how you can check that a quotient is correct.

Independent Practice and Problem Solving

Copy the quotient and correctly place the decimal point.

16. $\overset{237}{4\overline{)94.8}}$	**17.** $\overset{0084}{6\overline{)0.504}}$	**18.** $\overset{046}{8\overline{)3.68}}$	**19.** $\overset{145}{52\overline{)\$75.40}}$

Divide. Check by multiplying.

20. $5\overline{)68.5}$	**21.** $3\overline{)7.92}$	**22.** $46\overline{)58.88}$	**23.** $61\overline{)\$83.57}$
24. $8\overline{)0.032}$	**25.** $4\overline{)\$8.24}$	**26.** $59\overline{)2.006}$	**27.** $22\overline{)53.9}$
28. $8.46 \div 9$	**29.** $8.12 \div 4$	**30.** $7.52 \div 16$	**31.** $10.2 \div 85$
32. $6.24 \div 6$	**33.** $1.253 \div 7$	**34.** $\$65.28 \div 32$	**35.** $281.2 \div 74$

USE DATA For 36–38, use the table.

36. Eight lanes are usually marked in a pool. How wide is each lane?

37. Suppose 10 lanes are marked in a pool. If the total width of the pool is 25 meters, how wide is the space on each side of the pool outside of the lanes used?

38. **Pose a Problem** Look at Problem 36. Use the table to change the number and write a new problem. Trade problems with a classmate and solve.

Competition Pool Dimensions

Number of Lanes Marked	Combined Width of All Lanes Marked (in meters)
8	21.92
9	21.96
10	21.30

39. ***FAST FACT*** A fin whale is the second-largest whale. It is known for being the fastest-moving whale. It can travel almost 24 miles per hour for short amounts of time. About how far can it travel in one minute at this speed? (Hint: 24 = 24.0.)

40. **What's the Question?** Tickets for a state swim meet are \$8.00 for adults and \$4.50 for children. Mr. and Mrs. Bulabi spent \$29.50 for tickets. The answer is 3.

41. **Reasoning** Would you expect $72.43 \div 25$ to be greater than or less than 3? Explain.

42. **WRITE Math** How is dividing a decimal by a whole number the same as dividing a whole number by a whole number? How is it different?

CD ROM Technology
Use Harcourt Mega Math, The Number Games, *Buggy Bargains,* Level M.

 Extra Practice on page 204, Set B

Learn About ALGEBRA Inverse Operations

You can use division to solve multiplication equations.

Example

Natalie bought 9 kickboards for her swimming class. She paid $71.55 altogether. What was the cost of one kickboard?

Let c = the cost of a kickboard.
$9 \times c = \$71.55$

Because multiplication and division are inverse operations, if $9 \times c = \$71.55$ then $\$71.55 \div 9 = c$.

$\$71.55 \div 9 = c$ Solve this equation.
$\$7.95 = c$

So, the cost of one kickboard is $7.95.

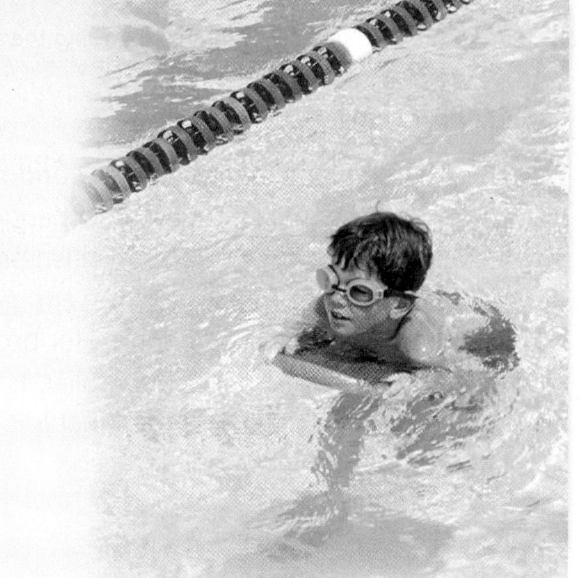

Try It

Use division to solve each equation.

43. $5 \times c = \$18.40$

44. $7 \times n = 16.8$

45. $3 \times a = 74.34$

Mixed Review and Test Prep

46. Which two class pets together received 10 votes? (Grade 4)

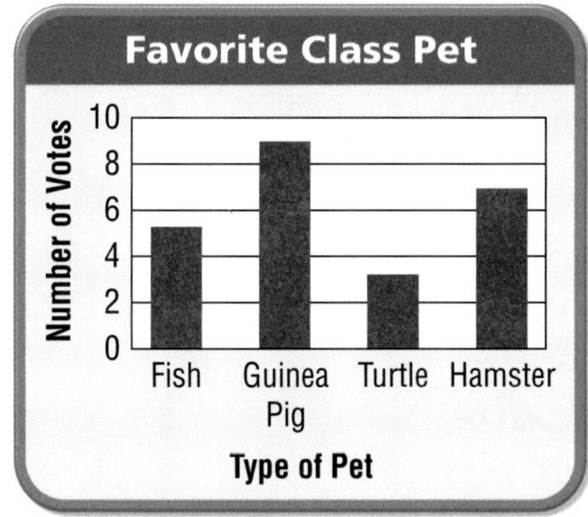

47. Nick ran 8.45 miles. Round this distance to the nearest tenth of a mile. (p. 150)

48. **Test Prep** Find $570.9 \div 33$.

A 0.0173 **C** 17.3

B 1.73 **D** 173

49. **Test Prep** Dan paid $40.00 for a monthly swimming pass. He swam 16 times that month. Which amount represents the cost of each swim?

A $0.25

B $2.50

C $25

D $250

Problem Solving Workshop
Skill: Evaluate Answers for Reasonableness

OBJECTIVE: Solve problems by using the skill *evaluate answers for reasonableness.*

Use the Skill

PROBLEM Jennifer's family went to London, England. Before going, the family members exchanged U.S. dollars for British pounds. They got 1.725 British pounds for every 3 U.S. dollars. Jennifer said the exchange rate was 1 U.S. dollar = 0.575 British pound. Her brother Jack said the exchange rate was 1 U.S. dollar = 0.0575 British pound. Whose statement was reasonable?

Jennifer	Jack
$3\overline{)1.725}$ = 0.575	$3\overline{)1.725}$ = 0.0575
−15	−15
22	22
−21	−21
15	15
−15	−15
0	0

Estimate $1.725 \div 3$.

Use compatible numbers to estimate. $1.8 \div 3 = 0.6$

Compare Jennifer's and Jack's numbers with the estimate. Jennifer's number, 0.575, is close to the estimate of 0.6. Jack's number, 0.0575, is not close to the estimate of 0.6. So, Jennifer's number is more reasonable.

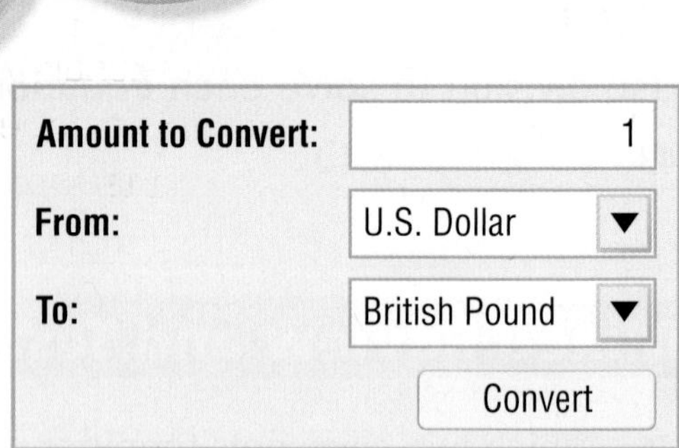

Many web sites offer a foreign exchange currency converter like the one shown here, which can convert U.S. dollars to more than 100 different foreign currencies.

Think and Discuss

Answer without doing the computation. Explain your reasoning.

a. Bob bought five identically priced books for \$14.75. He said the cost of one book was \$2.95. Is his statement reasonable?

b. Stella bought 3 bags of potting soil. Each bag weighs 0.79 kilogram. Stella said the total mass of the potting soil is 23.7 kilograms. Is her statement reasonable?

Guided Problem Solving Practice

1. Before going to Cancun, Mexico, Alan's family will exchange U.S. dollars for Mexican pesos. The exchange rate is 86.88 Mexican pesos for every 8 U.S. dollars. Alan says the exchange rate is 1 U.S. dollar = 1.086 Mexican pesos. His sister Ellen says the exchange rate is 1 U.S. dollar = 10.86 Mexican pesos. Whose statement is reasonable?

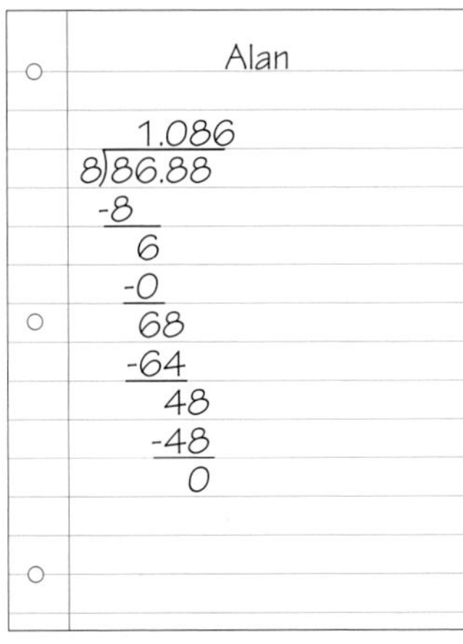

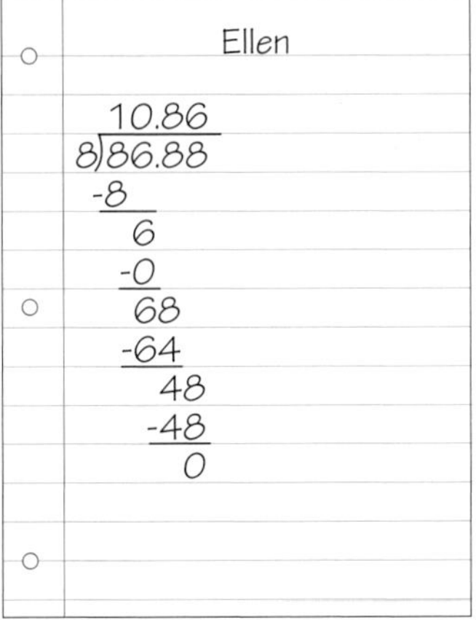

Divide using compatible numbers to estimate. What equation can you use to estimate the solution?

Compare Alan's statement with Ellen's statement. Whose number is closer to the estimate? Which statement is more reasonable?

2. **What if** Alan says the exchange rate is 1 U.S. dollar = 10.9 Mexican pesos and Ellen's statement stays the same? Whose statement is reasonable then?

3. Britney bought 0.97 kg of apples, 1.05 kg of bananas, and 0.57 kg of oranges. Britney says she bought 25.9 kg of fruit. Brad says that Britney bought 2.59 kg of fruit. Use estimation to find out whose statement is reasonable. **Explain.**

Mixed Applications

USE DATA For 4–7, use the table.

4. Tanesha says 1 U.S. dollar is equal to about 80 Hong Kong dollars. Andrew says 1 U.S. dollar is equal to about 8 Hong Kong dollars. Whose statement is reasonable? **Explain.**

5. George exchanged some U.S. currency for 23.568 in European euros. Then he traded the euros for 233.736 in Hong Kong dollars. How much did George exchange in U.S. dollars?

6. **Pose a Problem** Write a problem like Problem 4, using different numbers from the table.

7. **WRITE Math** George exchanged 5 U.S. dollars for some Japanese yen. **Explain** how you can find the number of yen George received.

Currency Exchange Rates (September 2006)

U.S. Dollars	Currency
2	2.691 Australian dollars
5	3.928 European euros
8	943.320 Japanese yen
12	321.281 Russian rubles
15	116.868 Hong Kong dollars

Extra Practice

Set A Find two estimates for the quotient. (pp. 196–197)

1. $2\overline{)33.08}$
2. $15\overline{)814.4}$
3. $22\overline{)545.15}$
4. $37\overline{)94.76}$

Use compatible numbers to estimate the quotient.

5. $75.2 \div 8$
6. $29.88 \div 6$
7. $15.41 \div 5$
8. $201.1 \div 68$
9. $637.5 \div 76$
10. $461.4 \div 6$
11. $611.2 \div 12$
12. $439.44 \div 11$
13. During a 5-day period, 6.2 inches of rain fell. Estimate the daily rainfall, if about the same amount of rain fell each day.
14. A bag of 12 apples costs $3.79. About how much does each apple cost?

Set B Copy the quotient and correctly place the decimal point. (pp. 198–201)

1. $\begin{array}{r} 132 \\ 3\overline{)39.6} \end{array}$
2. $\begin{array}{r} 0141 \\ 5\overline{)0.705} \end{array}$
3. $\begin{array}{r} 605 \\ 4\overline{)24.20} \end{array}$
4. $\begin{array}{r} 160 \\ 28\overline{)44.80} \end{array}$
5. $\begin{array}{r} 249 \\ 15\overline{)37.35} \end{array}$
6. $\begin{array}{r} 616 \\ 9\overline{)55.44} \end{array}$
7. $\begin{array}{r} 2220 \\ 13\overline{)288.60} \end{array}$
8. $\begin{array}{r} 0126 \\ 6\overline{)0.756} \end{array}$

Divide. Check by multiplying.

9. $24\overline{)4.008}$
10. $6\overline{)8.70}$
11. $24\overline{)42.48}$
12. $54\overline{)72.90}$
13. $6.24 \div 8$
14. $12.84 \div 6$
15. $9.65 \div 5$
16. $20.4 \div 68$
17. $21\overline{)9.072}$
18. $54.75 \div 5$
19. $15\overline{)105.75}$
20. $3.77 \div 2$
21. $7\overline{)0.049}$
22. $7\overline{)\$7.21}$
23. $14\overline{)70.56}$
24. $34\overline{)72.76}$
25. $5\overline{)5.25}$
26. $6\overline{)1.872}$
27. $9\overline{)\$45.36}$
28. $5\overline{)175.2}$
29. $453.84 \div 8$
30. $9.96 \div 12$
31. $\$5.28 \div 3$
32. $367.5 \div 30$
33. Melissa paid $6.24 for a box of 8 note cards. What was the price of each card?
34. Jason drove 54.6 miles in 1 hour. If he drove at a steady speed, how many miles did Jason drive each minute?

CD ROM **Technology**
Use Harcourt Mega Math, The Number Games, *Tiny's Think Tank*, Level S.

TECHNOLOGY CONNECTION

Calculator: Divide Decimals

On the balance beam in a gymnastics competition, Marti received a total of 50.58 points from 6 judges. Her official score was her point total divided by the number of judges. What was Marti's official score?

You can use a calculator to divide 50.58 by 6.

So, Marti's balance beam score was 8.43.

On the floor exercise, Marti received 47.075 points from 5 judges. What was Marti's score for the floor exercise? Divide 47.075 by 5.

9.415

So, Marti's official score for the floor exercise was 9.415.

Try It

Use a calculator to find the quotient.

1. 28.38 ÷ 6
2. 96.9 ÷ 40
3. 28.84 ÷ 14
4. 61.76 ÷ 32
5. 72.66 ÷ 21
6. 94.35 ÷ 25
7. 64.8 ÷ 72
8. 88.88 ÷ 64
9. 436.4 ÷ 16
10. 825.44 ÷ 44
11. 312.45 ÷ 50
12. 297.54 ÷ 38
13. 991.65 ÷ 601
14. 48.1 ÷ 65
15. 75.48 ÷ 444
16. 2.98 ÷ 80

17. Which results in a greater quotient, dividing 754.218 by 54, or dividing 864.64 by 64? **Explain** how you got your answer.

18. A crate of 24 bicycle helmets weighs 414.32 ounces. If the package includes 20 ounces of packing material, what is the weight of each helmet? **Explain** how you got your answer.

19. **Explore More** Michelle snowboarded down a 1.456-mile hill in 4.16 minutes. Using the formula, speed = distance ÷ time, **explain** how you could use a calculator to calculate her speed.

MATH POWER

Divide by Decimals

By the Box

At the warehouse club, Jeb bought a 7.5-pound bag of breakfast cereal. Into how many 1.5-pound boxes can he divide the cereal?

To solve the problem, you need to divide 7.5 by the decimal 1.5.

Remember

To divide by a decimal divisor:

- Make a whole-number divisor by moving the decimal point to the right.
- Move the decimal point in the divisor and dividend the same number of places to the right.

Examples

Divide 7.5 by 1.5.

Move the decimal point to the right to make a whole-number divisor.	$1.5\overline{)7.5}$
Move the decimal point in the dividend the same number of places.	$1.5\overline{)7.5}$
Place the decimal point for the quotient. Divide as you would normally.	$\begin{array}{r} 5. \\ 1.5\overline{)7.5} \\ \underline{-75} \\ 0 \end{array}$
So, Jeb will have 5 boxes.	

In some cases you need to add zeroes to the dividend.

Divide 2.8 by 0.35.

Move the decimal point to the right two places to create a whole-number divisor.	$.35\overline{)2.8}$
Move the decimal point in the dividend two places. Write in a zero.	$.35\overline{)2.80}$
Place the decimal point for the quotient and divide.	$\begin{array}{r} 8. \\ .35\overline{)2.80} \\ \underline{-280} \\ 0 \end{array}$

Try It

Find the quotient.

1. $0.7\overline{)4.2}$ **2.** $0.8\overline{)24.8}$ **3.** $2.4\overline{)19.2}$ **4.** $5.6\overline{)6.72}$

5. $0.44\overline{)0.088}$ **6.** $0.45\overline{)2.7}$ **7.** $0.16\overline{)32}$ **8.** $0.53\overline{)58.3}$

9. WRITE Math **Explain** why 0.8 divided by 0.4 has the same quotient as $8 \div 4$.

Chapter 8 Review/Test

Check Concepts

1. How can you use multiplication to check your answer when you divide decimals by whole numbers? KY Grade 6 (pp. 196–197)
2. What is the first step when you use paper and pencil to divide decimals by whole numbers? KY Grade 6 (pp. 198–201)

Check Skills

USE DATA For 3–7, use the table. KY Grade 6 (pp. 196–197)

Ski Lift Tickets		
Type of Ticket	**Cost**	**Days Used**
Weekend	\$145.50	Sat.–Sun.
Weekday	\$327.50	Mon.–Fri.
Weekly Pass	\$473.00	Sun.–Sat.

3. Estimate the cost of skiing per day on Saturday and Sunday.
4. How was the cost of a weekly pass calculated?
5. James said that it would cost him \$6.55 per day to ski each of the five days if he bought a weekday pass. Why is his answer incorrect?
6. What is the cost of skiing 1 weekday and 1 weekend day if the daily rate is same as the ticket amount divided by the number of days?
7. If the daily rate is the same as the ticket amount divided by the number of days, which is cheaper, skiing two weekdays and two weekend days, or skiing all five weekdays?

Copy the quotient and correctly place the decimal point. KY Grade 6 (pp. 198–201)

8. $\begin{array}{r}43\\3\overline{)12.9}\end{array}$ **9.** $\begin{array}{r}61\\7\overline{)42.7}\end{array}$ **10.** $\begin{array}{r}054\\6\overline{)3.24}\end{array}$ **11.** $\begin{array}{r}302\\12\overline{)36.24}\end{array}$ **12.** $\begin{array}{r}45\\17\overline{)76.5}\end{array}$

Divide. Check by multiplying. KY Grade 6 (pp. 198–201)

13. $5\overline{)8.35}$ **14.** $25\overline{)\$55.75}$ **15.** $6.24 \div 12$ **16.** $\$125.44 \div 32$ **17.** $247.5 \div 33$

Check Problem Solving

Solve. KY Grade 6 (pp. 202–203)

18. Lisa bought 6 medium cups of hot chocolate for a total of \$12.60. She said the cost of one cup was about \$2.10. Is her statement reasonable?
19. Mrs. Harris bought 4 bags of apples. The total weight of all of the bags was 7.8 pounds. Mrs. Harris estimated that each bag weighed about 3 pounds. Is her statement reasonable?
20. **WRITE Math** Mr. McHenry's class is going on a field trip. Mr. McHenry has collected a total of \$41.20 from 8 students. Matt said that each student turned in \$5.15. Is Matt's statement reasonable? **Explain.**

KENTUCKY Unit Review/Test
Chapters 5–8

Multiple Choice

1. Which pair of decimals is equivalent? KY MA-05-1.1.3 (p. 136)

   A. 3.11 and 3.011
   B. 8.9 and 8.90
   C. 53.6 and 536.0
   D. 12.07 and 12.007

2. The table shows the amount of rain, in millimeters, that fell during four different months.

Month	March	April	May	June
Rainfall (millimeters)	8.10	8.01	8.11	8.00

   Which month had the greatest rainfall? KY MA-05-1.1.3 (p. 138)

   A. March
   B. April
   C. May
   D. June

3. What is 38.452 rounded to the nearest tenth? KY MA-05-1.2.1 (p. 150)

   A. 38.4
   B. 38.45
   C. 38.5
   D. 40

4. For lunch, Jesse bought a sandwich for $3.25 and a fruit juice for $0.95. How much did he spend? KY MA-05-1.3.1 (p. 152)

   A. $3.10 C. $4.10
   B. $3.20 D. $4.20

5. Carlotta is hiking a trail that is 3.2 miles long. She already has hiked 2.7 miles. How much farther does Carlotta have to hike? KY MA-05-1.3.1 (p. 152)

   A. 0.5 miles C. 1.9 miles
   B. 0.7 miles D. 5.9 miles

6. Round 0.493 to the nearest tenth. KY MA-05-1.2.1 (p. 132)

   A. 10
   B. 1
   C. 0.5
   D. 0.49

7. Which of the following is the *best* estimate for 5.24×0.82? KY MA-05-1.2.1 (p. 178)

   A. 0.4 C. 40
   B. 4 D. 400

8. Which of the letters represents 2.4 on the number line? KY MA-05-1.1.1 (p. 132)

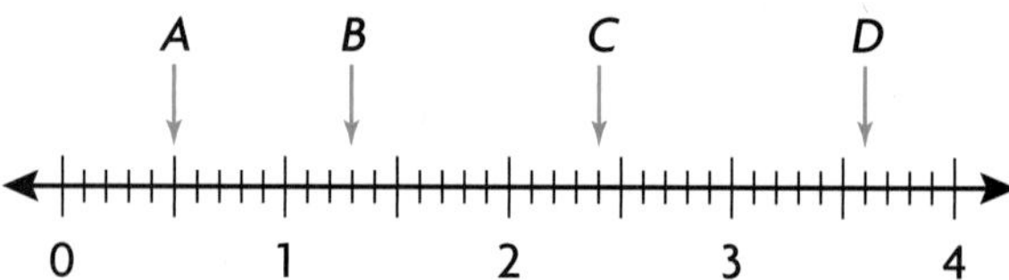

   A. A C. C
   B. B D. D

GO ONLINE Technology Use *Online Assessment.*

9. Carmen has five boxes to send to her brother in Radcliff, KY. Each one weighs the same amount. Together, the weight of the boxes is 30 pounds. Using the equation $5 \times b = 30$, what does b stand for in the equation? KY MA-05-5.3.1 (p. 108)

   A. weight of all the boxes

   B. weight of one box

   C. number of boxes

   D. number of labels

10. A day camp in Ashland has 360 campers. Each counselor will have a group of 17 campers. About how many counselors will the camp need? KY MA-05-1.2.1 (p. 72)

    A. 2

    B. 20

    C. 30

    D. 50

11. On Saturday, 39,138 fans attended a University of Kentucky basketball game. On Sunday, 34,722 fans attended a game. Which shows about how many more fans attended the Saturday game than the Sunday game? KY MA-05-1.2.1 (p. 16)

    A. about 8,000

    B. about 6,000

    C. about 4,000

    D. about 2,000

12. Mrs. DaVinci has a sticker sheet with 360 different stickers. She gives an equal number of stickers to each of the 15 students in her class. How many stickers will each student receive? KY MA-05-1.3.1 (p. 74)

    A. 375

    B. 345

    C. 26

    D. 24

Open Response WRITE Math

13. A small wedge of cheese costs $3.95. About how much does the whole wheel of cheese cost? Show your work. KY MA-05-1.2.1 (p. 178)

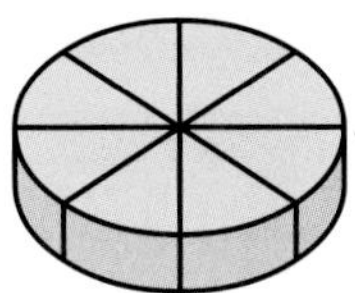

14. Simon caught fish in the tournament weighing 2.11 kg and 3.07 kg. Andrew caught fish weighing 2.56 kg and 2.87 kg. **Explain** how to find whose fish weighed more. KY MA-05-1.3.1 (p. 152)

15. Matt has a strawberry patch with 104 rows. He counted the first row and found 198 strawberries. What is the best estimate of the total number of strawberries in Matt's strawberry patch? **Explain** the method you used to solve this problem. KY MA-05-1.2.1 (p. 38)

THE WORLD ALMANAC FOR KIDS

The Olympics

The World's Fastest Runners

Every 4 years the world's fastest runners gather to compete in track events at the Summer Olympic Games. In most sports, the winners are the athletes with the highest scores. However, in track, runners try for the lowest number, which is the fastest time.

FACT · ACTIVITY

Olympic Times for the 400-Meter Run

Year	Gold Medalist	Country	Time in seconds
1968	Lee Evans	United States	43.86
1972	Vincent Matthews	United States	44.66
1976	Alberto Juantorena	Cuba	44.26
1980	Viktor Markin	USSR	44.60
1984	Alonzo Babers	United States	44.27
1988	Steven Lewis	United States	43.87
1992	Quincy Watts	United States	43.50
1996	Michael Johnson	United States	43.49
2000	Michael Johnson	United States	43.84
2004	Jeremy Wariner	United States	44.00

Use the table to answer the questions.

1. Who had the fastest 400-meter run?
2. How much faster was the fastest time than the slowest time?
3. What was the difference between Viktor Markin's time and Alberto Juantorena's time?
4. Between which two consecutive Olympic Games did the times increase the most?
5. Who ran faster, Lee Evans or Jeremy Wariner? How much faster?
6. **Pose a Problem** Write a problem like Problem 3 to compare two runners' times.

ALMANAC Fact

Summer Olympics 2004
Host City: Athens, Greece
Opening date: Aug. 13, 2004
Closing date: Aug. 29, 2004
Nations: 201
Athletes: 11,099
301 events in 28 sports

Running Long Distances

The marathon long-distance race, as we know it today, is based on a Greek legend. Pheidippides (fī • dip'ə • dēz'), a soldier, ran without stopping from the city of Marathon, Greece, to Athens, Greece. He was bringing news of the Athenian army's victory over Persia in the battle of Marathon.

Today, the Athens Marathon uses the same trail that Pheidippides ran. The race ends at the ancient Olympic stadium.

FACT • ACTIVITY

A marathon is about 26 miles long. The map shows the Athens Marathon.

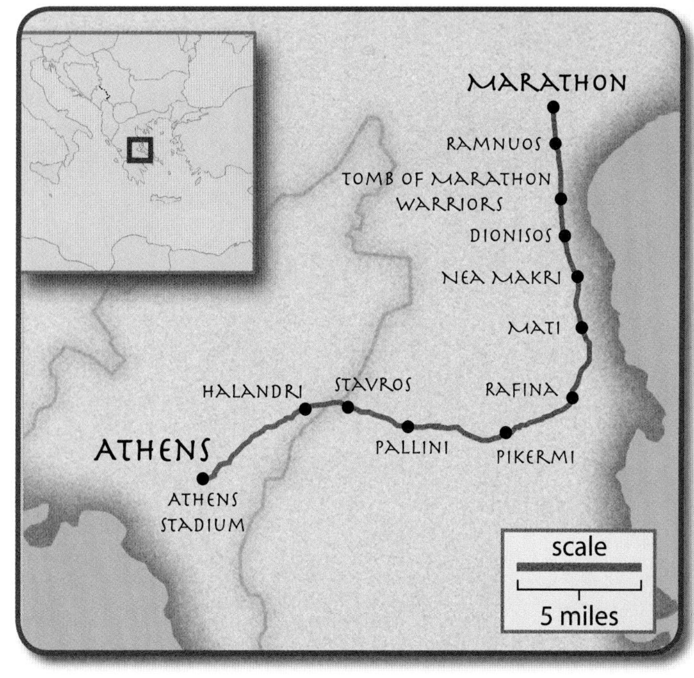

1. Use a map to help you design your own marathon route.
   - Find a town or city that is about 26 miles from where you live.
   - Draw a map of your marathon route. Place a mark every 5 miles.
2. A marathoner who completes the race in 4 hours runs 1 mile in 9.2 minutes. During a race, the runner should stop at a water station about every 30 minutes.
   - About how many miles can the runner race before he or she needs to stop for water?
   - How many water stations will you have on your route? Explain and show them on your map.
   - Place four first-aid stations on your route. How many miles are between each first aid station?

UNIT 3

Data and Graphing

Math on Location

with
Chapter Projects

1

Meteorology is the study of weather and climate. Data on the number of strikes of lightning are recorded.

2

Equipment used to collect data is moved by truck to locations where storms or tornadoes might occur.

3

Data from thousands of weather stations are collected and represented in many graphical forms.

VOCABULARY POWER

TALK Math

What math ideas are used in the **Math on Location**? What kinds of data could you collect at a weather station? How would you display this data?

READ Math

REVIEW VOCABULARY You will learn the words below when you learn about collecting and displaying data. How do these words relate to **Math on Location**?

mean the average of a set of data

line graph a graph that uses line segments to show how data change over time

circle graph a graph that shows how parts of the data are related to the whole and to each other

WRITE Math

Copy and complete a match graphic like the one below. Use what you know about graphs to match the name of a graph to the drawing that looks most like it.

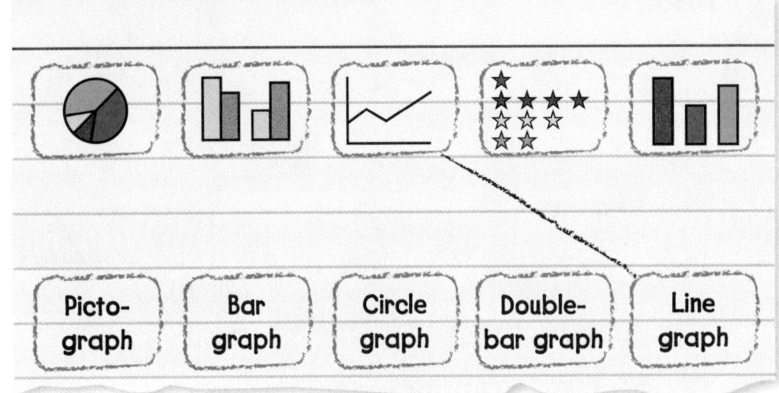

Technology
Multimedia Math Glossary link at
www.harcourtschool.com/hspmath

CHAPTER 9

Data and Statistics

FAST FACT

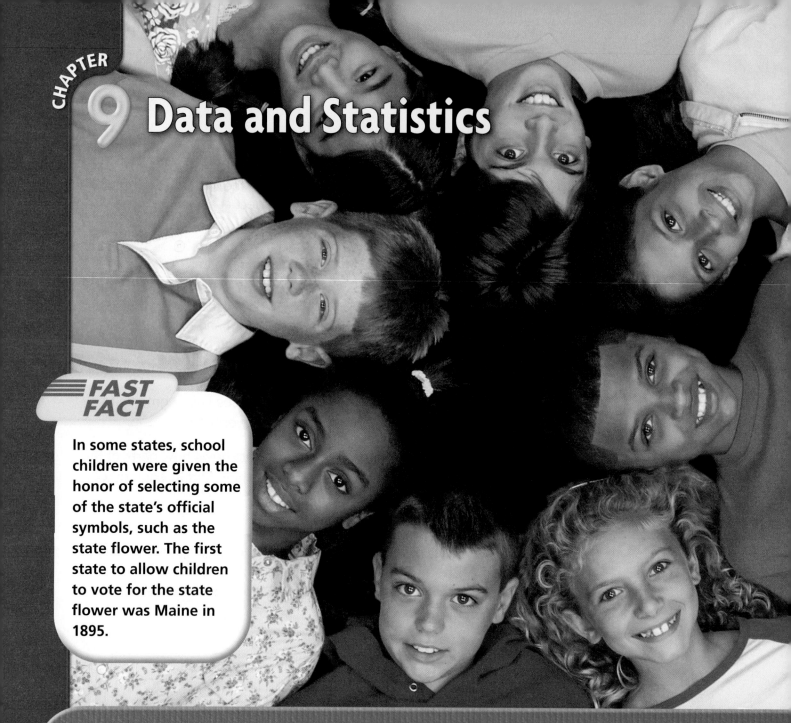

In some states, school children were given the honor of selecting some of the state's official symbols, such as the state flower. The first state to allow children to vote for the state flower was Maine in 1895.

Investigate

The three tables show the results of school children voting for the state flower in Mississippi, West Virginia, and Wisconsin. Compare the data for the votes in two of the states using either mean or median.

Wisconsin	
Flower	**Number of Votes**
Arbutus	27,068
Rose	31,024
Violet	67,178
White water lily	22,648

West Virginia	
Flower	**Number of Votes**
Goldenrod	3,162
Honeysuckle	3,663
Big laurel	19,131
Wild rose	3,387

Mississippi	
Flower	**Number of Votes**
Cape jasmine	2,484
Cotton blossom	4,171
Magnolia	12,745

Technology
Student pages are available in the Student eBook.

Show What You Know

Check your understanding of important skills needed for success in Chapter 9.

▶ Read Bar Graphs

For 1–3, use the bar graph.

1. List the endangered species in order from greatest to least.
2. Estimate the total number of endangered species in 2006.
3. Which type of animal had more endangered species, birds or reptiles? How many more endangered species did it have?

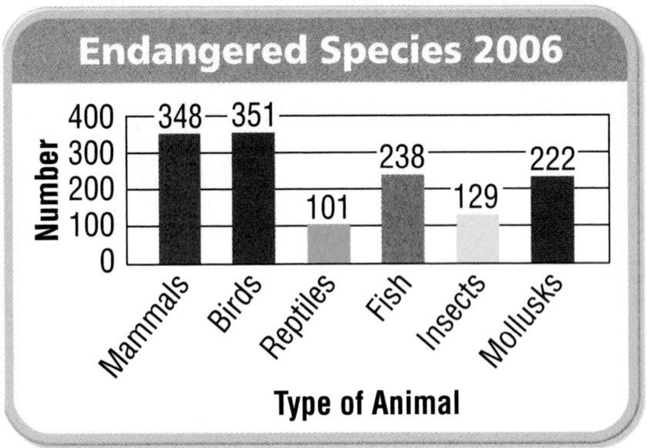

▶ Read Frequency Tables

For 4–6, use the frequency table.

4. Which bird has the greatest frequency?
5. What is the total number of birds shown in the data?
6. What is the difference between the number of Starlings and the number of Woodpeckers?

Bird Watching

Type of Bird	Frequency
Starling	18
Finch	9
Woodpecker	5
Warbler	13

VOCABULARY POWER

CHAPTER VOCABULARY

bar graph
circle graph
frequency table
line graph
line plot
mean
median
mode
outlier
pictograph
population
range
random sample
sample
survey
trend

WARM-UP WORDS

mean the average of a set of data

survey a method of gathering information about a group

trend a pattern over time, in all or part of a graph, in which the data increase, decrease, or stay the same

LESSON 1 Collect and Organize Data

OBJECTIVE: Collect data by using surveys and organize data in tables and line plots.

Quick Review

1. 18 + 9
2. 22 + 45
3. 350 + 120
4. 90 − 65
5. 275 − 150

Vocabulary

survey, sample, population, random sample, frequency table, line plot, range, outlier

Learn

Many states have state flowers, state birds, and state trees. Some states have state animals. Suppose you want to find what state animal Minnesota residents would choose.

You can use a **survey** to gather information about a group. Often, a part of the group, called a **sample**, is chosen to represent the whole group, or **population**.

A sample must represent the population fairly. In a **random sample**, each person in the population has an equal chance of being chosen.

▲ Lady Slipper Orchid

Example 1

Suppose a marketing company is hired to find which animal most residents of Minnesota would choose for a state animal. Which random sample best represents the population?

a 100 children	**b** 100 men
c 100 adults in southern Minnesota	**d** 100 Minnesota residents in different parts of the state

Choice **d** is the only one that represents the population fairly. Every Minnesota resident would have an equal chance of being selected.

Activity

Write a survey and collect data.

A Choose a topic to investigate. Select one of the following topics: pets, homework, or games.

B Decide what population you want to survey. How can you choose a random sample that is fair?

C Write a survey question. The question should be clear, easy to understand, and require only a single response.

D Make a recording sheet. Be sure to include your survey question so that you ask each person the same question. Survey a random sample of at least 25 students.

Pet Survey
How many pets do you have?

Number of Pets	Tally
0	𝍸 III
1	𝍸 II
2	𝍸 IIII
3	
4	
5	I

Shows that 7 people have one pet.

FAST TRACK KY MA-05-4.1.1 Students will analyze and make inferences from data displays (drawings, tables/charts, tally tables, pictographs, bar graphs, circle graphs, line plots, Venn diagrams, line graphs). DOK 3 *also MA-05-4.1.2;* **MA-05-4.1.3;** *MA-05-4.3.1*

Organizing Data

A **frequency table** shows the total for each category or group.

Example 2 Organize data in a frequency table.

Count by 5s in the tally table below to find each frequency.

Survey Question: Which animal would you choose as Minnesota's state animal—badger, mink, red fox, or river otter?

Minnesota State Animal	
Badger	HHT HHT HHT HHT HHT HHT HHT HHT HHT
Mink	HHT HHT HHT HHT HHT I
Red fox	HHT HHT HHT HHT HHT IIII
River otter	HHT HHT HHT HHT HHT

Minnesota State Animal Survey	
Animal	**Frequency**
Badger	45
Mink	26
Red fox	29
River otter	25

In the frequency table, the frequency shows the total for each type of animal.

A **line plot** gives you a visual picture of the data and can also be used to identify the range and any outliers. The **range** is the difference between the greatest number and the least number in a set of data. An **outlier** is a value that is separated from the rest of the data.

Example 3 Organize the pet survey data in a line plot. Find the range of the number of pets.

Pet Survey	
Number of Pets	**Frequency**
0	8
1	7
2	9
3	0
4	0
5	1

Step 1

Draw a number line from 0 to 5. Include a title. Graph an X for each response in the frequency table.

Step 2

Find the range. The greatest number of pets is 5. The least number of pets is 0.

So, the range is 5 − 0, or 5.

5 is an outlier since it is separated from the rest of the data.

Guided Practice

1. Complete the table. Find the missing frequencies.

Favorite Flower		
Type of Flower	**Tally**	**Frequency**
Rose	HHT HHT HHT HHT HHT HHT HHT III	■
Tulip	HHT HHT HHT I	■

A fruit juice company wants to survey children ages 10–14. Tell whether each sample represents the population. If it does not, explain.

2. a random sample of 100 children
3. a random sample of 100 children, ages 10–14
4. a random sample of 100 children at one school

5. TALK Math **Explain** how you could collect and organize data about choosing a mascot for a new school.

Independent Practice and Problem Solving

A toy company wants to find out if children ages 8–12 like the company's new action figures. Tell whether each sample represents the population. If it does not, explain.

6. a random sample of 300 girls, ages 8–12
7. a random sample of 300 adults
8. a random sample of 300 children, ages 8–12

Make a line plot. Find the range of hours.

9.

Homework Survey	
Number of Hours	**Frequency**
1	8
2	16
3	4
4	2

10.

Weekly Activity Survey	
Number of Hours	**Frequency**
1	3
2	9
3	10
4	12

For 11–14, use the tally table.

11. Make a frequency table of the data.
12. Which state bird has the greatest frequency?
13. What is the range of the data?
14. WRITE Math **What's the Question?** Twenty-one states have either a cardinal, western meadowlark, mockingbird, or robin as their state bird.

Most Common State Birds	
Bird	**Number of States**
Cardinal	卌 ||
Western Meadowlark	卌 |
Mockingbird	卌
Robin	|||

Mixed Review and Test Prep

15. Kurt bought 3 cans of soup for $5.07. How much did each can cost? (p. 180)
16. Find the quotient of 921 ÷ 3. (p. 62)
17. **Test Prep** Karen swam 20, 25, 17, 32, and 15 laps. Which is the range of the data?

A 5 **B** 10 **C** 17 **D** 22

 Extra Practice on page 234, Set A

Write a Conclusion

The northern cardinal is the most common choice of state bird. It can be spotted from Minnesota, South Dakota, and Maine southward through southern Florida. Barry used the data in the table to write a conclusion about the number of northern cardinals.

Northern Cardinals Counted

State	Frequency
California	2
Minnesota	1,318
Ohio	10,081
Pennsylvania	8,698
Texas	11,723

- First, I looked at the data in the table. The table shows the number of northern cardinals people counted in California, Minnesota, Ohio, Pennsylvania, and Texas.
- Next, I ordered the data in the table from least to greatest.

  2 ← least
  1,318
  8,698
  10,081
  11,723 ← greatest

- Last, I wrote a conclusion.

My Conclusion: Of the states listed, I would be most likely to see a northern cardinal in either Texas or Ohio.

Tips

- Review the data and any other related information you know.
- Look for relationships in the data.
- Then write a conclusion based on what you can infer from the data.

Problem Solving **For 1–2, use the data shown on the map.**

1. Write a conclusion about the number of northern cardinals in western states compared to eastern states.
2. Write a conclusion about the states that have the least number of northern cardinals counted.

2005 Northern Cardinal Bird Count

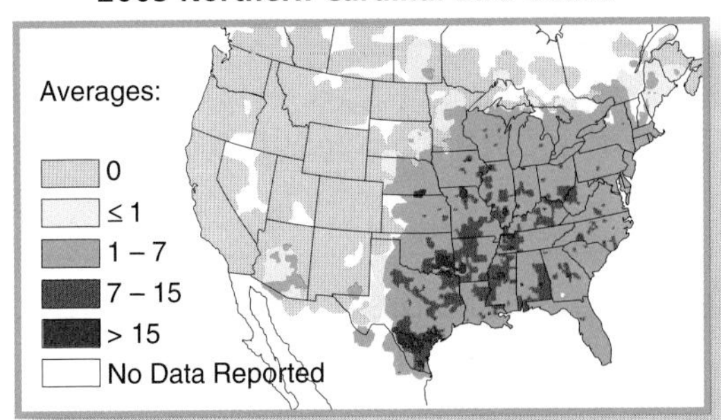

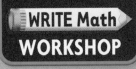

LESSON 2

Mean, Median, and Mode

OBJECTIVE: Describe data using the mean, median, and mode.

Quick Review

1. 80 ÷ 4
2. 120 ÷ 3
3. 49 ÷ 7
4. 144 ÷ 6
5. 72 ÷ 8

Vocabulary

mean

median

mode

Learn

PROBLEM The Little League World Series is held in Williamsport, Pennsylvania. What are the mean, median, and mode for the number of runs the West O'ahu team scored?

The **mean** is the average of a set of data.

Example 1

A Find the mean.

Step 1

Add to find the total number of runs.

7 + 7 + 10 + 2 + 6 = 32

Step 2

Divide the sum by the number of addends.

32 ÷ 5 = 6.4

So, the mean is 6.4 runs.

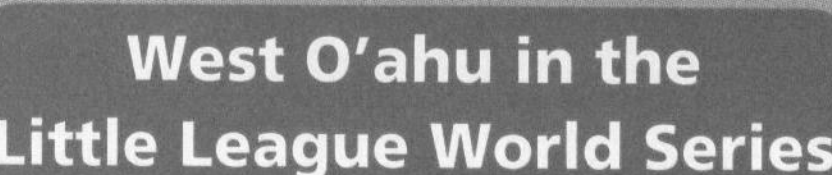

West O'ahu in the Little League World Series

Game	Number of Runs
1	7
2	7
3	10
4	2
5	6

▲ Little League World Series

The **median** is the middle number when a set of data is arranged in order.

B Find the median.

Step 1

Order the data from least to greatest.

2, 6, 7, 7, 10

Step 2

Find the middle number.

2, 6, 7, 7, 10

So, the median is 7 runs.

Math Idea

When there are two middle numbers, the median is the mean of those two numbers.

The **mode** is the number that occurs most often in a set of data. There may be one mode, more than one mode, or no mode at all.

C Find the mode.

Step 1

Order the data from least to greatest.

2, 6, 7, 7, 10

Step 2

Find the number that occurs most often.

2, 6, 7, 7, 10

The number 7 occurs twice. So, the mode is 7 runs.

KY MA-05-4.2.1 Students will determine and apply the mean, median, mode and range of a set of data. DOK 2 *also* MA-05-4.1.1

You can use a calculator to find the mean.

Example 2 **Use a calculator to find the mean.**

Find the mean for the following set of data: 6.8, 3.2, 7.9, 5.4, 3.2

So, the mean is 5.3.

You can find the mean, median, and mode for data shown on a graph.

Example 3 **Find the mean, median, and mode.**

Mean: $16 + 12 + 13 + 15 + 16 + 18 + 10 + 18 + 20 + 14 = 152$

$152 \div 10 = 15.2$

So, the mean is 15.2 runs.

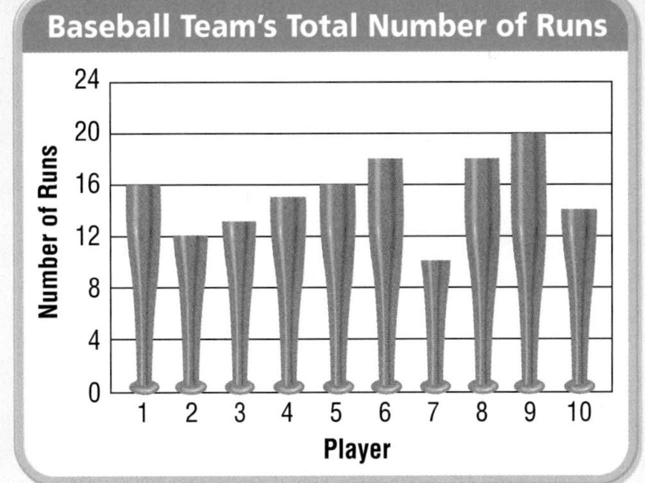

Median: 10, 12, 13, 14, 15, 16, 16, 18, 18, 20

↑

The median is between 15 and 16.

$(15 + 16) \div 2 = 15.5$

So, the median is 15.5 runs.

Mode: 10, 12, 13, 14, 15, 16, 16, 18, 18, 20

16 and 18 occur most often.

So, the modes are 16 runs and 18 runs.

More Examples

A Find the mean.

5.8, 4.2, 3.6, 3.8, 6.1, 2.6

$5.8 + 4.2 + 3.6 + 3.8 + 6.1 + 2.6 = 26.1$

$26.1 \div 6 = 4.35$ ← mean

B Find the median.

10, 4, 11, 4, 13, 12

Order the data.

4, 4, 10, 11, 12, 13

Add the two middle numbers. Then divide by 2.

$(10 + 11) \div 2 = 10.5$ ← median

C Find the mode.

13, 10, 12, 16, 11

Order the data.

10, 11, 12, 13, 16

No number occurs more than once, so there is no mode.

Guided Practice

1. Copy and complete the steps shown to find the mean of 12, 8, 15, and 9. Then explain each step.

Step 1: $12 + 8 + 15 + 9 = 44$

Step 2: $44 \div 4 = ■$

Find the mean, median, and mode for each set of data.

2. 19, 27, 32, 27
3. \$45, \$10, \$79, \$93, \$23
4. 8, 8, 14, 5, 38, 5
5. 8.7, 7.5, 7.4, 7.4, 9.2
6. 98, 87, 90, 93, 76, 87
7. 0.92, 0.52, 0.48, 0.85, 0.78
8. TALK Math **Explain** what the mean, median, and mode represent for a set of data.

Independent Practice and Problem Solving

Find the mean, median, and mode for each set of data.

9. 12, 8, 7, 10, 8
10. \$24, \$13, \$26, \$13
11. 64, 82, 70, 64
12. 680; 1,080; 499
13. 207, 316, 127, 119, 316
14. 11.2, 9.3, 10.3, 10.3, 2.9
15. 112, 130, 121, 109, 125
16. 12, 10, 7, 8, 6, 5, 15
17. 8.2, 7.9, 5, 4.2, 7.7, 6
18. 1.1, 1.09, 1.36, 1.2, 1.2
19. 524, 913, 499, 831
20. 18, 36, 29, 36, 27, 18, 32

Algebra Use the given mean to find the missing number in each data set.

21. 5, 10, 13, ■; mean: 9
22. \$16, \$24, ■; mean: \$17
23. 11, 14, 11, 20, ■; mean: 14

For 24–27, use the graph.

24. What is the mean number of wins for the top World Series teams?
25. What are the median and mode of the number of wins?
26. How many more wins have the New York Yankees had in the World Series than the Boston Red Sox?
27. **Reasoning** The Cincinnati Reds are ranked sixth with 5 wins in the World Series. Suppose you added the Cincinnati Reds' wins to the graph. How would the mean, median, and mode change?

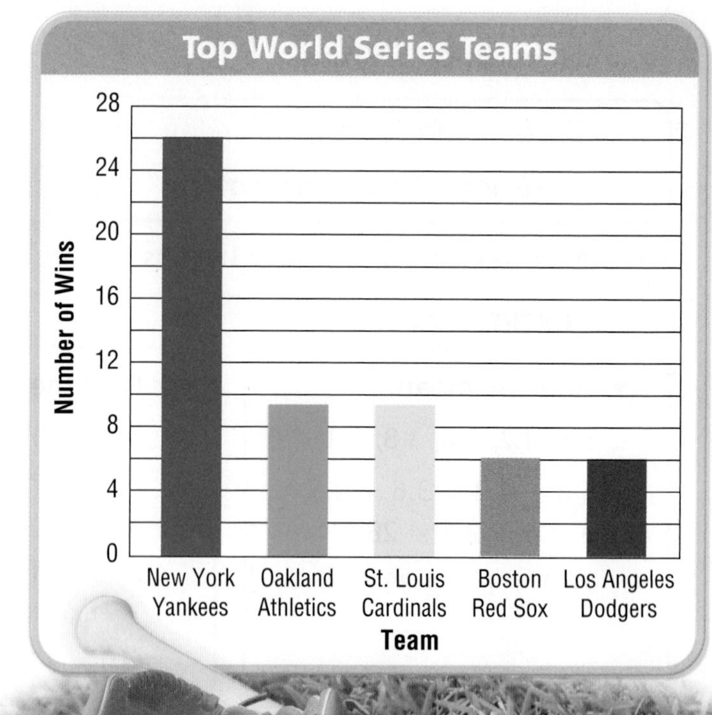

28. The admission to the National Baseball Hall of Fame museum is \$18.50 for adults and \$5.00 for children ages 7 to 12. What is the mean cost for 4 teachers and 50 fifth-grade students to visit the museum?
29. WRITE Math **What's the Error?** Lindsey said the median of 8, 3, 6, and 8 is 8. Find the median. What is Lindsey's error?

Extra Practice on page 234, Set B

Learn About The Most Useful Description of Data

This table shows the eight United States cities with the largest populations, based on the 2000 census.

Find the range, mode, median, and mean for the data. Which is most useful to describe the data? Explain.

A line plot can help you find the mode and the median.

Eight Largest Cities in the United States			
City	Population (in millions)	City	Population (in millions)
Chicago, IL	2.9	New York, NY	8.0
Dallas, TX	1.2	Philadelphia, PA	1.5
Houston, TX	2.0	Phoenix, AZ	1.3
Los Angeles, CA	3.7	San Diego, CA	1.2

Example

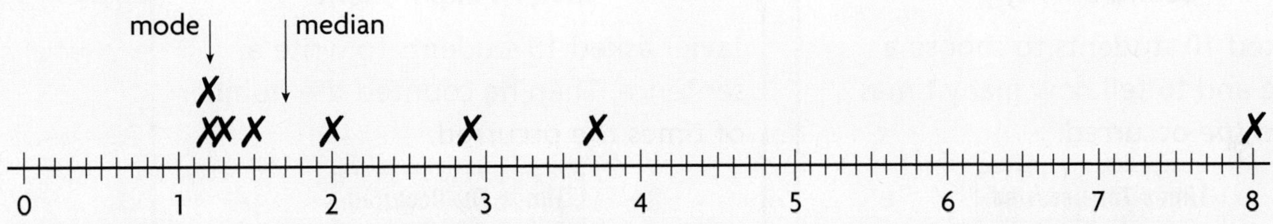

range: 8.0 − 1.2 = 6.8	mode: 1.2	median: (1.5 + 2.0) ÷ 2 = 1.75
The range is the difference between the greatest and least numbers. It is *not* useful to describe data.	The mode is the smallest population, so it is *not* the most useful to describe the data.	Most of the populations are closest to the median, so the median is most useful to describe the data.

mean: 2.9 + 1.2 + 2.0 + 3.7 + 8.0 + 1.5 + 1.3 + 1.2 = 21.9   21.8 ÷ 8 = 2.7

New York's population is an outlier which distorts the mean, so the mean is *not* the most useful to describe the data.

Try It

Find the range, mode, median, and mean. Tell which measure or measures are most useful to describe the data. Explain.

30. \$125, \$42, \$35, \$37, \$35, \$41

31. 9.5, 7.0, 5.4, 6.3, 9.5, 6.0, 6.7

Mixed Review and Test Prep

32. 3.7 × 8,920 = ▆ (p. 180)

33. What is the value of the expression $(28 \div r) \times 16$ for $r = 7$? (p. 96)

34. Test Prep What is the median for the set of data? 52, 22, 52, 30, 29

A 52 **B** 35 **C** 37 **D** 30

LESSON 3

Compare Data

OBJECTIVE: Compare two or more sets of data.

Quick Review

Find the median for each set of data.

1. 12, 8, 15, 21, 17
2. 7.5, 9.2, 8.6, 7.9, 9.5
3. 5, 5, 5, 9, 3
4. 32, 41, 37, 45
5. 4.2, 6.9, 5.3, 4.7

Learn

PROBLEM The word used most often in English is *the*. Leah and Javier collected data on the number of times the word *the* occurs. Are Leah's and Javier's results similar? To compare their data, you can calculate the mean.

Example 1

Leah's Survey

Leah asked 10 students to choose a sentence and to tell how many times the word *the* occurred.

Times *The* Occurred				
2	3	4	3	1
4	2	4	4	0

Mean: $27 \div 10 = 2.7$
The mean is 2.7 times.

Javier's Experiment

Javier asked 15 students to write a sentence. Then he counted the number of times *the* occurred.

Times *The* Occurred				
1	1	3	4	3
2	3	1	0	5
3	4	5	2	2

Mean: $39 \div 15 = 2.6$
The mean is 2.6 times.

The means for the two sets of data are similar.
So, Leah's and Javier's results are similar.

You can compare two sets of data by calculating the range and median.

Example 2 **The line plots below show the results from two battery experiments. Are the results similar?**

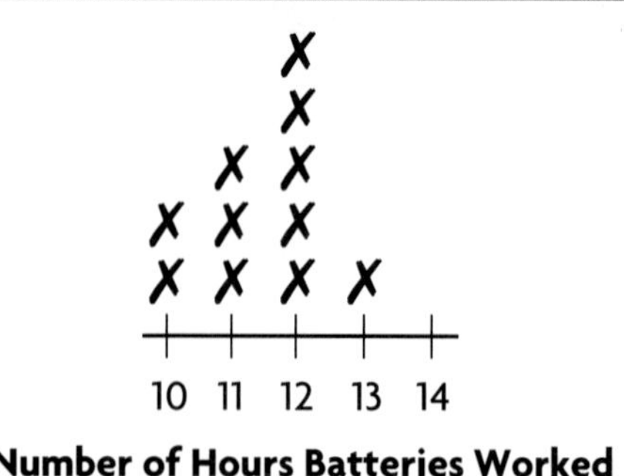

Number of Hours Batteries Worked

Range: 3 hours **Median:** 12 hours

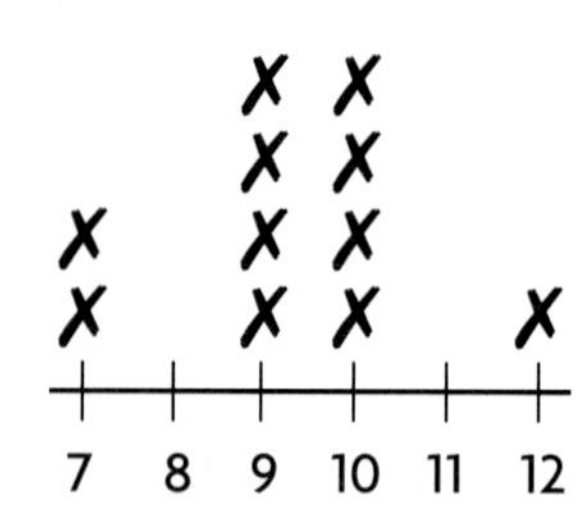

Number of Hours Batteries Worked

Range: 5 hours **Median:** 9 hours

The range and the median for the two sets of data are different.
So, the results from the battery experiments are not similar.

FAST TRACK

KY MA-05-4.1.1 Students will analyze and make inferences from data displays (drawings, tables/charts, tally tables, pictographs, bar graphs, circle graphs, line plots, Venn diagrams, line graphs). DOK 3 *also* MA-05-4.2.1; *MA-05-4.3.1*

Guided Practice

1. Jane collected data about the number of hours her classmates spent on homework. Mark collected the same type of data from his classmates. Explain how the medians from their results compare.

- **Jane's data: Median is 2.5 hours.**
- **Mark's data: Median is 1.25 hours.**

Compare the mean, median, and range of the data sets.

2.

A: Pages Students Read					
43	10	68	65	31	12
79	24	52	52	68	69

B: Pages Students Read					
32	53	68	12	52	37
15	72	60	52	22	68

3. TALK Math **Explain** how mean, median, and range help you compare two similar sets of data.

Independent Practice and Problem Solving

Compare the mean, median, and range of the data sets.

4.

A: Weights of Backpacks (pounds)							
0	3	1	8	3	2	8	1
5	4	2	2	3	4	0	0

B: Weights of Backpacks (pounds)						
2	9	8	10	9	4	5
10	2	7	10	6	10	6

For 5–6, use the double-bar graph.

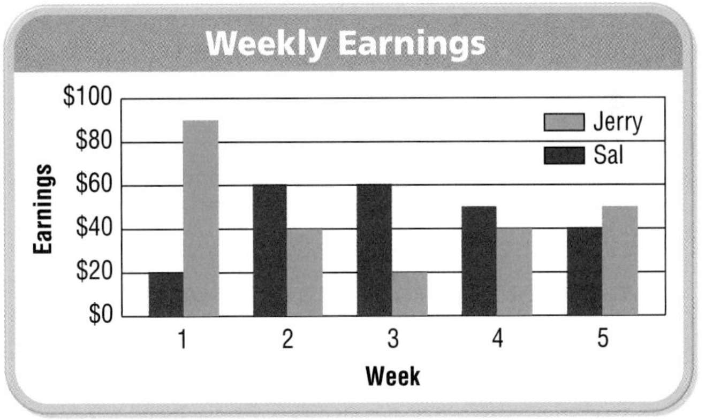

5. How do the ranges of the weekly earnings compare for Sal and Jerry?

6. **What if** Jerry got a bonus of $30 in week 3? How would the median for these sets of data compare then?

7. WRITE Math Explain why using the mean, median, mode, or range makes it easier to compare two sets of data.

Mixed Review and Test Prep

8. Mrs. Ricci is designing a garden in the shape of a circle. The diameter is 56 feet. What is the radius? (Grade 4)

9. Serena buys 6 yards of fabric for $35.79. About how much does one yard of fabric cost? (p. 198)

10. **Test Prep** Which shows how the median scores for the sets of data compare?

Bowling Team 1 Scores			
110	250	98	136

Bowling Team 2 Scores			
103	99	158	146

A $101 < 123$

B $123 < 123.5$

C $124.5 > 123.5$

D $124.5 > 123$

Extra Practice on page 234, Set C

Analyze Graphs

OBJECTIVE: Read, interpret, and analyze the data in graphs.

Quick Review

Write < or > for each ●.

1. 34 ● 48
2. 16 ● 19
3. 73 ● 71
4. 84 ● 121
5. 109 ● 98

Vocabulary

pictograph **bar graph**
circle graph **line graph**
trend

Learn

When you analyze graphs, you can answer questions, draw conclusions, and make predictions about the data.

A **pictograph** displays countable data with symbols or pictures. A key shows how many each symbol or picture represents.

2004–2005 Baseball Wins

UNC Wilmington	⚾ ⚾ ⚾ ⚾
UNLV	⚾ ⚾ ⚾ ◖
Georgia Tech	⚾ ⚾ ⚾ ⚾ ◖
George Mason	⚾ ⚾ ⚾ ◖
Key: ⚾ = 10 wins	

How many games did Georgia Tech win?

This key shows that each symbol represents 10 wins. A half symbol represents 5 wins.

For Georgia Tech, it shows ⚾ ⚾ ⚾ ⚾ ◖: $(4 \times 10) + 5 = 45$.

So, Georgia Tech had 45 wins.

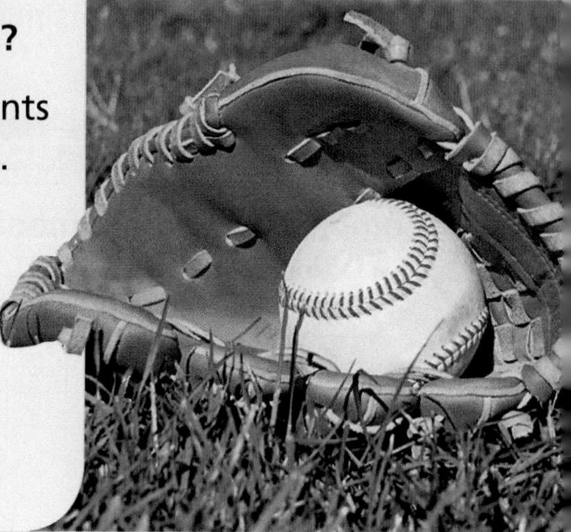

A **bar graph** uses horizontal or vertical bars to display countable data. You can use bar graphs to compare data. The graph below is a double-bar graph.

Which women's basketball team won the most games? Which men's team won the most games?

Look at the key. The different-colored bars represent the men's and women's basketball teams.

For the women, the longest bar is above the label for Michigan State. It shows that this team won 33 games.

For the men, the longest bar is for Duke. It shows that this team won 27 games.

So, Michigan State won the most women's games and Duke won the most men's games in the 2004–2005 season.

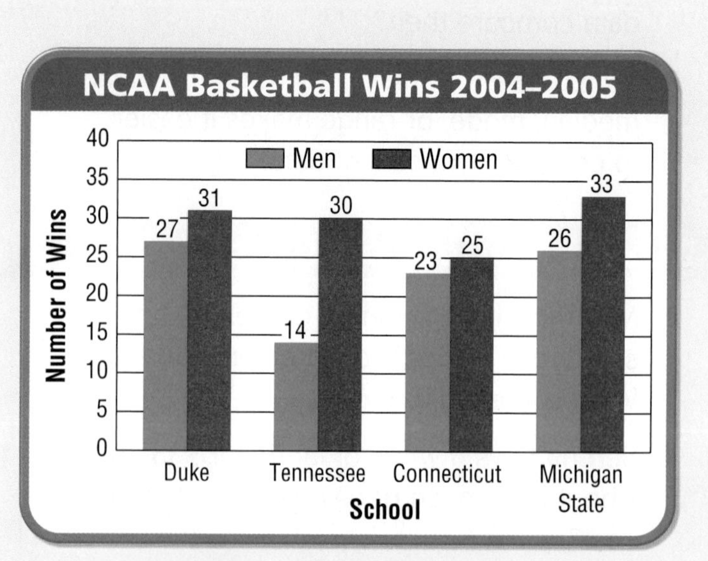

FAST TRACK

KY MA-05-4.1.1 Students will analyze and make inferences from data displays (drawings, tables/charts, tally tables, pictographs, bar graphs, circle graphs, line plots, Venn diagrams, line graphs). DOK 3 *also MA-05-4.3.1*

A **circle graph** shows how parts of the data are related to the whole and to each other.

How does the amount of time Eric spends swimming compare to the total time of his workout?

The circle graph represents the whole set of data. Each section in the circle graph represents a part of the whole.

Find the part of the circle graph that represents swimming. Eric swims for 1 hour.

The entire workout is 1 + 2 + 1 + 1, or 5 hours.

So, Eric spends 1 hour out of 5 hours, or $\frac{1}{5}$ of his workout swimming.

A **line graph** uses line segments to show how data change over time. A line graph may show a trend. A **trend** is a pattern over time, in all or part of a graph, in which the data increase, decrease, or stay the same.

How long will it take Sarah to run 5 miles?

To identify a trend, look at the direction of the line from one point to the next.

- If the line is going up from one point to the next, the pattern is increasing.
- If the line is going down from one point to the next, the pattern is decreasing.

The general pattern shown by the graph is increasing.

So, if the trend continues, Sarah will probably run 5 miles in 50 minutes.

Guided Practice

For 1–4, use the pictograph on page 226.

1. Thirty-five wins would be shown as ⚾⚾⚾◖. Which teams had this number of wins?
2. What if a fifth team had 55 wins? How would this number of wins be shown on the pictograph?
3. How many wins did UNC Wilmington have?
4. Which team had the most wins?

5. TALK Math Suppose you have a pictograph with a key that shows each symbol represents 8. Explain how you would determine the number of symbols you would need to show 20.

Independent Practice and Problem Solving

For 6–8, use the double-bar graph.

6. Which team had the greatest number of wins? How many more wins did the team have than losses?
7. Which two teams played the same number of games?
8. What was the total number of wins for all the teams?

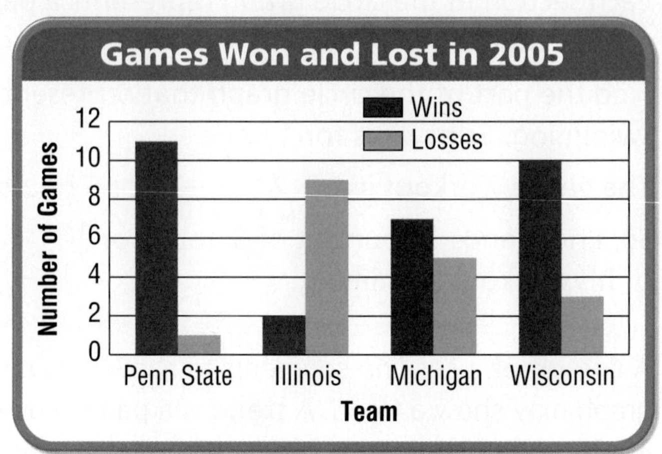

For 9–12, use the circle graph.

9. Which part of the workout takes the least time?
10. Which parts of the workout take the same amount of time?
11. Which part of the whole workout is leg exercises?
12. Which exercises take up $\frac{1}{9}$ of the workout?

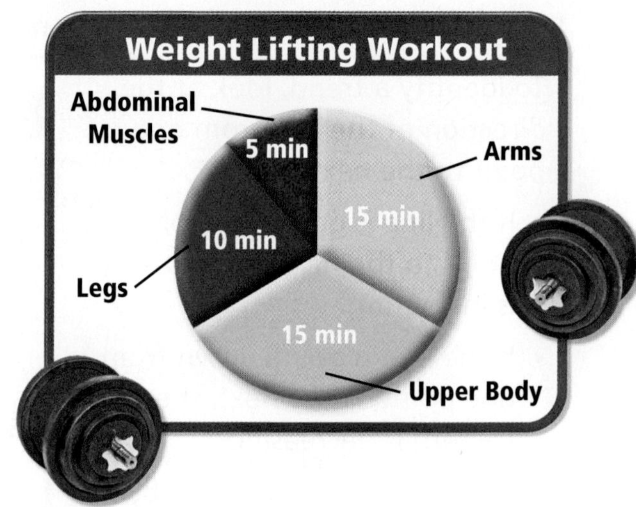

For 13–15, use the line graph.

13. Which part of the graph shows the greatest increase from one mile to the next?
14. How would you describe the trend shown in the graph from mile 2 to mile 3?
15. **Reasoning** Suppose the course from mile 7 to mile 10 is uphill. What trend do you predict the graph would show from mile 7 to mile 10?
16. **FAST FACT** Lance Armstrong retired from bicycle racing in 2005. His average speed during the 2005 season was 41.65 kilometers per hour. At this speed, how far could he travel in 3 hours? in n hours?

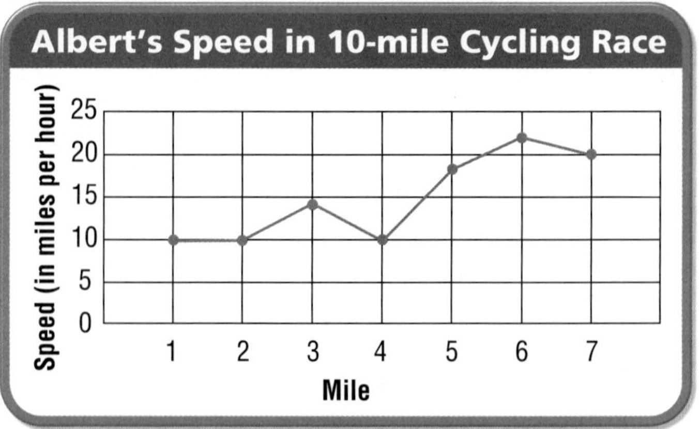

17. WRITE Math **Explain** how a line graph might show an increasing or decreasing pattern.

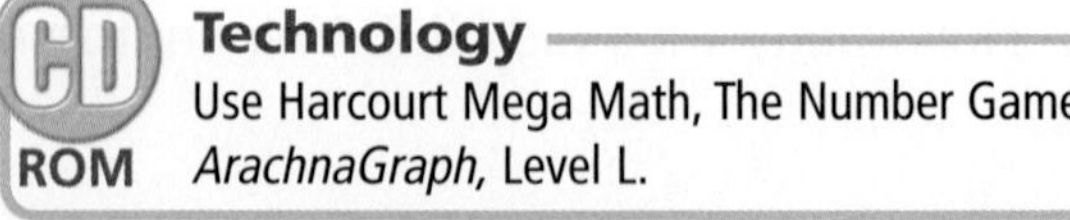

CD ROM
Technology
Use Harcourt Mega Math, The Number Games, *ArachnaGraph*, Level L.

 Extra Practice on page 234, Set D

Learn About Double-line Graphs

You can use a double-line graph to compare two sets of data. A key shows what each line represents.

Example **For the two cities, what is the difference in rainfall in March?**

Look at the graph and the key.

- Yuma's average is 0.3 inch for March.
- Reno's average is 0.7 inch for March.

Find the difference. $0.7 - 0.3 = 0.4$

So, the difference in rainfall amounts in March for the two cities is 0.4 inch.

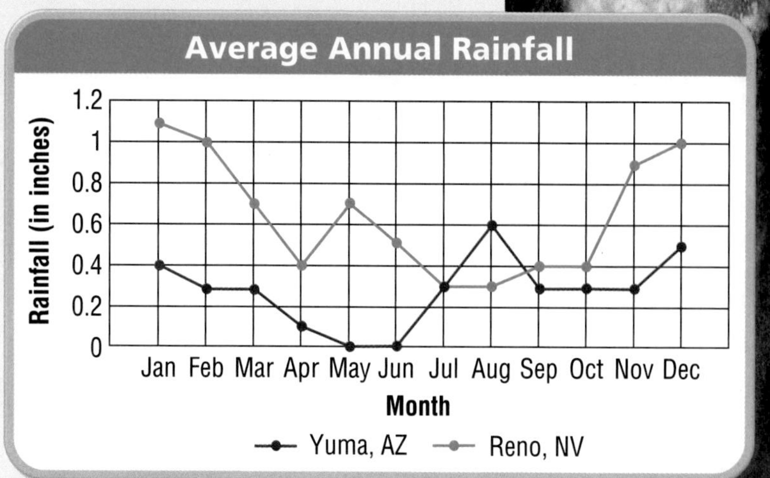

Try It

For 18–19, use the double-line graph.

18. Write a question that can be answered by using the data shown on the graph. Then, answer your question.

19. Based on the data shown on the graph, predict how the rainfall in Yuma and in Reno will compare during the first six months of next year.

Mixed Review and Test Prep

20. Lost Pine Trail is 2.6 miles long. Mesa Trail is 4.3 miles long. How much longer is Mesa Trail than Pine Trail? (p. 152)

21. Brad is buying film. Each roll of film costs $2. Write an expression that can be used to find the total cost of *n* rolls of film. (p. 92)

22. **Test Prep** A line graph shows a trend of people exercising more now than they did five years ago. Explain what the line graph might look like.

23. **Test Prep** Look at the double-bar graph at the top of page 228. Which statement about the data shown on the graph is **NOT** true?

A Penn State had the most wins.

B The median number of wins is 7.

C Wisconsin played the most games.

D The median number of losses is 4.

LESSON 5

Problem Solving Workshop
Strategy: Draw a Diagram

OBJECTIVE: Solve problems by using the strategy *draw a diagram.*

Learn the Strategy

Drawing a picture or a diagram can help you understand a problem and can make the solution visible. You can use different types of diagrams to show different types of problems.

A diagram can show relationships.

There are 14 students in the band, 9 students in chorus, and 4 students who are in band and chorus.

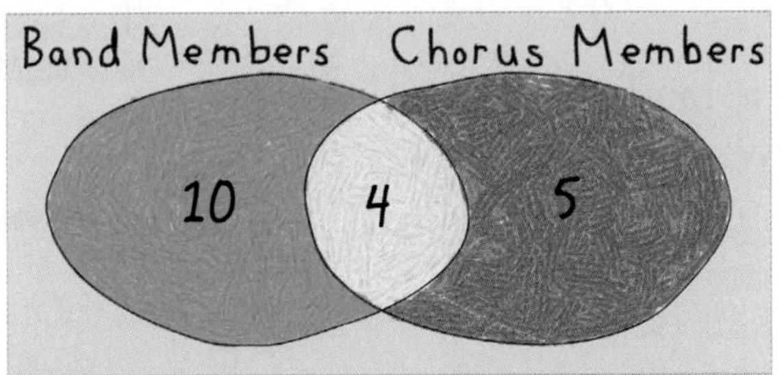

A diagram can show size.

Last week, D'Agastino's sold 3 more than twice as many cantaloupes as Vons.

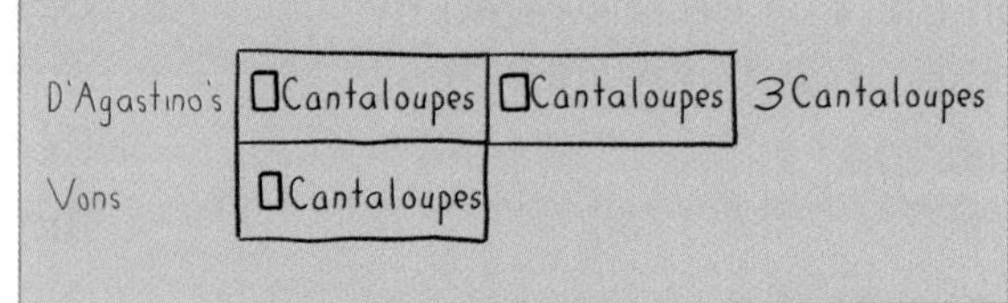

A diagram can show direction.

Mia walked 2 km east and 3 km south. Then she continued walking 1 km west to the lighthouse.

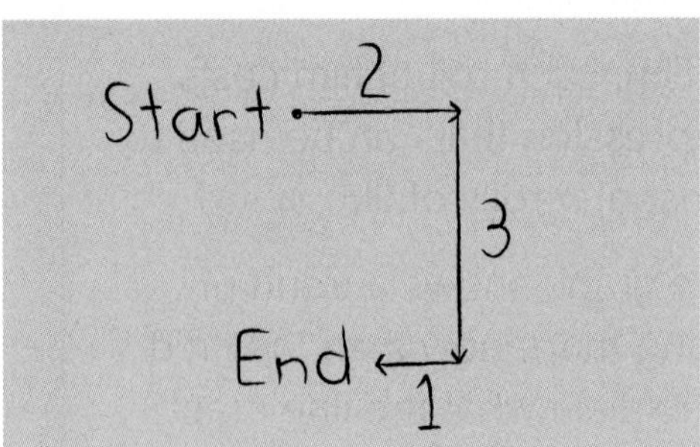

What are some questions that can be answered by using each of the diagrams shown above?

To draw a diagram, follow the information given in the problem. Keep the diagram simple. Label the parts to show what they represent.

FAST TRACK

KY MA-05-4.1.1 Students will analyze and make inferences from data displays (drawings, tables/charts, tally tables, pictographs, bar graphs, circle graphs, line plots, Venn diagrams, line graphs). DOK 3 *also MA-05-4.3.1*

Use the Strategy

PROBLEM The students in a fifth-grade class were asked to write a report. For data sources, 12 students used the Internet, 8 used an encyclopedia, and 13 used other reference books. Four students used the Internet and an encyclopedia, 5 used an encyclopedia and other reference books, 7 used the Internet and other reference books, and 2 used all three. How many students wrote reports?

Read to Understand
Plan
Solve
Check

Read to Understand

- **Generalize what you are asked to find.**
- **Is there information you will not use? If so, what?**

Plan

- **What strategy can you use to solve the problem?**
  You can draw a diagram to help you solve the problem.

Solve

- **How can you use the strategy to solve the problem?**

  a. Draw a Venn diagram with three overlapping ovals. Two students used all three sources, so write 2 in the part common to all three ovals.

  b. Four students used the Internet and an encyclopedia. Since 2 students used all three sources, subtract 2 from 4 to find the number of students who used an encyclopedia and the Internet: $4 - 2 = 2$. Write 2 in the part where only the Internet and encyclopedia ovals overlap. Use the same process to complete the other two middle parts.

  c. Look at the four parts of the oval labeled Internet. Since 12 students used the Internet, the sum of these parts must be 12. Since $12 - 9 = 3$, write 3 in the remaining part of the oval labeled Internet. Use the same process to complete the diagram. Then add all the numbers in the diagram to find how many students wrote reports: $3 + 2 + 1 + 5 + 2 + 3 + 3 = 19$.

  So, 19 students wrote reports.

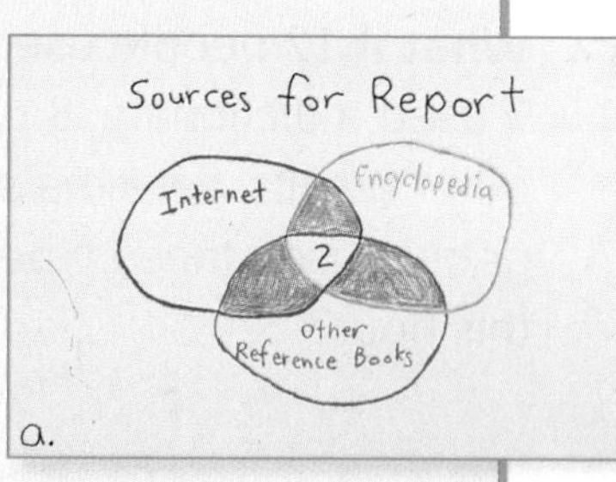

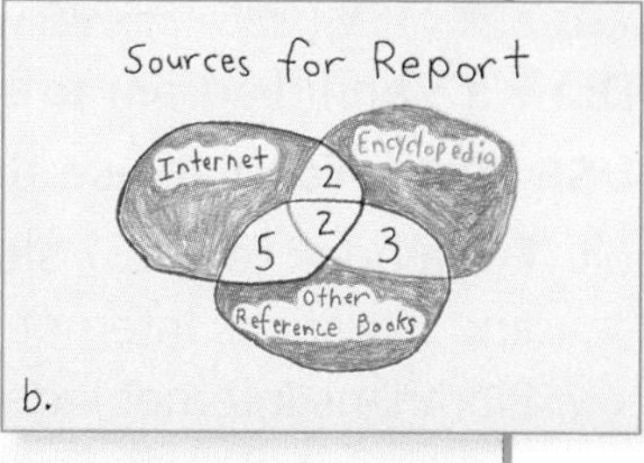

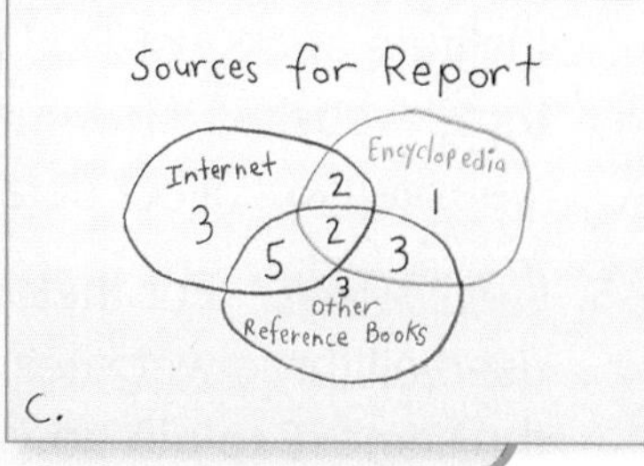

Check

- **What other strategy could you use to solve the problem?**

Read to Understand
Plan
Solve
Check

Guided Problem Solving

1. During one hour in a library, 7 people used an encyclopedia, 8 used a dictionary, 7 used an atlas, 2 used an encyclopedia and a dictionary, 3 used an encyclopedia and an atlas, 4 used a dictionary and an atlas, and 1 used all three. How many people used an encyclopedia, a dictionary, or an atlas during this hour?

   First, draw and label three overlapping ovals. In the part common to all three ovals, write the number of people who used all three types of books.

   Next, fill in the overlapping parts for each pair of book types.

   Last, fill in the remaining parts. Add all the numbers in the diagram to find the number of people who used these library books.

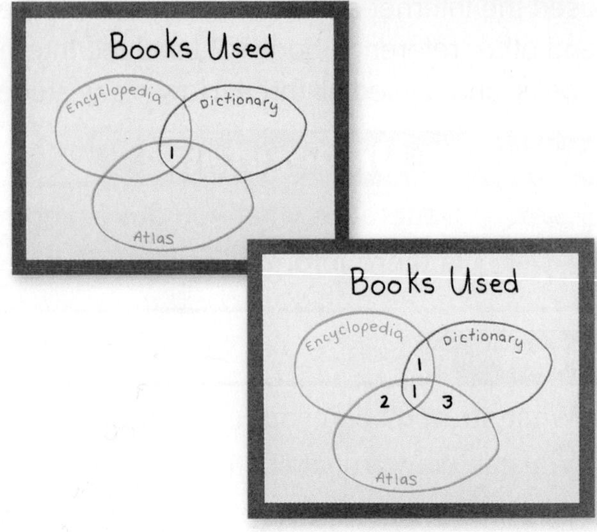

2. **What if** 12 people used an encyclopedia, 7 used a dictionary, 8 used an atlas, and all other results were the same? How many people used these types of books during this hour?

3. Five students wrote reports about U.S. Presidents, 8 wrote reports about U.S. first ladies, and 3 wrote reports about both U.S. Presidents and first ladies. How many students wrote reports?

Problem Solving Strategy Practice

Draw a Venn diagram to solve.

USE DATA For 4–5, use the picture.

4. For a book report, 7 students used KidsClick! and Librarians Internet Index, 5 students used Librarians Internet Index and Smithsonian Institute, and 5 students used Smithsonian Institute and KidsClick! Four students used all three websites. How many students used these websites to collect data?

5. WRITE Math For their next report, no student used all three websites, and all other results were the same. **Explain** how you could change your Venn diagram to find the number of students who used these websites.

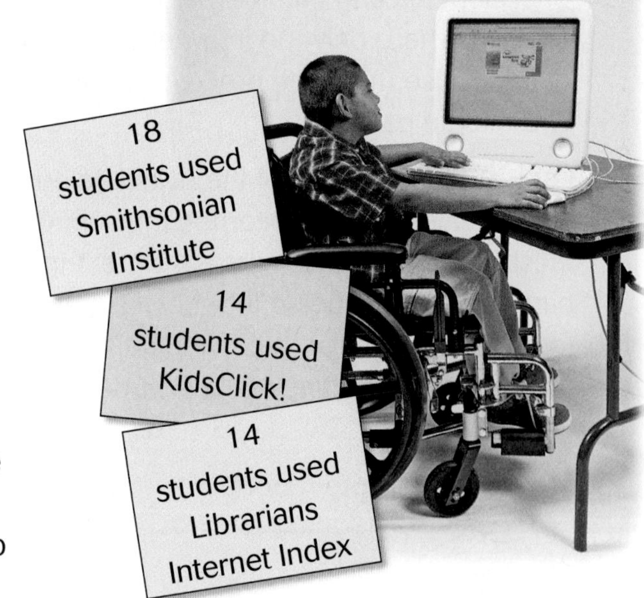

Mixed Strategy Practice

USE DATA For 6–10, use the information in the picture.

6. Samantha and Maria went to the book sale together. Samantha bought *Astronomy* and *Famous Women*. Maria bought *Insects* and *Almanac for Kids*. How much more did Maria spend on books than Samantha?
7. Ricardo spent $21.35 on two books. Which two books did he buy?
8. **Pose a Problem** Look back at Problem 7. Write a similar problem by changing the total cost and the number of books.
9. What is the median price of the books in the sale? What is the mode of the prices?
10. **Open-Ended** Write three number sentences that show different ways to buy three books for less than $35.00.

CHALLENGE YOURSELF

The owner of the store kept track of the number of books people bought so he could restock the books he sold.

11. During the sale, 8 people bought *Insects*, 8 bought *Astronomy*, 9 bought *World Geography*, 3 bought *Insects* and *Astronomy*, 5 bought *Insects* and *World Geography*, 6 bought *Astronomy* and *World Geography*, and 2 bought *Insects*, *Astronomy*, and *World Geography*. How many people bought these books?
12. At the end of the day, the store had the following sales. From 9 A.M. to 10:59 A.M., 12 books were sold; from 11 A.M. to 12:59 P.M., 30 books were sold; from 1 P.M. to 2:59 P.M., 18 books were sold; and from 3 P.M. to 4:59 P.M., 15 books were sold. During which time period did the sales decrease the most?

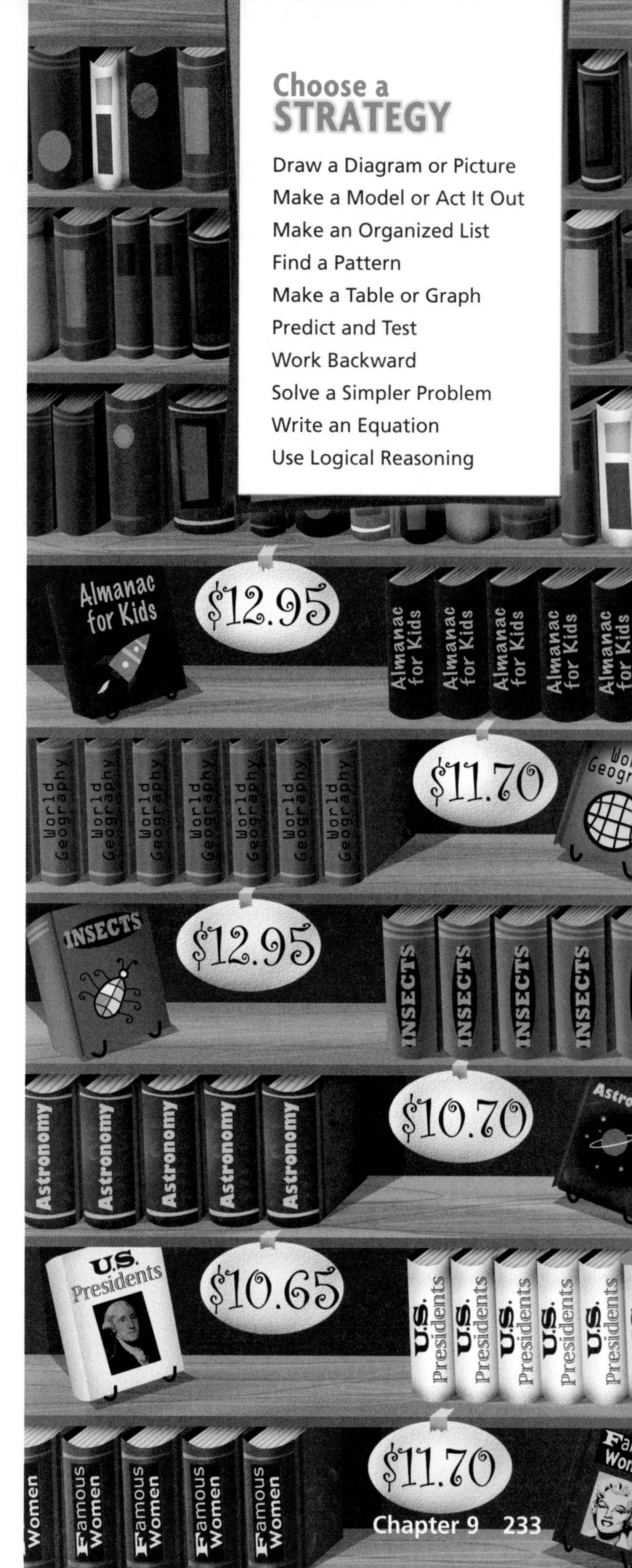

Extra Practice

Set A **A radio station wants to find out the number of teenagers who enjoy the station's music. Tell whether each sample represents the population. If it does not, explain.** (pp. 216–219)

1. a random sample of 500 adults
2. a random sample of 500 teenagers
3. a random sample of 500 teenage boys
4. Mrs. Washington's fifth grade class took a math quiz. Use the frequency table to find the range of the scores of the 12 students in the class.

Score	79	81	82	83	87	90	93	95
Number of Students	1	1	2	1	2	2	1	2

Set B **Find the mean, median, and mode for each set of data.** (pp. 220–223)

1. $15, $23, $18, $30
2. 6.2, 8.1, 4.5, 4.5, 6.2
3. 165, 212, 251, 208
4. 5, 17, 10, 5, 3, 8
5. 4, 3, 5, 5, 2, 5
6. 5.8, 7, 6.4, 11, 7
7. Simon is saving money to buy a new building set. He has seen the set at five different stores, at the following prices: $19.95, $18.99, $19.99, $18.99, and $18.49. Find the mean, median, and mode of these prices, rounding to the nearest cent.

Set C **Compare the mean, median, and range of the data sets.** (pp. 224–225)

1.

A: Number of Jelly Beans							
12	8	14	20	24	15	11	22
21	10	8	12	14	23	12	16

B: Number of Jelly Beans							
8	18	11	7	12	12	15	14
19	12	8	21	14	18	22	13

Set D **For 1–3, use the line graph.** (pp. 226–229)

1. How many hours did Carter practice in Week 4?
2. How many more hours did Carter practice in Week 6 than in Week 1?
3. What trend can you see in Carter's practice times?

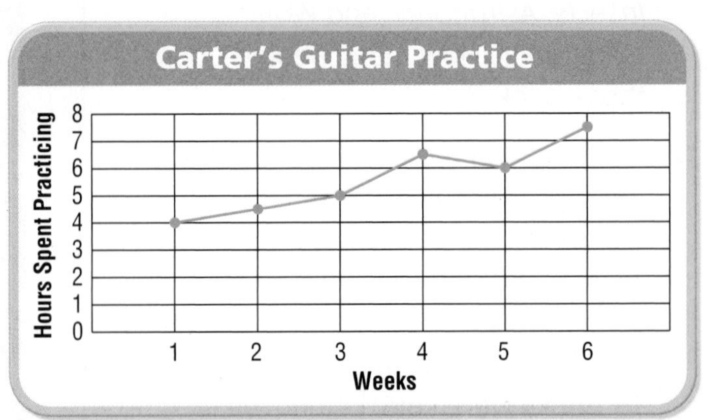

CD ROM **Technology** Use Harcourt Mega Math, The Number Games, *Arachna Graph*, Level L.

PRACTICE GAME

Mean of Means

Players

2 players

Materials

- Number cube (labeled even numbers 6-16)
- 18 red and 18 blue connecting cubes

	Player 1	Player 2
Mean of Round 1		
Mean of Round 2		
Mean of Round 3		
Mean of Round 4		
Mean of Round 5		
Mean for Rounds 1–5		

Start Playing

- Players copy the table shown above.
- The first player rolls the number cube 2 times and uses connecting cubes to model each number.
- If the stacks have an equal number of cubes, the number in one of the stacks is the mean. Record the mean in the table.
- If the stacks are not equal, make them equal by moving cubes from the taller stack to the shorter. Record the mean in the table.
- The next player repeats the process.
- Play continues for 4 more rounds.
- After the fifth round, players find the mean for rounds 1–5 and record the means in the table.
- The player with the greater mean for rounds 1–5 is the winner.

Box-and-Whisker Plot

Make the Grade

A class of 18 students took a math test. The table shows their scores. You can use a **box-and-whisker plot** to show how far apart and how evenly data are distributed.

Math Test Scores					
89	75	80	70	95	73
82	88	70	92	72	89
94	92	70	74	84	79

Step 1

Order the data from least to greatest. Circle the least value, or **lower extreme**, and the greatest value, or **upper extreme**.

70 70 70 72 73 74 75 79 80 82 84 88 89 89 92 92 94 95

Step 2

Find the median of the data. If the median is not one of the numbers written, write the median above the data in the middle and circle it.

81

70 70 70 72 73 74 75 79 80 | 82 84 88 89 89 92 92 94 95

Step 3

Find the median of the lower half of data. This median is called the **lower quartile**. Then find the median of the upper half of the data. This median is the **upper quartile**. Draw a number line. Then use the lower and upper extremes, the median, and the lower and upper quartiles to make a box-and-whisker plot like the one below.

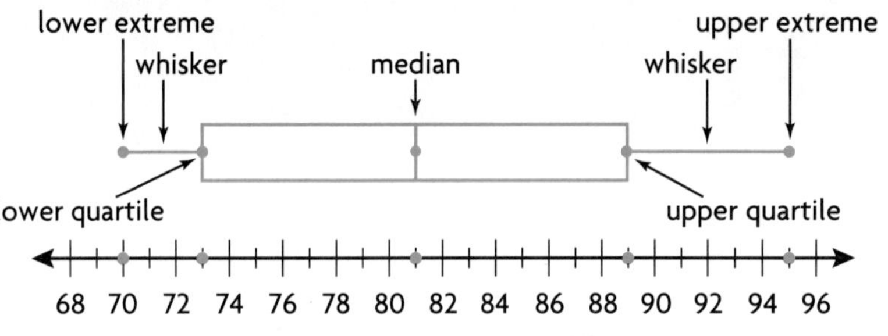

The lowest $\frac{1}{4}$ of the data are closer together than the greatest $\frac{1}{4}$ of the data. The middle $\frac{1}{2}$ of the data are evenly distributed.

Try It

Number of Tickets Sold				
33	47	50	31	49
48	40	40	42	35

1. Make a box-and-whisker plot for the data.
2. WRITE Math **Explain** how your data are distributed.

Chapter 9 Review/Test

Check Vocabulary and Concepts

Choose the best term from the box.

VOCABULARY
range
sample
survey
trend

1. Part of a group, chosen to represent the whole group. KY MA-05-4.1.1 (p. 216)
2. The difference between the greatest number and the least number in a set of data. KY MA-05-4.2.1 (p. 217)
3. A pattern over time, in all or part of a graph, in which the data increase, decrease, or stay the same. KY MA-05-4.1.1 (p. 227)

Check Skills

Find the mean, median, and mode for each set of data. KY MA-05-4.2.1 (pp. 220–223)

4. 47, 51.5, 38, 47, 32.3
5. 300, 400, 585, 214, 380
6. 2, 2, 8, 12, 4, 7, 7

Compare the mean, median, and range of the data sets. KY MA-05-4.2.1 (pp. 224–225)

7.

A: Weight of Grapes (ounces)							
32	34	33	16	18	21	37	42
30	16	28	34	20	28	34	40

B: Weight of Grapes (ounces)							
31	28	13	22	27	15	16	31
30	28	39	32	13	18	30	13

For 8–10, use the line graph. KY MA-05-4.1.1 (pp. 226–229)

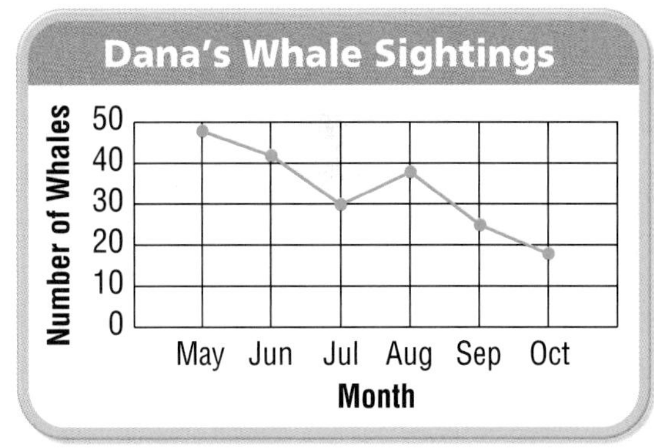

8. In which month did Dana have the least number of whale sightings?
9. About how many whales did Dana see during the months of September and October?
10. Which two months have a combined number of whale sightings that is about the same as the number of whale sightings in May?

Check Problem Solving

Solve. KY MA-05-4.1.1 (pp. 230–233)

11. Ms. Stein asked her students to name their favorite summer activities. 12 students named swimming, 10 named hiking, and 11 named traveling. 4 named hiking and swimming, 6 named swimming and traveling, and 3 named hiking and traveling. 2 students named all three activities. How many students are there in Ms. Stein's class? Draw a Venn diagram to find your answer.
12. WRITE Math Why do you have to subtract to find the correct numbers to put into a Venn diagram like the one you made in Problem 11? **Explain.**

GO ONLINE **Technology** Use *Online Assessment.*

Practice for the KCCT
Chapters 1–9

Number and Operations

1. Order the numbers in the table from least to greatest. KY MA-05-1.1.3 (p. 10)

648,912
521,767
690,124
703,815

A 521,767; 648,912; 690,124; 703,815

B 521,767; 690,124; 648,912; 703,815

C 690,124; 521,767; 648,912; 703,815

D 703,815; 690,124; 648,912; 521,767

Eliminate choices.

See item 1. Compare the numbers starting with the hundred thousands place. Then compare them using the ten thousands place. Keep comparing until you have decided the correct order.

2. Louisville, Kentucky has a population of two hundred forty-eight thousand, seven hundred sixty-two. Which is this number written in standard form? KY MA-05-1.1.1 (p. 4)

A 248,672

B 248,762

C 249,672

D 249,762

3. **WRITE Math** Divide 62 by 5. Show the remainder in two different ways. **Explain** how you found each answer.
KY MA-05-1.3.1 (p. 62)

Algebraic Thinking

4. What is the rule for the function table?
KY MA-05-5.1.2 (p. 112)

Input, x	100	70	60	15
Output, y	20	14	12	3

A add 80 to y

B subtract 80 from y

C multiply x by 10

D divide x by 5

5. Which is the value of the variable b?
KY MA-05-5.3.1 (p. 108)

$$34 \times b = 204$$

A 4

B 5

C 6

D 9

6. **WRITE Math** David drew a rectangle with a length of 6 inches. The area of any rectangle is found by multiplying length and width. Write an expression for the area of David's rectangle, using a variable. **Explain** how you chose the variable and what the variable represents.
KY MA-05-5.2.1 (p. 92)

Geometry

7. Howard made this square pyramid out of toothpicks. Now he wants to make a triangular pyramid. How many toothpicks will he need? KY Grade 4

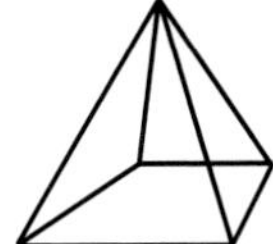

A 3

B 4

C 6

D 8

8. In the figure below, $\overleftrightarrow{LP}$ and $\overleftrightarrow{MQ}$ are lines. Which of the following names a pair of obtuse angles? KY Grade 4

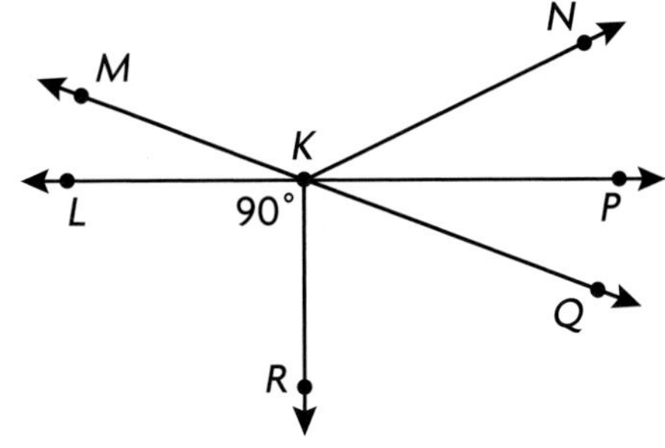

A $\angle RKM$, $\angle RKN$

B $\angle RKP$, $\angle PKM$

C $\angle LKN$, $\angle PKQ$

D $\angle NKP$, $\angle PKM$

9. **WRITE Math** Becka says that all squares are also parallelograms. Do you agree? **Explain.** KY Grade 4

Data Analysis and Probability

10. What is the range of the data?
KY MA-05-4.2.1 (p. 216)

14, 25, 18, 36, 11, 15, 17, 31

A 47 **C** 25

B 30 **D** 21

11. The bar graph shows the favorite sports of students in Jacob's class. Which fraction could be used to represent the students who prefer soccer? KY MA-05-4.1.1 (p. 226)

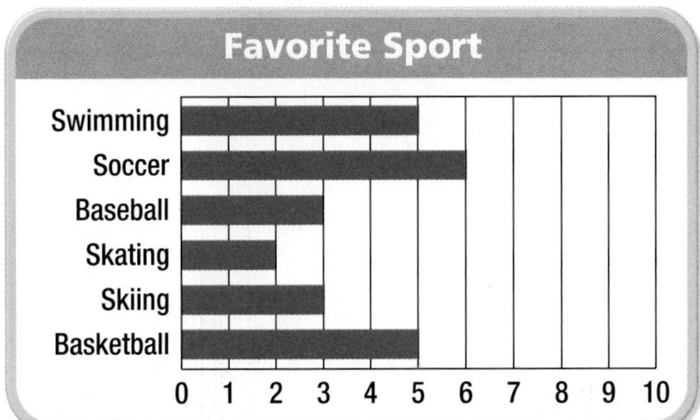

A $\frac{2}{24}$ **C** $\frac{5}{24}$

B $\frac{3}{24}$ **D** $\frac{6}{24}$

12. **WRITE Math** Kathryn counted the number of baskets she made each day for one week. Find the mean, median, and mode. How would the data change if Kathryn made 19 baskets during Day 8? **Explain.** KY MA-05-4.2.1 (p. 220)

Day	1	2	3	4	5	6	7
Baskets	19	10	20	10	16	15	22

CHAPTER 10 Make Graphs

Investigate

The bar graph shows the number of dairy cows in various states. What observations can you make about the data?

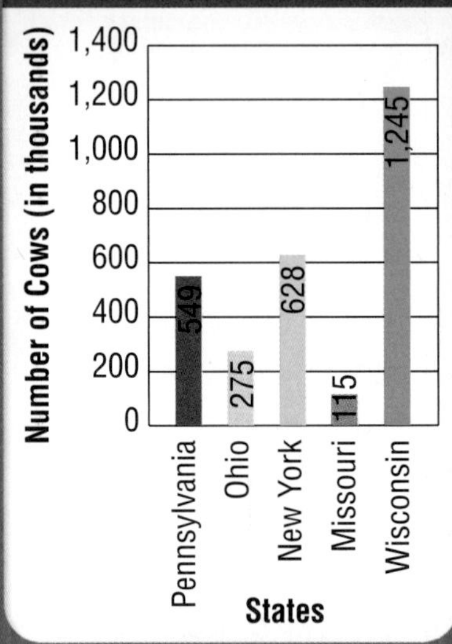

FAST FACT

Holstein cows account for 90% of all dairy cows in the United States. The average dairy cow produces about 2,000 gallons of milk per year.

GO ONLINE **Technology**
Student pages are available in the Student eBook.

Show What You Know

Check your understanding of important skills needed for success in Chapter 10.

▶ Identify Points on a Coordinate Grid

For 1–10, use the ordered pair to name the point on the grid.

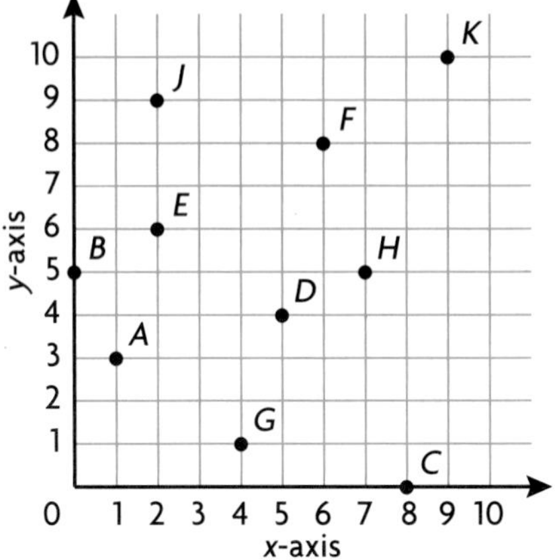

1. (1,3) **2.** (2,6)

3. (5,4) **4.** (4,1)

5. (6,8) **6.** (0,5)

7. (7,5) **8.** (2,9)

9. (9,10) **10.** (8,0)

▶ Extend Patterns

Write a rule for each pattern. Then find the missing numbers.

11. 0, 4, 8, 12, 16, ■, ■, ■

12. 0, 5, 10, 15, 20, ■, ■, ■

13. 90, 80, 70, 60, ■, ■, ■

14. 1, 3, 9, 27, ■, ■, ■

15. 3, 6, 12, 24, ■, ■, ■

16. 25, 50, 75, 100, ■, ■, ■

17. 48, 40, 32, 24, ■, ■, ■

18. 3, 7, 15, 31, ■, ■, ■

VOCABULARY POWER

CHAPTER VOCABULARY

categorical data
circle graph
double-bar graph
double-line graph
histogram
numerical data
ordered pair
stem-and-leaf plot
***x*-axis**
***x*-coordinate**
***y*-axis**
***y*-coordinate**

WARM-UP WORDS

categorical data data that includes groups or choices and that can be shown in any order in a graph

numerical data data that includes numbers and that can be ordered numerically

ordered pair a pair of numbers used to locate a point on a grid

Make Bar Graphs and Pictographs

OBJECTIVE: Represent data by making a bar graph, double-bar graph, and pictograph.

Quick Review

Find the next number in the pattern.

1. 0, 5, 10, ▇
2. 0, 10, 20, ▇
3. 0, 15, 30, ▇
4. 0, 25, 50, ▇
5. 0, 40, 80, ▇

Vocabulary

double-bar graph

Learn

The table shows the number of each type of bike sold at Kathy's Bike Shop.

You can make a bar graph of this data. Remember, a bar graph uses horizontal or vertical bars to display countable data.

Kathy's Bike Shop

Type of Bike	Number Sold
BMX	35
Mountain	80
Road	50
Trail	15

Example 1 Make a bar graph.

Step 1

Choose a title, labels, and a scale for the graph.

For this data, use a scale of 0–90 with an interval of 10.

Step 2

Draw the bars.

Use bars of equal width, and leave equal space between them. Use the data to determine the heights of the bars.

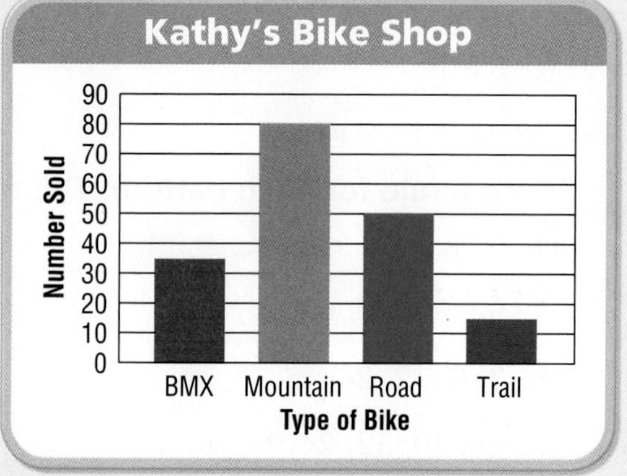

You can also make a pictograph of this data. Remember, a pictograph displays countable data with symbols or pictures.

Example 2 Make a pictograph.

Step 1

Choose a title and a key for the graph.

For the key, use 10 for each symbol since the data are multiples of 5 or 10.

Step 2

Draw the symbols.

Use a half symbol for data when necessary. For Trail Bikes, $15 = 10 + 5$ or $1\frac{1}{2}$ symbols.

Kathy's Bike Shop

BMX	
Mountain	
Road	
Trail	

Key: = 10 bikes sold

- How does the bar graph compare to the pictograph for this data?

FAST TRACK

KY MA-05-4.1.3 Students will construct data displays (pictographs, bar graphs, line plots, line graphs, Venn diagrams, tables). DOK 2 *also* MA-05-4.1.1

Double-Bar Graph

The table shows the sales of different types of bikes at the Cycle Center during May and June. Brenda wants to make a graph that she can use to compare sales for May and June.

A **double-bar graph** is used to compare similar kinds of data.

Cycle Center Sales

Type of Bike	May	June
BMX	20	12
Mountain	32	24
Road	18	36
Trail	10	10

Example 3 Make a double-bar graph.

Step 1

Choose a title, labels, and a scale.

For this data, use a scale of 0–40 with an interval of 4.

Step 2

Make a key.

Use one color for May and another color for June.

Step 3

Draw the bars.

Show a bar for May and a bar for June for each type of bike. Use the data in the table to determine the heights of the bars.

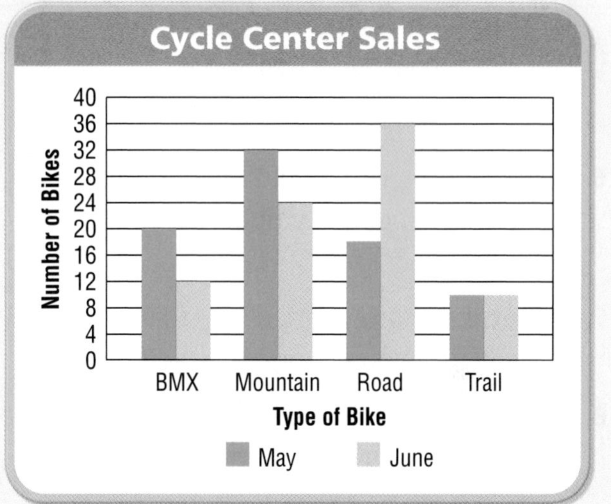

- How does a double-bar graph make it easier to compare similar data?

Math Idea
Two similar kinds of data can be shown as two single-bar graphs or as one double-bar graph.

Guided Practice

1. Copy the graph at the right. Draw bars on the graph for this data: Tina, 40 miles; Phillip, 52 miles.

For 2–4, use the bar graph you completed.

2. **What if** Emma rode her bike 40 miles? How would you change the graph?

3. What is another scale and interval you could use for this graph? Explain.

4. Describe how to make a double-bar graph of the data in the table and this data: Week 2: Marcus, 56 miles; Tina, 44 miles; Emma, 32 miles; Phillip, 48 miles.

5. TALK Math **Explain** what type of data you need to make a bar graph, a pictograph, or a double-bar graph.

Independent Practice and Problem Solving

For 6–11, use the graphs below.

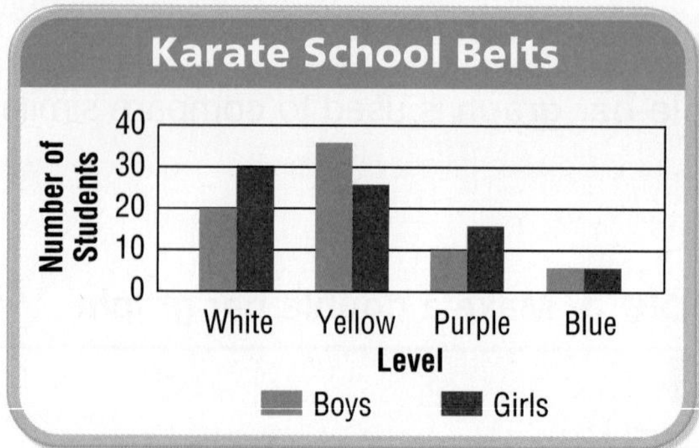

6. **Explain** how you would change the pictograph if each symbol represented 10 people.

7. **What if** the attendance were 150 in June? How would you change the pictograph?

8. **Explain** how you would change the pictograph to a bar graph.

9. How many sets of data does the Karate School Belts graph show?

10. What scale and interval are used in the double-bar graph?

11. **Explain** how the bars in the graph would change if the interval changed to 20.

Make the graph for each data set.

12. bar graph

Students' Pets	
Pet	**Number of Students**
Dog	15
Cat	12
Fish	5
Other	9

13. pictograph

Favorite Sport	
Sport	**Number of Votes**
Baseball	20
Soccer	32
Basketball	30
Volleyball	24

14. double-bar graph

Sport Shoe Sales		
Shoe	**July**	**August**
Tennis	40	45
Running	50	45
Basketball	25	35
Hiking	40	25

For 15–16, use the table.

15. Were more bikes sold in the fall or spring? How many more?

16. **Pose a Problem** Change the numbers for the spring bike sales. Then make a bar graph or a pictograph for the new spring data.

17. **Reasoning** What is the relationship between the heights of two vertical bar graphs of the same data if one uses an interval of 50 and the other uses an interval of 25?

18. WRITE Math **Explain** why a pictograph and a double-bar graph have a key.

Cycle Center Sales		
Bike Color	**Fall**	**Spring**
Red	400	750
Yellow	550	300
Blue	800	600
Black	650	700

 Extra Practice on page 264, Set A

Learn About Spreadsheets

You can use a spreadsheet to make a bar graph.

Step 1
Enter the data shown in the table in two columns on a spreadsheet. Highlight the data.

Step 2
Click **Insert**. Then click **Chart**. Choose **Column** to make a vertical bar graph and to see a preview of the graph.

Step 3
Click **Next** and fill in the labels for the graph.
Chart title: **Shell Collections**
Category (X) axis: **Name**
Category (Y) axis: **Number of Shells**

Step 4
Click **Next**. You can place the graph and data on the spreadsheet or you can place the graph on a new page. Click **Finish** to view the completed graph.

Shell Collections

Name	Number of Shells
Carol	25
Vicky	17
Brianna	34
Renata	42

Try It

Use a spreadsheet to make a bar graph for each data set.

19. Favorite Vacation

Location	Number of Students
Beach	28
Mountains	16
Theme Park	20

20. Trading Cards

Name	Number of Cards
Felix	60
Rita	45
Sandro	75
Sean	80

21. Music Camp

Week	Number of Students
1	32
2	56
3	24
4	35

Mixed Review and Test Prep

22. Draw a rectangle with 4 equal sides and 4 right angles. What is another name for this rectangle? (Grade 4)

23. A scientist records the following tree heights: 89 feet, 69 feet, 73 feet, 94 feet, and 85 feet. What is the median height? (p. 220)

24. Test Prep Which interval would you use to make a bar graph of the following data: 75 cm, 25 cm, 50 cm, 100 cm, and 110 cm?

A 1
B 2
C 25
D 110

LESSON 2

Make Histograms

OBJECTIVE: Represent data by making a histogram.

Quick Review

Find the next number in the pattern.

1. 5, 10, 15, 20, ■
2. 6, 9, 12, 15, ■
3. 4, 9, 14, 19, ■
4. 1, 11, 21, 31, ■
5. 28, 32, 36, 40, ■

Vocabulary

histogram

Learn

PROBLEM The data shows the ages of runners who preregistered for a 5K race. Make a graph of the data. How many runners are in the age group 16–30?

Ages of Runners									
32	17	26	24	35	13	19	23	27	41
38	9	16	28	8	37	18	59	40	43
52	29	12	10	25	28	32	39	46	24

Sometimes you want to show how often data occur. A **histogram** is a bar graph that shows the number of times data occur within intervals.

Activity

Follow the steps to make a histogram for the data above.

Step 1

Make a frequency table with intervals of 15. Start with 1. Record the number of times data occur for each interval, or age group.

Age Group	Frequency
1–15	5
16–30	13
31–45	9
46–60	3

Step 2

Make a histogram.

Choose an appropriate scale and interval for the vertical axis. Label the axis.

List the age groups, and label the horizontal axis.

Draw a bar for the number of runners in each age group. The bars should touch but not overlap.

Write a title for the graph.

So, 13 runners are in the age group 16–30.

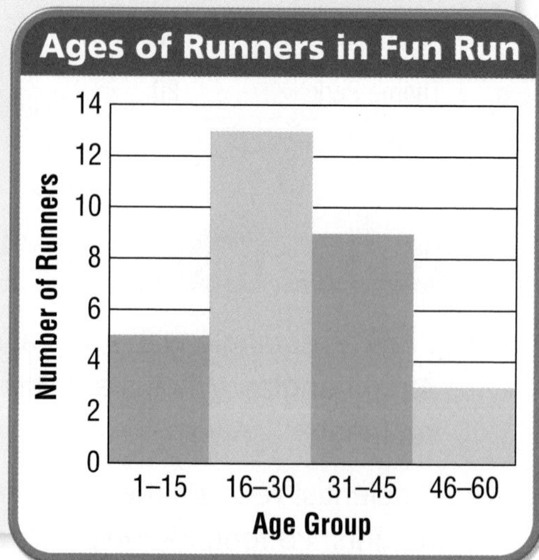

FAST TRACK

KY MA-05-4.1.3 Students will construct data displays (pictographs, bar graphs, line plots, line graphs, Venn diagrams, tables). DOK 2
also MA-05-4.1.1; *MA-05-4.3.1*

Guided Practice

For 1–3, use the table. The data shows the ages of children taking swimming lessons.

Ages of Children				
9	11	6	4	2
3	8	7	4	6
6	3	10	12	11
6	5	11	12	4

1. Use 3 years for each interval. List the intervals.
2. Make a histogram of the data.
3. How many children ages 4–6 take swimming lessons?
4. TALK Math **Explain** how a histogram and a bar graph are similar and how they are different.

Independent Practice and Problem Solving

For 5–6, use the table.

Practice Time (in minutes)					
25	32	20	35	37	33
28	42	36	32	23	41

5. What is a reasonable interval for the practice times?
6. Make a histogram of the data.

For 7–8, decide whether a bar graph or a histogram would better represent the data. Then make the graph.

7.

Color of Car	Number of Cars
Black	35
White	25
Red	10

8.

Height (in inches)	Number of Students
48–51	2
52–55	4
56–59	12

For 9–11 and 14, use the graph.

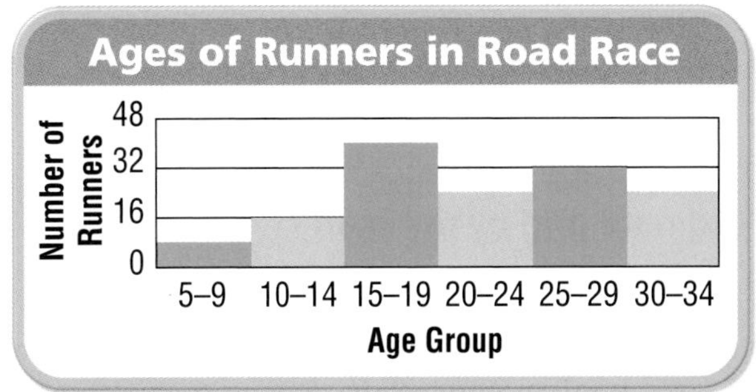

9. How many more runners are in the age group 25–29 than in the age group 5–9?
10. How many people ran in the road race?
11. WRITE Math Can you tell from the histogram how many people are 15 years old? **Explain.**

Mixed Review and Test Prep

12. Order from least to greatest: 0.6, 1.4, 0.09, and 1.37. (p. 138)
13. If y is a number that satisfies $4y - 2 = 18$, is y equal to 4 or to 5? (p. 108)
14. **Test Prep** How many people in the road race are 5–14 years old?

    A 16 **C** 32

    B 24 **D** 48

Extra Practice on page 264, Set B

LESSON 3

ALGEBRA

Graph Ordered Pairs

OBJECTIVE: Graph and name points on a coordinate grid using ordered pairs.

Quick Review

Ben rides 16 blocks south, 17 blocks west, and 12 blocks south. How many blocks does Ben ride?

Vocabulary

x-axis
x-coordinate
y-axis
y-coordinate
ordered pair

Learn

Reading a map of a city is like finding a point on a coordinate grid. The horizontal number line on the grid is the ***x*-axis**. The vertical number line on the grid is the ***y*-axis**.

Each point on the coordinate grid can be located by using an **ordered pair** of numbers. The ***x*-coordinate** is the first number in the ordered pair and tells the horizontal location. The ***y*-coordinate** is the second number and tells the vertical location.

NY Public Library
Empire State Building
y-axis
x-axis
0 1 2 3 4 5 6 7 8 9 10

(*x*,*y*)
x-coordinate ↑↑ *y*-coordinate

So, to get to the Empire State Building, start at (0,0). Move 3 units right and 2 units up. The Empire State Building is at (3,2).

- Explain how you could find the distance between the Empire State Building and the NY Public Library.

▲ Midtown Manhattan, New York City

You can graph a point on a coordinate grid by using an ordered pair.

Example **Graph the ordered pair (5,7).**

Start at (0,0).
Move 5 units to the right.
Move 7 units up.
Graph the point.

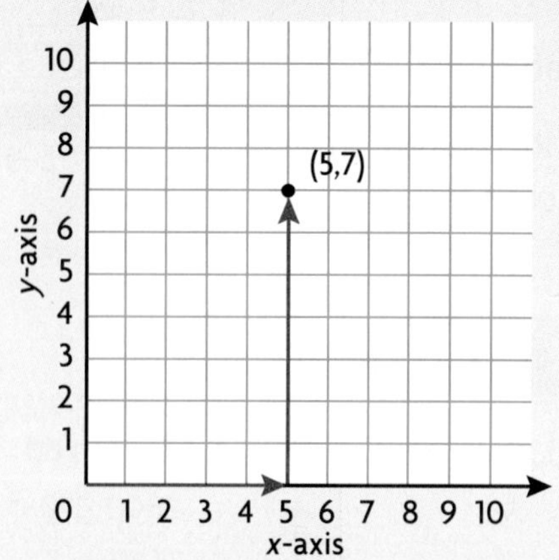

So, the point on the coordinate grid shows the ordered pair (5,7).

- The point (0,6) lies on one of the axes. Which axis?

Math Idea

The *x*-axis and the *y*-axis intersect at the point (0,0). Points that lie on the *x*-axis have 0 for the *y*-coordinate. Points that lie on the *y*-axis have 0 for the *x*-coordinate.

FAST TRACK KY MA-05-3.3.1 Students will identify and graph ordered pairs on a positive coordinate system scaled by ones, twos, threes, fives or tens; locate points on a grid; and apply graphing in the coordinate system to solve real-world problems. DOK 2 *also MA-05-4.3.1*

Guided Practice

1. Use the coordinate grid. Start at (0,0). Move 6 units to the right and 2 units up. What point is at (6,2)?

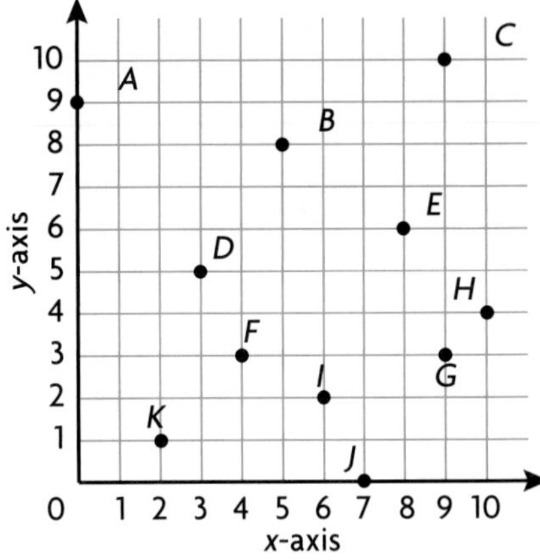

Use the coordinate grid. Write an ordered pair for each point.

2. *D*
3. *G*
4. *C*

Graph and label each point on a coordinate grid.

5. (0,9)
6. (8,6)
7. (10,4)

8. **TALK Math** Describe the path from (0,0) to point *K*.

Independent Practice and Problem Solving

Use the coordinate grid above. Write an ordered pair for each point.

9. *B*
10. *H*
11. *F*
12. *J*
13. *A*
14. *E*

Graph and label each point on a coordinate grid.

15. *J* (1,1)
16. *K* (0,4)
17. *L* (2,5)
18. *M* (3,4)
19. *P* (5,2)
20. *Q* (7,6)

For 21–23 and 27, use the map. Each unit represents 1 city block.

21. What ordered pair gives the location of Bryant Park?
22. The Grand Central Terminal is 3 blocks right of and 2 blocks up from the NY Public Library. What ordered pair gives the location of the Grand Central Terminal?
23. **Reasoning** Paulo walks from point *B* to Bryant Park. Raul walks from point *B* to Madison Square Garden. Who walks farther? **Explain.**
24. **WRITE Math** **Explain** why order is important when graphing an ordered pair on a coordinate grid.

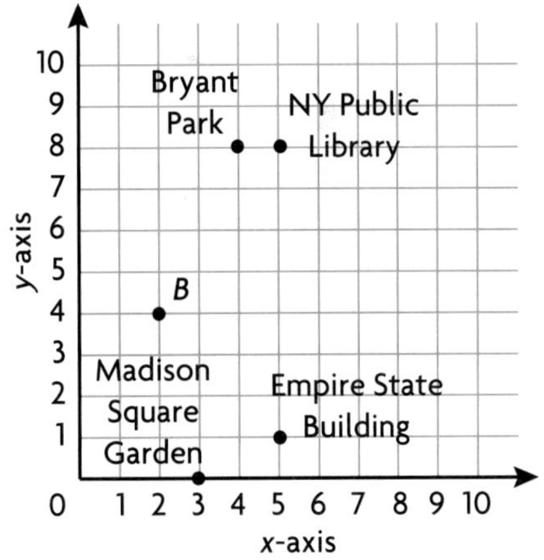

Mixed Review and Test Prep

25. A melon weighs 18 ounces. How much more or less than a pound does it weigh? (Grade 4)
26. What is a reasonable scale and interval for a bar graph of the building heights: 350 ft, 500 ft, 250 ft, 400 ft, and 650 ft? (p. 242)
27. **Test Prep** Use the map above. Suppose a pizzeria is located at point *B*. What ordered pair locates this point?

A (4,2) **C** (2,4)

B (3,4) **D** (4,4)

Extra Practice on page 264, Set C

LESSON 4

Make Line Graphs

OBJECTIVE: Represent data by making a line graph.

Quick Review

What scale would you use to graph the data?

1. 5, 9, 15, 6, 3
2. 28, 75, 36, 48, 31
3. 58, 69, 94, 86, 90
4. 12, 30, 25, 48, 41
5. 90, 120, 85, 125, 80

Vocabulary

double-line graph

Learn

A line graph is a good way to show data that changes over time.

Average Monthly Temperature in Philadelphia, PA

Month	Jan	Feb	Mar	Apr	May	Jun	Jul	Aug	Sep
Temperature (in °F)	30	33	42	52	63	72	77	76	68

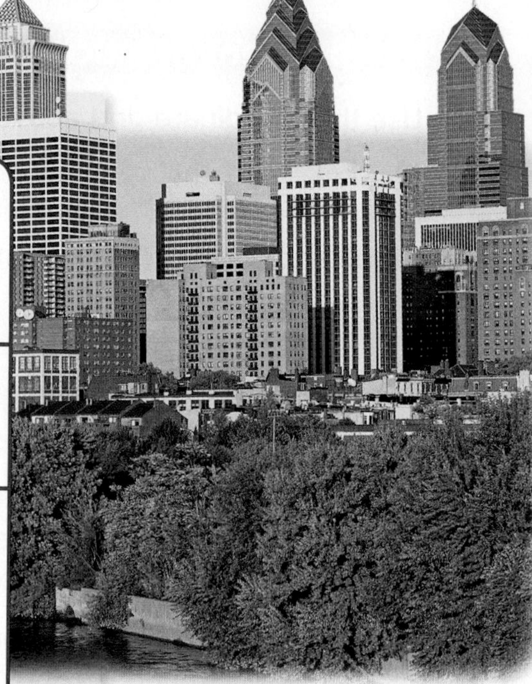

Example 1

Step 1

Choose an appropriate scale and interval for the data. Scales on graphs always start at zero. Since there are no temperatures between 0°F and 29°F, show a break in the scale.

Step 2

Write the months along the bottom of the graph. Label the horizontal and vertical axes. Write a title for the graph.

Step 3

Write related pairs from the data as ordered pairs. Graph the ordered pairs. Connect the points with straight line segments.

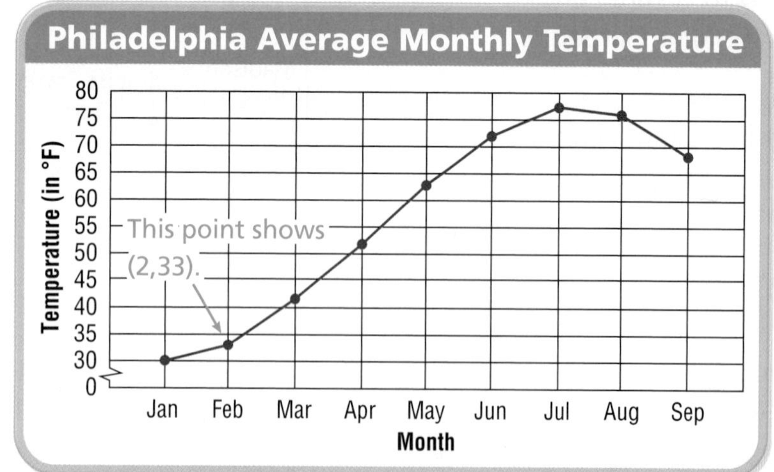

Math Idea

You can write related pairs of data as ordered pairs. In the set of data above, each month has a related temperature. For example, you would write the first related pair as (Jan,30), or (1,30) since January is the first month of the year.

FAST TRACK

KY MA-05-4.1.3 Students will construct data displays (pictographs, bar graphs, line plots, line graphs, Venn diagrams, tables). DOK 2
also MA-05-4.1.1; *MA-05-4.3.1*

Double-Line Graph

The table shows the average monthly temperatures for Long Beach, California. Make a graph to compare the data for Philadelphia from page 250 with the data for Long Beach.

Average Monthly Temperature in Long Beach									
Month	Jan	Feb	Mar	Apr	May	Jun	Jul	Aug	Sep
Temperature (in °F)	56	57	59	62	65	69	73	75	73

A **double-line graph** is one way to show two sets of related data for the same period of time.

Example 2 Make a double-line graph.

Step 1

Choose an appropriate scale and interval.

Step 2

Write the months along the bottom of the graph. Label the horizontal and vertical axes. Write a title for the graph.

Step 3

Make a key. Use one color for Philadelphia and another color for Long Beach.

Step 4

Using the appropriate color, graph the ordered pairs for Philadelphia and connect the points with straight line segments.

Use the other color to graph the ordered pairs for Long Beach and connect the points with straight line segments.

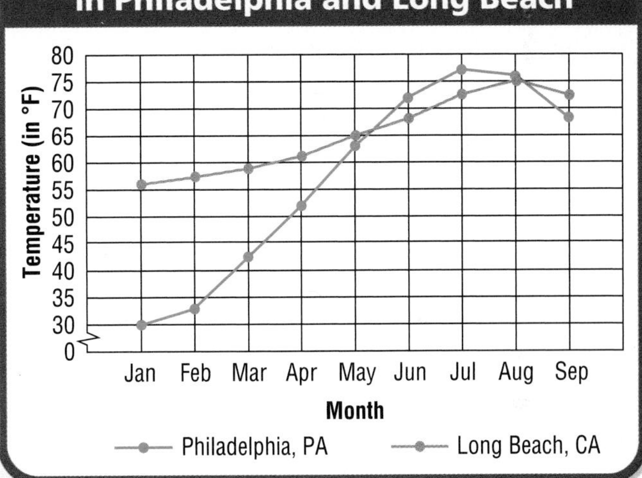

Guided Practice

1. Suppose you add the data at the right to the graph above. Would the lines go up or down for each city?

Average October Temperature	
City	**Temperature (in °F)**
Philadelphia	56
Long Beach	68

For 2–5, use the table.

Average Monthly Temperature in Tupelo, MS					
Month	Jan	Feb	Mar	Apr	May
Temperature (in °F)	40	44	54	62	70

2. What would be an appropriate scale and interval to use in graphing the data?
3. Write the related pairs as ordered pairs.
4. Make a line graph of the data.
5. TALK Math **Explain** when it is appropriate to show a break in the scale on a line graph.

Independent Practice and Problem Solving

For 6–8, use the table.

Daily Temperatures					
Day	Mon	Tue	Wed	Thu	Fri
High	80°F	84°F	78°F	78°F	85°F
Low	68°F	70°F	65°F	70°F	73°F

6. What would be an appropriate scale and interval to graph the data?
7. Write the related pairs for the high temperature and for the low temperature as ordered pairs.
8. Make a double-line graph of the data.

For 9–10, make a line graph or a double-line graph for each set of data.

9.

Skating Rink Sales					
Week	1	2	3	4	5
East Rink	$120	$150	$180	$170	$180
West Rink	$110	$130	$160	$170	$150

10.

Stock X Price				
Month	Jan	Feb	Mar	Apr
Price	$48	$55	$62	$38

For 11–13, use the graph.

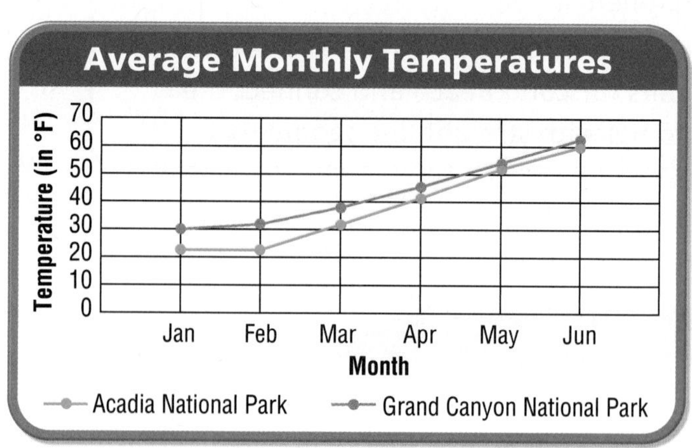

11. During which of the months shown is the temperature difference between the two national parks the greatest?
12. Which park has an average temperature represented by (Apr,45)?
13. WRITE Math **Explain** how graphing an ordered pair on a coordinate grid is similar to graphing an ordered pair on a line graph.

Technology
Use Harcourt Mega Math, The Number Games, *ArachnaGraph*, Levels I and J.

 Extra Practice on page 264, Set D

Mixed Review and Test Prep

For 14–17, use the data in the table.

Average Monthly Precipitation in Yosemite National Park						
Month	Jan	Feb	Mar	Apr	May	Jun
Precipitation (in inches)	6.2	6.1	5.2	3.0	1.3	0.7

14. What is the total average precipitation in Yosemite National Park for the first six months of the year? (p. 152)

15. What is the range in the number of inches of precipitation in Yosemite National Park for the first six months of the year? (p. 216)

16. **Test Prep** What would be an appropriate scale and interval to graph this data?

17. **Test Prep** Suppose you made a line graph of this data. Which best describes the line from January to June?

    A It goes up.

    B It goes down.

    C First it goes up, and then it goes down.

    D First it goes down, and then it goes up.

Problem Solving connects to Science

The Water Cycle

Water changes to water vapor by evaporation and then condenses to form rain. This process is called the water cycle. The ocean is an important part of this cycle and has a strong effect on climate. The ocean absorbs heat from the sun and then loses heat by evaporation, often causing precipitation and even storms. The overlay graph at the right uses two vertical scales to show monthly average temperatures and precipitation for Redding, California.

For 1–3, use the graph.

1. About how much precipitation falls in Redding, California, in February?
2. What is the average temperature for Redding, California, in February?
3. How does the overlay graph help you compare temperature and precipitation for each month?

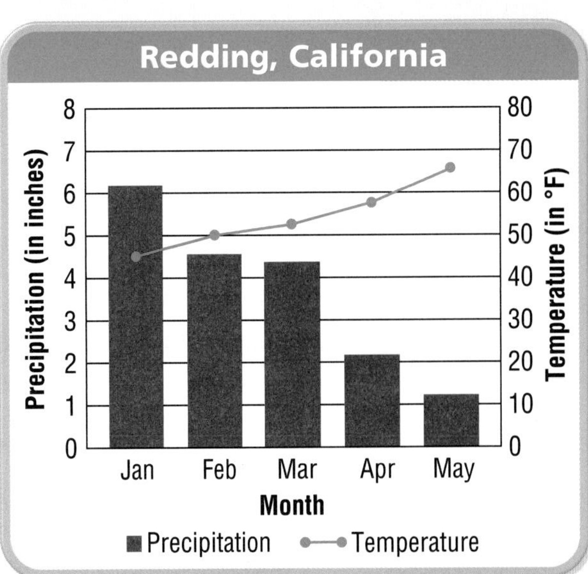

LESSON HANDS ON

5 Make Circle Graphs

OBJECTIVE: Represent data by making a circle graph.

Quick Review

Angie asks 10 students to choose their favorite color. Two choose green, 2 choose pink, and 3 choose red. The rest choose blue. How many students choose blue?

Investigate

Materials ■ circle graph pattern ■ hundredths circle

Remember that a circle graph shows how parts of the data are related to the whole and to each other.

You can use a circle graph pattern to make a circle graph.

A Survey 10 classmates to find out whether their favorite sea mammal is a sea otter, a dolphin, or a whale. Record the results in a table.

Favorite Sea Mammal	
Sea Mammal	Number of Votes
Sea otter	III
Dolphin	~~IIII~~
Whale	II

B Use your data and the circle graph pattern to make a circle graph.

- Since there are 10 sections in the graph, count one section for each of the 10 people you surveyed. Label and shade the sections. For example, if 3 students choose sea otters, count and shade 3 sections on the circle graph for sea otters.
- Repeat for the other two mammals in the survey. Shade the sections a different color for each survey choice.

C Choose a title for your circle graph.

Favorite Sea Mammal

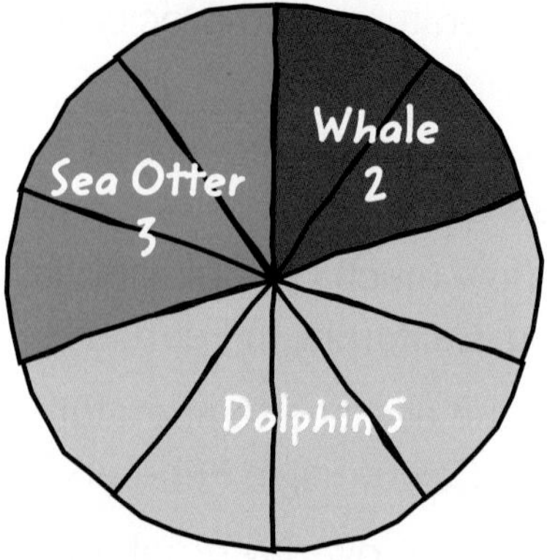

Draw Conclusions

1. What does the whole circle in the circle graph represent?
2. How does the circle graph show how the survey results for the different sea mammals relate to each other?
3. **Synthesis** How does the circle graph show the results of your survey? Explain.

FAST TRACK

KY MA-05-4.1.1 Students will analyze and make inferences from data displays (drawings, tables/charts, tally tables, pictographs, bar graphs, circle graphs, line plots, Venn diagrams, line graphs). DOK 3 *also* MA-05-4.1.3; *MA-05-4.3.1*

Connect

You can use a hundredths circle to make a circle graph.

Every Dollar Brad Earns	
Activity	**Amount**
Savings	$0.50
Lunch & Snacks	$0.20
Fun	$0.15
Other	$0.15

Step 1

Use the data in the table to decide how large to make the section for each of the four activities.

The hundredths circle shows 100 equal parts, so each part is 0.01 of the whole.

For each dollar Brad earns, he saves $0.50, so count 50 tick marks around the circle for Savings. Shade and label the section.

Step 2

Repeat for the other three activities shown in the table. Label each section. Shade the sections a different color for each activity.

Step 3

Choose a title for your graph.

TALK Math

Explain what the whole circle in the circle graph represents.

Practice

Use the data to make a circle graph.

1.

Music Lessons	
Instrument	**Number of Students**
Piano	6
Guitar	2
Violin	2

✓2.

Money From Each Dollar Earned	
Activity	**Part of Each Dollar**
Savings	0.4
Entertainment	0.5
Snacks	0.1

✓3.

Team Captain Election	
Name	**Number of Votes**
Will	20
Roland	60
Omar	20

4. **WRITE Math** Elsie has $10. **Explain** how to make a circle graph to show that Elsie spends $3 and saves the rest.

LESSON 6

Problem Solving Workshop
Strategy: Make a Graph

OBJECTIVE: Solve problems by using the strategy *make a graph.*

Learn the Strategy

You can make a graph to display data. The type of graph you make depends on the type of data you want to display.

Make a line graph for data that change over time.

George recorded the high temperature each day for 5 days.

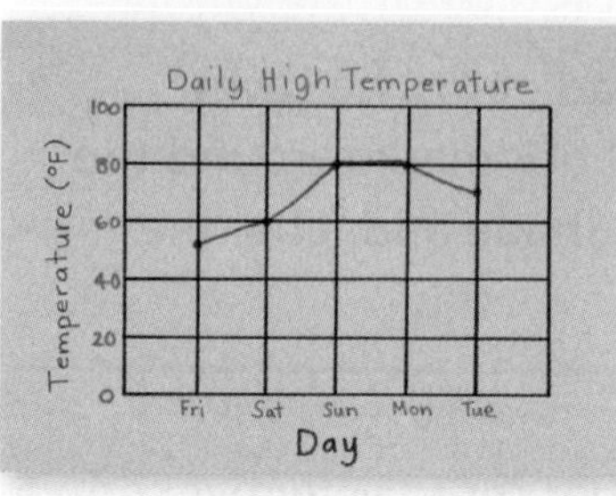

Make a circle graph for data that are related to the whole and to each other.

LaToya recorded the amount of time she spent on different activities during her workout.

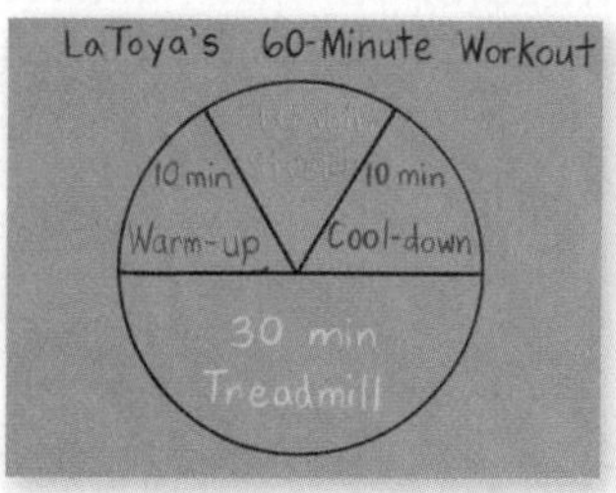

Make a stem-and-leaf plot for data that are clustered or grouped.

Mr. Ramirez recorded the number of magazines he sold in his store every day for two weeks.

Magazines Sold

Stem	Leaves
3	0 0 1 2 6 7
4	1 2 2 3 8
5	0 6 6

TALK Math

How would you determine which type of graph would best show a set of data?

To make a graph, start by analyzing the data you want to display. Then make the graph that best displays that type of data.

FAST TRACK

KY MA-05-4.1.3 Students will construct data displays (pictographs, bar graphs, line plots, line graphs, Venn diagrams, tables). DOK 2
also **MA-05-4.1.1**; *MA-05-4.3.1*

Use the Strategy

Read to Understand
Plan
Solve
Check

PROBLEM The members of a local bowling team recorded their scores from their last match. Did the greatest number of team members bowl in the 70s, 80s, or 90s?

Scores of Bowling Team Members			
72	74	81	90
76	82	91	87
80	80	73	92
70	79	83	85
85	96	82	72

Read to Understand

- **Classify and categorize what you are asked to find.**
- **Is there information you will not use? If so, what?**

Plan

- **What strategy can you use to solve the problem?**

  You can make a graph to help you solve the problem.

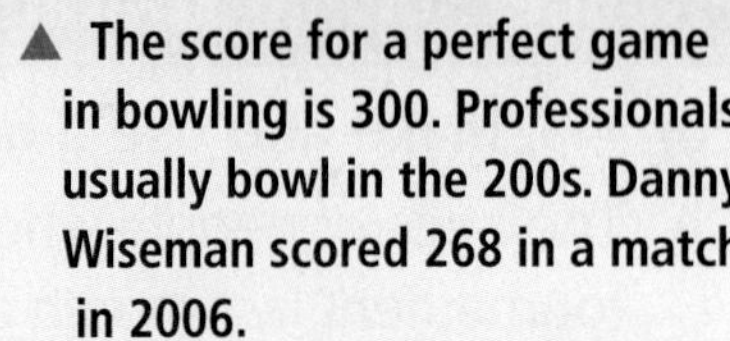

▲ The score for a perfect game in bowling is 300. Professionals usually bowl in the 200s. Danny Wiseman scored 268 in a match in 2006.

Solve

- **How can you use the strategy to solve the problem?**

  You can make a **stem-and-leaf plot** to help you see how data are clustered, or grouped.

  Group the data by the tens digits. Then, order the data from least to greatest.

  Use the tens digits as stems. Use the ones digits as leaves. Write the leaves in increasing order.

  The stem, 8, has the most leaves.

  So, the greatest number of team members bowled in the 80s.

Scores of Bowling Team Members

Stem	Leaves
7	0 2 2 3 4 6 9
8	0 0 1 2 2 3 5 5 7
9	0 1 2 6

9 | 6 represents 96.

The tens digit of each number is its stem.

The ones digit of each number is its leaf.

Check

- **What other type of graph would be appropriate for this data?**

Guided Problem Solving

1. Jason's golfing scores are 75, 72, 68, 70, 81, 74, 81, 80, 93, 77, 80, 83, 84, 94, and 87. Are his golfing scores most often in the 60s, 70s, 80s, or 90s?

   First, organize the data for a stem-and-leaf plot by grouping the data by the tens digits.

   Then, order the data from least to greatest. Use the tens digits as stems. Use the ones digits as leaves. Write the leaves in increasing order. Copy and complete the graph.

   Finally, find the stem with the greatest number of leaves.

Jason's Golfing Scores

Stems	Leaves
6	
7	
8	
9	

2. **What if** Jason scored 78 instead of 68 and all of the other scores remained the same? How would the stem-and-leaf plot change?

3. The points scored in each game by the Hampton High basketball team are 63, 67, 73, 55, 61, 53, 60, 63, 52, 61, and 64. Did the basketball team score least often in the 50s, 60s, or 70s? Make a graph to solve.

Problem Solving Strategy Practice

For 4–5, make and use a graph to solve.

4. The ages of people who bowled in a tournament last month are 11, 42, 30, 17, 26, 19, 30, 19, 22, 23, 19, and 18. Which age group had the most bowlers: 10–19, 20–29, 30–39, or 40–49?

5. The manager of the bowling alley wants to find out some information about the people who bowled last month. What is the mean age? What is the mode of their ages? What is the median age?

For 6–7, use the graph.

6. Mariah made a graph to show the total number of points she scored in the first ten basketball games she played in. Did she most often score less than 10 points, between 10 and 20 points, or more than 20 points?

7. WRITE Math Describe how you could make a stem-and-leaf plot to display the data in the graph.

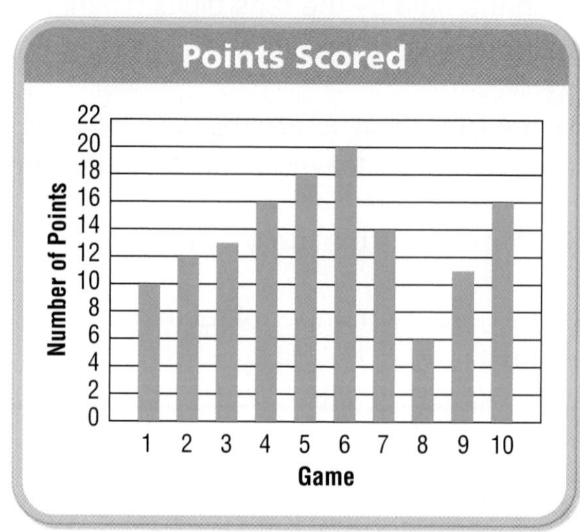

Mixed Strategy Practice

For 8–13, use the information in the graph.

8. What are the mean, median, and mode for the Home Run Derby winners from 1997–2006?

9. Is the number of home runs hit by the winner usually in the 10s, 20s, 30s, or 40s?

10. During which year was the number of home runs 10 more than in 1997?

11. **Pose a Problem** Look back at Problem 10. Write a similar problem by changing the year and the number.

12. The longest home run hit in the 2005 Home Run Derby was 517 feet. How many yards was this home run hit?

13. **Open-Ended** Write two equations that compare the number of runs for the Home Run Derby winners for 2005 and 2004.

CHALLENGE YOURSELF

The major league baseball Home Run Derby has 3 rounds of competition: round 1, semi-finals, and finals. In the 2005 Home Run Derby, 8 players hit 71 home runs in round 1. The average number of home runs for the 3 rounds was 35 less than the number of runs in round 1.

14. The number of home runs hit in the 2005 semi-finals was 8 less than the number of home runs hit in round 1 divided by three. How many home runs were hit in the semi-finals?

15. In the 2005 finals, the total number of home runs hit was 20 less than the average for the three rounds of competition. How many home runs were hit in the finals?

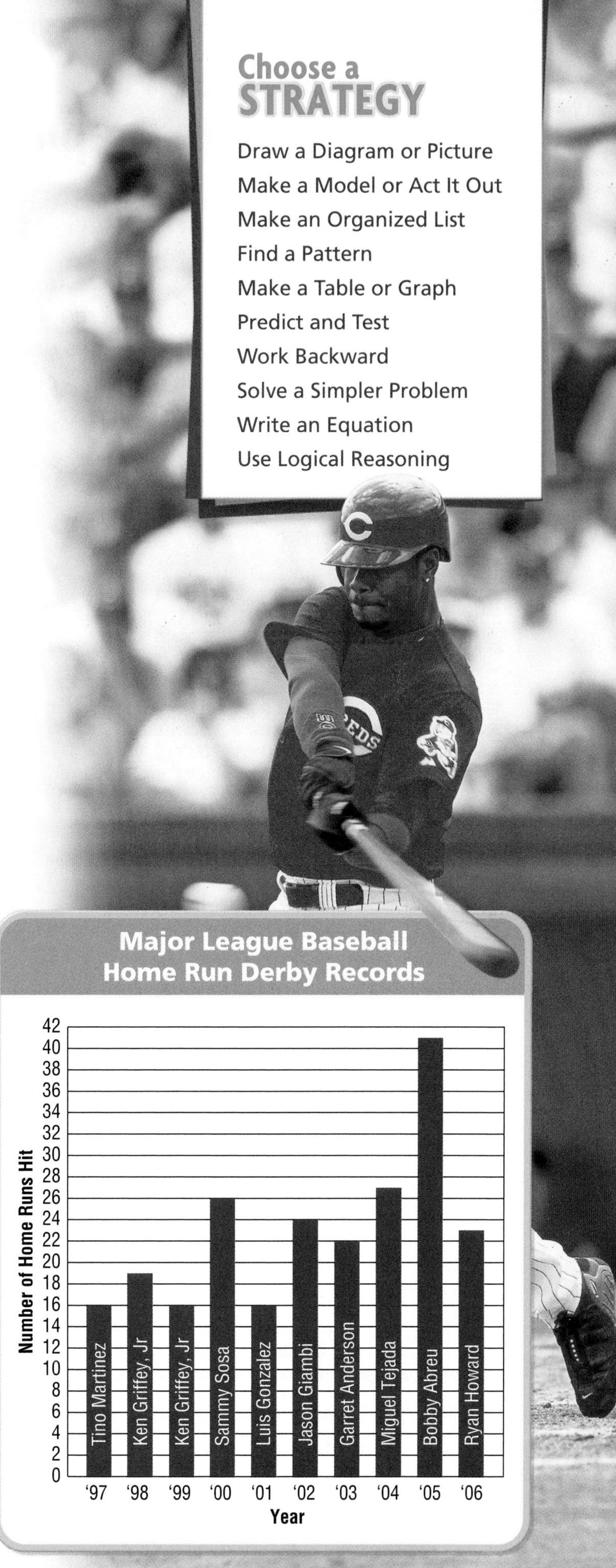

Choose the Appropriate Graph

OBJECTIVE: Compare the types of graphs that can be used for categorical data and numerical data and select an appropriate graph.

Quick Review

William wants to show the number of students in third, fourth, and fifth grade at his school. What type of graph could he use for this data?

Vocabulary

categorical data

numerical data

Learn

In a survey, questions that can be answered with words are categorical data. **Categorical data** includes groups or choices. The data is shown in any order in a graph. You can use a bar graph or a circle graph to show data that is categorical.

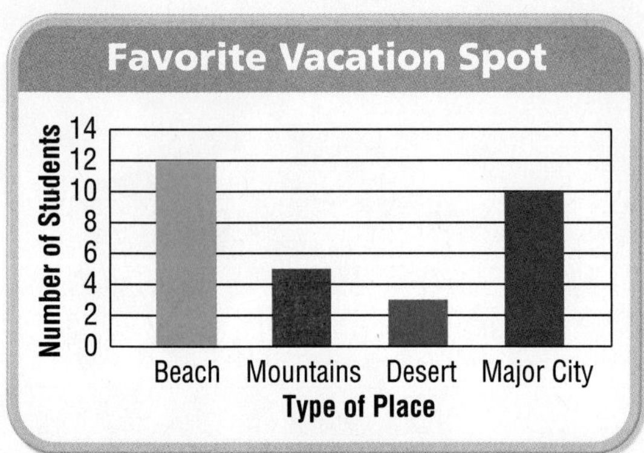

The horizontal axis on this bar graph shows different locations. The vertical axis shows the number of students who chose them as a favorite.

The parts on this circle graph show different types of big cats and the number of students who chose them as a favorite.

Numerical data includes numbers. The data is ordered numerically. You can use a line graph, a stem-and-leaf plot, a line plot, a bar graph, or a circle graph to show data that is numerical.

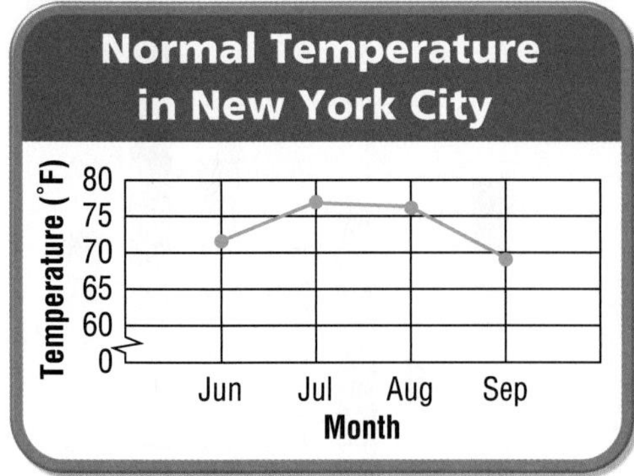

This line graph shows the numerical data for temperature and time.

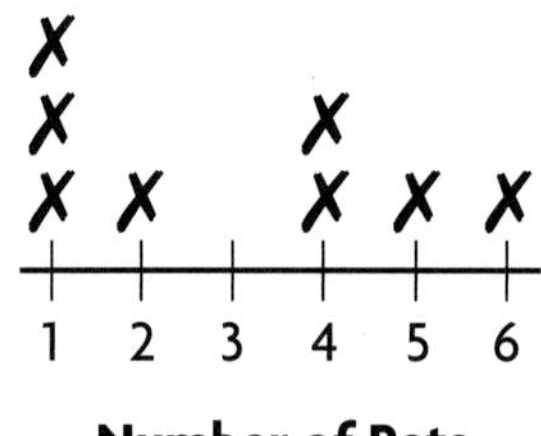

This line plot shows numbers of pets students have. For example, two students have 4 pets.

Student Heights (in inches)

Stem	Leaves
3	5 7 7 9
4	0 3 5 7 8
5	1 3 6

4 | 8 represents 48.

This stem-and-leaf plot shows a number for each student's height.

FAST TRACK KY MA-05-4.1.1 Students will analyze and make inferences from data displays (drawings, tables/charts, tally tables, pictographs, bar graphs, circle graphs, line plots, Venn diagrams, line graphs). DOK 3 *also MA-05-4.3.1*

What is the best graph for the data?

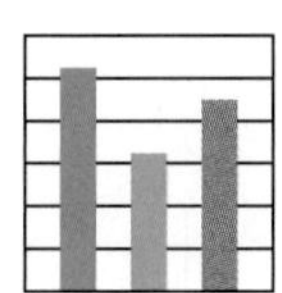

A bar graph or a double-bar graph compares data by category.

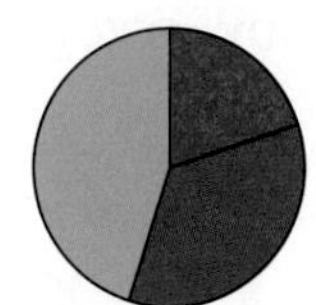

A circle graph compares parts of the whole to the whole and to each part.

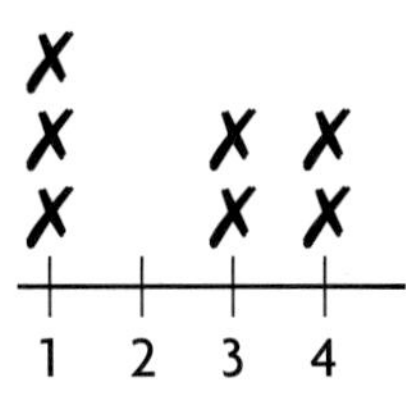

A line plot keeps count of data to show frequency.

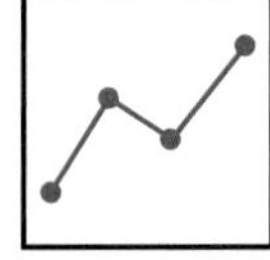

A line graph shows how data change over time.

Stem	Leaves
3	1 7
4	5

A stem-and-leaf plot organizes data by place value.

Moira, Neil, and Chuck each used a different way to display the rainfall data shown in the table. Who chose the best graph?

Average March Rainfall

City	Rainfall (in inches)
San Diego, CA	1.8
El Paso, TX	0.3
Lansing, MI	2.4

Moira's Bar Graph

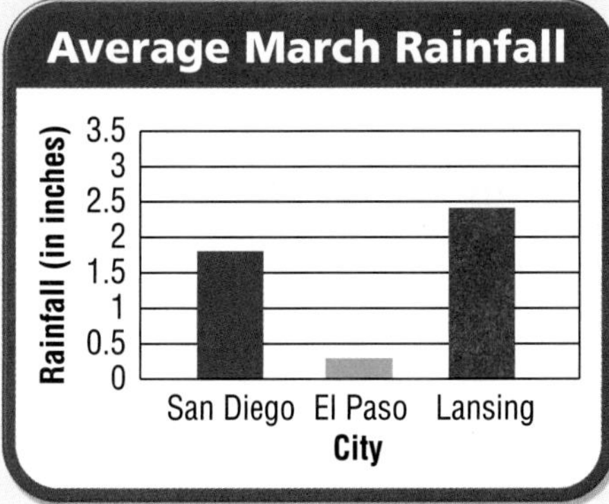

The data show the rainfall measured in different cities for the same month. So, a bar graph is a good way to display the data.

Neil's Stem-and-Leaf Plot

Average March Rainfall

Stem	Leaves
0	3
1	8
2	4

1 | 8 represents 1.8.

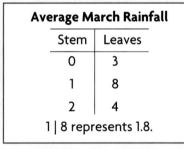

The data do not make sense organized by place value. This graph does not show which city had a given rainfall. So, a stem-and-leaf plot is *not* the best way to display the data.

Chuck's Line Graph

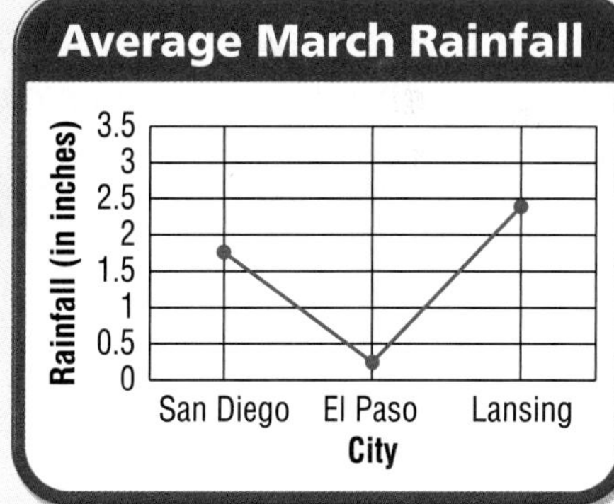

The data do not change over time. The average amount of rainfall is given for different cities, not one city. So, a line graph is *not* the best way to display the data.

So, Moira's bar graph is the best choice to display the data.

Guided Practice

Tell whether each graph or plot can show *categorical data*, *numerical data*, or *both*.

1. 

2. 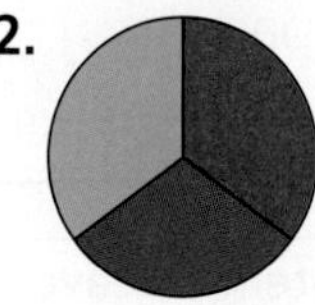

3. 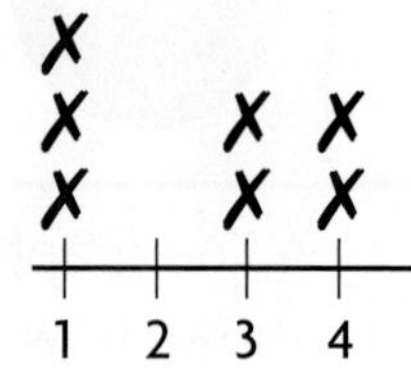

4.

Stem	Leaves
3	1
4	5

5. 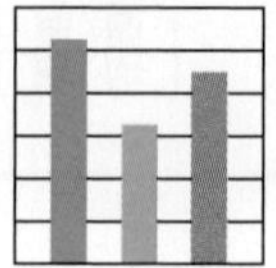

Choose the best type of graph or plot for the data. Explain your choice.

6. video game scores of 20 players
7. book sales each day for 5 days
8. how Jen spends the hours in one day

9. TALK Math **Explain** how you can determine if a graph shows numerical or categorical data.

Independent Practice and Problem Solving

Choose the best type of graph or plot for the data. Explain your choice.

10. numbers of students in six schools
11. minutes students spend practicing piano
12. high temperature each day for one week

Draw the graph or plot that best displays each set of data. Tell whether the data is *categorical* or *numerical*.

13.

Dog Weights (in pounds)							
35	32	48	89	93	125	12	17
132	116	78	41	56	92	36	87
10	15	38	45	76	99	82	105
56	72	39	14	23	83	97	112

14.

Henry's Allowance Budget	
Activity	**Amount**
Savings	$3
Entertainment	$5
Other	$2

15.

Skateboard Sales	
Month	**Sales**
April	$325
May	$450
June	$265

16.

Favorite Winter Activity	
Activity	**Number of Students**
Hockey	8
Skiing	17
Snowboarding	21

17. **Reasoning** Which graph would you make if you wanted to identify the median and mode from the graph?

18. WRITE Math **Explain** how you decide which type of graph is most appropriate for a set of data.

 Extra Practice on page 264, Set E

Learn About Continuous Data and Discrete Data

A graph can show data that is discrete or continuous. A graph that shows **continuous data** can be read between points. A graph that shows **discrete data** can only be read at its points.

Examples **Tell whether the graph shows *continuous* or *discrete* data.**

A

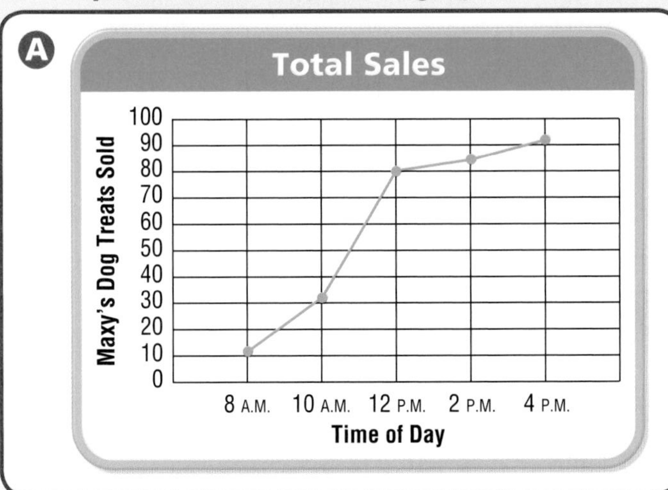

Time is continuous. Think: Were Maxy's dog treats sold between 8 A.M. and 10 A.M.? Since the answer is yes, this graph shows continuous data.

B

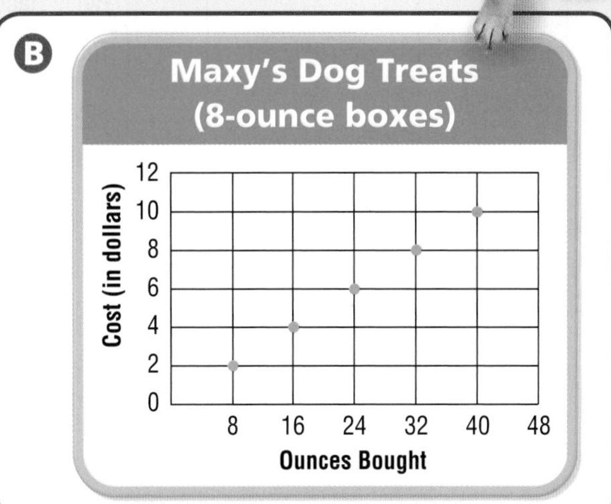

Think: Can I buy $1\frac{1}{2}$ boxes of Maxy's dog treats? Since the answer is no, this graph shows discrete data.

Try It

19. What question could you ask yourself to determine if a graph of a dog's weight over several months shows discrete or continuous data?

Select which of the two types of graphs shown above you would make to display each set of data. Explain.

20. a puppy's weight each month from 1 month to 6 months

21. the number of new tricks a puppy learns each month for 6 months

Mixed Review and Test Prep

22. What is the median of the data 9, 17, 6, 12, 15? (p. 220)

23. Kyle ran m miles yesterday. Today he ran 5.25 miles. If $m = 6.5$, how many miles did Kyle run in all? (p. 96)

24. **Test Prep** What type of graph would best display the data in the table? **Explain.**

Yearbook Sales				
Week	1	2	3	4
Amount	\$6	\$75	\$95	\$40

Extra Practice

Set A Make a graph for each data set. (pp. 242–245)

1.

Favorite Flavor	
Flavor	**Number of Votes**
Vanilla	24
Chocolate	30
Strawberry	26

2.

Field Day Activities	
Activity	**Number of Students**
Relay Race	20
Tug-of-War	16
Sack Race	18
High Jump	14

3.

Movie Ticket Sales	
Day	**Number Sold**
Thursday	36
Friday	42
Saturday	56
Sunday	20

Set B For 1–2, use the table. (pp. 246–247)

1. What is a reasonable interval for the ages of the campers?
2. Make a histogram of the data.

Ages of Campers					
12	4	13	7	11	6
18	11	10	5	16	18
5	14	7	15	10	12

Set C Graph and label each point on a coordinate grid. (pp. 248–249)

1. *F* (2,3) 2. *R* (6,4) 3. *M* (1,7) 4. *A* (5,2) 5. *B* (7,4) 6. *D* (3,3)

Set D For 1–2, make a line graph or a double-line graph for each set of data. (pp. 250–253)

1.

Show Attendance			
Day	**Monday**	**Tuesday**	**Wednesday**
Morning	120	150	130
Afternoon	140	140	120

2.

Free Throws Made					
Game	1	2	3	4	5
Number Made	12	15	22	18	16

Set E Draw the graph or plot that best displays each set of data. Tell whether the data is *categorical* or *numerical.* (pp. 260–263)

1.

Lunches Bought Today	
Lunch	**Number Bought**
Pizza	12
Chicken Nuggets	5
Chef Salad	4

2.

Class Grades on Math Test							
82	90	85	75	78	90	80	72
62	98	95	88	85	75	82	90
95	90	84	74	82	90	75	90

CD ROM **Technology**
Use Harcourt Mega Math, The Number Games, *ArachnaGraph*, Levels G, H.

TECHNOLOGY CONNECTION

*i*Tools: Graphs

Renee kept track of the number of points she scored in 5 games. She scored 11 points in Game 1, 4 points in Game 2, 14 points in Game 3, 20 points in Game 4, and 12 points in Game 5. How can Renee display the data in a graph?

Step 1	Click on *Graphs.*
Step 2	Since the greatest value is 20, click on the up arrow above the scale to set the scale from 0 to 20. Since there are 5 data values, enter 5 for the number of rows.
Step 3	Highlight the words in the data table and type new labels. Click in the data boxes to add new data.

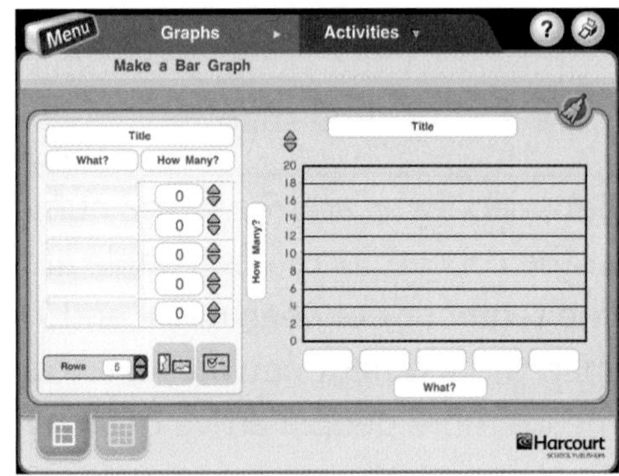

To make changes, you can go back to the Data Table, or you can make changes by typing directly on the graph.

Try It

For 1–4, follow the steps above to make an appropriate graph. Select the type of graph from the *Activities* menu.

1. Make a line graph for the following temperature data: Monday: 64°F, Tuesday: 74°F, Wednesday: 71°F, Thursday: 80°F, Friday: 73°F.
2. Make a bar graph for the number of people at each concert: pop: 290; jazz: 210; symphony: 225; hip-hop: 240.
3. Make a circle graph for a family's weekly budget. Use the following data: food: \$225; rent: \$285; utilities: \$75; car: \$100; entertainment: \$105.
4. **Explore More** Show your budget data for Exercise 3 as a bar graph. **Explain** how the bar graph is similar to and different from the circle graph.

GO ONLINE **Technology** *i*Tools are available online or on CD-ROM.

MATH POWER **Relationships in Graphs**

Line graphs can be used to show relationships.

Example

This graph shows the relationship between the number of people at a concert and time. It shows that the number of people sometimes increases, sometimes stays the same, and sometimes decreases during a 5-hour time span.

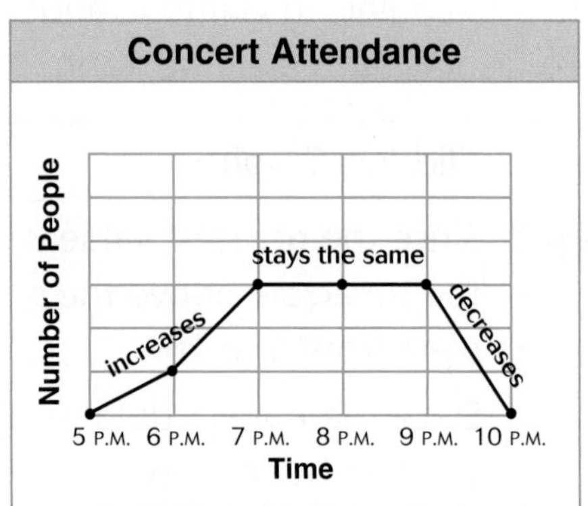

- Between 5 P.M. and 7 P.M. the number of people at the concert increases. People are arriving. The line segment between 6 P.M. and 7 P.M., is steeper than the segment between 5 P.M. and 6 P.M. This means more people arrive between 6 P.M. and 7 P.M. than between 5 P.M. and 6 P.M.
- Between 7 P.M. and 9 P.M. the number of people stays the same. The concert is on!
- Between 9 P.M. and 10 P.M. the number of people decreases. People are leaving the concert.

Try It

For each graph, describe what might be happening.

1. 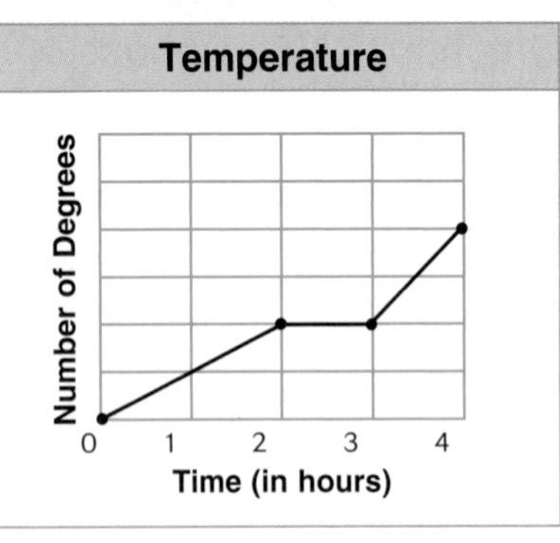

2. 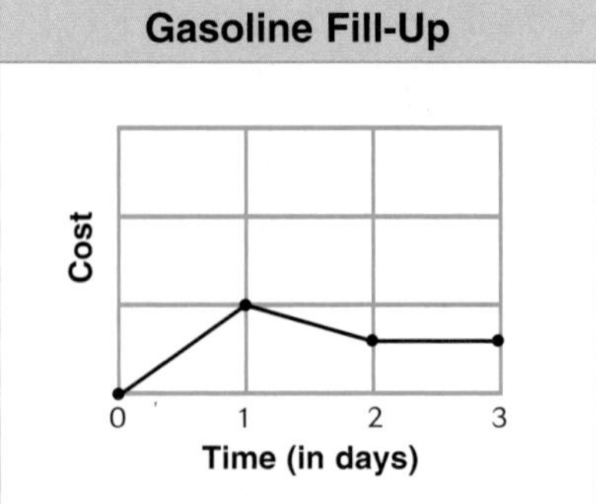

3. **WRITE Math** Make a graph to show the relationship between the total distance traveled on a car trip and the time it takes to make the trip. **Explain** what might be taking place when the graph shows an increase, a decrease, or stays the same.

Chapter 10 Review/Test

Check Vocabulary and Concepts

Choose the best term from the box.

VOCABULARY
double-bar graph
ordered pair
double line-graph
categorical data

1. A _?_ uses horizontal or vertical bars to display two sets of countable data. KY MA-05-4.1.3 (p. 242)
2. A(n) _?_ is used to locate points on a coordinate grid. KY MA-05-3.3.1 (p. 248)
3. _?_ are data that include groups or choices. KY MA-05-4.1.1 (p. 260)

Check Skills

Make a graph for each set of data. KY MA-05-4.1.3 (pp. 242–245, 250–253, 260–263)

4.

Frank's Flowers	
Type	Number Sold
Daisies	45
Tulips	50
Roses	75

5.

Rainfall	
Month	Amount (in in.)
April	15
May	12
June	10

6.

Weights of Cats (in pounds)			
15	14	18	21
21	24	18	15
16	14	17	20
22	24	15	13

Graph and label each point on a coordinate grid. KY MA-05-3.3.1 (pp. 248–249)

7. *A* (3,6) 8. *B* (5,1) 9. *C* (4,2) 10. *D* (6,3) 11. *E* (1,4)

Make a line graph or a double-line graph for each set of data. KY MA-05-4.1.3 (pp. 250–253)

12.

Video Rentals				
Month	Jan	Feb	Mar	Apr
Number	70	85	60	50

13.

Numbers of Rainy Days				
Month	Apr	May	Jun	Jul
Number	13	5	9	8

Check Problem Solving

Solve. KY MA-05-4.1.3 (pp. 256–259)

14. Karen kept track of the ages of people who rented ice skates at the park on Saturday. The ages are 12, 17, 15, 21, 14, 11, 19, 15, 13, 14, 20, 13, 11. Which age group had the most skate rentals: 10–12, 13–15, 16–18, or 19–21? Make a graph to solve.

15. WRITE Math Mark made a line graph to represent the number of pizzas sold at his restaurant each night for five nights. Why is a line graph the best way to display his data? **Explain.**

GO ONLINE **Technology** Use *Online Assessment.*

Unit Review/Test
Chapters 9–10

Multiple Choice

1. What is the median of Jonquil's test scores? KY MA-05-4.2.1 (p. 220)

Jonquil's Test Scores						
94	93	95	78	94	81	85

A. 85 C. 93

B. 87 D. 94

2. What is the mean of the scores for the 5 games played? KY MA-05-4.2.1 (p. 220)

The Hawks' Game Scores				
42	50	45	43	42

A. 42 C. 44

B. 43.5 D. 44.4

3. Which student had the highest mean test score? KY MA-05-4.2.1 (p. 220)

Name	Test 1	Test 2	Test 3	Test 4
Ally	87	93	99	95
Brad	95	90	91	91
Charles	87	92	88	90
Dill	74	100	92	98

A. Ally C. Charles

B. Brad D. Dill

4. What is the mode of the data? KY MA-05-4.2.1 (p. 220)

Number of Tickets Sold

Stem	Leaves
1	1 1 4
2	0 2 6 8
3	1 2 7 7 7
4	0 2 2 3 5

A. 11 C. 42

B. 37 D. 45

5. If the trend continues, about how long would it take Casey to walk 20 miles? KY MA-05-4.1.1 (p. 226)

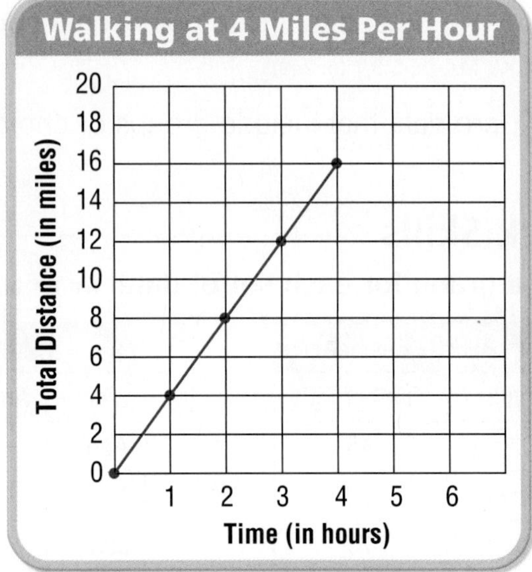

A. 4 hours C. 6 hours

B. 5 hours D. 20 hours

6. Ears of corn are stacked in a pyramid. There are 3 ears in the top row, 5 ears in the second row, 7 ears in the third row, and so on. How many ears will be in the eighth row of corn? KY MA-05-5.1.1 (p. 46)

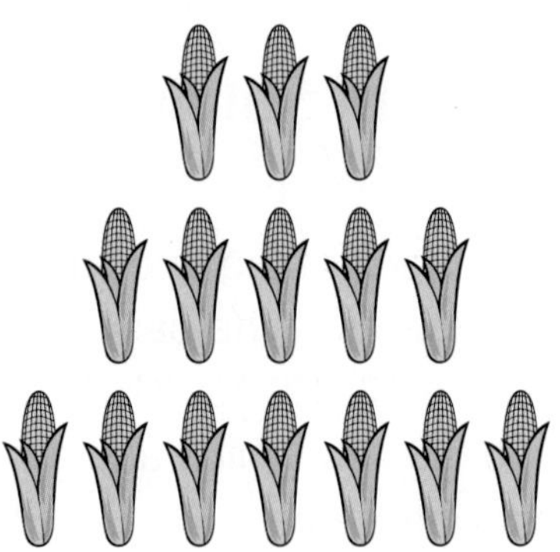

A. 13 C. 17

B. 15 D. 19

GO ONLINE Technology Use *Online Assessment.*

7. Cindy, Ricky, and John each practiced throwing a football. Cindy's average throw was 23.85 meters long. Ricky's throw was 23.25 meters long. John's throw was 23.58 meters long. Which orders the distances from greatest to least? KY MA-05-1.1.3 (p. 132)

A. 23.85; 23.58; 23.25

B. 23.85; 23.25; 23.58

C. 23.25; 23.58; 23.85

D. 23.25; 23.85; 23.58

8. For breakfast, Kate bought a bagel for $1.25, cream cheese for $0.95 and a glass of orange juice for $2.15. How much did Kate spend? KY MA-05-1.3.1 (p. 152)

A. $2.20

B. $3.10

C. $3.40

D. $4.35

9. Sue has taken 4 tests in math class. She has a mean test score of 89. Her mode is 88 and her highest score is 99. What are her 4 test scores? KY MA-05-4.2.1 (p. 220)

A. 99, 97, 88, 72

B. 81, 88, 88, 99

C. 85, 88, 88, 86

D. 99, 89, 88, 94

Open Response WRITE Math

10.

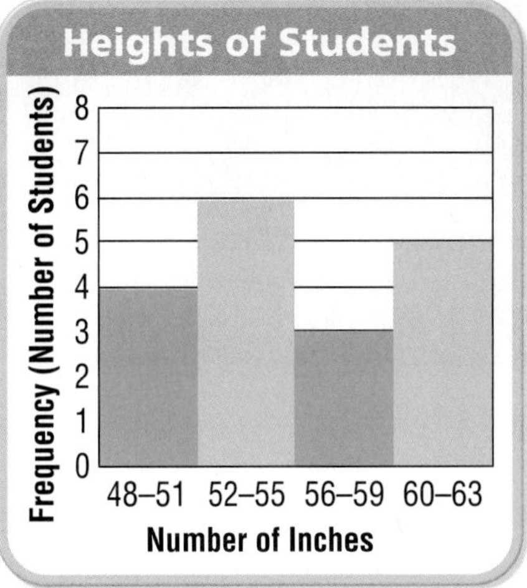

Look at the histogram. In which group do the heights of the most students fall? Where do the least fall? How would the histogram change if the following students' data were added? **Explain.** KY MA-05-4.1.3 (p. 246)

Jayne	56 inches
Carol	61 inches
Matt	59 inches

11. Use grid paper to make a line graph of the clock radio data.

Cal's Clock Radio Prices	
Year	**Price (dollars)**
1990	$35
1995	$32
2000	$29

Are the prices increasing or decreasing? If the trend continues, how much do you predict the radio will cost in 2010? **Explain.**

KY MA-05-4.1.3 (p. 250)

THE WORLD ALMANAC FOR KIDS

At the Library

Library Collections

There are more than 15,000 public libraries in the United States. Anyone with a current library card can borrow books from a public library. Many library systems have thousands of volumes. Volumes include books and magazines. However, most libraries also have music, movies, or recorded books that can be checked out to enjoy. Some libraries have special programs like reading contests.

FACT·ACTIVITY

Use the graph to answer the questions.

1. How many more volumes in millions does the Detroit Public Library hold than the Chicago Public Library?
2. How many volumes in millions do the New York and the Philadelphia libraries have combined?
3. WRITE Math **Explain** how you could find the mean number of volumes of the libraries in the graph.

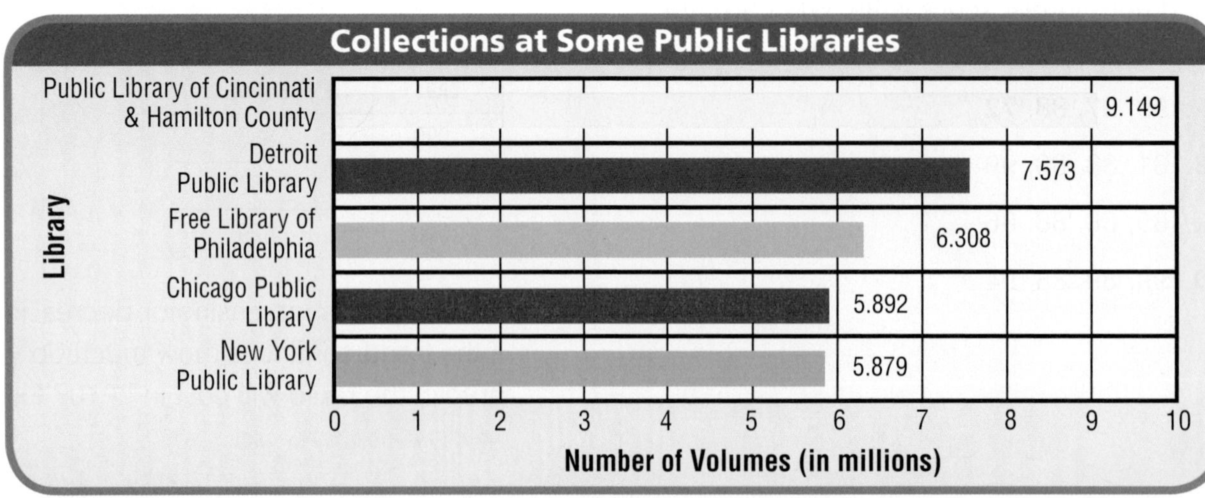

ALMANAC **Fact**

The Library of Congress in Washington, DC, is the largest library in the world. The collection has more than 134 million items contained on over 530 miles of bookshelves.

Keep Them Circulating

In 1731, Benjamin Franklin helped launch the Library Company, which became the first public library that circulated books. A book "circulates" when someone borrows it and then returns it. Circulation statistics show how many library books are checked out during a specific amount of time.

FACT·ACTIVITY

Use the table below to answer the questions.

1. Stack 10 books from your classroom in one pile. Measure the height of the stack with a yardstick. What is the mean height of one book?
2. If you could make one pile of all of the books in Cleveland's circulation, estimate how high would the stack would be.
3. Choose four of the circulation numbers. Round each to the nearest hundred thousand.
   - Decide what kind of graph would be best to compare the rounded amounts. Then make a scale for your graph. Draw your graph, but do not label it with the library names.
   - Switch graphs with a partner. Determine the four libraries on your partner's graph, and finish the graph.

Circulation for a Year in Some Ohio Libraries

Library	Circulation
Columbus	16,503,822
Cincinnati	14,344,449
Cuyahoga County	14,070,613
Dayton	6,363,468
Toledo	6,309,751
Cleveland	5,011,399

UNIT 4

Number Theory and Fraction Concepts

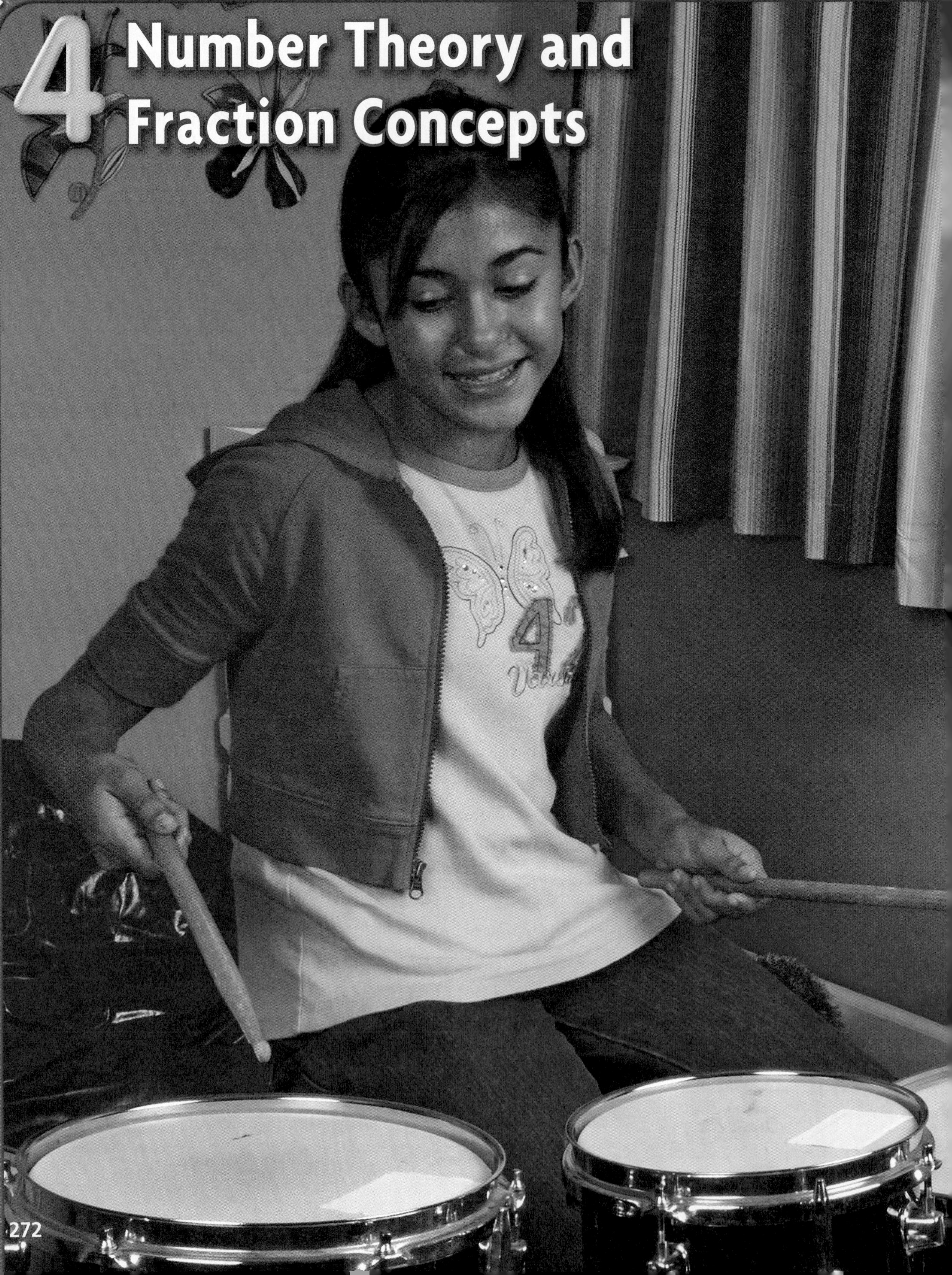

Math on Location

with
Chapter Projects

1

Beats of 3, 4, or 8 per measure form repeating patterns, or rhythms, on electronic drums.

2

Like patterns of factors, the rhythm is combined with another recorded, but different, rhythm.

3

Electronic equipment displays the recorded rhythms as patterns that can be viewed.

VOCABULARY POWER

TALK Math

What math is used in music in the **Math on Location**? How can you determine when two different rhythm patterns will share a single beat?

READ Math

REVIEW VOCABULARY You will learn the words below when you learn about factors and fractions. How do these words relate to **Math on Location**?

factor a number that is multiplied by another number to find a product

common factor a number that is a factor of two or more numbers

mixed number a number represented by a whole number and a fraction

WRITE Math

Copy and complete the table below. Use what you know about patterns.

Question	Rhythms
How many beats are in 7 measures?	2 beats per measure: 2, 4, 6, 8, 10, 12, **14**, 16, 18
When do two different rhythms share beats?	2, 3 beats per measure: 2, 4, **6**, 8, 10, **12**, 14, __, __ 3, **6**, 9, **12**, __, __, __
When do two different rhythms share beats?	3, 4 beats per measure: 3, 6, 9, __, __, __, __, __ 4, 8, __, __, __, __, __

Technology
Multimedia Math Glossary link at
www.harcourtschool.com/hspmath

CHAPTER 11

Number Theory

FAST FACT

Since 1959, the championship game of the Little League World Series has been played at Howard J. Lamade Stadium in Williamsport, Pennsylvania.

Investigate

The table shows some of the highest-scoring championship games since the Little League World Series began in 1947. Choose 3 games. Write the prime factorization for both scores of each game. Do the scores share any of the same prime factors?

Little League World Series Highest-Scoring Championship Games

Year	Winner	Score	Runner-Up
1998	New Jersey	12–9	Japan
1987	Taiwan	21–1	California
1971	Taiwan	12–3	Indiana
1959	Michigan	12–0	California
1947	Williamsport, PA	16–7	Lock Haven, PA

Technology
Student pages are available in the Student eBook.

Show What You Know

Check your understanding of important skills needed for success in Chapter 11.

▶ Multiplication and Division Facts

Find the product.

1. 3×7 **2.** 4×2 **3.** 8×5 **4.** 6×4

5. 7×9 **6.** 3×8 **7.** 6×9 **8.** 8×7

Find the quotient.

9. $18 \div 2$ **10.** $24 \div 3$ **11.** $28 \div 7$ **12.** $42 \div 6$

13. $54 \div 9$ **14.** $48 \div 8$ **15.** $36 \div 4$ **16.** $64 \div 8$

▶ Factors

Write all the factors for each number.

17. 10 **18.** 13 **19.** 20 **20.** 15

21. 32 **22.** 36 **23.** 72 **24.** 37

▶ Multiples

Write the first six multiples of each number.

25. 3 **26.** 5 **27.** 7 **28.** 10

29. 6 **30.** 12 **31.** 9 **32.** 15

VOCABULARY POWER

CHAPTER VOCABULARY

base
common factor
common multiple
composite number
divisible
exponent
factor
greatest common factor (GCF)
factor tree
least common multiple (LCM)
multiple
perfect square
prime factorization
prime number
square number

WARM-UP WORDS

common factor a number that is a factor of two or more numbers

common multiple a number that is a multiple of two or more numbers

exponent a number that shows how many times the base is used as a factor

LESSON 1 Multiples and the Least Common Multiple

OBJECTIVE: Identify multiples and the least common multiple of a set of whole numbers.

Quick Review

Count by

1. twos from 2 to 18.
2. fours from 8 to 32.
3. fives from 5 to 25.
4. sixes from 6 to 30.
5. sevens from 14 to 42.

Vocabulary

multiple **common multiple**
least common multiple (LCM)

Learn

The product of two or more whole numbers is called a **multiple**. When a number is a multiple of two or more numbers it is a **common multiple** of these numbers.

Example **Find common multiples of 4 and 6 for the set of numbers 4 to 30.**

multiples of 4: 4, 8, 12, 16, 20, 24, 28
multiples of 6: 6, 12, 18, 24, 30

So, the common multiples of 4 and 6 for this set of numbers are 12 and 24.

Math Idea
To find multiples of a number, just start with that number and skip-count by that number.
Example:
5, 10, 15, 20 and so on.

The least number, greater than zero, that is a multiple of two or more numbers is called the **least common multiple**, or **LCM**.

PROBLEM On a ferry line, a ferry leaves Hoboken, New Jersey, every 6 minutes and crosses the river to New York. On a different ferry line, a ferry leaves Hoboken for New York every 8 minutes. Both lines have ferries that leave Hoboken at 7:00 A.M. When will two ferries next leave from Hoboken at the same time?

Find the LCM of 6 and 8 for the set of numbers 6 to 60.

ONE WAY **Use a list.**

Step 1

Find common multiples.
6: 6, 12, 18, 24, 30, 36, 42, 48, 54, 60
8: 8, 16, 24, 32, 40, 48, 56

Step 2

Identify the least common multiple.
6: 6, 12, 18, 24, 30, 36, 42, 48, 54, 60
8: 8, 16, 24, 32, 40, 48, 56

ANOTHER WAY **Use a diagram.**

Place the multiples in the appropriate parts of the Venn diagram.

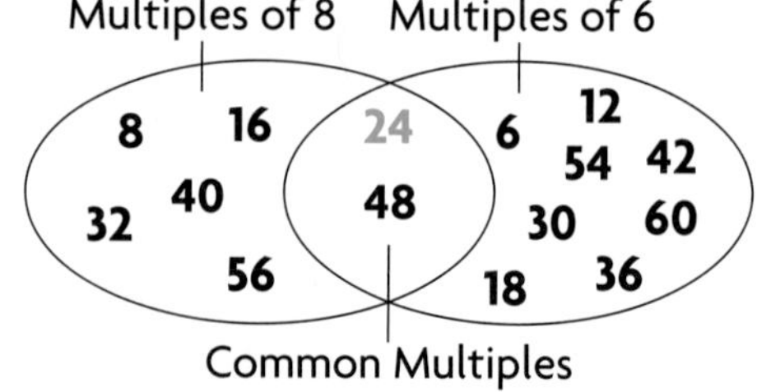

The least common multiple of 6 and 8 is 24. So, two ferries will next leave from Hoboken at the same time in 24 minutes, or at 7:24 A.M.

KY MA-05-1.5.1 Students will identify and determine composite numbers, prime numbers, multiples of a number, factors of a number and least common multiples (LCM), and will apply these numbers to solve real-world problems. DOK 2

Guided Practice

1. **Use these lists of multiples to find the least common multiple of 3 and 5.**

   3: 3, 6, 9, 12, 15, 18, 21, 24, 27, 30, 33
   5: 5, 10, 15, 20, 25, 30, 35

List the first ten multiples of each number.

2. 4 3. 7 4. 8 5. 2 6. 9

Write the least common multiple of each set of numbers.

7. 4 and 8 8. 3 and 7 9. 6 and 10 10. 3 and 4 11. 4, 8, and 12

12. TALK Math **Explain** how to use a Venn diagram to find the least common multiples of 6 and 9.

Independent Practice and Problem Solving

List the first ten multiples of each number.

13. 3 14. 9 15. 12 16. 6 17. 11

Write the least common multiples of each set of numbers.

18. 8 and 4 19. 9 and 12 20. 12 and 16 21. 7 and 5

22. 10 and 8 23. 12, 4, and 10 24. 7, 14, and 21 25. 6, 16, and 24

For 26–28, the diagram shows courses of Cars A, B, and C. All cars travel at the same speed.

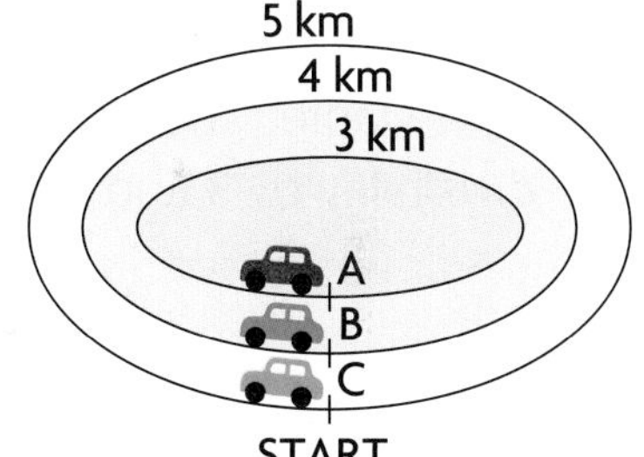

26. From Start, Cars A and B start together. Car A travels 4 laps. How many laps does Car B need to go to travel the same distance as Car A?

27. Cars B and C start together. After several laps both cars pass Start at the same time. How far has each car traveled the first time this happens?

28. Cars A, B, and C start together. After several laps, all three cars pass the starting line at the same time. How far has each car traveled when this first happens?

29. WRITE Math An unknown number and 10 have an LCM of 40. What is the unknown number? **Explain** how you found the unknown number.

Mixed Review and Test Prep

30. Kala's boat is 12.25 feet long. What is the length of her boat in inches? (Grade 4)

31. On a graph, what scale and interval would you use for these data: 10, 14, 21, 25, 32, 40, 51? (p. 242)

32. **Test Prep** Which set of numbers has an LCM of 54?

   A 6, 9, 27
   B 9, 18, 32
   C 3, 9, 24
   D 6, 9, 36

Extra Practice on page 300, Set A

LESSON 2 HANDS ON

Divisibility

OBJECTIVE: Identify numbers that are divisible by 2, 3, 5, 6, 9, and 10, and learn the divisibility rules.

Quick Review

In which problem does the quotient have a remainder of 0?

1. 64 ÷ 8 or 64 ÷ 6
2. 90 ÷ 11 or 90 ÷ 10
3. 125 ÷ 4 or 125 ÷ 5
4. 200 ÷ 3 or 200 ÷ 4
5. 144 ÷ 12 or 144 ÷ 7

Vocabulary

divisible

Investigate

Materials ■ calculator

A number is **divisible** by another number if the quotient is a whole number and the remainder is zero.

You can discover rules to determine divisibility without actually dividing.

A Make a table like the one shown at the right. Include the numbers 1,326; 952; 6,327; 57,460; and 2,235. Test them for divisibility by 2, 3 and 9. Use a calculator. Example:

1,326 ÷ 2 = 663 r0 ← divisible by 2

1,326 ÷ 3 = 442 r0 ← divisible by 3

1,326 ÷ 9 = 147 r3 ← not divisible by 9

Number	Divisible by			Sum of Digits	Sum Divisible by	
	2	3	9		3	9
1,326	yes	yes	no	12	yes	no
952						
6,327						

B Find the sum of the digits of the first number in the table. Check the sum of the digits for divisibility by 3 and 9. Example:

1,326 → 1 + 3 + 2 + 6 = 12 ← sum of the digits

12 ÷ 3 = 4 r0 ← sum divisible by 3

12 ÷ 9 = 1 r3 ← sum not divisible by 9

C Repeat for the other numbers. Complete your table.

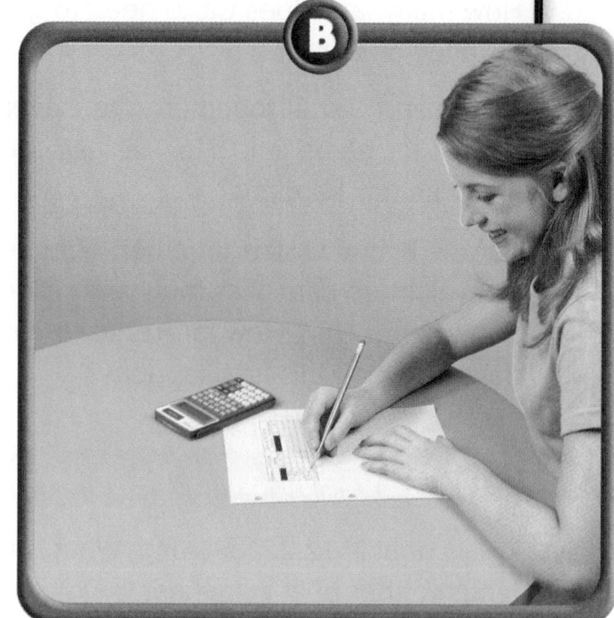

Draw Conclusions

1. If the sum of the digits of a number is divisible by 3, is the number divisible by 3? Write a rule for divisibility by 3.
2. If the sum of the digits of a number in your table is divisible by 9, is the number divisible by 9? Write a rule for divisibility by 9.
3. **Synthesis** Test some numbers that are divisible by both 2 and 3. Are they also divisible by 6? Write a rule for divisibility by 6. **Explain.**

Connect

The table shows divisibility rules for 2, 3, 5, 6, 9, and 10.

A number is divisible by		Examples
2	if the last digit is an even number.	534 ⟶ even, divisible by 2 227 ⟶ odd, not divisible by 2
3	if the sum of its digits is divisible by 3.	138 ⟶ $1 + 3 + 8 = 12$, divisible by 3 139 ⟶ $1 + 3 + 9 = 13$, not divisible by 3
5	if the last digit is 0 or 5.	245 ⟶ divisible by 5 544 ⟶ not divisible by 5
6	if the number is divisible by both 2 and 3.	474 ⟶ divisible by 6 679 ⟶ not divisible by 6
9	if the sum of its digits is divisible by 9.	792 ⟶ $7 + 9 + 2 = 18$, divisible by 9 158 ⟶ $1 + 5 + 8 = 14$, not divisible by 9
10	if the last digit is 0.	680 ⟶ divisible by 10 455 ⟶ not divisible by 10

You can use these rules to test the number 3,564 for divisibility.

Step 1

Look at the last digit. The last digit is 4, so
3,564 is divisible by 2.
3,564 is not divisible by 5.
3,564 is not divisible by 10.

Step 2

Find the sum of the digits.
$3 + 5 + 6 + 4 = 18$, so
3,564 is divisible by 3.
3,564 is divisible by 9.

Step 3

See if the number is divisible by both 2 and 3.
3,564 is divisible by 2.
3,564 is divisible by 3.
3,564 is divisible by 6.

So, 3,564 is divisible by 2, 3, 6, and 9.

TALK Math

Explain how to determine whether 6,825 is divisible by 6.

Practice

Test each number to determine whether it is divisible by 2, 3, 5, 6, 9, or 10.

1. 492 **2.** 8,037 **3.** 28,460 **4.** 43,705 **5.** 4,005

6. 27,400 **7.** 72,999 **8.** 8,128 **9.** 17,496 **10.** 5,675

Write *true* or *false*.

11. All even numbers are divisible by 2.

12. All odd numbers are divisible by 3.

13. All even numbers are divisible by 6.

14. All multiples of 9 are divisible by 9.

15. **WRITE Math** Write a 4-digit number that is divisible by both 6 and 9. **Explain** how you know without dividing that it is divisible by both 6 and 9.

LESSON 3

Factors and the Greatest Common Factor

OBJECTIVE: Identify factors and the greatest common factor of a set of whole numbers.

Quick Review

Write the missing number.

1. 7 × ■ = 21
2. ■ × 6 = 24
3. 10 × ■ = 70
4. 12 × ■ = 36
5. ■ × 8 = 72

Vocabulary

common factor

greatest common factor (GCF)

Learn

A number that is a factor of two or more numbers is called a **common factor**.

factors of 12: 1, 2, 3, 4, 6, 12
factors of 20: 1, 2, 4, 5, 10, 20

The common factors of 12 and 20 are 1, 2 and 4.

You can use common factors to solve problems.

PROBLEM Mr. Willis is making picture frames for Ami's Craft Store. He has one strip of framing wood that is 8 feet long and another that is 12 feet long. He wants to cut both strips of wood into smaller pieces that are all the same length for the sides of the frames without wasting any wood. What are the possible whole number lengths of each piece of wood?

Remember

A number multiplied by another number to find a product is called a factor.
For example:
6 × 2 = 12
6 and 2 are factors of 12.

ONE WAY Use a list.

Step 1	Step 2
List all factors of each number.	Identify the common factors.
8: 1, 2, 4, 8	**8:** 1, 2, 4, 8
12: 1, 2, 3, 4, 6, 12	**12:** 1, 2, 3, 4, 6, 12

The common factors of 8 and 12 are 1, 2, and 4.

ANOTHER WAY Use a diagram.

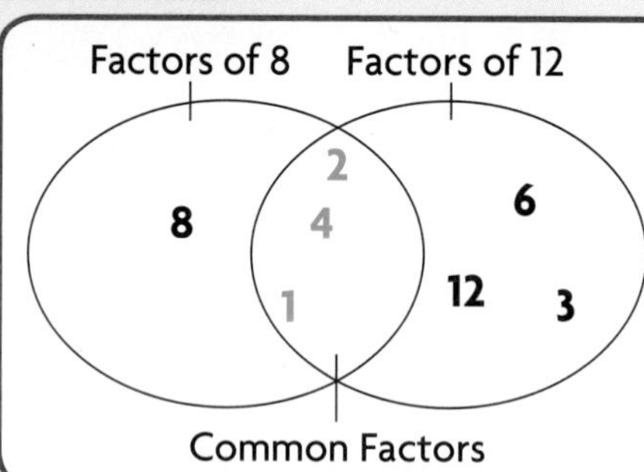

The common factors of 8 and 12 are 1, 2, and 4.

So, Mr. Willis can cut the wood in lengths of 1 foot, 2 feet, or 4 feet.

FAST TRACK

KY MA-05-1.5.1 Students will identify and determine composite numbers, prime numbers, multiples of a number, factors of a number and least common multiples (LCM), and will apply these numbers to solve real-world problems. DOK 2

Greatest Common Factor

To solve some problems, you may need to find the greatest factor possible. The **greatest common factor**, or **GCF**, is the greatest factor that two or more numbers have in common.

Example 1 Use the greatest common factor

At the craft store, Ami is gift wrapping the frames for her customers. She has one piece of ribbon that is 16 feet long and another that is 24 feet long. She needs to cut each ribbon into smaller pieces so that all pieces have the same length. What is the greatest whole-number length she can make each piece of ribbon?

Step 1	Step 2	Step 3
List all factors of each number.	Identify the common factors.	Identify the greatest common factor.
16: 1, 2, 4, 8, 16 **24:** 1, 2, 3, 4, 6, 8, 12, 24	**16:** 1, 2, 4, 8, 16 **24:** 1, 2, 3, 4, 6, 8, 12, 24	**16:** 1, 2, 4, 8, 16 **24:** 1, 2, 3, 4, 6, 8, 12, 24

The greatest common factor, or GCF, of 16 and 24 is 8.
So, the greatest length that Ami can make each piece is 8 feet.

Example 2 Use the greatest common factor

Ami has two more ribbons that she needs to cut. One is 20 feet long and the other is 30 feet long. What is the greatest length, in feet, that she can make each smaller piece so that all the pieces have the same length?

Step 1	Step 2	Step 3
List all factors.	Identify the common factors.	Identify the GCF.
20: 1, 2, 4, 5, 10, 20 **30:** 1, 2, 3, 5, 6, 10, 15, 30	**20:** 1, 2, 4, 5, 10, 20 **30:** 1, 2, 3, 5, 6, 10, 15, 30	**20:** 1, 2, 4, 5, 10, 20 **30:** 1, 2, 3, 5, 6, 10, 15, 30

The greatest common factor, or GCF, of 20 and 30 is 10.
So, the greatest length that Ami can cut is 10 feet.

- What is the greatest common factor of 12 and 28?

Guided Practice

1. Copy and complete the Venn diagram. What are the common factors of 14 and 21? What is the greatest common factor of 14 and 21?

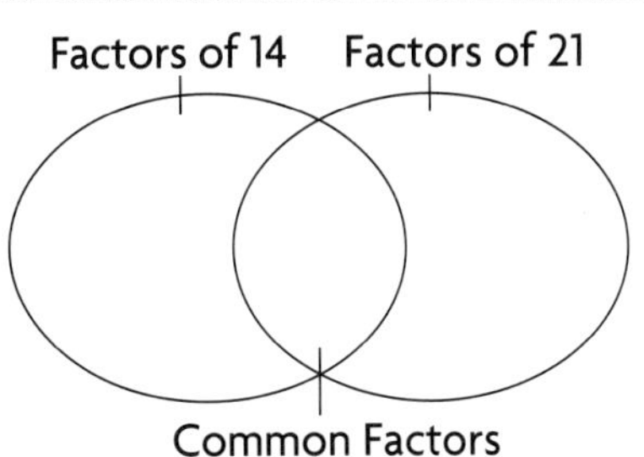

List the factors of each number.

2. 25
3. 10
4. 32
5. 18
6. 21

Write the common factors of each pair of numbers.

7. 12, 20
8. 12, 15
9. 16, 24
10. 9, 27
11. 14, 35

Write the greatest common factor for each pair of numbers.

12. 10, 15
13. 12, 16
14. 9, 18
15. 15, 24
16. 16, 40

17. TALK Math **Explain** how to find the greatest common factor of 12 and 30.

Independent Practice and Problem Solving

List the factors of each number.

18. 27
19. 16
20. 36
21. 11
22. 34
23. 50
24. 13
25. 54
26. 7
27. 42

Write the common factors for each pair of numbers.

28. 25, 50
29. 28, 35
30. 30, 45
31. 16, 18
32. 20, 24

Write the greatest common factor for each pair of numbers.

33. 16, 32
34. 10, 12
35. 20, 30
36. 27, 36
37. 24, 40
38. 18, 42
39. 24, 60
40. 18, 30
41. 40, 56
42. 14, 49

USE DATA For 43–46, use the table.

Bread Ingredients		
Recipe	**Flour**	**Liquid**
Country Sourdough	32 oz	12 oz
Whole Wheat	30 oz	9 oz
Coffee Cake	40 oz	16 oz

43. Marco wants to use a single scoop to measure both flour and liquid for making coffee cake. In whole ounces, what is the largest scoop size he can use to make the cake?
44. What is the largest scoop size Marco can use to make country sourdough bread? whole-wheat bread?
45. Marco adds 26 ounces of flour and 12 ounces of liquid to the whole-wheat recipe. How can Marco use 2 scoops to make the whole-wheat bread?
46. **Reasoning** Does the maximum scoop size double when you make a double recipe? **Explain.**
47. WRITE Math **What's the Question?** Marco made a recipe that called for 20 ounces of flour and 25 ounces of liquid. The answer is 5 oz.

Extra Practice on page 300, Set B

Mixed Review and Test Prep

48. Jan took 6 math tests this semester. Her scores were 72, 86, 78, 88, 94, and 92. What was her mean score? (p. 220)

49. **Test Prep** The greatest common factor of 18 and another number is 9. The second number is between 40 and 50. What is it?

50. Jan's math group received the following scores: 72, 92, 90, 83, 72, 80, 86, 67, 85? What was the median score for the group? (p. 220)

51. **Test Prep** Which number is not a common factor of 48 and 24?

A 24

B 16

C 8

D 6

Problem Solving connects to Social Studies

Another method for finding the greatest common factor was developed by Euclid. Euclid was a famous Greek mathematician who lived over 2,000 years ago. Euclid's method uses repeated division. Follow the steps to find the greatest common factor, or GCF of 72 and 42.

Step 1	Step 2	Step 3	Step 4
Divide the greater number by the lesser number.	Now divide the divisor from Step 1, 42, by the remainder from Step 1, 30.	Continue dividing divisors by remainders until the final remainder is 0.	The divisor in the last division is the GCF.
1 r30 42)72 (divisor: 42) −42 30 (remainder)	1 r12 30)42 −30 12	2 r6 12)30 −24 6	2 r0 6)12 −12 0

Since the remainder of 12 ÷ 6 is 0, the GCF of 42 and 72 is 6.

Use Euclid's method to find the GCF of each set of numbers.

1. 75, 200 **2.** 40, 96 **3.** 60, 108 **4.** 44, 110

5. 42, 105 **6.** 225, 90 **7.** 60, 150 **8.** 192, 72

9. **Reasoning** Explain how using Euclid's method for finding the GCF is different from using a Venn diagram.

LESSON 4 HANDS ON

Prime and Composite Numbers

OBJECTIVE: Identify factors and tell whether a number is prime or composite.

Quick Review

Write *true* or *false*.

1. 5 is a factor of 15.
2. 4 is a factor of 18.
3. 7 is a factor of 27.
4. 8 is a factor of 32.
5. 9 is a factor of 54.

Vocabulary

prime number composite number

Investigate

Materials ■ counters

A **prime number** has exactly two factors, 1 and itself. A **composite number** is a number that has more than two factors. The number 1 is neither prime nor composite.

You can use counters to represent whole numbers and their factors.

A Draw a table like the one shown at the right. Include numbers from 1 to 20.

Number	Arrays	Factors
1	1×1	1
2	$2 \times 1, 1 \times 2$	1, 2
3	$3 \times 1, 1 \times 3$	1, 3
4		

B For 4, you can make three different arrays: 4×1, 2×2, 1×4. The factors of 4 are 1, 2, and 4. Record this data in the table.

1×4 2×2 4×1

C Use the counters to represent numbers from 2 to 20. For each number, make every array possible. Record your results in the table.

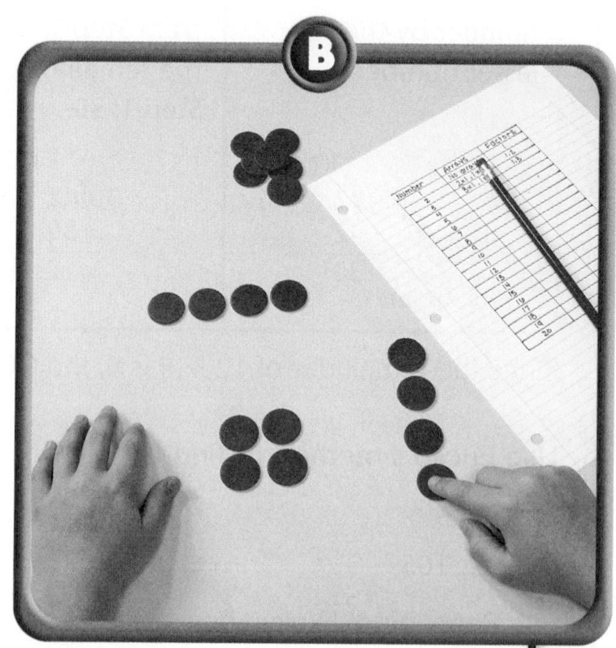

Draw Conclusions

1. Look at your table. Which numbers from 2 to 20 are prime numbers?
2. Which numbers from 2 to 20 are composite numbers?
3. **Comprehension** How can you use counters to determine whether a number greater than 20 is prime or composite? Explain.

FAST TRACK

KY MA-05-1.5.1 Students will identify and determine composite numbers, prime numbers, multiples of a number, factors of a number and least common multiples (LCM), and will apply these numbers to solve real-world problems. DOK 2

Connect

You can use the sieve of Eratosthenes to find prime numbers. This method for identifying primes was invented over 2,200 years ago by the Greek mathematician Eratosthenes. Copy the table. Follow the steps to circle all prime numbers from 1 to 60. Then write observations on what you discover.

1	2	3	4	5	6	7	8	9	10
11	12	13	14	15	16	17	18	19	20
21	22	23	24	25	26	27	28	29	30
31	32	33	34	35	36	37	38	39	40
41	42	43	44	45	46	47	48	49	50
51	52	53	54	55	56	57	58	59	60

Remember
A multiple is the product of two counting numbers. Multiples of 2:
$2 \times 1 = 2$, $2 \times 2 = 4$, $2 \times 3 = 6$,. . .

Step 1 Cross out 1, since it is not a prime number.

Step 2 Circle 2, since it is a prime. Cross out all other multiples of 2.

Step 3 Circle the next number that is not crossed out. Then cross out all of its remaining multiples.

Step 4 Repeat Step 3 until every number is either circled or crossed out.

- **Reasoning** Why are the multiples of any number not prime numbers?

TALK Math
Explain why the numbers that are not crossed out in the table are prime numbers.

Practice

Write prime or composite. You may use counters or draw arrays.

1. 25 **2.** 23 **3.** 32 **4.** 36

5. 48 **6.** 53 **7.** 71 **8.** 60

9. 95 **10.** 97 **11.** 144 **12.** 103

ERROR ALERT
- 1 is neither prime nor composite.
- 2 is the only even prime number.

13. True or false: the product of two prime numbers is a prime number. Explain. Use an example.

14. The combination to Erica's lock is 24, 35, and the greatest prime number between 30 and 40. What is the third combination number?

15. WRITE Math **Explain** why all prime numbers greater than 2 are odd numbers.

Problem Solving Workshop
Strategy: Make an Organized List

OBJECTIVE: Solve problems by using the strategy *make an organized list.*

Learn the Strategy

Making an organized list can help you look at data in several ways. You can use different types of lists to analyze different types of data.

An organized list can show all possibilities.

At Antonio's Pizza Place, you can choose from two types of crust and three different toppings. Antonio made a tree diagram to show all the possible pizzas you can order.

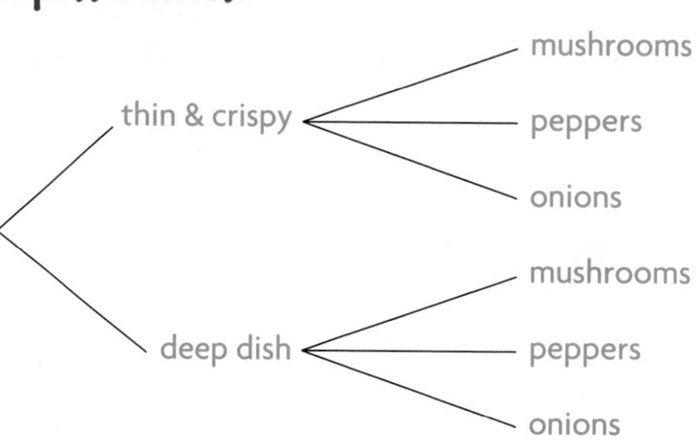

An organized list can help you sort information.

During the month of July, Emilee has gymnastics practice every other day and a gymnastics meet every Saturday. On July 7, she has practice and a meet. She made a list to see when both activities would occur on the same day.

So, practices and meets will both occur only on July 7 and July 21.

Practice is every other day.

1, 3, 5, **7**, 9, 11, 13, 15, 17, 19, **21**, 23, 25, 27, 29, 31

The first gymnastics meet is on July 7. Since there are 7 days in a week, list multiples of 7.

7, 14, **21**, 28

TALK Math

What additional questions can be answered by using each of the lists above?

Recording work in an organized way makes it easier to discover relationships and patterns among data.

Use the Strategy

PROBLEM For an art project, each student is making a rectangular mosaic design with 1-inch-square tiles. Students can use 22 tiles, 28 tiles, or 31 tiles in their designs. How many different rectangular arrays can a student make with 22 tiles? with 28 tiles? with 31 tiles?

Read to Understand

- **Visualize the problem situation.**
- **What information is given?**

Plan

- **What strategy can you use to solve the problem?**
  You can make an organized list to solve the problem.

Solve

- **How can you use the strategy to solve the problem?**
  List the data in a table to show all the possible rectangular arrays.

Step 1

List the number of tiles that can be used in the mosaic design.

Step 2

For each number of tiles used, list all the possible rectangular arrays.

Number of Tiles	Rectangular Arrays
22	1×22, 22×1, 2×11, 11×2
28	1×28, 28×1, 2×14, 14×2, 4×7, 7×4
31	1×31, 31×1

So, with 22 tiles students can make 4 different rectangular arrays. With 28 tiles students can make 6 different rectangular arrays, and with 31 tiles students can make 2 rectangular arrays.

Check

- **Look back at the problem. Do the answers make sense for the question in the problem? Explain.**

Guided Problem Solving

Read to Understand
Plan
Solve
Check

1. The students in design class are drawing floor plans on graph paper. They know that on their drawings, 1 unit square on the graph paper is equivalent to 1 square yard. In their plans, the rectangular spaces such as rooms, hallways, and closets must have areas of 5 unit squares, 9 unit squares, or 16 unit squares. How many possible rectangular spaces can the students choose from?

First, copy the table and list the areas for the rectangular spaces.

Then, list all the possible rectangular spaces that can be formed.

Finally, count the number of rectangular spaces.

Area of Space (in unit squares)	Rectangular Spaces
5	
9	
16	

✓2. **What if** the students could increase the area of each space by one unit square? How would the number of possible rectangular spaces change?

✓3. Toni and Hector are weaving pot holders using the colors red, white, green, and blue. If they use only two colors for each pot holder, how many ways can they combine two colors?

Problem Solving Strategy Practice

Use an organized list to solve.

4. Students at art camp must turn in a sketch every 3 days and a finished painting every 7 days. If art camp starts on June 1, when would the students have both assignments due on the same day?

5. Elliott is building a model. The top level has 1 block, and the next level has 3 blocks. The third level has 6 blocks and the fourth level has 10 blocks. If this pattern continues, how many blocks will be in the seventh level?

For 6–9, use the table of sculpture supplies to solve.

6. Each sculpture student can choose a tool, a material, and a finish from the list. How many choices do the students have?

7. If they can choose only a material and a tool, how many choices do they have?

8. Derek owns a complete set of tools. He only needs to choose the material and the finish. What are his choices?

9. Three students are doing a sculpture together. Ana does not want to use plaster and Rob does not want to use clay. Sheila wants to use paint. What material and finish did the students use?

Sculpture Supply List

Tool	Material	Finish
Hammer	Clay	Glaze
Scraper	Plaster	Paint
Sandpaper	Wood	
Paintbrush		

Mixed Strategy Practice

10. There are 7 art classes offered in the enrichment program. A class can have no more than 20 students. If there are 89 students in the program now, how many more can join?

11. Cara made twice as many bracelets as Keith, and Paulo made 7 more than Cara. If Paulo made 15 bracelets, how many bracelets did Keith make?

12. There are 12 boys and 6 girls in art class. If the same number of boys are at each table and the same number of girls are at each table, what is the greatest number of boys and girls that can be at a table if each table can seat 6?

Choose a STRATEGY

- Draw a Diagram or Picture
- Make a Model or Act It Out
- Make an Organized List
- Find a Pattern
- Make a Table or Graph
- Predict and Test
- Work Backward
- Solve a Simpler Problem
- Write an Equation
- Use Logical Reasoning

USE DATA For 13–15, use the graph.

13. Copy and complete the graph. Use the clues below to find the missing data in the graph.

    Clue 1: The most students are in drawing class.

    Clue 2: Design class has twice as many students as sculpture class.

    Clue 3: Crafts is the second-largest class.

    Clue 4: There are $\frac{1}{3}$ as many students in jewelry class as in sculpture class.

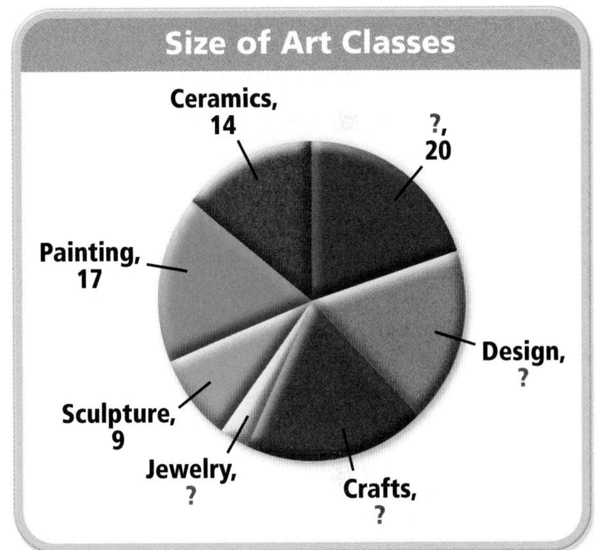

14. **Open-Ended** Next year the art classes will have a total of 125 students. Based on the clues in Problem 13, predict about how many students could be in each art class next year.

15. **Pose a Problem** Look back at Problem 13. Write a similar problem by changing the size of the ceramics class and the drawing class. Then solve the problem.

16. **WRITE Math** Write the numbers 2 to 15. Cross out all multiples of 2, not including 2. Cross out all multiples of 3, but not including 3. **Describe** the list of numbers that is left.

CHALLENGE YOURSELF

Before starting a project, the crafts teacher counted all the beads. She found that there were 235 purple beads, 180 red beads, 231 green beads, 198 yellow beads, and 203 blue beads.

17. A bracelet pattern requires two colors in groups of 3 and 11. Which two groups of beads can be divided evenly by both 3 and 11? **Explain** how you know.

18. Two colors of beads are divisible by one and themselves and by two other prime numbers. Which colors are these?

LESSON 6

Introduction to Exponents

OBJECTIVE: Write and evaluate powers of 10 using exponents.

Quick Review

Find each product.

1. $3 \times 3 \times 3$
2. $2 \times 2 \times 2 \times 2 \times 2$
3. $5 \times 5 \times 5$
4. $4 \times 4 \times 4 \times 4$
5. $6 \times 6 \times 6$

Vocabulary

base **exponent**

Learn

You can represent numbers by using exponents. In exponent form, numbers have a base and an exponent. The **base** is a number used as a repeated factor. The **exponent** is a number that shows how many times the base is used as a factor.

$$1{,}000 = \underbrace{10 \times 10 \times 10}_{\text{3 factors}} = 10^3$$

(3 is the exponent; 10 is the base)

PROBLEM In the United States, oil is used for many things including fuel, fertilizers, medicines, plastics, insulation, computers, asphalt, ink, glue, and chewing gum. Every 42 seconds, about 10^4 barrels of oil are used. What is the value of 10^4?

READ Math

The second and third powers have special names.

- Read 10^2 as "ten squared" or "the second power of 10".
- Read 10^3 as "ten cubed" or "10 to the third power".

Example Find the value of 10^4.

Step 1	Step 2	Step 3
Identify the exponent and base. 10^4 ← exponent; 10 ← base Read: "the fourth power of ten" or "ten to the fourth power."	Write the base as repeated factors. $\underbrace{10 \times 10 \times 10 \times 10}_{\text{4 factors}}$	Multiply. $10 \times 10 \times 10 \times 10 = 10{,}000$

So, about 10,000 barrels of oil are used every 42 seconds.

More Examples

A **Find the value of 10^5.**

$10^5 = 10 \times 10 \times 10 \times 10 \times 10$ ← Ten is used as a factor 5 times.

$= 100{,}000$

B **Write 100 in exponent form.**

10×10 ← Write as factors of 10.

10×10 ← Count the factors: 2.

10^2 ← Write in exponent form.

Hybrid cars use a combination of gasoline and electric power. They get about 50 miles to a gallon of gas. A traditional gas-powered car gets about 25 miles to a gallon of gas.▼

Guided Practice

1. Look at the expression at the right. If you wrote it in exponent form, what would be the base? What would be the exponent?

$$10 \times 10 \times 10 \times 10 \times 10 \times 10 \times 10$$

Write in exponent form. Then find the value.

2. 10×10
3. $10 \times 10 \times 10 \times 10$
4. $10 \times 10 \times 10$
5. $10 \times 10 \times 10 \times 10 \times 10$
6. TALK Math **Explain** how to find the value of 10^8.

Independent Practice and Problem Solving

Write in exponent form.

7. 100
8. 10,000
9. 100,000
10. 1,000,000

Find the value.

11. 10^5
12. 10^7
13. 10^9
14. 10^6

Algebra Find the value of *n*.

15. $10^7 = n$
16. $10 = 10^n$
17. $10 \times 10 \times 10 = 10^n$
18. $10^6 = n$

USE DATA For 19–22, use the table.

19. Which country produced a number of motor vehicles that is closest to 10^7?
20. Is the total number of motor vehicles produced by all 5 countries greater than or less than 10^8?
21. Which country produced fewer than 10^6 motor vehicles?
22. WRITE Math Is the number of motor vehicles produced in India closer to 10^5 or 10^6? **Explain** how you found the answer.

Motor Vehicle Production 2003

Country	Vehicles
United States	12,140,610
Canada	2,546,409
Japan	10,152,677
India	898,279
Russia	1,305,023

Mixed Review and Test Prep

23. Write the number 4,524,038 in words. (p. 4)
24. Round 13,509 to the nearest thousand. (p. 14)
25. **Test Prep** Which number represents $10 \times 10 \times 10 \times 10 \times 10 \times 10 \times 10 \times 10$?

   A 10^0
   B 10^8
   C 8^{10}
   D 10^{10}

Extra Practice on page 300, Set C

LESSON 7

Exponents and Square Numbers

OBJECTIVE: Write and evaluate repeated factors in exponent form and identify square numbers.

Quick Review

Write the missing factor.

1. $5 \times \blacksquare = 25$
2. $3 \times \blacksquare = 9$
3. $10 \times \blacksquare = 100$
4. $6 \times \blacksquare = 36$
5. $9 \times \blacksquare = 81$

Vocabulary

square number

perfect square

Learn

PROBLEM A frog egg starts as a single cell and then splits into 2 cells. Each of the two cells splits again. This process continues. After splitting 5 times, there are $2 \times 2 \times 2 \times 2 \times 2$ cells. Write this number in exponent form.

Exponents can be written with bases other than 10.

Example 1 Write $2 \times 2 \times 2 \times 2 \times 2$ in exponent form.

Step 1

Count the number of times the base is repeated.

repeated 5 times

$2 \times 2 \times 2 \times 2 \times 2$

exponent is 5

Step 2

Write the exponent and the base together.

2^5 ← exponent

↑ base

So, $2 \times 2 \times 2 \times 2 \times 2$ can be written in exponent form as 2^5.

Example 2 Write each in exponent form and in words.

A $3 \times 3 \times 3 \times 3$

Write: 3^4

Read: the fourth power of three, or three to the fourth

B $5 \times 5 \times 5$

Write: 5^3

Read: the third power of five, or five cubed

C 8×8

Write: 8^2

Read: the second power of eight, or eight squared

Example 3 Write each in exponent form and in words.

D 27

$27 = 3 \times 3 \times 3 = 3^3$

Read: the third power of three, or three cubed

E 49

$49 = 7 \times 7 = 7^2$

Read: the second power of seven, or seven squared

Math Idea

The zero power of any number, except zero, is 1.

$6^0 = 1$

FAST TRACK

KY MA-05-1.3.1 Students will analyze real-world problems to identify appropriate representations using mathematical operations, and will apply operations to solve real-world problems with the following constraints: a subtract, multiply, and divide whole numbers (less than 100,000,000), using technology where appropriate. DOK

Square Numbers

A **square number**, sometimes called a **perfect square**, is the product of a number and itself. A square number can be represented with the exponent 2.

Example: 25 = 5×5 or 5^2
↑
square number

Activity

Materials ■ color tiles

You can use color tiles to learn about square numbers.

A Make a table like the one below. Extend your table to the right to show 12 square numbers.

B Use the color tiles to make an array of each square number. Record the number of tiles you used in all.

C Complete your table. Show arrays with up to 12 tiles on each side.

Square Numbers

Model	■	■■ ■■	■■■ ■■■ ■■■	■■■■ ■■■■ ■■■■ ■■■■
Equal Factors	1×1	2×2	3×3	
Base	1	2	3	
Exponent Form	1^2	2^2		
Standard Form	1	4		

- Are square numbers all even, all odd, or both even and odd?
- **Analysis** Compare the last digit of a square number to its base. What pattern do you see?
- **Reasoning** Would the square of 137 be an even or odd number? **Explain** how you know without finding 137×137.

Guided Practice

1. What number in exponent form does this expression represent? $5 \times 5 \times 5 \times 5$

Technology
Use Harcourt Mega Math, Ice Station Exploration, *Arctic Algebra,* Levels V, W, X.

Write in exponent form and then write in words.

2. 6×6
3. $4 \times 4 \times 4$
4. $7 \times 7 \times 7 \times 7$
5. $3 \times 3 \times 3 \times 3 \times 3 \times 3$

Find the value.

6. 3^3
7. 9^2
8. 8^3
9. 11^2
10. 6^4

Compare. Write <, >, or = for each ●.

11. 3^2 ● 2^3
12. 3^3 ● 4^3
13. 8^2 ● 2^6
14. 5^3 ● 6^2

15. TALK Math **Explain** how to express $6 \times 6 \times 6 \times 6$ in exponent form and find its value.

Independent Practice and Problem Solving

Write in exponent form. Then find the value.

16. $9 \times 9 \times 9$
17. $2 \times 2 \times 2 \times 2 \times 2$
18. $8 \times 8 \times 8 \times 8$
19. $5 \times 5 \times 5 \times 5 \times 5 \times 5$

Find the value.

20. 7^2
21. 3^4
22. 2^8
23. 12^3
24. 5^3
25. 6^2
26. 4^5
27. 19^0
28. 10^4
29. 9^3

Compare. Write <, >, or = for each ●.

30. 2^4 ● 4^2
31. 3^5 ● 2^7
32. 9^3 ● 4^5
33. 5^6 ● 4^7

Algebra Find the value of n.

34. $2^4 = 4^n$
35. $3^4 = n^2$
36. $4^3 = n^2$
37. $8^2 = 4^n$

For 38–41, use the table.

38. A frog egg has split several times so it now has 128 cells. How many times has it split?

39. What number in exponent form represents the number of eggs after a frog egg splits 9 times? How many cells would a frog egg have after splitting 9 times?

40. After how many splits will a frog egg first have more than 1,000 cells?

41. **Pose a Problem** Use the information in the table to write a problem involving exponents. Have a classmate solve the problem.

42. WRITE Math Is 7^8 greater than 6^8? **Explain** how you know without doing any multiplying.

Frog Cells

Number of Splits	Cells	Exponent Form
Start	1	2^0
1	2	2^1
2	4	2^2
3	8	2^3

Extra Practice on page 301, Set D

Learn About Square Roots

Each square number has a square root. A **square root** is the base that was multiplied by itself to get a square number.

4 is the square root of 16, because $4^2 = 16$.

Example **Find the square roots of 1, 4, and 9.**

Step 1	Step 2
Break down each square number into repeated factors. $1 = 1 \times 1$ $4 = 2 \times 2$ $9 = 3 \times 3$	The square root is the base of each square number. The square root of 1 is 1. The square root of 4 is 2. The square root of 9 is 3.

Try It

Find the square root of each number.

43. 25 **44.** 49 **45.** 100 **46.** 144

47. 36 **48.** 64 **49.** 81 **50.** 121

51. What are the square numbers between 100 and 200? Find the square root of each of those square numbers.

52. The area of a square room is 169 sq. ft. What is the length of one side of the room? **Explain** how you know.

Mixed Review and Test Prep

53. If $n = 6$, what is the value of $5n + 2$? (p. 96)

54. **Test Prep** Which is less than 5^4?

A 4^5 C 3^5

B 7^4 D 10^4

55. What value for n makes the equation $3n = 12$ true? (p. 108)

56. **Test Prep** What is the greatest square number that is even and is less than 200? What is the value of this square number?

LESSON 8

Prime Factorization

OBJECTIVE: Find and write the prime factorization of a number by using exponents.

Quick Review

Write *prime* or *composite*.

1. 17
2. 70
3. 49
4. 93
5. 89

Vocabulary

prime factorization

factor tree

Learn

All composite numbers can be written as the product of prime factors. This is called the **prime factorization** of the number.

Remember

A **prime** number has exactly two factors, 1 and itself. A **composite** number has more than two factors.

PROBLEM The math club members write messages to each other in code. Each member's name is represented by a number. To identify someone in a message, you must find the prime factorization of the number. Kira received a message from 12. Who is 12?

Secret Chart of Prime Factorizations	
Kira	3 × 5
Alec	2 × 2 × 2
Grace	2 × 7
Sara	2 × 2 × 3
Alberto	5 × 2

You can use a diagram called a **factor tree** to find the prime factorization of a number. Since there is only one prime factorization of a number, you can start with any pair of factors of the number. Continue factoring until only prime factors are left.

ONE WAY

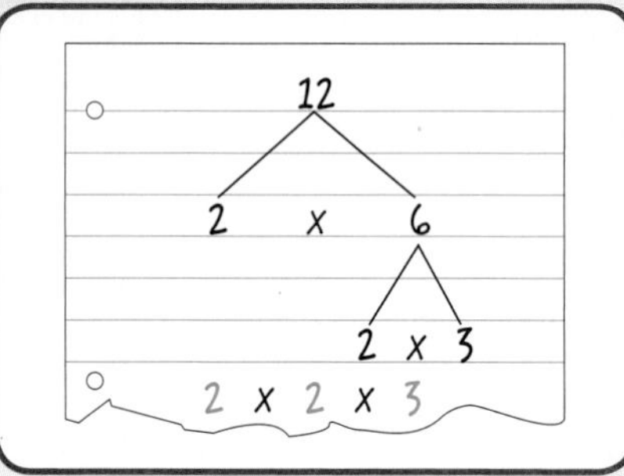

ANOTHER WAY

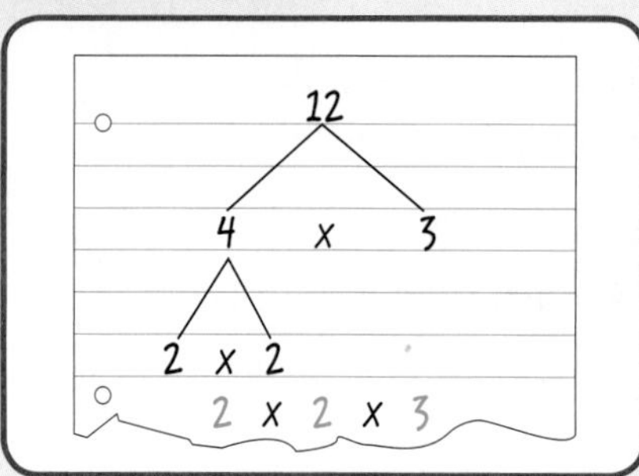

Look at the Secret Chart. The prime factorization of 12 is 2 × 2 × 3. So, Sara is 12.

Examples **Find the prime factorization.**

A

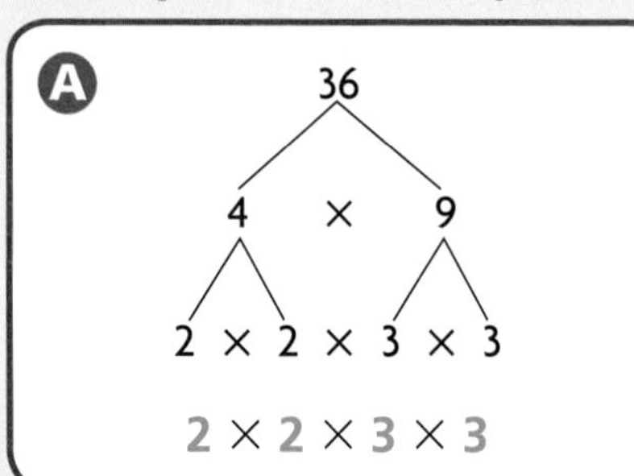

B

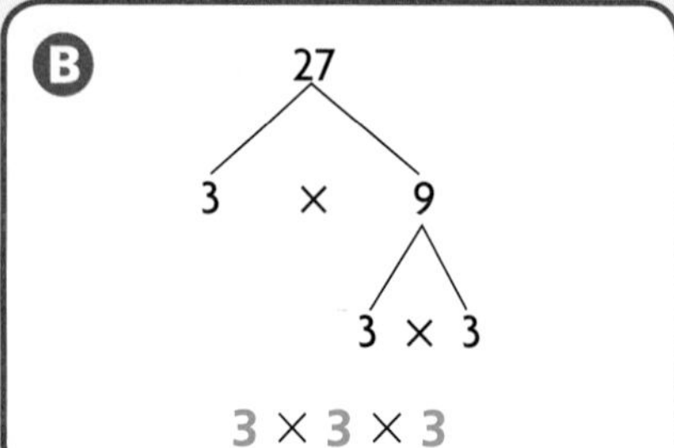

C

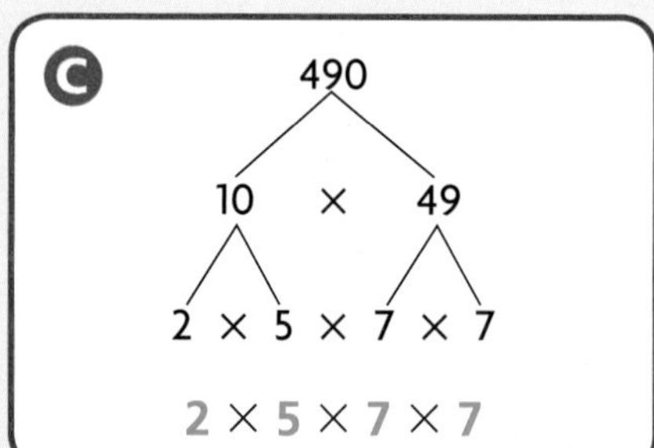

FAST TRACK

KY MA-05-1.5.1 Students will identify and determine composite numbers, prime numbers, multiples of a number, factors of a number and least common multiples (LCM), and will apply these numbers to solve real-world problems. DOK 2

Exponents in Prime Factorization

Sometimes you can use exponents to write the prime factorization of a number.

When a factor is repeated in a prime factorization, use the prime as the base and use the number of times it is repeated as the exponent.

$54 = 2 \times \underbrace{3 \times 3 \times 3}_{\text{factors}}$ ← 2 is a factor one time, and 3 is a factor three times.

$54 = 2 \times 3^3$

Examples

$8 = \underbrace{2 \times 2 \times 2}$

$8 = 2^3$

B

$45 = \underbrace{3 \times 3} \times 5$

$45 = 3^2 \times 5$

C

$128 = \underbrace{2 \times 2 \times 2} \times \underbrace{4 \times 4}$

$128 = 2^3 \times 4^2$

Notice that in Example B, the exponent 1 is not written with the 5.

- **Explain** how to write $3 \times 3 \times 3 \times 7$ using exponents.

Guided Practice

1. Draw a factor tree to find the prime factorization of 28. Write the prime factorization.

Find the prime factorization. You may use a factor tree.

2. 18
3. 70
4. 54
5. 8
6. ✓ 12
7. 16
8. 50
9. 36
10. 81
11. 125

Rewrite the prime factorization by using exponents.

12. $2 \times 3 \times 3$
13. $5 \times 2 \times 5 \times 2 \times 5$
14. ✓ $3 \times 7 \times 3 \times 11 \times 3$
15. $3 \times 5 \times 3 \times 5 \times 13$
16. $3 \times 3 \times 17 \times 3$
17. $5 \times 3 \times 3 \times 11 \times 11 \times 3$

Find the number for each prime factorization.

18. 3^4
19. $2 \times 2 \times 7 \times 2 \times 7$
20. $5^2 \times 3^4$
21. $3 \times 2 \times 13 \times 3$
22. 2×3^2
23. $7^2 \times 2^4$
24. $17 \times 2 \times 2 \times 2$
25. $11^2 \times 3$
26. TALK Math **Explain** how to find the prime factorization of 100 and express it using exponents.

Independent Practice and Problem Solving

Find the prime factorization. You may use a factor tree.

27. 48 **28.** 66 **29.** 63 **30.** 72 **31.** 9

32. 98 **33.** 96 **34.** 65 **35.** 56 **36.** 121

Rewrite the prime factorization by using exponents.

37. $19 \times 2 \times 2$ **38.** $2 \times 3 \times 5 \times 2 \times 5$ **39.** $11 \times 3 \times 2 \times 11 \times 2$

40. $3 \times 3 \times 3 \times 3 \times 7$ **41.** $5 \times 5 \times 5 \times 5$ **42.** $2 \times 7 \times 2 \times 7 \times 7 \times 7$

Find the number for each prime factorization.

43. 2^4 **44.** $5 \times 3 \times 3 \times 5$ **45.** $7^3 \times 2^2$ **46.** $2 \times 2 \times 13 \times 2$

47. 3×11^2 **48.** $5^3 \times 3^2$ **49.** $13^2 \times 2$ **50.** $2 \times 2 \times 2 \times 2 \times 2$

Algebra **Write a number for n that solves the equation.**

51. $5^2 \times n = 75$ **52.** $343 = 7^n$ **53.** $3^2 \times n^2 = 144$ **54.** $2^n = 128$

For 55–58, use the table.

The Crypto Lock Company has lock dials that look like clocks. The factors of the lock number tell the combination of the lock. Combination numbers are listed in order from least to greatest.

Crypto Lock Company

Lock	Lock Number	Factors
Ace	84	■, ■, ■, ■
Deluxe	140	■, ■, ■, ■
Super	■	■, ■, ■, ■
Mega	441	3, 3, 7, 7

55. The factors of the Ace 84 Lock are all prime. What four prime factors give the combination of the Ace 84 lock?

56. What are the four primes that unlock the Deluxe 140 lock?

57. None of the four prime factors in the Super Lock's combination are repeated. What is the greatest possible lock number the Super Lock could have? the least possible lock number?

58. **Pose a Problem** Use the information in the table to write a problem. Ask a classmate to solve it.

59. WRITE Math If a number is the product of a prime and a composite number, what is the fewest number of prime factors it could have? Explain.

 Extra Practice on page 301, Set E

Learn About Prime Factors and Codes

Computer security systems use large composite numbers as codes. Each composite number is the product of two secret primes. If you can find the primes, you can crack the code. The secret primes that computers use are *very large,* and could involve 100-digit numbers. These secret prime factors are just about impossible to find—even for a computer!

Example **Make your own secret computer security code.**

Step 1	Step 2	Step 3
Find two large primes. Examples: 61 ← prime 103 ← prime	Multiply the primes to get a composite number. Example: $61 \times 103 = 6{,}283$	Trade composite numbers with a classmate. Can you crack each other's codes?

Try It

60. Greg's composite number is 2,419. He identified one prime as 41. What is the other prime?

61. Sunil's composite number is 8,633. Both of his primes are less than 100 and greater than 88. What are they?

62. **Reasoning** Rita's composite number is 5,069. She identified one prime as 37. Is the second prime greater than or less than 100? **Explain.**

Mixed Review and Test Prep

63. What is the volume of a box that measures 12 cm by 8 cm by 3 cm? (Grade 4)

64. **Test Prep** Which numbers are two of the prime factors of 78?

A 13 and 2 **C** 39 and 4

B 2 and 6 **D** 6 and 13

65. A diagonal divides a rectangle into two right triangles. The area of the rectangle is 30 square inches. What is the area of each triangle? (Grade 4)

66. **Test Prep** What is the least number that is the product of two different primes that are cubed?

Extra Practice

Set A List the first ten multiples for each number. (pp. 276–278)

1. 6 **2.** 9 **3.** 5 **4.** 3 **5.** 7

Write the least common multiple for each pair of numbers.

6. 6 and 4 **7.** 3 and 9 **8.** 4 and 5 **9.** 8 and 4

10. 7 and 4 **11.** 5 and 6 **12.** 2 and 3 **13.** 10 and 12

14. Henry arrived at the train station at 10:00 A.M. A train arrives on Track 1 every 3 minutes. A train arrives on Track 2 every 4 minutes. What is the first time that Henry will see the trains on Tracks 1 and 2 at the same time?

15. Henry stayed at the train station until 10:55 A.M. How many times did he see the trains on Tracks 1 and 2 at the same time?

Set B List the factors of each number. (pp. 280–283)

1. 48 **2.** 17 **3.** 26 **4.** 52 **5.** 36

Write the common factors for each pair of numbers.

6. 42, 54 **7.** 12, 20 **8.** 24, 52 **9.** 44, 56 **10.** 14, 49

Write the greatest common factors for each pair of numbers.

11. 18, 24 **12.** 50, 64 **13.** 12, 36 **14.** 28, 42 **15.** 48, 72

16. Copy and complete the Venn diagram to find the greatest common factor of 36 and 81.

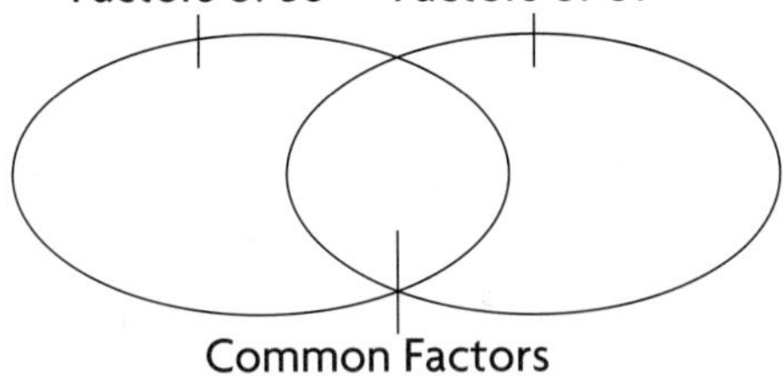

17. Jonas has saved 24 state quarters. Chantal has saved 32 state quarters. They want to display their quarters on plastic pages. Jonas and Chantal want to fill each page that they use. What is the largest number of quarters per page that they could both use?

18. Evan is going to make shelves for his DVDs and CDs. He has 30 DVDs and 40 CDs. He wants to fill each shelf exactly. All of the shelves are the same size. If each DVD and each CD are the same size, how many can he fit on a shelf so that they fit exactly?

Set C Write in exponent form. (pp. 290–291)

1. $10 \times 10 \times 10 \times 10$
2. $10 \times 10 \times 10$
3. $10 \times 10 \times 10 \times 10 \times 10 \times 10$
4. 100
5. 100,000
6. 100,000,000

Find the value.

7. 10^3
8. 10^9
9. 10^4
10. 10^7
11. 10^6
12. 10^5
13. 10^2
14. 10^8
15. A 2005–2006 survey found that there are about 10^7 pet reptiles in the United States. What is the value of 10^7?
16. More than 10^9 cell phones were in use worldwide in 2005. What is the value of 10^9?

Set D Write in exponent form. Then write in words. (pp. 292–295)

1. $3 \times 3 \times 3 \times 3$
2. $8 \times 8 \times 8 \times 8 \times 8$
3. $2 \times 2 \times 2$
4. 9×9

Write in exponent form. Then find the value.

5. $4 \times 4 \times 4 \times 4 \times 4$
6. $6 \times 6 \times 6 \times 6$
7. $7 \times 7 \times 7$
8. $5 \times 5 \times 5 \times 5$

Find the value.

9. 4^6
10. 12^0
11. 9^4
12. 6^3
13. 3^5

Compare. Write $<$, $>$, or $=$ for each ●.

14. 5^3 ● 2^6
15. 9^4 ● 7^5
16. 4^3 ● 3^4
17. 6^4 ● 3^7

Set E Find the prime factorization. You may use a factor tree. (pp. 296–299)

1. 108
2. 32
3. 51
4. 180
5. 84
6. 90
7. 630
8. 130
9. 125
10. 99

Rewrite the prime factorization by using exponents.

11. $2 \times 3 \times 5 \times 5 \times 2$
12. $3 \times 2 \times 7 \times 5 \times 2 \times 3$
13. $11 \times 3 \times 3 \times 3 \times 2$
14. $13 \times 3 \times 5 \times 3 \times 3$
15. $2 \times 3 \times 7 \times 3 \times 2 \times 2$
16. $17 \times 17 \times 3 \times 3 \times 3 \times 3 \times 3$

Find the number for each prime factorization.

17. $5 \times 3 \times 2 \times 2$
18. $5^2 \times 2^5 \times 3$
19. $3^2 \times 7^2$
20. $2^4 \times 3^3$

MATH POWER

Scientific Notation

SOLAR SYSTEM TRAVELER

Scientific notation is a way to express a very large number as the product of two factors. The first factor is a number greater than 1 and less than 10. The second factor is a power of 10 expressed as a exponent.

Earth lies about 93,000,000 miles from the Sun. Follow these steps to express this distance in scientific notation.

1. Put a decimal point at the end of the number.

   93,000,000.

2. Count the number of places the decimal point must be moved to the left to form a number greater than 1 but less than 10. This number is the first factor.

   9.3000000 ⟶ 9.3

   7 places

3. The second factor is a power of 10. Its exponent is the number of places you moved the decimal point.

   9.3×10^7

Examples

A Write 475,000 in scientific notation.

475,000. ⟵ 5 places

4.75×10^5

B Write 640,000,000 in scientific notation.

640,000,000. ⟵ 8 places

6.4×10^8

Try It

Write each number in scientific notation.

1. 47,000,000,000
2. 38,000
3. 910,000,000
4. 1,600,000
5. 520,000,000,000
6. 173,000
7. 219,000,000
8. 67,000

9. WRITE Math **Explain** how you would write 7.8×10^5 in standard form.

Chapter 11 Review/Test

Check Vocabulary and Concepts

Choose the best term from the box.

VOCABULARY
multiple
prime number
composite number
exponent
least common multiple (LCM)

1. The least number, greater than zero, that is a multiple of two or more numbers. KY MA-05-1.5.1 (p. 276)
2. A number with exactly two factors, 1 and itself. KY MA-05-1.5.1 (p. 284)
3. A whole number that has more than two factors. KY MA-05-1.5.1 (p. 284)
4. The product of two or more whole numbers. KY MA-05-1.5.1 (p. 276)

Check Skills

Write the least common multiple for each pair of numbers. KY MA-05-1.5.1 (pp. 276–277)

5. 3 and 12
6. 15 and 10
7. 2 and 11
8. 16 and 12
9. 7, 10, and 14

Write the greatest common factor for each pair of numbers. KY MA-05-1.5.1 (pp. 280–283)

10. 12, 48
11. 27, 63
12. 16, 68
13. 60, 81
14. 32, 48
15. 18, 27
16. 20, 45
17. 15, 35
18. 12, 36
19. 9, 15

Find the value. KY MA-05-1.5.1 (pp. 292–295)

20. 5^4
21. 11^2
22. 13^0
23. 8^4
24. 2^6
25. 6^3
26. 9^5
27. 12^3
28. 7^5
29. 3^7

Check Problem Solving

Solve. KY MA-05-4.4.1 (pp. 286–289)

30. Beverly is playing with her little sister. Her sister's dress-up doll has 3 shirts: white, pink, and blue. The doll has 4 skirts: white, red, brown, and black. How many different ways can Beverly mix and match shirts and skirts to make different outfits for the doll?

31. Jason's class is making designs with square tiles. Students can use 15 tiles, 17 tiles, or 24 tiles to make a rectangular array. How many different arrays could Jason make?

32. Grandma Maria visits Renee every 3 days. Grandma Sophia visits every Sunday. On February 4, both grandmothers visited Renee. On what other date in February will both of Renee's grandmothers visit?

33. WRITE Math Give an example of when you would use a tree diagram. Give an example of when you would use an organized list. **Explain.**

GO ONLINE **Technology** Use *Online Assessment.*

Practice for the KCCT
Chapters 1–11

Number and Operations

1. Sebastian is estimating the product of 39 and 42. Which of the following is the best estimate? KY MA-05-1.2.1 (p. 38)

   A 150

   B 160

   C 1,000

   D 1,600

2. Which of the numbers in the table below has a 6 in the ten-thousands place and a 2 in the hundreds place? KY MA-05-1.1.1 (p. 4)

Attendance at Baseball Stadiums	
Year	Number of People
2003	1,347,265
2004	1,265,463
2005	1,643,581
2006	1,467,281

   A 1,265,463

   B 1,347,265

   C 1,467,281

   D 1,643,581

3. WRITE Math Explain how to write the number 54,893 in expanded form. KY MA-05-1.1.1 (p. 4)

Algebraic Thinking

4. Ryan's fifth-grade class is taking a field trip to the Spring Flower Show. There are 28 students in Ryan's class. There are 7 adult chaperones on the field trip. Each chaperone has an equal group of students. Which numerical expression represents this situation? KY MA-05-5.2.1 (p. 92)

   A $28 \div 7$

   B $28 - 7$

   C 28×7

   D $28 + 7$

5. If $x = 5$, which of the following is true? KY MA-05-5.3.1 (p. 114)

   A $4x > 20$

   B $3x \leq 15$

   C $5x < 25$

   D $6x \geq 35$

Check your work.

See item 5. Look at each expression carefully. Be sure that the expression you chose uses the correct symbol.

6. WRITE Math What is the value of n in the equation below? **Explain.** KY MA-05-5.3.1 (p. 108)

$$6n + 14 = 32$$

Measurement

7. Jeff is planting a garden in the shape of a rectangle. He plans to put a fence around the perimeter of the garden. How many feet of fence will he need? KY Grade 4

18 feet

6 feet

A 24 feet C 96 feet

B 48 feet D 108 feet

8. Estimate the length of the leaf. KY Grade 4

A 1 inch C 3 inches

B 2 inches D 4 inches

9. WRITE Math How does the area of the base of a cube relate to the volume of the cube? Use an example. **Explain.** KY Grade 4

Data Analysis and Probability

10. Amy and her friends belong to a writing club. The pictograph shows how many pages each student wrote in one month. How many more pages did Charles write than Devyn? KY MA-05-4.1.1 (p. 226)

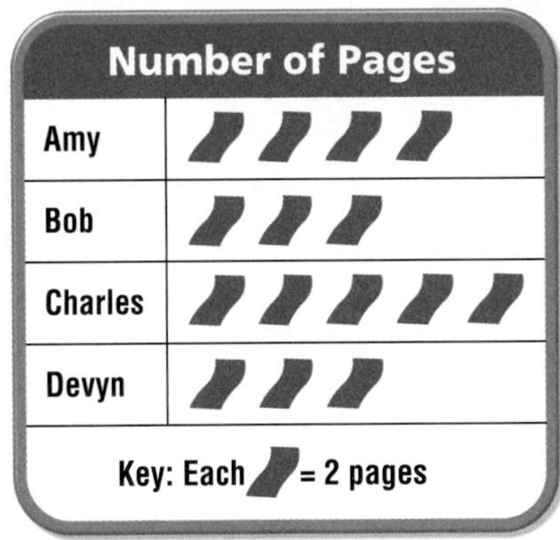

A 2 C 4

B 3 D 5

11. Which is the mean of the data? KY MA-05-4.2.1 (p. 220)

4, 16, 32, 33, 41, 47, 49, 74

A 27 C 37

B 31 D 42

12. WRITE Math Gwen and Daniel are comparing the number of times they can jump rope in one minute. What kind of graph could they use? **Explain** how they should make the graph. KY MA-05-4.1.3 (p. 258)

CHAPTER 12 Fraction Concepts

FAST FACT

Most electric guitars, like the famous Fender Stratocasters shown here, have 6 strings. Each string is capable of producing 22 different notes.

Investigate

Suppose you are writing the notes for one measure of music. The measure will be equivalent to one whole note. What combinations of different types of notes could you use that would be equivalent to one whole note? Tell how many of each note you used.

Note	Symbol	Fraction of Measure
Whole note	𝅝	$\frac{1}{1}$
Half note	𝅗𝅥	$\frac{1}{2}$
Quarter note	♩	$\frac{1}{4}$
Eighth note	♪	$\frac{1}{8}$
Sixteenth note	𝅘𝅥𝅯	$\frac{1}{16}$

Technology
Student pages are available in the Student eBook.

Show What You Know

Check your understanding of important skills needed for success in Chapter 12.

▶ Understand Fractions

Write the fraction for the shaded part.

1. 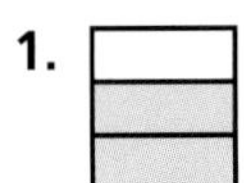
2. 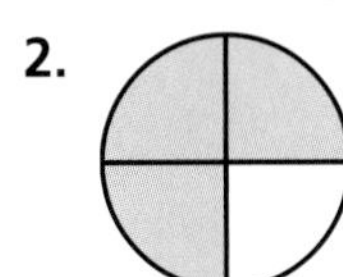
3. 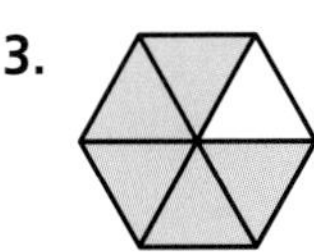
4. 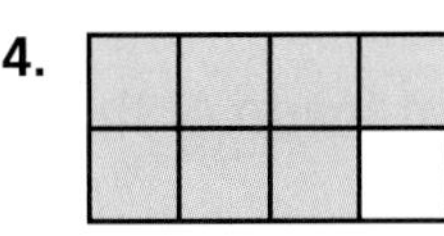

Write in words.

5. $\frac{2}{5}$
6. $\frac{1}{7}$
7. $\frac{4}{9}$
8. $\frac{1}{3}$

▶ Understand Mixed Numbers

Write a mixed number for each picture.

9. 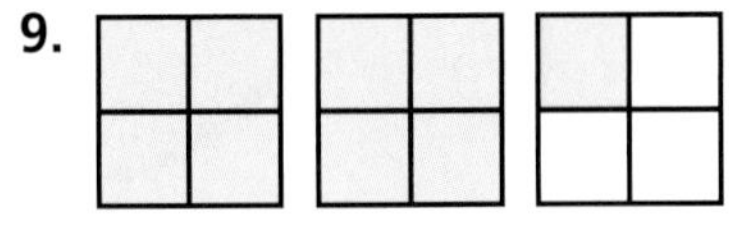
10. 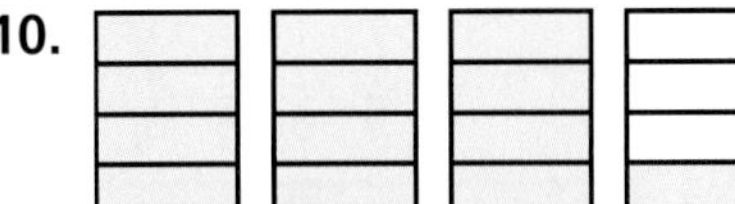
11. 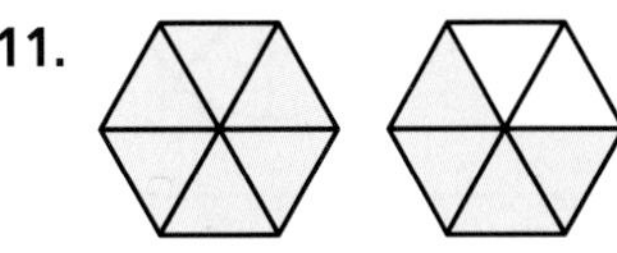

▶ Compare Fractions

Compare the fractions. Write <, >, or = for each ●.

12. $\frac{1}{4}$ ● $\frac{1}{3}$
13. $\frac{2}{4}$ ● $\frac{4}{8}$
14. $\frac{2}{3}$ ● $\frac{1}{2}$
15. $\frac{1}{2}$ ● $\frac{3}{8}$

VOCABULARY POWER

CHAPTER VOCABULARY

equivalent fractions
mixed number
simplest form

WARM-UP WORDS

equivalent fractions fractions that name the same amount or part

mixed number a number that is made up of a whole number and a fraction

simplest form A fraction is in simplest form when the numerator and denominator have only 1 as their common factor.

Understand Fractions

OBJECTIVE: Read, write, and represent fractions as part of a whole or as part of a group.

Quick Review

Identify the numerator and denominator.

1. $\frac{1}{2}$
2. $\frac{3}{4}$
3. $\frac{2}{5}$
4. $\frac{1}{10}$
5. $\frac{3}{8}$

Learn

PROBLEM Mike ordered a small pizza. The pizza was cut into 8 equal slices. Mike ate 6 of the slices. There are 2 slices left. What fraction of the pizza is left?

Examples Parts of a Whole

A Use an area model to show 8 equal parts with 2 parts shaded.

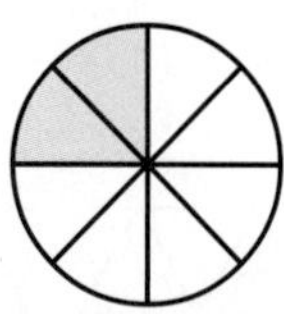

B Use a number line divided into 8 equal parts. The length of any 1 part is $\frac{1}{8}$. So, Point *A* names $\frac{2}{8}$.

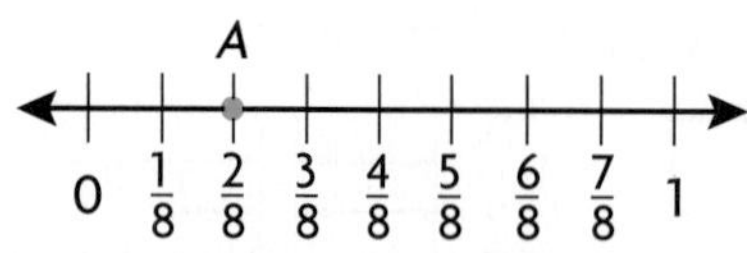

Remember
The numerator is the number above the bar. The denominator is the number below the bar.

Read: two eighths
two out of eight
two divided by eight

Write: $\frac{2}{8}$ ← number of slices left / ← total number of slices

So, $\frac{2}{8}$ of the pizza is left.

Example Parts of a Group

What fraction of the counters are red?

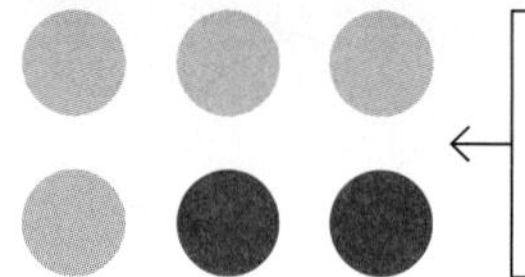

2 counters are red.
6 counters are in the group.

Read: two sixths
two out of six
two divided by six

Write: $\frac{2}{6}$

So, $\frac{2}{6}$ of the counters are red.

 FAST TRACK

KY MA-05-1.1.1 Students will: apply multiple representations (e.g., drawings, manipulatives, base-10 blocks, number lines, symbols) to describe commonly-used fractions, mixed numbers and decimals through thousandths; DOK 2

Guided Practice

1. Into how many equal parts is the rectangle divided? How many parts are green? Write a fraction for the part that is green.

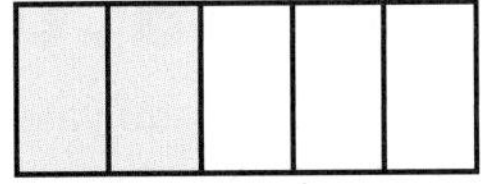

Write a fraction for the shaded part. Write a fraction for the unshaded part.

2. 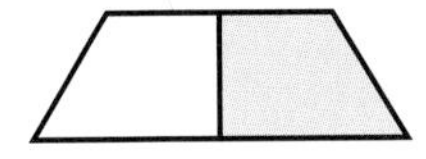

3. 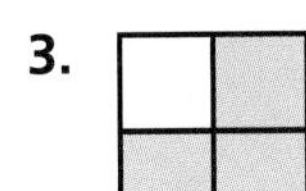

4. 

5. 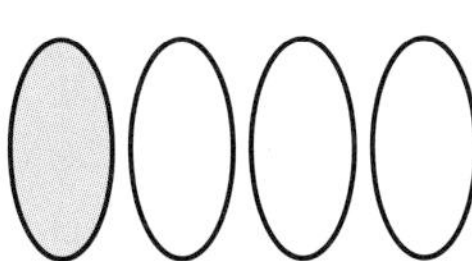

Write a fraction to name the point on the number line.

6. A
0 1

7. 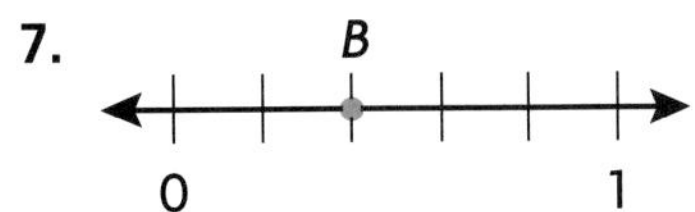

8. 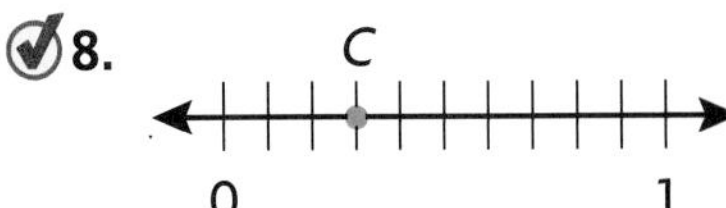

9. TALK Math **Explain** what the numerator and denominator of a fraction represent.

Independent Practice and Problem Solving

Write a fraction for the shaded part. Write a fraction for the unshaded part.

10. 

11. 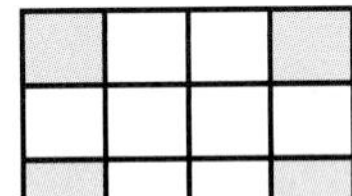

12. 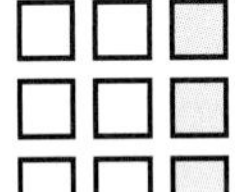

13. ○ ○ ○ ○
○ ○ ○ ○
○ ○ ○ ○

Write a fraction to name the point on the number line.

14. 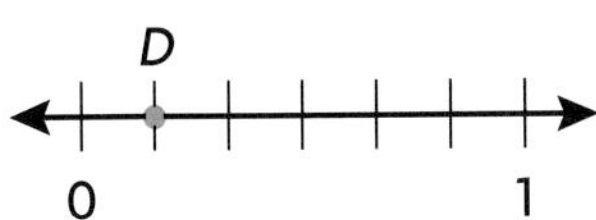

15. 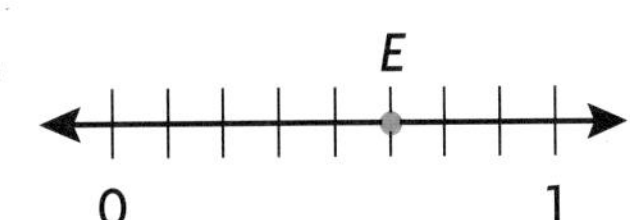

16. 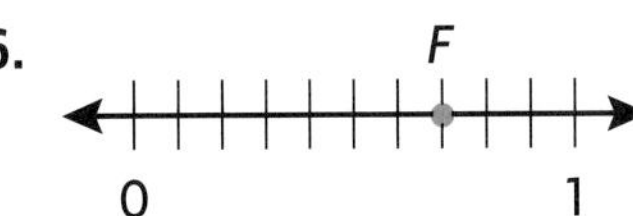

Write the fraction for each.

17. one out of seven
18. eight tenths
19. one third
20. four divided by eight

21. A basket of fruit had 2 peaches, 4 apples, and 4 bananas. Alex took 3 apples. What fraction of the fruit is left?

Mixed Review and Test Prep

22. The prime factorization for a number is $2^5 \times 3^3 \times 11^2$. What is the number? (p. 296)

23. Round 9,509,565 to the nearest million. (p. 14)

24. **Test Prep** What fraction of the stars are pink?

A $\frac{2}{3}$ B $\frac{1}{2}$ C $\frac{2}{5}$ D $\frac{3}{5}$

Extra Practice on page 330, Set A

LESSON 2

Equivalent Fractions

OBJECTIVE: Identify and write equivalent fractions.

Quick Review

Model each fraction.

1. $\frac{1}{4}$ **2.** $\frac{2}{3}$ **3.** $\frac{3}{5}$

4. $\frac{1}{8}$ **5.** $\frac{4}{12}$

Vocabulary

equivalent fractions

Learn

PROBLEM Eva wants to share $\frac{1}{2}$ of a cake with two friends. She divides half of the cake into three equal parts. Write two fractions to represent the part of the cake she is sharing with her friends.

Activity **Materials** ■ pattern blocks

You can use pattern blocks to model fractions. Let the hexagon equal 1 whole.

Step 1	Step 2	Step 3
Cover a hexagon with a trapezoid to show $\frac{1}{2}$. 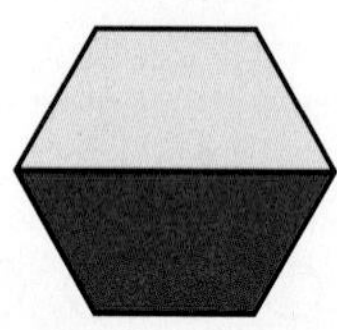	Cover another hexagon with triangles to show $\frac{3}{6}$. 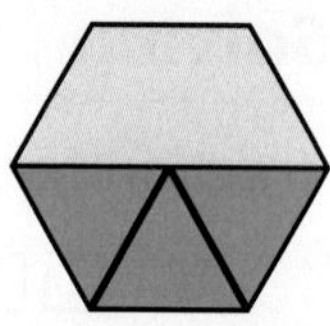	Compare the two hexagons. 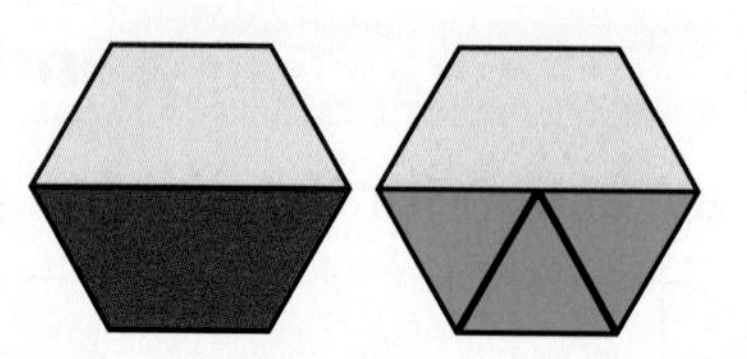

So, both $\frac{3}{6}$ and $\frac{1}{2}$ represent the part of the cake Eva is sharing with her friends.

The fractions $\frac{1}{2}$ and $\frac{3}{6}$ are called equivalent fractions. **Equivalent fractions** are fractions that name the same amount or part. The number lines at the right show that the fractions $\frac{1}{3}$ and $\frac{2}{6}$ are equivalent fractions because they are the same distance from 0.

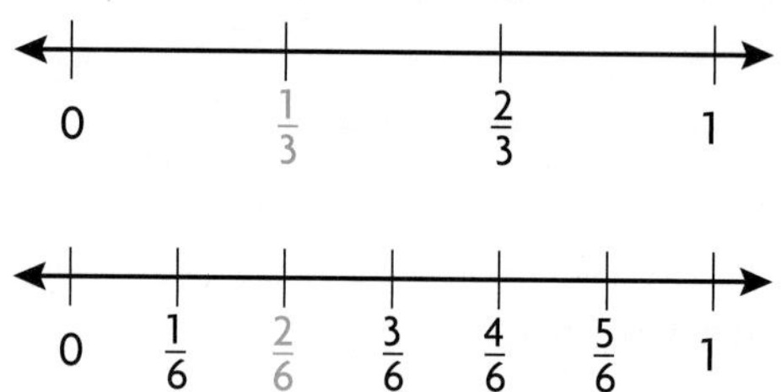

You can also find equivalent fractions by multiplying or dividing the numerator and the denominator by the same number.

ONE WAY **Use multiplication.**

$$\frac{6}{8} = \frac{6 \times 2}{8 \times 2} = \frac{12}{16}$$

So, $\frac{6}{8} = \frac{12}{16}$.

ANOTHER WAY **Use division.**

$$\frac{6}{8} = \frac{6 \div 2}{8 \div 2} = \frac{3}{4}$$

So, $\frac{6}{8} = \frac{3}{4}$.

- Are $\frac{3}{4}$ and $\frac{12}{16}$ equivalent fractions? Explain.

Math Idea

A fraction with the same numerator and denominator is equal to 1, such as $\frac{2}{2}$, $\frac{5}{5}$, $\frac{12}{12}$, or $\frac{96}{96}$.

FAST TRACK

KY MA-05-1.1.1 Students will: apply multiple representations (e.g., drawings, manipulatives, base-10 blocks, number lines, symbols) to describe commonly-used fractions, mixed numbers and decimals through thousandths; DOK 2 *also* MA-05-1.1.3

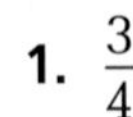

Guided Practice

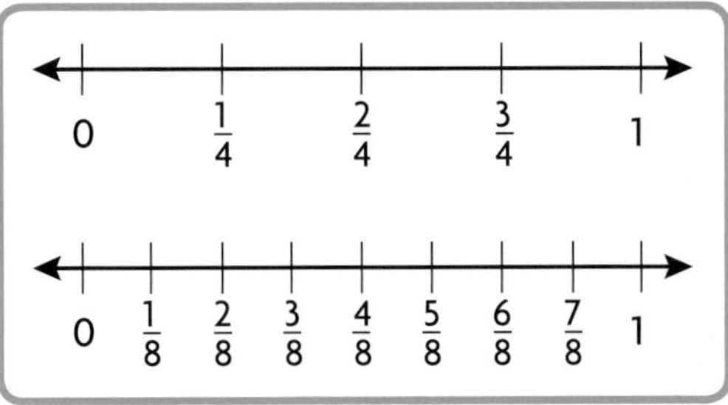

Use the number lines to name an equivalent fraction for each.

1. $\frac{3}{4}$ **2.** $\frac{2}{8}$ **3.** $\frac{2}{4}$ **4.** $\frac{6}{8}$

Write an equivalent fraction.

5. $\frac{1}{4}$ **6.** $\frac{5}{10}$ **7.** $\frac{1}{3}$ **8.** $\frac{5}{8}$ ✓**9.** $\frac{2}{5}$ ✓**10.** $\frac{5}{6}$

11. TALK Math **Explain** how to find an equivalent fraction for $\frac{6}{10}$.

Independent Practice and Problem Solving

Write an equivalent fraction.

12. $\frac{1}{5}$ **13.** $\frac{6}{10}$ **14.** $\frac{3}{6}$ **15.** $\frac{6}{9}$ **16.** $\frac{3}{8}$ **17.** $\frac{5}{15}$

18. $\frac{1}{9}$ **19.** $\frac{3}{10}$ **20.** $\frac{3}{12}$ **21.** $\frac{10}{12}$ **22.** $\frac{2}{3}$ **23.** $\frac{12}{16}$

Tell which fraction is *not* equivalent to the others.

24. $\frac{3}{4}, \frac{2}{3}, \frac{8}{12}$ **25.** $\frac{2}{5}, \frac{4}{10}, \frac{3}{15}$ **26.** $\frac{2}{6}, \frac{1}{4}, \frac{1}{3}$ **27.** $\frac{3}{4}, \frac{5}{6}, \frac{6}{8}$

Use the picture for 28–30.

28. Mark has these 24 marbles. Write four equivalent fractions to show how many of the marbles are blue.

29. What if Mark trades the six green marbles for six more blue marbles? Write three equivalent fractions to show how many blue marbles he has now.

30. WRITE Math Mark said that $\frac{1}{4}$ of his marbles are green. He said that was the same as $\frac{2}{8}$ of his marbles. Was Mark right? **Explain.**

Mixed Review and Test Prep

31. Kenya bought 3 shirts on sale for $9.95 each. Did she pay more or less than $25? **Explain.** (p. 38)

32. Jon cut a pizza into 12 equal slices. He ate 3 of the slices. His friends ate the rest of the pizza. What fraction of the pizza did Jon's friends eat? (p. 306)

33. Test Prep Which fraction is equivalent to $\frac{1}{3}$?

A $\frac{1}{6}$ **C** $\frac{2}{5}$

B $\frac{4}{12}$ **D** $\frac{2}{3}$

Extra Practice on page 330, Set B

LESSON 3

Simplest Form

OBJECTIVE: Write fractions in simplest form.

Quick Review

Write an equivalent fraction.

1. $\frac{1}{4}$ 2. $\frac{5}{7}$ 3. $\frac{3}{8}$

4. $\frac{4}{10}$ 5. $\frac{2}{3}$

Vocabulary

simplest form

Learn

PROBLEM The United States is divided into regions. Ten states are in the Northeast region. That is $\frac{10}{50}$ of the states. What is $\frac{10}{50}$ in simplest form?

A fraction is in **simplest form** when the numerator and denominator have 1 as their only common factor. You can divide by common factors to find the simplest form of $\frac{10}{50}$.

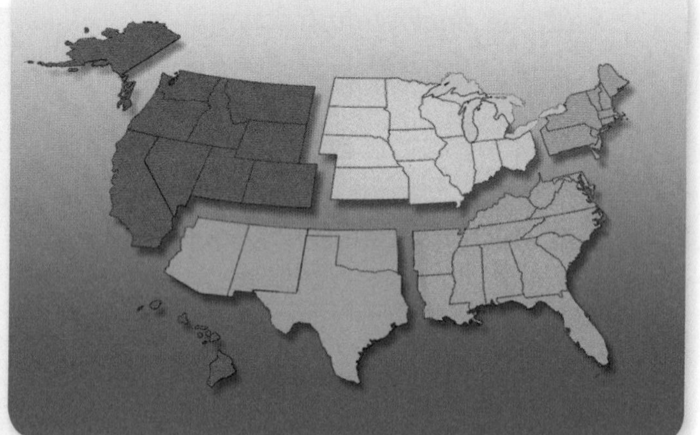

Example

Divide both the numerator and denominator by a common factor of 10 and 50.

Try 2. $\frac{10 \div 2}{50 \div 2} = \frac{5}{25}$ ← not in simplest form

Try 5. $\frac{5 \div 5}{25 \div 5} = \frac{1}{5}$ ← The numerator and denominator have 1 as their only common factor.

So, $\frac{10}{50}$ in simplest form is $\frac{1}{5}$.

Of the 50 states, $\frac{1}{5}$ of them are in the Northeast region.

More Examples Write the fractions in simplest form.

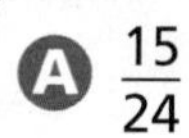

A $\frac{15}{24}$

$\frac{15 \div 3}{24 \div 3} = \frac{5}{8}$ simplest form

B $\frac{12}{12}$

$\frac{12 \div 12}{12 \div 12} = \frac{1}{1}$

$\frac{1}{1} = 1$ simplest form

C $\frac{45}{60}$

$\frac{45 \div 5}{60 \div 5} = \frac{9}{12}$

$\frac{9 \div 3}{12 \div 3} = \frac{3}{4}$ simplest form

- When do you have to divide by a common factor more than once to write a fraction in simplest form?

You can also use a calculator to find simplest form.

3 6 n 6 0 Simp Enter | 36/60 ▶S 18/30

Simp Enter | 18/30 ▶S 9/15

Simp Enter | 9/15 ▶S 3/5

KY MA-05-1.1.3 Students will compare (<, >, =) and order whole numbers, fractions and decimals, and explain the relationships (equivalence, order) between and among them. DOK 2

Use the Greatest Common Factor

You can use the greatest common factor, or GCF, to write a fraction in simplest form.

The Southeast, Southwest, and Midwest and Hawaii make up $\frac{30}{50}$ of the states. What is $\frac{30}{50}$ in simplest form?

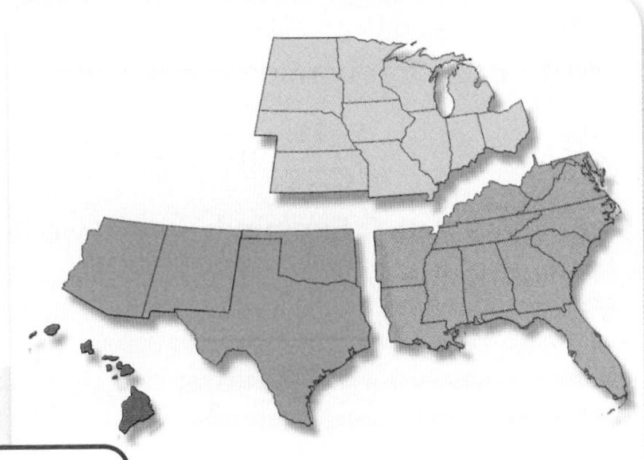

Example 2

Step 1

List the factors of 30 and 50. Find the GCF.

Factors of 30: 1, 2, 3, 5, 6, 10, 15, 30
Factors of 50: 1, 2, 5, 10, 25, 50

The GCF is 10.

Step 2

Divide the numerator and denominator by the GCF.

$$\frac{30 \div 10}{50 \div 10} = \frac{3}{5}$$

So, $\frac{30}{50}$ written in simplest form is $\frac{3}{5}$.

More Examples

D **Write $\frac{7}{10}$ in simplest form.**

$\frac{7}{10}$ 1 is the only common factor for 7 and 10.

So, $\frac{7}{10}$ is in simplest form.

E **Write $\frac{18}{36}$ in simplest form.**

$$\frac{18 \div 18}{36 \div 18} = \frac{1}{2}$$

So, $\frac{18}{36}$ in simplest form is $\frac{1}{2}$.

F **Write $\frac{35}{49}$ in simplest form.**

$$\frac{35 \div 7}{49 \div 7} = \frac{5}{7}$$

So, $\frac{35}{49}$ in simplest form is $\frac{5}{7}$.

- What is the GCF of 9 and 16? Write the fraction $\frac{9}{16}$ in simplest form.

To find the simplest form of a fraction, you can divide by common factors until 1 is the only common factor left, or you can divide by the GCF one time.

Guided Practice

Complete to write each fraction in simplest form.

1. $\frac{9}{12} = \frac{9 \div \blacksquare}{12 \div 3} = \frac{\blacksquare}{4}$
2. $\frac{4}{20} = \frac{4 \div 4}{20 \div \blacksquare} = \frac{1}{\blacksquare}$
3. $\frac{5}{11} = \frac{5 \div \blacksquare}{11 \div 1} = \frac{\blacksquare}{11}$

Name the GCF of the numerator and denominator.

4. $\frac{5}{12}$
5. $\frac{5}{10}$
6. $\frac{25}{45}$
7. $\frac{6}{9}$
8. $\frac{3}{12}$
9. $\frac{12}{18}$

Write each fraction in simplest form.

10. $\frac{4}{8}$
11. $\frac{6}{10}$
12. $\frac{5}{5}$
13. $\frac{7}{9}$
14. $\frac{24}{36}$
15. $\frac{10}{14}$

16. TALK Math **Explain** how you would find the simplest form of $\frac{12}{36}$ using the GCF.

Independent Practice and Problem Solving

Name the GCF of the numerator and denominator.

17. $\frac{10}{30}$
18. $\frac{4}{22}$
19. $\frac{11}{13}$
20. $\frac{9}{18}$
21. $\frac{12}{42}$
22. $\frac{18}{24}$

Write each fraction in simplest form.

23. $\frac{30}{45}$
24. $\frac{5}{5}$
25. $\frac{6}{16}$
26. $\frac{24}{32}$
27. $\frac{18}{30}$
28. $\frac{3}{7}$
29. $\frac{14}{16}$
30. $\frac{20}{100}$
31. $\frac{12}{25}$
32. $\frac{16}{32}$
33. $\frac{15}{75}$
34. $\frac{48}{54}$
35. $\frac{2}{6}$
36. $\frac{12}{15}$
37. $\frac{25}{100}$
38. $\frac{8}{20}$
39. $\frac{24}{26}$
40. $\frac{9}{30}$

Algebra Complete.

41. $\frac{1}{2} = \frac{\blacksquare}{6}$
42. $\frac{3}{4} = \frac{9}{\blacksquare}$
43. $\frac{\blacksquare}{20} = \frac{1}{4}$
44. $\frac{2}{\blacksquare} = \frac{10}{15}$
45. $\frac{4}{12} = \frac{\blacksquare}{3}$

USE DATA For 46–49, use the graph.

46. What fraction of the 50 states are part of the Southeast region? Write the fraction in simplest form.

47. What fraction of the 50 states are either in the Southwest or Northeast regions? Write the fraction in simplest form.

48. What region makes up one-fifth of the states?

49. **FAST FACT** Only five states border the Gulf of Mexico. What fraction of the states is this? Write the fraction in simplest form.

50. WRITE Math **What's the Question?** Six twenty-fifths of the 50 states make up this region.

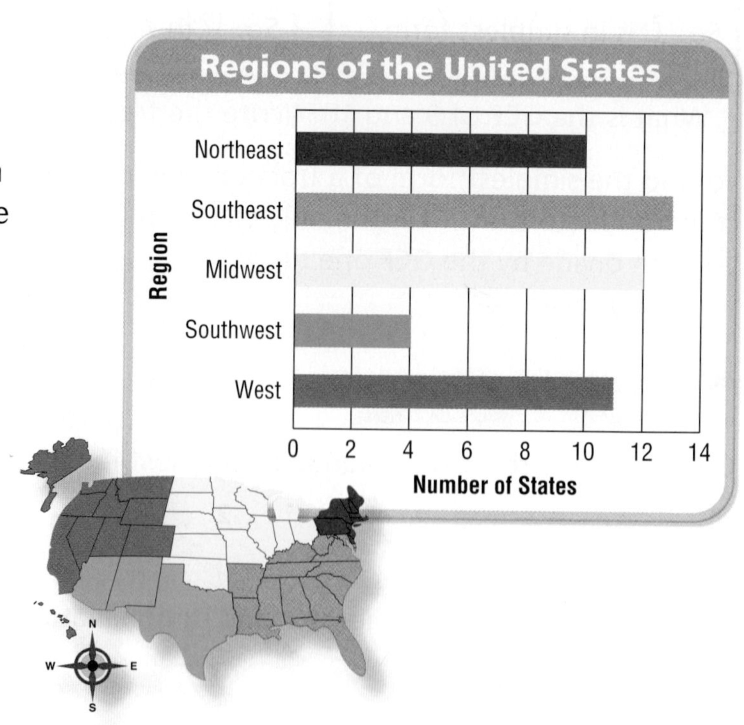

CD ROM **Technology** Use Harcourt Mega Math, Fraction Action, *Number Line Mine*, Level E.

 Extra Practice on page 330, Set C

Learn About Rounding Fractions to Benchmarks

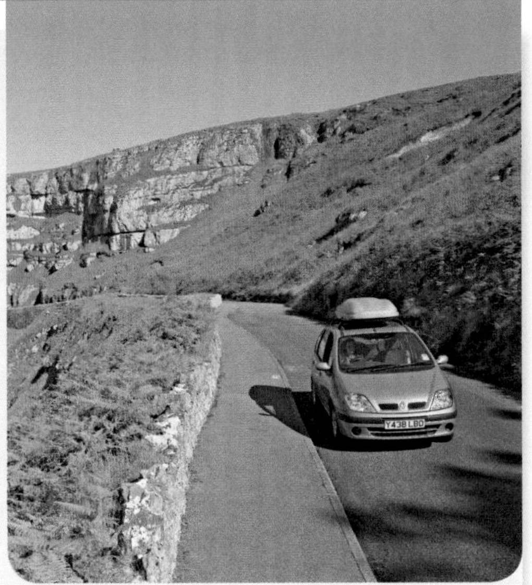

Cody's mom said they had traveled five-ninths of the way to the beach. Cody wanted to estimate about how far that was.

You can use benchmarks to estimate fractions by rounding to 0, $\frac{1}{2}$, or 1.

Round $\frac{5}{9}$.

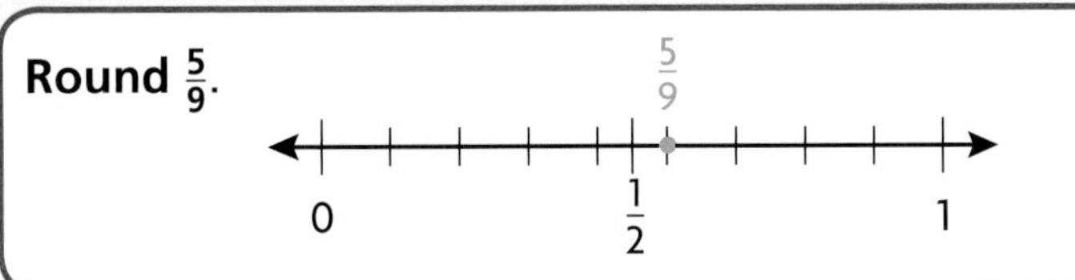

The fraction $\frac{5}{9}$ is closer to $\frac{1}{2}$. So, Cody estimated that they had traveled about halfway to the beach.

You can round fractions by comparing the numerator and denominator.

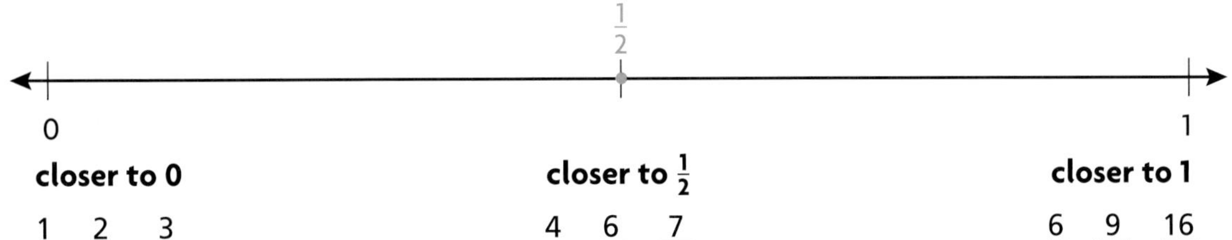

closer to 0	**closer to $\frac{1}{2}$**	**closer to 1**
$\frac{1}{6}$ $\frac{2}{11}$ $\frac{3}{15}$	$\frac{4}{7}$ $\frac{6}{11}$ $\frac{7}{16}$	$\frac{6}{7}$ $\frac{9}{10}$ $\frac{16}{18}$
Each numerator is much less than half the denominator, so the fractions are close to 0.	Each numerator is about half the denominator, so the fractions are close to $\frac{1}{2}$.	Each numerator is about the same as the denominator, so the fractions are close to 1.

Try It

Draw a number line and label the benchmarks 0, $\frac{1}{2}$, and 1. Then estimate each fraction by rounding to 0, $\frac{1}{2}$, or 1.

51. $\frac{5}{6}$ **52.** $\frac{2}{9}$ **53.** $\frac{5}{8}$ **54.** $\frac{2}{3}$ **55.** $\frac{1}{5}$

Mixed Review and Test Prep

56. Jo had 25 books. She bought 9 more and gave 15 to Ellen. Write an expression to show how many books Jo has now. (p. 92)

57. **Test Prep** Which fraction shows $\frac{24}{60}$ in simplest form?

A $\frac{4}{6}$ **B** $\frac{12}{30}$ **C** $\frac{2}{5}$ **D** $\frac{8}{20}$

58. By what number is each of the following numbers divisible? How do you know? (p. 278)

128, 342, 898, 434, 276

59. **Test Prep** Ten of 22 students bought lunch today. What fraction of the students bought lunch? Write the fraction in simplest form.

LESSON 4

Understand Mixed Numbers

OBJECTIVE: Rename fractions greater than 1 as mixed numbers and mixed numbers as fractions greater than 1.

Quick Review

Write each fraction in simplest form.

1. $\frac{4}{4}$
2. $\frac{10}{14}$
3. $\frac{10}{25}$
4. $\frac{4}{8}$
5. $\frac{9}{12}$

Vocabulary

mixed number

Learn

A **mixed number** is made up of a whole number and a fraction. A mixed number can be renamed as a fraction greater than 1. A fraction greater than 1 is sometimes called an *improper fraction*.

PROBLEM Ricardo is making fruit punch. He starts with one cup of orange juice. Then he adds $\frac{3}{4}$ cup more. He uses $1\frac{3}{4}$ cups of orange juice in all. $1\frac{3}{4}$ is a mixed number. How many $\frac{1}{4}$ cups of orange juice does Ricardo use in his fruit punch?

Example Use a number line.

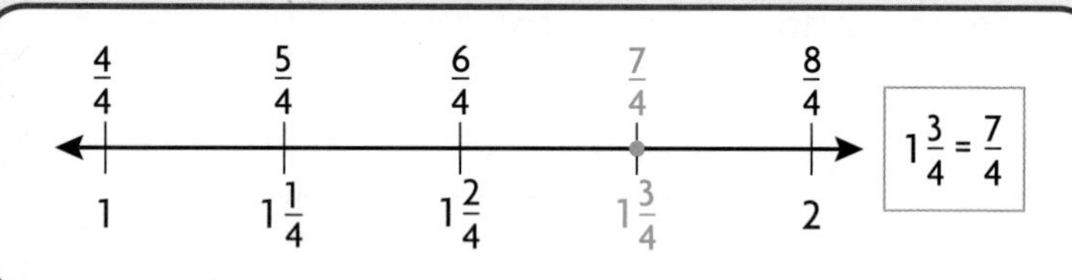

So, Ricardo uses seven $\frac{1}{4}$-cups of orange juice in his fruit punch.

You can use multiplication and addition to rename a mixed number as a fraction greater than 1. You can use division to rename a fraction greater than 1 as a mixed number.

Examples

A Use multiplication.

Rename $2\frac{5}{8}$ as a fraction.

$2 = \frac{(8 \times 2)}{8} = \frac{16}{8}$ Write the whole number as a fraction using the denominator, 8.

$2\frac{5}{8} = \frac{16 + 5}{8} = \frac{21}{8}$ Write the number of eighths as a fraction greater than 1.

So, $2\frac{5}{8} = \frac{21}{8}$.

B Use division.

Rename $\frac{21}{8}$ as a mixed number.

$$\begin{array}{r} 2 \rightarrow 2\frac{5}{8} \\ 8\overline{)21} \\ -16 \\ \hline 5 \end{array}$$

Divide the numerator by the denominator.

Use the remainder and the divisor to write a fraction.

So, $\frac{21}{8} = 2\frac{5}{8}$.

- When a mixed number is changed to a fraction, what is always true about the numerator and the denominator?

FAST TRACK

KY MA-05-1.1.1 Students will: apply multiple representations (e.g., drawings, manipulatives, base-10 blocks, number lines, symbols) to describe commonly-used fractions, mixed numbers and decimals through thousandths; DOK 2

Guided Practice

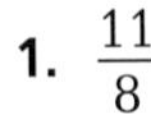

Use the number line. Write each fraction as a mixed number. Write each mixed number as a fraction.

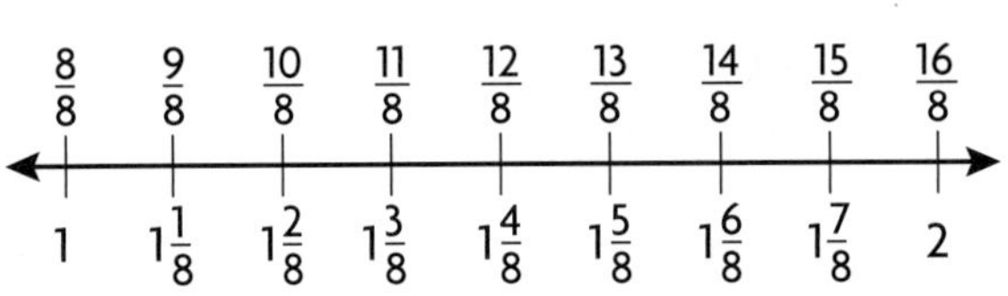

1. $\frac{11}{8}$ 2. $1\frac{1}{8}$ 3. $1\frac{5}{8}$

Write each mixed number as a fraction. Write each fraction as a mixed number.

4. $\frac{11}{4}$ 5. $\frac{6}{5}$ 6. $2\frac{7}{9}$ 7. $3\frac{2}{3}$ ✓8. $\frac{23}{10}$ ✓9. $4\frac{2}{5}$

10. **TALK Math** **Explain** how you can rename a mixed number as a fraction greater than 1.

Independent Practice and Problem Solving

Write each mixed number as a fraction. Write each fraction as a mixed number.

11. $1\frac{3}{5}$ 12. $2\frac{1}{3}$ 13. $\frac{9}{4}$ 14. $\frac{11}{10}$ 15. $\frac{13}{6}$ 16. $1\frac{3}{7}$

17. $\frac{8}{3}$ 18. $3\frac{5}{6}$ 19. $7\frac{1}{2}$ 20. $\frac{47}{15}$ 21. $\frac{25}{4}$ 22. $2\frac{7}{12}$

USE DATA Use the recipe for 23–25.

23. Cal is making one batch of energy squares. How many $\frac{1}{3}$-cups of honey will he use?
24. What is the amount of bran cereal in the recipe written as a fraction?
25. **WRITE Math** Cal has a $\frac{1}{2}$-cup measure. How many times must he fill it to measure out the right amount of peanut butter? **Explain.**

Mixed Review and Test Prep

26. How many angles does this pentagon have? (Grade 4)

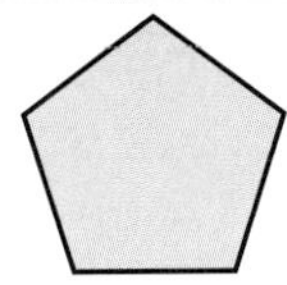

27. What is the prime factorization of 40? (p. 294)

28. **Test Prep** Which fraction is the same as $2\frac{3}{5}$?

A $\frac{5}{5}$
B $\frac{11}{5}$
C $\frac{12}{5}$
D $\frac{13}{5}$

LESSON

5 Compare and Order Fractions and Mixed Numbers

OBJECTIVE: Compare and order fractions and mixed numbers.

Quick Review

Tom had 12 fruit bars. He gave 6 bars to Mark and 2 bars to Marge. Write two equivalent fractions to describe the number of fruit bars that are left.

Learn

PROBLEM Greg plans to usher at $\frac{2}{3}$ of the symphony concerts. Sayre plans to usher at $\frac{3}{4}$ of the symphony concerts. Who will usher at more concerts? Compare $\frac{2}{3}$ and $\frac{3}{4}$.

ONE WAY **Use fraction bars to compare.**

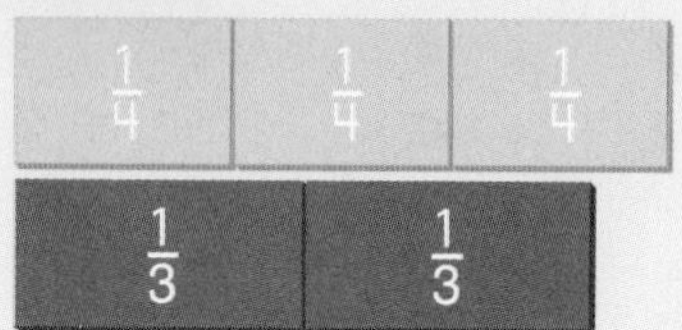

$\frac{3}{4} > \frac{2}{3}$

So, Sayre will be an usher at more concerts.

You can use equivalent fractions to rename unlike fractions so that they have like denominators for easy comparison.

ANOTHER WAY **Find like denominators.**

Step 1

Write the multiples of the denominators and then find a common multiple. Common multiples of the denominators are also known as *common denominators.*

Multiples of 3: 3, 6, 9, 12, 15, 18, 21, 24
Multiples of 4: 4, 8, 12, 16, 20, 24

12 and 24 are common denominators.

Step 2

Use equivalent fractions and rename each fraction using a common denominator.

$\frac{3}{4}$ can be renamed as $\frac{3 \times 3}{4 \times 3} = \frac{9}{12}$ or $\frac{3 \times 6}{4 \times 6} = \frac{18}{24}$

$\frac{2}{3}$ can be renamed as $\frac{2 \times 4}{3 \times 4} = \frac{8}{12}$ or $\frac{2 \times 8}{3 \times 8} = \frac{16}{24}$

Step 3

Compare the numerators of the renamed fractions.

Since $9 > 8$, or $18 > 16$, $\frac{3}{4} > \frac{2}{3}$.

Remember

To compare fractions with like denominators, you need only to compare the numerators. Since $5 > 2$, $\frac{5}{8} > \frac{2}{8}$.

FAST TRACK

KY MA-05-1.1.3 Students will compare (<, >, =) and order whole numbers, fractions and decimals, and explain the relationships (equivalence, order) between and among them. DOK 2 *also* MA-05-1.1.1

Order Fractions and Mixed Numbers

Tony ushered at $\frac{5}{6}$ of the concerts. Maria ushered at $\frac{4}{9}$ of the concerts, and Tanya ushered at $\frac{2}{3}$ of the concerts. Order the fractions $\frac{5}{6}$, $\frac{4}{9}$, and $\frac{2}{3}$ from least to greatest to find who ushered at the least number of concerts.

Example 1 Find a common denominator.

Step 1

Find a common denominator for 6, 9, and 3.

6: 6, 12, 18, 24, 30
9: 9, 18, 27, 36
3: 3, 6, 9, 12, 15, 18, 21

A common denominator is 18.

Step 2

Rename each fraction as an equivalent fraction with a denominator of 18.

$$\frac{5 \times 3}{6 \times 3} = \frac{15}{18}$$

$$\frac{4 \times 2}{9 \times 2} = \frac{8}{18}$$

$$\frac{2 \times 6}{3 \times 6} = \frac{12}{18}$$

Step 3

Compare the numerators. Put them in order from least to greatest.

Since $8 < 12 < 15$,

$$\frac{8}{18} < \frac{12}{18} < \frac{15}{18}.$$

The order from least to greatest is $\frac{4}{9}$, $\frac{2}{3}$, $\frac{5}{6}$.

So, Maria ushered at the least number of concerts.

- How can you order unit fractions from least to greatest?

Remember

A *unit fraction* is a fraction that has 1 as a numerator.

You can use the common denominators to order mixed numbers. First, compare the whole numbers. Then compare the fractions.

Example 2 Order mixed numbers.

Order $2\frac{2}{3}$, $3\frac{1}{6}$, $2\frac{3}{4}$ from greatest to least.

Step 1

Compare the whole numbers.

$$2\frac{2}{3} \quad 3\frac{1}{6} \quad 2\frac{3}{4}$$

Since $3 > 2$, $3\frac{1}{6}$ is the greatest.

Step 2

Use common denominators to compare the other two fractions, $\frac{2}{3}$ and $\frac{3}{4}$.

$$2\frac{2}{3} = 2\frac{8}{12} \qquad 2\frac{3}{4} = 2\frac{9}{12}$$

Since $9 > 8$, $2\frac{9}{12} > 2\frac{8}{12}$.

So, the order from greatest to least is $3\frac{1}{6}$, $2\frac{3}{4}$, $2\frac{2}{3}$.

- If you were ordering mixed numbers that all had different whole numbers, which parts of the mixed numbers would you compare?

Guided Practice

Compare the fractions. Write <, >, or = for each ●.

1.

$\frac{1}{5}$	$\frac{1}{5}$	$\frac{1}{5}$	$\frac{1}{5}$

$\frac{1}{3}$	$\frac{1}{3}$

$\frac{2}{3}$ ● $\frac{4}{5}$

2.

$\frac{1}{8}$	$\frac{1}{8}$	$\frac{1}{8}$	$\frac{1}{8}$	$\frac{1}{8}$

$\frac{1}{5}$	$\frac{1}{5}$	$\frac{1}{5}$	$\frac{1}{5}$

$\frac{4}{5}$ ● $\frac{5}{8}$

Compare. Write <, >, or = for each ●.

3. $\frac{1}{3}$ ● $\frac{2}{3}$
4. $\frac{2}{5}$ ● $\frac{3}{8}$
5. $3\frac{1}{4}$ ● $2\frac{13}{15}$
6. $1\frac{3}{4}$ ● $1\frac{9}{12}$
7. $5\frac{7}{21}$ ● $5\frac{3}{7}$
8. **TALK Math** **Explain** how to order the unit fractions $\frac{1}{6}$, $\frac{1}{2}$, and $\frac{1}{3}$ from least to greatest.

Independent Practice and Problem Solving

Compare. Write <, >, or = for each ●.

9. $\frac{1}{2}$ ● $\frac{1}{3}$
10. $\frac{3}{4}$ ● $\frac{6}{8}$
11. $\frac{5}{7}$ ● $\frac{3}{5}$
12. $\frac{2}{11}$ ● $\frac{1}{4}$
13. $3\frac{5}{7}$ ● $3\frac{7}{14}$

Write in order from least to greatest.

14. $\frac{1}{2}$, $\frac{3}{4}$, $\frac{1}{4}$
15. $\frac{3}{8}$, $\frac{1}{8}$, $\frac{7}{8}$
16. $1\frac{3}{8}$, $1\frac{1}{4}$, $1\frac{5}{6}$
17. $2\frac{2}{3}$, $3\frac{1}{8}$, $2\frac{3}{5}$
18. $1\frac{1}{4}$, $\frac{7}{8}$, $2\frac{1}{5}$

USE DATA For 19–21 use the table.

19. Janine collects animal-shaped flutes called ocarinas. List her flutes in order from longest to shortest.
20. Janine buys a turtle-shaped ocarina that is $6\frac{7}{8}$ inches long. Which flute in her collection has a greater length?
21. **WRITE Math** **Explain** how to determine which ocarina is between $6\frac{1}{2}$ inches and $6\frac{3}{4}$ inches long.

Ocarina Flutes	
Frog flute	$6\frac{3}{4}$ in. long
Monkey flute	$7\frac{1}{2}$ in. long
Armadillo flute	$6\frac{5}{8}$ in. long

Mixed Review and Test Prep

22. Julie has \$20 and spends an amount, y, on lunch. Write an expression she can use to find how much lunch money is left. (p. 92)
23. Hannah has collected 180 toy cars. If she separates them into 12 groups, how many will she have in each group? (p. 74)
24. **Test Prep** Ken practiced his trumpet $1\frac{2}{3}$ hours on Monday. He practiced $1\frac{5}{6}$ hours on Tuesday, and $1\frac{4}{9}$ hours on Wednesday. On which day did he practice the longest?

    A Monday
    B Tuesday
    C Wednesday
    D Thursday

 Extra Practice on page 331, Set E

Water Planet

READ Math WORKSHOP

Reading Skill **Visualize**

Earth's water moves through the environment as part of the water cycle. Most of the water is salt water located in the oceans and seas. The rest of the water is fresh water. The chart below shows the different places where the earth's fresh water is located. Where is most of the earth's fresh water located?

Earth's Fresh Water		
Ice caps and glaciers	Groundwater	Lakes, rivers, and water in soil and air
$\frac{47}{56}$	$\frac{1}{7}$	$\frac{1}{56}$

You can solve some problems by visualizing them. When you visualize a problem, you picture the problem in your mind.

Step 1 Read the problem carefully and visualize it.

Step 2 Think about how best to show the problem. You might draw a picture or make a chart or graph. You might use a model, such as fraction bars or counters.

About $\frac{3}{4}$ of Earth's surface is covered with water.

If all the Earth's water could be held in a 1-liter bottle, the contents would be divided as shown.

Problem Solving **Visualize to solve the problem.**

1. Solve the problem above.
2. Where is the least amount of Earth's fresh water located?
3. Compare the amount of fresh groundwater to the amount of fresh water in ice caps and glaciers.

Problem Solving Workshop
Strategy: Make a Model

OBJECTIVE: Solve problems by using the strategy *make a model*.

Learn the Strategy

Making a model can help you solve a problem. There are different types of models for different types of math problems.

A model can show fractions.

Joe asked his friends Matt and Ellen to help him paint his room. Each person was painting the same size wall. By lunchtime Joe had painted $\frac{3}{8}$ of his wall. Matt had painted $\frac{2}{3}$ of his wall, and Ellen had painted $\frac{3}{5}$ of her wall. Who had painted the greatest part of his or her wall?

Use fractions bars to show how much wall each person painted. Compare the fraction bars.

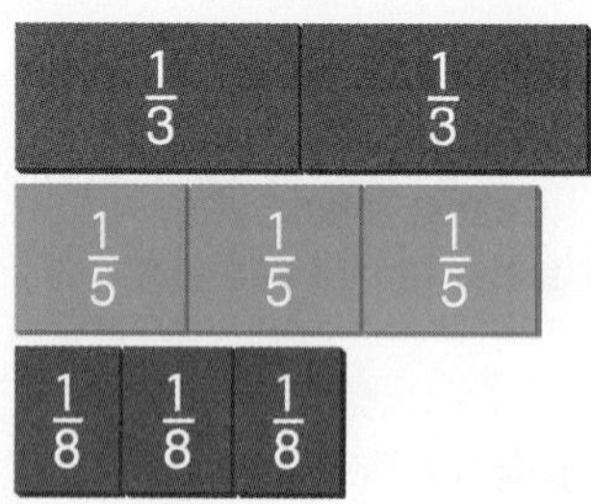

A model can help you estimate.

Enrollment at Bakersville Elementary School increased to 445. About how many students attend the school? Round your answer to the nearest hundred.

Locate 445 on the number line. Find the hundred that is closest to 445.

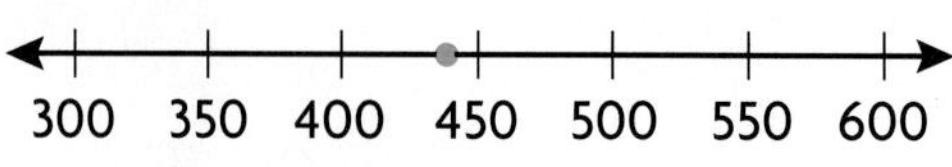

TALK Math

What other types of math problems can you model with a number line?

A model can show decimals.

Ira needs 0.8 meter of denim cloth to make a backpack. How many meters of denim cloth does Ira need to make 3 backpacks?

Shade 0.8 three times.

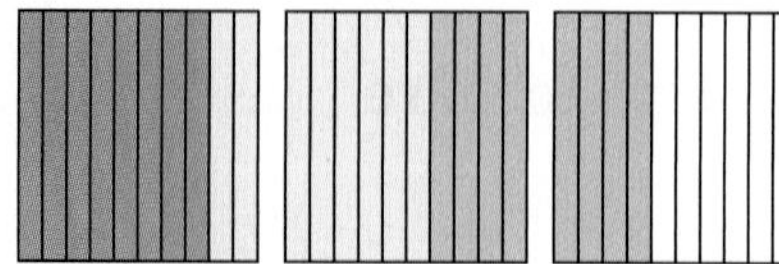

FAST TRACK

KY MA-05-1.1.1 Students will: apply multiple representations (e.g., drawings, manipulatives, base-10 blocks, number lines, symbols) to describe commonly-used fractions, mixed numbers and decimals through thousandths; DOK 2 *also* MA-05-1.1.3

Use the Strategy

PROBLEM Shelly and her friends are playing horseshoes at a family picnic. Mike's horseshoe lands $1\frac{5}{6}$ feet from the stake. Tonya tosses her horseshoe $2\frac{1}{4}$ feet from the stake. Rico's is $1\frac{7}{12}$ feet from the stake. Shelly's lands $1\frac{2}{3}$ feet from the stake. Whose horseshoe was closest to the stake? Whose horseshoe was farthest from the stake?

Read to Understand
Plan
Solve
Check

Read to Understand

- **Identify the details in the problem.**

Plan

- **What strategy can you use to solve the problem?**

You can use make a model to help you solve the problem.

Solve

- **How can you use the strategy to solve the problem?**

Compare the whole-number parts of the mixed numbers.

$1\frac{5}{6}, 2\frac{1}{4}, 1\frac{7}{12}, 1\frac{2}{3}$ Since $2 > 1$, $2\frac{1}{4}$ feet is the greatest distance.

Use fraction bars to compare the fractional parts of the other mixed numbers.

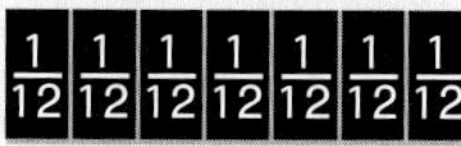

Since $\frac{7}{12}$ is the shortest, $1\frac{7}{12}$ feet is the least distance.

So, Rico's horseshoe was closest to the stake, and Tonya's was farthest from it.

Check

- **What other models could you use to solve the problem?**

Guided Problem Solving

1. Some of Shelly's friends decided to have a jumping contest. Who jumped the longest distance? Who jumped the shortest distance?

   First, compare the whole-number parts of the mixed numbers.

   $$3\frac{5}{12}, 3\frac{3}{4}, 4\frac{3}{8}, 3\frac{1}{2} \qquad 4 > 3$$

   Then, use fraction bars to compare the fractional parts of the mixed numbers that have the same whole number.

   Finally, find who jumped the longest distance and who jumped the shortest distance.

Length of Jump

Name	Length (in feet)
Amber	$3\frac{5}{12}$
Marcus	$3\frac{3}{4}$
Paul	$4\frac{3}{8}$
Shelly	$3\frac{1}{2}$

2. **What if** Shelly's jump was $3\frac{1}{6}$ feet long instead? Who would have made the longest and shortest jumps then? Explain.

3. Amber, Marcus, Paul, and Shelly line up to make their jumps. Shelly is not first. Amber has at least two people ahead of her. Paul was third. Give the order of the four.

Problem Solving Strategy Practice

Make a model to solve.

4. Mario bought 2 packs of invitations for a party. Each pack contains 10 invitations. Mario is inviting 7 classmates, 4 cousins, and 5 children from his neighborhood. What fraction of the invitations will Mario use?

5. Paul, Greg, and Hilda are meeting at Hilda's house before going to the park. Paul lives $8\frac{4}{5}$ miles from Hilda. Greg lives $8\frac{3}{4}$ miles from Hilda. Who lives closer to Hilda?

6. Tina's garden is 5 meters wide and 12 meters long. The flower section is the same width and twice as long as the vegetable section. How long is each section?

7. Steve bought 24 yellow balloons for a party. He returned 12 of the balloons and bought 9 red balloons. Then he decided to return 6 red balloons and buy 16 blue balloons. How many balloons does Steve have now?

8. WRITE Math **What's the Error?** Andy started out with 14 marbles. He gave 9 marbles to Claudia. Sue gave Andy 18 marbles. Then Andy gave Ryan 8 marbles. Andy says that he has 31 marbles now. Describe his error and use a model to show the solution.

Mixed Strategy Practice

Solve.

9. Hannah had a party and gave each of her friends some party favors. The favors included 7 yo-yos, 13 whistles, 6 kaleidoscopes, 9 maracas, and some marker sets. Altogether, Hannah handed out 41 favors. How many were marker sets?

10. Ryan sent 2 invitations to a party on Monday. On Tuesday, he sent 3 invitations, and on Wednesday, 5 invitations. On Thursday, he sent 8 invitations. If the pattern continued through Saturday, how many invitations will Ryan send in all?

USE DATA For 11–14, use the bar graph.

11. Santos, Alice, Otis, and Fred each voted for a different party theme. Alice voted for a Scavenger Hunt. Fred did not vote for a Hawaiian Luau or a Pirate Adventure. Otis did not vote for a Pirate Adventure. What theme did each student vote for?

12. The number of girls who voted for Fiesta Fun is three times as great as the number of boys who voted for it. How many boys voted for Fiesta Fun?

13. **Pose a Problem** Look back at Problem 12. Write a similar problem by changing the mathematical relationship between the numbers of girls and boys who voted for Fiesta Fun. Then solve the problem.

14. **Open-Ended** Use the data in the bar graph to write three different number sentences that use one or more operations.

CHALLENGE YOURSELF

A party supply store sells party favors for $0.75 each, hats for $0.45 each, and noisemakers for $0.60 each.

15. Trevor buys 12 party favors. He spends the same amount of money on hats as on party favors. He spends twice as much on noisemakers as on party favors. How many hats and noisemakers does he buy?

16. Heather paid $15.90 for party supplies. She spent $7.50 on party favors. She bought the same number of hats as noisemakers. How many hats and noisemakers did she buy?

Choose a STRATEGY

- Draw a Diagram or Picture
- Make a Model or Act It Out
- Make an Organized List
- Find a Pattern
- Make a Table or Graph
- Predict and Test
- Work Backward
- Solve a Simpler Problem
- Write an Equation
- Use Logical Reasoning

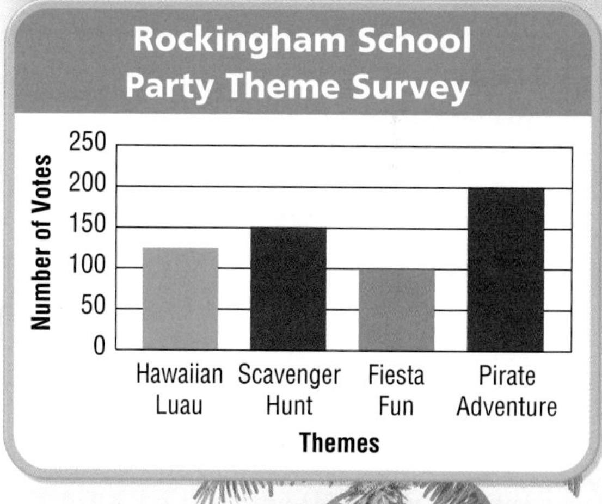

Relate Fractions and Decimals

OBJECTIVE: Name fraction and decimal equivalents.

Quick Review

Write a fraction for the shaded part. Write a fraction for the unshaded part.

1. 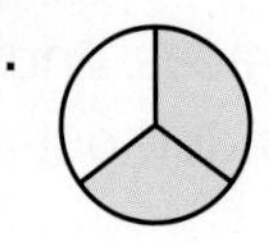 **2.** **3.** 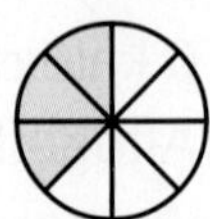

4. 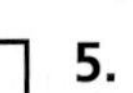 **5.**

Learn

PROBLEM One lap around the track is 0.4 kilometers. Mary jogs four laps, or 1.6 kilometers, each day. The distances can be expressed as either fractions, mixed numbers, or decimals.

How can you show the relationship between fractions and decimals?

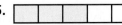

ONE WAY **You can use a number line.**

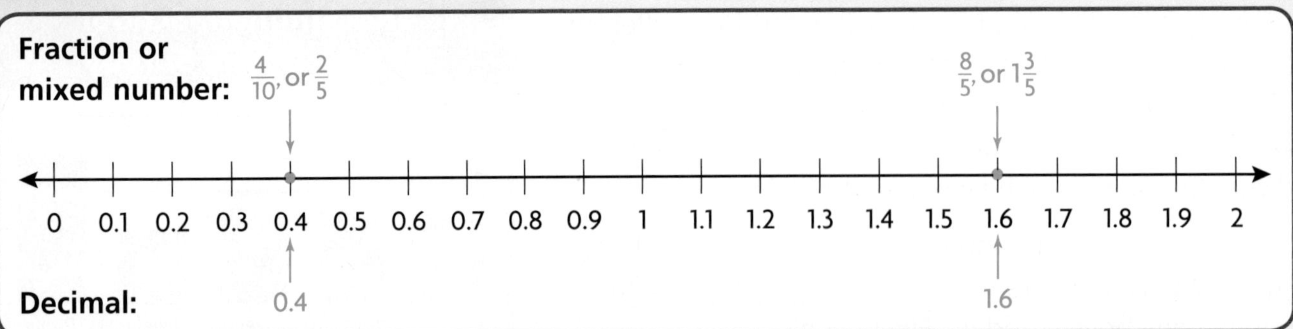

ANOTHER WAY **You can use a model.**

A Write a fraction and a decimal for the model.

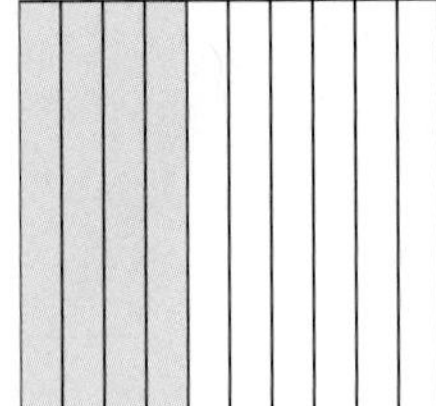

Four out of ten equal parts are shaded.

fraction
Four tenths, or $\frac{4}{10}$, is shaded.

decimal
Four tenths, or 0.4, is shaded.

B Write a mixed number and a decimal for the model.

 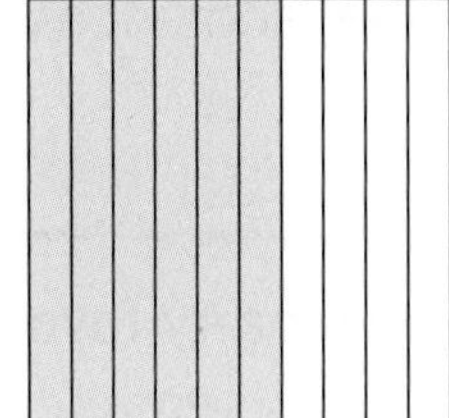

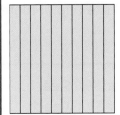

One whole plus six out of ten equal parts are shaded.

mixed number
One and six tenths, or $1\frac{6}{10}$, is shaded.

decimal
One and six tenths, or 1.6, is shaded.

- How would you explain the relationship between 0.25 and $\frac{1}{4}$ to a classmate?

FAST TRACK

KY MA-05-1.1.3 Students will compare (<, >, =) and order whole numbers, fractions and decimals, and explain the relationships (equivalence, order) between and among them. DOK 2 *also* MA-05-1.1.1

Using Place Value and Division

You can use place value to change a decimal to a fraction.
You can use division to change a fraction to a decimal.

Examples

C Decimal to Fraction

0.75 — Identify the place value of the last digit. The 5 is in the hundredths place.

$\frac{75}{100}$ — Use that place value for the denominator.

$\frac{75}{100} = \frac{3}{4}$ — Simplify.

So, $0.75 = \frac{3}{4}$

D Fraction to Decimal

$\frac{3}{5}$ — Divide the numerator by the denominator.

$$\begin{array}{r} 0.6 \\ 5\overline{)3.0} \\ -3.0 \\ \hline 0 \end{array}$$

Place the decimal point. Since 5 does not divide into 3, place a zero. Then divide as with whole numbers.

So, $\frac{3}{5} = 0.6$

READ Math

You can read a fraction in different ways. Example:

$\frac{3}{4}$: three fourths
three out of four
three divided by four

More Examples

E Write 0.625 as a fraction in simplest form.

0.625 — The 5 is in the thousandths place.

$0.625 = \frac{625}{1,000} = \frac{5}{8}$

So, $0.625 = \frac{5}{8}$

F Write $\frac{3}{4}$ as a decimal.

$$\begin{array}{r} 0.75 \\ 4\overline{)3.00} \\ -28 \\ \hline 20 \\ -20 \\ \hline 0 \end{array}$$

So, $\frac{3}{4} = 0.75$

G Write $4\frac{7}{8}$ as a decimal.

$$\begin{array}{r} 0.875 \\ 8\overline{)7.000} \\ -64 \\ \hline 60 \\ -56 \\ \hline 40 \\ -40 \\ \hline 0 \end{array}$$

Use division to rename the fraction $\frac{7}{8}$ as a decimal. Then add the whole number to the decimal.

So, $4\frac{7}{8} = 4.875$

Guided Practice

Write a decimal and a fraction for each model.

1. 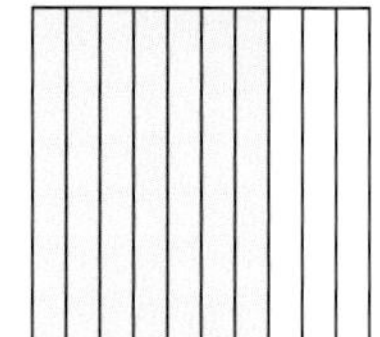

2. 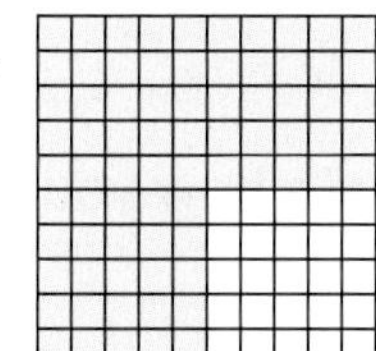

3. 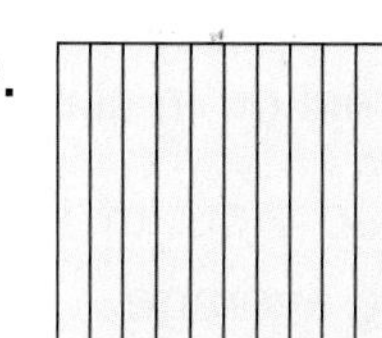 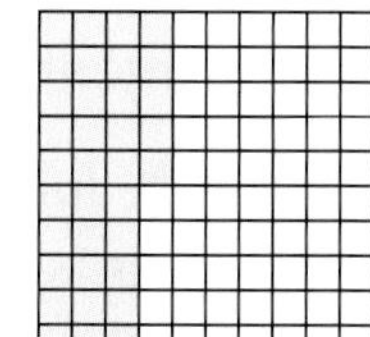

Identify a decimal and a fraction or mixed number for each point.

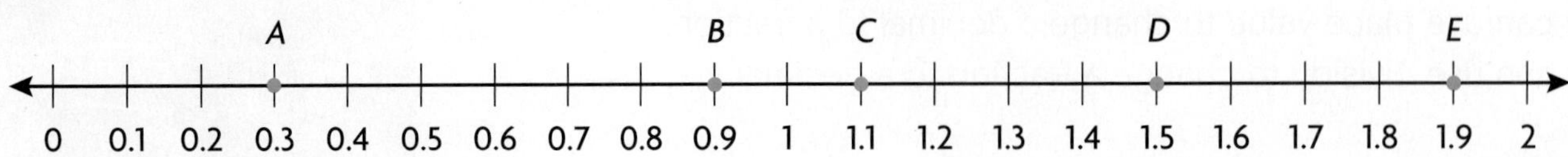

4. Point *C** **5.** Point *A* **6.** Point *E* **7.** Point *D* **8.** Point *B*

Write each decimal as a fraction or mixed number in simplest form.

9. 0.6 **10.** 0.45 **11.** 3.4 **12.** 3.84 **13.** 0.255

Write each fraction or mixed number as a decimal.

14. $\frac{4}{100}$ **15.** $\frac{7}{10}$ **16.** $3\frac{3}{8}$ **17.** $\frac{48}{100}$ **18.** $6\frac{2}{5}$

19. TALK Math **Explain** how to change a decimal to a fraction and a fraction to a decimal.

Independent Practice and Problem Solving

Write each decimal as a fraction or mixed number in simplest form.

20. 0.25 **21.** 0.4 **22.** 0.425 **23.** 7.83 **24.** 3.45

Write each fraction or mixed number as a decimal.

25. $\frac{10}{20}$ **26.** $3\frac{3}{15}$ **27.** $7\frac{10}{25}$ **28.** $\frac{3}{5}$ **29.** $\frac{333}{1,000}$

30. $6\frac{24}{25}$ **31.** $\frac{26}{50}$ **32.** $\frac{2}{8}$ **33.** $1\frac{589}{1,000}$ **34.** $1\frac{15}{25}$

Algebra Compare. Write <, >, or = for each ●.

35. 0.35 ● $\frac{1}{2}$ **36.** $\frac{3}{4}$ ● 0.8 **37.** 0.30 ● $\frac{3}{10}$ **38.** 0.55 ● $\frac{3}{7}$

39. A batting average of .333 means the player had about 333 hits for every 1,000 at-bats. Copy and complete the table to show equivalent fractions and decimals.

Fractions of Hits at Bat	Batting Average
■	.500
■	.250
$\frac{2}{5}$	■

40. **FAST FACT** Ty Cobb batted .420 in 1911. What fraction shows his batting average? Write the fraction in simplest form.

41. WRITE Math Julia had 4 out of 10 hits at bat. **Explain** how you would find her batting average.

 Extra Practice on page 331, Set F

Learn About Terminating and Repeating Decimals

To rewrite a fraction as a decimal, use long division or a calculator.

Use Long Division

Change $\frac{3}{8}$ to a decimal.

```
   0.375
8)3.000
 -24
   60
 - 56
    40
  - 40
     0
```

Divide the numerator by the denominator.

Use a calculator

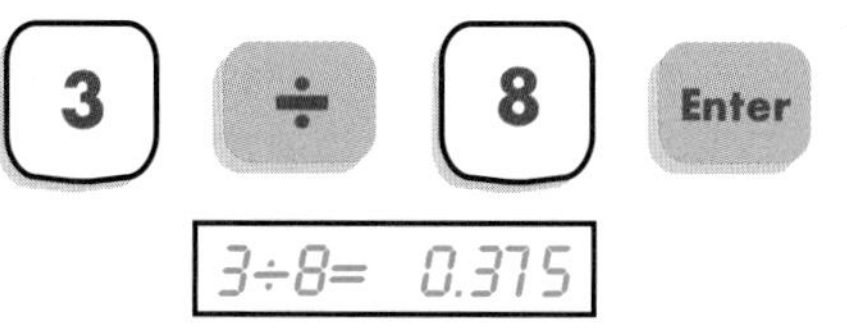

So, $\frac{3}{8} = 0.375$ is an example of a terminating decimal. A **terminating decimal** has a remainder of 0 in long division.

Use Long Division

Change $\frac{5}{6}$ to a decimal.

```
   0.833
6)5.000
 -48
   20
 - 18
    20
  - 18
     2
```

To write a repeating decimal, show the pattern and then three dots, or draw a bar over the repeating digits. 0.833... or $0.8\overline{33}$

Use a calculator

So, $\frac{5}{6} = 0.833\ldots$ is an example of a repeating decimal. When the remainder repeats and is not 0, the decimal is a **repeating decimal**.

Try It

Change each fraction to a decimal. Write whether the fraction is a *terminating decimal* or a *repeating decimal*.

42. $\frac{5}{12}$ **43.** $\frac{1}{9}$ **44.** $\frac{3}{5}$ **45.** $\frac{5}{8}$ **46.** $\frac{2}{11}$ **47.** $\frac{9}{24}$

Mixed Review and Test Prep

48. Chris has \$20. She would like to buy three T-shirts that cost \$7.29 each. Does she have enough money? **Explain.** (p. 170)

49. **Test Prep** Which fraction is NOT equivalent to 0.4?

A $\frac{1}{2}$ **B** $\frac{2}{5}$ **C** $\frac{4}{10}$ **D** $\frac{8}{20}$

50. Jen's softball team won $\frac{1}{3}$ of its games. What are three fractions equivalent to $\frac{1}{3}$? (p. 310)

51. **Test Prep** At basketball practice, Nick made $\frac{4}{5}$ of his free throws. What decimal is equivalent to $\frac{4}{5}$?

A 0.4 **B** 0.8 **C** 0.5 **D** 0.9

Extra Practice

Set A Write a fraction for the shaded part. Write a fraction for the unshaded part. (pp. 308–309)

1. 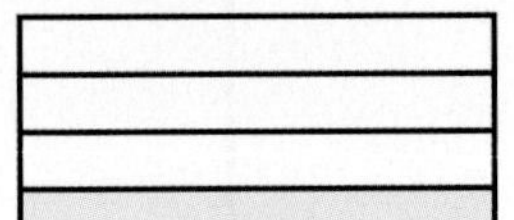
2. 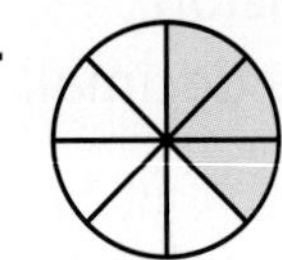
3. 
4. 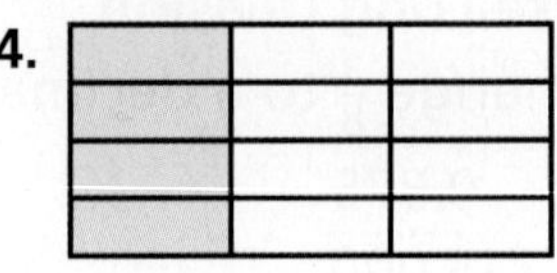

Write a fraction to name the point on the number line.

5. 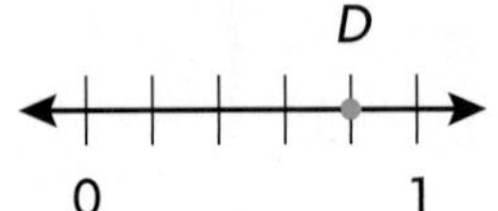

6. 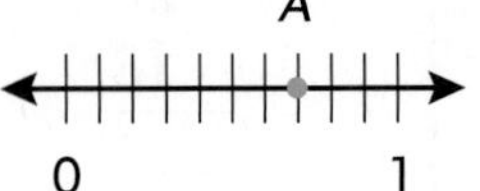

7. 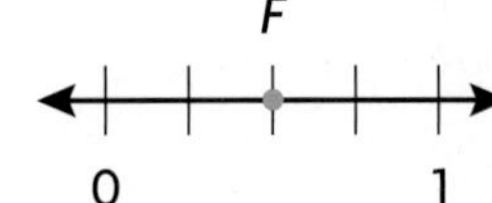

Write the fraction for each.

8. four out of five
9. seven eighths
10. one tenth
11. six divided by nineteen

Draw a model to show each fraction.

12. $\frac{3}{4}$
13. $\frac{1}{6}$
14. $\frac{2}{2}$
15. $\frac{9}{10}$
16. $\frac{2}{8}$
17. $\frac{2}{3}$

Set B Write an equivalent fraction. (pp. 310–311)

1. $\frac{3}{5}$
2. $\frac{1}{8}$
3. $\frac{4}{8}$
4. $\frac{4}{5}$
5. $\frac{3}{9}$
6. $\frac{6}{12}$
7. $\frac{4}{6}$
8. $\frac{2}{7}$
9. $\frac{4}{10}$
10. $\frac{3}{18}$
11. $\frac{2}{5}$
12. $\frac{3}{15}$
13. Kenisha has 6 cans of fruit. Two cans contain peaches. Write two fractions that represent the cans containing peaches.
14. Jake and Evan are playing with 4 red cubes and 8 blue cubes. Jake says that $\frac{1}{2}$ of the cubes are red. Evan says that $\frac{1}{3}$ are red. Who is correct? **Explain.**

Set C Write each fraction in simplest form. (pp. 312–315)

1. $\frac{30}{40}$
2. $\frac{4}{14}$
3. $\frac{3}{3}$
4. $\frac{4}{5}$
5. $\frac{12}{24}$
6. $\frac{40}{100}$
7. $\frac{5}{12}$
8. $\frac{18}{20}$
9. $\frac{8}{32}$
10. $\frac{50}{75}$
11. $\frac{18}{24}$
12. $\frac{7}{49}$
13. $\frac{10}{80}$
14. $\frac{9}{15}$
15. $\frac{16}{16}$
16. $\frac{25}{45}$
17. $\frac{15}{16}$
18. $\frac{75}{100}$

CD ROM **Technology**
Use Harcourt Mega Math, Fraction Action, *Fraction Flare Up*, Levels F, H, J.

Set D Write each mixed number as a fraction. Write each fraction as a mixed number. (pp. 316–317)

1. $\frac{13}{4}$ 2. $2\frac{1}{5}$ 3. $\frac{5}{3}$ 4. $\frac{29}{4}$ 5. $1\frac{1}{2}$ 6. $4\frac{3}{8}$

7. $\frac{49}{12}$ 8. $\frac{7}{3}$ 9. $3\frac{4}{5}$ 10. $\frac{21}{20}$ 11. $5\frac{1}{3}$ 12. $\frac{20}{9}$

13. $\frac{4}{3}$ 14. $1\frac{5}{6}$ 15. $\frac{43}{10}$ 16. $\frac{19}{3}$ 17. $3\frac{2}{9}$ 18. $8\frac{1}{2}$

19. Mrs. Walters is making a chocolate cake. The recipe calls for $2\frac{1}{2}$ cups of sifted flour. How many $\frac{1}{2}$ cups of flour will she need?

20. Edmund ran nine fourths around a $\frac{1}{4}$ mile track. How many miles did Edmund run? Write the distance as a mixed number and a fraction greater than 1.

Set E Compare. Write <, >, or = for each ●. (pp. 318–321)

1. $\frac{1}{3}$ ● $\frac{3}{5}$ 2. $\frac{1}{2}$ ● $\frac{2}{4}$ 3. $4\frac{5}{6}$ ● $4\frac{7}{12}$ 4. $2\frac{2}{9}$ ● $1\frac{1}{2}$ 5. $3\frac{3}{4}$ ● $3\frac{4}{5}$

6. $2\frac{1}{5}$ ● $2\frac{2}{3}$ 7. $1\frac{3}{4}$ ● $2\frac{1}{16}$ 8. $3\frac{2}{5}$ ● $3\frac{4}{10}$ 9. $4\frac{5}{12}$ ● $4\frac{3}{8}$ 10. $12\frac{3}{10}$ ● $12\frac{3}{5}$

Write in order from least to greatest.

11. $1\frac{5}{9}, 1\frac{2}{9}, 1\frac{7}{9}$ 12. $\frac{4}{5}, \frac{3}{5}, \frac{7}{10}$ 13. $\frac{1}{6}, \frac{1}{8}, \frac{1}{10}$ 14. $1\frac{3}{4}, \frac{1}{3}, 1\frac{5}{12}$ 15. $2\frac{1}{2}, 2\frac{5}{6}, \frac{3}{8}$

16. Toni has three cats: Lizzie, Kiki, and Lulu. Lizzie weighs $9\frac{1}{8}$ pounds, Kiki weighs $10\frac{1}{4}$ pounds, and Lulu weighs $9\frac{3}{4}$ pounds. Which cat weighs the least?

17. Ming gave his seedlings $\frac{3}{4}$ cup of water on Monday, $\frac{1}{2}$ cup of water on Tuesday, and $\frac{7}{8}$ cup of water on Wednesday. On which day did he give his seedlings the most water?

Set F Write each fraction as a decimal. (pp. 326–329)

1. $\frac{2}{5}$ 2. $\frac{11}{20}$ 3. $\frac{14}{100}$ 4. $\frac{6}{8}$ 5. $\frac{9}{10}$

6. $\frac{9}{20}$ 7. $\frac{6}{10}$ 8. $\frac{2}{5}$ 9. $\frac{13}{50}$ 10. $\frac{44}{100}$

Write each decimal as a fraction in simplest form.

11. 0.9 12. 0.03 13. 0.45 14. 0.75 15. 0.6

16. 0.14 17. 0.3 18. 0.52 19. 0.8 20. 0.99

MATH POWER **Solve for Unknowns**

Use the Clues

You can use what you know about equivalent fractions to solve.

Example 1

Find the unknown number. $\frac{6}{7} = \frac{■}{56}$

Clue: The unknown number is an even number greater than 40 but less than 60 whose digits have a sum of 12.

Step 1	Step 2
List all the even numbers greater than 40 but less than 60. 42, 44, 46, 48, 50, 52, 54, 56, 58	Find a number in the list whose digits have a sum of 12. $4 + 8 = 12$ So, the unknown number = 48.

Example 2

Find the unknown number. $\frac{2}{3} = \frac{■ - 8}{51}$

Step 1	Step 2	Step 3
Find a fraction equivalent to $\frac{2}{3}$ that has 51 as the denominator. So, divide 51 by 3. $51 \div 3 = 17$	Since $3 \times 17 = 51$, multiply: 2×17. $\frac{2 \times 17}{3 \times 17} = \frac{34}{51}$	Solve for the unknown number. $■ - 8 = 34$ $42 - 8 = 34$ So, the unknown number is 42.

Try It

Solve.

1. $\frac{4}{5} = \frac{■}{60}$

   Clue: The unknown number is an even number greater than 45 but less than 65.

2. $\frac{3}{4} = \frac{27}{■}$

   Clue: The sum of the digits is 9.

3. $\frac{7}{13} = \frac{28}{■}$

   Clue: The sum of the digits is 7.

4. **WRITE Math** **Explain** how you would find the unknown number in $\frac{■}{24} = \frac{2}{3}$.

Chapter 12 Review/Test

Check Vocabulary and Concepts

VOCABULARY
- common factor
- mixed number
- equivalent fractions
- simplest form

Choose the best term from the box.

1. __?__ are fractions that name the same amount or part. KY MA-05-1.1.3 (p. 310)
2. A fraction is in __?__ when the numerator and denominator have only 1 as their common factor. KY MA-05-1.1.3 (p. 312)
3. A number that is made up of a whole number and a fraction is a __?__. KY MA-05-1.1.1 (p. 316)

Check Skills

Write an equivalent fraction. KY MA-05-1.1.3 (pp. 310–312)

4. $\frac{1}{6}$ 5. $\frac{4}{12}$ 6. $\frac{2}{10}$ 7. $\frac{5}{8}$

Write each fraction in simplest form. KY MA-05-1.1.3 (pp. 312–315)

8. $\frac{8}{32}$ 9. $\frac{75}{100}$ 10. $\frac{27}{81}$ 11. $\frac{7}{11}$

Write each mixed number as a fraction. Write each fraction as a mixed number.
KY MA-05-1.1.1 (pp. 316–321)

12. $\frac{9}{2}$ 13. $1\frac{1}{4}$ 14. $5\frac{2}{3}$ 15. $\frac{10}{3}$

Compare. Write $<$, $>$, or $=$ for each ●. KY MA-05-1.1.3 (pp. 318–321)

16. $\frac{2}{3}$ ● $\frac{5}{6}$ 17. $1\frac{1}{2}$ ● $1\frac{5}{10}$ 18. $3\frac{1}{5}$ ● $2\frac{3}{7}$ 19. $1\frac{2}{3}$ ● $1\frac{4}{7}$

Write each fraction as a decimal. Write each decimal as a fraction in simplest form.
KY MA-05-1.1.1 (pp. 326–329)

20. 0.75 21. $\frac{19}{100}$ 22. 0.48 23. $\frac{2}{8}$

Check Problem Solving

Solve. KY MA-05-1.1.1; MA-05-1.1.3 (pp. 322–325)

24. Jen, Rick, and Katrina are making bead chains. Jen's chain is $4\frac{3}{8}$ feet long. Rick's chain is $4\frac{1}{2}$ feet long. Katrina's chain is $3\frac{3}{4}$ feet long. Whose chain is the longest?
25. **WRITE Math** Lin lives 0.9 mile from school. **Explain** how you could use a model to find the distance Lin travels to and from school during a 5-day week.

GO ONLINE **Technology** Use *Online Assessment.*

Unit Review/Test
Chapters 11–12

Multiple Choice

1. What fraction of the stars are shaded?
KY MA-05-1.1.1 (p. 308)

A. $\frac{3}{4}$
C. $\frac{2}{3}$
B. $\frac{3}{5}$
D. $\frac{2}{5}$

2. What is the value of 20^2?
KY MA-05-1.5.1 (p. 290)

A. 22
B. 40
C. 202
D. 400

3. Which of the following is a prime number?
KY MA-05-1.5.1 (p. 284)

A. 4
B. 9
C. 13
D. 15

4. What is the prime factorization of 48?
KY MA-05-1.5.1 (p. 296)

A. $2^3 \times 3^2$
B. $2^3 \times 3^1$
C. $2^3 \times 3^3$
D. $2^4 \times 3^1$

5. Which of the following shows the fraction modeled in simplest form?
KY MA-05-1.1.3 (p. 312)

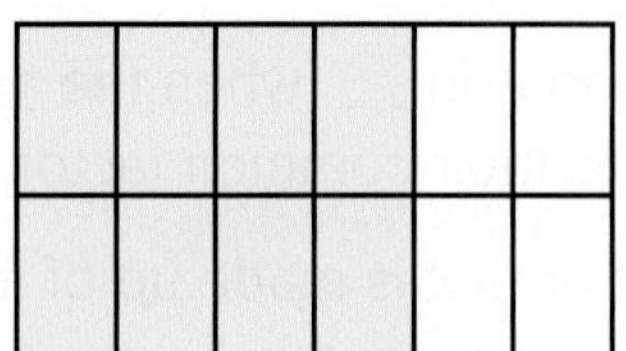

A. $\frac{2}{3}$
B. $\frac{1}{2}$
C. $\frac{8}{12}$
D. $\frac{3}{4}$

6. Which number line shows $2\frac{1}{4}$ represented by a point? KY MA-05-1.1.1 (p. 316)

A. 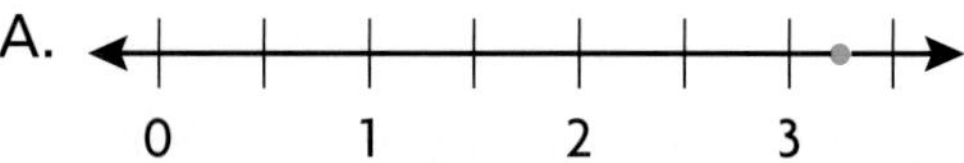

B. 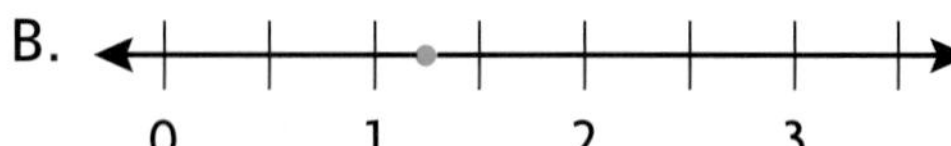

C. 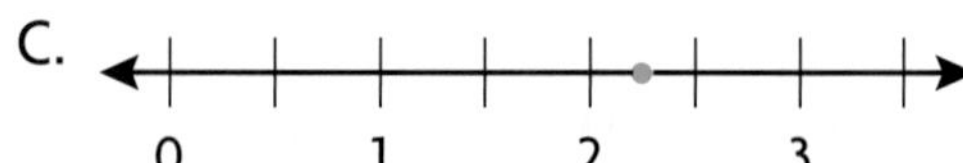

D. 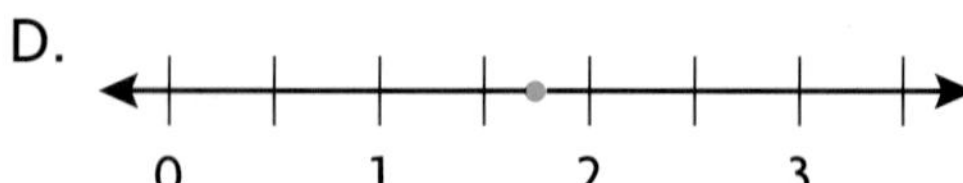

GO ONLINE **Technology** Use *Online Assessment.*

7. Which type of graph would best display the following data? KY MA-05-4.1.1 (p. 226)

Swim Team Size	
Grade	**Number of Swimmers**
Third Grade	18
Fourth Grade	20
Fifth Grade	26
Sixth Grade	24

A. bar graph

B. histogram

C. line graph

D. circle graph

8. What is the least common multiple of 14 and 8? KY MA-05-1.5.1 (p. 276)

A. 14

B. 28

C. 42

D. 56

9. Of the students surveyed, what is the most popular type of exercise? KY MA-05-4.1.1 (p. 226)

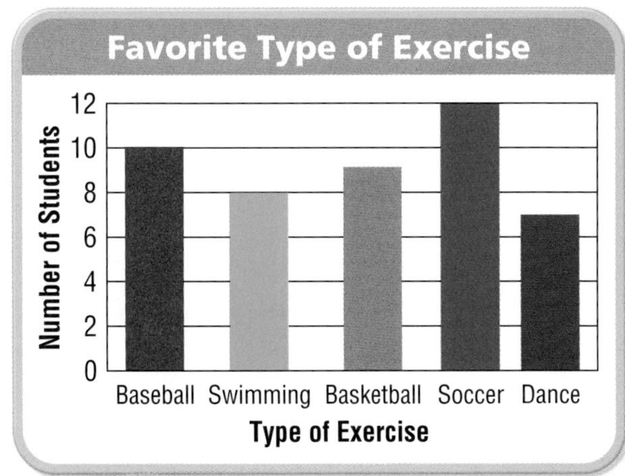

A. Dance

B. Soccer

C. Swimming

D. Baseball

Open Response WRITE Math

10. Draw a number line from 0 to 4 as shown.

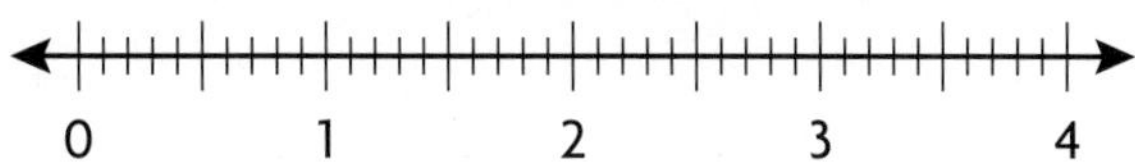

Place the following numbers on the number line: 1.4, 3.7, $2\frac{1}{5}$. KY MA-05-1.1.1 (p. 326)

11. Use any of the digits 1, 2, 3, or 5 to find the prime factorization of a number that is greater than 40 but less than 50. **Explain** how you found your answer. KY MA-05-1.5.1 (p. 296)

12. The basketball coach keeps score of the baskets and attempts made during each game. The table below shows the data for five players.

Player	Baskets made per attempt	Equivalent Decimal
Miles	$\frac{2}{4}$	■
Rona	$\frac{5}{10}$	■
Jerry	$\frac{7}{10}$	■
Erin	$\frac{3}{4}$	■
Dan	$\frac{3}{5}$	■

Copy the table and write an equivalent decimal for each fraction. Then place the players in order from most baskets made per attempt to fewest baskets made per attempt. You can use a number line or another model to solve. **Explain** how you found your answer. KY MA-05-1.1.3 (p. 326)

THE WORLD ALMANAC FOR KIDS

Music, Music, Music

Music to Our Ears

What type of music do you like? Rock? Country? Classical? Each type of music has its own fans who buy albums. An album that sells a million copies "goes platinum." Multi-platinum albums sell two million copies or more.

In 2005, about 705 million CDs were sold. That's more than 10.5 billion dollars' worth of music!

FACT·ACTIVITY

Albums That "Went Platinum"

Type of Music	Number
Jazz	1
R&B/Soul	5
Hip-Hop	10
Country	10
Rock	14
Pop	15

Use the table to answer the questions.

1. What fraction of the platinum albums are rock?
2. What kind of music is on $\frac{3}{11}$ of the total platinum albums?
3. Which two types of music together are on $\frac{1}{5}$ of the total platinum albums? Hint: There are two possible answers.
4. Write an inequality that compares the fraction of country and the fraction of pop albums that went platinum. Write the fractions in simplest form.
5. A store owner wants to display complete sets of every platinum pop CD on one shelf and every platinum country CD on another shelf. He wants to have the same number of CDs on the two shelves. What's the least number of CDs that can be on each shelf?
6. WRITE Math **Explain** how you found your answer for Problem 5.

ALMANAC Fact

Orchestras can range in size from small chamber orchestras to large symphony orchestras with as many as 120 musicians.

Many Players, One Orchestra

What do you call a large group of musicians? Both *orchestra* and *band* are correct, but the two musical groups are different. Orchestras have four sections: brasses, percussion, woodwinds, and strings. Bands do not have a string section.

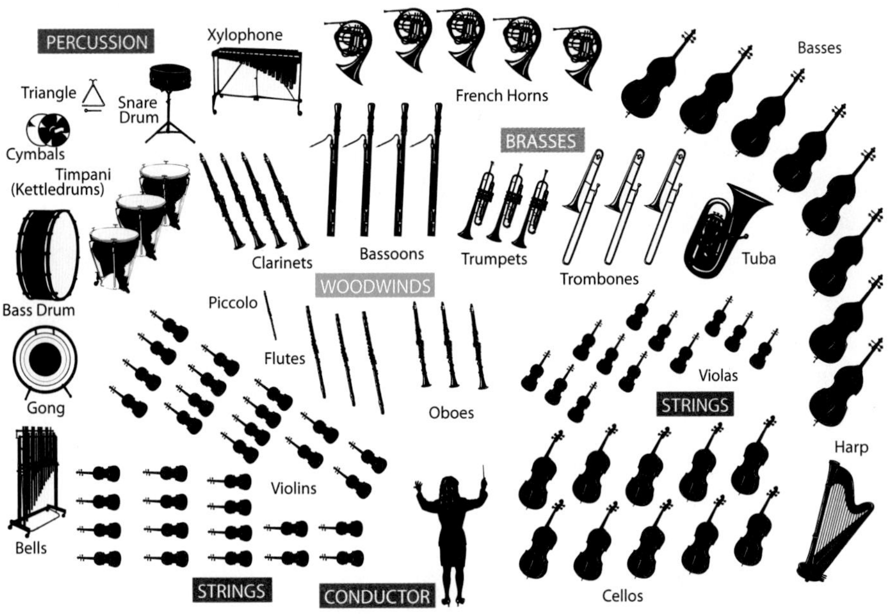

In an orchestra the strings include the violins, violas, cellos, basses, and a harp. The strings make up $\frac{63}{100}$ of the orchestra above.

FACT·ACTIVITY

1. Design your own musical group.
   - Decide the number of members that will be in your group.
   - Choose an instrument for each member. You may want to refer to the diagram above.
   - How many of each instrument will you need?
   - What fractions and decimals can you use to describe each part of your group?
2. Describe how the fractions will change if one member of your group is not able to perform.

UNIT 5 Fraction Operations

Math on Location

with
Chapter Projects

1

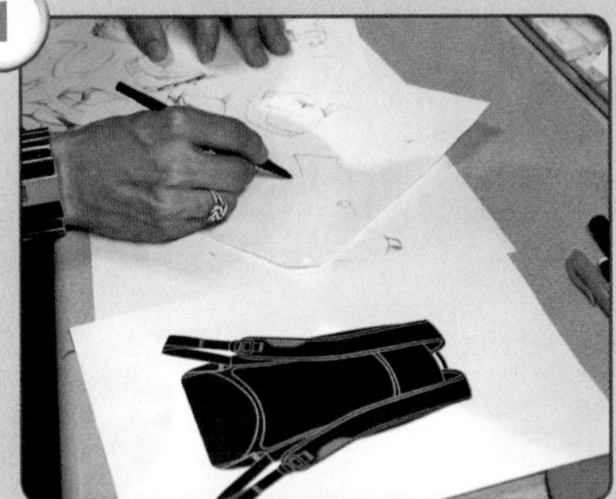

The designer's idea sketches and drawings show measurements in fractions and mixed numbers.

2

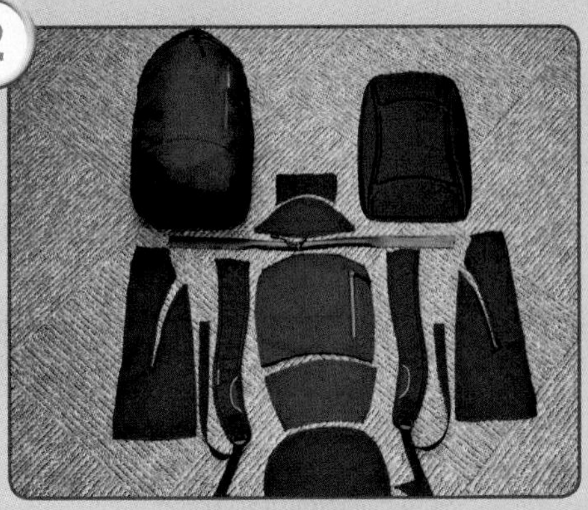

Patterns for all the pieces are used to cut and assemble a prototype for testing.

3

The designer looks at other finished backpacks to be able to explain the benefits of his design.

VOCABULARY POWER

TALK Math

What math is used in the **Math on Location**? What kinds of units and numbers do you need to use to measure and cut material in precise sizes?

READ Math

REVIEW VOCABULARY You learned the words below when you learned about fraction concepts. How do these words relate to **Math on Location**?

equivalent fractions fractions that name the same amount

simplest form the form of a fraction in which the numerator and denominator have only 1 as their common factor

WRITE Math

Copy and complete a word definition map like the one below. Use what you know about fractions.

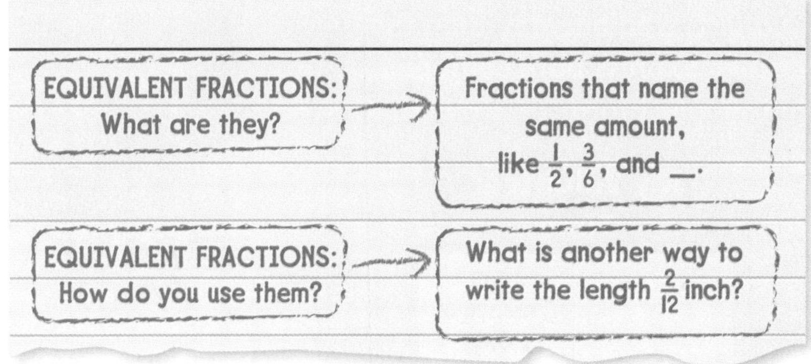

EQUIVALENT FRACTIONS: What are they?
Fractions that name the same amount, like $\frac{1}{2}$, $\frac{3}{6}$, and ___.
EQUIVALENT FRACTIONS: How do you use them?
What is another way to write the length $\frac{2}{12}$ inch?

Technology
Multimedia Math Glossary link at
www.harcourtschool.com/hspmath

CHAPTER 13

Add and Subtract Fractions

Investigate

Suppose you volunteer at the Adler Planetarium during the summer. Choose any two days. Write and solve an equation to show how much time you volunteered in all on those two days. Write and solve another equation to show how much longer you volunteered one day than the other. Express both solutions in simplest form.

My Volunteer Time

Day	Time (Fraction of a Day)
Monday	$\frac{1}{12}$
Tuesday	$\frac{1}{4}$
Wednesday	$\frac{5}{24}$
Thursday	$\frac{1}{8}$
Friday	$\frac{1}{6}$

FAST FACT

The Henry Moore Sundial Sculpture at the Adler Planetarium in Chicago is an example of an *equatorial sundial*. The dial plate is marked with hour lines. Each represents $\frac{1}{24}$ of a day.

GO ONLINE **Technology**
Student pages are available in the Student eBook.

Show What You Know

Check your understanding of important skills needed for success in Chapter 13.

▶ Equivalent Fractions

Write two equivalent fractions for each picture.

1. 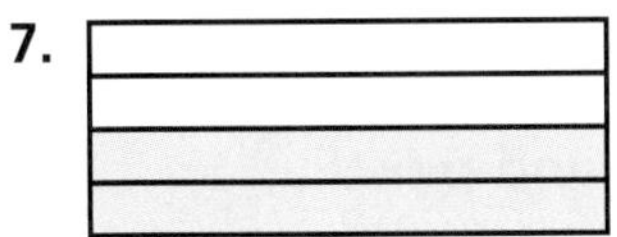
2. 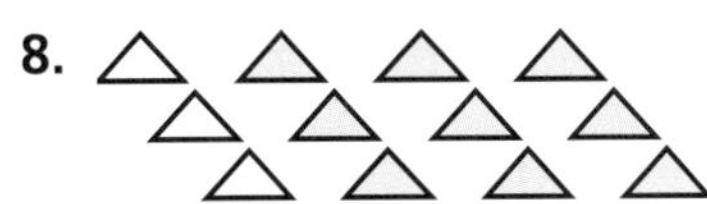
3. 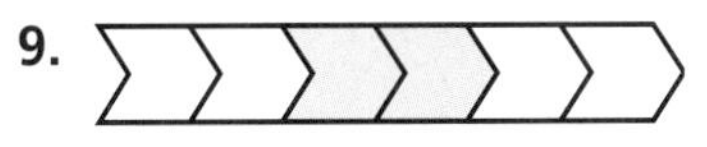
4.
5.
6.
7.
8.
9.

▶ Simplest Form

Write each fraction in simplest form.

10. $\frac{3}{6}$
11. $\frac{6}{8}$
12. $\frac{2}{6}$
13. $\frac{6}{9}$
14. $\frac{3}{12}$
15. $\frac{4}{10}$
16. $\frac{12}{15}$
17. $\frac{15}{20}$
18. $\frac{8}{16}$
19. $\frac{14}{21}$
20. $\frac{18}{24}$
21. $\frac{5}{30}$

VOCABULARY POWER

CHAPTER VOCABULARY

common multiple
equivalent fractions
least common denominator (LCD)
multiples

WARM-UP WORDS

common multiple a number that is a multiple of two or more numbers

equivalent fractions fractions that name the same amount or part

least common denominator (LCD) the least common multiple of two or more denominators

LESSON 1

Add and Subtract Like Fractions

OBJECTIVE: Add and subtract like fractions.

Quick Review

Write each fraction in simplest form.

1. $\frac{2}{10}$
2. $\frac{6}{8}$
3. $\frac{4}{8}$
4. $\frac{2}{6}$
5. $\frac{6}{9}$

Learn

PROBLEM Alaska's Columbia Glacier is one of North America's fastest moving glaciers. It moves at a rate of about 78 feet to 114 feet each day. Suppose the glacier moves 78 feet per day for two weeks. This is about $\frac{2}{10}$ mile. It then moves 114 feet per day for two weeks. This is about $\frac{3}{10}$ mile. How far in miles does the glacier move in four weeks?

Add. $\frac{2}{10} + \frac{3}{10}$

ONE WAY **Use a model.**

Shade 2 parts of a tenths model.

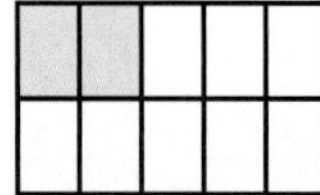

Shade 3 more parts.

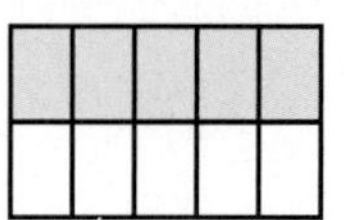

Write the fraction for the part that is shaded. $\frac{5}{10} = \frac{1}{2}$

ANOTHER WAY **Use paper and pencil.**

$$\frac{2}{10} + \frac{3}{10} = \frac{5}{10} = \frac{1}{2}$$

- Add the numerators.
- Write the sum over the denominator.
- Write the sum in simplest form.

So, the glacier moves about $\frac{1}{2}$ mile every 4 weeks.

Subtract. $\frac{3}{10} - \frac{2}{10}$

ONE WAY **Use a model.**

Shade 3 parts of a tenths model.

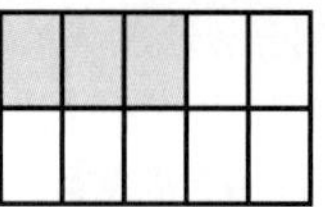

Subtract $\frac{2}{10}$. Draw a line through 2 parts.

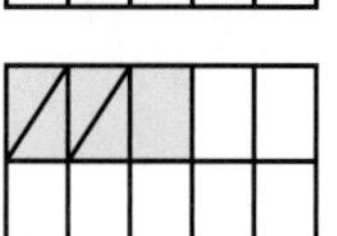

Write the fraction: $\frac{1}{10}$.

ANOTHER WAY **Use paper and pencil.**

$$\frac{3}{10} - \frac{2}{10} = \frac{1}{10}$$

- Subtract the numerators.
- Write the difference over the denominator.
- Check that the difference is in simplest form.

Guided Practice

1. Use a model to find $\frac{2}{8} + \frac{4}{8}$. Write the answer in simplest form.

FAST TRACK

KY MA-05-1.3.1 Students will analyze real-world problems to identify appropriate representations using mathematical operations, and will apply operations to solve real-world problems with the following constraints: add and subtract fractions with like denominators through 16, with sums less than or equal to one. DOK 2

Find the sum or difference. Write it in simplest form.

2. $\frac{1}{4} + \frac{2}{4}$
3. $\frac{3}{4} - \frac{1}{4}$
4. $\frac{5}{8} + \frac{3}{8}$
5. $\frac{2}{3} - \frac{1}{3}$
6. $\frac{7}{10} + \frac{1}{10}$
7. TALK Math Explain how to find $\frac{2}{12} + \frac{4}{12}$.

Independent Practice and Problem Solving

Find the sum or difference. Write it in simplest form.

8. $\frac{1}{10} + \frac{3}{10}$
9. $\frac{3}{6} - \frac{1}{6}$
10. $\frac{4}{8} + \frac{3}{8}$
11. $\frac{5}{7} - \frac{3}{7}$
12. $\frac{7}{12} + \frac{5}{12}$
13. $\frac{4}{4} - \frac{1}{4}$
14. $\frac{2}{7} + \frac{4}{7}$
15. $\frac{5}{8} - \frac{3}{8}$
16. $\frac{1}{3} + \frac{1}{3}$
17. $\frac{3}{8} - \frac{1}{8}$

Algebra Find the missing number for each ■.

18. $■ + \frac{4}{9} = \frac{7}{9}$
19. $\frac{3}{4} - ■ = \frac{1}{4}$
20. $1 - ■ = \frac{2}{3}$
21. $\frac{9}{12} + ■ = \frac{11}{12}$

USE DATA For 22–24, use the graph.

22. What fraction of students chose either spring or summer as their favorite season?
23. **Reasoning** Which two seasons were chosen by $\frac{2}{5}$ of all the students?
24. WRITE Math **What's the Error?** To find the difference in the number of students who chose summer and those who chose winter, Cara found $\frac{5}{10} - \frac{2}{10}$ and got 3. What is her error?

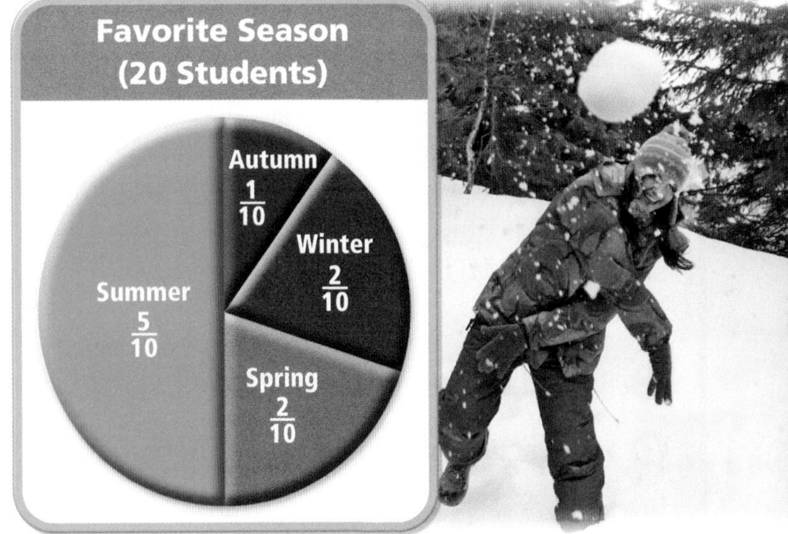

Mixed Review and Test Prep

25. A hockey team added 3 more players. Let p = the number of players originally on the team. Write an expression to show how many players are on the team now. (p. 92)
26. What is the fraction $\frac{10}{12}$ written in simplest form? (p. 312)
27. **Test Prep** Alex pours $\frac{1}{4}$ cup orange juice and $\frac{2}{4}$ cup pineapple juice into a measuring cup. He fills the rest of it with cranberry juice. How much cranberry juice does he put in the measuring cup?

   A $\frac{1}{4}$ cup
   B $\frac{3}{8}$ cup
   C $\frac{3}{4}$ cup
   D 3 cups

Extra Practice on page 358, Set A

LESSON HANDS ON

2 Model Addition of Unlike Fractions

OBJECTIVE: Add unlike fractions using fraction bars.

Quick Review

Find the sum or difference. Write it in simplest form.

1. $\frac{1}{4} + \frac{1}{4}$
2. $\frac{3}{8} - \frac{1}{8}$
3. $\frac{4}{8} + \frac{3}{8}$
4. $\frac{5}{10} - \frac{2}{10}$
5. $\frac{1}{5} + \frac{4}{5}$

Investigate

Materials ■ fraction bars

You can use fraction bars to add fractions with unlike denominators.

A Find $\frac{1}{2} + \frac{1}{4}$. Place one $\frac{1}{2}$ bar and one $\frac{1}{4}$ bar under a 1 whole bar.

1

$\frac{1}{2}$ $\frac{1}{4}$

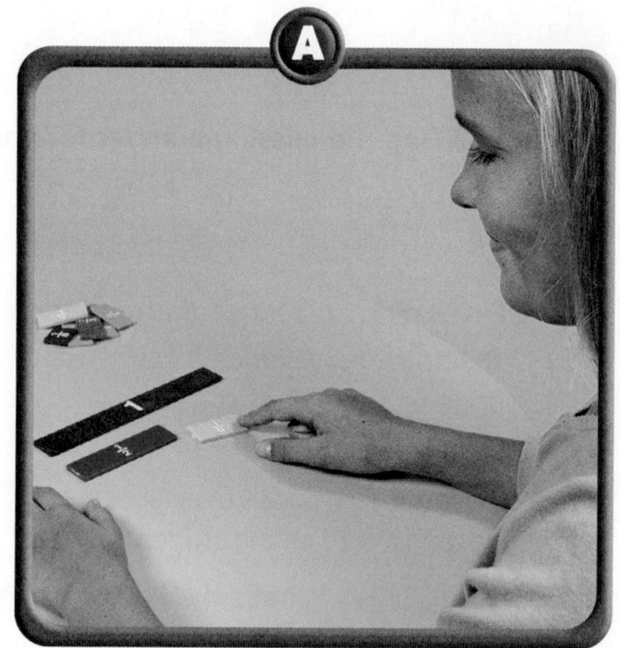

B Find like fraction bars that fit exactly under the sum $\frac{1}{2} + \frac{1}{4}$.

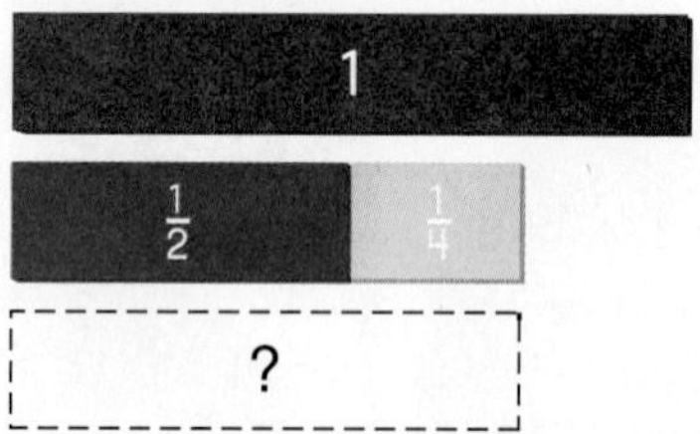

C Record the sum in simplest form.

D Use fraction bars to find $\frac{3}{5} + \frac{1}{2}$. Record the sum.

Draw Conclusions

1. What like fraction bars did you use to fit exactly under $\frac{1}{2} + \frac{1}{4}$? Could you have used any other like fraction bars? If so, which ones?
2. What like fraction bars did you use to find $\frac{3}{5} + \frac{1}{2}$? Is the sum greater than or less than 1?
3. **Analysis** In your model of $\frac{3}{5} + \frac{1}{2}$, how many $\frac{1}{10}$ bars equal $\frac{3}{5}$? How many equal $\frac{1}{2}$? What do you know about $\frac{3}{5}$ and $\frac{6}{10}$? about $\frac{1}{2}$ and $\frac{5}{10}$?

Connect

When you find the fraction bars that fit exactly under a sum, you are finding equivalent fractions.

Find: $\frac{2}{3} + \frac{1}{6}$.

Step 1

Place two $\frac{1}{3}$ fraction bars under a bar for 1. Then place one $\frac{1}{6}$ fraction bar beside the two $\frac{1}{3}$ bars.

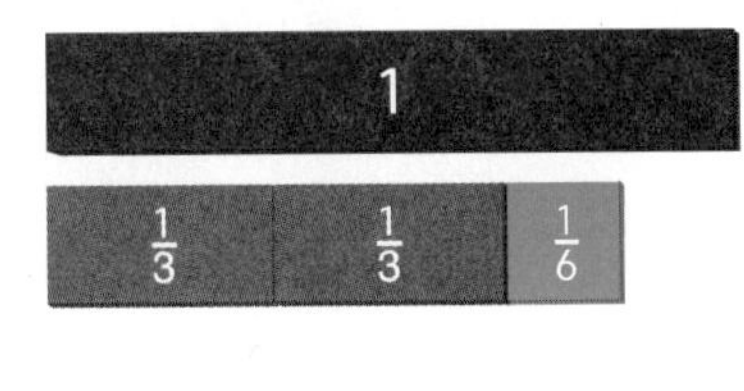

Step 2

Find like fraction bars that are equivalent to $\frac{2}{3}$ and $\frac{1}{6}$.

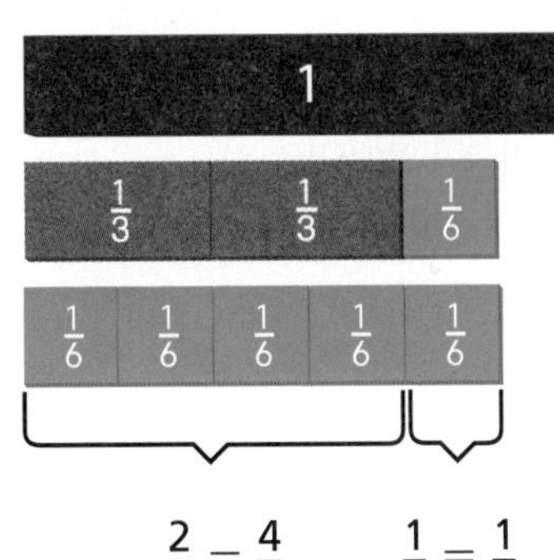

$\frac{2}{3} = \frac{4}{6}$ $\quad \frac{1}{6} = \frac{1}{6}$

Step 3

Add the like fractions.

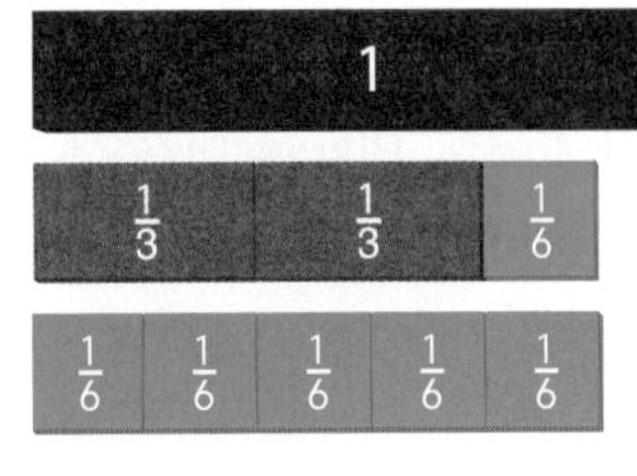

$\frac{4}{6} + \frac{1}{6} = \frac{5}{6}$

So, $\frac{2}{3} + \frac{1}{6} = \frac{5}{6}$.

TALK Math

Which like fractions would you use to find $\frac{1}{2} + \frac{3}{4}$?

Practice

Find the sum. Write it in simplest form.

1. 1/2 | 1/8 | 1/8 | 1/8

   $\frac{1}{2} + \frac{3}{8}$

2. 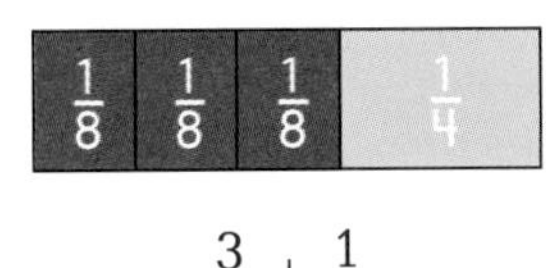

   $\frac{3}{8} + \frac{1}{4}$

3. 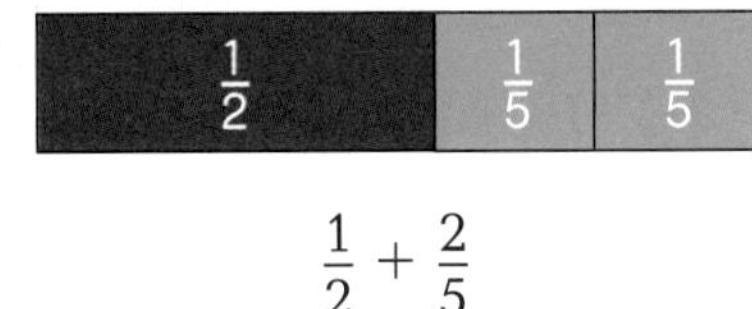

   $\frac{1}{2} + \frac{2}{5}$

Find the sum using fraction bars. Write it in simplest form.

4. $\frac{2}{5} + \frac{3}{10}$
5. ✓ $\frac{1}{4} + \frac{2}{12}$
6. $\frac{1}{2} + \frac{3}{10}$
7. $\frac{1}{2} + \frac{1}{3}$
8. $\frac{1}{4} + \frac{4}{12}$
9. $\frac{1}{3} + \frac{3}{6}$
10. $\frac{1}{5} + \frac{1}{10}$
11. $\frac{3}{4} + \frac{1}{3}$
12. $\frac{3}{4} + \frac{1}{6}$
13. $\frac{3}{5} + \frac{1}{2}$
14. $\frac{2}{3} + \frac{1}{4}$
15. ✓ $\frac{3}{4} + \frac{5}{6}$
16. **WRITE Math** **Explain** how to add $\frac{2}{8}$ and $\frac{3}{4}$ by using fraction bars.

LESSON 3 HANDS ON

Model Subtraction of Unlike Fractions

OBJECTIVE: Subtract unlike fractions using fraction bars.

Quick Review

Find the difference. Write it in simplest form.

1. $\frac{3}{4} - \frac{1}{4}$
2. $\frac{5}{8} - \frac{2}{8}$
3. $\frac{2}{3} - \frac{1}{3}$
4. $\frac{4}{5} - \frac{2}{5}$
5. $\frac{10}{10} - \frac{8}{10}$

Investigate

Materials ■ fraction bars

You can use fraction bars to subtract fractions with unlike denominators.

A Find $\frac{3}{4} - \frac{1}{8}$. Place three $\frac{1}{4}$ bars under a 1 whole bar. Then place one $\frac{1}{8}$ bar under the $\frac{1}{4}$ bars.

1		
$\frac{1}{4}$	$\frac{1}{4}$	$\frac{1}{4}$
$\frac{1}{8}$		

B Compare the bars. Find like fraction bars that fit exactly under the difference $\frac{3}{4} - \frac{1}{8}$.

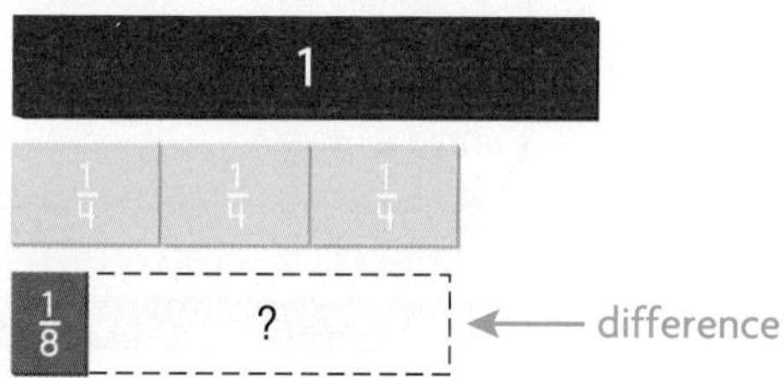

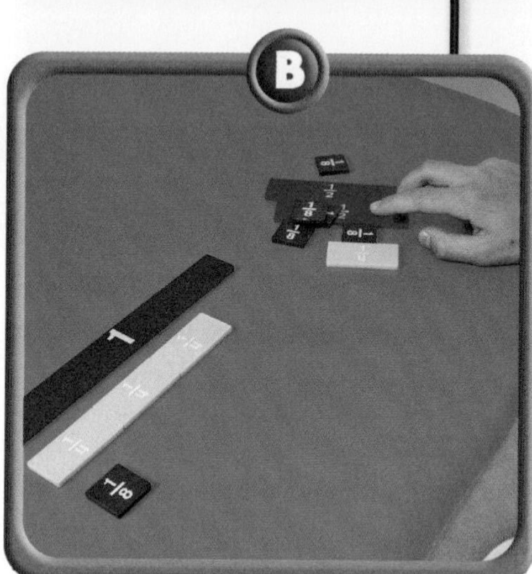

C Record the difference.

D Use fraction bars to find $\frac{1}{3} - \frac{1}{4}$.

Draw Conclusions

1. What like fraction bars did you use to fit exactly under the difference $\frac{3}{4} - \frac{1}{8}$?
2. What like fraction bars did you use to find $\frac{1}{3} - \frac{1}{4}$?
3. **Analysis** In your model of $\frac{1}{3} - \frac{1}{4}$, how many $\frac{1}{12}$ bars equal $\frac{1}{3}$? How many equal $\frac{1}{4}$? What do you know about $\frac{1}{3}$ and $\frac{4}{12}$? $\frac{1}{4}$ and $\frac{3}{12}$?

Connect

You can use fraction bars with like denominators to subtract fractions with unlike denominators.

Find: $\frac{2}{3} - \frac{1}{4}$.

Step 1

Place two $\frac{1}{3}$ bars under a 1 whole bar. Then place one $\frac{1}{4}$ bar under the two $\frac{1}{3}$ bars.

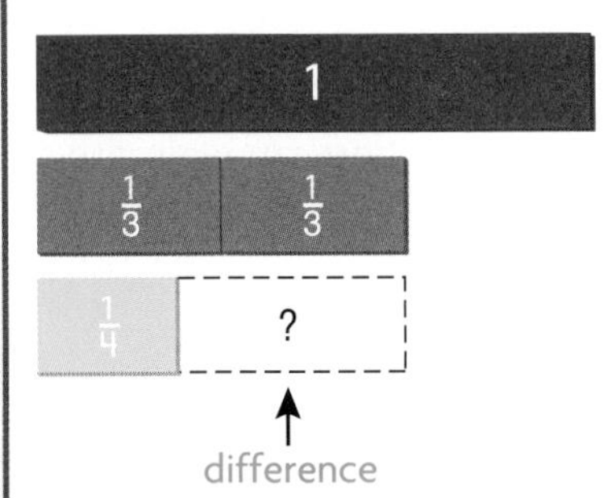

Step 2

Find like fraction bars that fit exactly under the difference $\frac{2}{3} - \frac{1}{4}$.

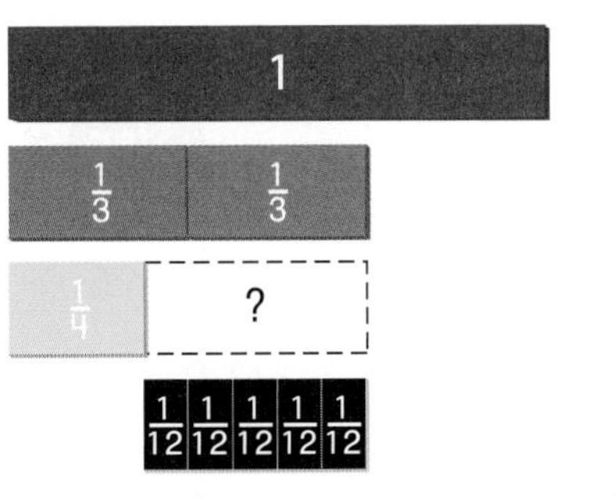

So, $\frac{2}{3} - \frac{1}{4} = \frac{5}{12}$.

Which like fractions would you use to find the difference $\frac{5}{6} - \frac{1}{2}$?

Practice

Use fraction bars to find the difference. Write it in simplest form.

1. $\frac{7}{10} - \frac{2}{5}$

2. $\frac{2}{3} - \frac{1}{6}$

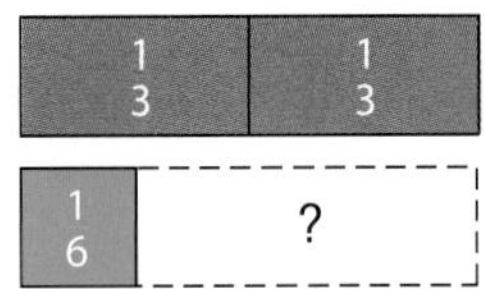

3. $\frac{1}{2} - \frac{3}{10}$

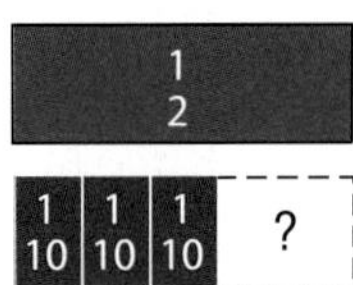

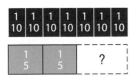

Find the difference using fraction bars. Write it in simplest form.

4. $\frac{3}{5} - \frac{3}{10}$
5. $\frac{5}{12} - \frac{1}{3}$
6. $\frac{1}{2} - \frac{1}{10}$
7. $\frac{3}{5} - \frac{1}{2}$
8. $\frac{7}{8} - \frac{1}{4}$
9. $\frac{2}{3} - \frac{3}{6}$
10. $\frac{3}{4} - \frac{1}{3}$
11. $\frac{5}{6} - \frac{1}{2}$
12. WRITE Math **Explain** how to use fraction bars to find $\frac{3}{4} - \frac{5}{8}$.

LESSON 4

Estimate Sums and Differences

OBJECTIVE: Estimate the sums and differences of fractions by using benchmark fractions.

Quick Review

Find the sum or difference. Write the answer in simplest form.

1. $\frac{3}{4} + \frac{1}{4}$
2. $\frac{2}{2} - \frac{1}{2}$
3. $\frac{2}{8} + \frac{3}{8}$
4. $\frac{5}{8} - \frac{1}{8}$
5. $\frac{2}{5} + \frac{3}{5}$

Learn

PROBLEM Kimberly is using different toppings for her banana split. First she pours $\frac{1}{6}$ cup fruit sauce on the ice cream. Then she puts $\frac{3}{8}$ cup of walnuts over the fruit sauce. Estimate the total amount of toppings Kimberly puts on her banana split.

Estimate. $\frac{1}{6} + \frac{3}{8}$

Step 1

The fraction $\frac{1}{6}$ is close to 0. Round to 0.

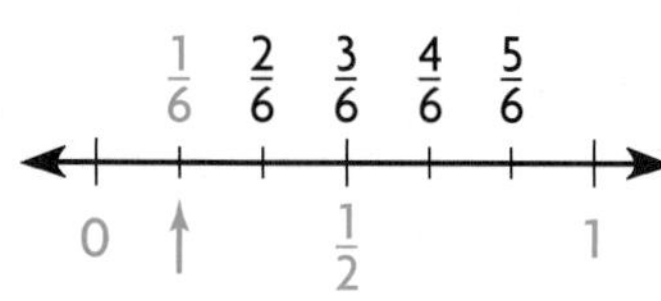

Step 2

The fraction $\frac{3}{8}$ is close to $\frac{1}{2}$. Round to $\frac{1}{2}$.

Step 3

Add the rounded fractions.

$$\begin{array}{r} \frac{1}{6} \rightarrow \quad 0 \\ +\frac{3}{8} \rightarrow +\frac{1}{2} \\ \hline \frac{1}{2} \end{array}$$

Math Idea

You can estimate sums and differences by rounding fractions to benchmark fractions such as 0, $\frac{1}{2}$, or 1.

So, Kimberly puts about $\frac{1}{2}$ cup of toppings on her banana split.

Example **Estimate.** $\frac{7}{8} - \frac{2}{5}$

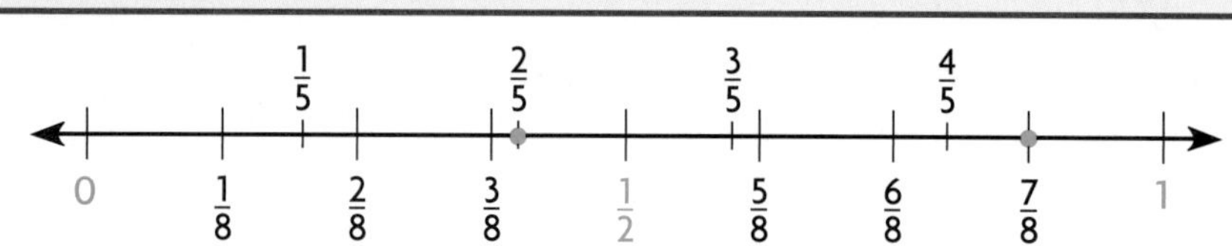

$\frac{7}{8}$ is between $\frac{1}{2}$ and 1, but closer to 1.

$\frac{2}{5}$ is between 0 and $\frac{1}{2}$, but closer to $\frac{1}{2}$.

$1 - \frac{1}{2} = \frac{1}{2}$

So, $\frac{7}{8} - \frac{2}{5}$ is about $\frac{1}{2}$.

Guided Practice

1. Look at the number line to complete.

   $\frac{3}{8}$ is between ▪ and ▪, but closer to ▪.

   $\frac{2}{3}$ is between ▪ and ▪, but closer to ▪.

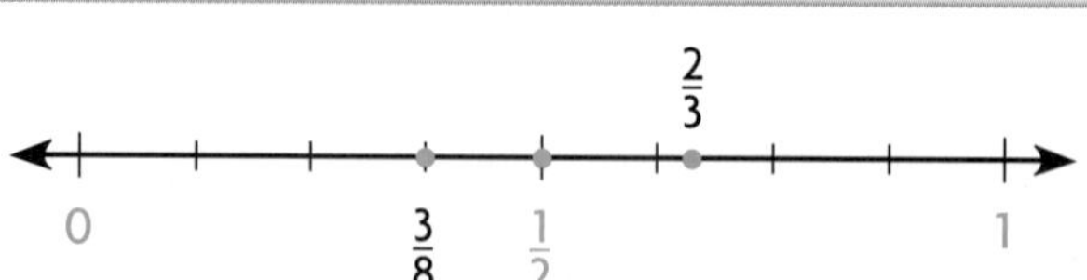

KY MA-05-1.2.1 Students will apply and describe appropriate strategies for estimating quantities of objects and computational results in real-world problems. DOK 2

Estimate each sum or difference.

2. $\frac{4}{6} - \frac{1}{8}$ 3. $\frac{7}{10} + \frac{1}{3}$ 4. $\frac{5}{6} + \frac{2}{5}$ 5. $\frac{9}{10} - \frac{2}{9}$ ✓6. $\frac{4}{6} + \frac{1}{9}$ ✓7. $\frac{4}{10} - \frac{1}{9}$

8. **TALK Math** Explain how you know that $\frac{5}{8} + \frac{6}{10}$ is greater than 1.

Independent Practice and Problem Solving

Estimate each sum or difference.

9. $\frac{5}{8} - \frac{1}{5}$ 10. $\frac{2}{6} + \frac{3}{8}$ 11. $\frac{6}{7} - \frac{3}{5}$ 12. $\frac{11}{12} + \frac{6}{10}$ 13. $\frac{9}{10} - \frac{1}{2}$

14. $\frac{3}{6} + \frac{4}{5}$ 15. $\frac{5}{6} - \frac{3}{8}$ 16. $\frac{1}{7} + \frac{8}{9}$ 17. $\frac{5}{12} - \frac{1}{10}$ 18. $\frac{3}{8} + \frac{3}{5}$

19. $\frac{1}{5} + \frac{5}{6}$ 20. $\frac{7}{12} - \frac{4}{10}$ 21. $\frac{3}{7} + \frac{8}{9}$ 22. $\frac{7}{8} - \frac{3}{5}$ 23. $\frac{10}{12} - \frac{1}{10}$

Estimate to compare. Write < or > for each ●.

24. $\frac{2}{3} + \frac{1}{9}$ ● 1 25. $\frac{3}{4} - \frac{1}{8}$ ● $\frac{1}{2}$ 26. $\frac{7}{12} + \frac{3}{5}$ ● 1 27. $\frac{7}{12} - \frac{1}{5}$ ● 0

28. Lisa and Valerie are picnicking in Roosevelt State Park in Mississippi. Lisa made a salad with $\frac{3}{4}$ cup of strawberries, $\frac{2}{3}$ cup of peaches, and $\frac{1}{8}$ cup of walnuts. About how many cups does this make?

29. **WRITE Math** **What's the Error?** Nick estimated that $\frac{5}{8} + \frac{4}{7}$ is about 2. What is his error?

30. ***FAST FACT*** At Trace State Park in Mississippi, there is a 25-mile mountain bike trail. If Tommy rode his bike $\frac{1}{3}$ of the trail on Saturday and $\frac{1}{5}$ of the trail on Sunday, about what fraction of the trail did he ride?

Mixed Review and Test Prep

31. Jon usually spends 45 minutes skating in the park. What fraction of an hour is this? (p. 308)

32. Which is the best estimate for the length of your arm? $\frac{1}{2}$ inch, $\frac{1}{2}$ foot, or $\frac{1}{2}$ yard? (Grade 4)

33. **Test Prep** Jake added $\frac{1}{8}$ cup of sunflower seeds and $\frac{4}{5}$ cup of banana chips to his sundae. Estimate the total amount that Jake added to his sundae.

A $\frac{1}{2}$ cup **C** $1\frac{1}{2}$ cups

B 1 cup **D** 2 cups

Technology Use Harcourt Mega Math, Fraction Action *Number Line Mine,* Level K.

Extra Practice on page 358, Set B

Use Common Denominators

OBJECTIVE: Use a common denominator to add and subtract unlike fractions.

Quick Review

Find a common multiple of each pair.

1. 2 and 4
2. 5 and 10
3. 4 and 6
4. 3 and 9
5. 6 and 10

Vocabulary

least common denominator (LCD)

Learn

PROBLEM The Pomo tribes who lived in California during the 1800s were highly skilled at weaving baskets. Suppose $\frac{1}{2}$ of a basket is woven in one month and $\frac{1}{4}$ of it is woven in the next two weeks. How much of the basket has been woven?

To add or subtract unlike fractions, rename them as like fractions with a common denominator.

Example 1 Add. $\frac{1}{2} + \frac{1}{4}$

Step 1

Multiply the denominators to find a common denominator.

$2 \times 4 = 8 \leftarrow$ common denominator

Step 2

Use the common denominator to write equivalent fractions. Then add.

$$\begin{array}{r} \frac{1}{2} = \frac{4}{8} \\ +\frac{1}{4} = +\frac{2}{8} \\ \hline \frac{6}{8} = \frac{3}{4} \leftarrow \text{simplest form} \end{array}$$

So, $\frac{3}{4}$ of the basket has been woven.

Suppose a Pomo basket weaver had a grass reed that was $\frac{5}{6}$ yard long. He needed only $\frac{3}{4}$ yard to complete a basket. How much of the reed was left when the basket was completed?

Example 2 Subtract. $\frac{5}{6} - \frac{3}{4}$

Step 1

Multiply the denominators to find a common denominator.

$6 \times 4 = 24 \leftarrow$ common denominator

Step 2

Use the common denominator to write equivalent fractions. Then subtract.

$$\begin{array}{r} \frac{5}{6} = \frac{20}{24} \\ -\frac{3}{4} = -\frac{18}{24} \\ \hline \frac{2}{24} = \frac{1}{12} \leftarrow \text{simplest form} \end{array}$$

So, the basket weaver had $\frac{1}{12}$ yard of grass reed left.

FAST TRACK

KY MA-05-1.1.3 Students will compare (<, >, =) and order whole numbers, fractions and decimals, and explain the relationships (equivalence, order) between and among them. DOK 2 *also* MA-05-1.1.1

The Least Common Denominator

You can use the least common denominator to write equivalent fractions. The **least common denominator (LCD)** is the least common multiple of two or more denominators.

Remember

To find the least common denominator, first find the least common multiple of the denominators.

Example 3 Add. $\frac{1}{4} + \frac{3}{8}$

A basket weaver bought shell beads and glass beads to weave into designs in her baskets. She bought $\frac{1}{4}$ pound of shell beads and $\frac{3}{8}$ pound of glass beads. How many pounds of beads did she buy?

ONE WAY **Use a common denominator.**

Multiply the denominators to find a common denominator.

$4 \times 8 = 32 \leftarrow$ common denominator

Use a common denominator to write equivalent fractions. Then add.

$$\begin{array}{r} \frac{1}{4} = \frac{1 \times 8}{4 \times 8} = \frac{8}{32} \\ + \frac{3}{8} = \frac{3 \times 4}{8 \times 4} = + \frac{12}{32} \\ \hline \frac{20}{32} = \frac{5}{8} \leftarrow \text{simplest form} \end{array}$$

ANOTHER WAY **Use the least common denominator (LCD).**

List multiples of each denominator.

Multiples of 4: 4, 8, 12, 16, 20, 24
Multiples of 8: 8, 16, 24, 32, 40, 48

The least common multiple is 8. So, the LCD of $\frac{1}{4}$ and $\frac{3}{8}$ is 8. Write equivalent fractions. Then add.

$$\begin{array}{r} \frac{1}{4} = \frac{1 \times 2}{4 \times 2} = \frac{2}{8} \\ + \frac{3}{8} \qquad\qquad + \frac{3}{8} \\ \hline \frac{5}{8} \leftarrow \text{simplest form} \end{array}$$

So, the basket weaver bought $\frac{5}{8}$ pound of beads.

More Examples

A **Add.** $\frac{1}{6} + \frac{1}{2}$

Use a common denominator.

$$\begin{array}{r} \frac{1}{6} = \frac{1 \times 2}{6 \times 2} = \frac{2}{12} \\ + \frac{1}{2} = \frac{1 \times 6}{2 \times 6} = + \frac{6}{12} \\ \hline \frac{8}{12} = \frac{2}{3} \end{array}$$

So, $\frac{1}{6} + \frac{1}{2} = \frac{2}{3}$.

B **Subtract.** $\frac{11}{12} - \frac{5}{8}$

Use the least common denominator.

$$\begin{array}{r} \frac{11}{12} = \frac{11 \times 2}{12 \times 2} = \frac{22}{24} \\ - \frac{5}{8} = \frac{5 \times 3}{8 \times 3} = - \frac{15}{24} \\ \hline \frac{7}{24} \end{array}$$

So, $\frac{11}{12} - \frac{5}{8} = \frac{7}{24}$.

Guided Practice

1. Copy the problem to the right. Show how to subtract unlike fractions by writing equivalent fractions using the least common denominator. Write the answer in simplest form.

$$\begin{array}{r} \frac{4}{5} = \frac{■}{30} \\ -\frac{2}{6} = -\frac{■}{30} \\ \hline \end{array}$$

Find the sum or difference. Write it in simplest form.

2. $\frac{3}{4} - \frac{1}{8}$
3. $\frac{2}{5} + \frac{3}{10}$
4. $\frac{1}{4} - \frac{1}{7}$
5. $\frac{5}{12} + \frac{1}{3}$
6. $\frac{9}{10} - \frac{1}{2}$
7. TALK Math **Explain** how you can use common multiples to add $\frac{7}{8}$ and $\frac{1}{3}$.

Independent Practice and Problem Solving

Find the sum or difference. Write it in simplest form.

8. $\frac{3}{5} + \frac{1}{4}$
9. $\frac{5}{8} + \frac{1}{5}$
10. $\frac{1}{12} + \frac{1}{2}$
11. $\frac{7}{10} + \frac{1}{5}$
12. $\frac{3}{4} - \frac{1}{2}$
13. $\frac{5}{6} - \frac{3}{8}$
14. $\frac{2}{7} + \frac{3}{10}$
15. $\frac{7}{8} - \frac{1}{6}$
16. $\frac{3}{7} - \frac{3}{14}$
17. $\frac{5}{12} - \frac{1}{4}$

Algebra Find the missing number for each ■. Write the answer in simplest form.

18. $\frac{5}{8} - ■ = \frac{3}{8}$
19. $\frac{1}{6} + ■ = 1$
20. $\frac{9}{10} - ■ = \frac{1}{5}$
21. $\frac{5}{12} + ■ = \frac{1}{2}$

USE DATA For 22–24, use the picture.

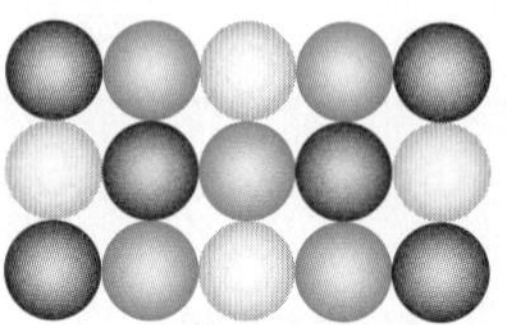

22. Sara is making a belt for a doll using the bead design shown. What fraction of the beads in her design are blue or red?
23. In making the belt, Sara wants to repeat the pattern of beads 3 times. She has a total of 21 red beads, 18 blue beads, and 19 white beads. Write a fraction that shows the number of beads she will have left over.
24. WRITE Math **What's the Question?** The answer is $\frac{2}{15}$ of the pattern.

Mixed Review and Test Prep

25. Thirty-five out of 50 students chose red as their favorite color in a survey. What fraction of students chose red? Write the answer in simplest form. (p. 312)
26. Write the fraction $\frac{27}{100}$ as a decimal. (p. 326)
27. **Test Prep** Which addition equation represents the fraction of beads that are green or yellow?

A $\frac{1}{4} + \frac{1}{8} = \frac{3}{8}$

B $\frac{1}{2} + \frac{1}{8} = \frac{5}{8}$

C $\frac{1}{2} + \frac{1}{4} = \frac{3}{4}$

D $\frac{3}{4} + \frac{2}{8} = 1$

 Extra Practice on page 358, Set C

Presenting Patterns

Graphic Aids

One of the oldest known American Indian crafts is basket-weaving. Different tribes used different materials, such as wood, grass, pine needles, or shoots of a willow tree, depending on what was available in their environment. The patterns and materials in the baskets could be used to identify which of the tribes had woven them.

These patterns, just like patterns in mathematics, often followed a rule, such as: *multiply by 5* or *add* $\frac{1}{4}$.

Look for the pattern in this list of fractions.

$$\frac{1}{4}, \frac{2}{4}, \frac{3}{4}, \frac{4}{4}, \frac{5}{4}$$

How do the values of these fractions change as the numerators increase? What is the pattern's rule?

You can use **graphic aids** to help you solve the problem. Choose a graphic aid that can help you show the problem or its solution. For example, you can use a number line to model the fractions.

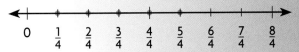

0, $\frac{1}{4}$, $\frac{2}{4}$, $\frac{3}{4}$, $\frac{4}{4}$, $\frac{5}{4}$, $\frac{6}{4}$, $\frac{7}{4}$, $\frac{8}{4}$

Think: To solve the problem, you might also use graphic aids such as drawing a fraction model.

These baskets show some of the different types of patterns used by American Indian craftsworkers.

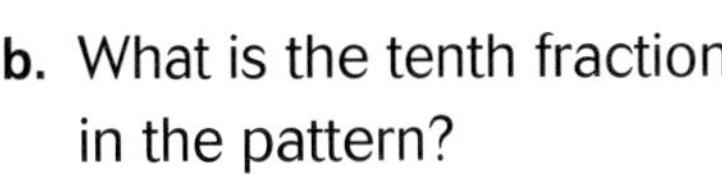

Problem Solving Use a graphic aid to solve the problem.

1. Solve the problem above.
2. a. How do the values of these fractions change as the denominators increase?

   $$\frac{1}{2}, \frac{1}{3}, \frac{1}{4}, \frac{1}{5}, \frac{1}{6}, \frac{1}{n}$$

   b. What is the tenth fraction in the pattern?

Problem Solving Workshop
Strategy: Compare Strategies

OBJECTIVE: Compare different strategies to solve problems.

Use the Strategy

PROBLEM In Natalie's science class, the students are observing the total monthly rainfall. At the end of each week, they record the amount of rain that fell. By the end of Week 3, there was a total of $\frac{5}{6}$ inch of rain. This was $\frac{2}{5}$ inch more than the amount recorded at the end of Week 2. During Week 2, $\frac{1}{3}$ inch more rain fell than the week before. What was the rainfall in Week 1?

Read to Understand

- **Summarize what you are asked to find.**
- **What information is given?**

Plan

- **What strategy can you use to solve the problem?**

  Often you can use more than one strategy to solve a problem. Use *make a model* and *work backward.*

Solve

- **How can you use the strategy to solve the problem?**

Make a Model

You can use fraction bars to find the missing data.

$\frac{1}{6}$	$\frac{1}{6}$	$\frac{1}{6}$	$\frac{1}{6}$	$\frac{1}{6}$

$\frac{1}{3}$	$\frac{1}{5}$	$\frac{1}{5}$	$\frac{1}{10}$

$$\frac{5}{6} = \frac{1}{3} + \frac{2}{5} + \frac{1}{10}$$

Work Backward

You can write an equation for the total rainfall.

Week 1 + Week 2 + Week 3 = Total

$$n + \frac{1}{3} + \frac{2}{5} = \frac{5}{6}$$

To work backward, start with $\frac{5}{6}$ and subtract.

$$n = \frac{5}{6} - \frac{2}{5} - \frac{1}{3}$$

$$n = \frac{25}{30} - \frac{12}{30} - \frac{10}{30}$$ ← Find a common denominator.

$$n = \frac{3}{30}, \text{ or } \frac{1}{10}$$

So, $\frac{1}{10}$ inch of rain fell in Week 1.

Check

- **What other strategy could you use to solve the problem?**

Guided Problem Solving

1. On Saturday, David worked on his science project for 1 hour. He spent $\frac{1}{2}$ hour reading his science journal and $\frac{2}{5}$ hour building a model. He then spent the rest of his time making note cards for the project. What part of the hour did David spend making note cards?

   First, use the *make a model* strategy.

   Then, use the *work backward* strategy.

   Finally, compare the answers.

2. **What if** David read his science journal for $\frac{3}{10}$ hour? What part of the hour did he spend making note cards?

3. David bought some supplies for the science project. He spent $2.99 for note cards, $1.24 for a glue stick, and $4.55 for color pencils. If David had $1.57 when he left the store, how much money did he have before his purchases?

Choose a STRATEGY

- Draw a Diagram or Picture
- Make a Model or Act It Out
- Make an Organized List
- Find a Pattern
- Make a Table or Graph
- Predict and Test
- Work Backward
- Solve a Simpler Problem
- Write an Equation
- Use Logical Reasoning

Mixed Strategy Practice

4. In Ms. Grant's science class, $\frac{1}{3}$ of the projects were about climate, $\frac{1}{6}$ were on earthquakes, and $\frac{1}{4}$ were on water and ecosystems. The rest of the projects were about hurricanes. What fraction of the science projects were about hurricanes?

5. Julia is building a rectangular base for the school's weather station. The perimeter is 1.2 meters. If the width is 0.2 meters, what is the length?

USE DATA For 6–9, use the table.

6. Using Monday's rainfall, list the four towns in order from least to greatest rainfall.

7. On what day did two cities have the same amounts of rainfall greater than zero? What were the two cities and what were the amounts of rainfall?

8. On what day did the sum of the rainfall for two cities equal the amount of rainfall for a third city? What were the cities and what were the amounts of rainfall?

9. WRITE Math **Explain** how you could use the *work backward* strategy to solve one of the problems above.

Kansas Rainfall During a Week in August

Day	City Rainfall (inches)			
	Hays	Hesston	Hutchinson	St. John
Monday	$\frac{2}{5}$	$\frac{3}{10}$	$\frac{9}{10}$	$\frac{7}{10}$
Tuesday	0	0	0	$\frac{1}{100}$
Wednesday	0	0	0	0
Thursday	$\frac{1}{5}$	0	$\frac{1}{2}$	$\frac{3}{10}$
Friday	$\frac{3}{20}$	$\frac{1}{10}$	$\frac{1}{20}$	0
Saturday	$\frac{1}{10}$	$\frac{1}{25}$	$\frac{1}{10}$	0
Sunday	0	$\frac{4}{5}$	$\frac{1}{100}$	$\frac{3}{10}$

Choose a Method

OBJECTIVE: Choose mental math, paper and pencil, or a calculator to add and subtract fractions.

Quick Review

Estimate the sum or difference.

1. $\frac{1}{2} + \frac{1}{7}$
2. $\frac{3}{5} - \frac{1}{10}$
3. $\frac{1}{6} + \frac{7}{8}$
4. $\frac{5}{8} - \frac{3}{5}$
5. $\frac{7}{12} + \frac{3}{5}$

Learn

PROBLEM Charles lives near the Barnegat Lighthouse in New Jersey. On Saturday, Charles spent $\frac{1}{5}$ of his day visiting the lighthouse and $\frac{3}{10}$ of his day playing baseball. What fraction of the day did Charles spend either visiting the lighthouse or playing baseball?

The Barnegat Lighthouse in Long Beach Island, New Jersey ▶

You can add or subtract fractions by using mental math, paper and pencil, or a calculator. Choose the method that works best with the fractions.

Use paper and pencil. Add. $\frac{1}{5} + \frac{3}{10}$ **Estimate.** $0 + \frac{1}{2} = \frac{1}{2}$

Step 1	Step 2
Use the LCD to write equivalent fractions. $\frac{1}{5} = \frac{2}{10}$, $+\frac{3}{10} = +\frac{3}{10}$	Find the sum. Write it in simplest form. $\frac{1}{5} = \frac{2}{10}$, $+\frac{3}{10} = +\frac{3}{10}$, $\frac{5}{10} = \frac{1}{2}$

So, Charles spent $\frac{1}{2}$ the day either visiting the lighthouse or playing baseball.

Use mental math. Subtract. $\frac{7}{24} - \frac{5}{24}$

Think: $7 - 5 = 2$ So, $\frac{7}{24} - \frac{5}{24} = \frac{2}{24} = \frac{1}{12}$.

ERROR ALERT

When entering a fraction into a calculator, be sure to enter the numerator before the denominator.

Use a calculator. Subtract. $\frac{2}{7} - \frac{3}{20}$

0

Guided Practice

1. Look at the problems at the right. Choose one to solve mentally. **Think:** Which fractions are easy to add or subtract mentally?

$\frac{1}{2} + \frac{2}{3}$ $\frac{3}{5} + \frac{4}{5}$ $\frac{5}{12} - \frac{1}{9}$

Choose a method. Find the sum or difference. Write it in simplest form.

2. $\frac{1}{7} + \frac{5}{7}$ **3.** $\frac{5}{6} - \frac{3}{8}$ **4.** $\frac{5}{9} + \frac{3}{8}$ **5.** $\frac{1}{2} - \frac{1}{3}$ **6.** $\frac{1}{5} + \frac{7}{10}$

7. TALK Math **Explain** which method you would choose to find $\frac{11}{12} - \frac{1}{8}$.

Independent Practice and Problem Solving

Choose a method. Find the sum or difference. Write it in simplest form.

8. $\frac{3}{7} + \frac{1}{8}$ **9.** $\frac{3}{4} - \frac{1}{2}$ **10.** $\frac{2}{3} + \frac{1}{4}$ **11.** $\frac{3}{19} - \frac{1}{10}$ **12.** $\frac{1}{8} + \frac{5}{8}$

13. $\frac{4}{9} - \frac{1}{6}$ **14.** $\frac{1}{3} + \frac{2}{5}$ **15.** $\frac{7}{20} - \frac{3}{10}$ **16.** $\frac{2}{15} + \frac{5}{11}$ **17.** $\frac{6}{7} - \frac{3}{7}$

Algebra **Find the value of** ***n*****.**

18. $\frac{n}{5} + \frac{2}{5} = \frac{4}{5}$ **19.** $\frac{1}{3} + \frac{n}{2} = \frac{5}{6}$ **20.** $\frac{n}{4} - \frac{1}{8} = \frac{5}{8}$

USE DATA **Use the graph for 21–24.**

21. What fraction of the day did Chad spend either sleeping or eating?

22. How much more of the day did Chad spend at sports camp than watching television?

23. **Reasoning** How many more hours did Chad spend sleeping than playing?

24. WRITE Math **Explain** how you can tell from looking at the graph that Chad spent more time mowing the lawn than watching television.

Mixed Review and Test Prep

25. Arlen uses $\frac{8}{5}$ pound of clay to make a vase. Is that more than or less than 2 pounds of clay? (p. 318)

26. Callie jogged $\frac{5}{8}$ mile, then walked another $\frac{2}{5}$ mile. What is a reasonable estimate of the total distance? (p. 348)

27. **Test Prep** At 2:00 P.M., a rain gauge showed $\frac{5}{8}$ inch of rain. Between noon and 1:00 P.M., $\frac{1}{4}$ inch of rain had fallen. Between 1:00 P.M. and 2:00 P.M., $\frac{1}{8}$ inch of rain had fallen. The rest fell between 8:00 A.M. and noon. How much rain fell between 8:00 A.M. and noon? Show your work.

Extra Practice on page 358, Set D

Extra Practice

Set A **Find the sum or difference. Write it in simplest form.** (pp. 342–343)

1. $\frac{3}{4} + \frac{1}{4}$
2. $\frac{5}{8} + \frac{1}{8}$
3. $\frac{7}{10} - \frac{3}{10}$
4. $\frac{3}{12} + \frac{1}{12}$
5. $\frac{5}{6} - \frac{1}{6}$
6. $\frac{6}{7} - \frac{3}{7}$
7. $\frac{2}{5} + \frac{2}{5}$
8. $\frac{8}{9} - \frac{7}{9}$
9. $\frac{1}{2} - \frac{1}{2}$
10. $\frac{1}{3} + \frac{2}{3}$

Set B **Estimate each sum or difference.** (pp. 348–349)

1. $\frac{3}{5} + \frac{1}{3}$
2. $\frac{4}{7} - \frac{1}{8}$
3. $\frac{4}{9} + \frac{7}{8}$
4. $\frac{9}{10} - \frac{1}{12}$
5. $\frac{2}{3} + \frac{2}{5}$

Estimate to compare. Write < or > for each ●.

6. $\frac{6}{7} + \frac{2}{5}$ ● $1\frac{1}{2}$
7. $\frac{5}{8} + \frac{2}{3}$ ● 1
8. $\frac{7}{9} - \frac{1}{12}$ ● 1
9. $\frac{4}{5} - \frac{1}{10}$ ● $\frac{1}{2}$
10. Gregory is learning sections of his violin solo for the orchestra concert. On Monday, he practiced $\frac{1}{5}$ of his solo. On Tuesday, he practiced another $\frac{3}{8}$ of his solo. About how much of his solo has Gregory practiced?

Set C **Find the sum or difference. Write it in simplest form.** (pp. 350–353)

1. $\frac{5}{8} - \frac{1}{4}$
2. $\frac{1}{7} + \frac{3}{5}$
3. $\frac{5}{9} + \frac{1}{3}$
4. $\frac{5}{16} - \frac{1}{4}$
5. $\frac{2}{3} - \frac{1}{2}$
6. $\frac{1}{3} + \frac{1}{5}$
7. $\frac{4}{5} - \frac{1}{4}$
8. $\frac{1}{2} + \frac{1}{5}$
9. $\frac{1}{2} - \frac{1}{4}$
10. $\frac{1}{6} + \frac{1}{2}$

Set D **Choose a method. Find the sum or difference. Write it in simplest form.** (pp. 356–357)

1. $\frac{3}{5} + \frac{1}{8}$
2. $\frac{5}{12} - \frac{1}{3}$
3. $\frac{4}{5} - \frac{1}{3}$
4. $\frac{1}{4} + \frac{5}{8}$
5. $\frac{5}{6} - \frac{1}{6}$
6. Jack baked lasagna for his family. They ate $\frac{3}{4}$ of it for dinner on Thursday. On Friday, Jack ate another $\frac{1}{6}$ of it for lunch. How much of the lasagna was left after Jack's lunch?

CD ROM **Technology**
Use Harcourt Mega Math, Fraction Action, *Fraction Flare Up*, Levels G, H.

PICK A PAIR

Who?
4 students

What?
- 32 index cards

$\frac{5}{6}$	$\frac{1}{6}$	$\frac{4}{6}$	$\frac{2}{6}$	$\frac{6}{7}$	$\frac{1}{7}$	$\frac{4}{7}$	$\frac{3}{7}$	$\frac{5}{8}$	$\frac{3}{8}$	$\frac{1}{8}$	$\frac{7}{8}$	$\frac{7}{9}$	$\frac{2}{9}$	$\frac{4}{9}$	$\frac{5}{9}$
$\frac{2}{5}$	$\frac{3}{5}$	$\frac{4}{5}$	$\frac{1}{5}$	$\frac{1}{10}$	$\frac{9}{10}$	$\frac{3}{10}$	$\frac{7}{10}$	$\frac{1}{3}$	$\frac{2}{3}$	$\frac{1}{4}$	$\frac{3}{4}$	$\frac{2}{7}$	$\frac{5}{7}$	$\frac{1}{2}$	$\frac{1}{2}$

How!

- Label the index cards as shown. Shuffle them and place them facedown on a flat surface in a 8-by-4 array.
- The first player turns over two cards. If the fractions displayed have a sum of 1, the player keeps the cards and takes another turn.
- If the fractions do not have a sum of 1, they are returned facedown to their original positions.
- The next player repeats the process. Play continues until all cards have been picked up.
- The player with the greatest number of cards is the winner.

Unit Fractions

Egyptian Unit Fractions

A **unit fraction** is a fraction with a numerator of 1. Ancient Egyptians represented values less than 1 as the sum of different unit fractions.

$$\frac{7}{8} = \frac{1}{2} + \frac{1}{4} + \frac{1}{8}$$

To express a fraction as an Egyptian fraction, you continually subtract the greatest unit fraction possible from the original fraction. When the difference is a unit fraction, you can stop subtracting.

Example

Express $\frac{7}{12}$ as Egyptian fractions.

Step 1

The greatest unit fraction less than $\frac{7}{12}$ is $\frac{1}{2}$.

Step 2

Find the equivalent fraction for $\frac{1}{2}$ and subtract.

$\frac{1}{2} = \frac{6}{12}$ $\frac{7}{12} - \frac{6}{12} = \frac{1}{12}$

Step 3

Since the difference is a unit fraction, stop subtracting. Use the unit fractions to write Egyptian fractions.

So, $\frac{7}{12} = \frac{1}{2} + \frac{1}{12}$.

Remember

The greatest unit fraction is $\frac{1}{2}$.

$\frac{1}{2} > \frac{1}{3} > \frac{1}{4} \ldots$

Try It

Express each fraction as an Egyptian fraction.

1. $\frac{3}{4}$ **2.** $\frac{2}{3}$ **3.** $\frac{2}{5}$ **4.** $\frac{5}{6}$ **5.** $\frac{4}{5}$ **6.** $\frac{8}{10}$

7. WRITE Math **Explain** how to express the Egyptian fraction $\frac{1}{2} + \frac{1}{3} + \frac{1}{12}$ as a single fraction.

Chapter 13 Review/Test

Check Concepts

1. What is the first step when you add fractions with like denominators, using paper and pencil? KY MA-05-1.3.1 (p. 342)

2. How can you estimate the sum or difference of two fractions? KY MA-05-1.2.1 (p. 348)

Check Skills

Find the sum or difference. KY MA-05-1.3.1 (pp. 342–343)

3. $\frac{6}{12} + \frac{6}{12}$
4. $\frac{1}{5} - \frac{1}{5}$
5. $\frac{7}{10} + \frac{1}{10}$
6. $\frac{6}{15} + \frac{8}{15}$
7. $\frac{9}{14} - \frac{2}{14}$
8. $\frac{3}{15} + \frac{4}{15}$
9. $\frac{11}{13} - \frac{5}{13}$
10. $\frac{16}{16} - \frac{12}{16}$
11. $\frac{9}{14} + \frac{5}{14}$
12. $\frac{5}{12} + \frac{3}{12}$
13. $\frac{3}{4} + \frac{1}{4}$
14. $\frac{2}{5} + \frac{1}{5}$
15. $\frac{6}{10} - \frac{3}{10}$
16. $\frac{9}{12} - \frac{7}{12}$
17. $\frac{12}{15} - \frac{9}{15}$
18. $\frac{4}{9} + \frac{4}{9}$
19. $\frac{7}{9} - \frac{4}{9}$
20. $\frac{13}{16} - \frac{9}{16}$
21. $\frac{4}{10} + \frac{5}{10}$
22. $\frac{11}{13} - \frac{3}{13}$
23. $\frac{5}{6} + \frac{1}{6}$
24. $\frac{8}{9} - \frac{4}{9}$
25. $\frac{12}{14} - \frac{7}{14}$
26. $\frac{1}{16} + \frac{4}{16}$
27. $\frac{8}{15} + \frac{6}{15}$

Check Problem Solving

Solve. KY MA-05-1.3.1 (pp. 354–355)

28. Annie used $\frac{7}{8}$ cup of blueberries to make muffins. She used $\frac{2}{8}$ cup less blueberries to make a blueberry tart. She used $\frac{4}{8}$ cup less blueberries to make a smoothie than to make a tart. What amount of blueberries did Annie use to make a smoothie?

29. WRITE Math **Explain** how you could use the strategy *work backward* to solve problem 28.

Technology Use *Online Assessment.*

Practice for the KCCT
Chapters 1–13

Number and Operations

1. Ian spent $\$29.59$ for a pair of jeans and $\$14.29$ for a shirt. Which is the best estimate of how much money he spent in all? KY MA-05-1.2.1 (p. 156)

   A $\$30.00$

   B $\$35.00$

   C $\$45.00$

   D $\$50.00$

Choose the answer.

See item 1. Make a reasonable estimate for each number. Some answer choices are clearly too high or too low. Choose from the choices that seem reasonable.

2. Which is the prime factorization of 36? KY MA-05-1.5.1 (p. 296)

   A $2^2 \times 3^2$

   B $2^1 \times 3^2$

   C $2^2 \times 3^1$

   D $2^3 \times 3^1$

3. **WRITE Math** Estimate the product of $2{,}341 \times 4$. To which place value could you round 2,341 to get the quickest estimate? Would this also be the most accurate estimate? **Explain.** KY MA-05-1.2.1 (p. 16)

Algebraic Thinking

4. Which equation could be a rule for this function table? KY MA-05-5.1.2 (p. 112)

x	y
3	15
6	30
8	40
11	55

   A $y = 2x + 9$

   B $y = x + 5$

   C $y = 3x$

   D $y = 5x$

5. Which is the value of the equation if $n = 20$? KY MA-05-5.3.1 (p. 96)

$$9 \times (n - 17)$$

   A 11

   B 17

   C 22

   D 27

6. **WRITE Math** When you use paper and pencil to multiply by a 2-digit number, you place a zero to the right of your second product. What does this zero represent? **Explain.** KY MA-05-1.3.1 (p. 44)

Geometry

7. Gerard is cutting geometric figures out of construction paper. Which could be the lengths of the sides of an equilateral triangle? KY Grade 4

   A 2 in., 3 in., 2 in.

   B 3 in., 3 in., 3 in.

   C 2 in., 3 in., 4 in.

   D 2 in., 4 in., 4 in.

8. Look at the figure below. KY Grade 4

   Which shows a 180° rotation of the figure?

   A

   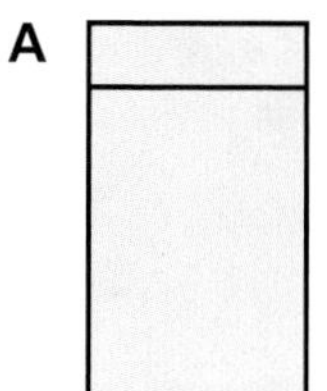

   B

   C

   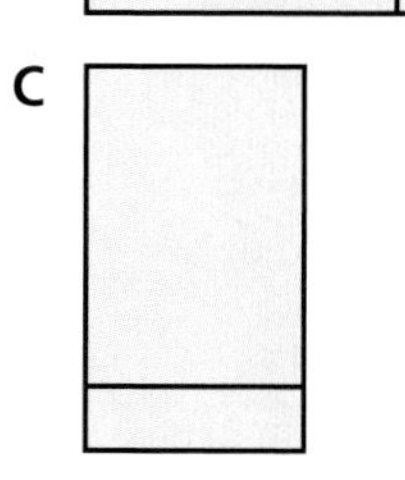

   D

   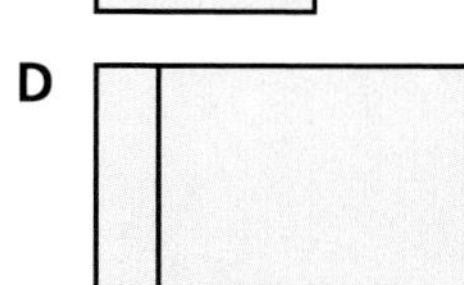

9. **WRITE Math** How do a ray, a line, and a line segment differ? **Explain.** KY Grade 4

Data Analysis and Probability

10. Mr. Thackeray commutes to a different location each weekday. The table below shows the distances he drives each day. What is the mean number of miles Mr. Thackeray drives each week? KY MA-05-4.2.1 (p. 220)

Miles Driven Each Week

Day	Number of Miles
Monday	13
Tuesday	25
Wednesday	32
Thursday	26
Friday	19

   A 19

   B 23

   C 25

   D 115

11. Pamela took a survey to find out what color her classmates wanted for the cover of the school yearbook. She wants to make a graph to show how the number of students who voted for each color compares to the total number of students who voted. Which would be the best type of graph for Pamela to make? KY MA-05-4.1.3 (p. 258)

   A line graph

   B bar graph

   C circle graph

   D histogram

12. **WRITE Math** What steps do you need to take to make a graph of the 8 A.M. temperature at your house each day for a week? Write at least three steps. **Explain.** KY MA-05-4.1.3 (p. 250)

CHAPTER 14

Add and Subtract Mixed Numbers

Investigate

The mountain-biking trails in Chequamegon National Forest are divided into six clusters. Suppose you want to ride half of the trails in the Delta Cluster. Choose three trails from the table. Calculate the total distance you will have ridden after biking the trails you chose.

Delta Cluster Trails

Trail	Length (miles)
South Fork	$8\frac{7}{10}$
West Fork	$11\frac{3}{10}$
Tall Pines	$12\frac{6}{15}$
Wilderness Lake	$10\frac{4}{5}$
Twin Bear	$18\frac{9}{10}$
Delta Hills	$15\frac{4}{5}$

FAST FACT

The Chequamegon National Forest covers more than 1,300 square miles in northern Wisconsin. There are about 200 miles of trails that can be used for hiking and mountain biking.

GO ONLINE **Technology** Student pages are available in the Student eBook.

Show What You Know

Check your understanding of important skills needed for success in Chapter 14.

▶ Understand Mixed Numbers

Write a mixed number for each picture.

1.

2.

3.

4.

5.

6.

▶ Add and Subtract Fractions

Write the sum or difference in simplest form.

7. $\frac{1}{5} + \frac{2}{5}$ **8.** $\frac{3}{8} + \frac{1}{8}$ **9.** $\frac{5}{6} - \frac{1}{6}$ **10.** $\frac{11}{12} - \frac{5}{12}$ **11.** $\frac{1}{3} + \frac{1}{6}$

12. $\frac{7}{10} - \frac{2}{5}$ **13.** $\frac{2}{3} - \frac{4}{9}$ **14.** $\frac{1}{6} + \frac{3}{4}$ **15.** $\frac{3}{10} + \frac{7}{15}$ **16.** $\frac{5}{7} - \frac{3}{5}$

VOCABULARY POWER

CHAPTER VOCABULARY

equivalent fractions
least common denominator (LCD)
mixed number
multiples
renaming

WARM-UP WORDS

equivalent fractions fractions that name the same number or amount

least common denominator (LCD) the least common multiple of two or more denominators

mixed number a number that is made up of a whole number and a fraction

LESSON 1 HANDS ON

Model Addition of Mixed Numbers

OBJECTIVE: Add mixed numbers with models.

Quick Review

1. $\frac{1}{3} + \frac{1}{3}$
2. $\frac{1}{5} + \frac{3}{5}$
3. $\frac{3}{8} + \frac{4}{8}$
4. $\frac{2}{4} + \frac{1}{4}$
5. $\frac{3}{6} + \frac{2}{6}$

Investigate

Materials ■ fraction bars

You can use fraction bars to model the addition of mixed numbers.

A Use fraction bars to model $1\frac{3}{4} + 2\frac{1}{8}$.

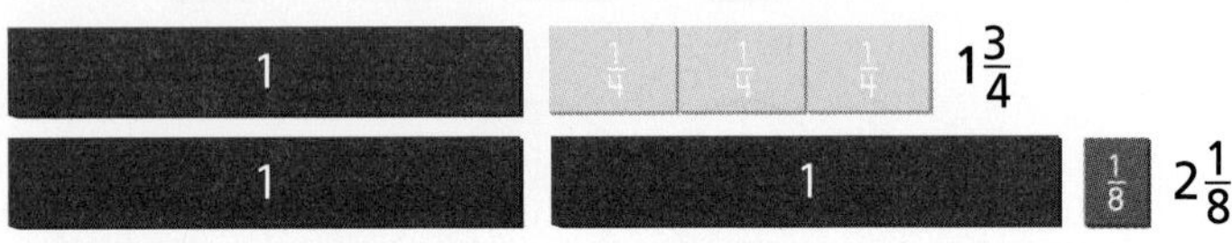

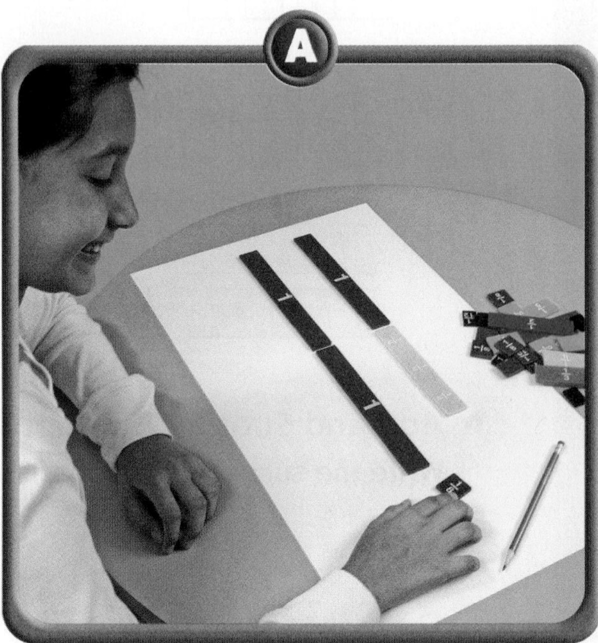

B Find like fraction bars for $\frac{3}{4}$ and $\frac{1}{8}$.

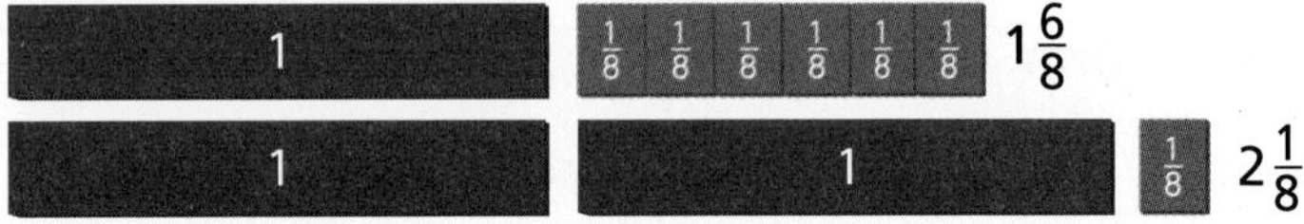

C Add the fractions, and add the whole numbers. Record your answer in simplest form.

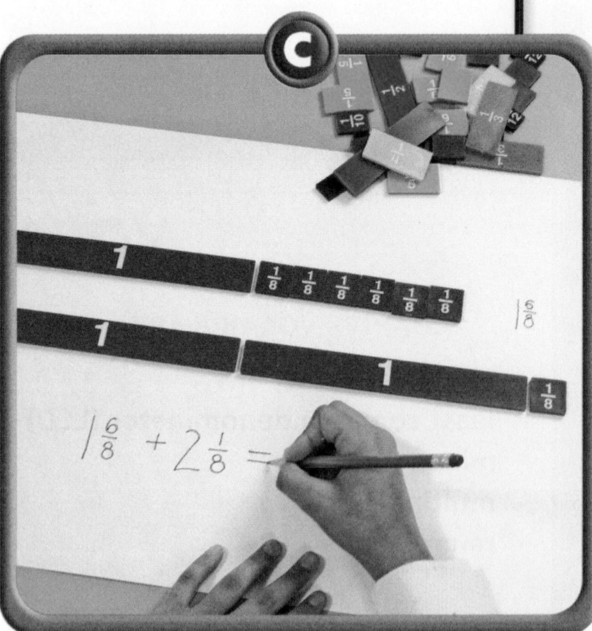

D Use fraction bars to find $1\frac{2}{5} + 1\frac{3}{10}$. Write the answer in simplest form.

Draw Conclusions

1. In Part B, explain why you replaced the $\frac{1}{4}$ fraction bars.
2. When adding mixed numbers, explain how you know whether your answer is in simplest form.
3. **Analysis** Explain why $\frac{1}{8}$ fraction bars were used for like fraction bars in Part B.

Connect

Sometimes, you need to rename the sum when you add mixed numbers.

Add. $2\frac{2}{3} + 2\frac{1}{2}$

Step 1

Model $2\frac{2}{3}$ and $2\frac{1}{2}$.

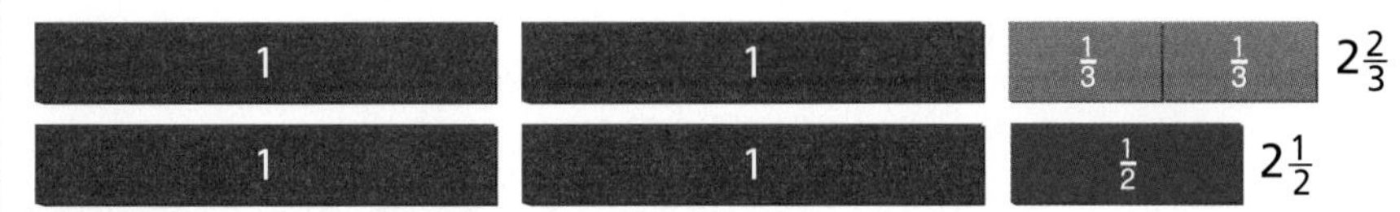

Step 2

Use like fraction bars.

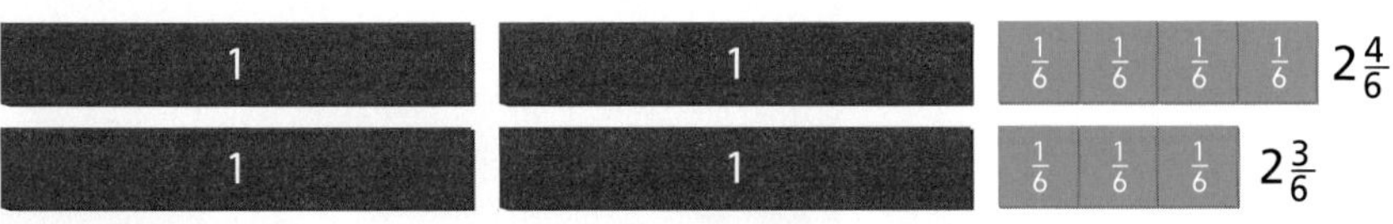

Step 3

Find the sum.

$2\frac{4}{6} + 2\frac{3}{6} = 4\frac{7}{6}$

$4\frac{7}{6} = 4 + 1 + \frac{1}{6}$ Rename $4\frac{7}{6}$.

$= 5\frac{1}{6}$

So, $2\frac{2}{3} + 2\frac{1}{2} = 5\frac{1}{6}$.

TALK Math

Explain how you could use $\frac{1}{12}$ fraction bars to find $2\frac{2}{3} + 2\frac{1}{2}$.

Practice

Use fraction bars to find the sum. Write the answer in simplest form.

1. $4\frac{5}{12} + 1\frac{1}{6}$

2. $1\frac{3}{6} + 2\frac{1}{6}$

3. $2\frac{2}{5} + 1\frac{1}{2}$

✓ **4.** $1\frac{1}{4} + 1\frac{1}{3}$

5. $3\frac{2}{6} + 2\frac{5}{6}$

6. $2\frac{5}{8} + 2\frac{3}{4}$

7. $5\frac{3}{4} + 2\frac{2}{3}$

✓ **8.** $2\frac{3}{10} + 3\frac{4}{5}$

9. **WRITE Math** **Explain** how fraction bars help you add mixed numbers.

LESSON 2 HANDS ON

Model Subtraction of Mixed Numbers

OBJECTIVE: Subtract mixed numbers with models.

Quick Review

Subtract. Write the answer in simplest form.

1. $\frac{3}{8} - \frac{1}{8}$
2. $\frac{5}{7} - \frac{2}{7}$
3. $\frac{7}{12} - \frac{1}{12}$
4. $\frac{4}{3} - \frac{1}{3}$
5. $\frac{7}{9} - \frac{1}{9}$

Investigate

Materials ■ fraction bars

You can use fraction bars to model the subtraction of mixed numbers.

A Use fraction bars to model $3\frac{3}{4} - 1\frac{5}{8}$.

B To subtract $1\frac{5}{8}$ from $3\frac{3}{4}$, find like fraction bars. Replace the three $\frac{1}{4}$ bars with $\frac{1}{8}$ bars until they are the same length.

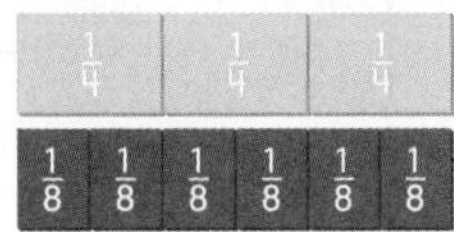

$\frac{3}{4} = \frac{6}{8}$

C Subtract the fractions, and subtract the whole numbers. Record your answer in simplest form.

D Use fraction bars to find $7\frac{5}{8} - 2\frac{3}{8}$. Write the answer in simplest form.

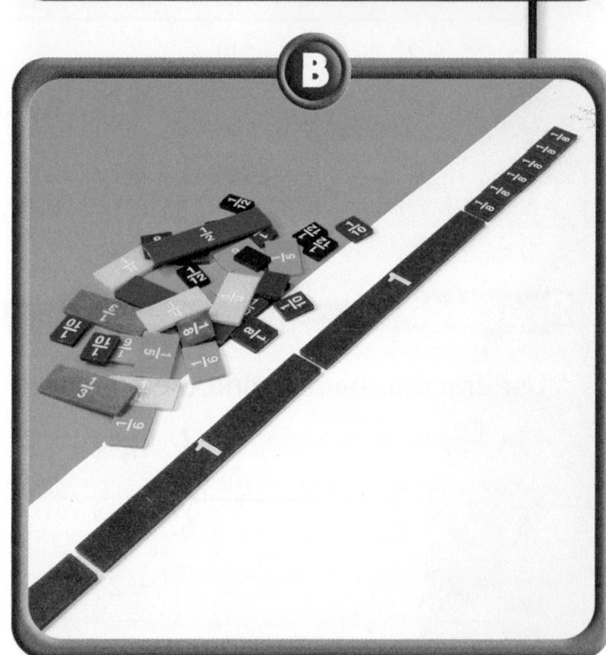

Draw Conclusions

1. Explain how you know which like fraction bars to use to model $\frac{3}{4}$ and $\frac{5}{8}$.

2. When subtracting mixed numbers, how do you know if your answer is in simplest form?

3. **Evaluation** How can equivalent fractions help you subtract?

Connect

When you add or subtract mixed numbers that have unlike denominators, you can think of equivalent fractions that have like denominators.

Subtract. $2\frac{7}{8} - 1\frac{1}{2}$

Step 1

Draw a picture. Show $2\frac{7}{8}$.

Step 2

Subtract $1\frac{1}{2}$.

Think: $\frac{1}{2}$ is equivalent to $\frac{4}{8}$.

So, $2\frac{7}{8} - 1\frac{1}{2} = 1\frac{3}{8}$.

- Draw a picture to find $3\frac{1}{2} - 1\frac{1}{3}$.

TALK Math

To find $3\frac{1}{2} - 1\frac{1}{3}$, what equivalent fractions would you use?

Practice

Use fraction bars, or draw a picture to find the difference. Write the answer in simplest form.

1. $2\frac{3}{5} - 1\frac{1}{5}$
2. $3\frac{7}{10} - 1\frac{5}{10}$
3. $4\frac{5}{6} - 2\frac{2}{3}$
4. $2\frac{1}{2} - 1\frac{3}{8}$
5. $2\frac{2}{3} - \frac{1}{6}$
6. $3\frac{5}{8} - 1\frac{1}{4}$
7. $2\frac{5}{6} - 2\frac{1}{3}$
8. $1\frac{7}{8} - \frac{1}{4}$
9. $6\frac{3}{4} - 2\frac{3}{12}$
10. $5\frac{3}{4} - 2\frac{1}{8}$
11. $3\frac{1}{2} - 1\frac{3}{10}$
12. $4\frac{1}{3} - 2\frac{1}{4}$
13. $3\frac{1}{2} - 1\frac{1}{4}$
14. $2\frac{3}{4} - 1\frac{3}{8}$
15. $5\frac{3}{4} - 2\frac{3}{6}$
16. $3\frac{4}{6} - 1\frac{1}{6}$

17. **WRITE Math** **Explain** how you find the difference between $3\frac{7}{8}$ and $1\frac{1}{2}$.

LESSON 3

Record Addition and Subtraction

OBJECTIVE: Find the sums and differences of mixed numbers.

Quick Review

Write a common multiple for each pair.

1. 4 and 6
2. 3 and 5
3. 8 and 10
4. 12 and 9
5. 15 and 20

Learn

PROBLEM Denise mixed $1\frac{4}{5}$ ounces of blue paint with $2\frac{3}{10}$ ounces of yellow paint. How many ounces of paint did Denise mix in all?

To find the sum of mixed numbers with unlike denominators, you can use a common denominator.

Example 1 Add. $1\frac{4}{5} + 2\frac{3}{10}$

Step 1

Find a common denominator. Write equivalent fractions.

$$\begin{array}{rcr} 1\frac{4}{5} & = & 1\frac{8}{10} \\ +2\frac{3}{10} & = & +2\frac{3}{10} \\ \hline \end{array}$$

Step 2

Add the fractions.

$$\begin{array}{rcr} 1\frac{4}{5} & = & 1\frac{8}{10} \\ +2\frac{3}{10} & = & +2\frac{3}{10} \\ \hline & & \frac{11}{10} \end{array}$$

Step 3

Add the whole numbers. Write the answer in simplest form.

$$\begin{array}{rcr} 1\frac{4}{5} & = & 1\frac{8}{10} \\ +2\frac{3}{10} & = & +2\frac{3}{10} \\ \hline & & 3\frac{11}{10} = 4\frac{1}{10} \end{array}$$

Simplest form

So, Denise mixed $4\frac{1}{10}$ ounces of paint in all.

- What other common denominator could you have used in Example 1?

Example 2

Subtract. $4\frac{2}{3} - 2\frac{1}{4}$

Step 1

Find the LCD. Write equivalent fractions.

$$\begin{array}{rcr} 4\frac{2}{3} & = & 4\frac{8}{12} \\ -2\frac{1}{4} & = & -2\frac{3}{12} \\ \hline \end{array}$$

Step 2

Subtract the fractions.

$$\begin{array}{rcr} 4\frac{2}{3} & = & 4\frac{8}{12} \\ -2\frac{1}{4} & = & -2\frac{3}{12} \\ \hline & & \frac{5}{12} \end{array}$$

Step 3

Subtract the whole numbers. Write the answer in simplest form.

$$\begin{array}{rcr} 4\frac{2}{3} & = & 4\frac{8}{12} \\ -2\frac{1}{4} & = & -2\frac{3}{12} \\ \hline & & 2\frac{5}{12} \end{array}$$

So, $4\frac{2}{3} - 2\frac{1}{4} = 2\frac{5}{12}$.

Guided Practice

1. Copy the problem. Write the equivalent fractions. Find the sum, and write it in simplest form if needed.

$$\begin{array}{rcl} 7\frac{2}{5} & = & 7\frac{\blacksquare}{20} \\ +4\frac{3}{4} & = & +4\frac{\blacksquare}{20} \\ \hline \end{array}$$

Find the sum or difference. Write the answer in simplest form.

2. $2\frac{3}{4} + 3\frac{3}{10}$
3. $9\frac{5}{6} - 2\frac{1}{3}$
4. $5\frac{3}{4} + 1\frac{1}{3}$
5. $10\frac{5}{9} - 9\frac{1}{6}$
6. $7\frac{2}{3} - 3\frac{1}{6}$
7. TALK Math **Explain** why you need to find equivalent fractions to add $4\frac{3}{6}$ and $1\frac{1}{8}$.

Independent Practice and Problem Solving

Find the sum or difference. Write the answer in simplest form.

8. $3\frac{2}{3} - 1\frac{1}{6}$
9. $1\frac{3}{10} + 2\frac{2}{5}$
10. $2\frac{5}{8} - 1\frac{1}{4}$
11. $2\frac{1}{2} + 2\frac{1}{3}$
12. $1\frac{5}{12} + 4\frac{1}{6}$
13. $8\frac{1}{2} + 6\frac{3}{8}$
14. $9\frac{2}{3} - 4\frac{4}{9}$
15. $8\frac{1}{6} + 7\frac{3}{8}$
16. $10\frac{1}{2} - 2\frac{1}{5}$
17. $5\frac{1}{4} + 9\frac{1}{3}$
18. $5\frac{6}{7} - 1\frac{2}{3}$
19. $2\frac{1}{3} + 4\frac{5}{6}$
20. $14\frac{7}{12} - 5\frac{1}{4}$
21. $3\frac{4}{9} + 3\frac{1}{2}$
22. $12\frac{3}{4} - 6\frac{1}{6}$

USE DATA For 23–25, use the table.

23. Gavin is mixing a batch of green paint for an art project. How much green paint did Gavin mix?
24. Gavin mixed $4\frac{3}{10}$ ounces of green paint with $3\frac{3}{8}$ ounces of blue to make turquoise. How much turquoise paint did he mix?
25. WRITE Math Gavin made 2 batches of purple paint and plans to store it in 10-ounce jars. **Explain** how to find the number of jars Gavin will need to hold the 2 batches of purple paint.

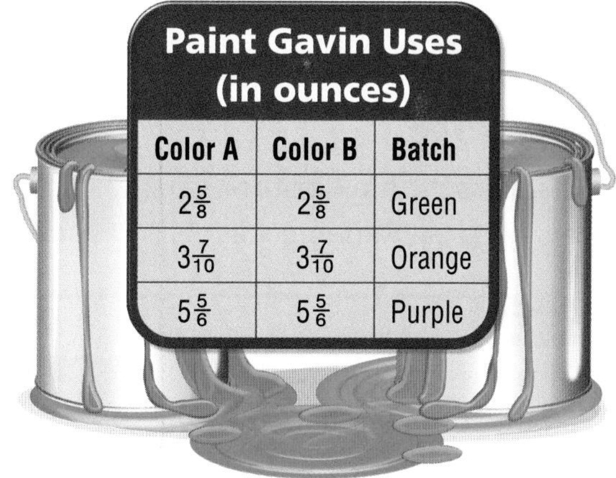

Paint Gavin Uses (in ounces)

Color A	Color B	Batch
$2\frac{5}{8}$	$2\frac{5}{8}$	Green
$3\frac{7}{10}$	$3\frac{7}{10}$	Orange
$5\frac{5}{6}$	$5\frac{5}{6}$	Purple

Mixed Review and Test Prep

26. What is the value of the expression $(9 \times 3) + (14 - 9)$? (p. 96)
27. Write $4 \times 4 \times 4 \times 4 \times 4$ using an exponent. (p. 292)
28. **Test Prep** Yolanda walked $3\frac{6}{10}$ miles and $4\frac{1}{2}$ miles. How many miles did Yolanda walk?

   A $7\frac{1}{10}$ miles
   B $7\frac{7}{10}$ miles
   C $8\frac{1}{10}$ miles
   D $8\frac{7}{10}$ miles

Extra Practice on page 380, Set A

LESSON 4

Subtraction with Renaming

OBJECTIVE: Model subtraction of mixed numbers by using renaming.

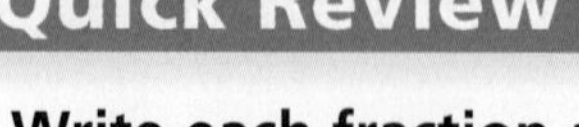

Quick Review

Write each fraction as a mixed number in simplest form.

1. $\frac{5}{4}$
2. $\frac{7}{3}$
3. $\frac{9}{2}$
4. $\frac{13}{3}$
5. $\frac{20}{7}$

Learn

PROBLEM Dean and Faith are using colorful streamers to decorate a table before a party. They have $2\frac{1}{3}$ yards of streamers. They use $1\frac{7}{12}$ yards. How many yards of streamers do Dean and Faith have left?

Sometimes, you need to rename whole numbers to subtract mixed numbers.

HANDS ON

Activity

Materials ■ fraction bars

Subtract. $2\frac{1}{3} - 1\frac{7}{12}$

Step 1

Model $2\frac{1}{3}$ using two whole bars and one $\frac{1}{3}$ bar.

Step 2

To subtract, think of the LCD for $\frac{1}{3}$ and $\frac{7}{12}$. Rename $\frac{1}{3}$ as $\frac{4}{12}$.

Step 3

Since $\frac{7}{12}$ is greater than $\frac{4}{12}$, rename one whole bar as $\frac{12}{12}$.

$2\frac{4}{12} = 1\frac{16}{12}$

Step 4

Subtract $1\frac{7}{12}$. Write the answer in simplest form.

$1\frac{16}{12} - 1\frac{7}{12} = \frac{9}{12} = \frac{3}{4}$

So, $\frac{3}{4}$ yard is left.

Guided Practice

1. Use the model for $2\frac{1}{3} - 1\frac{5}{6}$ to find the difference. Write it in simplest form.

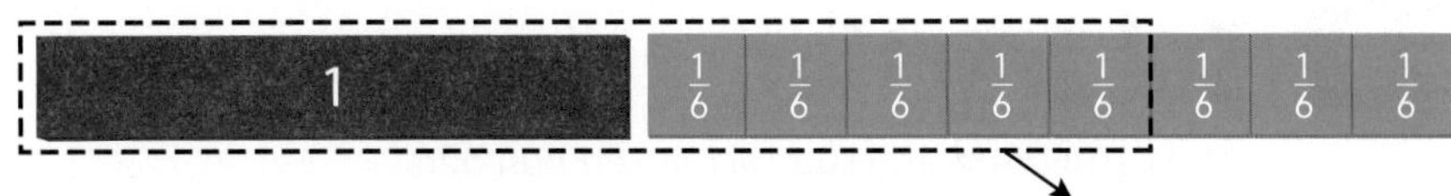

Use fraction bars to find the difference. Write the answer in simplest form.

2. $3\frac{1}{4} - 1\frac{3}{4}$
3. $2\frac{1}{5} - 1\frac{4}{5}$
4. $4\frac{1}{2} - 2\frac{5}{6}$
5. $2\frac{1}{2} - 1\frac{3}{4}$
6. TALK Math **Explain** how to find $1\frac{1}{5} - \frac{3}{10}$.

Independent Practice and Problem Solving

Use fraction bars to find the difference. Write the answer in simplest form.

7. $4\frac{2}{9} - 1\frac{6}{9}$
8. $5 - 3\frac{1}{2}$
9. $3\frac{1}{3} - \frac{5}{9}$
10. $6\frac{1}{3} - 4\frac{5}{6}$
11. $4\frac{7}{10} - 2\frac{4}{5}$
12. $5\frac{3}{8} - 2\frac{5}{8}$
13. $5\frac{2}{3} - 1\frac{11}{12}$
14. $4\frac{1}{2} - 3\frac{2}{3}$

USE DATA For 15–18, use the recipe.

15. For the party, Faith decided to reduce the amount of orange juice by $\frac{3}{4}$ quart. How much orange juice did Faith use?
16. Faith's recipe makes 5 quarts of fruit punch. If the cranberry juice is not included, how much punch is made?
17. Faith decided to reduce the amount of cranberry juice by $\frac{3}{4}$ quart from the original recipe. How much cranberry juice did she use? How much punch did Faith make in all?
18. WRITE Math **Explain** how to find how much more cranberry juice is needed than pineapple juice.

Fruit Punch
$2\frac{1}{4}$ qt orange juice
$\frac{3}{4}$ qt pineapple juice
$1\frac{2}{3}$ qt cranberry juice
$\frac{1}{3}$ qt apple juice

Mixed Review and Test Prep

19. Kira used $2\frac{1}{2}$ cups of water to make juice from juice concentrate. Write the number of cups Kira used as a fraction. (p. 316)
20. Edward drew a polygon that has 8 sides of equal length and 8 equal angles. What is the name of the polygon? (Grade 4)
21. **Test Prep** There are $5\frac{1}{2}$ ounces of banana in a small banana smoothie. A large smoothie has $8\frac{1}{4}$ ounces of banana. How much more banana does the large smoothie have?

    A $2\frac{3}{4}$ ounces
    B $2\frac{1}{4}$ ounces
    C $3\frac{3}{4}$ ounces
    D $3\frac{1}{4}$ ounces

Extra Practice on page 380, Set B

LESSON

5 Practice Addition and Subtraction

OBJECTIVE: Add and subtract mixed numbers.

Quick Review

Write in simplest form.

1. $8\frac{8}{12}$ **2.** $3\frac{6}{9}$

3. $18\frac{15}{18}$ **4.** $42\frac{13}{26}$

5. $7\frac{24}{28}$

Learn

PROBLEM Chelsea's softball bat weighs $25\frac{6}{12}$ ounces. She puts $1\frac{1}{8}$ ounces of tape on the bat handle. What is the total weight of Chelsea's bat?

Example 1 Add. $25\frac{6}{12} + 1\frac{1}{8}$ Estimate. $26 + 1 = 27$

Step 1	Step 2	Step 3
Find the LCD. Write equivalent fractions.	Add the fractions.	Add the whole numbers. Write the answer in simplest form.
$25\frac{6}{12} = 25\frac{12}{24}$ $+\ 1\frac{1}{8} = +\ 1\frac{3}{24}$	$25\frac{6}{12} = 25\frac{12}{24}$ $+\ 1\frac{1}{8} = +\ 1\frac{3}{24}$ $\frac{15}{24}$	$25\frac{12}{24}$ $+\ 1\frac{3}{24}$ $26\frac{15}{24} = 26\frac{5}{8}$

So, the total weight of Chelsea's bat is $26\frac{5}{8}$ ounces. Since $26\frac{5}{8}$ is close to the estimate of 27, the answer is reasonable.

ERROR ALERT

When you rename to subtract, remember to subtract 1 from the whole number.

Example 2 Subtract. $27\frac{1}{3} - 24\frac{1}{2}$ Estimate. $27 - 25 = 2$

Step 1	Step 2	Step 3
Find the LCD. Write equivalent fractions.	Rename one whole as a fraction to subtract.	Subtract and write the answer in simplest form.
$27\frac{1}{3} = 27\frac{2}{6}$ $-\ 24\frac{1}{2} = -\ 24\frac{3}{6}$	$27\frac{1}{3} = 26\frac{8}{6}$ $-\ 24\frac{1}{2} = -\ 24\frac{3}{6}$	$26\frac{8}{6}$ $-\ 24\frac{3}{6}$ $2\frac{5}{6}$

Example 3 Use a fraction calculator to add $4\frac{2}{5} + 3\frac{5}{8}$.

$8\frac{1}{40}$

Guided Practice

1. Estimate. Write equivalent fractions. Then find the sum and write it in simplest form.

$$\begin{array}{r} 6\frac{3}{4} = 6\frac{\blacksquare}{12} \\ +4\frac{5}{6} = 4\frac{\blacksquare}{\blacksquare} \\ \hline \end{array}$$

Estimate. Then write the sum or difference in simplest form.

2. $3\frac{1}{2} + 6\frac{1}{3}$
3. $9\frac{4}{9} - 4\frac{1}{3}$
4. $2\frac{2}{3} + 8\frac{3}{5}$
5. $7\frac{2}{5} - 2\frac{5}{8}$
6. TALK Math **Explain** how to subtract $4\frac{2}{5} - 1\frac{3}{4}$ using the LCD.

Independent Practice and Problem Solving

Estimate. Then write the sum or difference in simplest form.

7. $1\frac{5}{6} + 4\frac{2}{3}$
8. $13\frac{5}{9} - 9\frac{5}{6}$
9. $8\frac{3}{5} + 12\frac{4}{7}$
10. $12\frac{3}{8} - 10\frac{7}{10}$
11. $16\frac{5}{12} - 13\frac{9}{10}$
12. $31\frac{4}{5} + 19\frac{11}{15}$
13. $9 - 2\frac{4}{7}$
14. $28\frac{8}{15} + 7\frac{17}{20}$
15. $15\frac{1}{2} + 41\frac{2}{5}$
16. $47\frac{4}{5} - 29\frac{3}{10}$
17. $81\frac{3}{4} + 26\frac{9}{10}$
18. $132\frac{3}{8} - 101\frac{5}{6}$

USE DATA For 19–21, use the table.

19. On which day did Chelsea spend the most time at batting practice? The least? How much less?
20. Which amount of time is greater, the difference between Tuesday's and Wednesday's practices, or the difference between Thursday's and Friday's practices? By how much?
21. WRITE Math Chelsea needs to practice softball a total of 10 hours this week. How many more hours of practice will Chelsea need? **Explain** how you got your answer.

Chelsea's Batting Practice

Day	Number of Hours
Tuesday	$1\frac{5}{6}$
Wednesday	$2\frac{1}{3}$
Thursday	$2\frac{2}{5}$
Friday	$1\frac{7}{10}$

Mixed Review and Test Prep

22. Write an equivalent decimal for 14.04. (p. 136)
23. Dawn had the following scores on 5 math tests: 78, 100, 92, 87, and 75. What is the mean score? (p. 220)
24. **Test Prep** Ann played a $2\frac{3}{4}$-minute song and a song that is $6\frac{5}{12}$ minutes long. How many minutes long are the two songs?

    A $\frac{5}{6}$ minute
    B $3\frac{3}{4}$ minutes
    C $9\frac{1}{6}$ minutes
    D $10\frac{2}{4}$ minutes

Extra Practice on page 380, Set C

Problem Solving Workshop
Strategy: Use Logical Reasoning

OBJECTIVE: Solve problems by using the strategy *use logical reasoning.*

Learn the Strategy

Logical reasoning can help you solve problems based on what you know. You can use diagrams and tables to help you collect and organize information so that you are able to analyze all of the data you have.

A Venn diagram can show relationships.

Find all the factors that both 132 and 72 have in common.

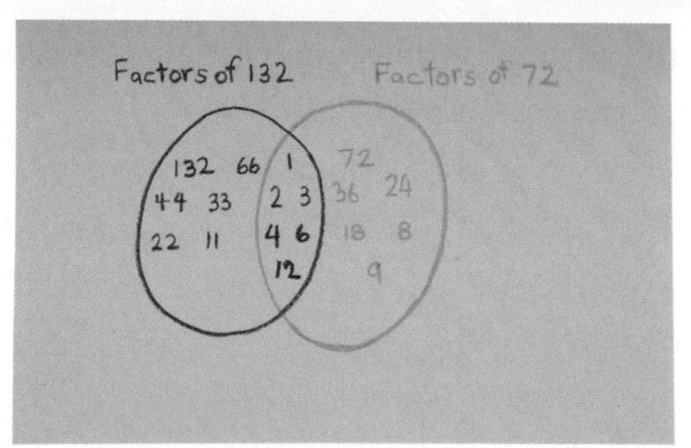

A table can help you organize information.

Tim and Alex play baseball. They each got at least one hit in each of their first five baseball games.

Tim's hits per game were 2, 2, 4, 3, 3.

Alex's hits per game were 3, 2, 2, 1, 1.

First 5 Baseball Games

	Game 1	Game 2	Game 3	Game 4	Game 5
Tim	2	2	4	3	3
Alex	3	2	2	1	1

TALK Math

What logical conclusions might you draw from the table?

To use logical reasoning, carefully review the information that you know and think about what must be true to reach a conclusion.

Use the Strategy

PROBLEM Carlos and Judy pitched all 6 innings in each of the 3 games their baseball team played. Carlos pitched $1\frac{2}{3}$ innings in Game 1 and $3\frac{2}{3}$ innings in Game 3. Carlos pitched a total of $8\frac{1}{3}$ innings in the three games. In Game 2, Carlos and Judy pitched the same number of innings. How many innings did Judy pitch in Games 1, 2, and 3?

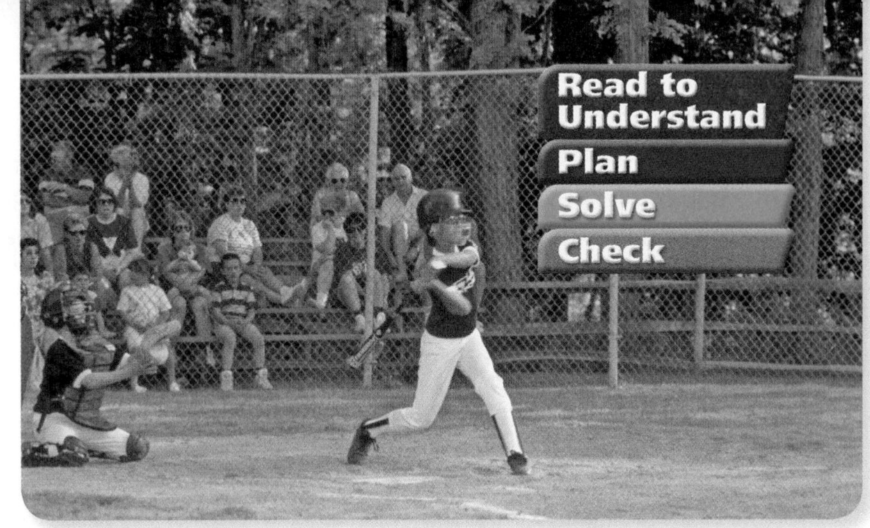

Read to Understand

- **What conclusions can you make from the problem?**
- **What are you asked to find?**

Plan

- **What strategy can you use to solve the problem?**

  You can use logical reasoning to help you solve the problem.

Solve

- **How can you use the strategy to solve the problem?**

  Make a table to help you organize the information in the problem.

  Use if/then statements to help you solve the problem.

  - If there are 6 innings in each game, then the total innings Carlos and Judy pitched for each game should equal 6.
  - If Carlos pitched $1\frac{2}{3}$ innings in Game 1, then Judy pitched $6 - 1\frac{2}{3}$, or $4\frac{1}{3}$, innings.
  - If Carlos pitched $3\frac{2}{3}$ innings in Game 3, then Judy pitched $6 - 3\frac{2}{3}$, or $2\frac{1}{3}$, innings.
  - If Carlos and Judy pitched the same number of innings in Game 2, then they each pitched half of 6 innings, or 3 innings $(3 + 3 = 6)$.

Pitcher	Game 1 Innings	Game 2 Innings	Game 3 Innings
Carlos	$1\frac{2}{3}$	■	$3\frac{2}{3}$
Judy	■	■	■

  So, Judy pitched $4\frac{1}{3}$ innings in Game 1, 3 innings in Game 2, and $2\frac{1}{3}$ innings in Game 3.

Check

- **How can you check your answer?**

Read to Understand
Plan
Solve
Check

Guided Problem Solving

1. Jeff, Molly, and Sam pitched all 6 innings in each of 2 games their baseball team played. Molly pitched $1\frac{1}{3}$ innings in Game 1 and $2\frac{2}{3}$ innings in Game 2. Jeff pitched 2 innings in Game 1 and a total of $3\frac{1}{3}$ innings in the two games. How many innings did Sam pitch in each of the two games?

   First, make a table to organize the information in the problem.

	Game 1 Innings	Game 2 Innings
Jeff		
Molly		
Sam		

   Then, write if/then statements to complete the table.

2. **What if** Jeff pitched $2\frac{1}{2}$ innings in Game 1? How many innings would Sam have pitched in this game?

3. Jordan, Linda, Bryce, and Carrie wrote down their longest hits during batting practice. The shortest of the 4 hits was $96\frac{1}{4}$ feet. Jordan hit the ball $5\frac{1}{4}$ feet farther than Linda but $2\frac{1}{2}$ feet less than Bryce. Carrie hit the ball $1\frac{5}{8}$ feet farther than Linda did. Of Bryce, Linda, Carrie, and Jordan, who hit the ball the farthest, and what distance was the ball hit?

Problem Solving Strategy Practice

Use logical reasoning to solve.

4. During the summer, 42 sixth graders played baseball or soccer. If 25 students played baseball and 30 students played soccer, how many students played both soccer and baseball?

5. Phil was watching a baseball game $2\frac{2}{3}$ hours before he had to clean his room. Charlie came over to Phil's house $\frac{1}{6}$ hour before Phil started watching the game and left $\frac{1}{2}$ hour before Phil had to clean his room. How many hours was Charlie at Phil's house?

6. Sarah, Lynn, Jan, and Trisha play baseball. Two of them have the same hat size. Lynn wears a size 7. Trisha's hat size is the largest. Sarah's hat size is $1\frac{2}{8}$ larger than Lynn's hat size. Jan's hat size is larger than Lynn's hat size. Which two players have the same hat size? What is their size?

Mixed Strategy Practice

7. A construction worker is building a 13-foot brick wall. After the first day, the wall was $2\frac{7}{12}$ feet tall. The second day, it was $5\frac{1}{6}$ feet tall. After the third day, the wall was $7\frac{3}{4}$ feet tall. If the worker continues building at this rate, will the wall be finished in five days? **Explain.**

8. Miranda is keeping only her favorite sports cards. At a yard sale, $\frac{4}{15}$ of her collection is sold. Miranda gives away $\frac{2}{5}$ of her collection to friends, and she keeps the rest. What fraction of her collection does Miranda keep?

9. **Pose a Problem** Look back at Problem 7. Write a similar problem by changing the number of feet of wall built each day.

Choose a STRATEGY

- Draw a Diagram
- Make a Model
- Make an Organized List
- Find a Pattern
- Make a Table or Graph
- Predict and Test
- Work Backward
- Solve a Simpler Problem
- Write an Equation
- Use Logical Reasoning

USE DATA For 10–12, use the data in the table.

10. The data in the "Games Back" column shows how far from first place each team is. How many games from first place are the Bulls?

11. **WRITE Math** The star player for the Beavers was injured for most of the season, but she came back for the last two games. If she plays for the Beavers next year, what conclusion can you reach about how the Beavers will do next season? **Explain.**

12. **Open Ended** Choose two data from the "Games Back" column, and describe how they were calculated. Explain why the two numbers are different and what that difference describes.

Little League Standings

	Win	Loss	Games Back	Win/Loss Streak
Cougars	10	2	0	Won 2
Jaguars	8	4	2	Won 1
Bulls	6	6	4	Lost 2
Owls	4	8	6	Lost 1
Beavers	2	10	8	Won 2

This box shows that the Beavers won the last 2 games.

CHALLENGE YOURSELF

For the softball throw event at Field Day, the lengths of a competitor's three throws are added together for a total distance. Kevin's total distance was $53\frac{1}{3}$ yards. Scott's total distance was $47\frac{2}{3}$ yards.

13. In the first two rounds, Kevin had throws of $17\frac{2}{3}$ yards and $18\frac{1}{2}$ yards. How far did Kevin throw the last ball?

14. Scott's first two throws totaled $30\frac{5}{6}$ yards, and his third throw was $2\frac{1}{2}$ yards longer than his first. How long was Scott's second throw?

Extra Practice

Set A **Find the sum or difference. Write the answer in simplest form.** (pp. 370–371)

1. $3\frac{1}{2} + 6\frac{5}{8}$

2. $9\frac{5}{6} - 2\frac{1}{2}$

3. $4\frac{1}{5} + 1\frac{2}{3}$

4. $7\frac{7}{9} - 3\frac{1}{3}$

5. $5\frac{3}{4} - 2\frac{1}{8}$

6. $2\frac{3}{4} + 5\frac{1}{3}$

7. $10\frac{4}{5} - 5\frac{3}{10}$

8. $8\frac{1}{2} + 6\frac{2}{3}$

9. $7\frac{3}{8} + 13\frac{1}{4}$

10. $14\frac{5}{12} - 8\frac{1}{6}$

11. $3\frac{2}{9} + 7\frac{1}{6}$

12. $11\frac{1}{2} - 6\frac{2}{5}$

13. Clarice bought $1\frac{1}{2}$ pounds of grapes and $1\frac{1}{4}$ pounds of cherries. How many pounds of fruit did she buy in all?

14. Mr. Grant weighed $5\frac{3}{4}$ pounds of apples and $3\frac{2}{3}$ pounds of pears. How many more pounds of apples did he have than pears?

Set B **Use fraction bars to find the difference. Write the answer in simplest form.** (pp. 372–373)

1. $7\frac{2}{5} - 5\frac{3}{5}$

2. $4\frac{1}{4} - 3\frac{2}{3}$

3. $4\frac{3}{8} - 1\frac{1}{2}$

4. $8 - 2\frac{1}{5}$

5. $12\frac{1}{5} - 6\frac{9}{10}$

6. $8\frac{1}{3} - 7\frac{3}{4}$

7. $7 - \frac{1}{3}$

8. $14\frac{3}{8} - 5\frac{10}{12}$

9. Wyatt measures a pencil and a piece of chalk. The pencil is $7\frac{1}{8}$ in. long and the chalk is $2\frac{3}{4}$ in. long. How much longer is the pencil?

10. Marla is $5\frac{1}{6}$ ft tall. Her younger brother is $4\frac{5}{6}$ ft tall. How much taller is Marla?

Set C **Estimate. Then write the sum or difference in simplest form.** (pp. 374–375)

1. $4\frac{1}{4} + 3\frac{1}{8}$

2. $22\frac{5}{9} - 10\frac{1}{4}$

3. $12\frac{1}{5} + 5\frac{1}{3}$

4. $18\frac{2}{7} - 7\frac{2}{3}$

5. $4\frac{2}{5} + 9\frac{4}{15}$

6. $16\frac{9}{10} - 4\frac{1}{10}$

7. $15\frac{1}{9} + 13\frac{5}{6}$

8. $5 - 3\frac{1}{5}$

9. Ingrid is baking chocolate chip cookies for the school bake sale. She uses $5\frac{1}{3}$ cups white sugar and $3\frac{3}{4}$ cups brown sugar. How much more white sugar than brown sugar does Ingrid use?

10. Mr. Finnigan bought $3\frac{1}{8}$ qt of lemonade and $6\frac{1}{4}$ qt of iced tea for the school picnic. He needs a total of at least $9\frac{1}{2}$ qt of lemonade and iced tea. Did Mr. Finnigan buy enough? **Explain.**

TECHNOLOGY CONNECTION

Calculator: Add Mixed Numbers

Nan's puppy weighs $2\frac{2}{3}$ pounds. Oscar's puppy weighs $4\frac{1}{4}$ pounds. How much do the two puppies weigh together?

Step	Instructions	Keys	Display
Step 1	Turn the calculator ON. Press the Frac button to access fraction mode.		U n/d n/d
Step 2	Enter $2\frac{2}{3}$. First, enter 2 as a whole number. Press 2 Unit.		2–
Step 3	Press 2 n for the numerator of $2\frac{2}{3}$. Then, press 3 d for the denominator.		$2\frac{2}{3}$
Step 4	Press + to add. Repeat the process to enter $4\frac{1}{4}$.		$2\frac{2}{3}+4\frac{1}{4}$
Step 5	Finally, press Enter to find the sum of the mixed numbers.	  	$2\frac{2}{3}+4\frac{1}{4}=6\frac{11}{12}$

To simplify fractions, press the Simp button. You may have to press the Simp button more than once for simplest form.

Try It

Use a calculator to find each sum or difference.

1. $4\frac{3}{7}+2\frac{1}{7}$ **2.** $5\frac{1}{8}+3\frac{3}{8}$ **3.** $7\frac{2}{5}+2\frac{1}{4}$

4. $6\frac{3}{4}-4\frac{1}{4}$ **5.** $10\frac{7}{8}-5\frac{5}{6}$ **6.** $7\frac{7}{9}-5\frac{1}{6}$

7. $8\frac{3}{10}+3\frac{2}{5}$ **8.** $12\frac{7}{12}-3\frac{3}{8}$ **9.** $20\frac{11}{15}-9\frac{3}{10}$

10. $6\frac{3}{5}-4\frac{6}{10}$ **11.** $32\frac{5}{8}+21\frac{3}{4}$ **12.** $5\frac{8}{9}+11\frac{5}{8}$

13. $8+3\frac{5}{13}$ **14.** $10-3\frac{2}{3}$ **15.** $25\frac{13}{20}+23\frac{7}{8}$

16. Explore More **Explain** how you could use the calculator in its decimal mode to check your answers to the problems above.

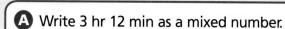

Mixed Numbers and Time

Part of an HOUR

At 1 P.M., a clerk told Risha that the train to New York City would leave in about $2\frac{1}{2}$ hours. To find the departure time, Risha thought:

- There are 60 minutes in 1 hour.
- $\frac{1}{2}$ of 60 is 30. So, my train leaves in 2 hours 30 minutes.
- If I add 2 hours 30 minutes to 1 P.M., the time will be 3:30 P.M.
- So, my train leaves at about 3:30 P.M.

Examples

A Write 3 hr 12 min as a mixed number.

$12 \text{ min} = \frac{12}{60} \text{ hr} = \frac{1}{5} \text{ hr}$

So, 3 hr 12 min as a mixed number is $3\frac{1}{5}$ hr.

Think:
60 min = 1 hr
1 minute = $\frac{1}{60}$ hr

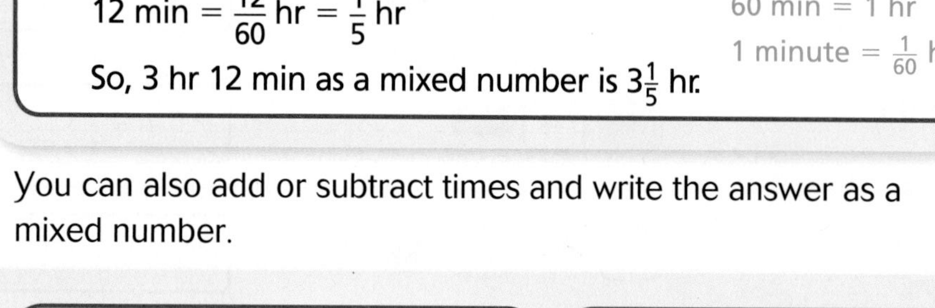

You can also add or subtract times and write the answer as a mixed number.

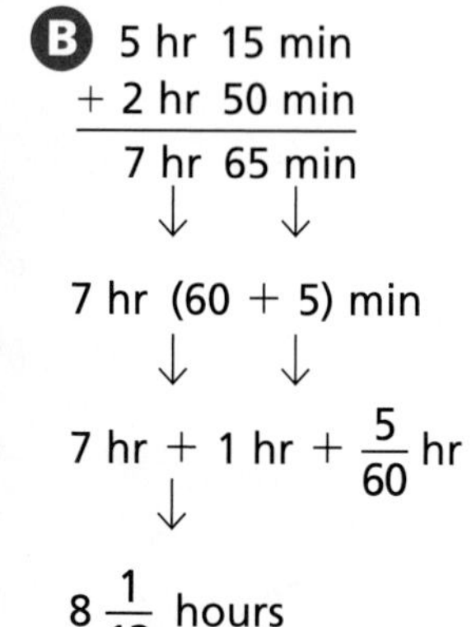

B

$$\begin{array}{r} 5 \text{ hr } 15 \text{ min} \\ +\ 2 \text{ hr } 50 \text{ min} \\ \hline 7 \text{ hr } 65 \text{ min} \end{array}$$

$\downarrow \quad \downarrow$

7 hr (60 + 5) min

$\downarrow \quad \downarrow$

$7 \text{ hr} + 1 \text{ hr} + \frac{5}{60} \text{ hr}$

$\downarrow$

$8\frac{1}{12}$ hours

C Regroup an hour into minutes to subtract.

$$\begin{array}{r} 4 \text{ hr } 22 \text{ min} \\ -\ 1 \text{ hr } 40 \text{ min} \\ \hline \end{array} \longrightarrow \begin{array}{r} 3 \text{ hr } (60 + 22) \text{ min} \\ -\ 1 \text{ hr } 40 \text{ min} \\ \hline \end{array}$$

$$\begin{array}{r} 3 \text{ hr } 82 \text{ min} \\ -\ 1 \text{ hr } 40 \text{ min} \\ \hline 2 \text{ hr } 42 \text{ min} \end{array} = 2\frac{42}{60} = 2\frac{7}{10} \text{ hr}$$

Try It

Write as a mixed number.

1. 2 hr 25 min
2. 1 hr 24 min
3. 6 hr 30 min
4. 3 hr 50 min

Solve. Write the answer as a mixed number.

5. 6 hr 10 min − 3 hr 55 min
6. 3 hr 42 min + 2 hr 38 min
7. **WRITE Math** **Explain** how to write 5 hr 48 min as a mixed number.

Chapter 14 Review/Test

Check Concepts

1. How can modeling problems with fraction bars help you add mixed numbers? KY Grade 6 (p. 366)
2. Use three steps to explain how to find the sum of two mixed numbers with unlike denominators. KY Grade 6 (p. 370)
3. Explain why the first mixed number in the problem $6\frac{1}{8} - 2\frac{5}{8}$ needs to be renamed. KY Grade 6 (p. 372)

Check Skills

Find the sum or difference. Write the answer in simplest form. KY Grade 6 (pp. 370–371, 372–373, 374–375)

4. $2\frac{2}{3} + 5\frac{1}{6}$
5. $1\frac{11}{12} - \frac{5}{6}$
6. $3\frac{5}{8} + 1\frac{1}{4}$
7. $8\frac{9}{10} - 2\frac{2}{5}$
8. $8\frac{3}{4} + 5\frac{1}{12}$
9. $9\frac{2}{3} - 2\frac{1}{6}$
10. $3\frac{1}{8} + 6\frac{7}{10}$
11. $16\frac{4}{7} - 8\frac{1}{3}$
12. $5 + 18\frac{1}{2}$
13. $7\frac{1}{4} - 4\frac{3}{4}$
14. $17\frac{1}{8} + 14\frac{2}{3}$
15. $7\frac{8}{9} - 3\frac{1}{6}$
16. $6\frac{1}{5} - 2\frac{3}{5}$
17. $10\frac{2}{15} - 4\frac{2}{3}$
18. $8\frac{2}{21} - 5\frac{6}{7}$
19. $11 - 4\frac{5}{6}$
20. $19\frac{3}{4} + 22\frac{5}{8}$
21. $10\frac{1}{25} - 3\frac{4}{5}$
22. $1\frac{1}{100} + 6\frac{13}{25}$
23. $9\frac{1}{2} - 5\frac{7}{10}$

Check Problem Solving

Solve. KY Grade 6 (pp. 376–379)

24. Julio lives $8\frac{1}{6}$ miles from school and 3 miles from the library. Trisha lives $2\frac{1}{3}$ miles closer to school than Julio and $4\frac{1}{2}$ miles farther from the library. Andy lives 3 miles farther from school than Trisha and $5\frac{2}{3}$ miles farther from the library than Julio. How far do Trisha and Andy each live from school and from the library?
25. **WRITE Math** Valerie spent a total of $4\frac{1}{4}$ hours working on her science project on Saturday and $1\frac{2}{3}$ hours less time on her social studies report. On Sunday, she spent a total of $2\frac{1}{2}$ hours working on her science project and $\frac{1}{4}$ hours less time on her social studies report. How much total time did Valerie spend working on her social studies report? **Explain** how you know.

Technology Use *Online Assessment.*

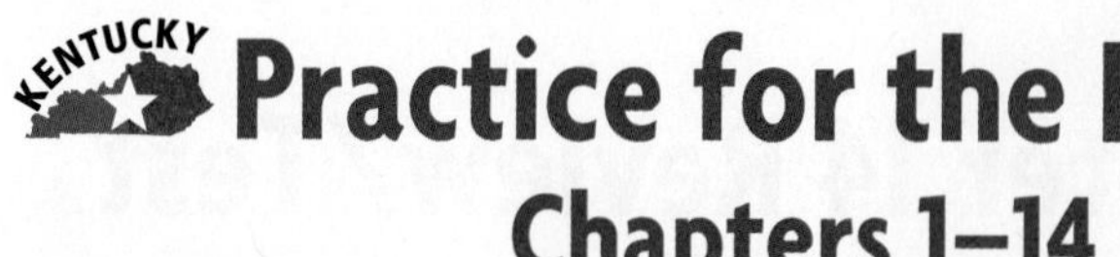

Practice for the KCCT
Chapters 1–14

Number and Operations

1. The attendance for a national park for four years is shown in the table below. Which of the following lists the years in order from least to greatest attendance? KY MA-05-1.1.3 (p. 10)

National Park Attendance	
Year	**Number of Visitors**
2003	67,898
2004	67,856
2005	68,992
2006	67,983

A 2006, 2004, 2005, 2003

B 2004, 2006, 2003, 2005

C 2005, 2003, 2004, 2006

D 2004, 2003, 2006, 2005

2. One copy of a magazine costs $3.85. Which of the following is the best estimate of the cost for 8 copies? KY MA-05-1.2.1 (p. 178)

A $20

B $22

C $32

D $43

3. **WRITE Math** Explain how to add the fractions $\frac{3}{9} + \frac{4}{9}$. KY MA-05-1.3.1 (p. 342)

Algebraic Thinking

4. What is the value of x in the following equation? KY MA-05-5.3.1 (p. 108)

$$x + 7 = 31$$

A 24 **C** 12

B 22 **D** 9

Check your work.

See item 4. Replace the variable in the equation with your answer. If the equation does not balance, check your computation.

5. Robyn made the coordinate grid below to show where her friends live. Name the ordered pair for Brett's house.

KY MA-05-3.3.1 (p. 246)

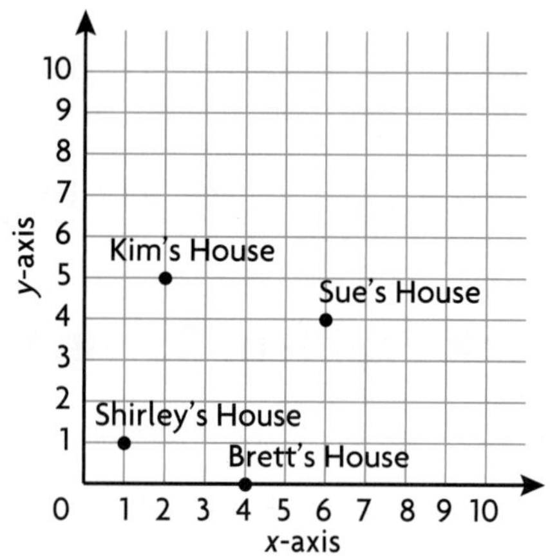

A (3,4) **C** (2,5)

B (4,0) **D** (1,1)

6. **WRITE Math** Is there more than one solution to the inequality $x > 10$? **Explain.**

KY MA-05-5.3.1 (p. 114)

Measurement

7. What is the area of the rectangle? KY Grade 4

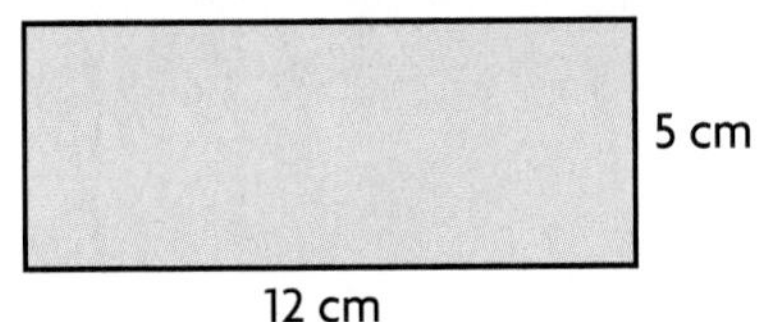

A 17 square centimeters

B 34 square centimeters

C 50 square centimeters

D 60 square centimeters

8. The table shows the amount of liquids needed for a science experiment. How many liters of water and vinegar are needed? KY Grade 4

Science Experiment	
Liquid	**Amount Needed**
Water	150 mL
Iodine	25 mL
Vinegar	50 mL
Salt Water	100 mL

A 20 L

B 2 L

C 0.2 L

D 0.02 L

9. WRITE Math What operation do you use to change millimeters to meters? **Explain.** KY Grade 4

Data Analysis and Probability

10. George tosses a number cube numbered 1 through 6. How many possible outcomes are there for tossing a 5? KY Grade 4

A 1

B 2

C 4

D 8

11. Jake made the tree diagram below to show all of the possible combinations available at his ice cream shop. How many different ice cream and topping combinations are possible? KY Grade 4

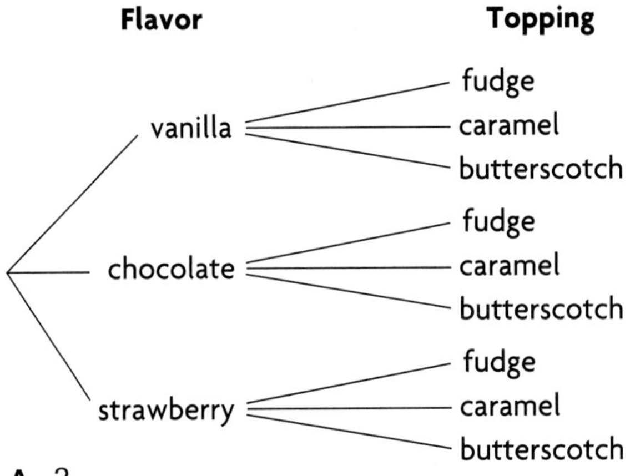

A 3

B 4

C 9

D 12

12. WRITE Math Are you more likely to get heads when you toss a coin or when you toss a 1 on a number cube? Write your answer as a fraction. **Explain.** KY Grade 4

CHAPTER

15 Multiply and Divide Fractions

FAST FACT

The 285-foot *Delta Queen* is one of only five authentic steam-powered paddleboats in the United States.

Investigate

The steam engine on a paddleboat turns a set of paddles in the water to propel the boat. Suppose a riverboat turns 260 metric tons of water with each revolution of its paddlewheel. If the paddles are evenly spaced around the paddlewheel, how much water does a partial turn of the wheel move? Choose two partial turns from the diagram. Calculate the amount of water moved for each.

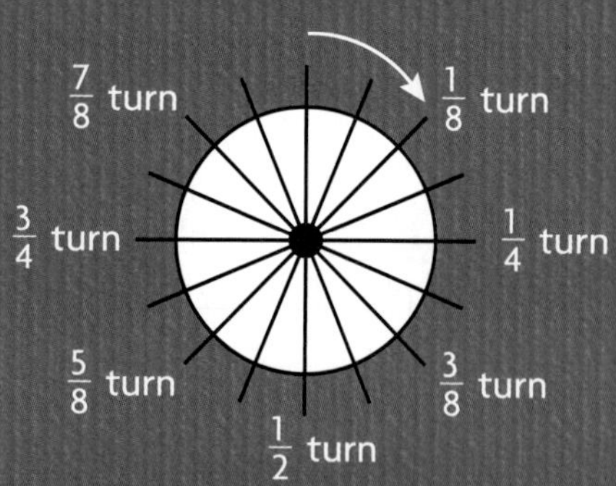

Technology
Student pages are available in the Student eBook.

Show What You Know

Check your understanding of important skills needed for success in Chapter 15.

Write Common Factors

Write the common factors for each pair of numbers.

1. 8 and 12 **2.** 10 and 20 **3.** 16 and 24 **4.** 21 and 42 **5.** 24 and 40

6. 30 and 45 **7.** 48 and 60 **8.** 40 and 100 **9.** 28 and 56 **10.** 75 and 125

Rename Fractions and Mixed Numbers

Rename each fraction as a mixed number or each mixed number as a fraction.

11. $\frac{4}{3}$ **12.** $1\frac{1}{2}$ **13.** $\frac{5}{2}$ **14.** $3\frac{1}{4}$ **15.** $\frac{10}{3}$

16. $2\frac{4}{5}$ **17.** $\frac{18}{7}$ **18.** $4\frac{3}{5}$ **19.** $6\frac{5}{6}$ **20.** $5\frac{4}{9}$

Parts of a Whole

Write a fraction to represent the group shown in red.

21. 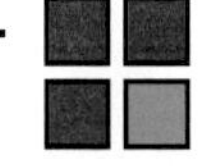 **22.** 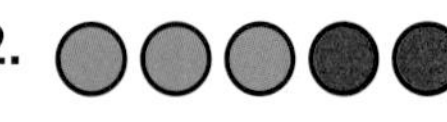 **23.** 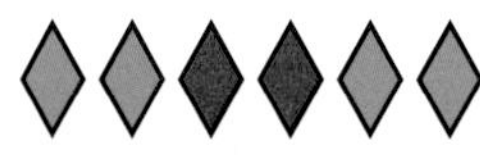

24. 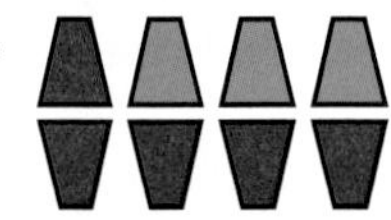 **25.** 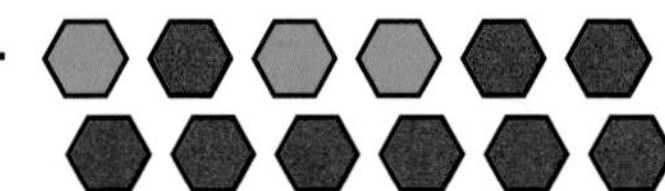 **26.** 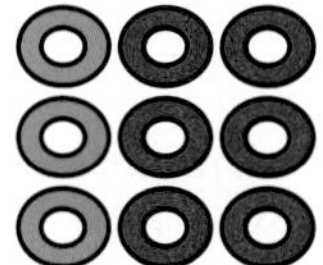

VOCABULARY POWER

CHAPTER VOCABULARY

fraction
mixed number
reciprocals

WARM-UP WORDS

fraction a number that names a part of a whole or a part of a group

mixed number a number that is made up of a whole number and a fraction

reciprocals two numbers are reciprocals of each other if their product is 1

LESSON HANDS ON

1 Model Multiplication of Fractions

OBJECTIVE: Use models to multiply fractions.

Quick Review

What fraction of the model is shaded?

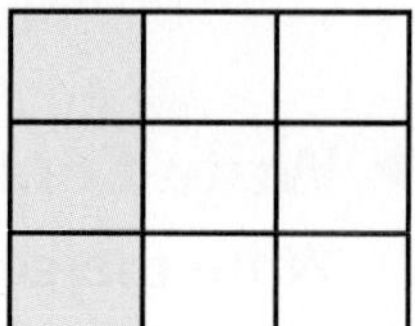

Investigate

Materials ■ yellow and blue crayons ■ paper

You can make a model to find $\frac{1}{3} \times \frac{1}{2}$.

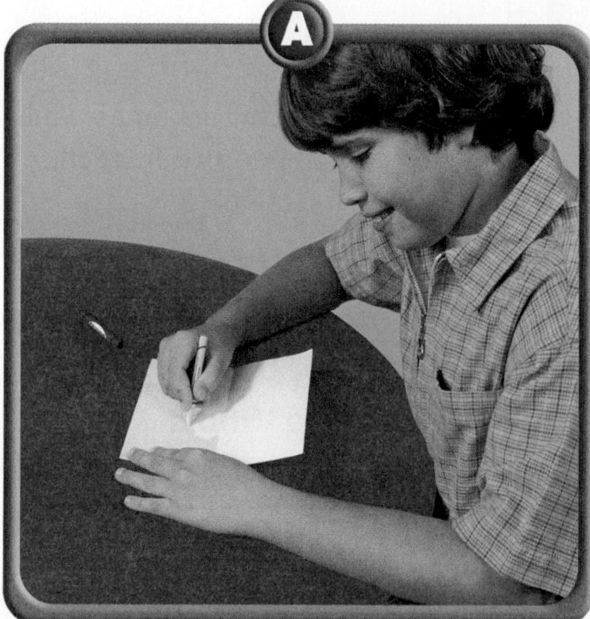

A Fold a rectangular piece of paper into 2 equal parts.

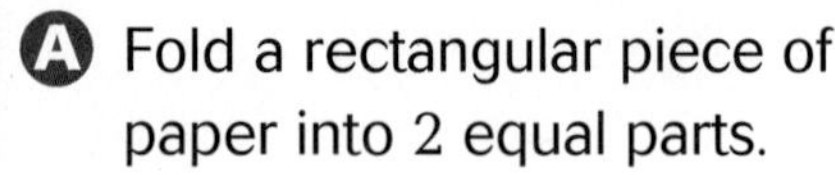

Shade $\frac{1}{2}$ yellow.

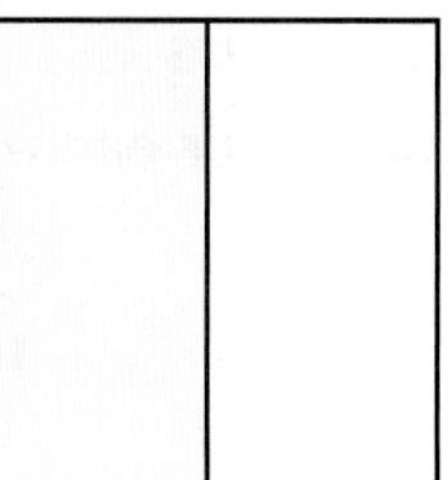

B Now fold the paper the other way into 3 equal parts.

To find $\frac{1}{3}$ of $\frac{1}{2}$, shade $\frac{1}{3}$ of the yellow section blue.

What fraction of the whole model is shaded twice? What is $\frac{1}{3} \times \frac{1}{2}$?

C Make a model to find $\frac{1}{2} \times \frac{1}{4}$.

Draw Conclusions

1. How many parts is your model folded into for $\frac{1}{2} \times \frac{1}{4}$? What is $\frac{1}{2} \times \frac{1}{4}$?
2. If you modeled $\frac{1}{3} \times \frac{2}{4}$, how many parts do you think your model would have? Explain your reasoning.
3. **Analysis** Look at the numerators and denominators of the factors and the product for $\frac{1}{3} \times \frac{1}{2}$. What relationships do you see?

Connect

You can also draw a picture to multiply fractions.

Example **Multiply.** $\frac{2}{5} \times \frac{1}{2}$

Step 1

Draw a rectangle.
Divide it into 2 equal parts.

Shade $\frac{1}{2}$.

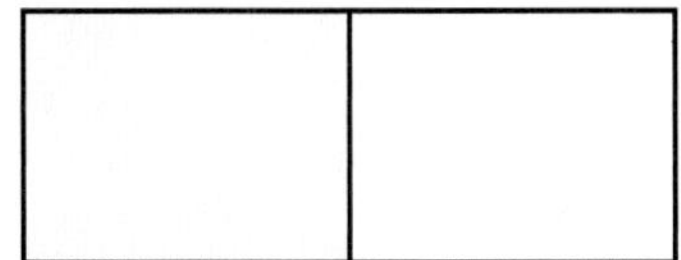

Step 2

Divide the rectangle the other way into 5 equal parts. Use a different color to shade $\frac{2}{5}$ of the parts that are already shaded.

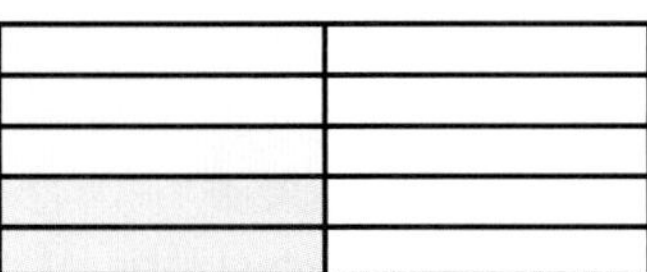

Step 3

Two-tenths of the model is shaded twice.

$\frac{2}{5} \times \frac{1}{2} = \frac{2}{10}$, or $\frac{1}{5}$.

TALK Math

Look at page 388. Is $\frac{1}{3} \times \frac{1}{2}$ greater than or less than $\frac{1}{2}$? Look at the Example above. Is $\frac{2}{5} \times \frac{1}{2}$ greater than or less than $\frac{1}{2}$? For both problems, **explain** why.

Practice

Write the product each model represents.

1. 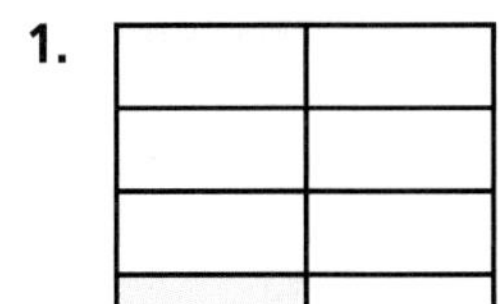

2. 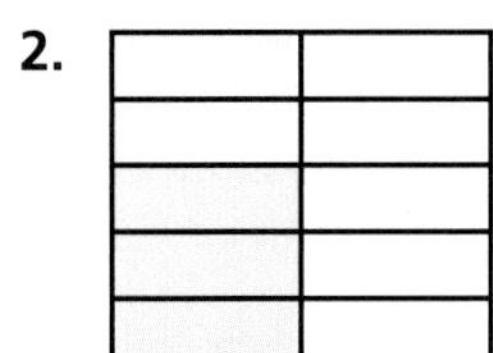

3. 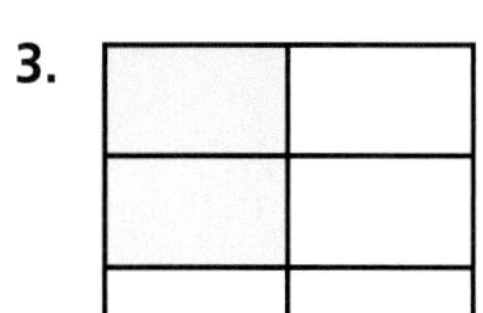

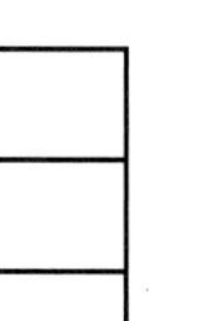

4. 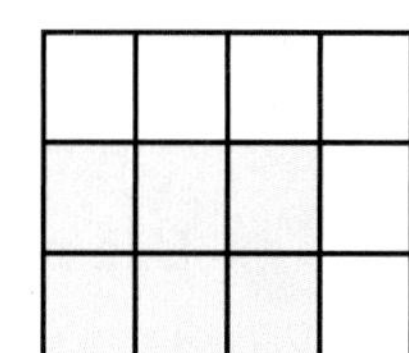

Find the product.

5. $\frac{1}{3} \times \frac{1}{4}$

6. $\frac{1}{4} \times \frac{2}{3}$

7. $\frac{1}{8} \times \frac{1}{2}$

8. $\frac{2}{3} \times \frac{1}{3}$

9. $\frac{1}{2} \times \frac{1}{2}$

10. $\frac{1}{4} \times \frac{3}{4}$

11. $\frac{2}{5} \times \frac{1}{4}$

12. $\frac{1}{2} \times \frac{4}{5}$

13. $\frac{1}{6} \times \frac{2}{3}$

14. $\frac{3}{4} \times \frac{1}{2}$

15. **WRITE Math** **Explain** why the product of two fractions that are less than 1 is always less than 1.

LESSON

2 Record Multiplication of Fractions

OBJECTIVE: Solve problems by multiplying fractions.

Quick Review

Write in simplest form.

1. $\frac{15}{20}$
2. $\frac{12}{18}$
3. $\frac{9}{15}$
4. $\frac{8}{16}$
5. $\frac{14}{20}$

Learn

PROBLEM In Maria's backyard, $\frac{2}{3}$ of the land is used for a garden. She grows vegetables in $\frac{1}{2}$ of the garden. What fraction of Maria's backyard is used for growing vegetables?

ONE WAY **Draw a picture.**

Multiply. $\frac{1}{2} \times \frac{2}{3}$

Step 1

Draw a rectangle. Divide it into 3 equal parts. Shade $\frac{2}{3}$.

Step 2

Divide the rectangle into 2 equal parts. Use a different color to shade $\frac{1}{2}$ of the parts that are already shaded.

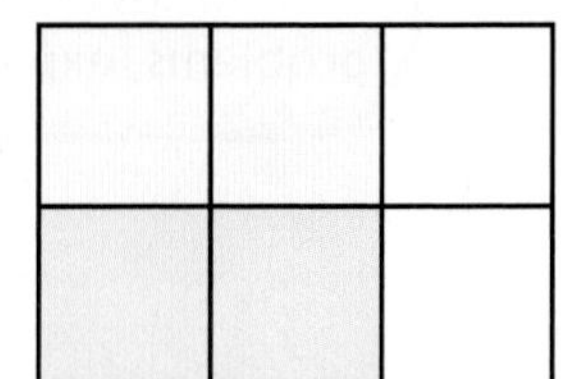

Step 3

Two-sixths of the model is shaded twice.

$\frac{1}{2} \times \frac{2}{3} = \frac{2}{6}$, or $\frac{1}{3}$

So, $\frac{2}{6}$, or $\frac{1}{3}$, of Maria's backyard is used for growing vegetables.

- Compare the numerator and denominator of the product, $\frac{2}{6}$, with the numerators and denominators of the factors. What relationship do you see?

ANOTHER WAY **Use paper and pencil.**

Multiply. $\frac{2}{5} \times \frac{3}{4}$

Step 1

Multiply the numerators.
Then multiply the denominators.

$\frac{2}{5} \times \frac{3}{4} = \frac{2 \times 3}{5 \times 4} = \frac{6}{20}$

Step 2

Write the answer in simplest form.

$\frac{6}{20} = \frac{6 \div 2}{20 \div 2} = \frac{3}{10}$

So, $\frac{2}{5} \times \frac{3}{4} = \frac{3}{10}$.

Guided Practice

1. Look at the model. How many parts are there? How many parts are shaded twice? What is $\frac{3}{4} \times \frac{3}{5}$?

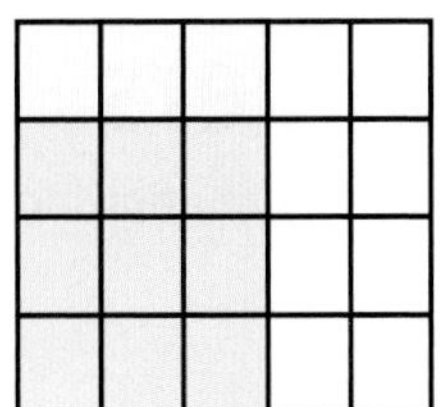

Find the product. Write the answer in simplest form.

2. $\frac{2}{5} \times \frac{2}{5}$
3. $\frac{5}{6} \times \frac{1}{10}$
4. $\frac{1}{8} \times \frac{1}{4}$
5. $\frac{3}{10} \times \frac{5}{6}$
6. $\frac{2}{3} \times \frac{3}{4}$
7. **TALK Math** **Explain** how to find $\frac{3}{4} \times \frac{2}{3}$.

Independent Practice and Problem Solving

Find the product. Write the answer in simplest form.

8. $\frac{1}{4} \times \frac{3}{4}$
9. $\frac{5}{8} \times \frac{7}{10}$
10. $\frac{1}{2} \times \frac{5}{12}$
11. $\frac{4}{9} \times \frac{2}{3}$
12. $\frac{2}{3} \times \frac{1}{6}$

Algebra **Evaluate each expression. Then write <, >, or = for each ●.**

13. $\frac{1}{2} \times \frac{3}{4}$ ● $\frac{1}{4} \times \frac{3}{4}$
14. $\frac{2}{3} \times \frac{2}{5}$ ● $\frac{2}{5} \times \frac{6}{9}$
15. $\frac{7}{8} \times \frac{1}{3}$ ● $\frac{5}{6} \times \frac{1}{2}$

16. Pat used $\frac{2}{3}$ of a raisin package to make 2 loaves of bread. Her family ate $\frac{1}{2}$ of the bread. What fraction of the raisin package did her family eat?

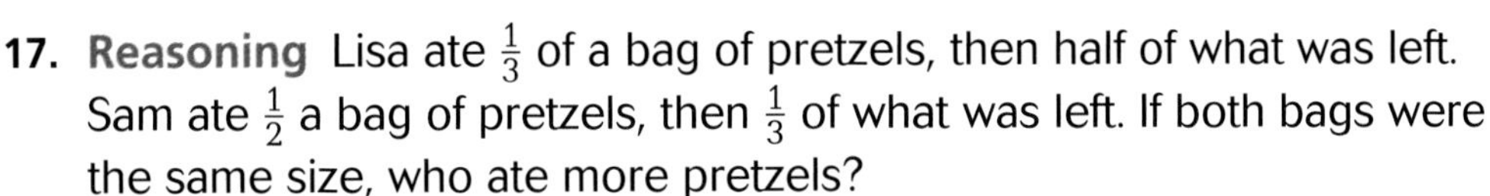

17. **Reasoning** Lisa ate $\frac{1}{3}$ of a bag of pretzels, then half of what was left. Sam ate $\frac{1}{2}$ a bag of pretzels, then $\frac{1}{3}$ of what was left. If both bags were the same size, who ate more pretzels?

18. **WRITE Math** **What's the Question** Maria uses $\frac{3}{8}$ of her garden to grow greens. She plants lettuce in $\frac{2}{9}$ of the greens garden. The answer is $\frac{1}{12}$.

Mixed Review and Test Prep

19. Greg's four kittens weigh 20 ounces, 14 ounces, 23 ounces, and 18 ounces. What is the median weight of Greg's kittens? (p. 220)

20. Liza has $6\frac{1}{2}$ feet of rope. She uses a piece $4\frac{1}{3}$ feet long. How many feet of rope does Liza have left? (p. 374)

21. **Test Prep** Bryan eats $\frac{2}{3}$ of $\frac{3}{8}$ of a pizza. What fraction of the pizza does Bryan eat?

   A $\frac{1}{12}$

   B $\frac{1}{8}$

   C $\frac{5}{24}$

   D $\frac{1}{4}$

Extra Practice on page 410, Set A

LESSON 3

Multiply Fractions and Whole Numbers

OBJECTIVE: Solve problems by multiplying fractions and whole numbers.

Quick Review

Write each product in simplest form.

1. $\frac{1}{2} \times \frac{1}{5}$
2. $\frac{3}{4} \times \frac{2}{3}$
3. $\frac{5}{6} \times \frac{1}{3}$
4. $\frac{1}{4} \times \frac{3}{8}$
5. $\frac{1}{4} \times \frac{3}{5}$

Learn

PROBLEM Simon, the candle maker, uses $\frac{5}{6}$ cup of wax for each white candle he makes. How many cups of wax does Simon need to make 5 candles?

Multiply. $5 \times \frac{5}{6}$

ONE WAY **Draw a picture.**

Step 1

Use circles to show 5 groups of $\frac{5}{6}$.

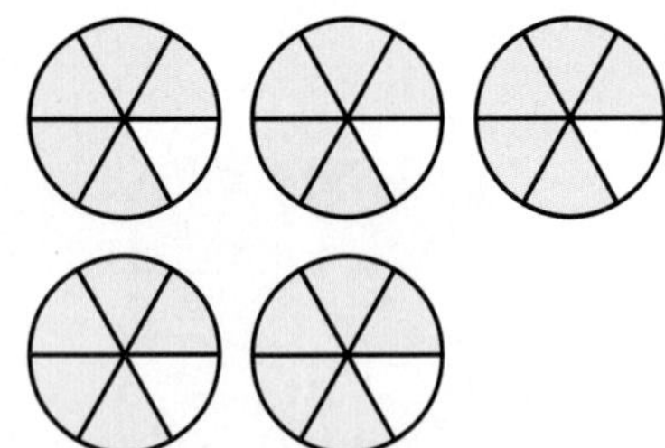

Step 2

Count the shaded sixths or use repeated addition to find the total amount.

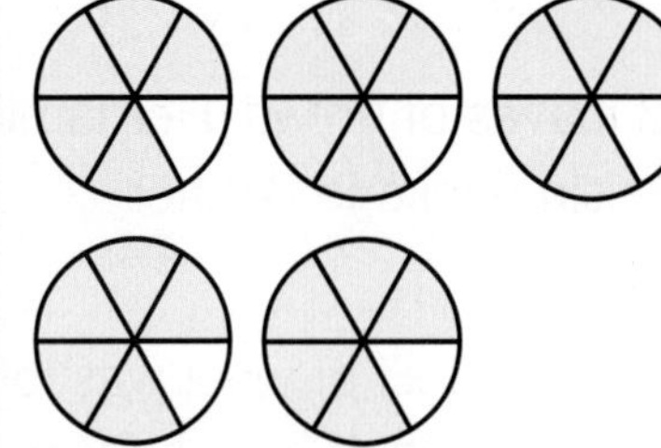

$\frac{5}{6} + \frac{5}{6} + \frac{5}{6} + \frac{5}{6} + \frac{5}{6} = \frac{25}{6}$

Step 3

Write the answer as a mixed number.

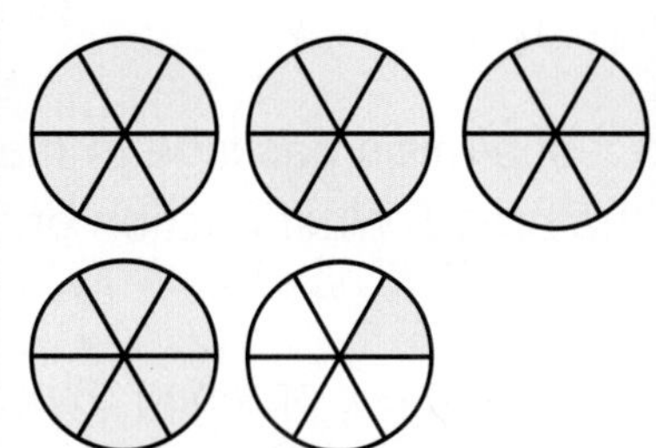

$\frac{25}{6} = 4\frac{1}{6}$

ANOTHER WAY **Use paper and pencil.**

Step 1

Write the whole number as a fraction.

$5 \times \frac{5}{6} = \frac{5}{1} \times \frac{5}{6}$

Step 2

Multiply the numerators. Then multiply the denominators.

$\frac{5}{1} \times \frac{5}{6} = \frac{5 \times 5}{1 \times 6} = \frac{25}{6}$

Step 3

Write the answer as a mixed number in simplest form.

$\frac{25}{6} = 4\frac{1}{6}$

So, Simon needs $4\frac{1}{6}$ cups of wax.

- What picture could you draw to find $\frac{4}{5} \times 5$?

Guided Practice

1. Use the picture to find the product $6 \times \frac{1}{3}$.

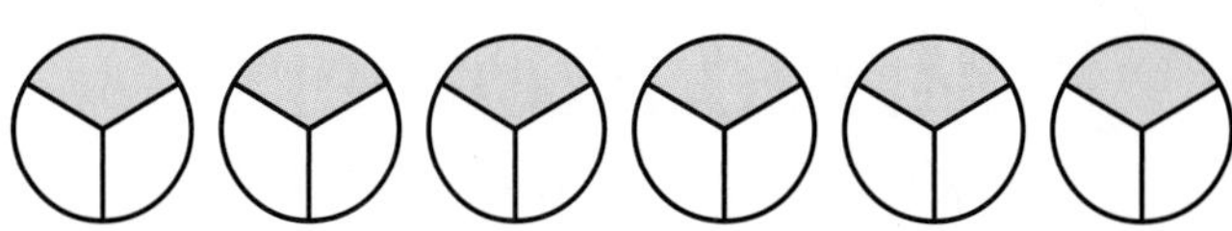

Find the product. Write it in simplest form.

2. $\frac{1}{4} \times 2$
3. $9 \times \frac{1}{6}$
4. $\frac{2}{3} \times 4$
5. $\frac{3}{8} \times 8$
6. $\frac{2}{9} \times 5$
7. $10 \times \frac{4}{5}$

8. **TALK Math** Explain how to find $3 \times \frac{3}{5}$.

Independent Practice and Problem Solving

Find the product. Write it in simplest form.

9. $\frac{5}{12} \times 4$
10. $7 \times \frac{3}{5}$
11. $\frac{1}{6} \times 15$
12. $4 \times \frac{2}{3}$
13. $7 \times \frac{4}{5}$
14. $8 \times \frac{3}{4}$
15. $6 \times \frac{1}{5}$
16. $5 \times \frac{3}{8}$
17. $5 \times \frac{1}{2}$
18. $7 \times \frac{5}{6}$
19. $5 \times \frac{1}{4}$
20. $\frac{2}{3} \times 9$
21. $\frac{3}{5} \times 4$
22. $6 \times \frac{5}{8}$
23. $12 \times \frac{3}{5}$
24. $\frac{1}{6} \times 3$
25. $5 \times \frac{7}{8}$
26. $\frac{1}{3} \times 12$

USE DATA For 27–28, use the table.

27. How many cups of wax does Simon need to make 10 blue candles?
28. How many more cups of wax does it take to make 6 orange candles than it takes to make 6 red candles?
29. **WRITE Math** Explain how you could use the product of $\frac{1}{2} \times 60$ to find the product $\frac{1}{4} \times 60$.

Simon's Candles

Color	Wax per Candle (in cups)
Purple	$\frac{1}{2}$
Red	$\frac{3}{8}$
Blue	$\frac{7}{8}$
Orange	$\frac{2}{3}$

Mixed Review and Test Prep

30. Roy spends $14.37 to buy 3 cartons of tennis balls. How much did each carton of tennis balls cost? (p. 198)
31. Tori ate $\frac{3}{8}$ of a fruit salad. Rob ate $\frac{1}{4}$ of the same fruit salad. Who ate more? (p. 318)
32. **Test Prep** Cassidy used $\frac{3}{4}$ of 3 gallons of paint for her room. How many gallons of paint did she use?

    A $1\frac{1}{4}$ gallons
    B $1\frac{3}{4}$ gallons
    C $2\frac{1}{4}$ gallons
    D $3\frac{3}{4}$ gallons

Extra Practice on page 410, Set B

Multiply with Mixed Numbers

OBJECTIVE: Multiply two mixed numbers.

Quick Review

Rename each mixed number as a fraction.

1. $3\frac{1}{2}$ **2.** $1\frac{2}{3}$

3. $2\frac{5}{6}$ **4.** $5\frac{1}{4}$

5. $4\frac{3}{5}$

Learn

PROBLEM A neighborhood park is on $1\frac{1}{2}$ acres of land. Dogs are allowed in $\frac{3}{4}$ of the park. How many acres of the park are dogs allowed in?

ONE WAY **Use a model.**

Multiply. $\frac{3}{4} \times 1\frac{1}{2}$

Step 1

Use 2 whole squares. Divide each square in half. Shade $1\frac{1}{2}$, or $\frac{3}{2}$, of the parts.

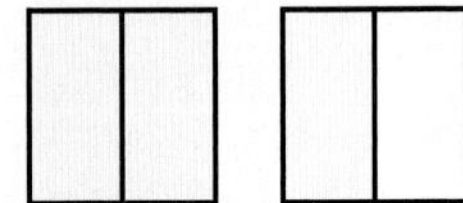

Step 2

Divide the squares into fourths the other way.

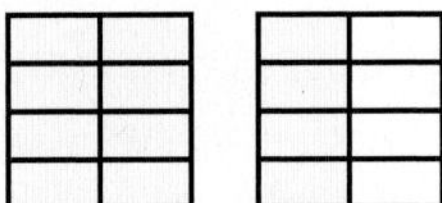

Step 3

Use another color to shade $\frac{3}{4}$ of the parts already shaded. Nine-eighths are shaded both colors.

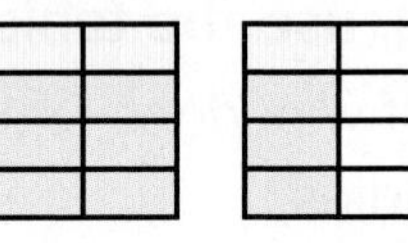

$\frac{3}{4} \times 1\frac{1}{2} = \frac{9}{8}$, or $1\frac{1}{8}$

ANOTHER WAY **Use paper and pencil.**

Multiply. $\frac{3}{4} \times 1\frac{1}{2}$

Step 1

Rename the mixed number as a fraction greater than 1.

Think: $1\frac{1}{2} = \frac{3}{2}$

$\frac{3}{4} \times 1\frac{1}{2} = \frac{3}{4} \times \frac{3}{2}$

Step 2

Multiply the numerators and the denominators.

$\frac{3}{4} \times \frac{3}{2} = \frac{3 \times 3}{4 \times 2} = \frac{9}{8}$

Step 3

Write the product as a mixed number in simplest form.

$\frac{9}{8} = 1\frac{1}{8}$

Remember

A mixed number can be written as a fraction.

$2\frac{3}{4} = 2 + \frac{3}{4}$

$= \frac{8}{4} + \frac{3}{4} = \frac{11}{4}$

So, dogs are allowed in $1\frac{1}{8}$ acres of the park.

- In Step 1, why do you rename the mixed number as a fraction greater than 1?

Multiply Two Mixed Numbers

To multiply two mixed numbers, follow the same steps you use to multiply a fraction and a mixed number.

ERROR ALERT

Remember to rename both mixed numbers as fractions when multiplying mixed numbers.

Example 1 **Multiply.** $2\frac{3}{4} \times 1\frac{2}{3}$

$2\frac{3}{4} \times 1\frac{2}{3} = \frac{11}{4} \times \frac{5}{3}$ Rename each mixed number as a fraction greater than 1.

$\frac{11 \times 5}{4 \times 3} = \frac{55}{12}$ Multiply.

$= \frac{55}{12}$, or $4\frac{7}{12}$ Write the product as a mixed number in simplest form.

When a numerator and a denominator have a common factor, you can simplify before you multiply.

Example 2 **Multiply.** $2\frac{4}{7} \times 1\frac{1}{6}$

$2\frac{4}{7} \times 1\frac{1}{6} = \frac{18}{7} \times \frac{7}{6}$ Look for a numerator and denominator with common factors. Find the GCF.

$= \frac{\overset{3}{\cancel{18}} \times \overset{1}{\cancel{7}}}{\underset{1}{\cancel{7}} \times \underset{1}{\cancel{6}}}$ The GCF of 6 and 18 is 6. The GCF of 7 and 7 is 7.

$= \frac{3}{1}$, or 3 Multiply.

Guided Practice

1. What does one column of Figure 1 represent?

Use Figures 1 and 2 to find the product $\frac{1}{3} \times 1\frac{1}{5}$.

Figure 1

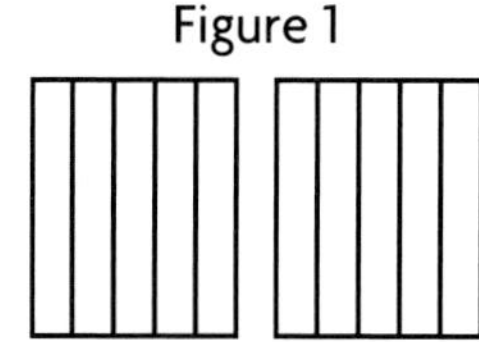

Figure 2

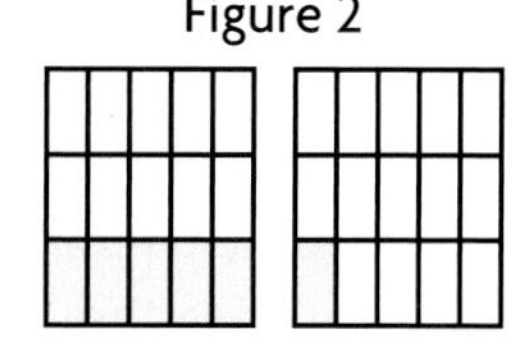

Find the product. Write it in simplest form.

2. $\frac{2}{3} \times 1\frac{3}{8}$
3. $\frac{3}{5} \times 2\frac{1}{2}$
4. $1\frac{1}{3} \times 1\frac{1}{2}$
5. $1\frac{1}{2} \times 2\frac{2}{3}$
6. $2\frac{1}{3} \times 6$
7. $1\frac{2}{9} \times \frac{1}{3}$
8. $1\frac{2}{3} \times 2\frac{1}{3}$
9. $1\frac{1}{7} \times 1\frac{1}{6}$
10. $2\frac{1}{5} \times 1\frac{1}{3}$
11. $3\frac{3}{4} \times 2$
12. TALK Math **Explain** how you would find $3 \times 2\frac{3}{4}$.

Independent Practice and Problem Solving

Make a model to find the product. Write it in simplest form.

13. $\frac{1}{2} \times 2\frac{1}{3}$ **14.** $\frac{2}{3} \times 1\frac{3}{4}$ **15.** $\frac{1}{4} \times 1\frac{1}{2}$ **16.** $\frac{1}{3} \times 1\frac{2}{3}$

Find the product. Write it in simplest form.

17. $3 \times 1\frac{1}{4}$ **18.** $1\frac{2}{5} \times \frac{1}{3}$ **19.** $2\frac{3}{5} \times 1\frac{1}{4}$ **20.** $\frac{5}{6} \times 1\frac{3}{4}$ **21.** $\frac{5}{12} \times 2\frac{1}{3}$

22. $1\frac{1}{4} \times 1\frac{3}{5}$ **23.** $4\frac{1}{2} \times 1\frac{1}{9}$ **24.** $2\frac{7}{8} \times 4$ **25.** $3\frac{1}{5} \times 1\frac{3}{8}$ **26.** $4\frac{3}{4} \times \frac{2}{3}$

27. $1\frac{2}{3} \times 6$ **28.** $3 \times 2\frac{1}{2}$ **29.** $\frac{7}{8} \times 1\frac{1}{2}$ **30.** $2\frac{1}{4} \times \frac{5}{6}$ **31.** $3\frac{1}{2} \times 1\frac{1}{4}$

32. $\frac{1}{2} \times 1\frac{1}{3} \times 1\frac{2}{3}$ **33.** $2\frac{1}{4} \times \frac{3}{10} \times 1\frac{2}{3}$ **34.** $2\frac{1}{3} \times 1\frac{1}{2} \times 1\frac{3}{4}$

Algebra **Find the missing number.**

35. Find *c* if ▲ = 2.
◆ = 4 × ▲
w = ▲ × 6
$\frac{◆}{w} = \frac{▲}{c}$

36. Find *s* if ▲ = 4.
◆ = 3 × ▲
w = 4 + ▲
$\frac{w}{s} = \frac{▲}{◆}$

37. Find *b* if ▲ = 6.
◆ = 2 × ▲
w = ▲ − 2
$\frac{b}{◆} = \frac{w}{▲}$

38. A beach is $3\frac{3}{4}$ miles long. Pets on a leash are allowed on $\frac{1}{2}$ of the beach. On how many miles of beach are leashed pets allowed?

39. Sheri has a large dog and one small dog. She feeds the smaller dog $3\frac{3}{4}$ pounds of food each week. She feeds the large dog $1\frac{1}{2}$ times more food each week. How many pounds of food does Sheri feed the larger dog each week?

40. Andy took his dog to the park for $1\frac{1}{4}$ hours on Friday. On Saturday, they were at the park $\frac{2}{3}$ of the time they were there on Friday. How many total hours did Andy and his dog spend at the park on Friday and Saturday?

41. **Reasoning** How can you use multiplication to find $2\frac{3}{8} + 2\frac{3}{8} + 2\frac{3}{8}$?

42. **What's the Error?** Kelly says that $1\frac{2}{3} \times 3\frac{1}{3}$ is $3\frac{2}{9}$. Describe the error Kelly might have made. What is the correct answer?

43. WRITE Math **Explain** how multiplying mixed numbers is different than adding mixed numbers.

 Extra Practice on page 410, Set C

Mixed Review and Test Prep

44. Philip lives $1\frac{1}{2}$ miles from the park. He walked to the park, $1\frac{3}{4}$ miles around the park, and then home. How many miles did Philip walk? (p. 370)

45. **Test Prep** Nathan has $2\frac{1}{2}$ pounds of clay. He used $\frac{3}{4}$ of the clay to make a model. How many pounds of clay did Nathan use for the model?

    A $1\frac{7}{8}$
    B $2\frac{3}{8}$
    C $3\frac{1}{4}$
    D $3\frac{3}{4}$

46. Evaluate $(17 + n) \div 5$, if $n = 3$. (p. 96)

47. **Test Prep** Cindy worked $1\frac{1}{3}$ hours on Tuesday. Tom worked $\frac{3}{4}$ times as long. How many hours did Tom work?

    A $2\frac{1}{6}$ hours
    B 1 hour
    C $3\frac{2}{5}$ hours
    D $3\frac{5}{6}$ hours

Problem Solving connects to Social Studies

The California Trail took many pioneers westward from its starting point in Missouri. Today, parts of the trail are preserved as the California National Historic Trail. The trail passes through 10 states from Missouri to California. Pioneers traveling along the California Trail could cover from 14 to 45 miles each day depending on the type of transportation they used.

Example

A pioneer family traveled $3\frac{1}{2}$ miles per hour using a team of horses. They traveled $6\frac{2}{3}$ hours each day for a week. How many miles did they travel in a week?

$3\frac{1}{2} \times 6\frac{2}{3} \times 7 = \frac{7}{2} \times \frac{20}{3} \times 7$ Rename each mixed number.

$\frac{7}{2} \times \frac{20}{3} \times 7 = \frac{980}{6}$ Multiply.

$\frac{490}{3} = 163\frac{1}{3}$ Write the product as a mixed number in simplest form.

So, the pioneer family traveled $163\frac{1}{3}$ miles in a week.

1. A pioneer family traveled $2\frac{1}{4}$ miles per hour using a team of oxen. They traveled 8 hours each day for a week. How many miles did they travel in a week?

2. A pioneer family walked $3\frac{3}{5}$ miles per hour. They walked $5\frac{1}{2}$ hours each day for a week. How many miles did they travel in a week?

LESSON HANDS ON

5 Model Fraction Division

OBJECTIVE: Model fraction division.

Quick Review

Write the product in simplest form.

1. $\frac{1}{2} \times \frac{1}{3}$
2. $\frac{2}{3} \times \frac{3}{8}$
3. $\frac{5}{6} \times \frac{1}{5}$
4. $10 \times \frac{3}{5}$
5. $\frac{3}{4} \times \frac{4}{5}$

Investigate

Materials ■ fraction bars

You can use a model to find $2 \div \frac{1}{5}$.

A Use two whole bars to model 2.

Place a $\frac{1}{5}$ bar under the whole bars.

B See how many $\frac{1}{5}$ bars are equal to 2 wholes.

1 | 1

$\frac{1}{5}$ | $\frac{1}{5}$ | $\frac{1}{5}$ | $\frac{1}{5}$ | $\frac{1}{5}$ | $\frac{1}{5}$ | $\frac{1}{5}$ | $\frac{1}{5}$ | $\frac{1}{5}$ | $\frac{1}{5}$

C Write a division number sentence to express what the model shows.

D Make a model to find $3 \div \frac{1}{4}$. Record the quotient.

Draw Conclusions

1. How is dividing fractions like dividing whole numbers?
2. How do the fraction bars help you understand dividing fractions?
3. **Analyze** How can you use the quotient for $2 \div \frac{1}{5}$ to find the quotient for $6 \div \frac{1}{5}$?

Connect

You can also use fraction bars to divide a fraction by a fraction.

Example Divide. $\frac{1}{2} \div \frac{1}{10}$

Step 1

Model $\frac{1}{2}$ and $\frac{1}{10}$ with fraction bars.

Step 2

See how many $\frac{1}{10}$ bars are equal to the $\frac{1}{2}$ bar.

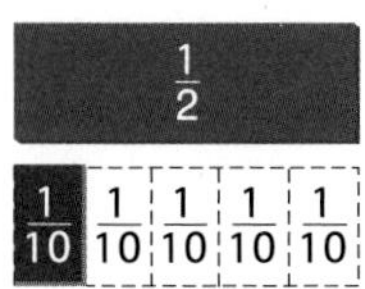

Five $\frac{1}{10}$ bars are equal to a $\frac{1}{2}$ bar.

Step 3

Write a number sentence to express what the model shows.

$$\frac{1}{2} \div \frac{1}{10} = 5$$

TALK Math

Find the product $\frac{1}{2} \times 4$ and the quotient $\frac{1}{2} \div \frac{1}{4}$. What do you notice?

Practice

Write a division number sentence for each model.

1. 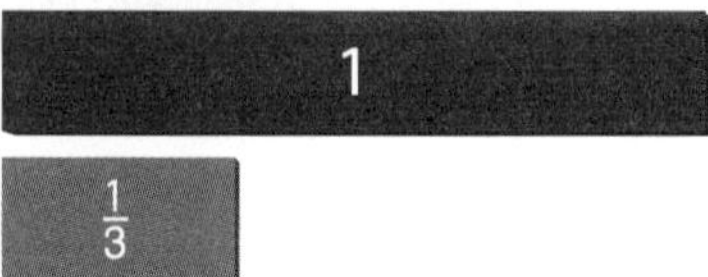

2. 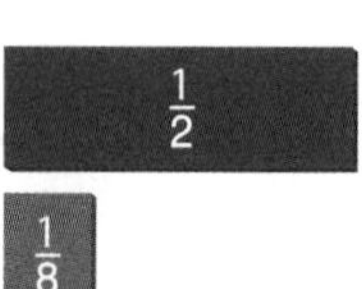

3. 

Use fraction bars to find the quotient.

4. $1 \div \frac{1}{6}$
5. $\frac{1}{3} \div \frac{1}{6}$
6. $\frac{1}{5} \div \frac{1}{10}$
7. $2 \div \frac{1}{8}$
8. $\frac{1}{6} \div \frac{1}{12}$
9. $\frac{1}{2} \div \frac{1}{6}$
10. $4 \div \frac{1}{5}$
11. $6 \div \frac{1}{3}$
12. $3 \div \frac{1}{4}$
13. $\frac{1}{3} \div \frac{1}{6}$
14. $6 \div \frac{1}{5}$
15. $2 \div \frac{1}{3}$
16. $\frac{1}{3} \div \frac{1}{12}$
17. $3 \div \frac{1}{6}$
18. $6 \div \frac{1}{4}$
19. $\frac{1}{4} \div \frac{1}{8}$

20. **WRITE Math** **Explain** how to use a model to find $3 \div \frac{1}{3}$.

LESSON 6

Divide Whole Numbers by Fractions

OBJECTIVE: Divide whole numbers by fractions.

Quick Review

1. $\frac{1}{2} \times 8$
2. $9 \times \frac{2}{3}$
3. $\frac{5}{6} \times 4$
4. $6 \times \frac{3}{8}$
5. $5 \times \frac{3}{10}$

Vocabulary

reciprocals

Learn

PROBLEM Students are painting a mural on a wall that is divided into three sections. It takes the students 4 hours to paint $\frac{2}{3}$ of the mural. If they spend the same amount of time painting each section, how many hours will it take the students to paint the mural?

Example 1 Use a common denominator to find $4 \div \frac{2}{3}$.

Step 1	Step 2	Step 3
Rename 4 with a denominator of 3. Think: $4 = \frac{12}{3}$ $4 \div \frac{2}{3} = \frac{12}{3} \div \frac{2}{3}$	Divide the numerators. Divide the denominators. $\frac{12}{3} \div \frac{2}{3} = \frac{12 \div 2}{3 \div 3}$ $= \frac{6}{1}$	Write the quotient in simplest form. $\frac{6}{1} = 6$

So, it will take the students 6 hours to paint the mural.

- Why is 3 used as the common denominator?
- Why do you use a common denominator to divide?

Example 2 Use multiplication to find $6 \div \frac{1}{3}$.

Step 1	Step 2
Write an equivalent multiplication problem with a missing factor. Think: $6 \div \frac{1}{3} = ■$ is equivalent to $\frac{1}{3} \times ■ = 6$	Find the missing factor. 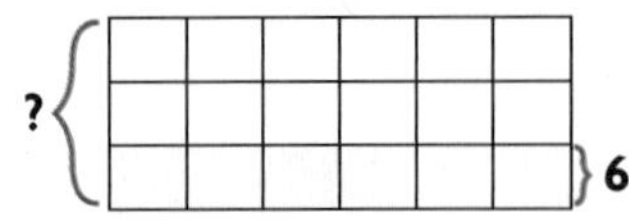 The model shows that $\frac{1}{3}$ of the missing number is 6. Since $\frac{1}{3} \times 18 = 6$, $6 \div \frac{1}{3} = 18$.

So, $6 \div \frac{1}{3} = 18$.

- How would you write an equivalent multiplication problem to find $4 \div \frac{2}{3}$ in Example 1?

Use Reciprocals to Divide

You can also divide using the reciprocal of the divisor. Two numbers whose product is 1 are **reciprocals.**

The reciprocal of $\frac{1}{8}$ is $\frac{8}{1}$, or 8.	The reciprocal of $\frac{5}{6}$ is $\frac{6}{5}$.	The reciprocal of 3, or $\frac{3}{1}$, is $\frac{1}{3}$.
$\frac{1}{8} \times \frac{8}{1} = \frac{8}{8} = 1$	$\frac{5}{6} \times \frac{6}{5} = \frac{30}{30} = 1$	$\frac{3}{1} \times \frac{1}{3} = \frac{3}{3} = 1$

You can write a related number sentence using the reciprocal and the inverse operation.

$\frac{1}{2} \times 2 = 1$ $\frac{1}{2}$ and 2 are reciprocals.

$1 \div \frac{1}{2} = 2$ or $1 \div 2 = \frac{1}{2}$

To divide a whole number by a fraction, write the whole number as a fraction and then multiply it by the reciprocal of the divisor.

Example 3 Use the reciprocal to find $4 \div \frac{3}{5}$.

Step 1	Step 2	Step 3
Write the whole number as a fraction.	Use the reciprocal of the divisor to write a multiplication problem.	Multiply. Write the answer as a mixed number in simplest form.
$4 \div \frac{3}{5} = \frac{4}{1} \div \frac{3}{5}$	$\frac{4}{1} \div \frac{3}{5} = \frac{4}{1} \times \frac{5}{3}$ reciprocals $\frac{3}{5} \times \frac{5}{3} = 1$	$\frac{4}{1} \times \frac{5}{3} = \frac{20}{3}$, or $6\frac{2}{3}$

So, $4 \div \frac{3}{5} = 6\frac{2}{3}$.

More Examples

A $6 \div \frac{1}{3}$

$\frac{6}{1} \times \frac{3}{1} = \frac{18}{1} = 18$ related multiplication sentence

So, $6 \div \frac{1}{3} = 18$.

B $9 \div \frac{3}{4}$

$\frac{9}{1} \times \frac{4}{3} = \frac{36}{3} = 12$ related multiplication sentence

So, $9 \div \frac{3}{4} = 12$.

Guided Practice

1. Use the reciprocal of $\frac{7}{8}$ to write a multiplication problem to find $2 \div \frac{7}{8}$.

Find the quotient. Write it in simplest form.

2. $8 \div \frac{2}{3}$
3. $5 \div \frac{1}{10}$
4. $6 \div \frac{3}{5}$
5. $4 \div \frac{7}{8}$
6. $2 \div \frac{3}{4}$
7. TALK Math **Explain** two ways you can find $3 \div \frac{1}{4}$.

Independent Practice and Problem Solving

Find the quotient. Write it in simplest form.

8. $6 \div \frac{5}{12}$
9. $7 \div \frac{1}{2}$
10. $6 \div \frac{1}{4}$
11. $3 \div \frac{3}{10}$
12. $9 \div \frac{3}{4}$
13. $1 \div \frac{5}{9}$
14. $2 \div \frac{4}{5}$
15. $10 \div \frac{5}{6}$
16. $6 \div \frac{2}{3}$
17. $4 \div \frac{2}{5}$

Algebra **Find the missing number for each ■.**

18. $\frac{1}{4} \times \frac{■}{1} = 1$
19. $9 \times \frac{1}{■} = 1$
20. $\frac{7}{10} \times \frac{■}{7} = 1$
21. $5 \div \frac{1}{■} = 20$
22. $9 \div \frac{■}{3} = 27$
23. The fifth grade is painting scenery. It takes the students 9 hours to paint $\frac{3}{4}$ of the scenery. At this rate, how long will it take them to complete the scenery?
24. The fifth grade class is making posters for a play. If each poster is $\frac{2}{3}$ yard long, how many posters can the students make from 12 yards of banner paper?
25. WRITE Math **Explain** how to use multiplication to find $3 \div \frac{5}{8}$.

Mixed Review and Test Prep

26. Jamie wants to fold a rectangular paper along a line of symmetry to make two congruent pieces. How many different ways can she fold the paper? (Grade 4)
27. Of the 25 bikes on display, $\frac{2}{5}$ are red. How many bikes are red? (p. 392)
28. **Test Prep** Ellen cut 4 feet of ribbon into $\frac{1}{2}$-foot pieces. How many pieces did Ellen cut the ribbon into?

    A 2 **B** $3\frac{1}{2}$ **C** $4\frac{1}{2}$ **D** 8

Technology
CD ROM Use Harcourt Mega Math, Fraction Action, *Fraction Flare Up*, Level P.

 Extra Practice on page 410, Set D

Write to Prove or Disprove

When you are given an equation, you may have to decide whether it is true or false. You must understand the reasoning used to write the equation to be able to decide its validity.

It took students 1 hour to paint $\frac{1}{10}$ of a mural at the playground. The students will paint another mural that is three times as large as the playground mural. Glen estimates it will take $3 \div \frac{1}{10}$, or 30 hours to complete the mural. Raven estimates it will take $3 \div \frac{3}{10}$, or 10 hours. Read about how the students proved whose statement was true and whose statement was false.

First, we checked their computations:

Glen: $3 \div \frac{1}{10} = \frac{3}{1} \times \frac{10}{1} = \frac{30}{1} = 30$

Raven: $3 \div \frac{3}{10} = \frac{3}{1} \times \frac{10}{3} = \frac{30}{3} = 10$

Both quotients are correct.

Next, we looked for an error in reasoning.

Looking back at the time it takes to paint the playground mural, we wrote the following equation: $1 \div \frac{1}{10} = 10$.

It takes 10 hours to complete the playground mural. Raven's equation must be false since the larger mural will take more time.

We think Glen correctly recognized that he could multiply the time for the smaller mural by 3 to estimate the time for the larger mural.

Tips

Tips for Writing to Prove or Disprove

- Decide whether an equation is true.
- Demonstrate why an equation is true or false.
- Compare statements for errors in reasoning.
- Explain why an error in reasoning may have occurred.

Problem Solving Write to prove or disprove.

1. It takes Dennis 4 hours to complete $\frac{2}{5}$ of a painting. He estimates it will take 15 hours to complete a painting that is 5 times as large.

2. It takes Sasha 8 hours to complete $\frac{2}{3}$ of a sculpture. She estimates it will take 4 hours to complete a sculpture that is half the size.

LESSON 7

Divide Fractions

OBJECTIVE: Divide with fractions.

Quick Review

1. $\frac{1}{2} \times \frac{1}{6}$
2. $\frac{1}{4} \times \frac{2}{3}$
3. $\frac{5}{6} \times \frac{2}{5}$
4. $\frac{3}{4} \times \frac{3}{8}$
5. $\frac{1}{2} \times \frac{7}{10}$

Learn

PROBLEM For the school play, the drama teacher has $\frac{3}{4}$ yard of ribbon for costumes. Each costume needs $\frac{1}{12}$ yard of ribbon for trim. How many costumes can the teacher trim using $\frac{3}{4}$ yard?

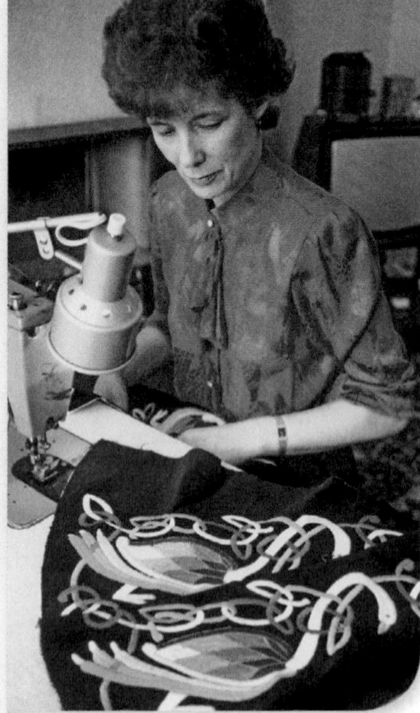

Divide. $\frac{3}{4} \div \frac{1}{12}$

ONE WAY **Use fraction bars.**

See how many $\frac{1}{12}$ bars are equal to three $\frac{1}{4}$ bars.

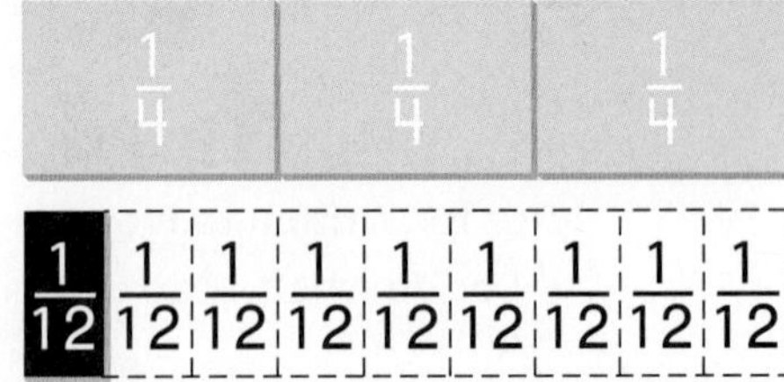

ANOTHER WAY **Use reciprocals.**

Step 1

Use the reciprocal of the divisor to write a multiplication problem.

$$\frac{3}{4} \div \frac{1}{12} = \frac{3}{4} \times \frac{12}{1}$$

reciprocals

$$\frac{1}{12} \times \frac{12}{1} = 1$$

Step 2

Multiply. Write the answer in simplest form.

$$\frac{3}{4} \times \frac{12}{1} = \frac{36}{4}, \text{ or } 9$$

$$\frac{3}{4} \div \frac{1}{12} = 9$$

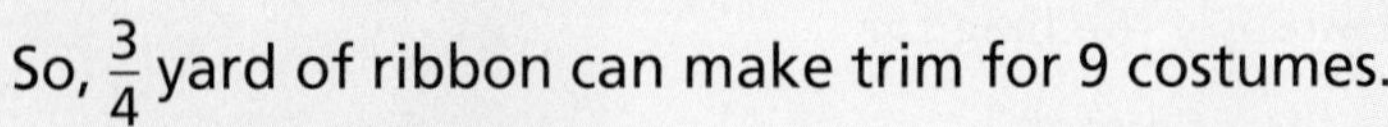

So, $\frac{3}{4}$ yard of ribbon can make trim for 9 costumes.

- How can you find the number of pieces of trim the teacher would have if each piece of trim were $\frac{1}{8}$ yard long?

Reciprocals and Mixed Numbers

You can use reciprocals to divide mixed numbers by fractions or by other mixed numbers. You can also use reciprocals to divide whole numbers by mixed numbers.

Example 1 **Divide.** $2\frac{1}{3} \div \frac{4}{9}$

Step 1	Step 2	Step 3
Write the mixed number as a fraction. $2\frac{1}{3} \div \frac{4}{9} = \frac{7}{3} \div \frac{4}{9}$	Use the reciprocal of the divisor to write a multiplication problem. $\frac{7}{3} \div \frac{4}{9} = \frac{7}{3} \times \frac{9}{4}$ (reciprocals: $\frac{4}{9}$ and $\frac{9}{4}$)	Multiply. Write the answer in simplest form. $\frac{7}{3} \times \frac{9}{4} = \frac{63}{12}$ $= \frac{21}{4}$, or $5\frac{1}{4}$

So, $2\frac{1}{3} \div \frac{4}{9} = 5\frac{1}{4}$.

Example 2 **Divide.** $2\frac{3}{4} \div 1\frac{1}{3}$

Step 1	Step 2	Step 3
Write the mixed numbers as fractions. $2\frac{3}{4} \div 1\frac{1}{3} = \frac{11}{4} \div \frac{4}{3}$	Use the reciprocal of the divisor to write a multiplication problem. $\frac{11}{4} \div \frac{4}{3} = \frac{11}{4} \times \frac{3}{4}$ (reciprocals: $\frac{4}{3}$ and $\frac{3}{4}$)	Multiply. Write the answer in simplest form. $\frac{11}{4} \times \frac{3}{4} = \frac{33}{16}$ $= 2\frac{1}{16}$

So, $2\frac{3}{4} \div 1\frac{1}{3} = 2\frac{1}{16}$.

- How is dividing by fractions different than dividing by mixed numbers? How is it similar?

Guided Practice

1. Use the model at the right to find $\frac{4}{6} \div \frac{1}{3}$.

   How many $\frac{1}{3}$ fraction bars fit into four $\frac{1}{6}$ fraction bars?

   What is $\frac{4}{6} \div \frac{1}{3}$?

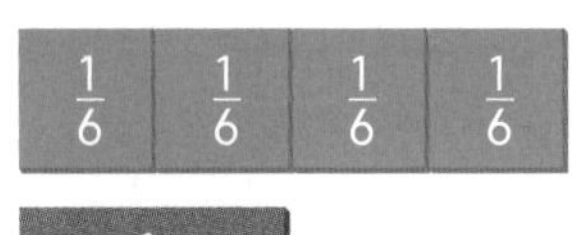

Write a division sentence for each model.

2.

3.

Divide. Write the answer in simplest form.

4. $\frac{3}{8} \div \frac{2}{3}$

5. $1\frac{1}{4} \div \frac{5}{6}$

6. $2\frac{1}{2} \div 1\frac{1}{3}$

7. $5 \div 2\frac{1}{8}$

8. $3\frac{1}{3} \div \frac{3}{8}$

9. TALK Math **Explain** how to use the reciprocal to find the quotient $2\frac{3}{4} \div 1\frac{1}{2}$.

Independent Practice and Problem Solving

Write a division sentence for each model.

10.

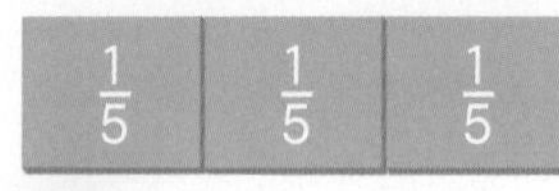

11.

Divide. Write the answer in simplest form.

12. $1\frac{3}{4} \div 2$

13. $\frac{5}{8} \div 4$

14. $1\frac{1}{2} \div \frac{3}{5}$

15. $\frac{5}{12} \div \frac{1}{3}$

16. $4\frac{1}{5} \div 3$

17. $3\frac{2}{3} \div 1\frac{1}{4}$

18. $1\frac{7}{8} \div \frac{1}{2}$

19. $2\frac{1}{6} \div 1\frac{2}{3}$

20. $6 \div 1\frac{1}{4}$

21. $1\frac{1}{2} \div 1\frac{3}{4}$

Algebra Copy and complete the function table.

22.

y	$\frac{1}{2}$	$\frac{5}{6}$	3
$y \div \frac{1}{8}$	■	■	■

23.

n	$\frac{3}{10}$	$\frac{4}{5}$	2
$n \div \frac{1}{5}$	■	■	■

24.

w	$\frac{1}{6}$	$\frac{2}{3}$	$1\frac{1}{6}$
$w \div \frac{1}{3}$	■	■	■

25. Simone has 12 yards of material to make costumes. She uses $4\frac{1}{2}$ yards for a dress. She uses the rest to make shirts. She needs $1\frac{1}{2}$ yards for each shirt. How many shirts can Simone make?

26. Kate has $7\frac{1}{2}$ yards of material to make capes for the school play. She uses $\frac{3}{4}$ yard to make each cape. How many capes can Kate make?

27. WRITE Math **Explain** how to find n if $\frac{5}{8} \div \frac{n}{3} = \frac{5}{8} \times \frac{n}{3}$. Then use that value for n to find the value of the expression $\frac{5}{8} \div \frac{n}{3}$.

 Extra Practice on page 410, Set E

Learn About ALGEBRA Inverse Operations

Multiplication and division are related operations. If $a \times b = c$, then $c \div b = a$ and $c \div a = b$. This relationship is true for fractions as well as for whole numbers. For example, if $2 \times 3 = 6$, then $6 \div 3 = 2$.

Examples **Use fraction circles to tell if the pair of number sentences is related.**

A $6 \times \frac{1}{3} = 2$.

Show six $\frac{1}{3}$ pieces.

How many wholes can you make?

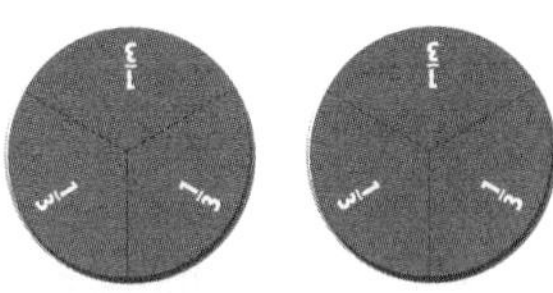

B $2 \div \frac{1}{3} = 6$.

Show two wholes.

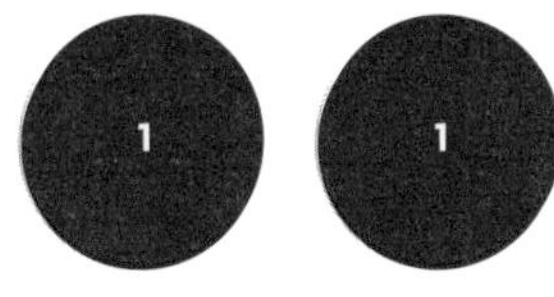

How many $\frac{1}{3}$ pieces can you make?

Since the models are similar, $6 \times \frac{1}{3} = 2$ and $2 \div \frac{1}{3} = 6$ are related number sentences.

Try It

Tell if the pair of number sentences is related.

28. $2 \times \frac{1}{2} = 1;\ 1 \div \frac{1}{2} = 2$

29. $8 \times \frac{1}{4} = 2;\ 8 \div 2 = 4$

30. $6 \times \frac{1}{3} = 2;\ 2 \div \frac{1}{3} = 6$

Mixed Review and Test Prep

31. Karl's last five bowling scores were 107, 136, 128, 107, and 109. What are the median and mode of his scores? (p. 220)

32. **Test Prep** An art teacher has $3\frac{1}{2}$ cups of paint powder. It takes $\frac{1}{3}$ cup of powder to make one jar of paint. How many jars of paint can the art teacher make?

33. If twelve $\frac{2}{3}$-cup servings of punch were used at a party, how many total cups of punch were used? (p. 392)

34. **Test Prep** Mona can ride a bike $8\frac{1}{2}$ miles in $\frac{3}{4}$ of an hour. How fast can she ride in miles per hour?

A $2\frac{5}{8}$ miles per hour

B $9\frac{1}{4}$ miles per hour

C $9\frac{2}{3}$ miles per hour

D $11\frac{1}{3}$ miles per hour

Problem Solving Workshop Skill: Choose the Operation

OBJECTIVE: Solve problems by using the skill *choose the operation.*

Use the Skill

PROBLEM The Mississippi Museum of Natural Science in Jackson has both indoor exhibits and outdoor habitats that display the different types of plants and animals found in the state. A class of 24 fifth-grade students went on a field trip to the museum. Of the students who went on the trip, $\frac{5}{8}$ were girls. How many of the students were girls?

▲ **The museum offers a hands-on program in which students can study the area's soil, plants, and water.**

The way numbers in a problem are related can help you choose the operation needed to solve the problem.

Add.	Combine amounts or groups.
Subtract.	Take away or compare amounts.
Multiply.	Combine equal amounts or groups.
Divide.	Separate into equal-sized groups; share equally; find out how many in each equal-sized group.

Since you are asked to find $\frac{5}{8}$ of the students, you can multiply to find how many of the students were girls.

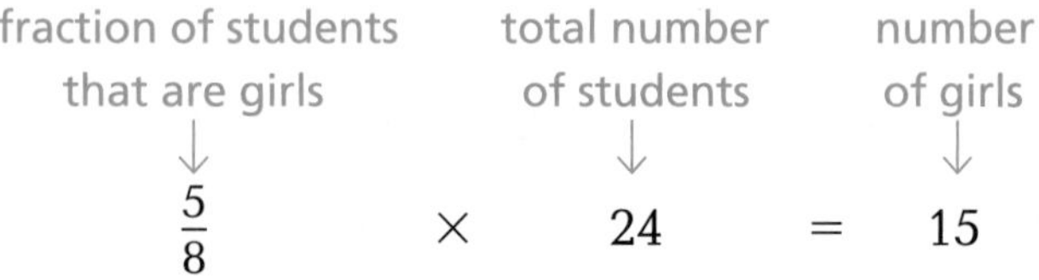

So, 15 of the students who went on the field trip were girls.

Think and Discuss

Decide how the numbers in the problem are related. Tell which operation you would use to solve the problem. Then solve.

At Jackson Elementary there are 120 fifth-grade students. Of the fifth-grade students, $\frac{1}{2}$ went on the field trip to the science museum, $\frac{1}{3}$ went on the field trip to the art museum, and $\frac{3}{4}$ went on the field trip to the history museum.

a. How many students went on each field trip?

b. What fraction of the students did not visit the art museum compared to the number that did not visit the history museum?

Guided Problem Solving

Tell which operation you would use to solve the problem. Then solve.

1. Mrs. Hall volunteers $\frac{1}{3}$ of the days each month at the Museum of Natural History and $\frac{1}{4}$ of the days each month at the Museum of Science. What fraction of the days each month does Mrs. Hall volunteer at both museums?

   Think: Which operation would you use to find the fraction of the days each month that Mrs. Hall volunteers at both museums?

Fraction of days at the Museum of Natural History		Fraction of days at the Museum of Science		Fraction of days at both museums
↓		↓		↓
$\frac{1}{3}$	$+$	$\frac{1}{4}$	$=$	■

2. **What if** Mrs. Hall volunteers $\frac{3}{8}$ of the days each month at the Museum of Natural History? What fraction of the days each month does Mrs. Hall volunteer at both museums?

3. Tanya has 10 fish in her aquarium. Of these fish, $\frac{2}{5}$ are goldfish. How many fish are goldfish?

Mixed Applications

USE DATA For 4–6, use the information at the right.

4. Carlos and Diane each attended one science program. Carlos attended the Hands-on Program, and Diane attended The Web of Life. How much longer did Carlos' program last than Diane's program? Tell which operation you will use to solve the problem. Then solve.

5. **Pose a Problem** Write a multistep problem that uses the information at the right. **Explain** the steps you would use to solve your problem.

6. **WRITE Math** The Web of Life video runs continuously for 3 hours. **Explain** how to find the number of times the video is shown during those 3 hours.

SCIENCE PROGRAMS
WETLANDS PROGRAM
Become a wetlands researcher.
Length of program: 1/2 hour
HANDS-ON PROGRAM
Use scientific skills and tools.
Length of program: 3/4 hour
THE WEB OF LIFE
Watch a science video.
Length of program: 1/3 hour

Extra Practice

Set A **Find the product. Write it in simplest form.** (pp. 390–391)

1. $\frac{2}{3} \times \frac{1}{3}$
2. $\frac{3}{4} \times \frac{4}{12}$
3. $\frac{1}{5} \times \frac{5}{10}$
4. $\frac{1}{2} \times \frac{2}{3}$
5. $\frac{2}{8} \times \frac{2}{4}$
6. $\frac{3}{6} \times \frac{2}{3}$
7. $\frac{1}{4} \times \frac{2}{5}$
8. $\frac{1}{2} \times \frac{5}{6}$
9. $\frac{1}{3} \times \frac{3}{8}$
10. $\frac{2}{5} \times \frac{1}{2}$

Set B **Find the product.** (pp. 392–393)

1. $6 \times \frac{1}{3}$
2. $\frac{2}{4} \times 5$
3. $4 \times \frac{3}{5}$
4. $\frac{1}{2} \times 7$
5. $8 \times \frac{2}{6}$
6. $\frac{1}{3} \times 9$
7. $\frac{3}{8} \times 10$
8. $7 \times \frac{2}{3}$
9. $15 \times \frac{3}{5}$
10. $\frac{5}{6} \times 9$

Set C **Find the product.** (pp. 394–397)

1. $\frac{1}{2} \times 2\frac{1}{5}$
2. $1\frac{2}{3} \times \frac{2}{6}$
3. $1\frac{3}{4} \times 2\frac{1}{2}$
4. $1\frac{3}{5} \times \frac{1}{3}$
5. $2\frac{1}{4} \times 1\frac{1}{8}$
6. A hiking trail is $7\frac{1}{8}$ miles long. Ramona hiked $\frac{3}{4}$ of the trail. How many miles did Ramona hike?
7. One lap around the lake is $3\frac{4}{5}$ miles long. Jake ran $\frac{1}{2}$ of a lap. How many miles did Jake run?

Set D **Find the quotient. Write it in simplest form.** (pp. 400–403)

1. $6 \div \frac{1}{2}$
2. $3 \div \frac{2}{3}$
3. $4 \div \frac{1}{8}$
4. $5 \div \frac{3}{10}$
5. $6 \div \frac{2}{5}$
6. $8 \div \frac{3}{4}$
7. $10 \div \frac{2}{5}$
8. $5 \div \frac{1}{2}$
9. $3 \div \frac{1}{6}$
10. $7 \div \frac{1}{5}$

Set E **Divide. Write the answer in simplest form.** (pp. 404–407)

1. $1\frac{1}{4} \div 4$
2. $2\frac{3}{6} \div \frac{1}{3}$
3. $2\frac{4}{10} \div \frac{1}{2}$
4. $\frac{6}{10} \div \frac{2}{5}$
5. $2\frac{2}{8} \div 1\frac{1}{4}$
6. Mariah has 15 yards of material to make curtains. She uses $2\frac{3}{4}$ yards to make each curtain. How many curtains can Mariah make?
7. Jen has $18\frac{1}{2}$ yards of material to make pillows for her friends. She uses $4\frac{1}{2}$ yards for each pillow. How many pillows can Jen make?

CD ROM **Technology**
Use Harcourt Mega Math, Fraction Action, *Number Line Mine*, Level L.

TECHNOLOGY CONNECTION

*i*Tools: Multiply Fractions

You can use the *Fractions* tool program to find the product of two fractions. For example, here is how to find $\frac{3}{4} \times \frac{2}{3}$.

Step 1	Click on *Fractions*. Then select *Multiply* from the *Activities* menu.
Step 2	Enter 3 for the *Number of columns.* This divides the rectangular box area into 3 unshaded columns.
Step 3	Shade $\frac{2}{3}$ of the area by dragging the orange arrow—below the box—to the right.
Step 4	Enter 4 for the *Number of rows*.
Step 5	Shade $\frac{3}{4}$ of the blue area by dragging up the orange arrow on the left.
Step 6	The area shaded green shows $\frac{3}{4}$ of $\frac{2}{3}$. You can see that 6 of the 12 rectangles are green. So, $\frac{3}{4} \times \frac{2}{3} = \frac{6}{12}$, or $\frac{1}{2}$.

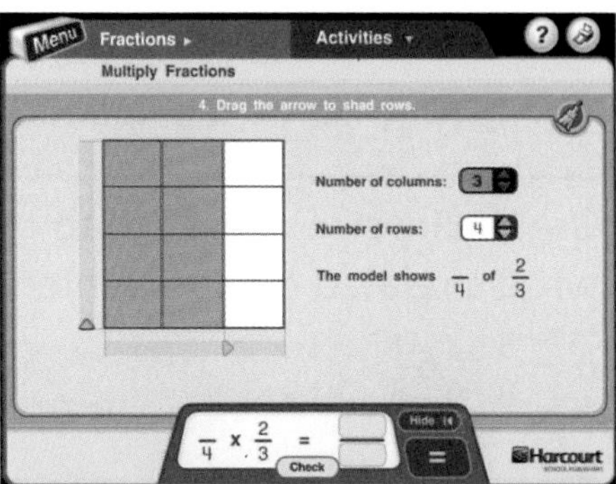

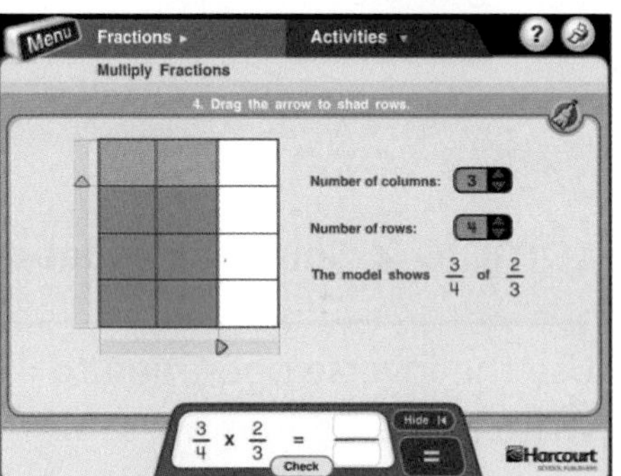

Try It

Follow the steps above to multiply. Write your answer in simplest form.

1. $\frac{1}{2} \times \frac{1}{3}$
2. $\frac{2}{5} \times \frac{1}{2}$
3. $\frac{3}{4} \times \frac{1}{3}$
4. $\frac{1}{4} \times \frac{1}{2}$
5. $\frac{1}{6} \times \frac{1}{3}$
6. $\frac{3}{5} \times \frac{5}{6}$
7. $\frac{3}{8} \times \frac{2}{3}$
8. $\frac{1}{6} \times \frac{3}{4}$
9. $\frac{4}{5} \times \frac{5}{8}$
10. $\frac{5}{9} \times \frac{1}{2}$
11. $\frac{7}{12} \times \frac{1}{4}$
12. $\frac{2}{3} \times \frac{3}{8}$

13. Explore More Multiply $\frac{1}{5} \times \frac{2}{3}$ and $\frac{2}{3} \times \frac{1}{5}$. How do the products compare? **Explain** how this is possible.

GO ONLINE **Technology**
*i*Tools are available online or on CD-ROM.

MATH POWER

Fraction Equations

GROW, BAMBOO, GROW

Bamboo plants grow incredibly fast. At noon a bamboo plant measured $6\frac{1}{8}$ feet in height. This was $\frac{5}{8}$ of a foot shorter than its height three hours later at 4 P.M. How tall was the plant at 4 P.M.?

To solve the problem, you can write the equation $h - \frac{5}{8} = 6\frac{1}{8}$ where h stands for the height of the plant at 4 P.M.

Example 1 **Solve the equation $h - \frac{5}{8} = 6\frac{1}{8}$.**

Use the inverse operation to write a related number sentence.

$h - \frac{5}{8} = 6\frac{1}{8}$

$6\frac{1}{8} + \frac{5}{8} = h$

Find the sum. Simplify.

$h = 6\frac{6}{8}$

$= 6\frac{3}{4}$

So, the plant was $6\frac{3}{4}$ feet tall at 4 P.M.

Example 2 **Solve the equation $s + 5\frac{2}{3} = 14\frac{3}{4}$.**

Use the inverse operation to write a related number sentence.

$s + 5\frac{2}{3} = 14\frac{3}{4}$

$14\frac{3}{4} - 5\frac{2}{3} = s$

Find the difference. Simplify.

$14\frac{9}{12} - 5\frac{8}{12} = s$

$9\frac{1}{12} = s$

So, in the equation $s + 5\frac{2}{3} = 14\frac{3}{4}$, $s = 9\frac{1}{12}$.

Try It

Solve the equation.

1. $a - \frac{2}{9} = \frac{4}{9}$

2. $n + \frac{5}{12} = \frac{11}{12}$

3. $2\frac{1}{8} = p - \frac{3}{8}$

4. $x + \frac{3}{10} = 5\frac{4}{5}$

5. $t - 3\frac{2}{7} = 8\frac{5}{7}$

6. $r - 6\frac{1}{2} = 9\frac{3}{8}$

7. $s + 7\frac{2}{5} = 10$

8. $q + 2\frac{1}{3} = 5\frac{1}{6}$

9. WRITE Math **Explain** why you need to rename to solve the equation $w + 3\frac{1}{2} = 5$.

Chapter 15 Review/Test

Check Vocabulary and Concepts

VOCABULARY
reciprocal
quotient

1. $\frac{3}{4}$ is the _____ of $\frac{4}{3}$. KY Grade 6 (p. 400)
2. What is the first step when you multiply with mixed numbers, using pencil and paper? KY Grade 6 (p. 394)

Check Skills

Find the product. Write it in simplest form. KY Grade 6 (pp. 390–391, 392–393, 394–397)

3. $\frac{1}{2} \times \frac{4}{10}$
4. $\frac{1}{3} \times \frac{4}{6}$
5. $\frac{6}{8} \times \frac{1}{3}$
6. $\frac{4}{8} \times \frac{1}{2}$
7. $6 \times \frac{1}{3}$
8. $\frac{1}{3} \times 9$
9. $\frac{2}{4} \times 5$
10. $\frac{1}{4} \times 1\frac{1}{2}$
11. $1\frac{2}{3} \times 1\frac{1}{4}$
12. $1\frac{1}{10} \times 2\frac{1}{2}$

Divide. Write the answer in simplest form. KY Grade 6 (pp. 404–407)

13. $\frac{4}{6} \div 5$
14. $1\frac{2}{3} \div 6$
15. $\frac{7}{8} \div \frac{1}{2}$
16. $\frac{3}{5} \div 4$
17. $2\frac{1}{4} \div 1\frac{1}{4}$
18. $1\frac{1}{8} \div 3$
19. $\frac{6}{7} \div \frac{1}{3}$
20. $2\frac{1}{5} \div 1\frac{2}{3}$
21. $1\frac{7}{8} \div 5$
22. $\frac{8}{9} \div \frac{1}{9}$

Check Problem Solving

Solve. KY Grade 6 (pp. 408–409)

23. Ryan spent $\frac{1}{4}$ of his time on reading homework and $\frac{1}{2}$ on math homework. He spent the remaining time on science homework. How much of his time did he spend on science homework? Solve. Write the operations you used.

24. The baseball team players practiced for 3 hours. They spent $\frac{2}{3}$ of the time on batting practice. How much time did they spend on batting practice? Solve. Write the operation you used.

25. **WRITE Math** Karen has 8 pints of punch. If each serving is $\frac{1}{2}$ pint. How many servings of punch does Karen have? **Explain.**

Unit Review/Test
Chapters 13–15

Multiple Choice

1. $\frac{3}{8} + \frac{4}{8} = \blacksquare$
   Write the answer in simplest form.
   KY MA-05-1.3.1 (p. 342)
   A. $\frac{12}{8}$
   B. $\frac{7}{8}$
   C. $\frac{7}{16}$
   D. $\frac{7}{64}$

2. Which sign should complete the sentence?
   KY MA-05-1.1.3 (p. 349)
   $\frac{2}{3} + \frac{1}{9} \bullet 1$
   A. $>$
   B. $<$
   C. $+$
   D. $=$

3. $\frac{3}{5} - \frac{1}{10} = \blacksquare$
   Write the answer in simplest form.
   KY MA-05-1.3.1 (p. 350)
   A. $\frac{3}{10}$
   B. $\frac{2}{5}$
   C. $\frac{1}{2}$
   D. $\frac{7}{10}$

4. Tony made a cherry pie for his family. His father and mother each ate $\frac{1}{4}$ of the pie. Tony ate the remaining pie. How much pie did Tony eat? KY MA-05-1.3.1 (p. 350)
   A. $\frac{3}{4}$
   B. $\frac{1}{3}$
   C. $1\frac{3}{4}$
   D. $\frac{1}{2}$

5. $\frac{4}{9} + \frac{2}{9} = \blacksquare$
   Write the answer in simplest form.
   KY MA-05-1.3.1 (p. 342)
   A. $\frac{1}{3}$
   B. $\frac{6}{9}$
   C. $\frac{2}{3}$
   D. $\frac{2}{9}$

6. Nadja is making a fruit salad. She used $\frac{2}{3}$ cup of grapes, $\frac{3}{4}$ cup strawberries, and $\frac{1}{8}$ cup of pineapple. About how many cups does this make? KY MA-05-1.3.1 (p. 350)
   A. 1 cup
   B. 2 cups
   C. 3 cups
   D. 4 cups

Technology Use *Online Assessment.*

7. What is the least common multiple of 16 and 12? KY MA-05-1.5.1 (p. 278)

   A. 3

   B. 4

   C. 36

   D. 48

8. What is 0.5 written as a fraction in simplest form? KY MA-05-1.1.3 (p. 326)

   A. $\frac{1}{5}$

   B. $\frac{1}{2}$

   C. $\frac{2}{3}$

   D. $\frac{5}{6}$

9. Which letter on the number line identifies the location of $1\frac{2}{3}$ KY MA-05-1.1.1 (p. 318)

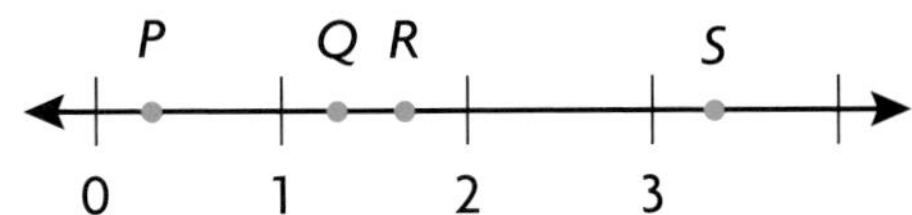

   A. P

   B. Q

   C. R

   D. S

Open Response WRITE Math

10. Mrs. Banek's class went on a field trip to a park. Before lunch they hiked $\frac{3}{4}$ mile. After lunch they hiked another $\frac{1}{3}$ mile. About how many miles did the class hike in all? Show your work. KY MA-05-1.2.1 (p. 348)

11. Find the mean of the following data. Explain how to find it. KY MA-05-4.2.1 (p. 220)
    207, 316, 127, 119, 316

12. On Friday, a tomato plant was $\frac{2}{3}$ foot tall. It had grown $\frac{1}{6}$ foot from Wednesday to Friday. It had grown $\frac{1}{12}$ foot from Monday to Wednesday. How tall was the plant on Monday? **Explain** your answer.
    KY MA-05-1.3.1 (p. 350)

13. What is the prime factorization of 96? Explain how to find it.
    KY MA-05-1.5.1 (p. 296)

THE WORLD ALMANAC FOR KIDS

The Planets

Around the Sun in One Year

It takes Earth about 365 days to orbit the sun. The farther away a planet is from the sun, the longer the planet's orbit takes. The closest planet to the sun, Mercury, orbits the sun in about 3 months, or $\frac{1}{4}$ of an Earth year. In 2006, scientists decided that Pluto should be called a "dwarf planet" instead of one of the main planets.

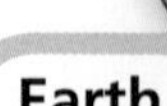

FACT·ACTIVITY

Use the table to answer the questions.

Planet Orbits—Time to Orbit the Sun

Planet	Earth	Jupiter	Mars	Mercury	Neptune	Saturn	Uranus	Venus
Time (in Earth years)	1	$11\frac{9}{10}$	$1\frac{9}{10}$	$\frac{1}{4}$	$164\frac{4}{5}$	$29\frac{2}{5}$	84	$\frac{4}{5}$

1. List the planets in order from least amount of time to greatest amount of time to orbit the sun.
2. How much longer than Earth does it take Mars to orbit the sun?
3. Which planet takes longer to orbit the sun, Saturn or Jupiter? How much longer?
4. Which planet takes about 7 times as long to orbit the sun as Jupiter?
5. How long in Earth years is $\frac{1}{2}$ of Neptune's orbit?
6. Jupiter's orbit is how many years longer than Mars' orbit?
7. **Pose a Problem** Write a problem similar to Problem 6, but change the planets. Ask a classmate to solve the problem.

ALMANAC Fact

If Earth were the size of a cherry, Jupiter, the largest planet, would be the size of a cantaloupe.

Space Adventure!

When you jump into the air, why don't you fly off into space? The force of *gravity* acting on your body is what keeps you on the ground. Every planet has gravity. A planet's gravitational pull depends on the planet's mass. The surface gravity of a planet determines an object's weight on the surface of the planet.

FACT·ACTIVITY

The table at right compares each planet's surface gravity to Earth's surface gravity. Suppose you are a space traveler. Your task is to design a space mission and then write a magazine article about the mission.

- Design a spacecraft and draw a picture of it. Decide how much your spacecraft will weigh.
- Estimate the total weight of the spacecraft on Earth. Include the weight of equipment, food, and a passenger.
- Choose three planets to visit. Make a table like the one below, and determine how much the total weight of your spacecraft will be on each planet.
- Write your story about your space adventure. Be sure to include the changes in the weight of your spacecraft.

Surface Gravity of Planets Compared to Earth's Surface Gravity

Planet	Number of Times Earth's Surface Gravity
Earth	1
Jupiter	$2\frac{1}{10}$
Mars	$\frac{2}{5}$
Mercury	$\frac{2}{5}$
Neptune	$1\frac{1}{10}$
Saturn	$\frac{3}{4}$
Uranus	$\frac{3}{4}$
Venus	$\frac{9}{10}$

Weight of Spaceship

Planet You Plan to Visit	Weight of Spacecraft on Earth	× Surface Gravity of Planet	= Weight of Spacecraft on Planet

UNIT 6

Ratio, Percent, and Probability

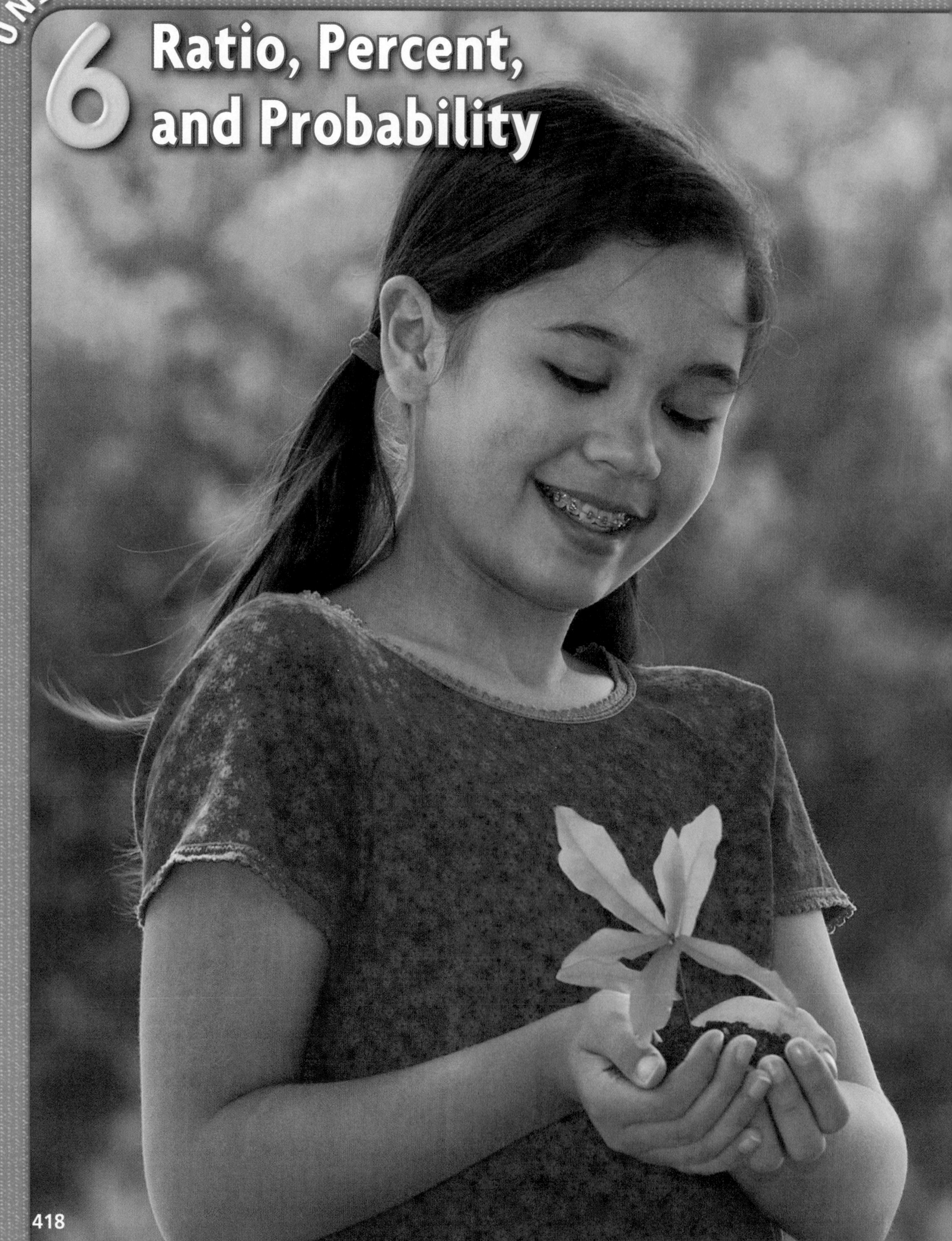

Math on Location

with
Chapter Projects

1

The engineering of the software that operates a robot minimizes the likelihood of failure.

2

Many interacting elements are put together to build the systems that make up a robot.

3

The robot is engineered with redundancy and backup systems to lessen its chances of failure.

VOCABULARY POWER

TALK Math

What math is used in the **Math on Location**? How might engineers reduce the likelihood of failure in building a robot?

READ Math

REVIEW VOCABULARY You learned the words below when you learned about ratio and probability. How do these words relate to **Math on Location**?

ratio the comparison of two quantities

likely having a greater-than-even chance of happening

unlikely having a less-than-even chance of happening

WRITE Math

Copy and complete a semantic map like the one below. Use what you know about probability to tell how likely it would be to roll a number cube labeled 1 through 6 in these ways.

Event	Probability
Roll a 1, 2, 3, or 4	likely
Roll a 6	unlikely
Roll a 3 or a 4	_____
Roll a number less than 7	_____
Roll a number greater than 1	_____
Roll a 1 or a 6	_____
Roll five 3s in a row	_____
Roll an odd number or an even number	_____

Technology
Multimedia Math Glossary link at
www.harcourtschool.com/hspmath

CHAPTER 16

Ratios and Percents

Investigate

A painter is mixing different paint colors. The formulas in the table show how many quarts of each color are needed for each of the paint colors. Choose two paint colors. If the painter uses 12 quarts of white paint, tell how many quarts of the other colors in the formula are needed to make each paint color.

Paint Color Formulas

Paint Color	Formula
Sea green	3 quarts white, 3 quarts yellow, 1 quart blue
Sky blue	4 quarts white, 1 quart blue
Lavender	6 quarts white, 1 quart blue, 1 quart red
Sun yellow	3 quarts white, 1 quart yellow

FAST FACT

In 2004, more than 809 million gallons of paint were sold for use in homes and buildings. More than one half of the paint was sold between the months of April and September.

GO ONLINE **Technology** Student pages are available in the Student eBook.

Show What You Know

Check your understanding of important skills needed for success in Chapter 16.

Relate Fractions and Decimals

Write a decimal and a fraction for the shaded part.

1. 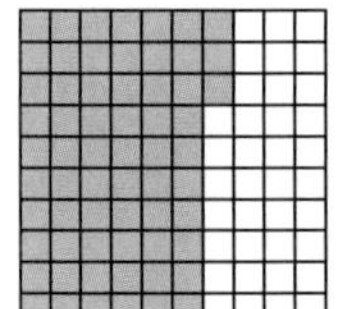

2. 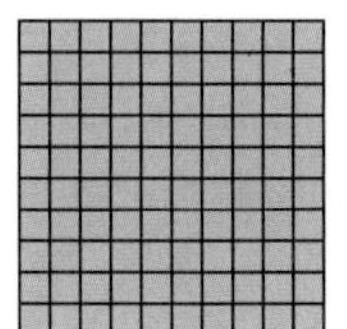 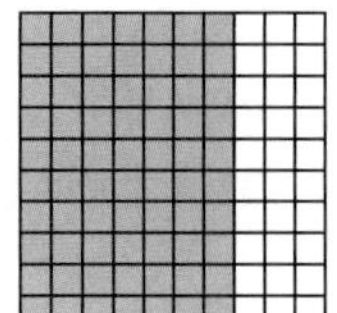

3. 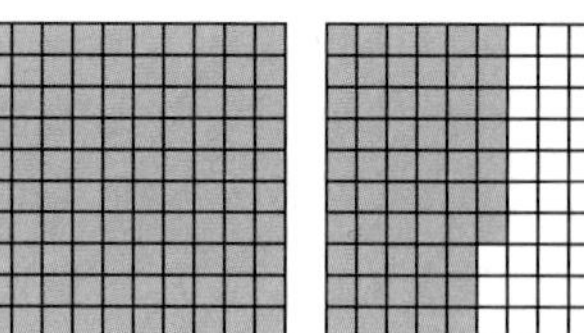

Write as a decimal.

4. $\frac{7}{10}$ **5.** $1\frac{13}{100}$ **6.** $\frac{3}{4}$ **7.** $3\frac{2}{5}$ **8.** $4\frac{8}{100}$

Write as a fraction or mixed number.

9. 1.5 **10.** 0.6 **11.** 7.44 **12.** 1.023 **13.** 18.001

Multiply Decimals by Whole Numbers

Find the product.

14. 0.25×4 **15.** 0.42×3 **16.** 0.76×5 **17.** 0.38×6 **18.** 0.84×9

19. 0.56×7 **20.** 0.19×8 **21.** 0.62×3 **22.** 0.47×9 **23.** 0.73×5

VOCABULARY POWER

CHAPTER VOCABULARY

equivalent ratios
map scale
percent
proportion
rate
ratio
scale drawing
unit rate

WARM-UP WORDS

equivalent ratios ratios that make the same comparisons

proportion an equation that shows that two ratios are equal

ratio the comparison of two quantities

Understand and Express Ratios

OBJECTIVE: Write part-to-part, part-to-whole, and whole-to-part ratios.

Quick Review

What fraction is blue?

1. ★★★
2. ☆★★★
3. ★☆
4. ★★★★★
5. ★★★

Vocabulary

ratio

Learn

PROBLEM Each of the 50 states has a state flag. The table shows the flags that have stars or eagles. How does the number of state flags with eagles compare with the number of state flags with stars?

The 50 State Flags		
Flags with Stars	AK, AR, AZ, CA, GA, ID, IL, IN, MA, ME, MN, MO, MS, NC, ND, NH, NV, OH, OR, RI, TN, TX, UT	23
Flags with Eagles	IA, IL, MI, ND, NY, OR, PA, UT	8

You can use a ratio to compare the number of flags. A **ratio** is the comparison of two quantities. A ratio can be written in three ways.

Write: 8 to 23 or 8:23 or $\frac{8}{23}$ ← first term, ← second term **Read:** eight to twenty-three

So, the ratio of state flags with eagles to state flags with stars is 8:23.

Math Idea

A ratio can compare a part to a part, a part to a whole, and a whole to a part. A ratio that compares a part to a whole also names a fraction.

Examples Write each ratio in three ways.

A Part to Part

state flags with stars to state flags with eagles

23 to 8 or 23:8 or $\frac{23}{8}$

B Part to Whole

state flags with stars to total number of state flags

23 to 50 or 23:50 or $\frac{23}{50}$

C Whole to Part

total number of state flags to state flags with stars

50 to 23 or 50:23 or $\frac{50}{23}$

Guided Practice

1. At the bottom of page 422, what is the ratio of stars to stripes on the third flag, the Ohio flag? $\frac{\text{number of stars}}{\text{number of stripes}} \rightarrow \frac{■}{■}$

Write each ratio in three ways. Then name the type of ratio.

2. stars to stripes
3. stripes to all figures
4. red to white
5. all figures to blue
6. stripes to stars
7. red stripes to blue stripes
8. TALK Math **Explain** why you need to write the numbers in a ratio in a certain order.

Independent Practice and Problem Solving

Write each ratio in three ways. Then name the type of ratio.

9. all figures to people
10. people to boats
11. boats to eagles
12. people to eagles
13. eagles to all figures
14. boats to all figures

USE DATA For 15 and 17, use the flags.

15. What is the ratio of stars to stripes on the 1777 United States flag?
16. **FAST FACT** In 1959, Alaska and Hawaii became the 49th and 50th states. The United States flag was then redesigned with 50 stars, one for each state, and 13 stripes, one for each original colony. Write the ratio of stars to stripes in three ways.
17. WRITE Math **Explain** which flags the ratio 15 to 20 might compare.

Three early versions of the United States flag

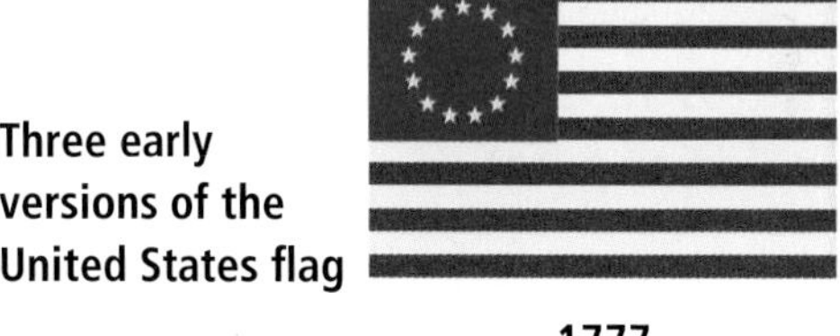

1777

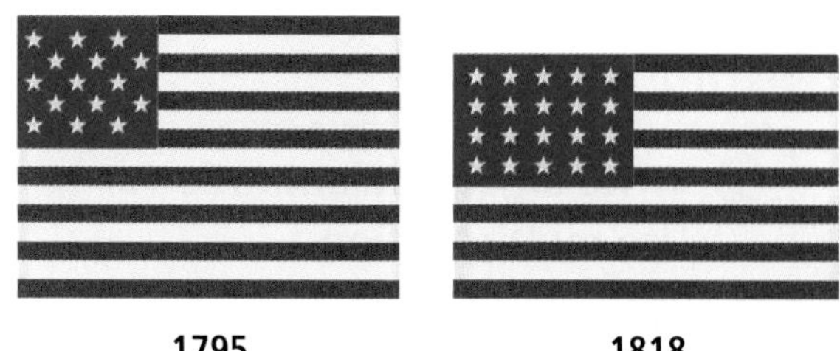

1795 1818

Mixed Review and Test Prep

18. Find the value of $a + 14$ if $a = 23$. (p. 96)
19. Hank ran $\frac{3}{4}$ mile each day. How far did Hank run in a week? (p. 390)
20. **Test Prep** Trent ate 2 slices of his pizza. There are 4 slices left. What is the ratio of slices eaten to all the slices?

A 2:4 **B** 4:2 **C** 6:4 **D** 2:6

Extra Practice on page 446, Set A

ALGEBRA

Equivalent Ratios and Proportions

OBJECTIVE: Identify and write equivalent ratios, and use proportional reasoning to solve problems.

Quick Review

1. 1×2
2. 3×2
3. 4×3
4. $8 \div 2$
5. $10 \div 5$

Vocabulary

equivalent ratios

proportion

Learn

PROBLEM Karen mixed paint in a ratio of 1 part blue to 2 parts red to make the color plum. Mike used a ratio of 3 parts blue to 6 parts red when he mixed his paint. Will Karen and Mike have the same color of paint?

Equivalent ratios are ratios that make the same comparisons.

Karen:	Mike:
1 part blue: 2 parts red	3 parts blue: 6 parts red

For 1 part blue, Karen used 2 parts red.	For each 1 part blue, Mike used 2 parts red.

Since the ratios 1:2 and 3:6 are equivalent, Karen and Mike mixed the same color of paint.

You can find an equivalent ratio by multiplying or dividing the first term and second term of the ratio by the same number.

Examples

A Write an equivalent ratio for $\frac{1}{4}$. Use multiplication.

Multiply the first term and the second term by the same number.

$$\frac{1}{4} = \frac{1 \times 3}{4 \times 3} = \frac{3}{12}$$

So, $\frac{1}{4}$ and $\frac{3}{12}$ are equivalent ratios.

B Write an equivalent ratio for $\frac{4}{8}$. Use division.

Divide the first term and the second term by the same number.

$$\frac{4}{8} = \frac{4 \div 4}{8 \div 4} = \frac{1}{2}$$

So, $\frac{4}{8}$ and $\frac{1}{2}$ are equivalent ratios.

Proportions

A paint set has a ratio of 2 paintbrushes to 12 pans of paint. In three of these paint sets, there is a ratio of 6 paintbrushes to 36 pans of paint, which is equivalent to 2:12.

These ratios can be used to write a proportion. A **proportion** is an equation that shows that two ratios are equal.

$$\frac{\text{number of brushes}}{\text{pans of paint}} \rightarrow \frac{2}{12} = \frac{6}{36} \leftarrow \frac{\text{number of brushes}}{\text{pans of paint}}$$

Activity

Materials ■ two-color counters

You can use counters to model proportions.

- Make the model shown here. Write the ratio of yellow counters to red counters.

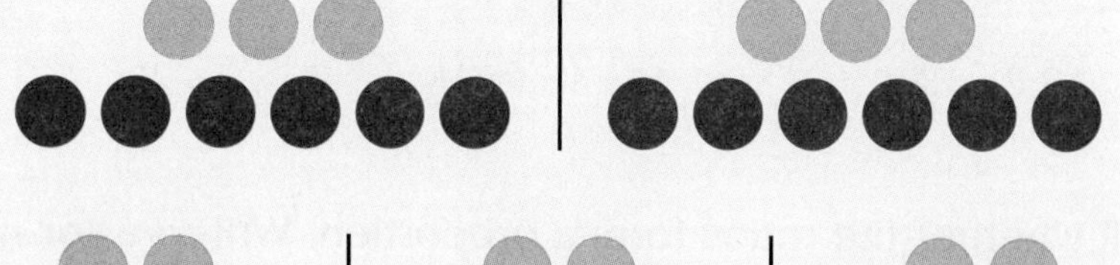

- Separate the yellow counters into two equal groups. Do the same with the red counters. Write the ratio of yellow to red in each group.

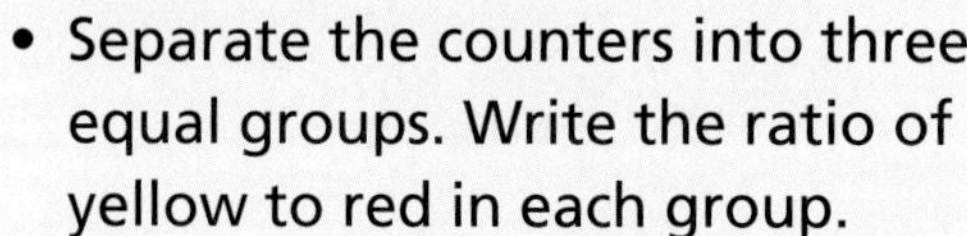

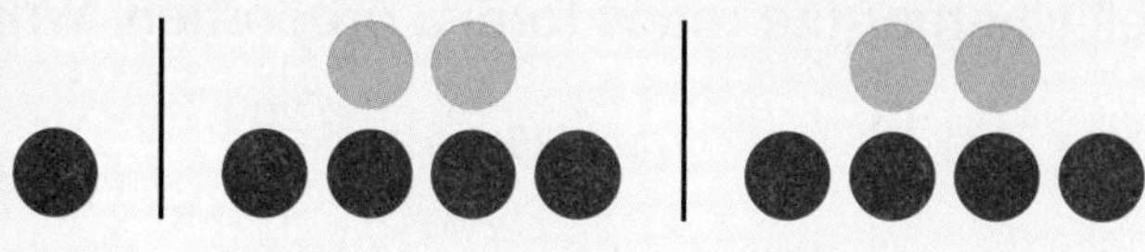

- Separate the counters into three equal groups. Write the ratio of yellow to red in each group.

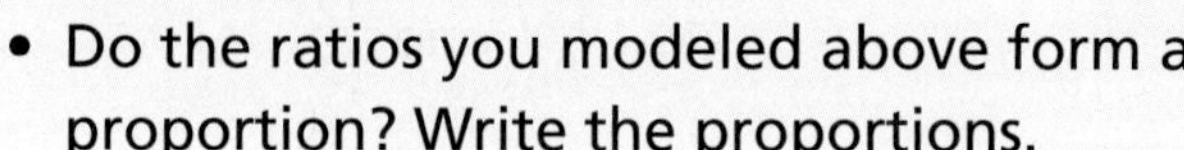

- Do the ratios you modeled above form a proportion? Write the proportions.

You can find an unknown value in a proportion by using multiplication or division.

Examples Find the unknown value.

C $\frac{9}{6} = \frac{n}{24}$ **Think:** What number times 6 equals 24?

$\frac{9 \times 4}{6 \times 4} = \frac{36}{24}$ Multiply both the first term and the second term by that number.

So, $n = 36$.

D $\frac{30}{66} = \frac{10}{n}$ **Think:** 30 divided by what number equals 10?

$\frac{30 \div 3}{66 \div 3} = \frac{10}{22}$ Divide both the first term and the second term by that number.

So, $n = 22$.

Guided Practice

Tell whether the ratios are equivalent. Write *yes* or *no*.

1. $\frac{2}{5}$ and $\frac{4}{10}$ **2.** 1 to 7 and 3 to 14 **3.** 8:4 and 4:2 **4.** $\frac{6}{9}$ and $\frac{9}{12}$

Write two equivalent ratios for each ratio. Use multiplication or division.

5. 1 to 5 **6.** 9:3 **7.** $\frac{3}{2}$ **8.** 4 to 6

Tell whether the ratios form a proportion. Write *yes* or *no*.

9. $\frac{1}{8}$ and $\frac{3}{20}$ **10.** $\frac{15}{5}$ and $\frac{45}{15}$ **11.** $\frac{16}{18}$ and $\frac{90}{140}$ **12.** $\frac{9}{12}$ and $\frac{3}{4}$

13. TALK Math **Explain** how you could write an equivalent ratio for 13:3.

Independent Practice and Problem Solving

Write two equivalent ratios for each ratio. Use multiplication or division.

14. 8 to 10 **15.** $\frac{20}{100}$ **16.** 33:6 **17.** $\frac{14}{4}$

18. 12:3 **19.** 16 to 18 **20.** $\frac{25}{7}$ **21.** 9 to 27

Tell whether the ratios form a proportion. Write *yes* or *no*.

22. $\frac{1}{3}$ and $\frac{13}{39}$ **23.** $\frac{4}{3}$ and $\frac{20}{16}$ **24.** $\frac{6}{15}$ and $\frac{30}{80}$ **25.** $\frac{6}{4}$ and $\frac{12}{8}$

26. $\frac{25}{70}$ and $\frac{100}{280}$ **27.** $\frac{9}{7}$ and $\frac{81}{63}$ **28.** $\frac{1}{8}$ and $\frac{1}{9}$ **29.** $\frac{121}{88}$ and $\frac{22}{14}$

Algebra Find the unknown value.

30. $\frac{6}{8} = \frac{x}{56}$ **31.** $\frac{7}{d} = \frac{49}{42}$ **32.** $\frac{v}{15} = \frac{10}{75}$ **33.** $\frac{136}{36} = \frac{34}{p}$

USE DATA For 34–35, use the directions on the paint can for making 1 gallon of Pumpkin Patch Orange.

34. For 4 gallons of Pumpkin Patch Orange, Mr. Lopez uses 8 parts red. How many parts yellow should he use?

35. Write a proportion to show the numbers of yellow to red parts you would need for 10 gallons of Pumpkin Patch Orange.

36. WRITE Math **What's the Error?** Nelson says that 2:3 and 3:4 form a proportion. **Explain** the error that Nelson made.

 Extra Practice on page 446, Set B

Learn About Graphs and Equivalent Ratios

When you graph equivalent ratios and connect the points with a line, a straight line is formed. Graphing the ratios can help you see the pattern and find other equivalent ratios.

Example

At a store, each gallon of paint costs $14. Jim buys three gallons of paint for $42. Andrea buys 2 gallons of paint for $28. How much do 4 gallons of paint cost?

Gallons of Paint	1	2	3	4
Cost	$14	$28	$42	■

Each column in the table names an ordered pair: (1,14), (2,28), (3,42) and so on. The ordered pairs are equivalent ratios.

Step 1

Draw a coordinate grid, and graph each ordered pair in the table.

Step 2

Graph a line through the points to 4 gallons of paint, and mark a point. Read the vertical scale to find the cost.

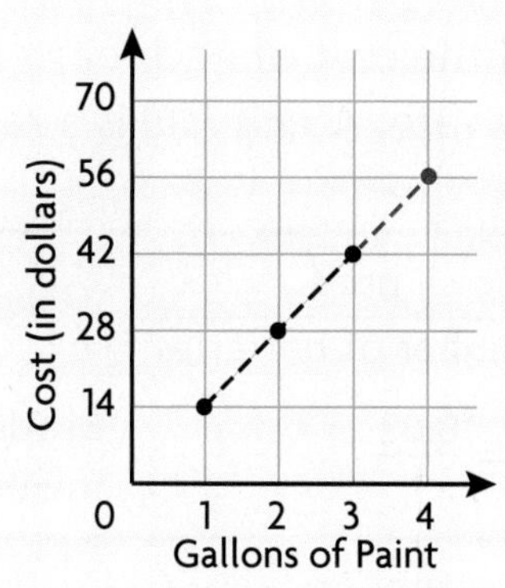

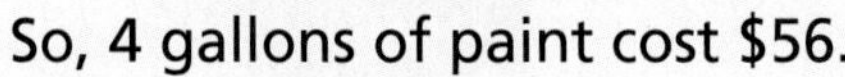

So, 4 gallons of paint cost $56.

Try It

Make a graph of the equivalent ratios. Then find the missing value.

37.

Gallons of Gas	1	2	3	4
Number of Miles	25	50	75	■

38.

Map Distance (in inches)	1	2	3	4
Actual Distance (in miles)	55	110	165	■

Mixed Review and Test Prep

39. What is the prime factorization of the number 106? (p. 298)

40. Test Prep To cook rice, the ratio is 2 cups of water to 1 cup of rice. Which ratio is equivalent to 2 to 1?

A 1:2 **C** 5:10

B 18:8 **D** 8:4

41. A necklace has 3 square beads and 4 round beads. What is the ratio of square beads to round beads? (p. 422)

42. Test Prep In the cafeteria, the ratio of chairs to tables is 8 to 1. The cafeteria has 32 tables. How many chairs are there?

A 4 **B** 8 **C** 246 **D** 256

LESSON 3

Ratios and Rates

OBJECTIVE: Find rates and unit rates.

Quick Review

1. 18×3
2. 12×6
3. $15 \div 5$
4. $36 \div 9$
5. $\$2.56 \div 4$

Vocabulary

rate

unit rate

Learn

A **rate** is a ratio that compares two quantities that have different units of measure.

$$\frac{\$14.88}{24} \begin{array}{l}\leftarrow \text{price} \\ \leftarrow \text{number of batteries}\end{array}$$

PROBLEM Mrs. Marquis bought a 24-pack of AA batteries for her photography class. At the rate $14.88 for 24 batteries, how much did Mrs. Marquis pay for each battery?

You can find the cost of each battery by finding the unit price, or unit rate. A **unit rate** is a rate that has 1 unit as its second term.

$\frac{14.88}{24} \begin{array}{l}\leftarrow \text{price} \\ \leftarrow \text{number of batteries}\end{array}$ Write the rate as a fraction.

$\frac{14.88 \div 24}{24 \div 24} = \frac{0.62}{1}$ Divide each term by 24 to find the unit cost.

So, the unit cost, or the cost of each battery, is $0.62.

Examples

A 288 miles on 12 gallons

$\frac{288}{12} \begin{array}{l}\leftarrow \text{miles} \\ \leftarrow \text{gallons}\end{array}$ Write the rate as a fraction.

$\frac{288 \div 12}{12 \div 12} = \frac{24}{1}$ Divide to find the unit rate.

$\frac{24}{1}$ ← 24 miles per gallon

B 82 words in 2 minutes

$\frac{82}{2} \begin{array}{l}\leftarrow \text{words} \\ \leftarrow \text{minutes}\end{array}$ Write the rate as a fraction.

$\frac{82 \div 2}{2 \div 2} = \frac{41}{1}$ Divide to find the unit rate.

$\frac{41}{1}$ ←.41 words per minute

C 150 miles in 3 hours

$\frac{150}{3} \begin{array}{l}\leftarrow \text{miles} \\ \leftarrow \text{hours}\end{array}$ Write the rate as a fraction.

$\frac{150 \div 3}{3 \div 3} = \frac{50}{1}$ Divide to find the unit rate.

$\frac{50}{1}$ ← 50 miles per hour

When an item comes in different sizes or quantities, you can compare unit rates to find the best buy.

Example Find the better buy for 35-mm film.

$3.12 for 24 exposures	$5.76 for 36 exposures
$\frac{3.12 \div 24}{24 \div 24} = \frac{0.13}{1}$	$\frac{5.76 \div 36}{36 \div 36} = \frac{0.16}{1}$

Since $\$0.13 < \$0.16$, the 24-exposure film is the better buy.

Guided Practice

Write each ratio in fraction form.

1. 240 miles in 4 hours
2. 130 miles in 2 hours
3. $1.50 for 2 pounds of apples

Write each ratio in fraction form. Then find the unit rate.

4. 30 pens in 5 packages
5. $64 for 8 hours of work
6. 18 dog walks in 6 days
7. 4.5 hours to write 6 pages
8. 770 miles in 14 hours
9. $2.16 for 12 juice boxes
10. TALK Math **Explain** how to find the unit price for a 24-ounce bottle of orange juice that costs $2.64.

Independent Practice and Problem Solving

Write each ratio in fraction form. Then find the unit rate.

11. $45 saved in 3 weeks
12. 50 minutes for 100 laps
13. 24 pages in 6 days
14. 190 seconds for 38 sit-ups
15. 96 grams in 2 cans
16. $3.24 for 12 eggs
17. 54 wheels on 3 semi-trucks
18. $8.20 for 20 stamps
19. 120 points in 8 games

USE DATA For 20–21, use the advertisement.

20. Mrs. Sharp buys a 5-pound package of ground turkey. What is the unit rate?
21. Which package of hamburger buns is the better buy?
22. **FAST FACT** One tablespoon of ketchup has 16 calories. How many calories are in 6 tablespoons of ketchup?
23. WRITE Math **Sense or Nonsense** Morris says he can do 300 jumping jacks in 50 seconds. Does this rate make sense? **Explain.**

2-pound package of ground turkey for **$7.98**

5-pound package of ground turkey for **$17.45**

package of 8 hamburger buns for **$1.44**

package of 12 hamburger buns for **$1.92**

32-ounce bottle of ketchup for **$2.56**

Mixed Review and Test Prep

24. What is the unknown value in the proportion $\frac{9}{12} = \frac{3}{n}$? (p. 424)
25. Find the product. $\frac{1}{5} \times \frac{1}{4}$. (p. 390)
26. **Test Prep** Roma buys 8 cups of limeade for $6.00. What is the unit rate?

    A $48.00 **C** $1.33
    B $6.00 **D** $0.75

Extra Practice on page 446, Set C

LESSON 4

Understand Maps and Scales

OBJECTIVE: Read and interpret a scale on a map

Quick Review

Write an equivalent fraction.

1. $\frac{1}{10}$
2. $\frac{2}{50}$
3. $\frac{4}{120}$
4. $\frac{3}{9}$
5. $\frac{5}{150}$

Vocabulary

scale drawing

map scale

Learn

A map is a scale drawing. A **scale drawing** is a reduced or enlarged drawing whose shape is the same as an actual object and whose size is determined by the scale. The ratio that compares the distance on a map to the actual distance is the **map scale**.

PROBLEM The map shows some of the streets in Mesa, Arizona. What is the actual distance from the corner of East McDowell Road and North Lindsay Road to the corner of North Lindsay Road and East Baseline Road?

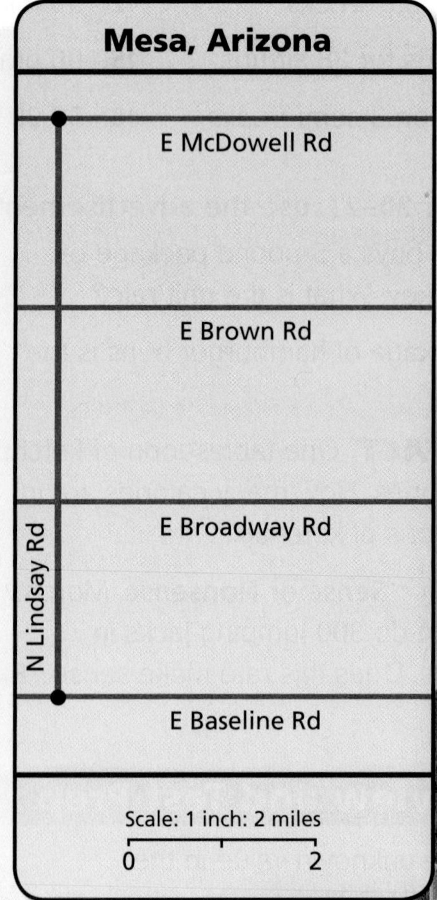

ONE WAY Use a table of ratios.

Step 1

Read the map scale, and write the ratio as a fraction. The map shows a scale of $\frac{1 \text{ inch}}{2 \text{ miles}}$.

Step 2

Use a ruler to measure the distance in inches from the corner of East McDowell Road and North Lindsay Road to the corner of North Lindsay Road and East Baseline Road. The distance is about 3 inches.

Step 3

Make a table to show the ratios.

Map Distance (in.)	1	2	3
Actual Distance (mi)	2	4	■

Complete the ratio table to find the actual distance when the map distance is 3 inches.

$$3 \times 2 = 6$$

So, the actual distance is about 6 miles.

Map Scale and Proportions

ANOTHER WAY **Use a proportion.**

Use the map to find the distance from Cimic to Waggoner.

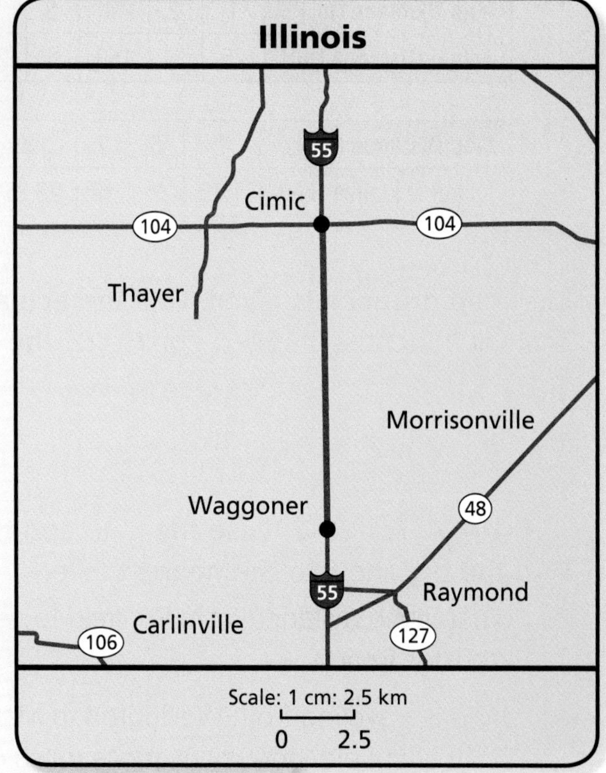

Step 1

Read the map scale, and write the ratio as a fraction.

$$\frac{1}{2.5} \begin{array}{l} \leftarrow \text{centimeter} \\ \leftarrow \text{kilometers} \end{array}$$

Step 2

Use a ruler to measure the distance from Cimic to Waggoner.

The distance is about 4 centimeters on the map.

Step 3

Use multiplication to find the actual distance.

$$\frac{1}{2.5} = \frac{4}{n} \qquad \frac{1 \times 4}{2.5 \times 4} = \frac{4}{10} \qquad n = 10$$

So, the distance from Cimic to Waggoner is about 10 kilometers.

Guided Practice

1. A map scale is 2 inches to 10 feet. Solve the proportion to find the actual distance. Think: $2 \times 6 = 12$, so $10 \times 6 = \blacksquare$. $\quad \begin{array}{l}\text{inches} \rightarrow \\ \text{feet} \rightarrow\end{array} \frac{2}{10} = \frac{12}{n}$

Copy and complete the ratio table.

2.

Map Distance (in.)	1	2.5	■	4	■
Actual Distance (mi)	50	■	150	■	500

3.

Map Distance (in.)	1	■	5.9	■	12.1
Actual Distance (ft)	6	18	■	54	■

4.

Map Distance (cm)	1	3	8	■	■
Actual Distance (km)	3.8	■	■	41.8	57

5.

Map Distance (cm)	2	4	■	■	12
Actual Distance (m)	120	■	360	480	■

The map distance is given. Find the actual distance. The scale is 1 inch:200 miles.

6. 4 in.
7. 2.5 in.
8. 3.6 in.
9. 0.25 in.

10. **TALK Math** **Explain** how you would find the actual distance from one city to another city if the measured distance on a map is 4 inches and the map scale is 1 inch:50 miles.

Independent Practice and Problem Solving

Copy and complete the ratio table.

11.

Map Distance (in.)	1	2	■	8	■
Actual Distance (mi)	25	■	150	■	275

12.

Map Distance (in.)	1	■	5	■	20
Actual Distance (ft)	2.4	7.2	■	24	■

13.

Map Distance (cm)	1	6	7	■
Actual Distance (km)	1.75	■	■	26.25

14.

Map Distance (cm)	3	4	■	■
Actual Distance (m)	75	■	137.5	210

The map distance is given. Find the actual distance. For 15–18, the scale is 2 inches:70 miles. For 19–22, the scale is 1 cm:9.2 km.

15. 1.2 in. **16.** 5 in. **17.** 0.8 in. **18.** 3 in.

19. 0.45 cm **20.** 6 cm **21.** 2.3 cm **22.** 9 cm

USE DATA For 23–25, use the map and the map scale. Find the distance, to the nearest mile.

23. What is the distance from Penfield to Webster Road?

24. John is traveling from Wellington to Mallet Creek. From Litchfield, how many more miles does he have to travel to get to Mallet Creek?

25. **Reasoning What if** the scale was 1 inch:3 miles? About how many inches would the distance from Wellington to Litchfield measure on the map?

26. WRITE Math Suppose you wanted to use a scale of 1 in:1 yd or 1 in:1 mi to make a map of your school. **Explain** which scale would be better.

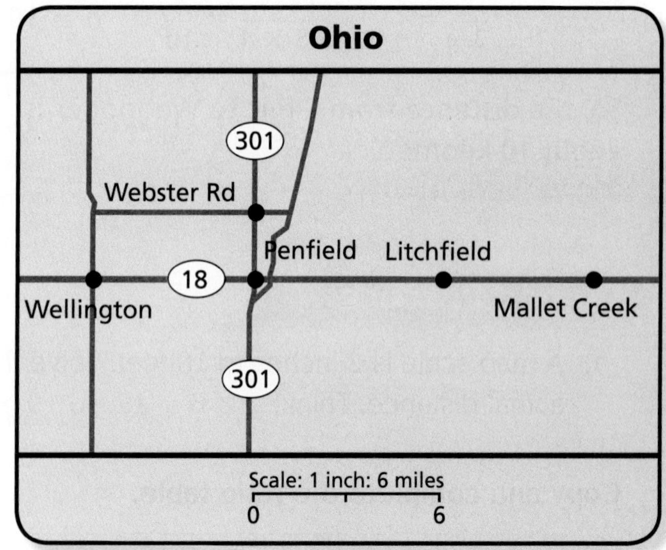

Mixed Review and Test Prep

27. A box that holds trading cards is 15 inches long, 7 inches wide, and 5 inches tall. What is the box's volume? (Grade 4)

28. A 12-ounce package of American cheese costs $2.79. What is the unit price to the nearest cent? (p. 428)

29. **Test Prep** Leah draws a map of her town, using a scale of 1 cm = 3 km. The actual distance between Leah's house and her school is about 7.5 kilometers. What is the distance on the map?

A 2 cm **C** 2.75 cm

B 2.5 cm **D** 3 cm

 Extra Practice on page 446, Set D

Cross Country

Sequence

Deanna flew from Sacramento, CA, to Albany, NY. From Sacramento, Deanna flew 525 miles. Then Deanna changed flights and flew another 2,100 miles. Her last flight was 145 miles. The map shows some possible flights. Which cities and in which order were the flights Deanna took from Sacramento, CA, to Albany, NY?

Knowing the sequence, or order, of the flight distances will help you solve the problem.

Read the problem, and put the distances in sequence.

First flight:	From Sacramento, 525 miles
Second flight:	2,100 miles
Third flight:	145 miles

Problem Solving **Use a sequence to solve the problems.**

1. Solve the problem above.
2. Edmund flew from Jackson, MS, to Columbus, OH. From Jackson, Edmund flew 350 miles. Then Edmund changed flights and flew 1,000 miles. The map shows some possible flights. Through which cities and in which order were the flights Edmund took from Jackson, MS, to Columbus, OH?

Problem Solving Workshop
Strategy: Make a Table

OBJECTIVE: Solve problems by using the strategy *make a table*.

Learn the Strategy

Making a table can help you record and group data so that a problem is easier to solve. You can use different types of tables to show different types of problems.

A table can display data.

Cliff made a table to record the morning and evening temperatures each day at the same time.

Daily Temperature Changes (in °F)

	Mon	Tue	Wed	Thu	Fri	Sat	Sun
6:00 A.M.	31°	29°	28°	32°	32°	29°	34°
6:00 P.M.	42°	44°	48°	52°	48°	46°	57°

A table can show relationships.

Mia sells T-shirts at Logo. She charges $6.50 for each T-shirt.

Logo Cost Chart

Number of T-Shirts	1	2	5	10
Total Price	$6.50	$13.00	$32.50	$65.00

A table can show frequency.

Times Computer Users Logged On

(from 9:00 A.M. to 2:59 P.M.)

9:10, 9:00, 12:20, 11:45, 2:00,

2:50, 9:05, 11:55, 2:45, 10:30,

2:15, 1:05, 12:00, 11:00, 9:00,

1:30, 2:15, 10:00, 9:50, 1:00

Times Computer Users Logged On

Time of Day	Frequency
9:00 A.M. – 9:59 A.M.	5
10:00 A.M. – 10:59 A.M.	2
11:00 A.M. – 11:59 A.M.	3
12:00 A.M. – 12:59 P.M.	2
1:00 P.M. – 1:59 P.M.	3
2:00 P.M. – 2:59 P.M.	5

When making a table to solve a problem, consider the best way to organize the given information. Read the problem carefully to identify what you are being asked to find. Design the table so that it will help you answer the question.

TALK Math

What questions can be answered using each of the tables shown?

Use the Strategy

PROBLEM At a science museum, Margo spent some time at a moon exhibit. She listened to a recording of Neil Armstrong's famous words "That's one small step for man, one giant leap for mankind." At the exhibit, Margo also read that Neil Armstrong, wearing his suit and backpack, weighed 360 pounds on Earth but only 60 pounds on the moon. How much would Margo weigh on the moon if she weighs 75 pounds on Earth?

Read to Understand

- **What details can you identify in the problem?**
- **What details will you use?**

Plan

- **What strategy can you use to solve the problem?**

You can make a table of equivalent ratios to help you solve the problem.

Solve

- **How can you use the strategy to solve the problem?**

Write the ratio, $\frac{360}{60}$, in a table. Then find equivalent ratios.

Think: How can I move from 360 to 75 using equivalent ratios?

$$75 = 60 + 15$$

Find equivalent ratios with 60 and 15 as the weights on Earth.

Divide 360 and 60 by 6 to get an Earth weight of 60.

$\frac{360 \div 6}{60 \div 6} = \frac{60}{10}$ ← weight on Earth / ← weight on the moon

Divide 60 and 10 by 4 to get an Earth weight of 15.

$\frac{60 \div 4}{10 \div 4} = \frac{15}{2.5}$ ← weight on Earth / ← weight on the moon

ADD

Weight on Earth (in pounds)	360	60	15	75
Weight on the Moon (in pounds)	60	10	2.5	■

Since 60 + 15 = 75, add 10 and 2.5 to find Margo's weight on the moon.

So, Margo would weigh 12.5 pounds on the moon.

Check

- **What other equivalent ratios could you use to solve the problem?**

Read to Understand
Plan
Solve
Check

Guided Problem Solving

1. At the science museum, Jacob learned that the more gravity a planet has, the more a person will weigh. Jacob weighs 85 pounds. He found out that his weight on Mars would be 32 pounds. Earth has more gravity than Mars. Jacob's science teacher found that he would weigh 72 pounds on Mars. How much does Jacob's science teacher weigh on Earth?

   First, make a table and enter the ratio of Jacob's weights.

   Then, decide how to go from 32 to 72.
   $72 = 64 + 8$ $32 \times 2 = 64$ $64 \div ■ = 8$

   Finally, complete the ratio table to find the science teacher's weight on Earth.

Weight on Mars (in pounds)	32	64		72
Weight on Earth (in pounds)	85	170		■

2. **What if** Jacob's science teacher would weigh 80 pounds on Mars? How much would he weigh on Earth?

3. Tania weighs 80 pounds on Earth and would weigh 77 pounds on Venus. Tania's father weighs 200 pounds. How much would Tania's father weigh on Venus?

Problem Solving Strategy Practice

Make a table to solve. For 5–6, use the information in the picture.

4. In one weightlifting competition, there are three age groups: youth, 17 years old and younger; juniors, 18–19 years old; and seniors, 20 years old or older. The ages of the competitors are 16, 25, 19, 17, 28, 22, 20, 19, 20, 15, 17, 18, 23, and 25. How many competitors are in each age group?

5. WRITE Math Since the moon has less gravity, a weightlifter would be able to lift more on the moon than on Earth. Suppose a weightlifter on Earth lifted 200 kg. What would be an equivalent mass to lift on the moon? **Explain** your answer.

6. At a weightlifting competition on the moon, the greatest masses lifted were 918 kg, 1,005 kg, and 1,206 kg. At a weightlifting competition on Earth, the greatest masses lifted were 215 kg, 192 kg, and 195 kg. The winner of each competition lifted the greatest mass. List the masses from Earth and the moon in order from greatest to least. Which mass is the greatest?

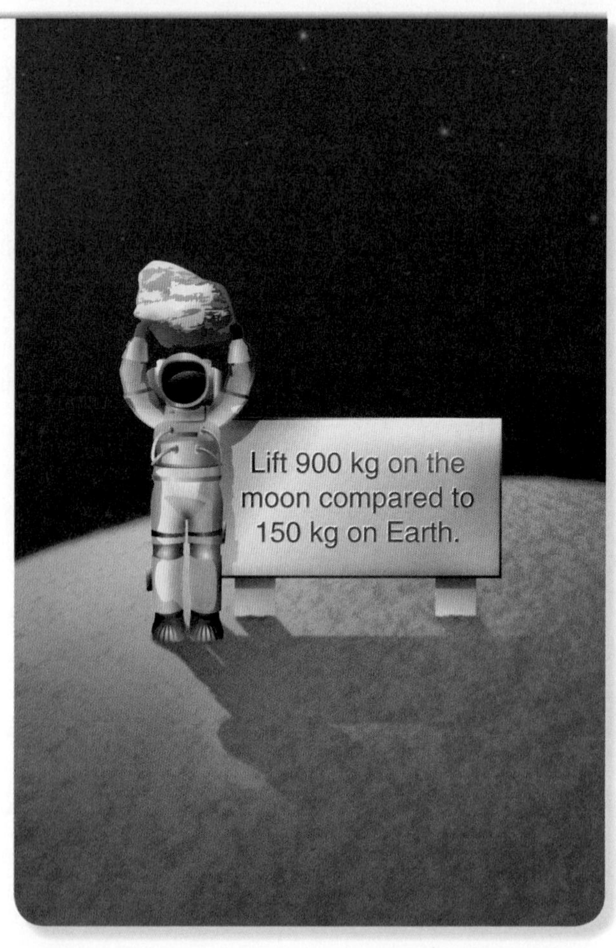

Lift 900 kg on the moon compared to 150 kg on Earth.

Mixed Strategy Practice

USE DATA For 7–10, use the information in the picture.

7. The diameter of Venus is 405 miles less than Earth's. Mercury's diameter is 1,186 miles less than that of Mars. Write the diameters of the first four planets, known as the inner planets, in order from greatest to least.

8. The diameter of Jupiter is 1,544 miles more than 11 times the diameter of Earth. What is the diameter of Jupiter?

9. A planet's orbit around the sun is not a perfect circle. So a planet's distance from the sun has a minimum and maximum distance shown in the picture. What are Earth's, Mars', and Saturn's average distances from the sun?

10. **Pose a Problem** Look back at Problem 8. Write a similar problem by changing the planets.

11. **Open-Ended** Suppose you wanted to make a model of the planets. How could you use the diameters of the planets to show the size of each planet in relation to the other planets?

CHALLENGE YOURSELF

The speed needed for an object to leave the gravitational field of a planet and travel into space is the planet's *escape velocity.* Neptune has an escape velocity of 52,794 mph. Earth's escape velocity is 25,055 mph.

12. Pluto, now named a dwarf planet, has an escape velocity that is 835.9 miles per minute less than Neptune's escape velocity in miles per minute. What is the escape velocity from Pluto in miles per minute and miles per hour?

13. The escape velocity from Saturn is 54,584 miles per hour greater than the escape velocity from Earth. The escape velocity from Jupiter is 53,465 miles per hour greater than the escape velocity from Saturn. What is the escape velocity from Jupiter?

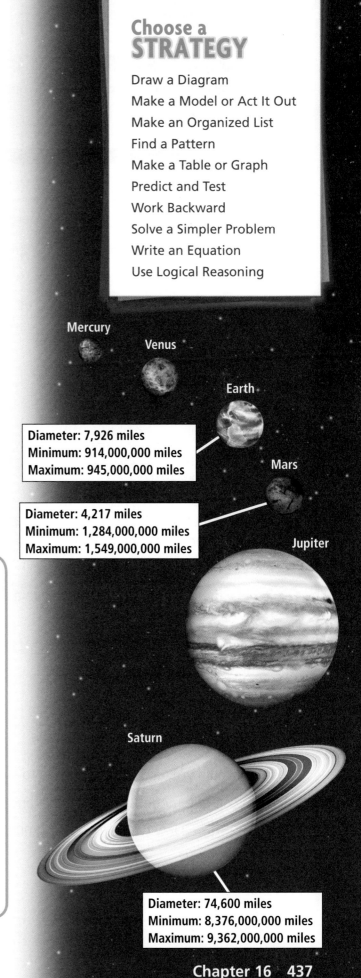

Choose a STRATEGY

- Draw a Diagram
- Make a Model or Act It Out
- Make an Organized List
- Find a Pattern
- Make a Table or Graph
- Predict and Test
- Work Backward
- Solve a Simpler Problem
- Write an Equation
- Use Logical Reasoning

Mercury

Venus

Earth

Diameter: 7,926 miles
Minimum: 914,000,000 miles
Maximum: 945,000,000 miles

Mars

Diameter: 4,217 miles
Minimum: 1,284,000,000 miles
Maximum: 1,549,000,000 miles

Jupiter

Diameter: 74,600 miles
Minimum: 8,376,000,000 miles
Maximum: 9,362,000,000 miles

LESSON HANDS ON

6 Understand Percent

OBJECTIVE: Model, read, and write percents.

Quick Review

Write an equivalent fraction with a denominator of 100.

1. $\frac{1}{4}$
2. $\frac{3}{10}$
3. $\frac{4}{5}$
4. $\frac{8}{25}$
5. $\frac{25}{50}$

Vocabulary

percent

Investigate

Materials ■ 10 by 10 grids ■ color pencils

You can use a 10 by 10 grid to explore percent.

Percent is the ratio of a number to 100. *Percent*, or %, means "per hundred."

A On one 10 by 10 grid, shade 5 squares. On four other grids, shade 10 squares, 25 squares, 50 squares, and 75 squares.

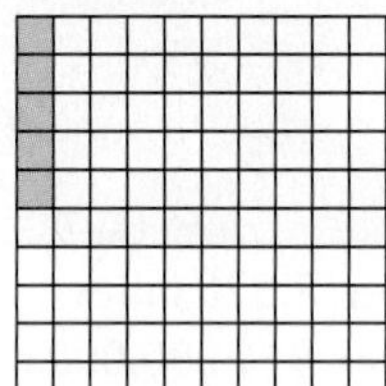

$\frac{5}{100}$; 0.05

B Write a fraction and a decimal below each model to show what part of the shaded squares are the total squares.

C Review the definition of *percent*. Write a percent below each of your models.

D Now use another 10 by 10 grid to show 30%.

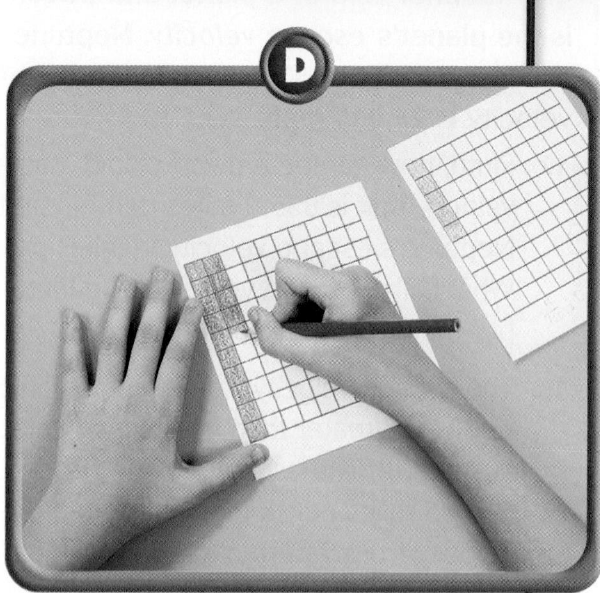

Draw Conclusions

1. Explain how you determined the percent for each model.
2. How would you use a 10 by 10 grid to show $\frac{1}{2}$?
3. Why can one model show $\frac{50}{100}$, 0.50, and 50%?
4. **Application** How would you show 200%, using 10 by 10 grids?

Connect

The table shows the results of a survey of 100 students. Students were asked which technology was the most important to them. You can use a fraction, a decimal, and a percent to represent each result.

Remember that *percent* means "per hundred." So, 26 out of 100, 0.26, or 26% of students chose notebook computers.

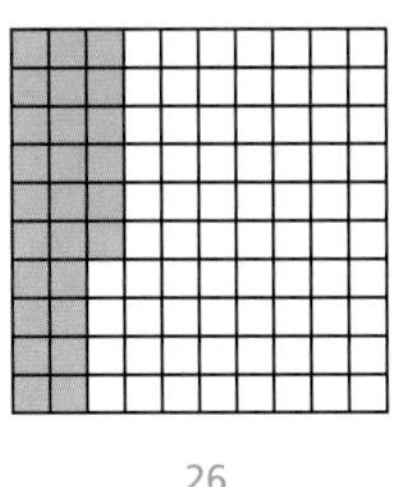

$\frac{26}{100}$
0.26
26%

Technology Survey

Technology	Number of Students
Notebook Computers	26
Portable MP3 Players	12
Personal Digital Assistants	5
Digital Cameras	4
Cell Phones	53

- Make a model for each type of technology, and label each model with a fraction, a decimal, and a percent.

TALK Math

Explain how you could model all of the data on one grid. How many squares would you shade?

Practice

Write a fraction and a percent to represent the shaded part.

1. 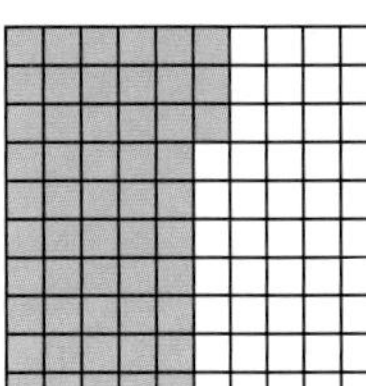

2. 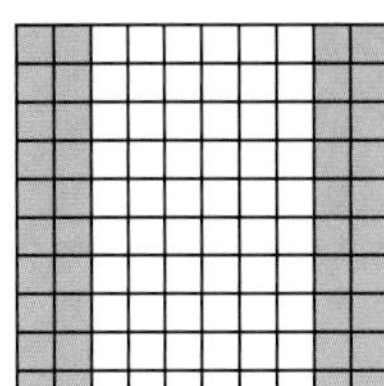

3. 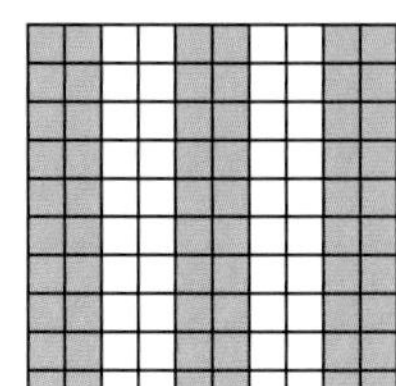

Write a decimal and a percent to represent the shaded part.

4. 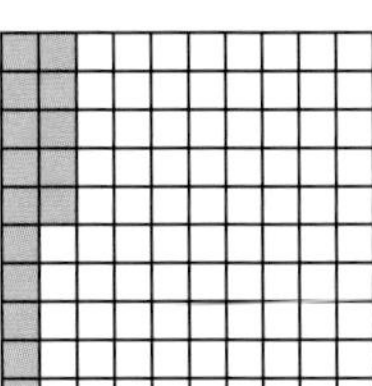

5. 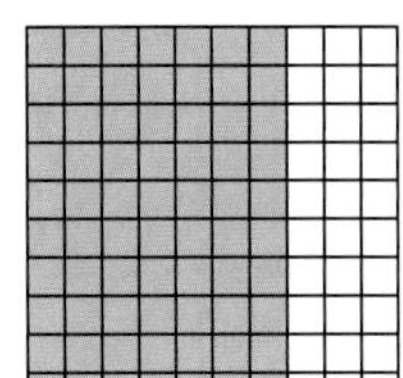

6. 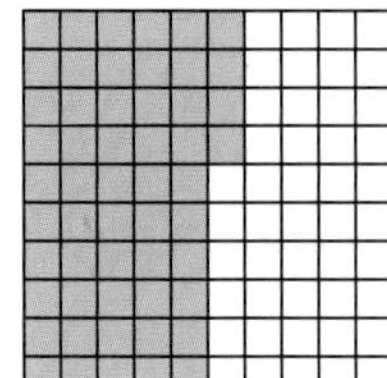

7. **WRITE Math** **Explain** why $\frac{1}{4}$, 0.25, and 25% are equivalent.

LESSON 7

Fractions, Decimals, and Percents

OBJECTIVE: Write equivalent forms of fractions, decimals, and percents.

Quick Review

Write each fraction in simplest form.

1. $\frac{2}{4}$ **2.** $\frac{4}{6}$ **3.** $\frac{6}{8}$

4. $\frac{2}{10}$ **5.** $\frac{35}{50}$

Learn

PROBLEM Asparagus is grown in every state in the United States. About 80% of all the asparagus grown in the United States is grown in California. What fraction of the asparagus grown in the United States is grown in California?

Example 1 Write the percent as a fraction in simplest form.

Step 1	Step 2
Write the percent as a fraction with a denominator of 100. $80\% = \frac{80}{100}$	Write the fraction in simplest form. $\frac{80 \div 20}{100 \div 20} = \frac{4}{5}$

So, $\frac{4}{5}$ of the asparagus in the United States is grown in California.

You can write a percent as a decimal.

Example 2 Write 80% as a decimal.

Step 1	Step 2
Write the percent as a fraction with a denominator of 100. $80\% = \frac{80}{100}$	Write the fraction as a decimal. $\frac{80}{100} = 0.80$

So, 80% written as a decimal is 0.80.

- How would you write 95% as a fraction and as a decimal?

More Examples

A Write 24% as a fraction.

$24\% = \frac{24}{100}$ Write the percent as a fraction with a denominator of 100.

$\frac{24 \div 4}{100 \div 4} = \frac{6}{25}$ Write the fraction in simplest form.

B Write 7% as a decimal.

$7\% = \frac{7}{100}$ Write the percent as a fraction with a denominator of 100.

$\frac{7}{100} = 0.07$ Write the fraction as a decimal.

Write Decimals and Fractions as Percents

You can use place value or multiplication to write a decimal as a percent.

Example 3

ONE WAY **Use place value.**

Write 0.75 as a percent.

Step 1

Use place value to express the decimal as a fraction.

$$0.75 \rightarrow \frac{75}{100}$$

Step 2

Since percent means "out of one hundred", write the fraction as a percent.

$$\frac{75}{100} = 75\%$$

ANOTHER WAY **Use multiplication.**

Write 0.04 as a percent.

Step 1

Multiply the decimal by 100.

$$0.04 \times 100 = 4$$

Step 2

Write the product as a percent.

$$0.04 \times 100 = 4\%$$

You can use equivalent fractions or division to write a fraction as a percent. Use equivalent fractions when the denominator of a fraction is a factor of 100. Use division when the denominator of a fraction is *not* a factor of 100.

Example 4

ONE WAY **Use equivalent fractions.**

Write $\frac{1}{4}$ as a percent.

Step 1

Write an equivalent ratio in fraction form with a denominator of 100.

$$\frac{1 \times 25}{4 \times 25} = \frac{25}{100}$$

Step 2

Since percent is a ratio of a number to 100, write the ratio as a percent.

$$\frac{25}{100} = 25\%$$

ANOTHER WAY **Use division.**

Write $\frac{3}{8}$ as a percent.

Step 1

Divide the numerator by the denominator.

$$\frac{3}{8} = 8\overline{)3} \qquad \begin{array}{r} 0.375 \\ 8\overline{)3.000} \end{array}$$

Step 2

Multiply 0.375 by 100. Write the product as a percent.

$$0.375 \times 100 = 37.5\%$$

- Write 0.05 as a fraction and as a percent.

Guided Practice

1. Write $\frac{1}{2}$ as a percent. $\frac{1 \times ■}{2 \times ■} = \frac{50}{100} = ■\%$

Write each percent as a decimal and as a fraction in simplest form.

2. 20%
3. 65%
4. 70%
5. 98%
6. 43%

Write each fraction or decimal as a percent.

7. $\frac{1}{5}$
8. 0.15
9. $\frac{3}{10}$
10. 0.80
11. 0.64
12. TALK Math **Explain** whether 0.04 is equivalent to 40%.

Independent Practice and Problem Solving

Write each percent as a decimal and as a fraction in simplest form.

13. 14%
14. 30%
15. 49%
16. 85%
17. 2%
18. 23%
19. 64%
20. 71%
21. 96%
22. 54%

Write each fraction or decimal as a percent.

23. $\frac{7}{10}$
24. 0.28
25. $\frac{2}{5}$
26. 0.03
27. $\frac{1}{8}$
28. 0.325
29. $\frac{5}{8}$
30. 0.011
31. $\frac{6}{20}$
32. 0.09

USE DATA For 33–37, use the table.

33. Write as a decimal the percent of American households that eat strawberries.
34. What fraction of strawberries in the United States does Hillsborough County produce? Write the fraction in simplest form.
35. **Reasoning** If you eat 8 medium strawberries one day, what fraction of vitamin C for that day do you still need?
36. Write a fraction that shows the 7- to 9-year-olds who *do not choose* strawberries as their favorite fruit.
37. WRITE Math **What's the Question?** The answer is 6%.

Facts About Strawberries
• If you eat 8 medium strawberries, you'll get 93% of the vitamin C you should have every day.
• 94% of households in the United States eat strawberries.
• 53% of 7- to 9-year-olds choose strawberries as their favorite fruit.
• Hillsborough County, Florida, produces about 15% of the strawberries in the United States.

CD ROM **Technology**
Use Harcourt Mega Math, Fraction Action, *Fraction Flare Up*, Level N.

Extra Practice on page 446, Set E

Learn About Percents: Less than 1%, Greater than 100%

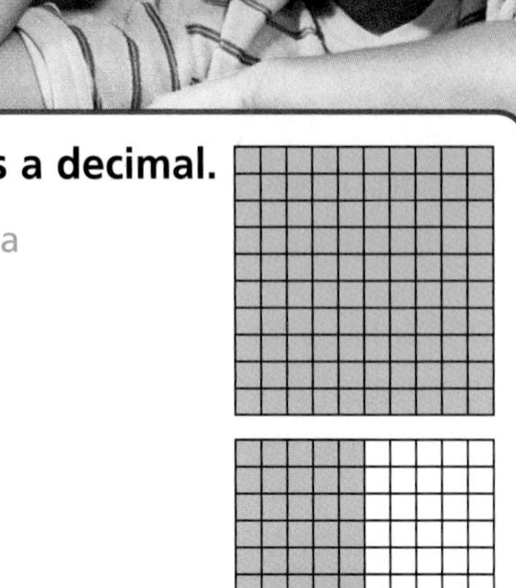

If you write a percent that is less than 1% as a decimal, the decimal will be less than 0.01. If you write a percent that is greater than 100% as a decimal, the decimal will be greater than 1.

Examples

A Write 0.5% as a decimal.

Write the percent as a fraction with a denominator of 100.

$\frac{0.5}{100}$

Divide.

$100\overline{)0.5} = 100\overline{)0.500}$ (quotient: 0.005)

So, 0.5% = 0.005.

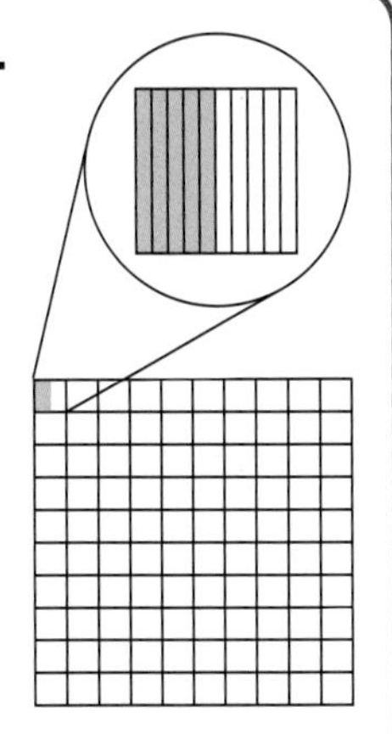

B Write 150% as a decimal.

Write the percent as a fraction with a denominator of 100.

$\frac{150}{100}$

Divide.

$100\overline{)150} = 100\overline{)150.0}$ (quotient: 1.5)

So, 150% = 1.5.

Try It

Write each percent as a decimal and as a fraction in simplest form.

38. 0.25% **39.** 0.80% **40.** 200% **41.** 175%

42. 130% **43.** 0.1% **44.** 105% **45.** 0.9%

Mixed Review and Test Prep

46. Bill drew a 10-by-10 grid to make a design for a tile floor. He colored 27 squares red. What percent of the squares are red? (p. 438)

47. Test Prep Sami correctly answered 85% of the questions on a math test. What is that percent written as a decimal?

A 0.85 **C** 85

B 8.5 **D** 850

48. Kay is practicing free throws at practice. She completed $\frac{12}{20}$ of the free throws. What decimal represents the number of free throws Kay completed? (p. 326)

49. Test Prep At the Rocking R Ranch, $\frac{9}{10}$ of the stalls have horses in them. What percent of the stalls are filled?

A 0.09 **C** 0.9

B 9% **D** 90%

LESSON 8 HANDS ON

Find Percent of a Number

OBJECTIVE: Find the percent of a number.

Quick Review

1. 0.6×12
2. 0.9×9
3. 1.3×4
4. 0.25×22
5. 0.48×317

Investigate

Materials ■ two-color counters

You can use two-color counters to model a percent of a number.

Monica likes to shop for bargains. She finds a $40 backpack marked "30% off." How can she find the amount she would save, 30% of 40?

A Let each counter represent 10%. Put down 10 red counters to represent 100%. Each 10% represents 4, since $10 \times 4 = 40$.

B Now flip over three of the counters. The three yellow counters show $3 \times 10\%$, or 30%.

C Since each counter represents 4, what is 30% of 40? How much would Monica save?

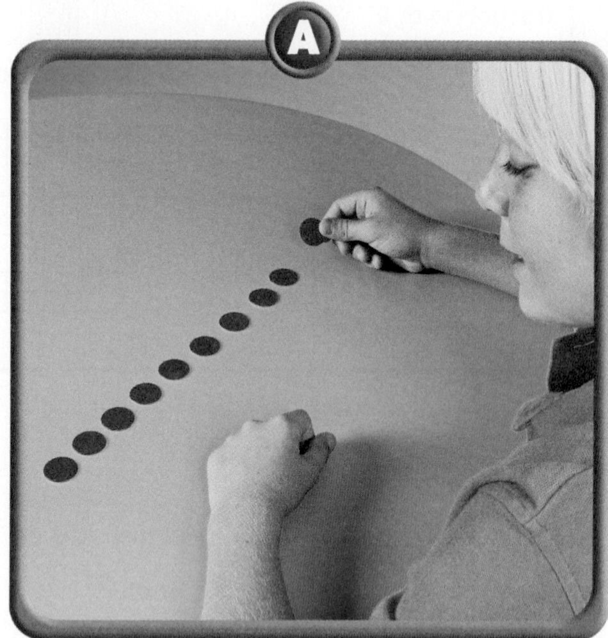

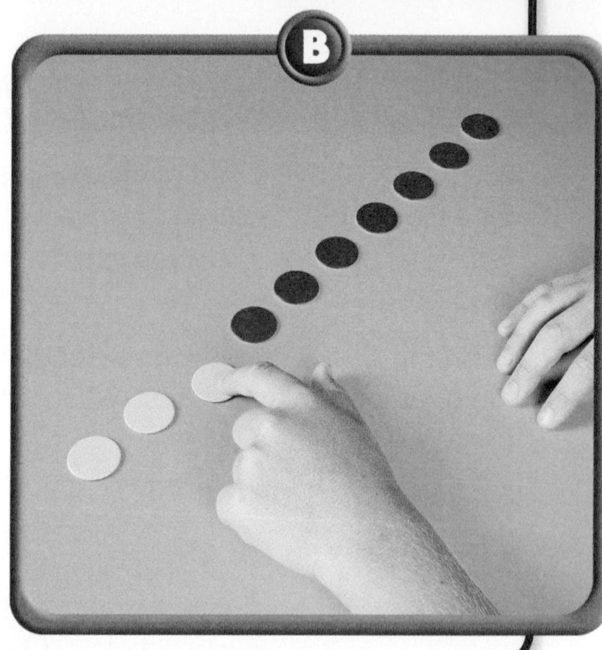

Draw Conclusions

1. What percent do the 3 yellow counters represent in your model?
2. What decimal could you write to represent the 3 yellow counters?
3. What fraction could you write to represent the 3 yellow counters?
4. **Comprehension** Explain how you would change the model to find 40% of 40.

Connect

You can write a percent as a fraction and then multiply to find a percent of a number.

Find 75% of 20.

Step 1	Step 2
Write 75% as a fraction in simplest form. $75\% = \frac{75}{100} = \frac{3}{4}$	Multiply. $\frac{3}{4} \times 20 = \frac{3}{4} \times \frac{20}{1} = \frac{60}{4} = 15$

So, 75% of 20 is 15.

TALK Math

Explain why it might be easier to find 25% of 80 using multiplication compared to using counters.

Practice

Complete the sentence. Then, find the percent of each number.

1. 60% of 50

10 counters represent 100%, or 50.
So, each counter represents 10%, or ■.

2. 20% of 80

10 counters represent 100%, or 80.
So, each counter represents 10%, or ■.

3. $20\% \text{ of } 15 = \frac{■}{■} \text{ of } 15$

$= \frac{■}{■} \times 15$

$= ■$

4. $25\% \text{ of } 48 = \frac{■}{■} \text{ of } 48$

$= \frac{■}{■} \times 48$

$= ■$

Find the percent of each number.

5. 30% of 30
6. 50% of 8
7. 75% of 24
✓**8.** 90% of 10
9. 20% of 25
10. 50% of 80
11. 25% of 16
✓**12.** 25% of 24

13. WRITE Math ▸ **Explain** how you would use a fraction to find 20% of 30.

Extra Practice

Set A Write each ratio in three ways. Then name the type of ratio. (pp. 422–423)

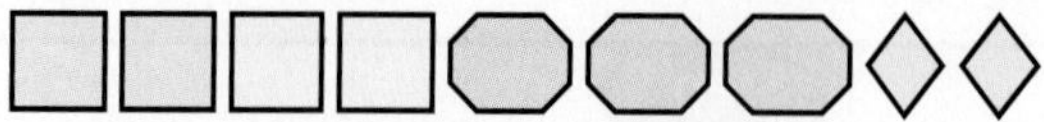

1. squares to rhombi
2. all figures to octagons
3. rhombi to all figures
4. octagons to blue squares
5. 8-sided figures to 4-sided figures
6. blue squares to yellow squares

Set B Write two equivalent ratios for each ratio. Use multiplication or division. (pp. 424–427)

1. $\frac{1}{3}$
2. 2 to 10
3. 20:12
4. $\frac{30}{660}$

Set C Write each ratio in fraction form. Then find the unit rate. (pp. 428–429)

1. 42 points in 2 games
2. 24 legs on 4 insects
3. $120 spent in 12 weeks
4. Nina buys a pack of 4 T-shirts for $48. How much does Nina pay for each T-shirt?

Set D The map distance is given. Find the actual distance. For 1–2, the scale is 1 in. = 60 mi. For 3–4, the scale is 2 cm = 16 km. (pp. 430–433)

1. $2\frac{1}{2}$ in.
2. $1\frac{1}{5}$ in.
3. 4 cm
4. 0.25 cm

Set E Write each percent as a decimal and as a fraction in simplest form. (pp. 440–443)

1. 12%
2. 32%
3. 4%
4. 22%
5. 98%

Write each fraction or decimal as a percent.

6. $\frac{4}{10}$
7. 0.67
8. $\frac{1}{4}$
9. 0.015
10. $\frac{2}{25}$
11. Bonnie surveyed the students in her class about their favorite season. The greatest number of students, 76%, said summer. Write this percent as a decimal.

CD ROM **Technology**
Use Harcourt Mega Math, Fraction Action, *Fraction Flare Up*, Level N.

SAVINGS ACCOUNT

Savers
2 players

Materials
- 10 index cards
- 2 number cubes labeled 1–6
- Paper and pencil

10%	25%	30%	40%	50%
60%	70%	75%	80%	90%

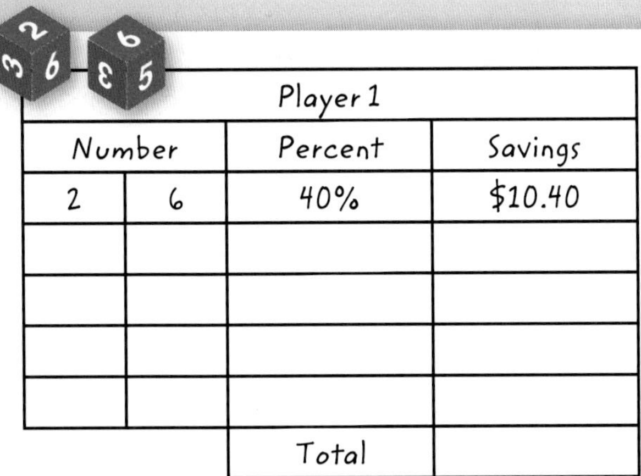

Player 1			
Number		Percent	Savings
2	6	40%	$10.40
		Total	

Player 2			
Number		Percent	Savings
5	4	25%	$13.50
		Total	

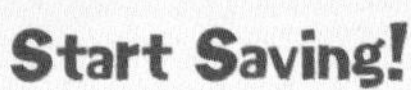

Start Saving!

- Players make one set of percent cards and two score cards as shown above.
- Players shuffle the percent cards and place them in a stack facedown on the table.
- Player 1 rolls each number cube one at a time to form a 2-digit number. The first number cube is used as the tens digit. The second number cube is used as the ones digit.
- Player 1 draws a percent card from the stack. Player 1 then calculates that percent of the number that was rolled and writes the percent as dollars and cents.
- Player 2 repeats the process. Play continues in this manner until all the percent cards have been used.
- Each player finds the total amount in his or her savings account. The player with the greater total amount of savings wins the game!

MATH POWER

Circle Graphs and Percent

CIRCULAR REASONING

The Cooking Club spent 20% of its \$60 budget on transportation, 30% on equipment, and the rest on food. How much did they spend on food?

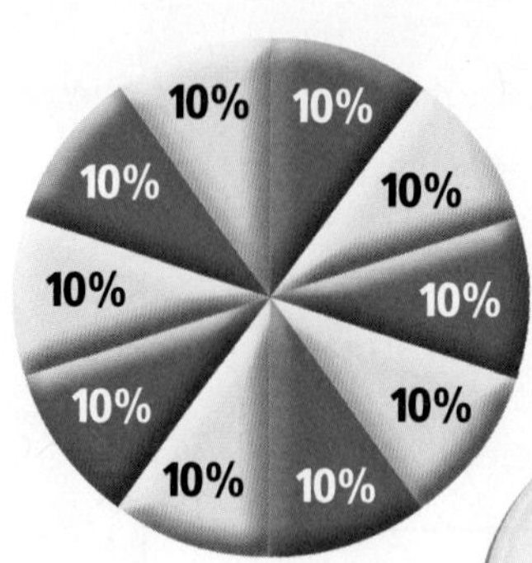

You can think of the entire circle graph as divided into ten sections. Each section represents 10%, or one-tenth of the \$60 budget.

Each 10% section: $\frac{1}{10} \times \$60 = \$6$

Remember

- Each tenth of the circle graph is equal to 10% of the total.

Examples

Count the sections to find the amount spent on food.

For transportation, 20% is equal to 2 sections.
For equipment, 30% is equal to 3 sections, or:

20% = 2 sections = 2 × \$6 = \$12
30% = 3 sections = 3 × \$6 = \$18

Subtract 20% and 30% from 100% to get the amount spent for food.

100% − (20% + 30%) = 50%

So the club spent 50% of its budget on food:

50% = 5 sections = 5 × \$6 = \$30

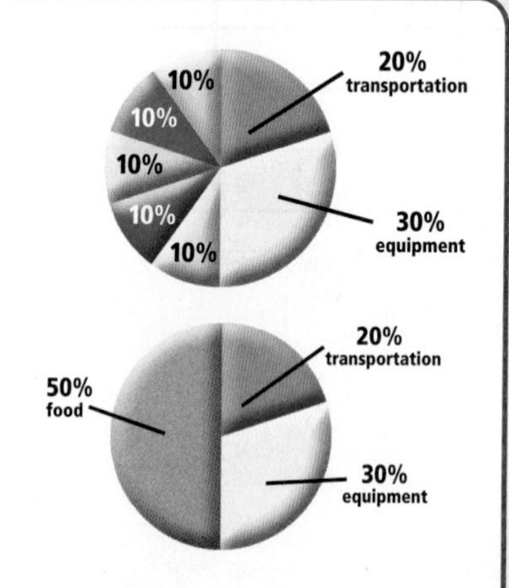

Try It

The circle graph shows the \$250 budget for the soccer team. Find each amount.

1. Amount spent on water
2. Amount spent on bus
3. Amount spent on shorts and socks
4. Amount spent on jerseys
5. Three items that make up exactly 50% of the budget
6. Three items that make up 70% of the budget
7. WRITE Math **Explain** how you can find the value of each 10% section of a circle graph.

Chapter 16 Review/Test

Check Vocabulary and Concepts

Choose the best term from the box.

VOCABULARY
ratio
percent
proportion
rate

1. An equation that shows that two ratios are equal. KY Grade 6 (p. 425)
2. A ratio that compares two quantities having different units of measure. KY Grade 6 (p. 428)
3. The ratio of a number to 100. KY Grade 6 (p. 438)

Check Skills

Write each ratio in three ways. Then name the type of ratio. KY Grade 6 (pp. 422–423)

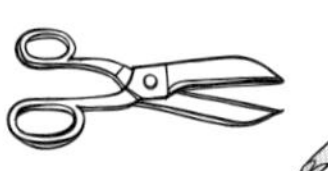  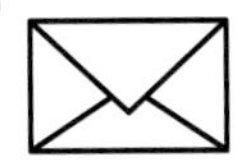 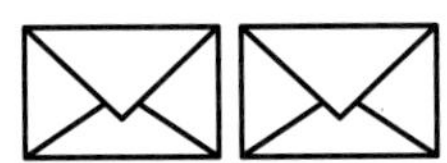    

4. pencils to all figures
5. scissors to envelopes
6. envelopes to all figures

Find the unknown value. KY Grade 6 (pp. 424–427)

7. $\frac{x}{14} = \frac{54}{42}$
8. $\frac{8}{54} = \frac{4}{v}$
9. $\frac{15}{p} = \frac{1}{5}$
10. $\frac{120}{10} = \frac{m}{2}$

Write each ratio in fraction form. Then find the unit rate. KY Grade 6 (pp. 428–429)

11. 1.6 miles in 2 hours
12. $2 for 10 bananas
13. 3 books in 2 days

The map distance is given. Find the actual distance. The scale is 1 cm = 15 km. KY Grade 6 (pp. 430–433)

14. 3 cm
15. 2.5 cm
16. 5 cm
17. 4.2 cm
18. 7 cm

Write each fraction or decimal as a percent. KY Grade 6 (pp. 440–443)

19. 0.014
20. $\frac{6}{50}$
21. 0.99
22. $\frac{3}{8}$
23. $\frac{4}{25}$

Check Problem Solving

Solve. KY Grade 6 (pp. 434–437)

24. There are 38 band members, 26 chorus members, 12 gardening club members, and 24 art club members at Roosevelt Elementary School. Make a table. Which club has the most members?

25. **WRITE Math** Use the table you made in problem 24. The computer club has 18 members. Each student belongs to only one club. How many students are in all of the clubs combined? **Explain.**

GO ONLINE **Technology** Use *Online Assessment.*

Practice for the KCCT
Chapters 1–16

Number and Operations

1. The Computer Super Store sold 1,206 computers in January and 984 computers in February. How many more computers did the store sell in January than in February? KY MA-05-1.3.1 (p. 20)

   A 222

   B 282

   C 322

   D 382

Check your work.

See item 1. Use addition to check your answer. The sum of the answer and the lesser value in the problem should equal the greater value in the problem.

2. Each shelf of Mr. Peterson's bookshelf can hold a maximum of 12 textbooks. He has a total of 67 textbooks. What is the least number of shelves Mr. Peterson will need? KY MA-05-1.3.1 (p. 74)

   A 5 C 7

   B 6 D 8

3. **WRITE Math** Jessie is shopping for new clothes. A pair of jeans costs $38.95, and a sweater costs $29.89. Jessie has a $50 bill. About how much money do the jeans and sweater cost? Does he have enough money to buy the jeans and the sweater? **Explain.** KY MA-05-1.2.1 (p. 156)

Algebraic Thinking

4. Manny earns $5 for every lawn that he mows in his neighborhood. Which expression represents the amount of money he makes for mowing a certain number, n, of lawns? KY MA-05-5.3.1 (p. 92)

   A $5 + n$

   B $5 \div n$

   C $5n$

   D $5 - n$

5. Which is the rule for the function table? KY MA-05-5.1.2 (p. 112)

Input	Output
x	y
5	17
14	26
51	63
142	154

   A add 7 to x

   B divide y by 3

   C subtract 12 from y

   D multiply x by 3

6. **WRITE Math** Explain how you find the rule of a function table. KY MA-05-5.1.2 (p. 112)

Geometry

7. Which term best describes the figure shown below? KY Grade 4

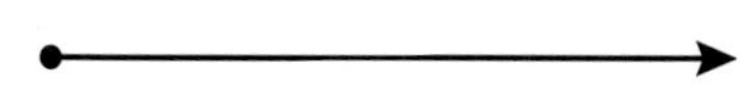

A line

B ray

C angle

D segment

8. The drawing below shows the outline of Xavier's backyard. Which of the following best describes the shape of the yard? KY Grade 4

A rectangle

B pentagon

C parallelogram

D trapezoid

9. WRITE Math Half of a figure and its line of symmetry are shown below. Complete the figure. **Explain** the process you used. KY Grade 4

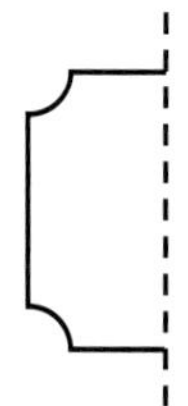

Data Analysis and Probability

10. Michael surveys 35 people about their favorite food. Pizza received 13 votes, spaghetti received 10 votes, chicken received 9 votes and macaroni and cheese received 3 votes. Which type of graph would be best to display the results of Michael's survey? KY MA-05-4.1.3 (p. 260)

A pictograph

B bar graph

C line graph

D double-bar graph

11. Which of the following should you NOT include when creating a bar graph? KY MA-05-4.1.3 (p. 242)

A scale

B title

C labels

D pictures

12. WRITE Math What is the mean of the data set shown? Explain how you find the mean of a data set. KY MA-05-4.2.1 (p. 220)

150, 175, 250, 125, 275, 225

CHAPTER 17 Probability

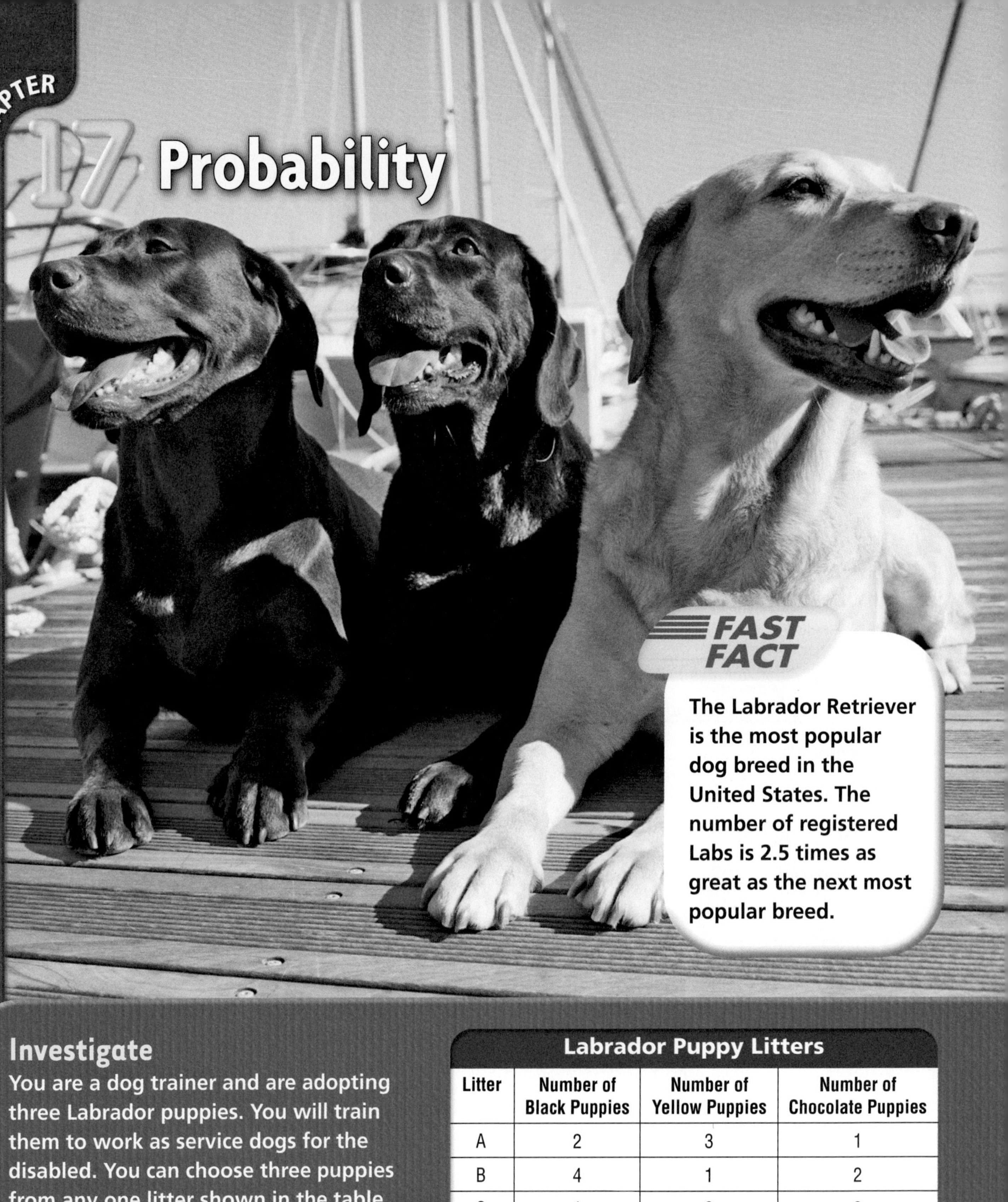

FAST FACT

The Labrador Retriever is the most popular dog breed in the United States. The number of registered Labs is 2.5 times as great as the next most popular breed.

Investigate

You are a dog trainer and are adopting three Labrador puppies. You will train them to work as service dogs for the disabled. You can choose three puppies from any one litter shown in the table. Find the different combinations of colors of three puppies in a litter. List all possible combinations.

Labrador Puppy Litters

Litter	Number of Black Puppies	Number of Yellow Puppies	Number of Chocolate Puppies
A	2	3	1
B	4	1	2
C	1	2	2
D	3	1	1

Technology
Student pages are available in the Student eBook.

Show What You Know

Check your understanding of important skills needed for success in Chapter 17.

▶ Simplest Form

Write each fraction in simplest form.

1. $\frac{10}{12}$ **2.** $\frac{5}{10}$ **3.** $\frac{6}{8}$ **4.** $\frac{12}{15}$ **5.** $\frac{4}{6}$

6. $\frac{2}{4}$ **7.** $\frac{4}{12}$ **8.** $\frac{8}{12}$ **9.** $\frac{9}{15}$ **10.** $\frac{2}{8}$

▶ Probability—More Likely, Less Likely, Equally Likely

A number cube labeled 1 through 6 is tossed. Tell whether the event has a *likely*, an *unlikely*, or an *equally likely* chance of happening as not happening.

11. tossing a number greater than 4

12. tossing an odd number

13. tossing a number less than 4

14. tossing the numbers 2, 3, 4, or 5

15. tossing an even number

16. tossing a number greater than 1

17. tossing a number between 1 and 5

18. tossing a 2

VOCABULARY POWER

CHAPTER VOCABULARY

arrangement
combination
equally likely
event
tree diagram
unlikely
experimental probability
Fundamental Counting Principle
likely
outcome
prediction
probability
sample space
theoretical probability

WARM-UP WORDS

outcome a possible result of an experiment

prediction a reasonable guess as to the outcome of an event

probability the likelihood that an event will happen

LESSON 1 Outcomes and Probability

OBJECTIVE: Describe outcomes of probability experiments.

Quick Review

Write each fraction in simplest form.

1. $\frac{2}{4}$
2. $\frac{3}{9}$
3. $\frac{6}{24}$
4. $\frac{4}{12}$
5. $\frac{5}{10}$

Vocabulary

outcome
equally likely
sample space
event
theoretical probability

Learn

Each color on a spinner represents an **outcome**, or possible result, of a single spin of the pointer.

The sections are the same size on all of the spinners. Spinner 2 has two blue sections and two red sections. On Spinner 2, an outcome of red and an outcome of blue are equally likely. Outcomes that are **equally likely** have equal chances of occurring.

The **sample space** is the set of all possible outcomes. The sample space for Spinner 1 is red, green, yellow, and blue. For Spinner 2, the sample space is red and blue. For Spinner 3, the sample space is blue.

Spinner 1

An **event** is a set of one or more outcomes. It can be any set that is part of the sample space. For Spinner 1, the pointer landing on blue is an event. The pointer landing on red or blue is also an event.

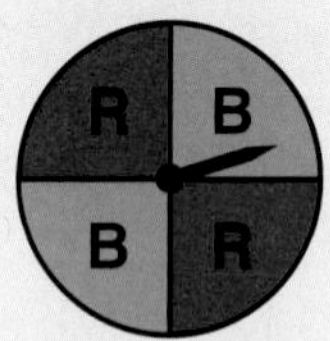

Spinner 2

The **theoretical probability** of an event, or P(event), is the ratio of the number of favorable outcomes to the number of all possible equally likely outcomes. You can express probability in words or as a fraction.

Probability of an event, or P(event) $= \frac{\text{number of favorable outcomes}}{\text{number of possible equally likely outcomes}}$

Spinner 3

Examples **Find the probability of the pointer landing on blue.**

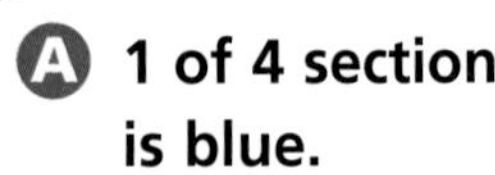

A **1 of 4 sections is blue.**

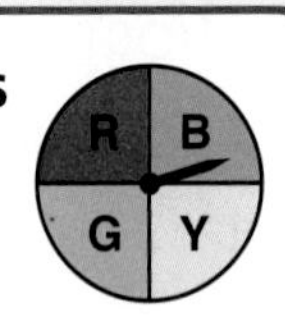

P(blue) = 1 out of 4 — in words

P(blue) $= \frac{1}{4}$ — fraction

The probability of the pointer landing on blue is $\frac{1}{4}$.

B **2 of 4 sections are blue.**

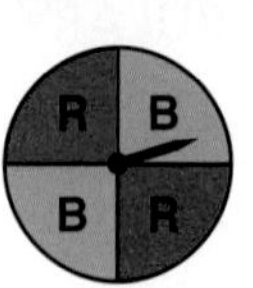

P(blue) = 2 out of 4 — in words

P(blue) $= \frac{2}{4}$ or $\frac{1}{2}$ — fraction

The probability of the pointer landing on blue is $\frac{1}{2}$.

C **4 of 4 sections are blue.**

P(blue) = 4 out of 4 — in words

P(blue) $= \frac{4}{4}$ or 1 — fraction

The probability of the pointer landing on blue is 1.

FAST TRACK

KY MA-05-4.4.1 Students will determine all possible outcomes of an activity/event with up to 12 possible outcomes. DOK 2 *also* MA-05-4.4.2

Probability and Likelihood

Probability may take on any value between 0 and 1. The more likely an event is, the closer its fraction of probability is to 1. The less likely an event is, the closer its fraction of probability is to 0.

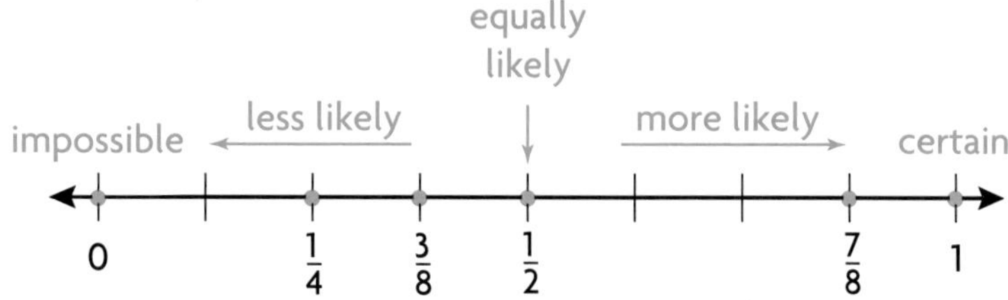

More Examples **Find the probability of each event. Describe how likely the event is.**

D **Tossing 2 or 4 on a number cube labeled 1 through 6**

2 favorable outcomes: 2 and 4

6 possible outcomes: 1, 2, 3, 4, 5, and 6

$$P(2 \text{ or } 4) = \frac{2 \text{ favorable outcomes}}{6 \text{ equally likely outcomes}} = \frac{2}{6} = \frac{1}{3}$$

Since $\frac{1}{3}$ is less than $\frac{1}{2}$, tossing either a 2 or a 4 is unlikely.

E **Pulling a yellow sock from the drawer**

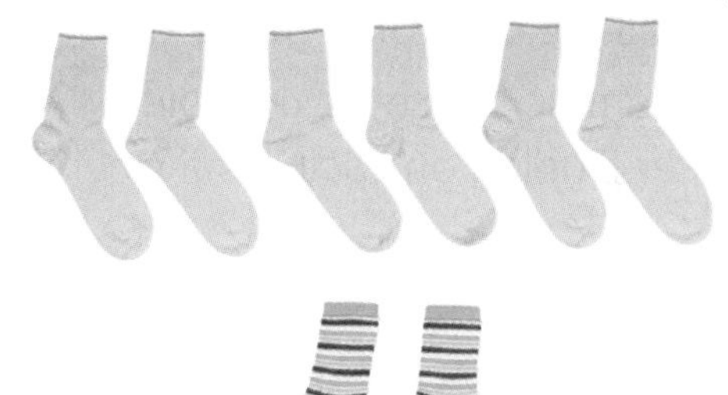

6 favorable outcomes: a yellow sock

8 possible outcomes: a yellow sock and a blue striped sock

$$P(\text{yellow}) = \frac{6 \text{ favorable outcomes}}{8 \text{ equally likely outcomes}} = \frac{6}{8} = \frac{3}{4}$$

Since $\frac{3}{4}$ is greater than $\frac{1}{2}$, pulling a yellow sock from the drawer is likely.

- What is the probability of pulling a red sock from the drawer in Example E?

Guided Practice

Write the probability as a fraction in simplest form.

1. 1 out of 5 = $\frac{1}{\blacksquare}$ **2.** 4 out of 8 = $\frac{1}{\blacksquare}$ ✓**3.** 2 out of 6 = $\frac{1}{\blacksquare}$

CD ROM **Technology**
Use Harcourt Mega Math, Fraction Action, *Last Chance Canyon,* Levels A, C.

Use the spinner to write the probability of spinning each event.

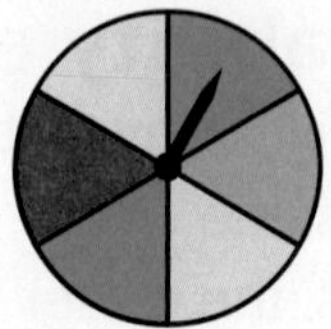

4. green
5. yellow
6. blue or red

7. TALK Math **Explain** why probability can never be greater than 1 or less than 0.

Independent Practice and Problem Solving

Use the bag of 18 marbles to write the probability of the event of pulling the marble described.

8. green
9. red
10. blue
11. green or blue
12. red or blue
13. red or green
14. red, green or blue
15. pink
16. red, green, blue, or yellow

Use a number cube labeled 1 through 6 to write the probability of tossing the number. Tell whether the event is likely, unlikely, certain, or impossible.

17. 4
18. a number less than 3
19. 2 or 3
20. a number less than 7
21. 0 or 1
22. a number greater than 2
23. 1, 2, 3, 4, or 6
24. a number less than 1

USE DATA For 25–29, use the spinner and the bar graph.

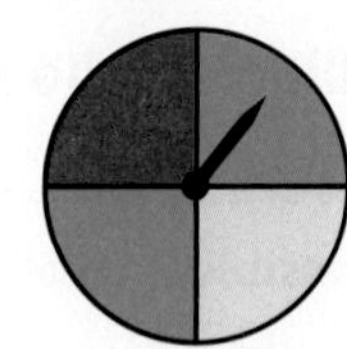

25. What is the sample space for the spinner? What is the probability of the pointer landing on each color?
26. Levi made the graph to show the results of spinning the pointer. How many times did he spin the pointer?
27. Which color did the pointer land on the most often? How does this result compare to the probability for that event?
28. Is the pointer more likely, less likely, or equally likely to land on red than yellow? How do you know?
29. **What's the Question?** When you spin the pointer on the spinner, the probability is $\frac{3}{4}$.
30. WRITE Math Make and color a spinner with at least 4 equal-sized sections. Name the sample space for your spinner. **Explain** why the sum of probabilities for all possible outcomes on your spinner should equal 1.

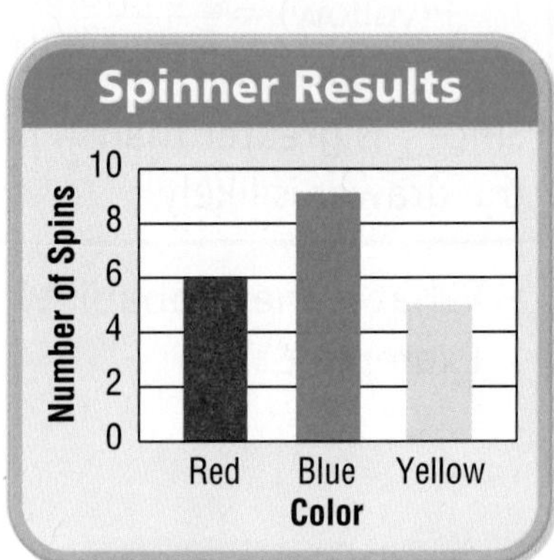

 Extra Practice on page 470, Set A

Learn About A Complement of an Event

The **complement** of an event is the set of all other possible outcomes in the sample space that are not outcomes of the original event.

Consider the event of the pointer landing on green on the spinner at the right.

$$P(\text{green}) = \frac{2}{6}, \text{ or } \frac{1}{3}$$

The complement of spinning green is ***not*** spinning green. This is the same as spinning orange or purple. The probability of the complement of green is written P(not green), and is read P of not green.

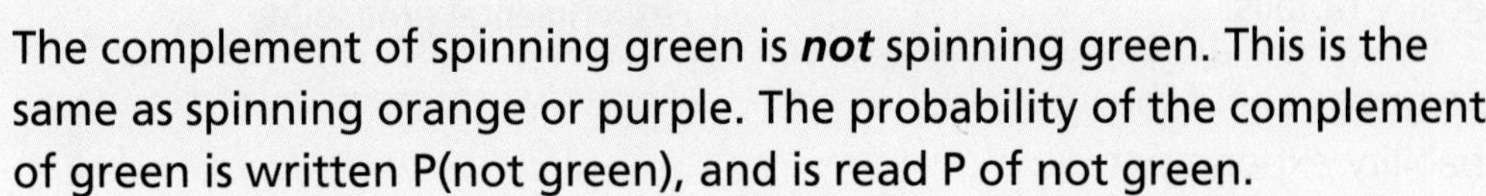

$$P(\text{not green}) = P(\text{orange or purple}) = \frac{4}{6}, \text{ or } \frac{2}{3}$$

The sum of the probabilities of an event, A, and its complement, not A, are equal to 1. You can find the probability of an event by subtracting the probability of its complement from 1.

$$P(A) + P(\text{not } A) = 1 \text{ or } P(A) = 1 - P(\text{not } A)$$

Try It

Use a number cube labeled 1 through 6 to identify the complement of each event and the probability of that complement.

31. 2

32. 6

33. 1 or 2

34. an odd number

35. an even number

36. less than 4

Mixed Review and Test Prep

For 39–40, use the spinner.

37. There are 128 students riding the bus. There are 3 buses in the lot. Each bus holds 38 students. How many students will have to wait for the next bus? (p. 62)

38. Dana rides 54 miles in 3 hours. At this rate, how far will she ride in 5 hours? (p. 428)

39. **Test Prep** Is the spinner most likely to land on blue, green, or red? **Explain.**

40. **Test Prep** What is the probability the pointer will land on green?

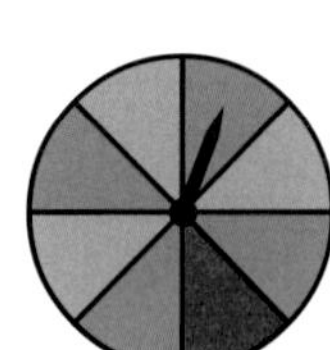

A $\frac{1}{8}$

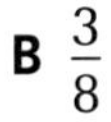

B $\frac{3}{8}$

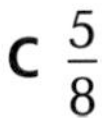

C $\frac{5}{8}$

D $\frac{3}{5}$

LESSON 2 HANDS ON

Probability Experiments

OBJECTIVE: Predict outcomes of probability experiments.

Quick Review

Gina tossed a number cube labeled 1 through 6. Is it likely or unlikely that she tossed a number that is less than 3?

Vocabulary

prediction

experimental probability

Investigate

Materials ■ 1 coin

When you toss a coin a single time, the probability of heads is equal to the probability of tails.

A **prediction** is a reasonable guess about the possible outcome of a probability experiment.

A Make a tally table with a row for heads and a row for tails. Use the table to record the results of the experiment.

B Toss or drop a coin 10 times. Predict the number of heads and the number of tails that you will toss. Use the tally table to record the actual results of 10 tosses.

C Find and record the total number of heads and the total number of tails.

D Do the experiment two more times. Toss the coin 10 times in each experiment and record the results in the tally table. Compare the outcomes of the three experiments with each other and with your original prediction.

Coin Experiment

	1	2	3	Total
Heads	||			
Tails	||||			

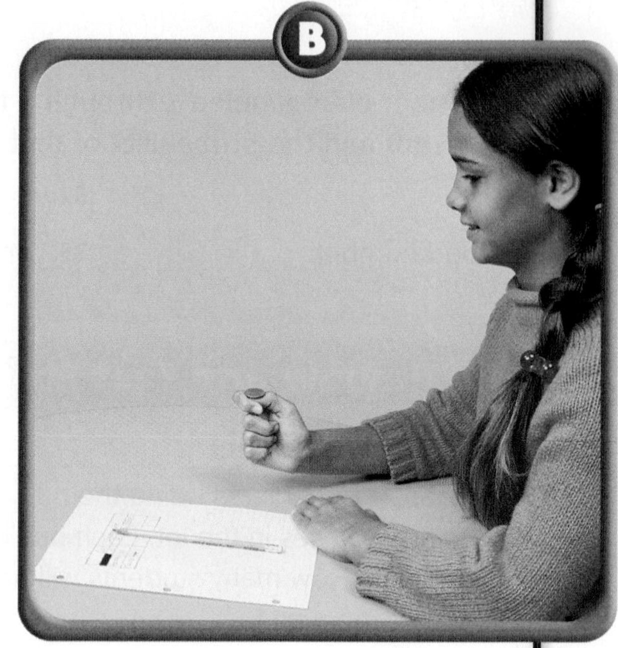

Draw Conclusions

1. Do you think that the coin you tossed will always land more often on either heads or tails? Why?
2. If you tossed 3 heads in a row, do you think the next toss is more likely to be tails? Why or why not?
3. **Evaluation** If you could toss the coin hundreds or thousands of times, about how many times do you think you would toss tails? Explain.

FAST TRACK

KY MA-05-4.4.2 Students will determine the likelihood of an event and the probability of an event (expressed as a fraction). DOK 2
also MA-05-4.1.2

Connect

The **experimental probability** of an event is the ratio of the number of times an event occurs to the total number of times the activity is performed.

Shawna's Experiment

	1	2	3	Total
Heads	||	𝍸 |	𝍸	13
Tails	𝍸 |||	||||	𝍸	17

$$\text{experimental probability} = \frac{\text{number of times an event occurs}}{\text{total number of trials}}$$

$$\text{experimental probability of heads} = \frac{13}{30}$$

You can use experimental probabilities to predict the outcomes of future experiments. Based on these results, a reasonable prediction for 60 coin tosses might be 2 × 13, or 26 heads.

TALK Math

Based on Shawna's results, what would be a reasonable prediction for tails in 90 tosses?

Practice

For 1–3, use the table.

1. Dylan pulled a marble from a bag, recorded its color, and put the marble back in the bag. He did this 25 times and recorded his results in the table. What is the experimental probability of Dylan's pulling a red marble? a blue marble? a green marble?

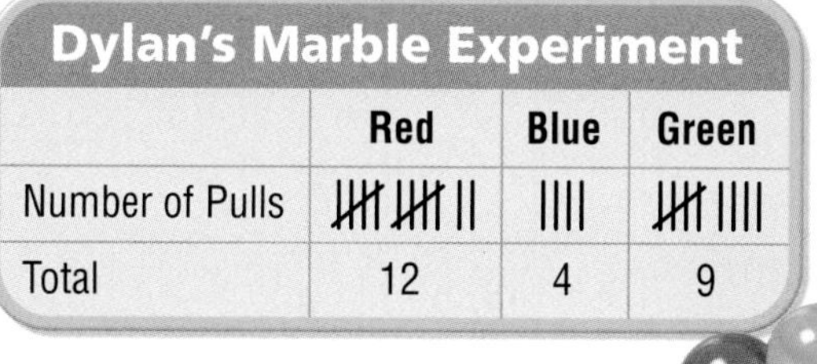

Dylan's Marble Experiment

	Red	Blue	Green
Number of Pulls	𝍸 𝍸 ||	||||	𝍸 ||||
Total	12	4	9

2. Predict how many times out of 50 pulls that Dylan might get a red marble from the bag.

3. Predict the number of times out of 50 pulls that Dylan might get a marble that is either red or blue. Compare this with your prediction of the number of times out of 50 pulls that Dylan might get a marble that is not green.

4. **WRITE Math** Combine the results of your coin experiments on page 458 with the results of one of your classmates. Then combine those results with the results of your entire class. Compare both combined results with the results that you got by yourself. How do the two combined results compare with your original prediction?

LESSON 3

Probability and Predictions

OBJECTIVE: Predict the results of probability experiments.

Quick Review

1. $\frac{4}{8} = \frac{■}{16}$
2. $\frac{3}{9} = \frac{9}{■}$
3. $\frac{4}{6} = \frac{24}{■}$
4. $\frac{9}{12} = \frac{■}{36}$
5. $\frac{10}{16} = \frac{■}{48}$

Learn

PROBLEM Bruce pulls one tile from a jar of colored tiles without looking. He records the color and puts the tile back. He performs the experiment 16 times. The table shows Bruce's results.

Tile Experiment

Tile Color	Number of Times Picked
Green	6
Red	7
Yellow	3

If this pattern continues, about how many times can Bruce expect to pull a green tile from the jar in his next 80 pulls?

To find the experimental probability, compare the number of times an event occurs with the total number of trials. You can use experimental probabilities and equivalent fractions to predict future trials.

Step 1

Write the experimental probability. Write the fraction in simplest form.

$$P(\text{event}) = \frac{\text{number of times an event occurs}}{\text{total number of trials}}$$

$$P(\text{green}) = \frac{\text{number of green tiles pulled}}{\text{total number of tiles pulled}}$$

$$= \frac{6}{16} = \frac{3}{8}$$

Step 2

Find an equivalent fraction. Multiply the numerator and the denominator by the same number to predict the number of future trials.

$$\frac{3}{8} \times \frac{■}{■} = \frac{■}{80}$$

$$\frac{3}{8} \times \frac{10}{10} = \frac{30}{80}$$

Think: By what number can I multiply the denominator to get the total number of future trials?

So, if the pattern continues, Bruce can expect to pull a green tile in about 30 of his next 80 pulls.

Example

The pointer on Karri's spinner lands on blue 8 out of 15 times. If she spins the pointer 45 more times, about how many times can Karri expect the pointer to land on blue?

$$P(\text{blue}) = \frac{8}{15} = \frac{■}{45} \qquad \frac{8}{15} \times \frac{3}{3} = \frac{24}{45}$$

So, if the pattern continues, Karri can expect the pointer to land on blue in about 24 out of 45 more spins.

KY MA-05-4.4.2 Students will determine the likelihood of an event and the probability of an event (expressed as a fraction). DOK 2

Guided Practice

Find the missing numbers to predict the outcomes of future trials.

1. 8 games won out of 14 games played
   How many wins in 35 games?

   $\frac{8}{14} = \frac{\blacksquare}{7} \qquad \frac{\blacksquare}{7} \times \frac{5}{5} = \frac{\blacksquare}{35}$

2. 12 orange marbles pulled out of 20 pulls
   How many orange marbles in 40 pulls?

   $\frac{12}{20} = \frac{\blacksquare}{5} \qquad \frac{\blacksquare}{5} \times \frac{8}{8} = \frac{\blacksquare}{40}$

Express the experimental probability as a fraction in simplest form. Then predict the outcomes of future trials.

3. 8 green tiles in 20 pulls; 35 pulls
4. 6 heads in 14 coin tosses; 28 tosses
5. 10 wins in 16 games; 40 games
6. TALK Math **Explain** the difference between experimental probability and theoretical probability.

Independent Practice and Problem Solving

Express the experimental probability as a fraction in simplest form. Then predict the outcomes of future trials. For 8–11, items are returned after each trial.

7. 10 losses in 15 games; 30 games
8. 9 red marbles in 24 pulls; 56 pulls
9. 6 dimes out of 15 coins; 45 coins
10. 14 blue tiles in 18 pulls; 36 pulls
11. 4 pink socks out of 10 socks; 30 socks
12. 21 wins in 36 games; 48 games

USE DATA For 13, use the tally chart and the spinner.

13. What is the experimental probability of the pointer landing on each color? How many of each color would you predict in 54 spins?
14. WRITE Math Ask 8 classmates which of the following games they like the best: checkers, chess, or cards. **Explain** how to use your results to predict how many students in your class like playing cards the best.

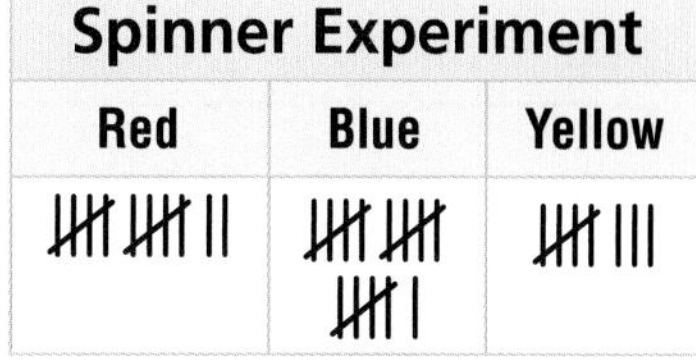

Spinner Experiment		
Red	Blue	Yellow
𝍸 𝍸 ||	𝍸 𝍸 𝍸 |	𝍸 |||

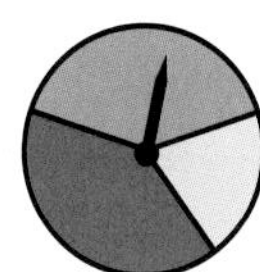

Mixed Review and Test Prep

15. Liz has 3 boxes that each have an equal number of red beads, and 1 box with 20 white beads. Write an expression for the total number of beads. (p. 92)
16. What is the probability of rolling a 2 on a number cube labeled 1 through 6? (p. 454)
17. **Test Prep** John won 12 of the 15 games he played in a tournament. Predict how many times he might win in 25 games.

    A 5 times
    B 15 times
    C 20 times
    D 25 times

Extra Practice on page 470, Set B

Problem Solving Workshop
Strategy: Make an Organized List

OBJECTIVE: Solve problems by using the strategy *make an organized list*.

Use the Strategy

PROBLEM The special at Kaye's Restaurant is a ham, tuna salad, or chicken salad sandwich, served with a side order of cottage cheese, applesauce, or chips. How many different choices of a sandwich and a side order are possible?

Read to Understand

- **What details can you identify?**
- **What are you asked to find?**

Plan

- **What strategy can you use to solve the problem?**
  You can make an organized list to help you solve the problem.

Solve

- **How can you use the strategy to solve the problem?**
  List the 3 sandwiches, and pair each with the 3 possible side orders.

ham, cottage cheese	tuna salad, cottage cheese	chicken salad, cottage cheese
ham, applesauce	tuna salad, applesauce	chicken salad, applesauce
ham, chips	tuna salad, chips	chicken salad, chips

Count the different choices.

So, 9 different choices of a sandwich and a side order are possible.

Check

- **Is your answer reasonable? Explain.**
- **How do you know the answer is correct?**

KY MA-05-4.4.1 Students will determine all possible outcomes of an activity/event with up to 12 possible outcomes. DOK 2

Guided Problem Solving

1. Jeff is ordering a frozen yogurt sundae for dessert. He can choose strawberry, vanilla, chocolate, or banana frozen yogurt, topped with fruit or chopped nuts. How many different choices of frozen yogurt and toppings are possible?

   First, list one flavor of frozen yogurt and pair it with each of the two toppings.

   Then, pair each of the other three flavors of frozen yogurt with each of the two toppings.

strawberry, fruit	vanilla, fruit	chocolate, ■	■, ■
strawberry, nuts	vanilla, ■	chocolate, ■	■, ■

   Finally, count the number of different choices.

2. **What if** the restaurant runs out of strawberry frozen yogurt? How many different choices of frozen yogurt and toppings will be possible?

3. Nia, Sam, and Toni are waiting in line to be seated at Kaye's Restaurant. How many different ways can they line up?

Choose a STRATEGY

Draw a Diagram
Make a Model or Act It Out
Make an Organized List
Find a Pattern
Make a Table or Graph
Predict and Test
Work Backward
Solve a Simpler Problem
Write an Equation
Use Logical Reasoning

Mixed Strategy Practice

USE DATA For 4–7, use the menu.

4. How many different choices of lunch items and drinks are possible?

5. Four students paid a total of $\$14.40$ for their lunch items. Two students got one item and two students got another item. Which lunch items did they have?

6. Rachel got one quarter and one nickel back in change after she paid for pizza and bottled water. How much money did Rachel give the server?

7. Luis, Megan, Dylan, and Kasey each had a different lunch item. Dylan had a taco. Megan did not have pizza or a chili dog. Kasey did not have pizza. What did each student have?

Mel's Café Lunch Menu

Lunch Item		Drink	
Chili dog	\$3.95	Fruit juice	\$2.25
Chicken nuggets	\$5.75	Milk	\$2.75
Pizza	\$2.75	Bottled water	\$2.95
Taco	\$3.25		

8. Dave wants either a taco or pizza for lunch, with juice or milk to drink. If he has apple pie or ice cream for dessert, how many lunch choices does Dave have?

9. Mel changed the menu at his café on July 6, July 15, and July 24. If the pattern continues, on what date will Mel change the menu again?

10. WRITE Math **What's the Question?** In the morning, there was $\$85$ in the cafe's cash register. By the end of the day, there was $\$649$. The answer is $\$564$.

LESSON

5 Tree Diagrams

OBJECTIVE: Find all possible outcomes of an event.

Quick Review

Tell whether spinning the event is *likely, unlikely, certain,* or *impossible.*

1. 2
2. an even number
3. an odd number
4. blue
5. 6

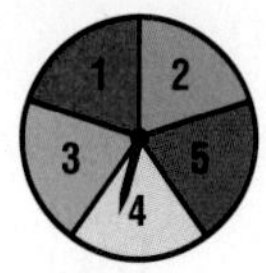

Vocabulary

tree diagram

Fundamental Counting Principle

Learn

PROBLEM Jerry wears a school uniform. He can wear a white, blue, or green shirt and he can choose black, tan, or navy pants. How many different uniform choices does Jerry have?

ONE WAY **Use a tree diagram.**

You can use a tree diagram to organize and show all possible choices. A **tree diagram** is a specific kind of organized list that shows all possible outcomes of an event.

Shirts	Pants	Outcomes
white	black	white shirt, black pants
	tan	white shirt, tan pants
	navy	white shirt, navy pants
blue	black	blue shirt, black pants
	tan	blue shirt, tan pants
	navy	blue shirt, navy pants
green	black	green shirt, black pants
	tan	green shirt, tan pants
	navy	green shirt, navy pants

Count the branches at the end of the tree diagram to find the number of total possible outcomes.

ANOTHER WAY **Use the Fundamental Counting Principle.**

You can multiply to find the number of total possible outcomes using the **Fundamental Counting Principle**. If one event has m possible outcomes, and another event has n possible outcomes, there are $m \times n$ total possible outcomes for the two events together.

3 shirt choices		3 pants choices		total number of uniform choices
3	$\times$	3	=	9

So, Jerry has 9 different uniform choices.

Math Idea

To find the total number of outcomes for 3 or more events, multiply the number of outcomes for each event. For example, if Jerry has 2 different ties that he can wear, then he has $3 \times 3 \times 2$, or 18 uniform choices.

 FAST TRACK

KY MA-05-4.4.1 Students will determine all possible outcomes of an activity/event with up to 12 possible outcomes. DOK 2

Guided Practice

1. Complete the tree diagram. Find the total number of possible outcomes for tossing two coins.

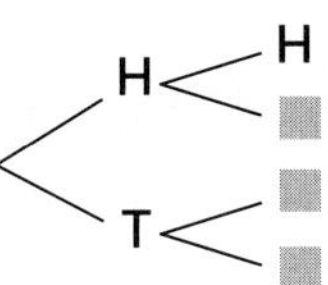

Draw a tree diagram or use the Fundamental Counting Principle to find the total number of possible outcomes.

2. choosing outfits with a pink or blue shirt and gray or tan shorts

3. tossing a number cube labeled 1 through 6 and spinning a spinner labeled 1 through 3

4. using two spinners, both with 3 equal sections colored red, blue, and yellow

5. TALK Math **Explain** how you could use part of a tree diagram to find a partial list of all possible choices.

Independent Practice and Problem Solving

For 6–9, use the cards and the spinner. Draw a tree diagram to find the total number of possible outcomes.

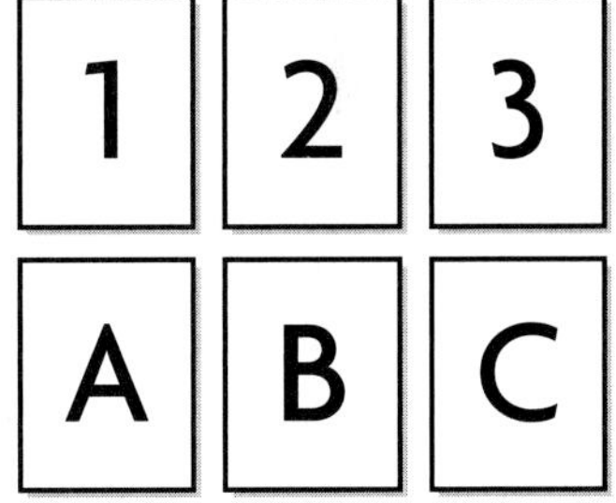

6. Draw a letter card at random and toss a coin.

7. Toss a number cube labeled 1 through 6 and draw a number card.

8. Mike puts the cards lettered *A*, *B*, and *C* in one bag and the cards numbered 1, 2, and 3 in another bag. He draws 1 card at random from each bag. Name all of the possible outcomes in his game.

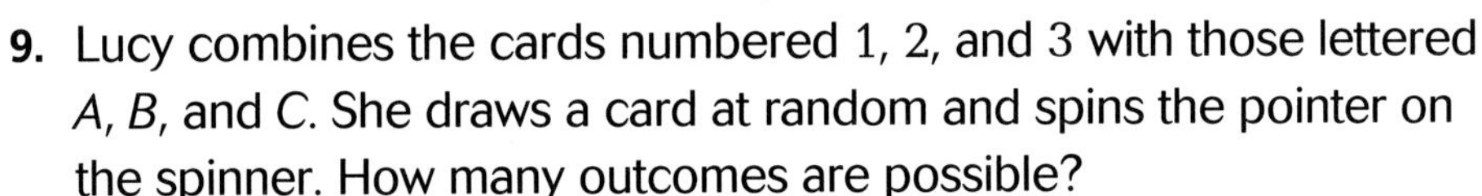

9. Lucy combines the cards numbered 1, 2, and 3 with those lettered *A*, *B*, and *C*. She draws a card at random and spins the pointer on the spinner. How many outcomes are possible?

10. WRITE Math Darren has 8 postcards and 3 different stamps. **Explain** how to use a tree diagram to find how many ways he can combine a postcard with a stamp.

Mixed Review and Test Prep

11. Rebecca needs 3 feet 4 inches of ribbon to use as trim for a scarf. How many inches of ribbon does she need? (Grade 4)

12. David drew a blue card 4 times in 9 draws. Predict how many times he might draw a blue card in 27 draws. (p. 458)

13. **Test Prep** Matt can choose vanilla, mint, or strawberry ice cream. He can have it in a cup or in a plain or waffle cone. How many ice cream choices does Matt have?

A 6

B 8

C 9

D 15

Extra Practice on page 470, Set C

LESSON 6

Combinations and Arrangements

OBJECTIVE: Find the number of possible combinations and arrangements of a set of items.

Quick Review

1. $2 \times 3 \times 2$
2. $2 \times 3 \times 4$
3. $2 \times 2 \times 4$
4. $3 \times 2 \times 5$
5. $3 \times 3 \times 3$

Vocabulary

combination

arrangement

Learn

PROBLEM Toni is designing a web page. She wants the background of her web page to change between two different colors. She will choose the combination of two colors from pink, blue, green, and violet. From how many different two-colored backgrounds can Toni choose?

A **combination** is a selection of different items in which the order is not important.

Example 1 Make a list.

Make a list of all possible outcomes. Choose one background color, then pair it with another background color.

The web page with the combination of the colors pink and blue will look identical to the web page with the color combination of blue and pink. Since order is not important, you only need to list one of the combinations from each pair.

pink and blue (p,b), or blue and pink (b,p) → pink and blue (p,b)
pink and green (p,g), or green and pink (g,p) → pink and green (p,g)
pink and violet (p,v), or violet and pink (v,p) → pink and violet (p,v)
blue and green (b,g), or green and blue (g,b) → blue and green (b,g)
blue and violet (b,v), or violet and blue (v,b) → blue and violet (b,v)
green and violet (g,v), or violet and green (v,g) → green and violet (g,v)

So, Toni can choose from 6 combinations of two-colored backgrounds for her web page.

- From how many two-colored web backgrounds can Toni choose if she only chooses from blue, green, and violet?

An arrangement is different than a combination. An **arrangement** is a selection of different items in which the order is important. To determine whether a selection is an arrangement, first decide if the order is important. If it is not, then the selection is a combination. If the order is important, then the selection is an arrangement.

KY MA-05-4.4.1 Students will determine all possible outcomes of an activity/event with up to 12 possible outcomes. DOK 2

A tree diagram can help you see and count all arrangements.

Example 2 **Use a tree diagram.**

Toni has 3 photographs that she wants to use on her web page. If she places 3 photos in a row, in how many ways can Toni arrange the photographs?

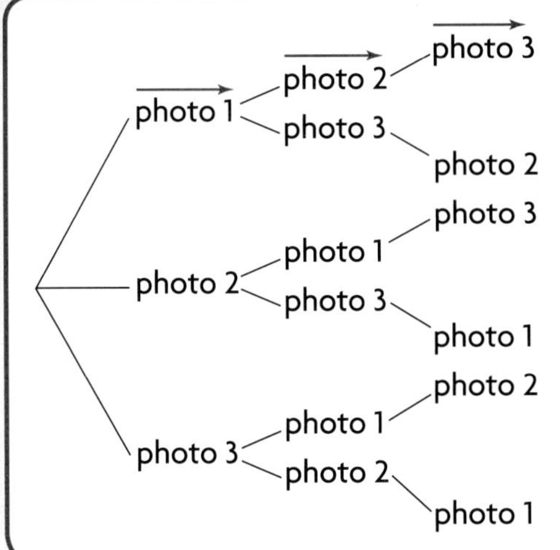

Each branch is an arrangement because the photo position is important. Once a photo is in place, it cannot be used again.

Each row of connected branches, going from left to right, shows a particular order in which the photos can be placed.

So, Toni can arrange the photographs in 6 different ways.

More Examples

A Arrangements in a list

What are all the possible arrangements of heads and tails with 2 coin tosses?

heads, heads (H,H)
heads, tails (H,T)
tails, heads (T,H)
tails, tails (T,T)

Order matters in an arrangement, so (H,T) and (T,H) are different.

There are 4 arrangements of 2 coin tosses.

B Combinations in a list

What are all the possible combinations of 2 coins using a quarter, dime, and penny?

quarter, dime (q,d)
quarter, penny (q,p)
dime, penny (d,p)

Order does not matter in a combination. The coins can be listed in any order.

There are 3 combinations of 2 coins.

Guided Practice

Complete the list to find the number of arrangements.

1. the different orders in which David can play songs A, B, and C on his portable music player

A, B, C	B, C, ■	■, ■, B
A, ■, B	B, ■, ■	■, ■, ■

number of ways David can play his songs: ■

Make a list or draw a tree diagram to find the total number of possibilities.

2. ways to arrange the numbers 4, 5, and 6

3. pizzas with choices of thick or thin crust and cheese or pepperoni topping

4. ways to place a math book, a science book, and an art book on a shelf

5. TALK Math How many 2-letter arrangements can be made from the letters in the word CAT? How does it compare with the number of arrangements that can be made using all 3 letters? **Explain.**

Independent Practice and Problem Solving

Make a list or draw a tree diagram to find the total number of possibilities.

6. sandwich combinations: turkey, chicken, or tuna salad; white or whole-wheat bread

7. swim race combinations: 25-meter, 50-meter, or 100-meter; backstroke, freestyle, or breaststroke

8. ways to arrange the letters of the word *SUM*

9. orders in which Jacob can walk his dogs Lucy, Daisy, and Thomas if each is walked alone

10. arrangements in which a green marble, a blue marble, and an orange marble are pulled from a bag without looking.

11. cat food combinations: dry, or moist; salmon, tuna, lamb, or chicken

12. The pet store offers a special to new dog owners. Any customer with a new dog or puppy can purchase 3 dog products for $25. The customer can choose 3 of the following 5 items: a sleeping basket, a supper dish, a dog collar, a training video, and a bag of dog food. The customer may choose only 1 of each type of item. Make a list that shows the total number of combinations that can be made choosing 3 of the 5 dog products.

13. WRITE Math **Sense or Nonsense** Josh says that there are usually more arrangements than combinations. Does Josh's statement make sense? **Explain.**

 Extra Practice on page 470, Set D

Learn About Permutations and Factorials

In probability, an arrangement is also called a **permutation**. A **permutation** is a selection of different items in which the order is important.

Example

You can use the Fundamental Counting Principle to find the total number of permutations of 3 objects.

Permutation of 3 objects: $3 \times 2 \times 1 = 6$

Notice that the factors in the product count down from 3 to 2 to 1. Once an item is chosen, there is one less item remaining in the set.

For example, if you have 3 books on a shelf, they can be in any order. However, once you have placed the first book, there are 2 choices for which book to place next.

Special mathematical notation called **factorials** are used to represent the products of factors that count down to 1. A factorial is written as a counting number with an exclamation point at the end.

Read: "3 factorial" $3! = 3 \times 2 \times 1 = 6$

▲ **Yosemite Falls in the Sierra Nevada Mountains in California is the highest measured waterfall in North America.**

Try It

Write the permutation to solve each problem. Evaluate the factorial.

14. The Clark family is visiting Yosemite National Park on their vacation. They plan to take five different hikes in the park. How many different ways can they arrange the hikes?

15. The Santos family plans to see six different waterfalls on their trip to Pennsylvania. How many different ways can they arrange the sites?

Mixed Review and Test Prep

16. Which type of graph best displays the data in the table? **Explain.** (p. 258)

Camp Attendance			
Camp	Tennis	Volleyball	Basketball
June	40	50	25
July	45	45	35

17. Nicole has 6 envelopes and 3 different stamps. How many possible choices does she have? (p. 464)

18. **Test Prep** There are 4 open seats together in one row at the movie theater. In how many different ways can Ray, Katie, Carmela, and Simon sit in the seats?

A 4

B 10

C 12

D 24

Extra Practice

Set A Use the bag of marbles to write the probability of the event of pulling the marble described. (pp. 454–457)

1. red
2. yellow
3. blue or yellow
4. green or red
5. blue or green
6. red, blue, or green

Use a number cube labeled 1 through 6 to write the probability of the event of tossing each number. Tell whether the event is likely, unlikely, certain, or impossible.

7. 3
8. 7 or 8
9. 1, 3, 4, or 5
10. a number less than 7
11. There are 4 white socks and 6 black socks in a drawer. Brad reaches into the drawer and picks one sock without looking. What is the probability that it is a black sock?
12. Amanda bought 12 apples. She bought 8 red apples and the rest are green apples. Amanda reaches into the bag without looking and picks an apple. What is the probability that she picks a green apple?

Set B Express the experimental probability as a fraction in simplest form. Then predict the outcome of future trials. For 1–2, items are returned after each trial. (pp. 460–461)

1. 8 pennies out of 20 coins; 30 coins
2. 7 red marbles in 28 pulls: 40 pulls
3. 8 blue sections in 24 spins; 45 spins

Set C Draw a tree diagram or use the Fundamental Counting Principle to find the total number of possible outcomes. (pp. 464–465)

1. tossing a coin and spinning a spinner labeled 1 through 5
2. tossing a number cube labeled 1 through 6 and drawing one of three cards labeled *A*, *B*, and *C*

Set D Make a list or draw a tree diagram to find the total number of possibilities. (pp. 466–469)

1. juice combinations: small, medium, or large; apple, grape, or orange
2. outfit combinations: tan or black pants; red, green, or purple shirt
3. ways to arrange the numbers 7, 8, and 2
4. ways to arrange Carl, Vince, Wendy, and Lily in a straight line
5. Kelly is trying to remember her friend's house number. She knows the digits are 0, 1, 8, and 4 in some order. How many different arrangements are there?
6. Rosa has 1 red, 1 pink, and 1 white tulip. How many ways can she arrange the tulips?

Technology
Use Harcourt Mega Math, Fraction Action, *Last Chance Canyon*, Levels D, E, J.

TECHNOLOGY CONNECTION

*i*Tools: Probability

Mario wanted to perform a coin toss experiment in which he would make 20 tosses.

Step 1	Click on *Probability*. Then select *Coin Toss* from the *Activities* menu.
Step 2	Click on the arrows to set the number of tosses to 20.
Step 3	Click on *GO* to start the coin tosses. Look at the table to see the results.

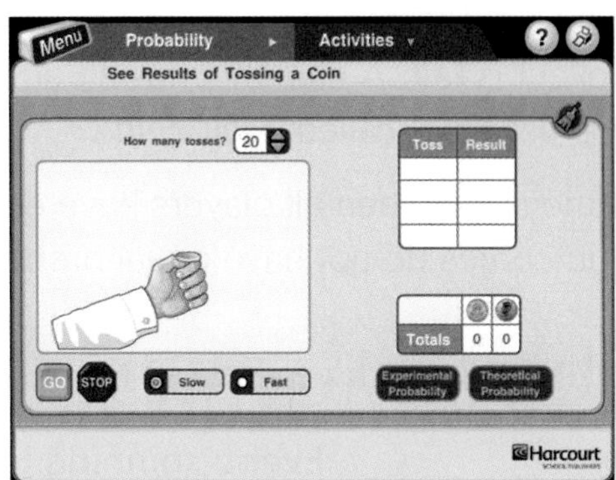

Click the broom to clear the workspace.

Try It

Predict the results of each coin toss experiment. Then follow the steps above to run the experiment. Record your results.

1. Run a coin toss experiment using 40 tosses.
2. Run a coin toss experiment using 48 tosses.
3. Run a coin toss experiment using 80 tosses.
4. Run a coin toss experiment using 100 tosses.
5. **WRITE Math** What result did you expect for each of your experiments? How did the results compare with your prediction? **Explain.**
6. **Explore More** How could you improve the accuracy of your coin toss experiment so your results more closely match your predictions? **Explain.**

GO ONLINE **Technology**
*i*Tools are available online or on CD-ROM.

MATH POWER **Fairness**

Playing Fair

When you toss a coin, you expect that the chance that the coin will land on heads or tails will be the same. Both probabilities should equal $\frac{1}{2}$. However, a damaged or altered coin might land more often on one side than the other.

When all outcomes of an event have an equal chance of occurring, the event is **fair**. A coin that has an equal probability of landing on heads or tails is called a fair coin.

A game is fair when all players have equal chances of winning. When the outcomes do not have equal probabilities, the event is unfair.

Examples **Decide whether the events are fair or unfair.**

Event: spinning blue, green, red, or yellow

- The probability of spinning blue, green, or yellow is $\frac{1}{5}$.
- The probability of spinning red is $\frac{2}{5}$.

The probabilities are not equal, so the event is unfair.

Event: spinning 1, 2, 3, 4, or 5

- The probability of spinning any number is $\frac{1}{5}$.

Since the probabilities are equal, the event is fair.

Try It

Decide whether each event is *fair* or *unfair*.

1. tossing an odd number on a number cube labeled 1 through 6
2. pulling a blue button from a jar with 4 blue, 2 green, and 4 red buttons
3. pulling a white sock from a drawer with 4 brown socks, 6 black socks, and 2 white socks
4. **WRITE Math** You are playing a game with 10 other classmates. Each player is assigned one number from 2 to 12. On each player's turn, he or she tosses two number cubes. The player whose number matches the sum of the two number cubes gets a point. The first player to get 10 points wins the game.

   Is the game fair? **Explain.** (Hint: List the different possible sums that make each sum for tossing two number cubes and count them to find their probabilities.)

Chapter 17 Review/Test

Check Vocabulary and Concepts

Choose the best term from the box.

VOCABULARY
probability
combination
arrangement
prediction

1. The likelihood that an event will happen. KY MA-05-4.4.2 (p. 458)
2. A reasonable guess about the possible result of a probability experiment. KY MA-05-4.4.2 (p. 458)
3. A selection of items in which the order is not important. KY MA-05-4.4.1 (p. 466)

Check Skills

Use the bag of marbles to write the probability of the event of pulling the marble described. Tell whether the event is *likely, unlikely, certain* or *impossible*. KY MA-05-4.4.2 (pp. 454–457)

4. red
5. green
6. blue or red
7. blue, red, or green

Express the experimental probability as a fraction in simplest form. Then predict the outcome of future trials. For Problem 8, the marble is returned after each trial. KY MA-05-4.4.2 (pp. 460–461)

8. 9 blue marbles in 27 pulls; 90 pulls
9. 10 wins in 12 games; 18 games
10. 4 white sections in 20 spins 50 spins

Make a list or draw a tree diagram to find the total number of possible outcomes. KY MA-05-4.4.1 (pp. 466–469)

11. sandwich combinations: tuna, cheese, ham, or roast beef; white or whole-wheat bread
12. ways to arrange the letters in the word *MATH*

Check Problem Solving

Solve. KY MA-05-4.4.1 (pp. 462–463)

13. Morgan ordered from Triangle Park Café's Pick Three Menu. From how many different combinations of appetizer, entrée and dessert can she choose if she can pick one of each?
14. The waiter tells Linn that the chicken is not available today. How many appetizer, entrée, and dessert choices are possible?
15. **WRITE Math** How many different combinations of letters can be made choosing one letter from the word PINK and one letter from the word BLUE? Make a list or draw a diagram.

Triangle Park Café's Pick Three Menu

Appetizer	Entrée	Dessert
Buffalo wings	Chicken	Cheesecake
Potato skins	Spaghetti	Pudding
Mozzarella sticks	Sirloin steak	Apple pie

GO ONLINE Technology Use *Online Assessment.*

Unit Review/Test
Chapters 16–17

Multiple Choice

1. Tory pulls one marble from the bag without looking. Which color is she most likely to choose? KY MA-05-4.4.2 (p. 456)

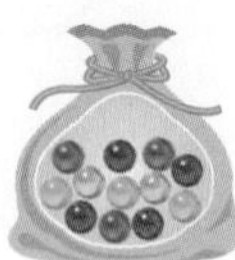

A. Green C. Red

B. Blue D. Purple

2. Simon tosses a number cube labeled 1 through 6. Which outcome is impossible for Simon to roll? KY MA-05-4.4.2 (p. 456)

A. Prime number

B. Odd number

C. Composite number

D. Multiple of 8

3. The table shows the number of times Jasmine pulled tiles from a bag.

Tile Pulls		
Red	**Green**	**Blue**
𝍸 |||	𝍸	||

What is the experimental probability of pulling a green tile from the bag? KY MA-05-4.4.2 (p. 460)

A. $\frac{1}{3}$

B. $\frac{2}{5}$

C. $\frac{1}{2}$

D. $\frac{5}{8}$

4. The pointer on a spinner lands on green 8 times in 20 spins. Predict how many times the pointer will land on green in 50 spins. KY MA-05-4.4.2 (p. 460)

A. 15 times

B. 20 times

C. 30 times

D. 40 times

5. How many outcomes are possible if Jack tosses the coin and spins the pointer on the spinner shown below? KY MA-05-4.4.1 (p. 456)

A. 25 C. 10

B. 15 D. 6

6. Polly has 9 letter cards that spell the word *EXCELLENT* when put together. If she chooses 1 card without looking, what is the probability that it will have the letter *L* on it? KY MA-05-4.4.2 (p. 466)

A. $\frac{7}{9}$

B. $\frac{3}{7}$

C. $\frac{2}{7}$

D. $\frac{2}{9}$

GO ONLINE **Technology** Use *Online Assessment.*

7. What fraction of the squares are shaded?
KY MA-05-5.1.1 (p. 308)

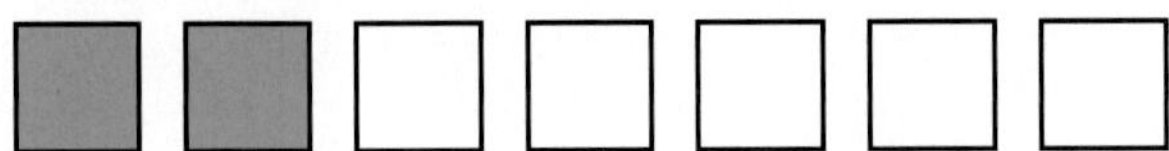

A. $\frac{2}{5}$

B. $\frac{2}{7}$

C. $\frac{5}{7}$

D. $\frac{5}{2}$

8. What is the mean of the scores for the 5 games played? KY MA-05-4.2.1 (p. 220)

Blue Darters' Game Scores				
44	53	67	57	44

A. 44

B. 53

C. 57

D. 67

9. What is 24.937 rounded to the nearest tenth? KY MA-05-1.2.1 (p. 150)

A. 24.9

B. 24.93

C. 24.94

D. 25

10. Jin's Movie Store ordered 8 boxes of new movies to sell. There are 24 movies in each box. How many movies are there in all?
KY MA-05-1.3.1 (p. 40)

A. 192

B. 52

C. 32

D. 16

Open Response WRITE Math

11. Ashton put 3 green tiles, 8 red tiles, and 4 blue tiles into a bag. She pulled one tile out of the bag without looking. What are the possible outcomes? **Explain.**
KY MA-05-4.4.1 (p. 462)

12. What are all the possible 3-digit numbers that can be made with the number cards shown below? **Explain** how you got your answer. KY MA-05-4.4.1 (p. 466)

6	7	8

13. What fraction represents the unshaded number of stars? Write your answer as a percent and as a decimal. **Explain** how you got your answers. KY MA-05-4.4.2 (p. 460)

THE WORLD ALMANAC FOR KIDS

Games and Probability

What Are the Chances of That?

Have you ever played Twister® or another game that uses a spinner? The way that a spinner is designed may determine who wins the game. For each spin in the game of Twister, there are 16 possible outcomes. Each outcome is 1 of 4 colors, left or right side, and hand or foot. You can calculate the probability of each different outcome, such as "Right hand, green!"

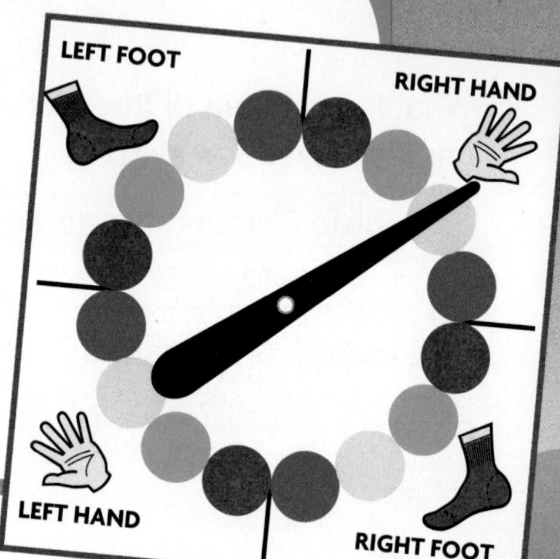

FACT·ACTIVITY

Use the spinner to answer the questions.

1. If each section is an equally likely outcome, what is the probability of spinning a particular color?
2. If each section is an equally likely outcome, what is the probability of spinning either left or right foot?
3. If each section is an equally likely outcome, what is the probability of spinning right foot combined with red, yellow, or blue?

Draw a spinner that matches both parts of the description.

4. a spinner with 6 equal sections; probability of spinning red: $\frac{1}{2}$
5. a spinner with 10 equal sections; probability of spinning an even number: $\frac{3}{10}$
6. a spinner with 3 equal sections; probability of spinning a 3: 0
7. a spinner with 8 equal sections; probability of spinning blue or green: $\frac{3}{4}$
8. **WRITE Math** Compare the spinner you drew and colored for Problem 7 with the Twister spinner. **Explain** why the probability of landing on blue is the same or different on the two spinners.

Spin It Yourself

Most board games use number cubes or spinners. Players advance game pieces around a board by moving them the number of spaces they roll or spin. The winner is usually the player who rolls or spins the highest numbers. In the game of Twister, the winner is only partly determined by outcomes on the spinner. A player with good balance and long arms and legs has a better chance of winning.

Many games require a mental or physical skill to win. If all of the players are equally skilled, all have about the same chance of winning the game. If one player has more skill than the others, he or she has a better chance of winning.

ALMANAC Fact

It has been estimated that about 65 million people around the world have played Twister since it was introduced in 1966.

Design a game that gives a player with more skill a better chance of winning the game. Use Kyle's game as an example.

- Decide on the materials to use (color tiles, marbles, number cubes, and so on).
- Write the rules. Will your game involve a physical activity, moving pieces on a board, answering questions, or a combination of these? Tell how to win the game.
- What skill would give a player a better chance of winning the game?
- WRITE Math Create a spinner game. Design the game and write the rules. Then make the spinner. Is your spinner fair? Why or why not?

Marble Game — Kyle

Place 1 yellow, 1 blue, 1 green, and 1 red marble in a bag. To play the game, draw a marble from the bag.

A player who draws a yellow marble takes 1 step forward.

A player who draws a blue marble takes 2 steps backward.

A player who draws a green marble must answer a question about video games correctly to move 3 steps forward.

A player who draws a red marble loses a turn.

To win the game, be the first player to reach the finish line.

UNIT 7

Geometry and Algebra

Math on Location

with
Chapter Projects

1

Precious and semi-precious gems are found on Earth as shapeless, dull stones.

2

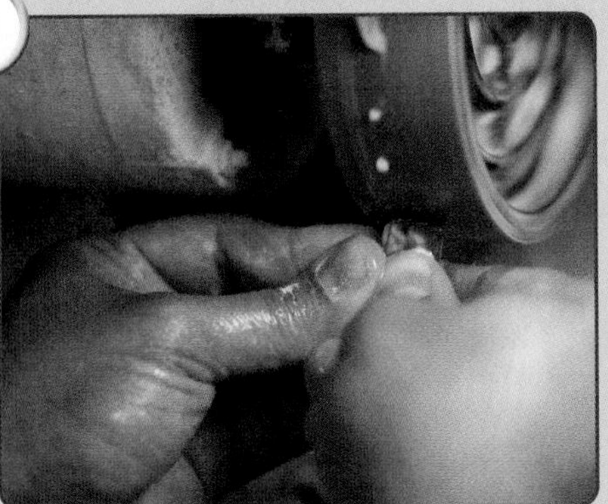

Flat faces, called facets, are precisely cut to form the gems into geometric shapes.

3

Colorful gems are used in jewelry that incorporates lines and angles in symmetric designs.

VOCABULARY POWER

TALK Math

What math do you see in the **Math on Location**? What kinds of angles and polygons can you identify in the jewelry shown?

READ Math

REVIEW VOCABULARY You learned the words below when you learned about angles, geometric figures, and patterns. How do these words relate to **Math on Location**?

angle a figure formed by two rays that have a common endpoint

equilateral triangle a triangle with three congruent sides

input/output table a table that uses a mathematical rule to generate numbers

WRITE Math

Copy and complete a chart like the one below. Use what you know about triangles to fill in the blanks.

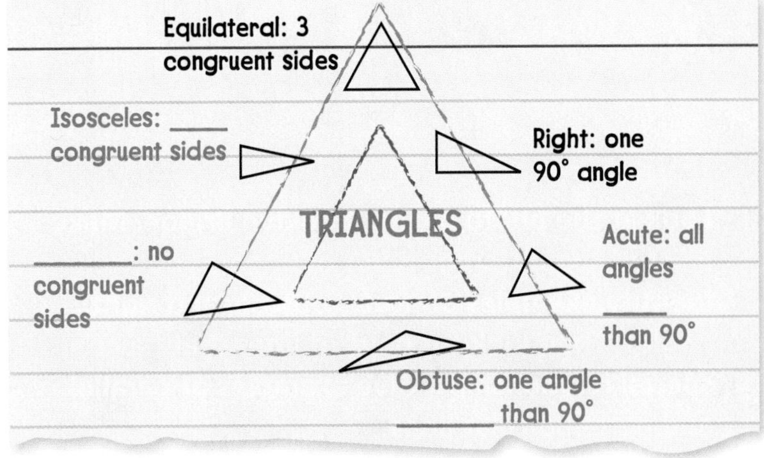

Technology
Multimedia Math Glossary link at
www.harcourtschool.com/hspmath

CHAPTER 18

Geometric Figures

FAST FACT

The Brooklyn Bridge, in New York City, NY, crosses the lower East River with a total length of 6,016 feet. The bridge took 13 years to build and opened in 1883.

Investigate

Look at the photo of the Brooklyn Bridge. Make a list of the different types of angles you see. Identify examples of acute, obtuse, and right angles. Then look for pairs of lines that have special relationships. Give examples of parallel and perpendicular lines.

Term	Example
Acute angle	
Obtuse angle	
Right angle	
Parallel lines	
Perpendicular lines	

Technology
Student pages are available in the Student eBook.

Show What You Know

Check your understanding of important skills needed for success in Chapter 18.

▶ Name Polygons

Name each polygon. Tell the number of sides and angles.

1. 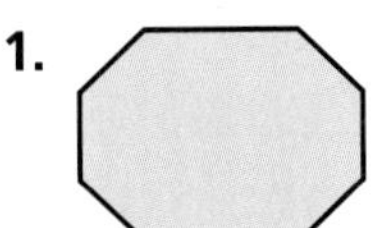
2. 
3. 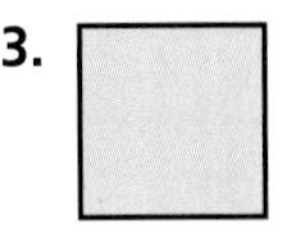
4. 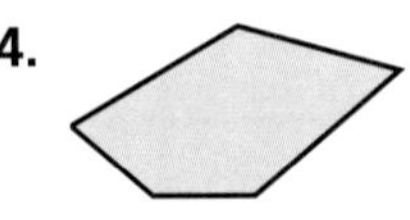
5. 
6. 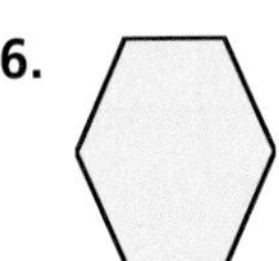
7. 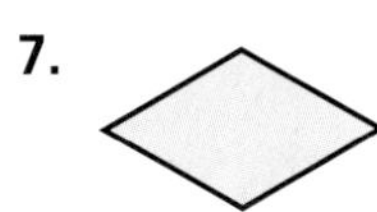
8. 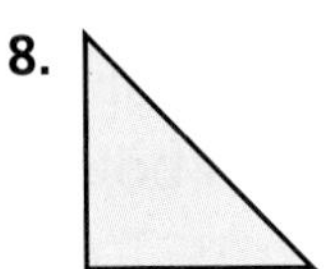

▶ Angles

Tell whether each angle is a *right angle, greater than a right angle,* or *less than a right angle.*

9.
10. 
11. 
12. 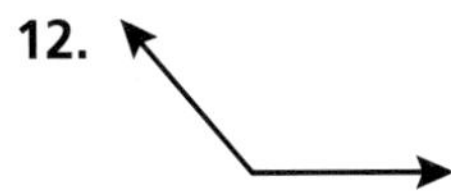

VOCABULARY POWER

CHAPTER VOCABULARY

acute angle
chord
circle
congruent
corresponding angles
corresponding sides
diameter
intersecting lines
line
line segment
line symmetry
obtuse angle
polygon
parallel lines
perpendicular lines
plane
point
protractor
radius
ray
regular polygon
right angle
rotational symmetry
skew lines
similar
straight angle
vertex

WARM-UP WORDS

acute angle an angle that measures less than 90°

polygon a closed plane figure formed by three or more line segments

similar having the same shape but not necessarily the same size

LESSON 1

Points, Lines, and Angles

OBJECTIVE: Identify and use the concepts of point, line, and angle and classify angles as acute, right, or obtuse.

Quick Review

Write the number of sides and angles for each figure.

1. 2.

3. 4.

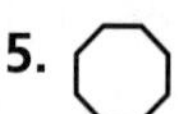

5.

Vocabulary

point	line
line segment	ray
plane	right angle
acute angle	obtuse angle
straight angle	parallel lines
intersecting lines	skew lines
perpendicular lines	

Learn

Points, lines, and planes are building blocks of geometry. These figures are represented and named in a special way.

A **point** is an exact location in space. Use a letter to name a point.	•*A* point *A*
A **line** is a straight path in a plane, extending in both directions with no endpoints. To name a line, use any two points that are on the line.	*B* *C* line *BC* or $\overleftrightarrow{BC}$ or line *CB* or $\overleftrightarrow{CB}$
A **line segment** is a part of a line between two endpoints. To name a line segment, use both endpoints.	*D* *E* line segment *DE* or $\overline{DE}$ or line segment *ED* or $\overline{ED}$
A **ray** is a part of a line. It begins at one endpoint and extends forever in one direction. To name a ray, use the endpoint and any other point that is on the ray.	*F* *G* ray *FG* or $\overrightarrow{FG}$
A **plane** is a flat surface that extends without end in all directions. To name a plane, name any three points on the plane, but not all on the same line.	*H* *I* *J* plane *HIJ*

Examples Name the labeled geometric figure in each picture.

A

The part labeled on the bicycle has two endpoints. So, the figure represented is line segment *MN*, or $\overline{MN}$.

B

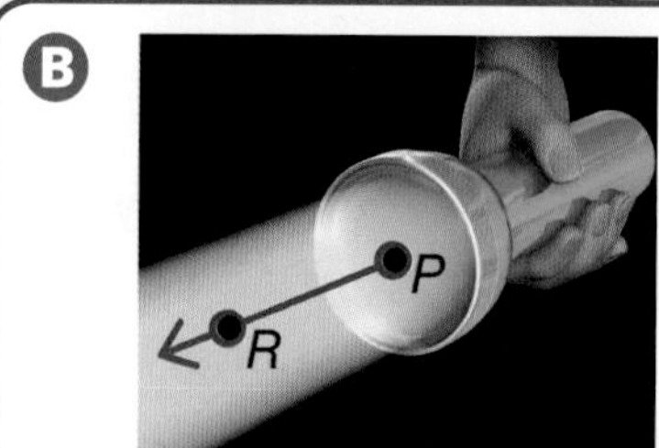

The beam from the flashlight has one endpoint. So, the figure represented is ray *PR* or $\overrightarrow{PR}$.

C

The wall is a flat surface. Three points are labeled on it. So, the figure represented is plane *STU*.

FAST TRACK KY MA-05-3.1.1 Students will describe and provide examples of basic geometric elements and terms [points, segments, lines (perpendicular, parallel, intersecting), rays, angles (acute, right, obtuse), sides, edges, faces, base vertices, radius, diameter] and will apply these elements to solve real-world and mathematical problems. DOK 2

Other Geometric Figures

Two rays that have a common endpoint, or vertex, form an angle. To name an angle, use three points, with the vertex in the middle, or use only the point at the vertex.

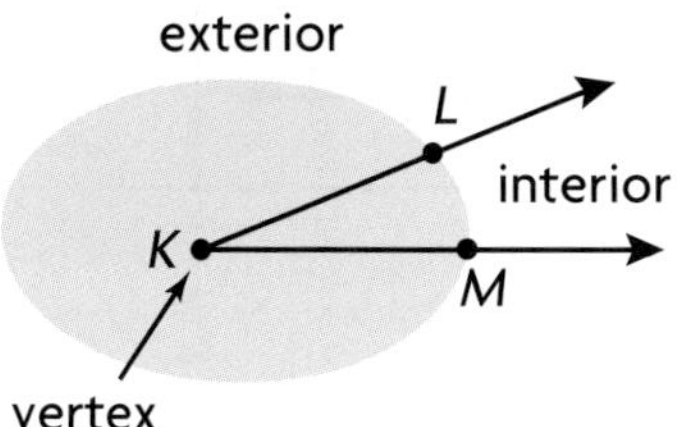

$\angle LKM$, $\angle MKL$, or $\angle K$

▼ The Seattle Public Library

You can classify angles by their size. The size of an angle is measured in degrees. The lengths of the rays that form an angle do not affect the measure of an angle.

A **right angle** is an angle that measures 90°.

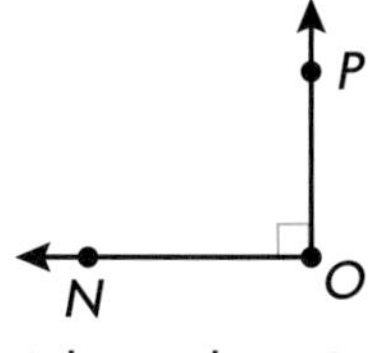

right angle *NOP*

An **acute angle** is an angle that measures less than 90°.

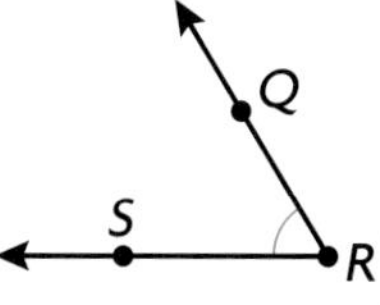

acute angle *QRS*

An **obtuse angle** is an angle that measures greater than 90° and less than 180°.

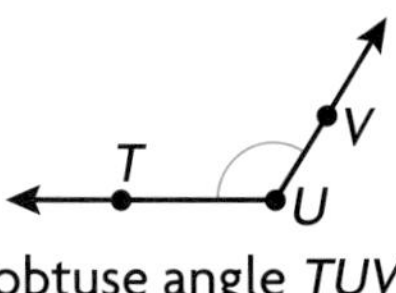

obtuse angle *TUV*

A **straight angle** is an angle that measures 180°.

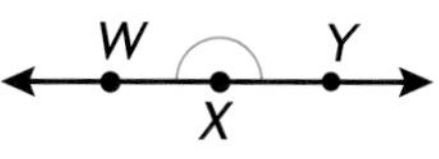

straight angle *WXY*

- On the photos of the Seattle Public Library, can you see examples of angles that appear to be right, acute, obtuse, or straight?

Lines can have different relationships with each other.

Parallel lines are lines in a plane that are always the same distance apart.

$\overleftrightarrow{BC} \parallel \overleftrightarrow{AZ}$

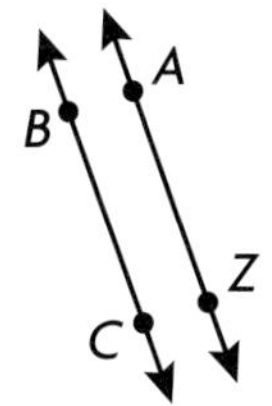

Intersecting lines are lines in a plane that cross at exactly one point.

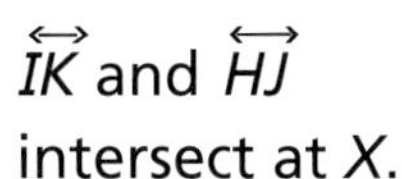
$\overleftrightarrow{IK}$ and $\overleftrightarrow{HJ}$ intersect at *X*.

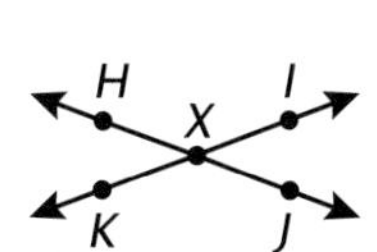

Perpendicular lines are two lines in a plane that intersect to form right angles.

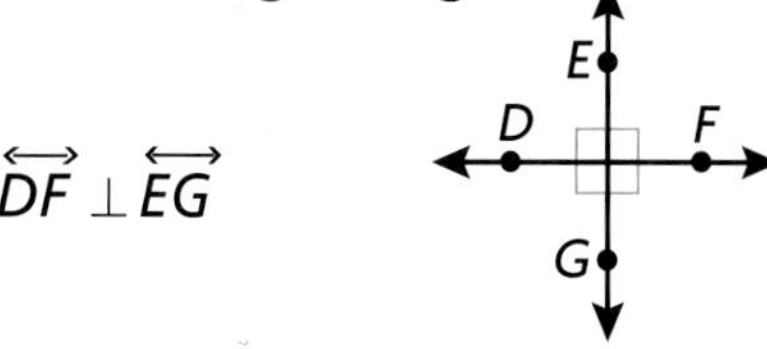

$\overleftrightarrow{DF} \perp \overleftrightarrow{EG}$

Skew lines are lines that are not in the same plane, are not parallel, and do not intersect.

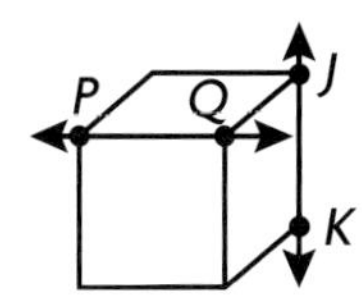

$\overleftrightarrow{JK}$ and $\overleftrightarrow{PQ}$ are skew lines.

- Draw and label line segments that are parallel, intersecting, and perpendicular.

Guided Practice

1. Name each angle, and identify it as right, acute, obtuse, or straight. Use grid paper to draw and label the kind of angle not shown.

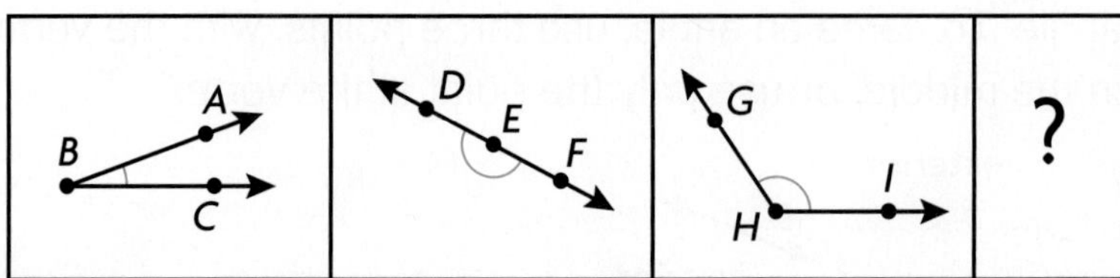

For 2–5, use the figure. Name an example of each.

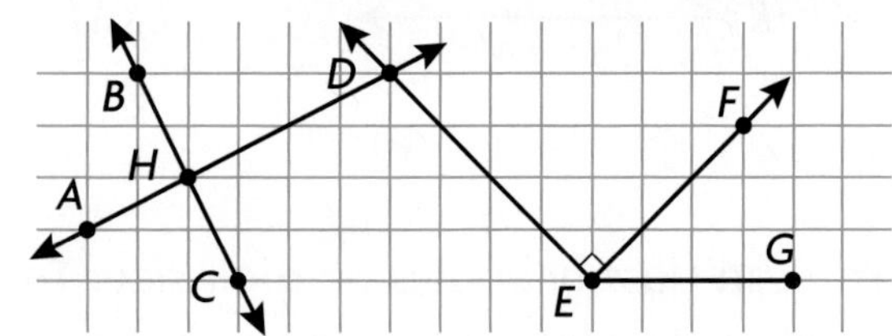

2. ray
3. point
4. line
5. intersecting lines

For 6–9, use the figure above. Classify each angle. Write *obtuse, acute, straight,* or *right*.

6. $\angle FED$
7. $\angle DEG$
8. $\angle FEG$
9. $\angle BHC$

10. **TALK Math** **Explain** how skew lines are different from parallel lines.

Independent Practice and Problem Solving

For 11–16, use the figure. Name an example of each.

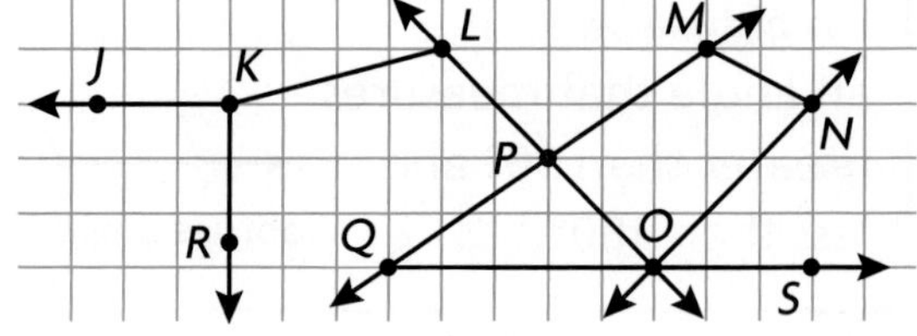

11. point
12. line segment
13. line
14. plane
15. vertex
16. angle

For 17–24, use the figure above. Classify each angle. Write *obtuse, acute, straight,* or *right*.

17. $\angle JKR$
18. $\angle LPQ$
19. $\angle NOS$
20. $\angle LOS$
21. $\angle QPM$
22. $\angle RKL$
23. $\angle SQM$
24. $\angle PMN$

USE DATA For 25–27, use the map.

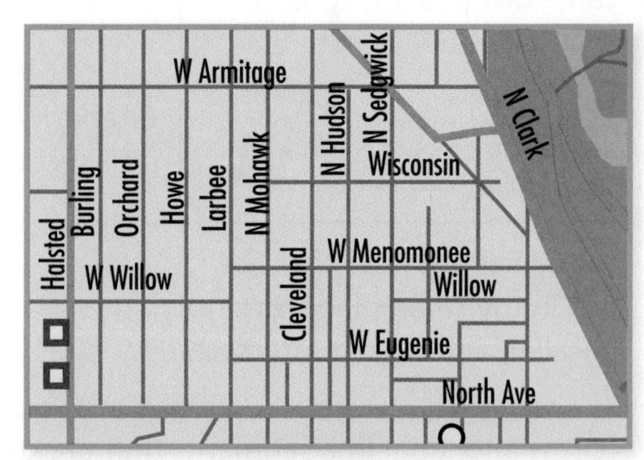

25. Name three streets that are parallel to Orchard.

26. Name three streets that are perpendicular to Halsted.

27. Find an acute angle that N. Clark forms with another street. What is the name of the other street?

28. **WRITE Math** **Explain** how intersecting and perpendicular lines are both similar and different.

CD ROM Technology
Use Harcourt Mega Math, Ice Station Exploration, *Polar Planes,* Levels A, B.

Extra Practice on page 506, Set A

Learn About Vertical Angles

Vertical angles are opposite each other and are equal.

Find the measures of $\angle AED$, $\angle CED$, and $\angle BEC$.

Step 1

Note that $\angle BEA$ and $\angle AED$ together make up a straight angle, $\angle DEB$.

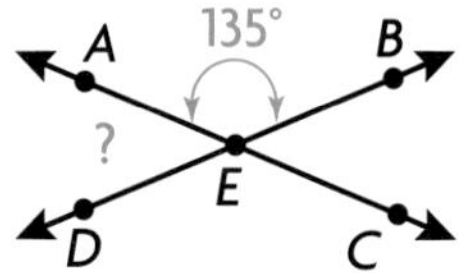

Step 2

Subtract the measure of $\angle BEA$ from 180° to find the measure of $\angle AED$.

$$180° - 135° = 45°$$

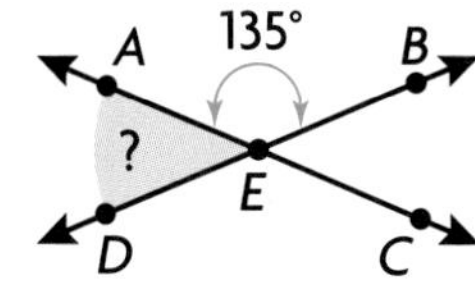

So, the measure of $\angle AED$ is 45°.

Step 3

$\angle AEB$ and $\angle DEC$ are vertical angles. $\angle AED$ and $\angle BEC$ are vertical angles. Vertical angles have equal measures.

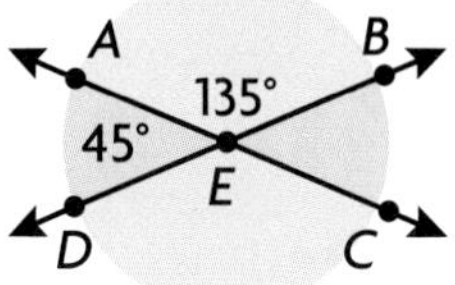

So, the measure of $\angle DEC$ is equal to 135° and the measure of $\angle BEC$ is equal to 45°.

Try It

Use the drawing to find the measure of each angle. Tell whether you used straight or vertical angles to find the measure of each angle.

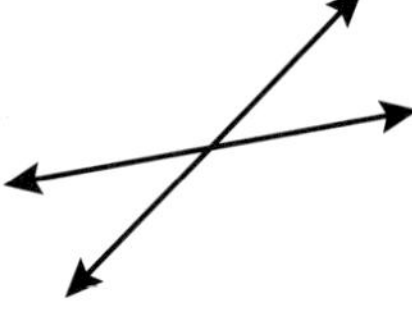

29. $\angle EGB$

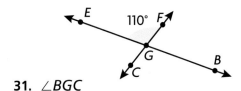

30. $\angle FGB$

31. $\angle BGC$

Mixed Review and Test Prep

32. Which number is greater, 3.25 or $3\frac{2}{5}$? (p. 440)

33. What is 20% of 50? (p. 447)

34. **Test Prep** Which is the greatest whole number of degrees an acute angle can have?

A 89°
B 179°
C 269°
D 359°

35. **Test Prep** Which of the following best describes the figure?

A intersecting lines
B parallel lines
C perpendicular lines
D acute angles

LESSON 2

Measure and Draw Angles

OBJECTIVE: Estimate, measure, and draw angles.

Quick Review

Classify each angle as *acute, right,* or *obtuse.*

1. 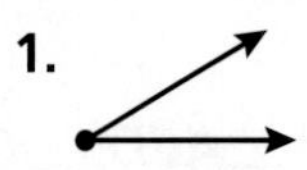
2. 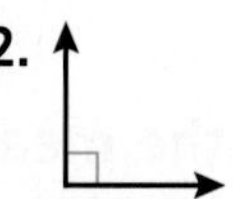
3. 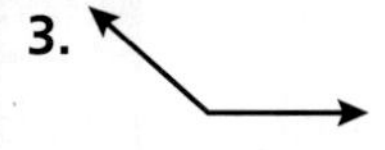
4. 
5. 

Vocabulary

protractor

Learn

To estimate the measure of an angle you can use benchmarks and what you know about acute, right, and obtuse angles.

Examples Estimate the measure of each angle.

A

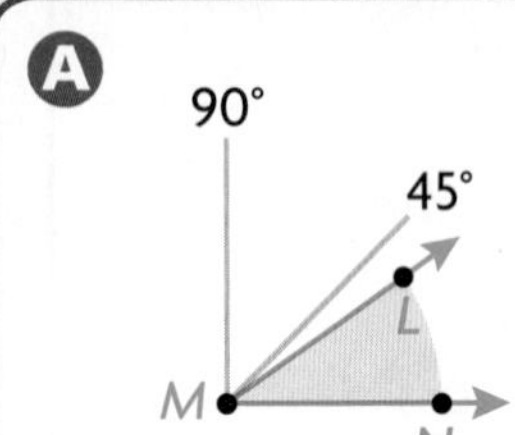

Angle *LMN* is an acute angle, so its measure is less than 90°.

A benchmark, 45°, is halfway between 0° and 90°.

So, the measure of $\angle LMN$ is about 45° or a little less than 45°.

B

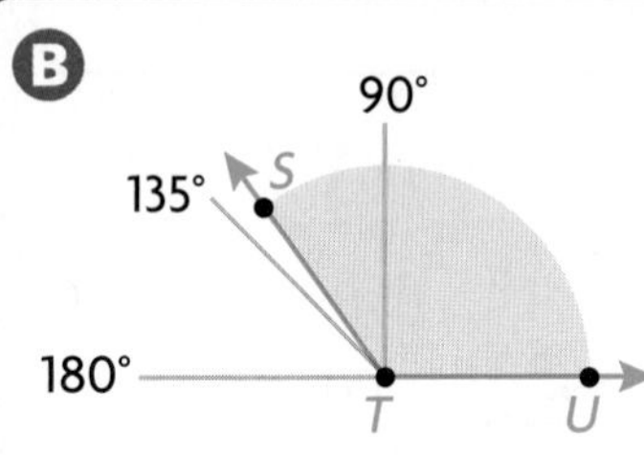

Angle *STU* is an obtuse angle, so its measure is greater than 90° and less than 180°.

A benchmark, 135°, is halfway between 90° and 180°.

So, the measure of $\angle STU$ is about 135° or a little less than 135°.

▲ Surveyors use a tool called a theodolite to measure angles.

You can use a protractor to measure angles. A **protractor** is a tool used for measuring or drawing angles.

Activity **Materials** ■ protractor

Measure $\angle JKL$.

1. Place the center point of the protractor on the vertex of the angle.
2. Place the base of the protractor along ray *KL*.
3. Read the scale that starts with 0° at ray *KL*. The measure of $\angle JKL$ is 60°.

Extend the rays if you need to.

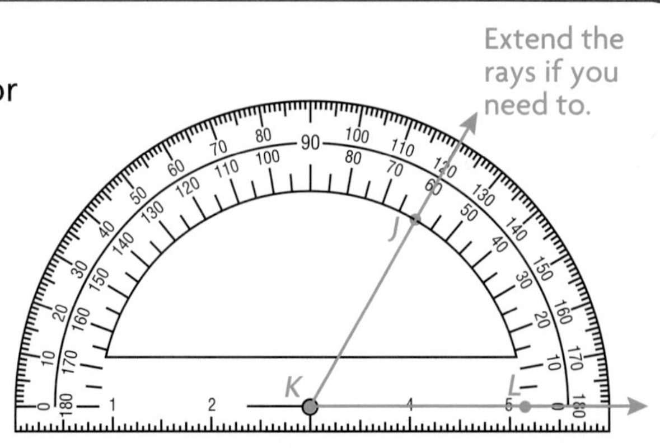

FAST TRACK

KY MA-05-2.1.1 Students will apply standard units to measure length (to the nearest eighth-inch or the nearest centimeter) and to determine: angle measures (nearest degree). DOK 2 *also MA-05-2.1.2;* MA-05-2.1.6; MA-05-3.1.1

Draw Angles

You can also use a protractor to draw angles of a given measure.

Activity **Materials** ■ protractor ■ straightedge

Use a protractor to draw ∠*FDE* with a measure of 60°.

Step 1

Use a straightedge to draw ray *DE*.

Step 2

Line up the ray with the protractor. Mark point *F* at 60°.

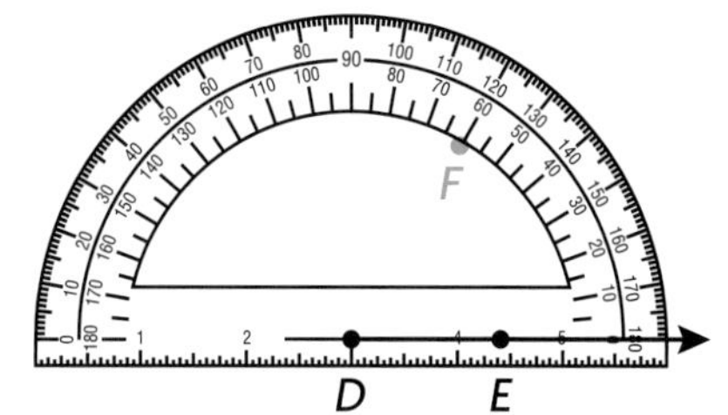

Step 3

Use a straightedge to draw ray *DF*.

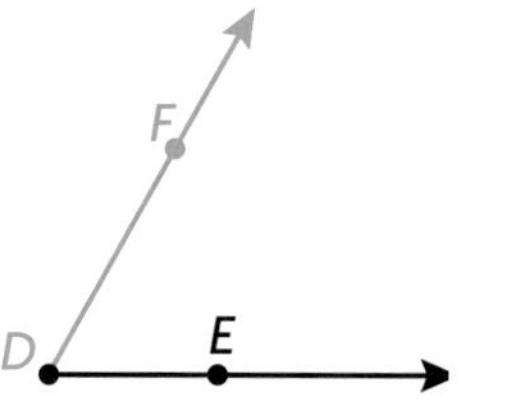

When angles appear to be equal, measure them with a protractor and then compare.

More Examples **Find the measure of each angle. How do ∠*ABC* and ∠*XYZ* compare?**

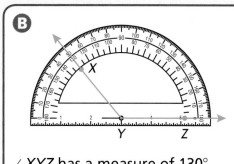

A

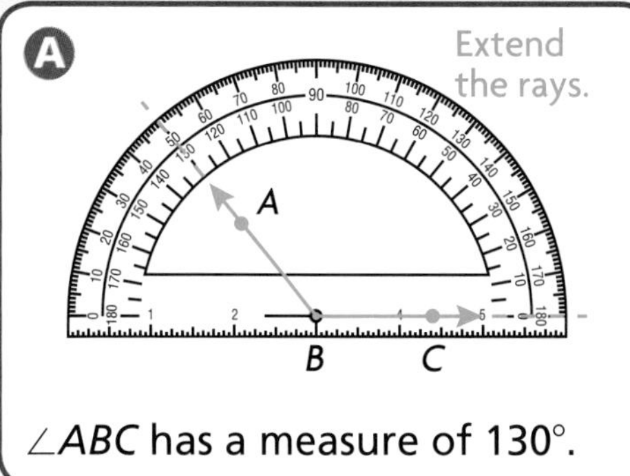

∠*ABC* has a measure of 130°.

B

X
Y
Z

∠*XYZ* has a measure of 130°.

So, ∠*ABC* and ∠*XYZ* both have the same measure, 130°.

ERROR ALERT

Remember that the measure of an angle is determined by the degree of rotation of a ray and not the length of the ray.

Guided Practice

1. Draw and label an angle with about the same measure as ∠*MOQ*, shown at the right.
   a. Is your angle acute, obtuse, or right? Estimate the measure of your angle.
   b. Use a protractor to find the measure of your angle. How does your estimate compare to the actual measure of the angle?
   c. Use a straightedge to draw ray *OP*. Use a protractor to find the measure of your new angle *QOP*.

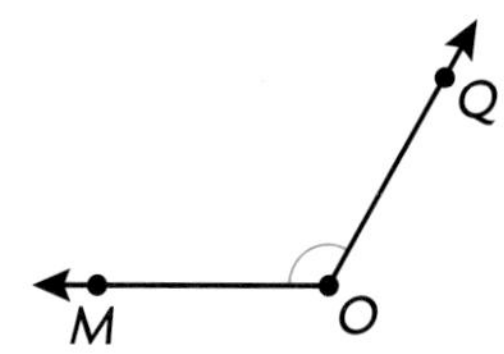

Estimate the measure of each angle. Then use a protractor to find the measure.

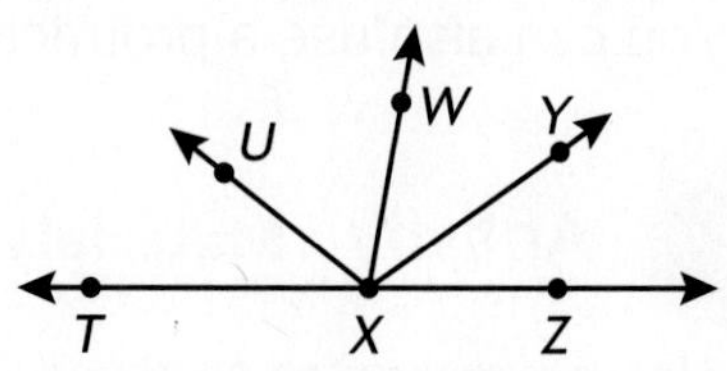

2. ∠*TXW** **3.** ∠*WXY* **4.** ∠*UXY*
5. ∠*YXZ* **6.** ∠*TXU* **7.** ∠*UXW*

Use a protractor to draw each angle. Classify each angle.

8. 45° **9.** 60° **10.** 125° **11.** 14°

12. TALK Math **Explain** how you can estimate and find the measure of ∠*WXZ* in the figure above.

Independent Practice and Problem Solving

Estimate the measure of each angle. Then use a protractor to find the measure.

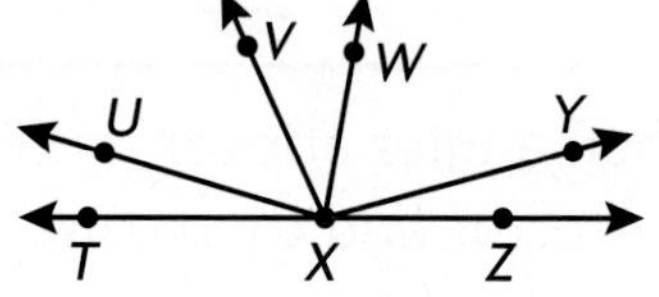

13. ∠*YXZ* **14.** ∠*VXT* **15.** ∠*WXZ*
16. ∠*VXU* **17.** ∠*VXW* **18.** ∠*UXT*
19. ∠*VXZ* **20.** ∠*UXY* **21.** ∠*TXZ*

Use a protractor to draw each angle. Classify each angle.

22. 35° **23.** 159° **24.** 16° **25.** 95°
26. 120° **27.** 44° **28.** 180° **29.** 135°

30. an angle whose measure is between 110° and 130°

31. an angle whose measure is less than 65°

USE DATA For 32–35, use the clocks.

32. Copy the angle made by the hands of the clock that shows 6:00. What is the measure of this angle? **Explain** how you know.

33. At what hours do the hands of a clock form a right angle?

34. Estimate the measure of the angle formed by the hands of the clock that shows 3:05. Then measure the angle.

35. Draw a clock like the ones at the right. Make the hands on the clock form an angle of 30°. What time is on your clock?

36. WRITE Math **What's the Error?** Tracy measured an angle as 50° that was actually 130°. Describe her error.

 Extra Practice on page 506, Set B

Mixed Review and Test Prep

37. If $n = 6$, what is the value of $5n - 2$? (p. 196)

38. **Test Prep** Which angle measure names an obtuse angle?

    A 45°

    B 85°

    C 90°

    D 110°

39. Find the product. $\frac{1}{4} \times \frac{2}{3}$ (p. 390)

40. **Test Prep** What is the approximate measure of the angle below?

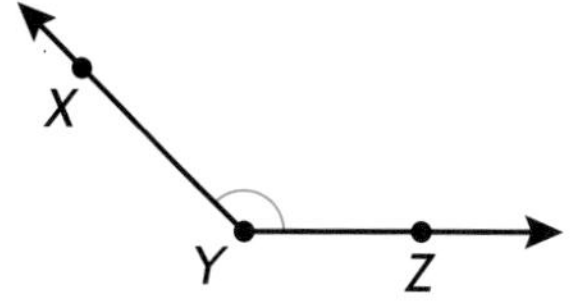

Problem Solving connects to Science

Why does Earth have seasons? The planet is tilted on its axis. To see how this causes the seasons, look at the diagrams, which show the sun's angle with Earth's axis.

Examples Northern Hemisphere

Winter
The axis is tilted away from the sun on the first day of winter, often on December 21.

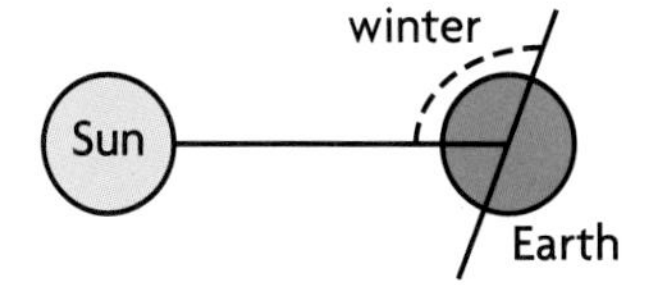

Spring and Fall
The axis is not tilted away from or toward the sun on the first day of spring and fall, often on March 20 and September 22.

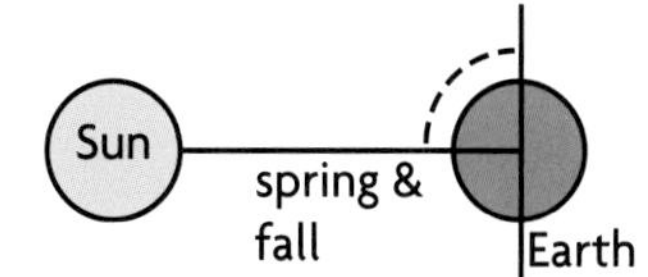

Summer
The axis is tilted toward the sun on the first day of summer, often on June 21.

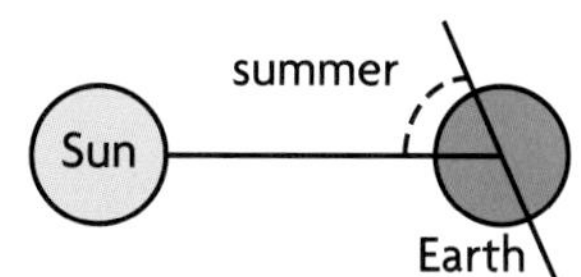

Use the diagrams to find the angle measures.

1. What is the marked angle on the shortest day of the year, the first day of winter?
2. What is the marked angle on the longest day of the year, the first day of summer?
3. What is the marked angle on the first day of spring and fall?

LESSON 3

Polygons

OBJECTIVE: Identify, classify, and draw polygons; find the sum of the angles in triangles and in quadrilaterals.

Quick Review

Find the measure of ∠*ABC*.

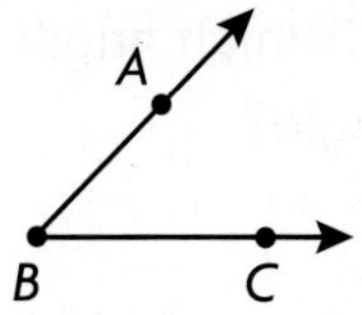

Vocabulary

polygon

regular polygon

Learn

PROBLEM The Castel del Monte in Apulia, Italy, was built sometime between A.D. 1240 and 1250. The main building and the center courtyard have 8 sides. Each of the 8 towers also has 8 sides. What polygon matches these features of Castel del Monte?

A **polygon** is a closed plane figure formed by three or more line segments. Polygons are named by the number of their sides and angles.

Polygon	Number of Sides and Angles
Triangle	3
Quadrilateral	4
Pentagon	5
Hexagon	6
Octagon	8
Decagon	10

▲ Courtyard view of Castel del Monte looking up

So, an octagon matches the Castel del Monte's main structure, courtyard, and towers.

In a **regular polygon**, all sides are congruent and all angles are congruent. A polygon that has sides and angles that are not congruent is not a regular polygon.

Examples Classify each figure.

	Polygon	Numbers of Sides and Angles	Name of Polygon	Types of Angles	Regular Polygon?
	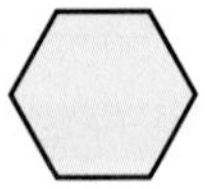	6 sides and 6 angles	hexagon	6 obtuse angles	Yes; the hexagon appears to have congruent sides and congruent angles.
		6 sides and 6 angles	hexagon	2 acute angles and 4 obtuse angles	No; the sides are not congruent and the angles are not congruent.
	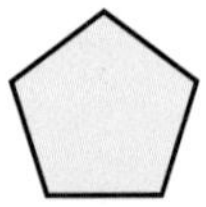	5 sides and 5 angles	pentagon	5 obtuse angles	Yes; the pentagon appears to have congruent sides and congruent angles.

FAST TRACK

KY MA-05-3.1.2 Students will describe and provide examples of basic two-dimensional shapes [circles, triangles (right, equilateral), all quadrilaterals, pentagons, hexagons, octagons] and will apply these shapes to solve real-world and mathematical problems. DOK 2 *also* MA-05-3.1.1

Sum of the Angles

If you add the measures of the three angles in any triangle, is the sum always the same?

Activity 1 **Materials** ■ protractor ■ isometric dot paper ■ straightedge

Step 1

Use isometric dot paper to draw a triangle. Label the angles *A*, *B*, and *C*.

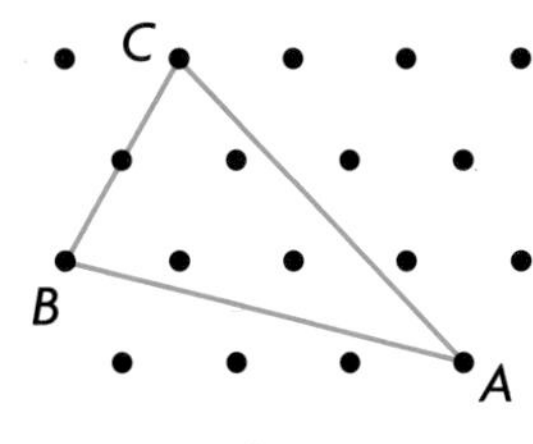

Step 2

Use a protractor to measure all 3 angles. Find the sum of the 3 angles.

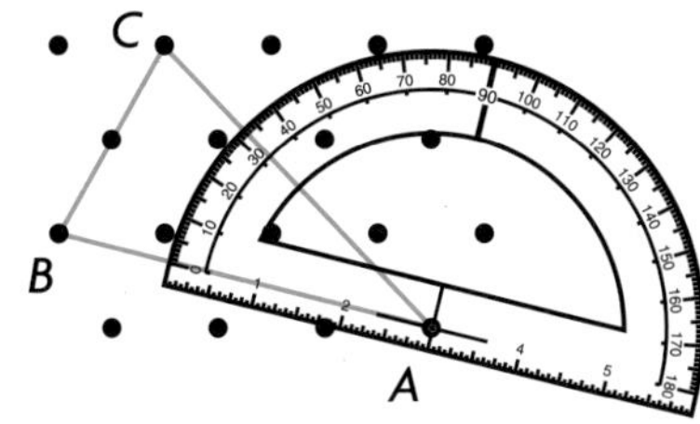

Step 3

In a table, record the measure of each angle and the sum of the angles. Then repeat Steps 1, 2, and 3 for three different-shaped triangles.

Triangle	∠*A*	∠*B*	∠*C*	Sum of the Angles
1				
2				

- Compare the sums of the angles of triangles 1–4. What conclusion can you draw about the sum of the angles in a triangle? **Explain.**

So, the sum of the angles in every triangle is always 180°.

Activity 2 **Find the sum of the angles in a quadrilateral.**

Step 1

Use isometric dot paper to draw a quadrilateral. Label the angles *A*, *B*, *C*, and *D*.

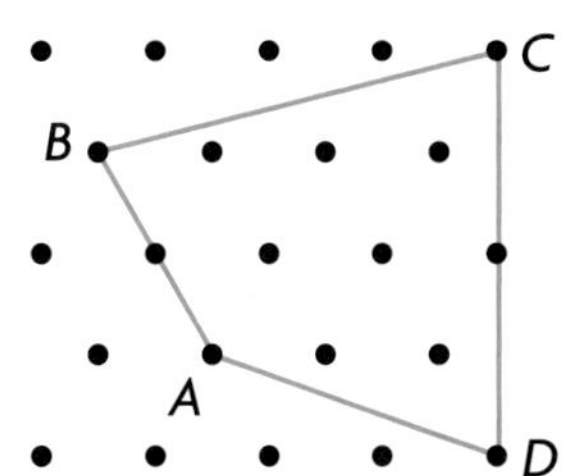

Step 2

Draw a line segment from *C* to *A* to make 2 triangles.

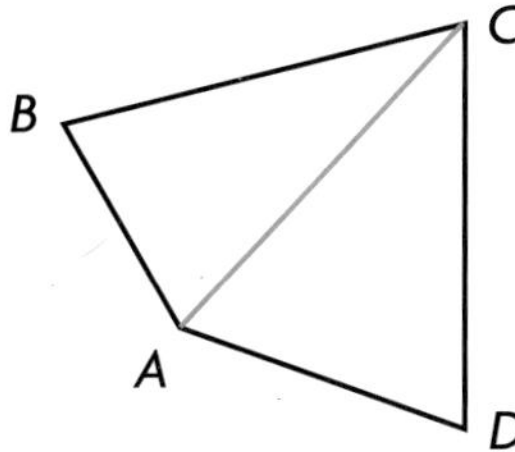

Step 3

The sum of the angles in a triangle is 180°. $180 \times 2 = 360$. Repeat Steps 1 and 2 for other quadrilaterals.

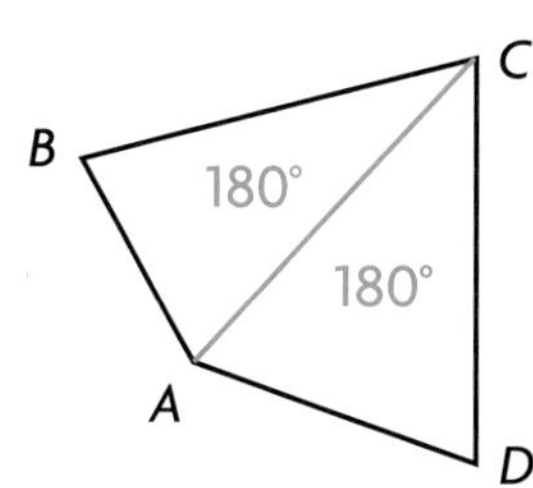

So, the sum of the angles in every quadrilateral is always 360°.

Guided Practice

1. Classify the polygon at the right.

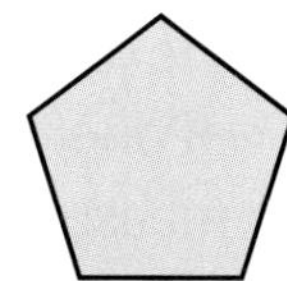

   a. How many sides and angles does this polygon have?

   b. Name the polygon.

   c. What types of angles does this polygon have?

   d. Is the polygon a regular polygon?

2. Make a quadrilateral similar to the one at the right. Draw a line segment from *F* to *H*.

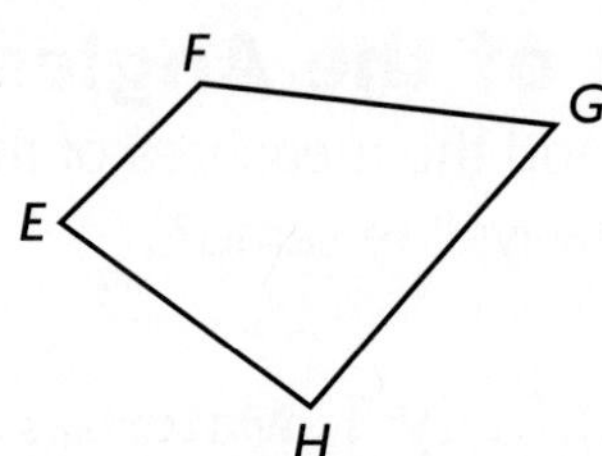

   a. What is the sum of the angles in each triangle?

   b. What is the sum of the angles in quadrilateral *EFGH*?

Name each polygon, and tell whether it is regular or not regular.

3. 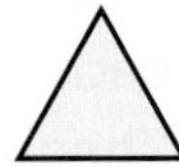

4. 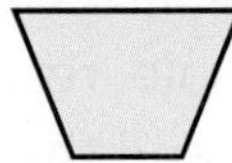

5. 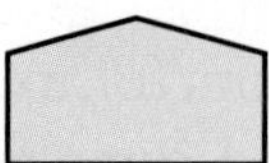

6. 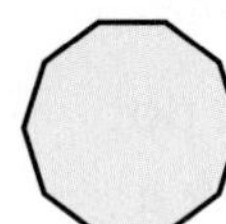

Tell if the given angles could form the figure named.

7. triangle; 90°, 75°, 15°

8. triangle; 30°, 60°, 80°

9. quadrilateral; 90°, 45°, 90°, 135°

10. quadrilateral; 110°, 110°, 70°, 70°

11. TALK Math **Explain** how you can show that the sum of the angles of a quadrilateral is 360°.

Independent Practice and Problem Solving

Name each polygon, and tell whether it is regular or not regular.

12. 

13. 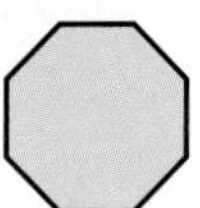

14. 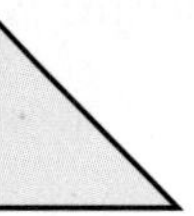

15. 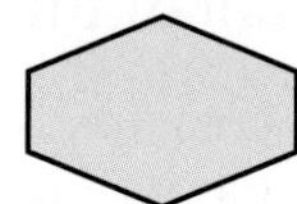

Tell if the given angles could form a triangle.

16. 45°, 60°, 45°

17. 50°, 70°, 60°

18. 82°, 68°, 10°

19. 20°, 33°, 127°

Tell if the given angles could form a quadrilateral.

20. 90°, 90°, 105°, 75°

21. 60°, 30°, 45°, 45°

22. 54°, 72°, 115°, 119°

23. 35°, 90°, 100°, 135°

USE DATA For 24–25, use the Castel del Monte floor plan.

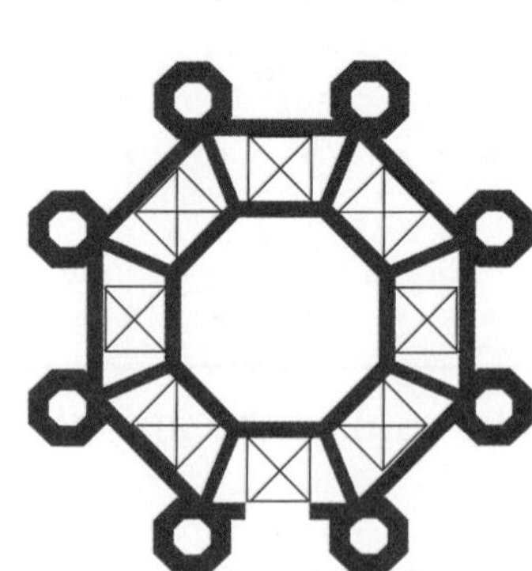

24. Which polygons in the drawings have 4 equal sides and 2 pairs of parallel sides? How many of these polygons are there?

25. What other regular polygons can you identify in the drawing? How many are there?

26. WRITE Math **Explain** how to determine if a polygon is a regular polygon.

27. In a triangle with angles labeled *A*, *B*, and *C*, the measure of angle *A* is 90°. The measures of angles *B* and *C* are equal. What is the measure of angle *B* and angle *C*?

28. A triangle has angles that all have the same measure. What is the measure of each angle?

 Extra Practice on page 506, Set C

Learn About Combining and Subdividing Figures

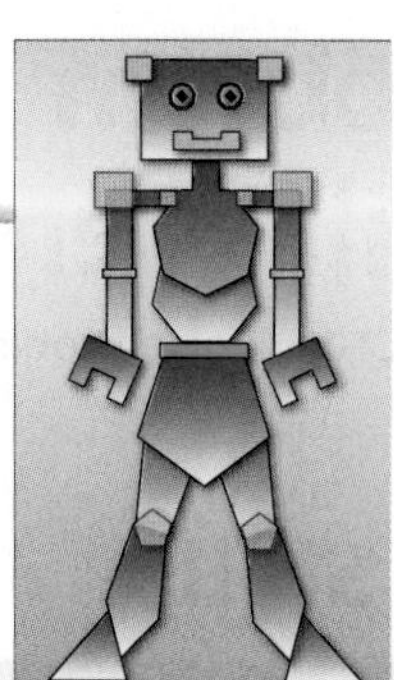

A computer graphic artist can create new shapes by combining or subdividing existing shapes or figures. A complex figure can be subdivided into basic polygons, or polygons can be combined to make a more complex figure.

A Combine triangle *A* and triangle *B* to make a new figure. What polygon will be formed?

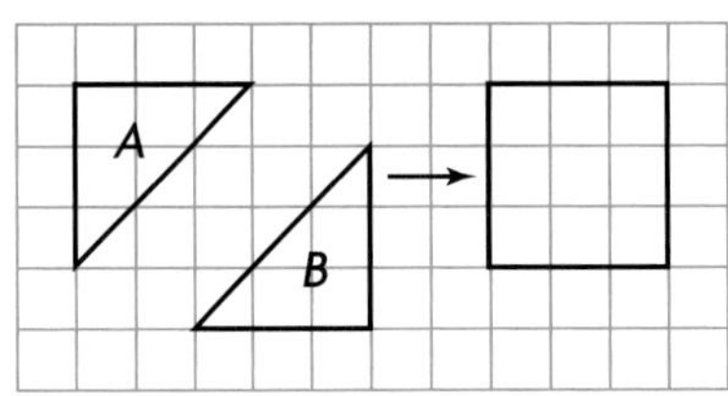

The polygon formed is a square.

B Subdivide Figure *C* to make new figures. What polygons will be formed?

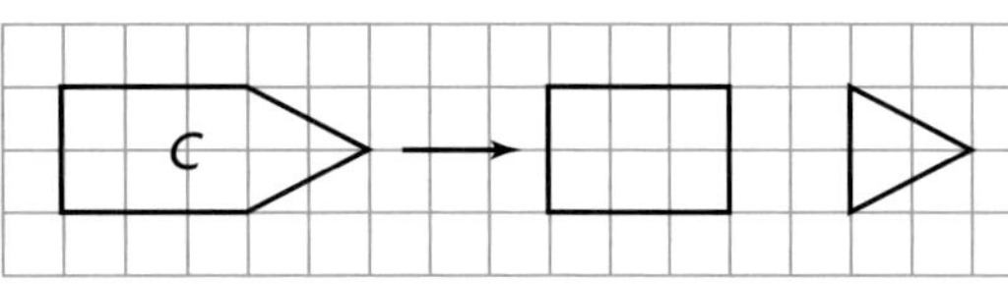

The polygons formed are a rectangle and a triangle.

Try It

Draw a new polygon or polygons by combining or subdividing the figures. Name the resulting polygons.

29. Subdivide.

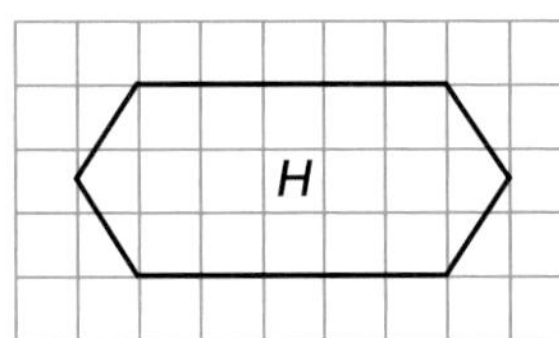

30. Combine.

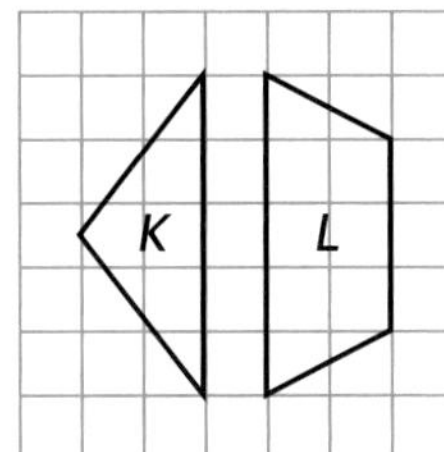

31. Subdivide.

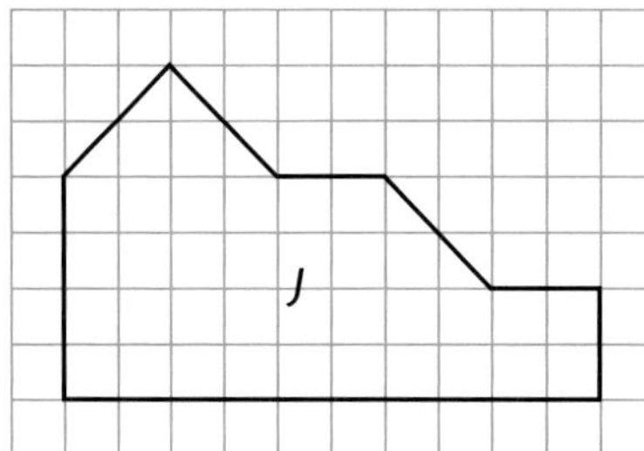

Mixed Review and Test Prep

32. What percent is equal to $\frac{5}{8}$? (p. 440)

33. **Test Prep** Which of the following angles could form a triangle? (p. 490)

A 70°, 50°, 50° **C** 45°, 90°, 50°

B 45°, 45°, 45° **D** 45°, 45°, 90°

34. What fraction is equal to 60%?

35. **Test Prep** Which polygon is not regular?

A **C**

B **D**

Problem Solving Workshop
Skill: Identify Relationships

OBJECTIVE: Solve problems by using the skill *identify relationships.*

Read to Understand
Plan
Solve
Check

▲ **Quilt made with regular hexagons**

Use the Skill

PROBLEM Felicia is making a quilt with regular hexagons. A regular polygon has sides that are the same length and angles that have the same measure. What is the measure of each angle of a regular hexagon?

Identifying relationships can help you solve problems. Look for a relationship in polygons between the number of sides and the number of triangles a polygon can be divided into.

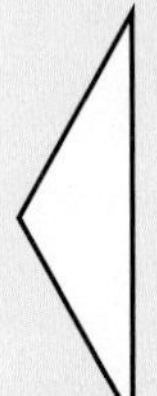
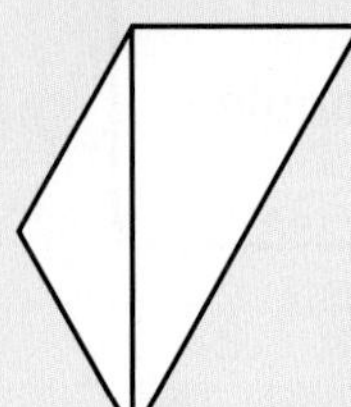
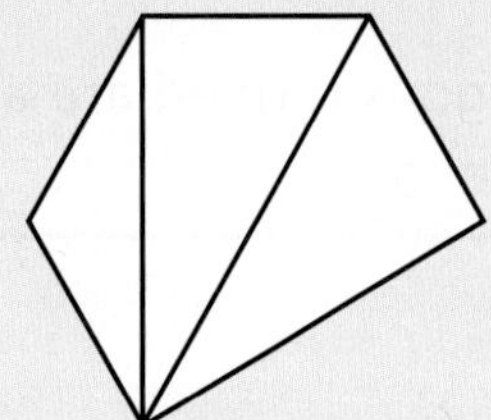
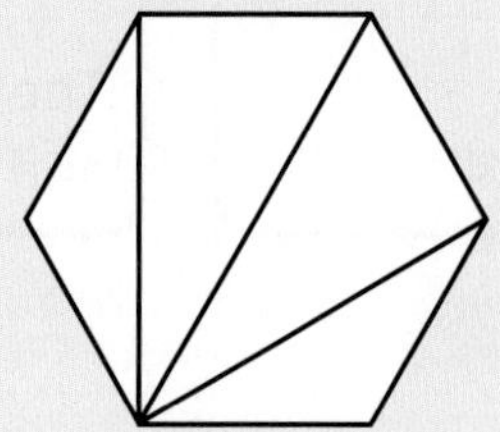

Make a table to help you find a relationship.

Polygon	Sides	Triangles	Sum of Angle Measures
Triangle	3	1	180°
Quadrilateral	4	2	$2 \times 180° = 360°$
Pentagon	5	3	$3 \times 180° = 540°$
Hexagon	6	4	$4 \times 180° = 720°$

Remember
The sum of the angle measures in a triangle is 180°.

The number of triangles in a polygon is always 2 fewer than the number of sides.

A hexagon can be divided into $6 - 2 = 4$ triangles. $4 \times 180° = 720°$

Since a regular hexagon has 6 congruent angles, the measure of each angle is $720 \div 6$, or 120°.

Think and Discuss

Jennifer is making a quilt using pink and blue squares. Solve each problem by identifying the relationship.

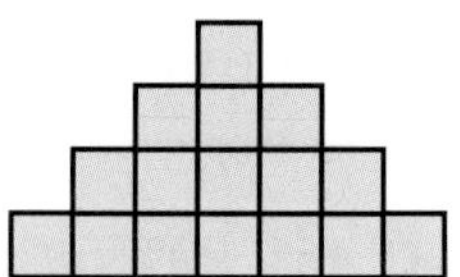
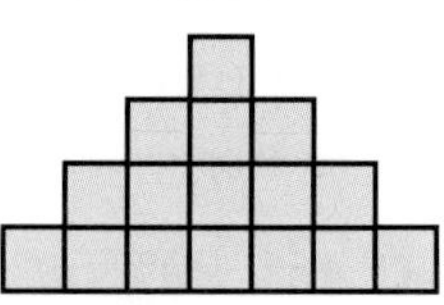

a. Jennifer continues the pattern in the picture. What rule describes the relationship between the row and the number of squares needed in each row?

b. For Jennifer's pattern, what rule describes the relationship between the number of pink squares and the number of blue squares in each row?

FAST TRACK

KY MA-05-3.1.1 Students will describe and provide examples of basic geometric elements and terms [points, segments, lines (perpendicular, parallel, intersecting), rays, angles (acute, right, obtuse), sides, edges, faces, bases, vertices, radius, diameter] and will apply these elements to solve real-world and mathematical problems. DOK 2

Guided Problem Solving

For 1–3, identify the relationship. Then solve.

1. What relationship can you find between the number of angles of a regular polygon and the size of its angles?

Regular Polygon	Number of Congruent Sides	Sum of Angles	Measure of Each Angle
Triangle	3	180°	■
Quadrilateral	4	360°	■
Pentagon	5	540°	■
Hexagon	6	720°	■
Octagon	8	■	■

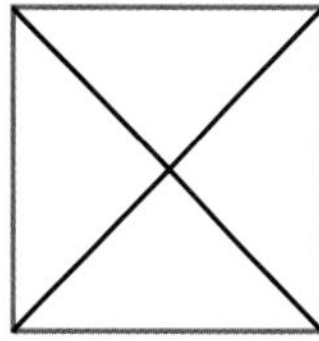

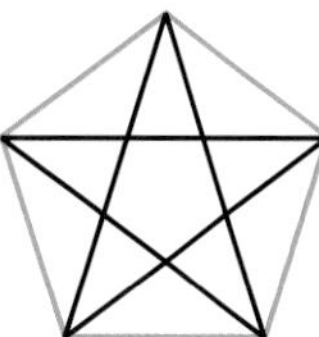

Think: The angles in a regular polygon are congruent.

✓2. **What if** you want to find the measure of each angle in a regular decagon? Write a number sentence that shows the number of triangles a decagon can be divided into. What is the measure of each angle?

✓3. Connect the vertices within a square and within a regular pentagon. A square and a regular pentagon are shown above. Count the lines within each figure. How many lines would you draw within a regular hexagon?

Mixed Applications

4. Mark, Ben, Jennifer, and Morgan are the first four people in line at the store. Mark is second in line. Morgan is not third in line. Jennifer is fourth in line. In what place is Ben in the line?

5. Mr. Wright needs 33 feet of wood to complete a fence. The wood is sold in 8-foot sections. How many sections must he buy?

6. A stop sign is a regular octagon. Each side is 10 inches long. What is the perimeter of the stop sign?

7. What is the sum of the angle measures in a one way sign? **Explain** your reasoning.

USE DATA For 8 and 9, use the table.

8. A town has $250 in its budget to purchase new road signs. The town plans to purchase 3 new stop signs, 1 yield sign, and 2 one way signs. Look at the table. Did the town put enough money in its budget for road signs? **Explain.**

9. **WRITE Math** Mrs. Reynolds purchased 10 of one type of road sign for $625.00. Which road sign did Mrs. Reynolds purchase? **Explain** your thinking.

Cost of Road Signs

Road Sign	Cost
Stop	$62.50
Yield	$34.50
One Way	$32.50

Circles

OBJECTIVE: Identify, describe, and draw a circle and its parts; relate the radius and the diameter.

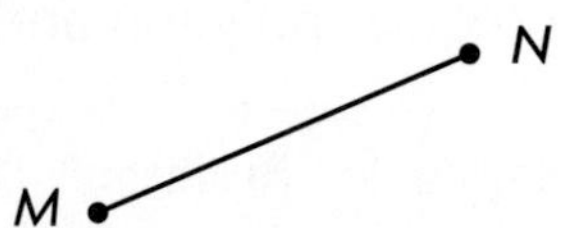

Name and identify the figure.

M N

Vocabulary

circle radius
diameter chord

Learn

A **circle** is a closed plane figure with all points on the figure the same distance from a point called the center of the circle. Circles are named by the center point.

Examples

A A line segment with one endpoint at the center of a circle and the other endpoint on the circle is called a **radius**. All radii in a given circle have the same length. So, $\overline{RE}$, $\overline{RC}$, and $\overline{RD}$ are radii.

B A line segment that passes through the center of the circle and has both of its endpoints on the circle is called a **diameter**. So, $\overline{CD}$ is a diameter.

C A line segment with its endpoints on the circle is called a **chord**. So, $\overline{AB}$ and $\overline{CD}$ are chords. A diameter is also a chord.

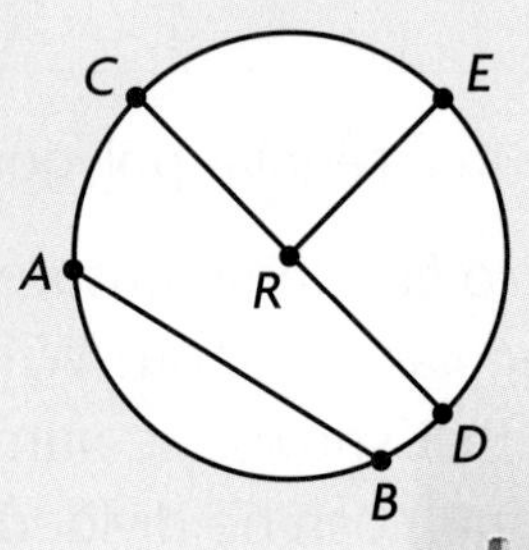

Math Idea
In any given circle, the length of a diameter measures twice the length of a radius.

▲ Capitol Records Building

Activity

Materials ■ compass ■ straightedge

Step 1	Step 2	Step 3	Step 4
Draw and label point *C*. Place the point of the compass on point *C*.	Open the compass to 6 cm. This will be the radius of the circle.	Use the compass to draw the circle.	Draw and label a radius, a diameter, and a chord of circle *C*.
 C	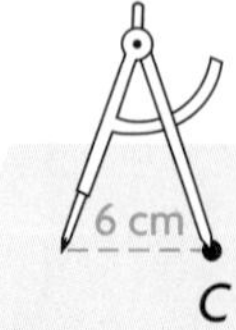 6 cm C	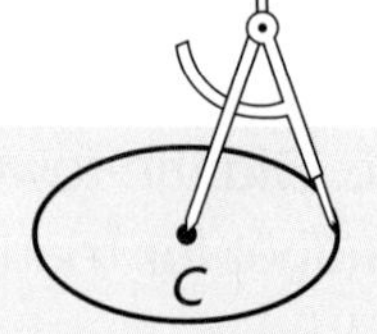 C	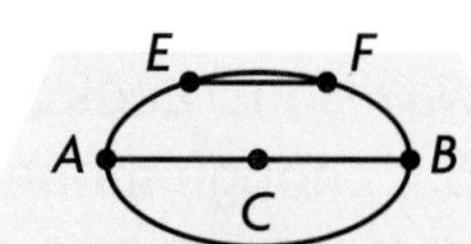 E F A B C

• In circle *C*, what is the length of the diameter?

KY MA-05-3.1.1 Students will describe and provide examples of basic geometric elements and terms [points, segments, lines (perpendicular, parallel, intersecting), rays, angles (acute, right, obtuse), sides, edges, faces, bases, vertices, radius, diameter] and will apply these elements to solve real-world and mathematical problems. DOK 2 *also* MA-05-2.1.1; *MA-05-2.1.2; MA-05-2.1.3;* MA-05-3.1.2

Angles Surrounding a Point

You can draw and measure the angles in a circle to find the sum of angles surrounding a point.

Activity

Materials ■ compass ■ ruler ■ protractor

Step 1

Use a compass to draw circle *O*. Draw radii *OP* and *OT*.

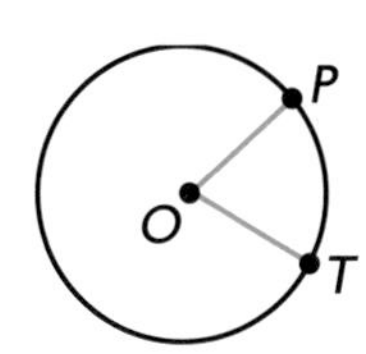

Step 2

Use a protractor to find the measure of your ∠*POT*.

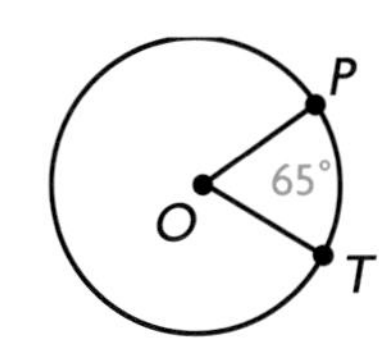

Step 3

Draw three or more radii. Find the measure of each angle.

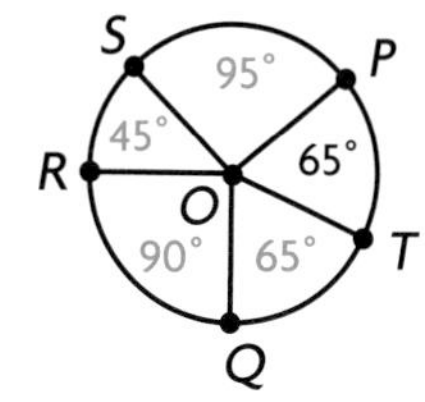

Step 4

Find the sum of the angles in the circle.

∠*POT* = 65°, ∠*TOQ* = 65°, ∠*QOR* = 90°, ∠*ROS* = 45°, ∠*SOP* = 95°

65° + 65° + 90° + 45° + 95° = 360°

The sum of the angles in every circle is 360°.

You can find an unknown angle measure in a circle without using a protractor.

Example **Find the measure of ∠*DAE*.**

Step 1

Find the sum of the angles that are given in the circle.

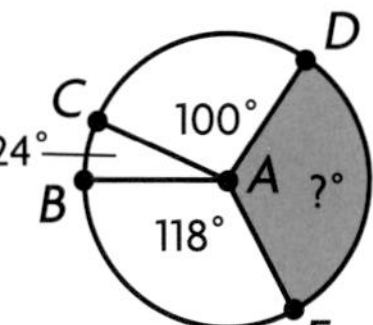

∠*CAB* = 24°
∠*CAD* = 100°
∠*BAE* = 118°
∠*DAE* = ?

24° + 100° + 118° = 242°

Step 2

Then, subtract the sum from 360° to find the measure of the unknown angle, ∠*DAE*.

360° − 242° = 118°

So, ∠*DAE* = 118°.

Guided Practice

1. For a–b, name the type of line segment described.
   a. A line segment with one endpoint at the center of a circle and the other endpoint on the circle
   b. A line segment with its endpoints on the circle

For 2–5, use the circle at the right.

2. Name the circle.
3. Name a radius.
4. Name a diameter.
5. Name a chord.

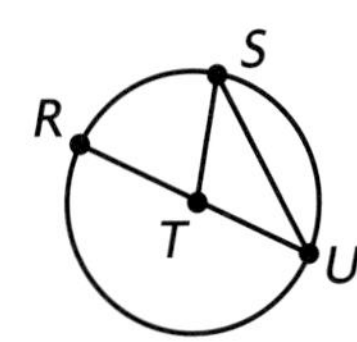

Complete 6–9. Then use a compass to draw each circle. Draw and label the measurements.

6. radius = 5 cm
diameter = ■

7. radius = ■
diameter = 8 in.

8. radius = 3.5 in.
diameter = ■

9. radius = ■
diameter = 16 cm

10. TALK Math **Explain** how a radius and a diameter of a circle are related.

Independent Practice and Problem Solving

For 11–15, use the circle at the right.

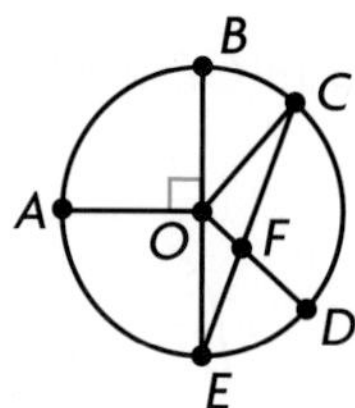

11. Name 5 radii.

12. Name a diameter.

13. Name a chord.

14. Name the circle.

15. If $\overline{AO}$ is 10 inches, what is $\overline{BE}$?

Complete 16–19. Then use a compass to draw each circle. Draw and label the measurements.

16. radius = ■
diameter = 9 cm

17. radius = 4.2 cm
diameter = ■

18. radius = 2 in.
diameter = ■

19. radius = ■
diameter = $6\frac{1}{2}$ in.

Find the unknown measure.

20. 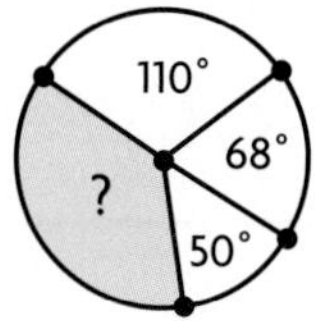

21. 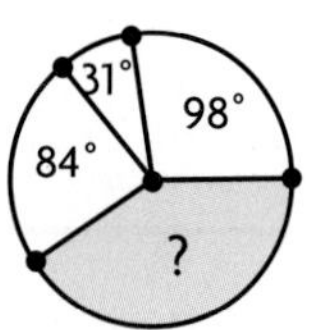

22. 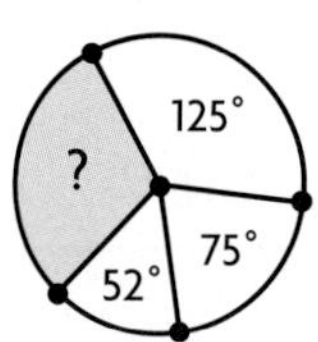

23. 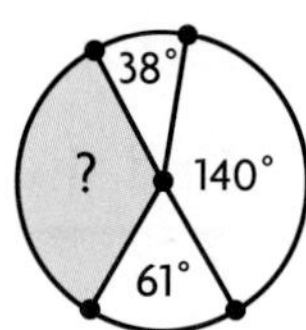

24. A music CD has a radius of 60 millimeters. What is the diameter of a CD?

25. **FAST FACT** Before music CDs, music was produced on a record. The diameter of a long play record was 10 inches. The diameter of a single was $3\frac{1}{8}$ inches shorter than the long play. What is the radius of a long play and a single?

26. WRITE Math A circle has 4 angles. The measures of 3 angles in the circle have a sum of 218°. **Explain** how you can find the measure of the fourth angle.

Mixed Review and Test Prep

27. One fourth of the voters voted for Diaz. Thirty percent voted for Smith. Who received more votes? **Explain.** (p. 440)

28. Tom earned quiz scores of 82, 96, 77, and 70. If his lowest score is thrown out, what is Tom's mean score? (p. 220)

29. **Test Prep** Which is the measure of ∠*AXC*?

A 145°

B 135°

C 125°

D 90°

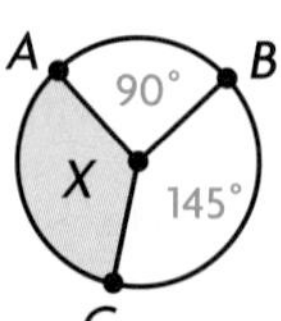

 Extra Practice on page 507, Set D

Draw to Explain

One way to solve a problem is to draw a diagram. A diagram helps you visually represent the information given in a problem.

The science club is planning a circular garden with a fountain at the center. Two of the sections of the garden measure 75° and 85°. The third section measures 20° greater than the fourth section. Explain how to draw a diagram of the garden to show the measure of each section.

Jo Ellen's group drew this diagram of the garden and wrote this explanation.

First, use a compass to draw a circle with center point P.

Next, use a straightedge and a protractor to draw and label the first two sections of 75° and 85°.

Then, use a protractor to try various angle measures for the third and fourth angles so the third angle is 20° greater than the fourth angle. The sum of the 4 measures equals 360°.

So, the angle measures of our garden are 75°, 85°, 110°, and 90°.

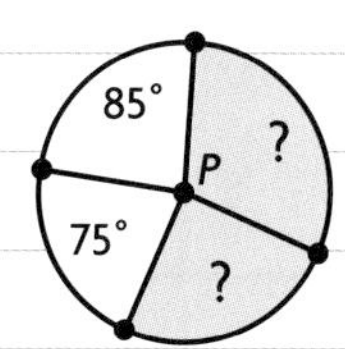

Tips

To draw a diagram to explain:

- Explain the steps you took to draw the diagram.
- Use appropriate tools and measure carefully.
- Label the diagram.
- Use correct math vocabulary in your explanation.
- In the last sentence, state the solution to the problem.

Problem Solving Make a diagram to explain your solution.

1. Draw a diagram of a circular garden that is divided into 5 equal sections. What is the measure of each angle?
2. Draw a diagram of a circular garden in which two of its four sections measure 95° and 115°. The third and fourth sections have the same measure. What are the four angle measures?

LESSON 6

Congruent and Similar Figures

OBJECTIVE: Identify congruent and similar figures

Quick Review

Name the angle below.

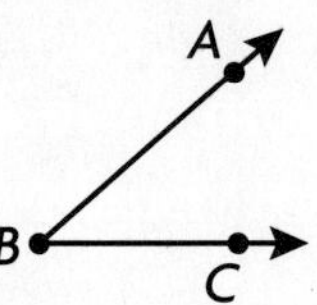

Vocabulary

congruent
similar
corresponding sides
corresponding angles

Learn

PROBLEM Susie's mother ordered a package of school pictures that included 4-inch × 6-inch photos and wallet-size photos that are 2-inch × 3-inch each. How do the wallet-size photos compare to each other? How do the wallet-size photos compare to the 4-inch × 6-inch photos?

Congruent figures have the same shape and size. The wallet-size photos are the same shape and size. So, these photos are congruent.

Similar figures have the same shape but may not have the same size. The wallet-size photos and the 4-inch × 6-inch photos are the same shape but are different sizes. So, these photos appear to be similar.

Figures can be congruent, similar, or neither. All congruent figures are similar, but similar figures may not be congruent.

Math Idea
Congruent figures have the same area.

More Examples

A

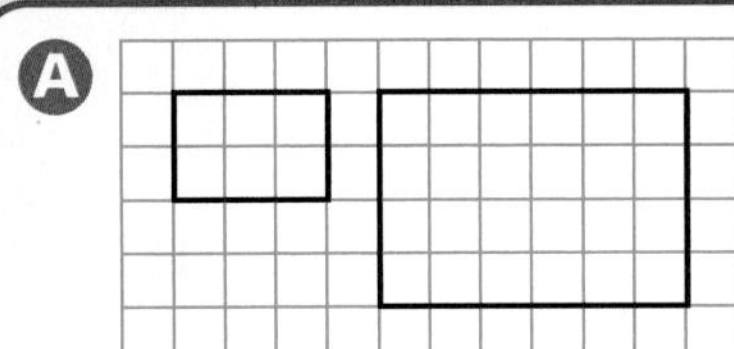

- Same shape
- Different sizes

The figures are similar but not congruent.

B

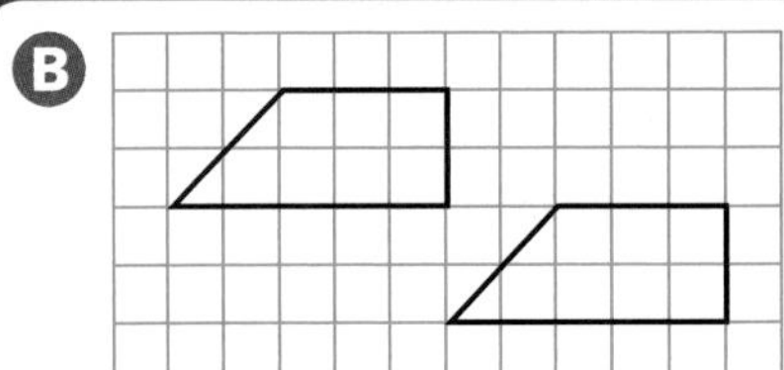

- Same shape
- Same size

The figures are congruent and similar.

C

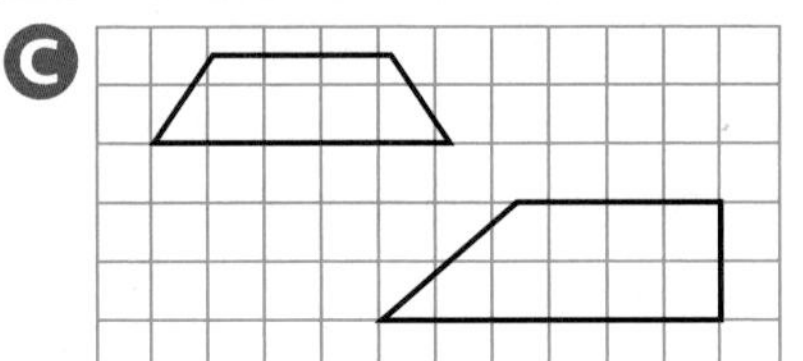

- Different shapes
- Different sizes

The figures are neither similar nor congruent.

KY MA-05-3.1.5 Students will identify and describe congruent and similar figures in real-world and mathematical problems. DOK 2

Corresponding Sides and Angles

Figures that are congruent or similar have corresponding sides and angles. **Corresponding sides** and **corresponding angles** are in the same relative position in different figures.

Examples

A Triangles *ABC* and *DEF* are similar.

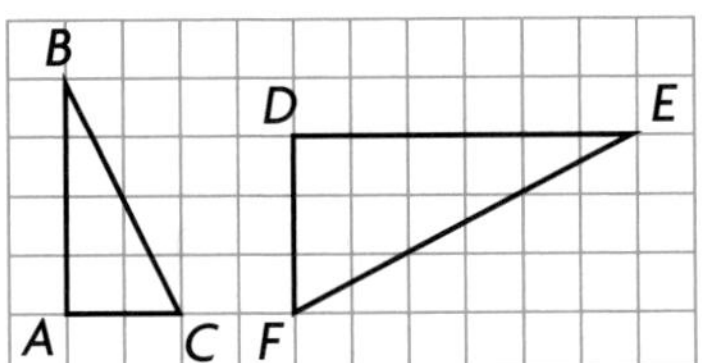

Corresponding Sides

$\overline{AB}$ corresponds to $\overline{DE}$.
$\overline{AC}$ corresponds to $\overline{DF}$.
$\overline{BC}$ corresponds to $\overline{EF}$.

Corresponding Angles

$\angle A$ corresponds to $\angle D$.
$\angle B$ corresponds to $\angle E$.
$\angle C$ corresponds to $\angle F$.

B Quadrilaterals *GHIJ* and *KLMN* are congruent.

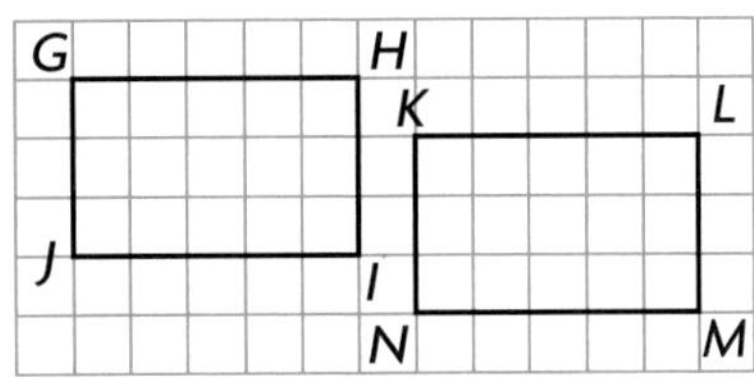

Corresponding Sides

$\overline{GH}$ corresponds to $\overline{KL}$.
$\overline{HI}$ corresponds to $\overline{LM}$.
$\overline{IJ}$ corresponds to $\overline{MN}$.
$\overline{JG}$ corresponds to $\overline{NK}$.

Corresponding Angles

$\angle G$ corresponds to $\angle K$.
$\angle H$ corresponds to $\angle L$.
$\angle I$ corresponds to $\angle M$.
$\angle J$ corresponds to $\angle N$.

Corresponding sides and angles of congruent figures have the same measure. Corresponding angles of similar figures have the same measure. Corresponding sides of similar figures have the same ratio.

Activity **Materials** ■ centimeter grid paper ■ ruler ■ protractor

Are the triangles below congruent or similar?

Step 1

The symbol for *triangle* is $\triangle$. Copy $\triangle STU$ and $\triangle WXY$ on grid paper.

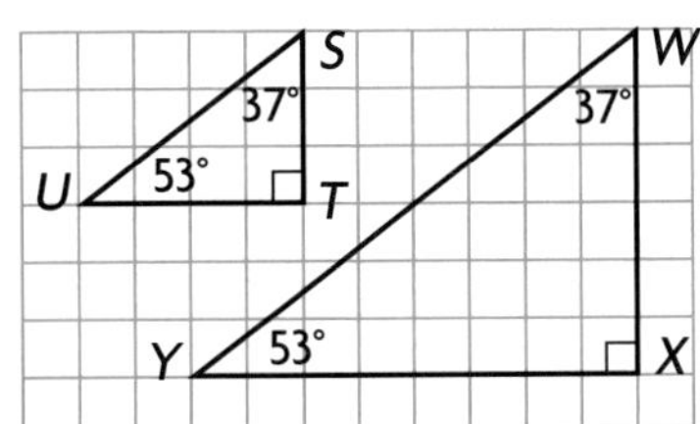

Step 2

Use a centimeter ruler to measure corresponding sides.

$\overline{ST} = 3$ cm $\overline{WX} = 6$ cm
$\overline{TU} = 4$ cm $\overline{XY} = 8$ cm
$\overline{SU} = 5$ cm $\overline{WY} = 10$ cm

Step 3

Write the ratios $\overline{ST}$ to $\overline{WX}$, $\overline{TU}$ to $\overline{XY}$, and $\overline{SU}$ to $\overline{WY}$ in the simplest form.

$\overline{ST}$ to $\overline{WX} \rightarrow \frac{3}{6}$, or $\frac{1}{2}$

$\overline{TU}$ to $\overline{XY} \rightarrow \frac{4}{8}$, or $\frac{1}{2}$

$\overline{SU}$ to $\overline{WY} \rightarrow \frac{5}{10}$, or $\frac{1}{2}$

So, $\triangle STU$ and $\triangle WXY$ are similar. Their corresponding angles have the same measure and their corresponding sides have the same ratio.

Guided Practice

1. Are the two figures at the right the same shape?
   Are the two figures the same size?
   Write the ratio of the corresponding sides in simplest form.
   Write whether the two figures appear to be *congruent, similar,* or *neither.*

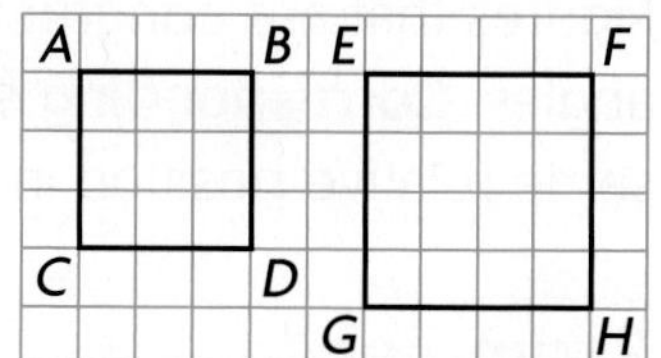

Write whether the two figures appear to be *congruent, similar,* or *neither.*

2. 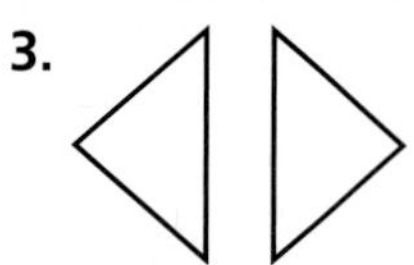

3. 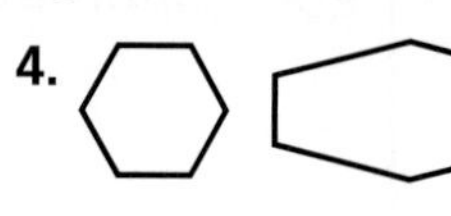

4. 

✓5. 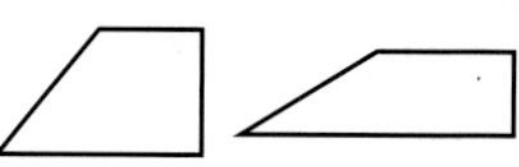

Use the triangles at the right. Identify the corresponding side or angle.

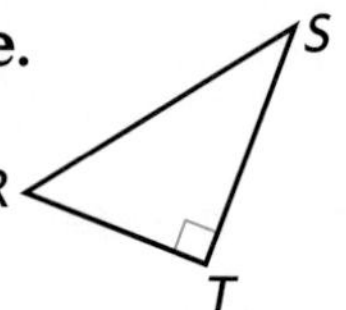

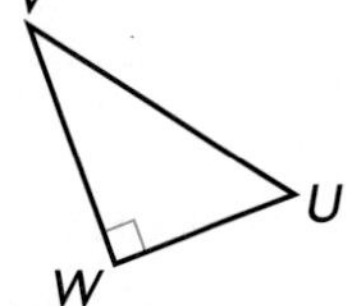

6. $\overline{ST}$
7. $\overline{RT}$
8. $\angle R$
✓9. $\angle T$

10. **TALK Math** **Explain** how you can decide whether two figures are congruent or similar.

Independent Practice and Problem Solving

Write whether the two figures appear to be congruent, similar, or neither.

11. 

12. 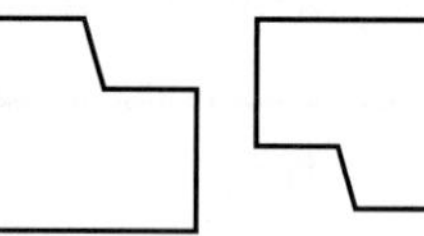

13. 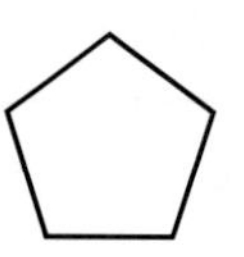

14. 

Identify the corresponding side or angle.

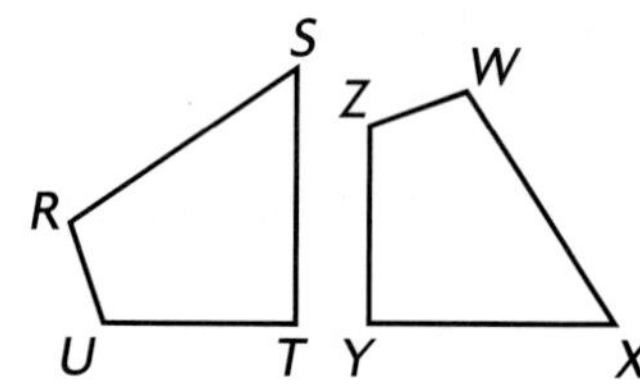

15. $\overline{ST}$
16. $\angle R$
17. $\overline{RU}$
18. $\angle U$
19. $\overline{SR}$
20. $\overline{TU}$
21. $\angle T$
22. $\angle S$

USE DATA For 23–25, use the figures shown.

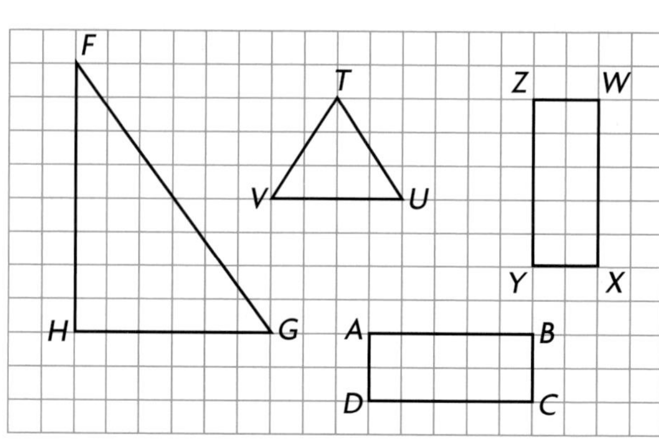

23. Copy the figures on centimeter grid paper. Use a centimeter ruler and a protractor to measure the sides and angles of each figure.

24. Do any of the figures appear to be congruent? Which figures? **Explain.**

25. Do any of the other figures appear to be similar? Which figures? **Explain.**

26. **WRITE Math** Draw a triangle *MNO* that is similar to triangle *FHG*. **Explain** how you know that they are similar.

Extra Practice on page 507, Set E

Learn About Constructing Congruent Angles

You can use a compass and a straightedge to copy any angle. Trace ∠ABC. Then construct ∠DEF so that it is congruent to ∠ABC.

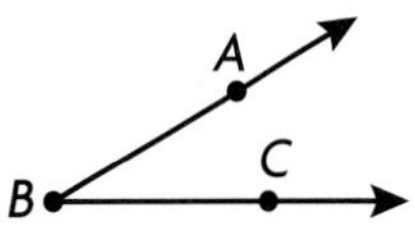

Step 1	Step 2	Step 3	Step 4	Step 5
Place the compass point on vertex *B*. Draw an arc through *A* and *C*.	Draw ray *EF*. Without changing the compass, draw an arc touching *F*.	Go back to ∠*ABC*. With the compass point on *C*, open the compass so it touches *A*.	Without changing the compass, draw an arc to make point *D*.	Use a straightedge to draw ray *ED*.

Try It

27. Draw ∠ABC with a measure of 60°. Then use a compass and a straightedge to construct an angle that is congruent to the given angle.

28. Draw ∠JKL with a measure of 110°. Then use a compass and a straightedge to construct an angle that is congruent to the given angle.

Mixed Review and Test Prep

29. Alex's yogurt stand sells 3 types of yogurt that can be served in a cup, a sugar cone, or a waffle cone. How many choices of yogurt and ways to serve yogurt do customers have? (p. 462)

30. **Test Prep** Which best describes the two figures below?

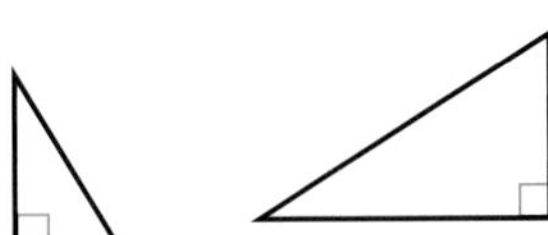

A congruent **C** regular polygons

B similar **D** quadrilaterals

31. At basketball practice, Samantha missed 3 out of 25 basketball free throws. What percent of her shots did Samantha make? (p. 438)

32. **Test Prep** Quadrilaterals *ABCD* and *EFGH* are congruent. The measure of ∠A is 45°. What is the measure of the corresponding angle, ∠E?

Symmetry

OBJECTIVE: Identify and describe line and rotational symmetry.

Quick Review

Write whether the figures appear to be *congruent*, *similar* or *neither*.

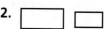

1. 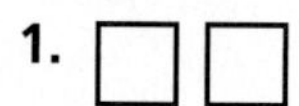
2. 
3. 
4. 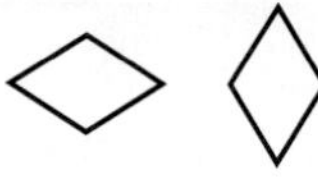
5. 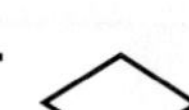

Vocabulary

line symmetry

rotational symmetry

Learn

In nature and in human-made objects, you can find examples of symmetry. The scallop's shell shown at the right is one example of symmetry in nature.

A figure that has **line symmetry** can be folded along a line so that the two parts match exactly.

Activity

Materials ■ isometric and square dot paper ■ ruler

How many lines of symmetry does each regular polygon have?

Step 1

Draw an equilateral triangle on isometric dot paper.

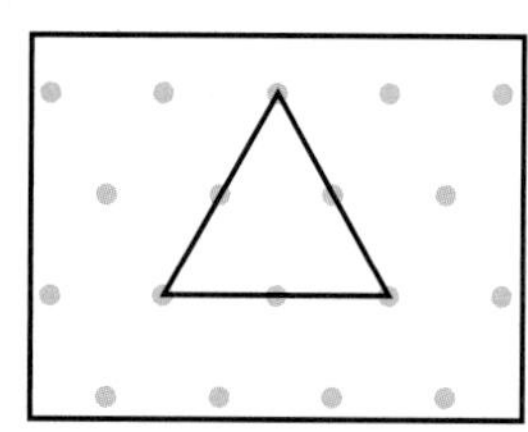

Step 2

Fold each polygon in different ways to test for line symmetry.

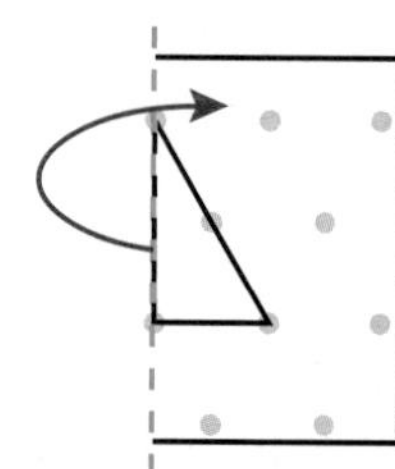

Step 3

Repeat Step 2 for a regular hexagon drawn on isometric dot paper and a square drawn on square dot paper.

For each polygon, record the number of lines of symmetry.

- How does the number of lines of symmetry compare to the number of sides on each regular polygon?

A figure has **rotational symmetry** if it can be rotated less than 360° around a central point and match the original figure.

Examples

A

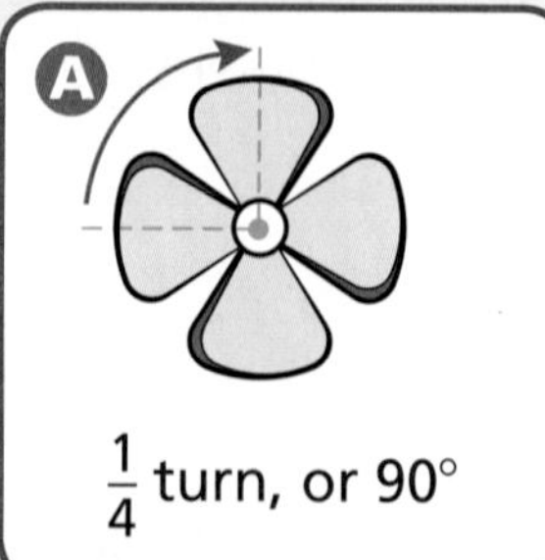

$\frac{1}{4}$ turn, or 90°

B

$\frac{1}{3}$ turn, or 120°

C

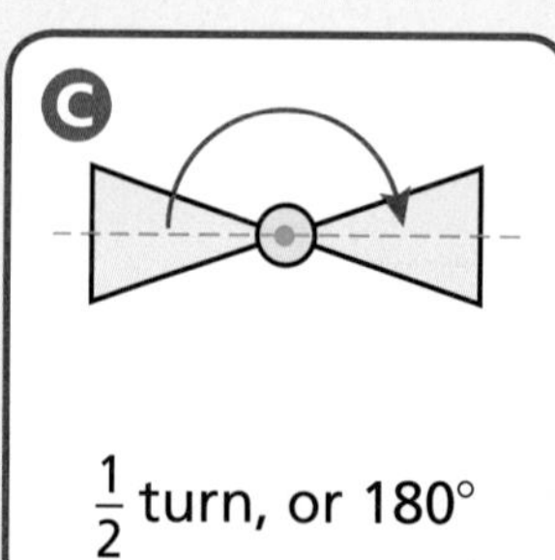

$\frac{1}{2}$ turn, or 180°

D

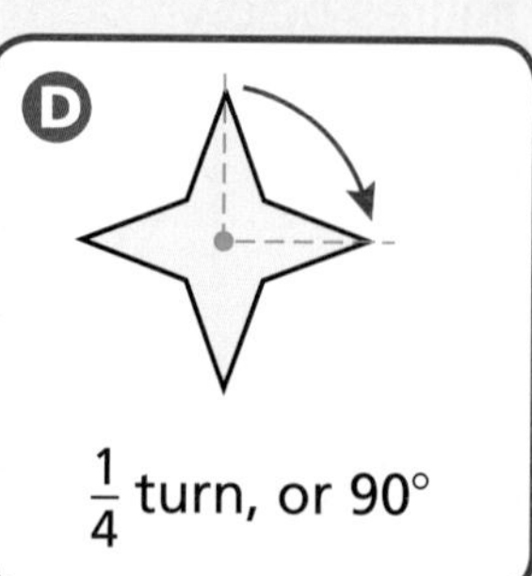

$\frac{1}{4}$ turn, or 90°

KY MA-05-3.2.1 Students will describe and provide examples of line symmetry in real-world and mathematical problems or will apply line symmetry to construct a geometric design. DOK 3

Guided Practice

Tell whether the parts on each side of the line match. Is the line a line of symmetry?

1. 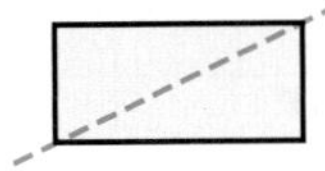
2. 
3. 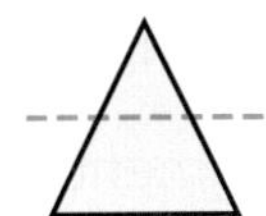
4. 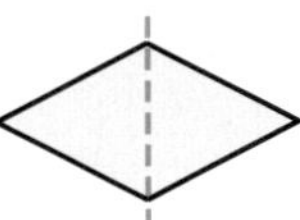

Trace each figure. Draw all lines of symmetry. Then tell whether each figure has rotational symmetry by writing *yes* or *no*.

5. 
6. 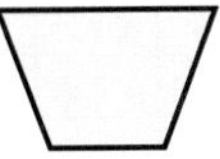
7. 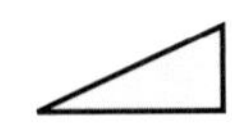
8. 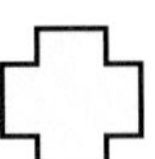

9. **TALK Math** **Explain** how you can find lines of symmetry for a figure.

Independent Practice and Problem Solving

Trace each figure. Draw all lines of symmetry. Then tell whether each figure has rotational symmetry by writing *yes* or *no*.

10. 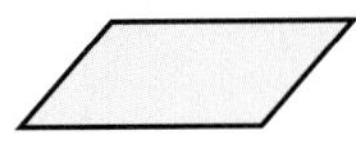
11. 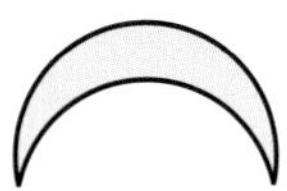
12. 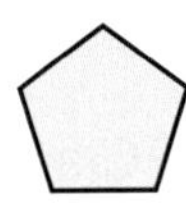
13. 

Each figure has rotational symmetry. Tell the fraction and the angle measure of the smallest turn that matches the original figure.

14. 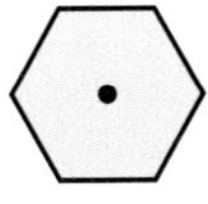
15. 
16. 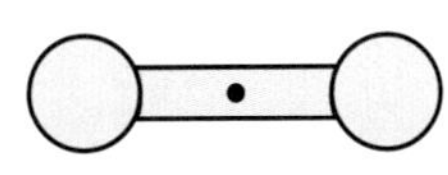
17. 

18. Della makes a design that has $\frac{1}{4}$-turn rotational symmetry. What angle measure describes the design's symmetry?

19. **WRITE Math** **Explain** how you can use a fraction to describe a figure with rotational symmetry.

Mixed Review and Test Prep

20. Ann has 250 dimes. She puts every 50 dimes in a coin roll. Write an equation to find the number of coin rolls, *c*, she will need. (p. 106)

21. John ate $\frac{3}{8}$ of a pizza. What fraction of the pizza did John not eat? (p. 346)

22. **Test Prep** Which letter has rotational symmetry?

A A
B X
C V
D B

Extra Practice on page 507, Set F

Extra Practice

Set A For 1–10, use the figure. Name an example of each. (pp. 482–485)

1. point
2. intersecting lines
3. ray
4. line segment
5. acute angle
6. vertex
7. obtuse angle
8. perpendicular lines
9. parallel lines
10. line

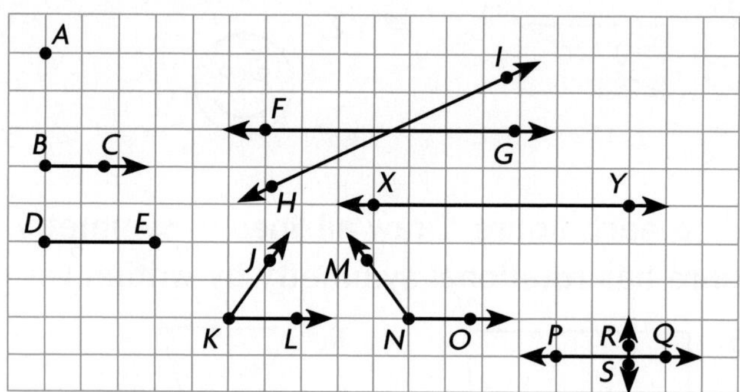

Set B Estimate the measure of each angle. Then use a protractor to find the exact measure. (pp. 486–489)

1. ∠*GBC*
2. ∠*JBG*
3. ∠*JBF*
4. ∠*JBC*
5. ∠*HBA*
6. ∠*FBA*

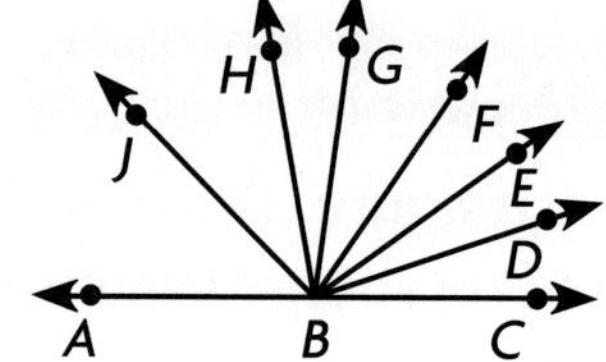

Use a protractor to draw each angle. Classify each angle.

7. 25°
8. 145°
9. 115°
10. 90°
11. an angle whose measure is between 50° and 85°
12. an angle whose measure is greater than 115° and less than 180°

Set C Name each polygon, and tell whether it is regular or not regular. (pp. 490–493)

1. 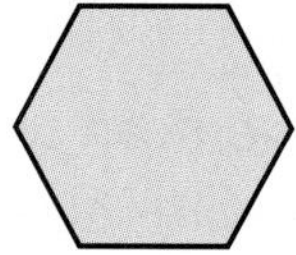
2. 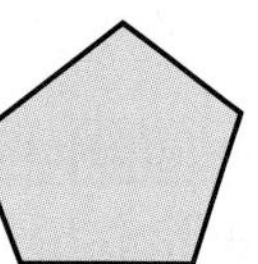
3. 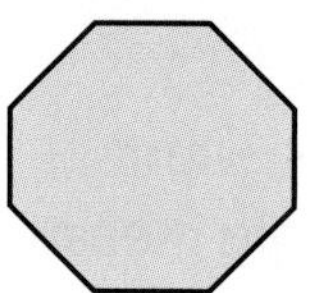
4. 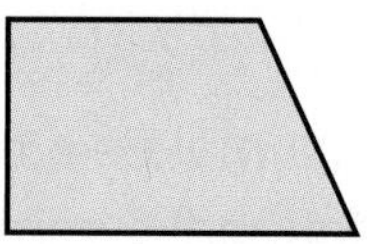

Tell if the given angles could form a triangle.

5. 25°, 68°, 87°
6. 45°, 45°, 70°
7. 60°, 30°, 90°
8. 20°, 116°, 39°

Tell if the given angles could form a quadrilateral.

9. 57°, 45°, 110°, 150°
10. 88°, 91°, 89°, 92°
11. 23°, 79°, 150°, 98°
12. 100°, 37°, 16°, 80°
13. Rachel drew a figure with 8 equal sides and 8 equal angles. What figure did she draw?
14. Two angle measures of a triangle are 60° each. What is the measure of the third angle?

Technology
Use Harcourt Mega Math, Ice Station Exploration, *Polar Planes,* Level D.

Set D For 1–6, use the circle at the right. (pp. 496–499)

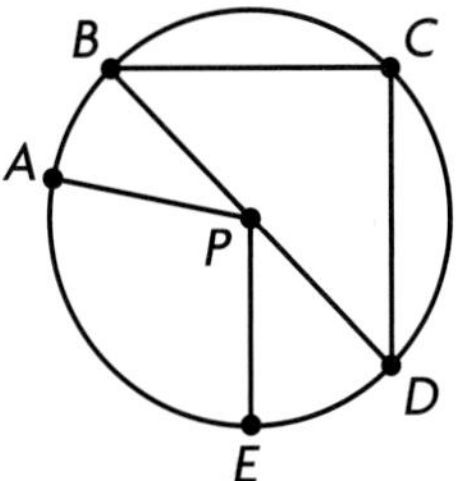

1. Name a chord.
2. Name the circle.
3. Name a diameter.
4. Name 4 radii.
5. If $\overline{EP}$ is 4 inches, what is $\overline{BD}$?
6. If $\overline{BD}$ is 6 inches, what is $\overline{EP}$?

Complete 7–10. Then use a compass to draw each circle. Draw and label the measurements.

7. radius: ■
   diameter: 8 cm
8. radius: 1.5 in.
   diameter: ■
9. radius: ■
   diameter: 2 in.
10. radius: 7 cm
    diameter: ■

Find the unknown measure.

11. 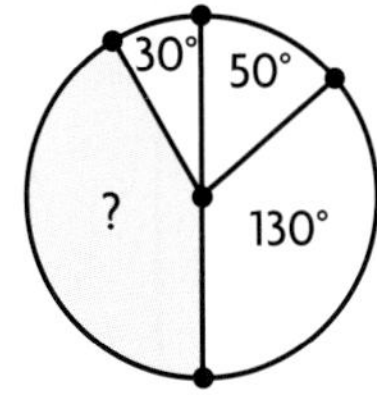

12. 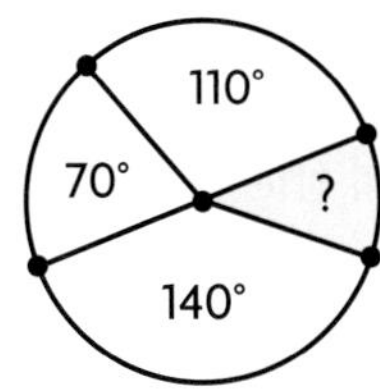

13. 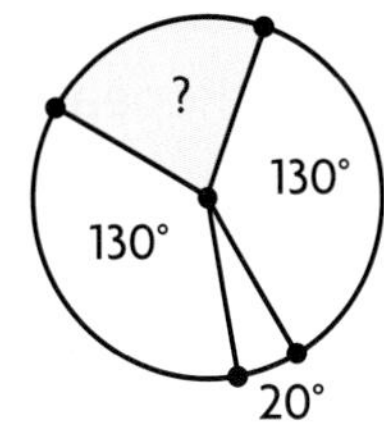

14. 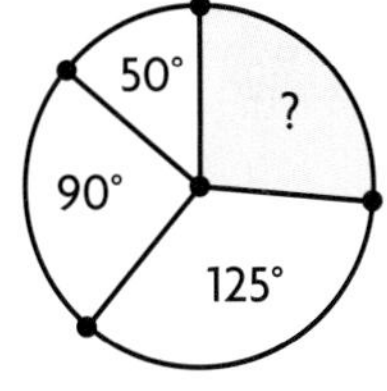

Set E Write whether the two figures appear to be *congruent*, *similar*, or *neither*. (pp. 500–503)

1. 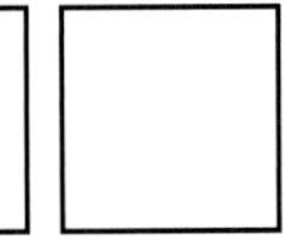
2. 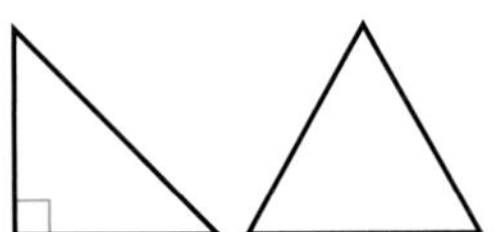
3. 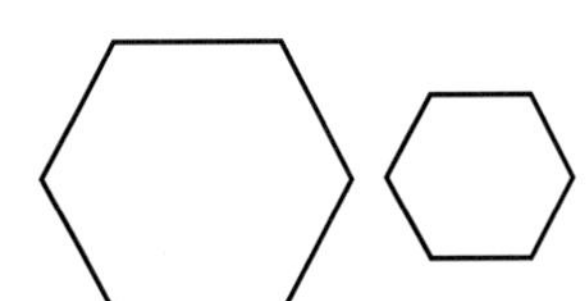
4. 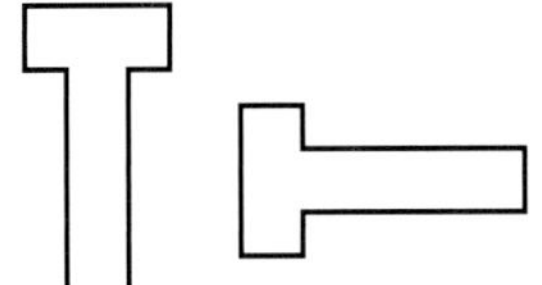

Name the angle or side that corresponds to the angle or side that is marked in blue.

5. 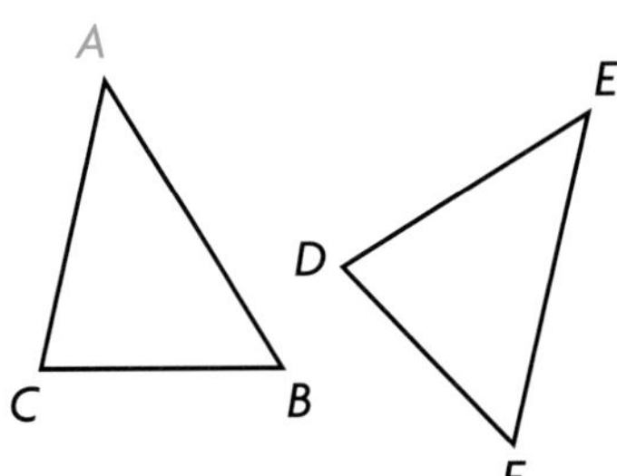

6. 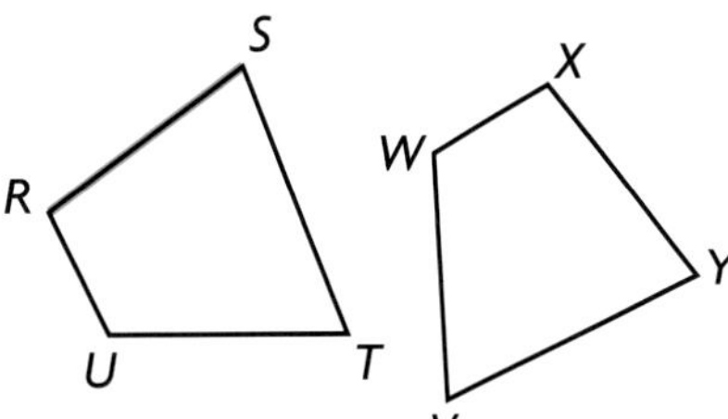

7. 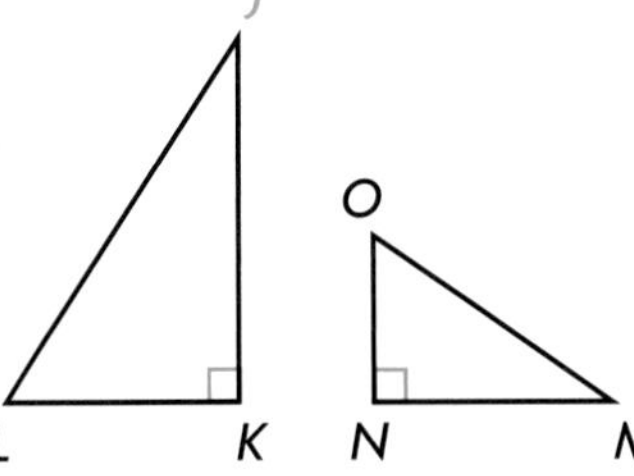

Set F Trace each figure. Draw lines of symmetry.

Tell whether each figure has rotational symmetry. Write *yes* or *no*. (pp. 504–505)

1. 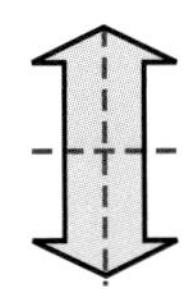
2. 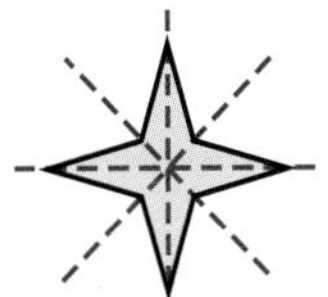
3. 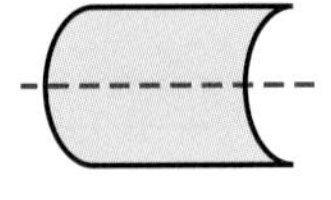
4. 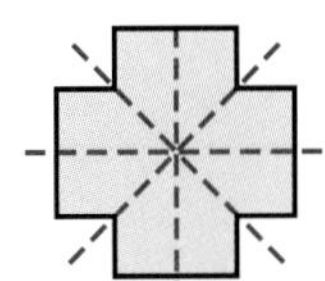

MATH POWER Diagonals in Polygons

A point where two sides of a polygon meet is called a vertex. A **diagonal** is a line segment that connects two vertices.

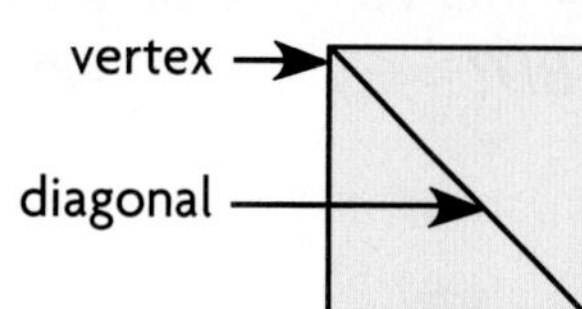

Example 1

Find the number of diagonals in an octagon by using a model.

Step 1 Choose a vertex. Draw line segments connecting it to every other vertex in the octagon.

Step 2 Choose a new vertex. Repeat Step 1. Continue in this manner until you have connected all the vertices with line segments.

Step 3 Count the line segments.

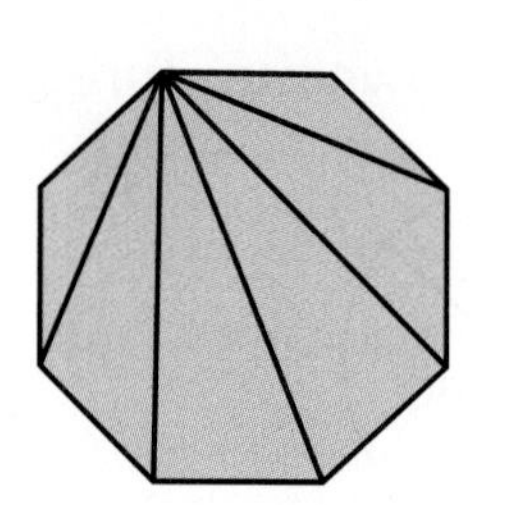

So, an octagon has 20 diagonals.

Example 2

Use a formula to find the number of diagonals in a hexagon.

Use the formula $\frac{n(n-3)}{2}$, where n = the number of sides in a polygon.

$$\frac{n(n-3)}{2} = \frac{6(6-3)}{2} = \frac{6 \times 3}{2} = \frac{18}{2} = 9$$

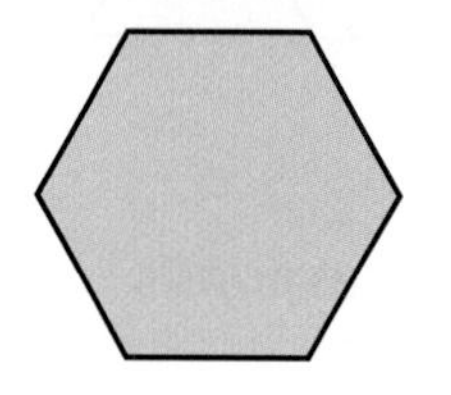

So, a hexagon has 9 diagonals.

Try It

Use the formula to find the number of diagonals in each polygon.

1. triangle
2. decagon
3. quadrilateral
4. pentagon
5. WRITE Math **Explain** why a rhombus, trapezoid, and parallelogram each have two diagonals.

Chapter 18 Review/Test

Check Vocabulary and Concepts

VOCABULARY
acute angle
congruent
obtuse angle

For 1–2, choose the best term from the box.

1. Figures that have the same size and shape are ? . KY MA-05-3.1.5 (p. 500)
2. A(n) ? is an angle that is greater than 90° and less than 180°. KY MA-05-3.1.1 (p. 483)

Check Skills

Use a protractor to draw each angle. KY MA-05-2.1.1 (pp. 486–489)

3. 55°
4. 140°
5. 31°
6. 128°

Name each polygon and tell if it is regular or not regular. KY MA-05-3.1:2 (pp. 490–493)

7. 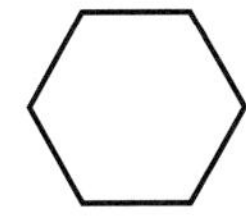
8. 
9. 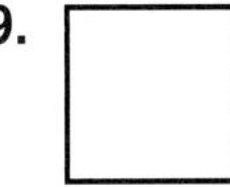
10. 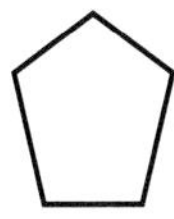

Tell if the given angles could form a quadrilateral. KY MA-05-3.1.1 (pp. 490–493)

11. 115°, 150°, 65°, 30°
12. 85°, 72°, 113°, 90°
13. 90°, 110°, 90°, 75°

Draw and label the following. KY MA-05-3.1.1 (pp. 496–499)

14. Circle *K* with radius 12 centimeters and chord *LM*
15. Circle *T* with diameter *SU* measuring 3 meters
16. Circle *F* with intersecting diameters *EG* and *CD*

Write whether the two figures appear to be *congruent*, *similar*, or *neither*. KY MA-05-3.1.5 (pp. 500–503)

17. 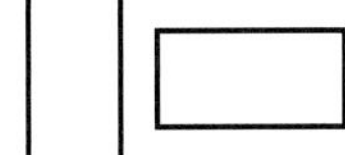
18. 
19. 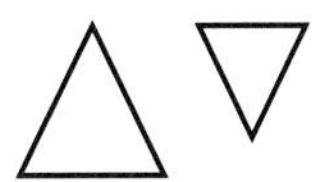

Check Problem Solving

Solve. KY MA-05-3.1.1 (pp. 494–495)

20. **WRITE Math** Chris is constructing a wooden puzzle. He cuts a piece shaped like a regular hexagon. What is the sum of the angle measures in Chris's piece? Suppose Chris cuts the hexagon into triangles. **Explain** how a rule that describes the relationship between the number of triangles and the number of sides in the hexagon can help solve this problem.

Technology Use *Online Assessment.*

Practice for the KCCT
Chapters 1–18

Number and Operations

1. The number of students in Amanda's school, when rounded to the nearest hundred, is 300. When rounded to the nearest ten, the number is 260. Which of these could be the exact number of students in Amanda's school? KY MA-05-1.2.1 (p. 14)

   A 252

   B 255

   C 267

   D 301

2. Jerry ordered a shipment of granola bars for his store. He ordered one carton each of blueberry, strawberry, and apple granola bars. Each carton holds 24 boxes, and each box holds 8 granola bars. How many granola bars did Jerry order? KY MA-05-1.3.1 (p. 40)

   A 192

   B 384

   C 576

   D 1,920

3. **WRITE Math** List the prime numbers between 10 and 20. Then, list the composite numbers between 10 and 20. **Explain** how you know that these numbers are prime or composite. KY MA-05-1.5.1 (p. 284)

Algebraic Thinking

4. Andrew and Jenny have a total of 140 marbles. Andrew has 115 marbles and Jenny has *m* marbles. How many marbles does Jenny have? KY MA-05-5.3.1 (p. 374)

   A 25 C 51

   B 39 D 76

Test Tip **Decide on a plan.**

See item 4. What number do you know? Use this number to find another number. Then use those numbers to find the answer.

5. Marissa and Nadine went shopping. Marissa spent $35 and Nadine spent *d* dollars. Together Marissa and Nadine spent $145. How much money did Nadine spend? KY MA-05-5.3.1 (p. 108)

   A $115

   B $110

   C $90

   D $75

6. **WRITE Math** Give the next number for each pattern. What are the differences between Pattern A and Pattern B? **Explain.** KY MA-05-5.1.1 (p. 46)

   Pattern A: 2, 6, 18, 54, ■

   Pattern B: 99, 88, 77, 66, ■

Geometry

7. How many angles does a rhombus have?
KY MA-05-3.1.2 (p. 490)

A 3
B 4
C 5
D 6

8. Which type of figure is shown?
KY MA-05-3.1.1 (p. 482)

A angle
B ray
C line segment
D line

9. WRITE Math Does this figure have line symmetry? Explain how you know if a figure has line symmetry. KY MA-05-3.2.1 (p. 504)

Data Analysis and Probability

10. The Shirt Shack graphed the sales of their T-shirts over 4 weeks. Which 2 weeks did they sell the most T-shirts? KY MA-05-4.1.1 (p. 242)

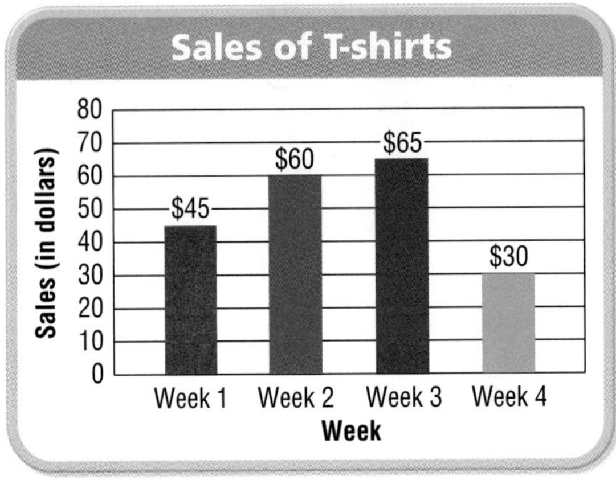

A Week 2 and Week 3
B Week 1 and Week 3
C Week 4 and Week 3
D Week 4 and Week 1

11. WRITE Math There are 12 boys and 10 girls in David's class. The teacher will choose one student to write on the board. Is it more likely that a boy or girl will be chosen? **Explain** how you know.
KY MA-05-4.4.2 (p. 454)

CHAPTER 19 Plane and Solid Figures

The Rock and Roll Hall of Fame and Museum in Cleveland, Ohio, is a composition of bold, geometric shapes. The architect, I.M. Pei, wanted the building's dramatic design to "echo the energy of rock and roll".

Investigate

Look for examples of plane and solid figures in the Rock and Roll Hall of Fame and Museum. Then, on a sheet of paper, draw your own building. Include plane and solid figures. Describe the properties of your figures.

Plane Figures	Solid Figures
triangles	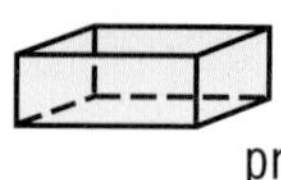 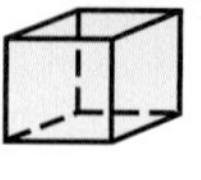 prisms
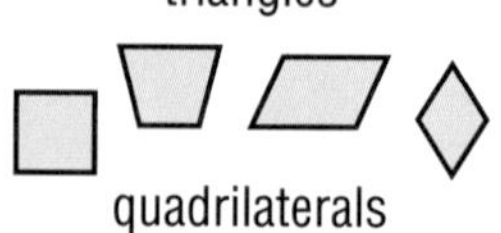 quadrilaterals	 pyramids
other plane figures	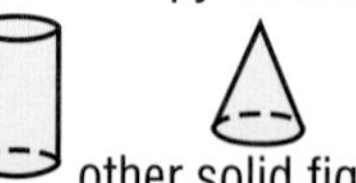 other solid figures

Technology
Student pages are available in the Student eBook.

Show What You Know

Check your understanding of important skills needed for success in Chapter 19.

▶ Measure and Classify Angles

Classify the angle. Write *acute, right,* or *obtuse*.

1. 

2. 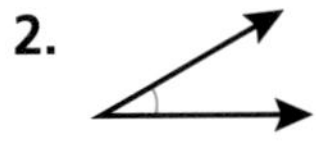

3. 

4. 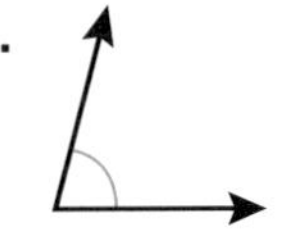

▶ Faces of Solid Figures

Name the plane figure that is the shaded face of the solid figure.

5. 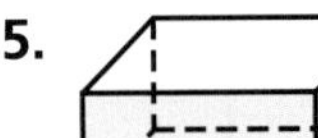

6. 

7. 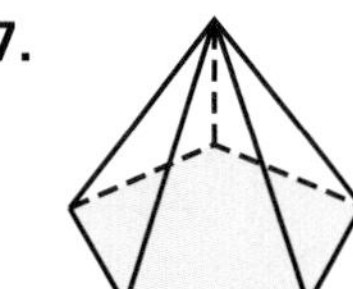

8. 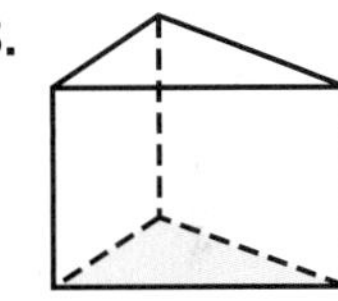

9. 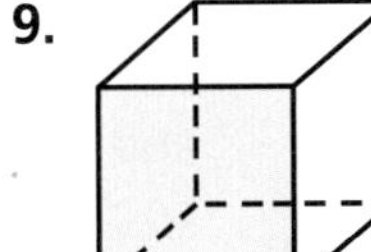

10. 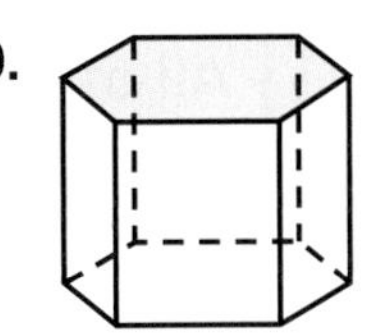

11. 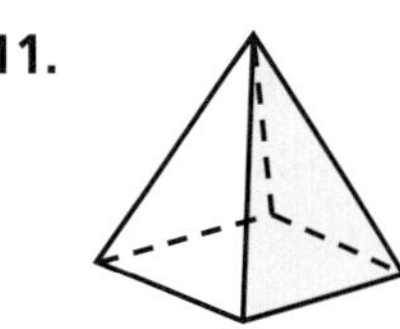

12. 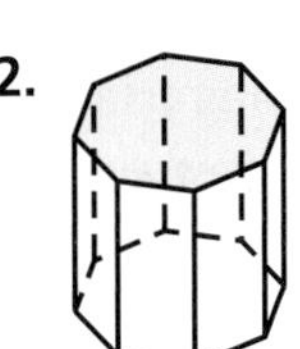

VOCABULARY POWER

CHAPTER VOCABULARY

acute triangle
base
edge
equiangular triangle
equilateral triangle
face
isosceles triangle
net
obtuse triangle
parallelogram
polyhedron
prism
pyramid
rhombus
right triangle
scalene triangle
trapezoid
vertex

WARM-UP WORDS

equilateral triangle a triangle with three congruent sides

prism a polyhedron that has two congruent and parallel polygons as bases with all other faces as rectangles

pyramid a polyhedron that has only one polygon base. All other faces are triangles that meet at a common vertex.

Classify Triangles

OBJECTIVE: Identify, describe, and classify types of triangles; find an unknown angle in a triangle.

Quick Review

Classify each angle as right, acute, or obtuse.

1. 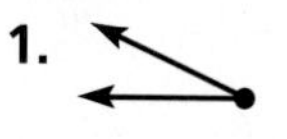
2. 
3. 
4. 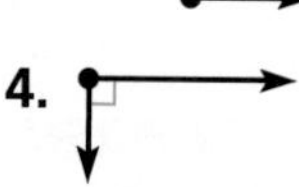
5. 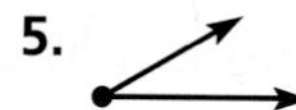

Vocabulary

isosceles triangle
scalene triangle
equilateral triangle
right triangle
acute triangle
obtuse triangle
equiangular triangle

Learn

PROBLEM The *Santa Maria* is one of the ships Christopher Columbus sailed to North America. The sail in the back of the ship was a triangle that had a right angle, but whose sides were all different lengths. What type of triangle was the sail?

You can classify triangles by the lengths of their sides. In the examples below, the slashes indicate congruent sides.

Examples

A 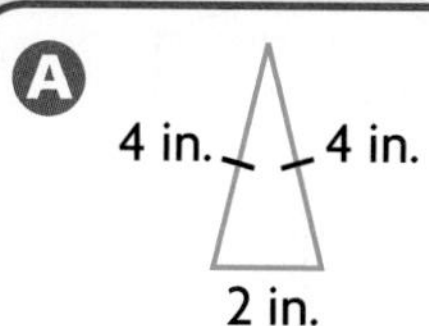

An **isosceles triangle** has exactly two congruent sides.

B 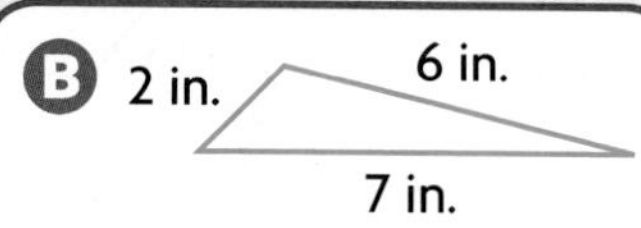

A **scalene triangle** has no congruent sides.

C 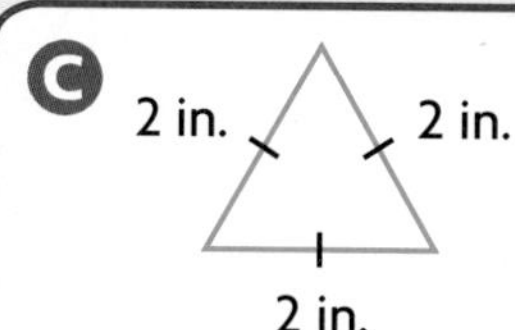

All of the sides of an **equilateral triangle** are congruent.

Math Idea
An equilateral triangle has 3 congruent sides and 3 congruent angles. An isosceles triangle has 2 congruent angles. A scalene triangle has no congruent angles.

You can also classify triangles by the measures of their angles.

Examples

D 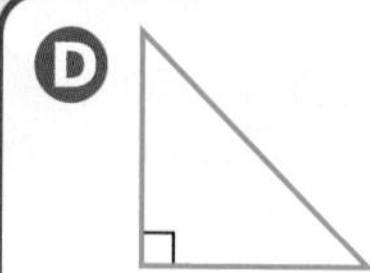

A **right triangle** has a right angle.

E 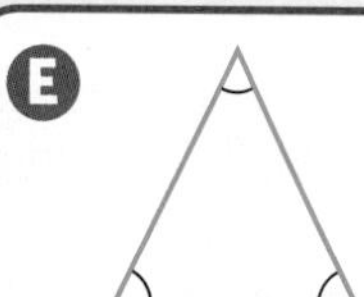

An **acute triangle** has three acute angles.

F 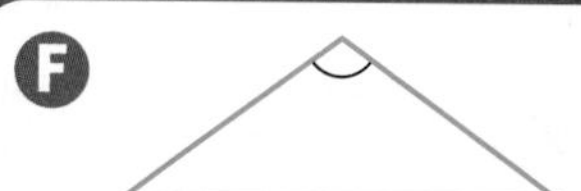

An **obtuse triangle** has one obtuse angle.

So, the sail was a scalene triangle and a right triangle.

An equilateral triangle is also known as an equiangular triangle. All of the angles of an **equiangular triangle** are congruent.

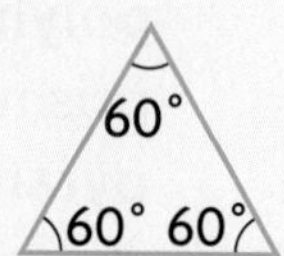

- Without actually measuring the angles, how can you determine whether a triangle has an obtuse angle?

This is a model of the *Santa Maria*.

FAST TRACK

KY MA-05-3.1.2 Students will describe and provide examples of basic two-dimensional shapes [circles, triangles (right, equilateral), all quadrilaterals, pentagons, hexagons, octagons] and will apply these shapes to solve real-world and mathematical problems. DOK 2 *also* MA-05-3.1.1

Finding an Unknown Angle

In a triangle, you can find the measure of an unknown angle if you know the measures of the other two angles.

Example

What is the measure of the unknown angle in the triangle below?

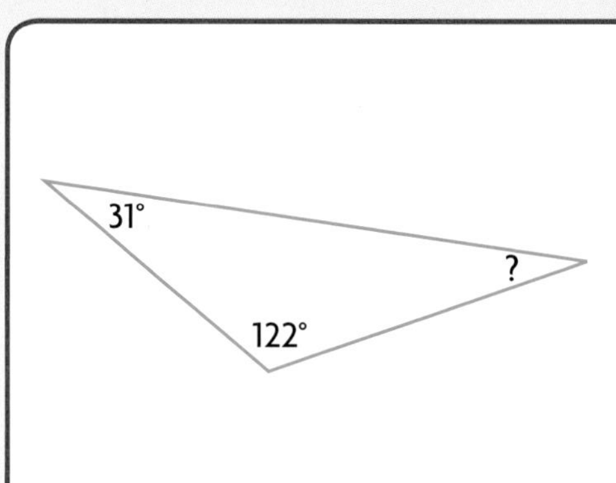

Step 1

Find the sum of the measures of the known angles.

$31° + 122° = 153°$

Step 2

Subtract the sum of the known angle measures from 180°.

$180° - 153° = 27°$

So, the measure of the unknown angle is 27°.

Remember

The sum of the measures of the interior angles of a triangle is always 180°.

Guided Practice

1. Copy triangle *ABC* at the right.

   a. Mark the congruent sides with slashes. Classify the triangle by the lengths of its sides.

   b. The triangle has 2 acute angles. Is the third angle a right angle, an acute angle, or an obtuse angle? Classify the triangle by the measures of its angles.

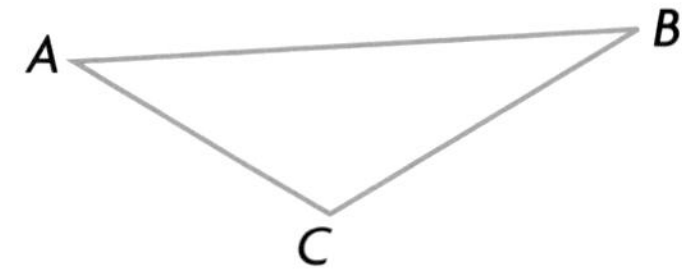

Classify each triangle. Write *isosceles, scalene,* or *equilateral*.

2. 3 cm, 3 cm, 3 cm

3. 6 in., 2 in., 6 in.

✓4. 2 cm, 7 cm, 8 cm

Classify each triangle. Write *acute, right,* or *obtuse*.

5.

6.

✓7.

8. **TALK Math** **Explain** the difference between an obtuse triangle and an acute triangle.

Independent Practice and Problem Solving

Classify each triangle. Write *isosceles*, *scalene*, or *equilateral*.

9. 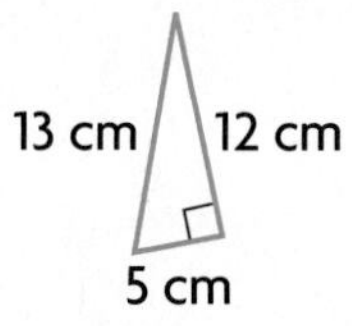

10. 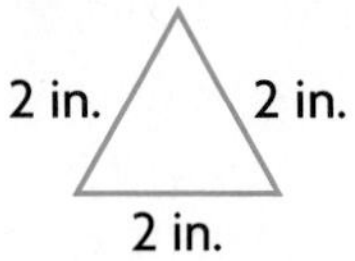

11. 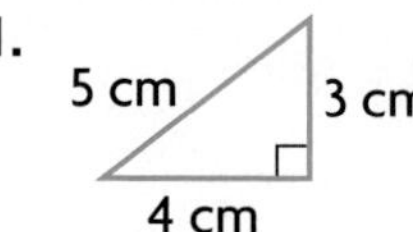

12. 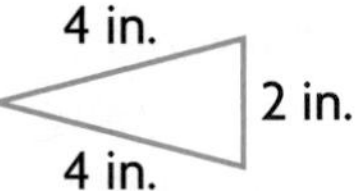

13. 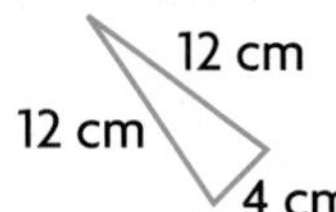

14. 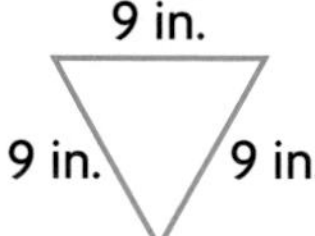

Classify each triangle. Write *acute, right,* or *obtuse*.

15. 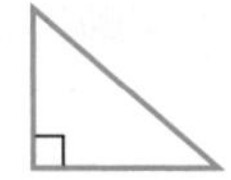

16. 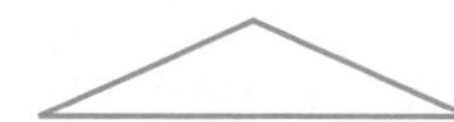

17. 

18. 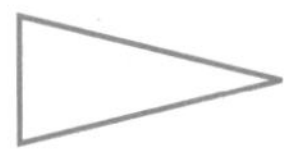

19. 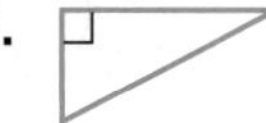

20. 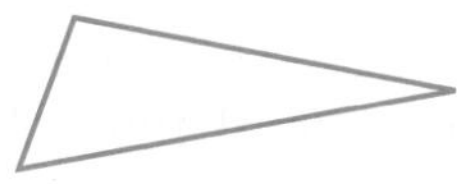

Algebra **Find the unknown angle measure for each triangle.**

21. 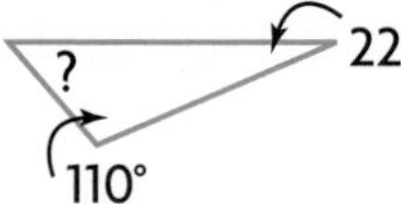

22. 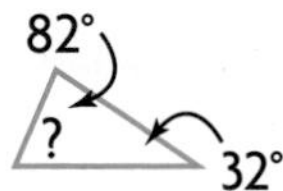

23. 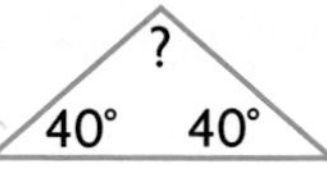

USE DATA **For 24–26, use the models of the sails.**

24. What type of triangle is the *Mayflower* sail?

25. What type of triangle is the *El Toro* sail?

26. Two of the angles in the *El Toro* lateen sail measure 83° and 64°. What is the measure of the third angle?

27. **Reasoning** Jade wants to draw a right triangle. She begins by drawing an angle that measures 70°. What are the measures of the other two angles Jade should draw?

28. The sides of a sail are 15 ft, 12 ft, and 9 ft. One of the angles of the sail is a right angle. Classify the triangular sail by the lengths of its sides and also by the measures of its angles.

29. **WRITE Math** **Explain** how an isosceles triangle can also be an acute triangle or an obtuse triangle.

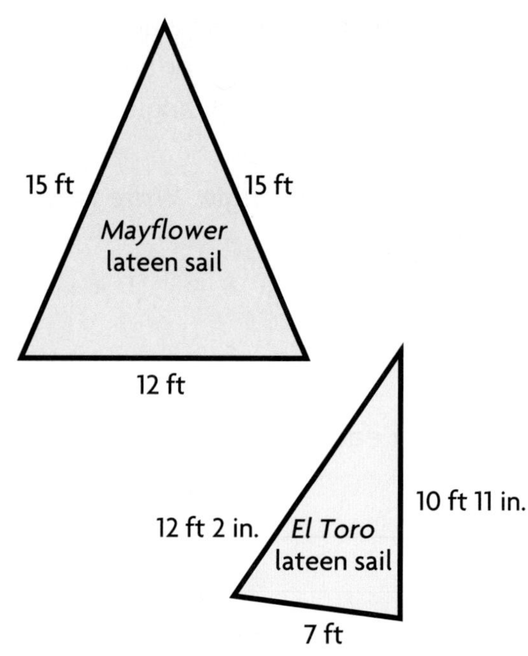

Technology
Use Harcourt Mega Math, Ice Station Exploration, *Polar Planes,* Levels E, F.

 Extra Practice on page 534, Set A

Learn About Triangles on a Geoboard

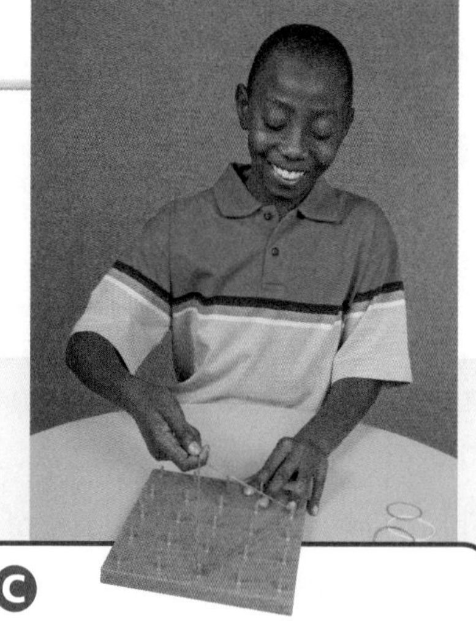

You have learned how a triangle can be named by the lengths of its sides and by the measures of its angles. Can you have a triangle that is obtuse and isosceles? How about a triangle that is acute and isosceles? How about a triangle that is right and equilateral?

Examples

Use a geoboard to try to make the triangles in the questions above. If it is not possible to make the triangle, explain why.

A

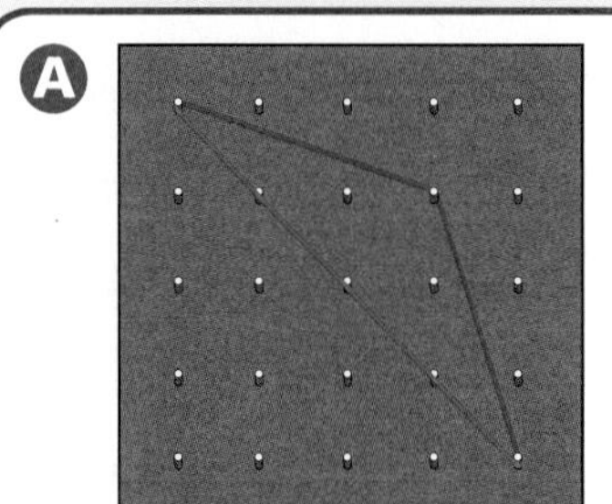

So, an obtuse isosceles triangle is possible.

B

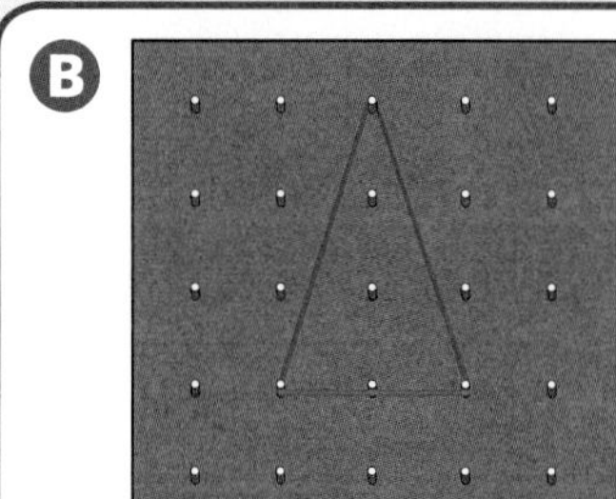

So, an acute isosceles triangle is possible.

C

An equilateral triangle has 3 congruent angles, and a right triangle has 1 angle that is 90°. It is not possible to have a triangle with three 90° angles.

So, a right equilateral triangle is not possible.

Try It

Use a geoboard to try to make each type of triangle. If it is not possible to make the triangle, explain why.

30. right scalene triangle

31. right isosceles triangle

32. obtuse scalene triangle

33. obtuse equilateral triangle

34. **Explain** why it is impossible to show a right equiangular triangle.

Mixed Review and Test Prep

35. Estimate the difference between 39,346 and 26,844. (p. 16)

36. Find 70% of 480. (p. 444)

37. **Test Prep** The measure of two angles in a triangle is 150°. What is the measure of the third angle?

A 30° **B** 35° **C** 90° **D** 210°

38. **Test Prep** A triangular picture frame has no congruent sides and 1 right angle. What type of triangle is the picture frame?

A rectangle

B acute and equilateral

C right and scalene

D obtuse and isosceles

LESSON 2

Classify Quadrilaterals

OBJECTIVE: Identify, describe, and classify quadrilaterals; find an unknown angle in a quadrilateral.

Quick Review

Sunny draws a pentagon. How many sides does the polygon have?

Vocabulary

trapezoid **parallelogram**

rhombus

Learn

In a recent year, Amish quilts were featured in United States stamps. Quilts use many shapes, such as quadrilaterals, in their designs.

This quilt was made by an Amish quilt maker in Pennsylvania.

There are five special types of quadrilaterals. On the quadrilaterals below, the sides with the same number of slashes are congruent.

general quadrilateral	**trapezoid**	**parallelogram**
A quadrilateral has 4 sides and 4 angles.	A **trapezoid** has exactly 1 pair of parallel sides.	A **parallelogram** has opposite sides parallel and congruent.
rectangle	**rhombus**	**square**
A rectangle has 4 right angles with opposite sides parallel and congruent.	A **rhombus** is a parallelogram with 4 congruent sides. The plural of *rhombus* is *rhombi*.	A square has 4 congruent sides and 4 right angles.

Example

Name the parallel and congruent sides. Then use the diagram to name the quadrilateral in as many ways as possible.

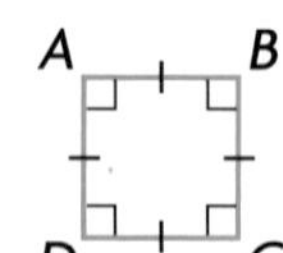

$\overline{AB}$ and $\overline{CD}$ are parallel; so are $\overline{AD}$ and $\overline{BC}$.
All angles are right angles.
Sides $\overline{AB}$, $\overline{BC}$, $\overline{CD}$, and $\overline{AD}$ are congruent.

Possible names: square, rectangle, rhombus, parallelogram, and quadrilateral

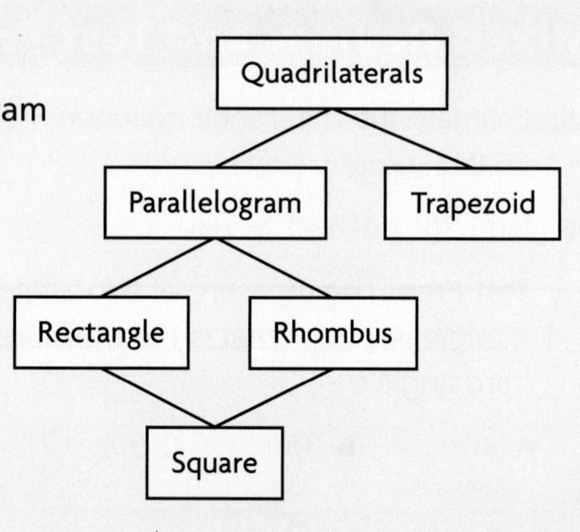

FAST TRACK

KY MA-05-3.1.2 Students will describe and provide examples of basic two-dimensional shapes [circles, triangles (right, equilateral), all quadrilaterals, pentagons, hexagons, octagons] and will apply these shapes to solve real-world and mathematical problems. DOK 2 *also* MA-05-3.1.1

Find the Unknown Angle

In a quadrilateral, you can find the measure of an unknown angle if you know the measures of the other three angles.

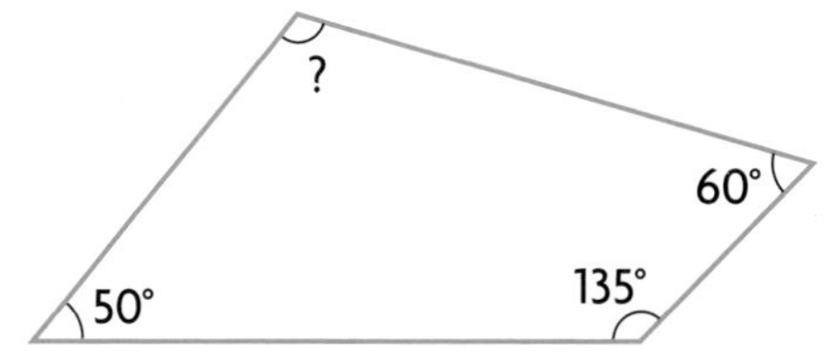

Example **What is the measure of the unknown angle in the quadrilateral above?**

Step 1	Step 2
Find the sum of the measures of the known angles. $50° + 135° + 60° = 245°$	Subtract the sum of the known angle measures from 360°. $360° - 245° = 115°$

So, the measure of the unknown angle is 115°.

Remember
The sum of the angles in a quadrilateral is always 360°.

For any type of quadrilateral, you can find the measure of an unknown angle by subtracting the sum of the known angles from 360°.

More Examples

A rectangle

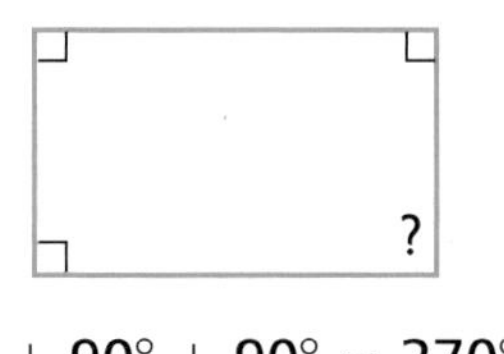

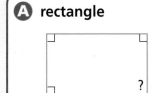

$90° + 90° + 90° = 270°$

$360° - 270° = 90°$

B parallelogram

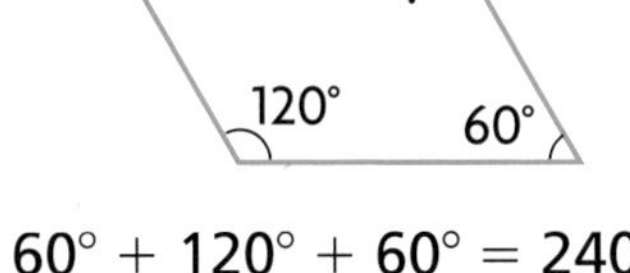

$60° + 120° + 60° = 240°$

$360° - 240° = 120°$

C rhombus

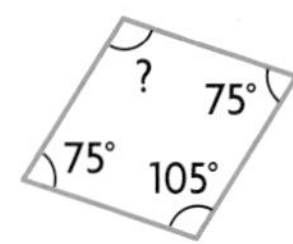

$75° + 105° + 75° = 255°$

$360° - 255° = 105°$

- What is the measure of an unknown angle in a quadrilateral with angles that measure 105°, 75°, and 105°? What type of quadrilateral could it be? Draw a picture of each type.

Guided Practice

1. Copy the quadrilateral at the right.

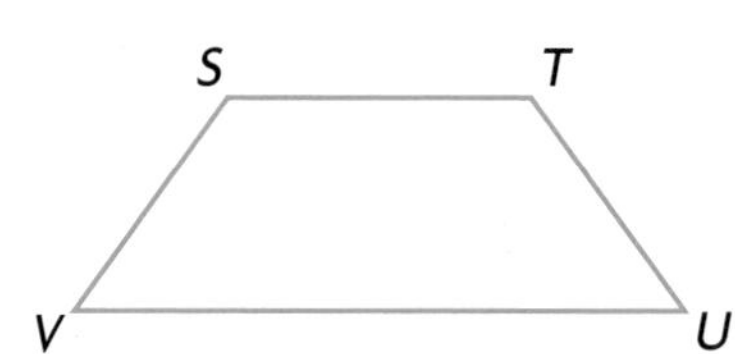

- Are any of the sides congruent? Mark the congruent sides. Then name them.
- Does the quadrilateral have perpendicular sides? Name them.
- Does the quadrilateral have parallel sides? Name them.
- Which term best describes quadrilateral *STUV—trapezoid, parallelogram, rectangle, rhombus,* or *square*?

Classify each figure in as many ways as possible. Write *quadrilateral, parallelogram, square, rectangle, rhombus,* or *trapezoid*.

2. 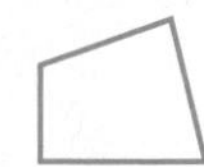

3. 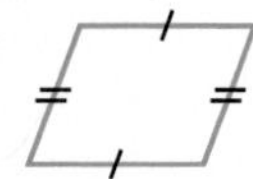

4. 

✓5. 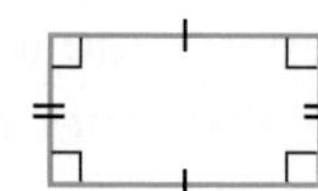

For each quadrilateral, name the parallel, perpendicular, and congruent sides.

6. 

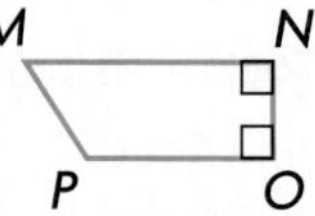

7. 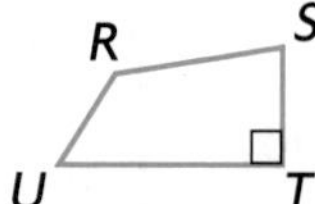

8. 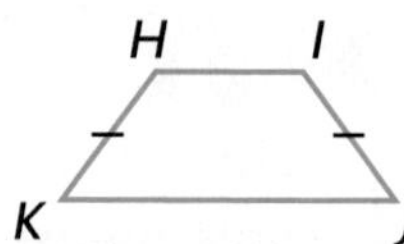

✓9. 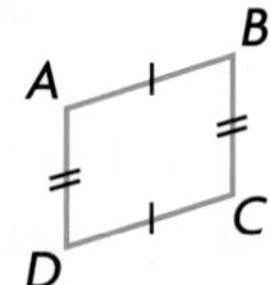

10. TALK Math **Explain** how a square and a rectangle are similar and how they are different.

Independent Practice and Problem Solving

Classify each figure in as many ways as possible. Write *quadrilateral, parallelogram, square, rectangle, rhombus,* or *trapezoid*.

11. 

12. 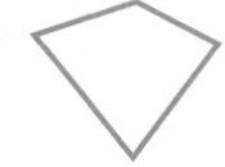

13. 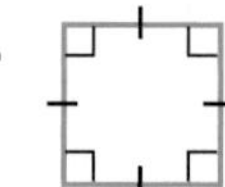

14. 

For each quadrilateral, name the *parallel, perpendicular,* and *congruent* sides.

15. 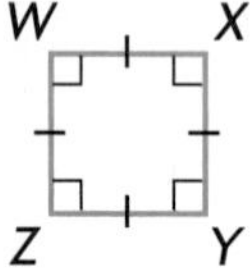

16. 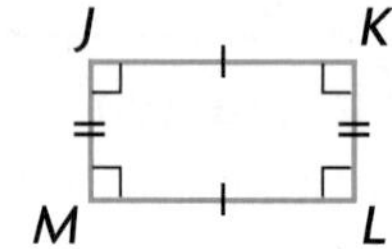

17. 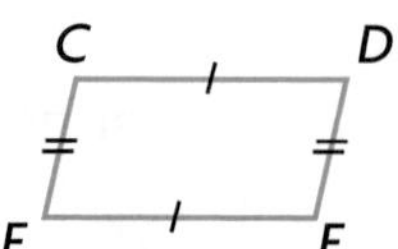

18. 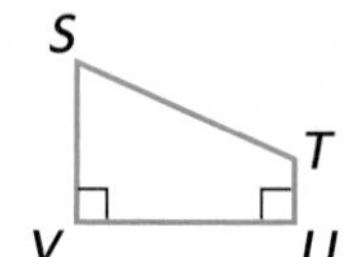

Algebra Find the unknown angle measure for each quadrilateral.

19. 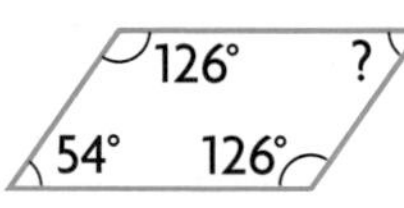

20. 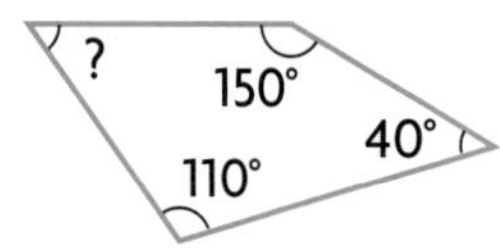

21. 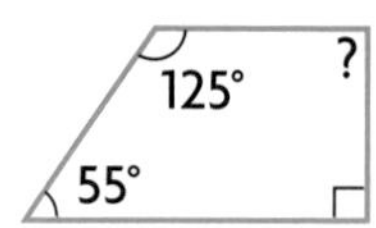

22. 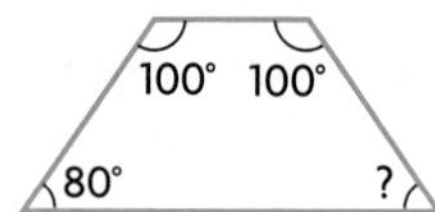

23. Draw and name a quadrilateral with 4 right angles and 2 pairs of congruent sides.

24. **Reasoning** Can you draw a quadrilateral that is both a rhombus and a rectangle? **Explain.**

25. **Algebra** All parallelograms have two pairs of congruent angles. If each angle in one pair is 48°, what is the measure of each of the unknown angles?

26. WRITE Math **Sense or Nonsense** The measure of an unknown angle in a quadrilateral always has to be equal to or less than 90°.

Extra Practice on page 534, Set B

Learn About Venn Diagrams

The Venn diagram below is one way to show how quadrilaterals are related.

As you read the Venn diagram, think about how you could apply the words *always*, *sometimes*, and *never* to describe how the quadrilaterals are related to one another.

Example

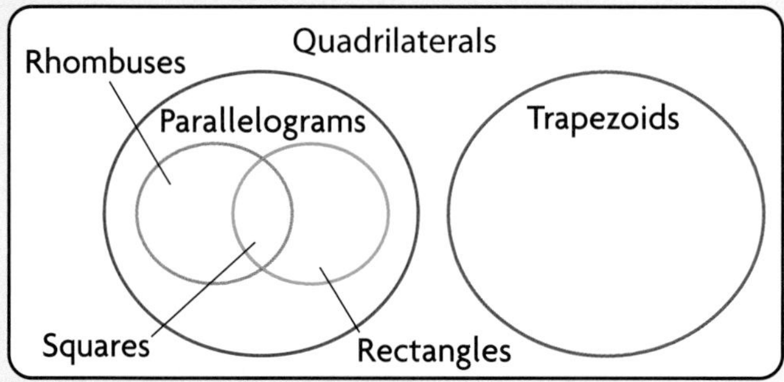

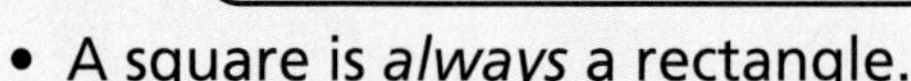

- A square is *always* a rectangle.
- A rectangle is *sometimes* a square.
- A rectangle is *never* a trapezoid.

Try It

Complete. Write *always, sometimes,* or *never.*

27. A rhombus is ___?___ a square.

28. A trapezoid is ___?___ a parallelogram.

29. A parallelogram is ___?___ a rectangle.

30. A rectangle is ___?___ a rhombus.

31. A rhombus is ___?___ a parallelogram.

32. A parallelogram is ___?___ a rectangle.

33. A trapezoid is ___?___ a quadrilateral.

34. A rhombus is ___?___ a trapezoid.

35. Write a problem that can be answered by using the Quadrilaterals Venn diagram above.

Mixed Review and Test Prep

36. In a card game, Alex must pick a number greater than 15 to win the game. The twenty cards are numbered from 1 to 20. What are Alex's chances of winning the game? (p. 454)

37. What quadrilateral could have angle measures of 90°, 135°, 90°, and 45°? (p. 491)

38. **Test Prep** A quadrilateral has 4 congruent sides and 2 pairs of congruent angles. What type of quadrilateral is it?

A rectangle

B trapezoid

C rhombus

D hexagon

LESSON 3 HANDS ON

Draw Plane Figures

OBJECTIVE: Draw and identify triangles and quadrilaterals.

Quick Review

Classify each triangle or quadrilateral.

1. 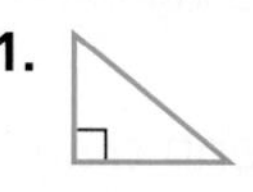

2. 

3. 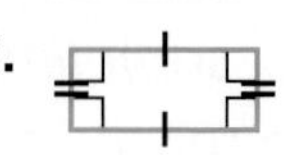

4. 

5. 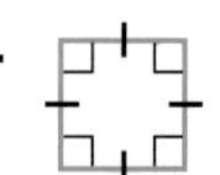

Investigate

Materials ■ straightedge ■ protractor

Draw triangle *ABC* so that it has two congruent sides and a right angle. Each congruent side should have a length of 2 inches.

A Use the protractor to draw a 90° angle. Mark a point at the vertex, and label the point *A*.

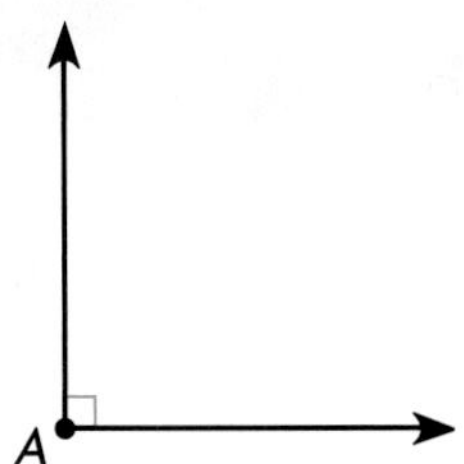

B Measure 2 inches from *A* along one of the rays, and mark a point. Label the point *B*.

C To draw the congruent side, measure 2 inches from *A* along the other ray, and mark a point. Label the point *C*.

D Draw a line to connect points *B* and *C*.

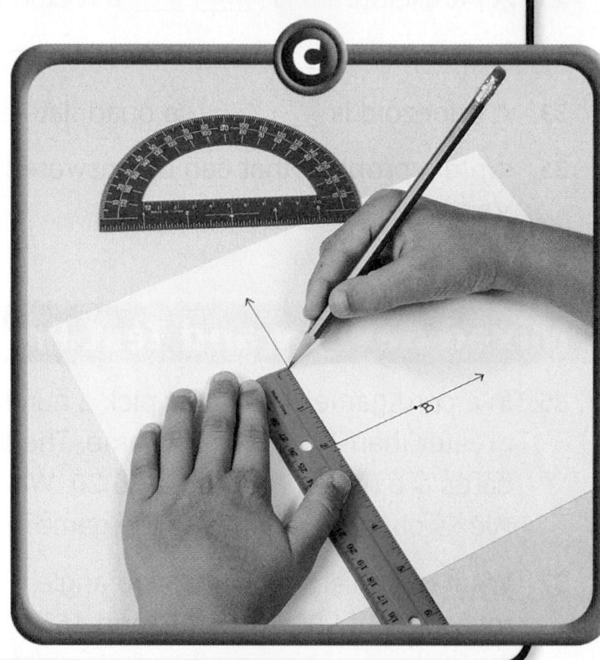

Draw Conclusions

1. What type of triangle is triangle *ABC*?
2. What is the measure of $\angle B$?
3. Without measuring, explain whether $\angle C$ is congruent to $\angle B$.
4. **Comprehension** Describe how you would draw a triangle with congruent angles and congruent sides.

 FAST TRACK

KY MA-05-3.1.2 Students will describe and provide examples of basic two-dimensional shapes [circles, triangles (right, equilateral), all quadrilaterals, pentagons, hexagons, octagons] and will apply these shapes to solve real-world and mathematical problems. DOK 2 *also* MA-05-3.1.1

Connect

You can use a ruler and a protractor to draw quadrilateral *ABCD* on a coordinate grid. Plot the points given and then connect the points. Use your protractor to measure the angles you have formed.

Given Points:

Point *A* (2,1), Point *B* (9,1), Point *C* (11,5), Point *D* (4,5)

Step 1

Plot the first point at (2,1) on the coordinate grid and label the point *A*.

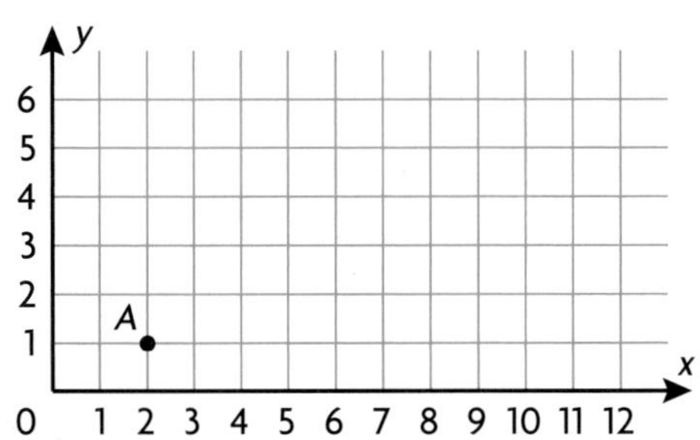

Step 2

Plot Point *B* at (9,1) on the grid. Draw a line to connect Points *A* and *B*.

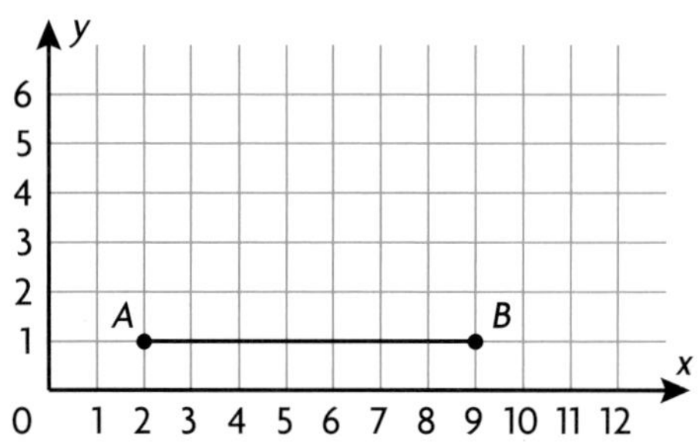

Step 3

Plot Point *C* at (11,5) and Point *D* at (4,5) and label them. Draw lines to connect Points *B*, *C*, and *D*.

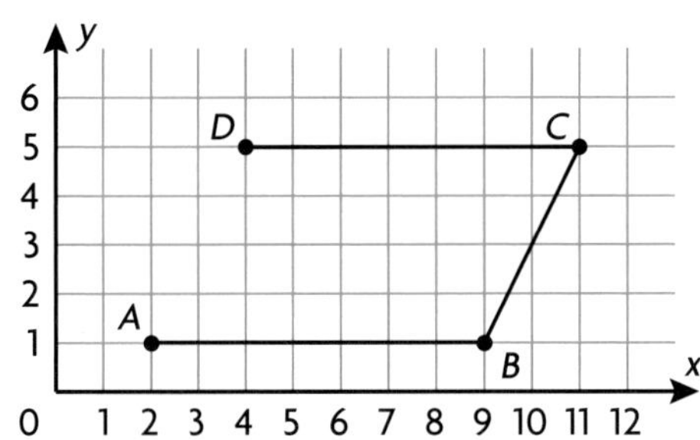

Step 4

Draw a line to connect Points *D* and *A*. Use your protractor to measure the four angles.

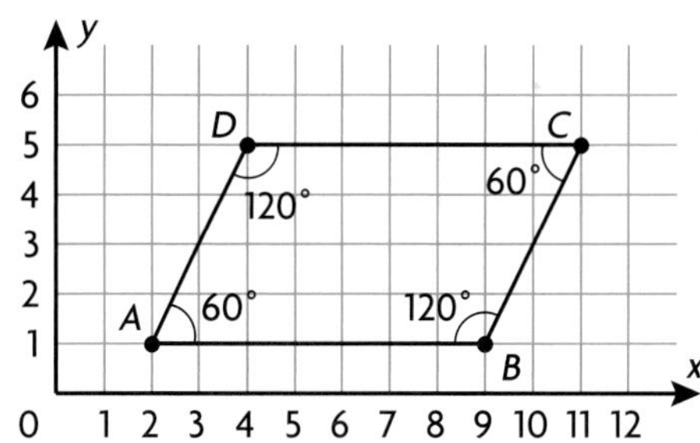

TALK Math

Classify the quadrilateral you drew. **Explain** how you identified it.

Practice

Draw each figure on a coordinate grid. Classify each figure.

1. a triangle with angles measuring 20°, 110°, 50°; no congruent sides
2. a quadrilateral with 4 right angles; 4 congruent sides each measuring 1 inch
3. **WRITE Math** **Explain** how you would use a ruler and a protractor to draw a rectangle on a coordinate grid.

LESSON 4

Solid Figures

OBJECTIVE: Identify, describe, and classify solid figures.

Quick Review

Name each figure.

1. △ **2.** 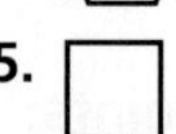 **3.** 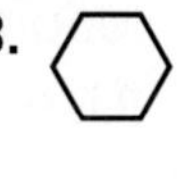

4. **5.** 

Vocabulary

polyhedron, prism, base, pyramid, face, edge, vertex

Learn

A **polyhedron** is a solid figure with faces that are polygons. Prisms and pyramids are polyhedrons.

A **prism** is a polyhedron that has two congruent and parallel polygons as **bases**. All the other faces in a prism are rectangles. A prism is named for the shape of its bases. A cube is a special rectangular prism.

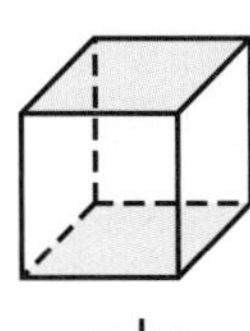
cube

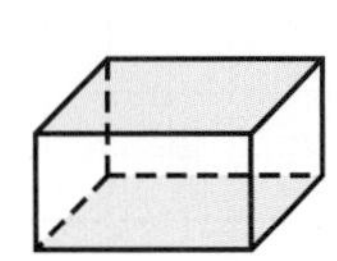
rectangular prism

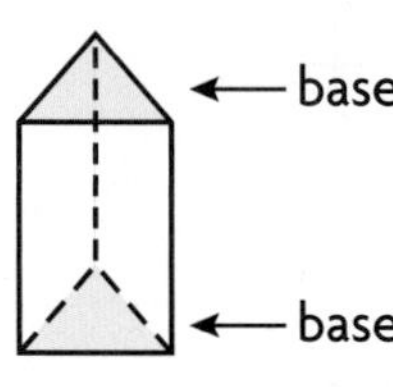

triangular prism

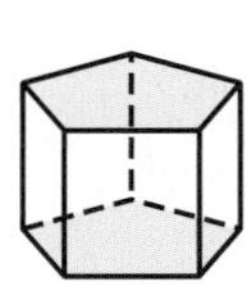
pentagonal prism

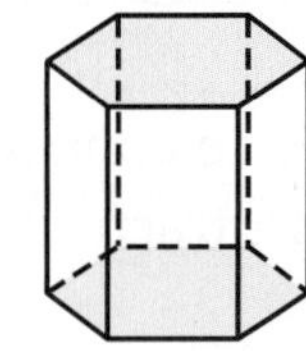
hexagonal prism

▲ The John F. Kennedy Library in Massachusetts suggests different solid figures in its design.

A **pyramid** is a polyhedron with only one polygon base. All the other faces are triangles that meet at a common vertex. The shape of its base names the pyramid.

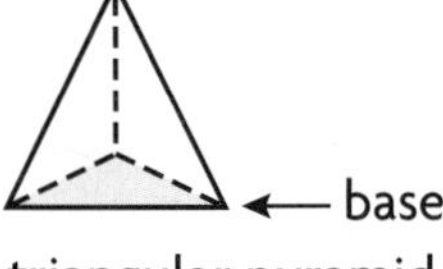

triangular pyramid

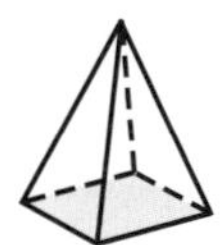
square pyramid

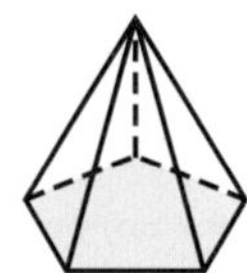
pentagonal pyramid

hexagonal pyramid

Some solid figures have curved surfaces. These solid figures are *not* polyhedrons.

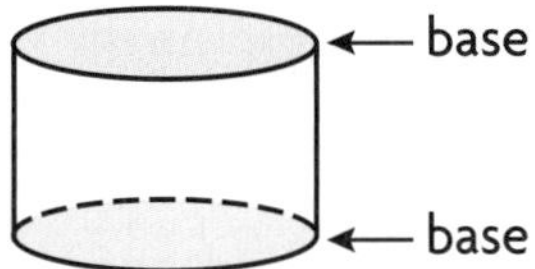

A **cylinder** has 2 congruent circular bases and 1 curved surface.

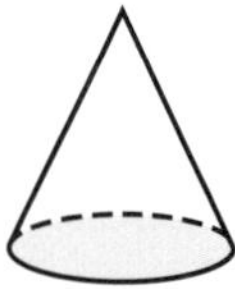

A **cone** has 1 circular base and 1 curved surface.

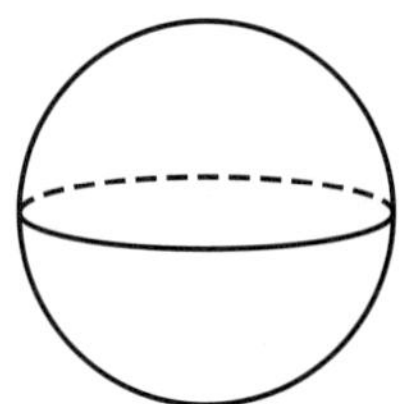

A **sphere** has no base and 1 curved surface.

FAST TRACK

KY MA-05-3.1.3 Students will describe and provide examples of basic three-dimensional objects (spheres, cones, cylinde pyramids, cubes, triangular and rectangular prisms), will identify three-dimensional objects from two-dimensior representations (nets) and will apply the attributes to solve real-world and mathematical problems. DOK 2 *also* MA-05-3.

Faces, Edges, and Vertices

Solid figures can be classified by the shape and the number of their bases, faces, edges, and vertices.

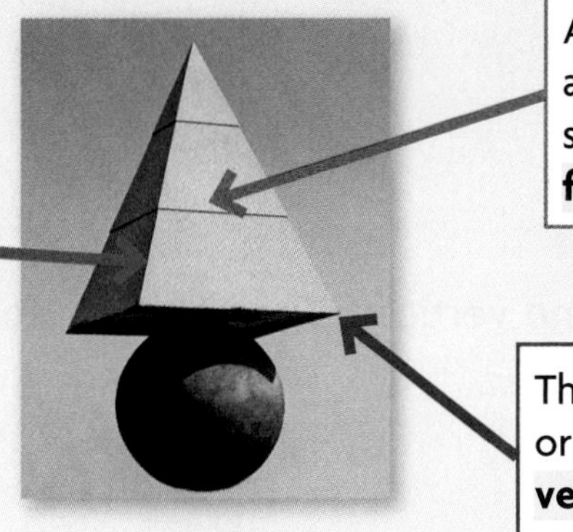

All the polygons that are flat surfaces of a solid figure are called **faces**.

The line where two faces meet is an **edge**.

The point where three or more edges meet is a **vertex**.

Examples

If the figure is a polyhedron, identify the number of faces, vertices, and edges. Then classify each solid figure.

A

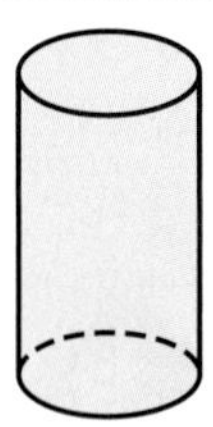

This figure has 2 circular bases. It is *not* a polyhedron.

Classify: cylinder

B

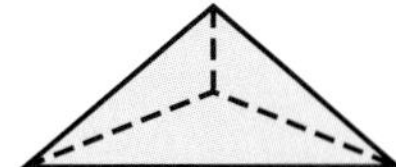

This figure has a triangular base.

Faces: 4 **Vertices:** 4
Edges: 6

Classify: triangular pyramid

C

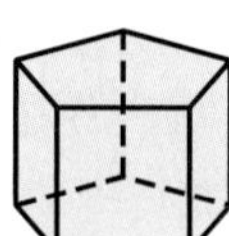

This figure has 2 pentagonal bases.

Faces: 7 **Vertices:** 10
Edges: 15

Classify: pentagonal prism

Guided Practice

Match each statement with the correct solid figure. Then, name each figure.

a 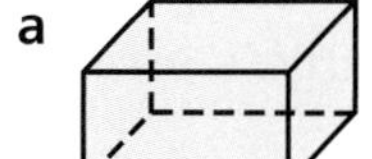 b 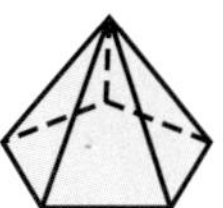 c 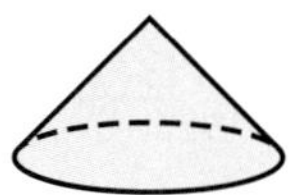

1. A polyhedron that has 2 congruent polygons as bases
2. A polyhedron with only one base
3. A solid figure with 1 circular base and 1 curved surface

Classify each solid figure. Write *prism*, *pyramid*, *cone*, *cylinder*, or *sphere*.

4. 
5. 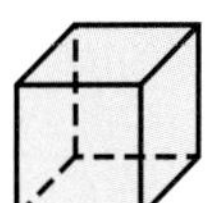
6. 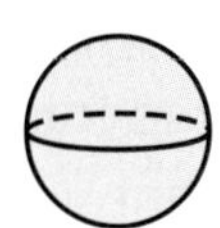
7. 

8. TALK Math **Compare** a prism and a pyramid. Tell how they are similar and how they are different.

Independent Practice and Problem Solving

Classify each solid figure. Write *prism*, *pyramid*, *cone*, *cylinder*, or *sphere*.

9. 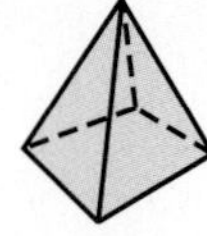

10. 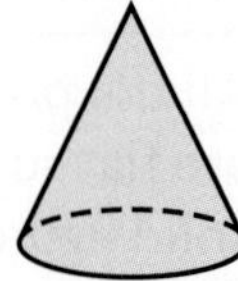

11. 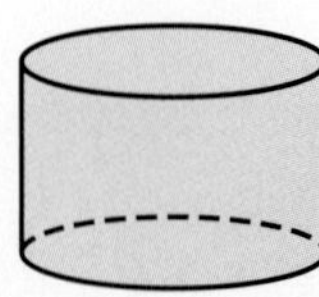

12. 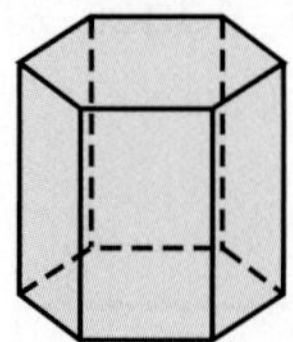

Write the number of faces, edges, and vertices. Then classify each solid figure.

13. 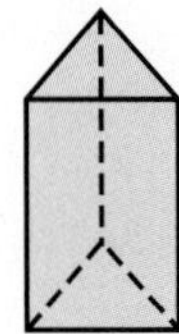

14. 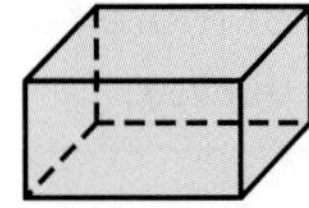

15. 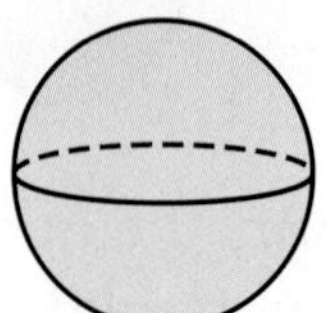

16. 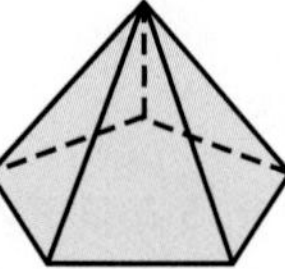

For 17–21, use the photo at the right.

17. What shape is suggested by the floor of the arena?

18. What shape is suggested by the outside walls of the arena?

19. How many faces, edges, and vertices does the arena have?

20. What kind of solid figure does the arena suggest?

21. ***FAST FACT*** The arena has congruent faces that are triangles. Each side of the base is 180 meters wide. The arena is 98 meters tall. What is the distance around the base of the arena?

▲ This arena in Memphis, Tennessee, has a square base.

22. **WRITE Math** **What's the Error?** Margo says that any polyhedron can be named if you know the number of faces it has. Describe Margo's error.

Mixed Review and Test Prep

23. What is $(3 \times 100{,}000) + (6 \times 10{,}000) + (2 \times 10)$ written in standard form? (p. 4)

24. One pair of congruent angles in a rhombus has a total measure of 72°. What is the total measure of the other pair of congruent angles in the rhombus? (p. 518)

25. **Test Prep** Which solid figure has a square as a base and 4 triangles as faces?

A cube

B cone

C triangular prism

D square pyramid

 Extra Practice on page 534, Set C

A City's Water

Classify and Categorize

In the late 1800s, the city of Boston built the Chestnut Hill Pumping Station. This is how the growing city got its drinking water. Large pumps inside the station pumped water from two nearby reservoirs. Reservoirs are places where water is stored.

How would you classify and categorize the solid figures you see in the Chestnut Hill Pumping Station building?

You can classify and categorize the information given in a problem to help you solve it. When you classify and categorize, you

- identify the items you want to classify.
- select an important item in the group.
- identify other items in the group that are like it and other items that are not like it.
- state a rule that describes the categories all the items belong in.

▲ The Chestnut Hill station also had a public park. People could ride around the reservoir in carriages.

Problem Solving **Classify and categorize to understand each problem.**

1. Answer the question above.

2. Use different types of solid figures to design and draw your own building.

Problem Solving Workshop
Strategy: Compare Strategies

OBJECTIVE: Compare different strategies to solve problems.

Use the Strategy

PROBLEM Taryn is building polyhedrons by using pieces of clay for the vertices and straws for the edges. How many pieces of clay and how many straws will she need to build a hexagonal prism?

Read to Understand

- **What do you visualize when you read the problem?**
- **What information is given?**

Plan

- **What strategy can you use to solve the problem?**

Often you can use more than one strategy to solve a problem. Use *find a pattern* and *make a model.*

Solve

- **How can you use each strategy to solve the problem?**

Find a Pattern

Copy and complete the table.

Figure	Number of Sides in Each Base	Number of Vertices	Number of Edges
Triangular Prism	3	6	9
Rectangular Prism	4	8	
Pentagonal Prism	5		
Hexagonal Prism			

The number of vertices is two times the number of sides in each base and the number of edges is three times the number of sides in each base.

Make a Model

Use clay and straws to make a model.

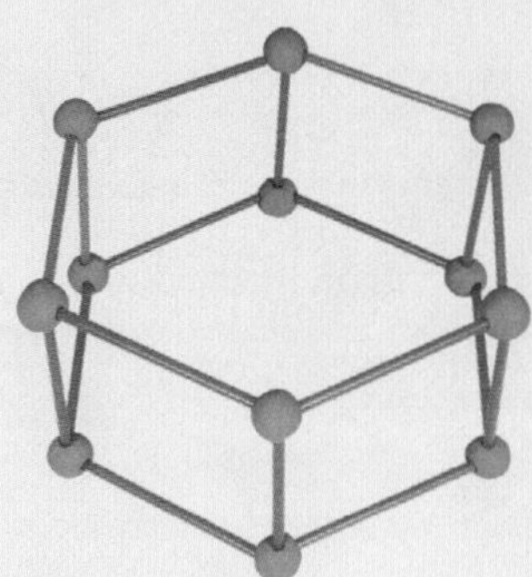

Count the number of pieces of clay and the number of straws used to make the model.

So, Taryn will need 12 pieces of clay and 18 straws.

Check

- **How do you know the answer is correct?**

KY MA-05-3.1.1 Students will describe and provide examples of basic geometric elements and terms [points, segments, lines (perpendicular, parallel, intersecting), rays, angles (acute, right, obtuse), sides, edges, faces, base vertices, radius, diameter] and will apply these elements to solve real-world and mathematical problems. DOK

Guided Problem Solving

1. Tyler is using pieces of clay and straws to make pyramids. How many pieces of clay and how many straws will he need to build an octagonal pyramid?

   First, use the *find a pattern* strategy.

   Then, use the *make a model* strategy.

   Finally, compare the answers.

2. **What if** Tyler had made an octagonal prism? How many pieces of clay and how many straws would he need?

3. Mackenzie used 12 straws as edges to build a pyramid. How many sides did the base of her pyramid have? How many vertices did it have?

Choose a STRATEGY

- Draw a Diagram
- Make a Model or Act It Out
- Make an Organized List
- Find a Pattern
- Make a Table or Graph
- Predict and Test
- Work Backward
- Solve a Simpler Problem
- Write an Equation
- Use Logical Reasoning

Mixed Strategy Practice

4. **WRITE Math** Charlotte makes glass jewelry boxes in the shape of pentagonal prisms. Each face of a box is made with a single piece of glass. How many pieces of glass does she need to make 3 jewelry boxes? **Explain** how you found your answer.

5. A park monument is built in the shape of an octagonal prism. For the weekend parade, each 25-foot vertical edge will be decorated with a banner. How many feet of banner paper will be needed?

USE DATA For 6–8, use the data in the diagram.

6. Sophia is designing a new bridge. It will be as tall and as wide as the George Washington Bridge shown at the right, but it will be only $\frac{3}{5}$ as long. What is the length of the bridge Sophia is designing?

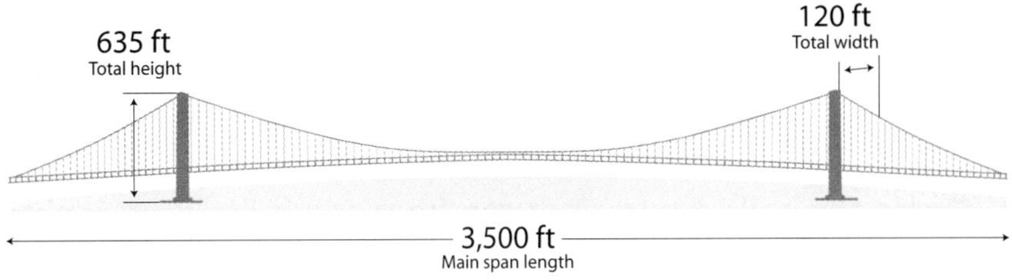

7. **Pose a Problem** Look back at problem 6. Write and solve a similar problem by changing the relationship of the dimensions of the new bridge to the George Washington Bridge.

8. Jason walked across the George Washington Bridge and back. Write and solve an equation that describes how far he walked.

9. **WRITE Math** Ava needs 0.7 yard of cloth to make a pillow cover. How many yards of cloth does Ava need to make 5 pillow covers? **Explain** how you can use the *make a model* strategy to solve the problem.

Nets for Solid Figures

OBJECTIVE: Identify and make nets for solid figures.

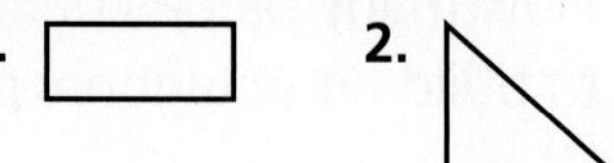

Name each polygon.

1. 
2.
3. 
4.
5.

Vocabulary

net

Learn

The wooden crate is a cube. You can make a model of this crate by making and folding a net. A **net** is a two-dimensional pattern that can be folded into a three-dimensional polyhedron.

Activity **Materials** ■ 1-inch grid paper ■ scissors ■ tape

A cube has 6 congruent square faces.

Step 1

Draw the net on grid paper. Cut it out.

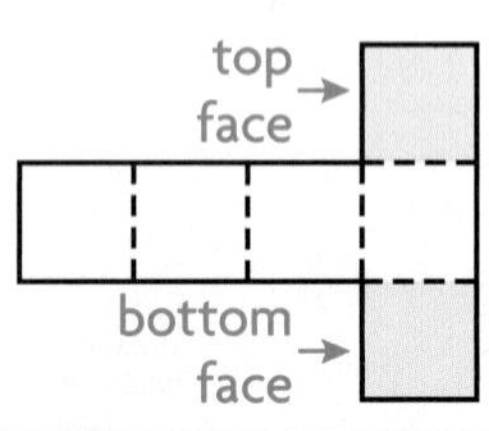

Step 2

Fold along the dashed lines.

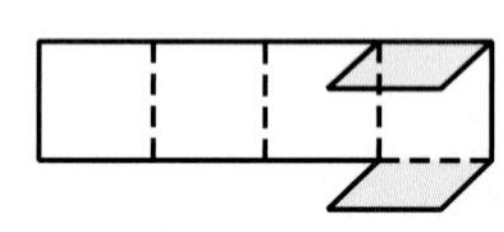

Step 3

Tape the edges together. Be sure there are no gaps and that none of the sides overlap.

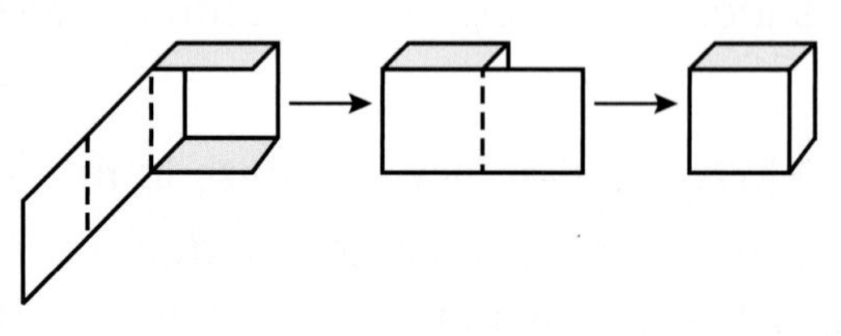

Examples

Name the solid figure that can be made by folding the net.

A

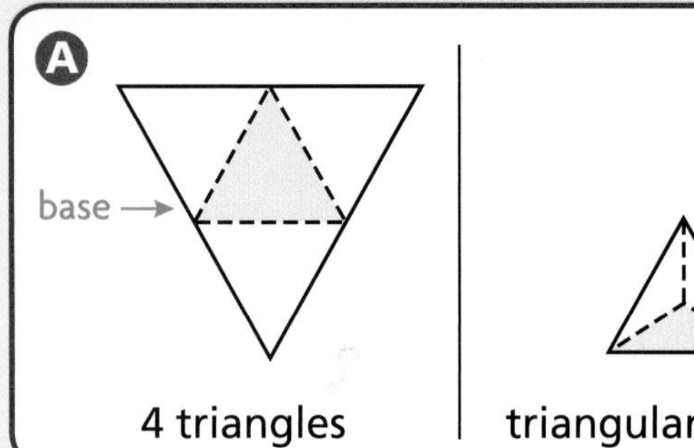

4 triangles | triangular pyramid

B

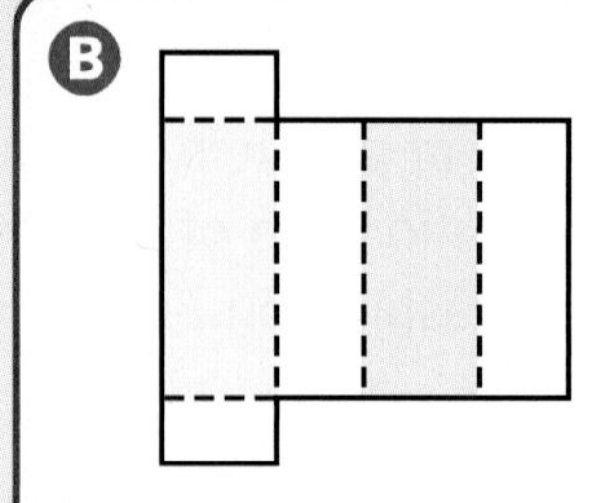

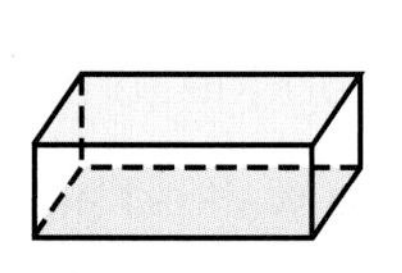

6 rectangles | rectangular prism

- **Explain** how identifying the shapes in a net can help you identify the solid figure that may be made by folding the net.

 FAST TRACK

KY MA-05-3.1.3 Students will describe and provide examples of basic three-dimensional objects (spheres, cones, cylinders, pyramids, cubes, triangular and rectangular prisms), will identify three-dimensional objects from two-dimensional representations (nets) and will apply the attributes to solve real-world and mathematical problems. DOK

Guided Practice

Match each solid figure with its net.

1. 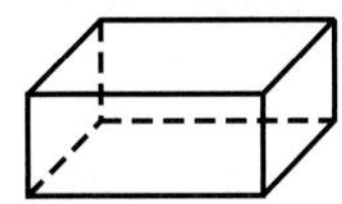

2. 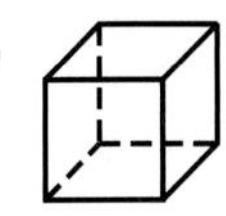

3. 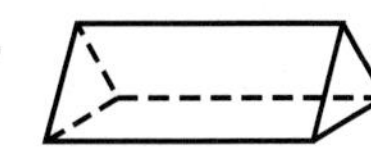

4. 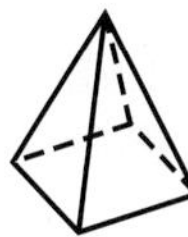

a 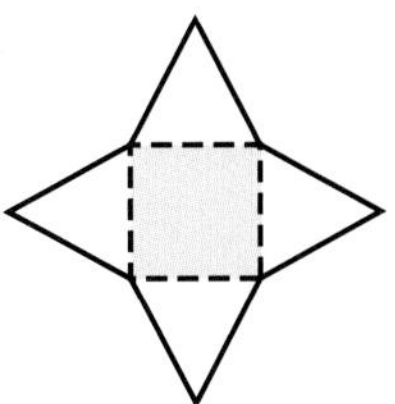

b 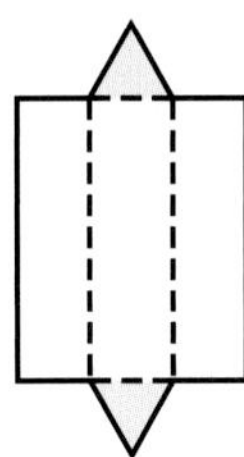

c 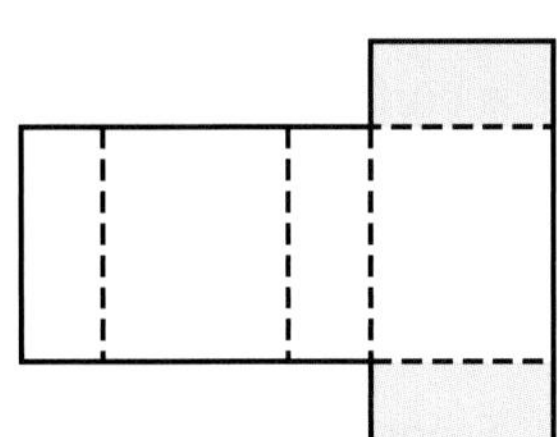

d 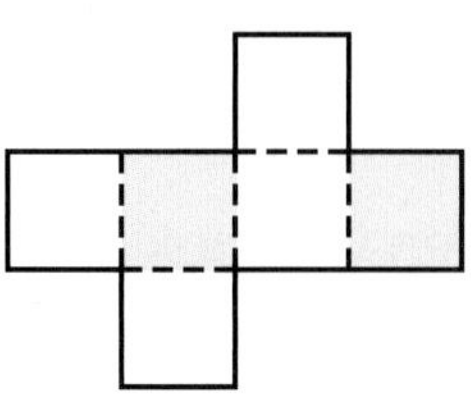

5. TALK Math What shapes will always appear in a net for a triangular prism? **Explain.**

Independent Practice and Problem Solving

Match each solid figure with its net.

6. 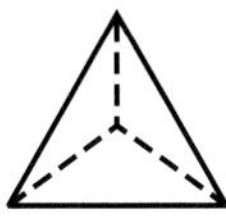

7. 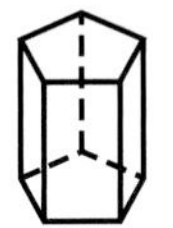

8. 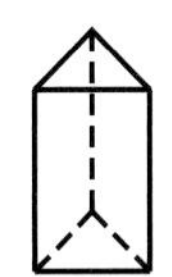

9. 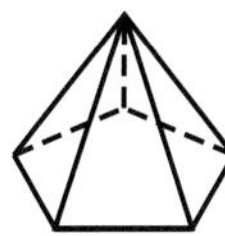

a 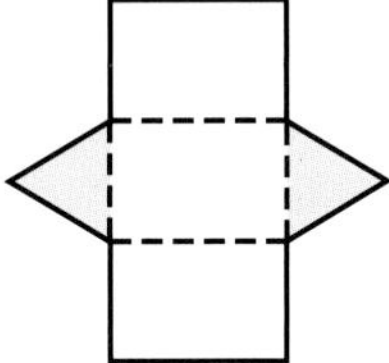

b 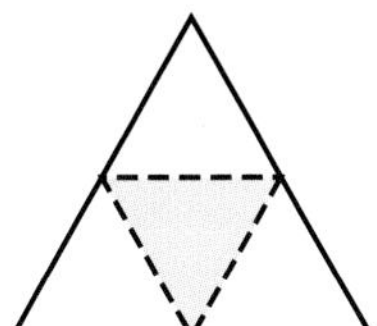

c 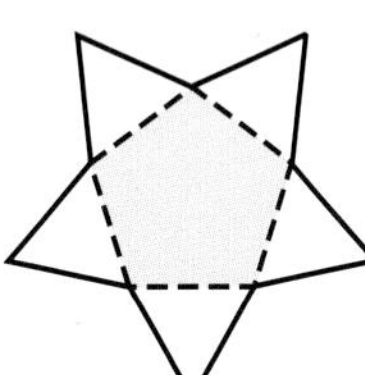

d 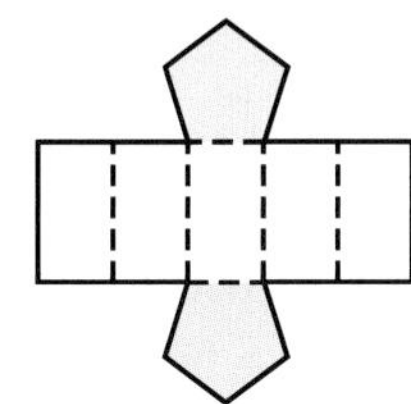

10. WRITE Math Copy the net at the right. Then cut it out and try to fold it to make a cube. **Explain** why the net cannot be folded to form a cube.

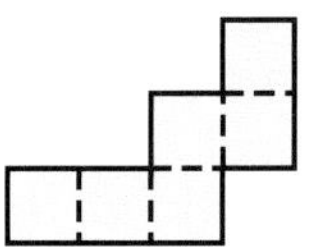

Mixed Review and Test Prep

11. What is the mode of the set of data? (p. 220)

12, 10, 11, 12, 15, 9

12. $1\frac{1}{8} + 2\frac{3}{4} =$ (p. 370)

13. What is the value of h in the equation $27 \times h = 135$? (p. 96)

14. Test Prep How many triangles does the net for a triangular pyramid contain?

A 2 **B** 3 **C** 4 **D** 5

LESSON 7 HANDS ON

Draw Solid Figures from Different Views

OBJECTIVE: Visualize and draw two-dimensional views of three-dimensional objects.

Identify the solid figure that has the base or bases described.

1. 2 circles
2. 1 square
3. 1 circle
4. 2 squares
5. 2 rectangles

Investigate

Materials ■ grid paper ■ tape ■ connecting cubes

When you look at solid figures from the top, front, and side, you see different two-dimensional figures.

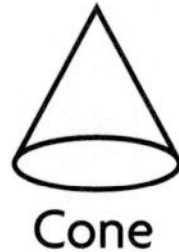
Cone

Top view

Front view
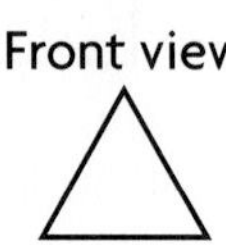

Side view
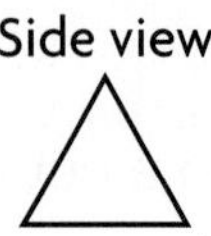

Copy the net shown below onto grid paper, and cut it out. Then fold the net, and tape the edges to make a rectangular prism.

A Look at the top of your rectangular prism, and draw the top view on grid paper.

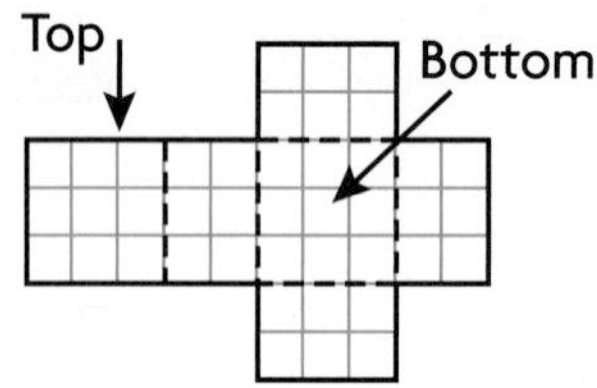

B Look at the front of your rectangular prism, and draw the front view.

C Look at the side of your rectangular prism, and draw the side view.

Draw Conclusions

1. How do the top, front, and side views of a rectangular prism compare?
2. How would the top view of a triangular prism compare to the top view of a rectangular prism?
3. **Application** Look at the top, front, and side views of the solid figure at the right. Identify the solid figure. **Explain** how the top, front, and side views helped you identify the solid figure.

Top view
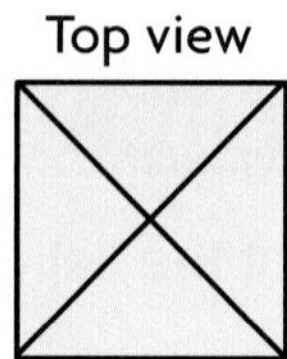

Front view
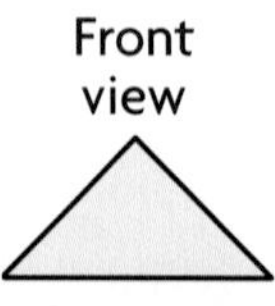

Side view
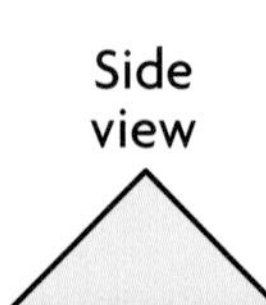

KY MA-05-3.1.3 Students will describe and provide examples of basic three-dimensional objects (spheres, cones, cylinders, pyramids, cubes, triangular and rectangular prisms), will identify three-dimensional objects from two-dimensional representations (nets) and will apply the attributes to solve real-world and mathematical problems. DOK

Connect

How would the solid figure at the right look if you viewed it from the top, front, and side? Use connecting cubes to build this solid figure. Then use grid paper to draw the different views.

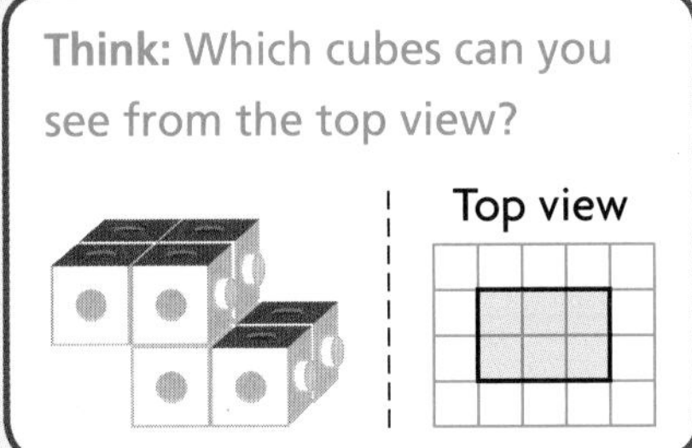

Think: Which cubes can you see from the top view?
Top view

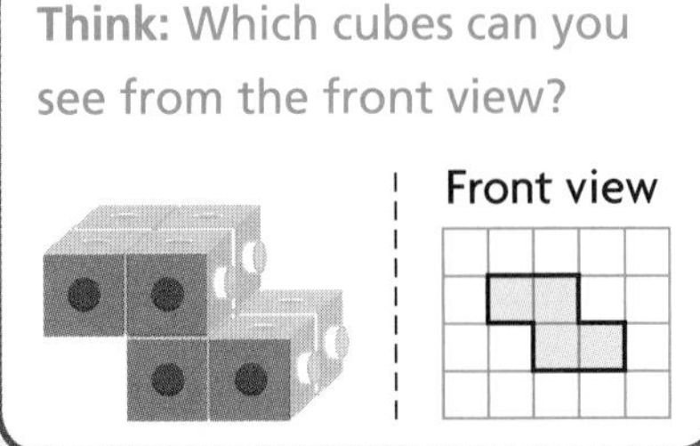

Think: Which cubes can you see from the front view?
Front view

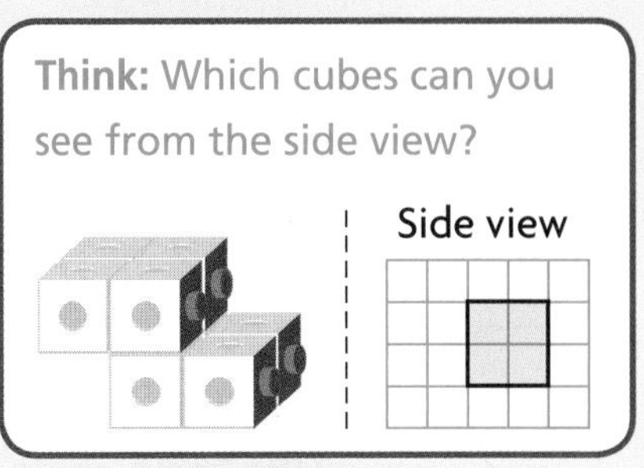

Think: Which cubes can you see from the side view?
Side view

TALK Math

How many cubes can you see from the left side view? How does this compare to the right side view?

Practice

Identify the solid figure that has the given views.

1. 

2. 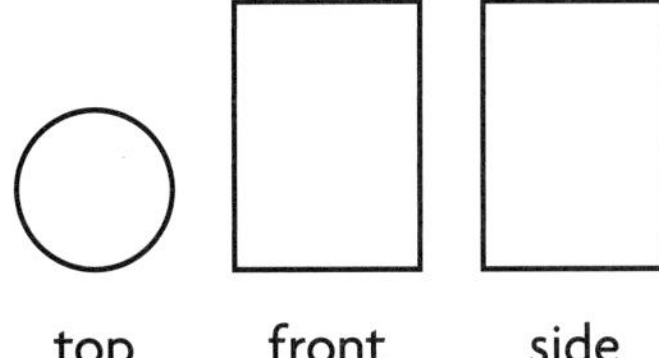

✓3. 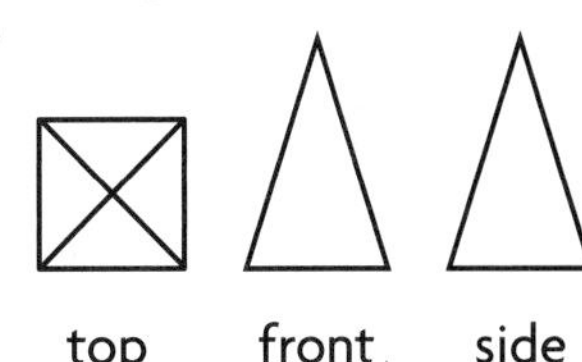

Use cubes to build the figure. On grid paper, draw the figure from the top, front, and side.

4. 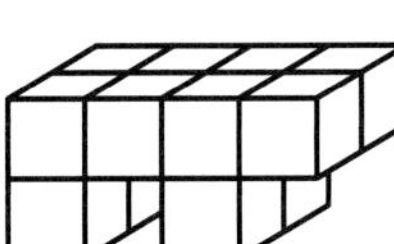

5. 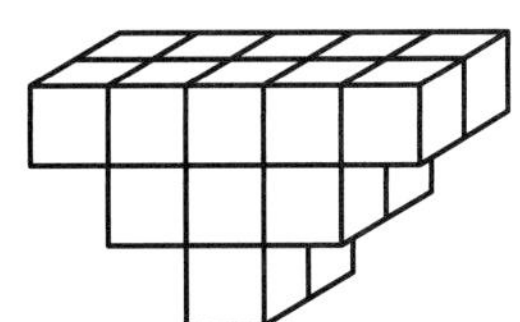

✓6. 

7. 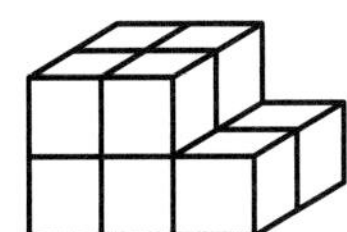

8. 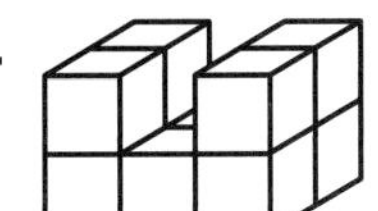

9. 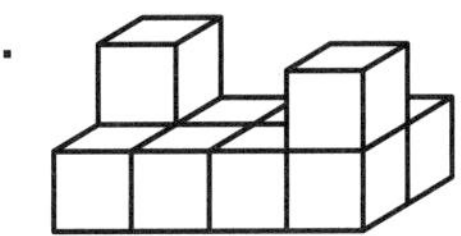

10. **WRITE Math** **Explain** which solid figures have a top view that is the same as the bottom view.

Extra Practice

Set A Classify each triangle. Write *isosceles, scalene,* or *equilateral.* (pp. 514–517)

1. 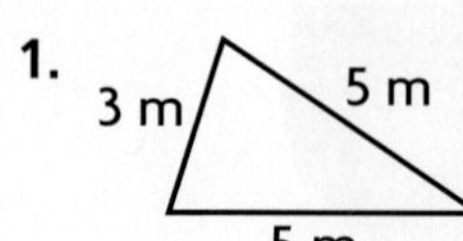

2. 8 in. 8 in. 6 in.

3. 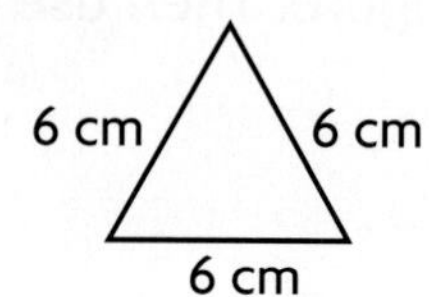

Classify each triangle. Write *acute, right,* or *obtuse.*

4. 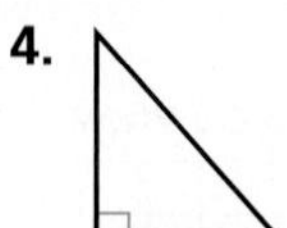

5.

6. 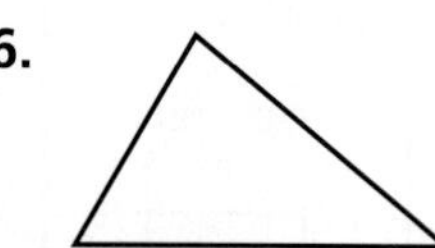

7. Two of the angles of a triangle measure 35° and 55°. What is the measure of the third angle?

Set B Classify each figure in as many ways as possible. Write *quadrilateral, parallelogram, square, rectangle, rhombus,* or *trapezoid.* (pp. 518–521)

1. 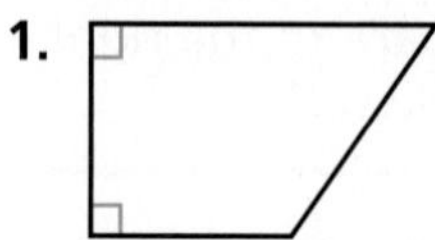

2.

3. 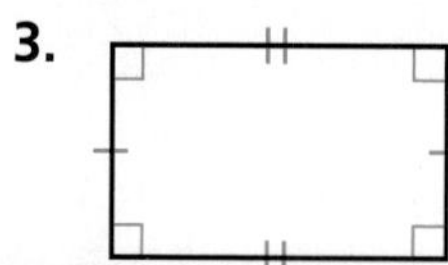

4. 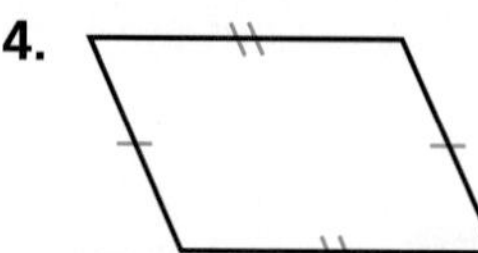

5. Three of the angles of a quadrilateral measure 90°, 60°, and 90°. What is the measure of the fourth angle?

Set C Classify each solid figure. Write *prism, pyramid, cone, cylinder,* or *sphere.* (pp. 524–527)

1. 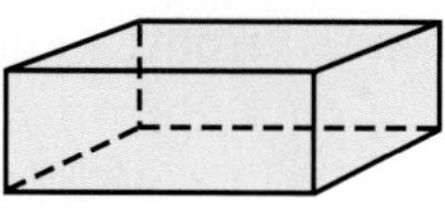

2. 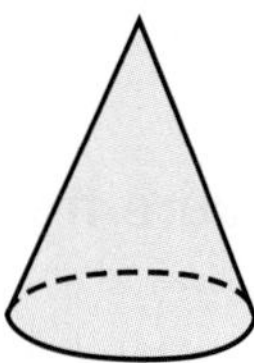

3. 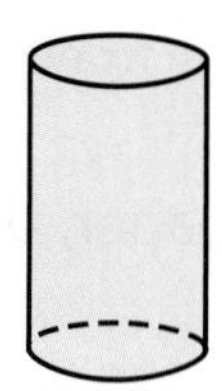

4. 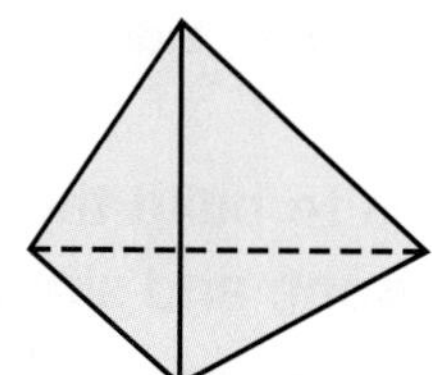

Set D Match each solid figure with its net. (pp. 530–531)

1. 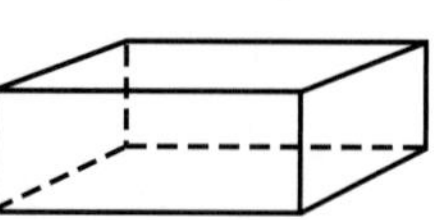

2. 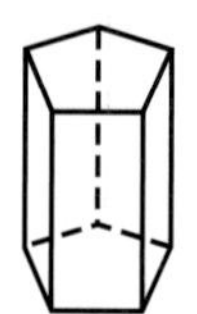

a. 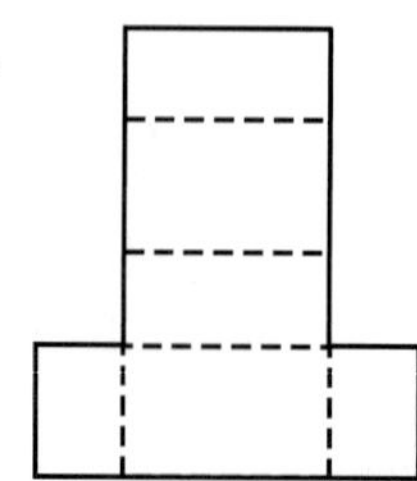

b. 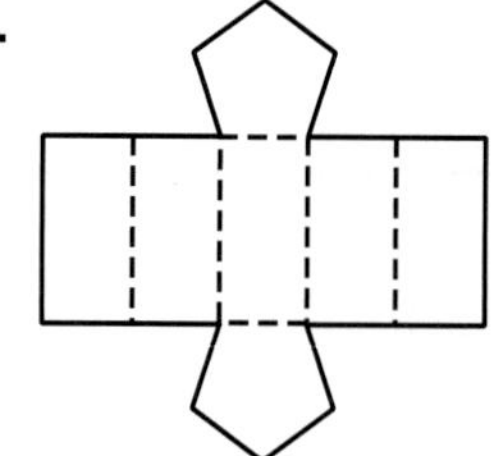

CD ROM **Technology**
Use Harcourt Mega Math, Ice Station Exploration, *Polar Planes,* Level G.

TECHNOLOGY CONNECTION

*i*Tools: Geometry

You can use the *Geometry* tool below to identify the attributes of different solid figures. How many faces does a square pyramid have? Do any of the faces appear to be congruent? Are any of the faces parallel to any of the other faces on the figure?

Step 1	Click on *Geometry*. Then click on the red pyramid from the solid figures on the left. To see the different faces on the pyramid, click the arrows around the STOP button at the bottom right corner of the screen.
Step 2	Enter the number of faces. Then, click on *Check*. Click on the broom to clear the workspace.

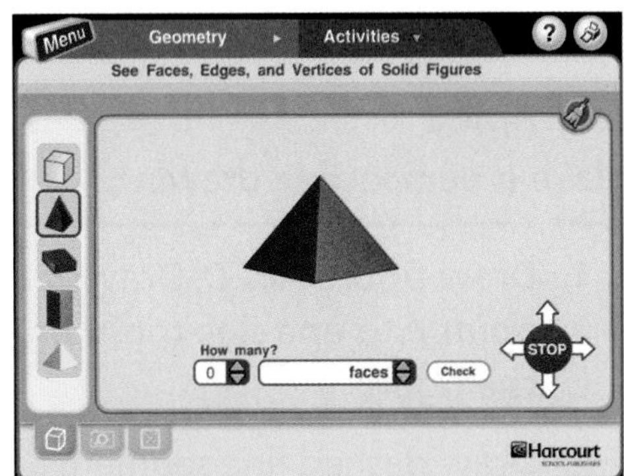

So, a square pyramid has 5 faces—4 faces that appear to be congruent, and no faces that are parallel.

Try It

Follow the steps above to complete the table.

Figure	Pairs of Parallel Faces	Number of Congruent Faces	Number of Vertices	Number of Edges
1.	■	■	■	■
2.	■	■	■	■
3.	■	■	■	■

4. **Explore More** If a pyramid has a base with 8 sides and 8 other faces that are congruent, will it have pairs of faces that are parallel? **Explain** how you know.

GO
ONLINE
Technology
iTools are available online or on CD-ROM.

Geometry

PERSPECTIVE DRAWING

Math Idea
A vanishing point is a point located in the distance from an object.

Perspective makes a three-dimensional drawing look real. A perspective drawing makes closer objects look larger and more distant objects appear to be smaller.

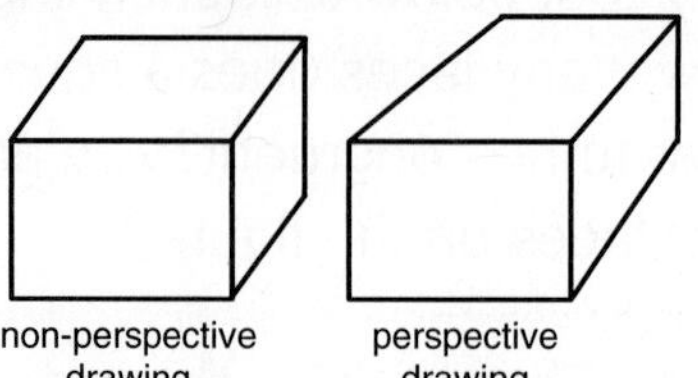

Examples

Make a perspective drawing.

1. Draw figure *ABCD*. Draw ***vanishing point P*** to one side (right or left) of the figure.
2. Draw dashed line segments $\overline{AP}$, $\overline{BP}$, and $\overline{CP}$ that connect the figure to *P*. Draw point *Q* anywhere on $\overline{BP}$.
3. Draw a horizontal line segment $\overline{QR}$ that meets $\overline{AP}$ as shown. $\overline{QR}$ should be parallel to $\overline{AB}$.
4. Draw vertical line segment $\overline{QS}$ that meets $\overline{CP}$ as shown. $\overline{QS}$ should be parallel to $\overline{BC}$.
5. Draw in edges from *A* to *R*, *B* to *Q*, and *C* to *S*. Erase point *P* and the dashed lines that remain to complete the drawing as shown.

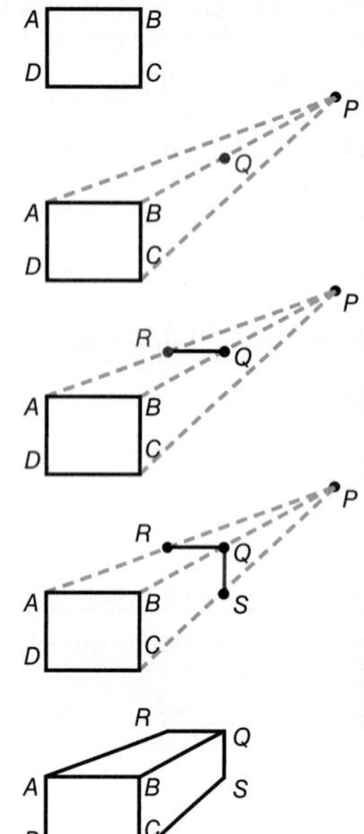

Try It

Copy each figure. Use the figure as a front face for a perspective drawing.

1 2 3

1. Draw figure 1 with a vanishing point on the right.
2. Draw figure 1 with a vanishing point on the left.
3. Draw figure 2. Choose a vanishing point.
4. Draw figure 3. Choose a vanishing point.
5. WRITE Math **Explain** why perspective makes a drawing look more real.

Chapter 19 Review/Test

Check Vocabulary and Concepts

For 1–2, choose the best term from the box.

VOCABULARY
prism
pyramid
scalene triangle

1. A _?_ has no congruent sides. KY MA-05-3.1.2 (p. 514)
2. A _?_ is a polyhedron with only one base. KY MA-05-3.1.3 (p. 524)
3. Explain how you can use a protractor to draw a right triangle. KY MA-05-3.1.1 (pp. 522–523)

Check Skills

Classify each triangle. Write *isosceles, scalene,* or *equilateral.* KY MA-05-3.1.3 (pp. 514–517)

4. 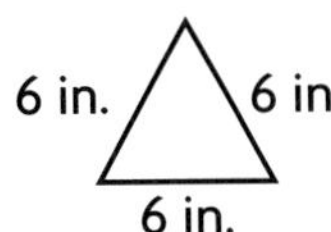

5. 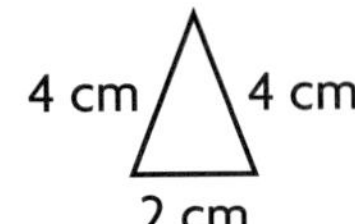

6. 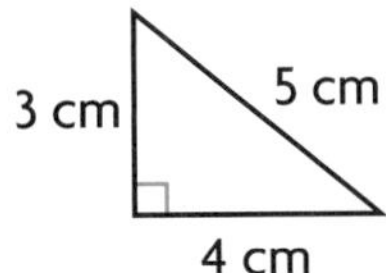

7. 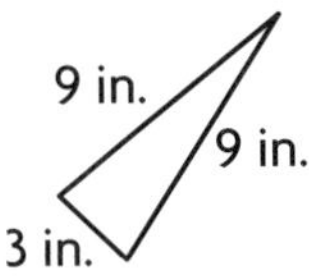

Classify each figure in as many ways as possible. Write *quadrilateral, parallelogram, square, rectangle, rhombus,* or *trapezoid.* KY MA-05-3.1.2 (pp. 518–521)

8. 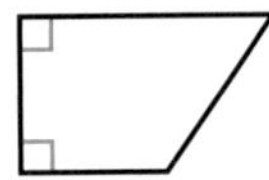

9. 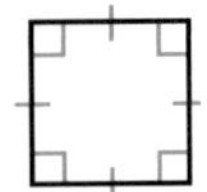

10. 

11. 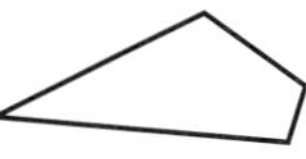

Classify each solid figure. Write *prism, pyramid, cone, cylinder,* or *sphere.* KY MA-05-3.1.3 (pp. 524–527)

12. 

13. 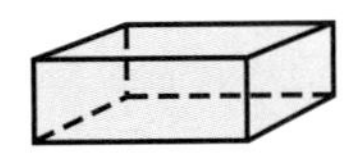

14. 

15. 

Match each solid figure with its net. KY MA-05-3.1.3 (pp. 530–531)

16. 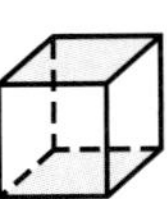

17. 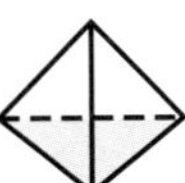

18. 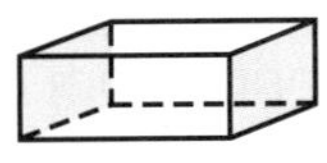

19. 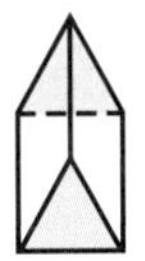

a. 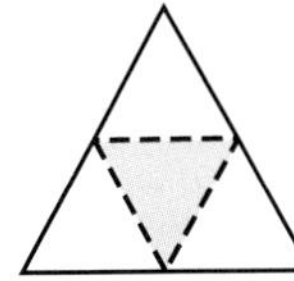

b. 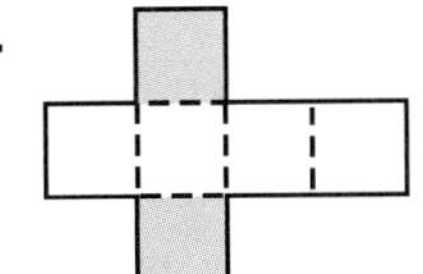

c. 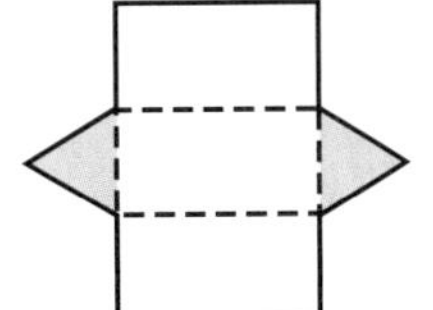

d. 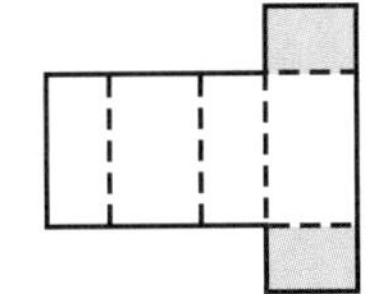

Check Problem Solving

Solve. KY MA-05-3.1.1 (pp. 528–529)

20. **WRITE Math** A tabletop terrarium is in the shape of a hexagonal prism. How many faces does it have? **Explain** how to solve.

Technology Use *Online Assessment.*

Practice for the KCCT
Chapters 1–19

Number and Operations

1. The aquarium lets groups of students meet the dolphins after each dolphin show. There were 5 groups that met the dolphins yesterday. There are 24 students in a group. How many students met the dolphins yesterday? KY MA-05-1.3.1 (p. 40)

   A 120

   B 104

   C 96

   D 80

Eliminate Choices

See item 2. Identify the item with the least price.

Eliminate the choices that do not start with this item.

Then choose the answer that shows the items correctly from least to greatest.

2. Ryan bought a drink for $2.95, a bag of popcorn for $2.75, and a box of candy for $2.80. Order the items by price from least to greatest. KY MA-05-1.1.3 (p. 138)

   A popcorn, drink, candy

   B candy, popcorn, drink

   C drink, candy, popcorn

   D popcorn, candy, drink

3. **WRITE Math** Sara solved this equation incorrectly: $4 + 3 \times 2 = 14$. What was her mistake? **Explain.** KY MA-05-5.3.1 (p. 108)

Algebraic Thinking

4. Gregory measured the height of his bean plant each week for 4 weeks. The plant measured 5 inches after the first week. The plant continued to grow 2 inches per week. Which table represents the data he collected? KY MA-05-4.1.3 (p. 216)

A

Bean Plant Growth	
Week	Height (in.)
1	2
2	4
3	6
4	8

B

Bean Plant Growth	
Week	Height (in.)
1	5
2	7
3	9
4	11

C

Bean Plant Growth	
Week	Height (in.)
1	5
2	6
3	7
4	8

D

Bean Plant Growth	
Week	Height (in.)
1	5
2	8
3	11
4	14

5. Marie added $1\frac{1}{4}$ cup of sugar to her batch of cookies. Write the amount of sugar as a decimal. KY MA-05-1.1.1 (p. 326)

   A 1.14

   B 1.25

   C 1.50

   D 1.75

6. **WRITE Math** Sam graphed the ordered pair (3,6). **Explain** how he knew where to plot the point on the coordinate grid. KY MA-05-3.3.1 (p. 248)

Geometry

7. Which shows an acute angle? KY MA-05-3.1.1 (p. 482)

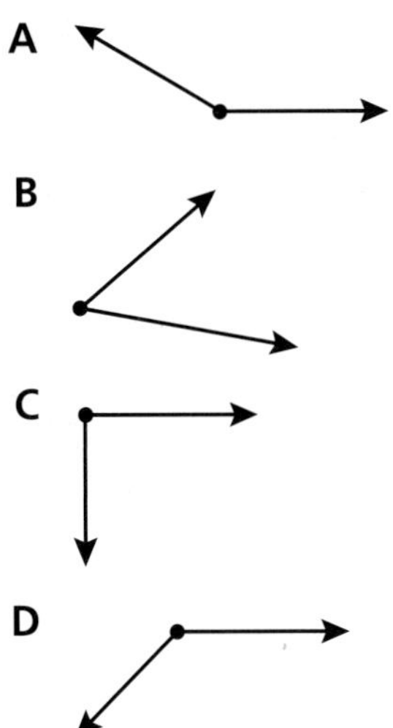

8. How many lines of symmetry does a square have? KY MA-05-3.2.1 (p. 504)

A 0

B 1

C 2

D 4

9. **WRITE Math** Can a rectangle be classified as a parallelogram and a quadrilateral? **Explain.** KY MA-05-3.1.2 (p. 518)

Data Analysis and Probability

10. Is it impossible, less likely, more likely, or certain that this spinner will land on red? KY MA-05-4.4.2 (p. 458)

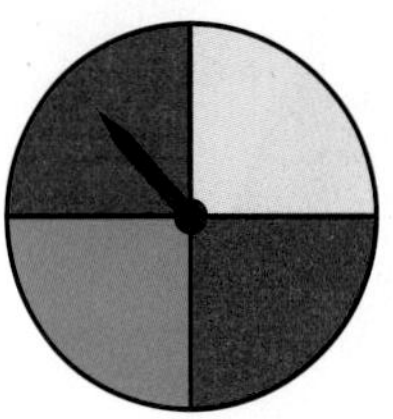

A impossible

B less likely

C more likely

D certain

11. Byron's family is making a snowman. They want to choose a scarf and a pair of mittens from those shown below to dress the snowman. How many combinations of scarves and mittens can they choose from? KY MA-05-4.4.1 (p. 462)

A 5

B 6

C 10

D 12

12. **WRITE Math** Marty's basketball team scored 72, 84, 78, 91, and 80 points in the last five games. What is the mean score? **Explain.** KY MA-05-4.2.1 (p. 220)

CHAPTER 20 Patterns

FAST FACT

Three different colors of marble trapezoids were used to make the tessellation in the atrium floor in the Bobst Library at New York University. The library opened in 1973.

Investigate

Use pattern blocks and colored paper to make your own tessellation.

A Trace a pattern block at the bottom right edge of a 3-inch square paper.

B Cut out the figure you traced.

C Translate the figure to the top of the opposite side of the square and tape it to the edge. Use this new figure to make a tessellation.

D Trace the new figure at least 8 times on a sheet of paper.

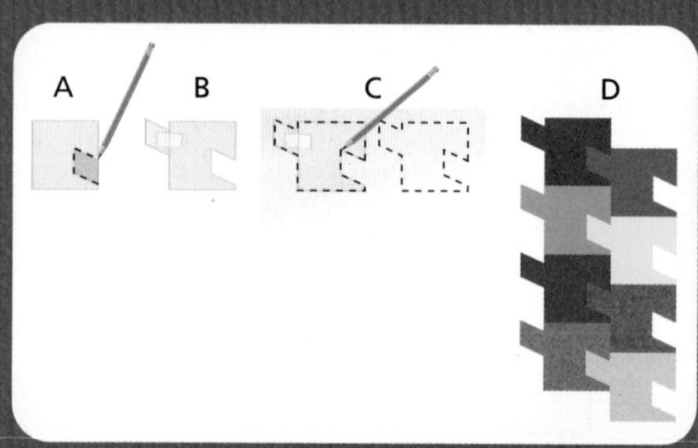

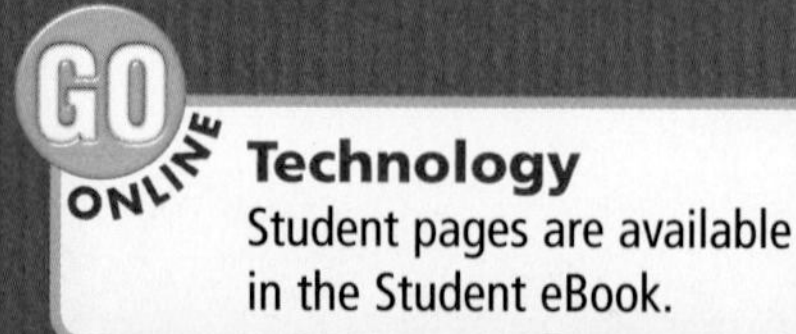

Technology
Student pages are available in the Student eBook.

Show What You Know

Check your understanding of important skills needed for success in Chapter 20.

▶ Translate Patterns

Rewrite the pattern using the letters A, B, C, or D in place of the figures.

1.

2.

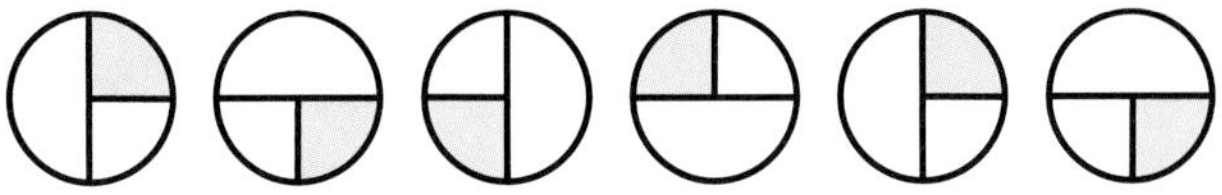

3.

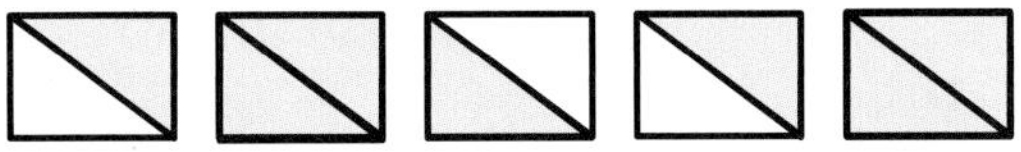

4.

5.

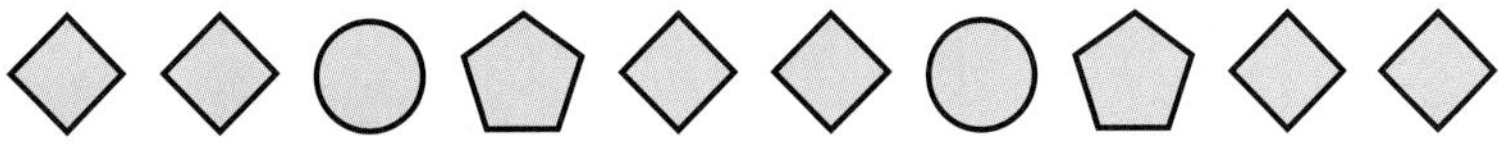

6.

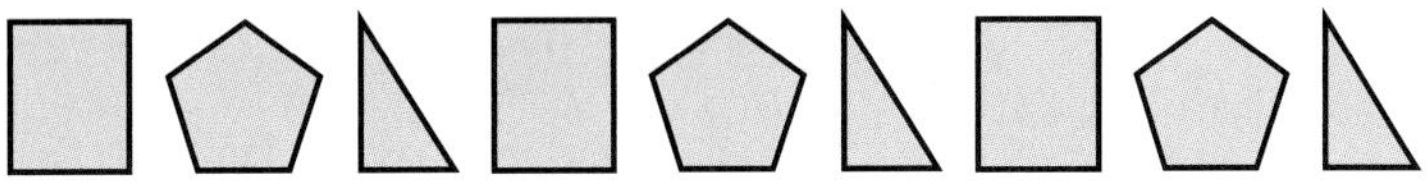

▶ Find a Number Pattern

Write the next 2 numbers in each pattern.

7. 1, 3, 5, 7, 9, ■, ■

8. 1, 4, 9, 16, 25, 36, ■, ■

9. 50, 45, 40, 35, 30, ■, ■

10. 2, 4, 6, 8, 10, ■, ■

VOCABULARY POWER

CHAPTER VOCABULARY

reflection
rotation
transformation
translation
tessellation

WARM-UP WORDS

transformation a figure moves to a new location without changing its size or shape

rotation a figure turns to a new position around a vertex, or point of rotation

tessellation a repeating pattern of closed figures that fit together to cover a surface, without any gaps or overlaps

1 Transformations

OBJECTIVE: Identify, describe, predict, and extend transformations.

Quick Review

Tell the number of sides in each polygon.

1. triangle
2. pentagon
3. decagon
4. octagon
5. quadrilateral

Vocabulary

transformation **translation**
reflection **rotation**

Learn

A movement of a figure to a new position by a translation, reflection, or rotation is called a **transformation**. You can carry out many transformations when you put together a jigsaw puzzle.

Examples

A **translation** is a slide. The figure slides to a new position along a straight line.

A **reflection** is a flip. The figure flips over a line to a new position.

A **rotation** is a turn. The figure turns to a new position about a vertex, or point of rotation.

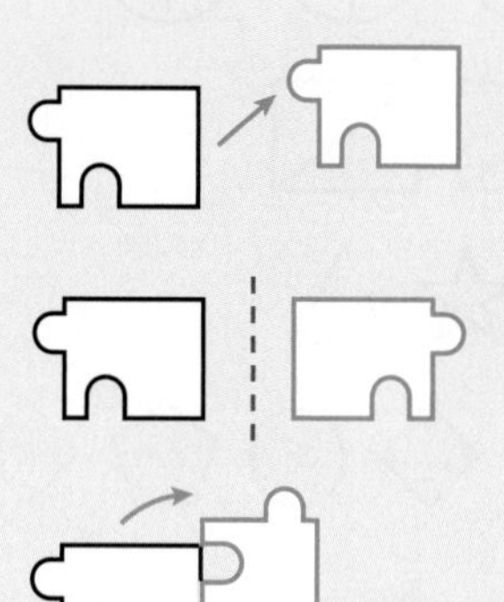

Math Idea
A rigid transformation, or movement of a figure, does not change its size or shape.

Activity

Materials ■ grid paper ■ scissors ■ tracing paper ■ straightedge

Draw a right triangle with a base of 5 units and a height of 3 units. Trace it and cut it out. Place the tracing over the original triangle on the grid paper. Transform the triangle as indicated.

TRANSLATION	ROTATION	REFLECTION
Translate each vertex 7 units right and 3 units down.	Rotate the triangle 90° clockwise about a point of rotation.	Reflect the triangle across a line of reflection.

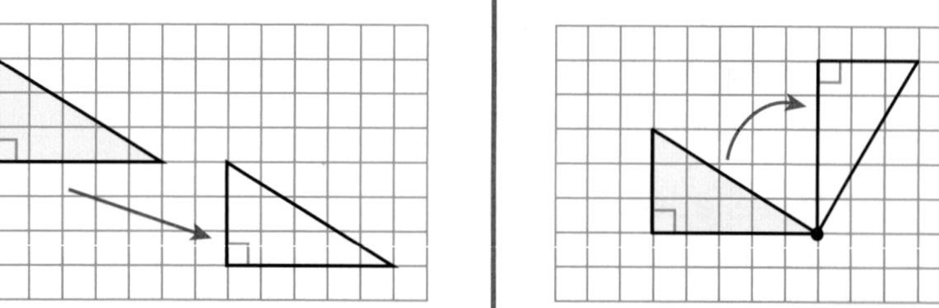

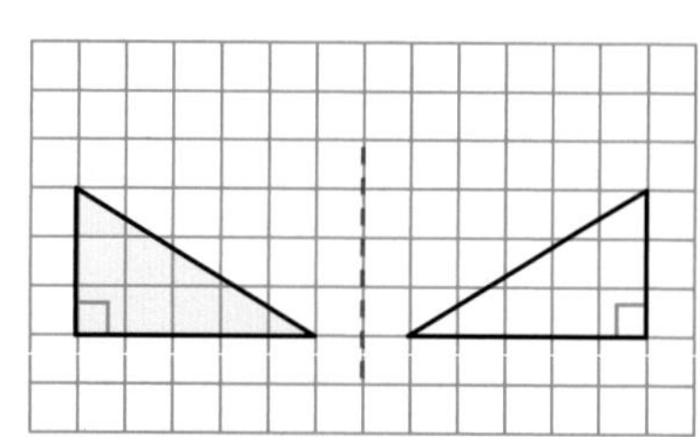

KY MA-05-3.2.2 Students will identify 90° rotations, reflections or translations of basic shapes within a plane. DOK 1

Activity

Materials ■ tracing paper

Predict how each figure was moved. Trace each figure on the left. Then test your prediction by translating, reflecting, and rotating your tracing to match each figure in its new position.

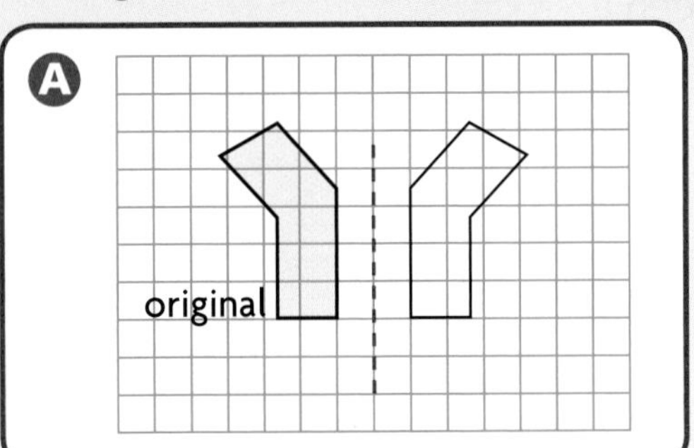

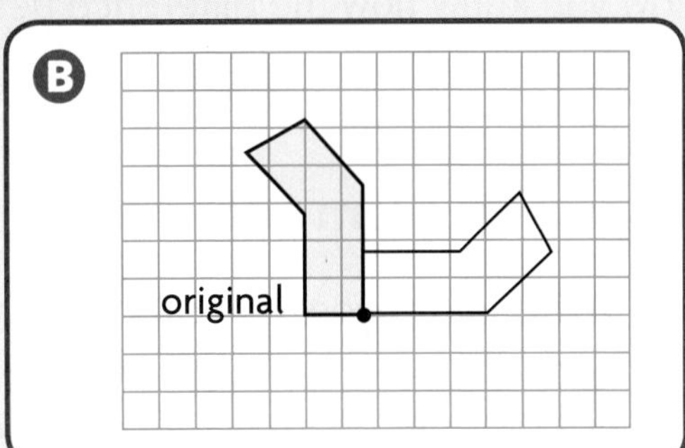

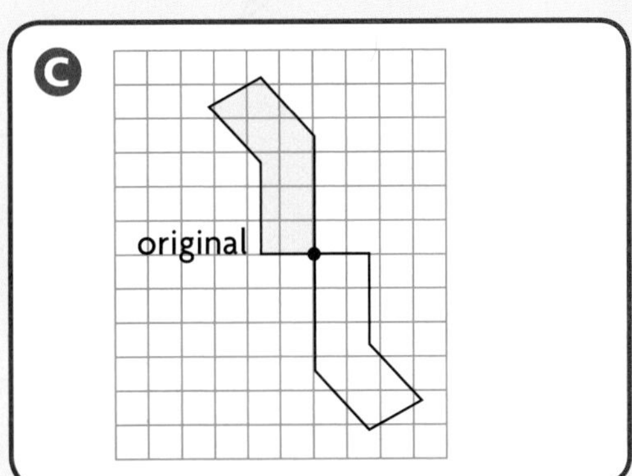

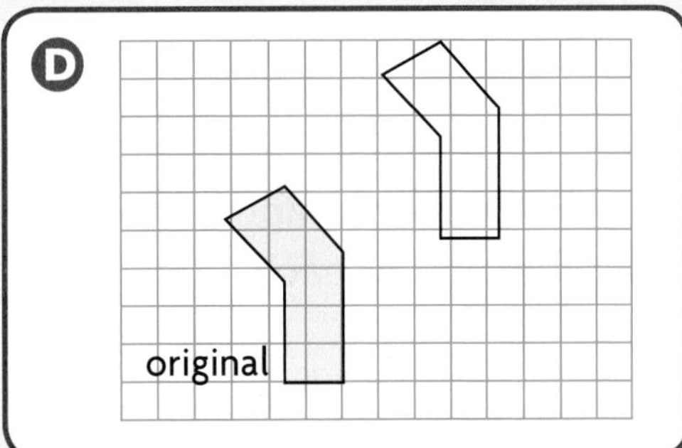

- What transformations did you use to match the figures in A–D?
- How is the original figure in A like the transformed figure? How is it different?

Guided Practice

Use the triangles on the grid to make predictions.

1. Predict which triangle could result from a translation of Triangle A.
2. Predict which triangle could result from a reflection of Triangle A.
3. Predict which triangle could result from a rotation of Triangle E.
4. Predict which triangle could result from a reflection of Triangle D.

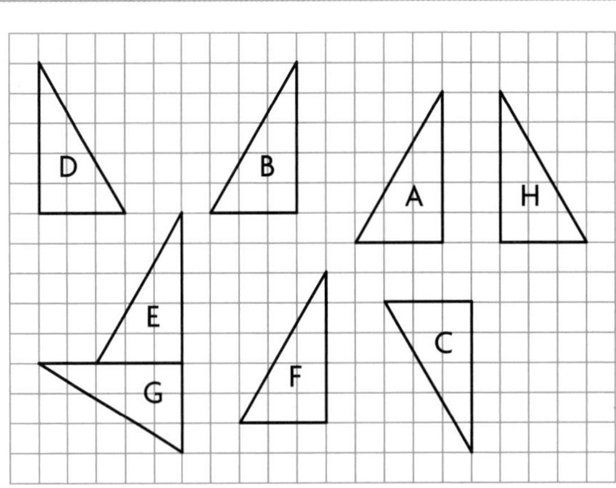

Name each transformation. Write *translation, reflection,* or *rotation*.

5. 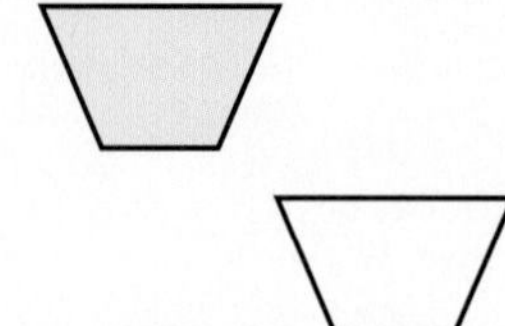

6. 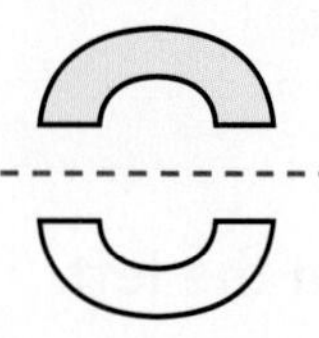

✓7. 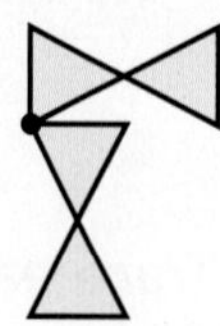

✓8. 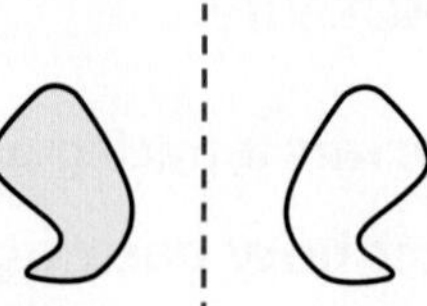

9. TALK Math **Explain** how you know how the difference between a translation and a reflection.

Independent Practice and Problem Solving

Name each transformation. Write *translation, reflection,* or *rotation*.

10. 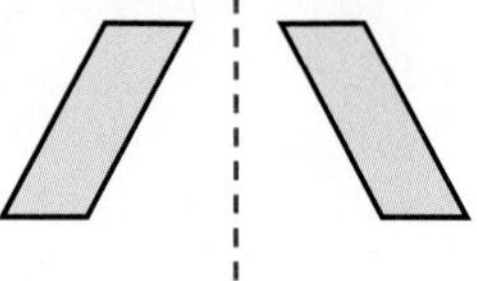

11. 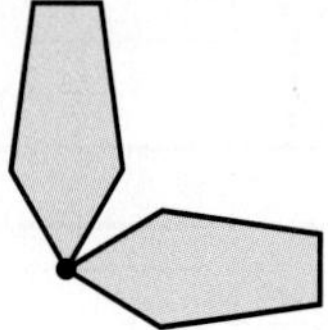

12. 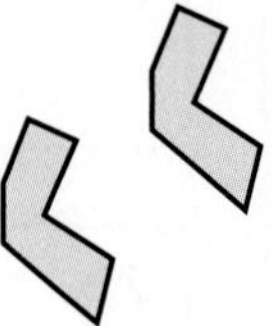

13. 

Copy each figure on grid paper. Then draw figures to show a translation, a rotation, and a reflection of each.

14. 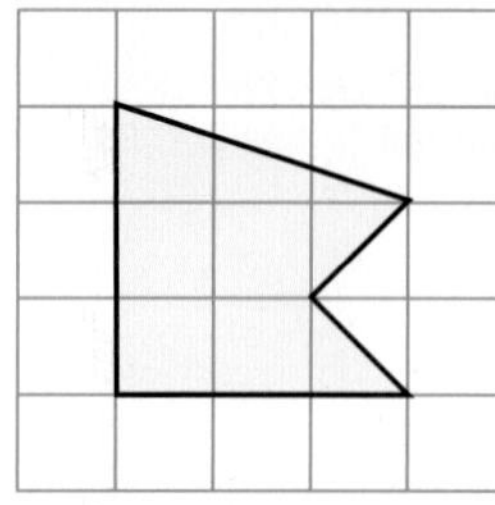

15. 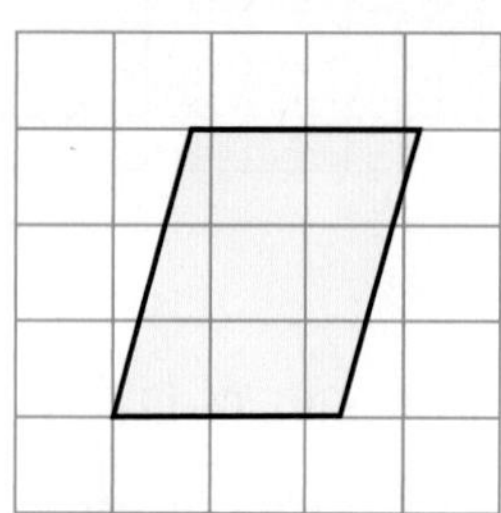

16. 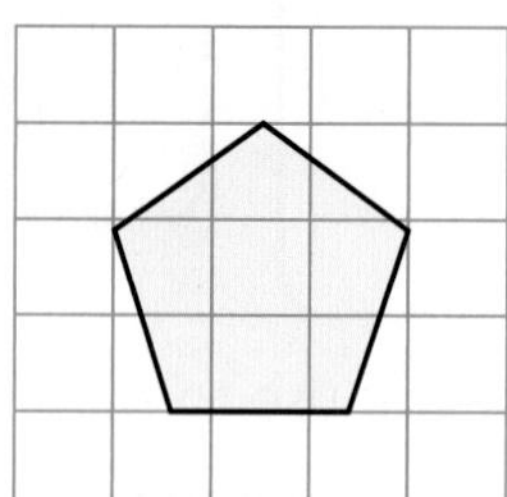

17. 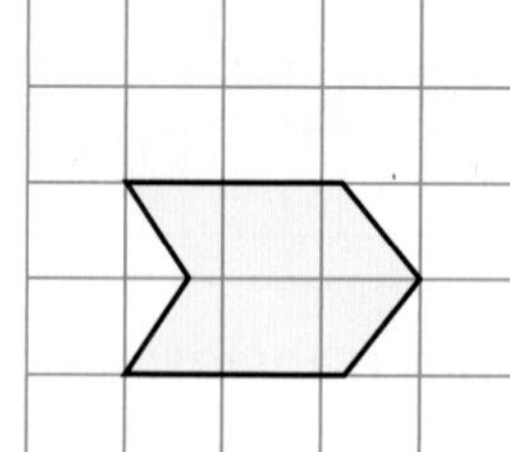

For 18–21, use the diagram.

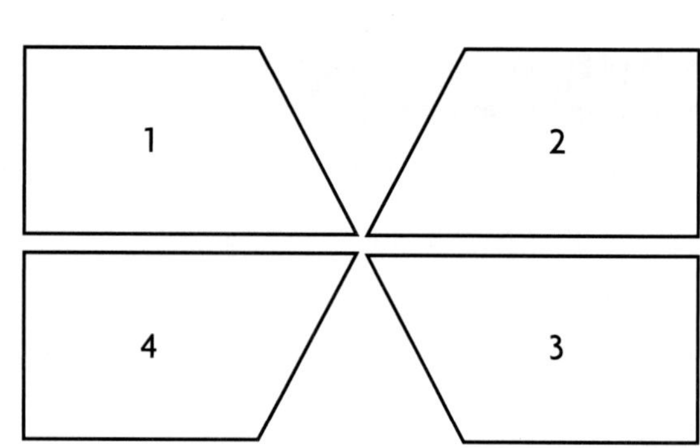

18. What is the only single transformation that will turn figure 1 into figure 3?

19. Describe how to transform figure 1 into
(a) figure 4, and
(b) figure 3, using more than one reflection.
Show each line of reflection.

20. How many ways can you think of to transform figure 1 into figure 4, using one or more transformations? List them.

21. WRITE Math Is the translation, reflection, and rotation of a figure always congruent to the original figure? **Explain.**

Learn About Transformations on a Coordinate Grid

You can use a coordinate grid to describe transformations.

Examples

Rotate the figure 180° clockwise about a vertex.

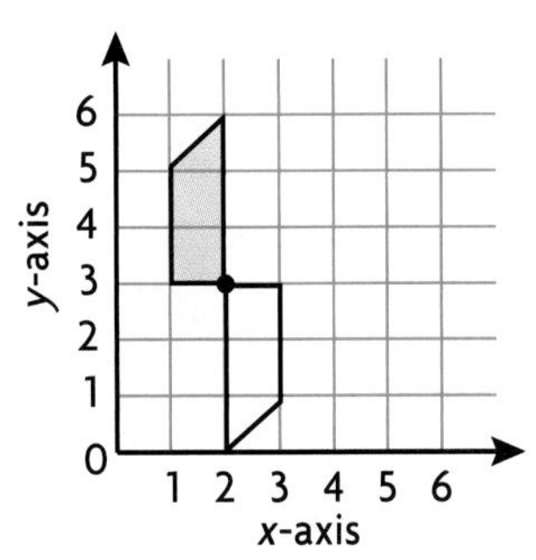

Original figure		New figure
(1,3)	→	(3,3)
(1,5)	→	(3,1)
(2,6)	→	(2,0)
(2,3)	→	(2,3)

Reflect the figure across a horizontal line of reflection.

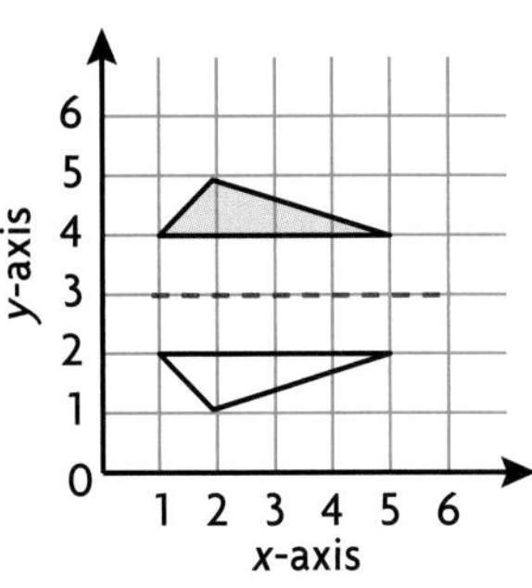

Original figure		New figure
(1,4)	→	(1,2)
(2,5)	→	(2,1)
(5,4)	→	(5,2)

Translate each vertex 1 unit right and 3 units up.

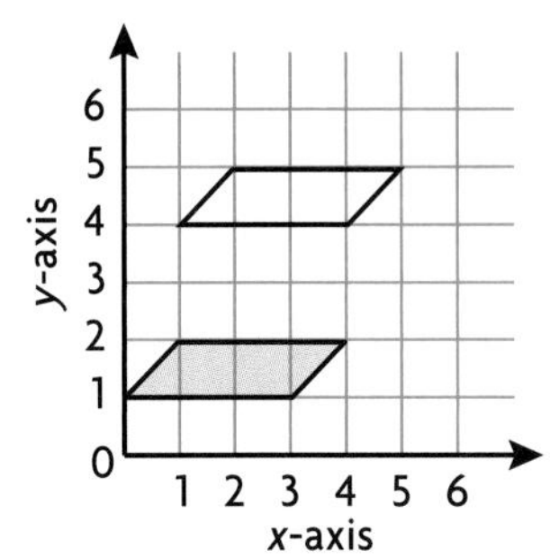

Original figure		New figure
(0,1)	→	(1,4)
(1,2)	→	(2,5)
(4,2)	→	(5,5)
(3,1)	→	(4,4)

Try It

Copy each figure onto a coordinate grid. Transform the figure according to the directions given. Give the new coordinates.

22. Translate 2 units right and 4 units up.

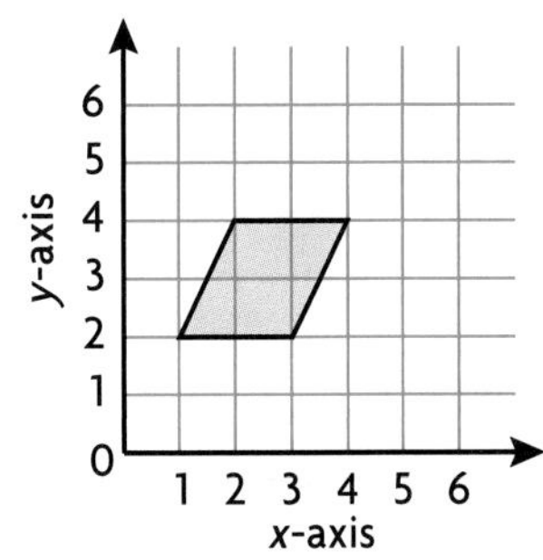

23. Reflect across the given line of reflection.

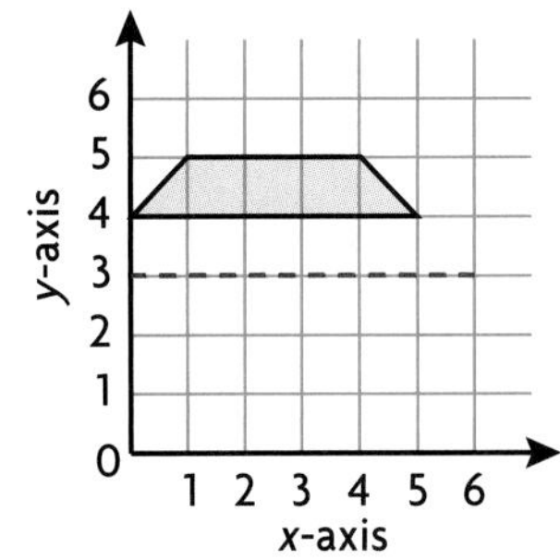

24. Rotate 180° about the given vertex.

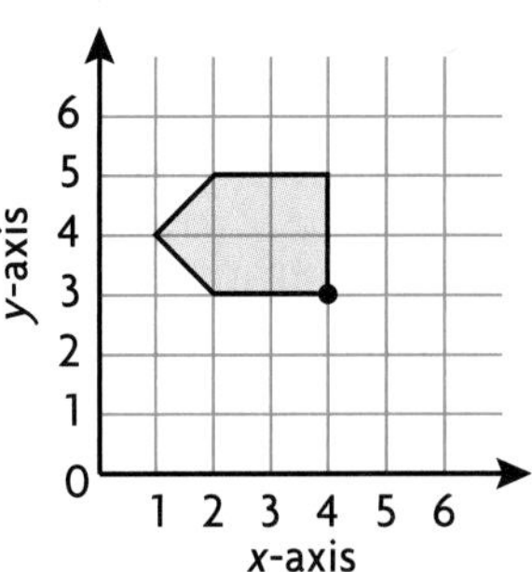

25. WRITE Math **Explain** how the coordinates of a figure change when you translate that figure.

LESSON HANDS ON

2 Tessellations

OBJECTIVE: Identify, describe, predict, and extend geometric tessellations.

Quick Review

A row of 6 one-inch tiles has a gap of 0.2 inch between tiles. How many gaps are there between tiles? What is the width of the row of six tiles?

Vocabulary

tessellation

Investigate

Materials ■ pattern blocks ■ scissors

Some designs are made by tracing one or more figures and then translating, reflecting, or rotating the figures. A **tessellation** is a repeating pattern of closed figures that fit together to cover a surface, without any gaps or overlaps.

Ⓐ Trace and cut out 6 triangles and 4 rhombuses.

Ⓑ Use translations, reflections, or rotations to make a tessellation. For example,

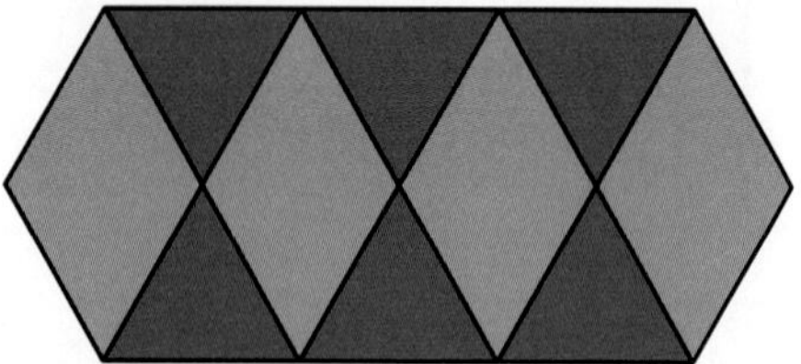

Ⓒ Try making different tessellations by using each figure by itself and by using the two figures together. Trace and cut out extra figures if you need them.

Draw Conclusions

1. In C, do your figures form a tessellation? Explain how you could extend the tessellation.
2. In C, what transformation or series of transformations did you use to make your tessellation?
3. **Application** Draw a quadrilateral of any size. Predict whether it will or will not form a tessellation. Explain how you can test to see if your quadrilateral forms a tessellation. Sketch your tessellation.

Connect

A paper company wants to design gift wrap with a regular polygon that tessellates. Use the charts and identify which polygons can be used to form a tessellation.

Polygon	Sides	Shape	Tessellates? (yes or no)
equilateral triangle	3		?
square	4		?
regular pentagon	5		?
regular hexagon	6		?

- Which polygon can the company use to design the gift wrap?
- Can you think of another shape that is not a regular polygon that the company could use to make the gift wrap? Draw it.

TALK Math

Explain how you can tell if a figure can be used to form a tessellation.

Practice

Predict whether the figure or figures will tessellate. Trace and cut out several copies of each figure and then test your predictions. Write *yes* or *no*.

1. 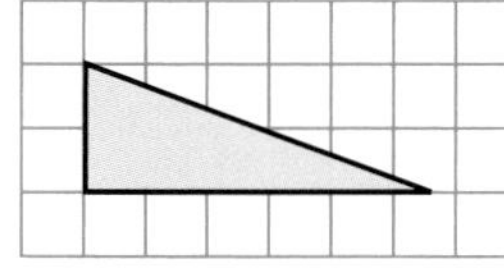

2. 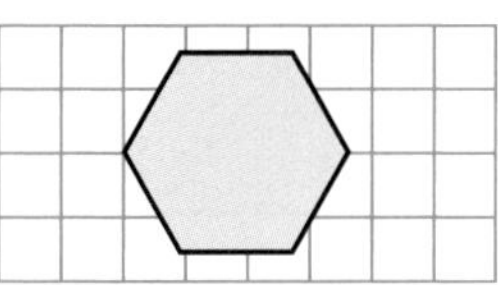

3. 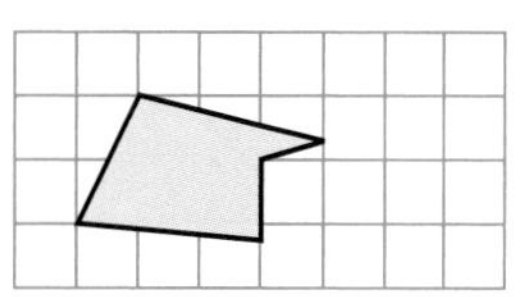

4. 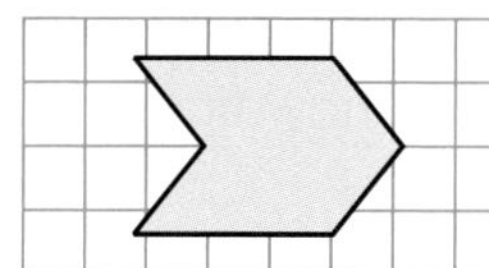

5. 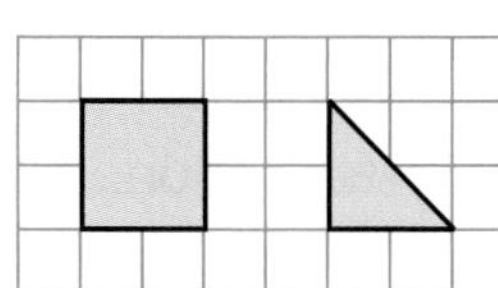

6. 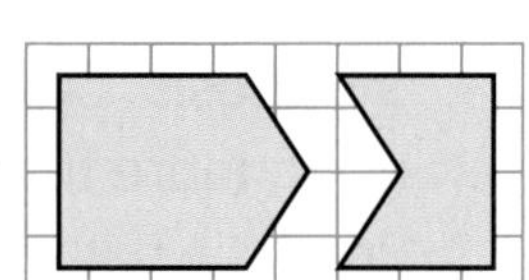

7. 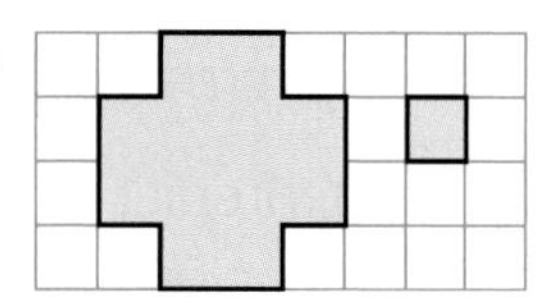

8. 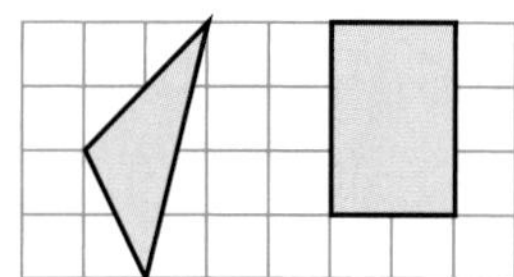

9. **WRITE Math** Draw three different figures that, when used together, will tessellate. **Explain** how you knew which type of figures to draw.

Technology
CD ROM Use Harcourt Mega Math, Ice Station Exploration, *Polar Planes,* Levels O and P.

LESSON 3 HANDS ON

Create a Geometric Pattern

OBJECTIVE: Use transformations to create and extend geometric patterns.

Quick Review

Nine small squares are arranged in a square in a 3 by 3 grid. Each small square measures 2.5 cm long on each side. What is the length of each side of the large square?

Investigate

Materials ■ grid paper ■ straightedge ■ tracing paper

A geometric pattern can be a series of repeating geometric figures that create a design. Patterns can include a variety of different figures and different types of transformations. You can make one type of pattern by using the following steps.

A Trace the triangle. Draw a vertical line of reflection along the right side of the figure.

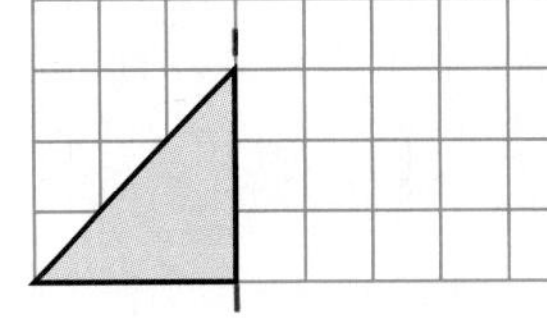

B Reflect the figure over the vertical line. Sketch the new figure.

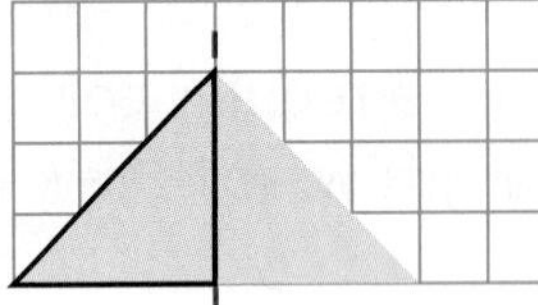

C Draw a new vertical line of reflection. Reflect the figure again. Sketch the new figure.

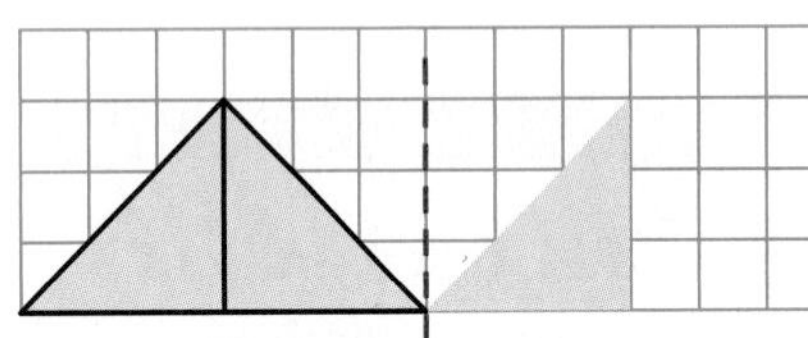

D Repeat the pattern five more times. Sketch each new figure.

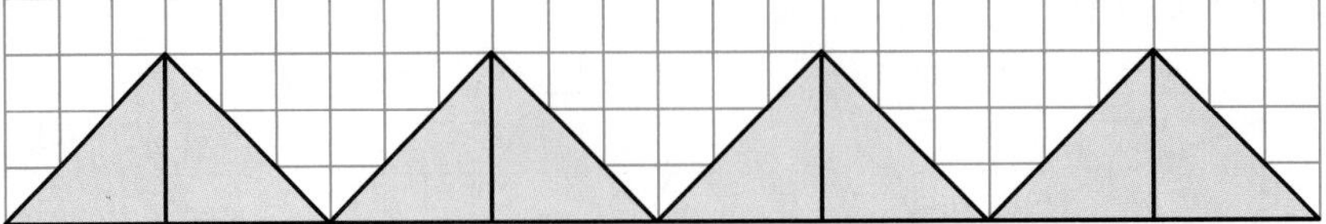

Draw Conclusions

1. Describe the pattern that you created.
2. If you continued the pattern, predict whether the 12th and 13th triangles would be connected by a line or a vertex.
3. **Synthesis** Create your own pattern by using more than one transformation. Predict what your pattern will look like. Then sketch the pattern. Explain the steps you used to create your pattern.

FAST TRACK KY MA-05-5.1.1 Students will extend patterns, find the missing term(s) in a pattern or describe rules for patterns (numbers, pictures, tables, words) from real-world and mathematical problems. DOK 3

Connect

Describe which transformations could have been used to create each pattern.

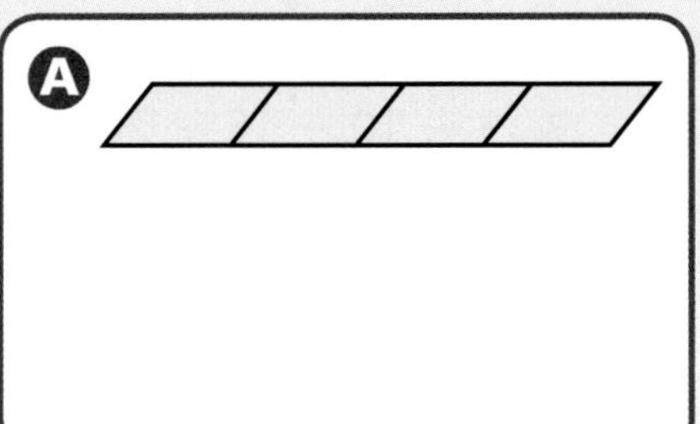

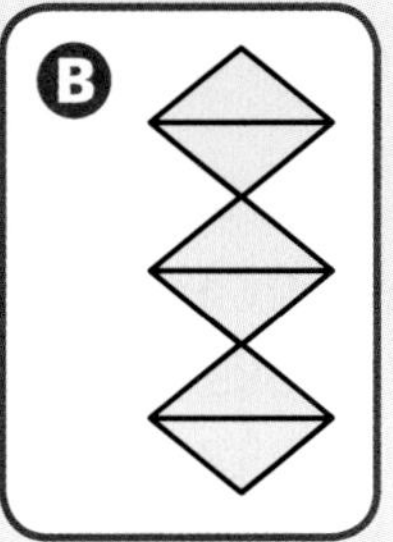

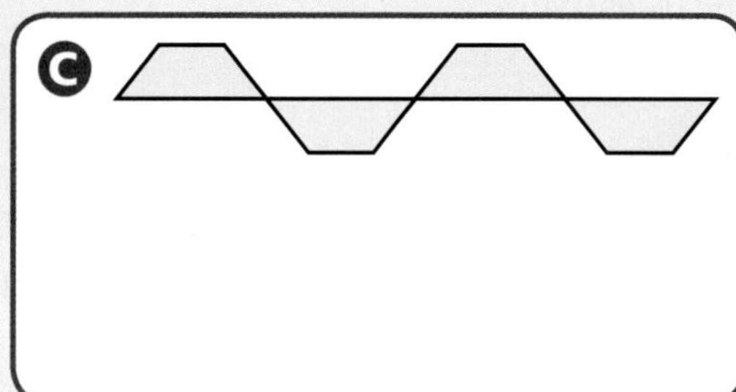

- How could only translations be used to create pattern A?
- How could only reflections be used to create pattern B?
- How could only rotations be used to create pattern C?

TALK Math

Explain how you can create a pattern by using just one kind of transformation.

Practice

Describe how each pattern might have been created.

1. 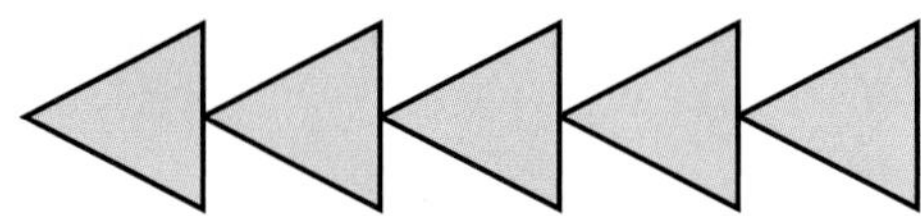

2. 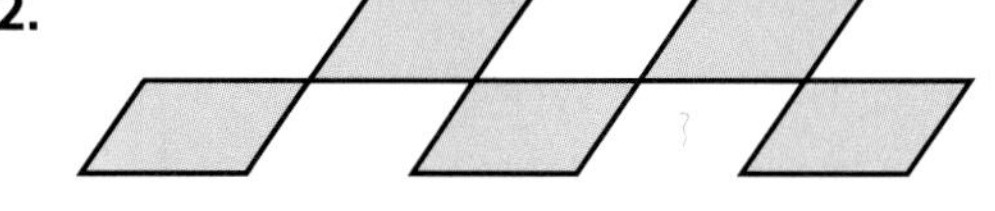

3. 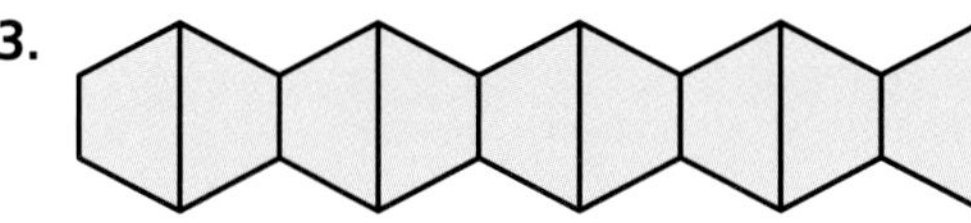

4. 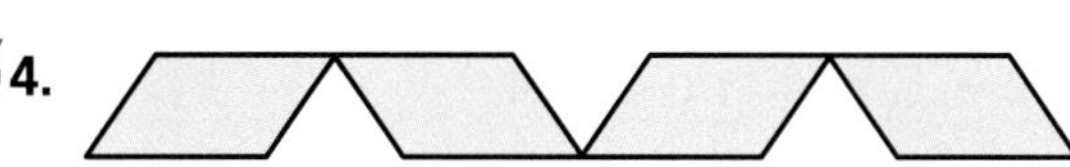

5. 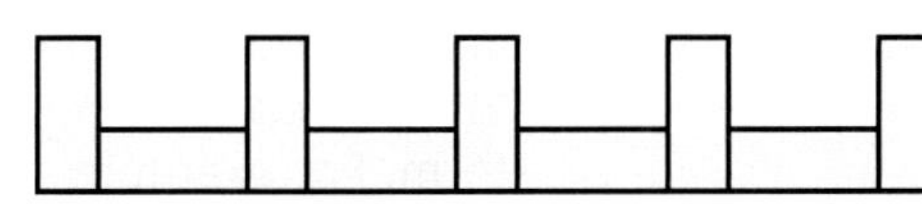

6. 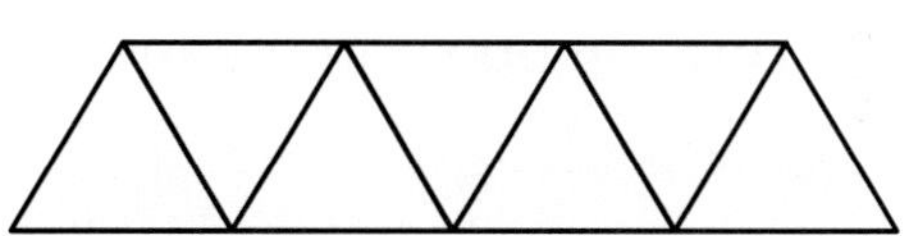

Trace each figure. Then transform it to create a pattern. Sketch your design.

7. Translate the figure horizontally three times. 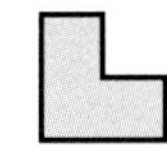

8. Reflect the figure over a vertical line three times. 

9. Draw a point of rotation. Rotate the figure clockwise $\frac{1}{2}$ turn five times. 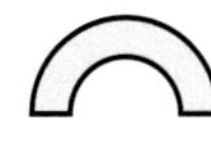

10. Reflect over a vertical line and then over a horizontal line. Do this three times. 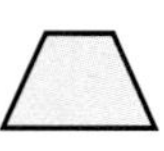

11. **Reasoning** A figure is rotated to the right to a different position. The new figure is positioned upside down and below the original figure. What type of rotation was used to transform the original figure? **Explain** how you know.

12. **WRITE Math** **Explain** how using transformations makes extending a geometric pattern simpler.

LESSON 4

Numeric Patterns

OBJECTIVE: Identify, describe, predict, and extend numeric patterns.

Quick Review

Find the total.

1. 1 + 3 + 5 + 7
2. 2 + 4 + 6 + 8
3. 5 + 10 + 15 + 20
4. 10 + 20 + 30 + 40
5. 120 + 60 + 30 + 15

Learn

PROBLEM Sam belongs to a book club. The first month, Sam received 1 book. The second month, he received 2 books, and the third month, he received 4 books. If Sam received 8 books in the fourth month, how many will he receive during the fifth and sixth months?

Example 1 Find a rule. Then find the next two numbers in the pattern. 1, 2, 4, 8, ■, ■

Step 1

Find a rule for the pattern.

Think: What rule changes 1 to 2?

Try **add 1** because 1 + 1 = 2

2 + 1 = 3, but 3 ≠ 4

The rule **add 1** doesn't work.

Try **multiply by 2** since 1 × 2 = 2.

2 × 2 = 4 and 4 = 4

The rule **multiply by 2** works.

Step 2

Now use the rule to solve the problem.

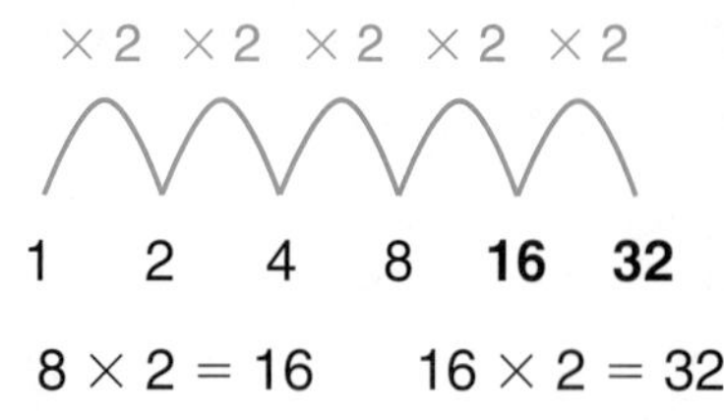

8 × 2 = 16   16 × 2 = 32

So, Sam will receive 16 books in the fifth month and 32 books in the sixth month.

Math Idea
Each number or figure in a pattern is called a term. For example, the first term in the pattern 3, 9, 27, 81 is 3.

Example 2 Find a rule. Then find the missing numbers in the pattern. 21, 25, 75, 79, ■, ■, 723, 727, 2,181

Step 1

Look at the first two numbers. Since they increase differently, try two operations.

Try **add 4, multiply by 3**, because 21 + 4 = 25 and 25 × 3 = 75.

75 + 4 = 79 and 79 × 3 = 237

The rule **add 4, multiply by 3** works.

Step 2

Now use the rule to solve the problem.

237 + 4 = 241 and 241 × 3 = 723

Check the last numbers in the pattern:

723 + 4 = 727 and 727 × 3 = 2,181

So, the missing numbers are 237 and 241.

KY MA-05-5.1.1 Students will extend patterns, find the missing term(s) in a pattern or describe rules for patterns (numbers, pictures, tables, words) from real-world and mathematical problems. DOK 3 *also MA-05-1.3.2*

Guided Practice

Identify the rule for each pattern.

1. 5, 10, 15, 20, ...
   Think: Does the pattern increase or decrease?
   Think: What operation is used in the pattern?

2. 4, 7, 10, 13, ...

3. 4, 16, 64, 256, ...

4. 567, 189, 63, 21, ...

Find the missing number in each pattern.

5. 5, 8, 11, 14, ■, 20

6. 1, 3, 9, ■, 81

7. 28, 21, ■, 10, 6, 3

8. TALK Math **Explain** how you found the missing number for Problem 6.

Independent Practice and Problem Solving

Identify the rule for each pattern.

9. 17, 21, 25, 29, ...

10. 12, 30, 75, 187.5, ...

11. 7, 13, 25, 49, ...

Find the missing number in each pattern.

12. 4, 12, 36, ■, 324

13. 84, 77, ■, 63, 56

14. 3, 15, 27, ■, 51

Find the mistake in each pattern. Write the correct number.

15. 2, 4, 6, 5, 10, 12, 14

16. 3, 6, 12, 24, 36, 96

17. 64, 32, 18, 8, 4, 2, 1

Write the first four terms in each pattern.

18. rule: subtract 6
    first term: 57

19. rule: add 12
    first term: 5

20. rule: multiply by 3, add 1
    first term: 2

21. ***FAST FACT*** Many biological organisms follow a Fibonacci Sequence growth pattern: 1, 1, 2, 3, 5, 8, 13... Find the next term in the pattern.

22. WRITE Math **Explain** how you found the mistake in Problem 15.

Mixed Review and Test Prep

23. Lillian flips a coin twice. What is the probability she will first get tails and then get heads? (p. 458)

24. **Test Prep** 7, 8, 10, 13, 17, 22, 28, ■,...
    - **A** 35
    - **B** 25
    - **C** 29
    - **D** 37

25. Walt flips a coin and gets heads 4 times in a row. What is the probability he will get heads on his next flip? (p. 458)

26. **Test Prep** 405, 135, 45, 15, ■, ...
    - **A** 10
    - **B** 7
    - **C** 6
    - **D** 5

Problem Solving Workshop
Strategy: Find a Pattern

OBJECTIVE: Solve problems by using the strategy *find a pattern.*

Use the Strategy

PROBLEM For a history project Kim and Josh are making a bulletin board about ancient wall paintings. For the border, they will use a pattern of shapes as shown below. They will need to identify the pattern unit that repeats and then continue the pattern 8 times on one side of the bulletin board. How many shapes in all will they need for one side of the bulletin board?

Read to Understand

- **Identify the details of the problem.**
- **What is the pattern?**

Plan

- **What strategy can you use to solve the problem?**

Find a pattern can help solve the problem.

Solve

- **How can you use the strategy to solve the problem?**

Identify the pattern unit in the pattern. Look for a pattern or a place in which the pattern unit starts to repeat itself.

The pattern in the top row could be a right triangle, then a reflected right triangle, followed by a trapezoid. The shapes in the pattern of the first row are reflected down across a horizontal line to make the pattern of the second row. A total of 6 shapes are needed for one pattern unit.

So, if this pattern continues and repeats itself 8 times for one side of the bulletin board, then a total of 48 shapes are needed.

Check

- **How can you check your results?**
- **What other strategy could you use to solve the problem?**

KY MA-05-5.1.1 Students will extend patterns, find the missing term(s) in a pattern or describe rules for patterns (numbers, pictures, tables, words) from real-world and mathematical problems. DOK 3

Guided Problem Solving

1. Another pattern Kim and Josh thought about using is shown below. What could be the next three shapes in the pattern?

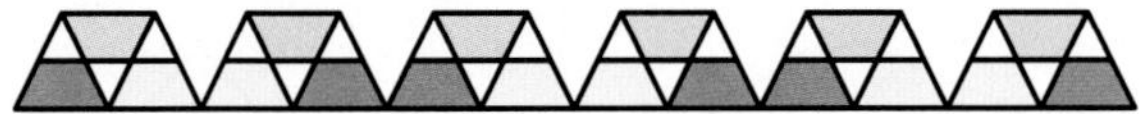

First, identify the details of the pattern.

Then, look for a sequence or a place in which the pattern starts to repeat itself.

Finally, look at the last shape in the pattern, and see where it appeared earlier in the pattern. What shape came after this shape? Repeat the next three shapes that came after this shape.

2. **What if** Kim changed the pattern in Problem 1 to be like the one below?

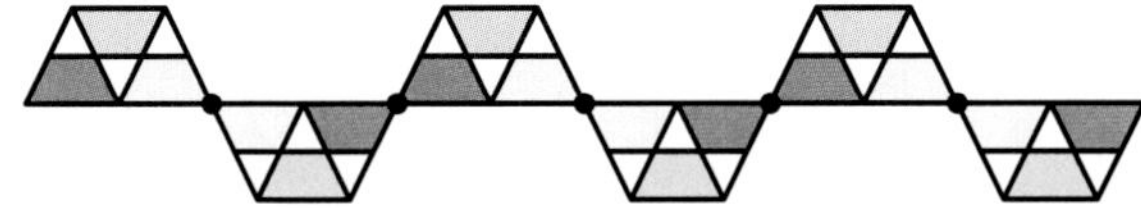

What could the next three shapes be?

3. Suri is painting a design that is a pattern of squares. She paints the squares black, white, black, gray, black, white, black, gray. What color could the next two squares be?

Choose a STRATEGY

- Draw a Diagram or Picture
- Make a Model or Act It Out
- Make an Organized List
- Find a Pattern
- Make a Table or Graph
- Predict and Test
- Work Backward
- Solve a Simpler Problem
- Write an Equation
- Use Logical Reasoning

Mixed Strategy Practice

4. Sarah draws a triangle on a coordinate grid and labels the vertices (1,3), (1,7), and (4,3). She uses the pattern of translating each vertex 4 units right to draw a second triangle. What would be the coordinates of Sarah's second triangle? Her third triangle?

5. In a pattern of shapes, the first shape had 4 squares, the next shape had 9 squares, and the next had 16. How many squares could be in the seventh shape?

6. Preston is building a triangular model with blocks. His top row has 1 block and his bottom row has 9 blocks. Each row has 2 more blocks than the previous row. How many blocks are in Preston's model? How many rows?

7. If the pattern below continues, how many squares could be in the next shape?

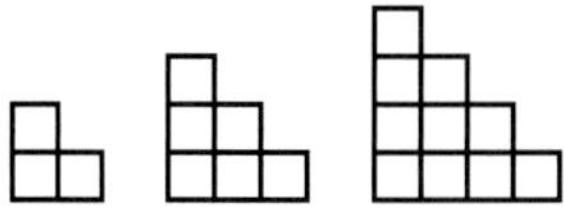

8. In Problem 7, what rule could you write to describe the pattern?

9. WRITE Math **Explain** how the pattern in Problem 5 is both a geometric pattern and a numeric pattern.

Extra Practice

Set A Name each transformation. (pp. 542–545)

1. 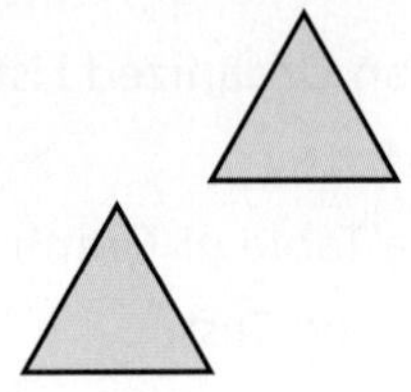
2. 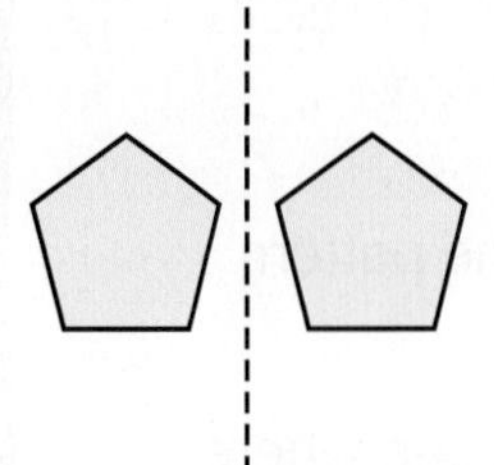
3. 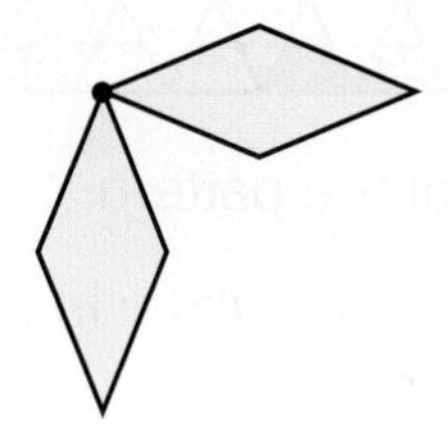
4. 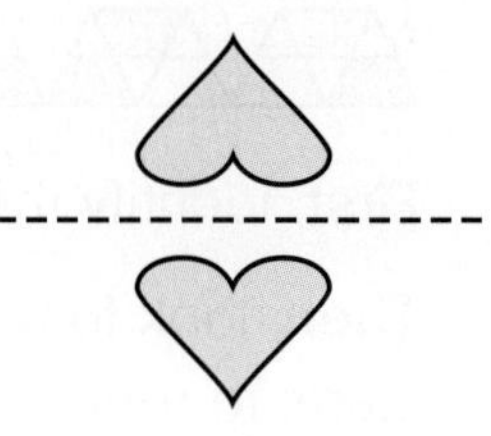

Copy each figure onto grid paper. Then draw figures to show a *translation*, a *rotation*, and a *reflection* of each.

5. 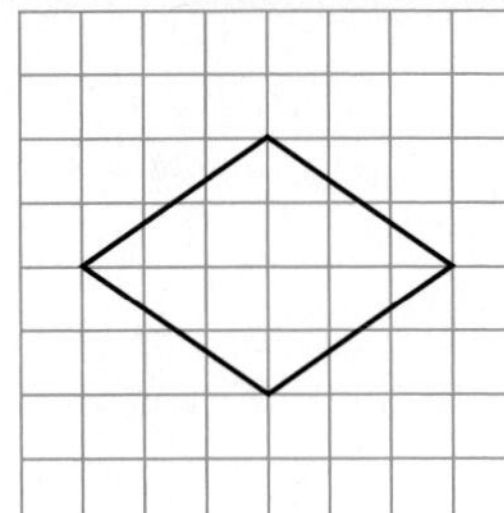
6. 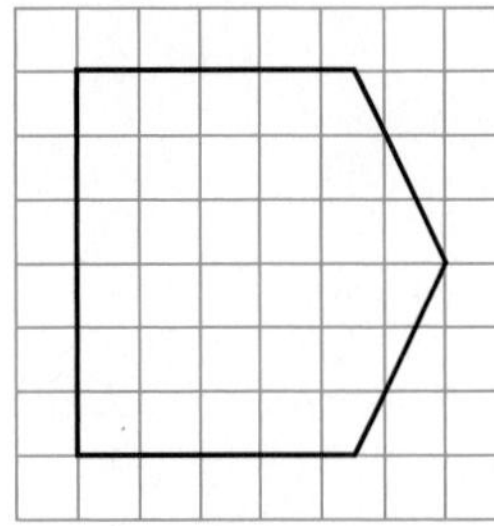
7. 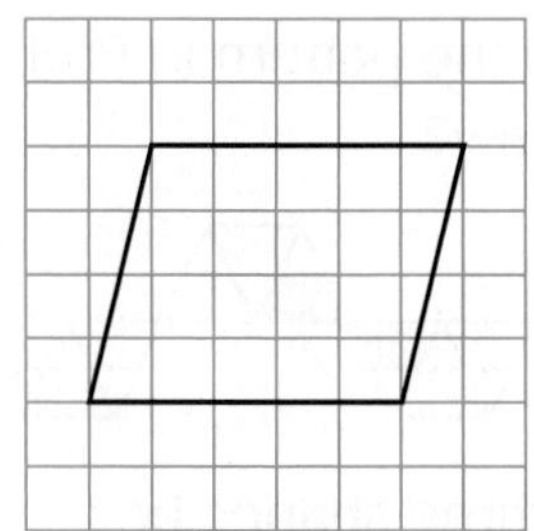
8. 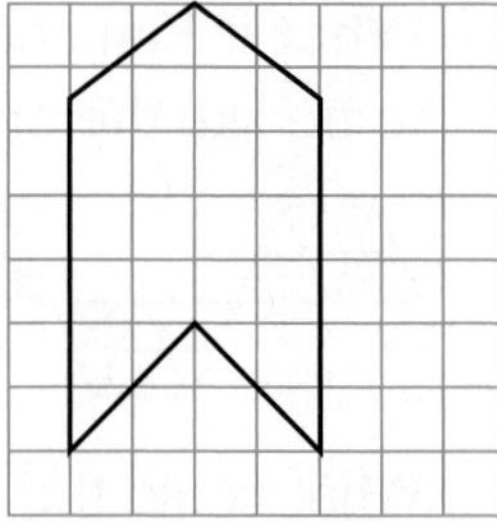

9. Use the figures on the right. Which figure could result if you reflected Figure A over a vertical line?

A 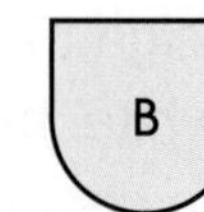 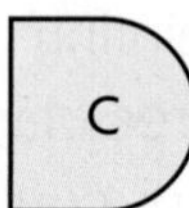 

Set B Identify the rule for each pattern. (pp. 550–551)

1. 8, 16, 24, 32, . . .
2. 3, 4.5, 6.75, 10.125, . . .
3. 4, 12, 10, 30, . . .

Find the missing number in each pattern.

4. 6, 12, 18, ■, 30
5. 4.5, 9, ■, 18, 22.5
6. 2, 8, 32, ■, 512

Find the mistake in each pattern. Write the correct number.

7. 1, 5, 9, 12, 17, 21
8. 5, 10, 15, 18, 25, 30
9. 35, 29, 21, 14, 7

Write the first four terms in each pattern.

10. rule: multiply by 2
first term: 8
11. rule: subtract 5
first term: 55
12. rule: add 1, multiply by 2
first term: 4

13. Janna wrote this pattern on the chalkboard: 2, 5, 8, 11. What is the rule for the pattern?
14. Erik wrote this pattern: 10, 14, 16, 22. Find his mistake. Write the correct number.

CD ROM **Technology**
Use Harcourt Mega Math, The Number Games, *Tiny's Think Tank*, Level J.

PRACTICE GAME

PATTERNS IN PLAY

Players
4 players

Materials
- 4 sets of 10 color tiles, each set a different color
- paper bag

Play!

- The first player chooses any five color tiles and places them on the table in a row. This is the pattern unit. The rest of the tiles are placed in a bag and mixed.
- All players draw five tiles randomly from the bag and place them in their own piles.
- The second player begins by trying to continue the first player's pattern by placing one of his or her 5 tiles.
- If the second player does not have the next tile in the pattern, he or she must draw tiles from the bag until the correct tile is drawn. The player then places that tile, and play passes to the next player.
- Play continues until a player cannot place the next tile in the pattern and the bag is empty.
- The player with the fewest tiles left in his or her pile is the winner.

MATH POWER **Transformations**

From Here to There

The *START* and *STOP* positions of a figure are shown below. In between, the figure has undergone three transformations: a reflection, a translation, and a rotation.

Example

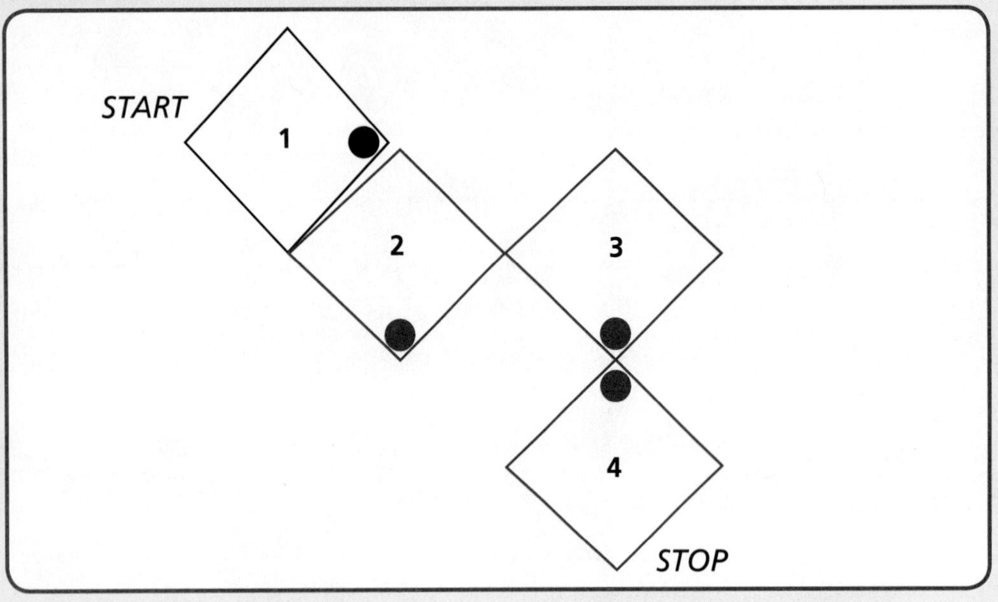

Try It

Describe three transformations that might have occurred between each START and STOP.

Hint: There is more than one way to get from START to STOP!

1. *START* 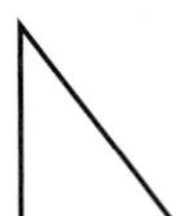 *STOP* 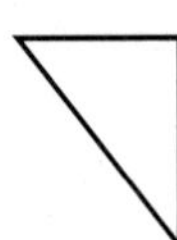
2. *START* 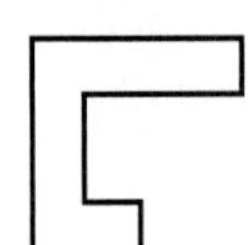 *STOP* 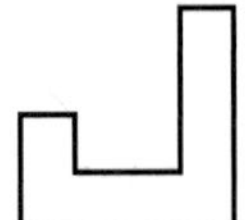
3. **Challenge** Draw a figure on another sheet of paper. Show three different transformations so that the position of the figure changes.
4. **WRITE Math** **Describe** a figure when rotated 180° can give same result when reflected vertically.

Chapter 20 Review/Test

Check Vocabulary and Concepts

Choose the best term from the box.

VOCABULARY
tessellation
rotation
translation
reflection

1. A figure slides to a new position along a straight line. KY MA-05-3.2.2 (p. 542)
2. A figure turns around a vertex to a new position. KY MA-05-3.2.2 (p. 542)
3. A figure flips over a line to a new position. KY MA-05-3.2.2 (p. 542)

Check Skills

Copy each figure on grid paper. Then draw figures to show a *translation*, a *rotation*, and a *reflection* of each. KY MA-05-3.2.2 (pp. 542–545)

4. 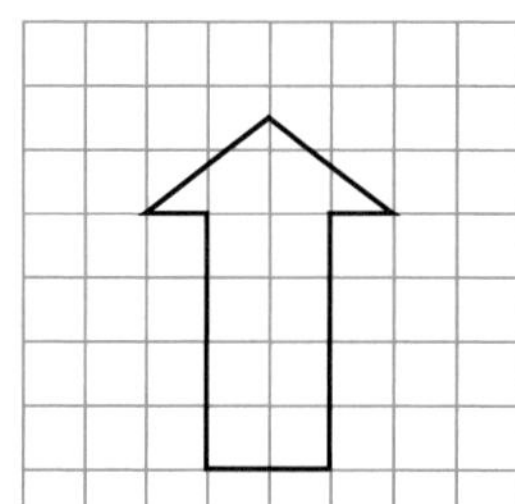

5. 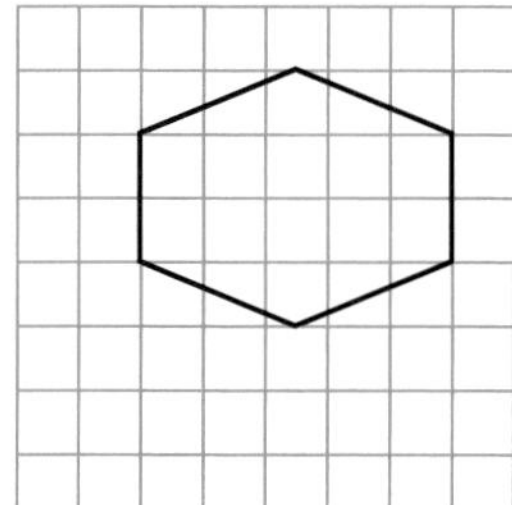

6. 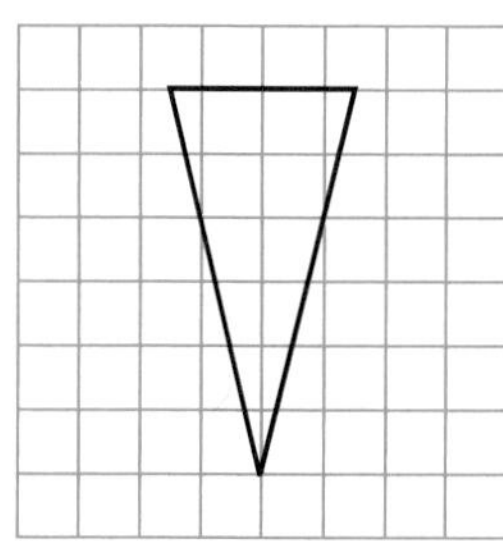

7. 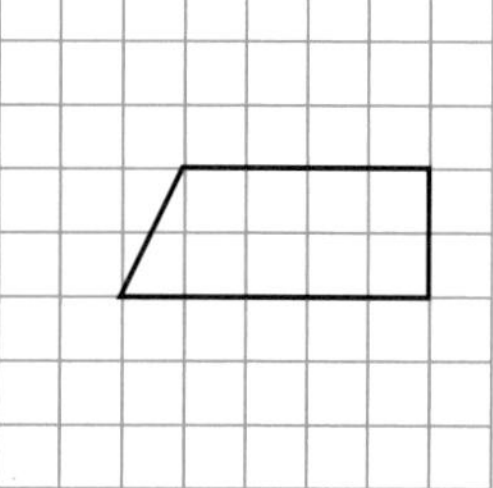

Identify the rule for each pattern. KY MA-05-5.1.1 (pp. 550–551)

8. 7, 9, 11, 13, . . .
9. 6, 12, 10, 20, . . .
10. 6, 7, 14, 15, . . .

Check Problem Solving

Solve. KY MA-05-5.1.1 (pp. 552–553)

11. Raquel is using tiles to cover her kitchen counter. She made the pattern on the right. What could be the colors of the next two tiles?

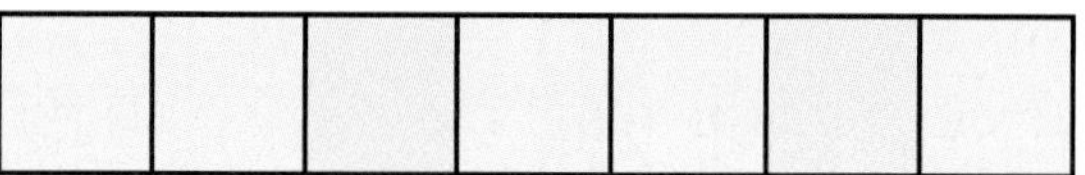

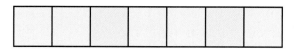

12. WRITE Math Parker and Tony painted a border around their bedroom using the pattern on the right. What could be the next three shapes in the pattern? **Explain.**

GO ONLINE **Technology** Use *Online Assessment.*

Practice for the KCCT
Chapters 1–20

Number and Operations

1. Alvin did a report on Antarctica. He found the land area to be about 14 million square kilometers. Which of the following rounds to 14 million? KY MA-05-1.2.1 (p. 14)

   A 13,472,180

   B 13,594,317

   C 14,613,989

   D 14,907,240

2. Allan ate $\frac{1}{6}$ of the apple pie and his brother Matt ate $\frac{3}{6}$ of the apple pie. How much of the pie did Allan and Matt eat? KY MA-05-1.3.1 (p. 342)

   A $\frac{2}{6}$

   B $\frac{3}{6}$

   C $\frac{4}{6}$

   D $\frac{6}{6}$

3. WRITE Math **Explain** how to add like fractions. KY MA-05-1.3.1 (p. 342)

Algebraic Thinking

Get the information you need.

See item 4. To solve this problem, find the pattern rule. Use the rule to extend the pattern.

4. The students in Mr. Mato's class made a border around the classroom using shapes. Each student wrote his or her name on one shape. Fred's name is on the 21st figure. Which shape did Fred use? KY MA-05-5.1.1 (p. 548)

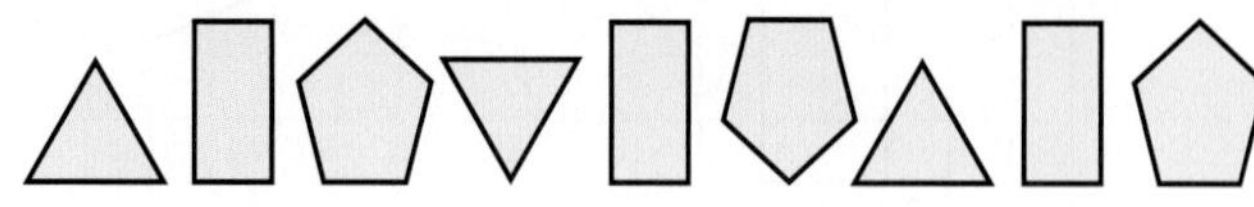

   A 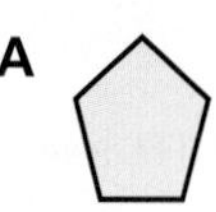

   C 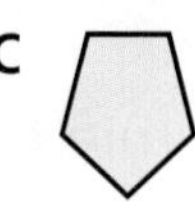

   B 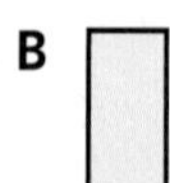

   D

5. Look at the function table. What is the value of x when $y = 18$? KY MA-05-5.1.2 (p. 112)

x	y
1	3
2	6
5	15
10	30

   A 3

   C 13

   B 6

   D 54

6. WRITE Math Write a situation that can be represented by the expression $4n \times 7$. **Explain** your choice. KY MA-05-5.2.1 (p. 92)

Geometry

7. Which figure has 4 angles, 2 pairs of parallel sides and no right angles?
KY MA-05-3.1.2 (p. 490)

   A rectangle

   B rhombus

   C trapezoid

   D square

8. How many lines of symmetry does this figure have? KY MA-05-3.2.1 (p. 504)

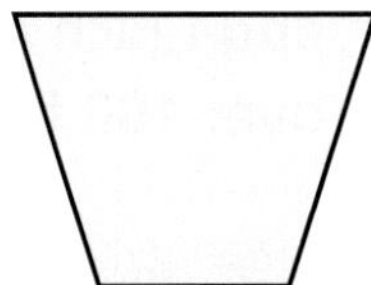

   A 6

   B 4

   C 2

   D 1

9. **WRITE Math** Billy has drawn a triangle and wants to draw another triangle that is a rotation of the original triangle. **Explain** how Billy should draw the rotated triangle.
KY MA-05-3.2.2 (p. 542)

Data Analysis and Probability

10. The stem-and-leaf plot below shows the scores on the last math quiz. Jill's score was the median. What was Jill's score?
KY MA-05-4.1.1 (p. 256)

Last Math Quiz Scores

Stem	Leaves
5	6
6	0 4
7	2 6 6 6 8
8	0 0 2 4 4 8 8
9	4 6

   A 40

   B 76

   C 78

   D 80

11. Eileen is playing a game with the spinner shown below. What is the probability that the spinner will land on red? KY MA-05-4.4.2 (p. 454)

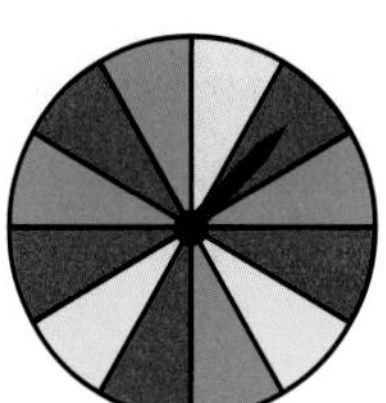

   A $\frac{1}{12}$

   B $\frac{1}{5}$

   C $\frac{1}{3}$

   D $\frac{5}{12}$

12. **WRITE Math** Jordan records the growth of her flower plants each week. **Explain** which type of graphs she could use to display her data. KY MA-05-4.1.1 (p. 260)

CHAPTER

21 Integers and the Coordinate Plane

FAST FACT

A kelp forest is home to a variety of animals. It is also a food source for many sea creatures. An uneaten kelp frond can grow more than 12 inches in one day and reach a length of over 100 feet!

Investigate

Suppose you are measuring the growth of 3 young kelp plants over 6 days. Each plant was 100 inches tall when you began. The table shows how many inches were gained or lost each week. Choose one of the kelp plants. Make a line graph to show the changing height of the plant.

Growth of Kelp Plants

Day	Plant A	Plant B	Plant C
1	$^-3$ in.	$^+2$ in.	$^-2$ in.
2	$^+6$ in.	$^-4$ in.	$^+4$ in.
3	$^-1$ in.	$^-2$ in.	$^-3$ in.
4	$^+5$ in.	$^+4$ in.	$^+2$ in.
5	$^+6$ in.	$^+5$ in.	$^+5$ in.
6	$^+3$ in.	$^+2$ in.	$^+7$ in.

GO ONLINE **Technology**
Student pages are available in the Student eBook.

Show What You Know

Check your understanding of important skills needed for success in Chapter 21.

▶ Compare and Order Whole Numbers

Compare. Use <, >, or = for each ●.

1. 15 ● 20 **2.** 132 ● 133 **3.** 95 ● 92 **4.** 78 ● 87 **5.** 121 ● 121

6. 211 ● 201 **7.** 415 ● 415 **8.** 59 ● 65 **9.** 11 ● 10 **10.** 475 ● 75

▶ Temperature

Write the Fahrenheit temperature reading for each.

11.

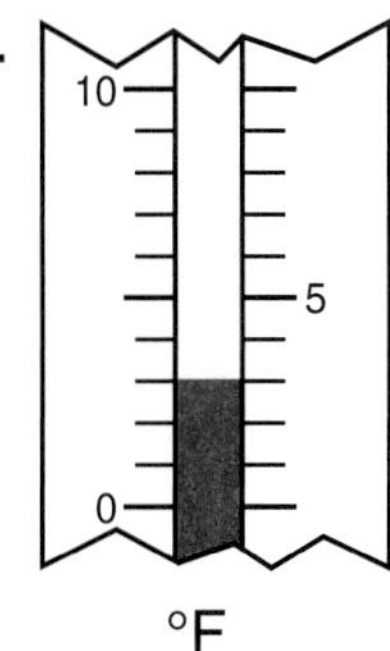

°F

12.

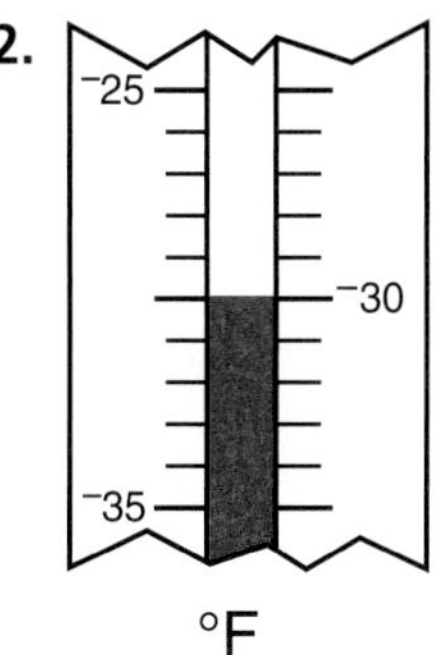

°F

13.

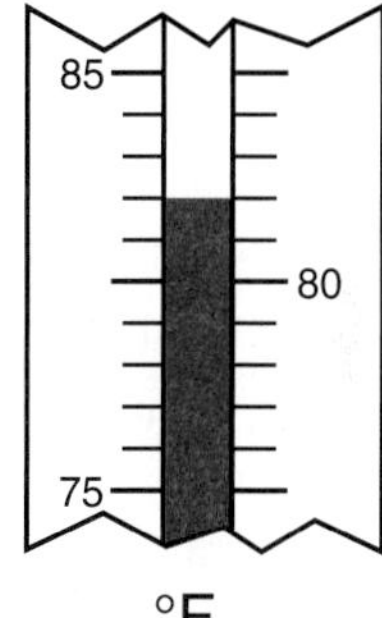

°F

14.

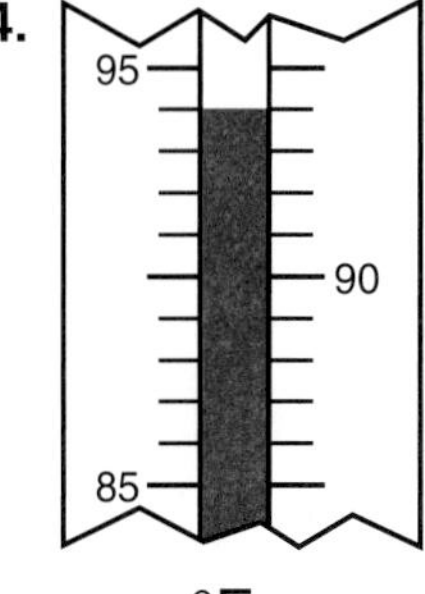

°F

15.

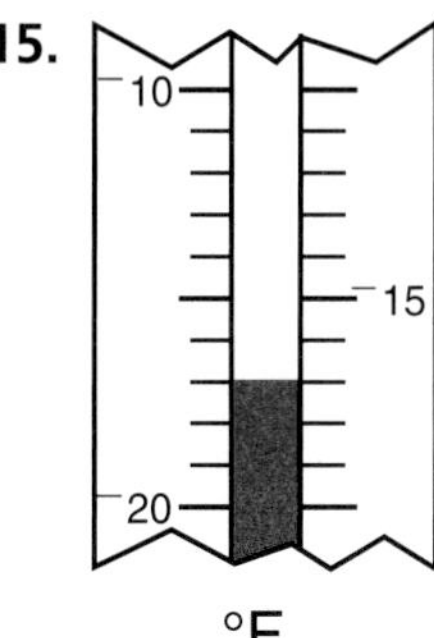

°F

16.

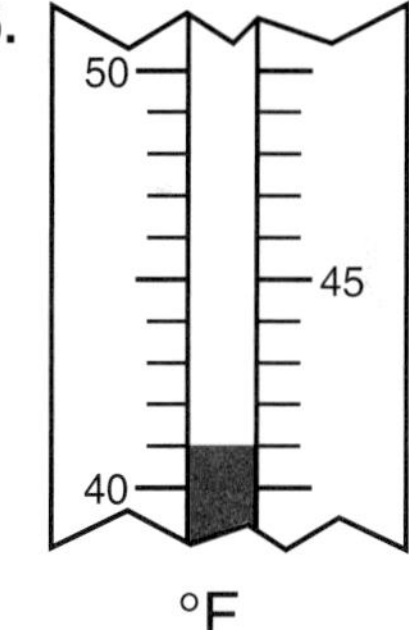

°F

VOCABULARY POWER

CHAPTER VOCABULARY

absolute value
coordinate plane
function
function table
integers
negative integers
ordered pair
origin
positive integer
***x*-axis**
***y*-axis**
***x*-coordinate**
***y*-coordinate**

WARM-UP WORDS

integers the set of whole numbers and their opposites

negative integer any integer less than zero

coordinate plane a plane formed by two intersecting and perpendicular number lines called axes

ALGEBRA

Graph Relationships

OBJECTIVE: Graph relationships from input-output tables.

Quick Review

Copy and complete the table.

Number of squares	1	2	3	4	5	6
Number of sides	4	8	12	■	■	■

Learn

PROBLEM Nick uses equilateral triangles to make quadrilaterals. Each side of an equilateral triangle is 1 unit. What is the relationship of the number of triangles to the perimeter of the quadrilateral? What is the perimeter of a quadrilateral that is made of 5 equilateral triangles?

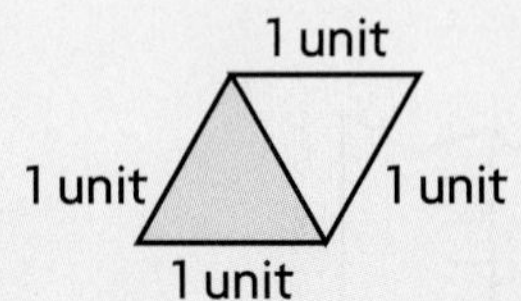

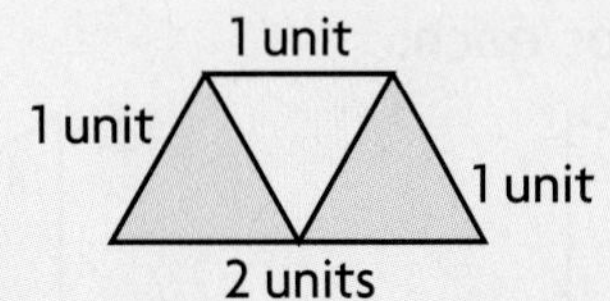

You can show the relationship in a table. An ordered pair represents a relationship on a grid.

Number of triangles, x	Perimeter, in units, y
2	4
3	5
4	6
5	■

The perimeter of each quadrilateral is 2 more than the number of equilateral triangles that make it up. The x-coordinate is 2 more than the y-coordinate.

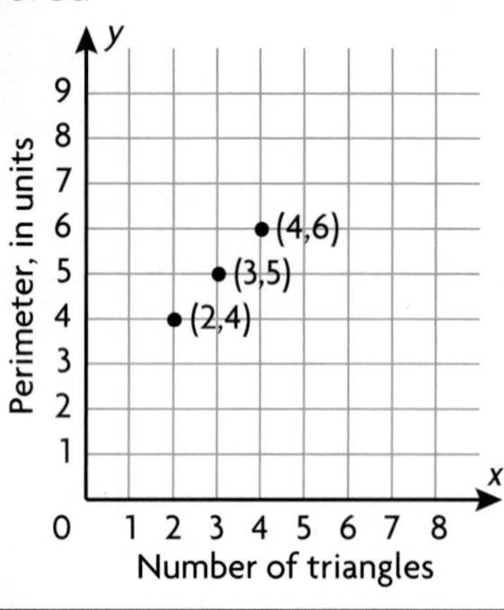

So, the perimeter of the quadrilateral is 7 units.

Example

Graph the relationship shown in the table.

Number of sides, x	3	6	9	12
Number of triangles, y	1	2	3	4

Write the ordered pairs for the data.

(3,1), (6,2), (9,3), (12,4)

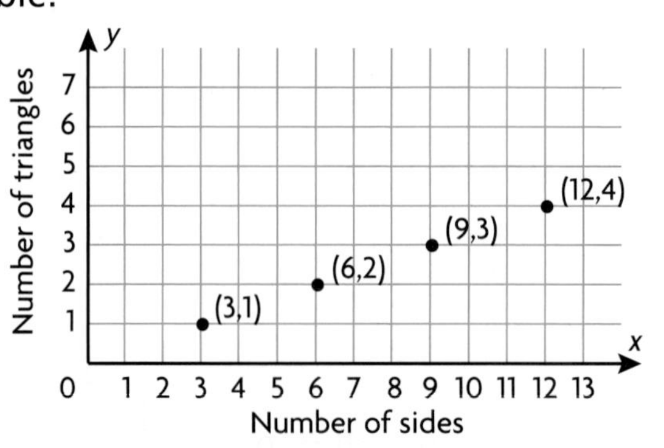

FAST TRACK

KY MA-05-3.3.1 Students will identify and graph ordered pairs on a positive coordinate system scaled by ones, twos, threes, fives, or tens; locate points on a grid; and apply graphing in the coordinate system to solve real-world problems. DOK 2 *also* MA-05-5.1.2; MA-05-5.1.3

Guided Practice

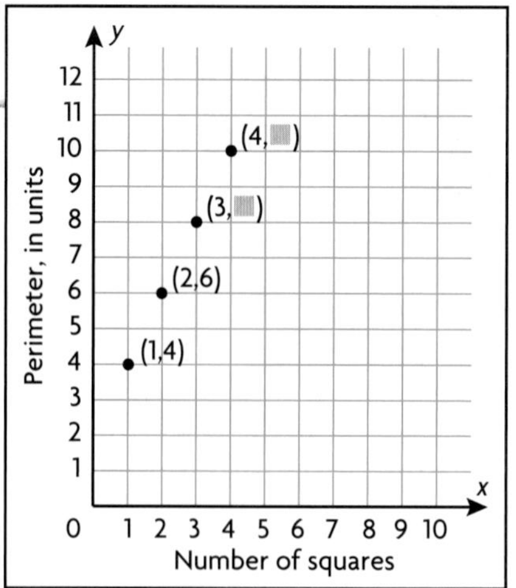

1. Use the table and the graph to complete the ordered pairs.

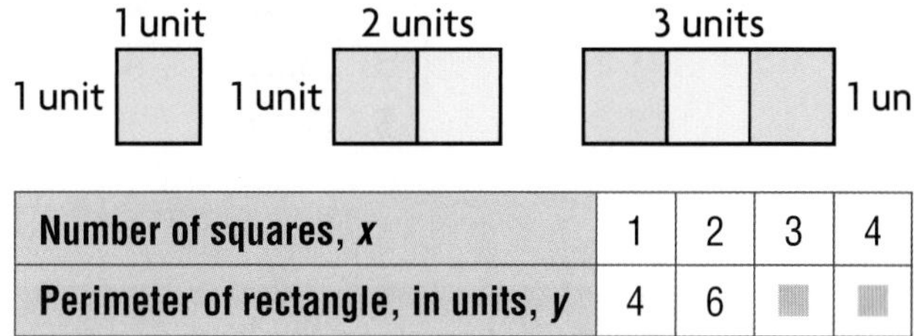

Number of squares, *x*	1	2	3	4
Perimeter of rectangle, in units, *y*	4	6	■	■

(1,4), (2,6), (3,■), (4,■)

Write the ordered pairs. Then graph them.

2.

Number of cars, *x*	1	2	3	4
Number of wheels, *y*	4	8	12	16

3.

Number of pentagons, *x*	1	2	3	4
Number of sides, *y*	5	10	15	20

4. TALK Math **Explain** what relationship is represented by the ordered pair (4,20) in Problem 3.

Independent Practice and Problem Solving

Write the ordered pairs. Then graph them.

5.

Number of cones, *x*	1	4	6	8
Number of vertices, *y*	1	4	6	8

6.

Number of cylinders, *x*	2	3	4	5
Number of flat bases, *y*	4	6	8	10

For 7–9, use the table.

Number of equilateral triangles, *x*	1	2	3	4
Number of interior angles of 60°, *y*	3	6	9	12

7. Write the ordered pairs in the table. Then graph each ordered pair.

8. **Reasoning** What does (3,9) mean in the graph for the table?

9. WRITE Math **What's the Error?** Nikki wrote the ordered pair (18,6) for 6 equilateral triangles with 18 interior angles of 60° in Problem 7. What is her error? What should she have written?

Mixed Review and Test Prep

10. Find the value of n in the equation $5 \times 105 = (5 \times 100) + (5 \times n)$. (p. 102)

11. The Hall family ate $\frac{2}{3}$ of one large pizza and $\frac{3}{4}$ of another large pizza. What fraction of a total large pizza is left? (p. 370)

12. **Test Prep** An ordered pair shows the relationship of the number of pentagons to the number of sides. If x represents 3 pentagons, what is the y-coordinate?

A 3 **B** 5 **C** 10 **D** 15

Extra Practice on page 580, Set A

LESSON 2

ALGEBRA

Equations and Functions

OBJECTIVE: Use function tables and equations to graph equations on a grid.

Quick Review

Graph the ordered pairs.

1. (3,5)
2. (0,6)
3. (8,2)
4. (7,7)
5. (1,0)

Learn

PROBLEM Erika is decorating an art frame with a rectangular pattern made of square tiles. Each side of a square tile is 1 inch. What is the perimeter of Erika's pattern if it has 4 tiles?

1 inch, 1 inch | 2 inches | 3 inches

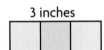

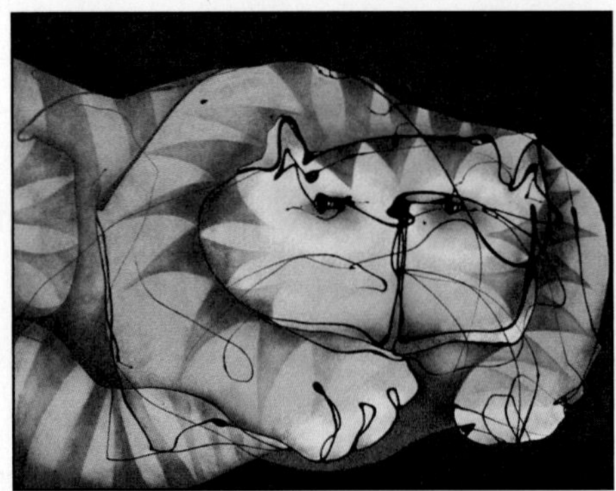
▲ "Green Cat" by Gerrit Greve

You can write an equation for the relationship. Then you can use the equation to make a function table and graph the ordered pairs.

Example 1

Step 1

Write an equation that shows the relationship. The length is greater with each additional tile, but the width always equals 1 inch. The length varies, but the width is constant.

Rule: Multiply the length by 2 and add 2.

Perimeter = **2 × length** + **2**

$y = 2x + 2$

Step 2

Use the equation to make a function table.

Length, x	1	2	3	4
Perimeter, y	4	6	8	■

$y = 2x + 2$
$y = 2 \times 4 + 2$
$y = 8 + 2$
$y = 10$

So, the perimeter of a rectangle pattern with 4 square tiles is 10 inches.

You can use the function table to write the ordered pairs.

(1,4), (2,6), (3,8), (4,10)

Graph the ordered pairs. The ordered pairs on the graph show the relationship of x and y using an equation.

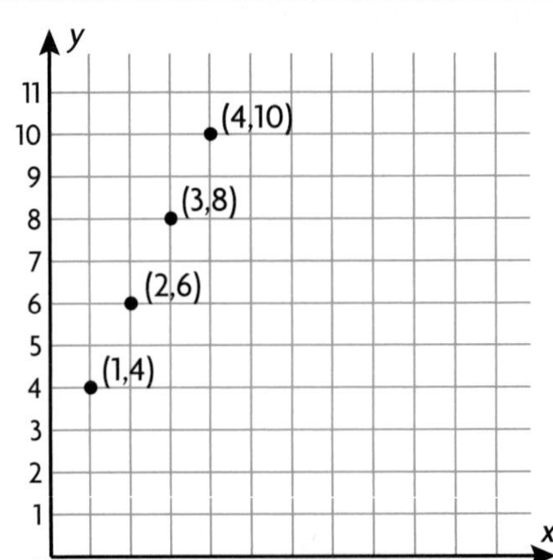

Math Idea

You can use an equation to make a function table to find the ordered pairs. Use the ordered pairs to graph the relationship.

FAST TRACK

KY MA-05-3.3.1 Students will identify and graph ordered pairs on a positive coordinate system scaled by ones, twos, threes, fives, or tens; locate points on a grid; and apply graphing in the coordinate system to solve real-world problems. DOK 2 *also* MA-05-5.1.2; MA-05-5.1.3

Example 2

Katie is 2 years older than her brother, Mike. Write and graph an equation that shows how much older than her brother Katie is.

Step 1

Write an equation that shows the relationship.
Rule: Add 2.

Katie's age	equals	Mike's age	plus	years older
↓	↓	↓	↓	↓
y	$=$	x	$+$	2

Step 2

Use the equation to make a function table.

x	2	3	4	5	6	7
y	4	5	6	7	8	9

Step 3

Write the data in the table as ordered pairs.

(2,4), (3,5) (4,6), (5,7) (6,8), (7,9)

Graph the ordered pairs.

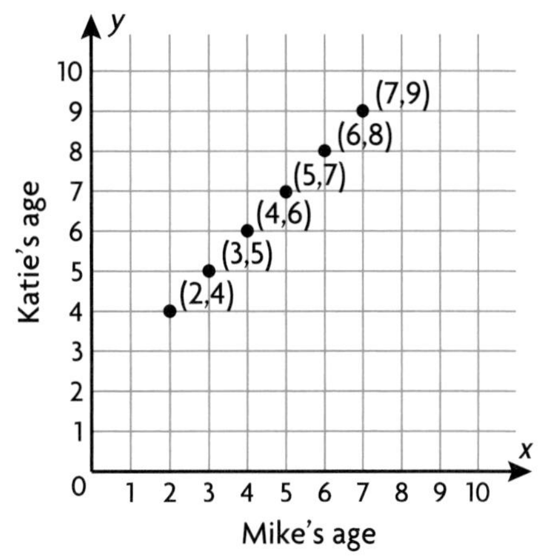

Example 3

Rich and Sam are saving the same amount from their weekly allowance to buy a computer. Their mom adds $5 to their total each week. Write and graph an equation that shows how much money they save weekly.

The amount saved each week by both children is the same. You can add or multiply the unknown amount to write the equation.

$x + x = 2x$ amount saved by Rich and Sam
$5 amount contributed by Mom
$y = 2x + 5$ total saved weekly

Use the equation to make a function table. Then use the table to write and graph the ordered pairs.

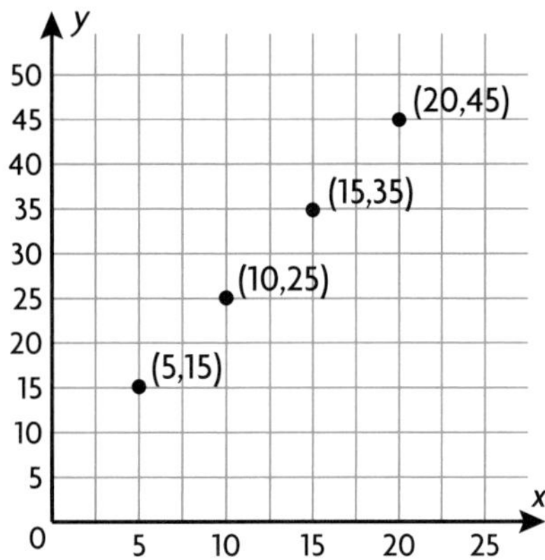

x	5	10	15	20
y	15	25	35	45

(5,15), (10,25), (15,35), (20,45)

Math Idea

For your graph, use an appropriate scale for your number set. You can skip-count by 2s, 5s, 10s, or even 100s if it works well with your data.

Guided Practice

1. Copy and complete the function table. Write the data in the table as ordered pairs.

Rule: Add 2.

Equation: $y = x + 2$

Input, x	1	2	3	4	■
Output, y	3	4	■	6	7

Find a rule to copy and complete the function table. Then write an equation.

2.

x	1	2	3	4	5
y	6	12	18	24	■

3.

f	0	1	2	3	4
g	■	4	8	12	16

4.

p	1	2	3	4	5
q	3	5	■	9	11

5. TALK Math **Explain** how you found the equation in Exercise 4.

Independent Practice and Problem Solving

Find a rule to copy and complete the function table. Then write an equation.

6.

b	5	4	3	2	1
c	9	7	5	3	■

7.

x	10	■	6	4	2
y	5	4	3	2	■

8.

w	4	3	2	1	0
z	20	■	10	5	■

9.

x	4	8	■	16	20
y	1	2	3	4	■

10.

f	■	1	2	3	■
g	3	6	9	12	15

11.

w	30	35	40	50	55
z	25	■	■	45	50

Use each equation to make a function table with at least four ordered pairs. Then graph the ordered pairs on a grid.

12. $y = x - 8$
13. $c = 2b + 2$
14. $m = 3k$
15. $q = 2p - 3$
16. $t = s - 1$
17. $g = 4f - 1$
18. $y = 3x - 4$
19. $z = 10 - w$

Gary makes \$3 more an hour than twice what Miles makes. Use this information for 20–22.

20. Write an equation to show the relationship between the amounts Gary and Miles make.

21. Make a function table with at least four values. Show Mile's salary as an input value and Gary's salary as an output value. Write the data as ordered pairs.

22. Make a graph that shows the relationship between Gary's salary and Miles's salary.

23. WRITE Math **Explain** why the equations $y = x + 4$ and $y = 4 + x$ are the same.

CD ROM **Technology**
Use Harcourt Mega Math, Ice Station Exploration, *Arctic Algebra*, Levels J, K, and L.

 Extra Practice on page 580, Set B

ALGEBRA

Learn About Functions with Fractions and Decimals

You can show fractions and decimals in function tables.

A fifth-grade class is making hand-held signs for a soccer game. Each sign requires a piece of wood that is $6\frac{1}{2}$ inches, or about 16.5 centimeters, long. The students need to make 5 signs. How much wood does the class need?

Examples

A Fractions

- Write an equation. → $y = 6\frac{1}{2}x$
- Use the equation to make a function table

Number of signs, x	1	2	4	5
Wood, in inches, y	$6\frac{1}{2}$	13	26	$32\frac{1}{2}$

B Decimals

- Write an equation. → $y = 16.5x$
- Use the equation to make a function table.

Number of signs, x	1	2	4	5
Wood, in centimeters, y	16.5	33.0	66.0	82.5

So, the class needs $32\frac{1}{2}$ inches, or about 82.5 centimeters, of wood to make 5 signs.

Try It

Make a function table with at least 4 values for each equation. Write the ordered pairs.

24. $y = \frac{1}{2}x$

25. $m = k + 1.25$

26. $h = g + \frac{1}{3}$

Mixed Review and Test Prep

27. What is the perimeter of a rectangle with a width of 2 inches and a length of 9 inches? (Grade 4)

28. Test Prep Which equation shows the relationship for the number of squares to the total number of sides of the squares?

A $y = x + 4$ **C** $y = 2x + 2$

B $y = 2x$ **D** $y = 4x$

29. Anna spent $13.47. Carson spent $9.87. How much did they spend in all? (p. 152)

30. Test Prep If you graph the equation $y = x - 7$, which of the following pairs would you graph?

A (3,4) **C** (4,3)

B (3,10) **D** (10,3)

LESSON 3

Problem Solving Workshop
Strategy: Write an Equation

OBJECTIVE: Solve problems by using the strategy *write an equation.*

Learn the Strategy

You can solve problems by writing and using equations.

Write an equation that shows a rule for a number pattern.

Jill sells tickets to the school fair. On day one, she sells 3 tickets. On day two, she sells 6 tickets. On day three, she sells 9 tickets, and on day 4, she sells 12 tickets. If the pattern continues, how many tickets will Jill sell on day 5?

Write the number pattern.

3, 6, 9, 12, ■

Find a rule.

3, 6, 9, 12, ■

+3 +3 +3 +3

Rule: Add 3.

Write an equation.

$12 + 3 = 15$

So, if the pattern continues, Jill will sell 15 tickets on the fifth day.

Write an equation to find the missing input or output of a function.

What is the missing *y*-value in the function table?

x	4	8	12	16	20
y	11	15	■	23	27

Each output value is 7 more than the input value.

Rule: Add 7.

Write an equation. $y = x + 7$

Solve the equation for $x = 12$.

$$y = 12 + 7 = 19$$

TALK Math

Explain how the equation $3b = 33$ would be different if Jenny bought a different number of beach balls.

Write an equation to model a situation with unknown value.

Jenny bought 3 beach balls that each cost the same amount. She spent $33 in all. What is the price of each beach ball?

Choose a variable for the unknown value.

Let *b* represent the price of each beach ball.

Write an equation. $3b = 33$

Think: What multiplied by 3 equals 33?

So, the price of each beach ball is $11.

FAST TRACK

KY MA-05-5.3.1 Students will model real-world and mathematical problems with simple number sentences (equations and inequalities) with a variable or missing value (e.g., 4 = 2 × N, ___ + 5 > 14) and apply simple number sentences to solve mathematical and real-world problems. DOK 2 *also* MA-05-5.2.1

Use the Strategy

PROBLEM A bus driver is paid at the hourly rate represented in the graph. How much does the bus driver earn in 4 hours?

Read to Understand

Reading Skill

- **What information is given?**
- **What conclusion can you draw from the graph about the amount of money earned as the number of hours worked increases?**

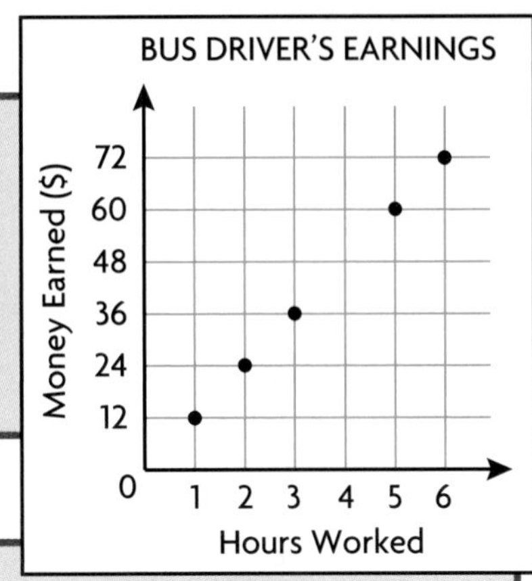

Plan

- **What strategy can you use to solve the problem?**

  You can write an equation to solve the problem.

Solve

- **How can you use the strategy to solve the problem?**

  First, write an ordered pair for each point on the graph.

  (1,12), (2,24), (3,36), (5,60), (6,72)

  Then, record the *x*- and *y*- value of each ordered pair in the function table. Write a rule for the function.

Hours worked, *x*	1	2	3	5	6
Money earned ($), *y*	12	24	36	60	72

Rule: Multiply the number of hours worked by 12.

Finally, use the rule to write and solve an equation.

$y = 12x$

$y = 12 \times 4$ Replace *x* with 4.

$y = 48$

So, the bus driver earns $48 in 4 hours.

Check

- **How can you use the graph to check the answer?**

Guided Problem Solving

1. The city bus system has different bus passes based on the age of the rider and the number of bus rides he or she needs to make. The price relationship between adult and student bus passes is represented in the graph. If the pattern continues, what is the price of a student bus pass if the price of an adult pass is $50?

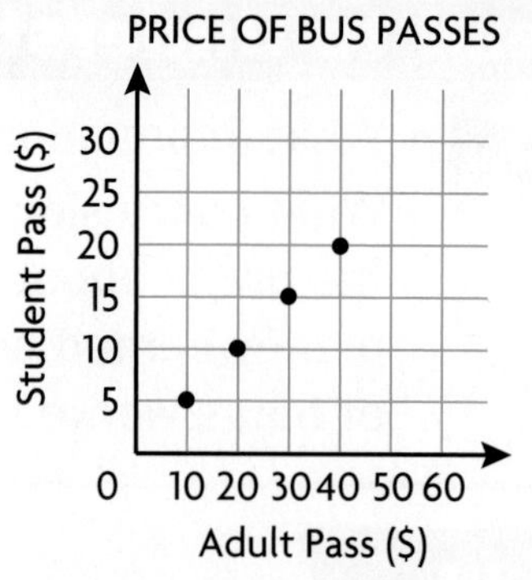

First, write an ordered pair for each point on the graph.

(10,5), (20,10), (30,■), (■, ■), (■, ■)

Then, record the *x*- and *y*-values of the ordered pairs in a function table. Write an equation for the function.

Adult pass ($), *x*	10	20	30	■	■
Student pass ($), *y*	5	10	■	■	■

2. **What if** the ordered pairs for the points on the graph were (10,5), (20,15), (30,25), (40,35), and (60,55)? What would the price of a student pass be if an adult pass were $50?

3. So far, Nancy has traveled 39 miles on a train to visit her grandmother. The total distance is 84 miles. How many more miles will Nancy travel to reach her grandmother's house?

Problem Solving Strategy Practice

Write an equation to solve.

4. George saves $30 each week by taking a train to work instead of driving his car. How much does George save in 9 weeks by taking the train instead of his car?

5. Carla pays $7 for a round-trip bus ticket to the beach. She parks her car at the bus station for $6 per hour. What is the total cost if Carla's car is parked for 5 hours?

6. Nick is taking a 12-mile ride to a museum in a taxicab. The cab driver charges a $3-fee plus $2 per mile. How much will the ride to the museum cost?

USE DATA For 7–8, use the function table.

7. The table shows the amount of money a ticket agent at a subway station earns working different numbers of hours. How much does the ticket agent earn working 3 hours?

Hours, *x*	1	2	3	4	5
Money earned ($), *y*	8	16	■	32	40

8. WRITE Math Make a graph of the data. **Explain** the relationship between the points on the graph and the function table.

Mixed Strategy Practice

Solve.

9. A trolley left the station with 7 people on board. At the first stop, 4 people got off the trolley and 12 people got on. At the second stop, 6 people got off the trolley and 5 people got on. How many people are on the trolley now?

USE DATA For 10–12, use the train schedule.

10. After riding the train, the Perez family arrived at the depot, then drove for 20 minutes to a restaurant. They were at the restaurant for 1 hour and 10 minutes. Then they drove for 2 hours and 15 minutes to arrive home at 4:25 P.M. At what time did the Perez family get off the train?

11. **Pose a Problem** Look back at Problem 10. Write and solve a new problem by changing the amount of time the Perez family spent driving and at the restaurant.

12. Rick and Kayla are planning to take one of the museum train rides on June 6, 7, 8, or 9. How many different combinations of dates and departure times are possible?

13. **Open-Ended Problem** Make up a schedule for any method of transportation. Write one or more equations to represent the relationship between the departure and arrival times.

Choose a STRATEGY

- Draw a Diagram or Picture
- Make a Model or Act It Out
- Make an Organized List
- Find a Pattern
- Make a Table or Graph
- Predict and Test
- Work Backward
- Solve a Simpler Problem
- Write an Equation
- Use Logical Reasoning

California State Railway Museum Train Schedule

Leave Depot	Arrive Depot
10:00 A.M.	10:40 A.M.
11:00 P.M.	11:40 P.M.
12:00 P.M.	12:40 P.M.
1:00 P.M.	1:40 P.M.

▲ The K4 steam locomotive is Pennsylvania's official state steam locomotive.

CHALLENGE YOURSELF

Train rides at the Mid-Continent Railway Museum in Wisconsin are $12 for adults and $7 for students ages 6 to 17. Rates for groups of 25 or more are $9 per adult and $6 per student.

14. Jim bought train tickets for 6 adults and 18 students. Ellen bought train tickets for 7 adults and 18 students. Who paid more for the train tickets, Jim or Ellen? **Explain.**

15. Kim bought 10 train tickets. She paid $85. How many of the tickets were for adults? How many were for students?

LESSON
4

Understand Integers

OBJECTIVE: Identify and represent positive and negative integers.

Quick Review

Identify the points on the number line.

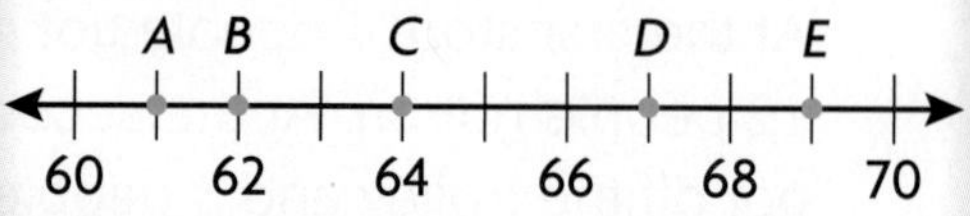
A B C D E
60 62 64 66 68 70

Vocabulary

integers **negative integer**
positive integer **absolute value**

Learn

PROBLEM The world's highest temperature, recorded in El Azizia, Libya, in 1922, was $^{+}136$°F. The lowest temperature, recorded in Vostok, Antarctica, in 1974, was $^{-}129$°F.

The numbers $^{+}136$ and $^{-}129$ are integers. **Integers** are the set of whole numbers and their opposites. Opposite integers are the same distance from 0 on a number line in opposite directions. The number $^{+}136$ is a **positive integer** because it is greater than 0. You read it as "positive one hundred thirty-six." The number $^{-}129$ is a **negative integer** because it is less than 0. You read it as "negative one hundred twenty-nine."

▲ The Amundsen-Scott South Pole Station near Vostok, Antarctica, is a science research facility. The average temperature there in July is $^{-}76$°F.

A number line shows numbers to the left and to the right of 0. You can show integers on a number line.

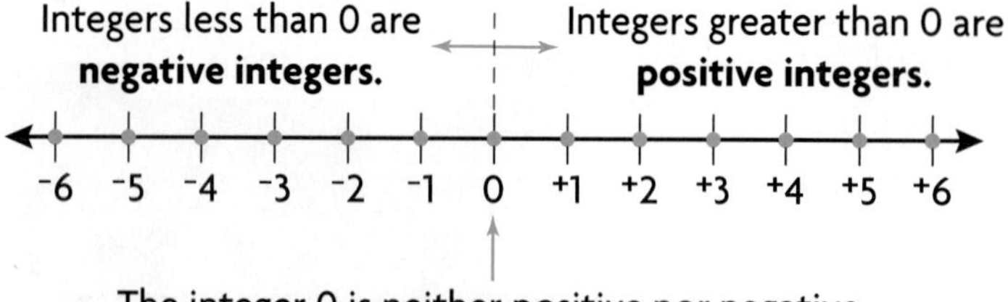
Integers less than 0 are
negative integers.
Integers greater than 0 are
positive integers.
-6 -5 -4 -3 -2 -1 0 +1 +2 +3 +4 +5 +6
The integer 0 is neither positive nor negative.

- Represent the integers $^{+}4$, $^{-}4$, 0, $^{-}1$, and $^{+}8$ on a number line.

Many situations can be represented as integers.

Situation	Integer
Death Valley, California, the lowest point in the United States, is 282 feet below sea level.	$^{-}282$
Larry deposits $25 in his bank account.	$^{+}25$
Sea level	0
The temperature is 18 degrees below 0.	$^{-}18$
Larry withdraws $30 from his bank account.	$^{-}30$
Mt. McKinley, Alaska, the highest peak in the United States, is 20,320 feet above sea level.	$^{+}20,320$

Math Idea

You can write integers in several ways. For example, positive three can be written as $^{+}3$, $+3$, or 3. Negative three can be written as $^{-}3$ or -3.

Opposite Numbers and Absolute Value

If you walk forward 2 steps, you are 2 steps from where you started. If you walk backward 2 steps, you are also 2 steps from where you started. In both cases the distance of 2 steps is traveled.

Integers that are opposites are the same distance from 0 on the number line, but in opposite directions. The integer $^{+}2$ is the same distance from 0 as the integer $^{-}2$. For every positive integer, there is an opposite, negative integer.

The number line shows opposite pairs of numbers. These opposites are graphed below:

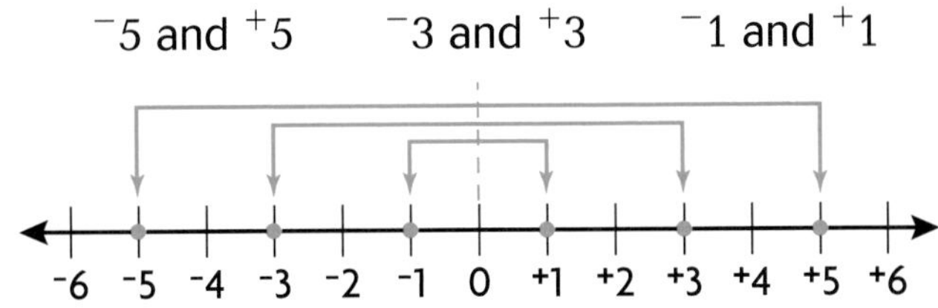

Opposite integers have the same absolute value.
The **absolute value** of an integer is its distance from 0 on a number line.

Write: $|^{-}5| = 5$. **Read:** The absolute value of negative five is five.
Write: $|^{+}5| = 5$. **Read:** The absolute value of positive five is five.

Examples

A Opposite

Name the opposite of $^{-}13$.

$^{-}13 \rightarrow {}^{+}13$

B Absolute Value

Use the number line to find $|^{+}6|$.

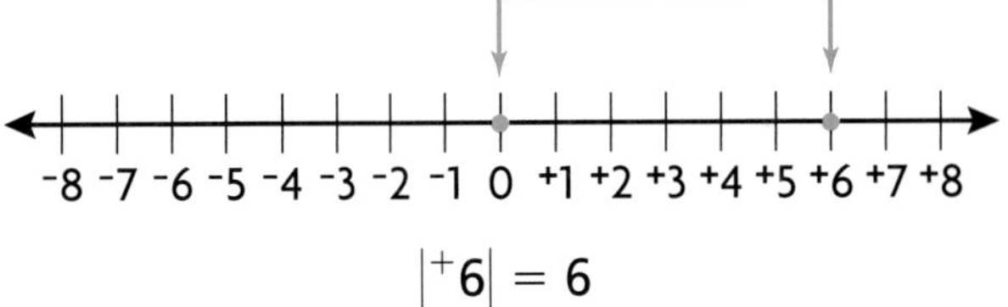

$|^{+}6| = 6$

C Opposite

Name the opposite of 6.

$^{+}6 \rightarrow {}^{-}6$

D Absolute Value

Use the number line to find $|^{-}7|$.

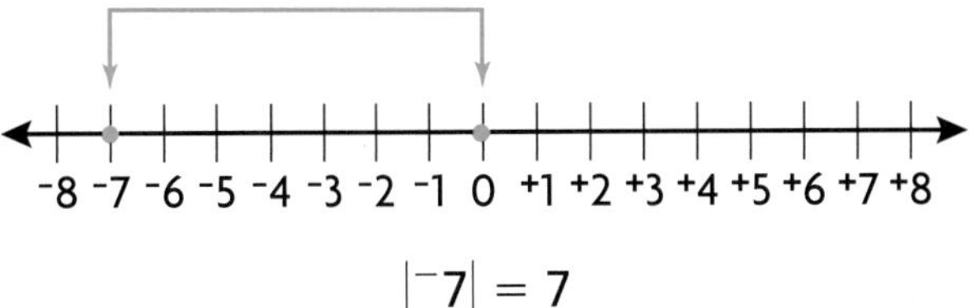

$|^{-}7| = 7$

Guided Practice

1. The number line shows the integer $^{+}2$. What is the opposite of $^{+}2$?

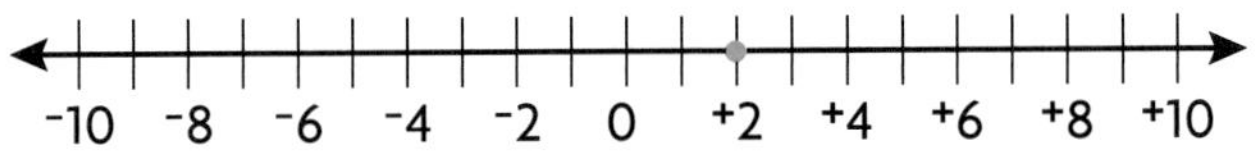

2. The number line shows the integer $^{-}8$. What is the opposite of $^{-}8$?

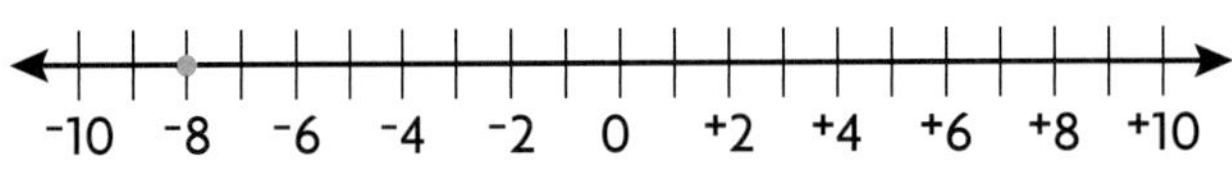

Identify the integers graphed on the number line.

3\. ✓4.

Write an integer to represent each situation.

5\. 30 feet above sea level

6\. a deposit of $18

✓7. 79 degrees below 0

8\. TALK Math **Explain** how to locate the integer $^{-}27$ and its opposite on a number line.

Independent Practice and Problem Solving

Identify the integers graphed on the number line.

9\. -10 -8 -6 -4 -2 0 +2 +4 +6 +8 +10

10\.

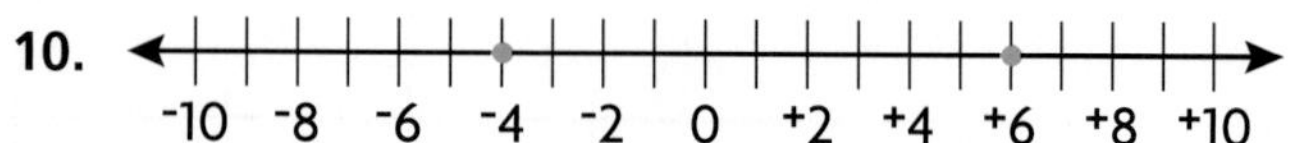

Write an integer to represent each situation.

11\. a gain of 10 yards

12\. 9 degrees above zero

13\. 8 feet below sea level

14\. no change in earnings

15\. a loss of 23 yards

16\. a profit of $100

Write the opposite of each integer.

17\. $^{+}6$

18\. $^{-}9$

19\. $^{-}14$

20\. $^{+}10$

21\. $^{+}51$

22\. $^{+}100$

23\. $^{-}365$

24\. $^{-}33$

25\. $^{+}430$

26\. $^{-}5{,}280$

Write the absolute value of the integer.

27\. $|^{-}100|$

28\. $|^{+}25|$

29\. $|^{-}36|$

30\. $|0|$

31\. $|^{-}10{,}000|$

For 32–34, use the number line.

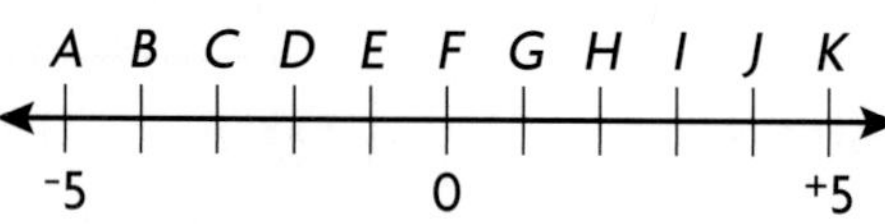

32\. Write the letter for each integer.

a. $^{-}4$ b. $^{+}3$ c. 0 d. $^{+}1$

33\. Write the letter for the opposite of each integer.

a. $^{-}3$ b. $^{+}2$ c. $^{-}2$ d. $^{+}5$

34\. Write the absolute value of the integer at each letter.

a. B b. D c. F d. K

35\. **Reasoning** Neil earns $17. He owes his brother $23. What integers represent the amount Neil has earned and the amount he owes?

36\. WRITE Math **Explain** three situations that the integer $^{-}13$ might represent.

Mixed Review and Test Prep

37. How many edges does a square pyramid have? (p. 524)

38. **Test Prep** Which integer is the opposite of $^{-}306$?

    A $^{-}603$
    B $^{-}306$
    C $^{+}306$
    D $^{+}603$

39. In the ordered pair (0,9), which number is the *x*-coordinate? (p. 248)

40. **Test Prep** Which integer represents 8 days before now if today is Day 0?

    A $^{+}80$
    B $^{+}8$
    C $^{-}8$
    D $^{-}80$

Problem Solving connects to Science

The Kelvin temperature scale is another way to measure temperature besides Celsius or Fahrenheit. The Kelvin scale does not use negative integers. Its units are the same size as the units on the Celsius scale. The temperature in kelvins can be found by adding 273.16 to the Celsius temperature. This is often rounded to 273.

When you write a temperature using the Kelvin scale, you do not need to use the degree symbol. It is conventional to say that water freezes at 273 kelvins.

The lowest temperature on the Kelvin scale is 0K, or "absolute zero." At absolute zero, all particles are completely at rest. They have zero heat energy. In theory, it is not possible for a system to have zero energy. The closest scientists have come to absolute zero in a laboratory is about $\frac{1}{2}$ of a billionth of 1K. This is nearly zero.

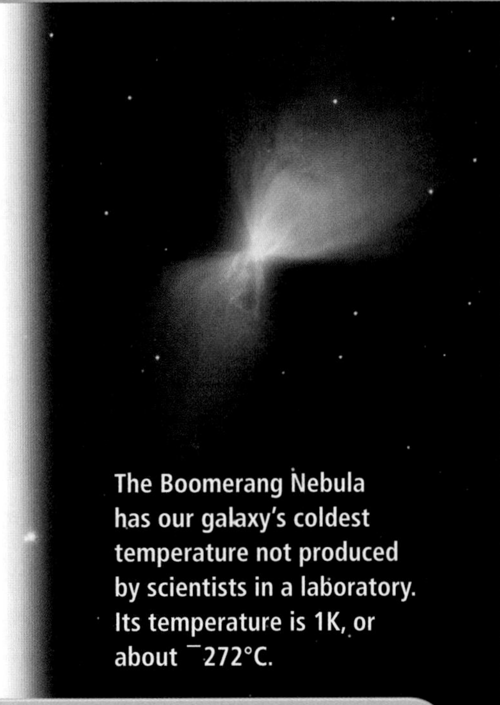

The Boomerang Nebula has our galaxy's coldest temperature not produced by scientists in a laboratory. Its temperature is 1K, or about $^{-}272$°C.

For 1–3, use the table.

1. Find the average temperature in kelvins for Mercury, Venus, and Earth.
2. Using the Celsius scale, write the absolute value of the temperature of each planet.
3. Using the Fahrenheit scale, write the integer that describes the temperature of each planet. Then write the absolute value of each integer.

Average Planet Temperatures

Planet	Celsius	Kelvin	Fahrenheit
Mercury	160°C	■	320°F
Venus	452°C	■	846°F
Earth	15°C	■	59°F
Mars	$^{-}63$°C	210K	$^{-}81$°F
Jupiter	$^{-}153$°C	120K	$^{-}243$°F
Saturn	$^{-}185$°C	88K	$^{-}301$°F
Uranus	$^{-}214$°C	59K	$^{-}353$°F
Neptune	$^{-}225$°C	48K	$^{-}373$°F

LESSON 5

Compare and Order Integers

OBJECTIVE: Identify, compare, and order integers.

Quick Review

Write the opposite of each integer.

1. $^{-}50$ **2.** 15 **3.** $^{-}3$
4. $^{-}67$ **5.** 22

Learn

PROBLEM Two black-vented shearwaters are diving for fish. One dives 20 meters below the surface, and the other dives 10 meters below the surface. Which dive is closer to the surface?

Example

Step 1

Name the integer that represents each situation.

the ocean's surface: 0
a dive of 20 meters below the surface of the ocean: $^{-}20$
a dive of 10 meters below the surface of the ocean: $^{-}10$

Step 2

Show the integers $^{-}20$, $^{-}10$, and 0 on a number line.

▲ **Black-vented shearwaters are seabirds that live off the coast of southern California.**

On the number line, $^{-}10$ is closer to 0 than $^{-}20$.

So, since $^{-}10 > {}^{-}20$, the second dive is closer to the surface.

Order the numbers $^{-}2$, $^{+}3$, $^{-}4$, and $^{+}4$ from least to greatest.

ONE WAY **Use a horizontal number line.**

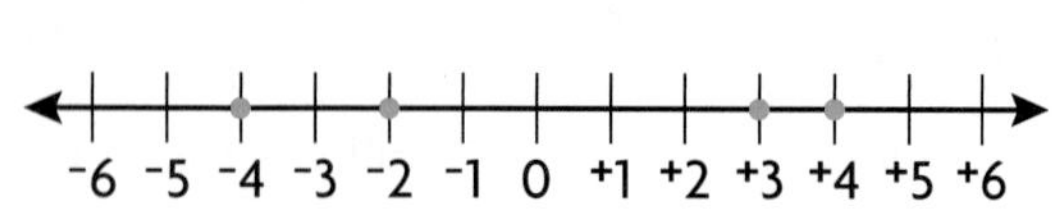

On a horizontal number line, the positive numbers are to the right of zero and the negative numbers are to the left of zero.

ANOTHER WAY **Use a vertical number line.**

On a vertical number line, the positive numbers are above zero, and the negative numbers are below zero.

So, the numbers from least to greatest are $^{-}4$, $^{-}2$, $^{+}3$, and $^{+}4$.

Guided Practice

1. Which integer is greater than $^{-}7$?

   a. $^{+}7$ b. $^{-}7$ c. $^{-}10$

2. Which integer is less than $^{-}7$?

   a. $^{+}10$ b. $^{+}7$ c. $^{-}8$

Compare. Write <, >, or = for each ●.

3. $^{+}6$ ● 0
4. $^{-}3$ ● $^{+}2$
5. $^{-}5$ ● $^{-}9$
6. $^{+}4$ ● $^{-}8$

7. **TALK Math** **Explain** how you would order 0, $^{-}2$, and $^{+}2$ from greatest to least.

Independent Practice and Problem Solving

Compare. Write <, >, or = for each ●.

8. $^{-}10$ ● $^{+}2$
9. $^{-}10$ ● $^{+}10$
10. $^{-}6$ ● $^{-}6$
11. $^{+}17$ ● $^{+}27$
12. $^{-}3$ ● $^{-}12$
13. 0 ● $^{+}7$
14. $^{-}20$ ● $^{-}2$
15. $^{+}112$ ● $^{-}113$
16. $^{-}322$ ● $^{-}323$
17. $^{-}14$ ● $^{+}15$

Order each set of integers from greatest to least.

18. $^{+}2, ^{-}6, ^{-}8$
19. $^{+}4, ^{-}4, ^{-}9$
20. $^{-}10, 0, ^{-}5, ^{+}7$
21. $0, ^{+}1, ^{-}1, ^{-}3$
22. $^{-}3, ^{-}2, ^{+}1, 0$

For 23–24, use the table.

23. Write each depth in the table as an integer. Order the integers from greatest to least.

24. **WRITE Math** The record for the greatest depth achieved by a freediver is 223 meters, held by Tom Sietas of Germany. Express the amount as a negative integer. **Explain** whether the integer is greater than or less than the integers in Problem 23.

Freediving Results

Name	Depth Below Surface
Audrey Mestre	115 meters
Angela Bandini	52 meters
Tanya Streeter	113 meters

▲ Competitive freediving is a sport in which divers try to reach the greatest depth on a single breath.

Mixed Review and Test Prep

25. What is the value of $4 \times n + 3$ if $n = 8$? (p. 96)

26. One beehive produced 22.8 kg of honey. Another hive produced 19.9 kg of honey. How much honey did both hives produce? (p. 152)

27. **Test Prep** Which integer is less than $^{-}38$?

   A $^{+}38$
   B 0
   C $^{-}37$
   D $^{-}39$

Extra Practice on page 581, Set D

ALGEBRA

Graph Integers on the Coordinate Plane

OBJECTIVE: Graph integers on the coordinate plane.

Quick Review

Identify the *x*-coordinate and *y*-coordinate in each ordered pair.

1. (1,6) **2.** (2,0)
3. (10,8) **4.** (9,9)
5. (7,12)

Vocabulary

coordinate plane **origin**

Learn

A **coordinate plane** is formed by two intersecting and perpendicular number lines. The point where the two lines intersect is called the **origin**, or (0,0).

Along the *x*-axis, the positive numbers are to the **right** of the *y*-axis and the negative numbers are to the **left** of the *y*-axis.

Along the *y*-axis, the positive numbers are **up,** or above the *x*-axis, and the negative numbers are **down,** or below the *y*-axis.

Start at the origin. Move 3 units to the left on the *x*-axis and 4 units up on the *y*-axis. The coordinates are (⁻3,4).

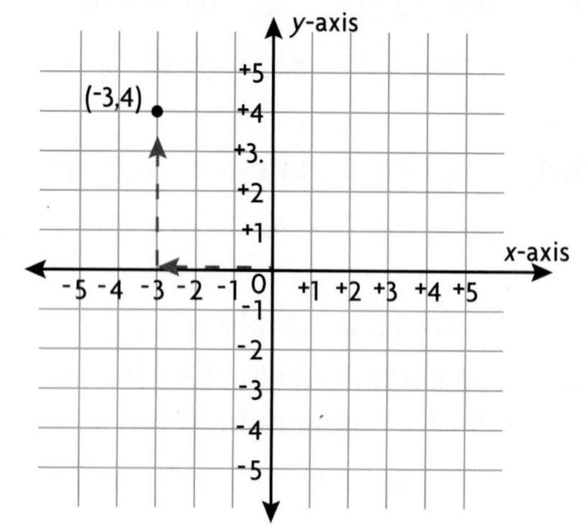

Examples

A Positive *x*-coordinate, negative *y*-coordinate

To graph (5,⁻2), start at the origin. Move 5 units to the ***right*** and 2 units ***down***.

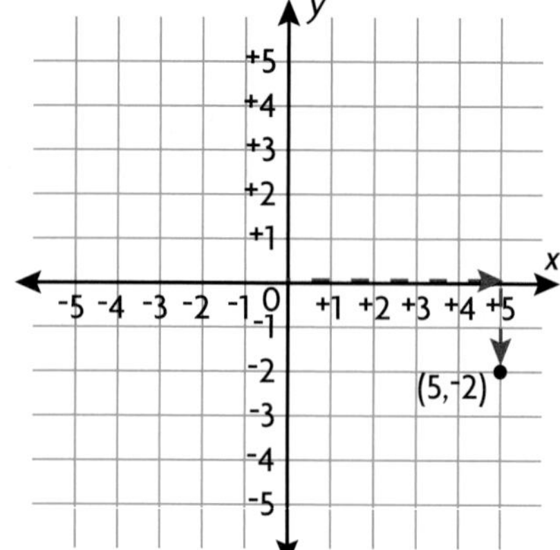

B Two negative coordinates

To graph (⁻3,⁻3), start at the origin. Move 3 units to the ***left*** and 3 units ***down***.

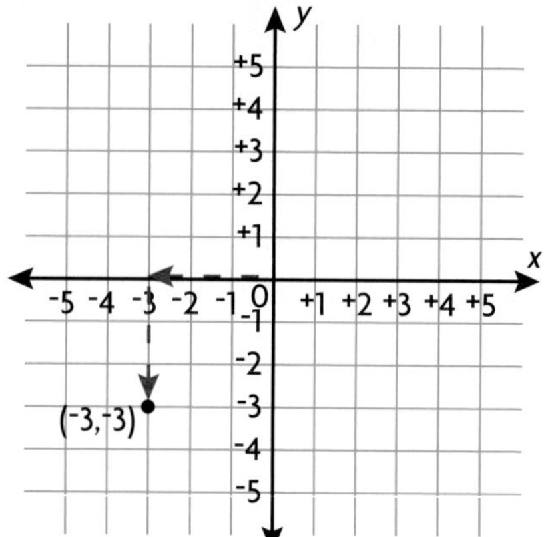

Guided Practice

Choose *right*, *left*, *up*, or *down* to fill in the blanks.

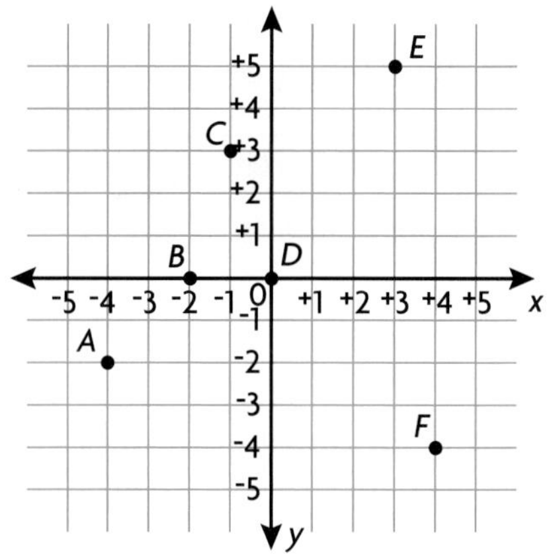

1. To graph $(^-1,^+1)$, start at (0,0), then go __?__ to $^-1$ and __?__ to $^+1$.

For 2–7, identify the ordered pair for each point.

2. point *A*
3. point *B*
4. point *C*
5. point *D*
6. point *E*
7. point *F*

8. **TALK Math** **Explain** how you would graph $(0,^-4)$ on a coordinate plane.

Independent Practice and Problem Solving

For 9–14, identify the ordered pair for each point.

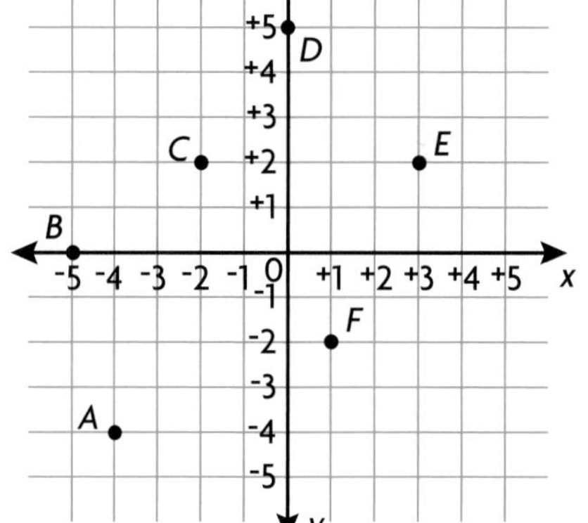

9. point *A*
10. point *C*
11. point *E*
12. point *F*
13. point *B*
14. point *D*

For 15–18, graph and label the ordered pairs on a coordinate plane.

15. *M* $(6,^-1)$
16. *N* $(^-2,2)$
17. *P* $(^-6,0)$
18. *Q* $(^-4,^-4)$

For 19–20, name the ordered pair that is described.

19. Start at the origin. Move 2 units to the right and 5 units down.
20. Start at the origin. Move 4 units to the left and 7 units up.
21. **Sense or Nonsense?** An ordered pair can never contain integers that are both negative. **Explain** why you agree or disagree.
22. **WRITE Math** Why is a coordinate plane more useful than a coordinate grid that only uses positive integers? **Explain.**

Mixed Review and Test Prep

23. Identify the integers 0, $^-8$, 9, and $^-2$ on a number line. Then order them from greatest to least. (p. 576)

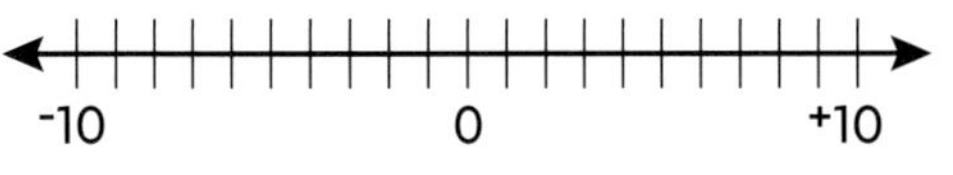

24. What does y equal if $x = 6$ for the equation $y = 3x + 5$? (p. 564)

25. **Test Prep** Start at the origin. Go to the left 2 units. Go down 2 units. What is the ordered pair?

 A (2,2) **C** $(^-2,2)$

 B $(2,^-2)$ **D** $(^-2,^-2)$

Extra Practice on page 581, Set E

Extra Practice

Set A Write the ordered pairs. Then graph them. (pp. 562–563)

1.

Number of hexagons, x	1	2	3	4
Number of sides, y	6	12	18	24

2.

Number of rectangles, x	1	2	3	4
Perimeter in inches, y	6	8	10	12

Set B Find a rule to copy and complete the function table. Then write an equation. (pp. 564–567)

1.

x	3	4	5	6	7
y	0	1	2	3	■

2.

x	10	8	6	■	2
y	■	16	12	8	4

3.

x	3	■	9	12	15
y	1	2	3	4	■

Use each equation to make a function table with at least 4 ordered pairs. Then graph the ordered pairs on a coordinate plane.

4. $y = x + 3$
5. $y = 4x - 1$
6. $y = x - 5$
7. $y = 3x + 2$
8. $y = 2x - 7$
9. $y = x + 1$
10. $y = x \div 2$
11. $y = 2x$
12. Val is 4 years younger than her brother Jeremy. Write an equation to show the relationship between the ages of Val and Jeremy.
13. Brian is 2 years older than Robin. Make a function table with at least four values. Use Robin's age as the input value and Brian's age as the output value. Then graph the ordered pairs.

Set C Identify the integers graphed on the number line. (pp. 572–575)

1. 2.

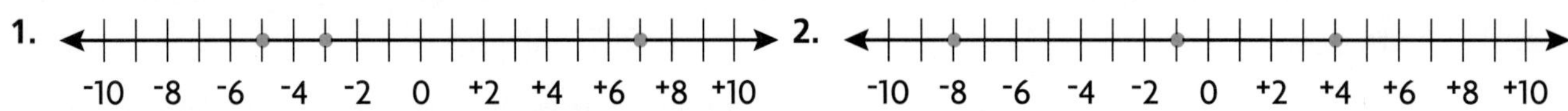

Write an integer to represent each situation.

3. 12 feet below sea level
4. a deposit of \$5
5. a loss of 10 yards

Write the opposite of each integer.

6. $^{+}3$
7. $^{-}7$
8. $^{-}15$
9. $^{+}42$
10. $^{-}38$

Write the integer's absolute value.

11. $|^{-}50|$
12. $|^{+}19|$
13. $|0|$
14. $|^{-}275|$
15. $|^{-}41|$

CD ROM **Technology**
Use Harcourt Mega Math, The Number Game, *ArachnaGraph*, Level H.

Set D Compare. Write <, >, or = for each ●. (pp. 576–577)

1. $^{-}7$ ● $^{+}5$
2. $^{-}4$ ● $^{-}2$
3. $^{+}8$ ● $^{-}8$
4. 0 ● $^{-}10$
5. $^{-}1$ ● $^{-}1$
6. $^{+}9$ ● $^{+}13$
7. $^{-}16$ ● $^{+}6$
8. $^{-}50$ ● $^{-}59$
9. $^{+}25$ ● $^{-}27$
10. $^{-}100$ ● $^{-}103$

Order each set of integers from greatest to least.

11. $^{+}3, ^{-}1, ^{+}5$
12. $^{-}4, ^{+}1, ^{-}6$
13. $^{-}8, ^{+}2, ^{-}9, ^{+}5$
14. $^{-}2, ^{-}3, 0, ^{+}4$
15. $0, ^{-}1, ^{-}5, ^{+}2$

16. The temperature at noon was 4 degrees above zero. At midnight, the temperature was 6 degrees below zero. Write each temperature as an integer. Then tell which integer is greater.

17. Tina scored 25 points the first time she played a video game. She lost 14 points in the second game. Write each score as an integer. Then tell which integer is greater.

18. Which of the integers $^{-}11$, $^{+}6$, 0, $^{+}3$, $^{+}11$, $^{-}3$, and $^{-}6$ are negative? positive? Name the opposite pairs.

19. If 0 stands for today, what integer stands for yesterday? What integer stands for tomorrow?

Set E For 1–9, identify the ordered pair for each point. (pp. 578–579)

1. point *E*
2. point *T*
3. point *M*
4. point *S*
5. point *V*
6. point *C*
7. point *K*
8. point *B*
9. point *D*

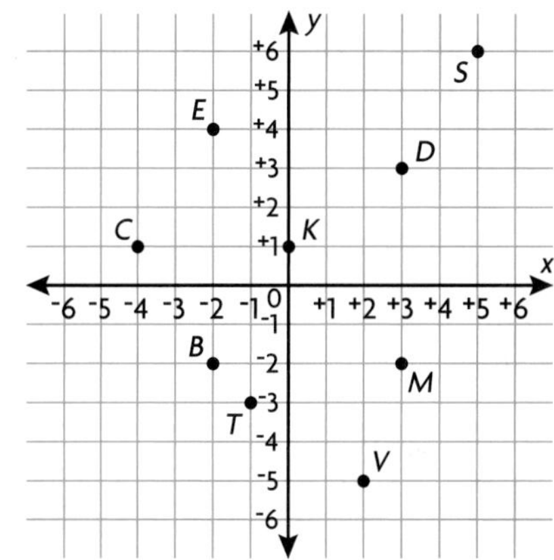

For 10–13, graph and label the ordered pairs on a coordinate plane.

10. $Y\ (^{-}3, ^{+}4)$
11. $H\ (0, ^{-}5)$
12. $B\ (^{+}7, ^{-}1)$
13. $J\ (^{-}4, ^{-}2)$

Name the ordered pair that is described.

14. Start at the origin. Move 5 units to the left and 3 units up.

15. Start at the origin. Move 2 units to the right and 4 units down.

16. Start at the origin. Move 2 units to the right and 3 units down.

17. Start at the origin. Move 4 units to the left and 4 units up.

18. Start at the origin. Move 2 units to the left. Then move 3 units down and 4 more units to the left.

19. Start at the origin. Move 5 units to the right. Then move 4 units up and 3 units left.

MATH POWER

Graphing Equations

A Point in Common

Some equations contain two variables. To find the value of each variable, replace the first variable with a value. Then solve the equation to find the value of the second variable.

Examples

What values of x and y make the equation $4 - x = y$ true?

A $4 - x = y$

Make a table. List 3 values for x.

x	y
0	
1	
2	

Solve the equation for y.

x	y
0	4
1	3
2	2

What values of x and y make the equation $y = x + 2$ true?

B $y = x + 2$

Make a table. List 3 values for x.

x	y
0	
1	
2	

Solve the equation for y.

x	y
0	2
1	3
2	4

Use the ordered pairs in the tables to graph each equation. Then, use a ruler to connect the points in each equation to make two lines. The lines intersect at the common solution. The point (1,3) is common, so it is a solution to both equations.

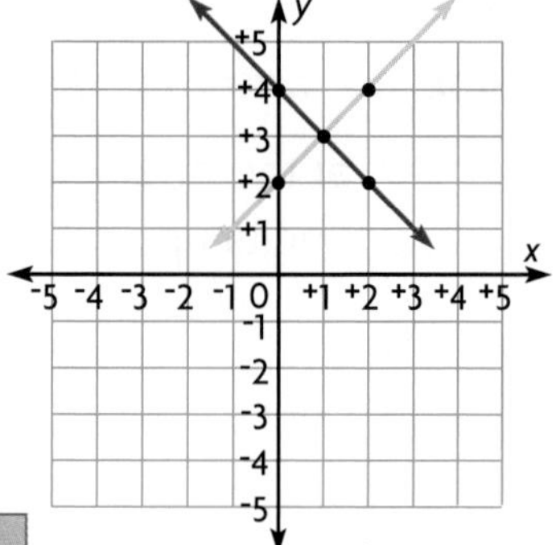

Try It

Complete the tables for each pair of equations. Then graph the equations to find a common solution.

1.

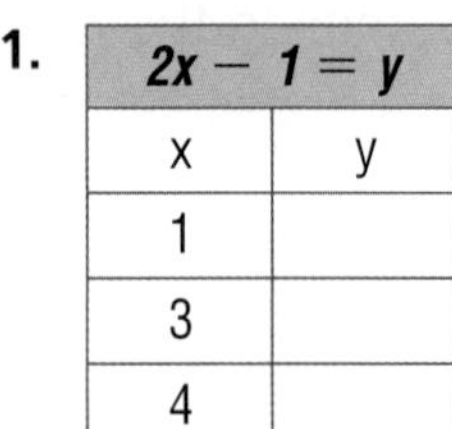

$2x - 1 = y$	
x	y
1	
3	
4	

$x + 1 = y$	
x	y
0	
1	
3	

2.

$5x - 3 = y$	
x	y
1	
3	
4	

$3x + 1 = y$	
x	y
0	
1	
3	

3. **WRITE Math** **Explain** how you could find a common solution of two equations by simply looking at a graph of the equations.

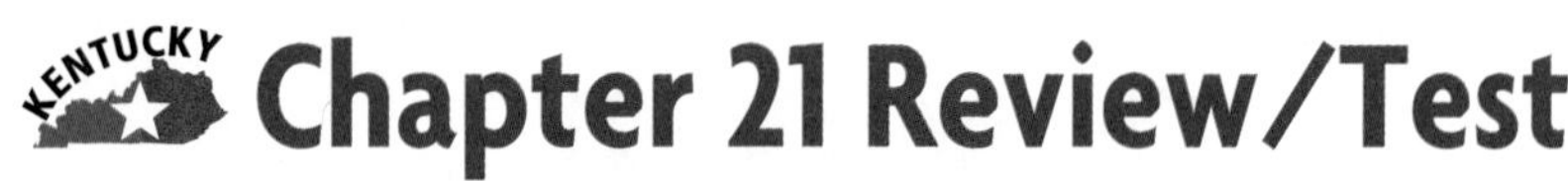

Chapter 21 Review/Test

Check Vocabulary and Concepts

Choose the best term from the box.

VOCABULARY
positive integer
negative integer
absolute value
origin

1. The point on a coordinate plane with the ordered pair (0,0). KY Grade 6 (p. 578)
2. A whole number that is greater than zero. KY Grade 6 (p. 572)
3. The _?_ of an integer is its distance from 0 on a number line. KY Grade 6 (p. 572)

Check Skills

Use each equation to make a function table with at least 4 ordered pairs. Then graph the ordered pairs on a coordinate grid. KY MA-05-3.3.1 (p. 562)

4. $y = x - 4$
5. $t = 2s - 1$
6. $c = 3b + 1$
7. $y = 8 - x$

Write the opposite of each integer. KY Grade 6 (p. 572)

8. $^{+}5$
9. $^{+}33$
10. $^{-}1$
11. $^{-}9$
12. $^{+}300$

Compare. Write <, >, or = for each ●. KY Grade 6 (p. 576)

13. $^{-}8$ ● $^{+}6$
14. $^{-}3$ ● $^{-}5$
15. $^{+}2$ ● $^{-}4$
16. $^{-}12$ ● 0
17. $^{+}3$ ● $^{-}9$

For 18–22, graph and label the ordered pairs on a coordinate plane. KY Grade 6 (p. 578)

18. $A(^{-}2,^{+}3)$
19. $B(^{-}5,0)$
20. $C(^{+}4,^{-}1)$
21. $D(^{-}3,^{-}1)$
22. $E(^{-}4,^{+}5)$

Check Problem Solving

For 23–24, use the graph. KY MA-05-3.3.1 (p. 562)

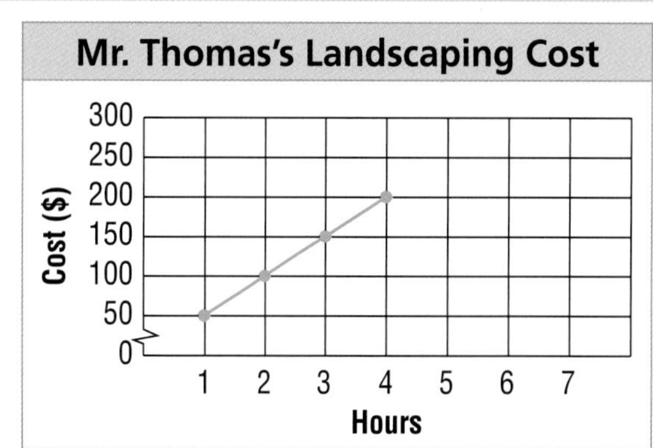

23. Mr. Thomas is a landscaper. The graph shows the amount he charges hourly for labor on each job. What is the labor cost for a job that takes 6 hours?
24. Mr. Thomas charged Mrs. Cho for 1 hour of labor plus the cost of 6 bags of mulch. If each bag of mulch costs \$4, what was Mrs. Cho's total bill?

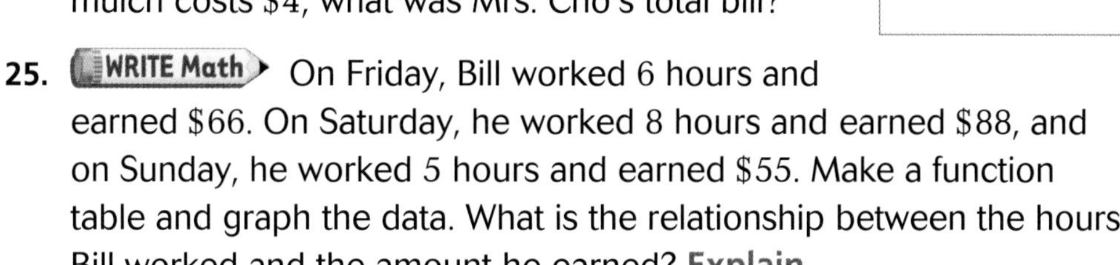

25. WRITE Math On Friday, Bill worked 6 hours and earned \$66. On Saturday, he worked 8 hours and earned \$88, and on Sunday, he worked 5 hours and earned \$55. Make a function table and graph the data. What is the relationship between the hours Bill worked and the amount he earned? **Explain.**

GO ONLINE **Technology** Use *Online Assessment.*

Unit Review/Test
Chapters 18–21

Multiple Choice

1. Which of the following best describes the figure below? KY MA-05-3.1.1 (p. 482)

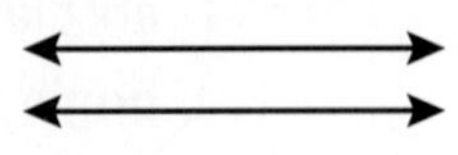

A. acute angles

B. right angles

C. parallel lines

D. perpendicular lines

2. What is the unknown angle measure for the quadrilateral below?
KY MA-05-3.1.1 (p. 518)

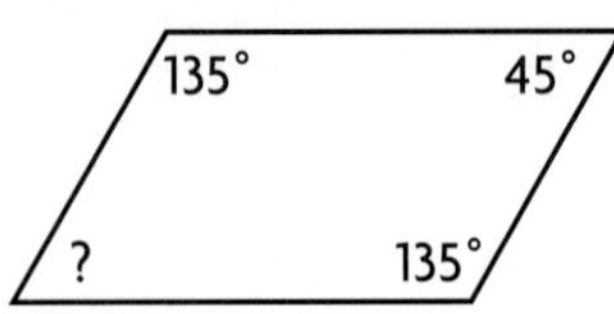

A. 45°   C. 180°

B. 75°   D. 270°

3. Which line segment is a diameter of the circle? KY MA-05-3.1.1 (p. 496)

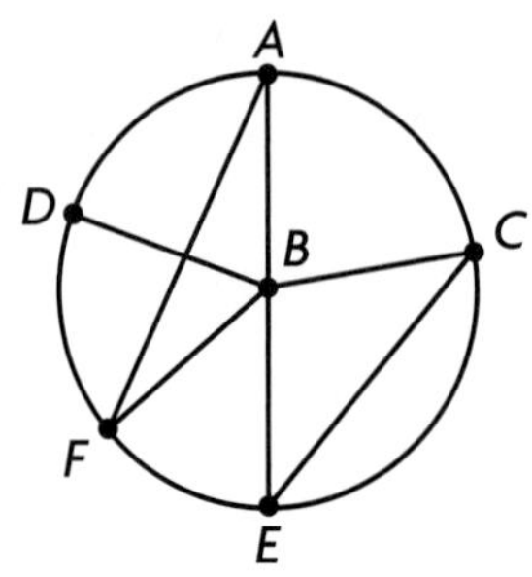

A. $\overline{FA}$ C. $\overline{DC}$

B. $\overline{AE}$ D. $\overline{EB}$

4. Which figure below has 6 vertices?
KY MA-05-3.1.1 (p. 524)

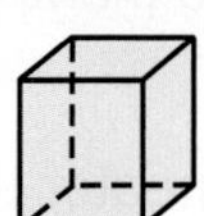
Figure *L*

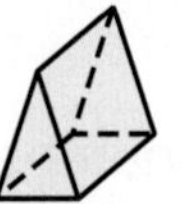
Figure *M*

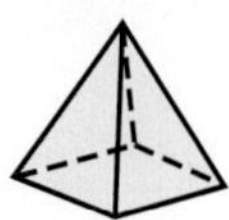
Figure *P*

Figure *Q*

A. Figure *L*   C. Figure *P*

B. Figure *M*   D. Figure *Q*

5. Which figure always has parallel sides?
KY MA-05-3.1.1 (p. 518)

A. Triangle   C. Pentagon

B. Quadrilateral   D. Rhombus

6. Which statement about the triangles shown below is **NOT** true? KY MA-05-3.1.5 (p. 500)

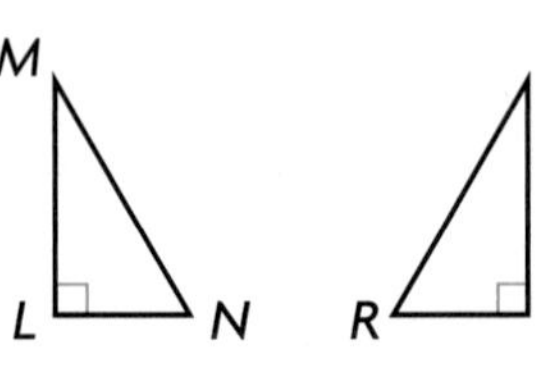

$\Delta LMN \cong \Delta TSR$

A. $\overline{LM} \cong \overline{RT}$ C. $\angle M \cong \angle S$

B. $\overline{MN} \cong \overline{SR}$ D. $\angle L \cong \angle T$

Technology Use *Online Assessment.*

7. Which of the following is a prime number?
KY MA-05-1.5.1 (p. 284)

A. 18

B. 19

C. 20

D. 21

8. $\frac{2}{7} + \frac{3}{7} = \blacksquare$
Write the answer in simplest form.
KY MA-05-1.3.1 (p. 342)

A. $\frac{6}{7}$

B. $\frac{5}{7}$

C. $\frac{6}{49}$

D. $\frac{5}{49}$

9. How many outcomes are possible if Sawyer tosses the coin and spins the pointer on the spinner below?
KY MA-05-4.4.1 (p. 456)

A. 5

B. 8

C. 10

D. 14

Open Response WRITE Math

10. Write a rule for the pattern. What might the next figure in the pattern be? **Explain.**
KY MA-05-5.1.1 (p. 548)

  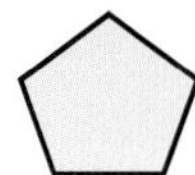 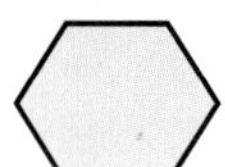

11. Draw an equilateral triangle. Explain how to use a protractor to measure the angles.
KY MA-05-3.1.1 (p. 486)

12. What transformation is represented in the diagram? **Explain** how you know.
KY MA-05-3.1.3 (p. 542)

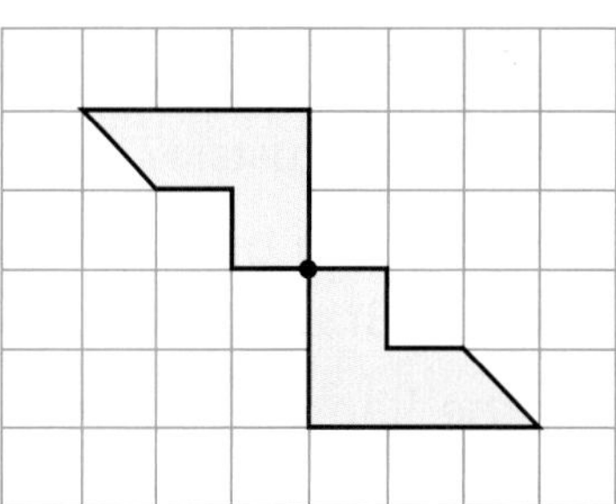

13. Write an equation for the relationship shown in the table. Graph the equation.

x	3	4	5	6	10
y	5	6	7	8	$\blacksquare$

What is y when $x = 10$? **Explain.**
KY MA-05-3.3.1 (p. 564)

THE WORLD ALMANAC FOR KIDS

Flags of the World

The Geometry of Flags

Every nation has its own unique flag. Most flags are made up of different colors, shapes, lines, and angles. Many flags use only the colors red, white, and blue. Some use rectangular bars of these colors. Some use stars and stripes, like the United States flag.

FACT·ACTIVITY

Use the pictures of the flags to answer.

1. How many rectangles can you find in the flag of Austria?
2. What kind of quadrilateral is the yellow shape in Brazil's flag?
3. For the flag of Laos, use *w* for the width of the blue stripe and *d* for the diameter of the circle. Write a number sentence comparing *d* and *w,* using <, >, or =.
4. How many acute angles are in the Czech Republic flag?
5. A student says she can draw only one line of symmetry on the flag of Laos. Is she correct?
6. WRITE Math Describe the Jamaican flag, using geometric terms and concepts.

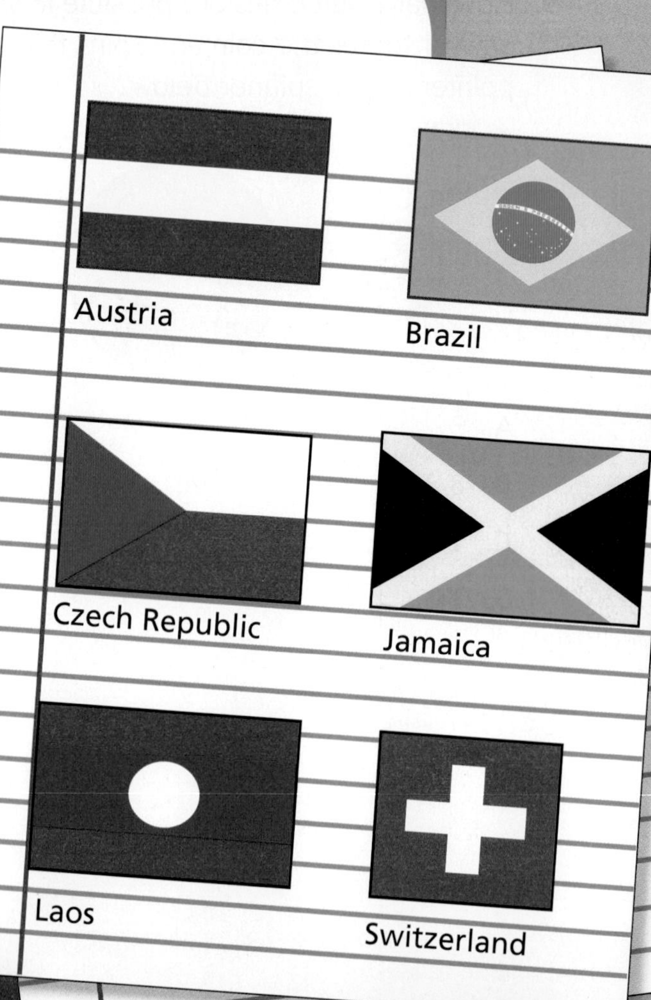

Flying in front of the United Nations building in New York City are flags of the 191 member countries.

Flag Shapes and Sizes

Flag designs can be simple or complex. Libya's flag is just one solid color. There is a picture of an eagle on the flag of American Samoa. The flag of the British Indian Ocean Territories contains the flag of Britain in the upper left corner. Most flags are rectangles, but Nepal has a different shape for its flag.

Libya

American Samoa

British Indian Ocean Territories

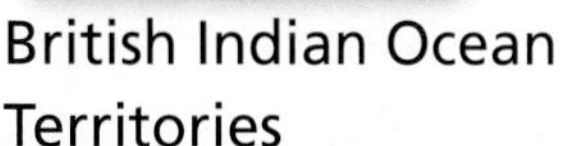

Nepal

FACT·ACTIVITY

Label a coordinate plane like the one at the right.

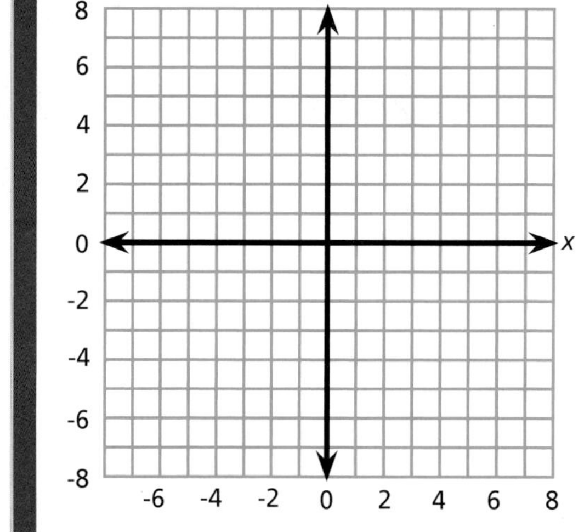

1. Use the directions below to make a flag. Then name the country whose flag has this shape and design.
   - Plot the following points and connect them in order: (5,5), (5,−5), (−5,−5), (−5,5), and back to (5,5).
   - Now plot the following points, and connect them in order: (1,3), (1,1), (3,1), (3,−1), (1,−1), (1,−3), (−1,−3), (−1,−1), (−3,−1), (−3,1), (−1,1), (−1,3), and back to (1,3).
2. Design a flag on the coordinate plane, using polygons. Name the polygons.
   - How many acute, obtuse, and right angles are in your flag?
   - Are there any congruent figures in your flag?
   - Is your flag symmetrical?
3. Using ordered pairs, write directions for drawing your flag. See if a classmate can draw your flag by using your directions.

UNIT 8

Measurement

Math on Location

with
Chapter Projects

1
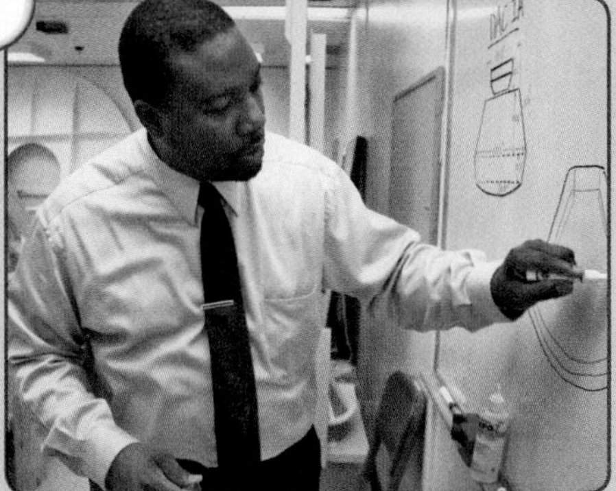

Dimensions, weight, and capacity are critical for the design of a space capsule.

2
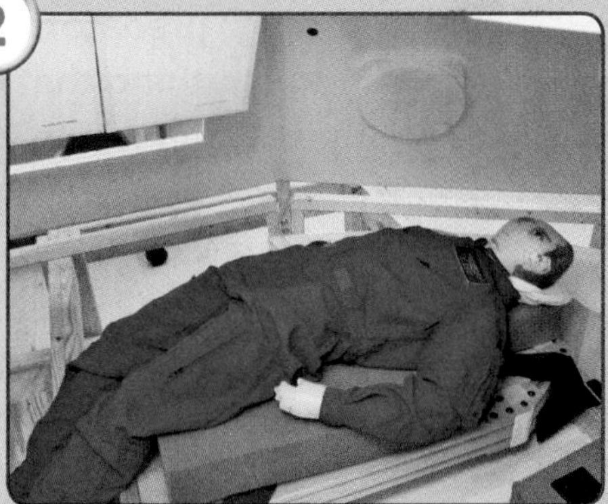

A life-size model of a human is placed in the model of the capsule to judge how much space is necessary.

3

This rendering shows 2- and 3-dimensional shapes in one possible Orion Space Capsule design.

VOCABULARY POWER

TALK Math

What math is used in the **Math on Location**? What types of measurements would you need to build a life-sized model for a space capsule?

READ Math

REVIEW VOCABULARY You learned the words below when you learned about measurement. How do these words relate to **Math on Location**?

capacity the amount a container can hold when filled

formula a set of symbols that expresses a mathematical rule

area the number of square units needed to cover a surface

WRITE Math

Copy and complete word association trees like the ones below. Use what you know about measurement units and formulas to identify what type of measurement is described.

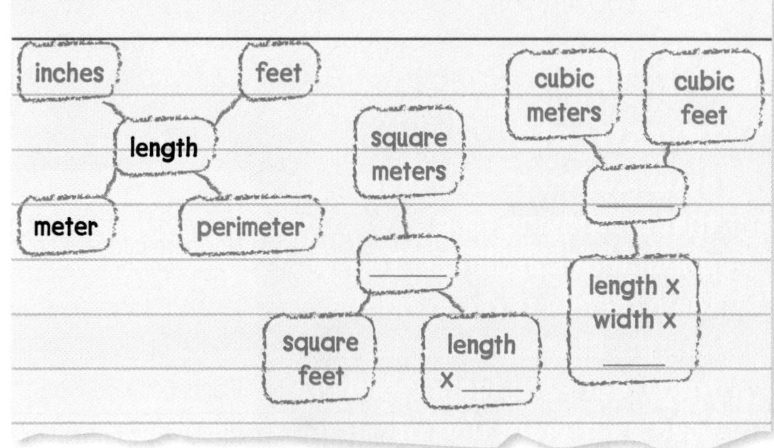

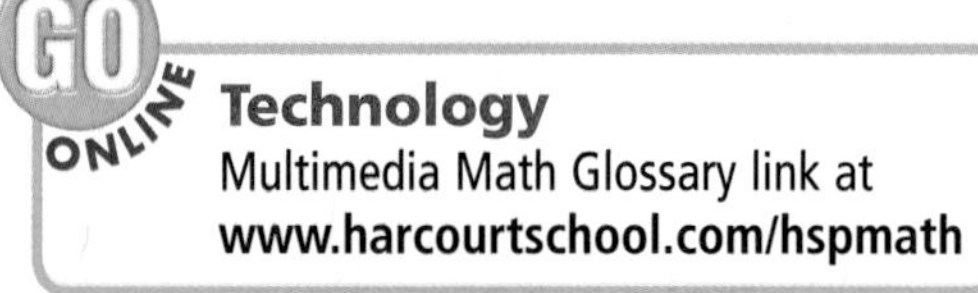

Technology
Multimedia Math Glossary link at
www.harcourtschool.com/hspmath

CHAPTER 22

Customary and Metric Measurements

FAST FACT

Green frogs are "sit and wait" predators, eating anything that comes within reach. They are carnivores that eat a variety of prey including flies, snails, spiders, moths, and even small snakes.

Investigate

Suppose you're on a team that is studying frog populations in Illinois. The team members recorded the lengths of several species of frogs, but each team member used a different unit of measure. Choose any three frogs. Order their lengths from greatest to least.

Frog Lengths

Frog	Length
Northern Leopard Frog	60 mm
Green Frog	0.72 dm
Pickerel Frog	0.065 m
Plains Leopard Frog	5.4 cm
Strecker's Chorus Frog	37 mm
American Bullfrog	0.12 m
Spring Peeper	2.5 cm

GO ONLINE **Technology** Student pages are available in the Student eBook.

Show What You Know

Check your understanding of important skills needed for success in Chapter 22.

▶ Customary Tools

Choose the tool you would use to measure each.

1. the weight of a bag of oranges
2. the length of a desk
3. the amount of milk needed to make pancake batter
4. the height of a box

A 

B 

C 

▶ Metric Tools

Choose the tool you would use to measure each.

5. the temperature of a classroom
6. the mass of a box of salt
7. the length of a room
8. the width of a door

D 

E 

F

VOCABULARY POWER

CHAPTER VOCABULARY

capacity
Celsius (°C)
centimeter (cm)
elapsed time
Fahrenheit (°F)
foot (ft)
inch (in.)
kilometer (km)
meter (m)
mile (mi)
millimeter (mm)
ounce (oz)
pound (lb)
precision
ton (T)
yard (yd)

WARM-UP WORDS

inch (in.) a customary unit for measuring length or distance; 12 inches = 1 foot

meter (m) a metric unit for measuring length or distance; 1 meter = 100 centimeters

precision a property of measurement that is related to the unit of measure used; the smaller the unit of measure used, the more precise the measurement is

LESSON 1 HANDS ON

Customary Length

OBJECTIVE: Estimate and measure using appropriate customary units and determine which measurement is more precise.

Quick Review

1. 2 × 12
2. 60 ÷ 5
3. 84 ÷ 3
4. 1,760 × 2
5. 25 × 3

Vocabulary

precision

Investigate

Materials ■ ruler ■ yardstick ■ classroom objects to measure

An inch (in.) is about the length of a paper clip.	A foot (ft) is about the length of a piece of notebook paper.	A yard (yd) is about the length of a baseball bat.	A mile (mi) is about how far you can walk in 20 minutes.

You can use *customary units*, such as inches, feet, or yards, to measure length.

	Estimate	Measurement
book		
width of door		
desk to wall		

Customary Units of Length
1 foot (ft) = 12 inches (in.)
1 yard (yd) = 3 feet
1 mile (mi) = 5,280 feet
1 mile (mi) = 1,760 yards

A Choose three different objects or distances in your classroom to measure.

B Make a table to record your estimated lengths and your actual measurements.

C Choose an appropriate customary unit for measuring each length. Estimate the length of each object or distance and record your estimates.

D Choose an appropriate tool for measuring each object or distance. Measure and record the lengths.

Draw Conclusions

1. How did you decide which measurement tool to choose to measure each object or distance?
2. Compare the units you used with those your classmates used. What can you conclude? Explain.
3. **Analysis** Which customary unit is best to measure the distance from your home to your school? Explain.

FAST TRACK

KY MA-05-2.1.6 Students will estimate weight, length, perimeter, area, angle measures and time using appropriate units of measurement. DOK 2 *also MA-05-2.1.3; MA-05-2.2.2*

Connect

The **precision** of a measurement is related to the unit of measure you choose. The smaller the unit, the more precise the measurement will be. For example, inches are more precise than feet. Quarter inches are more precise than half inches.

Measured to the nearest $\frac{1}{4}$ inch, the pencil is about $4\frac{3}{4}$ inches long.
Measured to the nearest $\frac{1}{8}$ inch, the pencil is about $4\frac{5}{8}$ inches long.
Measured to the nearest $\frac{1}{16}$ inch, the pencil is $4\frac{11}{16}$ inches long.
So, the most precise measurement for the pencil is $4\frac{11}{16}$ inches.

TALK Math

Explain why measuring the pencil to the nearest $\frac{1}{16}$ inch is more precise than measuring it to the nearest $\frac{1}{8}$ inch.

Practice

Estimate the length of the crayon. Then measure the length

1. to the nearest $\frac{1}{2}$ inch
2. to the nearest $\frac{1}{4}$ inch
3. to the nearest $\frac{1}{8}$ inch
4. to the nearest $\frac{1}{16}$ inch
5. In Exercises 1–4, which measurement is most precise? **Explain.**

Tell which measurement is more precise.

6. $2\frac{3}{4}$ inches or $2\frac{7}{8}$ inches
7. 2 feet or $22\frac{1}{4}$ inches
8. $8\frac{1}{4}$ inches or $8\frac{1}{2}$ inches
9. $8\frac{3}{4}$ feet or 3 yards
10. $5\frac{1}{4}$ inches or $5\frac{3}{8}$ inches
11. $11\frac{3}{4}$ inches or 1 foot

Estimate the length in inches. Then measure to the nearest $\frac{1}{16}$ inch.

12.

13.

14. **WRITE Math** **Explain** how you would measure the length of your math book to the nearest $\frac{1}{16}$ inch.

Technology
Use Harcourt Mega Math, Ice Station Exploration, *Linear Lab,* Levels C, D, E, F, G.

LESSON 2 HANDS ON

Metric Length

OBJECTIVE: Estimate and measure using appropriate metric units and determine which measurement is more precise.

Quick Review

1. 6×100
2. 58×100
3. 400×100
4. 730×10
5. $3{,}000 \times 10$

Vocabulary

millimeter (mm)
meter (m)
centimeter (cm)
kilometer (km)
decimeter (dm)

Investigate

Materials ■ metric ruler ■ meterstick ■ classroom objects to measure

A **millimeter (mm)** is about the thickness of a dime.	A **centimeter (cm)** is about the width of a crayon.	A **decimeter (dm)** is about the width of an adult's hand.	A **meter (m)** is about the width of a door.	A **kilometer (km)** is about how far you can walk in 10 minutes.

A Choose three different objects or distances in your classroom to measure.

B Make a table to record your estimated lengths and your actual measurements.

C Choose an appropriate metric unit for measuring each length. Estimate the length of each object or distance and record your estimates.

D Choose an appropriate tool for measuring each object or distance. Measure and record the lengths.

Metric Units of Length
1 centimeter (cm) = 10 millimeters (mm)
1 decimeter (dm) = 10 centimeters (cm)
1 meter (m) = 100 centimeters
1 kilometer (km) = 1,000 meters

	Estimate	Measurement
book		
desk		
desk to door		

Draw Conclusions

1. Which unit did you choose to measure the length of each object or distance? Explain your choice.
2. Compare the units you used with those your classmates used. What can you conclude? Explain.
3. **Application** Would you use kilometers to measure any lengths in your classroom? Explain.

FAST TRACK

KY MA-05-2.1.6 Students will estimate weight, length, perimeter, area, angle measures and time using appropriate units of measurement. DOK 2 *also MA-05-2.1.3; MA-05-2.2.2*

Connect

The smaller the unit, the more precise the measurement will be. When you measure to the nearest millimeter, the measurement is more precise than when you measure to the nearest centimeter.

Measured to the nearest centimeter, the yarn is about 8 centimeters long.

Measured to the nearest millimeter, the yarn is about 78 millimeters long.

So, the more precise measurement for the length of the yarn is 78 millimeters.

TALK Math

Explain how the number of millimeters in this problem is related to the number of centimeters.

Practice

Estimate the length of the eraser in centimeters. Then measure the length

1. to the nearest centimeter.
2. to the nearest millimeter.

Write the appropriate metric unit for measuring each.

3. height of a flagpole
4. thickness of a CD case
5. distance from Boston to Dallas

Estimate and measure each.

6. 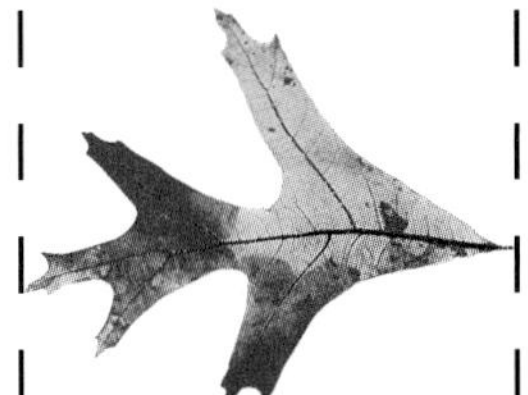

7. 

8. 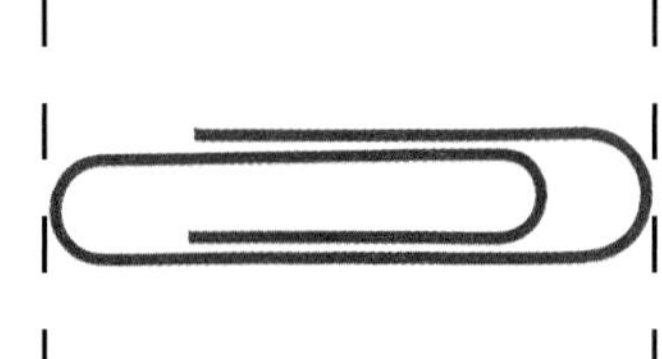

9. **WRITE Math** **Explain** which unit would be the most appropriate for measuring the width of a postage stamp: millimeter, centimeter, meter, or kilometer.

LESSON 3

Change Linear Units

OBJECTIVE: Identify and convert linear units of measurement.

Quick Review

1. 12 × 4
2. 350 × 10
3. 80 × 100
4. 5,280 ÷ 3
5. 6,200 ÷ 10

Learn

PROBLEM Matt needs 36 feet of chain for a swing set. The chain is sold by the yard. How many yards of chain does he need?

Example 1 Change customary units of length.

A To change smaller units to larger units, divide.

number of ft	÷	number of ft in 1 yd	=	total number of yd
↓		↓		↓
36	÷	3	=	12

So, Matt needs 12 yards of chain.

B How many inches are in 7 feet?

To change larger units to smaller units, multiply.

number of ft	×	number of in. in 1 ft	=	total number of in.
↓		↓		↓
7	×	12	=	84

Customary Units of Length
1 foot (ft) = 12 inches (in.)
1 yard (yd) = 3 feet
1 mile (mi) = 5,280 feet
1 mile = 1,760 yards

You can use multiplication and division to change metric units of length.

Example 2 Change metric units of length.

C How many meters are in 400 centimeters?

number of cm	÷	number of cm in 1 m	=	total number of m
↓		↓		↓
400	÷	100	=	4

D How many millimeters are in 12 centimeters?

number of cm	×	number of mm in 1 cm	=	total number of mm
↓		↓		↓
12	×	10	=	120

Metric Units of Length
1 centimeter (cm) = 10 millimeters (mm)
1 decimeter (dm) = 10 centimeters (cm)
1 meter (m) = 100 centimeters
1 kilometer (km) = 1,000 meters

FAST TRACK

KY MA-05-2.2.3 Students will convert units within the same measurement system [U.S. customary (inches, feet, yards, miles; ounces, pounds, tons), metric (millimeters, centimeters, meters, kilometers; grams, kilograms), money, or time] and use the units to solve problems. DOK 2 *also MA-05-2.1.3*

Add and Subtract Measurements

You may need to change units to add and subtract measurements.

Example 3 Add measurements.

Matt needs to glue two pieces of wood together. The first piece is 2 feet 8 inches wide. The second piece is 1 foot 9 inches wide. How wide will the glued piece of wood be?

Find 2 ft 8 in. + 1 ft 9 in.

Step 1	Step 2	Step 3
Add like units. 2 ft 8 in. + 1 ft 9 in. 3 ft 17 in.	Think: 12 in. = 1 ft Since 17 in. is more than 1 ft, rename 17 in. as 1 ft + 5 in. 3 ft 17 in. = 3 ft + (1 ft + 5 in.)	Combine like units. 3 ft + (1 ft + 5 in.) = (3 ft + 1 ft) + 5 in. = 4 ft 5 in.

So, the glued piece of wood will be 4 feet 5 inches wide.

Example 4 Subtract measurements.

Find 5 ft 6 in. − 2 ft 4 in.

Think: Subtract like units.

```
  5 ft 6 in.
− 2 ft 4 in.
  3 ft 2 in.
```

- **What if** you subtracted 3 feet? Explain.

Guided Practice

1. 14 ft = ■ in.
   Think: I am changing from a larger unit to a smaller unit, so I multiply.

2. 160 mm = ■ cm
   Think: I am changing from a smaller unit to a larger unit, so I divide.

Change the unit.

3. 7 yd = ■ ft
4. 6 ft = ■ in.
5. 3,520 yd = ■ mi
6. 45 ft = ■ yd
7. 9 cm = ■ mm
8. 50 dm = ■ cm
9. 4,600 m = ■ km
10. ✓ 800 cm = ■ m

Find the sum or difference.

11. 5 ft 2 in. + 3 ft 7 in.
12. 8 yd 2 ft − 6 yd 1 ft
13. 4 ft 10 in. + 2 ft 3 in.
14. ✓ 5 ft 3 in. − 2 ft 7 in.

15. TALK Math **Explain** how to change 3.8 meters to millimeters.

Independent Practice and Problem Solving

Change the unit.

16. 48 in. = ■ ft **17.** 12 yd = ■ ft **18.** 3 mi = ■ ft **19.** 42 ft = ■ yd

20. 6 mi = ■ yd **21.** 9 ft = ■ in. **22.** 5,000 m = ■ km **23.** 18 m = ■ dm

24. 46 cm = ■ mm **25.** 300 cm = ■ dm **26.** 41 km = ■ m **27.** 520 mm = ■ cm

Find the sum or difference.

28. 6 ft 9 in. + 5 ft 3 in.

29. 9 yd 2 ft − 6 yd 2 ft

30. 3 ft 8 in. + 4 ft 6 in.

31. 6 ft 7 in. − 2 ft 3 in.

32. 4.2 km + 9.6 km **33.** 720 mm − 48 cm **34.** 81 cm + 55 cm **35.** 137 mm − 45 mm

Algebra **Find the missing measurement.**

36. 5 in. + ■ = 1 ft **37.** 13 ft + ■ = 5 yd **38.** 47 cm + ■ = 1 m **39.** 25 mm + ■ = 4 cm

USE DATA **For 40–42, use the table.**

40. How many feet higher is Mt. Whitney than Mt. Olympus? How many meters higher?

41. About how many kilometers high is Mt. McKinley?

42. About how many miles high is Mt. Hood?

43. **Reasoning** Is 80 cm the same as 0.8 m? **Explain** why or why not.

44. WRITE Math **Sense or Nonsense** Karen says that she lives 2.3 km, or 230 meters, from the school. Does Karen's statement make sense? **Explain.**

Mountains of the United States

Mountain	Height in feet	Height in meters
McKinley	20,320	6,194
Whitney	14,494	4,418
Hood	11,239	3,426
Olympus	7,965	2,428

Mixed Review and Test Prep

45. The low temperatures for the last four days were 4°F, $^{-}2$°F, $^{-}9$°F, and 0°F. Order the temperatures from least to greatest. (p. 572)

46. **Test Prep** There are 27 feet of one kind of fabric left for sale. How many inches of the fabric are there?

A 2.7 in. **C** 9 in.

B 270 in. **D** 324 in.

47. The equation $d = 8h$ shows the amount in dollars, d, Kevin earns in h hours. How much does Kevin earn for 15 hours of work? (p. 108)

48. **Test Prep** Mark ran 0.545 kilometers. How many meters did he run?

A 54 m **C** 545 m

B 54.5 m **D** 5,450 m

 Extra Practice on page 614, Set A

Pose a Problem

Different problems can be posed using a given set of data. To do this, you may want to change the units in the data. Ms. Thomas asked her class to use the data in the table to write a problem that involved the lengths of the swing sets.

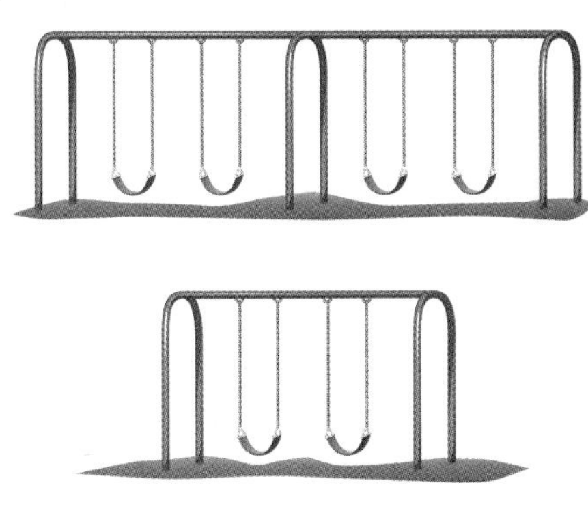

Swing Sets		
Size	Length (ft)	Width (ft)
Large A	27	24
Large B	21	30
Medium A	21	25
Medium B	12	24
Small A	20	21
Small B	17	23

First, I wrote this problem about the data. "In his backyard Mr. Torres has a space that is 7 yd long and 8 yd wide for a swing set. Which swing sets can fit in the space in his backyard?"

Size	Length	Width
Large A	9 yd	8 yd
Large B	7 yd	10 yd
Medium A	7 yd	8 yd 1 ft
Medium B	4 yd	8 yd
Small A	6 yd 2 ft	7 yd
Small B	5 yd 2 ft	7 yd 2 ft

Then, I converted the lengths of the swing sets to yards so that I can better compare the given lengths to an exact space described in my problem.

Solution: Mr. Torres can use the Medium B, the Small A, or the Small B swing set.

Tips

To pose a problem:

- Understand what your problem will be about.
- Study the data.
- Complete all the computations needed to solve the problem.
- Solve the problem to check that you have written it so that others can solve it.

Problem Solving **Pose a problem using the swing-set data in the following ways.**

1. Convert the length and width of one swing set from feet to inches.
2. Compare the lengths, in inches, of the two swing sets in the large, medium, or small group.

LESSON 4

Customary Capacity and Weight

OBJECTIVE: Convert customary capacity and weight units.

Quick Review

1. 8 × 5
2. 4 × 12
3. 4 × 25
4. 8 × 20
5. 16 × 5

Learn

PROBLEM Shelby is baking one dozen loaves of banana bread for a bake sale. She needs 1 cup of yogurt for each loaf. She has 2 quarts of yogurt. How many pints of yogurt does she need to buy to have enough to bake a dozen loaves?

Customary Units of Capacity
1 cup (c) = 8 fluid ounces (fl oz)
1 pint (pt) = 2 cups
1 quart (qt) = 2 pints
1 quart (qt) = 4 cups
$\frac{1}{2}$ gallon (gal) = 2 quarts
1 gallon (gal) = 4 quarts

cup (c) pint (pt) quart (qt) gallon (gal)

Example 1 Change customary units of capacity.

Step 1

Find the number of cups in 2 quarts.

Think: 2 quarts = ■ cups

To change larger units to smaller units, multiply:

number of quarts	×	number of cups in 1 quart	=	total cups
↓		↓		↓
2	×	4	=	8

Shelby has 8 cups of yogurt.

Step 2

Find how many cups of yogurt Shelby needs to buy.

Shelby needs 12 cups of yogurt. She has 8 cups.

12 − 8 = 4

Shelby needs to buy 4 cups of yogurt.

Step 3

Find how many pints are in 4 cups.

Think: 4 cups = ■ pints

To change smaller units to larger units, divide.

number of cups	÷	number of cups in 1 pint	=	total pints
↓		↓		↓
4	÷	2	=	2

So, Shelby needs to buy 2 more pints of yogurt.

- Shelby decides to double the number of loaves. What is the total number of pints of yogurt she will need? **Explain.**

FAST TRACK

KY MA-05-2.2.3 Students will convert units within the same measurement system [U.S. customary (inches, feet, yards, miles; ounces, pounds, tons), metric (millimeters, centimeters, meters, kilometers; grams, kilograms), money, or time] and use the units to solve problems. DOK 2 *also* MA-05-2.1.1; *MA-05-2.1.2; MA-05-2.1.4; MA-05-2.2.*

Customary Weight

Changing customary units of weight is similar to changing customary units of capacity.

Example 2 Change customary units of weight.

Steve is making 16 packets of trail mix. If he fills each packet with 3 ounces of mix, how many pounds of trail mix will he use in all?

Customary Units of Weight
1 pound (lb) = 16 ounces (oz)
1 ton (T) = 2,000 pounds

Step 1

Find how many ounces of trail mix are in 16 packets.

Think: 16 packets = ■ ounces of trail mix

number of packets	×	number of ounces in 1 packet	=	total ounces
↓		↓		↓
16	×	3	=	48

Step 2

Find the number of pounds in 48 ounces. When you convert from smaller units to larger units, divide.

Think: 48 oz = ■ lb

number of ounces	÷	number of ounces in 1 pound	=	number of pounds
↓		↓		↓
48	÷	16	=	3

A slice of bread weighs about 1 ounce.

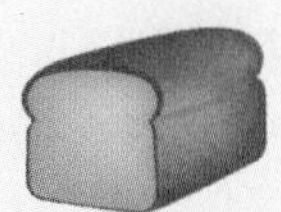

A loaf of bread weighs about 1 pound.

A compact car weighs about 1 ton.

So, Steve will use 3 pounds of trail mix.

Multiply to convert larger units of weight to smaller units of weight.

Example 3

Ross had 36 ounces of raisins. He used 2 pounds of raisins to make carrot muffins. How many ounces of raisins does Ross have left?

Step 1

Find the number of ounces in 2 pounds.

Think: 2 lb = ■ oz

number of pounds	×	number of ounces in 1 pound	=	number of ounces
↓		↓		↓
2	×	16	=	32

Step 2

Subtract.

36 oz − 32 oz = 4 oz

So, Ross has 4 ounces of raisins left.

Guided Practice

1. 12 cups = ■ quarts

   Think: I am changing from a smaller unit to a larger unit, so I divide.

2. 4 pounds = ■ ounces

   Think: I am changing from a larger unit to a smaller unit, so I multiply.

Change the unit.

3. 8 pt = ■ qt
4. 6,000 lb = ■ T
5. 3 c = ■ fl oz
6. 6 pt = ■ c
7. 32 oz = ■ lb
8. 12 qt = ■ gal
9. $2\frac{1}{2}$ lb = ■ oz
10. 8 c = ■ qt
11. TALK Math **Explain** how to change 4 gallons to quarts.

Independent Practice and Problem Solving

Change the unit.

12. 8 lb = ■ oz
13. 36 qt = ■ gal
14. 7 pt = ■ c
15. 5 gal = ■ qt
16. 40 fl oz = ■ c
17. 4 T = ■ lb
18. 80 oz = ■ lb
19. 2 gal = ■ pt
20. 3 pt = ■ fl oz
21. 12 qt = ■ pt
22. 32 c = ■ qt
23. $1\frac{1}{2}$ T = ■ lb

Find the sum or difference.

24. 3 lb 9 oz + 4 lb 12 oz
25. 1 gal 3 qt + 2 gal 2 qt
26. 7 lb 15 oz − 5 lb 12 oz
27. 3 qt 3 c + 1 qt 2 c

Algebra Find the missing measurement.

28. 2 pt + ■ pt = 1 gal
29. 30 oz + ■ oz = 3 lb
30. 20 fl oz + ■ fl oz = 1 qt

USE DATA For 31–32, use the list.

Baking Items
1 gal applesauce
2 lb walnuts
4 fl oz lemon juice
1 pt blueberries
3 qt milk

31. Tom and Angela are baking muffins. They need $\frac{1}{2}$ cup of lemon juice to make lemon blueberry muffins. Do Tom and Angela have enough lemon juice? **Explain.**
32. Tom and Angela use 8 ounces of walnuts in their muffins. How many ounces of walnuts do Tom and Angela have left?
33. **Reasoning** Mark needs to make 3 gallons of fruit punch for a party. He uses 6 quarts orange juice, 3 quarts cranberry juice, 2 quarts apple juice, and 1 quart grape juice. Will he have enough punch? **Explain.**
34. WRITE Math **What's the Error?** Judy added 2 quarts of water to 2 pints of juice concentrate. She says she ended up with 1 gallon of juice. Describe and correct her error.

Extra Practice on page 614, Set B

Learn About Mixed Measures

Mixed measures use more than one unit of measurement. You can convert mixed measures to a single unit of measurement.

Jordan has 2 gallons and 3 quarts of paint. She plans to mix the paint and put it into pint containers for her art classes. How many pints of paint can she make?

Step 1	Step 2
Change gallons to quarts.	Change quarts to pints.
Think: 1 gal = 4 qt	Think: 1 qt = 2 pt
$2 \times 4 = 8$ quarts	$11 \times 2 = 22$ pints
$8 + 3 = 11$ quarts in all	2 gal 3 qt = 22 pt

So, Jordan can make 22 pints of paint.

Try It

Change the units.

35. 2 pt 5 fl oz = ■ fl oz

36. 1 T 250 lb = ■ lb

37. 3 lb 12 oz = ■ oz

38. 1 lb 6 oz = ■ oz

39. 5 pt 1 c = ■ fl oz

40. 6 qt 1 c = ■ fl oz

41. 4 lb 7 oz = ■ oz

42. 2 gal 2 qt = ■ c

43. 4 gal 1 pt = ■ pt

Mixed Review and Test Prep

44. Joel used a triangular prism in a science experiment about light. How many faces does the prism have? (p. 524)

45. A piece of string is 5 feet 6 inches long. Grace cuts 3 feet off the string. How many inches of string are left? (p. 596)

46. **Test Prep** Miguel uses 3 ounces of cheese in each casserole he makes. How many pounds of cheese does he need to make 32 casseroles? **Explain.**

47. **Test Prep** Derrick made 8 quarts of lemonade for a picnic. How many cups of lemonade did he make?

A 4 **C** 32

B 16 **D** 64

LESSON 5

Metric Capacity and Mass

OBJECTIVE: Convert metric capacity and mass units.

Quick Review

1. 250 × 4
2. 1,000 × 3
3. 1,000 ÷ 2
4. 1,000 ÷ 4
5. 1,000 ÷ 10

Learn

PROBLEM Kelly and his family need to take water on their camping trip. Their water bottles each hold 1,000 milliliters. If they take enough water to fill their water bottles 30 times, how many liters of water will Kelly's family need to take?

Metric Units of Capacity
1 liter (L) = 1,000 milliliters (mL)
1 kiloliter (kL) = 1,000 liters

1 mL

1 L

Example 1 Change milliliters to liters.

Each bottle holds 1,000 milliliters of water.
The family needs enough water to fill 30 bottles.

30 × 1,000 = 30,000

The family needs 30,000 milliliters of water.

Find the number of liters in 30,000 milliliters.

Think: 30,000 milliliters = ■ liters

number of milliliters	÷	number of milliliters in 1 liter	=	number of liters
↓		↓		↓
30,000	÷	1,000	=	30

So, Kelly's family needs to take 30 liters of water.

Remember
To change smaller units to larger units, divide. To change larger units to smaller units, multiply.

Example 2 Change liters to milliliters.

How many milliliters are in 6 liters?

Think: 3 liters = ■ milliliters

number of liters	×	number of milliliters in 1 liter	=	number of milliliters
↓		↓		↓
6	×	1,000	=	6,000

So, there are 6,000 milliliters in 6 liters.

KY MA-05-2.2.3 Students will convert units within the same measurement system [U.S. customary (inches, feet yards, miles; ounces, pounds, tons), metric (millimeters, centimeters, meters, kilometers; grams, kilograms), money, or time] and use the units to solve problems. DOK 2 *also* MA-05-2.1.1; *MA-05-2.1.2; MA-05-2.1.4*

Metric Units of Mass

Changing metric units of mass is similar to changing metric units of capacity.

Metric Units of Mass
1 gram (g) = 1,000 milligrams (mg)
1 kilogram (kg) = 1,000 grams

Example 3 Change kilograms to grams.

Kelly's father bought 2 kilograms of trail mix. He needs to know how many grams of trail mix he has so he can divide it equally among the family members.

Find how many grams are in 2 kilograms.

Think: 2 kg = ▪ g

number of kilograms	×	number of grams in 1 kilogram	=	number of grams
↓		↓		↓
2	×	1,000	=	2,000

So, there are 2,000 grams in 2 kilograms.

- If there are 4 members in Kelly's family, how many grams of trail mix will each member get?

Example 4 Change milligrams to grams.

How many grams are in 12,000 milligrams?

Think: 12,000 mg = ▪ g

number of milligrams	÷	number of milligrams in 1 gram	=	number of grams
↓		↓		↓
12,000	÷	1,000	=	12

So, there are 12 grams in 12,000 milligrams.

Guided Practice

1. 6,000 milliliters = ▪ liters
   Think: you are changing from smaller units to larger units, so divide.
2. 7 grams = ▪ milligrams
   Think: you are changing from larger units to smaller units, so multiply.

Change the unit.

3. 6 kL = ▪ L
4. 7,000 mL = ▪ L
5. 3 kg = ▪ g
6. 2 L = ▪ mL
7. 2,000 g = ▪ kg
8. 4,000 mL = ▪ L
9. 4,000 L = ▪ kL
10. ✓ 10 g = ▪ mg
11. ✓ 9,000 g = ▪ kg
12. TALK Math **Explain** how to change 62,000 milliliters to liters.

Independent Practice and Problem Solving

Change the unit.

13. 3 L = ■ mL
14. 7,000 mg = ■ g
15. 25 kg = ■ g
16. 16,000 mL = ■ L
17. 9,000 L = ■ kL
18. 3 kL = ■ L
19. 12,000 mg = ■ g
20. 9 g = ■ mg
21. 85,000 mL = ■ L
22. 5 L = ■ mL
23. 6,000 L = ■ kL
24. 5,000 mL = ■ L

Find the sum or difference.

25. 9.8 kg − 6.2 kg
26. 12.6 L + 24.9 L
27. 335 g + 516 g
28. 750 mL − 207 mL
29. 900 mg − 625 mg
30. 10.6 kL + 15.8 kL

Algebra Find the missing measurement.

31. 20 mg + ■ mg = 1 g
32. 200 mL + ■ mL = 1 L
33. 360 g + ■ g = 1 kg
34. 1 kg − ■ g = 400 g
35. 2 g − ■ mg = 1,300 mg
36. 750 L + ■ L = 1 kL

USE DATA For 37–39, use the list.

37. Kelly's mother made one batch of peanut and pretzel mix. How many more grams does she need to add to the snack mix to make 2 kilograms?

38. Kelly plans to take juice on the camping trip. Which will hold more juice, 8 cans or 2 bottles? How much more?

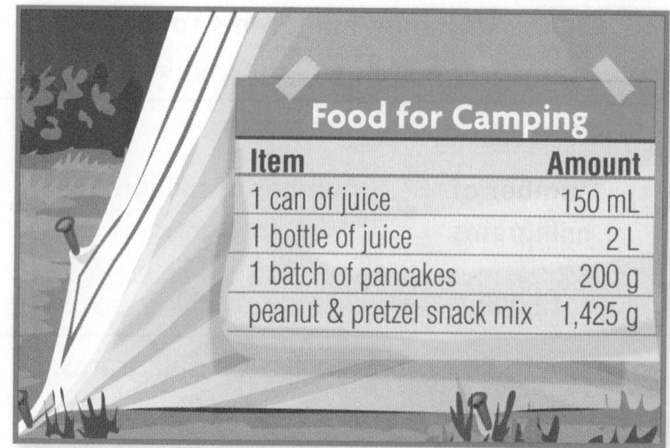

Food for Camping

Item	Amount
1 can of juice	150 mL
1 bottle of juice	2 L
1 batch of pancakes	200 g
peanut & pretzel snack mix	1,425 g

39. Kelly's father made 4 batches of pancakes from 3 kilograms of pancake mix. How many more batches can Kelly's father make?

40. Erin's water bottle holds 1600 milliliters of water. Dylan's water bottle holds 1.5 liters of water. Whose water bottle has the greater capacity? How much greater?

41. ***FAST FACT*** You can sweat about 500–1,000 milliliters of water while hiking for 1 hour under the summer sun. About how many liters of water would you have to drink to replace the amount you would lose if you hiked in the sun for 3 hours?

42. **WRITE Math** The prefix *milli-* means a multiple of 0.001. The prefix *kilo-* means a multiple of 1,000. **Explain** how these prefixes relate milliliters to liters and liters to kiloliters.

 Extra Practice on page 612, Set C

Learn About Metric Conversion

You can use decimal patterns to convert metric measures. Move the decimal point to the right 1, 2, or 3 places when you multiply by 10, 100, or 1,000. Move it to the left when you divide.

Examples

A If a large water jug holds 5.75 liters of water, how many milliliters does it hold?

Change liters to milliliters.

Think: 1 L = 1,000 mL

$5.75 \times 1{,}000 = 5{,}750.$ Move the decimal point 3 places to the right.

So, 5.75 liters is the same as 5,750 milliliters.

B If a water bottle holds 1,250 milliliters of water, how many liters does it hold?

Change milliliters to liters.

Think: 1,000 mL = 1 L

$1{,}250 \div 1{,}000 = 1.250$ Move the decimal point 3 places to the left.

So, 1,250 milliliters is the same as 1.25 liters.

Try It

Use patterns to change the unit.

43. 500 mL = ■ L

44. 7.5 kg = ■ g

45. 0.015 kL = ■ L

46. 4.05 g = ■ mg

47. 800 L = ■ kL

48. 0.09 g = ■ mg

49. 0.32 L = ■ mL

50. 50 mg = ■ g

51. 25 mL = ■ L

Mixed Review and Test Prep

52. Fifty different students attended a soccer camp each week for 4 weeks. What was the total number of students who attended the camp? (p. 42)

53. **Test Prep** A punch bowl holds 4,000 mL of punch. How many liters of punch are in the bowl if it is half full?

A 8 liters **C** 4 liters

B 6 liters **D** 2 liters

54. Alejandro's puppy weighed 12 pounds. How many ounces does the puppy weigh if he gained 8 ounces? (p. 599)

55. **Test Prep** How many grams are in a 40-kilogram bag of potatoes?

A 4 grams **C** 4,000 grams

B 400 grams **D** 40,000 grams

Problem Solving Workshop
Skill: Estimate or Actual Measurement

Read to Understand
Plan
Solve
Check

OBJECTIVE: Solve problems by using the skill *estimate or actual measurement*.

Use the Skill

Luke and Melissa each have 475 centimeters of lace trim.

Sometimes you need an *actual measurement*, sometimes an *estimate*.

PROBLEM 1
Luke wants to make 3 cushions that take 898 mm of trim each, and 2 cushions that take 745 mm of trim each. Does he have enough trim?

Luke can *estimate* by rounding each length up to the nearest centimeter.

898 mm → 900 mm = 90 cm   three pieces: $3 \times 90 \rightarrow$ 270 cm
745 mm → 750 mm = 75 cm   two pieces: $2 \times 75 \rightarrow$ 150 cm
420 cm

Since 420 cm < 475 cm, Luke has enough trim.

PROBLEM 2
Melissa wants to use all of her lace to make five cushions that all need the same length of trim. How many centimeters long should each piece of trim be?

Melissa wants to use all 475 cm of trim, so she divides to find the *actual* length for each cushion.

$475 \div 5 = 95$ cm   Divide.

So, each piece of trim should be 95 cm long.

Think and Discuss

Tell whether you need an estimate or an actual measurement. Explain your reasoning. Then solve.

a. Benji is buying some wallpaper border. It comes in rolls 10 meters long. He needs 16 meters of border for one room and 18 meters for another. Will Benji have enough border if he buys 3 rolls?

b. Jan has 675 mm of nylon cord. She uses 405 mm for a necklace and 217 mm for a bracelet. How much cord does Jan have left?

FAST TRACK

KY MA-05-2.1.6 Students will estimate weight, length, perimeter, area, angle measures and time using appropriate units of measurement. DOK 2 *also MA-05-2.1.3*

Guided Problem Solving Practice

Tell whether you need an estimate or an actual measurement. Then solve.

1. Tanya and George each have a 10-meter roll of paper to use to make posters for an upcoming school play.

PROBLEM 1

Tanya wants to make two 75-cm-long posters, two 170-cm-long posters, and one 260-cm-long poster. Does she have enough paper?

Round each length up to the next meter.

75 cm → 1 m	two posters → 2 m
170 cm → 2 m	two posters → 4 m
260 cm → ■ m	one poster → ■ m
	■ m

PROBLEM 2

George wants to use all of the paper to make four posters that are all the same length. How many centimeters long should each poster be?

Multiply to find the number of centimeters in 10 meters. Then divide to find the length of each poster in centimeters.

10×100 cm $= 1{,}000$ cm

$1{,}000 \div 4 =$ ■ cm

2. **What if** the roll of paper were 8 meters long? Would Tanya have enough paper? How many centimeters long would each of George's posters be?

3. Jennifer went jogging last week. She jogged 2.65 kilometers on Tuesday and twice as far on Wednesday. How far did Jennifer jog last week?

Mixed Applications

USE DATA For 4–7, use the poster.

FABRIC SALE
cotton
$3.00 per meter
denim
$4.00 per meter
silk
$5.00 per meter
All fabric sold in lengths of whole meters only.

4. Britney needs 375 centimeters of denim for some curtains she is making. How much will Britney pay for the fabric?

5. Brad wants to buy a piece of cotton 400 centimeters long. He says that he will pay $120 for the fabric. Do you agree with Brad? **Explain.**

6. Malcolm has $14. He needs 150 centimeters of silk and 85 centimeters of denim. Does Malcolm have enough money? **Explain.**

7. WRITE Math Tanesha paid $25 for 500 centimeters of one type of fabric. **Explain** how you can find the type of fabric Tanesha bought.

LESSON 7

Elapsed Time

OBJECTIVE: Identify and convert measurements involving elapsed time.

Quick Review

1. 2 min = ■ sec
2. 48 hr = ■ days
3. 5 wk = ■ days
4. 6 days = ■ hr
5. 180 min = ■ hr

Learn

PROBLEM To prepare for the talent show, Mark's band wanted to practice for at least $2\frac{1}{4}$ hours. They started practice at 3:25 P.M. and finished at 5:48 P.M. Did Mark's band reach their goal?

Example 1

ONE WAY **Use a clock.**

Count forward from the starting time to the ending time.

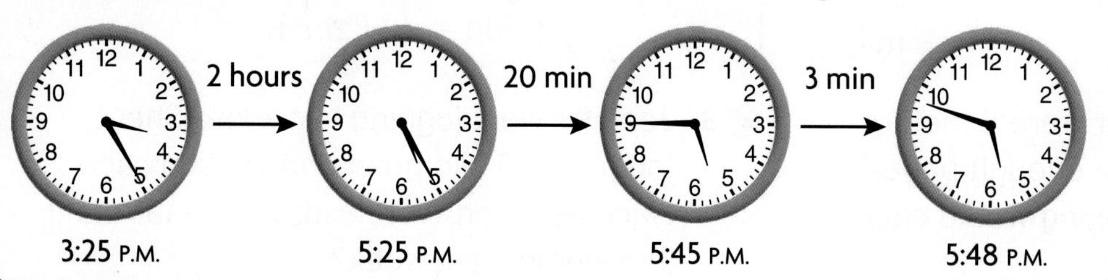

ANOTHER WAY **Use subtraction.**

5 hr 48 min ← ending time
− 3 hr 25 min ← starting time
2 hr 23 min ← elapsed time

Since 2 hr 23 min is more than $2\frac{1}{4}$ hr, or 2 hr 15 min, Mark's band reached their goal.

Example 2

Music camp begins on June 17 and ends on August 16. How many weeks and days does the camp last? First count the weeks. Start with June 17 and count to August 12. Then count the days until you get to August 16.

June

Sun	Mon	Tue	Wed	Thu	Fri	Sat
		1	2	3	4	5
6	7	8	9	10	11	12
13	14	15	16	17	18	19
20	21	22	23	24	25	26
27	28	29	30			

July

Sun	Mon	Tue	Wed	Thu	Fri	Sat
				1	2	3
4	5	6	7	8	9	10
11	12	13	14	15	16	17
18	19	20	21	22	23	24
25	26	27	28	29	30	31

August

Sun	Mon	Tue	Wed	Thu	Fri	Sat
1	2	3	4	5	6	7
8	9	10	11	12	13	14
15	16	17	18	19	20	21
22	23	24	25	26	27	28
29	30	31				

So, music camp lasts for 8 weeks 4 days.

FAST TRACK KY MA-05-2.2.1 Students will determine elapsed time. DOK 3
also MA-05-2.1.1; MA-05-2.2.3

Guided Practice

Use the calendar for item 1.

March						
Sun	Mon	Tue	Wed	Thu	Fri	Sat
	1	2	3	4	5	6
7	8	9	10	11	12	13
14	15	16	17	18	19	20
21	22	23	24	25	26	27
28	29	30	31			

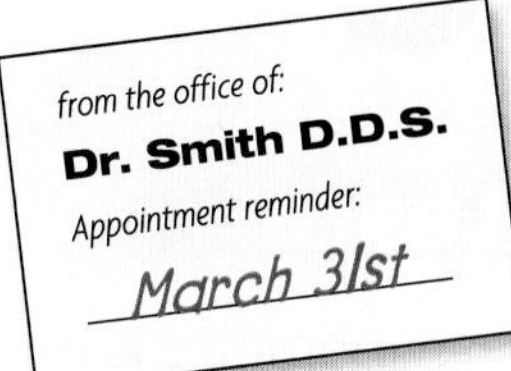

1. On March 10, Claire made a dental appointment for March 31. How many weeks away is Claire's appointment?

Write the time for each.

2. Start: 9:10 A.M.
   Elapsed time: 2 hr 15 min
   End: ■

3. Start: ■
   Elapsed time: 2 hr
   End: 1:15 P.M.

4. Start: May 3, 1 P.M.
   Elapsed time: ■
   End: May 5, 2:30 P.M.

5. TALK Math **Explain** how to find how long a movie lasts that starts at 1:35 P.M. and ends at 3:40 P.M.

Math Idea
Rename units of time whenever possible.
For example:
3 min 85 sec = 4 min 25 sec

Independent Practice and Problem Solving

Write the time for each.

6. Start: 11:38 A.M.
   Elapsed time: 3 hr 10 min
   End: ■

7. Start: ■
   Elapsed time: 2 hr 37 min
   End: 10:52 P.M.

8. Start: 7:41 P.M.
   Elapsed time: ■
   End: 8:50 P.M.

Add or subtract.

9. 2 days 12 hr + 5 days 4 hr

10. 6 min 46 sec + 1 min 32 sec

11. 5 hr 40 min − 2 hr 27 min

12. 2 wk 3 days + 1 wk 5 days

13. WRITE Math The bus leaves at 7:35 A.M. It takes you 12 minutes to reach the bus stop. **Explain** how to find what time you should leave if you want to arrive at the bus stop 5 minutes early.

Mixed Review and Test Prep

14. Alicia paid $5.90 for two hamburgers. If the tax was $0.52, how much did each hamburger cost without tax? (p. 152)

15. Grady has a 2-pound jar of peanut butter. He uses 12 ounces to make sandwiches. How many ounces of peanut butter are left? (p. 600)

16. **Test Prep** The concert started at 7:30 P.M. and lasted for 2 hours 45 minutes. What time did the concert end?

    A 9:30 P.M.
    B 9:45 P.M.
    C 10:15 P.M.
    D 10:45 P.M.

Extra Practice on page 614, Set D

LESSON 8

Temperature

OBJECTIVE: Measure temperature and solve problems involving temperature.

Quick Review

1. 230 mm = ■ cm
2. 2 kL = ■ liters
3. 1 g = ■ mg
4. 2 m = ■ cm
5. ■ km = 30,000 m

Vocabulary

Fahrenheit (°F)

Celsius (°C)

Learn

Temperature is measured with a thermometer. Degrees **Fahrenheit (°F)** are the customary units for measuring temperature. In the metric system, temperature is measured in degrees **Celsius (°C)**.

HANDS ON **Activity** **Read a thermometer.**

Materials ■ thermometer

- Use a thermometer to measure and record the temperature inside your classroom.
- Use the same thermometer to measure and record the temperature outside. Place the thermometer in the shade for several minutes before reading it.
- Use your data to find the difference in temperature.

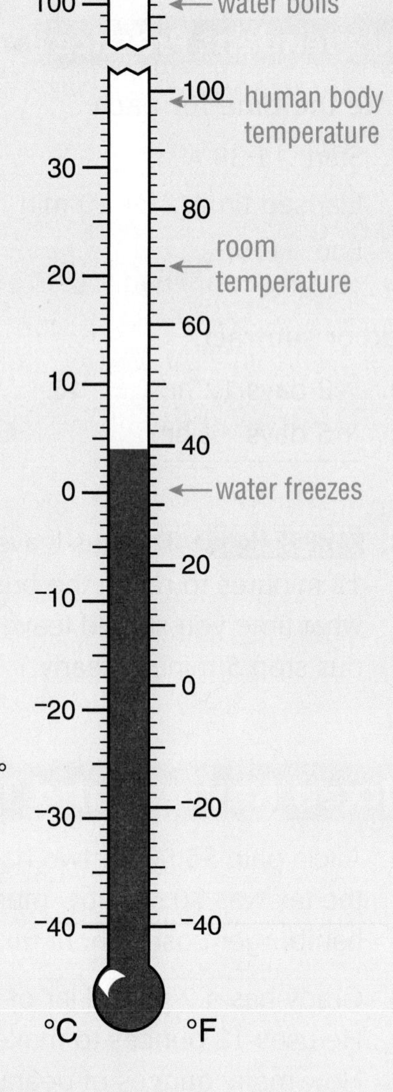

Example **Calculate changes in temperature.**

When Marsha left her cabin, the temperature outside was $^{-}5$°F. By noon, the temperature was 18°F. By how many degrees Fahrenheit had the temperature changed?

Step 1

First, find the change in temperature from 0°F to 18°F.

The change in temperature was 18°F.

Step 2

Then, find the change in temperature from 0 to $^{-}5$°F.

The change in temperature was 5°F.

Step 3

Add the two changes.

18°F + 5°F = 23°F

So, the change in temperature from $^{-}5$°F to 18°F was 23°F.

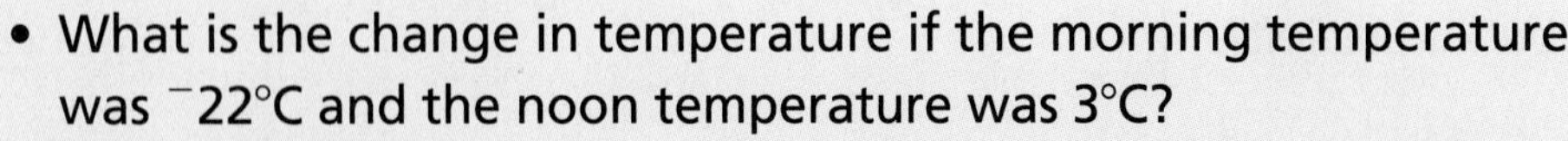

- What is the change in temperature if the morning temperature was $^{-}22$°C and the noon temperature was 3°C?

FAST TRACK KY MA-05-2.1.1 Students will apply standard units to measure length (to the nearest eighth-inch or the nearest centimeter) and to determine: temperature (Fahrenheit and Celsius) DOK 2 *also MA-05-2.1.2*

Guided Practice

Find the change in temperature.

1. What is the change in temperature from 0 to $^{-}8$°F?
2. What is the change in temperature from 0°C to 20°C?
3. What is the change in temperature from $^{-}8$°F to 20°F?

Find the change in temperature.

4. 30°C to 15°C
5. 80°F to 45°F
6. 102°F to 95°F
7. $^{-}5$°F to 15°F
8. 0°C to 25°C
9. $^{-}25$°C to 10°C
10. TALK Math **Explain** how you found the change in temperature for Exercise 7.

Independent Practice and Problem Solving

Find the change in temperature.

11. 7°C to 30°C
12. 36°F to 98°F
13. 50°C to $^{-}5$°C
14. $^{-}4$°F to 16°F
15. 68°F to 14°F
16. $^{-}25$°C to 5°C
17. 72°F to 94°F
18. $^{-}20$°C to 36°C

USE DATA For 19–21, use the graph.

19. Which month had the highest average temperature? The lowest? How many degrees Fahrenheit separate the two?
20. How many degrees Fahrenheit below freezing was the coldest month? How many degrees Fahrenheit above freezing was the warmest month?
21. WRITE Math **Explain** how to find how many degrees warmer June's average temperature is than May's.

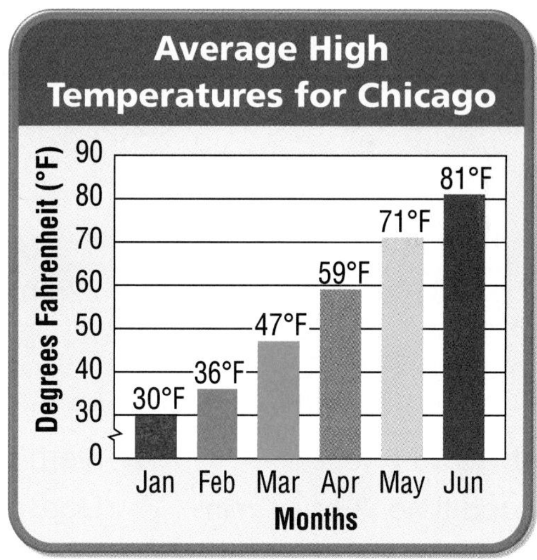

Mixed Review and Test Prep

22. Mark drew a circle with a radius of 5.8 cm. What was the diameter of the circle that Mark drew? (p. 496)
23. How many right angles does a rectangle have? (p. 490)
24. **Test Prep** What is the change in temperature from $^{-}8$°C to 12°C?

    A 8°C **C** 20°C
    B 12°C **D** 30°C

Extra Practice on page 614, Set E

Extra Practice

Set A Change the unit. (pp. 596–599)

1. 36 in = ■ ft
2. 12 ft = ■ yd
3. 2 mi = ■ ft
4. 16 yd = ■ ft

Find the sum or difference.

5. 5 ft 6 in. + 3 ft 7 in.
6. 4 yd 2 ft − 1 yd 2 ft
7. 4 yd 1 ft + 5 yd 2 ft
8. 8 ft 8 in. − 4 ft 3 in.

Set B Change the unit. (pp. 600–603)

1. 3 T = ■ lb
2. 6 lb = ■ oz
3. 3 gal = ■ pt
4. 8 qt = ■ pt

Find the sum or difference.

5. 3 gal 3 qt + 4 gal 2 qt
6. 8 lb 10 oz + 3 lb 14 oz
7. 6 lb 8 oz − 2 lb 12 oz
8. 4 qt 2 c − 2 qt 3 c
9. The cookie recipe Lee is following lists fluid ounces rather than cups. The recipe calls for 4 fl oz of milk and 2 fl oz of vegetable oil. Rewrite the recipe using cups.

Set C Change the unit. (pp. 604–607)

1. 8,000 mL = ■ L
2. 7 g = ■ mg
3. 4 kL = ■ L

Find the sum or difference.

4. 600 g − 310 g
5. 225 mL + 442 mL
6. 7.4 kg − 4.8 kg

Set D Write the time for each. (pp. 610–611)

1. Start: 12:15 P.M.
   Elapsed time: 3 hr 14 min
   End: ■
2. Start: 9:27 A.M.
   Elapsed time: ■
   End: 1:35 P.M.
3. Start: ■
   Elapsed time: 2 hr 15 min
   End: 5:42 P.M.
4. Sean's astronomy club met in a field behind their school at 10:15 P.M. They watched a meteor shower for 3 hours and 20 minutes, and left. What time did the club leave the field?

Set E Find the change in temperature. (pp. 612–613)

1. 65°F to 84°F
2. 14°C to 22°C
3. 76°F to 38°F
4. 20°C to ⁻3°C
5. ⁻5°C to 26°C
6. 46°F to 64°F

Technology
Use Harcourt Mega Math, Ice Station Exploration, *Linear Lab*, Levels H, I, J.

PRACTICE GAME

2 Steps Forward, 1 Step Back

Players

2 students

Materials

- game pieces
- game cards

Start

Finish

Start Playing

- Shuffle the game cards and place them facedown in a pile.
- Each player selects a different game piece and places it on START.
- Player 1 draws a card from the pile.
- Player 1 reads it and decides whether it is ***true*** or ***false***. Player 2 checks the answer.
- If the answer is correct, Player 1 moves 2 steps forward on the board.
- If incorrect, Player 1 moves 1 step back on the board.
- Player 2 draws a card and repeats the process. The game continues until a player reaches FINISH.
- The first player to reach FINISH wins.

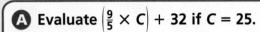

MATH POWER

Fahrenheit & Celsius

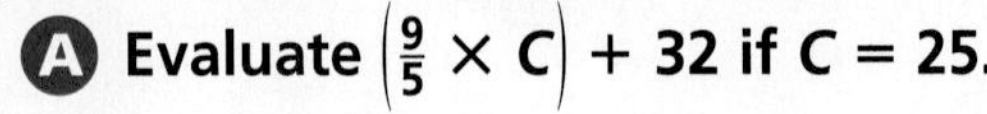

Swim Meet

The manager at the San José Swim Club must keep the temperature of the pool water at least 76°F so that competition can be held. When the teams arrive, the pool temperature is 25°C. Is the pool water warm enough?

You can use the expression $\left(\frac{9}{5} \times C\right) + 32$ to convert from degrees Celsius to degrees Fahrenheit.

Remember

°F = degrees Fahrenheit

°C = degrees Celsius

Examples

A **Evaluate $\left(\frac{9}{5} \times C\right) + 32$ if $C = 25$.**

Replace C with 25. $\quad \left(\frac{9}{5} \times C\right) + 32 = \left(\frac{9}{5} \times 25\right) + 32$

Operate inside parentheses.

Add. $\quad = 45 + 32$

So, 25°C = 77°F. $\quad = 77$

Since 77°F > 76°F, the temperature of the water is warm enough.

You also can convert from °F to °C. Use the expression $\frac{5}{9} \times (F - 32)$ to convert from degrees Fahrenheit to degrees Celsius.

B **Evaluate $\frac{5}{9} \times (F - 32)$ if $F = 82$.**

Replace F with 82. $\quad \frac{5}{9} \times (F - 32) = \frac{5}{9} \times (82 - 32)$

Operate inside parentheses.

Multiply. Round. $\quad = \frac{5}{9} \times 50$

So, 82°F ≈ 28°C. $\quad = 27\frac{7}{9} \approx 28$

≈ means "is approximately equal to."

Try It

Convert to degrees Fahrenheit or degrees Celsius. Round to the nearest degree.

1. 30°C = ■ °F
2. 85°F = ■ °C
3. 0°C = ■ °F
4. 113°F = ■ °C
5. WRITE Math **Explain** how to convert 32°F to degrees Celsius.

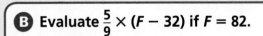

Chapter 22 Review/Test

Check Vocabulary and Concepts

VOCABULARY
Fahrenheit
centimeter
millimeter
Celsius

Choose the best term from the box.

1. Degrees used in the customary system of temperature measurement. KY MA-05-2.1.1 (p. 612)
2. Degrees used in the metric system of temperature measurement. KY MA-05-2.1.1 (p. 612)
3. About the width of a crayon. KY MA-05-2.1.6 (p. 594)

Check Skills

Change the unit. KY MA-05-2.2.3 (pp. 596–599; 604–607)

4. 36 in. = ■ ft
5. 10,560 ft = ■ mi
6. 4 yd = ■ ft
7. 4 mi = ■ yd
8. 6 kg = ■ g
9. 4,000 g = ■ kg
10. 5,500 g = ■ kg
11. 15 kg = ■ g

Find the sum or difference. KY MA-05-2.1.1 (pp. 600–603)

12. 4 lb 6 oz − 1 lb 10 oz
13. 4 gal 2 qt + 3 gal 2 qt
14. 5 qt 1 c − 3 qt 2 c
15. 6 lb 8 oz + 2 lb 10 oz

Write the time for each. KY MA-05-2.2.1 (pp. 610–611)

16. Start: 11:20 A.M.
    Elapsed time: 4 hr 52 min
    End: ■
17. Start: 8:48 P.M.
    Elapsed time: ■
    End: 11:15 P.M.
18. Start: ■
    Elapsed time: 6 hr 20 min
    End: 3:45 A.M.

Check Problem Solving

Solve. KY MA-05-2.1.6 (pp. 608–609)

19. Carmen has 3 meters of ribbon. She wants to make hair ribbons for 6 friends. What is the longest Carmen can cut each hair ribbon, if she makes them all the same length? Tell whether you should estimate or use an actual measurement. Then solve.
20. WRITE Math Samuel wanted to run 2 km. He ran 480 meters four times. Did he meet his goal? Should you estimate or use an actual measurement? **Explain.**

Practice for the KCCT
Chapters 1–22

Number and Operations

1. Linda expected about 8,000 people to attend her ballet company's spring production. The table shows how many people attended each show. What is the difference between the number of people Linda expected and the actual number of people? KY MA-05-1.3.1 (p. 16)

Spring Production	
Show	**Number Attending**
Friday evening	2,074
Saturday matinee	2,120
Saturday evening	3,097
Sunday matinee	1,982

A 1,237 **C** 1,327

B 1,273 **D** 1,732

2. Preston is making a collage of his favorite photographs. He wants to use $\frac{1}{2}$-inch-wide decorative tape around each photograph. The tape is sold in the widths shown in the table. Which tape should Preston choose? KY MA-05-1.1.3 (p. 310)

Tape Design	Solid	Flowers	Stripes	Balloons
Width	$\frac{5}{8}$ inch	$\frac{5}{16}$ inch	$\frac{3}{8}$ inch	$\frac{8}{16}$ inch

A solid

B flowers

C stripes

D balloons

3. **WRITE Math** What are the common factors of 56 and 72? **Explain** how you know. KY MA-05-1.5.1 (p. 278)

Algebraic Thinking

4. What is the missing number in the pattern? KY MA-05-1.3.3 (p. 172)

$$1 \times 0.09 = 0.09$$
$$10 \times 0.09 = 0.9$$
$$■ \times 0.09 = 9$$
$$1{,}000 \times 0.09 = 90$$

A 10 **C** 1,000

B 100 **D** 10,000

5. Judith is learning how to write Chinese characters. Each week she practices more than the week before. Which function rule could be applied to the hours she practiced for the first four weeks? KY MA-05-5.1.2 (p. 566)

Practicing Chinese Characters	
Week (w)	**Number of Hours (h)**
1	3
2	5
3	7
4	9

A $h = 2w$

B $h = 3w$

C $h = 2w + 1$

D $h = 3w + 1$

6. **WRITE Math** What is the next number in this number pattern: 4, 12, 36, 108, ■? **Explain** how you found your answer. KY MA-05-5.1.1 (p. 46)

Geometry

7. Which is an equiangular triangle? KY MA-05-3.1.2 (p. 514)

A
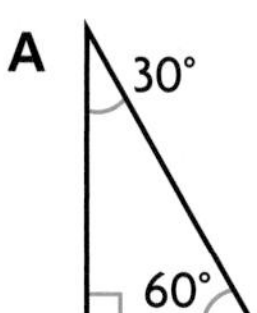

B
60°
60° 60°

C
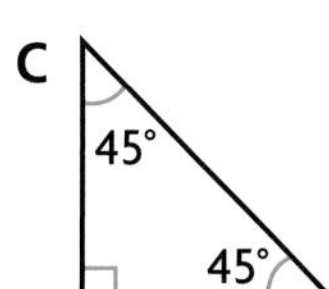

D
70°
60° 50°

8. What kind of transformation is shown? KY MA-05-3.2.2 (p. 542)

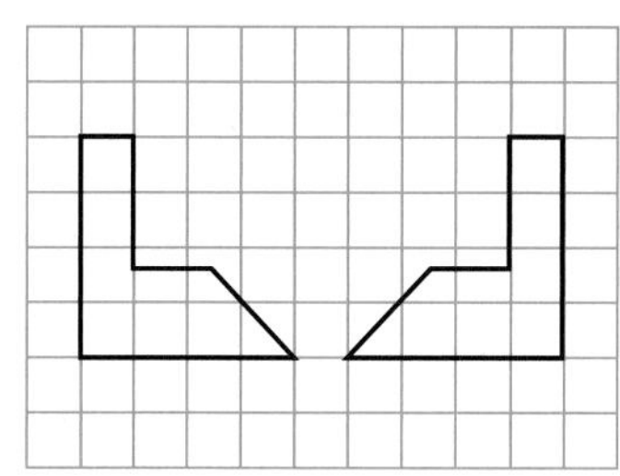

A reflection C tessellation

B translation D rotation

9. **WRITE Math** Angel drew a circle with a diameter of 14 cm. Paula drew a circle with a radius of 8 cm. Which circle is larger? **Explain** how you know. KY MA-05-3.1.1 (p. 496)

Data Analysis and Probability

Check your work.

See item 10. What method did you use to solve? Check the work you already did. Then, try another method and see if you get the same answer.

10. Tai made cookies for his class picnic. The types of cookies and colors of icing he used are shown in this tree diagram. How many possible combinations are there? KY MA-05-4.4.1 (p. 462)

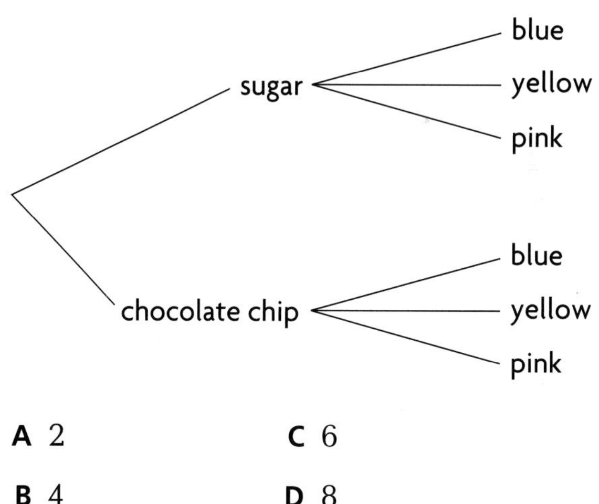

A 2 C 6

B 4 D 8

11. **WRITE Math** **Explain** how to find the median of this set of numbers. KY MA-05-4.2.1 (p. 220)

11, 8, 14, 12, 14, 16

CHAPTER 23 Perimeter

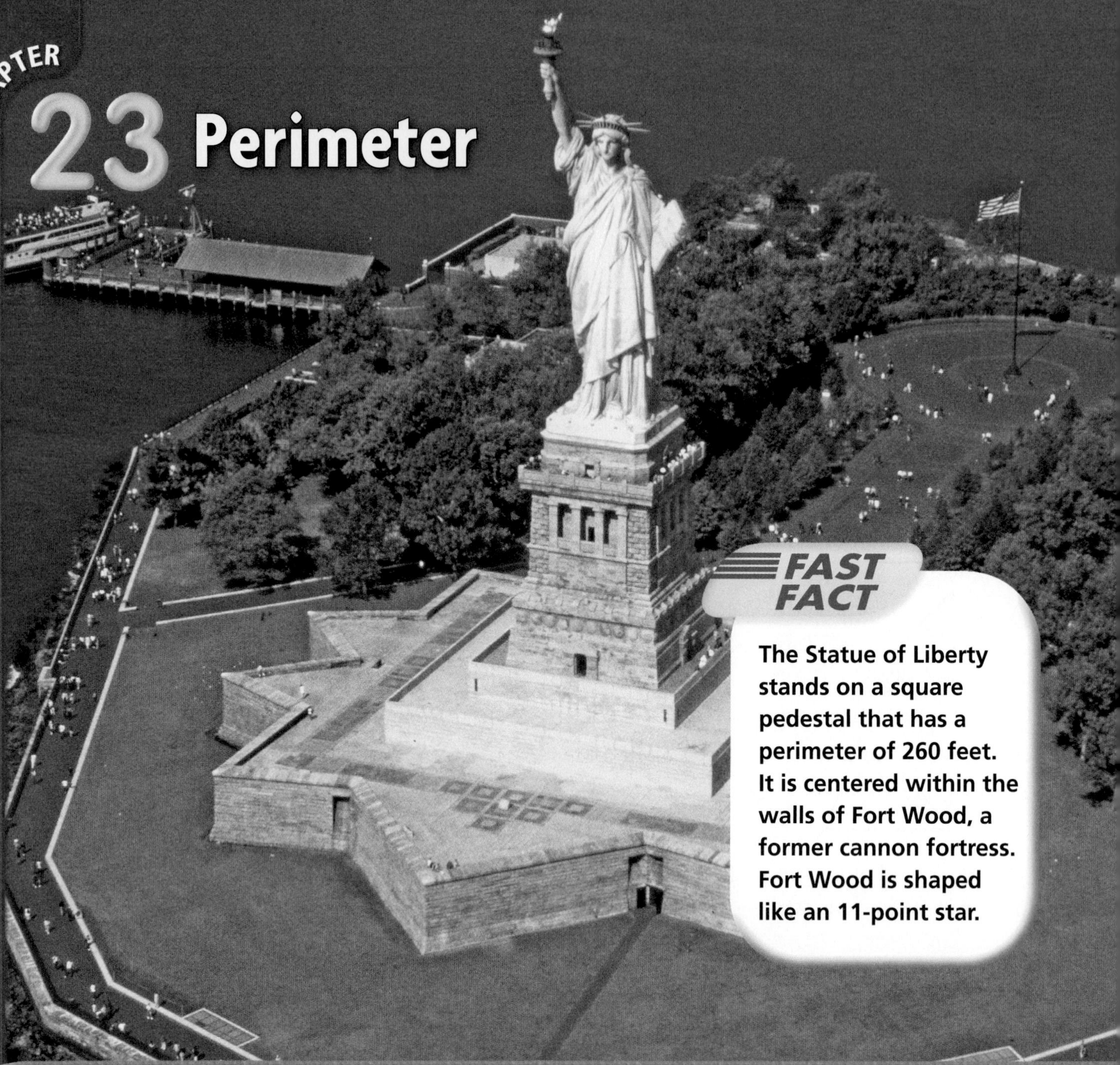

FAST FACT

The Statue of Liberty stands on a square pedestal that has a perimeter of 260 feet. It is centered within the walls of Fort Wood, a former cannon fortress. Fort Wood is shaped like an 11-point star.

Investigate

Suppose you are making a scale model of the Statue of Liberty and will begin by making the square pedestal. The table shows model sizes as a fraction of the size of the real statue, along with the scale model's pedestal side length. Choose a model size. What will the perimeter of the pedestal be in your model?

Statue of Liberty Scale Model Sizes

Model Size	Length of Pedestal Side
$\frac{1}{20}$	3.250 feet
$\frac{1}{40}$	1.625 feet
$\frac{1}{100}$	0.650 feet
$\frac{1}{130}$	0.500 feet
$\frac{1}{200}$	0.325 feet

Technology
Student pages are available in the Student eBook.

Show What You Know

Check your understanding of important skills needed for success in Chapter 23.

▶ Perimeter—Count Units

Find the perimeter of each figure.

1. 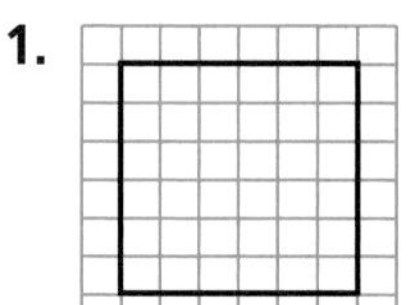

2. 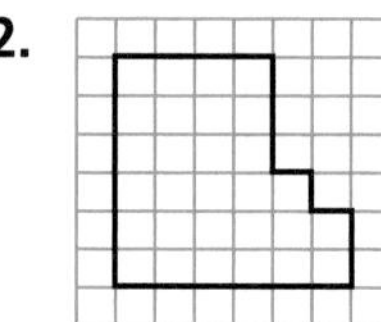

3. 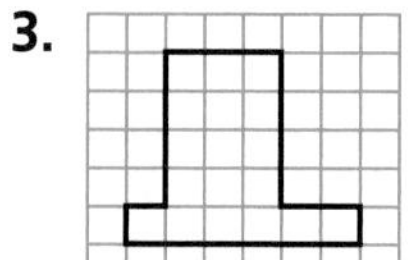

4. 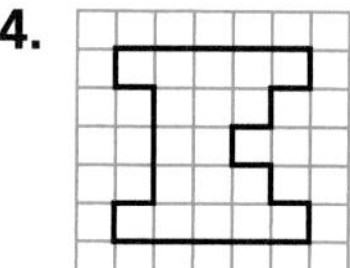

5. 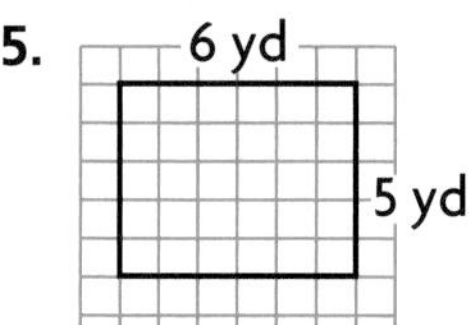

6. 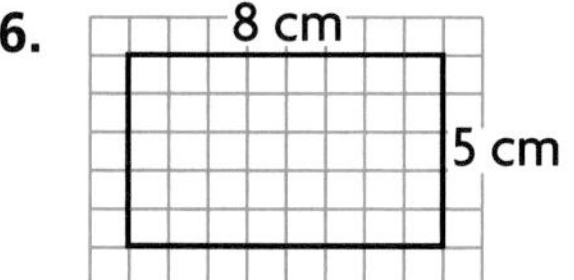

7. 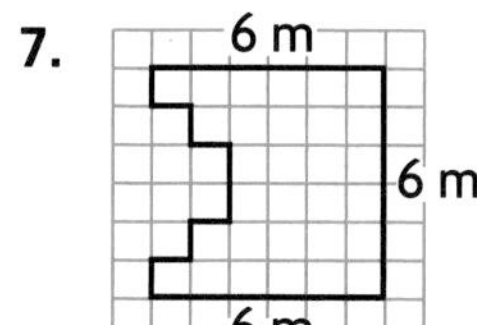

8. 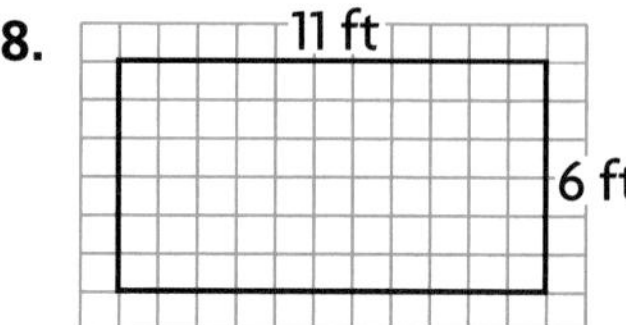

▶ Choose the Appropriate Unit and Estimate Length

Choose the appropriate unit.

9. height of a room
inches or **feet**

10. length of your finger
inches or **feet**

11. width of a baseball field
yards or **miles**

12. length of a pencil
centimeters or **meters**

13. distance biked in 1 hour
meters or **kilometers**

14. width of a room
centimeters or **meters**

VOCABULARY POWER

CHAPTER VOCABULARY

circumference
perimeter
pi

WARM-UP WORDS

perimeter the distance around a closed plane figure

circumference the distance around a circular object

pi the ratio of the circumference of a circle to the diameter of a circle; an approximate decimal value of pi is 3.14.

LESSON HANDS ON

1 Estimate Perimeter

OBJECTIVE: Estimate perimeter.

Quick Review

Estimate by rounding to the nearest whole number.

1. 4.74
2. 5.2 + 6.8
3. 3.84 + 1.9
4. 5.8 + 7.1
5. 7.2 + 15.14

Vocabulary

perimeter

Investigate

Materials ■ metric ruler ■ string ■ paper

The **perimeter** is the distance around a closed plane figure. You can estimate the perimeter of some figures by tracing around the figure and measuring its outline with string and a ruler.

A Trace the outline of your shoe on a sheet of paper. Make the outline as close to the shape and size of your shoe as you can.

B Lay a piece of string around the tracing of your shoe. Align the string carefully in order to get a good estimate of the perimeter. Mark the string where it meets itself after outlining the entire perimeter of your shoe.

C Now lay the string in a straight line, and use a ruler to measure the marked section in centimeters. Record your answer.

A

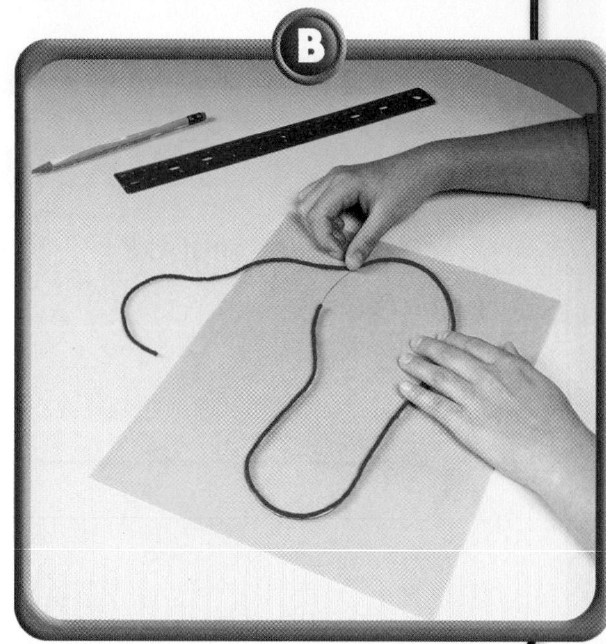
B

Draw Conclusions

1. Compare the estimated perimeter of your shoe with those of your classmates. How different are the measurements? What is the range? Are any the same?
2. **Comprehension** What does it mean to estimate a measurement?
3. Measure the string that you used to estimate the perimeter of your shoe with a customary ruler. Then measure your actual shoe with a cloth tape measure. Why might the two measurements be different? Which do you think is more accurate?

FAST TRACK

KY MA-05-2.1.6 Students will estimate weight, length, perimeter, area, angle measures and time using appropriate units of measurement. DOK 2 *also* MA-05-2.1.1; *MA-05-2.1.3*

Connect

You can use a ruler to measure the perimeter of polygons.

A Find the perimeter in centimeters.

4 cm

4 cm

4 cm

4 cm + 4 cm + 4 cm

So, the perimeter is 12 cm.

B Find the perimeter in inches.

$1\frac{1}{4}$ in.

$1\frac{1}{4}$ in.

$1\frac{1}{4}$ in.

$1\frac{1}{4}$ in.

$1\frac{1}{4}$ in. + $1\frac{1}{4}$ in. + $1\frac{1}{4}$ in. + $1\frac{1}{4}$ in.

So, the perimeter is 5 in.

TALK Math

Explain how you can use a ruler to find the perimeter of any polygon.

Practice

1. On a sheet of paper, trace around the outline of your hand with your fingers closed. Draw a line at the bottom of your outline to make a closed figure. Then use string and a ruler to estimate the perimeter in centimeters.

✓ 2. Using a string and a ruler, estimate the perimeter of the cover of your math book in centimeters. Then using a ruler only, estimate the perimeter by measuring each side and adding the lengths together.

Find the perimeter of each polygon in centimeters.

3.

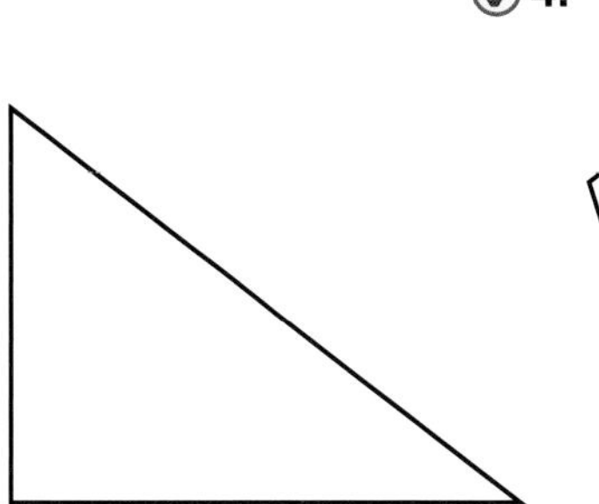

✓ 4.

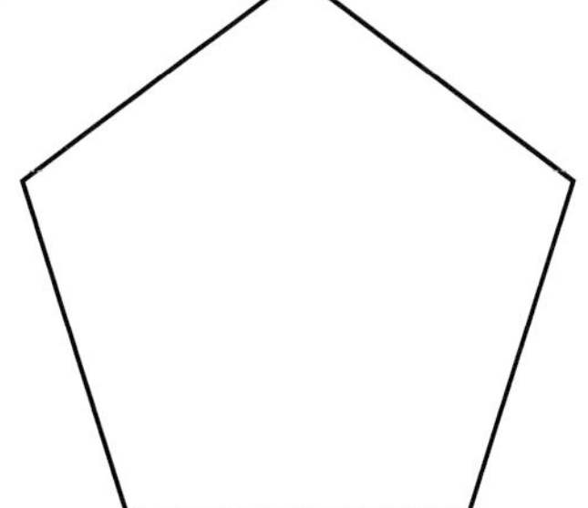

5.

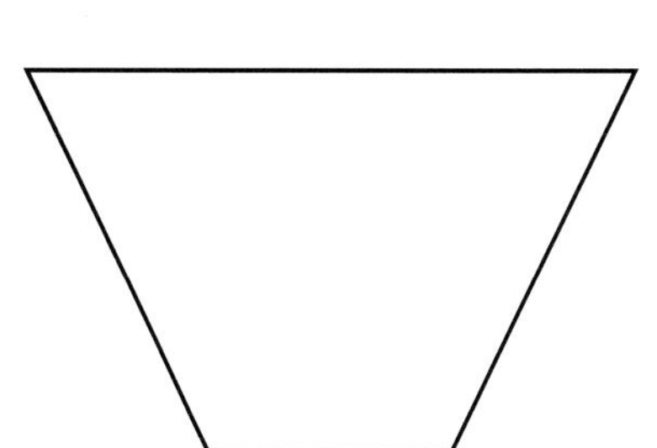

6.

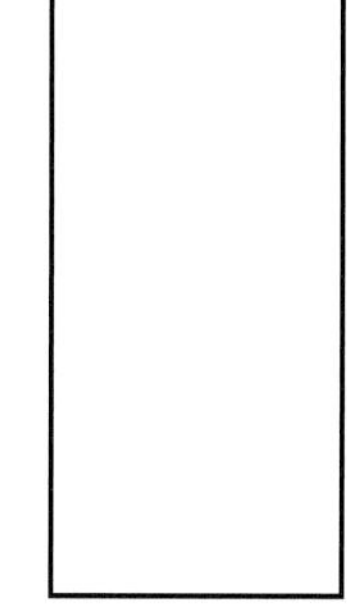

7. **WRITE Math** **Explain** how you can estimate the perimeter of a regular polygon.

LESSON 2

Find Perimeter

OBJECTIVE: Find the perimeter of polygons.

Quick Review

Name the number of sides for each figure.

1. square
2. triangle
3. hexagon
4. octagon
5. trapezoid

Learn

PROBLEM The Pentagon building, located near Washington, D.C., is a regular polygon. The length of each outer wall is 922 feet. What is the perimeter of the Pentagon?

▲ The Pentagon is one of the world's largest office buildings.

ONE WAY **Use addition.**

You can find the perimeter of a polygon by adding the lengths of its sides.

$922 + 922 + 922 + 922 + 922 = 4{,}610$

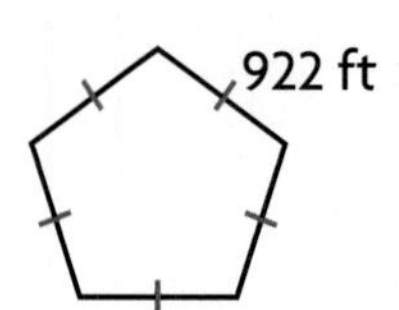

ANOTHER WAY **Use multiplication.**

If the polygon is a regular polygon, multiply the length of one side by the number of sides to find the perimeter.

$5 \times 922 = 4{,}610$

So, the perimeter is 4,610 feet.

More Examples **Find the perimeter of each figure.**

A

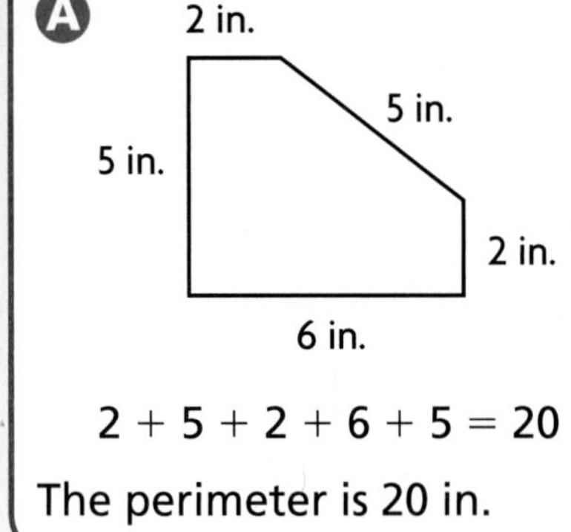

$2 + 5 + 2 + 6 + 5 = 20$

The perimeter is 20 in.

B

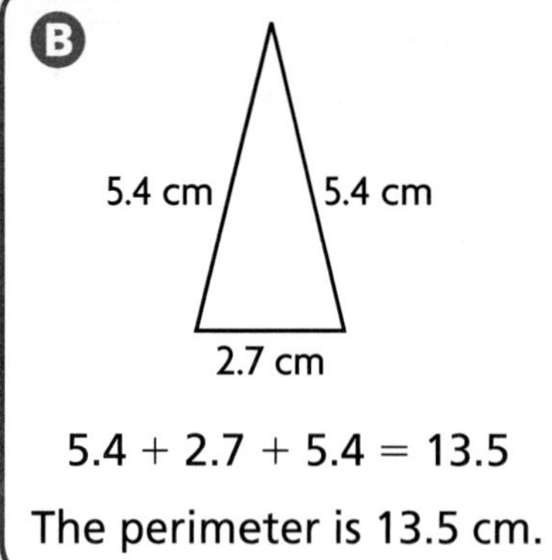

$5.4 + 2.7 + 5.4 = 13.5$

The perimeter is 13.5 cm.

C

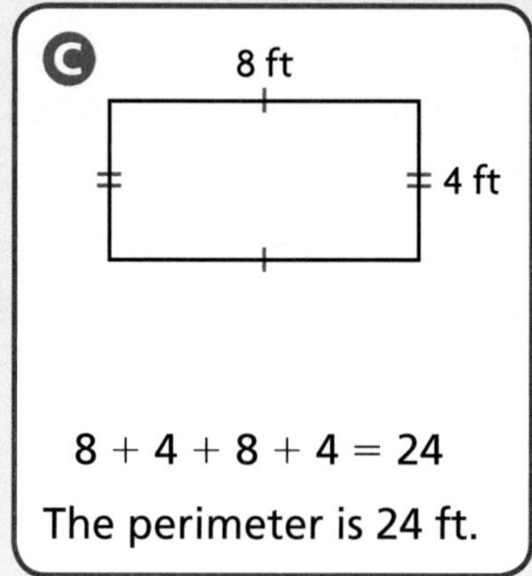

$8 + 4 + 8 + 4 = 24$

The perimeter is 24 ft.

- In Examples B and C, how could you use both multiplication and addition in one equation to find the perimeter?

Guided Practice

1. Find the perimeter of the square.

$10 + ■ + ■ + ■ = ■$ cm or $■ \times 10 = ■$ cm

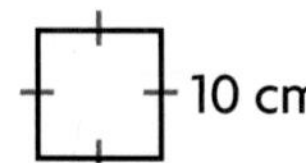

FAST TRACK

KY MA-05-2.1.1 Students will apply standard units to measure length (to the nearest eighth-inch or the nearest centimeter) and to determine: perimeter; DOK 2 *also MA-05-2.1.2;* MA-05-2.1.6

Find the perimeter of each polygon.

2. 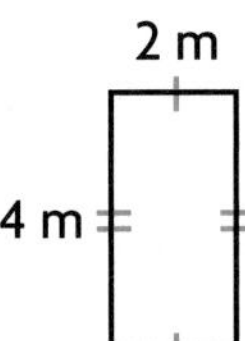

3. 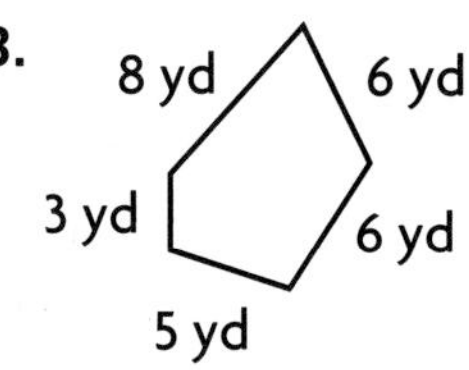

✓4. 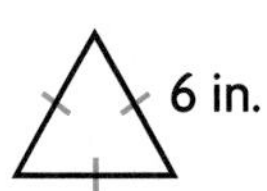

✓5. 8 ft
4 ft

6. TALK Math **Explain** how to find the perimeter of a square.

Independent Practice and Problem Solving

Find the perimeter of each polygon.

7. 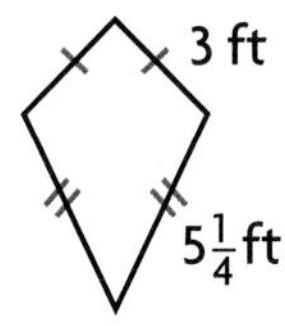

8. 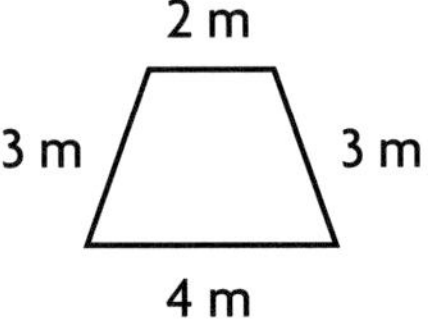

9. 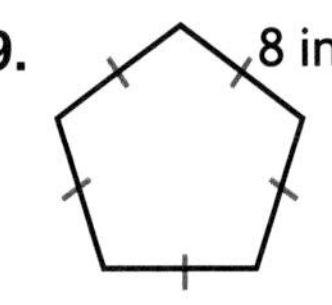

10. 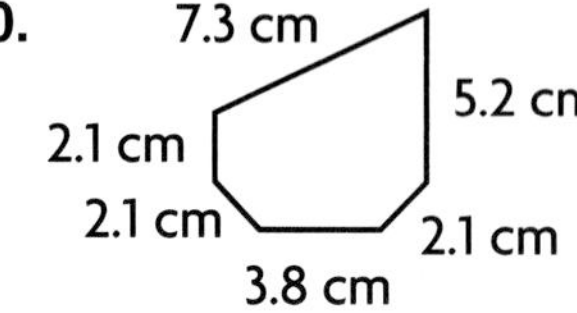

11. 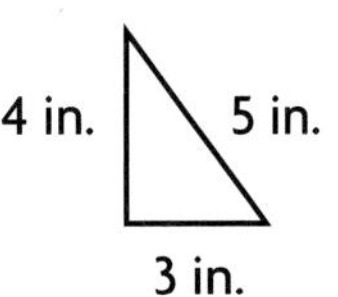

12. 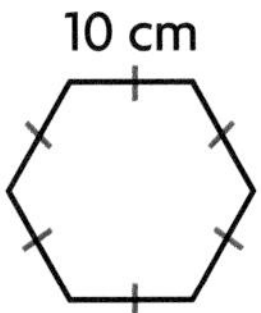

13. 8.3 m
1.9 m
6.8 m
7.2 m
3 m

14. $3\frac{1}{4}$ yd
$1\frac{1}{2}$ yd

15. Dora made a scale model of the Pentagon building. The length of each side of the model is 9.2 centimeters. What is the perimeter of Dora's Pentagon model?

16. WRITE Math **What's the Error?** Denzel labeled one side of a rectangle 3 cm and another side 5 cm. Denzel said that the perimeter of his rectangle is 8 cm. What did he do wrong?

Mixed Review and Test Prep

17. Which quadrilateral has 4 sides of equal length and 4 right angles? (p. 518)

18. Scott made a quadrilateral. Three of the angles of his quarilateral have a measure of 112°, 98°, and 52°. What is the measure of the fourth angle? (p. 490)

19. **Test Prep** The neighborhood pool is enclosed by a fence. What is the length of the fence that encloses the pool?

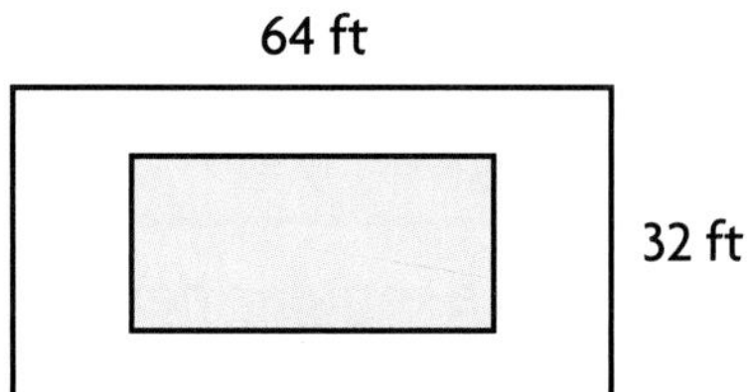

A 96 ft
B 160 ft
C 192 ft
D 2,048 ft

Extra Practice on page 632, Set A

CD ROM **Technology**
Use Harcourt Mega Math, Ice Station Exploration, *Arctic Algebra*, Level CC.

Algebra: Perimeter Formulas

OBJECTIVE: Find the perimeter of polygons by using formulas.

Quick Review

Ann has a picture frame that is 15 in. long and 9 in. wide. She wants to put some wood trim around the entire outside edge. How many inches of trim does Ann need?

Learn

You can find the perimeter of a polygon by using a formula.

Activity **Materials** ■ metric ruler

- Draw a square, a rectangle, and a parallelogram. Make a table for your data.

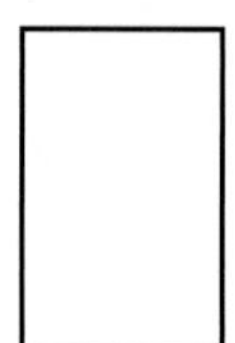

- Measure and record the lengths of the sides of each figure. Then record each perimeter.
- Look for a relationship between the lengths of the sides and the perimeter. Generate a formula for finding the perimeter of each figure, and record it.

▲ The Lincoln Memorial was built between 1915 and 1922.

Example

The base of the Lincoln Memorial, in Washington, D.C., is 188 feet long and 118 feet wide. What is the perimeter of the Lincoln Memorial's base?

$P = l + w + l + w$, or $2l + 2w$ $\quad$ P = perimeter
$P = (2 \times 188) + (2 \times 118)$ $\quad$ l = length
$P = 376 + 236$ $\quad$ w = width
$P = 612$

So, the perimeter of the Lincoln Memorial's base is 612 feet.

Remember

The opposite sides of a rectangle are equal in length.

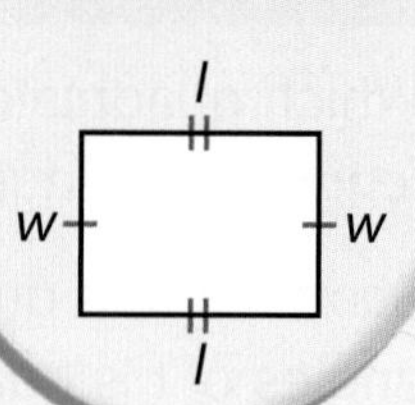

More Examples

A Perimeter of a regular hexagon

s = length of side
P = (number of sides) $\times s$
$P = 6 \times 2$
$P = 12$ ft

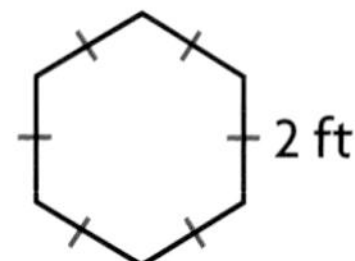

B Perimeter of a parallelogram

a = length of side 1 $\quad$ b = length of side 2
$P = 2a + 2b$
$P = (2 \times 5) + (2 \times 3)$
$P = 16$ cm

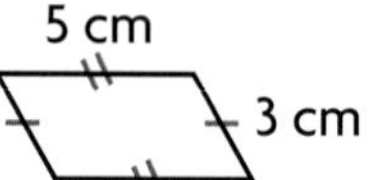

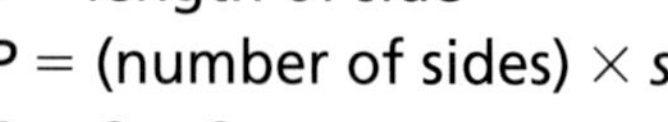

FAST TRACK

KY MA-05-2.1.1 Students will apply standard units to measure length (to the nearest eighth-inch or the nearest centimeter) and to determine: perimeter; DOK 2 *also MA-05-2.1.2; MA-05-2.2.2*

Guided Practice

Find the perimeter of each polygon by using a formula.

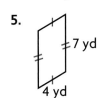

1. 6 m, 4 m
$P = 2a + 2b$
$P = (2 \times 6) + (2 \times \blacksquare)$
$P = \blacksquare$

2. 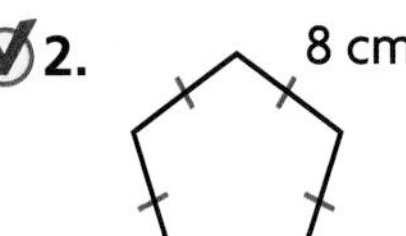

3. 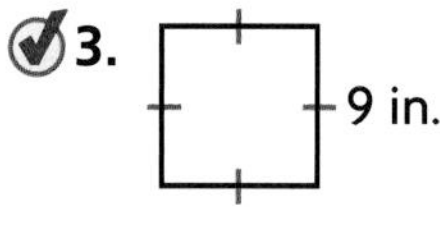

4. TALK Math **Explain** why you can use the same formula, $P = 2l + 2w$, for finding the perimeter of a rectangle and a square.

Independent Practice and Problem Solving

Find the perimeter of each polygon by using a formula.

5. 7 yd, 4 yd

6. 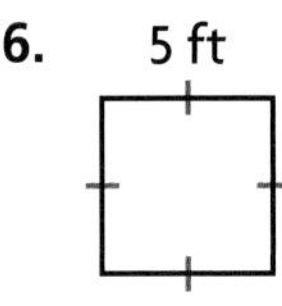

7. 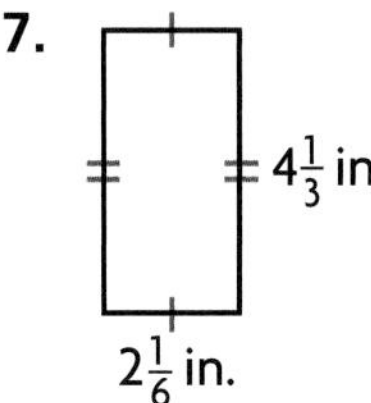

8. 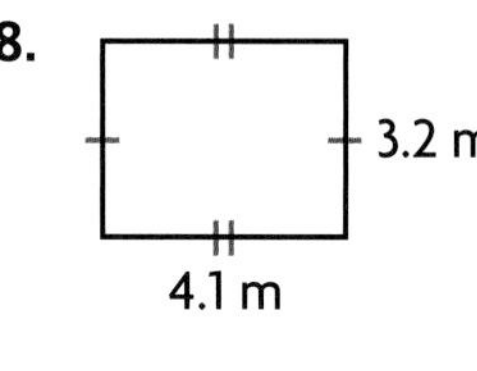

Find the perimeter of each regular polygon by using a formula.

9. $3\frac{1}{8}$ in.

10. 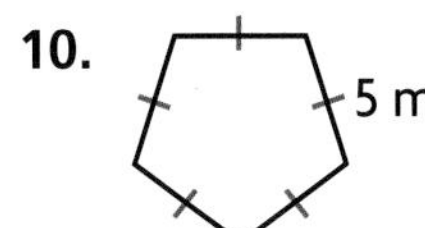

11. 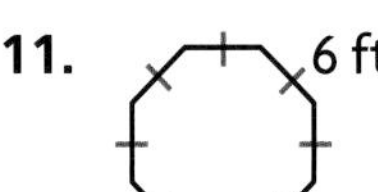

12. 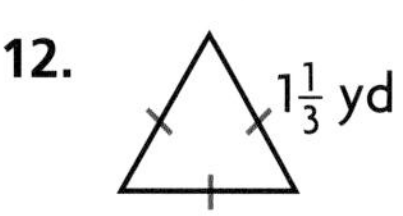

13. ***FAST FACT*** A sculpture of Abraham Lincoln is in the central chamber of the Lincoln Memorial. The central chamber is rectangular, and is 74 feet long and 60 feet wide. What is the perimeter of the central chamber?

14. **Algebra** The perimeter of a rectangle is 24 in. and the width is 3 in. What is the length of the rectangle?

15. WRITE Math **Explain** how to find the length of the sides of an equilateral triangle that has a perimeter of 84 m.

A worker at the Lincoln Memorial cleans the statue of Abraham Lincoln in the central chamber.

Mixed Review and Test Prep

16. What is the median of these scores?
89, 65, 72, 88, 57, 91 (p. 220)

17. What is the measure of a right angle? (p. 482)

18. **Test Prep** For which polygon could you use the formula $P = 2l + 2w$ to find its perimeter?
   - **A** triangle
   - **B** rectangle
   - **C** pentagon
   - **D** octagon

Extra Practice on page 632, Set B

Problem Solving Workshop
Skill: Make Generalizations

OBJECTIVE: Solve problems by using the skill *make generalizations*.

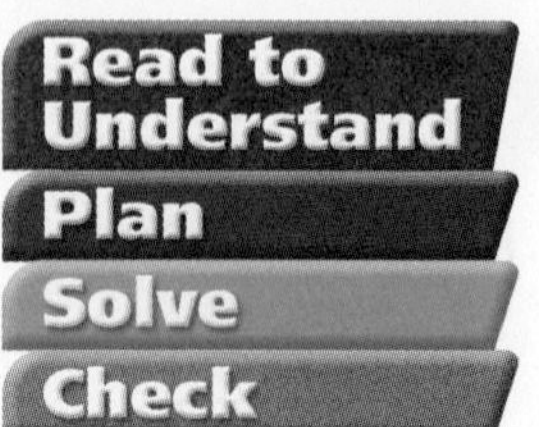

Use the Skill

PROBLEM Trump World Tower and Leighton House are skyscrapers in New York City. Both buildings are rectangular prisms. The base of Trump World Tower is 145 feet long and 78 feet wide. The perimeter of the base of Leighton House is 112 feet less than the perimeter of the base of Trump World Tower. What is the perimeter of the base of Leighton House?

▲ Trump World Tower

Sometimes you need to *make generalizations* to solve a problem. When you generalize, you make a statement that is true about a whole group of similar situations or objects.

What You Know	Generalization	Conclusion
Trump World Tower and Leighton House are rectangular prisms.	Rectangular prisms have rectangular bases.	Leighton House has a rectangular base.
Trump World Tower is 145 ft long and 78 ft wide.	The perimeter of a rectangle is $(2 \times \text{length}) + (2 \times \text{width})$.	The perimeter of the base of Trump World Tower is $(2 \times 145 \text{ ft}) + (2 \times 78 \text{ ft})$, or 446 ft.
The perimeter of the base of Leighton House is 112 ft less than the perimeter of the base of Trump World Tower.	To find an amount less than a given amount, subtract.	The perimeter of the base of Leighton House is 446 ft − 112 ft, or 334 ft.

So, the perimeter of the base of Leighton House is 334 ft.

Think and Discuss

Make a generalization. Then solve the problem.

a. A plane figure has 5 congruent sides. The perimeter of the figure is 90 ft. What is the length of each side?

b. A quadrilateral has a perimeter of 24 cm. Three of its sides each have a measure of 6 cm. What is the length of the fourth side?

c. The base of Leighton House has a length of 112 feet. If the perimeter is 334 feet, what is its width?

▲ Leighton House

KY MA-05-2.1.1 Students will apply standard units to measure length (to the nearest eighth-inch or the nearest centimeter) and to determine: perimeter; DOK 2 *also MA-05-2.1.3*

Guided Problem Solving

Make generalizations to solve.

1. Donna bought two boxes of cereal that are rectangular prisms. The base of the corn flakes box is 12 in. long and 4 in. wide. The perimeter of the base of the oat cereal box is 4 in. more than the perimeter of the base of the corn flakes box. What is the perimeter of the base of the oat cereal box?

   Make a table similar to the one on page 628. Write what you know about the cereal boxes. Then make a generalization and draw a conclusion.

   The perimeter of the base of the oat cereal box is ■ in.

2. **What if** the base of the cornflakes box was 10 in. long and 3 in. wide? What would the perimeter of the base of the oat cereal box be if it was still 4 in. greater than the perimeter of the corn flakes box?

3. Two tissue boxes are congruent cubes. If the perimeter of the base of one tissue box is 16 in., what is the length of one side of the base of the other tissue box?

Mixed Applications

USE DATA For 4–7, use the pictures.

4. The Pyramid of Menkaure is a square pyramid. The Pyramid of Khafre is the same shape. What is the length of each side of the base of the Pyramid of Khafre?

5. The Pyramid of Khufu is also a square pyramid with an original height of about 481 ft. What is the length of each side of the base of the Pyramid of Khufu?

6. The Pyramid of Menkaure has three smaller square pyramids standing along its south wall. The base of the largest of these three pyramids has a perimeter that is 800 ft less than the perimeter of the base of the Pyramid of Menkaure. What is the length of each side of the base of the largest of these three pyramids?

7. WRITE Math Kim says the length of each side of the base of the Pyramid of Menkaure is greater than the length of each side of the base of the Pyramid of Khufu. Is Kim's statement reasonable? **Explain.**

LESSON 5 HANDS ON

Circumference

OBJECTIVE: Find the circumference of a circle.

Quick Review

1. 3.2 × 5
2. 7.82 × 3
3. 2.4 ÷ 6
4. 0.08 ÷ 4
5. 14.7 ÷ 7

Vocabulary

circumference

pi

Investigate

Materials ■ metric ruler ■ string ■ cans

The distance around a circular object is its **circumference**.

A Wrap a string around a can. Mark the string where it meets itself after outlining the perimeter of the can.

B Use the ruler to measure the marked section of the string in centimeters. This is an estimate of the circumference, *C*, of the can.

C Trace the base of the can, and measure the diameter, *d*, of the circle.

D Divide the circumference by the diameter. Round your answer to the nearest hundredth of a centimeter. Make a table like the one below to record your answers.

E Repeat the steps with two different-sized cans.

Can	Circumference (*C*)	Diameter (*d*)	$C \div d$
Example	15.7 cm	5 cm	
1			
2			
3			

Draw Conclusions

1. What relationship do you find when you divide the circumference by the diameter of the can?
2. Does this relationship of the circumference to the diameter change according to the size of the circles? Explain.
3. **Application** How could you estimate the circumference of a circle without using the string method?

FAST TRACK

KY MA-05-3.1.1 Students will describe and provide examples of basic geometric elements and terms [points, segments, lines (perpendicular, parallel, intersecting), rays, angles (acute, right, obtuse), sides, edges, faces, bases, vertices, radius, diameter] and will apply these elements to solve real-world and mathematical problems. DOK 2 *also MA-05-2.1.*

Connect

The ratio of the circumference of a circle to its diameter is the same value for circles of all sizes. This value is called **pi** (π). The approximate decimal value of π is 3.14.

You can use the formula $C = \pi \times d$ to find the circumference of a circle.

Circumference of a Circle

$C = \pi \times d$

Circumference $\approx 3.14 \times$ diameter

The $\approx$ symbol means "is approximately equal to."

Examples **Find the circumference of each circle. Round to the nearest hundredth.**

Remember
The diameter of a circle is twice its radius.
$d = 2 \times r$

A

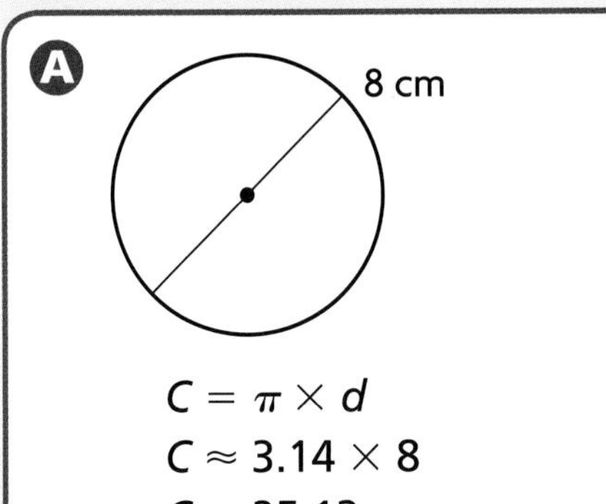

$C = \pi \times d$
$C \approx 3.14 \times 8$
$C \approx 25.12$

So, the circumference is about 25.1 cm.

B

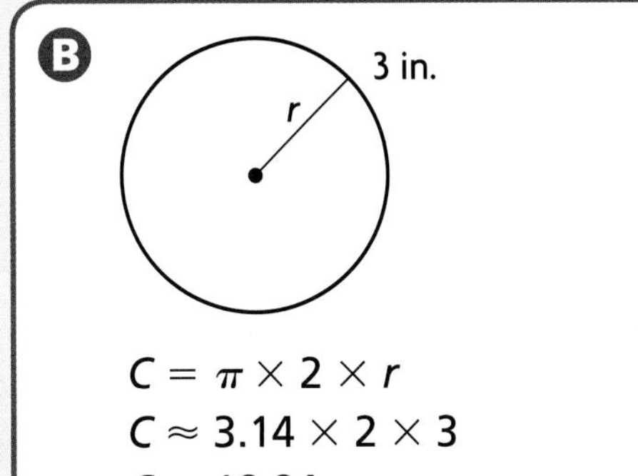

$C = \pi \times 2 \times r$
$C \approx 3.14 \times 2 \times 3$
$C \approx 18.84$

So, the circumference is about 18.8 in.

TALK Math
Explain the relationship between the radius and circumference of any circle.

Practice

For 1–3, complete the table.

	Object	C	d	$C \div d$
1.	plate	34.54 cm	11 cm	■
2.	coaster	15.7 cm	■	3.14
3.	pizza	■	30 cm	3.14

4. Leah has a circular cushion. She wants to put some ribbon around the cushion. If the diameter of the cushion is 32.3 cm, how much ribbon will border Leah's cushion?

To the nearest hundredth, find the circumference of a circle that has

5. a diameter of 8 m.
6. a radius of 5 ft.
7. a diameter of 6.7 cm.
8. a radius of 1 in.

9. **Reasoning** If you know the circumference of a circle, how can you find its diameter?

10. **WRITE Math** **Explain** why you use the $\approx$ symbol instead of the equal sign when you are finding the circumference of a circle.

Extra Practice

Set A Find the perimeter of each polygon. (pp. 624–625)

1. 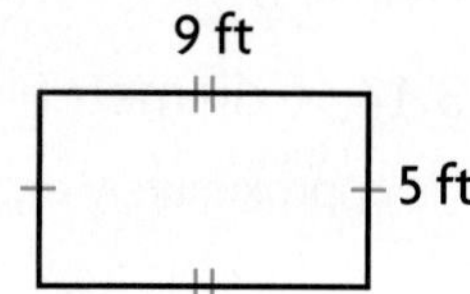

2. 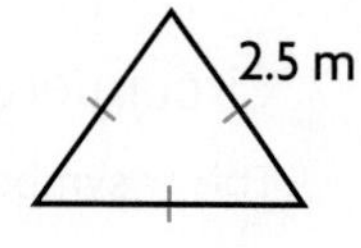

3. 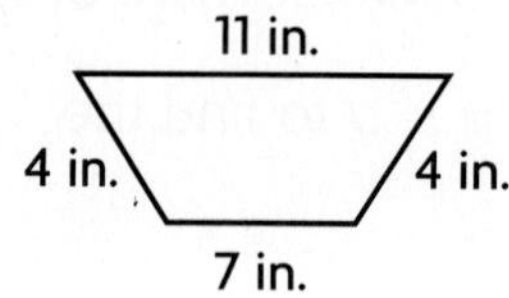

4. 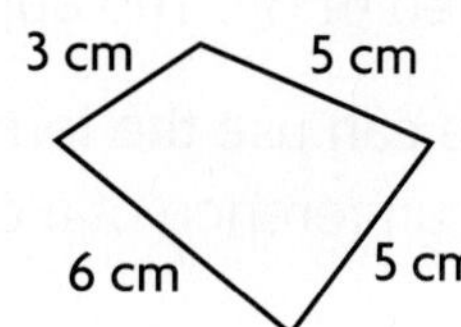

5. 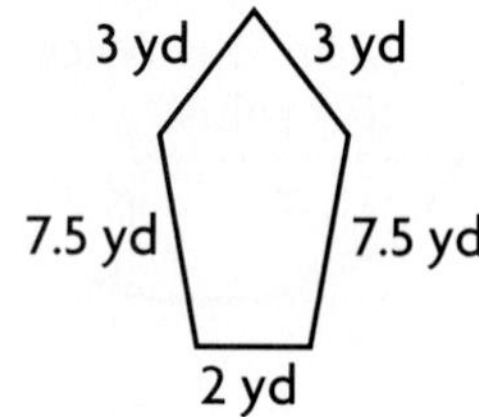

6. 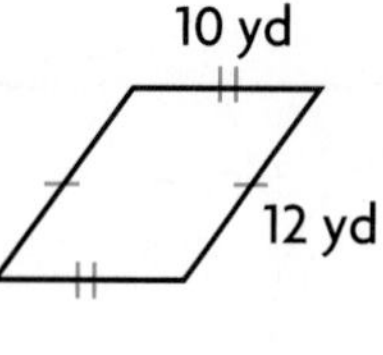

7. 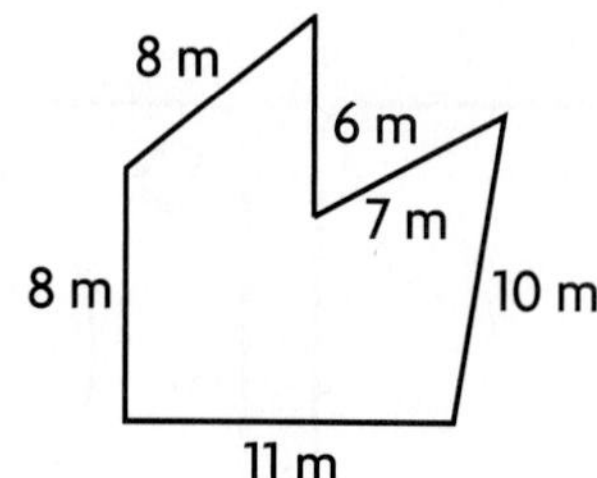

8. 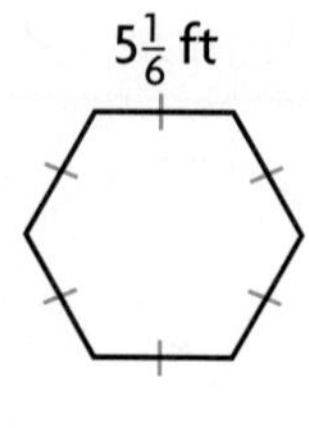

9. Roxie is putting a wallpaper border around her room. Her room is a square prism and each wall is 12 feet in length. What is the perimeter of Roxie's room?

10. A stop sign is a regular octagon. Each side measures $12\frac{1}{2}$ inches. What is the perimeter of a stop sign?

Set B Find the perimeter of each polygon by using a formula. (pp. 626–627)

1. 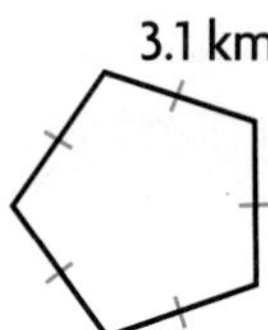

2. 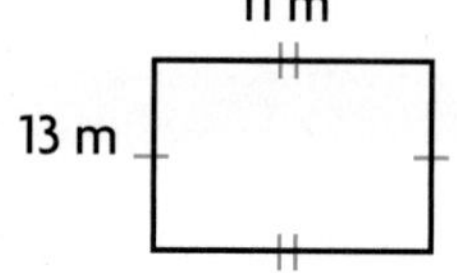

3. 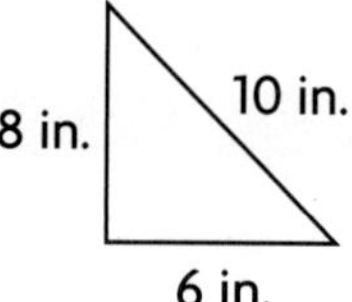

4. 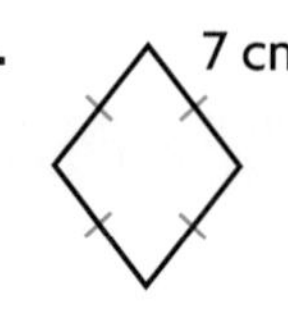

5. 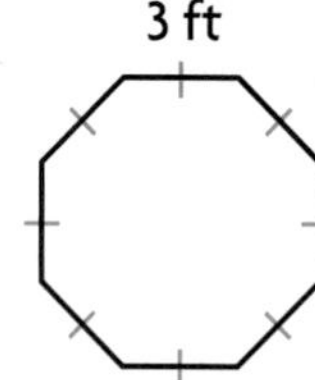

6. 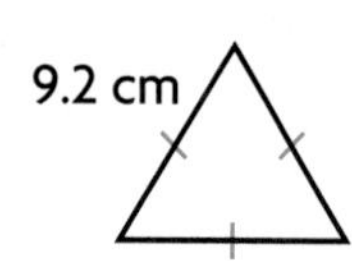

7. 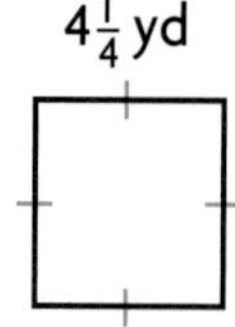

8. 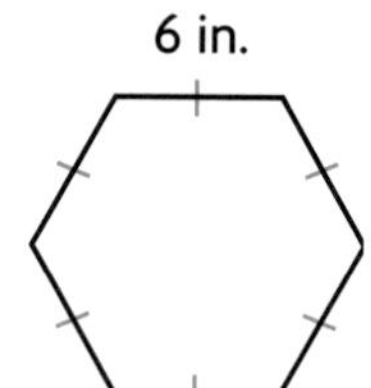

9. The screen at the movie theatre downtown is a rectangle that is 46 feet long and 18 feet high. What is the perimeter of the movie screen?

10. George placed a small fence around the perimeter of his square garden. He used a total of 20 feet of fencing. What is the length of each side of George's garden?

CD ROM **Technology**
Use Harcourt Mega Math, Ice Station Exploration, *Arctic Algebra*, Level CC

TECHNOLOGY CONNECTION

Calculator: Polygon Sides

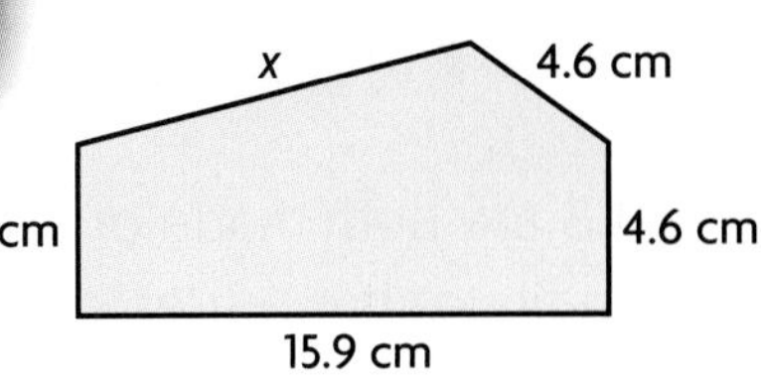

The perimeter of the figure is 42.6 cm. Use the calculator memory key to find the length of the unknown side *x*.

Step 1 Turn on the calculator and press MR/MC to clear the memory. Enter the length of the perimeter into the memory using the ▸M and Enter keys.

Step 2 Find the total length of the 3 congruent sides by multiplying 4.6 by 3. Use the ▸M − keys to subtract this product from the memory total.

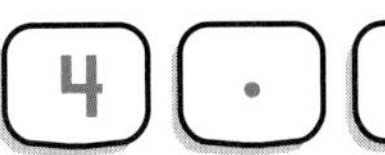

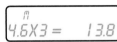

Step 3 Use the ▸M − keys to subtract the bottom side, 15.9, from the total. Use the memory recall key, MR/MC, to display the final memory total.

The unknown side measures 12.9 cm.

Try It

Use the calculator to find each unknown side.

1. $P = 21.2$ cm

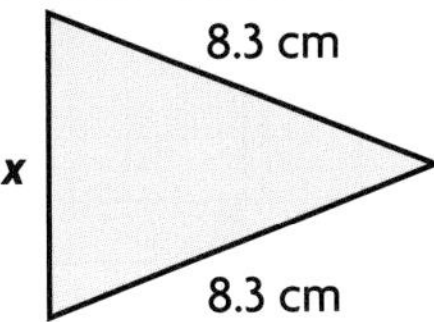

2. $P = 56$ m

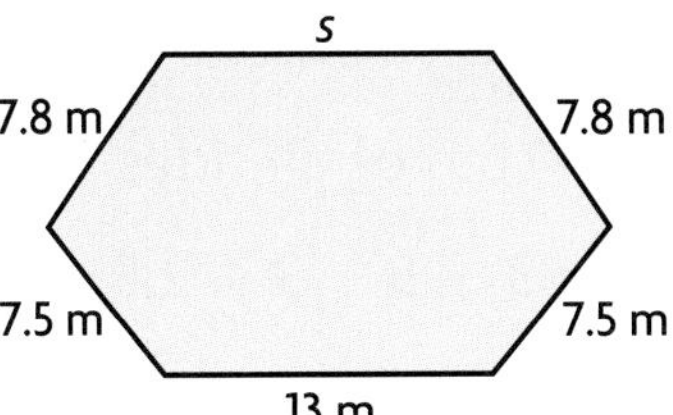

3. $P = 29$ ft

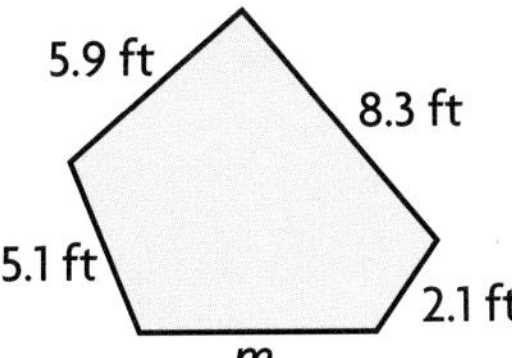

4. $P = 97.1$ in.

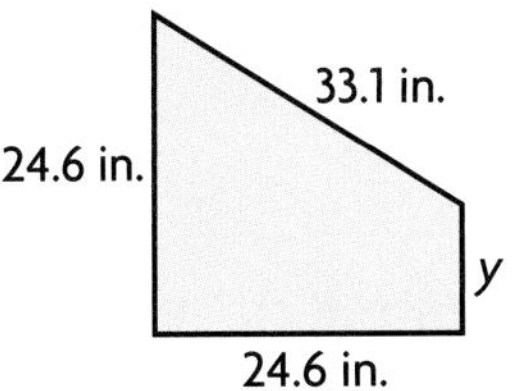

5. **Explore Math** The smallest side of a 6-sided figure measures 3.5 cm. Each successive side measures 1.25 cm greater in length than the previous side. What is the length of the figure's largest side? What is the total measure of the figure? **Explain** how you got your answers.

MATH POWER **Geometry**

Perimeter on a Grid

Figures A and B are both made of exactly 12 grid squares. Which figure has a greater perimeter?

You can count units to find the perimeter of a figure. Each grid square has a length and width of 1 unit.

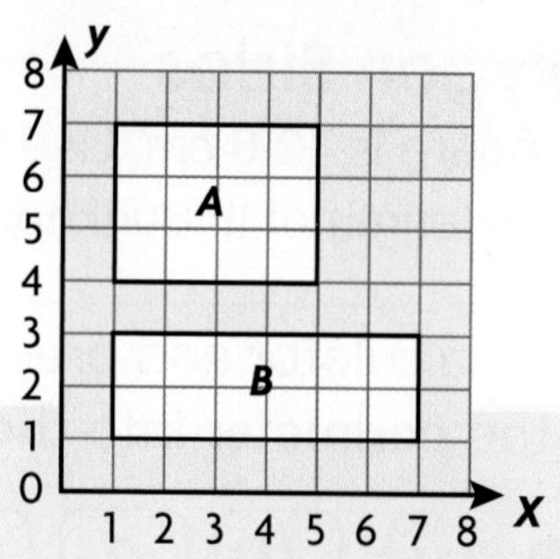

Remember

- Perimeter is the distance around a figure.

Examples

Find the perimeter of Figure *A* and Figure *B*.

Figure *A* is 4 units by 3 units. So:

P = sum of all sides

$P = 4 + 3 + 4 + 3 = 14$

Figure *B* is 6 units by 2 units. So:

$P = 6 + 2 + 6 + 2 = 16$

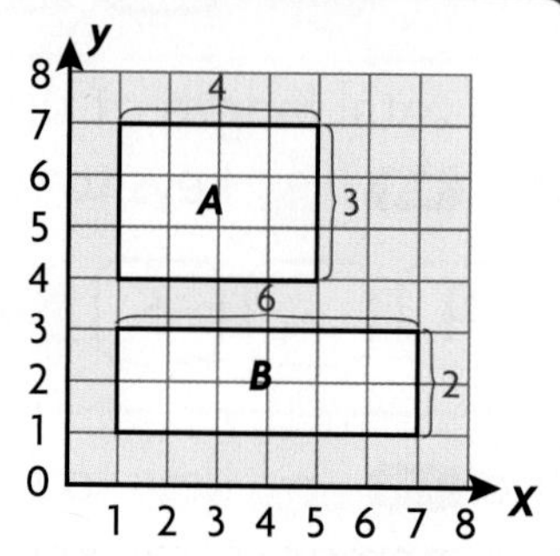

So the perimeter of Figure *B* is greater.

Estimate the perimeter of Figure C.

Estimate the length of the diagonal side:

diagonal: between 2 and 3 units → about 2.5 units

Now count boxes to find the perimeter:

P = sum of all sides

$P = 3 + 5 + 3 + 2.5 + 2 + 3 \rightarrow$ about 18.5 units

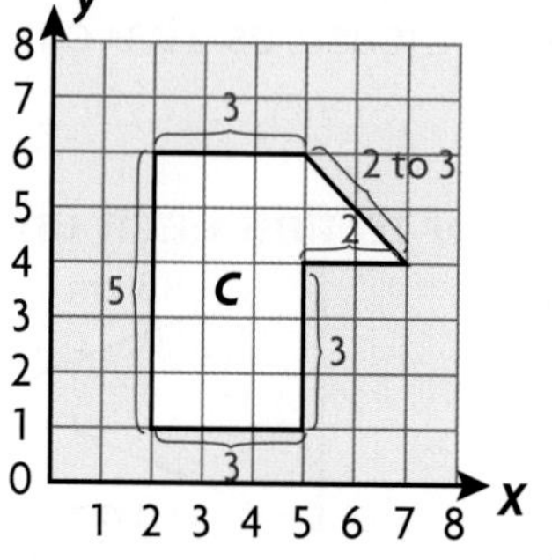

Try It

Solve. Estimate if necessary.

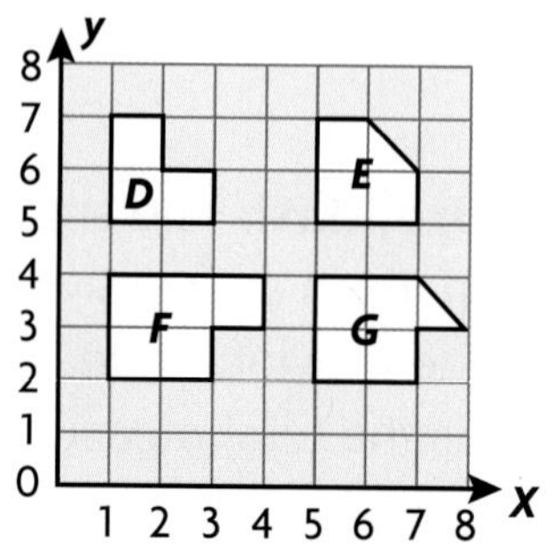

1. Find the perimeter of Figures *D* and *F*. Which perimeter is greater?
2. Estimate the perimeter of Figures *E* and *G*. Which perimeter is greater?
3. Rank the figures by perimeter size from greatest to smallest.
4. WRITE Math Compare Figures *F* and *G* in perimeter size. **Explain** how you know which Figure has a greater perimeter.

FAST TRACK KY MA-05-2.1.1 Students will apply standard units to measure length (to the nearest eighth-inch or the nearest centimeter) and to determine: perimeter; DOK 2

Chapter 23 Review/Test

Check Vocabulary and Concepts

Choose the best term from the box.

1. The distance around a circular object. KY MA-05-3.1.1 (p. 630)
2. The distance around a figure. KY MA-05-2.1.1 (p. 622)

VOCABULARY
- perimeter
- circumference
- pi
- diameter

Check Skills

Find the perimeter of each polygon. KY MA-05-3.1.1 (pp. 624–625)

3. 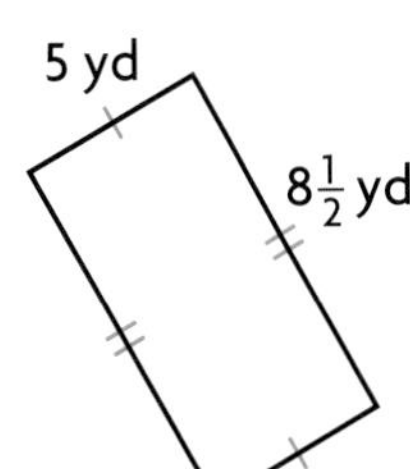

4. 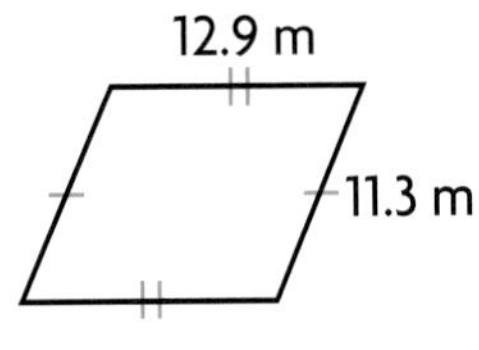

5. 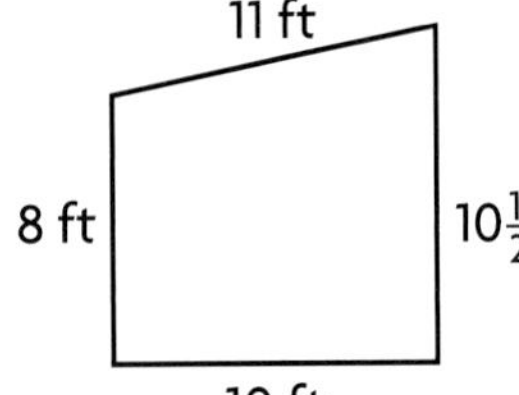

6. 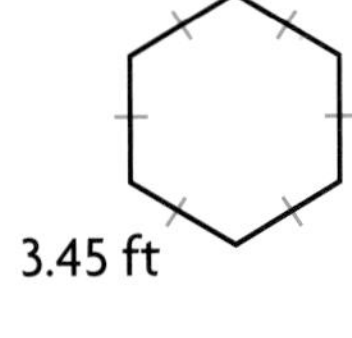

Find the perimeter of each regular polygon by using a formula. KY MA-05-3.1.1 (pp. 626–627)

7. $3\frac{1}{8}$ mi.

8. 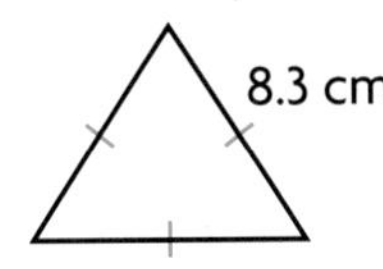

9. 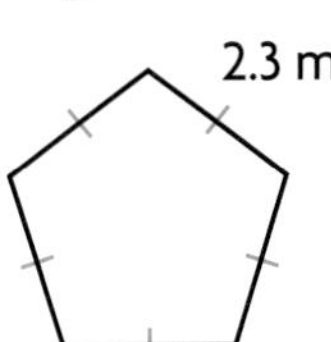

10. 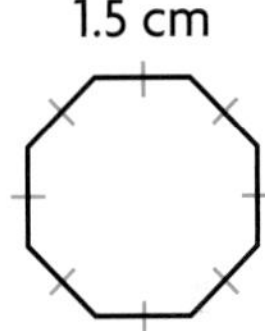

Check Problem Solving

Solve. KY MA-05-3.1.1 (pp. 628–629)

11. A company sells rectangular tarps to cover athletic fields. The tarp to cover a soccer field is 160 feet wide and 360 feet long. This tarp is the same size as a football field. What is the perimeter of a football field?

12. Luke's school bought a tarp to cover the infield of their softball field. The tarp is a square with a perimeter of 1,600 yards. What is the length of each side of the tarp?

13. A square field tarp has sides that are each 330 feet long. A smaller square tarp has sides that are each $\frac{1}{2}$ the length of the larger tarp. What is the perimeter of the smaller tarp?

14. WRITE Math Two rectangles have the same perimeter. Is it possible that the two rectangles have different side lengths? Give an example. **Explain.**

GO ONLINE **Technology** Use *Online Assessment.*

Practice for the KCCT
Chapters 1–23

Number and Operations

1. Nathan had $\frac{5}{8}$ of a sandwich left after lunch. He then ate $\frac{2}{8}$ of the sandwich. How much of the sandwich does Nathan have left? KY MA-05-1.3.1 (p. 342)

   A $\frac{4}{12}$

   B $\frac{2}{4}$

   C $\frac{3}{8}$

   D $\frac{4}{8}$

2. Felix and his friends went hiking. They hiked from the parking lot to the rest area. Then they hiked back to the parking lot. Which best compares the two distances from the parking lot to the rest area? KY MA-05-1.1.3 (p. 318)

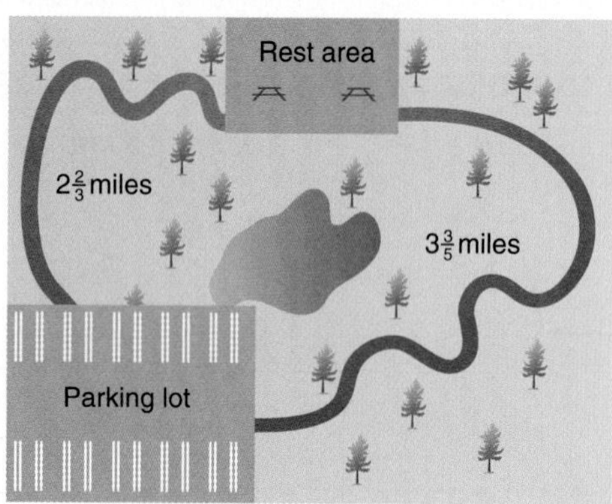

   A $3\frac{3}{5} < 2\frac{2}{3}$

   B $3\frac{3}{5} = 2\frac{2}{3}$

   C $2\frac{2}{3} > 3\frac{3}{5}$

   D $2\frac{2}{3} < 3\frac{3}{5}$

3. **WRITE Math** Is 23 a prime number? **Explain** how you know. KY MA-05-1.5.1 (p. 284)

Algebraic Thinking

4. Which is the value of k? KY MA-05-5.2.1 (p. 108)

$$8 \times k = 1{,}960$$

   A 104

   B 245

   C 366

   D 1,952

5. Which equation shows the relationship between x and y in this function table? KY MA-05-5.1.2 (p. 564)

Input	Output
x	y
3	10
4	13
6	19
8	25

   A $y = 3x + 1$

   B $y = 4x - 2$

   C $y = 5x - 5$

   D $y = x + 7$

6. **WRITE Math** Martin wrote this number pattern. If the pattern continues, what might the next two numbers be? **Explain** how you found your answer. KY MA-05-5.1.1 (p. 550)

   1, 5, 4, 8, 7, 11, 10, ■, ■

Measurement

7. Violet is gluing a ribbon around the perimeter of her rectangular jewelry box. The box is 8 in. long and 4 in. wide. How much ribbon does Violet need? KY MA-05-2.1.1 (p. 624)

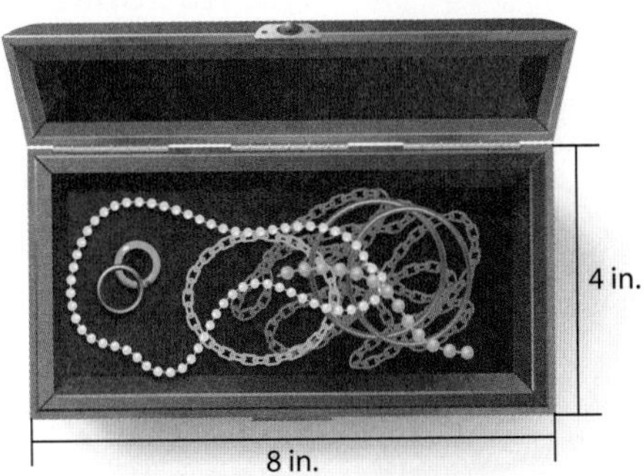

A 12 inches
B 20 inches
C 24 inches
D 32 inches

Understand the problem.

See item 7. The distance around a figure is the perimeter. Use the picture to help you solve the problem.

8. Susie's dance recital ended at 7:25 P.M. The recital lasted for 2 hours 10 minutes. At what time did the recital begin? KY MA-05-2.2.1 (p. 610)

A 9:15 P.M.
B 5:35 P.M.
C 5:15 P.M.
D 5:05 P.M.

9. WRITE Math **Explain** how to find the perimeter of a square where one side of the square is 10 ft. KY MA-05-2.1.1 (p. 624)

Data Analysis and Probability

10. Ron has a bag containing 5 green, 1 blue, 2 yellow, and 4 red marbles. He reaches into the bag and pulls a marble without looking. What is the probability that Ron will pull a green or red marble? KY MA-05-4.4.2 (p. 454)

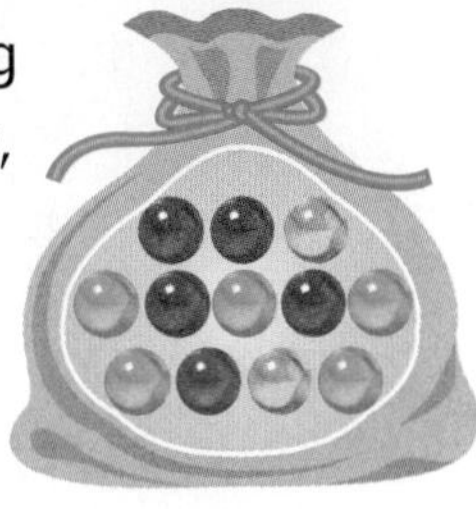

A $\frac{1}{3}$
B $\frac{1}{2}$
C $\frac{7}{12}$
D $\frac{3}{4}$

11. Hector surveyed the fourth-grade class at his school about their favorite type of music. The survey results are shown on the bar graph. How many students did Hector survey? KY MA-05-4.1.1 (p. 216)

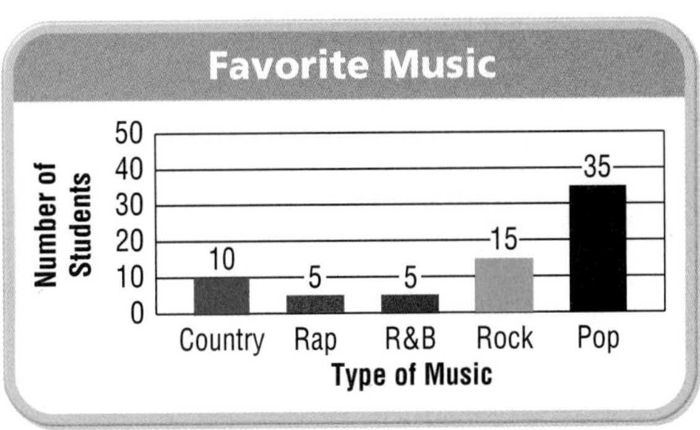

A 35
B 40
C 70
D 85

12. WRITE Math How can you find the median of this data set? **Explain.** KY MA-05-4.2.1 (p. 220)

32, 50, 34, 47, 20, 41, 45

CHAPTER 24 Area and Volume

FAST FACT

The National Hockey League, founded in 1917, is made up of 30 teams from the United States and Canada. It takes about 12,200 gallons of water to make the $1\frac{1}{4}$-inch-thick ice on a hockey rink.

Investigate

You are an NHL coach preparing the ice rink for practice. Suppose you want to divide the rink into smaller sections to practice drills. Describe a way to divide the rink into two or more smaller sections, and give the area of each.

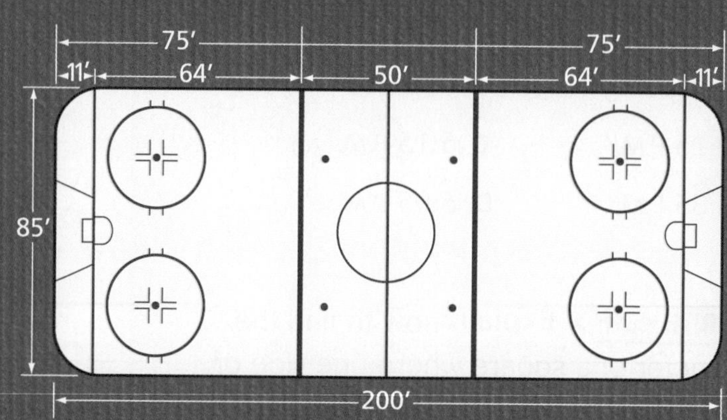

GO ONLINE **Technology** Student pages are available in the Student eBook.

Show What You Know

Check your understanding of important skills needed for success in Chapter 24.

Area

Find the area of each figure.

1. 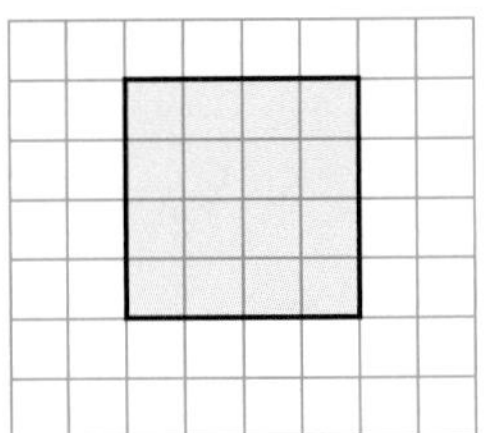
2. 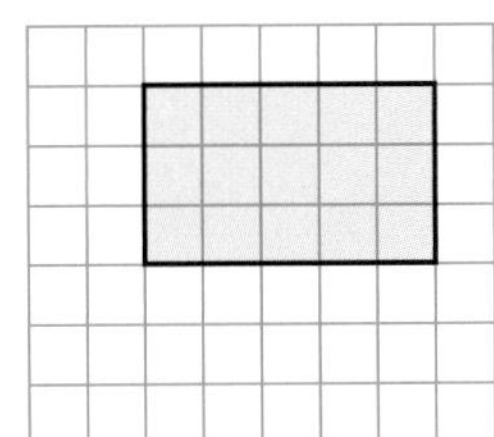
3. 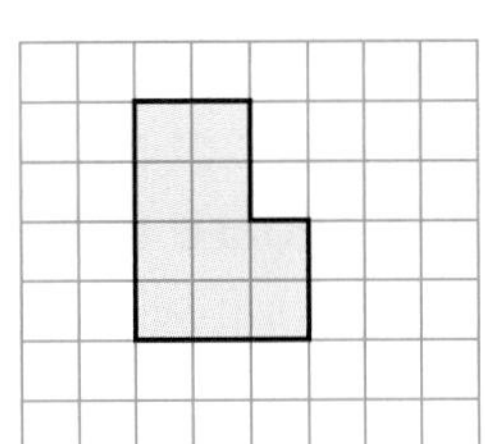
4. 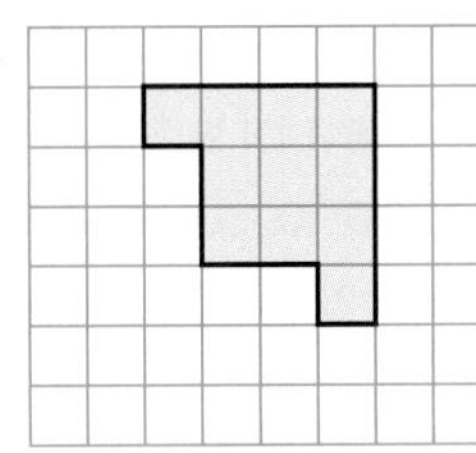
5. 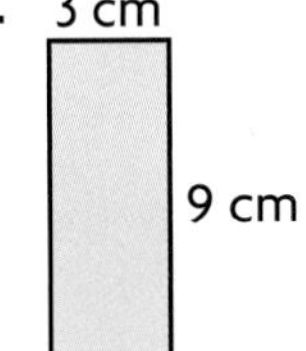

6. 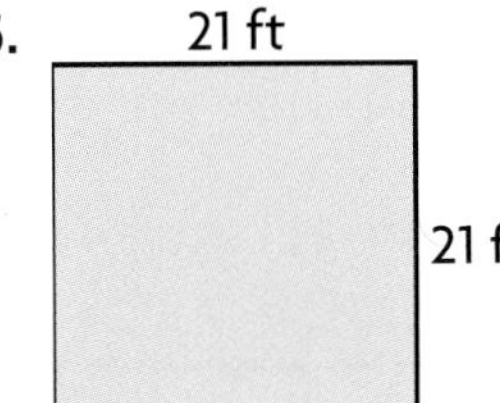

7. 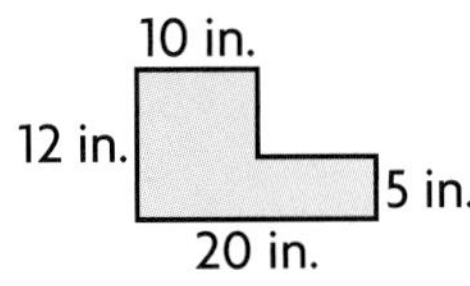

8. 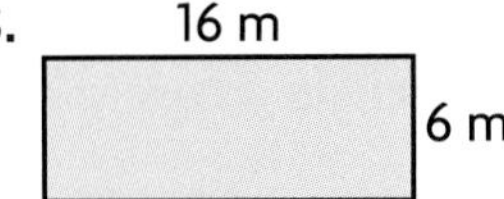

Multiply with Three Factors

Find the product.

9. $4 \times (4 \times 15)$
10. $(2 \times 6) \times 4$
11. $3 \times (5 \times 5)$
12. $8 \times 8 \times 8$
13. $8.4 \times (2 \times 3)$
14. $3.6 \times (4 \times 10)$
15. $(7 \times 5.7) \times 1$
16. $3.3 \times (2 \times 6)$
17. $7 \times 4 \times 7$
18. $(1.9 \times 2) \times 5$
19. $5.5 \times (3 \times 8)$
20. $4 \times 11 \times 7$

VOCABULARY POWER

CHAPTER VOCABULARY

area
base
cubic unit
height
perimeter
square unit
surface area
volume

WARM-UP WORDS

area the number of square units needed to cover a surface

base a polygon's side or a solid figure's face by which the figure is measured or named

height the length of a perpendicular from the base to the top of a plane figure or solid figure

Estimate Area

OBJECTIVE: Estimate the area of plane figures.

Quick Review

Find the sum.

1. $11 + 12\frac{1}{4}$
2. $10\frac{1}{2} + 5\frac{1}{2}$
3. $3\frac{3}{4} + 6$
4. $15 + 18$
5. $9\frac{1}{4} + 10\frac{2}{4}$

Vocabulary

area square unit

Learn

PROBLEM Joseph and Bonnie are putting together a jigsaw puzzle. How can they estimate the area of one puzzle piece?

The **area** of a figure is the number of square units needed to cover a surface. A **square unit** is a square that is 1 unit long and 1 unit wide.

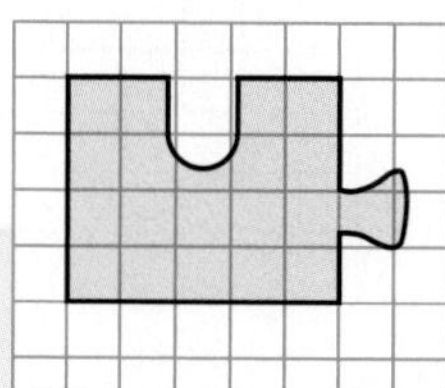

HANDS ON Activity

Materials ■ centimeter grid paper

Copy the diagram of the puzzle piece shown above. Each square on the grid is a one-centimeter square.

Step 1

Count the number of full squares. There are 14 full squares.

Step 2

Count the number of additional squares that are more than half full. There are 5. Do not count the squares that are less than half full.

Step 3

Add the numbers of squares you counted. $14 + 5 = 19$

So, the area of the puzzle piece is about 19 square centimeters, or 19 cm^2.

READ Math

Area is measured in square units, such as square feet (ft^2), square centimeters (cm^2), square inches ($in.^2$), and square miles (mi^2).

Joel and Natalie completed a circular puzzle. They traced it on a grid so they could estimate its area. Each square on the grid is a one-inch square.

Count the squares. There are 52 full green squares and 8 almost-full orange squares.

There are 8 almost half-full yellow squares. Combine them to make almost 4 full squares.

Find the sum of the squares counted.

$52 + 8 + 4 = 64$

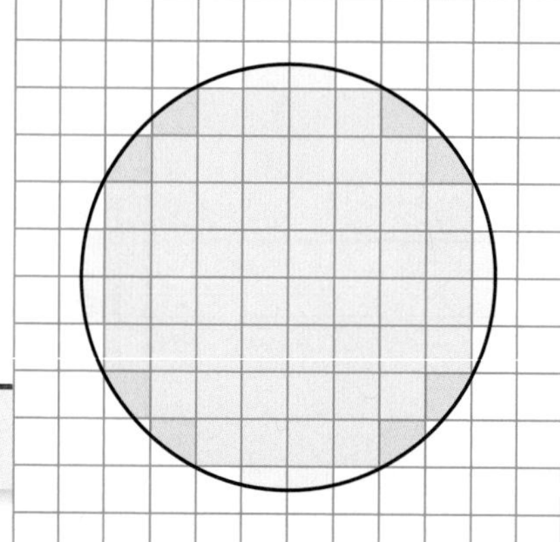

So, the area of the puzzle is about 64 $in.^2$

FAST TRACK KY MA-05-2.1.6 Students will estimate weight, length, perimeter, area, angle measures and time using appropriate units of measurement. DOK 2 *also* MA-05-2.1.1; *MA-05-2.1.3*

Guided Practice

Estimate the area of the shaded figure.

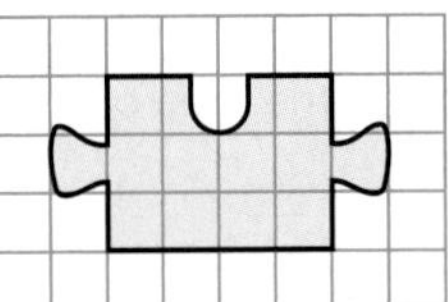

□ = 1 cm^2

1. How many full squares are there?
2. How many additional squares are more than half full?
3. What is the estimated area?

Estimate the area of the shaded figure. Each square on the grid is 1 $in.^2$

4. 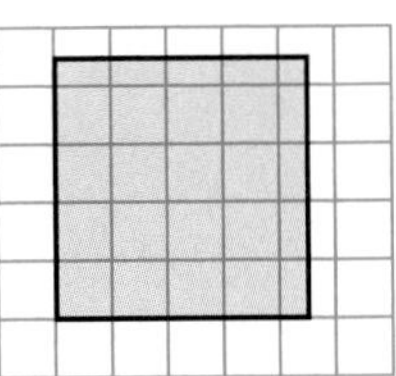

✓5. 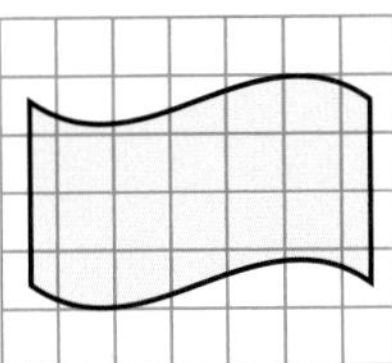

✓6. 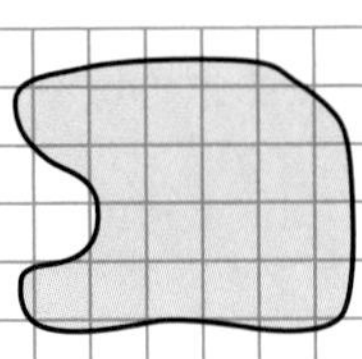

7. TALK Math **Explain** how to estimate the area of the figure in Problem 5.

Independent Practice and Problem Solving

Estimate the area of the shaded figure. Each square on the grid is 1 cm^2.

8. 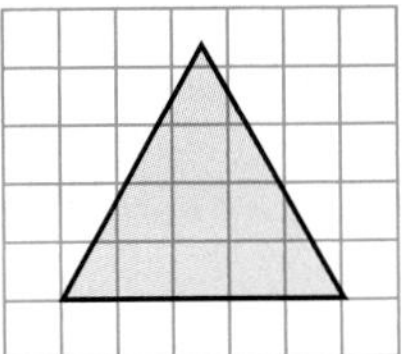

9. 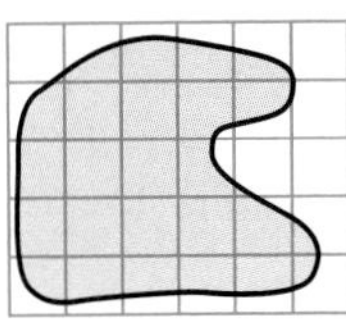

10. 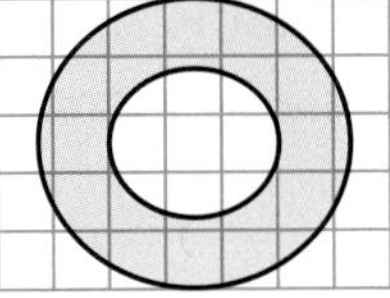

11. **FAST FACT** One of the world's largest jigsaw puzzles has more than 18,000 pieces. A model of the puzzle is shown on the grid. If each square on the grid represents 1 ft^2, estimate its actual area.

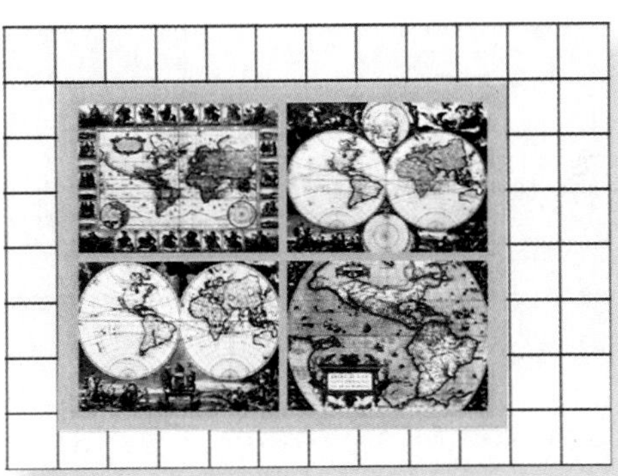

12. WRITE Math **Explain** how you can estimate the area of the center of the doughnut shape in Problem 10.

Mixed Review and Test Prep

13. What is the value of the expression $(6 + n) - 3$ if $n = 9$? (p. 96)

14. Mia buys a sweater with a price of $15. The computer multiplies the price by 1.07 to find the total cost including tax. If Mia pays the clerk with a $20 bill, how much change should she receive? (p. 184)

15. **Test Prep** Which of the following is the best estimate of the area of the figure?

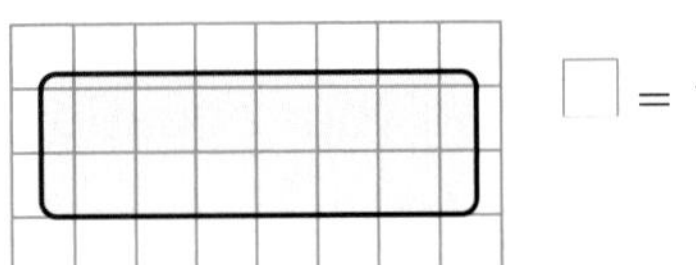

□ = 1 ft^2

A about 6 ft^2
B about 9 ft^2
C about 11 ft^2
D about 13 ft^2

Extra Practice on page 674, Set A

ALGEBRA

Area of Squares and Rectangles

OBJECTIVE: Find the area of squares and rectangles by using formulas.

Quick Review

Find the product.

1. 6×6
2. 10×8.5
3. 13×4
4. 0.7×0.8
5. 9×14

Learn

PROBLEM In art class, Mina is drawing plans for a flower garden. Mina's plans are for a garden that is 7 yards by 9 yards. What is the area of Mina's garden?

Use square units to find the area.

Activity

Materials ■ grid paper

Step 1

Let each square on the grid represent 1 square yard. Draw a rectangle that is 7 squares by 9 squares and shade it.

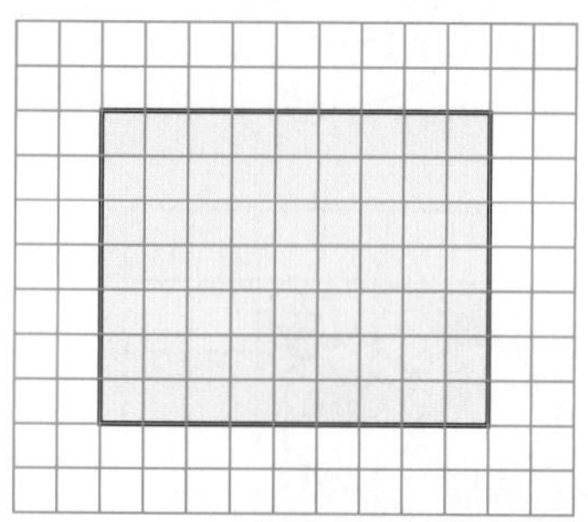

Step 2

Count the number of squares. Record your answer in square yards.

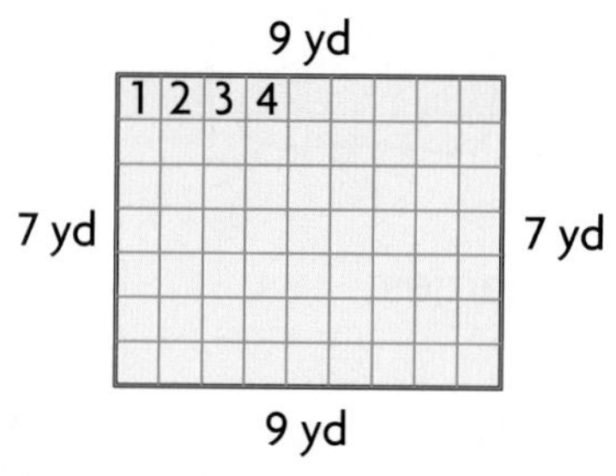

Area = 63 square yards, or 63 yd^2

So, the area of Mina's garden is 63 yd^2.

Example Write an equation.

Look at the relationship of the length and width of the rectangle to the area. What equation can you write to find the area?

Area = 7 rows of 9 squares each

Find the area using your equation.

Area $= 7 \times 9 = 63$

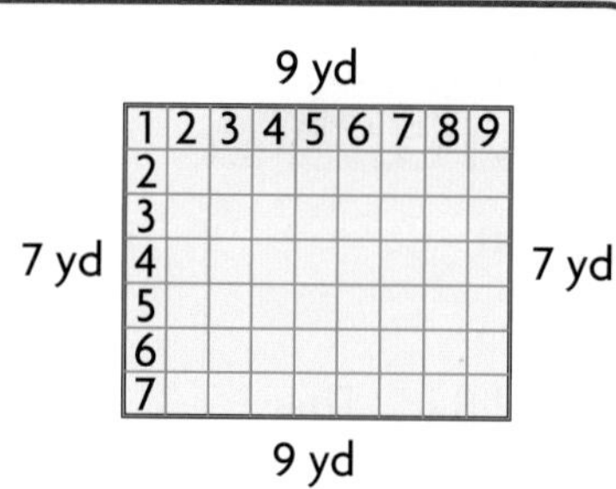

- How do the length and width of a rectangle relate to its area?

FAST TRACK

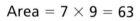

KY MA-05-2.1.1 Students will apply standard units to measure length (to the nearest eighth-inch or the nearest centimeter) and to determine: area (figures that can be divided into rectangular shapes); DOK 2 *also MA-05-2.1.3*

Use Formulas

You can use these formulas to find the area of a rectangle or a square.

Examples

A **Area of a rectangle**

$A = l \times w$, or $A = lw$

A = area, l = length, w = width

$A = 1\frac{1}{3} \times \frac{2}{3}$

$A = \frac{4}{3} \times \frac{2}{3}$

$A = \frac{8}{9}$

$1\frac{1}{3}$ yd

$\frac{2}{3}$ yd

So, the area of the rectangle is $\frac{8}{9}$ yd^2.

B **Area of a square**

$A = s \times s$, or $A = s^2$

A = area, s = side

$A = 6.2 \times 6.2$

$A = 38.44$

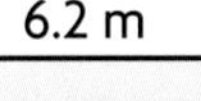

6.2 m

6.2 m

So, the area of the square is 38.44 m^2.

C **Area of a polygon**

Find the area of a polygon by dividing it into two or more simpler polygons.

Sophie's design for a garden is divided into a rectangle and a square. The area of the whole garden is equal to the sum of the areas of each part.

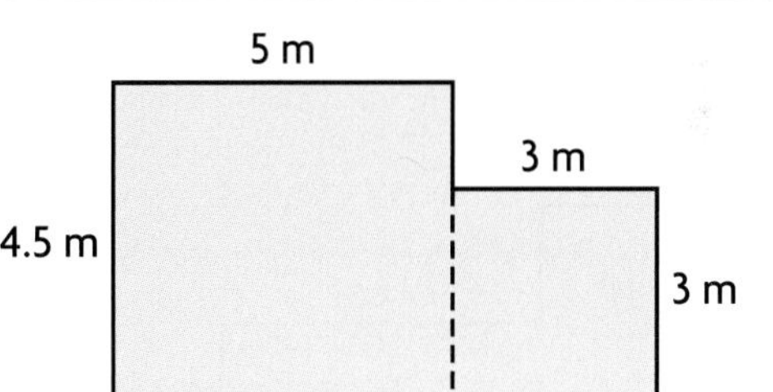

Parts of Garden		Whole Garden
Area of Rectangle	**Area of Square**	**Area of Whole Garden**
$A = (4.5 \times 5)$	$A = (3 \times 3)$	$A = (4.5 \times 5) + (3 \times 3)$
$A = 22.5$	$A = 9$	$A = 22.5 + 9 = 31.5$
The area is 22.5 m^2.	The area is 9 m^2.	The area is 31.5 m^2.

So, the area of the garden is 31.5 m^2.

Guided Practice

Find the area of each figure. Each square is 1 yd^2.

1.

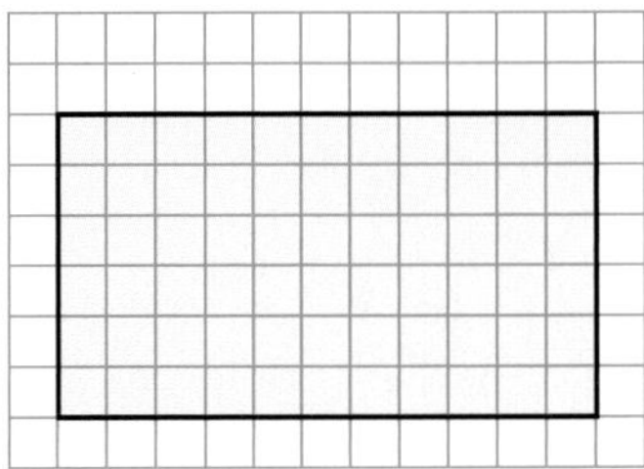

2.

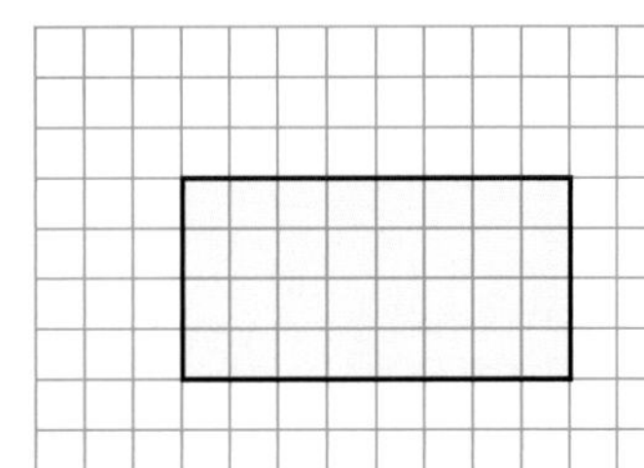

3.

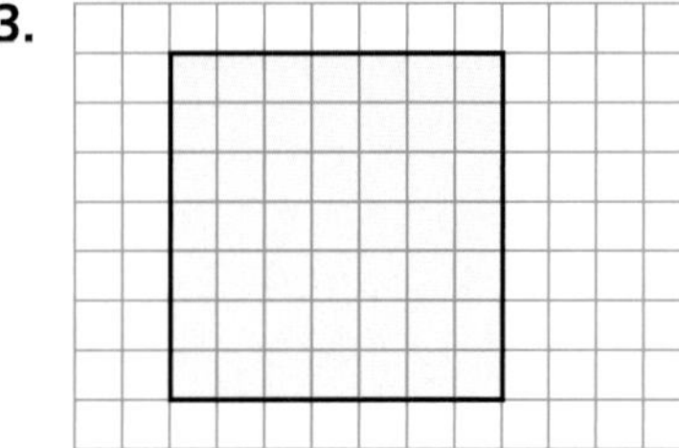

Find the area of each figure.

4. 3.3 m; 3.3 m

5.

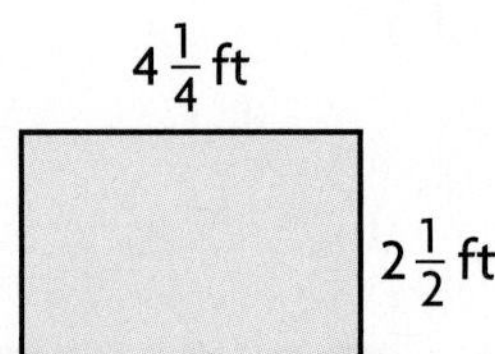

6. 6 km; 12.4 km; 9.6 km; 12.4 km

7. TALK Math **Explain** how to use the formula for the area of a rectangle to find the area of a square.

Independent Practice and Problem Solving

Find the area of each figure.

8.

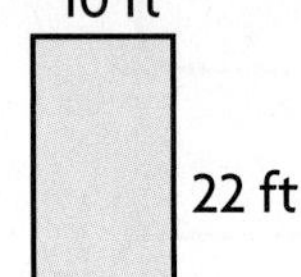

9.

10.

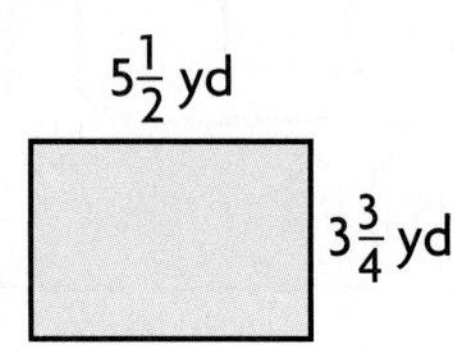

11.

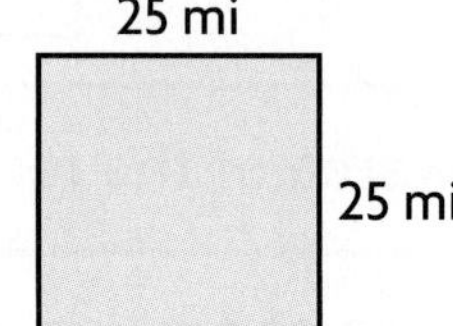

12.

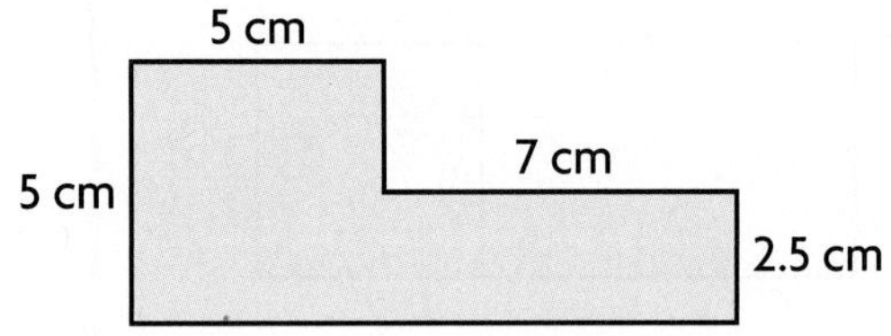

13.

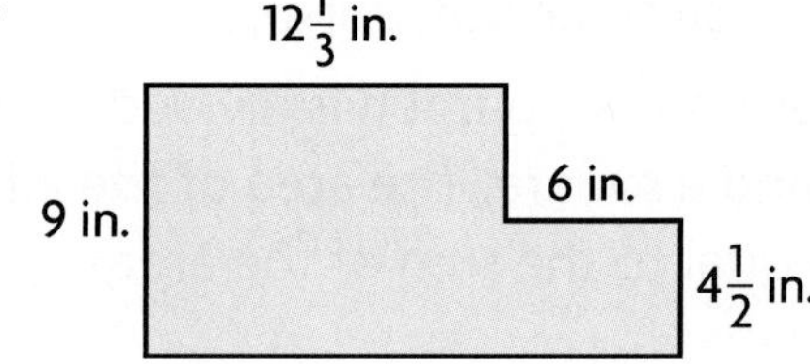

For each square or rectangle, find the area.

14. $s = 5.1$ m
$A = ■$

15. $s = 7$ in.
$A = ■$

16. $l = 3\frac{2}{5}$ ft
$w = 2$ ft
$A = ■$

17. $l = 4.3$ km
$w = 5.0$ km
$A = ■$

USE DATA Use the table for 18–21.

Wood Panel	Length	Width
Oak	60 in.	36 in.
Maple	68 in.	42 in.
Cherry	65 in.	48 in.

18. Brent plans to stain an oak panel. What is its area?

19. Which panel has an area of about 2,800 $in.^2$?

20. **Reasoning** Maddie's office wall is 8 feet tall and 10 feet wide. Can three cherry panels be placed against the wall? **Explain.**

21. WRITE Math **Sense or Nonsense** Ron says that the cherry panel has the greatest area. Does his statement make sense? **Explain.**

CD ROM **Technology**
Use Harcourt Mega Math, Ice Station Exploration *Polar Planes,* Level R.

 Extra Practice on page 674, Set B

Learn About Converting Units of Area

You can draw a diagram to find out how many smaller units of area make up a larger unit of area. For example, how can you show the number of square feet in a square yard?

Example

Step 1

Draw a square with sides labeled 1 yard.

1 yd

1 yd

Step 2

Divide the square into feet by dividing it into three equal rows and columns.

(Remember: 1 yd = 3 ft)

3 ft

3 ft

Step 3

Count the number of squares you made.

3 ft

1	2	3
4	5	6
7	8	9

3 ft

So, there are 9 square feet in 1 square yard.

Try It

Convert units of area to answer the questions.

22. Draw a diagram to find the number of square inches in 1 square foot. **Explain.**

23. How many square centimeters are in 1 square meter?

24. You want to carpet a room that has an area of 504 ft^2. How many square yards of carpeting will you need?

Mixed Review and Test Prep

25. Estimate the area of the trapezoid.
(p. 640)

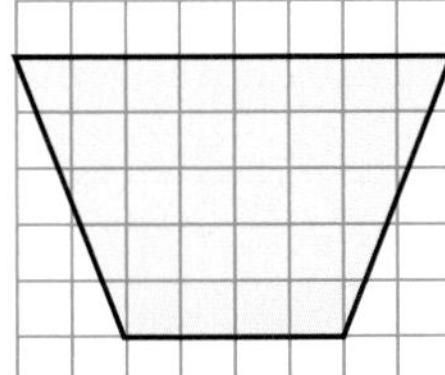

$\square = 1\ m^2$

26. Hope found that the height of a rectangular wall is 8 feet. If the wall's perimeter is 36 feet, what is its width? (p. 626)

27. **Test Prep** How many tiles that are 1 ft^2 are needed to cover a 14 ft × 20 ft patio?

A 68 tiles
B 140 tiles
C 280 tiles
D 560 tiles

28. **Test Prep** What is the area of an $8\frac{1}{2}$ in. × 11 in. sheet of paper?

A 39 $in.^2$
B $93\frac{1}{2}$ $in.^2$
C 99 $in.^2$
D $108\frac{1}{2}$ $in.^2$

LESSON 3

ALGEBRA

Relate Perimeter and Area

OBJECTIVE: Identify how perimeter and area are related.

Quick Review

Find the missing measurement.

1. $l = 6$ ft
   $w = 12$ ft
   $A = \blacksquare$
2. $l = 8.2$ m
   $w = 5.5$ m
   $A = \blacksquare$

Learn

PROBLEM The students at Central Valley School are painting a rectangular panel for a class play. The panel has the greatest possible area for a perimeter of 16 feet. What are the length and the width of the panel?

HANDS ON

Activity

Materials: ■ dot paper

You can use models to find the rectangle with the greatest area.

Step 1

On dot paper, draw rectangles with perimeters of 16 units.

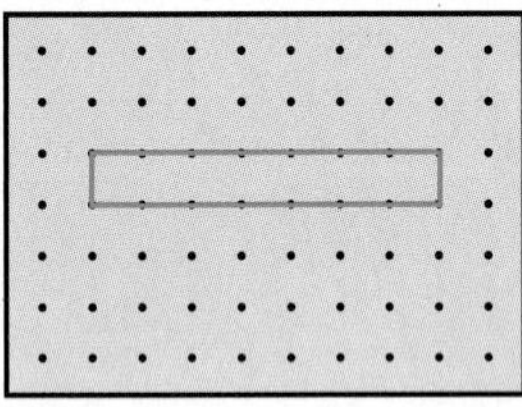

1×7

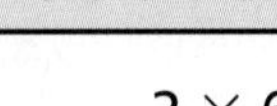

2×6

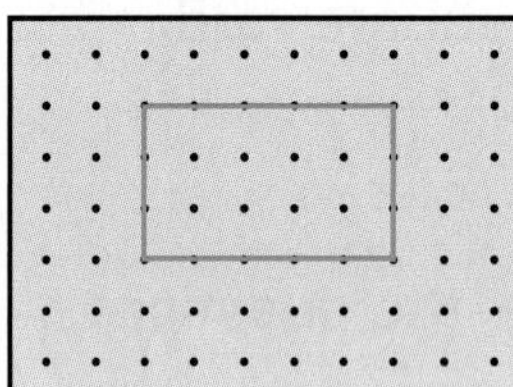

3×5

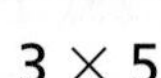

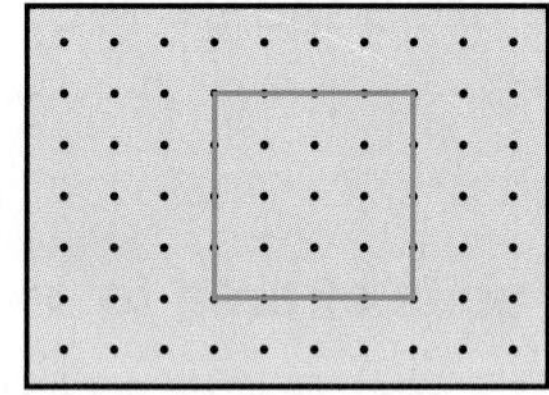

4×4

Step 2

Find and record the area of each rectangle. Each square unit represents 1 square foot.

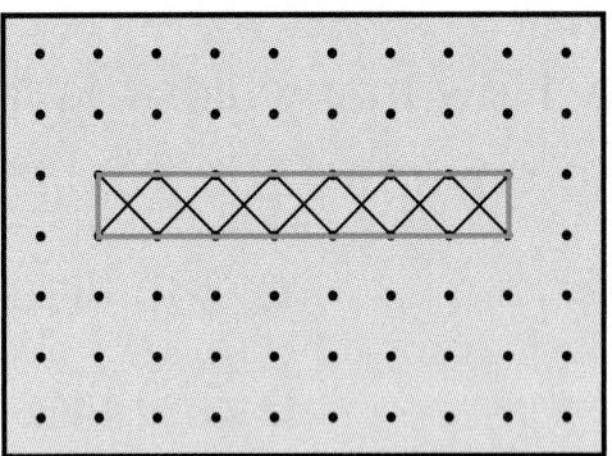

$A = 7 \text{ ft}^2$

Step 3

Make a table to record the length, width, perimeter, and area of each rectangle. Which length and width have the greatest area?

Length (ft)	Width (ft)	Perimeter (ft)	Area (ft^2)
7	1	16	7

So, to have the greatest area, the panel should be a square with 4-ft sides. The area is 4 ft $\times$ 4 ft, or 16 ft^2.

- If the panel had a perimeter of 12 ft, what length and width would have the greatest area?

Math Idea

For a given perimeter, a square has the greatest area of all possible rectangles.

KY MA-05-2.1.1 Students will apply standard units to measure length (to the nearest eighth-inch or the nearest centimeter) and to determine: perimeter and area; DOK 2 *also MA-05-2.1.3*

Anna's father wants to plant a garden and enclose it with a brick border. He wants to use the least possible number of bricks. The area of the garden will be 36 m^2. Which rectangle with this area will have the least perimeter?

Activity

Materials: ■ color tiles ■ grid paper

You can use models to find the rectangle with the least perimeter.

Step 1

Use 36 tiles or grid paper to make different rectangles with areas of 36 m^2. Let each tile represent 1 square meter.

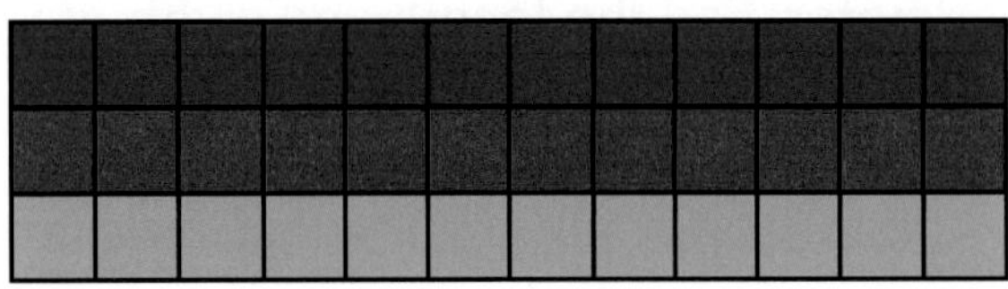

Step 2

Copy and complete the table to record your results. (Hint: To find all the possible whole number lengths and widths, find all the factors of 36.)

Length (m)	Width (m)	Perimeter (m)	Area (m^2)
36	1	74	36
18	2	■	36
12	■	■	36
9	■	■	36
6	■	■	36

So, the least perimeter is 24 m. The garden should be a square with sides of 6 m.

- As rectangles with the same areas get closer to becoming a square, what happens to their perimeters?

Math Idea
For a given area, a square has the least perimeter of all possible rectangles.

Example

Anna's father made another garden with an area of 20 m^2. Using whole numbers only, what rectangle has the least perimeter for this area?

Use tiles and make a table. Use factors of 20 as lengths and widths.

Length (m)	Width (m)	Perimeter (m)	Area (m^2)
20	1	42	20
10	2	24	20
5	4	18	20

So, the least perimeter is 18 m. The length of the rectangle is 5 meters and the width is 4 m.

- Why isn't this garden shaped in the form of a square?

Guided Practice

For 1–3, use the rectangles at the right.

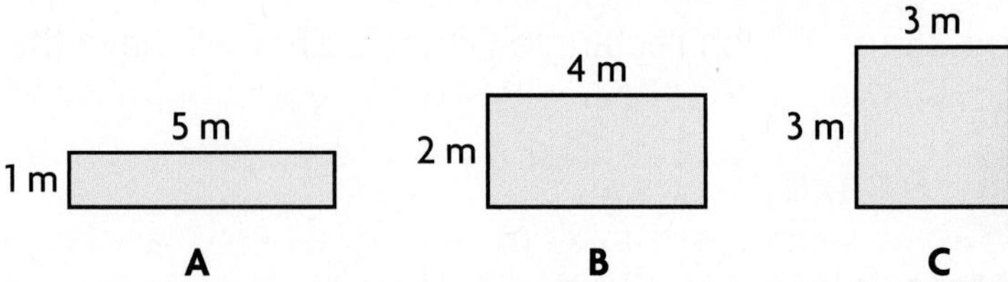

1. What is the perimeter of each rectangle?
2. Which rectangle has the greatest area?
3. What is the shape of the rectangle with the greatest area?

For the given perimeter, find the length and width of the rectangle with the greatest area. Use whole numbers only.

4. 8 in.   5. 28 m   6. 34 ft   7. 10 cm   ✓8. 44 yd

For the given area, find the length and width of the rectangle with the least perimeter. Use whole numbers only.

9. 28 cm^2 10. 32 km^2 11. 64 $in.^2$ 12. 54 ft^2 ✓13. 49 mi^2

14. TALK Math **Explain** what happens to the area of a rectangle with a given perimeter as the difference between the length and width increases.

Independent Practice and Problem Solving

For the given perimeter, find the length and width of the rectangle with the greatest area. Use whole numbers only.

15. 60 yd   16. 54 cm   17. 4 mi   18. 100 ft   19. 46 mm

For the given area, find the length and width of the rectangle with the least perimeter. Use whole numbers only.

20. 40 $in.^2$ 21. 9 km^2 22. 15 m^2 23. 45 ft^2 24. 100 cm^2

25. Copy and complete the table to find the areas of rectangles with a perimeter of 10 m. Describe the patterns you see.

Width (m)	0.5	1	1.5	2	2.5
Length (m)	■	■	■	■	■
Area (m^2)	■	■	■	■	■

26. **Pose a Problem** about a swimming pool with a length of 40 m and a width of 20 m.

27. Using 100 ft of fencing, what is the greatest area that can be fenced? the least area? Use whole numbers.

28. WRITE Math **What's the Error?** Jay says that with a given perimeter, the rectangle with the greatest width has the greatest area. What error did Jay make?

 Extra Practice on page 674, Set C

Learn About Pentominoes

A pentomino is a shape made from five squares of the same size. Each square must touch the entire side of another square.

Do all pentominoes have the same perimeter?

Example

Materials: ■ grid paper

Use grid paper to draw at least three more examples of different pentominoes. Then find their perimeters. Reflecting and rotating a pentomino does not count as a different pentomino.

$P = 12$ units $P = 12$ units

In the drawings at the right, four pentominoes have perimeters of 12 units, but one pentomino has a perimeter of 10 units.

So, not all pentominoes have the same perimeter.

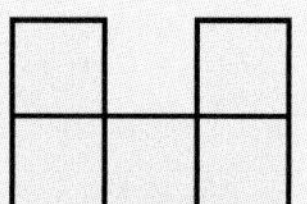

$P = 12$ units $P = 10$ units $P = 12$ units

Try It

Use logical reasoning to answer the questions.

29. Do all pentominoes have the same area? **Explain.**

30. Draw as many different pentominoes as you can. Then share your pentominoes with a classmate. How many different pentominoes are there?

Mixed Review and Test Prep

Use the diagram of the patio for 31–32.

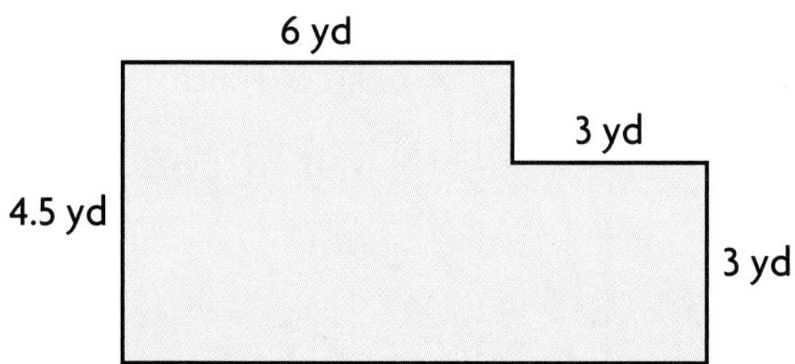

31. What is the area of the patio? (p. 642)

32. To place a rail around the outside of the patio, how much railing would you need? (p. 626)

33. **Test Prep** What is the greatest possible area for a rectangle with a perimeter of 22 m?

A 10 m^2 **C** 28 m^2

B 24 m^2 **D** 30 m^2

34. **Test Prep** What is the least possible perimeter for a rectangle with an area of 144 ft^2?

A 12 ft   **C** 48 ft

B 24 ft   **D** 148 ft

ALGEBRA

Area of Triangles

OBJECTIVE: Find the area of triangles by using a formula.

Quick Review

Find the product.

1. $\frac{1}{2} \times 8$
2. $\frac{1}{2} \times 20$
3. $\frac{1}{2} \times 15$
4. $\frac{1}{2} \times 4.2$
5. $\frac{1}{2} \times (2 \times 5)$

Vocabulary

height

base

Learn

PROBLEM The Sign Shop makes banners, flags, and signs. Mario's neighborhood wants a triangular banner to advertise an upcoming street fair. The banner will have a base of 4 feet and a height of 8 feet. How much fabric will be needed for the banner?

Activity

Materials ■ grid paper ■ scissors

Step 1

Draw a model of the banner on grid paper. Label the height and the base.

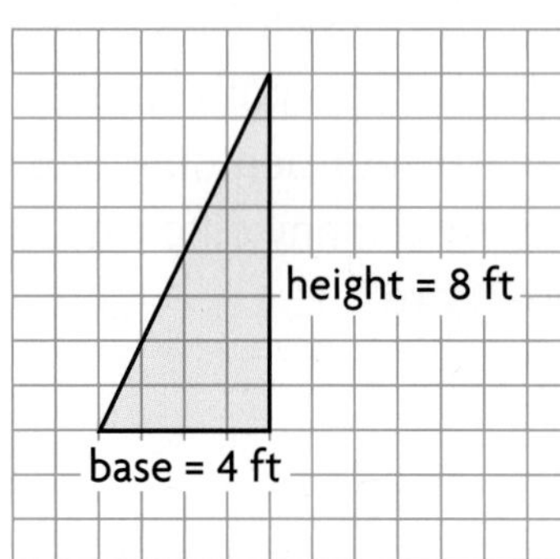

The **height** is the length of a line segment perpendicular to the **base** of the triangle.

Step 2

Draw a rectangle around the triangle as shown. Find the area of the rectangle.

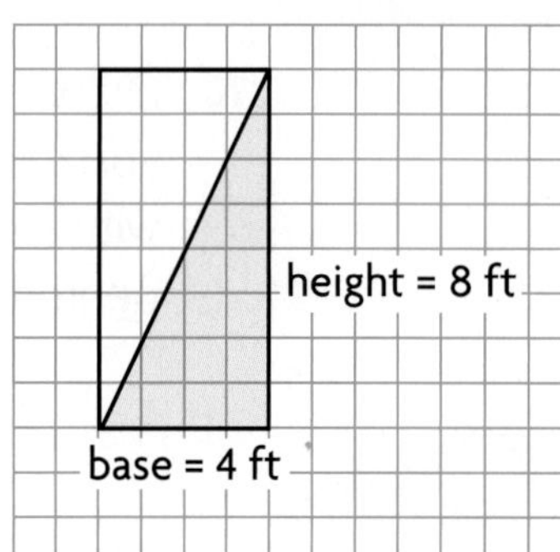

Rectangle:

$A = \text{base} \times \text{height}$

$A = bh$

$A = 4 \times 8$

$A = 32$

Step 3

Cut out the rectangle. Cut it in half to make two congruent triangles.

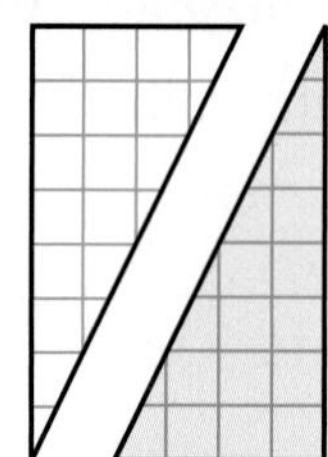

The area of the triangle is half the area of the rectangle.

Triangle:

$A = \frac{1}{2} \times \text{base} \times \text{height}$

$A = \frac{1}{2} \times b \times h$, or $\frac{1}{2}bh$

$A = \frac{1}{2} \times 4 \times 8$

$A = 16$

So, the amount of material needed for the banner is 16 ft^2.

- How do the base and height of the banner relate to the length and width of the rectangle in Step 2?

Other Triangles

The Sign Shop is making a sign in the shape shown at the right. What is the area of the sign?

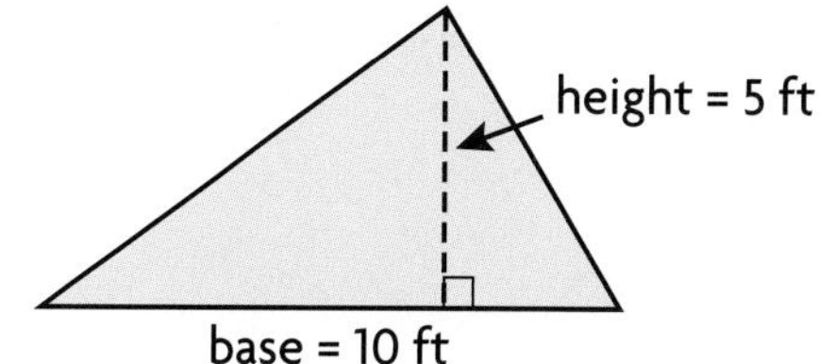

Activity

Materials ■ grid paper ■ scissors

Step 1

Draw and shade a model of the triangle inside a rectangle.

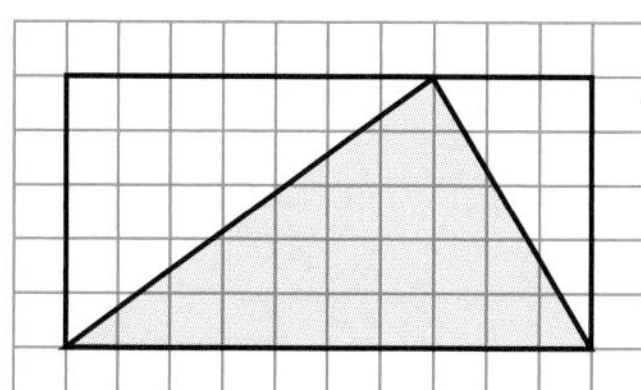

Step 2

Cut out the rectangle and then the shaded triangle.

Step 3

The parts of the rectangle that are not shaded fit exactly over the shaded triangle. So, the area of the triangle is half the area of the rectangle.

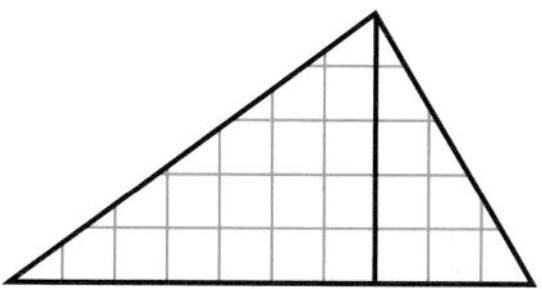

$A = \frac{1}{2} \times b \times h$

$A = \frac{1}{2} \times 10 \times 5 = 25 \text{ ft}^2$

So, the area of the sign is 25 ft^2.

Math Idea

You can use the formula $A = \frac{1}{2} \times b \times h$ to find the area of any triangle.

More Examples

A **Find the area.**

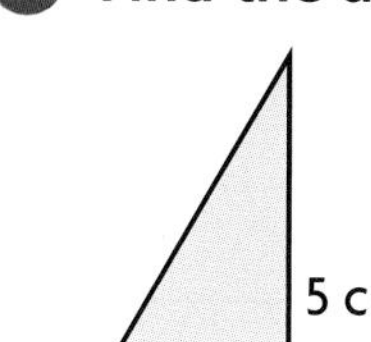

$A = \frac{1}{2}bh$

$A = \frac{1}{2} \times 3 \times 5 = 7.5$

The area is 7.5 cm^2.

B **Find the area.**

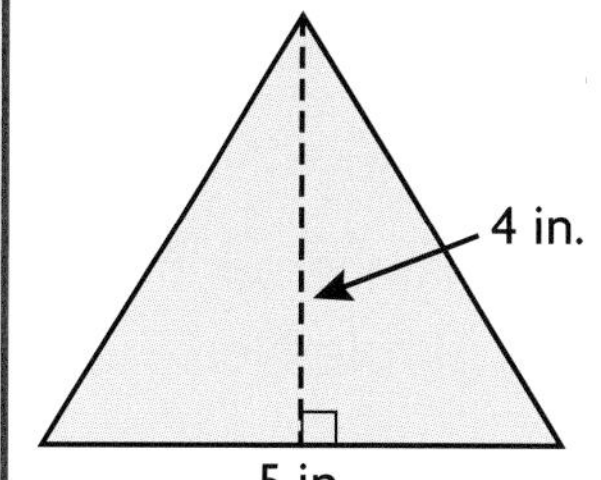

$A = \frac{1}{2}bh$

$A = \frac{1}{2} \times 5 \times 4 = 10$

The area is 10 in.^2

Guided Practice

Find the area of each triangle.

1.

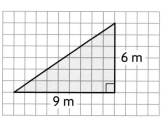

2.

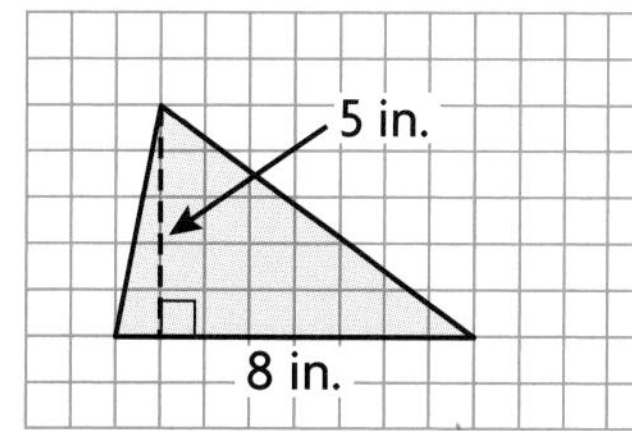

3.

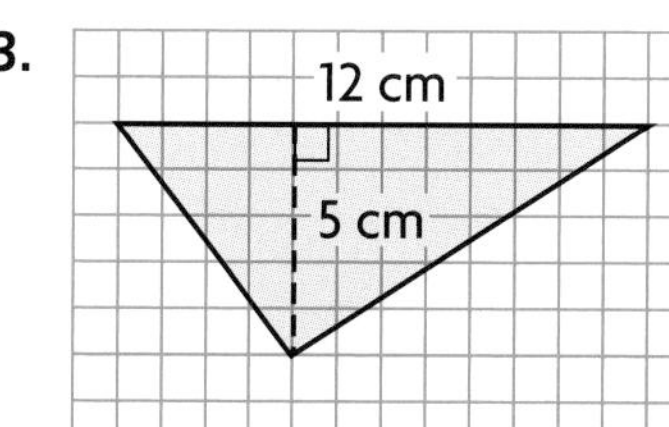

Find the area of each triangle.

4. 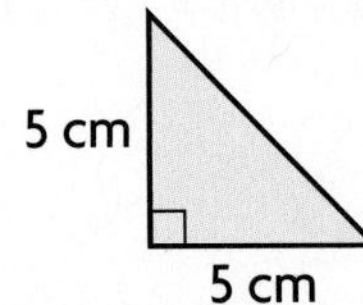

5. 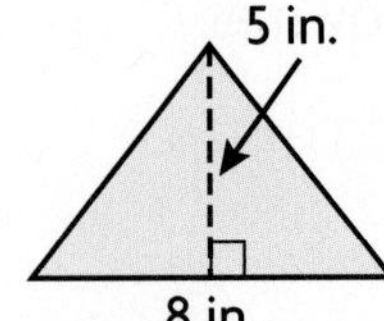

6. 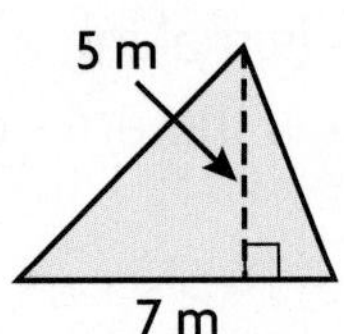

7. TALK Math **Explain** the relationship between the area of a rectangle and the area of a triangle.

Independent Practice and Problem Solving

Find the area of each triangle.

8. 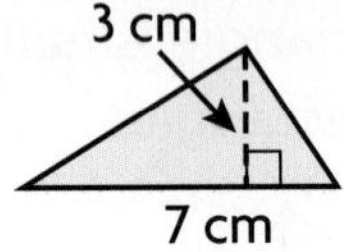

9. 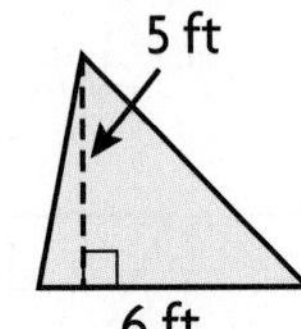

10. 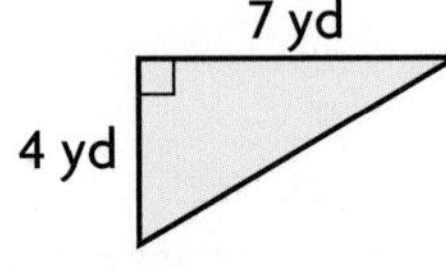

11. 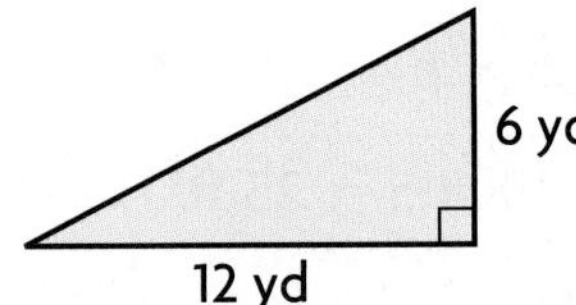

12. 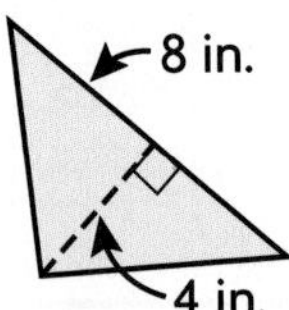

13. 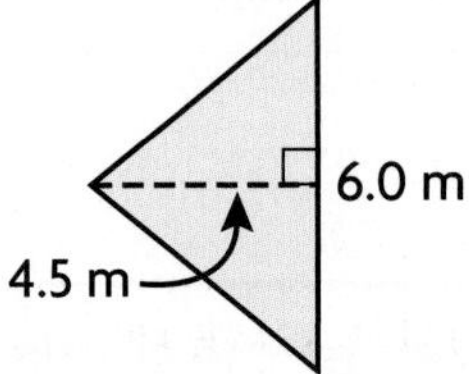

14. base (b) = 14 ft
height (h) = 8 ft
Area (A) = ■

15. base (b) = 7 in.
height (h) = 11 in.
Area (A) = ■

16. base (b) = 6 m
height (h) = 10 m
Area (A) = ■

For 17–18, use the diagram.

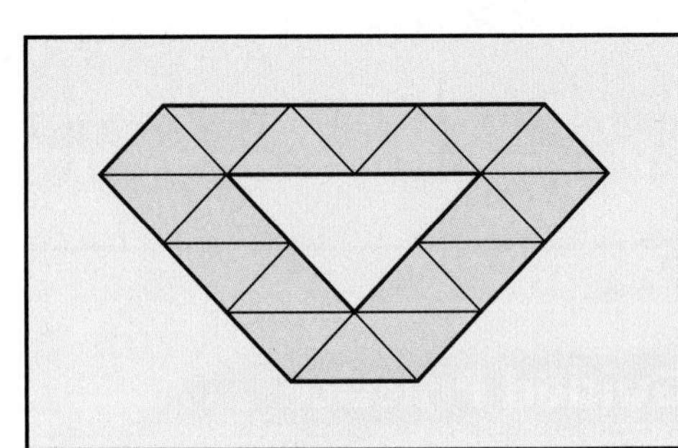

17. To fill the middle of the pattern, Natalie bought white tiles the same size and shape as the purple tiles. How many white tiles did she buy?

18. **Reasoning** The tiles in the pattern are right isosceles triangles. The two shorter sides of each triangle are each 1 in. long. Find the area of the purple part.

19. WRITE Math **What's the Error?** A triangle has a base of 4 m and a height of 8 m. Kara says its area is 32 m^2. Describe and correct her error.

 Extra Practice on page 464, Set D

Learn About Different Triangles, Same Size

Do two non-congruent triangles with the same base and height have the same area? Use grid paper to find out.

Example

Materials ■ centimeter grid paper

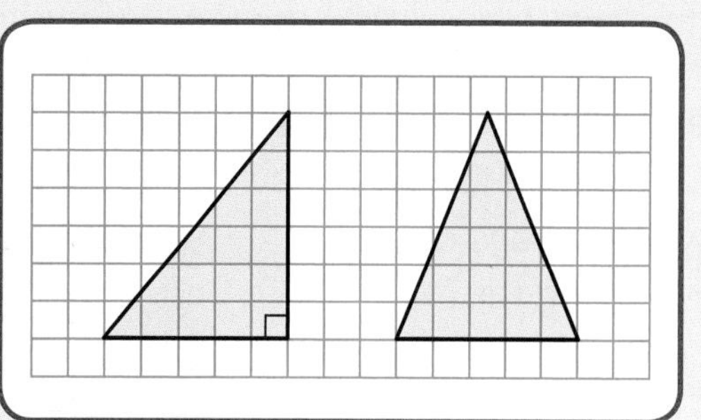

Use grid paper to draw a right triangle with a base of 5 cm and a height of 6 cm.

Then try to draw a different triangle with the same base and height. Do the triangles have the same area?

So, two non-congruent triangles with the same base and height can have the same area.

Try It

Use models drawn on grid paper to answer the questions.

20. Draw another triangle with a base of 5 cm and a height of 6 cm. Does this triangle have the same area as the first two triangles? **Explain.**

21. Draw two different triangles, each with an area of 12 cm^2. Do both triangles have the same perimeter?

Mixed Review and Test Prep

22. Mrs. Ryan wants to fence a rectangular area of 50 ft^2 for her dog. Using whole numbers, what is the length and width of a fence with the least perimeter? (p. 646)

23. **Test Prep** What is the area of the triangle?

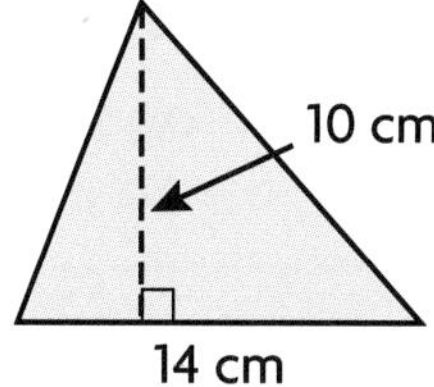

A 24 cm^2 **C** 100 cm^2
B 70 cm^2 **D** 140 cm^2

24. Trey tosses a number cube labeled 1 through 6. What is the probability of tossing a 5? (p. 454)

25. **Test Prep** What is the area of the triangular garden shown below?

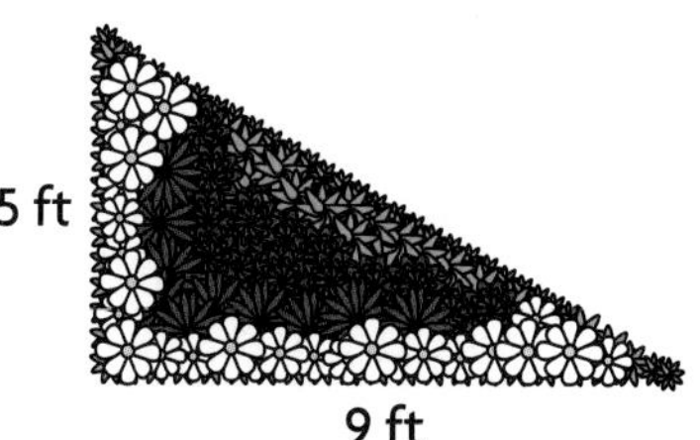

A 22.5 ft^2 **C** 45 ft^2
B 36.5 ft^2 **D** 90 ft^2

LESSON 5

ALGEBRA

Area of Parallelograms

OBJECTIVE: Find the area of parallelograms.

Quick Review

Find the area of each rectangle.

1. 5 in. × 11 in.
2. 4 ft × 12 ft
3. 6.2 cm × 5.3 cm
4. 10.5 m × 13 m
5. 35 km × 40 km

Learn

PROBLEM Jeremy's dog goes to a dog run shaped like a parallelogram. The dog run is covered with sand. One bag of sand covers 1 square meter. How many bags of sand does it take to cover the dog run?

The lengths of the base and height of the dog run are shown below. Find the area of the parallelogram.

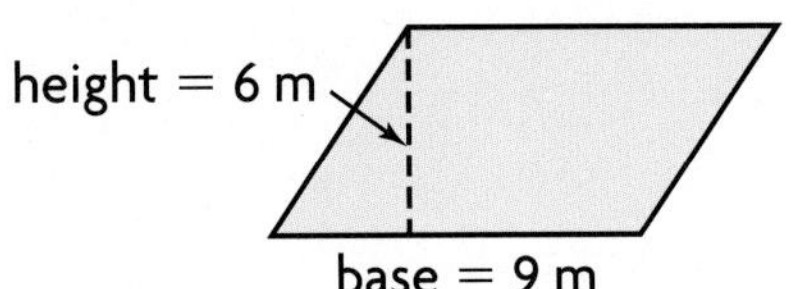

Remember

A *parallelogram* is a quadrilateral whose opposite sides are parallel and congruent.

ONE WAY **Use the area of a rectangle.**

You can use grid paper and what you know about the area of a rectangle to find the area of a parallelogram.

Step 1

Draw a diagram of the parallelogram on grid paper and cut it out. Draw a line segment to form a right triangle as shown.

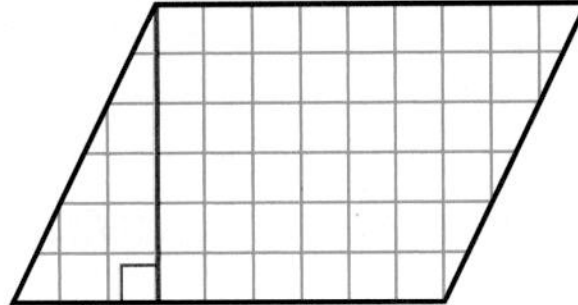

Step 2

Cut out the right triangle on the left, and move it to the right of the parallelogram to form a rectangle.

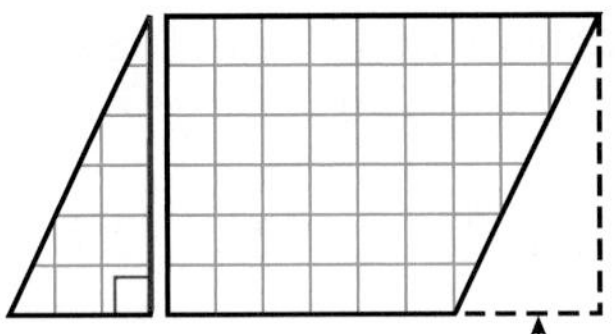

Step 3

Count the grid squares to find the area of the parallelogram. Each square represents 1 square meter.

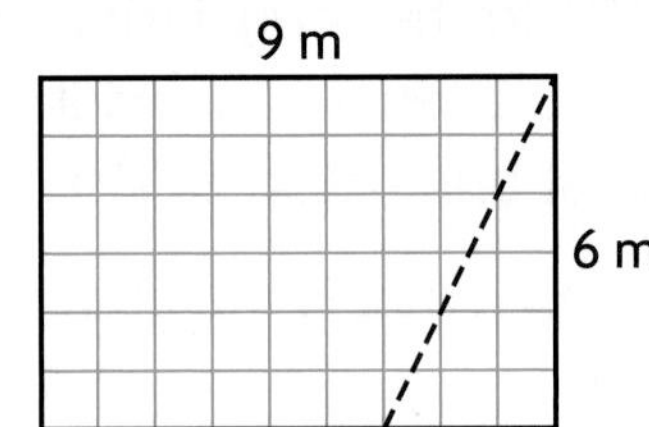

There are 6 rows of 9 squares, or 54 squares.

So, the area is 54 m^2. It takes 54 bags of sand to cover the dog run.

- How do the base and height of the parallelogram in Step 1 relate to the length and width of the rectangle in Step 3?

The area of a parallelogram is equal to the area of a rectangle with the same base (length) and height (width).

Area of a rectangle = length × width $A = l \times w$

Area of a parallelogram = base × height $A = b \times h$

ERROR ALERT

The slanted side of a parallelogram is *not* its height. The height must form a 90° angle with the base.

More Examples **Find the area.**

A

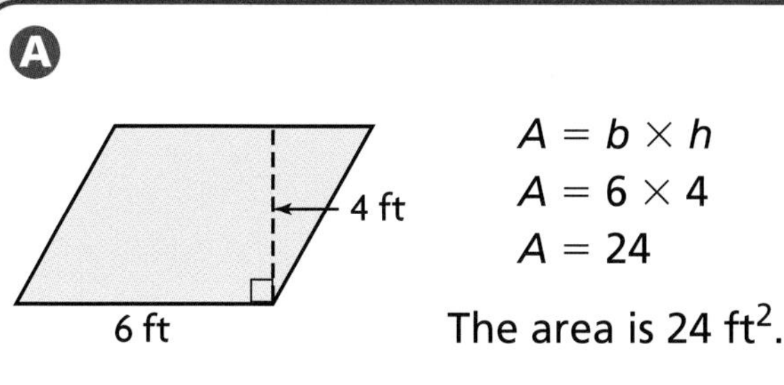

$A = b \times h$

$A = 6 \times 4$

$A = 24$

The area is 24 ft^2.

B

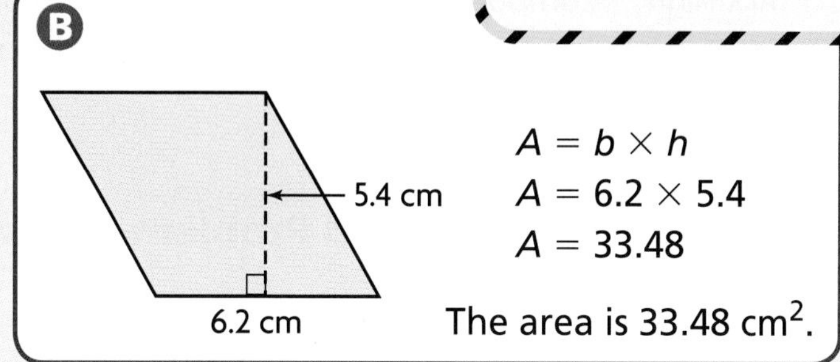

$A = b \times h$

$A = 6.2 \times 5.4$

$A = 33.48$

The area is 33.48 cm^2.

ANOTHER WAY **Use the area of a triangle.**

What would the area of the dog run be if the base were 11 m and the height were 5 m?

Step 1

Draw a 5 m × 11 m parallelogram on grid paper and cut it out.

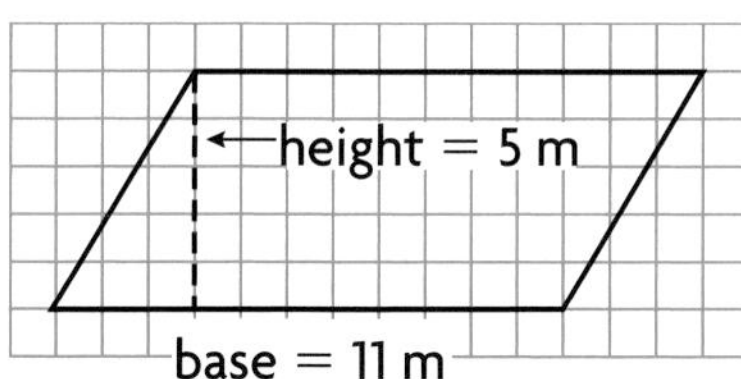

Step 2

Cut the parallelogram on a diagonal to form two congruent triangles.

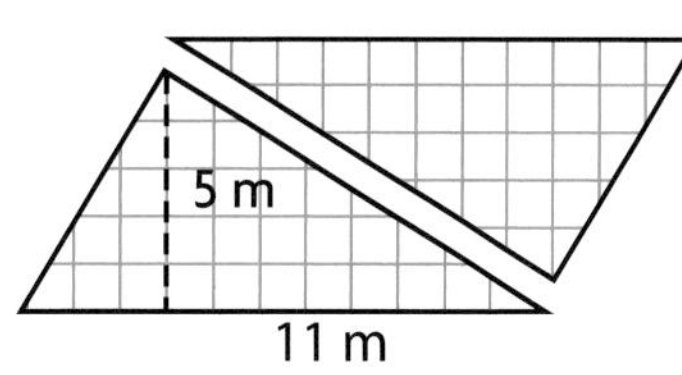

Step 3

Find the area of one triangle.

$A = \frac{1}{2} \times 11 \times 5$

$A = 27.5$

The area of the two congruent triangles is 2×27.5, or 55 m^2.

So, the area of the dog run would be 55 m^2.

- How is the area of the triangle related to the area of the parallelogram?

Guided Practice

Write the base and height of each parallelogram. Then find its area in square units.

1. 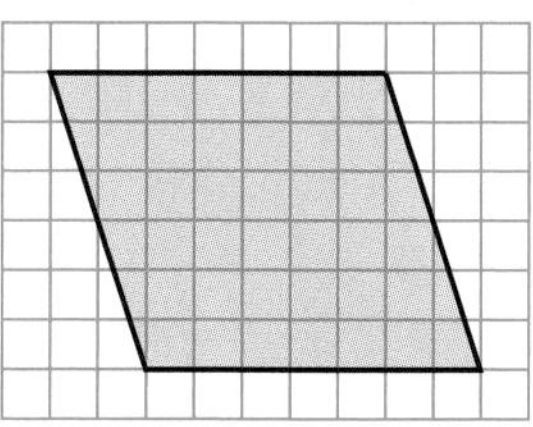

2. 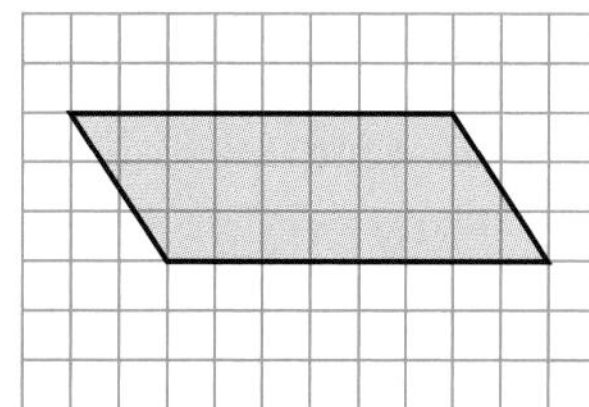

3. 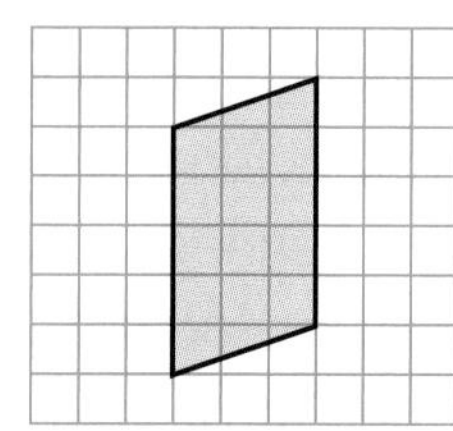

Find the area of each parallelogram.

4. 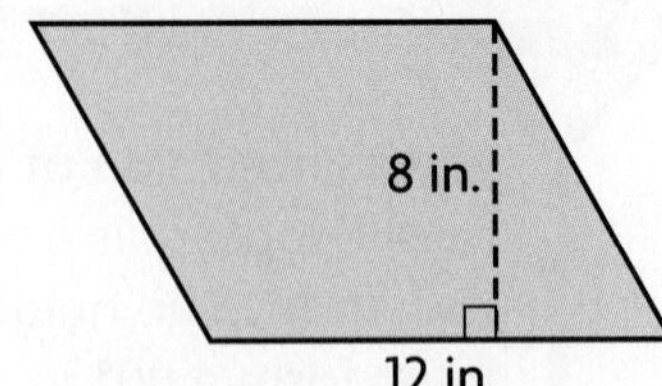

5. 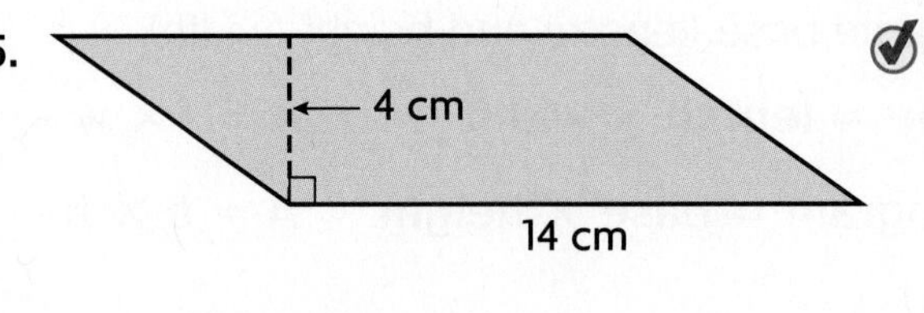

6. 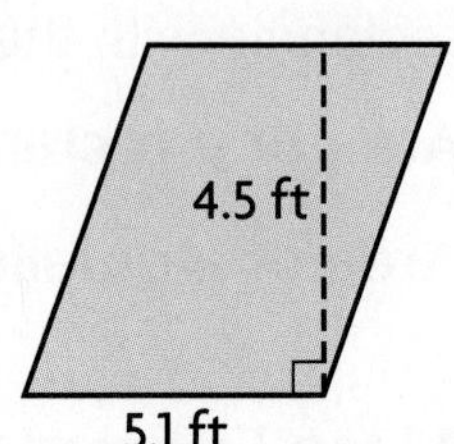

7. TALK Math Compare the area of any triangle with a base of 5 in. and a height of 6 in. to the area of a parallelogram with the same base and height.

Independent Practice and Problem Solving

Find the area of each parallelogram.

8. 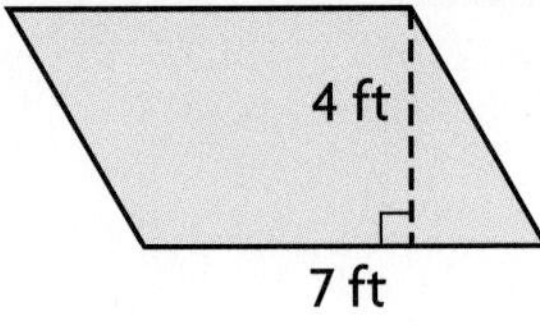

9. 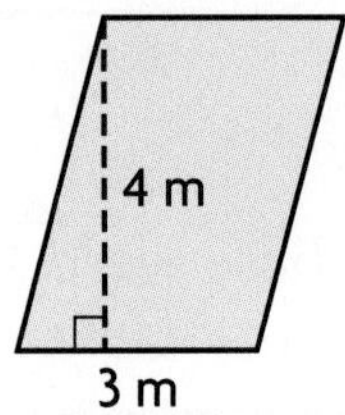

10. 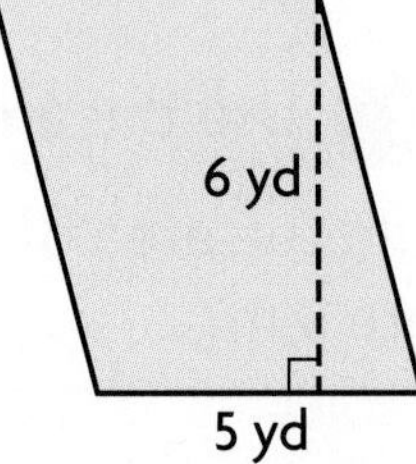

11. 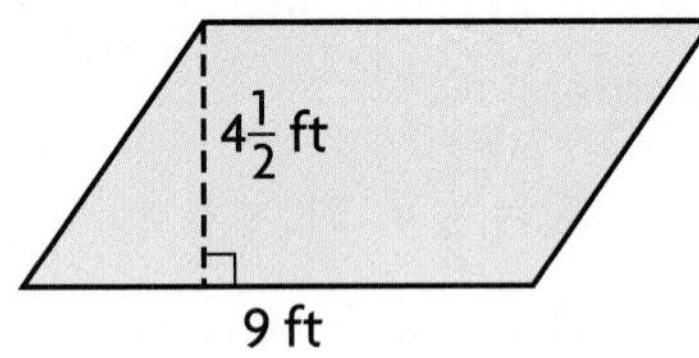

12. 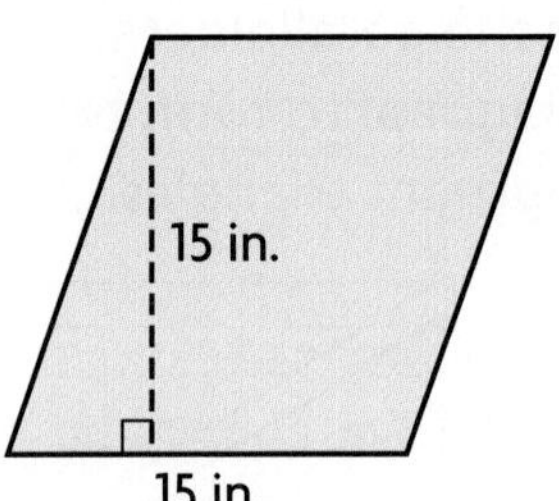

13. 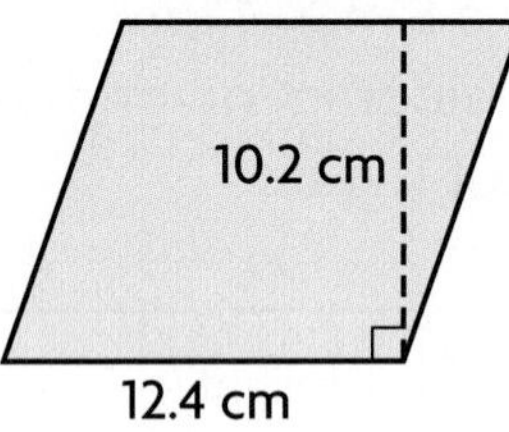

Solve.

14. A playground is shaped like a parallelogram with a base of 34 m and a width of 20 m. The playground is divided into two congruent triangles. What is the area of each triangle?

15. **Reasoning** The base of a parallelogram is two times its height. If the base is 12 cm, what is its area?

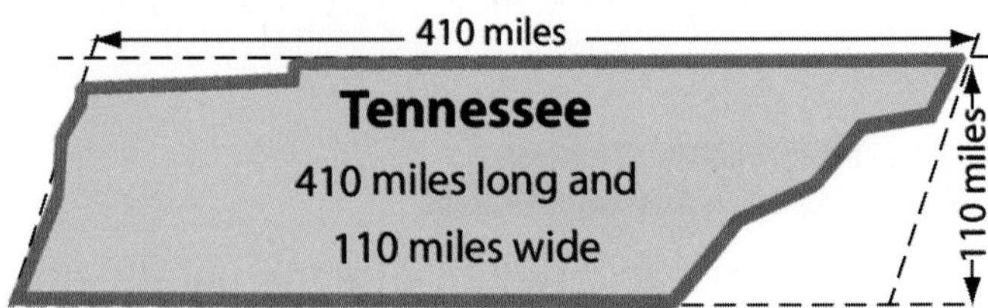

16. WRITE Math **What's the Question?** The base of a parallelogram is 7 yd. The area is 28 yd^2. The answer is 4 yd.

17. **FAST FACT** The state of Tennessee has an area of 42,169 mi^2, and is shaped roughly like a parallelogram. It is about 410 miles long and about 110 miles wide. Sid estimated the area of Tennessee to be about 40,000 mi^2. How could Sid have estimated the area? What is the difference between Sid's estimate and the actual area?

 Extra Practice on page 675, Set E

Learn About — ALGEBRA Area of Trapezoids

You can use grid paper and what you know about the area of a parallelogram to find the area of a trapezoid.

Example

Materials: ■ grid paper ■ scissors

Draw these two identical trapezoids on grid paper. Label them and cut them out.

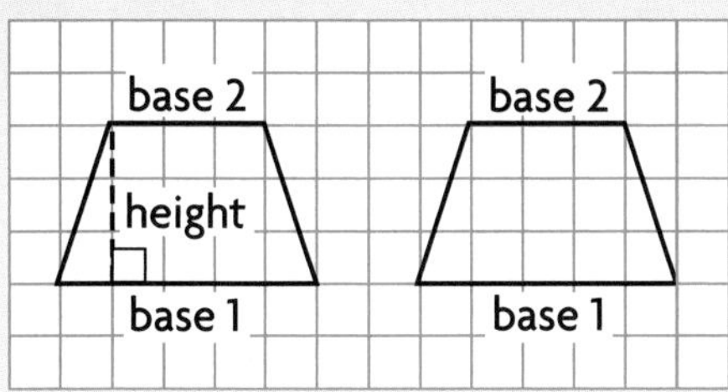

Arrange the trapezoids to form a parallelogram.

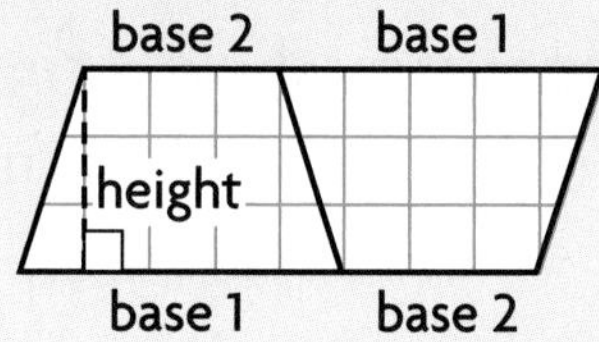

Try It

Use the trapezoids to answer the questions.

18. What is the base of the parallelogram?

19. What is the height of the parallelogram?

20. What is the area of the parallelogram?

21. How do the areas of the trapezoids relate to the area of the parallelogram?

22. Find the area of one trapezoid. Explain how you found your answer.

23. Write a formula for the area of a trapezoid.

Mixed Review and Test Prep

24. Mr. Alonzo's sailboat has a triangular sail. The base of the sail is 5 yd and the height of the sail is 7 yd. What is the area of the sail? (p. 650)

25. Test Prep What is the area of the parallelogram?

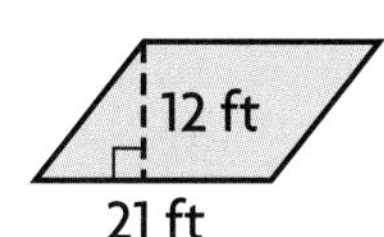

A 66 ft^2

B 126 ft^2

C 240 ft^2

D 252 ft^2

26. Mr. Arnold has $80 to spend on art supplies. He buys 3 canvases for $10.98 each, a brush for $7.50, and 8 tubes of paint for $4.69 each. About how much money will Mr. Arnold have left? (p. 184)

27. Test Prep The parking lot shown below is divided into two equal parallelograms. What is the area of the entire parking lot? Show your work.

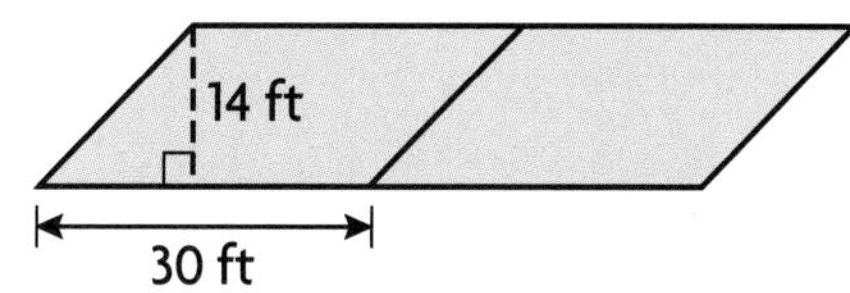

Problem Solving Workshop
Strategy: Solve a Simpler Problem

OBJECTIVE: Solve problems by using the strategy *solve a simpler problem.*

Learn the Strategy

Solving a simpler problem can help you understand a more complex problem.

A simpler problem may show a figure divided into simpler figures.

Find the area of the figure.

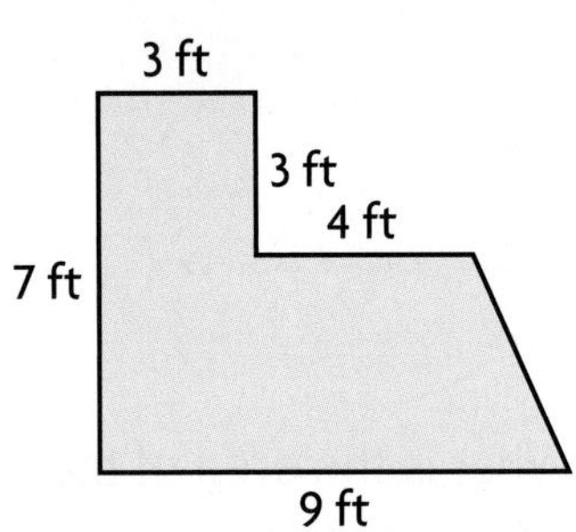

Divide the more complex figure into simpler figures. Find the area of each of the figures. Add all the areas.

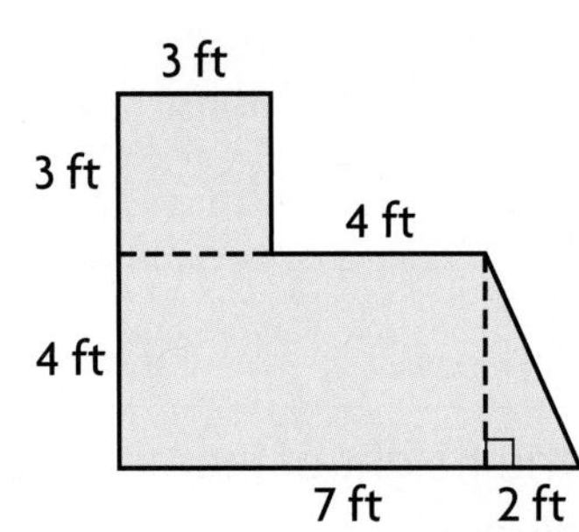

Area of square

$3 \times 3 = 9 \text{ ft}^2$

Area of rectangle

$4 \times 7 = 28 \text{ ft}^2$

Area of triangle

$\frac{1}{2} \times 2 \times 4 = 4 \text{ ft}^2$

Total area

$9 + 28 + 4 = 41 \text{ ft}^2$

A simpler problem may use friendlier numbers for computing.

There were 365 people at an outdoor benefit concert. They each paid \$30 for a ticket. How much money did the benefit make from ticket sales?

Rewrite 365 as 300 + 60 + 5, multiply each addend by 30, and add the partial products.

$$\begin{array}{r} 365 \\ \times\ 30 \\ \hline \end{array} \quad = \quad \begin{array}{rl} 300 + 60 + 5 & \\ \times \qquad\qquad 30 & \leftarrow 30 \times (300 + 60 + 5) \\ \hline 150 & \leftarrow 30 \times 5 \\ 1{,}800 & \leftarrow 30 \times 60 \\ +\ 9{,}000 & \leftarrow 30 \times 300 \\ \hline 10{,}950 & \end{array}$$

So, the benefit made \$10,950 from ticket sales.

TALK Math

Which property is being used in the problem on the right? How does that property make problems easier to solve?

Use the Strategy

PROBLEM Lisa and her friends are making sun catchers. Lisa is making a design out of three colors. What is the area of each color of Lisa's sun catcher design shown at the right? What is the area of the entire figure?

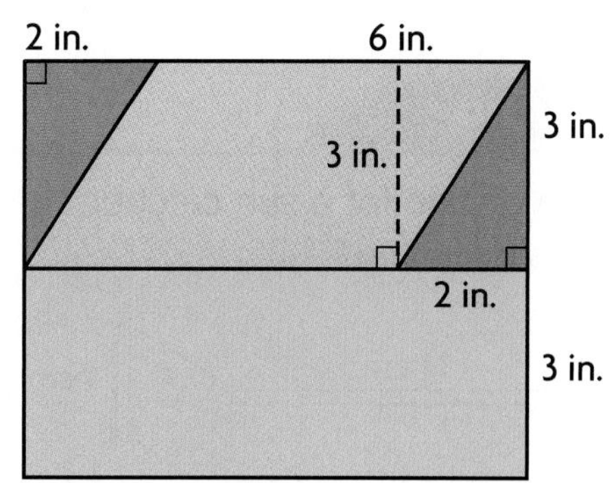

Read to Understand

- **How can you use graphic aids to break the problem into simpler parts?**
- **What information will you use?**

Plan

- **What strategy can you use to solve the problem?**

  You can *solve a simpler problem* to help you find the area of the design.

Solve

- **How can you use the strategy to solve the problem?**

  Find the area of each figure in the sun catcher design.

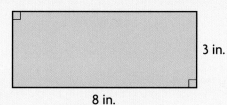

$A = l \times w$

$A = 8 \times 3$

$A = 24 \text{ in.}^2$

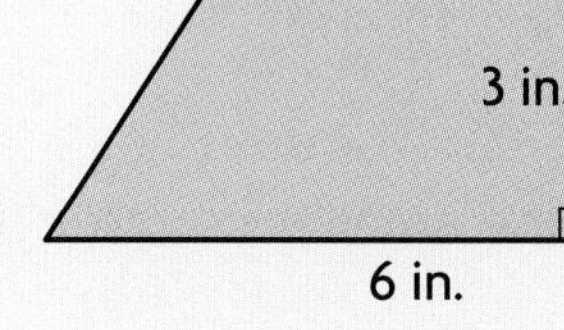

$A = b \times h$

$A = 6 \times 3$

$A = 18 \text{ in.}^2$

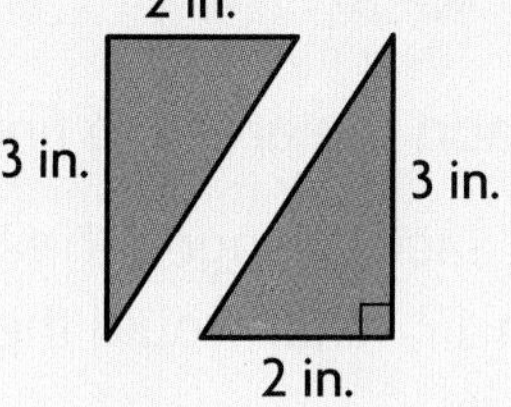

$A = \frac{1}{2} \times b \times h$

$A = \frac{1}{2} \times 2 \times 3$

$A = 3 \text{ in.}^2$

Total area for both triangles = $2 \times 3 = 6 \text{ in.}^2$

Then add the areas: $24 + 18 + 6 = 48$

So, the total area of the sun catcher design is 48 in.^2

Check

- **Look back at the problem. Is the answer reasonable? Explain.**

Guided Problem Solving

Read to Understand
Plan
Solve
Check

1. Jack made a spaceship design for a sun catcher. What is the area of the spaceship?

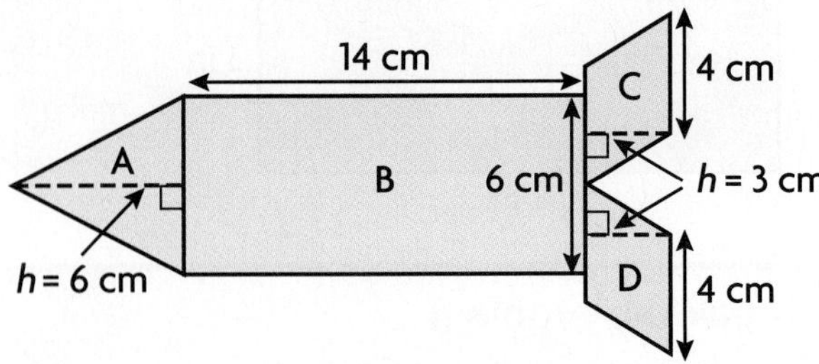

First, divide the diagram of the spaceship into simpler figures.

Then, find the area of each figure.

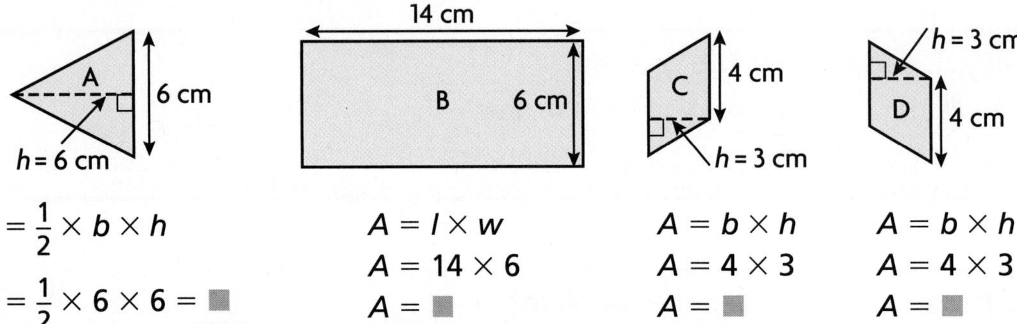

$A = \frac{1}{2} \times b \times h$

$A = \frac{1}{2} \times 6 \times 6 = \blacksquare$

$A = l \times w$
$A = 14 \times 6$
$A = \blacksquare$

$A = b \times h$
$A = 4 \times 3$
$A = \blacksquare$

$A = b \times h$
$A = 4 \times 3$
$A = \blacksquare$

Finally, add the areas to find the total area of the spaceship.

2. **What if** Jack changed the length of the rectangle to 10 cm in Problem 1? What would the area of the spaceship be?

3. Fran's sun catcher has 6 rows of 5 squares. Each square has 3 rows of 3 smaller squares. How many of the smaller squares are in Fran's sun catcher?

Problem Solving Strategy Practice

Use the strategy *solve a simpler problem* to solve.

4. Brett designed the figure at the right for a sun catcher. What is the area of the figure?

5. **Reasoning** Divide the figure in Problem 4 into different simpler figures. Use these simpler figures to check your answer to Problem 4.

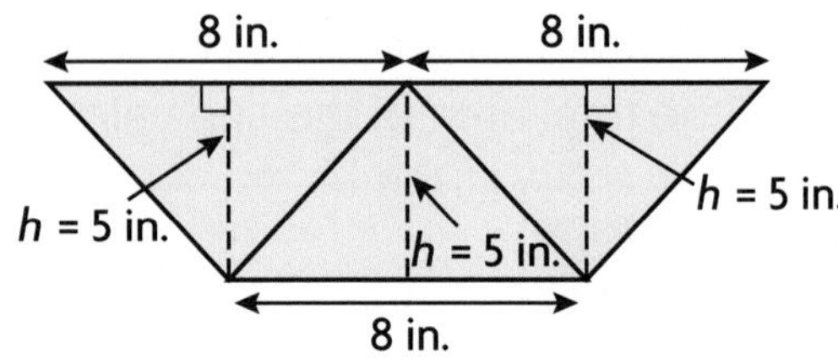

6. Myra bought sun catcher plastic for $16.50, 3 patterns for $8.50 each, 7 feet of chain for $7.25 per foot, and 4 bottles of stain for $2.35 each. How much did Myra spend in all?

7. WRITE Math **What's the Error?** Each student's art supplies cost $24.32. Janet says that if there are 50 students, the supplies will cost $121.60. Find and correct her error.

Mixed Strategy Practice

Solve.

8. Meg made a sun catcher with alternating green and purple squares. She started with a green square. The finished sun catcher has 7 rows of 5 squares each. How many squares of each color are there?

9. Juliet worked on a sun catcher for 45 minutes, starting at 11:35 A.M. Then Jim worked on the sun catcher for 1 hour 5 minutes. At 2:55 P.M., Mavis started to work on the sun catcher. How much time elapsed between the time that Jim stopped working on the sun catcher and the time Mavis started?

10. **Pose a Problem** Look back at Problem 9. Write a similar problem by changing the time that Mavis started to work on the sun catcher.

USE DATA For 11, use the picture of the sun catcher at the right.

11. **Reasoning** Mike, Ricardo, Kathy, and Betsy made the sun catcher shown to the right together. Betsy made 6 more squares than Kathy. Ricardo made 3 fewer squares than Betsy. Kathy made 8 squares. How many squares did each person make?

CHALLENGE YOURSELF

A rectangular sun catcher is made up of three figures: a parallelogram with a right triangle on each side of it.

The triangles are congruent. The area of the sun catcher is 54 sq in.

12. The base of the parallelogram is 7 in. The height is 6 in. What is the base of each triangle?

13. Greg made another rectangular sun catcher with the same area. The perimeter is 30 in. What is the length and width of the sun catcher?

Choose a STRATEGY

- Draw a Diagram or Picture
- Make a Model or Act It Out
- Make an Organized List
- Find a Pattern
- Make a Table or Graph
- Predict and Test
- Work Backward
- Solve a Simpler Problem
- Write an Equation
- Use Logical Reasoning

LESSON 7 HANDS ON

Surface Area

OBJECTIVE: Find the surface areas of rectangular and triangular prisms.

Quick Review

Name each polygon.

1. 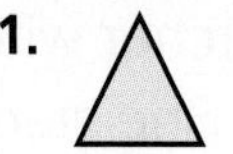
2. 
3.
4. 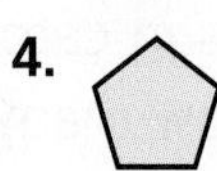
5. 

Vocabulary

surface area

Investigate

Materials ■ centimeter grid paper ■ scissors

You can use a net to find the surface area of a rectangular prism. **Surface area** is the sum of all the areas of the faces of a solid figure.

A On centimeter grid paper, draw and label the net shown below.

B Cut out the net and fold it on the lines to make a rectangular prism.

C Unfold the prism and lay it flat. Find the area of each face, *A–F*. Record the length, width, and area of each face in a table.

D Find the surface area of the prism.

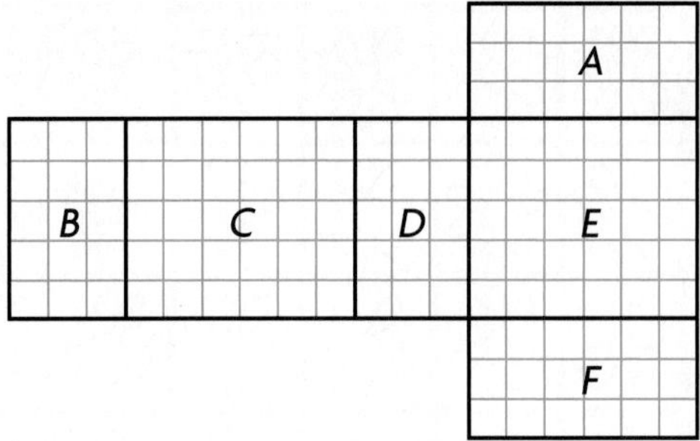

E A cube measures 5 centimeters on each edge. Repeat the steps above to find its surface area.

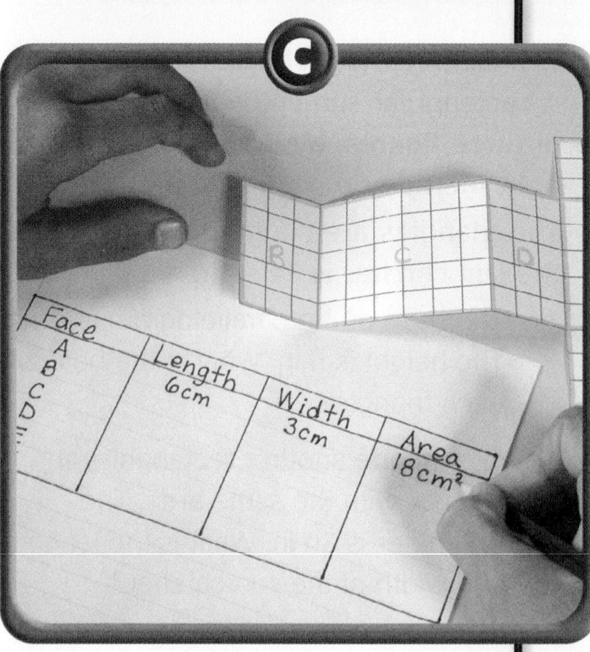

Draw Conclusions

1. Which faces of the rectangular prism are congruent? Do they have the same area?
2. Copy and complete the following expression for finding the surface area of a rectangular prism.

   ■ × (area of front) + ■ × (area of top) + ■ × (area of side)

3. **Synthesis** What expression could you write to find the surface area of a cube?

Connect

You can also use a net to find the surface area of a square pyramid.

Step 1

Copy the net on centimeter grid paper.

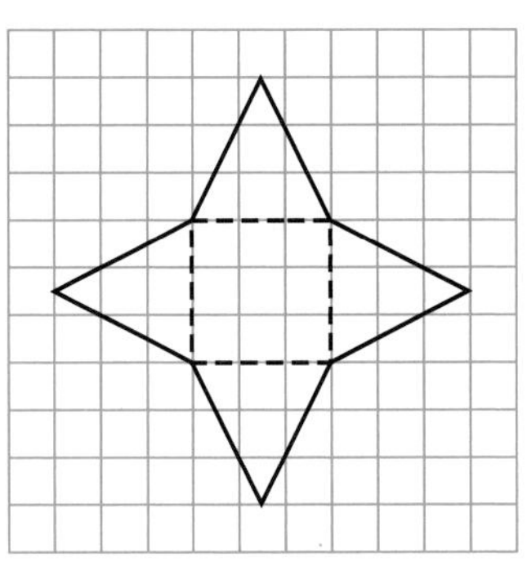

Step 2

Cut out the net and fold it on the lines to make a square pyramid.

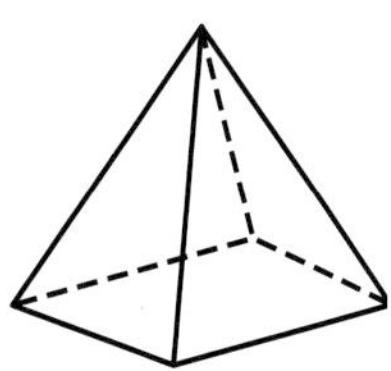

Step 3

Unfold the prism. Add the areas of the faces to find the surface area.

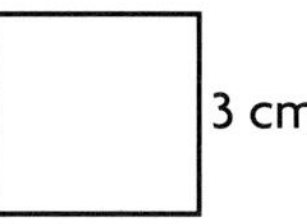

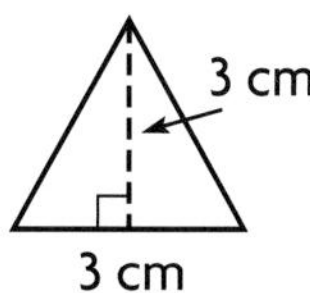

$A = b \times h$

$A = 3 \times 3 = 9$

$A = \frac{1}{2} \times b \times h$

$A = \frac{1}{2} \times 3 \times 3 = 4.5$

$9 + 4.5 + 4.5 + 4.5 + 4.5 = 27$

So, the surface area of the square pyramid is 27 cm^2.

TALK Math

Explain how to use a net to find the surface area of a square pyramid.

Practice

Use the net to find the surface area of each figure in square units.

1. Which faces are congruent?

   What is the area of each face?

   What is the surface area of the prism?

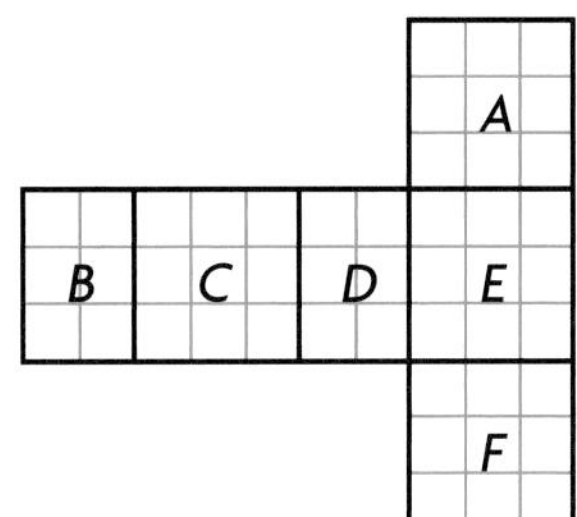

2.

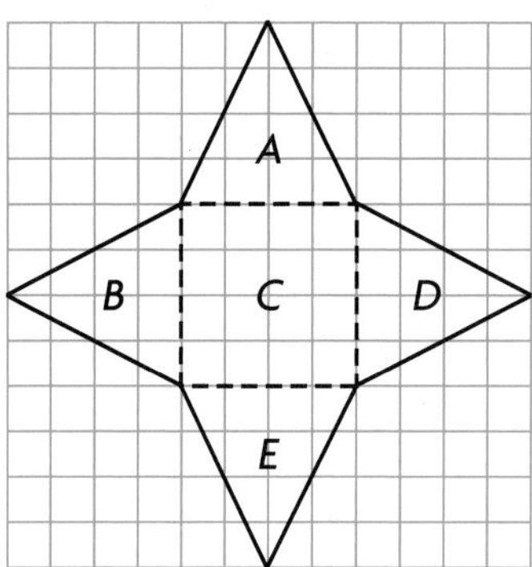

Find the surface area.

3.

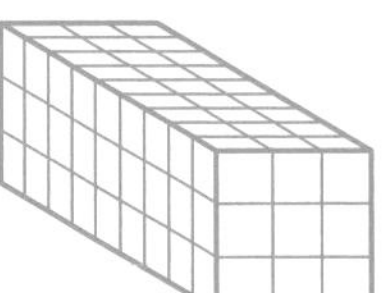

4.

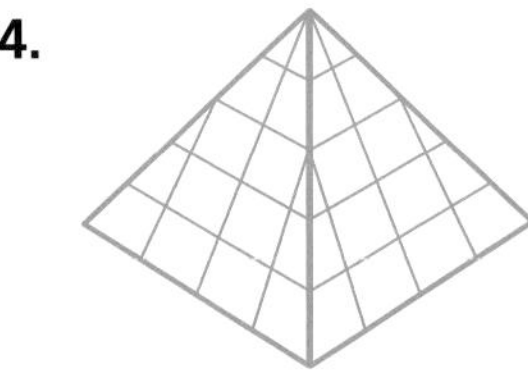

square pyramid

5.

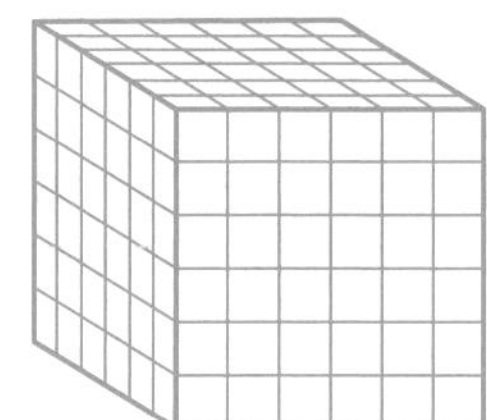

6. **WRITE Math** **Explain** the difference between *area* and *surface area*.

LESSON 8

ALGEBRA

Find Volume

OBJECTIVE: Find the volume of rectangular prisms.

Quick Review

Find the area of each rectangle.

1. $l = 3.5$ m, $w = 4$ m
2. $l = 2$ m, $w = 2.4$ m
3. $l = 9$ m, $w = 18$ m
4. $l = 12.7$ m, $w = 10$ m
5. $l = 15$ m, $w = 35$ m

Vocabulary

volume

cubic unit

Learn

PROBLEM Tony wants to estimate the amount of storage space in this cabinet. The cabinet is $4\frac{1}{8}$ feet long, $2\frac{7}{8}$ feet wide, and $8\frac{1}{4}$ feet high. About how much storage space does the cabinet have?

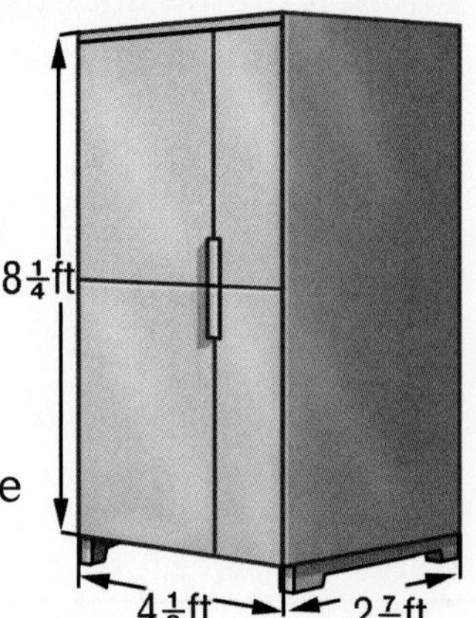

To estimate the amount of storage space, you need to estimate the cabinet's volume. **Volume** is the amount of space a solid figure occupies. It is measured in **cubic units**.

Activity **Materials** ■ centimeter cubes

You can use centimeter cubes to make a model of the cabinet to help you estimate the volume. Let each side of a cube represent one foot.

Step 1

One Dimension

Make a row of 4 cubes.

4

length: $4\frac{1}{8}$ ft is about 4 ft

Step 2

Two Dimensions

Make 3 rows of 4 cubes to make 1 layer.

width: $2\frac{7}{8}$ ft is about 3 ft

Count the number of cubes in one layer.

Step 3

Three Dimensions

Make 8 layers of 12 cubes to complete the prism.

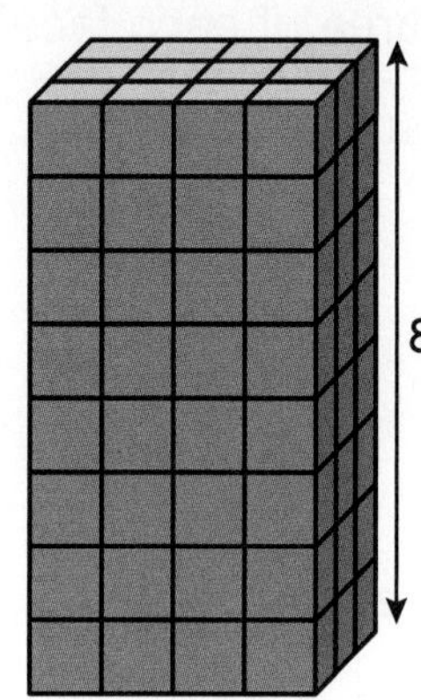

height: $8\frac{1}{4}$ ft is about 8 ft

Count the total number of cubes that make the prism.

So, the volume of the storage cabinet is about 96 cubic feet, or 96 ft^3.

Find Volume

Tony makes storage cabinets. One cabinet he made was 5 feet long, 2 feet wide, and 4 feet high. How much storage space does this cabinet have?

Step 1

Make a layer of centimeter cubes for the base of the rectangular prism.

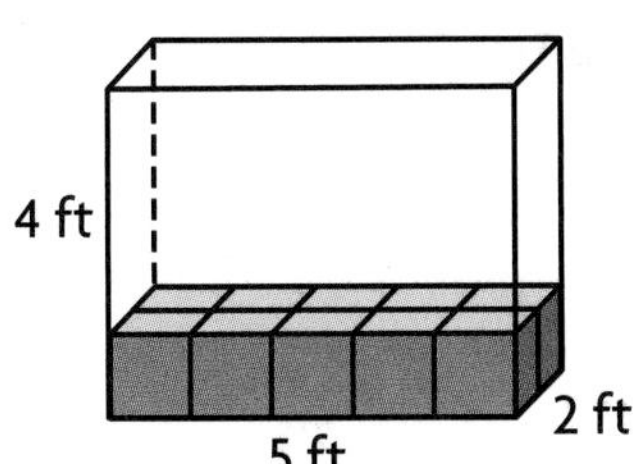

How many cubes does it take to make the base?

Step 2

Make three more layers of cubes to complete the prism.

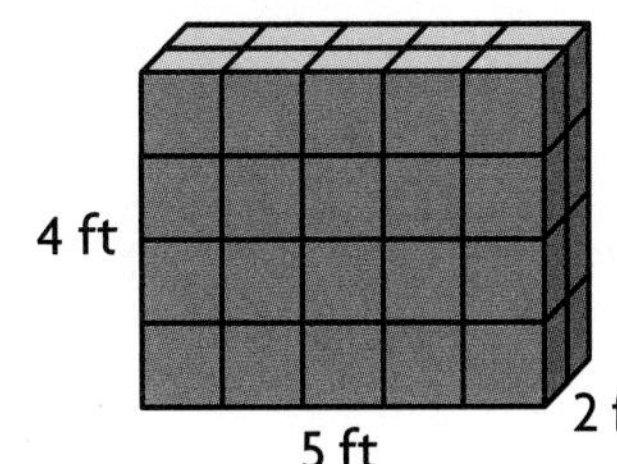

How many centimeter cubes did you use in all?

Step 3

Look at the table. What relationship do you see? What formula can you write for the volume of a rectangular prism?

Length	Width	Height	Volume
5	2	4	40
4	3	6	72
8	4	3	96

Volume = length × width × height

$V = l \times w \times h$, or $V = lwh$

$V = 5 \times 2 \times 4 = 40$

So, the volume of Tony's 5 ft × 2 ft × 4 ft storage cabinet is 40 ft^3.

Examples

A Volume of a rectangular prism

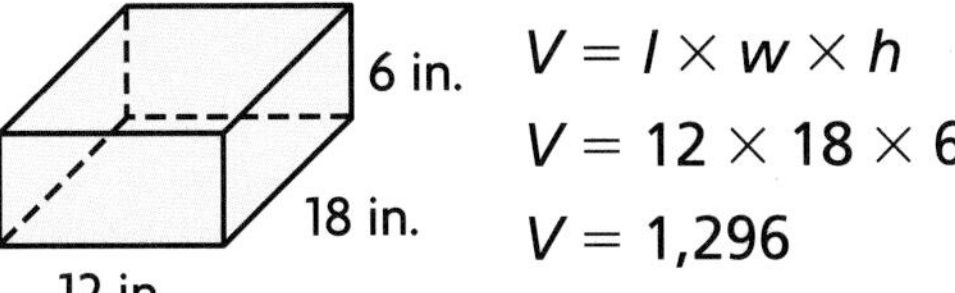

$V = l \times w \times h$

$V = 12 \times 18 \times 6$

$V = 1{,}296$

So, the volume is 1,296 $in.^3$

B Volume of a cube

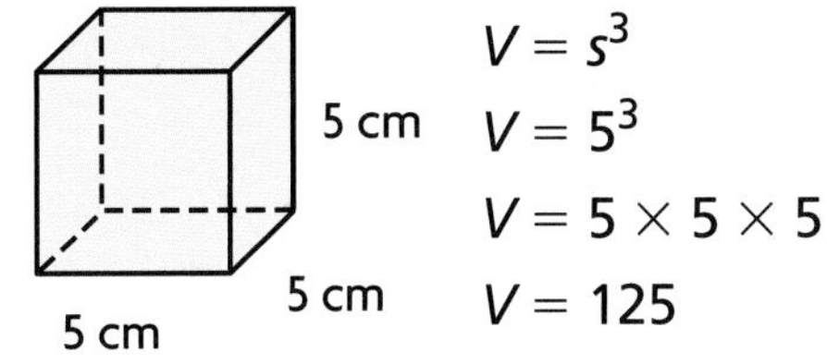

$V = s^3$

$V = 5^3$

$V = 5 \times 5 \times 5$

$V = 125$

So, the volume is 125 cm^3.

Guided Practice

For 1–4, use the rectangular prism at the right.

1. What is the length?
2. What is the width?
3. What is the height?
4. What is the volume?

Find the volume of each rectangular prism.

5. 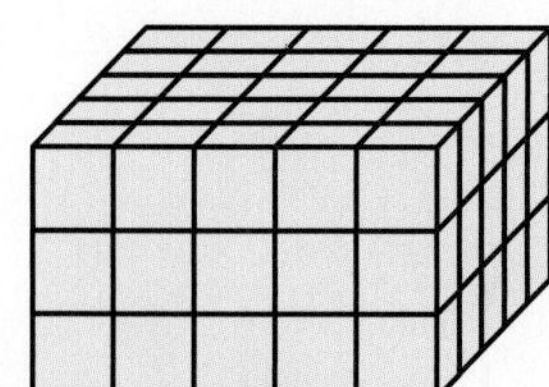

6. 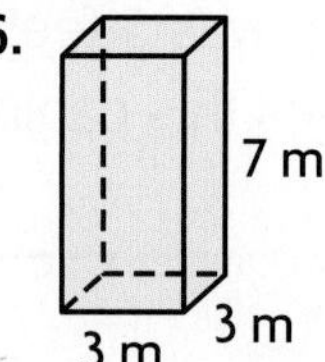

7. 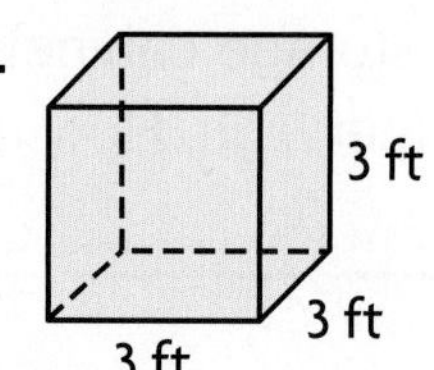

8. TALK Math When finding the volume of a rectangular prism, does the order in which you multiply the dimensions affect your answer? **Explain.**

Independent Practice and Problem Solving

Find the volume of each rectangular prism.

9. 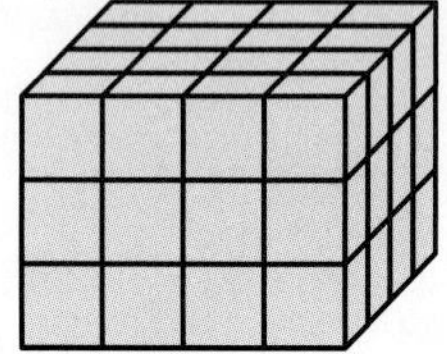

10. 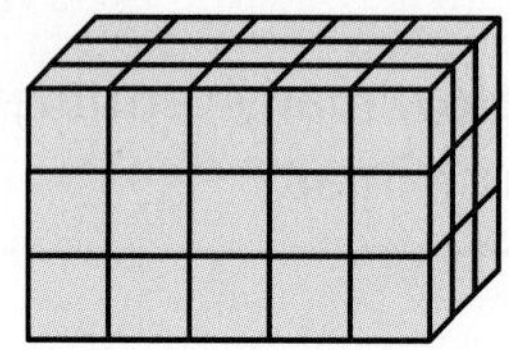

11. 

12. 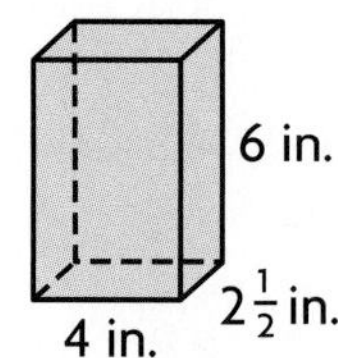

13. 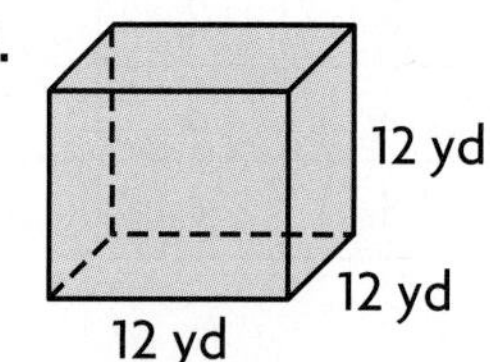

14. 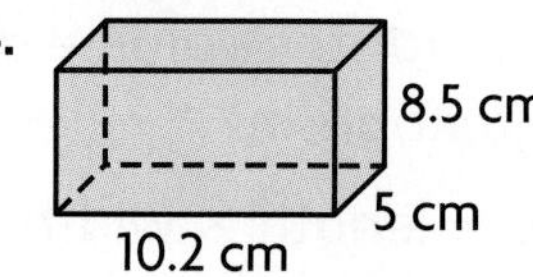

15. 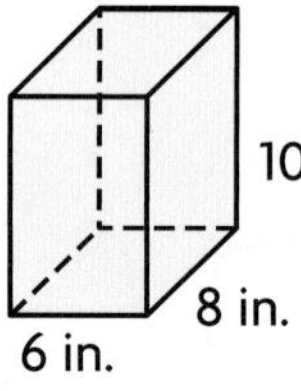

16. 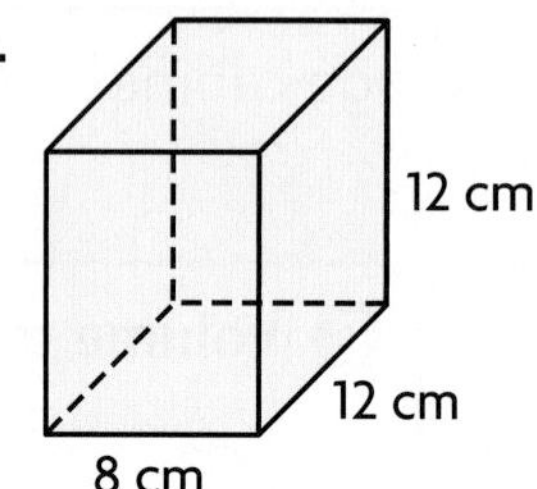

17. 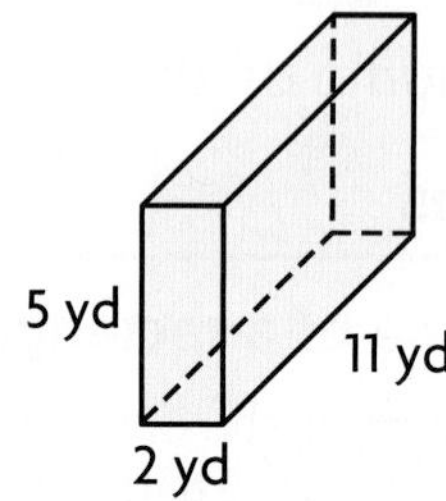

USE DATA **Use the table for 18–20.**

18. How many cubic meters of water does it take to completely fill an Olympic pool?

19. Which of the three pools has the greatest volume?

20. Suppose the lap pool is filled to a depth of 1 meter when it is closed for the winter. What is the volume of the water left inside the pool?

Swimming Pool Dimensions

Pool	Length	Width	Depth
Olympic pool	50 m	25 m	2 m
Lap pool	50 m	20 m	2.2 m
Pool for young swimmers	25 m	25 m	2 m

21. **Reasoning** A rectangular prism has a volume of 60 m^3, a length of 6 m, and a width of 5 m. What is its height?

22. WRITE Math **Explain** the difference between an inch, a square inch, and a cubic inch.

 Extra Practice on page 675, Set F

Learn About

ALGEBRA

Volume of Triangular Prisms

You can use what you know about finding the volume of a rectangular prism to find the volume of a right triangular prism.

Math Idea

The volume of a triangular prism is half the volume of a rectangular prism of the same length, width, and height.

$V = \frac{1}{2} \times l \times w \times h$

Example

The volume of this rectangular prism is 120 cm³. Imagine you cut it in half to form two congruent triangular prisms. How could you find the volume of one triangular prism?

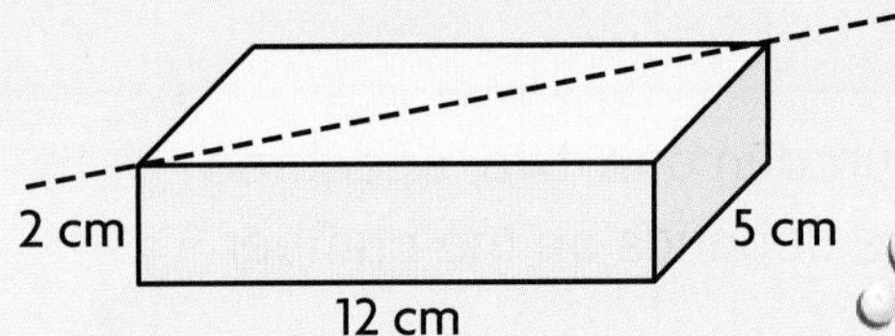

This process works for any triangular prism that has length, width, and height equal to the length, width, and height of a rectangular prism.

Volume, rectangular prism $= l \times w \times h$

Volume, triangular prism $= \frac{1}{2} \times l \times w \times h$

$V = \frac{1}{2} \times 12 \times 5 \times 2$

$V = 60 \text{ cm}^3$

Try It

Use the formula to find the volume of each triangular prism.

23.

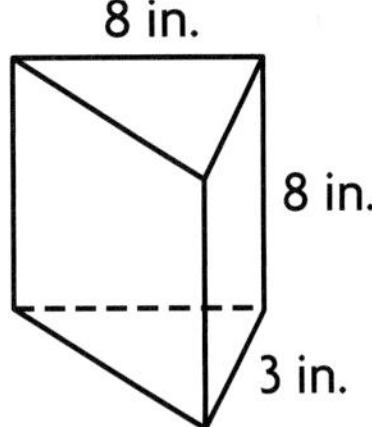

24.

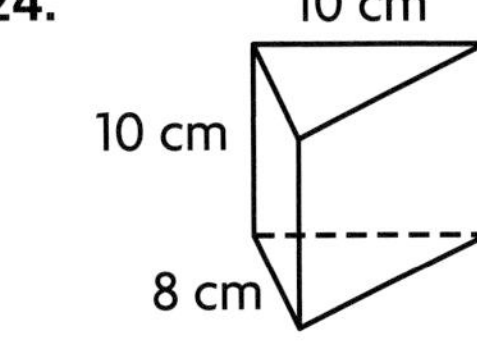

25.

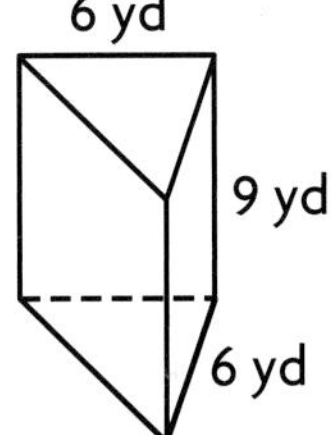

Mixed Review and Test Prep

26. What is the surface area of the prism shown by this net? (p. 530)

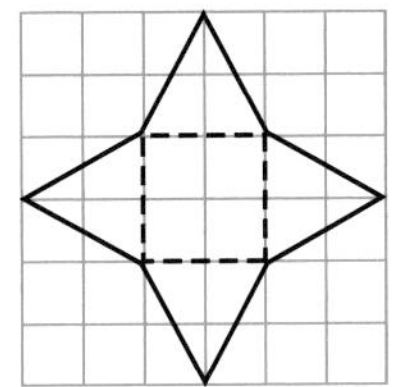

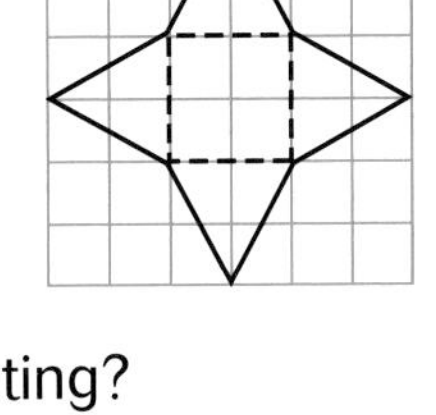

27. The area of a painting is 154 in.² Its length is 14 in. What is the width of the painting? (p. 646)

28. **Test Prep** Compare the volumes of two boxes. Box A has a length of 3 ft, a height of $2\frac{1}{2}$ ft, and a width of 2 ft. Box B has a length of $3\frac{1}{2}$ ft, a height of 2 ft, and a width of $2\frac{1}{2}$ ft. Which box has a greater volume? **Explain** your answer.

29. **Test Prep** What is the volume of the prism below?

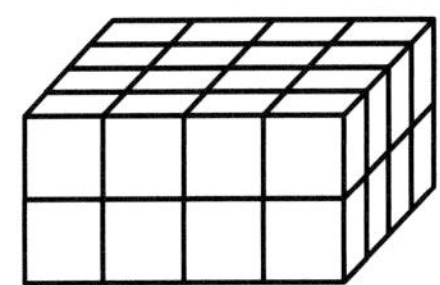

A 16 units³

B 24 units³

C 32 units³

D 64 units³

Relate Perimeter, Area, and Volume

OBJECTIVE: Identify the appropriate units of measure for perimeter, area, and volume.

Quick Review

1. 36 in. = ■ ft
2. 36 in. = ■ yd
3. 2 yd = ■ ft
4. 2 m = ■ cm
5. 75 cm = ■ m

Learn

Geometric figures can be measured in one, two, and three dimensions. The unit you choose depends on the number of dimensions you are measuring.

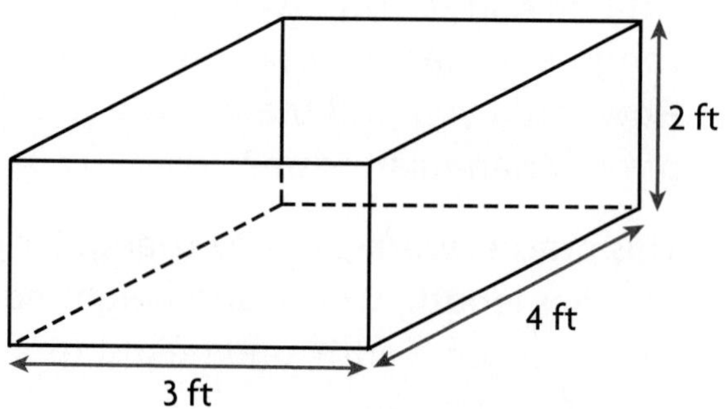

PROBLEM Mari and her dad want to build a frame for her cats' bed pillow, with the dimensions shown. What units should they use to measure the perimeter of the frame? The area of the base of the frame? The volume for the entire frame?

Perimeter is the distance around a figure.	**Area** is the measure of the flat surface of a figure.	**Volume** is the measure of the space a figure occupies.
	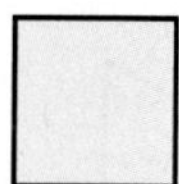	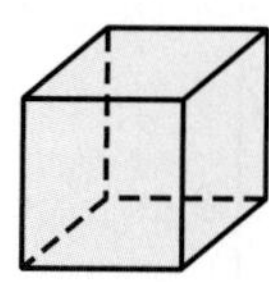
Its measure is in one dimension, *length*. Use linear units such as in., ft, yd, mi, cm, m, or km.	Its measure is in two dimensions, *length* and *width*. Use square units such as $in.^2$, ft^2, yd^2, mi^2, cm^2, m^2, or km^2.	Its measure is in three dimensions, *length*, *width*, and *height*. Use cubic units such as $in.^3$, ft^3, yd^3, mi^3, cm^3, m^3, or km^3.

So, Mari and her father should use feet to measure the perimeter of the frame.

They should use square feet to measure the area of the base of the frame.

They should use cubic feet to measure the volume of the frame.

- How are the units used to measure perimeter, area, and volume different?

Mari and her father are ready to build the frame. What are the perimeter, area, and volume of the frame?

Activity

Materials ■ centimeter grid paper ■ centimeter cubes

Let each ☐ equal 1 square foot.

Step 1

Draw a 3 × 4 rectangle on grid paper. Count to find the perimeter of the rectangle.

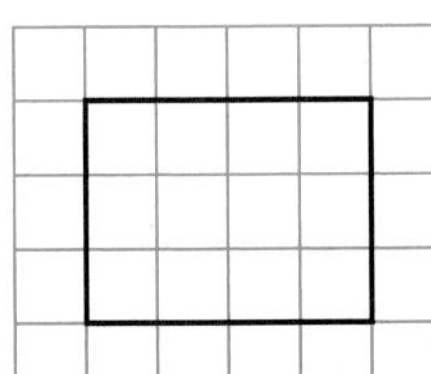

The perimeter of the frame, measured in linear units, is 14 ft.

Step 2

Shade the squares to show the area of the rectangle. Count the number of shaded squares to find the area.

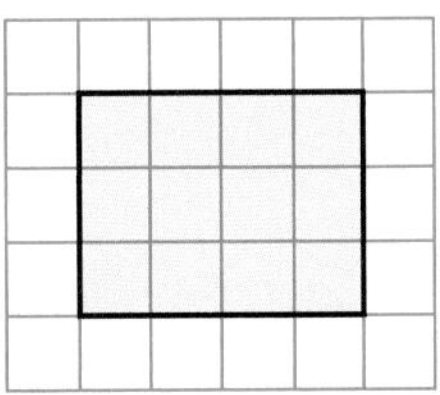

The area of the base of the frame, measured in square units, is 12 ft^2.

Step 3

Use centimeter cubes to build a 2-layer prism on the rectangle. Count the number of cubes to find the volume of the prism.

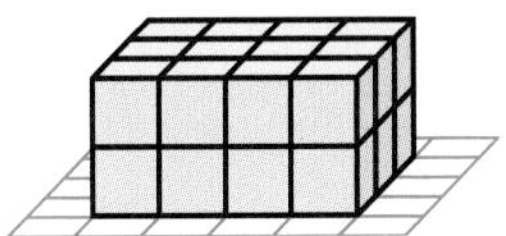

The volume of the frame, measured in cubic units, is 24 ft^3.

Guided Practice

Tell the type of unit you would use for measuring each. Write *linear*, *square*, or *cubic*.

1. volume
2. area
3. length
4. perimeter
5. fence to enclose a garden
6. matting for a picture frame
7. space inside a cabinet
8. size of a playground

Write the unit you would use for measuring each.

9. volume of this prism

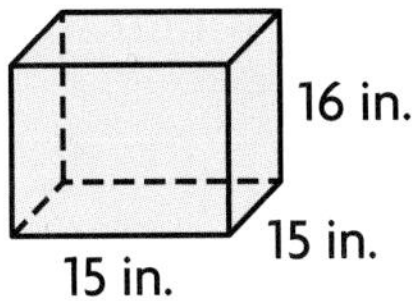

10. perimeter of this trapezoid

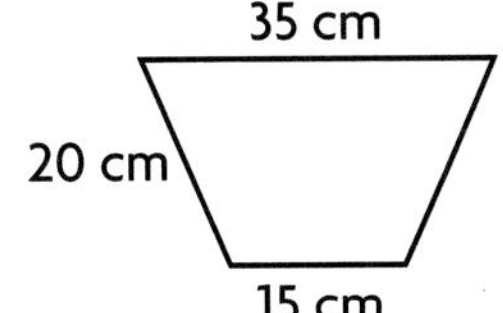

✓11. area of this triangle

8 in.
14 in.

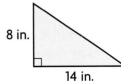

✓12. perimeter of this regular hexagon

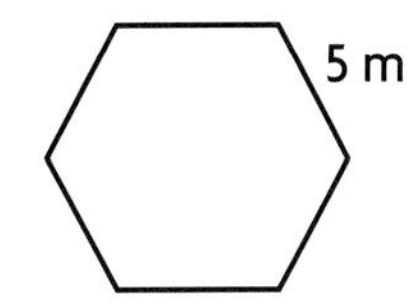

13. TALK Math Describe how you would use formulas to find the perimeter, area of the base, and volume of the frame.

Independent Practice and Problem Solving

Tell the type of unit you would use for measuring each. Write *linear, square,* or *cubic*.

14. carpet needed to cover a floor

15. amount of air in a room

16. distance around a picture frame

17. tile needed to cover a wall

Write the unit you would use for measuring each.

18. perimeter of this triangle

2.5 cm 2.5 cm 2.5 cm

19. volume of this prism

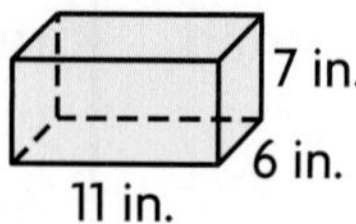

20. volume of this prism

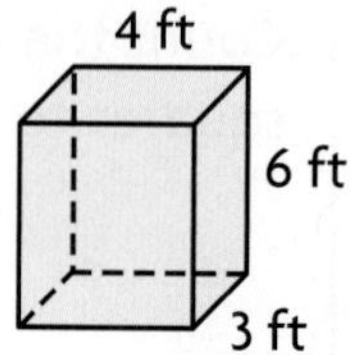

21. area of this parallelogram

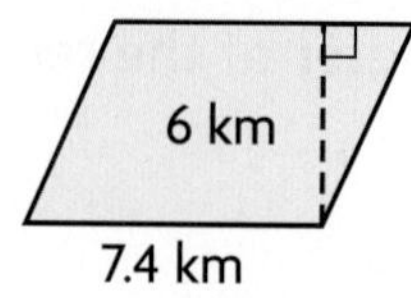

For 22–24, use the picture of the aquarium.

22. What is the aquarium's volume?

23. What is the surface area of the top surface of the water in the aquarium?

24. ***FAST FACT*** The sum of the lengths of all of the fish in an aquarium should be no more than 1 inch of fish for every 10 square inches of the top surface area of the water. For example, an aquarium with a water surface area of 120 square inches should have $120 \div 10$, or 12 inches of fish. How many fish and of what lengths would you recommend for the aquarium shown?

25. WRITE Math **Explain** what units you would use to find the area of a wall that you planned to paint.

Mixed Review and Test Prep

26. Tanya cut out square pieces of fabric to make a pillow. Each square measured 14 in. on a side. What was the perimeter of each square piece of fabric? (p. 624)

27. Cody drew a triangle with a base of 8 cm and a height of 16 cm. What was the area of the triangle that Cody drew? (p. 650)

28. **Test Prep** Susanne plans to cover a box with fabric as a gift for her aunt. The box measures 8 in. × 4 in. × 3 in. What units should she use to decide how much fabric she will need?

A inches

B square inches

C feet

D cubic inches

 Extra Practice on page 675, Set G

READ Math WORKSHOP

Building with Measurements

Generalize

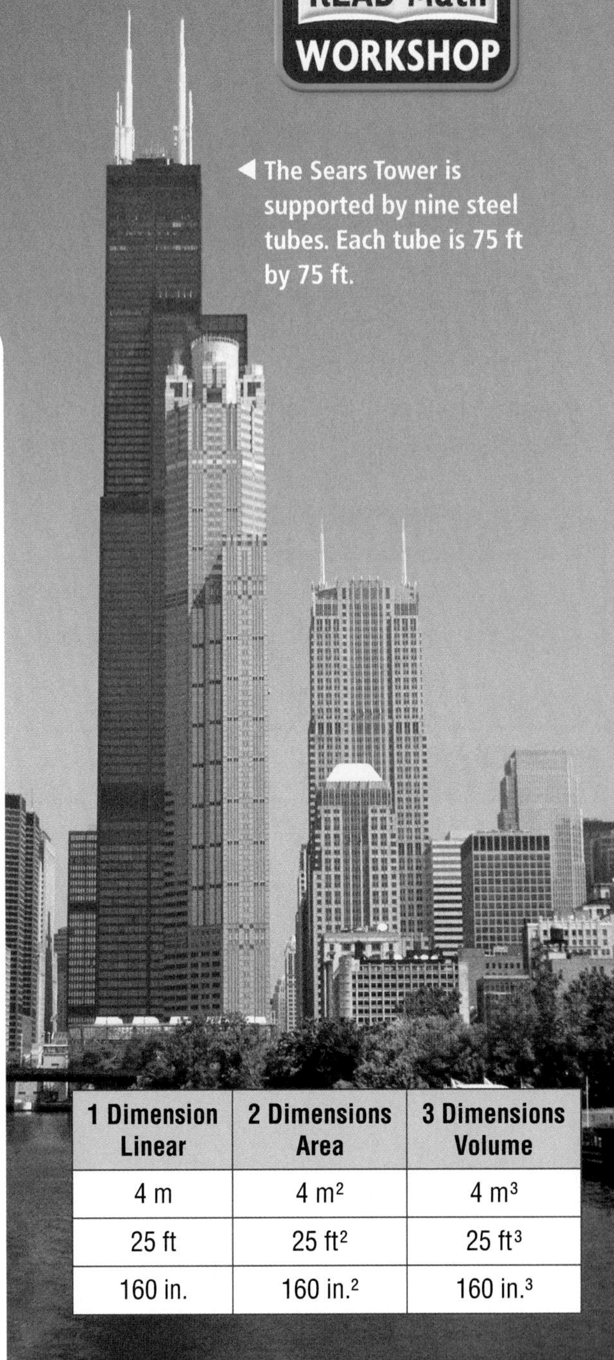

◀ The Sears Tower is supported by nine steel tubes. Each tube is 75 ft by 75 ft.

The Sears Tower in Chicago is one of the tallest buildings in the world. It rises to a height of 1,450 ft and occupies a "footprint," or area, of about 50,625 ft^2. To dig the 100-ft deep hole in which the foundation sits, about 180,000 yd^3 of soil and rock was removed.

Architects and builders work with measurements such as height, perimeter, area, and volume every day. They use a variety of linear, square, and cubic units. As part of their job, they must clearly communicate both the measurement and the unit of measure. For example, 5 ft is not the same as 5 ft^2 or 5 ft^3.

Think about the exponents used to show whether a measurement is linear, square, or cubic. What generalization can you make about the exponent used to identify each type of measurement?

To help solve the problem, you can compare measurements of length, area, and volume in a table like the one at the right. What does the table tell you about the exponents used to represent each type of measurement?

1 Dimension Linear	2 Dimensions Area	3 Dimensions Volume
4 m	4 m^2	4 m^3
25 ft	25 ft^2	25 ft^3
160 in.	160 $in.^2$	160 $in.^3$

Problem Solving Make a generalization to solve the problem.

1. Solve the problem above.
2. The measurement at the right has been partially erased. Even so, what generalization can you make about the measurement? **Explain.**

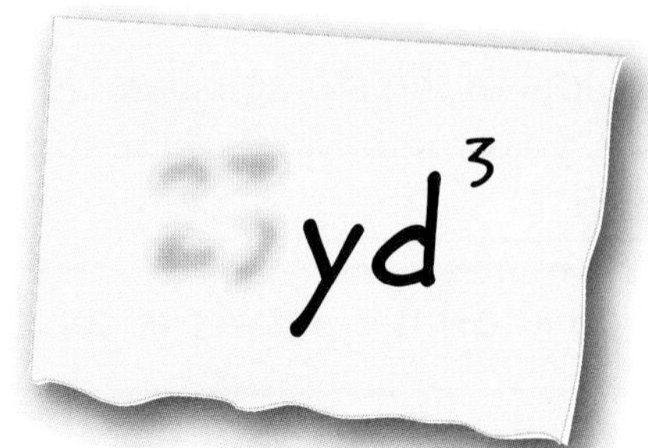

Problem Solving Workshop
Strategy: Compare Strategies

OBJECTIVE: Solve problems by comparing different strategies.

Use the Strategy

PROBLEM Paula is building a storage chest. She drew a picture to show what the storage chest would look like. She included measurements to show the length, width, and height. How can Paula find how much space her storage chest will occupy?

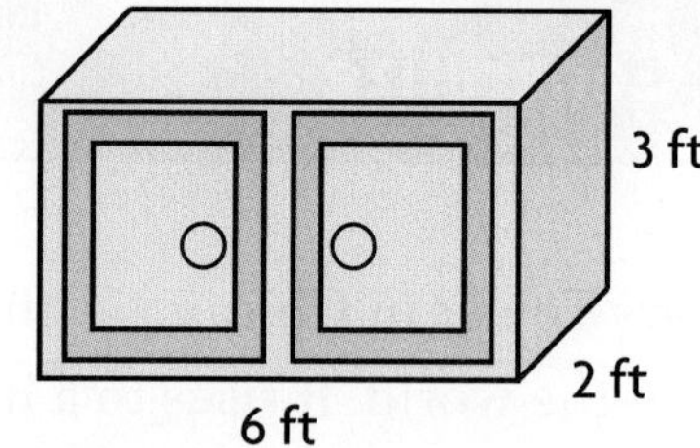

Read to Understand

- **What does the diagram tell you about the shape and size of the storage chest?**
- **What information will you use?**

Plan

- **What strategies can you use to solve the problem?**
  You can use *make a model* or *write an equation.*

Solve

- **How can you use each strategy to solve the problem?**

Make a Model Use cubes to make a model of the storage chest. Let each cube represent 1 cubic foot.

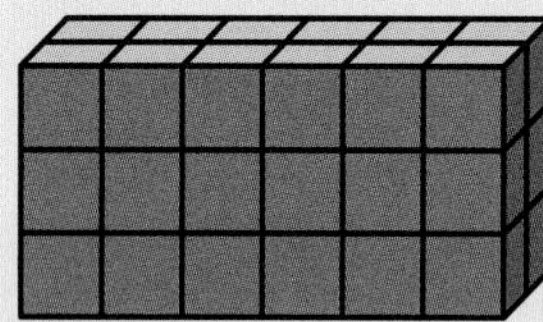

2 rows of 6 cubes = 12 cubes
3 layers of 12 cubes = 36 cubes
36 cubes = 36 ft^3

Write an Equation Use the formula for finding the volume of a rectangular prism to write an equation.

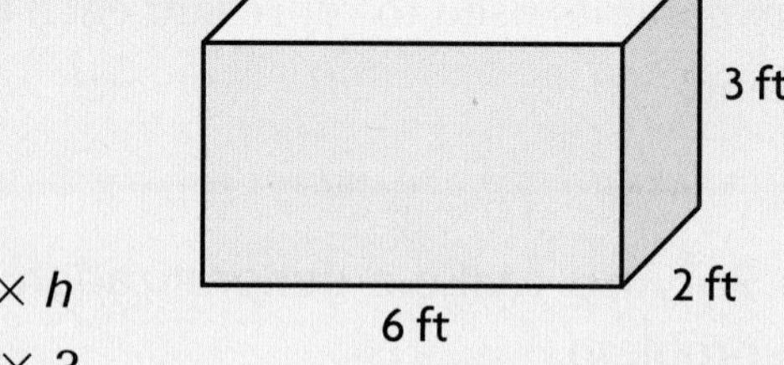

$V = l \times w \times h$
$V = 6 \times 2 \times 3$
$V = 36 \text{ ft}^3$

So, the volume of the storage chest is 36 ft^3.

Check

- **How do you know the answer is correct?**

Guided Problem Solving

1. Greg drew this diagram of a jewelry box he wants to make for his sister. What is the volume of the jewelry box?

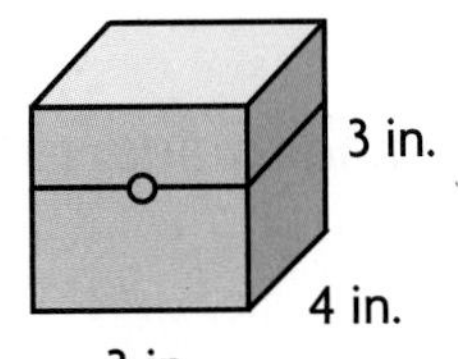

First, use the strategy *make a model* to solve the problem. Use cubes to model the length, width, and height of the jewelry box. Count or compute the number of cubes needed to make the model.

Then, use the *write an equation* strategy to solve the problem. Use the formula for finding the volume of a rectangular prism to write an equation.

$V = l \times w \times h$
$V = 3 \times 4 \times 3$
$V = \blacksquare$

Finally, compare the answers from both strategies.

2. **What if** the width of the jewelry box in Exercise 1 was 3 in.? What would the volume be?

3. Tashi is repairing tiles on a kitchen floor. The floor is in the shape of a rectangle. The area of the floor is 156 ft^2. The length is 13 ft. What is the width of the floor?

Choose a STRATEGY

- Draw a Diagram or Picture
- Make a Model or Act It Out
- Make an Organized List
- Find a Pattern
- Make a Table or Graph
- Predict and Test
- Work Backward
- Solve a Simpler Problem
- Write an Equation
- Use Logical Reasoning

Mixed Strategy Practice

Make a model or write an equation to solve.

4. Tony drew the diagram at the right for a storage chest he wants to make. How much space will the chest occupy?

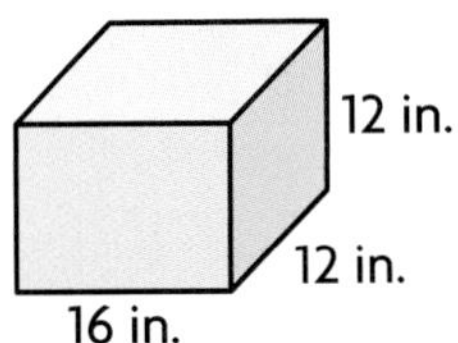

5. Isabel is installing a square window. Each side of the window is 14 in. long. What is the area of the window?

USE DATA Use the table for 6–7.

6. **Reasoning** The tool box that Chen bought has a length of 20 in. The height is 8 in. and the width is 9 in. What is the volume of his tool box?

7. The sales clerk gave Luis $4.75 back in change when he bought the tool box that has a volume of 1,320 $in.^3$ How much money did Luis give the clerk?

Tool Boxes

Length (in.)	Width (in.)	Height (in.)	Price
20	9	8	$58.25
18	8	10	$62.25
22	10	6	$65.25

8. **WRITE Math** Cora made a bookcase with 4 shelves. The shelves are one inch thick and one foot apart. The first shelf rests on a base that is 4 in. above the floor. The fourth shelf is also the top of the bookcase. Find the height of the bookcase. **Explain** your reasoning.

Extra Practice

Set A **Estimate the area of the shaded figure. Each square on the grid is 1 cm^2.** (pp. 640–641)

1. 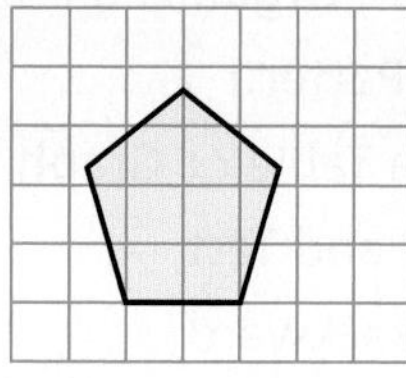

2. 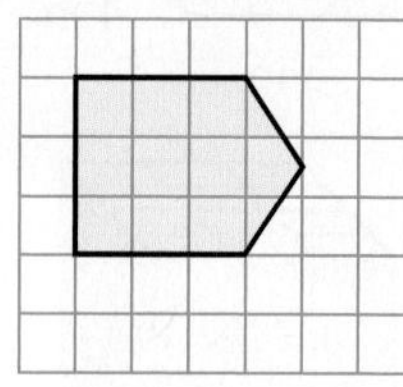

3. 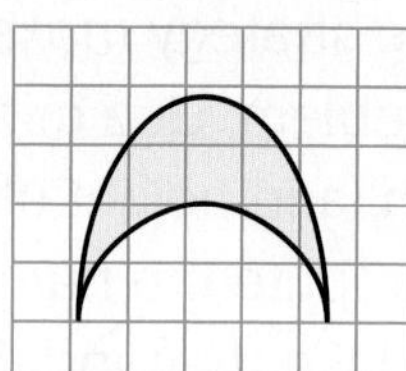

Set B **Find the area of each figure.** (pp. 642–645)

1. 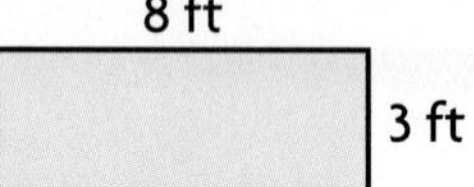

2. 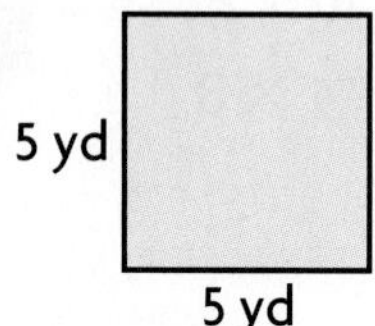

3. 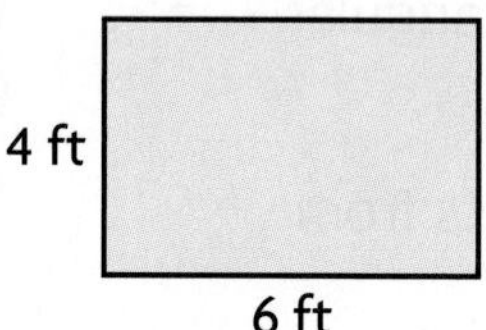

4. 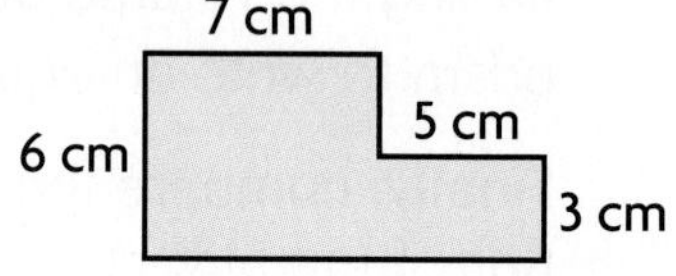

For each square or rectangle, find the area.

5. **Square**
   $s = 4.5$ yd
   $A = ■$

6. **Square**
   $s = 7.2$ m
   $A = ■$

7. **Rectangle**
   $l = 3.5$ km
   $w = 4$ km
   $A = ■$

8. **Rectangle**
   $l = 5$ in.
   $w = 8\frac{1}{2}$ in.
   $A = ■$

9. Jess measured one side of a square to be 6 in. long. What is the area of the square?

10. Ethan measured a rectangle. The length is 2.4 ft and the width is 3.6 ft. What is the area of the rectangle?

Set C **For the given perimeter, find the length and width of the rectangle with the greatest area. Use whole numbers only.** (pp. 646–649)

1. 30 ft
2. 16 in.
3. 24 yd
4. 40 m
5. 12 mi

For the given area, find the length and width of the rectangle with the least perimeter. Use whole numbers only.

6. 25 ft^2
7. 18 mi^2
8. 14 cm^2
9. 24 m^2
10. 42 ft^2

Set D **Find the area of each triangle in square units.** (pp. 650–653)

1. 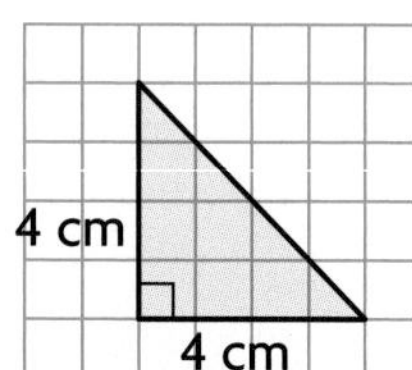

2. 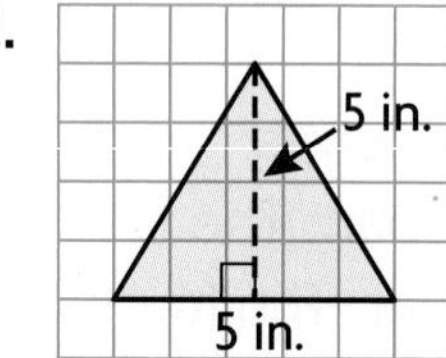

3. 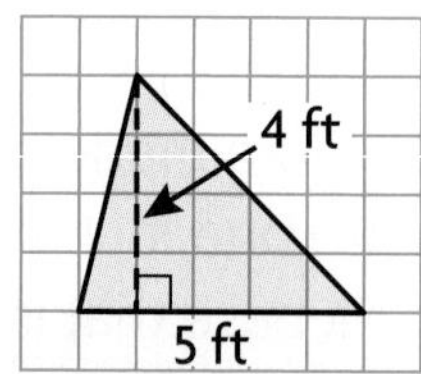

Technology
Use Harcourt Mega Math, Ice Station Exploration, *Polar Planes*, Level Q.

Find the area of each triangle.

4. 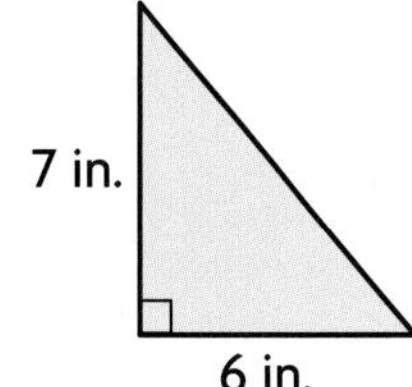

5. 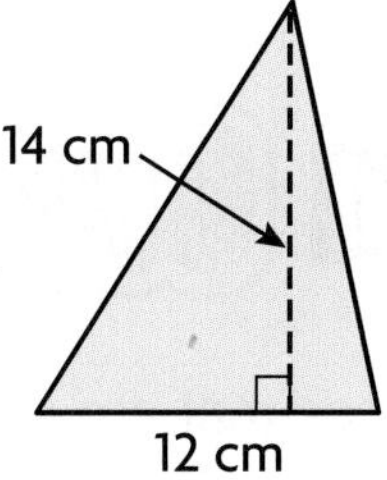

6. 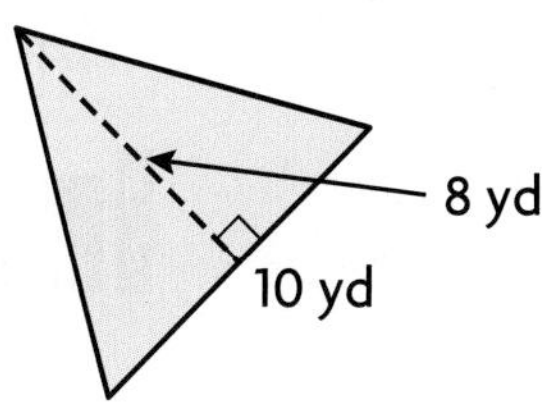

Set E Find the area of each parallelogram. (pp. 654–657)

1. 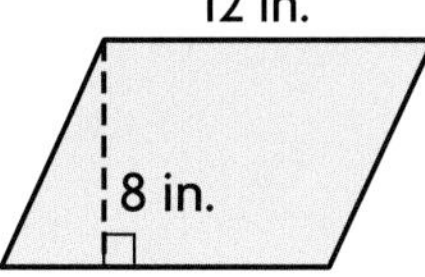

2. 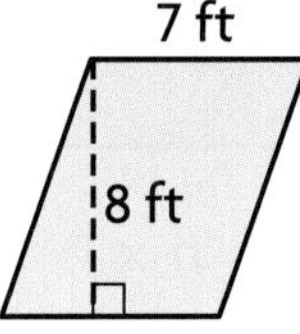

3. 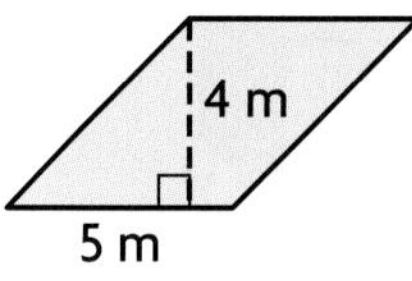

Set F Find the volume of each rectangular prism. (pp. 664–667)

1. 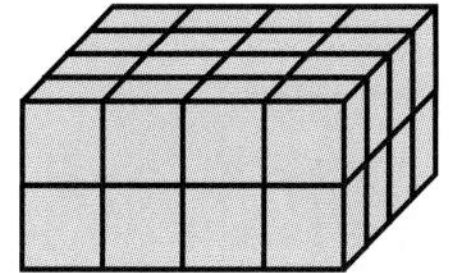

2. 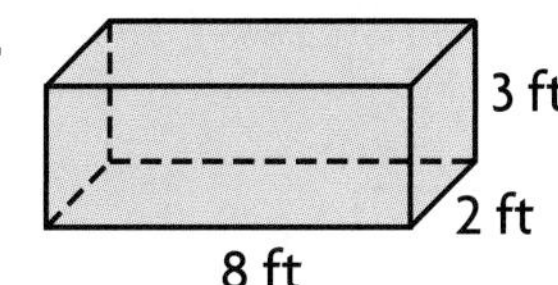

3. 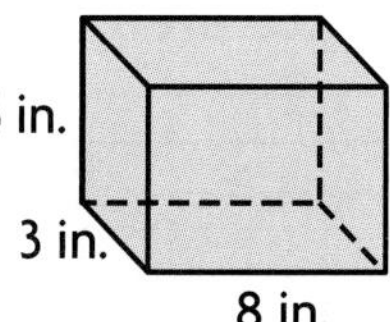

Set G Tell the type of unit you would use for measuring each.

Write *linear, square,* or *cubic.* (pp. 668–671)

1. rope needed to tie a boat to the dock
2. tile needed to cover a kitchen floor
3. amount of space in a fish tank
4. amount of chain link used to build a fence
5. Kimmie is measuring a ribbon to use on the edge of a quilt. Which unit should she use?
6. George is buying a new rug for his living room. Which unit should he use?

Write the units you would use for measuring each.

7. area of this square

9 ft

8. volume of this prism

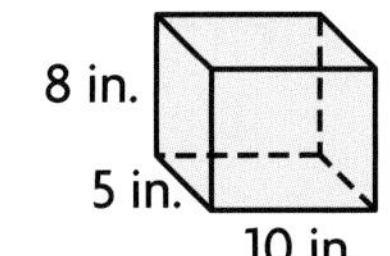

9. perimeter of this parallelogram

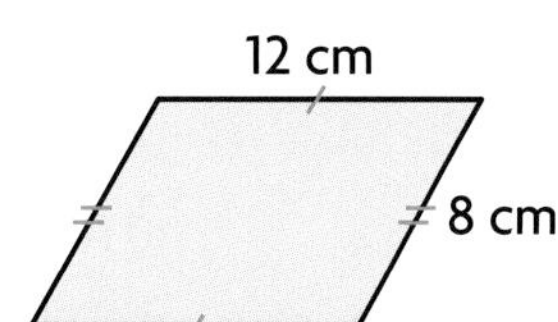

10. surface area of this prism

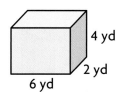

4 yd
2 yd
6 yd

Surface Area and Volume

Inside and Outside

A rectangular prism has 3 pairs of opposite faces that are congruent. You can find the surface area of a rectangular prism by finding the area of each unique face, multiplying each area by 2, and finding the sum of the products.

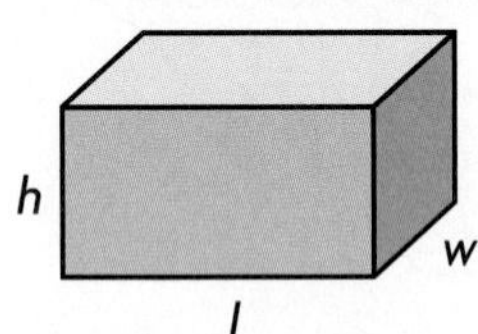

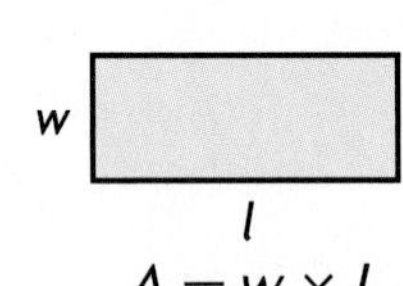

$A = w \times l$

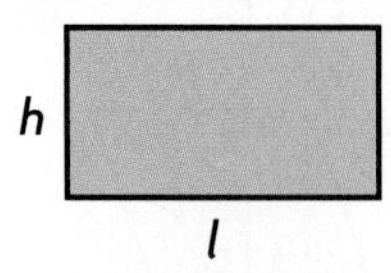

$A = h \times l$

h

w

$A = h \times w$

To find the volume of a rectangular prism, use the formula $V = l \times w \times h$.

Warm Up

Find the surface area and volume of the rectangular prism.

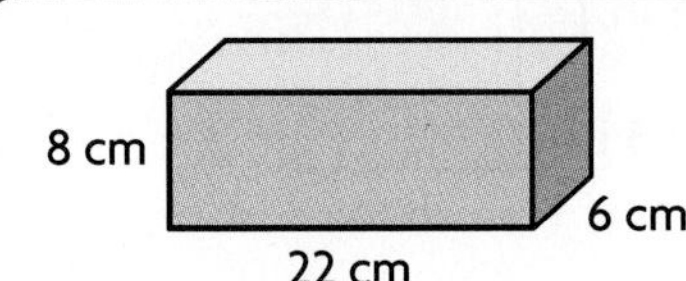

6 cm

22 cm

$6 \times 22 = 132$

8 cm

22 cm

$8 \times 22 = 176$

8 cm

6 cm

$8 \times 6 = 48$

Multiply the areas of each face by 2, and then add the products to find the surface area of the rectangular prism.

$2 \times 132 \text{ cm}^2 = 264 \text{ cm}^2$ $\quad 2 \times 48 \text{ cm}^2 = 96 \text{ cm}^2$ $\quad 2 \times 176 \text{ cm}^2 = 352 \text{ cm}^2$

$S = 264 \text{ cm}^2 + 96 \text{ cm}^2 + 352 \text{ cm}^2 = 712 \text{ cm}^2$

Volume, $V = l \times w \times h = 22 \text{ cm} \times 8 \text{ cm} \times 6 \text{ cm} = 1{,}056 \text{ cm}^3$

Try It

Find the surface area and volume of each rectangular prism.

1.

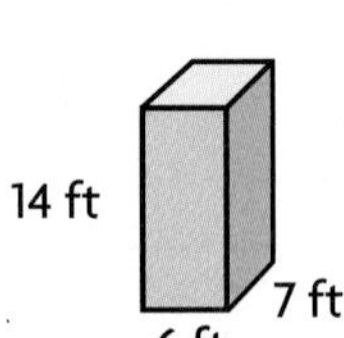

2.

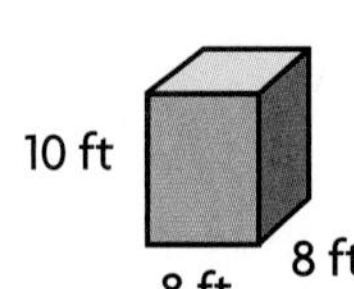

3.

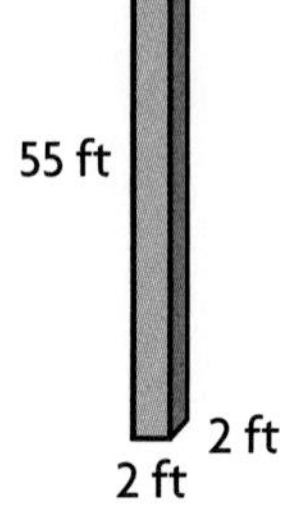

4. **WRITE Math** Compare the surface areas and volumes of the figures in Problems 1–3. Which figure, if any, would require the most fabric to be covered? Which figure, if any, would hold the greatest number of centimeter cubes? **Explain** your answer.

Chapter 24 Review/Test

Check Vocabulary and Concepts

Choose the best term from the box.

VOCABULARY
area
square units
height
base
surface area
volume

1. The area of a figure is the number of _?_ needed to cover it. KY MA-05-2.1.1 (p. 640)
2. The _?_ is the length of a perpendicular from the base to the top of a plane figure. KY MA-05-2.1.1 (p. 640)

Check Skills

Find the area of each figure. KY MA-05-2.1.1 (pp. 642–645, 650–653, 654–657)

3. 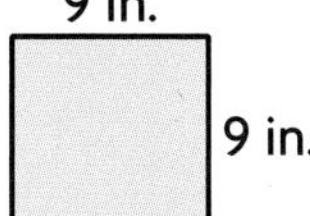

4. 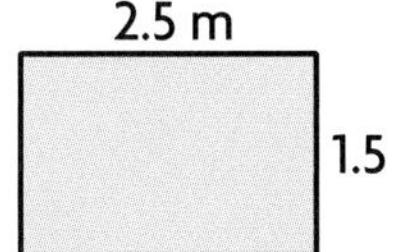

5. 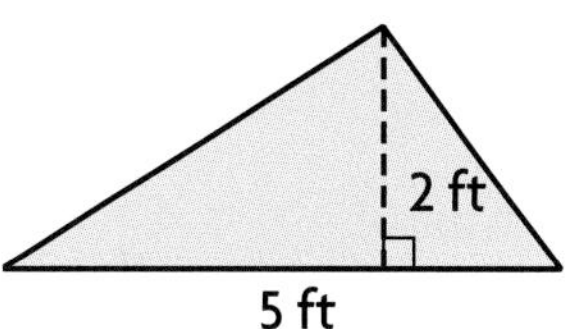

6. 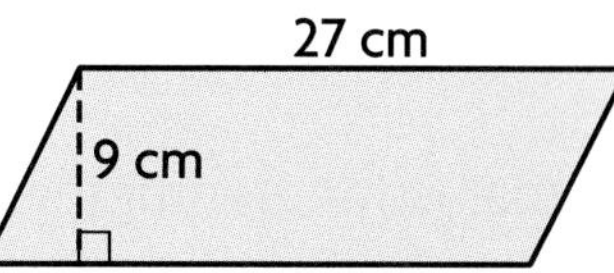

For the given area, find the length and width of the rectangle with the least perimeter. Use whole numbers only. KY MA-05-2.1.1 (pp. 646–649)

7. 32 ft^2
8. 18 cm^2
9. 24 m^2
10. 14 mi^2
11. 72 km^2

Find the volume of each rectangular prism. KY Grade 6 (pp. 664–667)

12. 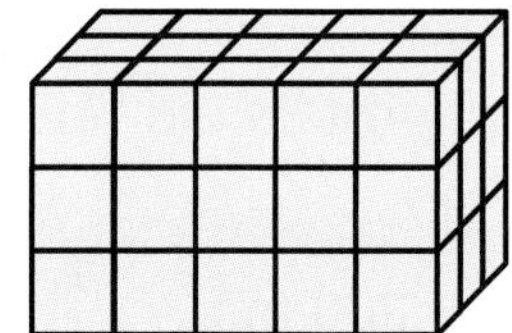

13. 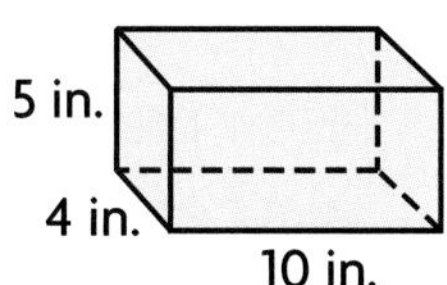

14. 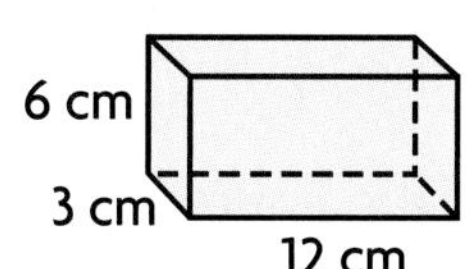

15. 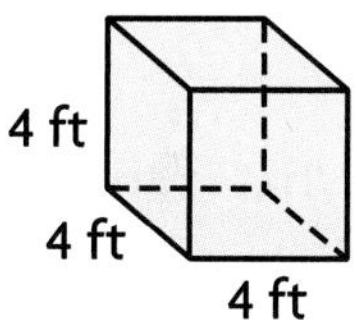

Tell the type of unit you would use to measure each. Write *linear*, *square*, or *cubic*. KY Grade 6 (pp. 668–671)

16. string to make a necklace
17. space in a shoebox
18. wallpaper to cover a wall
19. length of a pencil
20. floor space for a rug

Check Problem Solving

Solve. KY Grade 6 (pp. 664–667)

21. Emma put her sister's present in the gift box below. What is the volume of the gift box?

22. WRITE Math Mr. Jenkins built a storage cabinet that measured 4 ft × 2 ft × 6 ft. **Explain** how to find the volume of the storage cabinet.

Technology Use *Online Assessment.*

Unit Review/Test
Chapters 22–24

Multiple Choice

1. Which is the *best* estimate of the perimeter of the trapezoid? KY MA-05-2.1.1 (p. 622)

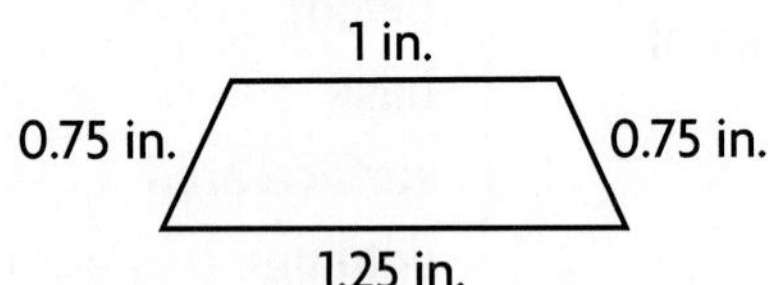

A. about 2 in.
B. about 4 in.
C. about 6 in.
D. about 8 in.

2. What is the perimeter of the rectangle below? KY MA-05-2.1.1 (p. 626)

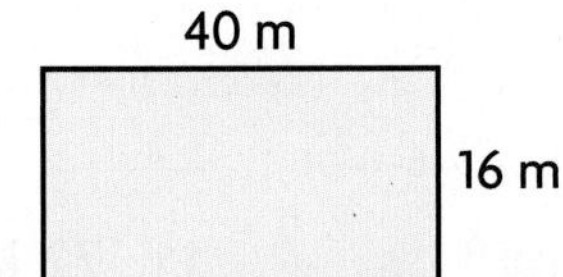

A. 56 m
B. 96 m
C. 112 m
D. 640 m

3. What is the total area of the figure below? KY MA-05-2.1.1 (p. 642)

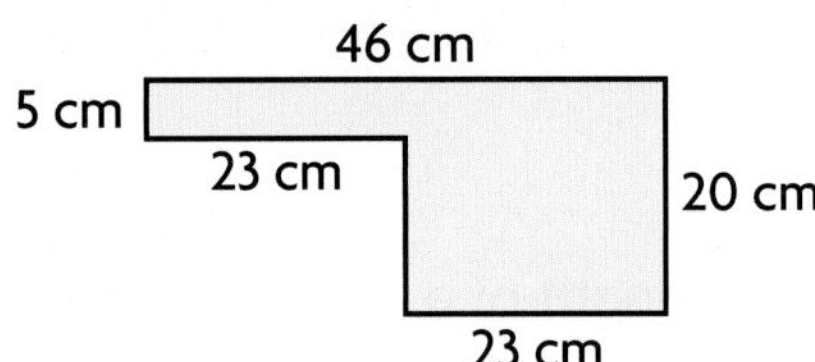

A. 117 cm
B. 132 cm
C. 575 cm^2
D. 690 cm^2

4. What is the area of the rectangle? KY MA-05-2.1.1 (p. 642)

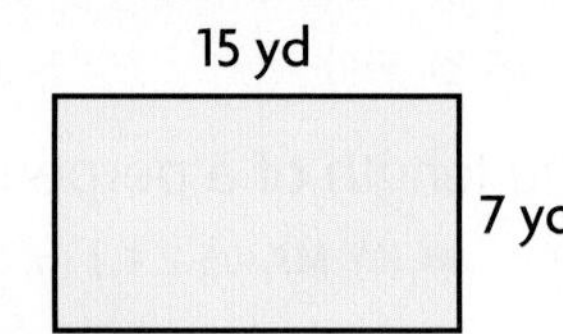

A. 22 yd^2
B. 105 yd^2
C. 210 yd^2
D. 1,575 yd^2

5. The table shows the amount of protein Brian ate for one day.

Meal	Grams of Protein
Breakfast	6
Lunch	12
Dinner	15

How many milligrams of protein did Brian eat? KY MA-05-2.2.3 (p. 604)

A. 33 mg
B. 330 mg
C. 3,300 mg
D. 33,000 mg

6. Doug has books that are 3 in. wide. He will set them side by side on a shelf that is 2 ft long. How many books will fit on the shelf? KY MA-05-2.2.3 (p. 596)

A. 4
B. 5
C. 8
D. 10

GO ONLINE **Technology** Use *Online Assessment.*

7. Which figure below has 4 vertices? KY MA-05-3.1.3 (p. 524)

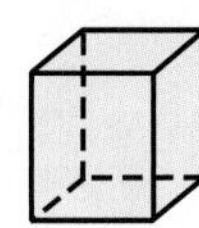
Figure *L*

Figure *M*

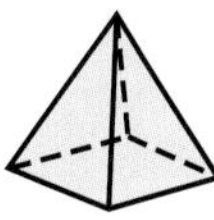
Figure *P*

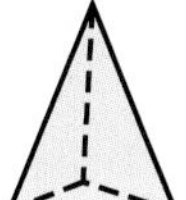
Figure *Q*

A. Figure *L*
B. Figure *M*
C. Figure *P*
D. Figure *Q*

8. What is the mean of the scores of the 5 math tests Jake took? KY MA-05-4.2.1 (p. 220)

Jake's Math Scores				
94	97	86	92	81

A. 85
B. 86
C. 90
D. 92

9. Enrique begins practicing his drums at 2:25 P.M. He needs to practice for at least 35 minutes. What is the earliest time he can stop? KY MA-05-2.2.1 (p. 610)

A. 2:10 P.M.
B. 2:50 P.M.
C. 3:00 P.M.
D. 3:05 P.M.

10. Min's dad works in Lexington. He takes a taxi twice a day. The first trip costs $0.54 and the second trip costs $1.14. How much does he spend in 5 days? **Explain.** KY MA-05-1.3.1 (p. 152)

Open Response WRITE Math

11. Suppose you have a choice of the flat gold bars shown in the table. Each has the same perimeter and thickness. You want the largest gold bar—the one with the greatest area. Which gold bar should you choose? **Explain** your reasoning. KY MA-05-2.1.1 (p. 646)

Gold Bar	Length (inches)	Width (inches)	Perimeter (inches)	Area (square inches)
A	5	1	12	■
B	4	■	12	■
C	3	■	12	■

12. Explain what two numbers make this expression true. KY MA-05-1.1.3 (p. 10)

$$652{,}526 < 652{,}5\_9 < 652{,}542$$

THE WORLD ALMANAC FOR KIDS

Playing in the Water

Built to Thrill

Have you ever been to an amusement park? In the country of Denmark, there is an amusement park that has been open since 1583. That's almost 200 years before the United States of America was founded! Early amusement parks in the United States began in Connecticut, Ohio, New York, and Pennsylvania. Lake Compounce Amusement Park in Bristol, Connecticut, was built in 1846.

Today many amusement parks have water rides, and some have only water features, such as log flumes, water slides, and wave pools.

FACT · ACTIVITY

1. Thunder Falls, a water slide in Aurora, Ohio, is 10 stories tall. If 1 story is 10 feet, how many feet tall is the slide? How many inches tall is the slide?
2. The park in Aurora also has a gigantic wave pool called Tidal Wave Bay. It is 325 feet wide and 220 feet long. In yards, about how wide and how long is Tidal Wave Bay?
3. The ground space needed for a water slide to be built is called the footprint. Use the footprint shown at the right to estimate the perimeter and area.
4. WRITE Math **Explain** how the numbers would change if you estimated the area and perimeter in yards instead of feet.

Footprint

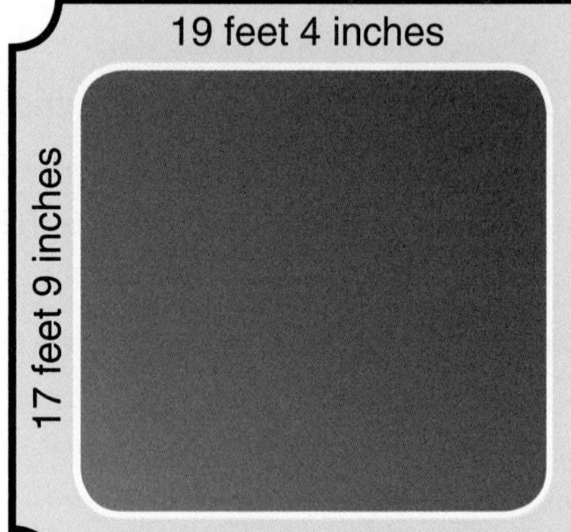

ALMANAC Fact

Paul Boynton, nicknamed "The Fearless Frogman," helped design a park in Chicago, Illinois, in 1894. In a water ride there, people rode in cars that slid down a ramp into a lake.

Make Waves!

Many water parks have wave pools, as well as water rides. The largest wave pools in the world have surface areas from 75,000 to 140,000 square feet. Hydraulic pumps can make waves that are 9 feet tall, allowing people to surf in a wave pool!

FACT·ACTIVITY

Design a splash area for a wave pool. One of the largest pools holds 350,000 gallons of water—equal to about 1,733 cubic yards. Your pool splash area should have a rectangular footprint and the same depth throughout.

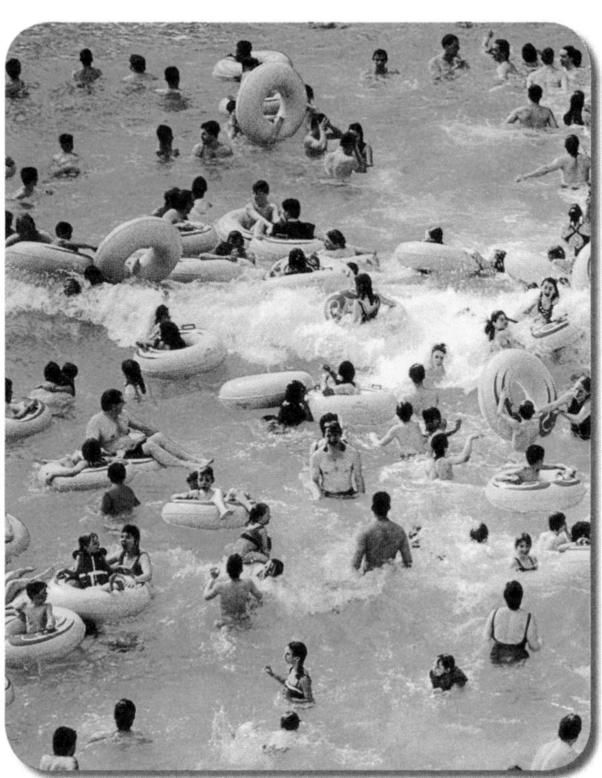

- Using any depth up to 2 yards, and whole numbers for length and width, what dimensions give you a volume that is close to 1,733 cubic yards? What is that volume?
- What if your wave pool splash area were long and narrow, with the same depth? How close could you come to having a wave pool with a volume of 1,733 cubic yards?
- What would the dimensions be if you kept a depth of 2 yards but made your pool's splash area a square?

Student Handbook

Review the Core Content for Assessment

These pages provide review of key concepts for your grade.

Review the Core Content for Assessment

Read and Write Numbers Through Millions

KY MA-05-1.1.1 Students will apply multiple representations (e.g., drawings, manipulatives, base-10 blocks, number lines, expanded form, symbols) to represent whole numbers (0 to 99,999,999). DOK 2

This place-value chart shows the number 5,084,000 written in standard form and expanded form.

MILLIONS	THOUSANDS			ONES		
Ones	Hundreds	Tens	Ones	Hundreds	Tens	Ones
5,	0	8	4,	0	0	0
5,000,000	0	80,000	4,000	0	0	0

The place value of the digit 5 in 5,084,000 is millions.

The value of 5 in 5,084,000 is $5 \times 1{,}000{,}000 = 5{,}000{,}000$.

Example

A number can be written in standard, word, or expanded form.

Standard Form: 5,930,026

Word Form: five million, nine hundred thirty thousand, twenty-six

Expanded Form: 5,000,000 + 900,000 + 30,000 + 20 + 6

ERROR ALERT

As you read a large number, remember to correctly name the place value of each digit.

Try It

Write the number in a different form.

1. 825,000
2. eight million, fifty-nine thousand
3. 9,000,000 + 100,000 + 200 + 50
4. 199,004
5. seventeen thousand, three hundred eleven
6. 6,000,000 + 9,000 + 80 + 2
7. 486,314
8. three million, eight hundred thousand, twelve

9. Read the problem below. **Explain** why B cannot be the correct answer choice. Then choose the correct answer. **COMMON ERROR**

   Which is another way to write the number Three million, two hundred thousand, one hundred and twenty-five?

   A 3,200,125 **C** 3,000,125

   B 32,020,125 **D** 2,300,125

Review the Core Content for Assessment

Compare Fractions and Decimals

KY MA-05-1.1.3 Students will compare (<, >, =) and order whole numbers, fractions and decimals, and explain the relationships (equivalence, order) between and among them. DOK 2

To compare fractions with common denominators, compare the numerators. To compare decimals, use place value.

Examples

You can use place value to compare 0.57 and 0.564.

A Compare $\frac{1}{4}$ and $\frac{3}{4}$.

Since the fractions have common denominators, you can compare their numerators.

Since $1 < 3$, $\frac{1}{4} < \frac{3}{4}$.

Step 1

Line up the decimal points. Begin at the left. Compare the tenths.

0.57

0.564 The tenths are the same.

Step 2

Compare the hundredths.

0.57

0.564 $7 > 6$

ERROR ALERT

When comparing fractions, the denominator stays the same.

So, 0.57 > 0.564, or 0.564 < 0.57.

Try It

Compare. Write <, > or = for each ●.

1. $\frac{4}{8}$ ● $\frac{3}{8}$
2. $\frac{1}{10}$ ● $\frac{3}{10}$
3. $\frac{5}{7}$ ● $\frac{5}{7}$
4. $\frac{4}{6}$ ● $\frac{2}{6}$
5. $\frac{7}{21}$ ● $\frac{11}{21}$
6. $\frac{9}{15}$ ● $\frac{9}{15}$
7. $\frac{3}{8}$ ● $\frac{4}{8}$
8. 0.2 ● 0.2
9. 0.5 ● 0.5
10. 0.32 ● 0.32
11. 0.93 ● 0.95
12. 0.72 ● 0.7
13. 0.45 ● 0.41
14. 0.81 ● 0.84

15. Read the problem below. **Explain** why D cannot be the correct answer choice. Then choose the correct answer.

COMMON ERROR

Rochelle and Jardine are making tomato sauce. Rochelle's recipe calls for $\frac{3}{4}$ cup of tomato paste, and Jardine's recipe calls for $\frac{1}{4}$ cup of tomato paste. Which shows the correct relationship between these fractions?

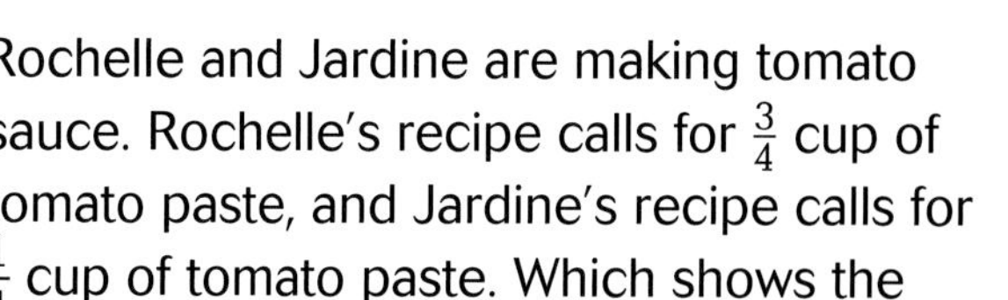

A $\frac{3}{4} < \frac{1}{4}$

B $\frac{3}{4} > \frac{1}{4}$

C $\frac{1}{4} > \frac{3}{4}$

D $\frac{3}{8} > \frac{1}{4}$

Review the Core Content for Assessment

Multiply Whole Numbers

KY MA-05-1.3.1 Students will analyze real-world problems to identify appropriate representations using mathematical operations, and will apply operations to solve real-world problems with the following constraints: add, subtract, *multiply*, and divide whole numbers (less than 100,000,000), using technology where appropriate. DOK 2

To multiply a whole number by a 1-digit number, multiply the ones and tens. Repeat the same steps for all the digits.

To multiply a whole number by a 2-digit number, multiply by the ones, then by the tens. Add the partial products.

Examples

A A labeling machine can label 471 juice bottles in an hour. How many bottles can the machine label in 5 hours?

Multiply the ones. Then multiply the tens and hundreds. Regroup as needed.

$$\begin{array}{r} \scriptstyle 3 \\ 471 \\ \times \quad 5 \\ \hline 2{,}355 \end{array}$$

So, the machine can label 2,355 bottles in 5 hours.

B A farmer planted 203 rose bushes in each of 36 rows. How many rose bushes in all did he plant?

Multiply by the ones and then by the tens. Add the partial products.

$$\begin{array}{rl} \scriptstyle 1 & \\ 203 & \\ \times \;\; 36 & \\ \hline 1218 & 6 \times 203 \\ +\,6090 & 30 \times 203 \\ \hline 7{,}308 & \end{array}$$

So, the farmer planted 7,308 rose bushes.

ERROR ALERT

When multiplying by tens, be sure to use a place-holder zero to align the places.

$$\begin{array}{r} \scriptstyle 1 \\ 203 \\ \times \;\; 36 \\ \hline 1218 \\ +\,6090 \\ \hline 7{,}308 \end{array}$$

Try It

Solve.

1. A toy company makes wooden blocks. A shipping carton holds 783 blocks. How many blocks can the company ship in 17 shipping cartons?

2. Marc has 22 bags of marbles. Each bag contains 365 marbles. How many marbles does Marc have in all?

3. Read the problem below. **Explain** why A cannot be the correct answer choice. Then choose the correct answer.

Venetia calculates that her heart beats about 72 times per minute. How many times will it beat during a 45-minute class period?

A 648 times **C** 3,240 times

B 3,230 times **D** 32,400 times

Review the Core Content for Assessment

Divide Whole Numbers

KY MA-05-1.3.1 Students will analyze real-world problems to identify appropriate representations using mathematical operations, and will apply operations to solve real-world problems with the following constraints: add, subtract, multiply, and *divide* whole numbers (less than 100,000,000), using technology where appropriate. DOK 2

To divide a 3-digit number, use estimation or place value to place the first digit. Then divide. If the divisor is greater than the number to be divided, place a zero in the quotient. Repeat the steps until the remainder is zero or less than the divisor.

Examples

A Juanita has 112 pencils that she wants to share equally with 7 friends. How many pencils will each friend receive?

$$\begin{array}{r} 16 \\ 7\overline{)112} \\ -7 \\ \hline 42 \\ -42 \\ \hline 0 \end{array}$$

Divide the tens. Multiply. Subtract. Bring down the 2 ones. Divide the 42 ones.

So, each friend will receive 16 pencils.

B Nigel has 348 stickers to put into an album. Each page holds 27 stickers. How many pages will Nigel fill and how many stickers will be left over?

Place the first digit in the tens place.

$$\begin{array}{r} 12 \text{ r}24 \\ 27\overline{)348} \\ -27 \\ \hline 78 \\ -54 \\ \hline 24 \end{array}$$

When you have a remainder, compare it to the divisor. $24 < 27$, so you can stop dividing.

So, Nigel will fill 12 pages with 24 stickers left over.

ERROR ALERT

When you solve a division problem with a remainder, the way you interpret the remainder depends on the situation. You may have to drop the remainder, round the quotient to the next greater number, or use the remainder as part of the answer.

Try It

Solve.

1. Mr Becker spent $408 for a set of 8 dining chairs. How much did a chair cost?
2. Jackie bought 31 packages of trading cards. The total number of trading cards is 558. How many cards come in each package?
3. Read the problem below. **Explain** why A cannot be the correct answer choice. Then choose the correct answer.

There are 292 people invited to a wedding reception. If each table seats 8 people, how many tables will be needed?

A 36 **C** 360

B 37 **D** 2,304

Review the Core Content for Assessment

Add and Subtract Decimals

KY MA-05-1.3.1 Students will analyze real-world problems to identify appropriate representations using mathematical operations, and will apply operations to solve real-world problems with the following constraints: add and subtract decimals through hundredths. DOK 2

Add. 38.92 + 15.45 Estimate. 38 + 15 = 53

Step 1

Line up the decimal points to align place-value positions. Add the hundredths.

```
  38.92
+ 15.45
      7
```

Step 2

Add the tenths. Regroup as needed.

```
   1
  38.92
+ 15.45
     37
```

Step 3

Add the ones and tens. Place the decimal point in the sum.

```
   1
  38.92
+ 15.45
  54.37
```

Examples

 Subtract. 17.25 − 6.43

```
    6 12
   17.25
 −  6.43
   10.82
```

B Add. 7.1 + 5.96 + 2.80

```
    1
    7.10
    5.96
 +  2.80
   15.86
```

ERROR ALERT

Place zeros to make equivalent decimals if the decimals do not have the same number of decimal places.

2.7 = 2.70

Try It

Find the sum or difference.

1. \$4.79 + \$2.25
2. 8.34 − 2.56
3. 32.08 + 59.63
4. 82.39 − 54.8
5. 23.09 + 15.47 + 7.8
6. 46.75 − 5.36

7. Read the problem below. **Explain** why C cannot be the correct answer choice. Then choose the correct answer. **COMMON ERROR**

Subtract. 56.78 − 39.01

A 17.65 **C** 17.76

B 17.69 **D** 17.77

Review the Core Content for Assessment

Prime and Composite Numbers

 KY MA-05-1.5.1 Students will identify and determine *composite numbers, prime numbers,* multiples of a number, factors of a number and least common multiples (LCM), and will apply these numbers to solve real-world problems. DOK 2

A prime number has exactly two factors, 1 and itself. A composite number is a number that has more than two factors. You can use arrays to decide if a number is prime or composite.

Examples

A Is 3 prime or composite?

Use counters or draw an array. Show all the possible ways to represent 3.

OOO 1×3 3×1

The number 3 has exactly two factors, 1 and 3. So, it is a prime number.

B Is 9 prime or composite?

Show all the possible arrays to represent 9.

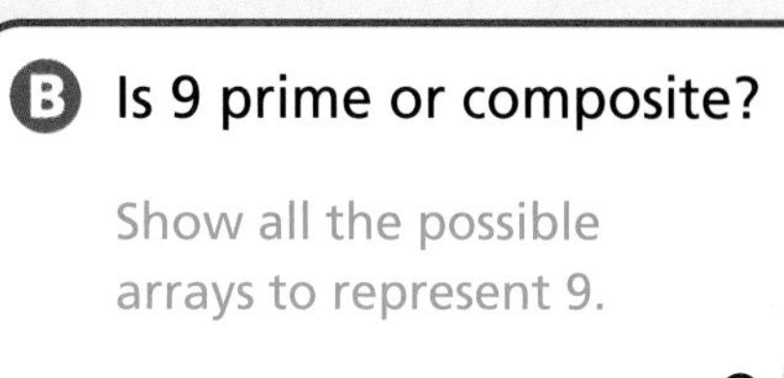

The number 9 has more than two factors; 1, 3, and 9. So, it is a composite number.

Remember that an odd number can also be composite.

For example, 21 is both odd and composite. Its factors are 1, 3, 7, and 21.

Try It

Use counters or a drawing to show all arrays for each number. Write *prime* or *composite*.

1. 11
2. 14
3. 35
4. 8
5. 7
6. 4
7. 15
8. 18
9. 22
10. 29
11. 12
12. 25
13. 6
14. 5
15. 23
16. 49
17. 17
18. 21

19. Read the problem below. **Explain** why A cannot be the correct answer choice. Then choose the correct answer.

Look at the numbers below.

4, 12, 15, 20

Each number is an example of which kind of number?

A Prime
B Composite
C Even number
D Odd number

Review the Core Content for Assessment

Multiples and Factors

KY MA-05-1.5.1 Students will identify and determine composite numbers, prime numbers, *multiples of a number, factors of a number* and least common multiples (LCM), and will apply these numbers to solve real-world problems. DOK 2

Multiples of 4: 4, 8, 12, 16, 20, 24, 28, 32, 36, 40,...

Multiples of 5: 5, 10, 15, 20, 25, 30, 35, 40,...

A number that is a multiple of two or more numbers in a set is called a common multiple. The common multiples of 4 and 5 are 20 and 40.

The least common multiple (LCM) of 4 and 5 is 20, because it is the least multiple that both numbers have in common.

Factors of 8: 1, 2, 4, 8

Factors of 12: 1, 2, 3, 4, 6, 12

A number that is a factor of two or more numbers is called a common factor. The common factors of 8 and 12 are: 1, 2, and 4.

The greatest common factor (GCF) of 8 and 12 is 4 because it is the greatest factor that both numbers have in common.

Examples

A Find the least common multiple of 2 and 3.

Multiples of 2: 2, 4, 6, 8, 10, 12,...

Multiples of 3: 3, 6, 9, 12, 15,...

Common multiples: 6, 12

LCM: 6

B Find the greatest common factor of 16 and 24.

16: 1, 2, 4, 8, 16

24: 1, 2, 3, 4, 6, 8, 12, 24

Common factors: 1, 2, 4, 8

GCF: 8

ERROR
ALERT
Remember that every number has 1 and itself as factors.

Try It

Write multiples for each set of numbers. Then find the least common multiple.

1. 5, 8
2. 6, 10
3. 3, 7

Write the factors for each set of numbers. Then find the greatest common factor.

4. 18, 27
5. 6, 15
6. 12, 20

7. Read the problem below. **Explain** why B cannot be the correct answer choice. Then choose the correct answer. Which group shows all the numbers that are common factors of 30 and 54?

COMMON ERROR

A 1, 2, 3, 6, 10

B 2, 3, 6

C 1, 2, 3, 6

D 1, 2, 3, 5, 6, 9, 10, 15, 18, 27, 30, 54

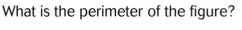

Review the Core Content for Assessment

Use Formulas to Find Perimeter

KY MA-05-2.1.1 Students will apply standard units to measure length (to the nearest eighth-inch or the nearest centimeter) and to determine perimeter. DOK 2

You can use a formula to find the perimeter of a polygon.

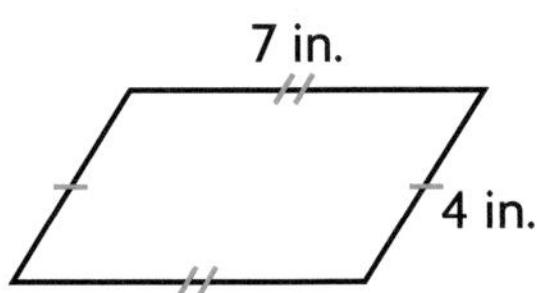

The figure is a parallelogram.

a, b = side lengths

$P = 2a + 2b$

$P = (2 \times 7) + (2 \times 4)$ Replace the variables with the given lengths.

$P = 14 + 8$

$= 22$

The perimeter is 22 inches.

ERROR ALERT

Be sure to account for all the sides of a figure when finding its perimeter.

Examples

A Find the perimeter.

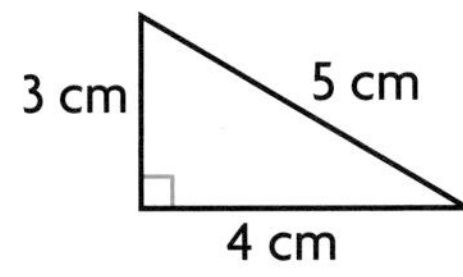

a, b, c = the side lengths

$P = a + b + c$

$P = 3 + 4 + 5$

$P = 12$ cm

So, the perimeter of the right triangle is 12 centimeters.

B Find the perimeter.

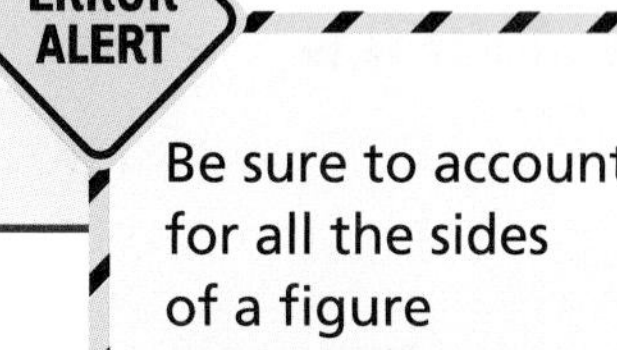

s = length of a side

$P = 5 \times s$ 5 is the number of sides.

$P = 5 \times 7\frac{1}{3}$

$P = 36\frac{2}{3}$

So, the perimeter of the regular pentagon is $36\frac{2}{3}$ feet.

Try It

Write a formula to find the perimeter. Solve.

1. 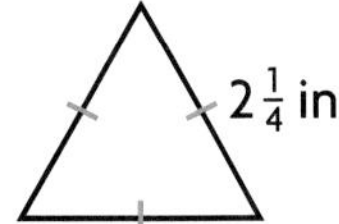

2. 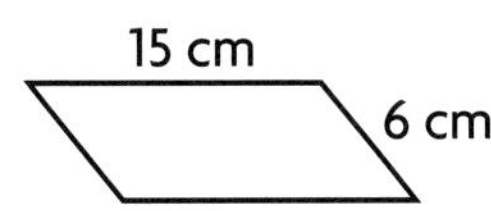

3.  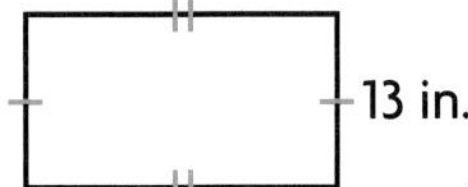

4.  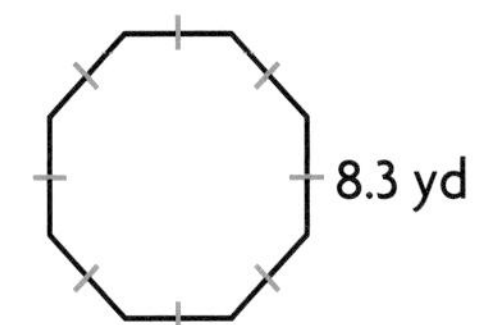

5. Read the problem below. **Explain** why B cannot be the correct answer choice. Then choose the correct answer.

What is the perimeter of the figure?

A 9 yd

B 18 yd

C 36 yd

D 81 yd

Review the Core Content for Assessment

Use Formulas to Find Area

KY MA-05-2.1.1 Students will apply standard units to measure length (to the nearest eighth-inch or the nearest centimeter) and to determine: area (figures that can be divided into rectangular shapes) DOK 2

You can use formulas to find area.

Area of a Rectangle

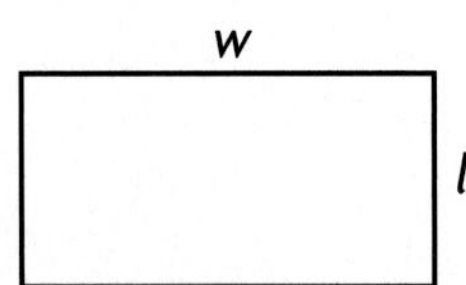

Area = length × width

$A = l \times w$

Area of a Square

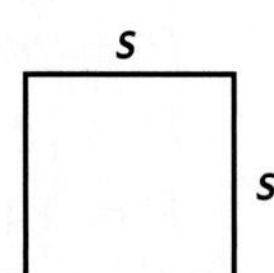

Area = side × side

$A = s^2$

ERROR ALERT

Square units are used to measure area.

Examples

A Find the area.

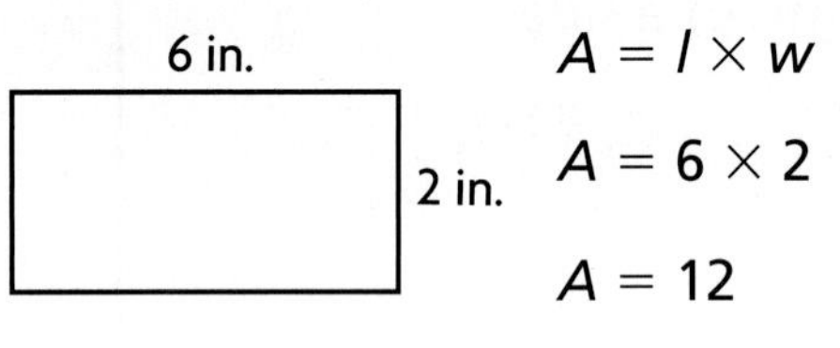

$A = l \times w$

$A = 6 \times 2$

$A = 12$

So, the area is 12 in.^{2}

B Find the area.

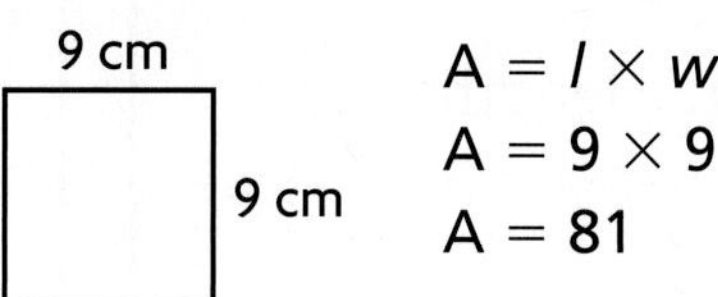

$A = l \times w$

$A = 9 \times 9$

$A = 81$

So, the area is 81cm^2.

Try It

Find the area.

1\.

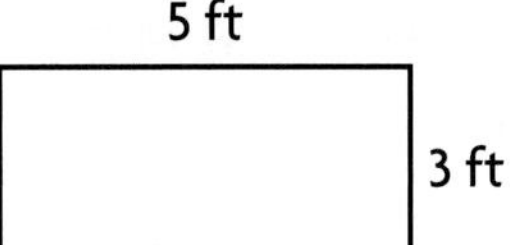

2\.

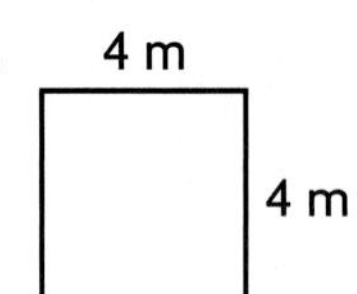

3\.

16 in.

3 in.

4\.

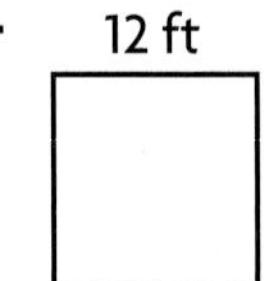

5\. Read the problem below. **Explain** why D cannot be the correct answer choice. Then choose the correct answer.

COMMON ERROR

What is the area of a storage cabinet that is 6 feet long and 4 feet high?

A 10 ft^2

B 10 ft^3

C 24 ft^2

D 24 ft^3

KENTUCKY Review the Core Content for Assessment

Elapsed Time

KY MA-05-2.2.1 Students will determine elapsed time. DOK 3

You can use subtraction to find elapsed time if you know the starting time and ending time.

Start: 1:15 P.M.
End: 4:50 P.M.

4 hr 50 min	← ending time
− 1 hr 15 min	← starting time
3 hr 35 min	← elapsed time

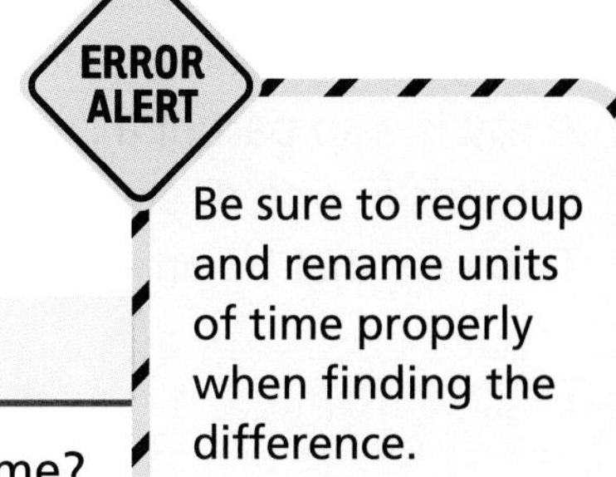

ERROR ALERT
Be sure to regroup and rename units of time properly when finding the difference.

Examples

A What is the ending time?

Start: 9:28 A.M.
Elapsed time: 2 hr 42 min

9 hr 28 min
+2 hr 42 min
11 hr 70 min — 70 min is 1 hr 10 min.

12 hr 10 min, or 12:10 P.M.

So, the ending time is 12:10 P.M.

B What is the elapsed time?

~~2~~ (1) wk ~~4~~ (11) days
−1 wk 5 days
6 days

Regroup 1 week as 7 days and rename. Subtract.

So, the elapsed time is 6 days.

Try It

Solve.

1. **Start:** ■
   Elapsed time: 2 hr 37 min
   End: 10:52 P.M.

2. **Start:** July 6, 3 P.M.
   Elapsed time: ■
   End: July 9, 5:15 P.M.

3. 4 days 12 hr
   +2 days 13 hr

4. 4 min 20 sec
   −1 min 35 sec

5. Read the problem below. **Explain** why C cannot be the correct answer choice. Then choose the correct answer. COMMON ERROR

   Find the elapsed time.

   Start: 8:45 A.M.
   End: 11:25 A.M.

   A 2 hr 20 min **C** 2 hr 80 min
   B 2 hr 40 min **D** 3 hr 20 min

Review the Core Content for Assessment

Lines, Segments, Rays and Angles

KY MA-05-3.1.1 Students will describe and provide examples of basic geometric elements and terms [*points, segments,* lines (perpendicular, parallel, intersecting), *rays,* angles (acute, right, obtuse), sides, edges, faces, bases, vertices, radius, diameter] and will apply these elements to solve real-world and mathematical problems. DOK 2

A **line** is a straight path. It extends in two directions in one plane and has no endpoints.

A **segment** is part of a line. A line segment has two endpoints.

A **ray** is also part of a line. A ray has only one endpoint, and extends in one direction.

Two rays that begin at the same point form an **angle**.

ERROR ALERT

Lines, segments, and rays can be defined by the number of their endpoints. A line has no endpoints, a ray has one endpoint and a line segment has two endpoints.

Examples

1 Describe the properties of a line, a line segment and a ray.

In how many directions does it extend? It extends in 2 directions.

Does it have endpoints? No.

What is its name? Line *RS* or $\overleftrightarrow{RS}$.

How many endpoints does it have? 2

What is its name? Line *DG* or $\overline{DG}$.

In how many directions does it extend? 1

How many endpoints does it have? 1

What is its name? Ray *XY* or $\overrightarrow{XY}$.

2 Describe different angles.

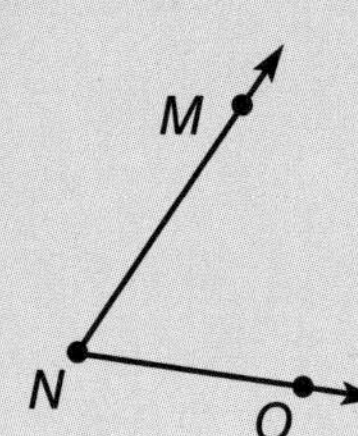

The angle at the left is formed by ray *NM* and ray *NO*. Its name is $\angle MNO$.

The rays come together at the vertex. What is the vertex? Point N.

An *acute* angle measures less than 90°.

A *right* angle measures exactly 90°.

An *obtuse* angle measures more than 90°.

Try It

For 1–6, use the figure to give examples of each.

1. A line
2. A line segment
3. A ray
4. An acute angle
5. An obtuse angle

6. Read the problem below. **Explain** why A cannot be the correct answer choice. Then choose the correct answer. **COMMON ERROR**

   How many endpoints does ray *ST* have?

   A 2 **C** 1

   B 0 **D** 3

Review the Core Content for Assessment

Line Relationships

KY MA-05-3.1.1 Students will describe and provide examples of basic geometric elements and terms [points, segments, *lines (perpendicular, parallel, intersecting)*, rays, angles (acute, right, obtuse), sides, edges, faces, bases, vertices, radius, diameter] and will apply these elements to solve real-world and mathematical problems. DOK 2

Lines and line segments can be parallel, perpendicular, or intersecting. Lines that intersect form an angle. A right angle measures exactly 90°. An acute angle is greater than 0° and less than 90°. An obtuse angle is greater than 90° and less than 180°.

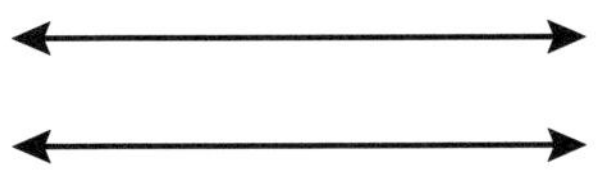

Parallel lines never intersect.

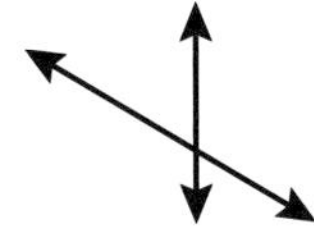

Intersecting lines cross at one point.

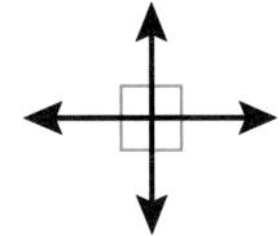

Perpendicular lines intersect to form four right angles.

Line segments can form polygons such as triangles or squares. They can also form three-dimensional figures such as pyramids or prisms. When figures are the same size and shape, they are congruent.

Example

Are the triangles congruent?

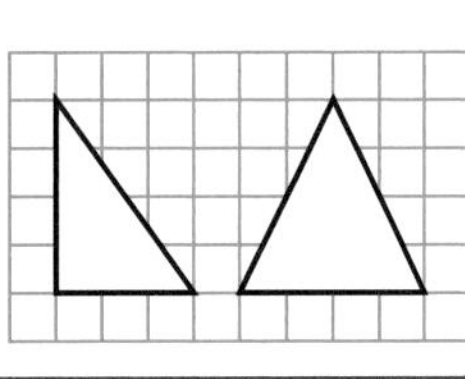

The triangles have the same height, but they are not the same shape.

So, the triangles are **not** congruent.

ERROR ALERT

A geometric figure may be named by more than one name. For example, perpendicular lines are also intersecting.

Try It

1. **Tell which statement about the rectangular prism shown below is true.**

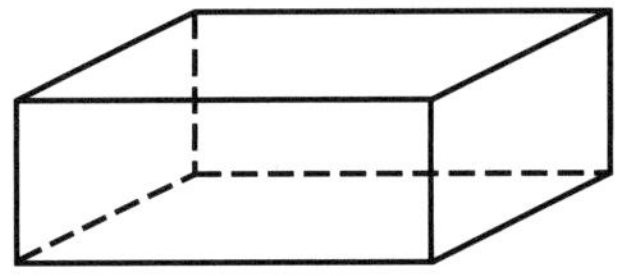

A The figure has only 1 pair of perpendicular faces.

B The figure has 6 congruent faces.

C The figure has 3 pairs of parallel faces.

D The figure has 2 pairs of congruent faces.

2. Read the problem below. **Explain** why F cannot be the correct answer choice. Then choose the correct answer.

COMMON ERROR

Which statement about the rectangles is true?

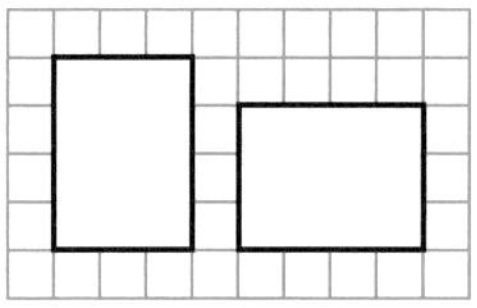

F The rectangles have no intersecting line segments.

G The rectangles are congruent.

H The rectangles have all acute angles.

J The rectangles each have just one pair of parallel sides.

Review the Core Content for Assessment

Nets

KY MA-05-3.1.3 Students will describe and provide examples of basic three-dimensional objects (spheres, cones, cylinders, pyramids, cubes, triangular and rectangular prisms), will *identify three-dimensional objects from two-dimensional representations (nets)* and will apply the attributes to solve real-world and mathematical problems. DOK 2

A net is a pattern for a three-dimensional object. The net can be folded along dotted lines to form the three-dimensional shape.

Examples

A Use the net to form a three-dimensional object.

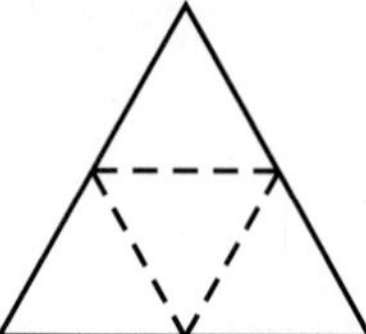

Fold along the dotted lines.

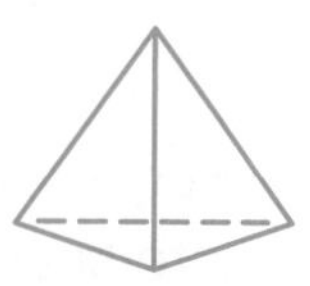

It is a triangular pyramid.

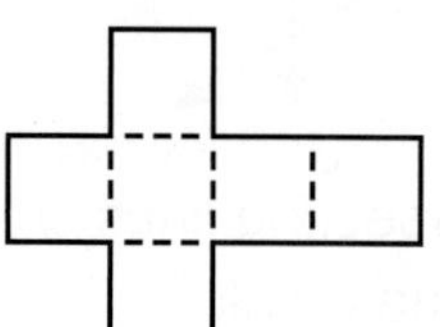

Fold along the dotted lines.

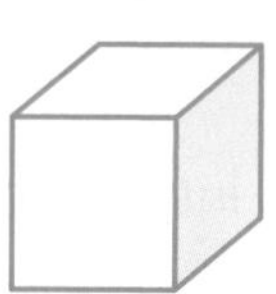

It is a cube.

B Determine the number of sides of the solid object from the net.

How many triangles are in net #1 above? 4

How many sides are there on the triangular pyramid? 4

How many squares are in net #2 above? 6

How many sides are there on the cube? 6

The number of polygons in a net is equal to the number of sides on the three-dimensional figure it forms.

ERROR ALERT

Each polygon in a net represents a side to a three-dimensional shape. When a net is folded, the sides should not overlap.

Try It

Match each figure to its net.

a) 

b) 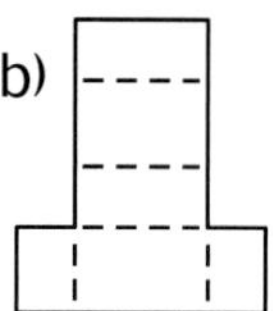

c) 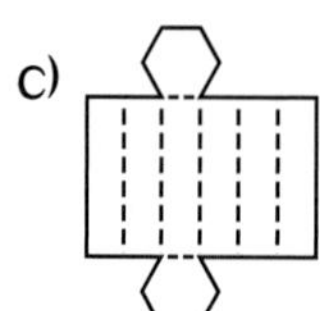

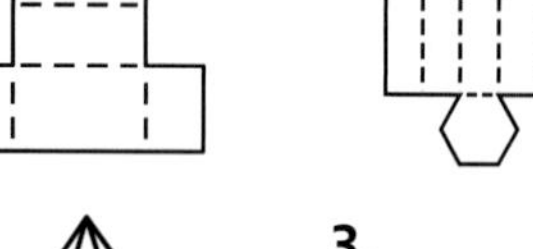

1. 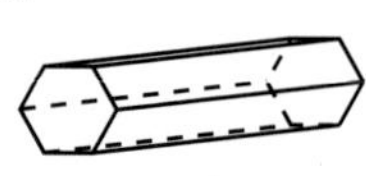

2. 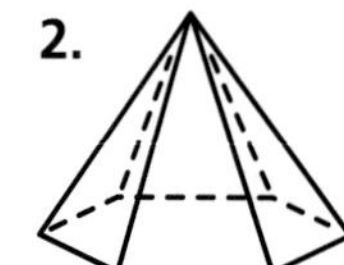

3. 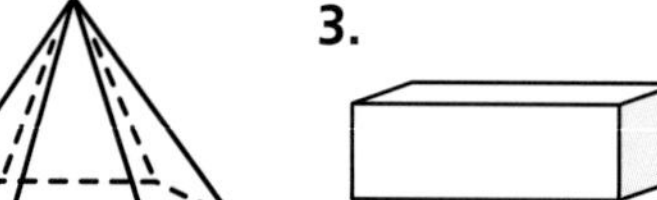

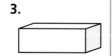

COMMON ERROR

4. Read the problem below. **Explain** why D cannot be the correct answer choice. Then choose the correct answer.

How many sides will be on the solid object that is made from this net?

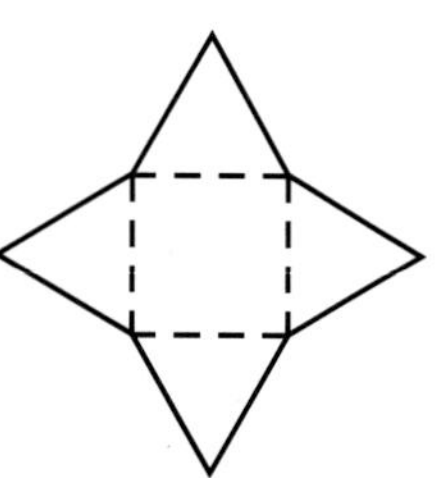

A 3 **C** 5

B 4 **D** 6

Review the Core Content for Assessment

Congruence

 KY MA-05-3.1.5 Students will identify and describe congruent and similar figures in real-world and mathematical problems. DOK 2

Plane shapes and solid figures are **congruent** if they have the same size and shape.

Examples

A Which figure appears to be congruent to Parallelogram A?

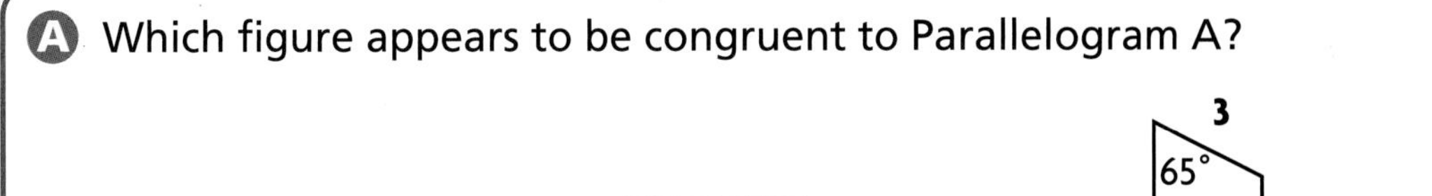

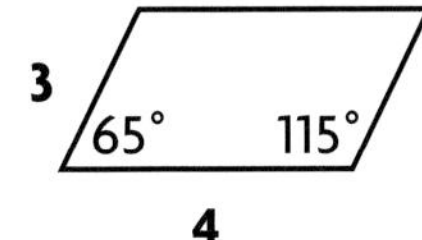

Parallelogram A

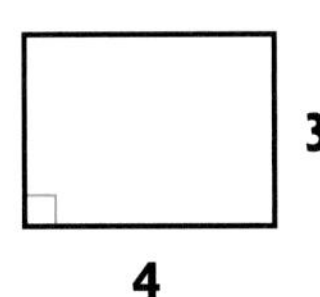

Figure 1

Same number of sides and same side lengths, but angles are not congruent.

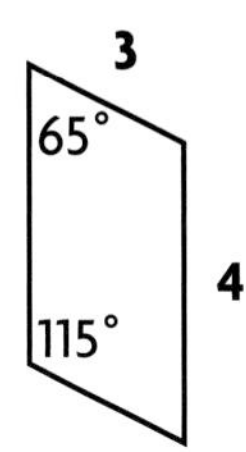

Figure 2

Sides and angles are congruent, figure has been turned but is still congruent.

B Which 2 solid figures appear to be congruent?

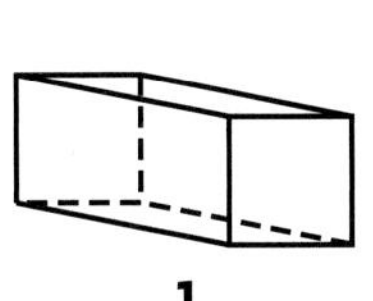

1

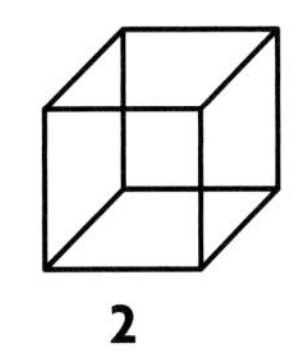

2

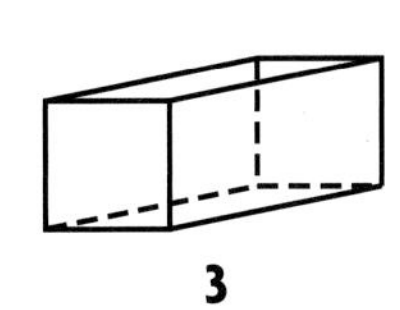

3

4

Figures 1 and 3 appear to be congruent. Both are rectangular prisms with 2 square faces. Both are more than twice as long as they are wide. Figure 2 has all square faces. Figure 4 has the same length but a rectangular face.

ERROR ALERT

All the sides and faces of a solid figure must be congruent for two figures to be congruent.

Try It

Which figures appear to be congruent?

1. 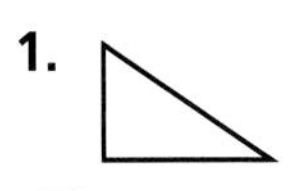 Figure 1 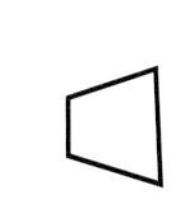 Figure 2  Figure 3 Figure 4

2. Read the problem below. **Explain** why A cannot be the correct answer. Then choose the correct answer.

Which solid figure below appears congruent to the shape to the right?

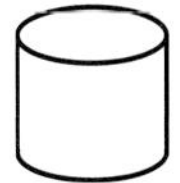 Figure 1 Figure 2  Figure 3 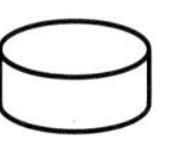 Figure 4

A Figure 1
B Figure 2
C Figure 3
D Figure 4

Review the Core Content for Assessment

Symmetry

KY MA-05-3.2.1 Students will describe and provide examples of line symmetry in real-world and mathematical problems or will apply line symmetry to construct a simple geometric design. DOK 3

A figure has **line symmetry** if a line can separate the figure into two *congruent* parts.

A figure has **rotational symmetry** if it can be rotated less than 360° about a central point and still match the original position.

Examples

A How many lines of symmetry does each figure have?

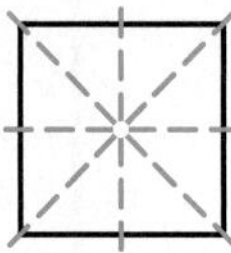

Square

Yes, 4 lines of symmetry

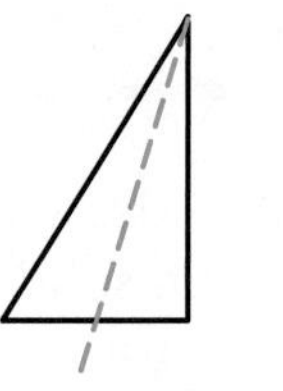

Scalene triange

No, sides do not line up when folded along the line. No lines of symmetry.

B Does the figure have rotational symmetry? How far must it be turned so that it appears the same as it does in the first position?

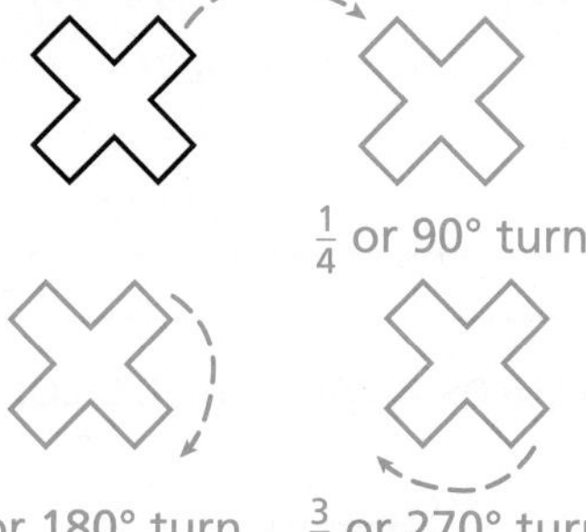

It has rotational symmetry. It can be given $\frac{1}{4}$ turn, $\frac{1}{2}$ turn or $\frac{3}{4}$ turn and look exactly the same.

ERROR ALERT

A line of symmetry divides a figure into two parts with sides that match up exactly when the figure is folded on the line.

Try It

Draw all possible lines of symmetry for each figure. Indicate if it also has rotational symmetry.

1. 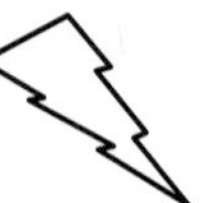
2. 
3. 
4. 
5. 
6. 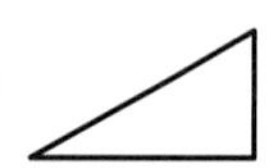

7. Read the problem below. **Explain** why C cannot be the correct answer choice. Then choose the correct answer. **COMMON ERROR**

Which lines are lines of symmetry?

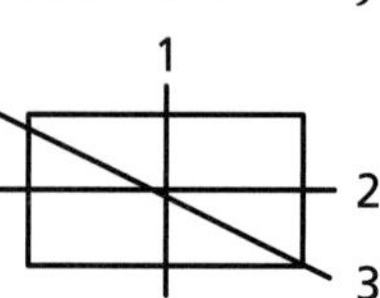

A 1, 2 **B** 1, 3

C 2, 3 **D** 1 only

Review the Core Content for Assessment

Transformations: Translations, Reflections, and Rotations

KY MA-05-3.2.2 Students will identify 90° rotations, reflections or translations of basic shapes within a plane. DOK 1

The examples below show three different types of **transformations,** or movements of figures in a coordinate grid.

- A **translation,** or slide, is a movement of a figure along a straight line.
- A **reflection,** or flip, moves a figure by flipping it over a line.
- A **rotation,** or turn, moves a figure by turning it around a vertex, or point of rotation.

ERROR ALERT

Don't confuse a translation with a reflection. A reflection can change the orientation of a figure.

Examples

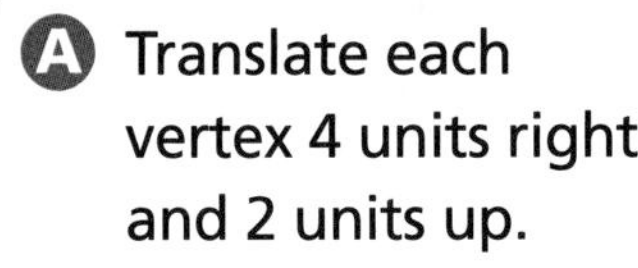

A Translate each vertex 4 units right and 2 units up.

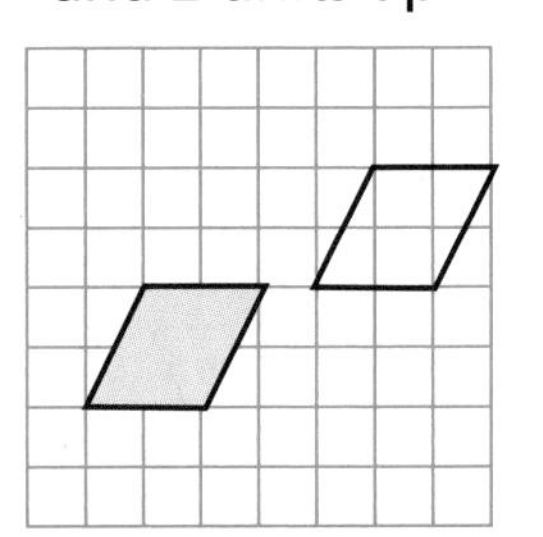

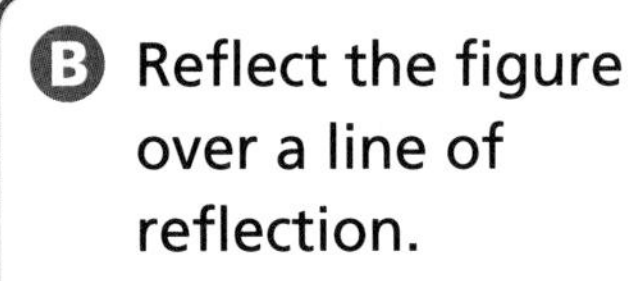

B Reflect the figure over a line of reflection.

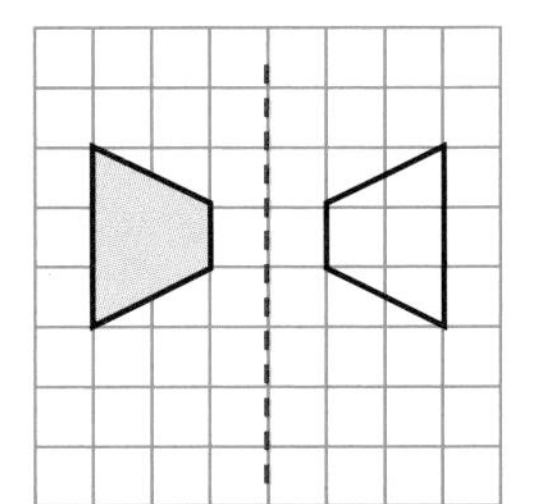

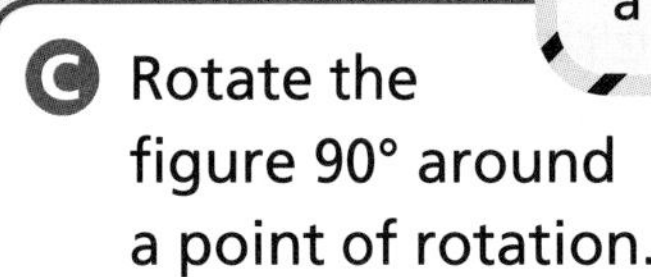

C Rotate the figure 90° around a point of rotation.

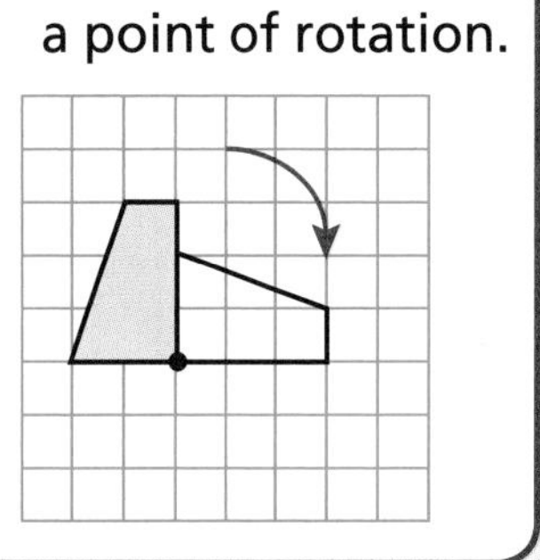

Try It

Copy each figure on grid paper. Then draw figures to show a translation, a rotation, and a reflection of each.

1. 

2. 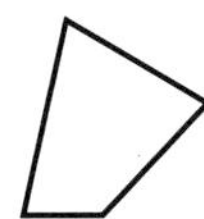

3. 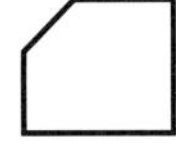

4. 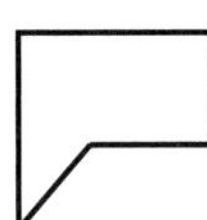 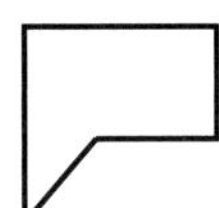

5. 

6. 

7. **Explain** why A is not correct. Then choose the correct answer.

COMMON ERROR

Which best describes how the figure shown below was transformed?

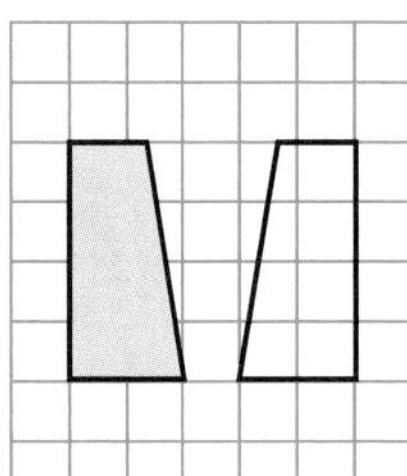

A Translation
B Reflection
C Rotation
D Not here

Review the Core Content for Assessment

Ordered Pairs

KY MA-05-3.3.1 Students will identify and *graph ordered pairs on a positive coordinate system* scaled by ones, twos, threes, fives, or tens; locate points on a grid; and apply graphing in the coordinate system to solve real-world problems. DOK 2

An **ordered pair** is a pair of numbers that is used to locate a point on a coordinate grid. Each ordered pair has an *x*-coordinate and a *y*-coordinate.

- The *x*-coordinate is written first and tells the horizontal distance of the point from point (0,0).
- The *y*-coordinate is written second and tells the vertical distance of the point from point (0,0).

ERROR ALERT

Don't confuse the *x*-coordinate and the *y*-coordinate in an ordered pair. The *x*-coordinate is always the first number of the pair.

Examples

A The point (4,3) is 4 units to the right of (0,0) and 3 units up.

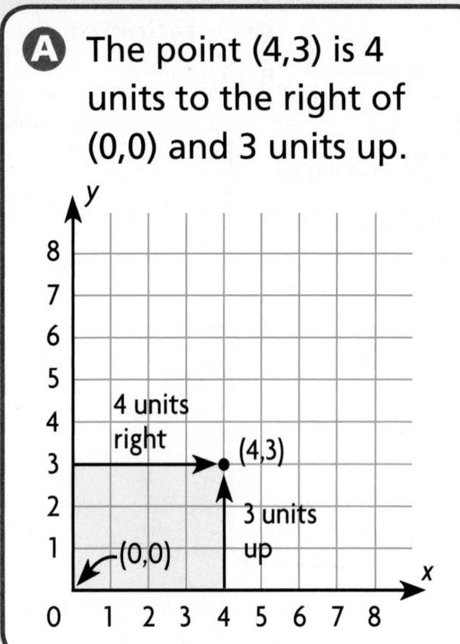

B The point (7,5) is 7 units to the right of (0,0) and 5 units up.

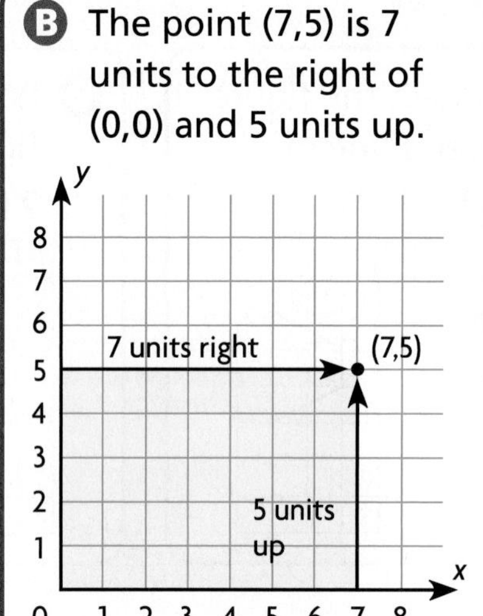

C The point (2,6) is 2 units to the right of (0,0) and 6 units up.

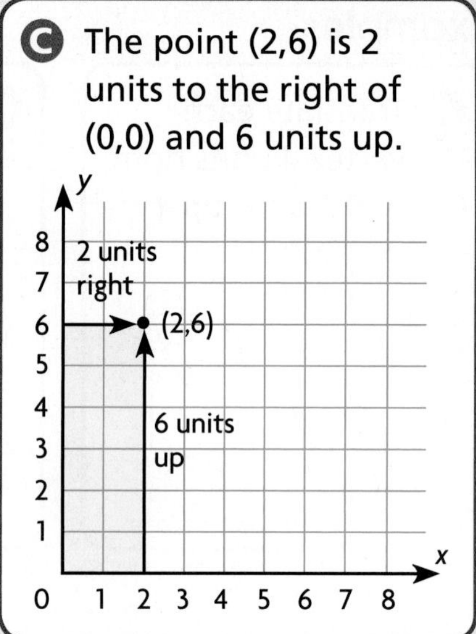

Try It

Identify each point on the coordinate grid. Write an ordered pair.

1. point *A*
2. point *B*
3. point *C*
4. point *D*
5. point *E*

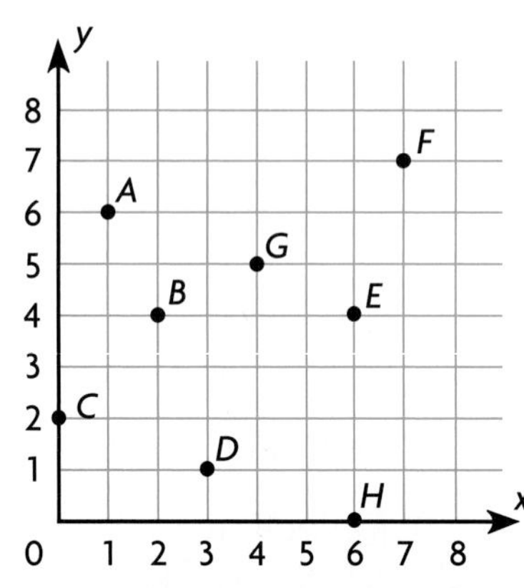

6. Read the problem below. **Explain** why *D* is not correct. Then choose the correct answer.

COMMON ERROR

Which two ordered pairs can be connected by a vertical line?

A (4,7) and (7,4) **C** (7,4) and (6,5)

B (4,7) and (4,1) **D** (7,4) and (3,4)

Review the Core Content for Assessment

Write Ordered Pairs

KY MA-05-3.3.1 Students will identify and graph ordered pairs on a positive coordinate system scaled by ones, twos, threes, fives, or tens; *locate points on a grid;* and apply graphing in the coordinate system to solve real-world problems. DOK 2

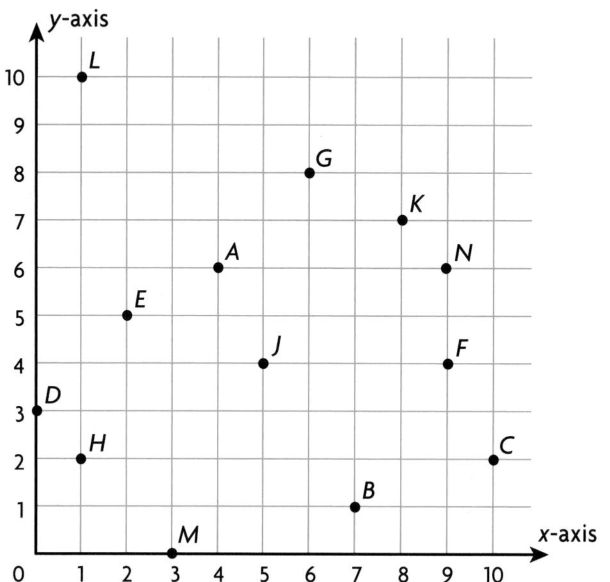

Each point on a coordinate grid can be located by using an ordered pair of numbers.

The first number in an ordered pair is the *x*-coordinate. It tells the distance to move in a horizontal direction from (0,0).

The second number in an ordered pair is the *y*-coordinate. It tells the distance to move vertically.

Point *A* is 4 spaces to the right of (0,0) so its *x*-coordinate is 4. It is 6 spaces above the *x*-axis, so its *y*-coordinate is 6. The ordered pair for point *A* is (4,6).

Examples

A What is the ordered pair for point *B*?

To get to point *B*, move 7 units right and 1 unit up. The ordered pair for point *B* is (7,1).

B Which point has coordinates (3,0)?

To get to (3,0), move 3 units right. Since the *y*-coordinate is 0, do not move up. Point *M* has coordinates (3,0).

ERROR ALERT

Move right first. Then move up.

Try It

Use the coordinate grid above. Write an ordered pair for each point.

1. *F*
2. *G*
3. *H*
4. *J*
5. *K*
6. *L*

Use the coordinate grid above. Identify the point with the given coordinates.

7. (0,3)
8. (9,6)
9. (10,2)

10. Read the problem below. **Explain** why *C* cannot be the correct answer choice. Then choose the correct answer.

What are the coordinates of point *E*?

A (0,5)

B (2,5)

C (5,2)

D (2,0)

Review the Core Content for Assessment

Pictographs

KY MA-05-4.1.1 Students will analyze and make inferences from data displays (drawings, tables/charts, tally tables, *pictographs*, bar graphs, circle graphs, line plots, Venn diagrams, line graphs). DOK 3

Pictographs display countable data with symbols or pictures. Pictographs use a key to tell what the symbols in the graph are to represent.

Examples

A Make a pictograph. *In August, a store sold 20 floor lamps, 50 table lamps, and 35 chandeliers.*

Draw the outline of the graph. Places for 3 groups should be shown.

Choose a title and key. *August Lighting Sales*. Each symbol will represent 10 pieces of equipment.

Draw the symbols and make a key.

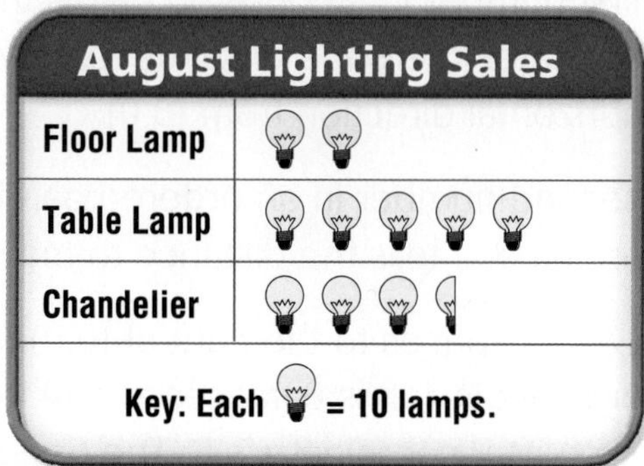

August Lighting Sales
Floor Lamp
Table Lamp
Chandelier
Key: Each = 10 lamps.

B Interpret a pictograph.

Beach Attendance

Month	
June	✹ ✹ ✹
July	✹ ✹ ✹ ✹
August	✹ ✹ ✹ ✹
September	✹ ✹

Key: Each ✹ = 300 people.

How many people does each symbol represent? 300

How many people went to the beach in June? $300 \times 3 = 900$

Which month had the fewest people at the beach? September

ERROR ALERT

The key of a pictograph tells how many units 1 symbol represents. Use the key to convert between the symbols and units.

Try It

Use the pictograph to answer 1–5.

Photography Class Attendance

Month	
September	📷 📷 📷 📷
October	📷 📷
November	📷 📷 📷 📷 📷
December	📷 📷

Key: Each 📷 = 4 people.

1. How many people attended in October?
2. How many attended in November?
3. Which month had the highest attendance?
4. Which months had the lowest attendance?
5. Read the problem below. **Explain** why C cannot be the correct answer choice. Then choose the correct answer. **COMMON ERROR**

How many more people attended photography class in November than in December?

A 12 **C** 3

B 6 **D** 2

Review the Core Content for Assessment

Bar Graphs

KY MA-05-4.1.1 Students will analyze and make inferences from data displays (drawings, tables/charts, tally tables, pictographs, *bar graphs*, circle graphs, line plots, Venn diagrams, line graphs). DOK 3

Bar graphs use bars to show data and make comparisons.

Scale: a series of numbers placed at fixed distances on a graph.

Interval: the distance between one number and the next on the scale of a graph.

Examples

Interpret a bar graph.

Which item sold the greatest amount? Look at the largest bar and read the label for that bar. Cookies sold about 30.

How many cupcakes were sold? From the top of the cupcake bar, move left. Find the number at the same height. 24

How many more cookies were sold than muffins? There were about 30 cookies sold and about 12 muffins. So, 30 –12 = 18.

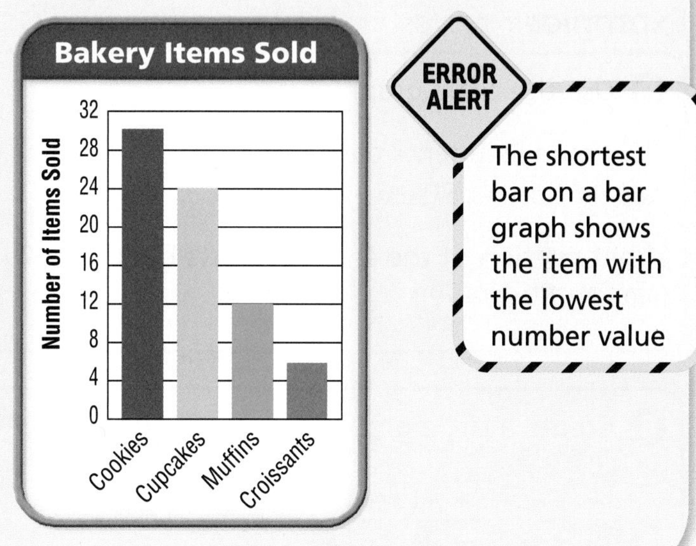

Try It

Use the bar graph to answer questions 1–5.

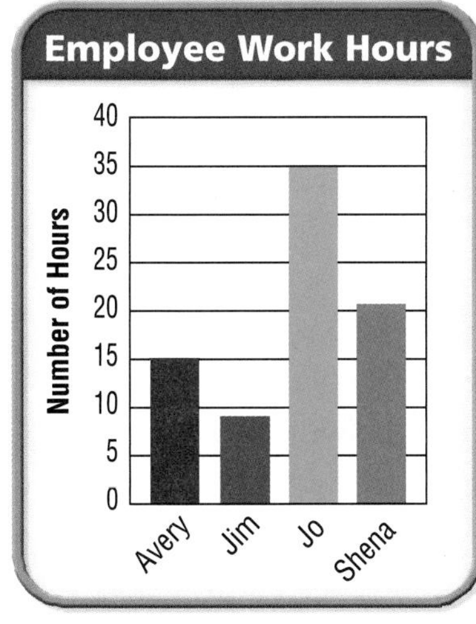

1. What are the scale and interval of the graph?
2. Approximately how many hours did Shena work?
3. How many more hours did Shena work than Avery?
4. Who worked more than 30 hours?
5. Read the problem below. **Explain** why B cannot be the correct answer choice. Then choose the correct answer.

   Which employee worked the fewest hours?

   A Jim
   B Jo
   C Avery
   D Shena

Review the Core Content for Assessment

Circle graphs

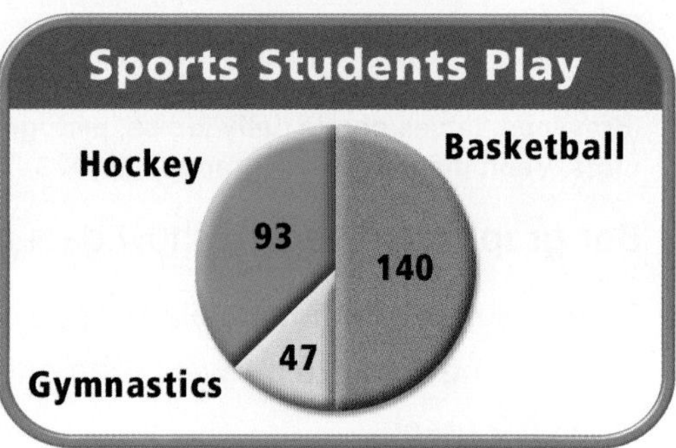

KY MA-05-4.1.1 Students will analyze and make inferences from data displays (drawings, tables/charts, tally tables, pictographs, bar graphs, *circle graphs*, line plots, Venn diagrams, line graphs). DOK 3

Circle graphs shows data as a whole made up of different parts.

This circle graph shows the number of students that play different types of sports

Examples

A Use the circle graph above.

How many students play sports?

Add the number of students in each sport 93 + 47 + 140 = 280

What portion of the students plays basketball?

140 out of 280 = $\frac{140}{280} = \frac{1}{2}$, or 50%

ERROR ALERT

Each section of a circle graph represents a part of the whole data set.

B Create a circle graph.

8 people were asked what they eat for breakfast. Create 8 sections in a circle graph.

Breakfast Foods Eaten	
Type of Food	Number of People
Eggs	1
Toast	5
Cereal	2

Shade each section to represent a food type. Then add labels.

Try It

Use the circle graph above to answer questions 1–4.

1. How many total students ate breakfast?
2. How many students ate cereal?
3. How many more students ate toast than eggs?
4. Read the problem below. **Explain** why A cannot be the correct answer choice. Then choose the correct answer.

COMMON ERROR

Which portion of the students chose to eat toast?

A $\frac{5}{5}$ B $\frac{3}{5}$

C $\frac{5}{8}$ D $\frac{3}{8}$

Review the Core Content for Assessment

Line Graphs

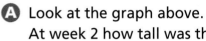

KY MA-05-4.1.1 Students will analyze and make inferences from data displays (drawings, tables/charts, tally tables, pictographs, bar graphs, circle graphs, line plots, Venn diagrams, *line graphs*). DOK 3

A line graph is used to show how data change over time. This line graph shows the height of a plant at the end of each week.

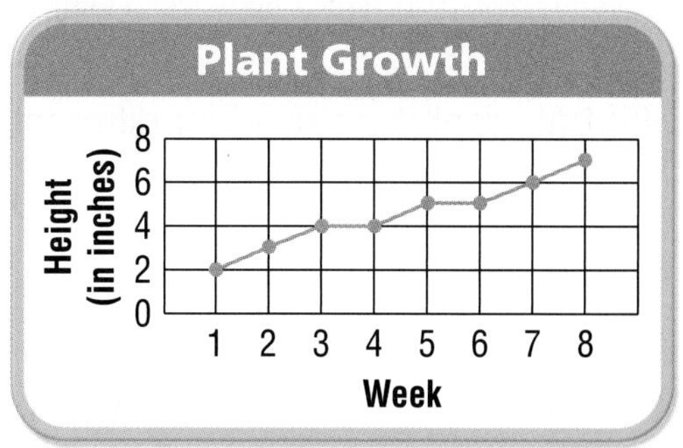

Examples

A Look at the graph above. At week 2 how tall was the plant?

Move in a vertical direction above week 2. The value is 3.

So, at week 2, the plant was 3 inches tall.

B Look at the graph above. Between which two weeks, did the plant show no growth?

The line is flat between weeks 3 and 4 and between weeks 5 and 6.

So, there was no growth between weeks 3 and 4 and between weeks 5 and 6.

ERROR ALERT

Be sure to understand and read the scale of a graph correctly.

Try It

Solve. Use the graph above.

1. How tall was the plant at the end of week 6?
2. What does the ordered pair (1,2) represent on the graph?
3. How much did the plant grow between weeks 1 and 7?
4. How much did the plant grow between the ends of weeks 2 and 5?
5. Read the problem below. **Explain** why D cannot be the correct answer choice. Then choose the correct answer.

Use the line graph above. At the end of Week 10, the plant had reached its final height of 12 inches. At the end of which week had the plant reached half its height?

A Week 5

B Week 6

C Week 7

D Week 8

 Review the Core Content for Assessment

Choose the Best Graphs

KY MA-05-4.1.3 Students will construct data displays (pictographs, bar graphs, line plots, line graphs, Venn diagrams, tables). DOK 2

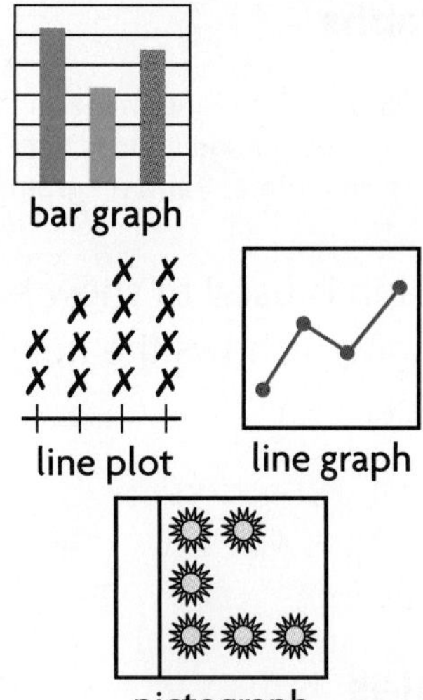

Different graphs are used for different purposes.

- **Line plots** keep count of data and show frequency.
- **Line graphs** show how data values change over time.
- **Pictographs** are good for visualizing data by category.
- **Bar graphs** work best for comparing categories of data.

Port Arthur, Texas	Sep	Oct	Nov	Dec	Jan
Rainfall (in inches)	6.10	4.67	4.75	5.25	5.69

What is the best graph for showing rainfall totals for Port Arthur, Texas?

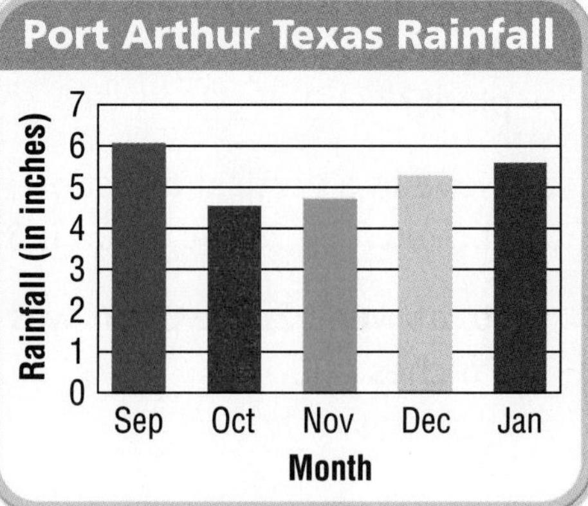

Step 1

Look at the data set. Is it:

- comparing categories?
- keeping track of data that changes in small intervals of time?
- keeping a tally count of data?
- hard to visualize?
- a part that is being compared to a whole?

Step 2

Draw a conclusion.

- The data compares rainfall in each month.

Choose a graph type.

- A **bar graph** fits the data best. Draw the graph.

ERROR ALERT

Don't use a circle graph to try to show how data changes over time.

Try It

Choose the best type of graph for the data.

1. sales totals for 5 different stores
2. number of votes for types of music
3. tally for the number of 3 species of frogs observed in a pond
4. record of plant growth over 3 months
5. the stock price of XYZ Company over the last year
6. Read the problem below. **Explain** why B does not name an appropriate type of graph. Then choose the correct answer.

   What is an appropriate type of graph to show the price of gasoline over a two-year period?

   A a bar graph **C** a line plot

   B a circle graph **D** a line graph

Review the Core Content for Assessment

Mean and Median

KY MA-05-4.2.1 Students will determine and apply the *mean, median,* mode and range of a set of data. DOK 2

Example

Find the mean and median. 10, 21, 17, 21, 23, 16, 11

Step 1

Mean

To find the mean, add the data values. Then divide the sum by the number of addends.

10 + 21 + 17 + 21 + 23 + 16 + 11 = 116
116 ÷ 7 = 17

So, the mean is 17.

Step 2

Median

To find the median, order the data from least to greatest.

10, 11, 16, 17, 21, 21, 23

Find the middle number.

Note: If there is an even number of values, add the two middle numbers, and divide by 2.

So, the median is 17.

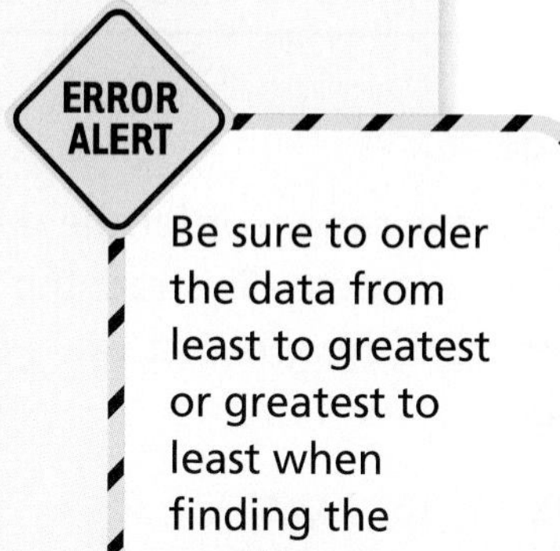

Be sure to order the data from least to greatest or greatest to least when finding the median.

Try It

Find the mean and median.

1. 5, 9, 11, 12, 8
2. 17, 25, 13, 17
3. \$38, \$20, \$82, \$78, \$38, \$44
4. 33, 26, 33, 24, 15, 29, 15
5. 304, 693, 279, 611
6. 147, 115, 97, 141, 115
7. 7.4, 6.3, 6.2, 6.2, 7.1
8. \$0.72, \$0.32, \$0.28, \$0.65, \$0.58

9. Read the problem below. **Explain** why B cannot be the correct answer choice. Then choose the correct answer.

Which is the median of the data?
18, 23, 14, 23, 11

A 11

B 14

C 18

D 23

Review the Core Content for Assessment

Range and Mode

KY MA-05-4.2.1 Students will determine and apply the mean, median, *mode* and *range* of a set of data. DOK 2

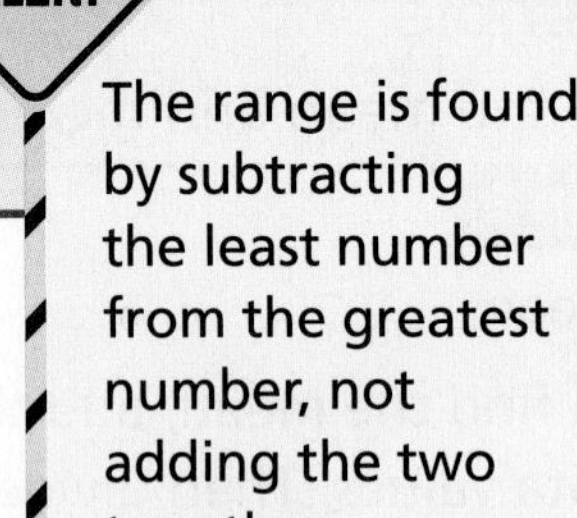

The range is found by subtracting the least number from the greatest number, not adding the two together.

Example

Find the range and mode. 10, 21, 17 21, 23, 16, 11

Step 1

Range

To find the range, order the data from least to greatest. Subtract the least value from the greatest value to get the range.

10, 11, 16, 17, 21, 21, 23

Range: 23 − 10 = 13

So, the range is 13.

Step 2

Mode

To find the mode, order the data from least to greatest. Find the number that occurs most often.

10, 11, 16, 17, 21, 21, 23 ← 21 occurs twice.

So, the mode is 21.

Try It

Find the mode and range.

1. 5, 9, 11, 12, 8
2. 17, 25, 13, 17
3. \$38, \$20, \$82, \$78, \$38, \$44
4. 33, 26, 33, 24, 15, 29, 15
5. 304, 693, 279, 611
6. 147, 115, 97, 141, 115
7. 7.4, 6.3, 6.2, 6.2, 7.1
8. \$0.72, \$0.32, \$0.28, \$0.65, \$0.58

COMMON ERROR

9. Read the problem below. **Explain** why D cannot be the correct answer choice. Then choose the correct answer.

   Which is the range of the data?
   18, 23, 14, 23, 11

   A 11

   B 12

   C 18

   D 34

 Review the Core Content for Assessment

Combinations and Arrangements

KY MA-05-4.4.1 Students will determine all possible outcomes of an activity/event with up to 12 possible outcomes. DOK 2

To decide whether a selection is a combination or an arrangement, first decide if the order is important. If order is not important, the selection should be a combination. If order is important, then the selection should be an arrangement.

ERROR ALERT

Do not list any combination that reverses the pairs already listed.

Examples

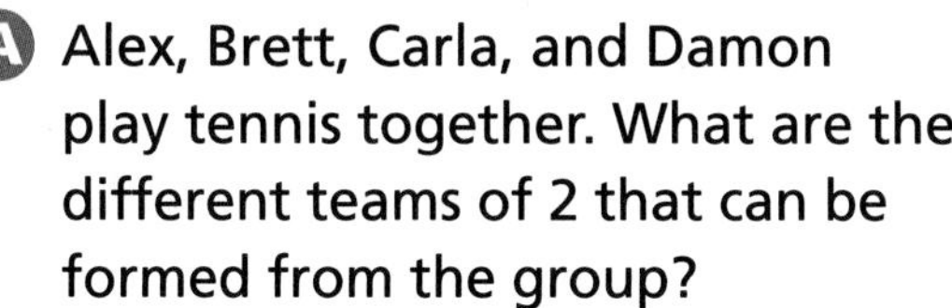

A Alex, Brett, Carla, and Damon play tennis together. What are the different teams of 2 that can be formed from the group?

Order does not matter. Find the number of combinations. Remember: The team of Alex and Brett is the same as the team of Brett and Alex.

Make a list of all the combinations.

A and B	B and C
A and C	B and D
A and D	C and D

So, there are 6 different combinations.

B Greg, Haley, and Ivy are seated in a row with 3 seats. What are the different ways they can be seated?

Make a list of all the arrangements.

G, H, I	H, G, I	I, G, H
G, I, H	H, I, G	I, H, G

Order does matter. Find the number of arrangements.

Or, make a tree diagram.

Seat 1	Seat 2	Seat 3
G	H	I
	I	H
H	G	I
	I	G
I	G	H
	H	G

So, there are 6 different arrangements.

Try It

Make a list or draw a tree diagram to find the total number of choices.

1. ways to arrange the letters X, Y, Z
2. ways to have a hamburger with 2 of the following: ketchup, mayonnaise, relish, mustard
3. ways to have a pizza with 2 of the following: mushrooms, sausage, olives, ham, pepperoni
4. ways to arrange a red book, a green book, a blue book, and a yellow book on a shelf
5. Read the problem below. **Explain** why D cannot be the correct answer choice. Then choose the correct answer.

COMMON ERROR

At the bus stop there are 6 people waiting to get on the bus. There are only 2 seats left on the bus. How many different pairs of the 6 people can sit in the seats?

A 6 different pairs **C** 15 different pairs

B 12 different pairs **D** 30 different pairs

Review the Core Content for Assessment

Probabilities as Fractions

KY MA-05-4.4.2 Students will determine the likelihood of an event and the probability of an event (expressed as a fraction). DOK 2

The probability of an event is the number of favorable outcomes divided by the total number of possible outcomes. Any probability can be expressed as a fraction.

$$\text{Probability of an event} = \frac{\text{number of favorable outcomes}}{\text{total number of possible outcomes}}$$

To find a probability, write the number of favorable outcomes as the numerator. Write the total number of possible outcomes as the denominator.

ERROR ALERT

Remember to include *all* favorable outcomes, not just some of them.

Example

In his closet, Doug has 3 black shirts, 5 white shirts, 2 grey shirts, and 2 blue shirts. If he takes one shirt without looking, what is the probability that Doug will select a black or a white shirt?

Step 1

Find the number of favorable outcomes and total outcomes.

favorable outcomes = black + white = 3 + 5 = 8

total possible outcomes = black + white + grey + blue = 3 + 5 + 2 + 2 = 12

Step 2

Express the probability as a fraction. Simplify, if necessary.

$$\text{Probability} = \frac{\text{favorable outcomes}}{\text{total possible outcomes}}$$

$$\text{Probability} = \frac{8}{12} = \frac{2}{3}$$

The probability of choosing a black or white shirt is $\frac{2}{3}$.

Try It

Express each probability as a fraction.

1. Marnie is trying to guess Nick's birthday. What is the probability that Nick was born during the spring?
2. What is the probability that Nick's birthday comes before July?
3. What is the probability that Nick was *not* born on a Friday, Saturday, or Sunday?
4. Read the problem below. **Explain** why A is not correct. Then choose the correct answer.

A bag contains 6 red, 4 blue, 3 yellow, 5 green and 2 white marbles. What is the probability of drawing a red, blue, or white marble?

A $\frac{1}{2}$ **C** $\frac{2}{3}$

B $\frac{3}{5}$ **D** $\frac{7}{10}$

Review the Core Content for Assessment

Whole Number Patterns

KY MA-05-5.1.1 Students will extend patterns, find the missing term(s) in a pattern or describe rules for patterns (numbers, pictures, tables, words) from real-world and mathematical problems. DOK 3

Number patterns can be described by rules. The rule can be used to extend or complete the pattern, or create a new pattern.

ERROR ALERT

A rule for a numeric pattern must fit *all* of the numbers in the pattern.

Examples

A Identify a rule for the pattern:

48, 46, 44, 42, 40...

What will change 48 to 46?

Try **subtract 2** because 48 – 46 = 2.

Test the rule on the other numbers in the sequence:

48, 46, 44, 42, 40

–2 –2 –2 –2

The rule is **subtract 2**.

B Find a rule and use it to fill in the missing number.

2, 8, 14, ■, ■, 32, 38...

What will change 2 to 8? Try **multiply by 4**.

Test the rule: 8 × 4 = 32, not 14. It does not work.

Try another rule: **add 6**. Test the rule: 8 + 6 = 14; 32 + 6 = 38. The rule works. The rule is "add 6."

Find the unknown numbers:

14 + 6 = 20, 20 + 6 = 26

The series of numbers is 2, 8, 14, 20, 26, 32, 38...

Try It

Describe the rule for the number patterns. Use the rule to create a new pattern.

1. 5000, 1000, 200, 40, 8
2. 111, 110, 55, 54, 27

Find a rule and fill in the missing numbers or extend the pattern by 2 numbers.

3. 5, 15, , 135, 405
4. 7, 14, 28, , 112,
5. 2, 4, 5, 10, 11, 22,...
6. 30, 26, 22, 18, 14,...

7. Read the problem below. **Explain** why C cannot be the correct answer choice. Then choose the correct answer. **COMMON ERROR**

Which pattern does the rule **add 7** belong to?

A 1, 8, 15, 22, 29..

B 2, 14, 98, 686, 4802...

C 2, 9, 15, 22, 28...

D 28, 21, 14, 7, 0

Review the Core Content for Assessment

Write and Solve Equations

KY MA-05-5.2.1 Students will model verbal descriptions of real-world and mathematical problems using a variable or a missing value in an expression. DOK 2

You can use an equation to represent a problem situation.

Example 1

Write an equation. Tell what the variable represents.

Keiko has 4 times as many red marbles as yellow marbles. She has 24 red marbles. Choose a variable. Let y = the number of yellow marbles Keiko has.

$$4 \times y = 24, \text{ or } 4y = 24$$

You can use mental math to solve an equation.

Example 2

Solve. $n + 14 = 21$

$n + 14 = 21$
$n = 7$

Think: What number plus 14 equals 21?

Check: $7 + 14 = 21$
$21 = 21$ ✔

To check, replace the variable in the original equation.

When you solve an equation, be sure the numbers are in the correct position.

Try It

Write an equation for each. Tell what the variable represents.

1. Lauren had 4 markers. After Randy gave her markers, she had 7 total.
2. Ty has 48 photos. He put an equal number of photos on each of 8 pages in an album.

Solve each equation. Check your solution.

3. $p - 7 = 4$
4. $\$14 + w = \$23$
5. $3 \times t = 21$
6. $d \div 6 = 9$

7. Read the problem below. **Explain** why C cannot be the correct answer choice. Then choose the correct answer.

Solve. $x - 18 = 6$

A 3

B 12

C 16

D 24

Review the Core Content for Assessment

Algebraic Expressions

KY MA-05-5.3.1 Students will model real-world and mathematical problems with simple number sentences (equations and inequalities) with a variable or missing value (e.g., $4 = 2 \times N$, ___ $+ 5 > 14$) and apply simple number sentences to solve mathematical and real-world problems. DOK 2

Find the value of an expression by replacing the variable with a number. Then follow the **order of operations** to find the value of the expression.

Evaluate $(14 - p) \times 4 \div 6$ if $p = 5$.

$(14 - p) \times 4 \div 6$	Replace p with 5.
$(14 - 5) \times 4 \div 6$	Operate inside the parentheses. Subtract.
$9 \times 4 \div 6$	Multiply.
$36 \div 6$	Divide.
6	

So, $(14 - p) \times 4 \div 6 = 6$ if $p = 5$.

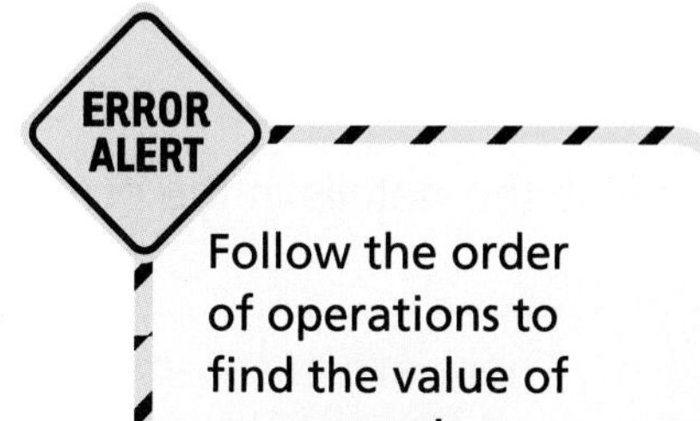
ERROR ALERT
Follow the order of operations to find the value of an expression.

Examples

A If $n = 4$, what is the value of $3 \times n - 7$?

$3 \times n - 7$
$3 \times 4 - 7$
$12 - 7$
5

So, if $n = 4$, $3 \times n - 7 = 5$.

B Evaluate $7 \times (54 \div b)$ if $b = 6$.

$7 \times (54 \div b)$
$7 \times (54 \div 6)$
7×9
63

So, $7 \times (54 \div b) = 63$ if $b = 6$.

Try It

Evaluate the algebraic expression for the given value of the variable.

1. $5n - 2$ if $n = 3.2$
2. $(14 + d) \div 7$ if $d = 35$
3. $\frac{x}{4} + 7 \times 3$ if $x = 20$
4. $8b + 2$ if $b = \frac{1}{8}$
5. Read the problem below. **Explain** why B cannot be the correct answer choice. Then choose the correct answer.

COMMON ERROR

If $a = 5$, what is the value of $(9 + a) \times 2$?

A 8 **C** 28
B 19 **D** 190

KENTUCKY KCCT Test-Taking Strategies

Tips for Taking Math Tests

Being a good test-taker is like being a good problem-solver. When you answer test questions, you are solving problems. Remember to **READ TO UNDERSTAND**, **PLAN**, **SOLVE**, and **CHECK**.

Read to Understand

Read the problem.

- Look for math terms and recall their meanings.
- Reread the problem and think about the question.
- Use the details in the problem and the question.

1. There are 460 campers and counselors at Summit Camp. Each table in the dining hall can seat 12 people. How many tables are needed?

   A 40   C 38

   B 39   D 4

Test Tip **Understand the problem.**

The critical information is that there are 460 campers and counselors. List all the given relationships and express them as equations. Use this information to begin solving the problem. Be sure to answer the question asked. The answer is **B**.

- Each word is important. Missing a word or reading it incorrectly could cause you to get the wrong answer.
- Is there information given that you do not need?
- Pay attention to words that are in all CAPITAL letters or *italics* and to words like *round*, *best*, *about* and *least to greatest*.

2. In 1995, Mariko ran the 100-yard dash in 12.40 seconds. In 1996, she ran it in 12.343 seconds. In 1997, she ran it in 12.6 seconds. In 1998, she ran it in 12.502 seconds. In what year was Mariko's fastest time?

   A 1995   C 1997

   B 1996   D 1998

Test Tip **Look for important words.**

The word *fastest* is important. The fastest runner takes the *least* amount of time. So, the least number of seconds is her fastest time. The answer is **B**.

Plan

Think about how you can solve the problem.

- Can you solve the problem with the information given?
- Pictures, charts, tables, and graphs may have the information you need.

3. Lisa made a line graph showing how much her plant grew each week.

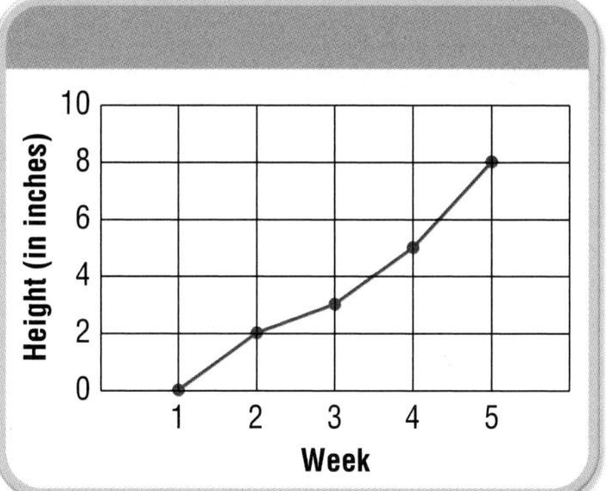

Between which two weeks did the plant grow the most?

A Weeks 1 and 2 C Weeks 3 and 4

B Weeks 2 and 3 D Weeks 4 and 5

Test Tip **Get the information you need.**

You need to find the two weeks between which the height of the plant increased the most. Find the difference from one week to the next and identify the two consecutive weeks with the greatest difference in height. The answer is **D**.

- You may need to write and solve an equation.
- Some problems have two steps or more.
- In some problems you need to look at relationships instead of computing an answer.
- If the path to the solution isn't clear, choose a problem solving strategy and use it to solve the problem.

4. A gravel path surrounds a rectangular grass field. The field is 60 feet long and 40 feet wide. The path is 3 feet wide. What is the area covered by the path?

A 300 ft^2 C 600 ft^2

B 309 ft^2 D 636 ft^2

Test Tip **Decide on a plan.**

Using the strategy *draw a diagram* will help you find the dimensions of the larger rectangle so you can find the area. Match the description in the problem and label the diagram. First find the area of the field and the path. Then subtract the area of the field. The answer is **D**.

Solve

Follow your plan, working logically and carefully.

- Estimate your answer. Are any answer choices unreasonable?
- Use reasoning to find the most likely choices.
- Make sure you solved all steps needed to answer the problem.
- If your answer does not match any of the answer choices, check the numbers you used. Then check your computation.

5. What is the prime factorization of 30?

A 3×10 C $2 \times 3 \times 5$

B 5×6 D $2^2 \times 5$

Eliminate choices.

Think about the meaning of *prime factorization*. You can eliminate the choices in which all the factors are not prime numbers. The answer is **C**.

- If your answer still does not match any of the choices, look for another form of the number, such as a decimal instead of a fraction.
- If answer choices are given as pictures, look at each one by itself while you cover the other three.
- If answer choices are statements, relate each one to the problem.
- Change your plan if it isn't working. Try a different strategy.

6. Andrew and Judy collect stamps. Andrew has half as many stamps as Judy. Let s represent the number of stamps that Andrew has. Which expression can be used to find the number of stamps that Judy has?

A $\frac{s}{2}$ C $s + 2$

B $2s$ D $s - 2$

Test Tip **Choose the answer.**

You need to determine how the number of stamps Andrew has is related to the number of stamps Judy has. The problem states, "Andrew has half as many stamps as Judy." So, Judy has two times the number of stamps Andrew has. Look at the answer choices and choose the answer that describes Judy's stamps in relation to Andrew's. The answer is **B**.

Check

Take time to catch your mistakes.

- Be sure you answered the question asked.
- Check that your answer fits the information in the problem.
- Check for important words you might have missed.
- Be sure you used all the information you needed.
- Check your computation by using a different method.
- Draw a picture when you are unsure of your answer.

7. At the market, Ms. Ruiz bought $\frac{1}{3}$ pound of Swiss cheese, $\frac{1}{4}$ pound of cheddar cheese, and $\frac{1}{2}$ pound of goat cheese. How much cheese did Ms. Ruiz buy?

A $\frac{1}{2}$ pound

B $1\frac{1}{12}$ pounds

C $1\frac{7}{12}$ pounds

D $3\frac{1}{2}$ pounds

Test Tip **Check your work.**

If your answer does not match any of the choices, check your computation. The answer is **B**.

Tips for Short-Answer and Extended-Response Items

- Plan to spend from 3 to 5 minutes on each Short-Answer item and from 5 to 15 minutes on each Extended-Response item.
- Read the problem carefully and think about what you are asked to do. Plan how to organize your response.
- Short-Answer items will ask you to find a solution to a problem. Extended-Response items will ask you to use problem solving and reasoning skills to apply something you have learned.
- Think about how you solved the problem. You may be asked to use words, numbers, or pictures to explain how you found your answer.
- Leave time to look back at the problem, check your answer, and correct any mistakes.

Getting Ready for the KCCT

Number Properties and Operations

1. Ryan looked at the distances of four hiking trails. Kettle Creek Loop Trail is 39,072 feet long, Jackson Trail is 29,568 feet long, Black Forest Trail is 44,880 feet long and Mid State Trail is 44,352 feet long. Which shows the distances ordered from **least** to **greatest**? KY MA-05-1.1.3

   A. 39,072; 29,568; 44,880; 44,352

   B. 44,880; 44,352; 39,072; 29,568

   C. 29,568; 39,072; 44,352; 44,880

   D. 39,072; 29,568; 44,352; 44,880

2. The table below lists the elevations of some cities in Kentucky.

City	Elevation (in feet)
Jenkins	1,526
Cumberland	1,440
Whitley City	1,357
Pine Knot	1,420

   Which is the difference between the **greatest** and the **least** elevations? KY MA-05-1.3.1

   A. 377 feet

   B. 269 feet

   C. 199 feet

   D. 169 feet

3. What are **all** the prime numbers between 50 and 60? KY MA-05-1.5.1

   A. 53 and 59

   B. 51, 53 and 57

   C. 53 and 57

   D. 50, 51 and 59

4. Melissa wrote down the amount of time she spent at voice lessons. KY MA-05-1.3.1

Melissa's Voice Lessons (in hours)			
Day	Monday	Tuesday	Friday
Time Spent	$\frac{3}{16}$	$\frac{8}{16}$	$\frac{4}{16}$

   Which is the total amount of time that Melissa spent at voice lessons?

   A. $\frac{1}{16}$ hour

   B. $\frac{10}{16}$ hour

   C. $\frac{15}{16}$ hour

   D. 1 hour

5. Which shows the decimals ordered from least to greatest? KY MA-05-1.1.3

   5.82, 0.852, 2.508, 5.008

   A. 5.82, 5.008, 0.852, 2.508

   B. 2.508, 0.852, 5.008, 5.82

   C. 0.852, 2.508, 5.008, 5.82

   D. 0.852, 2.508, 5.82, 5.008

6. Ms. Barr is collecting money for the field trip. The field trip costs $47.50 per student. There are 58 students. Which is the **best** estimate of the total amount of money Ms. Barr needs to collect? KY MA-05-1.2.1

   A. about $300

   B. about $3,000

   C. about $30,000

   D. about $300,000

Number Properties and Operations

7. Kentucky, Georgia and Texas have the largest number of counties in the United States. Kentucky has 123 counties, Georgia has 159 counties and Texas has 254 counties. Which state has the third most counties? KY MA-05-1.1.3

   A. Florida
   B. Georgia
   C. Kentucky
   D. Texas

8. Each shelf of a DVD stand can hold nine DVDs. Alexis has 100 DVDs. How many shelves does the DVD stand need to fit all of Alexis' DVDs? KY MA-05-1.3.1

   A. 9 shelves
   B. 10 shelves
   C. 11 shelves
   D. 12 shelves

9. Julia wants to write all the prime numbers between 60 and 70. Which numbers should Julia write? KY MA-05-1.5.1

   A. 63, 69
   B. 61, 67
   C. 61, 63, 67, 69
   D. 60, 62, 64, 66, 68

10. Leslie listed the factors of 32. Which is Leslie's list? KY MA-05-1.5.1

   A. 1, 2, 4, 8, 16, 32
   B. 1, 2, 4, 8, 16
   C. 1, 2, 4, 6, 8, 16, 32
   D. 32, 64, 96, 128

11. Giovanna wants to decorate the classroom bulletin board with a $\frac{3}{4}$ in. wide border. Which fraction is larger than the width of the border Giovanna wants to use? KY MA-05-1.1.3

   A. $\frac{3}{5}$ in.
   B. $\frac{11}{16}$ in.
   C. $\frac{7}{9}$ in.
   D. $\frac{6}{10}$ in.

12. Adriana bought 18 packs of balloons for the school dance. There are 25 balloons in each pack. How many balloons did Adriana buy? KY MA-05-1.3.1

   A. 350
   B. 400
   C. 450
   D. 500

13. Anthony has yellow, brown, and green blocks. Which represents the fraction of blocks that are yellow or green? KY MA-05-1.1.1

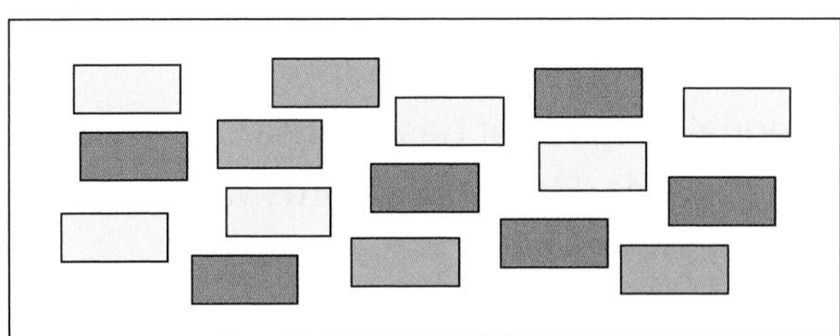

   A. $\frac{1}{2}$
   B. $\frac{4}{9}$
   C. $\frac{5}{8}$
   D. $\frac{3}{4}$

Getting Ready for the KCCT

Number Properties and Operations

14. Kentucky has 8 electoral votes and 6 seats in The House of Representatives. What is the least common multiple of 6 and 8? KY MA-05-1.5.1

A. 12

B. 24

C. 36

D. 48

15. Joseph read that the wingspan of a Tiger Swallowtail Butterfly can stretch to 16.25 cm, and that the wingspan of a Queen Alexandria Birdwing Butterfly can stretch to 32 cm. Which is the difference between the Tiger Swallowtail Butterfly's wingspan and the Queen Alexandria Birdwing Butterfly's wingspan? KY MA-05-1.3.1

A. 14.75 cm

B. 14.25 cm

C. 15.75 cm

D. 48.25 cm

16. Robert wants to give 5 friends an equal number of baseball cards. He has 225 cards. How many cards will each friend receive? KY MA-05-1.3.1

A. 35 cards

B. 45 cards

C. 55 cards

D. 230 cards

17. Which shows all the factors of 63? KY MA-05-1.5.1

A. 1, 4, 7, 9, 63

B. 1, 4, 3, 9, 21, 63

C. 1, 7, 9, 63

D. 1, 3, 7, 9, 21, 63

18. Louie collects models.

What fraction of the models are cars? KY MA-05-1.1.1

A. $\frac{4}{5}$

B. $\frac{2}{3}$

C. $\frac{1}{2}$

D. $\frac{1}{4}$

Number Properties and Operations

19. Which shows the decimals ordered from **least** to **greatest**? KY MA-05-1.1.3

0.80, 0.76, 0.89

A. 0.89, 0.76, 0.80

B. 0.76, 0.80, 0.89

C. 0.80, 0.89, 0.76

D. 0.76, 0.89, 0.80

20. The highest point in Kentucky is Black Mountain, which is 4,139 ft. The lowest point in Kentucky is the Mississippi River, which is 257 ft. What is the difference of these two heights? KY MA-05-1.3.1

A. 4,396 ft

B. 3,982 ft

C. 3,882 ft

D. 3,802 ft

21. Which fraction names the unshaded part? KY MA-05-1.1.1

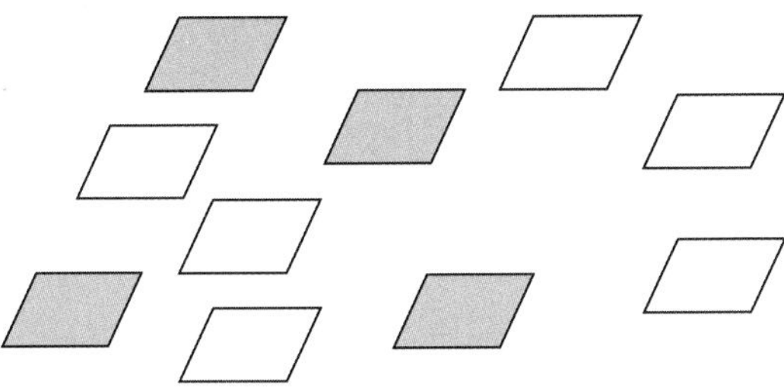

A. $\frac{2}{5}$

B. $\frac{1}{2}$

C. $\frac{5}{9}$

D. $\frac{3}{5}$

22. The estimated population of three Kentucky towns are shown below.

2006 Estimated Population	
Florence	26,900
Jeffersontown	25,900
Paducah	25,700

About how many people live in the three towns combined? KY MA-05-1.2.1

A. about 99,000 people

B. about 79,000 people

C. about 70,000 people

D. about 69,000 people

23. Which are all the factors of 54? KY MA-05-1.5.1

A. 1, 2, 3, 4, 6, 9, 27, 18, 54

B. 1, 3, 6, 9, 18, 54

C. 1, 2, 3, 6, 9, 18, 27, 54

D. 1, 2, 6, 9, 27, 54

KENTUCKY Getting Ready for the KCCT

Measurement

1. Rae sketched the layout of her house. What is the perimeter of Rae's house?
KY-MA-05-2.1.1

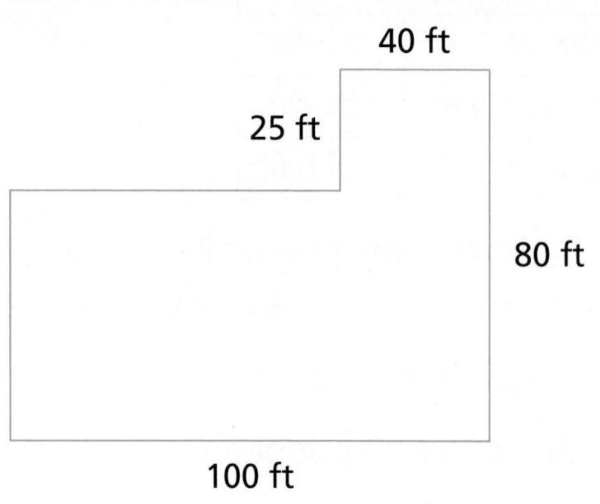

A. 245 ft
B. 305 ft
C. 360 ft
D. 440 ft

2. Anne wants to build a garden around her oak tree. She placed her outline on a grid.

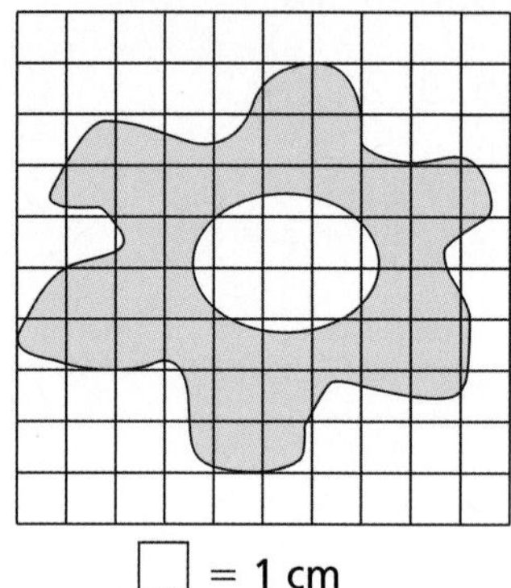

What is the **best** estimate of the area of the garden around the oak tree?
KY-MA-05-2.1.6

A. about 10 cm^2
B. about 20 cm^2
C. about 40 cm^2
D. about 50 cm^2

3. Isadora can't decide which laundry detergent to buy.

Detergent	Weight
Lavender	95 oz
Jasmine	33 oz
Vanilla	15 oz
Spring	50 oz

If Isadora decides to buy the jasmine and lavender laundry detergent, how many pounds of detergent will she have?
KY-MA-05-2.2.3

A. 5 lbs
B. 8 lbs
C. 11 lbs
D. 15 lbs

4. Crystal built a square stable for her horse. What is the area of the stable?
KY-MA-05-2.1.1

A. 148 ft^2
B. 592 ft^2
C. 1,184 ft^2
D. 1,369 ft^2

5. Patrick arrived at band practice at 1:20 P.M. His mom picked him up after practice at 3:30 P.M. How long was band practice?
KY-MA-05-2.2.1

A. 2 hr 10 min
B. 2 hr 50 min
C. 4 hr 40 min
D. 4 hr 50 min

Geometry

1. Which describes the figures below?

KY-MA-05-3.1.5

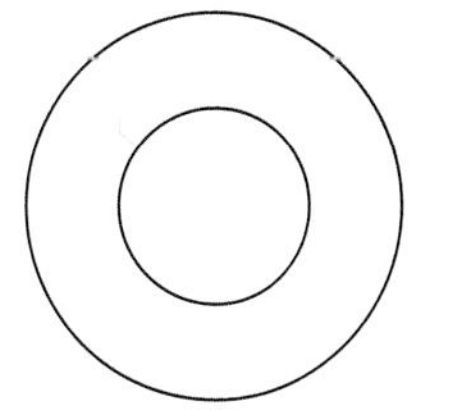

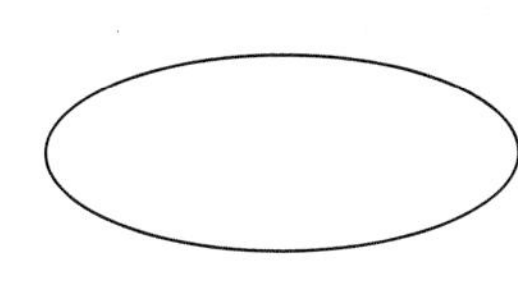

A. congruent

B. similar

C. both congruent and similar

D. neither congruent or similar

2. What type of transformation is shown?

KY-MA-05-3.2.2

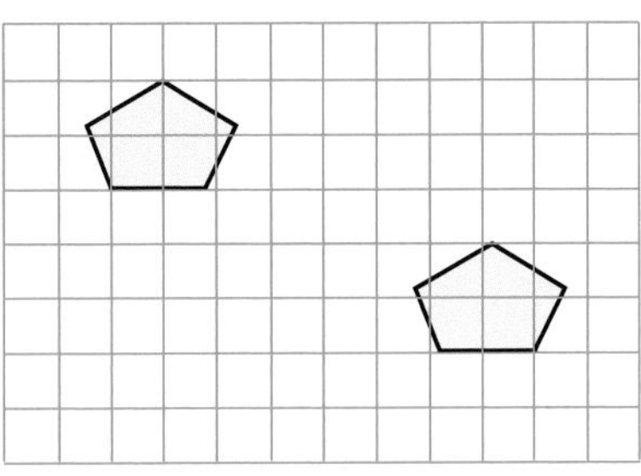

A. translation

B. tessellation

C. reflection

D. rotation

3. What are the coordinates of Point *B*?

KY-MA-05-3.3.1

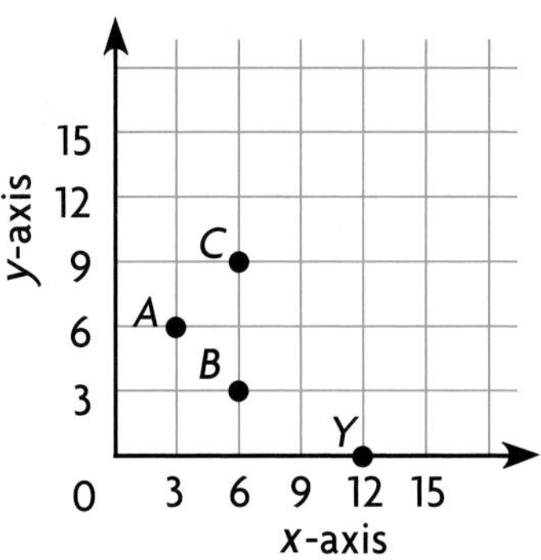

A. (0,12)

B. (6,9)

C. (6,3)

D. (3,6)

4. Which type of lines are shown?

KY-MA-05-3.1.1

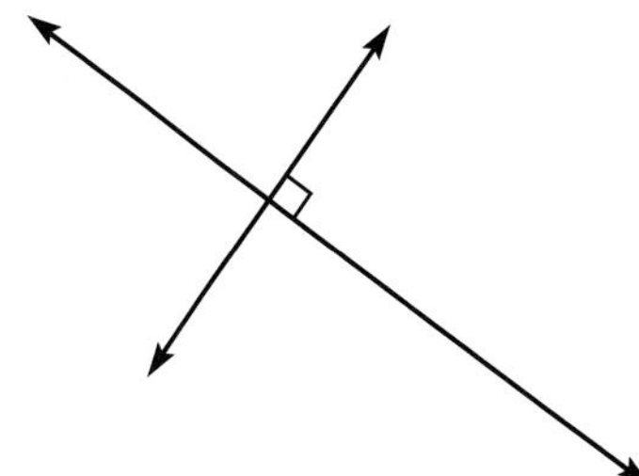

A. acute angles

B. parallel lines

C. perpendicular lines

D. intersecting lines

Geometry

5. What type of transformation is shown? KY MA-05-3.2.2

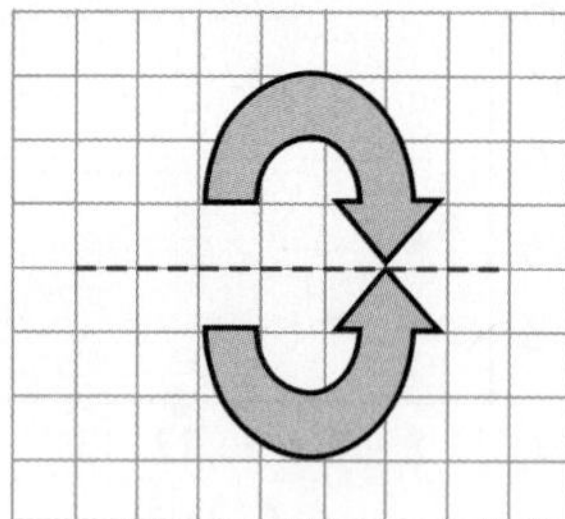

A. rotation

B. translation

C. tessellation

D. reflection

6. Which lines appear to be parallel? KY MA-05-3.1.1

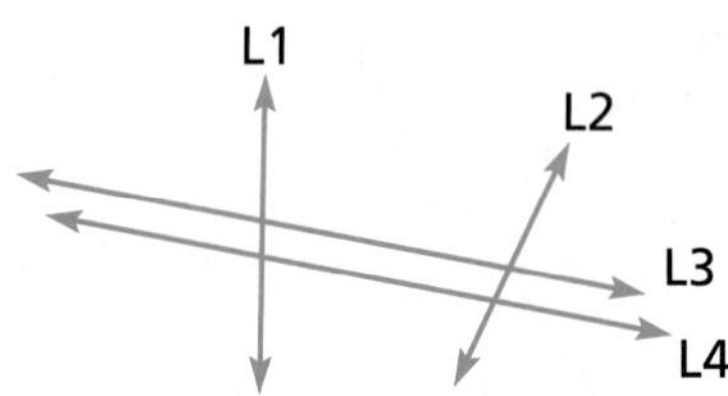

A. L1 and L2

B. L2 and L3

C. L3 and L4

D. L4 and L1

7. Which of the figures below has at least four lines of symmetry? KY MA-05-3.2.1

A. 

B. 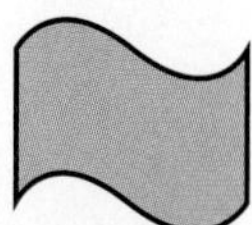

C. 

D. 

8. Phoebe drew the figure below.

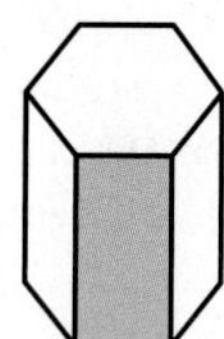

How many faces, vertices and edges does the figure have? KY MA-05-3.1.1

A. faces: 6; vertices: 10; edges: 12

B. faces: 8; vertices: 12; edges: 12

C. faces: 8; vertices: 12; edges: 18

D. faces: 6; vertices: 10; edges: 18

9. Gilberto drew the design below for a stained glass door.

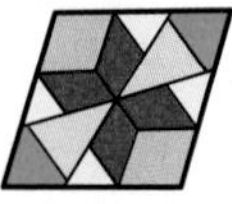

Which best describes the shape of the design? KY MA-05-3.1.2

A. rhombus

B. square

C. trapezoid

D. rectangle

Data Analysis and Probability

1. Craig has a number cube labeled 1 through 6. What is the probability of tossing a factor of 6? KY MA-05-4.4.2

A. $\frac{1}{6}$ C. $\frac{3}{6}$

B. $\frac{2}{6}$ D. $\frac{4}{6}$

2. Marvin wants to find out the likelihood of the spinner landing on an odd number.

Is it *certain, more likely, less likely* or *impossible* that Marvin will spin an odd number? KY MA-05-4.4.2

A. certain

B. more likely

C. less likely

D. impossible

3. Angie listed her Math test scores.

95, 94, 90, 82, 90, 85, 100, 85, 89

What is the mean of Angie's test scores? KY MA-05-4.2.1

A. 88 C. 92

B. 90 D. 94

4. Marge recorded the number of people in the different sections of the Ambler Symphony Orchestra in a bar graph.

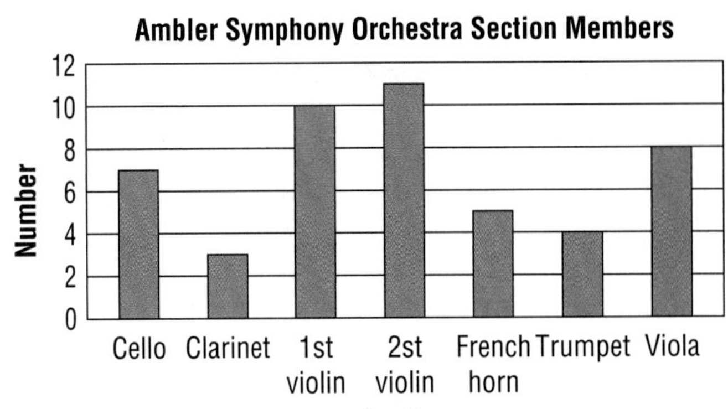

Which two sections combined have the same number of members as the viola section? KY MA-05-4.1.1

A. cello and clarinet

B. clarinet and French horn

C. trumpet and 1st violin

D. trumpet and clarinet

5. Francis has different lengths of nails in his toolbox.

4.5, 2.5, 3.5, 4.5, 2.5, 3.25, 2.5

What is the mode of the lengths of the nails in Francis' toolbox? KY MA-05-4.2.1

A. 2.5

B. 3.25

C. 3.5

D. 4.5

Getting Ready for the KCCT

Algebraic Thinking

1. Joy received 56 roses. She wants to give 8 of her friends an equal number of roses. Which equation can Joy use to determine how many roses each of her friends get? KY MA-05-5.3.1

   A. $r = 56 \div 8$

   B. $r = 56 - 8$

   C. $r = 8 \times 56$

   D. $r = 8 + 56$

2. Which is the rule for the input/output table. KY MA-05-5.1.2

Input	2	3	4	5
Output	18	25	32	39

   A. multiply by 6, add 7

   B. multiply by 7, add 4

   C. add 4, multiply by 3

   D. add 20, subtract 2

3. Dr. Gonzales bought dog treats for $8.50. He also bought some toys for his dog. He spent a total of $25. Which equation can Dr. Gonzales use to find how much he spent on toys for his dog? KY MA-05-5.3.1

   A. $\$8.50d = \$25$

   B. $d - \$25 = \$8.50$

   C. $\$25 \div d = \$8.50$

   D. $\$8.50 + d = \$25$

4. Mr. Tuano challenged the class to find the next number in the pattern:

   16 17 15 16 14 15 13 14

   What is the next number in the pattern? KY MA-05-5.1.1

   A. 16

   B. 15

   C. 12

   D. 10

5. The tiles in a garden are arranged in a pattern. If there were 8 rows, how many tiles would there be in all? KY MA-05-5.1.1

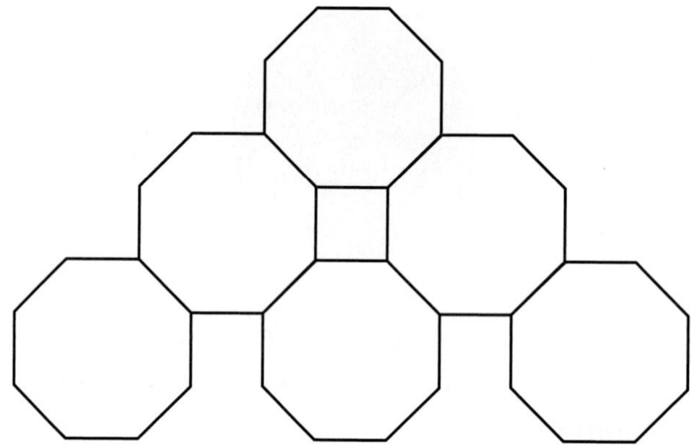

   A. 8

   B. 19

   C. 28

   D. 36

6. Denise told Paul that the combined ages of her parents are 82. Denise's dad is 44 years old. If Paul used m to represent his mom's age in the equation $m + 44 = 82$, how old is Denise's mom? KY MA-05-5.3.1

   A. 28

   B. 36

   C. 38

   D. 40

Open Response

1. Ryan uses only cubes, square pyramids, and triangular prisms to arrange a model city. The resulting model has a total of 31 faces, 54 edges and 35 vertices. How many of each figure does Ryan use? KY MA-05-3.1.3

2. Scott counted the number of paintings he studied each month at the University of Kentucky Art Museum. What are the mean, median, and mode for the number of paintings he studied? How would the data change if Scott studied 5 paintings less each month? KY MA-05-4.2.1

Paintings Viewed					
Jan.	Feb.	March	April	May	June
20	15	18	25	18	12

3. Melissa drew a rectangle with the following measurements:

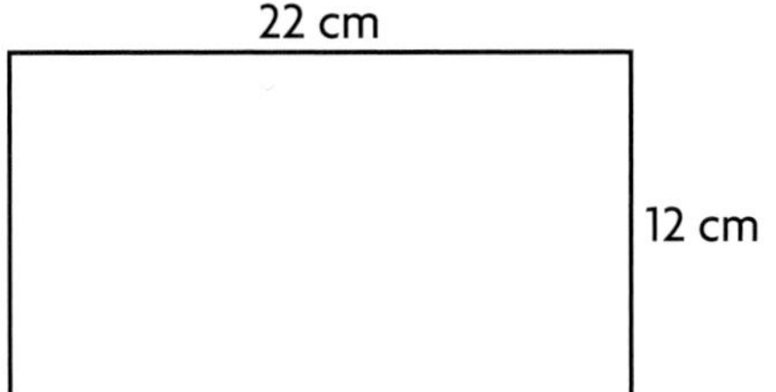

What is the area and the perimeter of Melissa's rectangle? If she wants to draw another figure with the same area but a different perimeter, what could the measurements be? KY MA-05-2.1.1

4. Tim has a bag of red, blue, and green marbles.

What is the probability that Tim will pull a red or a blue marble? Write the probability as a fraction. KY MA-05-4.4.2

Addition and Subtraction Facts

	K	L	M	N	O	P	Q	R
A	5 + 6	9 −3	8 +6	10 − 7	18 − 9	7 +9	11 − 4	0 +9
B	12 − 4	9 +9	14 − 5	8 −5	9 +4	11 − 6	5 +3	16 − 9
C	6 +5	0 +8	9 −6	4 +4	13 − 6	3 +6	12 − 3	7 +4
D	6 +3	14 − 6	8 +8	7 −7	13 −5	5 +8	9 +7	11 −8
E	4 +6	17 − 9	10 −5	6 +6	8 −4	1 +9	8 +7	12 −9
F	8 +5	4 +7	11 − 3	3 +7	10 −2	9 +0	12 − 8	7 +2
G	5 +7	13 − 4	6 +8	20 −10	8 −0	6 +9	14 − 7	4 +8
H	6 +7	11 − 7	9 −9	9 +8	16 − 8	8 +10	17 −10	7 −3
I	13 − 7	14 −9	5 +5	9 +10	10 − 6	3 +9	9 −7	7 +6
J	11 − 2	9 +5	15 − 7	10 +10	13 − 9	7 +8	11 − 5	8 +4

Multiplication Facts

	K	L	M	N	O	P	Q	R
A	5×6	5×9	7×7	9×10	7×5	12×2	10×6	6×7
B	6×6	0×6	2×7	12×8	9×2	3×5	5×8	8×3
C	7×0	5×1	4×5	9×9	6×8	8×11	11×7	10×5
D	1×7	9×4	0×7	2×5	9×7	10×9	3×3	12×7
E	5×7	1×9	4×3	7×6	11×3	3×8	4×2	10×10
F	10×12	5×5	6×4	9×8	0×8	9×6	11×2	12×6
G	5×3	4×6	6×3	7×9	12×5	0×9	5×4	12×11
H	7×1	6×9	1×6	4×4	3×7	11×11	4×8	12×9
I	7×4	2×4	8×6	3×4	11×5	2×9	8×9	7×8
J	8×0	3×9	12×12	8×5	4×7	6×2	9×5	8×8

Division Facts

	K	L	M	N	O	P	Q	R
A	$7\overline{)56}$	$5\overline{)40}$	$6\overline{)24}$	$6\overline{)30}$	$6\overline{)18}$	$7\overline{)42}$	$8\overline{)16}$	$9\overline{)45}$
B	$3\overline{)9}$	$10\overline{)90}$	$1\overline{)1}$	$1\overline{)6}$	$10\overline{)100}$	$3\overline{)12}$	$10\overline{)70}$	$8\overline{)56}$
C	$6\overline{)48}$	$12\overline{)60}$	$4\overline{)32}$	$6\overline{)54}$	$7\overline{)0}$	$3\overline{)18}$	$9\overline{)90}$	$11\overline{)55}$
D	$2\overline{)16}$	$3\overline{)21}$	$5\overline{)30}$	$3\overline{)15}$	$11\overline{)110}$	$9\overline{)9}$	$8\overline{)64}$	$9\overline{)63}$
E	$4\overline{)28}$	$2\overline{)10}$	$9\overline{)18}$	$1\overline{)5}$	$7\overline{)63}$	$8\overline{)32}$	$2\overline{)8}$	$9\overline{)108}$
F	$8\overline{)24}$	$4\overline{)4}$	$2\overline{)14}$	$11\overline{)66}$	$8\overline{)72}$	$4\overline{)12}$	$7\overline{)21}$	$6\overline{)36}$
G	$12\overline{)36}$	$5\overline{)20}$	$7\overline{)28}$	$7\overline{)14}$	$4\overline{)24}$	$11\overline{)121}$	$9\overline{)36}$	$11\overline{)132}$
H	$9\overline{)27}$	$3\overline{)27}$	$7\overline{)49}$	$4\overline{)20}$	$9\overline{)72}$	$5\overline{)60}$	$8\overline{)88}$	$10\overline{)80}$
I	$4\overline{)44}$	$8\overline{)48}$	$5\overline{)35}$	$8\overline{)40}$	$5\overline{)10}$	$2\overline{)12}$	$10\overline{)60}$	$9\overline{)54}$
J	$10\overline{)120}$	$12\overline{)72}$	$9\overline{)81}$	$4\overline{)16}$	$1\overline{)7}$	$12\overline{)60}$	$12\overline{)96}$	$12\overline{)144}$

Multiplication and Division Facts

	K	L	M	N	O	P	Q	R
A	$2\overline{)18}$	8×4	$5\overline{)15}$	10×6	8×1	$3\overline{)24}$	$6\overline{)12}$	5×8
B	8×2	$7\overline{)77}$	$9\overline{)81}$	4×10	7×12	$1\overline{)6}$	$8\overline{)80}$	4×9
C	$12\overline{)36}$	11×5	7×7	$10\overline{)90}$	$5\overline{)45}$	6×7	$8\overline{)16}$	9×9
D	10×2	$4\overline{)32}$	$9\overline{)99}$	7×8	12×3	$9\overline{)108}$	$11\overline{)88}$	12×4
E	8×10	12×9	$12\overline{)84}$	$2\overline{)20}$	9×0	10×11	$3\overline{)36}$	$10\overline{)100}$
F	$4\overline{)44}$	$12\overline{)72}$	7×11	12×6	$7\overline{)56}$	$9\overline{)45}$	10×3	9×7
G	$12\overline{)144}$	$6\overline{)60}$	9×2	8×12	$12\overline{)108}$	$11\overline{)44}$	5×10	$7\overline{)84}$
H	6×5	8×8	$11\overline{)33}$	$5\overline{)55}$	6×11	12×5	$11\overline{)132}$	$6\overline{)42}$
I	$8\overline{)96}$	$10\overline{)120}$	11×8	10×9	$5\overline{)60}$	11×4	10×10	$10\overline{)80}$
J	11×6	12×11	$4\overline{)40}$	$7\overline{)35}$	3×6	$8\overline{)56}$	9×8	12×12

Table of Measures

METRIC	CUSTOMARY
Length	
1 centimeter (cm) = 10 millimeters (mm)	1 foot (ft) = 12 inches (in.)
1 meter (m) = 1,000 millimeters	1 yard (yd) = 3 feet, or 36 inches
1 meter = 100 centimeters (cm)	1 mile (mi) = 1,760 yards, or 5,280 feet
1 meter = 10 decimeters (dm)	
1 kilometer (km) = 1,000 meters	
Capacity	
1 liter (L) = 1,000 milliliters (mL)	1 tablespoon (tbsp) = 3 teaspoons (tsp)
1 metric cup = 250 milliliters	1 cup (c) = 8 fluid ounces (fl oz)
1 liter = 4 metric cups	1 pint (pt) = 2 cups
1 kiloliter (kL) = 1,000 liters	1 quart (qt) = 2 pints, or 4 cups
	1 gallon (gal) = 4 quarts
Mass/Weight	
1 gram (g) = 1,000 milligrams (mg)	1 pound (lb) = 16 ounces (oz)
1 kilogram (kg) = 1,000 grams	1 ton (T) = 2,000 pounds

TIME
1 minute (min) = 60 seconds (sec)
1 hour (hr) = 60 minutes
1 day = 24 hours
1 week (wk) = 7 days
1 year (yr) = 12 months (mo) or about 52 weeks
1 year = 365 days
1 leap year = 366 days
1 decade = 10 years
1 century = 100 years
1 millennium = 1,000 years

SYMBOLS

Symbol	Meaning	Symbol	Meaning
$=$	is equal to	$\perp$	is perpendicular to
$\neq$	is not equal to	$\parallel$	is parallel to
$>$	is greater than	$\overleftrightarrow{AB}$	line *AB*
$<$	is less than	$\overrightarrow{AB}$	ray *AB*
$\geq$	is greater than or equal to	$\overline{AB}$	line segment *AB*
$\leq$	is less than or equal to	$\angle ABC$	angle *ABC*
2^3	the third power of 2, or 2 to the third power	$\triangle ABC$	triangle *ABC*
		$^{+}8$	positive 8
10^2	ten squared	$^{-}8$	negative 8
10^3	ten cubed	$\lvert 4 \rvert$	the absolute value of 4
10^4	the fourth power of 10, or 10 to the fourth power	$^\circ$	degree
		°C	degrees Celsius
$\sqrt{}$	positive square root	°F	degrees Fahrenheit
(2,3)	ordered pair (*x*,*y*)	π	pi
1:3	the ratio of 1 to 3	P(4)	the probability of the outcome 4
%	percent		
$\approx$	is approximately equal to		

FORMULAS

Perimeter		Area	
Polygon	P = sum of the lengths of the sides	Rectangle	$A = l \times w$, $A = lw$
		Square	$A = s^2$
Rectangle	$P = (2 \times l) + (2 \times w)$ or $2l + 2w$	Parallelogram	$A = b \times h$, or $A = bh$
Square	$P = 4 \times s$, $P = 4s$	Triangle	$A = \frac{1}{2} \times b \times h$, or $A = \frac{1}{2}bh$
Circumference		**Volume**	
$C = \pi \times d$		Rectangular prism	$V = l \times w \times h$
Other			
Celsius (°C) $C = \frac{9}{5} \times (F - 32)$		Fahrenheit (°F) $F = (\frac{9}{5} \times C) + 32$	
Diameter $= 2r$		Distance traveled $d = rt$	

Glossary

a add, map	ē equal, tree	m move, seem	o͞o pool, food	û(r) burn, term
ā ace, rate	f fit, half	n nice, tin	p pit, stop	yo͞o fuse, few
â(r) care, air	g go, log	ng ring, song	r run, poor	v vain, eve
ä palm, father	h hope, hate	o odd, hot	s see, pass	w win, away
b bat, rub	i it, give	ō open, so	sh sure, rush	y yet, yearn
ch check, catch	ī ice, write	ô order, jaw	t talk, sit	z zest, muse
d dog, rod	j joy, ledge	oi oil, boy	th thin, both	zh vision, pleasure
e end, pet	k cool, take	ou pout, now	t͟h this, bathe	
	l look, rule	o͝o took, full	u up, done	

ə the schwa, an unstressed vowel representing the sound spelled *a* in above, *e* in sicken, *i* in possible, *o* in melon, *u* in circus

Other symbols:
- • separates words into syllables
- ′ indicates stress on a syllable

A

absolute value [ab•sə•lo͞ot′ val′yo͞o] **valor absoluto** The distance of an integer from zero on a number line (p. 573)

acute angle [ə•kyo͞ot′ ang′gəl] **ángulo agudo** An angle that has a measure less than a right angle (less than 90°) (p. 483)
Example:

The Latin word for needle is *acus*. This means "pointed" or "sharp." You will recognize the root in the words *acid* (sharp taste), *acumen* (mental sharpness), and *acute*, which describes a sharp or pointed angle.

acute triangle [ə•kyo͞ot′ trī′ang•gəl] **triángulo acutángulo** A triangle that has three acute angles (p. 514)

addends [ad′endz] **sumandos** Numbers that are added in an addition problem (p. 17)

addition [ə•dish′en] **suma** The process of finding the total number of items when two or more groups of items are joined; the opposite of subtraction (p. 20)

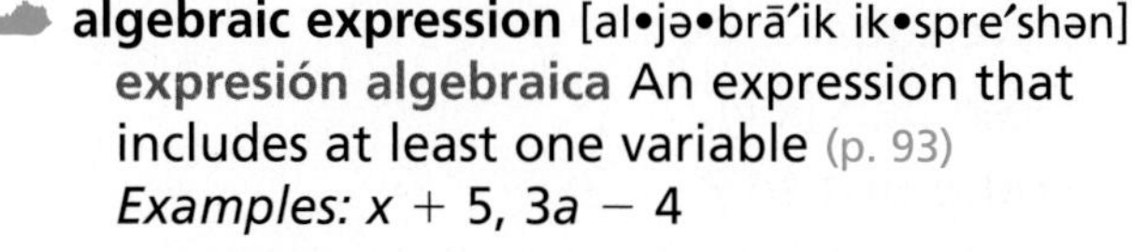

algebraic expression [al•jə•brā′ik ik•spre′shən] **expresión algebraica** An expression that includes at least one variable (p. 93)
Examples: $x + 5$, $3a - 4$

angle [ang′gəl] **ángulo** A figure formed by two rays that meet at a common endpoint (p. 483)
Example:

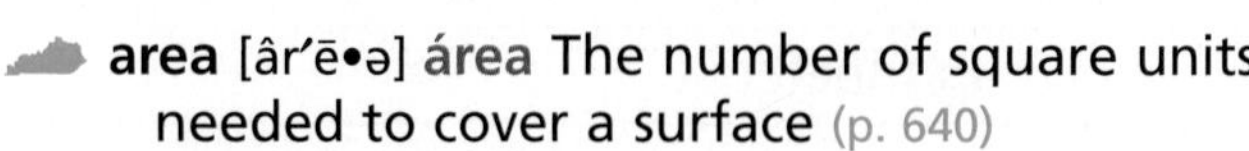

area [âr′ē•ə] **área** The number of square units needed to cover a surface (p. 640)

arrangement [ə rānj′•mənt] **ordenación** A selection of different items in which the order is important (p. 467)

Associative Property of Addition [ə•sō′shē•ə•tiv prä′ pər•tē əv ə•di′shən] **propiedad asociativa de la suma** The property that states that when the grouping of addends is changed, the sum is the same (p. 100)
Example: $(5 + 8) + 4 = 5 + (8 + 4)$

Associative Property of Multiplication [ə•sō′shē•ə•tiv prä′pər•tē əv mul•tə•plə•kā′shən] **propiedad asociativa de la multiplicación** The property that states that the way factors are grouped does not change the product (p. 100)
Example: $(2 \times 3) \times 4 = 2 \times (3 \times 4)$

bar graph [bär graf] **gráfica de barras** A graph that uses horizontal or vertical bars to display countable data (p. 226)
Example:

base [bās] (arithmetic) **base** A number used as a repeated factor (p. 290)
Example: $8^3 = 8 \times 8 \times 8$. The base is 8.

base [bās] (geometry) **base** In two dimensions, one side of a triangle or parallelogram which is used to help find the area. In three dimensions, a plane figure, usually a polygon or circle, which is used to partially describe a solid figure and to help find the volume of some solid figures. See *height* (p. 524)
Examples:

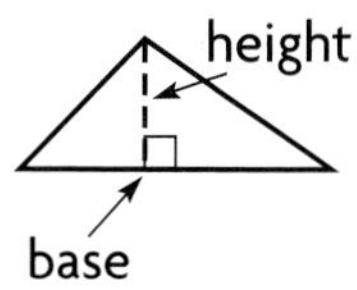

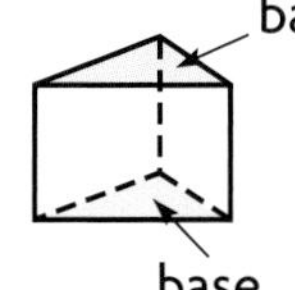

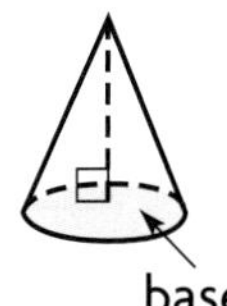

benchmark [bench′märk] **punto de referencia** A familiar number used as a point of reference (p. 7)

billion [bil′yən] **millardo** 1,000 millions; written as 1,000,000,000 (p. 8)

box-and whisker plot [bäks•ənd•hwis′kər graf] **diagrama de caja y brazos** A graph that shows how far apart and how evenly data are distributed (p. 236)

capacity [kə•pa′sə•tē] **capacidad** The amount a container can hold (p. 600)
Example: $\frac{1}{2}$ gallon = 2 quarts

categorical data [ka•tə•gor′i•kəl dā′tə] **datos categóricos** When graphed, data that shows groups or choices in any order (p. 260)

Celsius (°C) [sel′sē•us] **Celsius (°C)** A metric scale for measuring temperature (p. 612)

centimeter (cm) [sen′tə•mē•tər] **centímetro (cm)** A metric unit for measuring length or distance; 0.01 meter = 1 centimeter (p. 594)

chord [kôrd] **cuerda** A line segment with endpoints on a circle (p. 496)
Example:

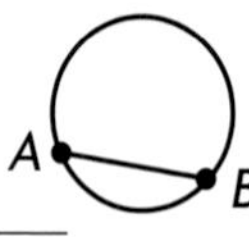

$\overline{AB}$ is a chord.

circle [sər′kəl] **círculo** A closed figure with all points on the figure the same distance from the center point (p. 496)
Example:

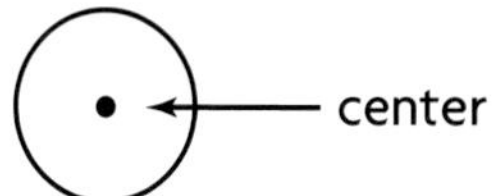

circle graph [sər′kəl graf] **gráfica circular** A graph that shows how parts of the data are related to the whole and to each other (p. 227)
Example:

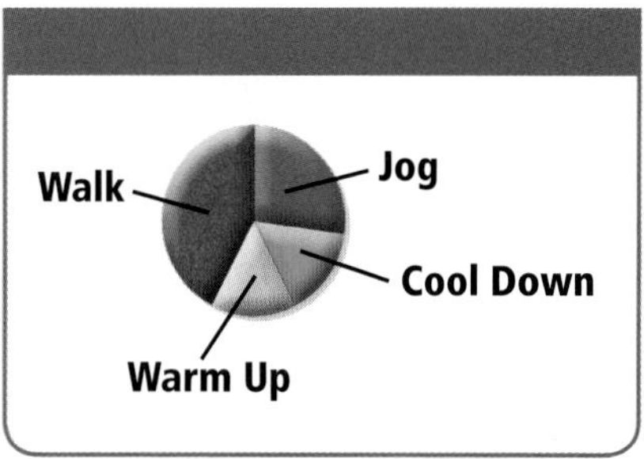

circumference [sər•kum′fər•əns] **circunferencia** The distance around a circle (p. 630)

combination [käm•bə•nā′•shən] **combinación** A selection of different items in which the order is not important (p. 466)

common factor [kä′mən fak′tər] **factor común** A number that is a factor of two or more numbers (p. 280)

common multiple [kä′mən mul′tə•pəl] **múltiplo común** A number that is a multiple of two or more numbers (p. 276)

Commutative Property of Addition [kə•myo͞o′tə•tiv prä′pər•tē əv ə•di′shən] **propiedad conmutativa de la suma** The property that states that when the order of two addends is changed, the sum is the same (p. 100) *Example:* 4 + 5 = 5 + 4

Commutative Property of Multiplication [kə•myōō′tə•tiv prä′pər•tē əv mul•tə•plə•kā′shən] **propiedad conmutativa de la multiplicación** The property that states that when the order of two factors is changed, the product is the same
Example: $4 \times 5 = 5 \times 4$ (p. 100)

compass [kum′pəs] **compás** A tool used to construct circles and arcs (p. 496)

compatible numbers [kəm•pa′tə•bəl num′bərz] **números compatibles** Numbers that are easy to compute mentally (p. 16)

complement [kom′plə•mənt] **complemento** In probability, the complement of an event is a new event consisting of all outcomes in the sample space that are not outcomes of the original event. The sum of the probability of an event and its complement is 1 (p. 457)
Example: The number cube is labeled 1 through 6.

Event: rolling a 2 ⟶ $P(2) = \frac{1}{6}$

Complement: not rolling a 2 ⟶ P(not 2) $\frac{5}{6}$

$P(2) + P(\text{not } 2) = \frac{1}{6} + \frac{5}{6} = 1$

composite number [käm•pä′zət num′bər] **número compuesto** A number having more than two factors (p. 284)
Example: 6 is a composite number, since its factors are 1, 2, 3, and 6.

cone [kōn] **cono** A solid figure that has a flat, circular base and one vertex (p. 524)
Example:

congruent [kən•grōō′ənt] **congruente** Having the same size and shape (p. 500)

continuous data [kən•tin′yōō•əs dā′tə] **datos continuos** Data that can take on any number within a selected range, usually given by measurements (e.g., time, distance) (p. 263)

coordinate plane [kō•ôr′də•nət plān] **plano de coordenadas** A plane formed by two intersecting and perpendicular number lines called axes (p. 578)
Example:

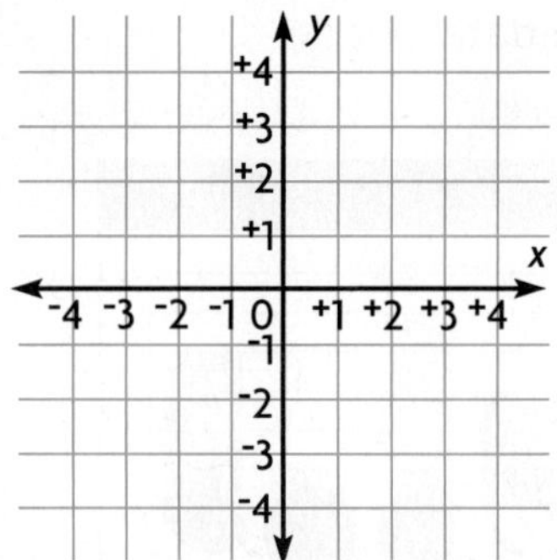

corresponding angles [kôr•ə•spän′ding ang′gəlz] **ángulos correspondientes** Angles that are in the same relative position in congruent or similar figures (p. 501)
Example:

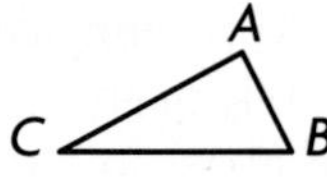

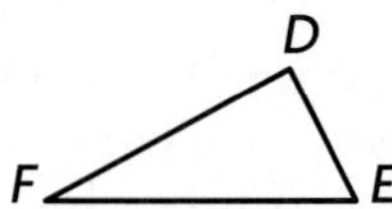

∠A and ∠D are corresponding angles.

corresponding sides [kôr•ə•spän′ding sīdz] **lados correspondientes** Sides that are in the same relative position in congruent or similar figures (p. 501)
Example:

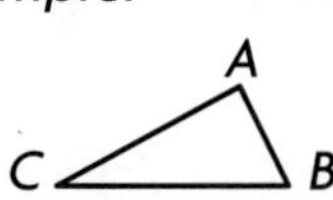

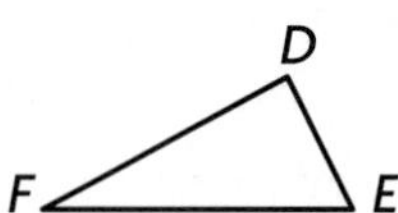

$\overline{CA}$ and $\overline{FD}$ are corresponding sides.

cube [kyōōb] **cubo** A solid figure with six congruent square faces (p. 524)
Example:

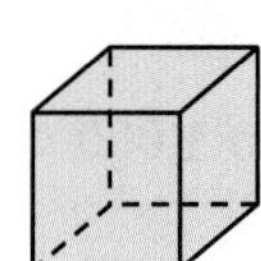

cubic unit [kyōō′bik yōō′nət] **unidad cúbica** A unit of volume with dimensions 1 unit × 1 unit × 1 unit (p. 664)

cup (c) [kup] **taza (t)** A customary unit used to measure capacity (p. 600)
Example: 8 ounces = 1 cup

cylinder [si′lən•dər] **cilindro** A solid figure that has two parallel bases that are congruent circles (p. 524)
Example:

Kentucky Mathematics Vocabulary

data [dā′tə] **datos** Information collected about people or things, often to draw conclusions about them (p. 216)

decagon [dek′ə•gän] **decágono** A polygon with 10 sides (p. 490)
Examples:

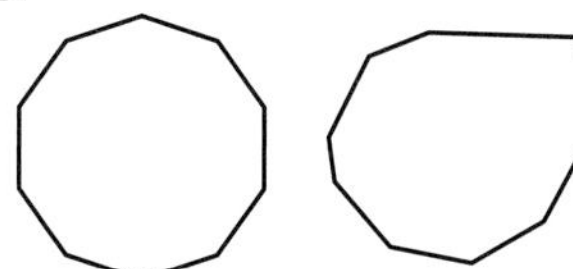

decimal [de′sə•məl] **decimal** A number with one or more digits to the right of the decimal point (p. 132)

decimal point [de′sə•məl point] **punto decimal** A symbol used to separate dollars from cents in money, and the ones place from the tenths place in decimal numbers (p. 132)

decimal system [de′sə•məl sis′təm] **sistema decimal** A system of computation based on the number 10 (p. 132)

decimeter (dm) [de′sə•mē•tər] **decímetro (dm)** A unit of length in the metric system; 10 decimeters = 1 meter (p. 594)

degree (°) [di•grē′] **grado (°)** A unit for measuring angles or for measuring temperature (p. 483)

denominator [di•nä′mə•nā•tər] **denominador** The number below the bar in a fraction that tells how many equal parts are in the whole (p. 308)
Example: $\frac{3}{4}$ ← denominator

diagonal [di•a′gə•nəl] **diagonal** A line segment that connects two non-adjacent vertices of a polygon (p. 508)
Example:

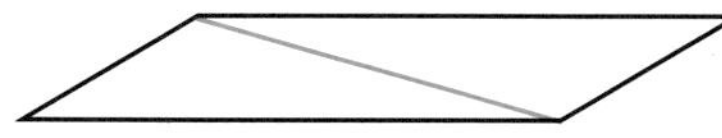

diameter [dī•am′ə•tər] **diámetro** A line segment that passes through the center of a circle and has its endpoints on the circle (p. 496)
Example:

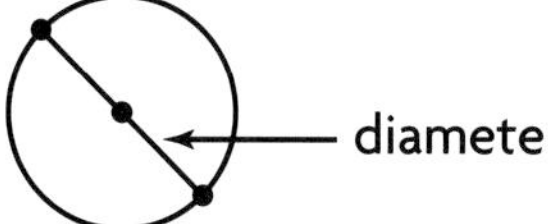

difference [dif′ər•əns] **diferencia** The answer to a subtraction problem (p. 16)

digit [di′jit] **dígito** Any one of the ten symbols 0, 1, 2, 3, 4, 5, 6, 7, 8, 9 used to write numbers (p. 4)

discrete data [dis•krēt′ dā′tə] **datos discretos** Data that is not continuous. The number of correct problems on a given test is an example of discrete data. (p. 263)

Distributive Property [di•strib′yə•tiv prä′pər•tē] **propiedad distributiva** The property that states that multiplying a sum by a number is the same as multiplying each addend in the sum by the number and then adding the products (p. 40)
Example: $3 \times (4 + 2) = (3 \times 4) + (3 \times 2)$
$3 \times 6 = 12 + 6$
$18 = 18$

dividend [di′və•dend] **dividendo** The number that is to be divided in a division problem (p. 60)
Example: 36 ÷ 6; $6\overline{)36}$ The dividend is 36.

division [də•vi′zhən] **división** The process of sharing a number of items to find how many groups can be made or how many items will be in a group; the operation that is the opposite of multiplication (p. 60)

divisible [di•viz′ə•bəl] **divisible** A number is divisible by another number if the quotient is a counting number and the remainder is zero (p. 278)
Example: 18 is divisible by 3.

divisor [də•vī′zər] **divisor** The number that divides the dividend (p. 60)
Example: 15 ÷ 3; $3\overline{)15}$ The divisor is 3.

double-bar graph [du′bəl bär graf] **gráfica de doble barra** A graph used to compare two similar kinds of data (p. 226)
Example:

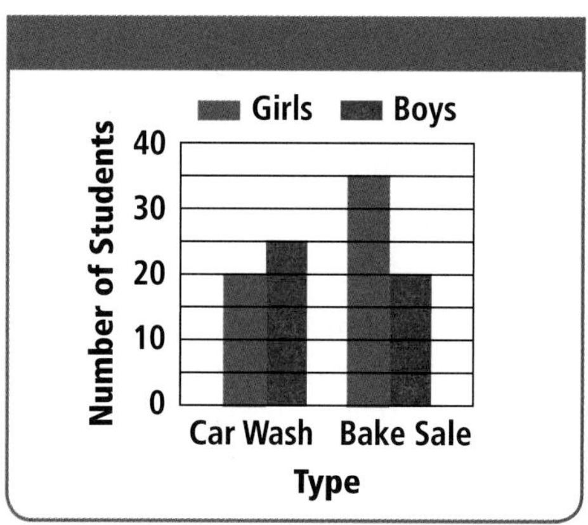

double-line graph [du′bəl līn graf] **gráfica lineal doble** A line graph that represents two sets of data. (p. 229)

edge [ej] **arista** The line made where two faces of a solid figure meet (p. 525)
Example:

edge

elapsed time [i•lapst′ tīm] **tiempo transcurrido** The time that passes between the start of an activity and the end of that activity (p. 610)

equally likely [ē′kwəl•lē lī′klē] **igualmente probable** Having the same chance of occurring (p. 454)

equation [i•kwā′zhən] **ecuación** An algebraic or numerical sentence that shows that two quantities are equal (p. 106)

equiangular triangle [ē′kwə•ang′gyə•lər trī′ang•gəl] **triángulo equiangular** A triangle with three congruent angles (p. 514)
Example:

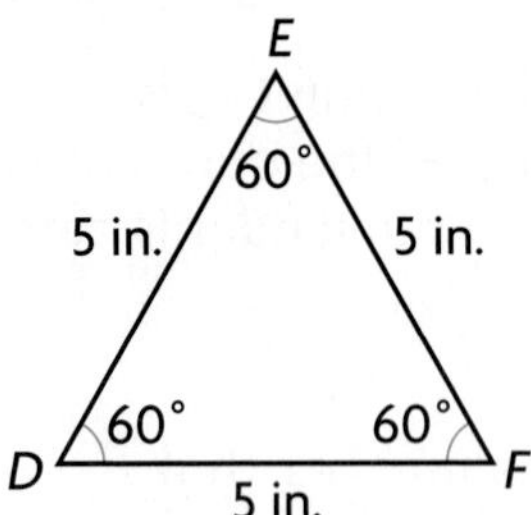

Δ*DEF* is equiangular.

equilateral triangle [ē•kwə•la′tə•rəl trī′ang•gəl] **triángulo equilátero** A triangle with three congruent sides (p. 514)
Example:

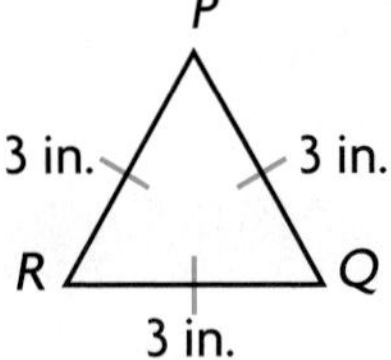

equivalent [ē•kwiv′ə•lənt] **equivalente** Having the same value

equivalent decimals [ē•kwiv′ə•lənt de′sə•məlz] **decimales equivalentes** Decimals that name the same number or amount (p. 136)
Example: 0.4 = 0.40 = 0.400

equivalent fractions [ē•kwiv′ə•lənt frak′shənz] **fracciones equivalentes** Fractions that name the same amount or part (p. 310)
Example: $\frac{3}{4} = \frac{6}{8}$

equivalent ratios [ē•kwiv′ə•lənt rā′shē•ōz] **razones equivalentes** Ratios that name the same comparison (p. 424)
Example:

The ratio of yellow to red is $\frac{2}{4}$ or $\frac{1}{2}$.
The ratios $\frac{2}{4}$ and $\frac{1}{2}$ are equivalent.

$$\frac{2}{4} = \frac{1}{2}$$

estimate [es′tə•māt] *noun* **estimación (s)** A number close to an exact amount (p. 16)

estimate [es′tə•mət] *verb* **estimar (v)** To find a number that is close to an exact amount (p. 16)

evaluate [ē•val′yo͞o•wāt] **evaluar** To find the value of a numerical or algebraic expression (p. 96)

event [i•vent′] **suceso** A set of one or more outcomes (p. 454)

expanded form [ek•spand′id fôrm] **forma desarrollada** A way to write numbers by showing the value of each digit (p. 4)
Example: 832 = 800 + 30 + 2

experimental probability [ek•sper•ə•men′tal prä•ba•bil′ə•tē] **probabilidad experimental** The ratio of the number of times an event occurs to the number of times the activity is performed (p. 459)

exponent [ek′spō•nənt] **exponente** A number that shows how many times the base is used as a factor (p. 290)
Example: $10^3 = 10 \times 10 \times 10$;
3 is the exponent.

Exponent comes from the combination of the Latin roots *ex* ("out of") + *ponere* ("to place"). In the 17th century, mathematicians began to use complicated quantities. The idea of positioning a number by raising it "out of place" is traced to René Descartes.

expression [ek•spre′shən] **expresión** A mathematical phrase or the part of a number sentence that combines numbers, operation signs, and sometimes variables, but does not have an equal sign (p. 92)

The males of some types of penguins incubate their eggs for **60 days** while the females feed and then return at hatching time.

Some penguins live in regions where the temperatures can be as high as 100°F.

Others live where the temperatures can be as low as -100°F.